WOMEN

WOMEN

NAIM ATTALLAH

QUARTET BOOKS
LONDON   NEW YORK

First published by Quartet Books Limited 1987
A member of the Namara Group
27/29 Goodge Street, London W1P 1FD

Copyright © by Naim Attallah 1987

British Library Cataloguing in Publication Data

    Attallah, Naim
    Women.
    1. Women – Social conditions
    I. Title
    305.4'2 HQ1121

    ISBN 0-7043-2625-6

Typeset by Reprotype Limited, Peterborough, Cambs
Printed and bound in Great Britain
by Hazell, Watson & Viney Limited, Aylesbury, Bucks

*For
Maria*

Contents

Acknowledgements

A large number of people helped to ease both the writing of this book and the short time the whole process took between concept and publication. The idea itself had its origin, tongue-in-cheek, when Pickles, the Editorial Director of Quartet Books, suggested over lunch that, since I liked women and expressed a keenness to try my hand at writing, it was women I should write a book about. I promptly rose to the bait, but his contribution did not end there. Later on I was to seek his views on many aspects of the book, and his editorial advice has been invaluable.

David Elliott of Quartet Books has been extremely supportive throughout the whole endeavour. It was his insistence and faith in the project that together convinced me I should publish the book myself rather than under the imprint of another publishing house. His wording of the initial press release on the book amused Veronica Horwell of the *Observer*, who wanted to know the identity of the writer of the 'blurb' which, she said, 'is currently causing so many giggles'. David Elliott is always to be relied upon to liven up the proceedings whenever the going grows dull.

Jennifer Bradshaw, my own editor, organized the historical background research, oversaw the transcription and typing for the taped interviews, edited the transcripts and finally collated the vast quantity of material that goes to make up the bulk of the book. Her task has been the most daunting of all, since time was of the essence from the start.

The team she assembled to carry through all the necessary work consisted of Alison Andrews, Florence Clifton, Janice Furness, David Hendy, Alicia Jackson, Dr Honor Levi, L. A. P. McCall, Ann Menzies and Dr Anna Paterson. Phillip Mallett of the University of St Andrews also made a significant contribution to the book with his encyclopedic knowledge of Victorian women. The transcribers of all the tapes were Norma Porter and her husband Harry, whose lives were unquestionably changed in the process and who now suffer severe withdrawal symptoms.

ACKNOWLEDGEMENTS

Chris Parker and Rosemary Graham read the proofs with great diligence; and Gary Grant, assisted by Georgia de Chamberet, produced the book well on schedule and to a very high standard. Peter Ford cast a critical eye over and cross-checked each portion of text as it reached completion. Anna Groundwater showed a boundless enthusiasm for the book in her handling of the publicity. Linda Brandon and Lady Alethea Savile researched and edited the biographies, and were helped in the final stages by Zelfa Hourani. Annie Faure, in Paris, not only spent many hours on the telephone arranging my appointments, she also drove me to each destination and displayed immense patience in waiting while I completed the interviews. Christina Oxenberg, in New York, defined whom I should see there, put the list together and helped me with making the contacts. My cook, Charlotte Millward, prepared many delicious lunches and created the informal ambience essential for conversation.

My list of thanks is rather lengthy because of the many kindnesses shown to me by people in general and friends in particular. In this context, each of these must also be mentioned:

Jan Amory, Beatriz Aristimuno, Elizabeth Arkus, Leila Badawi, Julian Bourne, Liz Brewer, Joan Juliet Buck, Charlotte Chandler, Alexandra Chapman, Tina Chow, Michelle Conquillat, Theo Cowan, Fleur Cowles, Susan Crosland, Lucien Dahdah, Abir Dajani, Ron Daniels, Sylvia Deutsch, June Ducas, Princess Elizabeth of Yugoslavia, Shirley Eskapa, Sarah Giles, Lady Annabel Goldsmith, Katya Grenfell, Jane Harker, Omar Hamze, Romain Hart, Mamoun Hassan, Marie Helvin, Reinaldo Herrera, Stuart Holland, Angela Huth, Alice Jay, Denys Johnson-Davies, Janette Kitching, Ros de Lanerolle, Candida Lord, Lyn Nesbitt, Rabbi Julia Neuberger, Catherine Norden, Penny Papreka, Diana Potter, Tim Pringle, Michael Rubinstein, Lucinda Scott, Andrea von Stumm, Sven Uffe-Reumert, Joan Vass, Marilyn Warnick, Anna Wintour, Janie Ironside Wood and Michael Deakin.

A vast debt of gratitude is owed, above all, to the women who consented to be interviewed by me and whose words go to make up the very heart of the book. The generosity of their response and the time and effort they put in are beyond calculation.

Lastly, I would like to pay a special tribute to my wife, Maria, without whose tolerance, advice and warm support the book would never have been possible.

WOMEN

Prelude

My childhood was a protected one. An only son among three girls, I grew up in Haifa, in what was then called Palestine, in a family predominantly female. My father was ill-tempered and authoritarian. His moods were unpredictable and contradictory, but most of the time he inspired fear. His mother had been only eighteen when he was born, and, as her husband had died during her pregnancy, she lived with us, as did her unmarried sister. When I was five, they went to live in Nazareth because my father could no longer put up with them. They had been very kind to me and I missed them greatly. My grandmother on my mother's side lived in the same house, but in a flat directly below us. I hardly knew her and can remember nothing endearing about her.

I was a frail and sickly child. I had pleurisy and bouts of dysentery and was also anaemic. Our house was like a hospital: there were doctors and nurses constantly coming and going. In desperation, my father even called in a rabbi to circumcise me in the belief this would improve my health. If that did provide the answer, it was not apparent until many years later.

As a child, I was never allowed to venture beyond the house unless accompanied by my mother or my sisters, in case something terrible should happen to me. I was never taught to swim or ride a bicycle, nor allowed to play games which involved any risk of accident. I was pampered at home by everyone but my father, though he, too, was very protective. I led a restricted life, not unlike a prisoner who enjoys every physical comfort but lacks the most coveted quality of all: freedom. The only solace I found was with my sisters. We were very close and forged a warm relationship which has lasted throughout the years.

During the summer, I remember I would sit on our balcony for hours on end, looking across the street, marvelling at the life below me: the passing cars, men and women going to work, and children at play. When I first went to school, it was to the convent with my sisters. My eldest sister would take me by the hand and we would walk up the near-by

1

mountain road and there, three hundred yards beyond, stood the convent. The nuns looked after me well, and I still have the fondest memories of those early days. Perhaps they were not entirely formative, but they were certainly valuable enough to instil in me a faith and spiritual purpose I have never wholly lost.

My mother, who is still alive, was entirely dominated by my father. She was sixteen when she married, and my eldest sister was born a year later. Life seems to have passed her by. She had known no other man but my father, lived no other life beyond him and her family and, I suspect, had no aspirations beyond seeing her children grown up and married. She loved me devotedly and remains an integral part of my life, but was not, I believe, a major influence.

My father and I held little in common. In practice, he had been an orphan because his mother could not afford to support him and consequently sent him to a German orphanage in Jerusalem. During the First World War, he naturally fought on the German side, and was taken prisoner by the Allies. The ravages of war, on top of his Germanic upbringing, made him a hard and complex man. He never mellowed, even in old age, and his relationship with me was always a difficult one. But for all that, he was proud and supportive of me from a very early age. When he died a dozen years ago, my mother found among his most treasured belongings poems and stories I had written at the age of nine and which he had kept all these years.

This apart, his influence on me was a negative one. I am the opposite of what he was and stood for. He was a profound pessimist and his everyday life seemed shrouded in an atmosphere of gloom. He lacked ambition and a sense of adventure, and consequently opted always for security. I remember him as a man intolerant of anyone who could not share his opinions, but his saving grace was an appreciation of fine art, of which he became a collector – an enthusiasm I was later to inherit. I always respected him because he was my father, but was never able to feel that I loved him enough. And yet, ironically, love was to prove the guiding spirit of my life.

It all began at the age of fifteen, in the midst of the tragic conflict that befell Palestine. I was sent to Nazareth to live with my grandmother and her sister. Nazareth was then an Arab city and considered a safe refuge at the beginning of the hostilities. It was there that I really came to know my grandmother and her sister. This was the period of my life, lasting about two years, that I regard as the most rich and satisfying. My grandmother cared for me untiringly, nursed me when I was ill and loved me unselfishly. In return, I loved her with the same dedication and commitment, and her memory is so engraved on my heart that, even now, hardly a day passes without something happening to remind me of her.

She lived in a traditional oriental house she had inherited from her father. It had two vast rooms, an outside kitchen and a lavatory at the bottom of the garden. We slept on the floor of one of the rooms on mattresses. My grandmother grew all the vegetables and fruits we needed and we had a lot of hens. It was like a small farm in the middle of town.

Close by there was a convent in which there lived an enclosed order of nuns, only one of whom was permitted access to the outside world. We had no watch or clock, but were able to keep track of the time through the night as the nuns would ring a bell every half-hour. My grandmother and her sister would rise with the morning star to attend to the hens.

There was a deep well in the garden, but its water was only used for watering the plants and for washing. Drinking water we usually fetched from the Fountain of Mary at the other end of town, in a large earthenware jar. There, at the fountain, I would stare wonderingly at Bedouin women carrying water-jars that rested on rolled circles of cloth on their heads. Their gait had the poise of a graceful flower undulating in a gentle breeze.

Across the garden, we could see the hills of Galilee and, when the full moon rose from behind the hills, we would sit in the garden and my grandmother and her sister would tell me stories of the Ottoman occupation, of their childhood and of the acts of courage for which my father's family were renowned.

I felt happy and comfortable in the company of these two old ladies who were in some measure to shape my future life. They were simple people whose wisdom derived from nature and the land. They understood the important things in life. I recall seeing my grandmother's sister plant an olive tree, and asking her why, since it would take so long to bear fruit. 'They planted and we ate,' she replied; 'we now plant that they may eat.' They taught me a good deal, and above all they gave me confidence through love. I found myself irresistibly drawn to them, and their environment became mine.

My life thereafter was much influenced by women. My days with my grandmother ended when I came to England to study. She died a few years later, and her sister died soon after. And the house in which they had lived, and of which I had all those memories, was sold by my father, who seems to have felt neither a particular attachment nor a sense of history. He cared very little for the land or for his family roots, while I cared a great deal for them. The attachment I felt to the land was certainly a reflection of my deep attachment to my grandmother. I was to see the house only once again after the death of my father, but the magic and the dreams had departed. The garden which used to bloom had become barren, the tall trees were drooping with age and neglect.

Impoverished students occupied my childhood home, above which the new owners had built another storey.

When I first arrived in London, I lived in Oakley Gardens, Chelsea. My landlady was called Eva, a diminutive figure with a slightly hunched back. She was about forty and I was about eighteen. She was a pious woman who looked after a blind man and his wife; I remember she had a Persian cat. There were three other lodgers, one of whom was my uncle. He was also a student, but was eleven years older than me. We all lived in perfect harmony. Eva took special care of me, for I was the youngest and least experienced. She helped me with my English and even did my laundry. We used to go for long walks every evening along the Chelsea Embankment, on to Sloane Square and back along the King's Road. Like so many of my generation, I was very interested in the last war, and she used to tell me about the terrible times she had lived through during the Blitz. She became my friend and mentor, and I grew very fond of her. We remained in close contact until her death a decade ago.

Looking back on my life, I realize that women have always been instrumental in whatever I have achieved. I owe that achievement to my mother, my sisters, the nuns who first taught me, to my grandmother and her sister, to that kindly landlady, and above all to my wife, whose love, loyalty and support have been without question the greatest influence. I met her when she was seventeen and I was twenty-six. At the outset, there was nothing special in our relationship, except that she was Polish and I was Palestinian. Her name was Maria and we seemed to get on well and, most important of all, appeared to be naturally comfortable in one another's company. We married a few months after we met and set up home in a large bed-sitter in Holland Park. We had no money, no furniture and no prospects of better things to come. Our joint earnings were just enough to keep our heads above water, but there were no holidays and no luxuries, and we worked hard. Several years later our son Ramsay was born.

Having been in the company of women all my life, I have always felt a need, almost a compulsion, to learn about them, and to understand their dreams and aspirations. During recent years, however, my interest has become focused more precisely. The social evolution of women in our time has been very swift. Women are no longer content merely to play supportive roles, but with new-found confidence are prepared to determine their own futures. I find these women particularly fascinating and consider myself fortunate, through undertaking this book, to have encountered so many at such a crucial time.

4

Introduction

To write a book on women is a difficult enough venture; to do it convincingly is immeasurably challenging. At the outset, the scale of the project was undefined, as were my expectations. I was to tackle a vast subject which has over the years been examined almost to saturation point. It is also one which has confounded and divided people. While conscious that I might lack formal qualifications for such an undertaking, I knew that this would be more than compensated for by enthusiasm and energetic resolve.

The first problem was one of interviews and how best to persuade women to talk to me freely and candidly. This was an all-important matter if the book was to have any depth or real value. The women I wanted to see were not, for the most part, easily accessible. Arranging the interviews drew exhaustively on my reserves of patience – unfortunately not one of my best qualities. Sometimes I found the whole exercise most exasperating, and, despite my initial drive, my spirit was in constant danger of weakening.

To start with, progress was good in the United Kingdom, but far less so in the United States. There, contrary to popular belief, such contacts cannot be established straightforwardly. In New York particularly no value is placed on the niceties of answering letters or returning telephone calls, and very few appointments are made in advance. I was often asked to telephone nearer the suggested date, only to be told, when I complied, that notice was too short. I had to use every device I could think of to secure an appointment: pleading, cajoling, even using other people's names; yet when I was successful, the perplexities would evaporate, the bad memories vanish and an unexpected serenity set in.

Another problem was where to hold the interviews. What I needed was somewhere quiet enough to record on my pocket-sized machine, but all too often I ended up in a crowded restaurant, competing with background music, the chink of glasses, noisy air-conditioning and other people's conversation. One woman in New York, who had at first suggested neutral ground, eventually agreed to come to my apartment. She felt so at ease there that, to my surprise, she seemed to know instinctively where everything was and proceeded to help herself to drink and cake while I was on the telephone to London.

Film agents are perhaps the most intractable. Their exaggerated sense of their own importance tends to bring out the worst in me and undermine my rational nature. Their decisions are not always made for the benefit of those they represent. Indeed, not once did I interview anyone in New York through the intermediary of an agent. The situation is much the same in Paris. It is impossible to find anyone in the office before 11a.m. Whatever one tries seems inadequate, but eventually someone in authority becomes available. Then, just as hope revives, the whole process is apt to repeat itself. Had it not been for the occasional success, I might have failed in my endeavour.

Most of the interviews with film stars were set up through personal contacts. The only useful role played by agents was in arranging time and place. As for literary agents, I tried to avoid them for fear of confrontation. Certainly, there were some helpful ones, but these were in a minority – unlike those who are revered by the literary establishment. But making an appointment did not mean I could relax. Even at the last moment, problems could still arise. Every telephone call might be to cancel the arrangement. I alternated between a sense of dejection and the need to come to terms with the situation. At times I needed to resign myself to the inevitable even as I sought renewed conviction that the project was worthwhile.

When this book was in the early stages in June 1986, I planned to interview 50 women. Once I had done so, I began to realize that the number needed to be increased to at least 100 to give the book a wider perspective. By the time I had reached that objective, I had come to think that perhaps women were more interesting than men. Almost every woman had a different viewpoint and expressed deeply felt convictions; their honesty, their courage, their very mysteriousness were impressive. They rarely became ill at ease with any of my questions, taking everything in their stride with remarkably good humour. The exceptions were few and even they remained courteous and restrained.

The number of interviews continued to escalate. Every time I read a newspaper or browsed through a magazine, I saw the possibility of another interview. My customary self-discipline faltered and I realized I could go on indefinitely. To call a halt, the magic number 250 was chosen, but in the end even that number grew by a further 39.

Those who declined to be interviewed amounted perhaps to no more than 10 per cent, while about another 15 per cent never replied at all. I found politicians to be the least predictable, and in some instances rather curious in their response. One MP replied:

> Please forgive me if I do not greet your request with cries of delight. I must have done a dozen similar ones, this year alone. I am not a radical or a feminist, have not met prejudice, only encouragement, am happily married and love my job, and I'd much rather discuss the National Health Service or the state of the economy. However, if you are still keen to do an interview, may I ask if the company is willing to pay for my time? I would expect £50 for up to one hour's interview, and could meet you when the Commons return in October.

Her letter was dated 9 September 1986. I replied on 21 November, ignoring the request for a fee and asking again whether it would be possible to meet. The reply came on a postcard dated 1 December: 'I'm sorry but I can see no purpose in meeting at present.'

Another MP was more courteous though somewhat puzzling when she wrote: 'I sympathize with the basic purpose of this book, but feel that, personally, I am in grave danger of being seen first and foremost as a woman MP, rather than as an MP.' A third MP replied on 20 November 1986, asking the name of the publishers of the book. On receiving the information, she wrote again, but this time through her private secretary, that she was at present 'fully booked until the middle of next year and would not be able to give you an interview before then'. But then there were many other MPs who never replied. Trade unionists were also especially difficult to reach, as were journalists who earn their keep by being extremely rude to others. For its part, the Salvation Army proved to be far too bureaucratic to be accessible, as did the Civil Service.

Writers in general provided a contrast by being most co-operative, as were serious journalists. I relish the reply of one well-known writer, also an early feminist, who wrote back: 'Unfortunately I am already so far behind in my schedule for work which I am morally obliged to do, because I have taken payment for it, that to take time off work for someone else for free would be inexcusable.' There was also the television personality who apologized since she herself had plans to write something about women one day and might well want to include her own experiences. A newscaster turned glamour personality agreed a date and then, through her agent, cancelled the interview on the same grounds. Another newscaster was more adventurous: 'I don't really think I can help you much with your book,' she wrote. 'I am anti the feminist movement, have no axe to grind – don't feel life has treated me badly and therefore don't think I would have anything to contribute.'

There were others who were perfectly charming in declining, but just occasionally I detected a patronizing tone. In general, though, I have had no cause or reason to complain, and it is certainly not my intention to appear ungracious in recounting these events and experiences. I have learnt a great deal about other people and about myself, and I feel very grateful to those women who agreed to talk to me. All the interviews I conducted face to face, with one exception. Diana Vreeland insisted that the interview with her must be done on the telephone or by letter. (I opted for correspondence to avoid the possibility of misquoting her.) The French interviews were all conducted in French and then translated into English, giving as exact a version of the original conversation as possible.

Writing this book has given me a great deal of pleasure. I have met and spoken to a host of interesting, successful and energetic women. I hope very much that something of this remarkable experience will be shared by all those who read its pages. Although there is still much that divides men and women, I feel sure that there is more common ground than is widely supposed. If the pages that follow contribute in a small way towards a clearer understanding between the two, then I cannot have wished for more.

BACKGROUNDS IN HISTORY

1
Women in Myth and Literature

That familiar figure, the visitor from space, were he to rely on the literature of the past for his idea of womankind, might well retreat precipitately, thanking his gods for having discovered the truth in time to avoid contact with such a strange monster. It is nothing unusual to find women erotic, incontinent, perverse and irrational. Where they are represented as virtuous, they are impossibly so, extremism being the hallmark of this literary imitation. The mirror held up to nature distorts, and always shows the same little girl in one of two nursery poses:

> When she is good, she is very, very good
> But when she is bad, she is horrid.

It would, of course, be equally possible to write about how men have often fared badly at the hands of writers, and to select quotations to demonstrate the thesis. Within the present context, however, it is the position of women that concerns us. If we accept that literature is, in one sense, a barometer for deep-set social attitudes, then the view of women as occupying a lower shelf in the evolutionary scale becomes striking in its uniformity. The conviction is embedded in the classical as well as the Hebraic and Christian traditions. Plato ascribed it to their being created second: there was an initial creation, and those who proved inadequate or cowardly were reborn as women at a second creation. The Old Testament takes much the same line: women are an afterthought. God, knowing Adam to be in need of a companion, created all the animals and brought them before him to be named – 'but for Adam there was not found an help meet for him'. Therefore Adam provides, from his own body, the material out of which Eve is made: 'She shall be called woman because she was taken out of man.' The roots of the words 'man' and 'woman' may be quite different, but the pattern is set. St Paul has no problem with seeing man's superiority established on the grounds that Adam was formed first, or with the

11

oddity of Adam's sin being entirely calculating whereas Eve's was that of being foolishly deceived by Satan. The hierarchy of the sexes is established in Genesis. 'The *sons* of God saw the *daughters* of men that they were fair': men are divine, but women only human.

Nevertheless, in the earliest days of Christianity we find Priscilla and Aquila instructing an Alexandrian Jew, Apollos – a man already familiar enough with the doctrine to be preaching. 'They took him unto them, and expounded unto him the way of God more perfectly' (Acts 18:36). Women were not, however, to be allowed to make such a contribution for long. St Paul makes it clear (I Timothy 2:11 and 12) that the business of women is to be silent and to learn, certainly not to teach: 'I suffer not a woman to teach nor to usurp authority over the man.' More than a thousand years later, Thomas Aquinas argued the exclusion of women from Holy Orders on the grounds that 'in the female sex, no eminence of degree can be signified'. Some six centuries after that Pope Pius XI declared:

> False and harmful to the Christian tradition is the so-called method of 'co-education' ... There is not in nature itself, which fashions the two quite different in organism, in temperament, in abilities, anything to suggest that there can be or ought to be promiscuity, and much less equality, in the training of the two sexes.

To Pius it seemed clear that the difference between the sexes should be 'maintained and encouraged' – to act otherwise being to act against nature. 'True emancipation will not involve false liberty and unnatural equality with the husband' – the notions of liberty and equality being coupled with 'false' and 'unnatural' without hesitation. Renaissance authors, such as Erasmus or Sir Thomas More, could be more sympathetic than this towards the education of women, but for others associated with Protestant reform, the message was basically the same. 'Never any good came out of female domination,' stated Martin Luther, '[for] God created Adam master and lord of living creatures, but Eve spoiled all.' In 1558, John Knox went further in his infamous 'The First Blast of the Trumpet Against the Monstrous Regiment of Women':

> Nature doth paint them ... to be weak, frail, impatient, feeble and foolish; and experience hath declared them to be inconstant, variable, cruel, and lacking the spirit of counsel.

With the secondary position of women accepted, Christian writers attended to the problems of their sexual nature. The early Church Fathers were clearly anxious about women, their anxieties mainly focusing on their supposed role as temptresses and the consequent need to promote modesty as a counterbalance and to prevent, as far as possible, all sexual activity. St Jerome lamented the many young women being lost to the Church because of their immodest behaviour:

> As they walk the streets they try to attract attention and with stealthy nods and winks draw after them troops of young men ... their dress is only a piece of transparent purple with the lilac cape they call a Marforte fluttering from their shoulders.

Widows were no better in his view: 'See their red lips and their plump sleek skins: you would not think they had lost a husband, you would think they were looking for one.' In this, Jerome was directly echoing St Paul's assumption that women are irredeemably committed to sexuality, as in his advice to Timothy to refuse community refuge to young widows because, 'when they have begun to wax wanton against Christ, they will marry'.

Sexual irregularity was, in fact, linked to almost every weakness with which women were charged. In the fourth century, Clement of Alexandria complained bitterly about how women wear silk and so reveal not only their superficiality but also their shape:

> These flimsy and luxurious things are proof of a shallow character, for, with the scanty protection they afford they do nothing more than disgrace the body, inviting prostitution. The folds of such a garment clinging to the body and following its contours very flexibly take its shape and outline the woman's form.

A century earlier, the influential Tertullian had been upset about the way women sought to make themselves attractive and condemned them for dying their hair with saffron (gentlemen, it seems, preferring blondes even then). It is obvious to him that 'salvation, in the case of women, depends chiefly on the observance of chastity'. 'They carefully have their cheeks painted,' he complains, 'and then deny that they have ever excited lust.' And since salvation depends on chastity, damnation must be inextricably linked with female incontinence: 'The judgement of God upon your sex endures even today; and with it inevitably endures your position of criminal at the bar of justice. You are the gateway to the Devil.'

To remain a virgin is best, as the Church Fathers explained; though the term 'father' seems inappropriate for one, like Paulinus of Nola, who prayed: 'Christ, instruct the newly married pair through your holy bishop. Aid their pure hearts through his chaste hands, so that they may both agree on a compact of virginity.' But where the spirit was willing the flesh might be weak, and should this prove to be so, the duty of

13

such couples was equally clear: to 'be the source of consecrated virgins'.

For St Paul, a woman 'shall be saved in childbearing' – so long, of course, as she continues 'in faith and charity and holiness with sobriety'. Pope Pius XII reiterated the theme in his 'Address to Women of Catholic Action' (26 October 1941): 'A cradle consecrates the mother of the family; and more cradles sanctify and glorify her before her husband and children, before Church and homeland.' Virgin and Mother are the two high points of feminine achievement, the former being preferable, but the combination being presented as the ideal; and not as a remote metaphysical ideal, but one put forward as a fact maintained stubbornly by faith through two millennia.

Clement of Alexandria taught that 'pleasure sought for its own sake, even within the marriage bonds, is contrary to both law and reason'. And his was a comparatively liberal view, for did not the fourth-century religious teacher Aphraates, from the Church of Edessa, consider that only those who renounced married life could enter into communion with the Church, baptism being 'reserved as a privilege for celebates'? To his credit, St Augustine opposed the zealots who slighted women for having been raped while imprisoned as witnesses to the Faith. That he was obliged to do so itself speaks volumes.

There were occasions when the Church Fathers took a reasonably even-handed view. Lactantius, writing in his *Divine Institutes*, remarked in passing that the Christian Church, unlike the civil power, did not confine the sin of adultery to women. Yet the civil view in fact reflected the one taken of divorce in Deuteronomy, where provision is made for a man to divorce his wife because 'he hath found some uncleanness in her' but no corresponding provision is made for a wife. The Decalogue recorded in Exodus 20 brackets a neighbour's wife with his servants, between his house and his ox, as things not to be coveted. Women may have been honoured as mothers, but their social status remained subordinate.

The Hebraic tradition itself provides a crop of startling views, as vigorous as anything to be found in early Christian writing. The Menahoth, a tractate of the Babylonian Talmud dealing with the ritual of the Temple, commends this prayer: 'Blessed art thou who hast not made me a women.' The various books of the Talmud repeatedly lump women together with slaves and minors as exempt from various duties. In the Hagigah, a list of those excused appearance at the Temple puts women alongside 'the deaf, imbeciles, minors, slaves, hermaphrodites, those of unknown sex, the lame, the blind, the sick and the aged'. One of the midrashim in the Genesis section of the Midrash Rabbah offers an explanation for why Eve was created from Adam's rib rather than from some other part of his body: being hidden, the rib promotes modesty. Other parts, such as head, eye, ear, heart or foot, would have produced pride, coquetry, eavesdropping, jealousy and gad-about habits. As it is, the same text characterizes women as 'greedy, eavesdroppers, lazy, jealous, querulous and garrulous'. It therefore comes as no surprise that the Rabbinic tradition advised men to 'talk not much with womankind ... He that talks with womankind brings evil upon himself and ... at the last will inherit Gehenna.' Even this was a good deal more gallant than the observation in the Talmud that, 'Woman is a pitcher full of filth with its mouth full of blood.' An unusual image of woman as temptress, perhaps, though we are assured that 'all speed after her'.

Since the Christian tradition grew out of the Hebraic, it is hardly surprising that the Preacher's cry, 'Vanity of vanities, all is vanity,' should have commended itself to the early Church Fathers, who applied it with fervour to women. The complaint was of falsification – a sort of physical hypocrisy, or pretending to be what one is not:

Dignity in dress comes not from adding to what is worn but from eliminating all that is superfluous. The unnecessary luxuries that women wear, in fact, like tail-feathers must be clipped off, because they give rise only to shifting vanity and senseless pleasure. Because of such vanity and pleasure, women become flighty and vain as peacocks, and even desert their husbands.

Not only was this patriarchal attitude ubiquitous, it was also absurdly literal-minded and governed by a real fear of sexuality:

It is absolutely forbidden them [women] to add artificial hair, for it is unholy for them to add someone else's hair to their own. In such a case, on whom does the priest lay his hands? They deceive their husbands by all this extra hair, and at the same time offend the Lord as far as they can by dressing themselves up like harlots to distort the truth.

From top to toe, nothing escapes the eagle eye of the Church. Having dealt with the dangers of false hair at one end of the body, the turn of the feet follows:

There are women who manifest a very similar vanity in their footwear ... It is a matter of shame to have sandals plaited with the costliest gold, and even worse to decide, as some do, to have nails hammered into the soles in a circular pattern. Many even engrave love messages on them so they mark the earth in recurring patterns as they walk and stamp the eroticism of their own heart upon it with their footprints!

15

The mythical material of the pre-Christian tradition, which impinges freshly on the Western imagination at the Renaissance, did nothing to unbalance the preferences and prejudices established as natural up to and during the Middle Ages. The tales of classical mythology positively introduced new elements into the already unholy mixture. Renaissance men who pondered the myths of the ancient world found they confirmed that not only were women vain and illogical, but they were also, by all accounts, unreliable, violent and prone to terrifying acts of vengeance.

At the root of the mythic stories lay the familiar belief in feminine depravity. Scylla, for love of Minos, cuts from her father's head a lock of the golden hair that is the source of his strength, so irresistibly mirroring Delilah's betrayal of Samson when she cuts off his hair to deliver him to blindness, slavery and death. Procne, informed that her husband has deceived her and raped and mutilated her sister Philomela, kills her own son Itys and serves him to his father as a meal. Medea, in revenge for the murder of Aeson, persuades the daughters of Pelias to cut their father up and boil the pieces, promising it will restore his youth. The Danaides, at their father's behest, murder forty-nine of their fifty husbands on their wedding night. Orpheus is torn to pieces by the Thracian women whose advances he rejected.

To Pandora, the first woman, are attributed all the woes of mankind. As Hesiod has it:

> From her has sprung the race of womankind,
> The deadly race and tribes of womankind,
> Great pain to mortal men with whom they live,
> Helpmeets in surfeit – not in dreadful need.
> Just as in ceilinged hives the honeybees
> Nourish the drones, partners in evil deeds,
> And all day long, until the sun goes down,
> They bustle and build up white honeycombs,
> While they who stay inside the ceilinged hives
> Fill up their bellies from the others' work,
> So women are a curse to mortal men –
> As Zeus ordained – partners in evil deeds.

Pandora is a parallel figure to the temptress Eve, and the box she opens reflects the carnal knowledge of women and the immensity of evil it brought to men. The sort of devastation she was blamed for was acted out on smaller stages by countless other female mythological figures. A war afflicting whole peoples is fought over Helen of Troy. Zeus is almost continually deceived by goddesses such as Aphrodite, Thetis and, most of all, by Hera, his sister and wife, their marriage being a kind of permanent war. Gods like Zeus were apt to take further revenge, and

16

disputes such as theirs had a way of getting out of hand and spreading chaos amid mortals and immortals indiscriminately.

On the positive side, it is true, the Muses merge into an indissoluble choir to preside over music and poetry, and the Graces, smiling divinities attendant on Aphrodite, spread joy in the hearts of men whenever they are present. But such collective images are readily offset by those other groups – always female – whose names have passed into the language as stereotypes: the Furies, monstrous spirits of vengeance who took away from men all peace of mind and led them into misery and misfortune; the Gorgons, with their brazen claws, enormous teeth and heads covered with hissing serpents; the Harpies, tempest goddesses with faces like old hags and bodies of birds, who plundered other people's food, soiling with excrement what they did not carry away, spreading famine and filth; and the Sirens, sea-monsters avid for the blood of unsuspecting men whom they charmed with music before killing them brutally. Thus Odysseus, about to set sail again, was warned by Circe:

Thou shalt arrive where the enchanter Sirens dwell, they who seduce men. The imprudent man who draws near them never returns, for the Sirens, lying in the flower-strewn fields, will charm him with sweet song; but around them the bodies of their victims lie in heaps.

The monstrous Sirens and Harpies who devour innocent travellers were but an extreme manifestation of the sexual magic by which individuals like Aphrodite, Hera, Calypso or Circe could ensnare any man. These were sexually mature women and were, as such, regarded as destructive and evil. Only virgins emerge as helpful in classical mythology. While Penelope wins the highest admiration for her chastity, Homer charges the ghost of Agamemnon to haunt Clytemnestra for her infidelity and part in his murder.

Whether they were virginal and domestic like Penelope, or carnal and destructive like Aphrodite, the mythical women of the ancient world formed archetypal images of human females. Unable to cope with any multiplicity of characteristics united in one female, men allotted to women one of two basic roles. And the extra gloss of sexual depravity, with its attendant acts of savagery, betrayal and revenge, which classical mythology puts on many of its women, has remained powerful. The narrative patterns established then shaped the literary forms of a more modern era.

From time to time literature has recorded generous tributes to women – to individual women, at least – but almost invariably where they have conformed to a required domestic or religious ideal: Church, children and kitchen mark the boundaries of the respectable heroine's

17

world. Presuppositions about masculine and feminine qualities have made it difficult to delineate heroines of any other sort. The qualities required to make a hero have been defined exclusively for men. 'As anything intrepid, free, and in a prudent degree bold, becomes a man, so what is soft, tender and modest renders your sex more amiable,' explains Samuel Richardson.

Amiability, of course, is not the stuff of heroes. True, there are women in the Old Testament who are presented as heroines, such as Deborah, the opponent of Sisera, but she sees herself specifically as a mother – 'I am a mother in Israel' – and never entered the imagination of Western Europe with the same thoroughness as Jezebel or Delilah, who, like the Gorgons and Sirens, became embodiments of feminine attributes. It is always hard, in any case, to make virtuous characters interesting, though some writers have succeeded, as Jane Austen did with the virtuous Eleanor in *Sense and Sensibility*. Even she, however, seems to have found the very proper Fanny of *Mansfield Park* something of a struggle. When Dryden's Cleopatra announces, 'Nature meant me for a harmless household dove,' we yearn after Shakespeare's 'serpent of Old Nile' who would drink a man to his bed before the ninth hour.

The assumption has been that sexuality is so consuming and central an interest to women that they have little time or inclination left for anything else (anything more useful than reproduction being a by-product). Byron, who was certainly acquainted with a great many women, said:

> Love is of man's life a thing apart:
> 'Tis woman's whole existence.

That may look like an ungenerous and essentially male view. For a female view, we might turn to George Eliot's discussion of the proper function of a woman in *The Mill on the Floss*, where it is defined as making 'reasons for husbands to stay at home, and still stronger reasons for bachelors to go out'. This may be a long way from the cheerful directness of Dorothy Parker, but its movement is in that direction. 'If all the young ladies who attended the Yale promenade dance were laid end to end,' said Parker, 'no one would be the least surprised.' The prophet Lemuel's mother, who prompted him to ask rhetorically, 'Who can find a virtuous woman? For her price is above rubies,' would certainly have expressed none.

Bold imaginative heroines who set out to defy the domestic ideal, or appear to do so for a time, are usually rewarded with a husband if virtuous, but otherwise with death. Viola and Rosalind stride respectively through *Twelfth Night* and *As You Like It* dressed, the one as a page, the other as a shepherd, until, in the end, they find true love. And all the ladies of France in *Love's Labours Lost*, each the most becoming, beguiling and feminine of creatures, can look forward to appropriate husbands. But let one fault appear, or even the suspicion of one, and all changes. Such faults usually take the form of sexual failings, and the change is sudden: death, the threat of death or exile. Hermia is advised in *A Midsummer Night's Dream*:

> To you your father should be as a god;
> One that composed your beauties, yea and one
> To whom you are but a form in wax
> By him imprinted, and within his power
> To leave the figure or disfigure it.

Her father has suggested death as an alternative to marrying a man of *his* choice. Duke Theseus, more charitable, proposes merely that she

> Live a barren sister all her life
> Chanting faint hymns to the cold fruitless moon.

Othello's Desdemona dies because, it is supposed, 'She turned to folly and she was a whore.' The Duchess of Malfi dies because she chooses a husband for herself.

Two centuries later, the genre is maybe different but the punishment for opposing orthodoxy remains the same. Flaubert's Madame Bovary and Tolstoy's Anna Karenina suffer death to atone for dishonour. Mrs Gaskell represents the same view in *Ruth*, the eponymous heroine having been seduced at the age of sixteen and abandoned, pregnant, in a remote Welsh inn. After she has attempted suicide and is at the point of death, a deeply religious and kindly visitor considers 'it would be better for her to die at once'. Ruth is 'depraved' through seeming to think she has a right to have a baby. A stern moral code is in operation: Ruth, after leading a life of exemplary goodness and charity, must expiate her sin by dying of typhus. Esther, in the same author's *Mary Barton*, turns when utterly destitute to prostitution to support her baby. She, too, is required to die, once she has 'come to see the place familiar to her innocence', but not before it has been made clear that her failure has produced a startling change: 'A face which was so different from the old recollection of her dazzling beauty' that her niece does not recognize her.

Certainly literature contains any number of portraits of good women, from Herbert's Teresa of Avila and Milton's 'late espousèd saint' to Jonson's 'gentlewoman noble and virtuous', but their values are those of exceptional piety or of actual or potential wives and mothers. Effective women, as opposed to good ones, generally stride through the dramatic world dressed as men, like the heroines in Shakespeare's comedies, or else destroy the innocent and trusting, as does Thackeray's Becky Sharp, likened to a Siren with a tail 'writhing and diabolically hideous and slimy, flapping amongst bones, or curling round corpses'. For every bold and enterprising Britomartis, there are two retiring, timid figures in the mould of David Copperfield's child-bride Dora. Even the brave Rosalind exclaims:

> And – in my heart
> Lie there what hidden women's fear there will –
> We'll have a swashing and a martial outside.

Timidity is supposedly native to women, is indeed part of their attraction for such men as Edmund Burke, who declared: 'The beauty of women is considerable owing to their weakness or delicacy, and is even enhanced by their timidity, a quality of mind analogous to it.' Among grown humans, women are the children, devoted only to pleasure – 'children of a larger growth' as Lord Chesterfield said; consequently 'a man only trifles with them, plays with them, humours them and flatters them, as he does with a sprightly and forward child'. 'Most women,' Pope explained, 'have no characters at all':

> Pleasure the sex, as children birds, pursue,
> Still out of reach, yet never out of view;
> Sure, if they catch, to spoil the toy at most,
> To covet flying, and regret when lost.

Bernard Mandeville in 1709 requires a female interlocutor, Lucinda, to acknowledge that, 'Women are shallow creatures, a sound and penetrating judgement belongs only to men.' The idea of shallowness, with its implications that women are fools, is found in both fiction and non-fiction. And since women are empty-headed, only empty-headed suitors are appropriate for them. As Swift puts it:

> For such is all the sex's flight,
> They fly from learning, wit and light:
> They fly, and none can overtake
> But some gay coxcomb, or a rake.

Authors, from the end of the Middle Ages on, were never reluctant to point out the dangers to men in all of this. Young men were constantly warned that association with women was a sure path to intellectual atrophy. 'It has often been objected to female company,' wrote William Alexander in 1779, 'that it so enervates and relaxes the mind, and gives it such a turn for trifling, levity and dissipation, as render it altogether unfit for that application which is necessary to become eminent in any of the sciences.' In 1711, an essay in the *Spectator* remarked:

> If we observe the conduct of the fair sex, we find that they choose rather to associate themselves with a person who resembles them in the light and volatile humour which is natural to them. When we see a fellow loud and talkative, full of insipid life and laughter, we may venture to pronounce him a female favourite.

The twenty-three-year-old John Keats seemed determined not to fall into such loud insipid company: 'These things combined with the opinion I have of the generality of women – who appear to me as children to whom I would rather give a sugar plum than my time – form a barrier against matrimony which I rejoice in.' He must have had a very forbearing sister, since it was to her he was writing!

Intellectual endeavour is generally regarded as either beyond women or else unbecoming and destructive of their beauty or femininity, and the notion that women do themselves a grave disservice by entering into any sort of intellectual or political arena has flourished. As Lady Bradshaig wrote to the novelist Samuel Richardson:

> I do not approve of great learning in women. I believe that it rarely turns out to their advantage. No further would I have them to advance, than to what would enable them to write and converse with propriety, and make themselves useful in every stage of life. I hate to hear Latin out of a woman's mouth. There is something in it, to me, masculine.

As central as stupidity to the presentation of women are hypocrisy, double-dealing and sheer love of mischief. Shakespeare set the tone in *As You Like It*, with the usual sexual implications:

> Take thou no scorn to wear the horn;
> It was a crest ere thou wast born.
> Thy father's father wore it;
> And thy father bore it.

Harriet, in Etherege's *The Man of Mode*, is made to explain that she will certainly make fools of others, 'if it be but for the dear pleasure of dissembling'. Another girl in another play, Berinthia in Vanbrugh's *The Relapse*, lists the 'entertaining qualities' of women as 'hypocrisy, invention, deceit, flattery, mischief and lying'. A straight list of *dramatis personae* is enough to make the point: Cockwood, Loveit, Fidget, Squeamish, Rampant, Hoyden, Frail, Pert, Trull, Doxy, Froth, Plyant, Wishfort, Fainall, Mincing. And then there is perhaps the most shameless hypocrite of all, Fielding's Shamela:

> As soon as I had breakfasted, a Coach and Six came to the Door, and who should be in it but my Master. I immediately run up into my room, and stript, and washt, and drest my self as well as I could, and put on my prettiest round-ear'd Cap, and pulled down my Stays, to show as much as I could of my Bosom (for Parson Williams says that is the most beautiful part of a woman), and then I practised all my Airs before the Glass, and then I sat down and read a Chapter in the Whole Duty of Man.

As may be expected, vanity, too, plays a large part in the hypocrisy, especially in that constantly recurring theme, the use of cosmetics. The face of Philotime in *The Faerie Queene* may seem 'wondrous faire', but is,

> ... wrought by art and counterfetted show,
> Thereby more lovers unto her to call.

In disgust, Hamlet exclaims to Yorick's skull: 'Get you to my lady's chamber, and tell her, let her paint an inch thick, to this favour she must come.' The simple Irish song, 'The Mountains of Mourne', explains of the complexions of London ladies, likened to roses and cream, that,

> If at these roses you ventured to sip,
> The colour would all come away on your lip.

The mockery, denunciations and snide observations all stem from an inescapable dilemma. Looked upon primarily as sexual beings, women have been simultaneously prized and rejected for identical qualities. While Marlowe's Doctor Faustus cries:

> Was this the face that launch'd a thousand ships
> And burnt the topless towers of Ilium?
> Sweet Helen, make me immortal with a kiss,

Shakespeare explains tersely in the prologue to *Troilus and Cressida* that the whole bloodthirsty shambles of the Trojan War may be ascribed to the fact that:

The ravish'd Helen, Menelaus' queen,
With wanton Paris sleeps; and that's the quarrel.

Again and again the ambivalence appears. Hamlet reproaches his mother for living

> In the rank sweat of an enseamed bed,
> Stew'd in corruption, honeying and making love
> Over the nasty sty.

King Lear uses these terms to revile women's sexuality:

> Down from the waist they are Centaurs,
> Though women all above:
> But to the girdle do the gods inherit,
> Beneath is all the fiends':
> There's hell, there's darkness, there's the sulphurous pit,
> Burning, scalding, stench, consumption...

Beauty and chastity in women are incompatible. 'Those she [Nature] makes fair she scarce makes honest,' says Celia in *As You Like It*, 'and those she makes honest she makes very ill-favourably.' 'Nowhere,' complains John Donne, 'lives a woman chaste and fair'; and if you were to find such a paragon, there would be no point in telling him, since, by the time he reached her, she would have been 'False ... to two, or three'.

Swift, as we might expect, took a dim view of the appetites and tricks of women. First, there is the dreadful smell which the maids of honour give off in Brobdignag, which becomes apparent to Gulliver because of their carnal natures:

> They would often strip me naked from top to toe, and lay me at full length in their bosoms; where with I was much disgusted; because, to say the truth, a very offensive smell came from their skins ... the handsomest among these maids of honour would sometimes set me astride upon one of her nipples, with many other tricks, wherein the reader will excuse me for not being over particular.

The Queen of Laputa is represented as twice running off with an elderly, deformed and violent footman who beats her. This, the reader infers, is the sort of foolish thing women do. The women of Laputa in general, Gulliver assures us, are 'very fond of strangers', so it is not surprising that he envisages a scheme for raising taxes to be assessed on women in accordance with their own estimate of their beauty, whereas, 'constancy, chastity, good sense and good nature were not rated, because they would not bear the charge of collecting'.

Images of women easily corrupted have adhered to tradition with the vigour of ivy. The result has been a lengthy appraisal of the benefits of chastity. On Saturday, 23 June 1711, the London public was able to read in the *Spectator*:

Nothing makes women more esteemed by the opposite sex than chastity; whether it be that we always prize those most who are hardest to come at, or that nothing beside chastity, with its collateral attendants, truth, fidelity and constancy, gives the man a property in the person he loves, and consequently endears her to him above all things.

Significantly, the rarity value of chastity and the idea of property came together here: chaste women were rewarded by allowing their property to be transferred to their husbands. David Copperfield's mother, for example, found herself in just such a position with her second husband, Mr Murdstone, as she was forced through the grades of ownership:

'It is very hard,' said my mother, 'that in my own house – '
'*My* own house?' repeated Mr Murdstone. 'Clara...'
'*Our* own house, I mean,' faltered my mother, evidently frightened –
'I hope you know what I mean, Edward – it's very hard that in *your* own house...'

Milton puts both sides of the case for chastity with vigour and conviction:

... chastity:
She that has that is clad in complete steel...
No savage fierce, bandite, or mountaineer,
Will dare to soil her virgin purity.

Always provided, of course, that such a woman chooses to exercise this 'strength of heaven' – otherwise she is apt to lose eternity, because when lust

Lets in defilement to the inward parts,
The soul grows clotted by contagion,
Imbodies and imbrutes, till she quite lose
The divine property of her first being.

This is much the same idea as is to be found in Pope's *The Rape of the Lock*, where Belinda's sylphs desert her when they spy an image of a human lover lurking in her heart.

The rationale was clear enough in any number of writers on social themes in the eighteenth century. 'Public whoring,' Bernard Mandeville stated, 'is neither as criminal in itself nor so detrimental to the society as private whoring.' Doctor Johnson provided us with the reason when he wrote: 'Confusion of progeny constitutes the essence of the crime.' As a result, the double standard was constantly applied, notably by Johnson, who took the view that a man 'did his wife no very material injury ... if, for instance, from a mere wantonness of appetite, he steals privately to her chambermaid. I would not receive home a daughter who had run away from her husband on that account.' A writer to the *Gentleman's Magazine* confirmed the attitude quite frankly: 'I think there is no harm in seducing a girl who is not entitled to expect me for a husband. If she allows liberties in such expectations, she is a fool.'

Many women, naturally enough, pointed out the unreasonableness and iniquity of laying constant siege to female chastity and then blaming those who succumbed. Certainly, whatever degree of chastity was desirable in theory, practice was rather different and preferences ran somewhat counter to orthodoxy:

> I care not for these ladies
> Who must be wooed and won.
> Give me sweet Amaryllis,
> The wanton country maid.

There is even an inescapable device to ensure the submission of the chastest girl. Not even the staunchest refusal is proof against imagination, as Dryden makes clear:

> Fancy, the kindest Mistress of the two,
> Fancy had done what Phillis wou'd not do!
> Ah, Cruel Nymph, cease your distain,
> While I can dream you scorn in vain;
> Asleep or waking you must ease my pain.

The best defence, of course, was modesty, and that is what is constantly recommended. On Thursday, 20 September 1711, the *Spectator* published this:

You are to know Sir, that a Jezabel (so called by the neighbourhood from displaying her pernicious charms at her window) appears constantly dressed at her sash, and has a thousand little tricks and fooleries to attract the eyes of all the idle young fellows in the neighbourhood.

At much the same time (6 July 1713), the *Guardian* made an analogous point about a fashion for displaying the breast:

> Every man is not sufficiently qualified with age and philosophy to be an indifferent spectator of such allurements. The eyes of young men are curious and penetrating, their imaginations are of a roving nature, and their passions under no discipline or restraint.

Addison joined the campaigning, writing in the same issue of the *Guardian* that Spartan girls were only clothed in dresses slashed to reveal their limbs until 'the shape of their limbs and the complexion of their bodies had gained their ends'. At that point, their 'garments were closed up, and stitched together with the greatest care imaginable'. 'Nothing,' added Addison, appealing to his female readers' vanity, 'bestows so much beauty on a woman as modesty.' He even makes an extravagant claim for its efficacy in reinstating 'the widow in her virginity'. If the nineteenth century could not take quite such a polite and sanguine view, it certainly continued to emphasize the same essential trust in modesty:

> Know, she who in her dress reveals
> A fine and modest taste, displays
> More loveliness than she conceals.

The castigation of vanity and the advocacy of modesty both helped to reinforce the natural hierarchy of the sexes. Edmund Spenser put the matter as clearly as anyone when he made these equivalencies:

> The one imperfect, mortall foeminine;
> Th' other immortall, perfect, masculine.

This hierarchical view, if not universal, has been extremely widespread and has altered little in the course of time. Nikos Kazantzakis's novel *Zorba the Greek* gives us a character who ascribes his deafness to the fact that his father insulted the Virgin Mary, and exclaims, 'God be praised! She might have made me blind or an idiot, or hunchbacked, or even – God Almighty preserve us! – she might have made me a girl.'

There have even been women who took a similar view, among them Lady Mary Wortley Montagu, who said, 'My only consolation for being of that Gender has been the assurance it has given me of never being marry'd to any one amongst them.'

26

Other women of her time, if they did not lament their natural state, certainly saw their duty in submissive obedience and the tact required by etiquette. 'She who marries ought to lay it down for an indisputable maxim, that her husband must govern absolutely and entirely.' However clever a woman might be, her prime duty was to avoid the exposure of her husband's ignorance. 'When he judges wrong,' says Lady Sarah Pennington, 'never flatly contradict, but lead him insensibly into an opinion in so discreet a manner, that it may seem entirely his own.' This was very much the view taken by the literary men of the time. Fielding offers this advice to a friend about choosing a wife:

> Superior judgement may she own thy lot
> Humbly advise, but contradict thee not.

And Pope, addressing Martha Blount in the second of his *Moral Essays*, speaks approvingly of

> She who ne'er answers till a husband cools
> Or, if she rules him, never shows she rules
> Charms by accepting, by submitting sways.

This portrayal of the proper relations between the sexes has been one of the most enduring literary concerns. Dr James Fordyce's view, voiced in 1776, that 'Providence designed women for a state of dependence and consequently of submission,' was still being passionately argued for in the nineteenth century by Sir James Fitzjames Stephens in opposition to John Stuart Mill. The arguments have a familiar ring. 'It is true,' thunders Sir James, 'that the actually existing generation of women do not dislike their position.' The whole idea, moreover, offends his common sense, and he insists with quiet reasonableness that 'to establish by law rights and duties which assume that people are equal when they are not is like trying to make clumsy feet look handsome by the help of tight boots'. 'Men and women are not equals,' Sir James states flatly. He goes on to imagine a situation where

... men and women are made as equal as law can make them and ... public opinion followed the law. Let us suppose that marriage became a mere partnership dissoluble like another; that women were expected to earn their living just like men; that the notion of anything like protection due from one sex to the other was thoroughly rooted out; that men's manners to women became identical with their manners to men; that the cheerful concessions to acknowledged weakness, the obligation to do for a woman a thousand things which it would be insulting to offer to do for a man, which we inherit from a different order of ideas, were totally exploded.

What, he asks, would the result of all this be? It would, he claims, be that 'women would become men's slaves and drudges, that they would be made to feel their weakness and to accept its consequences to the very utmost'.

Such an attitude would certainly have commended itself to Priscilla Wakefield, who, at the end of the eighteenth century, tells her readers that, 'as a more rational education prevails, women will be better acquainted with their relative situation and as their ideas are more defined they will perceive that there can be but one head or chief in any family'. Even calls for better education were, it seems, merely to enforce women's obedience, and to help to convince them of their naturally inferior status.

There were literary attempts to help with explaining this inferiority. One widely held view was that women have no souls, but are a species of animal – pleasant enough, but spiritless. Dryden speaks of them as 'ferae nature', wild game – something to be hunted, and Swift mentions in passing that the Laputians would 'praise a woman or any other animal'. Samuel Butler expressed the probability succinctly:

> The souls of women are so very small,
> That some believe they've none at all.

Other views have been much more elaborate and have divided women into various types. An account provided in the *Spectator* in the early eighteenth century may at least be said to allow that women do have souls, though that does not give quite the comfort anticipated:

In the beginning God made the souls of womankind out of different materials, and in a separate state from their bodies.

The souls of one kind of women were formed out of those ingredients which compose a swine. A woman of this make is a slut in her house and a glutton at her table. She is uncleanly in her person, a slattern in her dress, and her family is no better than a dunghill.

A second sort of female was formed out of the same materials that enter into the composition of a fox. Such a one is what we call a notable discerning woman, who has an insight into every thing whether it be good or bad. In this species of females there are some virtuous and some vicious.

A third kind of women were made up of canine particles. These are what we commonly call scolds, who imitate the animal out of which

28

they were taken, that are always busy and barking, that snarl at every one who comes in their way, and live in perpetual clamour.

The fourth kind of women were made out of the earth. These are your sluggards, who pass away their time in indolence and ignorance, hover over the fire a whole winter, and apply themselves with alacrity to no kind of business but eating.

The fifth species of females were made out of the sea. These are women of variable uneven tempers, sometimes all storm and tempest, sometimes all calm and sunshine. The stranger who sees one of these in her smiles and smoothness, would cry her up for a miracle of good-humour; but on a sudden her looks and her words are changed, she is nothing but fury and outrage, noise and hurricane.

The sixth species were made up of the ingredients which compose an ass, or beast of burden. These are naturally exceeding slothful, but, upon the husband's exerting his authority, will live upon hard fare, and do everything to please him. They are however far from being averse to venereal pleasures, and seldom refuse a male companion.

The cat furnished materials for a seventh species of women, who are of a melancholy, froward, unamiable nature, and so repugnant to the offers of love that they fly in the face of their husband when he approaches them with conjugal endearments. This species of women are likewise subject to little thefts, cheats, and pilferings.

The mare with a flowing mane, which was never broke to any servile toil and labour, composed an eighth species of women. These are they who have little regard for their husbands, who pass away their time in dressing, bathing, and perfuming; who throw their hair into the nicest curls, and trick it up with the fairest flowers and garlands. A woman of this species is a very pretty thing for a stranger to look upon, but very detrimental to the owner, unless it be a king or a prince who takes a fancy to such a toy.

The ninth species of females were taken out of the ape. These are such as are both ugly and ill-natured, who have nothing beautiful in themselves, and endeavour to detract from or ridicule every thing which appears so in others.

The *Spectator* may not have taken an especially comforting view of women's souls, but even that was rather better than having none at all, which is the condition of women to be inferred from judgements made in the Scottish courts even in the early twentieth century. When the Scottish universities returned Members of Parliament, and women graduates tried to exercise their right to vote, the courts declared that, 'only men could vote for Parliament and that the word "person" accordingly meant "male person"'. If prejudice and custom account in part for the way women have been presented in literature, another source of inequity is the law itself. The solemnization of matrimony in the Established Church, for example, calls attention to the fact that 'they two shall be one flesh'. But plainly, the flesh that counts is the husband's as the law has made clear:

> By marriage, the husband and wife are one person in law; that is, the very being, or legal existence of the woman is suspended during the marriage ... A woman's personal property, by marriage becomes absolutely the husband's.

In fact, the law scarcely seems to have protected women at all. Here is what William Alexander has to say on double standards of adultery: 'He may riot with impunity in adulterous amours; if the wife retaliates by copying his example, he immediately procures a divorce and may turn her out without subsistence.' There were husbands who dispensed with the formalities of a divorce and took their wives to market with a halter about their necks and, just like cattle, sold them. Thomas Hardy opens his novel *The Mayor of Casterbridge* with such a sale, the husband drunkenly exclaiming:

> 'I don't see why men who have got wives, and don't want 'em, shouldn't get rid of 'em as these gipsy fellows do their old horses ... Why shouldn't they put 'em up and sell 'em by auction to men who are in need of such articles?'

He need not have been so defensive. Selling a wife was popularly believed to be a perfectly legal and valid form of divorce. It was never formally sanctioned by the judiciary, but the sales created their own aura of legality: market tolls were paid, minimum prices set, witnesses found, and the halter symbolically handed over to the new buyer. The idea must have appealed to many a husband, for one popular song went,

> Bought a wife on Sunday,
> Brought her home on Monday,
> Beat her well on Tuesday,
> Sick she was on Wednesday,
> Dead she was on Thursday,
> Buried she was on Friday,
> Glad I was on Saturday,
> And now I'll buy another.

The Victorian critics who were shocked by Hardy's tale would have regarded such a rhyme as fanciful, but it was not all that far removed

30

from practices at the top end of the market, where Byron tells us of fashionable daughters: 'Some are soon bagged and some reject three dozen.'

What, therefore, was the ideal? That has hardly changed: submission, domesticity, service, chastity and, of course, beauty. 'Of average height with a build like a soft-drink bottle – plenty on top and a lot more on the bottom – Norma was the curvy kind of young woman most men dream of.' Not very sophisticated perhaps, but not such a far cry either from that 'serpent of old Nile', Shakespeare's Cleopatra, whose appearance 'beggared all description'. As Enobarbus says:

> ... she makes hungry where most she satisfies,
> For vilest things become themselves in her.

Quite how such overwhelming sexuality is to be made compatible with domesticity is not clear, but there can be no question about the desirability of the stay-at-home wife. 'A good wife,' Sir Thomas Overbury tells us,

> is a man's best moveable, a scion incorporate with the stock bringing sweet fruit. She frames her nature into his howsoever: the hyacinth follows not the sun more willingly. Stubbornness and obstinacy are herbs that grow not in her garden.

Literature is packed with such views, from the biblical examples of Miriam, Sarah, Rebeccah and Ruth to John Ferne's expostulation: 'I had rather have hard something sayd of gentle and meek women, for it is evil examples to let them understand of such sturdye manlye women as those have been which erewhile thou hast tolde of.' And here is the judgement of a writer in the late eighteenth century: 'The same applause which we involuntarily bestow upon honour, courage, and spirit in *men* we as naturally confer upon chastity, modesty and gentleness in women.'

The eighteenth century is, in fact, a good period for the expression of ideals about womankind, sometimes flippant, but sometimes serious and moving. The young Pope asks rhetorically, through the mouth of grave Clarissa:

> Say, why are beauties praised and honoured most,
> The wise man's passion and the vain man's toast?
> Why deck'd with all that land and sea affords?
> Why angels call'd and angel-like ador'd?
> How vain are all these glories, all our pains,
> Unless good sense preserves what beauty gains;

31

> That men may say, when we the front box grace,
> 'Behold the first in virtue as in face.'

George, Lord Lyttelton composed in 1734 a monody on the death of his wife Lucy which provides what certainly appears to be a heart-felt tribute to what he regarded as the wholly admirable qualities of a much-loved companion. She was, as may be seen from the extract, retiring, modest, beautiful, quite without vanity, religious, a chaste wife and a loving mother. It is an almost perfect example of what is so often presented as an ideal:

> O shades of Hagley, where is now your boast?
>   Your bright inhabitant is lost,
> You she preferr'd to all the gay resorts
> The pomp of cities and the pride of courts.
> Her modest beauties shunn'd the public eye
>   To your sequestered dales
>   And flow'r embroider'd vales
> From an admiring world she chose to fly;
> With Nature there retir'd and Nature's God,
>   The silent paths of wisdom trod,
> And banished every passion from her breast,
>   But those, the gentlest and the best,
> Whose holy flames with energy divine
> The virtuous heart enliven and improve,
> The conjugal, and the maternal love.

Such a paradigm of womanhood has changed little. The 'widowed' Tennyson, mourning his friend Hallam, portrays imaginatively his view of a wife's relationship to her husband. It is a portrait enshrining much the same attitude, not at all polemical or passionate, but drawing attention to exactly those qualities for which women have always been valued – their service, their devotion, their acknowledgement of man's superiority and their emotional fervour:

> For him she plays, to him she sings
>   Of early faith and plighted vows;
>   She knows but matters of the house,
> And he, he knows a thousand things.

> Her faith is fixt and cannot move,
>   She darkly feels him great and wise,
>   She dwells on him with faithful eyes,
> 'I cannot understand: I love.'

A century earlier, it was being explained that, 'Women were formed to temper Mankind, and soothe them into tenderness and compassion.' And a century before that, Ben Jonson was announcing 'That Women are but Men's shadowes':

> At morne and even, shades are longest;
> At noon, they are short, or none:
> So men at weakest, they are strongest,
> But grant us perfect, the're not known.

Why this was so is explained by Sir Thomas Overbury in the early seventeenth century: 'A very woman is a dough-baked man, or a she meant well towards man, but fell two bows short, strength and understanding.' Not that men lamented this shortcoming in all respects. Professor Higgins may have asked plaintively, 'Oh why can't a woman be more like a man?' but he was certainly not looking for too many signs of self-assertion. Submission is all. The classic statement turns up in Shakespeare's *Taming of the Shrew*:

> Thy husband is thy lord, thy life, thy keeper,
> Thy head, thy sovereign; one that cares for thee...
> And craves no other tribute at thy hands
> But love, fair looks, and true obedience...
> I am ashamed that women are so simple
> To offer war where they should kneel for peace,
> Or seek for rule, supremacy and sway,
> When they are bound to serve, love and obey.

This part of the projected ideal is unchanging: 'I lighted,' says Uncle Agostini in *Zorba the Greek*, 'on a good docile woman who gave me only sons. I've never seen her raise her eyes to me in defiance.' What men have longed for, in fact, is that 'angel in the house' of whom Coventry Patmore tells:

> The best things that the best believe
> Are in her face so kindly writ
> The faithless, seeing her, conceive
> Not only heaven, but hope of it.

There has certainly been a continuous chorus of praise. Women are allowed to be 'wonderful' – provided they will conform. That is why the very poet who tells us with great liberality that:

> Female and male God made the man;
> His image is the whole not half,

goes on to explain at once, with perfect confidence and equanimity:

> Man must be pleased; but him to please
> Is woman's pleasure.

Woman's pleasure, indeed, is the root of the trouble. What is required is both motherhood and chastity. To that ideal, every honour will be paid:

> Mother and maiden
> Was never none but she;
> Well may such a lady
> God's mother be.

Behind this hope lies the stubborn fear, voiced by Pope, that 'Every woman is at heart a rake'; and, as Kipling suggested, the belief that all women are really alike:

> The colonel's lady and Judy O'Grady
> Are sisters under the skin.

The plaintive cry of men, re-echoed over the centuries, is finally voiced by Thomas Campion:

> Lost is our freedom
> When we submit to women so
> Why do we need 'em
> When in their best they work our woe?

In the unfolding literature of our own days, how much is shown to be changing and how much remains unchanged in men's perception of women and vice versa? This is a vast and complex area of study, and one in which individual readers must make their own discoveries and judgements. The voices of the women whose views and testimonies make up the bulk of the book reflect both contributions to and indicators of the shifts, advances and dissensions involved in this never-ceasing process.

2
Women and Muslim Society

The Qur'an opens with the words: 'In the name of God the merciful, the compassionate ...' Although the word for God in Arabic, Allah, has a feminine ending, it is treated grammatically as masculine. However, the word for 'compassion' or 'mercy', *rahma*, is derived from the same root as *rahim*, meaning 'womb'. Some Muslim scholars regard the 'Lord of the Universe' as embracing both masculine and feminine qualities while transcending both. Nevertheless, in popular belief, Allah is certainly masculine. The writer Nawal el-Saadawi tells in *The Hidden Face of Eve: Women in the Arab World* of how she once asked innocently in class why Allah was masculine not feminine, only to be threatened with failure in her exams unless she stopped asking impious questions. When she reached home, her relatively liberal, open-minded father explained that Allah might only be addressed as masculine because of the 'superiority of males over females'.

For Muslims, the Qur'an is the word of God. To read it with full comprehension requires a great deal of linguistic sophistication, but its many-layered meanings also make it accessible at simpler levels. Yet the Qur'an is not the only source of Islamic faith and practice. There is also the Hadith, a body of literature relating the Sayings of the Prophet Muhammad as reported by his Companions. The society in which the Prophet lived in seventh-century Arabia differed fundamentally from most present-day Muslim societies. The customs forbidden by the Qur'an and the Hadith, and those left untouched, were concerned with the life of the original Muslim community. The problem facing modern Muslims has always been to interpret the message of the Prophet for situations he could never have envisaged and in societies of far greater complexity than his own.

Although in Arabic, as in English, the masculine is said to embrace the feminine, the Qur'an often expresses itself explicitly to 'believing men and believing women', implying that the spiritual status and duties of men and women are the same. In principle, men and women have

35

equal rights to education, over property and within marriage. In practice, many women in Muslim countries suffer grossly unjust laws and customs – these injustices apparently being sanctioned by the Qur'an as well as by the words and example of the Prophet himself. The Hadith may help with the Qur'an's interpretation, but many apocryphal or contradictory sayings retain a firm hold in popular attitudes and belief.

An important difference as to how the story of Adam and Eve is treated in the Qur'an and Genesis is that the former does not hold Eve solely responsible for the Fall of Man. It contains no account of Eve acting as Satan's instrument in seducing Adam away from God and calling down the curse of original sin, but shows Adam and Eve as equally responsible and possessing equal hope of salvation. Nevertheless women continue to suffer a stigma derived from traditional stories in which women and the devil are allies in a war against godliness and men.

Because of their generalized or equivocal expression, many Qur'anic precepts are open to interpretation. Even where a verse is explicit, scholars may still disagree about its intention, hence its application. In the Qur'an, the testimony of one man is taken as equal to that of two women, although there are those who will argue that this is not what is meant. Yet the effect of such ambivalence is that Islam often comes to look like a monolith of static ideas divorced from historic reality; but then traditional attitudes always were a powerful influence on the development of Muslim law, the Shariah, which was finally codified between 400 to 500 years after the Prophet's death.

The scholars responsible for the development and application of Muslim law over the centuries at times showed themselves capable of revising their opinions, on occasion as a result of experience in countries with different traditions. Muslim law is not necessarily more rigidly unchanging than Muslim society, though the law tends to lag behind social change. At a time like the present, on the other hand, the resurgence of Islamic fundamentalism as a political force inevitably means that Islam and its laws become inextricably linked with attempts to return to less sophisticated traditions in a general reaction to Western materialism. Just as inevitably, the reaction of fundamentalism represents a set-back to the liberalization of the status and rights of women in many Muslim countries.

Central to the story of the birth of Islam are two remarkable women: Khadija, the Prophet's first wife and disciple; and Aisha, the girl who became his youngest wife and the source for much of the Hadith. Khadija was a rich trader who employed Muhammad, then twenty-five and penniless, as agent on one of her caravans. Impressed by his intelligence, integrity and quiet authority, she proposed to him through a woman friend intermediary, and they married, even though she was forty and twice widowed and had rejected many of the wealthiest noblemen of Mecca.

To begin with, Muhammad ran their business, but in time, and despite the six children she bore him, Khadija shouldered more and more of the burden. When her husband's long spiritual search culminated in his first revelation, it was her reassurance that quelled his doubts. She became his mainstay during his first eleven years as a prophet, their spiritual rapport being such that he had many revelations in her presence. There is no indication of Muhammad showing susceptibility to the charms of other women during the twenty-five years of his marriage to Khadija, even though he could, as one of the leading men of Mecca, have enjoyed his pick of well-born virgins. After her death, he made nine more marriages, and some Muslim writers of earlier periods claimed great feats of sexual prowess for him, featuring Muhammad as superlative in all things and extolling him as a model for all men.

This helps to reflect one of the main differences in attitude between the ethical traditions of Christianity and Islam. In Christianity, following the celibate example of its founder, sexual feelings are part of man's sinful nature and therefore impure. In Islam, sex is a divine gift of enjoyment and so not overshadowed by any sense of guilt. One oft-quoted Saying of the Prophet runs to the effect that the three things he loved most in life were perfume, women and the pleasure to be found in prayer.

Muhammad was conscientious about treating his wives equally, spending the nights with each in turn and encouraging them to develop their individual talents. Sawdah, the elderly widow of one of the first Muslims, worked fine leather goods. Zaynab, a war-widow, was revered as 'Mother of the Poor' for her generosity. Umm Salama, another war-widow, acted as an imam for women and was an astute political adviser to Muhammad. The youngest, Aisha, became so knowledgeable in religious matters that he told his followers to consult her when he was away, although she was then still only a teenager.

After he had made his nine marriages, a revelation came to him that forbade him to marry again or to supplant any of his existing wives. He had married Aisha when he was about fifty-five and she six. She joined his household, with all her toys, four years or so later. In due course, Muhammad realized that, despite himself, he loved Aisha more than his other wives. When Amr Ibn al-As, later conqueror of Egypt, asked Muhammad who was closest to his heart, the Prophet answered, 'Aisha'. When the other wives complained that he spent most of his time in her apartment, he could only say, 'She is the only woman in whose company I receive my revelations.' Accepting that Aisha had his heart, the wives agreed he should spend his last illness in her apartment. He died in her arms, leaving her childless and only eighteen years old.

37

None of the Prophet's wives ever remarried, which meant, for Aisha, spending almost fifty years alone. Yet she was already accustomed to being consulted by men many years her senior on all religious matters; and when her father, Abu Bakr, having become Islam's first caliph, died only two years after Muhammad, it was she, rather than her less able elder brother, Abd al-Rahman, whom he elected to administer his estate and entrusted with his younger children. Thus may a woman be seen as occupying a position of respect and independent responsibility, not only in the lifetime of the Prophet, but also during Islam's founding years.

Certain Muslim jurists have seemed to argue that women possess two distinct rights in marriage: one to sexual fulfilment and another to children. Sexuality not being tainted with sin in Islam, sexual pleasure shared between husband and wife is one of the foundations of marriage. Sexual dissatisfaction alone may, for men and women alike, provide grounds for divorce. It is in their understanding of female sexuality that Muslim cultures show certain broad divergences. The twelfth-century scholar, al-Ghazali, did not consider the sexual act to be one of male aggression, or action, and female submission, or passivity. Men and women, he thought, differed only in the 'pattern of ejaculation'. 'The woman's ejaculation is a much slower process and during the process her sexual desire grows stronger and to withdraw from her before she reaches her pleasure is harmful to her.'

Al-Ghazali also cited the Prophet's view that it was a major fault in a man to have sex with his partner without first 'caressing, [being] tender with her in words and gestures and [lying] down beside her for a while so that he does not harm her, by using her for his satisfaction, without letting her get satisfaction from him'. Many Muslims today would be astonished at such advice, and more readily in agreement with the Pakistani commentator, Abul A'la Maududi, who wrote in 1939 that not only are men active and women passive sexually, but that 'man being the active partner has been justly regarded as superior by Islam'.

An example of the selective interpretation of the Qur'an to suit personal fancy may be found in the history of concubinage in the Muslim world. Muhammad Asad, a famous scholar and convert to Islam, takes the view that neither the Qur'an nor the example of the Prophet sanctioned men to take their slave women as concubines. Sex outside marriage is unlawful in Islam, and, he held, the edicts of the Qur'an forbade a man to have sex even with his slave woman, unless he married her. Asad's view runs directly counter to both popular opinion and the practice of many eminent Muslims in history, caliphs among them. Yet the Qur'an is explicit in its condemnation of extra-marital sex, and the penalty it lays down for fornication is 100 lashes for both the man and the woman. Such a penalty may, however, only be exacted in the unlikely event of there being four reliable eye-witnesses to actual coition.

Within four generations of the Prophet's death came the birth of the Abbasid dynasty and the founding of Baghdad. As they encountered influences more sophisticated than their own desert culture, so the conquering Arabs began to use their new wealth to seclude and 'consume' women to a degree hitherto unthinkable. When the caliphate moved to Baghdad, the noblewomen of the court found themselves confined to harems guarded by eunuchs, and heavily veiled in the Persian and Byzantine style. The women of the aristocracy, potentially the most educated and influential of their society, were thus removed from the public world. But far more attractive to certain caliphs than their wives were their concubines. Wives brought demanding relatives along with them and, in the event of divorce, acquired fortunes as settlement. Slave women, by contrast, had no relatives to bother with and could be discarded at a whim (although the law forbade the sale of a woman who had borne her master's child). And so it came about that all but three of the Abbasid caliphs were the sons of slave women, including the great Harun al-Rashid himself.

Nevertheless, while the negative effect of the harem was to close much of the outside world to women, in its positive aspects it gave them almost unfettered powers of command within their sphere and opened up avenues of independence and enterprise. Under the supremacy of Muslim medicine, not outstripped in Europe until the eighteenth century, women were trained in the medical schools of the medieval Muslim empire, and often joined their fathers and brothers in group practice. Such women were the equals of men in their medical knowledge, and, although a male doctor could enter the harem only in the direst emergency, women doctors were allowed to treat any patient who came to them. The income of a woman doctor was usually less than her male counterpart's, but it afforded her substantial independence. And while none of the surviving Arab medical treatises is directly credited to a woman, women undoubtedly contributed much to contemporary understanding of obstetrics and gynaecology. They certainly acted as surgeons and instructors in medical schools.

In other spheres, too, there were exceptions to the rule that women could succeed only under the dominance of men. The protection of the family allowed a few women to excel as lawyers, among them Amat al-Wahid, who studied law under her father, a prominent jurist, and herself became renowned as a brilliant judge. Accomplished poets, men as well as women, were in great demand, and successful extemporizers and praise-singers at court could win fame and fortune. There was even at the court of al-Mutawakkil a poetess, al-Fadl, who defied convention and freely took lovers. When a man challenged her and said, 'I prefer a horse that has not been broken in. What a difference between an untouched pearl and one that has been pierced and threaded into a necklace,' she retorted, 'But it is not pleasant to ride a horse that has not yet been disciplined by the bridle nor known a rider. And pearls are useless unless they have been pierced and arranged on a thread.' There were other women, royal and bourgeois, who paid with their lives for incurring the merest breath of such scandal.

The profane world of al-Fadl had its sacred counterpart in the story of Rabi'ah al-Adawiyyah, who, having lived a life of desperate poverty as a humble slave labourer, became one of the most renowned and influential of Sufis (Muslim mystics), 'on fire with love and ardent desire ... consumed with her passion for God'. Her position in the popular Muslim canon compares approximately with that of St Teresa of Avila in Christian tradition. Frequently honoured as a 'man in spirit', her watchword was 'The Neighbour, not the house', by which she meant she sought God, not paradise.

Despite its corruption, the brilliance and glitter of the medieval Arab world is still celebrated by Muslims, while its secluded though often powerful and glamorous women have come to represent a bastion of privileged femininity. The wealthy women of the later Ottoman era, though subject to rigorous exclusion from public life, were none the less objects of envy for Lady Mary Wortley Montagu, wife of the British Ambassador in Istanbul. 'Turkish Ladys are perhaps freer than any ladys in the Universe,' she wrote in 1718. Their complete independence in running the harem often created the impression it was they who excluded men from their world rather than the other way about. The so-called master of the house could seem no more than a guest in his wife's domain, for should he espy the slippers of a woman visitor outside the door, he must not even enter his wife's apartment. Lady Mary noted that, provided they had trusted confederates, these Turkish noblewomen had greater opportunities than Englishwomen to take lovers if they wished. Even so, she said, despite the legality of polygamy and concubinage in Turkey, 'No Man of Quality makes use of this Liberty [and] no Woman of Rank would suffer it.'

One young Turkish woman, who escaped from the harem to the 'freedom' of Paris early in the twentieth century, noted with great disappointment: 'I suppose we Turkish women, who have so much time to devote to culture, become unreasonably exacting.' But being so superbly educated meant that such women found the world of the harem over-constricted. The young Fatma Aliye, later the most famous woman writer of the closing years of the Ottoman era, was fortunate in attracting the attention of the well-known author, Ahmet Mithat, who fostered her ambition to write for publication. This in itself was considered almost indecent in an aristocratic girl, and it was not until she had persuaded her far less talented husband, the aide-de-camp to the Sultan, to let her publish a translation of a French novel that her gifts were unlocked. Her father later declared: 'If my daughter ... had been educated ... in a more systematic manner, she could have been a genius.' He not only helped her to negotiate with publishers, but also solicited her advice about his own work. Her central feminist interest, which provided the themes of all her novels and articles, was focused more precisely when she became editor of one of the first Turkish newspapers of its kind, the *Newspaper for Ladies*, and encouraged other Ottoman women to publish books through the paper's printing house.

It was in Egypt that the veil finally began to fall away from the faces of Muslim gentlewomen. In 1923, Huda Shaarawi, the daughter of a Circassian concubine and recent widow of a respected pasha, unveiled her face among the crowds on Cairo's railway station. This daring act was the leading public gesture to be made in her work as founder and leader of the Egyptian Feminist Union (EFU). As an association of aristocratic women, the EFU succeeded during its very first year in persuading Egypt's Islamic court to institute a minimum marriageable age of sixteen for girls and eighteen for boys. It subsequently struggled for many years to achieve reforms in the marriage and divorce laws and in the control of women's working conditions.

The founder of the Egyptian feminist movement had herself been forced to marry her elderly guardian when she was only thirteen, though was able to leave him after a year when he returned to the concubine he had agreed to put aside on their marriage – a stipulation insisted on by Huda's concubine mother. Towards the end of her life, Huda was awarded the highest state decoration of Egypt for services to the nation, but not until almost ten years after her death did Egyptian women win the vote – in 1956, the same year as the women of Switzerland! Her action in unveiling her face in the 1920s had, however, created a symbol considerably more powerful than the bra-burning of Western feminists in the 1960s. The veil thereafter became the main indicator of the advance or regression of the cause of women's rights in all Muslim societies.

Both Huda Shaarawi and her mother had been powerless to prevent her child marriage to her elderly guardian. The development of Muslim law has tended to emphasize the feminine need for protection, some-times at the expense of an equally important right to financial independence and education. The schools of Muslim law, moreover, feature a wide range of opinions as to when a woman needs a guardian. At one extreme, they say 'always'. Others maintain it is only necessary if she is inexperienced or a minor, or if she is either very rich or very poor and hence in peril of exploitation. Still other jurists consider that a grown woman should be as free as any man to negotiate contracts or to marry.

And all exponents of these differing positions cite the Qur'an as their authority. The Muslim apologist will therefore see the practice of child marriage as an example of social custom conveniently distorting Islamic law to its own ends. The barbaric practices of clitoridectomy or infibulation in pre-pubescent girls, still prevalent in some Muslim societies, will no doubt be seen to fall under a similar heading – a carry-over from the customs of the North African desert tribes. This at once raises the question of why it continues to be tolerated when Muslim law has dealt so sternly and confidently with other matters.

One indispensable feature of Muslim marriage is the *mahr*, a payment of goods or services from the groom to the bride. Without it, no marriage can be valid. The Qur'an insists that the payment be made to the bride herself, not to her male relatives, and emphasizes that a woman should control her own affairs. The nature of the *mahr* is a matter for agreement between the parties, and is usually a substantial settlement of money or property. A woman who divorces her husband must return the *mahr*, but one divorced by her husband may keep it. A *mahr* of high value is sometimes set to deter a man from divorcing his wife casually.

In quite recent times, certain Muslim jurists have ruled that a woman's entitlement to a *mahr* is in virtue of her making herself sexually available to her husband. This tendency to reify women and subordinate their needs to those of men is not uncommon, both in the application and the popular understanding of Muslim law. Jurists seem to perceive no contradictions in ignoring a woman's right to sexual fulfilment and denying the ideal of marriage as a haven of mutual love.

The Muslim divorce laws allow a man to divorce his wife simply by pronouncing the formula for repudiation before two witnesses. For a woman to obtain a divorce, however, the intervention of the courts is required. More often than not, it is then denied at the discretion of the judge, unless the woman is in demonstrable physical danger.

The Qur'an maintains an equity between men and women in its injunctions to be chaste and modest in mode of dress, but the traditions of the veiling of women and the harem mentality have always gone hand in hand in Muslim tradition. The modern mind is, of course, aware of how the zones of sexual attraction shift according to whatever is revealed or concealed by current female styles of fashion. The pre-occupation of the fundamentalists in Islam with pressing women to readopt the veil may therefore seem decidedly naïve. It also carries other implications. On the one hand, the 'chaste' style depersonalizes women; on the other, the erotic charge represented by women in the imagination of men simply takes on other aspects.

Middle Eastern society is suffused with an intense sexuality. In popular belief, neither men nor women are in full control of their sexual passions, while men fear women as agents of chaos and destruction. There is, in fact, a Hadith to the effect that, when a man and woman are alone together, Satan is also present. At the same time, where strict segregation is the order of the day, the competitive display of beauty and wealth is an important aspect of women's ranking of other families and of prospective brides for their menfolk. In societies in transition between the extended family of the harem and fresh social structures dictated by the need of rapidly expanding economies for a desegregated workforce, considerable tensions seem inevitable between cultural patterns and the realities of working lives. A woman entrusted with the reconstruction of shattered limbs or the design of a skyscraper may still not be trusted with her own sexuality. Even though she may be a sophisticated and successful professional at work, she is obliged to remain content to be guarded by her menfolk at home.

In those countries especially obsessed with female virginity, the conflict between tradition and distorted fantasies about the nature of Western freedom has sometimes meant that young women equate liberation exclusively with sexual experiment. This has led to the bizarre phenomenon of wealthy young brides-to-be consulting plastic surgeons to ensure they are able, on their wedding night, to put on an essential display of 'innocence' with a restructured hymen.

Throughout the Middle East, it has been mainly through the professions that women have first made their ways into the modern workforce. Such women, who almost invariably come from powerful or respected families, never find themselves mistaken for secretaries or asked 'But can you type?' Medicine and science are feminine; secretarial work is not. In the tradition-bound countries of the Gulf, the typing pool remains overwhelmingly male. Working women have therefore tended to congregate into élite professions. Even in countries where the harem is retained, opportunities exist for women to run women-only banks, shops and clinics; but it also stays true that a large pool of educated women, because of the pressures of family prejudice, never take up any occupation outside the house.

In theory at least, the working woman enjoys equality in pay and opportunity. Yet in many Muslim countries a wife still has to seek her husband's formal consent before she can be employed. There are women who are ministers of state or internationally renowned scholars who nevertheless may not marry or travel abroad without the written consent of the men who are their legal guardians.

The repercussions of the revolution in Iran have had an effect whose impact has been felt throughout the Muslim world. Many examples could be cited to illustrate what the Iranian revolution has meant for the lives of girls and women within that country. Like the fundamentalist strains of Christianity, Muslim fundamentalism makes a claim to being the 'purest' form of Islam: the one least corrupted by outside influences. Unlike the Western Christian democracies, moreover, Islamic states have seldom managed to evolve the clear-cut division within the legislature between the religious and the secular arms of government that has come to enshrine the principle of freedom of conscience within both the Anglo-Saxon and Roman schools of law.

The Muslim community embraces a broad group of societies that stand at many different stages of cultural and political development. Turkey looks towards Europe, has plans for applying to join the EEC and features a vigorous campaign for women's rights, spearheaded by the Foundation for the Advancement and Promotion of the Turkish Woman, of which Semra Özal, the wife of the prime minister, is president. Iran attempts to re-create a medieval ideal. The oil-rich states of Arabia embrace many of the most up-to-date and most positive features of modern technology to make life better for their peoples. Those countries not endowed with oil are faced by great problems of endemic poverty and, in Egypt, by horrendous and apparently insoluble problems of city overcrowding.

All of this leads within Muslim society to endless contradictions and tensions that must inevitably have many direct effects on the status and position of all Muslim women. The viewpoint of the sophisticated, educated woman is one thing, but fundamentalism continues to make its political advance through the special appeal it holds for the poor and dispossessed, for whom Huda Shaarawi's emblematic removal of her veil in 1923 might as well be an event lying far in the future. In the long run, the influence of the fundamentalists may turn out to be strictly sectarian. In the complex web between the advancement and retreat of feminist issues in Muslim societies, there still seems to be a basis for long-term optimism.

The history of Islam has recorded the presence of powerful and even aggressive women, albeit that popular culture sees them as sources of a dangerous energy that needs curbing by their menfolk lest it undermine the social fabric. The Muslim world as a whole, however, cannot afford to dispense with women's skills and the contributions they are making to economic growth. Their origins in the harem tradition offer them significant advantages of self-confidence in their own feminine authority and help them to see themselves as active agents for social change rather than as the mere recipients of favours and privileges that could be arbitrarily withdrawn at any time unless they behave. In the same way as it is for women in the world at large, the future of women in Muslim societies is going to be largely determined by the efforts they are themselves making today towards a more liberated life.

3
Women in the Middle Ages

In the Middle Ages, the Christian Church laid much emphasis on the equality of the sexes: 'All human souls are equal before God,' ran the oft-repeated protestation. It might therefore be thought that women were in a well-protected position, the Church being arbiter of standards of behaviour across the whole of Christendom and its authority resting firmly on divine sanction. Though rulers might try to limit the Church's role in the political affairs of their domains, they could not get by without its literate personnel to staff their bureaucracies; neither would they question the universal authority of an organization which, through parish church and roaming priest, touched on the lives of every man, woman and child. The Church had, as the most influential voice in the West, thrown in its lot on the side of equality between men and women; or so it seemed. It is not necessary to probe too far beneath the surface, however, before coming across the deep-riven distrust of the female sex that had come to dominate Christian thinking and which conjured up a world-view that placed women second to men in the divinely ordained scheme.

The churchmen's view of women was reinforced by reference to the Bible, especially as interpreted by the Church Fathers. Genesis was held to show Eve as having been readier than Adam to succumb to temptation. The message was clear: as instigator of the Fall, Eve needed to be set under Adam's authority, for without his discipline she would remain a moral danger. Her soul, and the souls of her daughters, may have been equal to a man's, but she was still best kept at arm's length under a watchful eye. Behind this concept of women as inferior in morals and intellect lay the Pauline pronouncements on marriage:

Wives, submit yourselves unto your husbands, as unto the Lord. For the husband is head of the wife, even as Christ is head of the Church ... Husbands, love your wives, even as Christ also loved the

45

Church ... Let everyone of you in particular so love his wife even as himself; and the wife see that she reverence her husband.

[Ephesians 5:22–33; cf. I Corinthians 6]

This hierarchical blueprint soon became wisdom. It provided the justification for Humbert of Romans's argument that a woman should not preach because

of her lack of intelligence which women have in smaller quantity than men ... the subjection imposed on her ... the fact that her appearance will provoke lust ... and because of the memory of the first woman who ... taught but once and turned the whole world upside down.

Following the expansion of theological studies in the twelfth century, such attitudes towards women grew to be fundamentals of Christian thinking throughout the rest of the Middle Ages. There were medieval theologians who had their doubts and who even suggested that Mary's part in the Incarnation compensated for the harm wrought by Eve. Nevertheless it was the Fall that continued to dominate theological concepts of women, and the image of woman as the moral inferior to man never ceased to shape the Church's attitude in regulating her life.

An aspect of this discrimination was the male cleric's horror of the flesh. 'There is nothing which degrades the manly spirit more,' wrote St Augustine, 'than the attractiveness of females and contact with their bodies.' The celebate ethos of the Church cast woman in the permanent role of temptress. James of Voragine believed it edifying to tell how, when Titus asked the Apostle Peter why he had not healed his daughter Petronilla, he replied it was because she was too beautiful to live. Such extremes of austerity extended to sexual contact in marriage. Carnality was evil, and marriage, the remedy, was in one sense an admission of failure: that of man to resist the physical impulses inevitably aroused by women. It was necessary for the sexual act to occur every now and then for the propagation of mankind, but, for St Jerome, there was nothing to choose between married couples who made love for pleasure and adulterers:

He who is too ardently amorous of his wife is also an adulterer. With regard to the wife of another, in truth, all love is disgraceful; and with regard to one's own wife, excessive love is. The wise man must love his wife with judgement, not with passion. Let him curb his transports of voluptuousness and not let himself be urged precipitately to indulge in coition. Nothing is more vile than to love a wife like a mistress.

46

Such assumptions were put into force through decrees which laid down clearly defined standards of behaviour. The most common regulations concerned the frequency of intercourse between married couples. Feast days, Sundays, the whole of Lent, and during pregnancies or menstruation, were the usual forbidden times, but the list was occasionally supplemented by a ban during the days on either side of a religious festival or in the daylight hours. A couple who observed all the exhortations about sexual restraint and regular attendance at church would hardly have been able to make love at all.

The restrictions stemmed from the fundamental view that sexual relations of all kinds were unclean and should be avoided except for procreation. 'Who does not know,' thundered Pope Innocent III (1160–1216), 'that conjugal intercourse is never committed without itching of the flesh, and heat, and foul concupiscence, whence the conceived seeds are befouled and corrupted?' Men, no less than women, were exposed to this fearful moral guardianship, but the very notion of sin originated with Eve's misbehaviour: ever since then it had always been women who led men astray.

Absolute chastity was therefore the ideal. For lesser mortals, who simply could not avoid temptation, there existed the option of marriage, although some churchmen thought that even marriage was too carnal a matter for the Church to involve itself with. The Church therefore needed to ensure that marriage took an acceptable form. The twelfth-century canonists, or ecclesiastical lawyers, formulated a series of church laws and received the vigorous backing of the Papacy in their campaigns. In 1234, Pope Gregory IX promulgated his *Decretals*, the whole fourth book of which was given over to propounding the canon law of marriage. The stress was on marriage as a holy act, which at once brought it within the jurisdiction of the church courts. One of the cornerstones of the guide-lines was that the consent of both parties was necessary to any marriage.

'It is evident,' declared the canonist, Gratian of Bologna, 'that no woman should be coupled to anyone except of her own free will.' It soon became clear that this made the consent of any third party – parent, lord or whoever – unnecessary; which, in turn, had a crucial implication: should a young couple flout the wishes of parents and marry, perhaps secretly, and if it was then proven in a church court that they had both consented, then the marriage remained an indissoluble bond. As a sacrament, marriage was seen as an unequivocal declaration of intent that could only be broken by the death of one or other partner. The doctrine of indissolubility became one more cornerstone of the Church view on marriage, to be added to the doctrine of consent.

In principle, the doctrines provided women with a safeguard. A woman's consent was as important as the man's; bigamy and concubinage were held in check; and the married woman gained a degree of protection through the imposition of certain obligations on her husband. A man, after all, was enjoined to 'love his wife as his own self'. It was not, however, that such doctrines reflected any high estimate of a woman's worth. Canon law could never be a liberalizing force, for the theology it was based on saw women as essentially inferior and in constant need of male tutelage. As the Church's grip on secular affairs tightened through the Middle Ages, so women's limited rights were eroded further, always under cover of affording their weakness a necessary protection. The Church generated an ideal of spiritual love more through concern with the effects of a woman's behaviour on others than through any interest in her actual soul: a woman may have been the mother of God, but did this redeem her role as the source of original sin? The Church clearly thought not. It was always far more at ease with the image of the divine Mary than with that of the seductive Eve. But whether or not the laity agreed with its view was a very different matter.

To those who possessed land and power, the relationship of the sexes was, in any case, too important to be left to churchmen. The ideals of mutual consent and indissolubility could not be left unchallenged in a world that saw marriage as a means for transferring property or mending political fences.

It was land that lay at the root of the problem. In a society where (in theory) land was granted in return for military services, women landholders were an anomaly. The law of primogeniture, by which the eldest son inherits, became customary practice to maximize the chances of a mature male holding the property. A last will and testament might grant a small proportion of the land to a wife or daughter, but the assumption was still that a man, not a woman, needed to be in control. Since military duties could be exchanged for money payment, a female might, in the absence of a male heir, inherit the family land, but her rights over it would be limited. As soon as she married, her husband assumed full control of her estate for as long as the marriage lasted; and, if he fathered a child that lived, he could keep the estate for all his life. Similarly, a widow's remarriage conveyed all her holdings to her new husband. In short, land inherited by a woman invariably passed to the man she married.

It was a system that left no room for a free 'marriage market'. Whoever owned the land would wish to see that it did not fall into the hands of an enemy; or at least that it could provide a full share of service, military or otherwise. Control of marriages was therefore written into feudal law: kings had the right to regulate the marriages of their lords, lords the right to regulate those of their tenants.

It was accepted that important heiresses could be bought, sold, exchanged and distributed as commodities – to be purchased by the highest bidder or granted by the king, as favour or reward, to a courtier or captain.

The heiresses themselves were given little choice. They could be married off at the tenderest age. One twelfth-century register of 'Rich Widows and of Orphaned Heirs and Heiresses' that circulated among the English aristocracy noted a 'widow' aged ten, and her brother's 'wife' aged five. When the fifty-year-old Earl of Oxford, still awaiting a son, married the twelve-year-old Agnes in 1162, only to repudiate her within a year, the young heiress appealed to the Pope for validation of her marriage. The earl responded by locking her up, though the Pope eventually found in her favour and commanded the earl to treat Agnes as his wife before God, threatening eternal punishment of any dereliction. In the end, the couple had several children and an heir to the earldom was secured. Uncomfortable though the marriage must have been, Agnes's desire to maintain it is quite understandable: committed to the earl's family from her infancy, she could have seen no future elsewhere.

Perhaps what made the earl accept Agnes in the end was not the wrath of the Pope but her proving herself capable of carrying an heir. This was a noblewoman's chief role in marriage. A lord's concern was to perpetuate the line from which he came. Sons were precious commodities, much more so than daughters, and, for fear of accidents, a wife would be well advised to have more than one son. Thus, in effect, fertility became the main measure of a marriage's worth. When Edward IV of England was reproached by his mother for marrying Elizabeth Woodville, he is said to have replied, '... and whereas you object that she has been a wife and is now a widow, and hath already children, why, by God's blessed lady, I that am a bachelor have some children too, and so for our better comfort each of us hath proof that neither of us is like to be barren'.

Clearly, for those who were infertile, the point of marriage would be lost, and it was usually the woman who was discarded. It was largely because Eleanor of Aquitaine had produced only two daughters in fifteen years that Louis VII of France divorced her in 1152, though it took the king two more marriages before he fathered a son. But the treatment of wives as marketable sources of land and heirs, who could be exchanged like faulty goods, flew in the face of the Church's ideal of free consent and the indissolubility of the marriage bond. Some half-hearted attempts to conform were put forward. In his Coronation Charter of 1100, Henry I promised that 'if the wife of one of my tenants shall survive her husband, she shall have her dower ... and I will not give her in marriage unless she herself consents ... and I require that my barons shall act likewise towards the widows of their men'. And King John made the same promise in Magna Carta over a century later. Neither monarch kept it.

The opportunities in the marriage market were too tempting to resist. And, in case a wife proved to be barren, divorce in some form or another needed to be available as well. This must be a tactful process, done with as little disturbance as possible to the political arrangements that had gone with the original marriage. Monogamy might be preferable, since it reduced the chances of conflict over inheritance, but a man could need to find cause to repudiate his wife.

Strictly speaking, the Church never gave way on this point. No *valid* marriage could ever be annulled in the Middle Ages. Therefore reasons had to be found for why it had been invalid in the first place. It might, for instance, be claimed that a marriage was invalid because one of the partners had previously contracted a marriage elsewhere; but 'divorce' by this means could oblige a husband to be married to a person with whom he had been pre-contracted. On the other hand, if a dispensation had previously been received to marry within the forbidden degrees of incest (and, since these extended to sixth cousins, this was nothing uncommon), it was only necessary to declare to the Pope that one's conscience would no longer allow the incestuous union to continue, whatever the terms of the original dispensation. Naturally this device proved to be the more popular one since it allowed the 'divorcee' total freedom to remarry. Indeed, it became a positive incentive to make an incestuous marriage in the first place. A man then knew he would have little trouble in obtaining an annulment if his wife failed to live up to his expectations. Whatever the option taken, the way was made clear for a nobleman to sacrifice as many wives as he wished in the search for an heir.

The matter of 'divorce' was the area where the Church gave most ground. It proclaimed the sanctity of marriage as a life-long union of two hearts, but consideration of land and family fortunes left no room for mere questions of love. It was true that laymen were forced to acknowledge that the wishes of the bride really should be taken into account, but noblemen had the money and the influence to bend the rule: political and dynastic considerations carried a greater weight than any loyalty to religious advice. This is not to say that medieval marriage became a constant battleground between two opposing hierarchies. Both Church and laity approved of the actual ceremony of marriage, and saw reproduction as one of its principal functions. But this left women with little to celebrate. Brides could rarely exert their right of consent to a choice of partner, and their married lives were consumed by the rearing of heirs. In such circumstances, lofty ideals of spiritual love were unlikely to ring true. It was only in widowhood that a woman might gain some freedom. As one fourteenth-century grandmother prayed:

> O good Lord, how is it that widows have a greater reward than married folk? How much better and more comfortable an estate we widows have than we had in marriage.

This widow had reason to be grateful, for she was in sole control of the lands her husband had left her and had no responsibility for the maintenance of his heir or for the repayment of his debts. Her prayer is nevertheless more a testimony to the injustices of a medieval marriage than one to the joys of a medieval widowhood. Much of the land she now enjoyed had been hers before marriage, and she became mistress of her own household only after years of subjection as a mere appendage to a husband she barely knew.

The scope for a life beyond the confines of the household a woman married into was almost non-existent. Women who lived among the merchant classes, or within leading town families, might have an opportunity to engage in trade, such as selling cloth or silk, but only where they were unmarried girls or widowed. Those in control of property possessed the same powers as men for making grants by charter, and had their personal seals; but, again, only if they were without a husband who could otherwise assume control. No married, unwidowed woman could act independently to sell, give away or bequeath her personal property. Even single women of standing played little overt part in public affairs: no matter how rich a female landlord, she would never be summoned to royal councils or allowed to serve as representative in any parliament.

For a woman of noble birth, the only real vocation besides marriage and motherhood was in fact the cloister. Historians have for long acknowledged the contributions women made as nuns and abbesses to the religious life of the Middle Ages. In this they echo various contemporary commentators who saw virtue in women's capacity to triumph over 'essential weaknesses'. Addressing the nuns of Godstow in 1284, Archbishop Peckham of Canterbury expressed his belief that, the more fragile the sex, the more worthy their virginal penitence. But women's houses never attracted the same degree of patronage as those of men. A female's virginity may have been held in high esteem by the Church, but most patrons felt sure that, in the end, no woman's moral probity was comparable to that of a man. Even the nunneries they did manage adequately could never be entirely self-sufficient, for the ban on female ordination obliged them to rely, for all sacraments, on male chaplains. And having made the nunneries reliant on their help, the monks did their best to minimize moral hazards to themselves and ensured that double monasteries lacked no sturdy wall between their two halves.

The fear of nuns felt by so many monks is illustrated in a tale by Alfred of Rievaulx concerning events in the two houses that stood side by side at Walton, Yorkshire, in the late twelfth century. A nun's 'impudent' eye had caught that of a brother. When their clandestine affair was discovered, she was thrashed and imprisoned. Later the monk was delivered by the brethren to the nuns, who forced his mistress to castrate him. It was clear that, however hard women might try to live chastely, the carnal passions lurking beneath the surface constantly threatened to ensnare innocent men. Even as it paid homage to Mary, so the Church could never forget Eve. Women who resorted to the cloister escaped the arranged marriages of the secular world only to be exposed to the full force of clerical suspicion.

But nuns at least had the chance to read and write, though usually only in the vernacular and without benefit of the lavish libraries their male counterparts possessed. There were among them some distinguished scholars, such as Hildegard of Bingen, famous for her prophetic visions and musical compositions, who became an indefatigable correspondent with theologians, emperors and popes before her death in 1179 as abbess of Rupertsberg. A laywoman's chances to become accomplished in any way were far more limited. Some authorities believed, in any case, that teaching a woman to write would only enable her to enter into secret correspondence. Reading, however, was not discouraged since it could be an aid to religious practice. Women thus often read of earthlier loves between women like themselves and men (not quite) like their husbands, and some of this literature was more explicit than the Victorian editions of chivalric romances would have us believe. One common theme of the original genre was the high-born lady who chooses to take the initiative with her lover.

Nevertheless, many of the pre-Christian tales, like those Geoffrey of Monmouth turned into Arthurian legend, indicate how the essence of chivalry was rape. 'Orders of chivalry' were aristocratic clubs which neither admitted women nor had their interests at heart, though there was also, of course, the tradition of mystical love. Nowhere was this stronger than with the troubadour poets of Provence during the twelfth century, the theme of their work being a love never satisfied by physical embrace. Sordello, an Italian who lived and wrote as a Provençal, expressed how love was at its purest when unrequited:

> Thus lady, I commend to thee
> My fate and life, thy faithful squire,
> I'd rather die in misery
> Than have thee stoop to my desire.

For the troubadour, no lust existed in the highest form of love between a woman and a man. The woman became a remote, unattainable ideal of beauty and virtue. By this standard, the tribulations of Heloïse, shut up in a nunnery, able only to write to Abelard, isolated and castrated in a monastery, are seen as an enviable experience. Naturally it went without saying that true love could never exist in marriage, where family decision, not the power of personal attraction, remained paramount.

What modern critics and historians call 'courtly love' is a term that covers a great variety of medieval attitudes, concepts and literary fashions. Alongside the literature that talked of passion satisfied, there grew up a body of other work to celebrate the impossibility of such a liaison. Scores of writers cover the ground in between, and most of what they wrote implied an attitude towards women that was not entirely flattering. At one extreme lay a tradition that saw, in a woman's seductive nature, the excuse for honouring the sexual athleticism of bold knights; at another was one that denied a woman any capacity at all for sexual desire.

Adultery, whether imagined or real, was bound to be a dominant theme when family considerations, rather than impulses of the heart, dictated the choice of marriage partner and women everywhere were given to men they barely knew and probably rarely liked. In an arranged marriage, the situation of a wife was certainly more difficult than that of her husband. Not only did she bring land to the husband, but she was also required to bear an heir. To ensure the smooth passage of property from one generation to the next, the paternity of this heir needed to be beyond doubt; the bride must be a virgin on the day she married, and during her marriage was to be faithful. In short, fornication and adultery could not be tolerated among women of substance. Hence the chastity belt, or so-called 'girdle of Venus', which wives or daughters were obliged to wear when a husband or father was away from home. And for those who escaped such indignity, there were always the watchful eyes of servants, neighbours or family friends, who would place the interests of the household and its lineage above those of the wife.

In such a world, the image of a woman entrapped by marriage took on a special poignancy, and the literature of 'courtly love' must have provided a ready supply of flights of fancy for the victim. In *Yonec*, one of the twelfth-century romances of Marie de France, a heroine speculates on ladies who 'found lovers, handsome and courteous, worthy and brave, and were blamed for it by none'; yet the tone was wishful for, like many heroines, she was already married and knew her situation to be helpless. The elaboration of the concept of a marital fidelity which left no place for other relationships brought with it the elevation of infidelity into a fine art.

But while the need to protect inheritance coincided neatly with the Church's condemnation of extra-marital sex, this was never allowed to interfere with the exploits of pleasure-seeking husbands. In this they obviously had to resort to low-born women, high-born women being closely and jealously guarded. It came to be perfectly accepted that a rich man might take a mistress. As Henry Grosmont, Duke of Lancaster and one of the most cultured noblemen of the fourteenth century, explained, while he loved the scent of fine ladies, he preferred to kiss the low-born, because they were more responsive.

A man with no mistress might go to the town to visit a prostitute, but at the beginning of the Middle Ages this was not easy. Although the existence of prostitutes was admitted, they were forbidden to reside within a town's walls. As time progressed, however, prostitution came more and more to be seen as a normal part of a nation's life. Brothels were identified, supervised and even owned by the public authorities. Within their grounds, a man was free to visit with no fear of being charged with adultery. One thirteenth-century commentary on the customs of Toulouse discussed adultery and asked whether 'a married man [who] enters a house where commonly are found women for money ... believing to have relations with an unmarried woman, when in fact it was a married woman ... commits adultery'; to which the answer was, 'No, since the place excuses the same.' Adultery, it was commonly believed, was primarily a female offence.

To begin with, brothels were scattered throughout a town, but then it came to be accepted that defined areas were needed, beyond which no prostitute could live or work. 'A cesspool is necessary to a palace if the whole place is not to smell,' declared Thomas Aquinas, and the public authorities soon put such reasoning into action. A series of bath-houses along the south bank of the Thames was officially classified as marking the red-light district of medieval London from the reign of Henry II. When, at Montpellier in the 1490s, an order of parliament closed down many private brothels because the women there debauched young children 'and gave a bad example to the girls and married women and widows who have their gardens near the said stews', a red-light district was created in their stead to ensure the strict segregation of the 'dishonest' from the 'honest'. Otherwise, the authorities claimed, 'honest' women might witness both the material and the pleasurable rewards of sin, and abandon the connubial bed for the street. What made women so vulnerable in the eyes of the town elders was their reputation for carnality. For a sex ruled by passion rather than reason, authorized red-light districts were the only guarantee of virtue against temptation.

Once brothels were accepted, secular and ecclesiastical authorities alike felt that it was only sensible to take advantage of the opportunities they offered for profit. A brisk trade in brothel ownership developed, and few speculators betrayed any moral qualms. In London, the prostitutes of Southwark came to be known as 'Winchester Geese' because the house from which they operated was owned by the Bishop of Winchester, who used some of the profits to found New College in the University of Oxford. In Germany, the Bishop of Würtzburg regarded a brothel under his control as an attractive gift to bestow on a young priest seeking office. And, in Rome, the papacy itself drew an income of some 20,000 ducats a year from the brothels it owned. All across Europe, brothel owners did everything they could to maximize the yield on their investment. When the rape of a prostitute was finally acknowledged as a crime, it was not because of any concern for her comfort, but through the wish to protect a valuable asset.

It was nevertheless the needs of those with land and power that proved crucial to the acceptance of prostitution. Arranged marriages which forged political alliances and directed the passage of property among the aristocracy had created a multitude of unhappy couples. While it was accepted that husbands might find an extra-marital dalliance desirable, women could never be allowed an illicit affair for fear of jeopardizing the inheritance through an illegitimate birth. Medieval society offered its response: men might enjoy the services of 'public' women, while the virtue of honest women was protected by the careful siting of brothels.

What of the prostitutes themselves? Some became unexpectedly rich. One, Françoise of Florence, who worked in Marseille, drafted a will in 1361 in which she made legacies to several charities, including the considerable sum of forty florins to a poor girl. Another, Thomasa of Barcelona, left goods of such value that the local clergy disputed the rights of her inheritance. Most prostitutes were of very humble origin indeed. More often than not, they came from neighbouring towns or, even more commonly, from the countryside. Here, in the hamlets, villages and small trading posts, the peasantry lived far removed from the world of the grand marriage alliance, discreet affairs and chivalrous romance.

The women of the peasantry led a mundane existence: a life-cycle of betrothal, marriage, motherhood and widowhood in which daily routines were geared towards raising children and keeping together a modest family holding. The one experience they shared with the aristocracy was the Church's attitudes to sex and marriage and view on the sinfulness of natural desire. Nevertheless there is considerable evidence for a 'happy innocence' still existing among the rural poor of the Middle Ages – an attitude to sexual freedom that any aristocratic woman might envy. From the Dark Ages on, popular literature throve on tales of casual sex among the ordinary folk, and women were certainly not always portrayed as the passive recipients of men's lusts.

Boccaccio's *Decameron*, written between 1348 and 1353, recounts the stories told among ten young Florentines, seven of whom were women. These tell of men deceived, and even of a wife indulging her lover in the presence of her husband. One of the women described how a young nun, caught in bed with her lover, was reproved by an abbess who had come fresh from the arms of a priest. Boccaccio defends his material as being 'freer, maybe than liketh your squeamish hypocritical prudes, who weigh words rather than deeds and study more to appear than to be good'.

Chaucer's *Canterbury Tales*, a collection of stories told this time by some thirty pilgrims of varied social standing, are, if anything, even more bawdy. 'The Miller's Tale' tells how a young wife deceives her elderly husband in some elaborate trickery with her student lodger. While the lovers rush to bed, 'Busy in solace and the quest for fun', Absalon, a rival suitor, attempts to serenade her from beneath a window. He refuses to go away without a kiss, so she flings open the window and,

> Dark was the night as pitch, as black as coal,
> And at the window out she put her hole,
> And Absalon, so fortune framed the farce,
> Put up his mouth and kissed her naked arse.

In the prologue to 'The Wife of Bath's Tale', we are advised that,

> Virginity is indeed a great perfection,
> And married continence, for God's dilection;

but, asks the story-teller,

> Tell me to what conclusion or in aid
> Of what were generative organs made?
> And for what profit were those creatures wrought?
> Trust me, they cannot have been made for naught.

The Wife of Bath has decided that,

> In wifehood I will use my instrument
> As freely as my Maker me it sent.

Yet her companions are as little shocked by this description of the way she managed her five husbands as they are by her self-confessed taste for casual sex:

56

So help me God I was a lusty one,
Fair young and well-to-do, and full of fun! ...
I ever followed natural inclination
Under the power of my constellation ...
For as I may be saved by God above,
I never used discretion when in love
But ever followed on my appetite,
Whether the lad was short, long, black or white.
Little I cared, if he was fond of me,
How poor he was, or what his rank might be.

It would seem that Chaucer's England was quite unabashed at an outspokenness surpassing that of Boccaccio's Italy, though when the *Decameron* was banned by the Church, it was not for its explicit content. In a permitted expurgated version, priests and monks became lawyers or magicians and nuns became noblewomen, yet the accounts of sexual abandon stayed in place. Even so, both books were written by men who were neither poor nor truly country-dwelling, so we have to question whether their stories may be taken as truly reflecting the behaviour of the broad mass of women. In fact, the bawdy sexual licence they portray rarely gives the women concerned anything much to celebrate.

The life of a peasant woman continued to be regulated by a primitive code of conduct based on shame, modesty and honour, these deemed to be held by every woman in finite quantities. The amount she possessed could never increase, but might be diminished, and she would constantly fear the judgement of men on her reputation. To be called 'whore' was the greatest insult a woman could suffer. Yet this was the accusation a woman involved in an illicit affair might well be risking. The Church based its ideas on a certain equality of sexual behaviour between men and women: fornication and adultery were mortal sins in which both parties were culpable. Lay opinion differed. In the transition from religious ideal to popular practice, there emerged a double standard of sexual morality, lax for men but strict for women.

Such views were readily institutionalized. In her study of Languedoc prostitution, Leah Lydia Otis found that most urban law codes considered adultery to be an offence committed by a married woman and her lover; only towns with a strong ecclesiastical presence punished the adultery of the husband. This explains the reluctance of many towns to punish the rape of a prostitute. Where a penalty was imposed, it was invariably lighter than that inflicted when an 'honest' woman was assaulted. Not that the rape of an 'honest' woman was taken especially seriously. And if women were treated badly as victims, the role of victim was, even so, the only one they were allowed in the administration of justice, for they filled no public office. Once it was accepted that women were the weaker sex, guided by passion and prone to irrationality, then giving them public responsibilities was simply out of the question.

If peasant women could expect neither sympathy for crimes committed against them nor interest in their individual talents, did married life offer them any refuge? As we might expect, the percentage of permanently single women in rural English communities was very low: no greater than 15 per cent, perhaps half that, to judge by the figures given in the English Poll Tax of 1377. Clearly, if the aristocracy were marrying with an eye to a dynastic alliance or building up the landed estate, the peasantry had corresponding reasons. For them, too, marriage involved far more than an agreement between two individuals. When a young girl married, the business was arranged by relations – sometimes her mother or aunts, usually brothers, uncles or, most commonly, her father. The bride could count herself lucky if ever consulted. Large amounts of land might not necessarily be at stake, but this made it all the more important that what little there was should not go astray.

Moreover, the local lord, who ultimately owned the land, was also keen to keep the family tenement as a viable unit of cultivation, and so defined the freedoms of his tenants in ways that safeguarded his own rights. The best way to achieve this would be to see the property pass to an eldest son; a daughter would do, but she must be married to someone suitable who could assume control. The choice of a woman's marriage partner was therefore something a lord often claimed for himself, very much according to the aristocratic pattern. As a result, a young woman's life was governed on two fronts: by her parents and by their landlord.

The early age for marriage reflected the situation. Fifteen or sixteen was common, though parents who wished to make sure their lord had no pretext to intervene might arrange for a daughter to be married as young as six or seven. Generally, as soon as a girl began to menstruate, match-makers would begin to take an interest; and, whatever her age, her new husband became – in the eyes of the village community as well as of the lord of the manor – the responsible tenant of the holdings and head of the household. There were exceptions to these manipulations of the marriage market. Wherever a landlord's control was lacking, peasant farmers would find it easier to follow their own wishes; and if they were reasonably well off, this sometimes involved an equal division of property between all offspring, daughters as well as sons. In such cases, the choice of marriage partner was not so crucial to the future of the entire family holding, and women became more likely to marry whom they pleased.

It followed that, in a society which saw men in their mid twenties marrying girls of fifteen, a large and far from ephemeral group were the widows. Common law entitled them to a third of a husband's property, as dower or 'free bench'; and they often received more. So long as their landlord was not too pressing in forcing a remarriage, the holding was effectively theirs to do with as they pleased, and any son and heir would have to wait his turn. This circumstance brought an independence unequalled at any other stage in a woman's life, and such opportunities were rarely wasted. Looking after the poultry, milking the cows and winnowing the grain were regarded as traditional womanly tasks, but there were other opportunities to be grasped. Selling bread or milk, cheese-making and cloth-working, all saw a good proportion of women practitioners, though their pay was rarely equal to a man's. In brewing, women were as common as men at times. According to the *Livre de Métiers*, a widow often exercised her deceased husband's trade, though remarriage could lose her the right to train apprentices.

Most women, however, worked in the home. A widow might remarry, and with her new husband there came the task of preserving the household he now commanded. The possible daily routines into which she now fell may be summarized from 'The Ballad of the Tyrannical Husband'. Having lit the fire, the wife would milk the cows and take them to pasture. After making some butter and cheese, she fed the poultry and took the geese to the green. She also worked on carding wool, spinning and beating flax, and every two weeks she baked and brewed. Day after day she would fetch the water and prepare the food. And the ballad by no means covers all possible tasks. The ploughman in 'Pierce the Ploughman's Crede' holds the plough, but it is his wife, goad in hand, who drives the team. In fact a wife's duties often took her into the fields to tackle a variety of manual tasks, including the back-breaking job of picking up stray grain as soon as harvest was over.

The fact that wives took on such roles has been seen as proof that marriage was very much a partnership. Dividing their responsibilities, both husband and wife worked to support the household, and at the end of the day they sat down at table to eat together. Marriage contracts and instructional poems outlined the economic benefits to each partner: a son was advised to search for a wife who would be meek, courteous and wise. Such a woman should be cherished, for it was 'better to eat homely fare in peace than have a hundred fine dishes served with strife'. A prospective wife was required to be faithful, respectable in public, and able to manage the household tasks in an orderly way. Certainly the contribution of a wife to the domestic economy did not go completely unrecognized, and a husband was admonished to offer her respect and protection. Yet it was no partnership of equals. The protection of the law was a two-edged sword, for while it was the wife's duty to obey, it was the husband's legal right to *ensure* her obedience. One manor court declared, when a woman was brought before it, that 'henceforth her husband shall punish her'. The man who murdered his wife committed a felony, but the woman who murdered her husband committed treason – and would be burned at the stake 'for killing her lord and master'.

It was in her duty to bear children, however, that the medieval wife experienced her biggest obstacle to equality. Even as the aristocratic lady was obliged to provide her husband with an heir to the landed estate, so the peasant woman was duty-bound to provide children who would eventually assist with the running of the household and support the couple in their dotage. A woman's capacity to have children was highly prized, but child-bearing, with its attendant duties of nurturing and training, also enslaved her. Even in childbirth, she was at the mercy of many erroneous medical notions and much harmful folklore. The risks to both mother and child could consequently be great. Women had markedly shorter life expectancies than men: childbirth, as the coroners' records reveal, was often a cause of early death. And few women faced this threat on only one occasion. It has been calculated, for the sixteenth century, that married women were likely to give birth to between six and seven children on average, and the figure was probably not much lower in earlier times. Those children who survived would then have to be fed, watched over and taught.

Although a mother's influence over her children was great, it was never strong enough to topple her husband from his position as head of the household. To the medieval peasantry, the family of flesh and blood and the house of wood, stone or daub were one and the same: if a husband owned the property, he also ruled the family. There is no doubt that many wives were treated with affection, but should a husband choose to resort to violence, he was quite within his rights.

Life among the rural poor in the Middle Ages offered a woman no more freedom from her subordination to men than did a life in the palaces of the rich and famous. A man might take a mistress, but his wife must do nothing to 'provoke lust' or put the paternity of an heir in doubt and threaten the future of an inheritance (no matter how modest). A woman's public life was subordinated to the private role men required of her. There would always be individuals – Marie de France, Margery Kempe, Joan of Arc – who stepped outside this state of affairs, but the lives of the vast mass of women are hidden from the public records by their restriction to a private life of marriage and motherhood.

Faced with a lack of sympathy on the part of the existing order, many women turned to a rejection of it altogether. An exceptional number joined the Cathar heresy which swept across southern Europe in the thirteenth century; they were also among the preachers of the Waldensian movement; and they played a directing role in the movements of the Beguines and Beghards, who called for a return to apostolic poverty. But women's rejection of the role allotted to them by society took its most extreme form in a turning to witchcraft. The activities of witches were a subject for wild and lurid speculation, running though a vast array of abominable behaviour. From this there emerged the familiar imagery of flying witches, the casting of spells and the mixing of potions, child-eating, bestiality and frenzied couplings with Satan himself. How much of this was imaginary is hard to tell, but the central theme remains the night-time 'Sabbat' in which witches gathered to worship the devil through orgiastic dances and engage in violently sexual acts.

Witchcraft was a ritual inversion of Christianity and all it stood for. The Church had spread an ideal which denied women the freedom to express sexual desires and created a fearful guilt among those who succumbed; witchcraft celebrated the animal side in human nature. The orgy at the centre of every Sabbat was no mere human debauch, as it would have been in the ancient world, but an outburst of eroticism that went hand in hand with apostasy. The unbridled sexuality was combined with a sacrilegious parody of divine service, Christianity being systematically burlesqued in this 'return of the repressed'. Witchcraft, in this sense, was something more than the widespread anti-clericalism that took hold in Europe during the later Middle Ages: it was the end-product of a tension between conscious beliefs and ideals on the one hand and unconscious desires and resentments on the other. Its main practitioners were women, simply because they had much less to lose by a rejection of orthodoxy.

Yet the witches were always outnumbered by the witch-hunters. For every true witch uncovered there were hundreds of false allegations and obsessional outbursts from people who saw the hand of witchcraft in every conceivable crime and disaster. After the *Malleus Maleficarum* (*The Hammer of Witchcraft*) was first printed in 1486, listing the misdeeds of witches and the ways of convicting them, it rapidly became a bestseller. The Church's determination to stamp out witchcraft touched a nerve in all lay people. The masses may not have been susceptible to theological argument, but the cause of morality could be served by dangling the devil incarnate, and all his followers, before their very eyes. Were not witches living proof of the carnal weakness of the female sex as a whole – a weakness that all men must fear and guard against? The records of inquisitions show how little girls involved in witchcraft were sometimes flogged but seldom executed; not yet nubile, they did not as yet possess the carnality that lured good men to their doom, and so were no real threat and not really witches. Such a view was in accord with what the medieval Church had taught: the lust a woman aroused turned a man's eye from the path of heaven.

The climate of fear and tension created by this anti-sexuality spread throughout society. It was responsible for the image in literature of the evil, witch-like woman, the temptress of men and sower of discord; it led to the setting up of red-light districts so that the 'adultery' committed by prostitutes was prevented from corrupting entire towns; and it proved the spur to building an unbreakable wall between nuns and monks who were supposed to be sharing the same vocation. A woman's one redeeming feature, it seemed, was her ability – like the divine Mary – to be a mother, but everyone knew what preceded mother-hood, so that even this was but another aspect of that dangerous quality – like Eve's – which lured men away from perfection.

Clerical views were not accepted without question: men and women continued to make love outside as well as within marriage. There were even lawyers of note, such as Peter Dubois, who were prepared to stand up and claim that the Church's attitude to women had been instituted by the 'old and decrepit'. But any relations between the sexes in the Middle Ages were overshadowed by immense feelings of guilt, and men pre-ferred to cope by shutting women off from the mainstream of society and refusing to trust them an inch. The medieval bifurcation of women into spiritual or profane beings – the divine Mary or the seductive Eve – was a theological construction. But at a time when the Church played such a large part in people's lives, its destructive influence was unavoid-able. As the witch-hunting crazes show no less than the exclusion of a woman from public life, in this state of affairs, women were very much the losers.

In the end, however, it was a more basic force which proved decisive in restricting a woman's freedoms in the Middle Ages. Day in, day out, a man was less concerned with the carnal nature of his wife than he was with the future of his family and household. A wife or daughter were crucial to his considerations: a wife brought him land, helped him to work his farm and run the home, and provided him with an heir; a daughter's marriage might remove some land from his control, but could be used to build a closer alliance with another family group. In this way, a woman's life was shaped by her capacity to bear children and the inseparable bond between marriage and property. The household she lived in represented something more than man, wife and children: it was the line, the stock, traversing generations, the symbol of wealth and power. The interests of past and future generations therefore pressed down on a woman. It was a burden that proved heavier in aristocratic circles, where more land and family prestige were at stake in marriage; but even peasant families had pride and did all they could to protect or enrich their humble inheritance. Women's freedom to choose whether or not to marry, when to marry and whom to marry, was sacrificed to considerations of family advantage at all levels.

There were still some freedoms to be gained, even within the confines of a domestic life. The shrewish wife, belabouring her husband with a distaff, is a literary and iconographic stereotype we should discount; but there is plenty of evidence of women refusing to be meek and helpless. The historian Susan Stuard reminds us that life spent in the home and away from public life may have lessened the harsh demands of day-to-day existence, even if at the price of lower social status:

> Does a peasant woman or town-bred spinster feel bitter resentment if relieved of fieldwork or excluded from a guild by an adequate supply of male labour? ... Does a Provençal duchess shut out from the administration of her own lands by her husband's growing corps of bureaucrats enjoy the courtly songs and poems composed in her honour by lesser noblemen?

The story of young Agnes, locked up after her marriage to the aged Earl of Oxford, and the wife in 'The Ballad of the Tyrannical Husband' suggest that life at home was far from cosy. In any case, women were never allowed to choose for themselves between a life of comfort or a life of status. From the moment of her birth, a woman's days were determined by a vast array of relatives, neighbours, lords, employers, theologians and priests. Between them they defined a role for women that rarely went beyond the part of wife and mother, virgin or whore, nun or witch. The Church's vision of a corrupt and inferior sex did not need wholesale acceptance to bring this about: the power of the family, the lineage and the household had done its work.

4
Women in Victorian England

The most cherished themes of Victorian literature were the sanctity and dignity of the family. No one in Victorian England who attended at church or chapel, read a newspaper or a periodical, or whiled away the evenings with a novel, could avoid hearing of the family as the essential moral centre of English life. At the highest level, it was an article of faith for the Christian believer that the family had been divinely ordained for the welfare and education of mankind, and in times of dispute, especially over such issues as the reform of the law on divorce, it was to Christian teaching that all sides looked for an answer. Politically, the family was hailed as 'the unit upon which a constitutional Government has been raised which is the envy and admiration of mankind', and it was a commonplace that the secret of national greatness lay in those virtues such as truthfulness, obedience, and subordination of self to the needs of others, which were first taught and practised within the family.

Only a little less grandly, it was the family portrait, in words or pictures, that revealed the Victorians to themselves as they wished to be seen. In Dean Stanley's celebrated *Life of Dr Arnold*, for example, the account of Arnold's religious and political convictions is rounded out with a description of the great man in gentler and more domestic mood – walking quietly beside his wife's pony, at work in his study with his numerous children, gathering the family and servants together for prayers and readings from the scriptures. Arnold's dream, writes Stanley, was of 'a whole house transplanted entire from earth to heaven': the 'very idea of family life' was invested in his eyes with 'a peculiar sense of solemnity'. In such sentiments Arnold and his biographer were at one with their age. Even – perhaps especially – for an agnostic like James Froude, home remained 'the one last reality of which universal instinct was assured'.

At the still, serene centre of the Victorian home was the wife and mother, and almost all that was written in praise of marriage and family was addressed to her, expounding her duties to her husband, children and nation; all of these depended on whether she was wise and virtuous, or foolish and faithless. The best known of these writings, and the most eloquent, was Ruskin's lecture 'Of Queens' Gardens', delivered in 1864 and published a year later in *Sesame and Lilies*. (It is perhaps in no way surprising that second-hand copies so often turn out to be old prize-books from girls' schools.)

Ruskin began his lecture by dissociating himself from those who insisted too vehemently on women's inferiority (a man could not be 'helped effectively by a shadow, or worthily by a slave'), and from those who sought to discuss the 'mission' and the 'rights' of women without reference to the key question of 'the relations of the womanly to the manly nature' – this being a glance at the writings of some of the first feminists, whose challenge lies in the background of Ruskin's lecture.

His own account of the relations of the womanly and manly nature divides into two parts. First, their natures are inherently and designedly different: 'Each has what the other has not: each completes the other, and is completed by the other: they are in nothing alike, and the happiness and perfection of both depends on each asking and receiving from the other what the other only can give.' Secondly, these differences are properly reflected in the existing division of functions within society. The man's power is 'active, progressive, defensive', he is 'the doer, the creator, the discoverer', equipped by his nature to carry out 'rough work in open world'. The woman's power is not inferior but complementary: 'for rule, not for battle ... not for invention or creation, but for sweet ordering, arrangement, and decision'. Her nature, more tender and less assertive than the man's, will be most fully expressed within the home, and through her duties as a wife and mother.

To describe the world reserved for men in honorific terms, as the arena of invention and discovery, was to do what custom and good manners required. But if Ruskin was to persuade the women in his audience that they should seek fulfilment only in the home, it was desirable to shift his ground a little. After all, the world of masculine activity is not good, but brutal and corrupting, and in his daily traffic with it the Victorian male must be 'wounded or subdued; often misled; and always hardened'. By contrast, home is a 'sacred place', a refuge from the 'terror, doubt, and division' of an 'inconsistently-minded, unknown, unloved, or hostile society'. Here, and only here, could the woman find protection from the dangers which her husband bravely faced on her account in the outside world. Her husband's house was therefore her proper sphere, both preserving her and preserved by her: 'Within his house, as ruled by her ... need enter no danger, no temptation, no cause of error or offence.' It was accordingly her duty to renounce any ambition or desires which might tempt her out into the world and away from the home she alone could preserve as 'the place of Peace'. It was her reward to know that 'a true wife, in her husband's house, is his servant', but 'in his heart ... she is queen'.

Ruskin's fervour was evidently gratifying, and the lecture was a huge success. But it was the eloquence that was remarkable, not the message. That had been anticipated in the 1830s and 1840s in a host of manuals and handbooks, mostly written by women, setting out the duties of the mothers, wives and daughters of England. But Mrs Ellis, Mrs Sandford, Mrs Lewis and their like were not concerned to make women into Queens, but to instruct those who were rising into the middle class how to be recognized as Ladies. For their benefit, what came to be known as the doctrine of 'separate spheres' was elaborated in detail. For Mrs Ellis, as for Ruskin, men belonged to the world of 'action' and wielded 'power', women to the world of 'feeling' where they could hope to exercise 'influence'. And she agreed that men were occasionally led to suppress their better feelings when caught up in the 'fierce conflict of worldly interests' outside the home. It was therefore the woman's task to maintain the home as an emblem on earth of the divine peace and order, where her husband could replenish those better feelings.

For her to leave home to undertake paid work on her own account would be to betray a sacred duty. Moreover, and hardly less important, it would also be to lose caste as a Lady: 'So soon as a woman begins to receive money,' warned Mrs Ellis, '[she is] transformed into a trades-woman, and must find her place in society as such.' Her proper work – that is, the only work she could perform with propriety – was in the home, and accordingly Mrs Ellis exhorted her readers to value more highly the various tasks of the home. But if paid work was demeaning, Good Works were not: indeed, the more a woman was involved in charitable work, the greater her status as a Lady. Lucy Aikin noted in 1841 that visiting the sick and poor had become 'a fashion and a rage' among middle-class women, and so, too, had the other tasks of Victorian philanthropy – raising funds, organizing bazaars, formation of sewing circles and the like. Such activities were outlets for energies which might otherwise have gone unused, and were exempt from the prejudices associated with paid employment. The 'whole law of woman's life' was 'a law of love', as Mrs Ellis explained. What could be more fitting than that she display her allegiance to this law outside as well as within the home?

This, then, was the idiom which helped to define the image of Victorian womanhood. Occasionally the idiom shifted and a harsher side showed through. Mrs Ellis reminded her readers that, as women, they must accept they were inferior to men: 'You may have more talent, with higher attainments ... but this has nothing whatever to do with your position as a woman, which is, and must be, inferior to his as a man.' Here she reflected the long tradition of Christian moralists who had insisted that the dependence of women was enjoined both by the scriptures and by the laws of nature. Both their relative physical weakness and their moral frailty demanded that they be subject at all times to male guidance or restraint, and the only claim a woman had on society was that she be handed safely from the custody of her father to that of her husband. This view hardly sits easily alongside Ruskin's elevation of women as a source of moral authority, yet the two views are often enough to be found in the same texts. But, on balance, the more flattering view was the one more frequently expressed. To Charles Kingsley, for example, the woman was 'the natural, and therefore divine, guide, purifier, inspirer, of the man', and many an essay and sermon elaborated on the wonders of the way the hand that rocked the cradle ruled – via male intermediaries – the world.

But there were those who refused to be disarmed by this rhetoric. 'This has ever been the flattering language of man,' warned one American feminist, 'since he laid aside the whip as a means of subjection.' And when women in the mid century looked at the law of the land, as in an age of legal reform they were bound to do, they were dismayed and angered at what they saw. Most of them learned it, as Lady Caroline Norton put it, 'piecemeal', as a series of affronts and anomalies.

Marriage was in this respect a great teacher. In effect, a woman surrendered her legal being when she married. By virtue of a legal fiction supposing the absolute coincidence of need and interest between man and wife, she and her husband became a single legal entity. 'By marriage,' explained Sir William Blackstone in his *Commentaries on the Laws of England*, 'the husband and wife are one person in law: that is, the very being or legal existence of the woman is suspended during the marriage, or at least is incorporated or consolidated into that of her husband, under whose wing, protection, and *cover*, she performs everything.' Feminist critics learned to put it more succinctly: 'My wife and I are one person, and I am he.'

The consequences of this system of coverture were far-reaching. A single woman had control over her property and earnings, but on her marriage they passed under the common law to her husband, unless she had previously been protected by a settlement in equity. Millicent Fawcett, later one of the leaders of the suffragist movement, heard the man who had robbed her in the street charged with stealing from the person of Millicent Fawcett a purse and a sum of money, *'the property of Henry Fawcett'*.

The children of the marriage were similarly held to be the property of the father; the mother might at any time be denied access to them, or discover that her husband had given them into the care of his mistress. Even after the Custody of Infants Act (1886), according to which the well-being of the child was to determine all questions of custody, the father remained during his lifetime their sole legal guardian, and had the right to nominate a guardian to replace him in the event of his predeceasing the mother. These provisions were not merely theoretical. In the 1870s, a woman in Scotland obtained a separation from her husband on grounds of his brutality towards her, only to find the custody of her children granted to him, on the assumption that it might 'introduce a soothing influence to cheer the darkness or mitigate the bitterness of his lot'. Such judgements were not uncommon.

As with her property and her children, so, too, with her person: in theory a woman's body was the property of her husband. In 1840, the Courts in England declared that the right of protection could be interpreted to allow a man to imprison his wife ('to restrain her from liberty for an indefinite time'). It was not until 1891 that a woman who had been imprisoned by her husband was ordered by the Courts to be released, thus effectively ending a man's right to restrict his wife's movements. But the underlying assumption, of a man's right to own his wife's person, remained in the law of divorce, which throughout the nineteenth century allowed the husband to demand damages of his wife's lover, for, in effect, trespass on his property. Needless to say, there was no corresponding claim that a wife could have made.

The career of Lady Caroline Norton gives some idea of the scale of the injuries a husband could legally inflict on his wife. In 1836, her husband brought an action against Lord Melbourne, the Whig prime minister, whom he accused of adultery with his wife. Melbourne was acquitted, and Norton's case dismissed. The marriage continued to deteriorate, and the couple eventually separated, Norton however retaining custody of the children. His wife only learned of the illness of one of her children when it was too late; she arrived to find him in his coffin. Her influential friends were instrumental in pushing through an Act in 1839, enabling innocent wives at least to visit their children, and in some cases to have custody of those aged under seven. But Lady Caroline's troubles were not over. Libelled by the *British and Foreign Quarterly Review*, largely on the basis of an article she had not written, she found she was unable to sue. She had no legal existence, and therefore could not have been libelled; although her husband could have sued on her behalf, and could of course have been awarded damages. She began to write in order to publicize her case and found that, since her earnings as a married woman belonged to her husband, so her publishers handed them over. It was not until Norton's death in 1875 that she became free to remarry.

Such cases attracted a good deal of publicity, and by the mid century there were several well-informed and articulate critics of the idea that women, once married, had no legal existence. But the responses to this were largely pragmatic, which perhaps helps to explain why so little attention was paid to another aspect of the official view of Victorian womanhood: the denial of women's sexual existence. Yet in each case the supposition was the same: that a woman existed merely contingently. 'In men,' claimed W. R. Greg in an article on prostitution, 'the sexual desire is inherent and spontaneous ... In the other sex [fine phrase!], the desire is dormant, if not non-existent, till excited; always till excited by undue familiarities; almost always till excited by actual intercourse.'

William Acton in his *The Functions and Disorders of the Reproductive Organs* (1857), gave medical support to Greg's view that 'a modest woman' wished no sexual gratification for herself, and submitted to her husband 'only to please him'. Acton writes: 'The best wives, mothers, and managers of households, know little or nothing of sexual indulgence. Love of home, children, and domestic duties are the only passions they feel.'

The point Mrs Ellis made in general terms, that 'the love of woman appears to have been created solely to minister; that of man to be ministered unto', was to be carried into the bedroom as well as elsewhere in the home. Yet neither Greg nor Acton saw any injustice in these arguments; on the contrary, they congratulated women on what Greg termed 'the kind decision of nature' to spare them the torments of desire, much as Blackstone had congratulated them on the kindness of the law in relieving them of the burdens of legal existence and responsibility. Women were also among those who held this view. The novelist Mrs Craik (*John Halifax, Gentleman*) noted that women were 'mercifully constituted with less temptation to sin than men'. In Victorian fiction, the woman who falls almost always does so out of love or vanity, almost never from sexual desire.

Here as elsewhere, however, women's fortunate exemption from the complexities of male experience brought with it certain duties. It was their task to save men from themselves: to inspire them to purity outside marriage, and moderation within it. In doing so, they would lessen the strain imposed on men by their coarser natures, and help to preserve the order of society. For, as Greg pointed out, if the passions of women were as strong as men's, society would be destroyed in a welter of 'sexual irregularities'. (Typically, Victorian writers view male sexuality as an all but unstoppable force: women's sexuality is then construed as a necessary check to it.) In Greg's and Acton's view, a woman who made sexual demands on her husband, thereby stimulating the coarser element in his nature, was as failing in her duties as both wife and member of society as the woman who took paid work: she was to be classed with the 'loose, or at best, low and vulgar women' who threatened society, and not with those 'best wives, mothers, and managers of households' who sustained it.

What, then, was the relation of the ideal set out in literature to the social reality of the lives actually lived by Victorian women? In the area of sexuality, this question is obviously difficult to answer. Our great-great-grandparents did not on the whole leave much written evidence on their sexual experience and we are constrained to guess. There is always the temptation for the present-day historian to write with the confidence of one who has come through to a sexually healthier age. But this is unwarranted; the mere availability of sex clinics, manuals and therapists does not obviously declare our greater sexual happiness, however much we might applaud them, and it is not hard to suppose that there were a great many Victorian men and women who discovered for themselves the possibilities of sexual pleasure.

There were some doctors who took differing views from those of Acton. George Drysdale, for example, had argued in his *The Elements of Social Science* (1854) that 'ignorance of the necessity for sexual intercourse to the health and virtue of both man and woman, is the most fundamental error in medical and moral philosophy'. (He put this sentence in italics, but took great care to publish the book anonymously.) This was, in print anyway, a minority view, but Drysdale's book was still being issued fifty years later, in its thirty-fifth edition. He was also attacked for giving advice on birth control, and for his advocacy of free love in preference to marriage, which he saw as an instrument in the degradation of women. He advised women to use the vaginal sponge as a means of contraception, and no doubt this worked against the level of innocence/ignorance assumed by such as Greg and Acton.

It seems that public opinion in this area may have outrun that of the medical profession, for while contraception remained a taboo subject throughout the century, works giving advice on birth control sold well, and family size began to decrease from around the 1870s: those who would not tolerate discussion of birth control were apparently able to practise it. The reduced risk of pregnancy, and its associated dangers of death in childbirth, must have done something to increase the chance of women looking without fear at their sexual lives. Isabella Beeton wrote her book on household management while coping with the death of her first child at three months and her second at three years; she herself died of puerperal fever after giving birth to her fourth child. Such cases were not uncommon, and many women must have lived in terror. Knowing that she might give birth six or more times must have given many a woman cause for fear; childbirth mortality ran at a rate of about 160 per 1,000 in the 1870s (as high as 219 per 1,000 in Liverpool, down to 125 per 1,000 in healthier Scotland), and a similar number of children died between one and five years of age. As one medical reformer, the statistician William Farr, put it: 'The mother when she looks at her baby is asked to think of its death.'

There was therefore every reason to promote discussion about medical reform and birth control, about the registration of midwives, and so on. Dentists and veterinary surgeons were required to register long before midwives, and those who advocated birth control were execrated and punished. (As Annie Besant discovered: her *The Law of Population* was not prosecuted, but she was declared unfit to act as a parent and lost custody of her daughter, the *Saturday Review* commenting that her position was like the advocates of 'prostitution or infanticide as useful and praiseworthy practices', and that she could hardly feel aggrieved at the outcome.) And there were those, even in the medical profession, who held that pain and danger in childbirth were part of God's decree, and that attempts to eliminate pain by anaesthesia were ungodly. Tyler Smith, writing in the *Lancet*, pointed out that etherization might stimulate feelings of sexual arousal, and went on to conclude that 'to the women of this country the bare possibility of having feelings of such a kind excited ... would be more shocking even to anticipate, than the endurance of the last extremity of physical pain'. This last extremity presumably meant death, and few doctors can have been quite so ready to propose death rather than dishonour even to their female patients, yet the example gives some idea of medical hostility to the idea of female sexuality.

There was an increasing tendency among doctors to view all specifically female functions as pathological. Insanity was assumed to be related to the female menstrual cycle, and a whole range of so-called 'nervous disorders' was attributed to the reproductive system. The methods of treatment were severe and included heavy doses of mercury-based drugs and opium, and bleeding with leeches, which, a Dr Bennet suggested, should be counted as they dropped off after engorgement with blood, in case some of them should be 'lost' in the uterus itself. He remarked: 'I think I have scarcely ever seen more acute pain than that experienced by several of my patients under these circumstances.' In 1835, Dr Sims, a gynaecologist, described the treatment as 'murderous' and ventured to suggest that 'it would be better to trust entirely to nature than to the hazardous skill of the doctors'.

But treatment was vigorously pursued, and during the 1860s a spate of clitoridectomies was performed to relieve conditions ranging between epilepsy and sterility which were held to result from unnatural sexual arousal. In the *Lancet* in 1866, such drastic surgery was defended on the grounds that 'a healthy organ was made the subject of an unnatural use'; prevention of masturbation by removal of the clitoris, difficult though it must have been to sanction on medical grounds, was therefore believed to be entirely justified on moral grounds. After all, as the *Lancet* went on to point out: '... since the clitoris was not part of the generative system its removal was not harmful to women's biological functions'.

Perhaps the most sensible way to view women's sexual lives in the nineteenth century is to suppose that a current of mutual understanding between men and women, which must have existed, was working against an empire-building mood in a medical profession that mistrusted female sexuality. It should not, of course, be forgotten that ignorance also played its part (Annie Besant recommended mid-period as the 'safe' time), along with understandable fear, and it seems reasonable to conclude that many men and women would have been drawn to accept the image of female sexuality offered them by Greg and Acton, and to have formed their expectations of married life along these lines.

So far as the restrictions imposed by the domestic ideal were concerned, these were, by the middle of the century, beginning to be questioned by a number of women, Florence Nightingale among them. In 1852, she addressed herself to the issue of why women had been given 'passion, intellect, moral activity ... and a place in society where no one of the three can be exercised'. Women, she complained, were compelled to 'act the farce of hypocrisy, the lie that they are without passion', with even the passionate communion they looked for in marriage denied them by husbands anxious not to trouble the presumed innocence of their wives. The 'conventional frivolities' known as the 'duties' of women required that their intellectual activities be regarded as 'merely selfish amusement', to be laid aside at the whim of 'every trifler more selfish than themselves'. Even the moral energies which might have found an outlet in philanthropic work were thwarted by the official wisdom that women had no need to understand the society in which this work was to be carried out. Women were expected to find their life's Mission (with a grand M) within the family, but the family was 'too narrow a field for the development of an immortal spirit', and married women too often found that 'the sacred hearth' was in reality only sacred 'to their husband's sleep, their sons' absence in the body and their daughters' in mind'. The truth was that there was 'no longer unity between the woman as inwardly developed, and as outwardly manifested', and if women were not to perish inwardly, the outer conditions of their lives must be changed.

Florence Nightingale described herself as one 'wandering alone in the bitterness of life', but to a large extent her frustrations were in keeping with the spirit of the age. Like their male counterparts, middle-class women wanted to share in the benefits of an expanding economy and, far more importantly, wanted to contribute to it.

Both the Protestant and the liberal traditions provided good grounds for arguing that the helpless dependence of women was not feminine and adorable, but degrading. The Protestant faith had been founded on the conviction that it was the duty of each individual to work out his or her own salvation, and this naturally led to the claim that each person, man or woman, was bound to contribute to the work that needed to be done in the world. To many feminists, and especially to those who had to face the opposition of family and friends, this belief was to prove an indispensable source of comfort and inspiration.

At the same time, the Protestant emphasis on individual responsibility accorded closely with one of the main principles of nineteenth-century liberalism: the principle, as John Stuart Mill explained it, 'that conduct alone, entitles to respect: that not what men are, but what they do, constitutes their claim to deference'. This principle was easily applied to women. If a claim to respect could not be inherited at birth, then it could not be acquired by marriage. Only work successfully accomplished could confer status; and, that being so, it was clearly unjust to deny women the chance to undertake such work.

Yet another assault on the adequacy of the domestic ideal came in the Census returns of 1851. These showed the increasing percentage of women over men throughout the century. But the domestic ideal offered no place to the single woman who wished or needed to be self-supporting; she had either to exist on the margins of society – for example, as a governess or a lady's companion – or sink out of it altogether into those trades allowed to 'women' but prohibited to 'ladies'. The problem attracted a good deal of attention, much of it unsympathetic. Men were urged to be more charitable, and to marry earlier; women who could not find husbands at home were advised to set out *en masse* for the colonies, where they might hope to be more successful. These proposals did not, for the most part, recommend themselves to the women in question, who argued instead that the real solution was twofold: to provide more and better paid work for women, and to remove the stigma of social and sexual failure attaching to those who remained single.

It was not until the end of the 1850s that enough like-minded women had banded together to make it possible to speak of a 'feminist movement' in England. By 1869, with the publication of John Stuart Mill's essay on *The Subjection of Women*, the movement had unquestionably come of age. In calling for an end to the subjection of women, Mill argued first that the community as a whole would benefit from the resulting increase in the number of its useful citizens. It could hardly be in anyone's interests to leave half the moral and intellectual resources of the nation undeveloped: to place women on an equal footing with men would be to double 'the mass of mental faculties available for the higher service of humanity'. Secondly, marriage itself could only be strengthened by removing the inequalities between men and women,

74

which were surely harmful to married life, reducing it, in many cases, merely to a 'school of despotism' in which men learned to be selfish and women to be cunning. Marriage between equals, on the other hand, would be a school of mutual improvement: 'The moral regeneration of mankind will only really commence, when the most fundamental of the social relations is placed under the rule of equal justice, and when human beings learn to cultivate their strongest sympathy with an equal in rights and in cultivation.'

More than a century of subsequent debate has done remarkably little to impair the status of Mill's essay, and it is easy to underestimate the extent to which it was a work both of and for its age. Two points are worth emphasizing. First, Mill's feminism is closely related to his individualism. Mill considered his to be an age of mediocrity in which only a small minority had the courage to question the ideas and values approved by society at large. Women especially, trained from childhood to a life of submission, were too often ready to surrender to public opinion. But, secondly, Mill held that challenge and diversity were the preconditions of moral intellectual progress: the liberation of women was necessary because it would enable them to contribute to this diversity and so bring closer the goal of a society in which there would be 'as many possible independent centres of improvement as there are individuals'. This aspect of Mill's argument has found only occasional echoes in subsequent feminist writing. Indeed, modern feminism, in emphasizing a 'shared sisterhood' or 'feminine consciousness', runs counter to Mill's, which was intended to liberate the greatest variety of individuality rather than bring about a sense of collective identity.

The feminists of the 1850s and 1860s, confident that an age which had freed the slaves and extended the franchise must eventually yield to the force of argument, sought to modify the effects of the previously unchallenged domestic ideology. The position of women in society was to be transformed by the development of new opportunities in higher education and the consequent opening up of areas of employment previously reserved for men. The legal position of married women was also to be improved, and, more problematically, attitudes towards sexuality were to be changed. Taken collectively, these campaigns amounted to an assault on the principle of male supremacy, and opposition to them was bitter and passionate. But, for all their vigour, these early feminists did not think of themselves as demanding a revolution. Like Mill, they looked only for the more equitable treatment of women within the existing framework of society; and, again like Mill, they seemed to have assumed throughout that personal life, in and out of marriage, would somehow adjust itself spontaneously to the changes they hoped to introduce. They were undoubtedly too optimistic, but one of the remarkable features of the social history of

Victorian England is the extent to which marriage was still seen, even at the end of the period, as the ideal way of life – the goal of man's labours and the summit of woman's expectations.

The first activity which helped to crystallize the conditions that made a feminist movement possible into a positive campaign for change was the effort to improve the education offered to middle-class girls. Initial attention focused on the desperate position of the governess. Ill-trained, if trained at all, entering the profession only because it allowed her to remain a 'lady', she was both more and less than a servant; more, because she wanted to maintain the idea of her status (one notch above that of the distressed gentlewoman, the daughter of an impoverished middle-class family); less, because her status was temporary and marginal. In 1848, lectures in London to aid the governess to improve her knowledge led on to the foundation of Queen's and Bedford Colleges. And out of the impetus of these developments, Miss Buss and Miss Beale pioneered girls' day schools in London and Cheltenham, and later the Girls' Public Day School Trust.

At the same time, moves to open up higher education for middle-class girls led on to the foundation of Girton College under Emily Davies, a shrewd and determined woman who, like many of her kind, blended an appearance of compliance with an unshakable resistance on the main points. She insisted that her young ladies behave as such, so as not to bring down charges of 'manliness' on their heads (they wore long gloves whenever in public, even while reading their essays), yet she also refused to be drawn into Cambridge campaigns to change the syllabus. Her girls were to do exactly the same work as men, and to be judged on the same terms. ('Different', she felt sure, would be seen by men as 'inferior'.)

By the later stages of the century, with increased provision for working-class children following the Education Act of 1870, and with more and better schools for the middle class, teaching had become a significant profession. In 1850, around 21,000 governesses endured low status and worse pay; by 1900, women represented 172,000 out of the country's 230,000 teachers, about half of them trained and certificated, and earning about 75 per cent of the male rate. The National Union of Teachers (NUT) was also one of the first professional unions, and gradually began to recruit women members, though slowly. The education campaign was then successful in a practical way, and a significant wedge was driven into male convictions about women's incapacity and dependence.

The moderation with which the feminists argued their case was largely ignored by their opponents, who called on the authority of science to prove, from first principles, that any movement towards sexual equality would be attended by dangerous consequences. George Romanes, for example, taking his cue from Darwin's discussion of secondary sexual characteristics such as the plumage of birds and the horns of mammals, sought to classify 'the secondary sexual characteristics of a mental kind' which distinguished men and women. It appeared that men excelled in creativity, self-control and tenacity of purpose; women in refinement, self-denial and patience under pain or disappointment. Men were intellectually superior, and more often capable of the heroic or civic virtues; religious feeling, sympathy and the 'gentler or domestic' virtues were 'the natural heritage of women in all but the lowest grades of culture'. Despite the revealing slip between 'natural' and 'cultural', it was Romanes's case that these differences were not the result of education, but of the process of evolution, and, in the last analysis, of the smaller size and lesser efficiency of women's brains. Even under the most favourable conditions, it would require 'many centuries for heredity to produce the missing five ounces of brain'. (A summary of our present-day understanding of the relative differences between the brains of women and men will be found in the Appendix at the end of the book.)

The argument that caused the feminists most concern, however, was that put forward by Dr Henry Maudsley, in an article in the *Fortnightly Review* on 'Sex in Mind and Education', that higher education would be damaging to women's health. Maudsley derived his case from the principle of the conservation of energy, which he supposed (incorrectly) to apply to the human body. In women, and especially young women, the demands made on the body's store of energy by menstruation were so great, argued Maudsley, as to leave no surplus for serious study: 'When nature spends in one direction, she must economize in another direction.' Women were the prisoners of their biology and any attempt to 'rebel ... against the tyranny of their organization' – for example, by studying for a university degree – would be likely to leave them permanently weakened, and possibly incapable of motherhood. At best, they could expect to become the mothers of 'a puny, enfeebled, and sickly race'.

The next issue of the *Fortnightly Review* published a reply from Elizabeth Garrett Anderson, arguing strongly that women were less likely to suffer from such well-conducted schemes of education as were beginning to become available than they were from 'the depressing influence of dullness' at home. More significantly, however, she rejected Maudsley's account of women's nature. Maudsley had argued that menstruation left women 'for a quarter of each month during the best years of life ... more or less sick and unfit'. But, replied Mrs Garrett Anderson, women knew this to be untrue: healthy women were, as a rule, able to disregard their menstrual periods almost completely. Domestic servants, for example, continued to work as usual, and were expected to do so; and, with regard to 'mental work', it was 'within the experience of many women' that menstruation was less an occasion of weakness than 'an aid, the nervous and mental powers being in many cases greater at those times'.

By the end of the century, the campaign to win higher education for women had taken the feminists further than they could reasonably have anticipated in the 1850s. The educated woman was still likely to think of marriage as the most desirable goal open to her, but she entered it with more confidence and self-knowledge. She had, according to one self-styled 'woman of the day', a new 'realization of her nature's complexity', and a new 'prescience that no man will ever learn it thoroughly'.

After education, the next most important challenge concerned the legal position of women. This campaign necessarily took place over a broad front, since so many of the laws of the land were touched on. But two areas were obviously vital: those concerned with women's political representation, or the absence of it; and those relating to the principles of 'coverture', which denied married women a legal existence.

The campaign for women's suffrage was slow-moving and encumbered by difficulties from the outset. It needed to operate in part through men, and though it had some notable supporters – Russell Gurney, John Stuart Mill and Henry Fawcett among them – it met powerful opposition. Gladstone, in particular, was implacably opposed. He criticized in the House of Commons measures that would deny a convicted criminal the vote, calling it too much that a man should 'bear for life the brand of electoral incapacity', but was happy, or rather determined, that women should be so branded. Technically, a certified lunatic was not allowed to vote, but it was open to allow him to do so during an interval of sanity; women were to be allowed no such intervals.

Some sense of the extreme nature of the refusal was focused after the 1867 Reform Bill, when the franchise was extended to male householders in the boroughs. Part of the deal with the newly enfranchised was that the rates were to be increased. Women householders found that their rates were also increased, but without their being included in the deal. When the law wrote 'men', exacting duties, the term included women; when it wrote 'men', conferring privileges, the term excluded women. In Salford, the names of 1,600 ratepayers, some of them women, were put on the register, and then removed by the revising barrister. The matter went to appeal, and Justice Byles considered it axiomatic that the possession of a name such as Mary or Hannah was enough to cause a name to be removed from the list. Would it not be proper, he asked, to remove a name that was obviously that of a dog or a horse?

None the less there were advances in the period following the 1867 Act. From 1871 to 1883, annual Bills for women's suffrage were introduced and lost, but the issue was kept in the forefront. Women obtained the municipal franchise, and about 14,000 voted in the municipal elections of 1871. During the decade of the 1870s, many joined in local government activity through school and Poor Law boards. Local government reorganization in 1894 created rural, parish and district councils to which women could be elected, and from 1907 this was also true of the county council: Elizabeth Garrett Anderson became the first woman mayor in her home town of Aldeburgh.

Throughout the fifty years preceding the First World War, women's organizations continued to work for the suffrage. As well as the opposition of men – on the grounds that women could not be entitled to the vote simply by virtue of their sex – there were other problems. Liberals, Gladstone excepted, were more likely to favour women's suffrage, but feared that the woman's vote would be a Tory vote; the Tories regarded any extension of the franchise in any direction as too liberal to consider. There were also divisions within the women's movements, mainly strategic: Emily Davies stood aloof, for example, so as to avoid damaging publicity for her campaigns in education.

There were disputes, too, about whether or not married women should be treated separately. A proposal that only single women should receive the vote, since married women were subject to coverture and anyway represented through their husbands, was seen as including a slight on married women, and many suffragists opposed the idea. Those who fought against women's suffrage warned that women were hysterical, and that a parliament elected by women would go to war on the basis of sentimental ideas. Yet, in truth, it was the women's arguments that were quiet and rational, the men's that were typically strident.

As with the campaign to increase women's educational opportunities, women found the male medical world hostile. Sir Almroth Wright expressed in 1913 what many had argued before: that a woman's actions (and therefore her use of the franchise) were subject to 'the reverberation of her physiological emergencies'. Others feared a clerical authority over women's minds. They were 'priest-ridden', argued Goldwin Smith in 1874, and if allowed the vote would soon bring about the end of 'free government, and with it liberty of opinion'.

There were women who shared these fears. Those who signed 'An Appeal Against Female Suffrage' in 1889 were rather the wives of famous men than famous women themselves (though a young Beatrice Webb signed, and later regretted having done so). Their arguments were based on the 'separate spheres' principle: change in society had gone as far as the moral and physical constitution of women could allow. To enfranchise unmarried women would be to give the vote to, among others, the wicked and fallen; to enfranchise married women would be to bring discord between husband and wife. Women should remain content with their 'special' contribution through their family roles (men, on this argument, seem not to have had a family role). Faced with arguments as flexible as these, and in some cases so frankly self-serving and/or offensive, it was not surprising that women should have been divided about tactics, and that the violence, verbal and actual, should have prompted many to join Mrs Pankhurst's Women's and Social Political Union in 1903, committed to the suffrage as the first and only goal, and prepared eventually to use violent tactics to force the pace of change. How far their efforts did so, and how far change might have come about anyway, is still an open question; but perhaps the reluctance to concede that violence may have won the day is one of the vestiges of the (male) belief that (male) legislators could not ever have been so wholly dishonest in their arguments and tactics as the suffragettes claimed.

The campaign to improve the legal position of married women, especially in terms of their rights to own property, was more successful, though hardly less impassioned on the side of the opponents of women's rights. A married woman was classed together with criminals, lunatics and minors as being legally incompetent and irresponsible. On her marriage, the control of and income from a woman's *real property* (that is, her property in freehold land) passed under the common law to her husband, though he could not dispose of it without her consent. Her *personal property* (that is, all other forms of property, including leasehold land, money from earnings or investments and personal belongings such as jewellery) passed absolutely into her husband's control and disposal. He could, if he wished, make a will devising all his personal property, including whatever he had received from her on marriage, away from her and her children; if he died intestate, she could never recover more than half.

The Married Women's Property Act (1870) allowed a married woman to retain earnings or property acquired *after* her marriage, but all that she owned on marriage was to pass, as before, into her husband's ownership and control. But, even in this form, the Act represented a substantial gain in that the earnings of about three quarters of a million working wives were now to be protected. Continual pressure from campaigners led, after twelve years, to the passage of a further Act which allowed women to keep possession of what they owned at the time of their marriage. The Married Women's Property Act (1882) in effect extended to all women the benefits of a settlement in equity. Married women were at last to have the same property rights, and roughly the same responsibilities, as those who stayed single. In one major area, the legal fiction of the non-existence of women was at an end, and on one point at least supporters and opponents of the Acts were agreed: the new legislation would bring into being a new kind of woman.

The women who campaigned for access to higher education and for the reform of the property laws were for the most part able to fight on ground of their own choosing, but this was not to be the case with their challenge to the double standard of sexual morality formally embodied in English law by the Divorce and Matrimonial Causes Act of 1857. Since the Restoration, marriages in England had been nominally indissoluble, but it was possible for a man with enough money and influence to secure a divorce by following an established but cumbersome procedure. The Act of 1857 simplified this procedure and cut the cost, thus extending a privilege of the very rich to the merely well-to-do. However, it remained much easier for a man to divorce his wife than for a woman to divorce her husband: a man could seek a divorce on the simple grounds of his wife's adultery, whereas a woman had to prove adultery aggravated by desertion (for a period of two years), or by cruelty, incest, sodomy or bestiality. The husband could be awarded damages against his wife's lover; no such award could be made to the wife divorcing her husband. In short, the purpose of the Act was to tidy up the procedures by which men were permitted to divorce their wives, and not to introduce into the law any new principle of equality between men and women. (The inequalities were not, in fact, removed until 1923, when the grounds for divorce were made the same for both parties.)

The main basis of opposition was the double standard itself: the rule of chastity for women, but licence for men. Gladstone argued, both in and out of Parliament, that the law should not admit a principle of inequality between men and women where there could be no inequality in the sight of God. Henry Drummond observed caustically that, in this matter, a male House of Commons was 'very much in the position of Turks legislating for the inhabitants of the seraglio'. But theirs was a lost cause. Supporters of the Bill replied that laws had to reflect the needs of society, and while the chastity of women was essential for the safe transmission of property, that of men was not. As Lord Cranworth explained, 'The adultery of the wife might be the means of palming off spurious offspring upon the husband, while the adultery of the husband could have no such effect with regard to the wife.' This argument took no account of the fact that an unfaithful wife was not held to be any less guilty even when there was no question of 'spurious' issue, and it was clearly not the only reason for clinging to the double standard. Some of the arguments put forward in its defence were coarser and more revealing. Men's sexuality, it was argued, was such that they, unlike their wives, could not be required to forgo adultery. Sexual licence among men was, and always had been, universal. Moreover, while a sensible woman did not trouble herself unduly about her husband's infidelity, it was not possible for a man to forgive a similar lapse by his wife: 'The infidelity of the wife inflicts upon the husband so much larger an amount of suffering than ... the infidelity of the husband inflicts upon the wife.'

The passage of the Divorce and Matrimonial Causes Act did not end the debate about the double standard. From the beginning of the century, there had been widespread concern about the effects of prostitution, leading to calls for state intervention along continental lines: that is to say, for a system of regulation which would accept prostitution as a necessary and permanent fact of society and provide for the regular medical inspection of the women involved so as to protect the health of their male clients.

Victorian observers were convinced that prostitution, especially in London, was quite extensive. The police estimated that there were around 10,000 prostitutes, others suggesting between 50,000 and 80,000. Whatever the true figure, prostitution was evidently highly visible. Even the *Theatrical Journal* in 1844 described the theatres as 'great public brothels', and when the theatres got rid of prostitutes, they moved into the casinos and pleasure gardens that were coming into vogue in the 1850s; and thence, from the 1870s, to music halls such as the Alhambra and, later, the Empire, both in Leicester Square.

The hypothetical 'typical' prostitute was neither a girl who made her way to the metropolis in the hope of finding wealthy clients nor an underage girl ensnared into a brothel (underage meaning, until 1875, under twelve, and until 1885, under thirteen; the age of consent then being set at sixteen in 1885). Nor, on the whole, was she an innocent who had been seduced by a member of the middle class. Typically, she was an unskilled worker, the daughter of a family of unskilled workers, often coming from a home disrupted by the death of one parent; her first sexual experience being with a man more or less of her own class, or just a little above it, at about the age of sixteen; and her move into prostitution being casual and gradual, as often as not to supplement a meagre income as a maid of all work, seamstress, hat-maker or whatever.

Few Victorian prostitutes were attached to brothels, though there were some famous brothels with a high-class clientele; and relatively few were managed by pimps. Most women left prostitution after a few years, generally to marry (only rarely did they oblige public sentiment by throwing themselves into the Thames). Prostitution was, in short, a briefly held career, chosen for economic motives against a background of limited choice. The exploitation of women that led to its existence was at the level of social organization rather than at the level of immediate sexual use of working women by middle-class men. Although virtually all confessed prostitutes were, of course, working class, so were a great many of their customers, especially (as one would expect) in the naval and garrison towns.

This latter point needs emphasizing if prostitution is not to be sentimentalized, whether by those who choose to attack middle-class sexual profligacy rather than the existence of extreme degrees of poverty among young women, or by those (like Freud) who have held that the Victorian male, so conditioned by the idea of feminine purity (represented by his mother and sister as well as his wife) could achieve sexual pleasure uninhibited by guilt only with a paid partner of a lower class. The Victorian prostitute took up a casual career as the best bargain she could make in a harsh society, and it was materfamilias as well as paterfamilias who exploited her economically before she became available for sexual exploitation.

In the 1860s, demands for the regulation of prostitution were stepped up following reports that as many as a quarter of the men in the home forces were suffering from venereal diseases; and in 1864 the first Contagious Diseases Act passed quietly into English law, to be revised and extended in 1866, and again in 1869. In their final form, these Acts provided that, where either a registered doctor or a member of the newly formed *police des moeurs* suspected that a woman was a 'common prostitute' plying her trade within a ten-mile radius of one of eighteen naval and garrison towns, he was to lay this information before a Justice of the Peace, who could then summon her to attend for medical examination at one of the hospitals set up for this purpose under the Acts. If the woman was then found to be diseased, she might be detained for up to nine months for treatment; and refusal to attend the hospital could be answered by forcible examination or imprisonment. The aim of the Acts was not to stamp out prostitution (which was not in itself a crime), but to ensure that the women who serviced the armed forces were clean and healthy – a fact clearly recognized by those women who voluntarily came forward for inspection and presented themselves to their clients as officially licensed 'Queen's Women'.

On 1 January 1870, the feminists launched their challenge to the Contagious Diseases Acts with the publication in the *Daily News* of the 'Women's Protest', signed by 124 women, including Josephine Butler, Harriet Martineau and Florence Nightingale. This marked the beginning of a long and bitter campaign. Mrs Butler went before a Royal Commission set up to investigate the working of the Acts to denounce them as an 'outrageous piece of sex legislation', 'a regulating of vice for the facilitating of its practice'. And in the *Shield*, the journal of the repeal movement, she quoted a woman who had suffered under them:

It is *men, men, only men*, from the first to the last, that we have to do with! To please a man I did wrong at first, then I was flung about from man to man. Men police lay hands on us. By men we are examined, handled, doctored, and messed on with. In the hospital it is a man again who makes prayers and reads the Bible for us. We are had up before magistrates who are men, and we never get out of the hands of men till we die!

The Royal Commissions of 1870–1 blandly dismissed feminist opposition: 'There is no comparison to be made between prostitutes and the men who consort with them. With the one sex the offence is committed as a matter of gain; with the other it is an irregular indulgence of a natural impulse.' The insouciance of such arguments infuriated Mrs Butler and her colleagues in the repeal movement, and increasingly, as she had foreseen it must, the campaign against the Acts took on the more general character of a 'revolt and rebellion ... against men'. The laws regulating marriage and the laws regulating vice were seen to point towards the same harsh fact: the sacrifice of the rights of women to the interests and even the appetites of men.

This analysis marks a watershed in the history of the women's movement in England. The feminists of the 1850s and 1860s had been pragmatic and reformist rather than systematic and radical: prepared to challenge the ideal of the domestic ideal for all women, but not to call into question the sanctity and dignity of marriage itself. Inevitably the debate reflected sharply divided views of human nature, and a recognition that the movement for the freedom of women had precipitated a challenge on sexual issues which could no longer be evaded. In the closing two decades of the nineteenth century, the social and sexual conventions which had safeguarded marriage came under scrutiny as never before. The pioneers of the age of the 'New Woman' remained in the minority, however, and perhaps inevitably there was large-scale regrouping of moral reformers campaigning for 'social purity'. For most women at the turn of the century, as for most women fifty years earlier, it was still the case that their true power lay in their ability to influence the minds and actions of the men to whom they belonged.

WOMEN SPEAK

1
The Early Influences

'The female image still projected to young girls tells them that the best way they can enjoy power is by manipulating a male person who claims it, some older male of whom the father is of course the prototype'
– Elizabeth Janeway, 'Incest: A Rational Look at the Oldest Taboo', in *Ms.* (November 1981)

'My upbringing was such that I cannot easily converse with men as though they were normal human beings. They are too special for this. God knows how much knowledge and insight and sense and nonsense I've missed because of this'
– Jessamyn West, *To See the Dream* (1956)

Jenny Agutter: It is a terrible thing to say, but I think one of the reasons my mother and father felt it was all right for me to go to ballet school, and indeed to start acting, was that education, because I was a girl, was of lesser consequence. They probably imagined I would marry and settle down, and therefore they would not have to worry much about my education. Of course, they were entirely wrong. My brother was the one who got married and settled down, and, of course, I carried on with the work. I really think that they felt that starting as a child in films would be all right, and that I would just fall into a situation where I married. Oddly enough, looking at my mother's life, she was a very independent woman who went off and jointed the WAAFs, and even forged her papers to make out she was older. She worked in various different things before she married, and seemed a very independent person. So why she would expect anything different of me, I don't know.

Maria Aitken: I had a rather eccentric upbringing. My father was a Member of Parliament, and we lived in the country, so he was always away in Westminster, and he also worked for a newspaper in London. So I have this curious situation with my mother's father educating me in a hut at the bottom of the garden in the most esoteric way. I used to go every day for my lessons – I had no school holidays – every day until I was eleven. And he taught me what he liked rather than what was on any school curriculum, so whenever school inspectors came, I would dazzle them with logic or philosophy. I never learned any mathematics, I never learned any history. The only English literature I learned was Robert Browning and Bulldog Drummond. I had an extraordinary mixture which equipped me in some ways but not in others. I was also brought up like a boy by him, because of my brother, so I learned to play cricket, brook jumping, endless ball games, fielding practice. It was a curious start.

I was certainly brought up to feel I was clever, that therefore there was nothing I could not achieve academically, and that I would be expected to achieve it. And I would be expected to do something in public life, but certainly not acting. And so, perversely, I chose the profession which defied all the logic of that upbringing, which depended on things that, it was always made clear, I really didn't have – in other words, looks or whatever. So I think I turned the whole thing on its head and tried terribly hard to achieve in an area where I was not obviously equipped at all.

Lady Penelope Aitken: I was a child of the British Raj and my parents were absent a great deal of the time. As soon as I became more or less articulate and could read, I was sent back from India to school in England and my parents stayed in India. There's absolutely nobody I can pinpoint in my life because I think that when one is removed from one's parents one becomes a sort of rebel. So although I would love to think there had been some great inspiring influence, I would say I pretty well just grew like Topsy. I didn't want to be a débutante. I was eventually brought out, but didn't like it at all. I wanted to be an actress, but my parents absolutely turned their axe on that. In my day, you see, you weren't able to forge ahead and do what you wanted. And because I had a great deal of opposition as I grew up, I cast myself off fairly young. I made young friends and travelled abroad. I stayed with friends in Germany and in Holland. I really was a bit of a wanderer, ahead of my generation, I think. I see what the young do now, but I was doing very much the same then, a couple of generations earlier.

Baria Alamuddin: My father and mother divorced when I was one year old, so the biggest influence in my life up to now has been my mother. She's the image I always try to follow, because she was among the very few educated women of her time. She was a Palestinian Jordanian, and when she came to the American University in Beirut she was the first Jordanian woman to study there. I was always influenced by her beauty, her charm, her intelligence, everything she did. I don't know that I still try, but I copied her for a long time, and I always stop and ask, would my mother like this, would my mother like that? There was no other person in my life.

Madeleine L. H. Alatas: I think there was no one person who influenced me most. I think it was a combination of people and places, responsibilities and lifestyles, changing from one country to another. My parents were divorced when I was very young, so I travelled between both of them and their houses. Intellectually, the person who influenced me most was my father. Emotionally, the person who influenced me most was my mother. I was brought up in a very peculiar way. There is something in America called the 200 families who have a peculiar way of bringing people up. It means that you learn other languages besides American or English, and you grow up exposed to a lifestyle that is unreal. It's a fairytale lifestyle – it's Palm Beach, Newport, Southampton, St Moritz, wherever – and there's no possession that means anything. And no place that means anything. You learn very quickly not to make attachments to anyone or anything. You become self-sufficient and independent. The idea of becoming mother, wife, whatever, was irrelevant. I was going to grow up, manage my trust, get degrees, and be able to fend for myself. I think my father's dream was that I would be something like his sister, who is a famous politician, and was a senator, congresswoman, editor of *Vogue* for a while, but now is an ambassador. Both my grandmothers were known as dollar princesses in the United States. They were the ones who had the money, not the men. So the women in our families were treated slightly differently from normal.

I had a tradition to live up to in the sense of very powerful women – strong, opinionated women – that was my father's point of view. My mother's point of view was that, as a woman, you must never lose sight of your femininity, and that you should be protected by men, never threatened. Her point of view was an easy one, because she was known as one of the most beautiful women in the world. She never went into competition on an intellectual basis, she was simply there and automatically incited someone to take care of her. For me, it was a bi-polar influence, north and south. By the time I was eighteen, I was sick and tired of that world. I realized how artificial it was, and got very bored with it. I found I was seeing the same people in New York as I'd see in Stadt, as I'd see in St Moritz, as I'd see in Morocco. It was always the same crowd, always with the same problems, always self-focused, focused inwardly. And I realized that there was a whole world out there that challenged me. I was interested, I suppose, in proving to my father that I was capable of standing on my own two feet and fighting my own battles.

Jan Amory: I was in an all-girls school at first. Boys were not really around at the time when I was growing up. When I reached a certain age, I felt I had missed out through my father dying so young. Because of that, although my mother was strong, I had to take on masculine as well as feminine strengths. In other words, I had to become aggressive to a degree where I could protect myself but be feminine too. I had to be both.

I guess I had no one but my mother to influence me in the growing-up period, as my father died when I was two months old, though my grandfather, who was a Russian émigré, also had a lot of influence. My mother was a very strong woman with fixed ideas who was very opinionated and whom I admired and was a little bit afraid of, maybe, I don't like to think I was, but I may have been. She was very strict. After I graduated from college, I decided that, nice as my mother's friends were, I didn't feel there was enough of a mixture. And so I made up my mind to try to create a bit of a salon at my house and have small, interesting dinners. So, at Pat Lawford's one evening, I ran into the Mailers and found Norman's girlfriend enchanting, though she was not at all sophisticated. Norman was seated next to me at dinner and he asked me what did I think of his girlfriend. I said, well, I think she is a good egg. Apparently he had asked a lot of women the same question, and later that evening, when they got home, he said you know, a lot of women at that dinner told me how beautiful you were, how sexy you were, but there's one girl that called you a good egg. I think that's going to be your best friend.

Adèle Anderson: My father is the one I remember most. He's been married many times, so I didn't really know my mother after the age of four, and what little I did know I didn't like very much. I have a marvellous stepmother now, but what I remember most as a child is my father. He gave love in the only way he knew how, which was to give me a good education and to make sure I had enough to eat, but there was none of the closeness and love I see between parents and children now. I remember wanting that. It's only quite recently that he and I've become much closer.

I wanted to be a girl from the age of three. When I was three I said to my father, when I finish being a boy, I'm going to be a lady. I got very upset because he said it wasn't possible, but I went away to single-sex schools for many years and it all got rather pushed down because there wasn't an outlet. I also got immersed in religion because I went to a cathedral school and used to sing in the choir. It was only when I reached puberty that it all came out again. I didn't enjoy doing the things that boys do. I can't look back and say that I had a desperately unhappy childhood, because I didn't. I was just dissatisfied because I knew really that what I wanted was to be something completely different. I suppose I figured out that I was going to have to wait until it was up to me to do something about it because I certainly wasn't going to get any support from my parents. I didn't have a good time at school, I must admit. I got bullied an awful lot, and I was subject to terrible tantrums, uncontrollable rages, because there was so much inside me and the only way I could let it out was to scream, tear my hair, and generally make an absolute idiot of myself. I ran away from school once, but that was more bravado than because I was desperately unhappy. And when I got to fifteen, my father took me away from school, having decided that it probably would be a much better idea for me to be in a mixed environment. Then I found that terribly difficult to cope with because I hadn't been used to it. It wasn't until I became a woman that I realized I had a lot to learn. I only knew what I had been feeling inside. Being a woman was quite different from the way I had maybe envisaged it.

Dr Swee Chai Ang: As a child, I think I was most influenced by my mother. She is one of the very rare women who are very much ahead of their time. She comes from a family where my grandfather had three wives and women are nobodies. My mother at the age of eight wanted to go to school. My grandfather thought it was useless for a girl to go to school, so my mother walked to the nearest school and got herself registered. When my grandfather took a fourth wife, my mother packed her bags and left home. I think she was only about eighteen then. And at that time, the Second World War broke out and Japan was invading South-East Asia and my mother left her job as a teacher and became an organizer to mobilize people to resist the Japanese invasion. She was captured, tortured and put in a prisoner-of-war camp for five years. She met my father who was also in prison at that time, and after the war they married. Although it was her desire for me to become a doctor, so I could help people who suffer, somehow she also influenced me in her political views. So, in a way, I'm very much like my mother. I hate to see things which are unjust, things which are unfair.

Lady Elizabeth Anson: Unfortunately I had a split home; my parents were divorced. My mother was a gentle person, so probably the influence, as a small child, came from my nanny, who is still alive. And I think I was probably very influenced, because we were close, by my brother Patrick. My nanny was a strong personality, and she was the person I was always with. We had to split holidays as far as my parents were concerned, but nanny was always with us – so one listened more to what she said probably than to anybody. I think she wanted me to be educated and then get married. In those days, nobody of my age actually forged a career; I was a one-off to start a business at the age when I did.

I wasn't more protected, because it was a very male-orientated situation when it was my father's turn to have us. My grandfather had been widowed. He did then remarry, but my father wasn't married, and so there was my father, my grandfather, my brother and then basically, the male staff in the house, like the butler and the gamekeeper, who played a great part in our lives. I was the only woman, so they didn't really look on me as a woman. I mean, I had to join them.

Beatrice Aristimuno: I have been influenced by both my parents, because they are both very strong characters. I always thought I would be like my father, and now, after thirty years, I am more and more like my mother, which I never thought I would be because I never got on with her. My parents are very different. My father is Venezuelan, born in Belgium and brought up in England, so he is very British, very cold. My mother is Argentinian, was raised in Hungary and lived in Vienna, and married a Thurn und Taxis. The language she speaks best is Hungarian. She is Central European, but also has Irish blood. They got together, and I'm one of the results, and now I realize I am more and more like her. She worked when she was young. She lived in Budapest, and during the war worked against the Germans and the Russians to get people out of Hungary. She got married to Thurn und Taxis, divorced, and then went back to Argentina, where she built knitting factories; she used to employ all the Hungarians who lived in Argentina at that time. Then she came to Paris, and worked for Dior. She met my father a month later and they married; she then went to Venezuela and had children. But she probably could have done many, many things.

Elisabeth Barillé: I was influenced principally by male authors, and when I think about it, I feel a little sorry that they are all male, as I would have liked to have women in my Pantheon too. As it is, it is writers like Montherlant, Drieu la Rochelle, Gide, Barrès, a whole generation that is being rediscovered, where women writers don't figure at all. If I was influenced by women, it was in my life. I had a great deal of contact with my mother, more close conversation with her than my father, but my intellectual formation was due to men, the models with whom I identified were men.

94

Dame Josephine Barnes: My father was a minister of religion, but had had a very hard time. His father had died when he was thirteen and left his mother to bring up four children on her own. And he always had the ambition, rather like Hardy's Jude the Obscure, to go to university. He worked very hard as a young man – but didn't go to university then, but became a minister of religion. He then went to the First World War, where he had a terrible time. He was at the Battle of the Somme, he saw Hill 60 blow up, and, as a padre, of course he had to minister to the thousands of British and Germans who were dead or dying. He spent all his time conducting funerals. That shook him very badly, and he eventually got appendicitis, and was invalided out. Then my mother came into some money, so he took my mother and five children to Oxford: went up as an undergraduate at the age of forty-four, and got his degree. We were three boys and two girls, and he saw to it that all his five children went to university – four of us to Oxford, while my sister read a degree in classics and archaeology at Cardiff. So his was quite an influence.

Josephine Barstow: I was born in Sheffield, and the first part of my childhood was spent in Yorkshire. I was pretty unhappy for the first eight years of my life, I seem to remember. I was very unhappy at school, and bullied, and all that. We moved down to London on my eighth birthday, and I went to a new school and seemed to get a new lease of life. I remember, at the age of eight, thinking I am never going to be as happy as this again, I've got to enjoy being eight. And part of the acceptance into North London life was that I was accepted by all the boys in the area and was a kind of little goddess in a masculine society for a short period of my life, which I enjoyed enormously.

One of the reasons I chose singing as a career was that I felt it was something I could do, but it also seemed a profession in which one could be active as a woman without having to fight any battles as a woman. One didn't have to establish oneself as anything different from the men already in the profession, because you were needed as much as anybody of the masculine gender. And I know that was something of which I was conscious very early on. But at fifteen to sixteen I wasn't positively career-orientated, I was much too conventional; I thought in terms of having a husband and all of that stuff, because that was the way little girls used to think. So I just followed the trend. I wasn't a trail-blazer at all, although I was a rebel later on. It never struck me that I would go off and do something on my own. The theatre is not a thing you do on your own, you are part of a team. I became theatre-struck at about the same time as I was in love with this English teacher, and used to go to the theatre practically every night in London. But I knew that I wasn't going to be an actress, and one day the two things in my life connected. I knew I could sing and I suddenly decided, very dramatically, as I've always done things in my life, that I was going to be an opera singer. I was brushing my hair at the time. I remember it absolutely clearly. I was then sixteen or seventeen, I rushed downstairs to my mother and dramatically announced, floods of tears everywhere, that I'd decided I was going to be an opera singer.

Jennifer Bartlett: I had a normal southern California upbringing. I was expected to marry at the age of twenty-three, which I did, to an appropriate person. I can remember that, when I was accepted for graduate school at Yale, my father was quite disturbed and said, well I won't pay for it, but then Yale did, so it wasn't a problem.

Rotraut Lisa Ursula Beiny: My parents were both interested in one thing: studying. My mother always said, get out of the kitchen, I don't want you to be a housewife and be dependent on a man. You must be independent and have a profession. You must be able to take care of yourself. We left Germany, where my father had been in a concentration camp, and so became refugees. When I was a little child – they are still vivid memories – we went over the border to Czechoslovakia; then, when Hitler invaded Czechoslovakia, over the border to Poland; and then we came to England. My mother is not Jewish, so that is how we managed to get out. And then we were interned as enemy aliens. I was in Holloway Prison for two days, a little child, and then I was in an orphanage. Then we went to the Isle of Man, and when we came out I hadn't really been to school and was, by this time, eight years old. I had started to learn English before we were interned and then my schooling was interrupted. In fact I never learned to read properly until I was eleven. Of course, my father influenced me in many of my ideas, because he had been through so much. He was a brilliant man, a genius, who had been a lawyer in Germany. But, of course, he couldn't practise law here, so he had to do something else, and that was why he founded this business. My father always said there was only one thing to be in life – No 1. If you were No 2 in school, he slapped your face. My father believed in being No 1. He didn't understand anything else. He was a Prussian and believed in discipline; when he came into a room, he expected you to stand and so on. You ate what you were served. You couldn't leave anything on your plate. My brother used not to eat some things, and he was caned. I'm afraid I learned to eat everything – everything and anything – and this was a useful lesson later on in life.

Christine Bogdanowicz-Bindert: I was never really told what to do or what not to do, but my perception, as a child, was that I was never doing well enough. I was rarely first in class, always second or third. And I would go home and be told you could have been first. That, I think, has influenced me all my life. That's basically where all my drive and ambition have come from. I always have to prove that really I should have been first, whereas I was second and third. I think in retrospect, and even now, the reason I am not No 1, however one defines this, is that my interests are broad. Although I am a banker, I have a lot of other things that I'm interested in. And I think, if you really want to be absolutely top in one area, you must do only one thing in life. I'm interested in a broad spectrum of things, from politics to culture, and I have an accomplished personal life which I place, not above everything, but at least equal to everything.

Francesca Braschi: My grandmother influenced me most. She is a very dynamic woman. My grandmother is South American. And in South America everything is very conservative, very traditional, so you can imagine when my grandmother was my age, you couldn't do half the things you can today. She had a lot of money, and she saw that there was a lot of poverty, so instead of being on these big haciendas doing nothing or sewing, she said, we've got to do something. So she dedicated her life to helping the poor, and abandoned children. She had farms throughout South America to take in abandoned children and educate them. Because of that, she spoke in the United Nations – another great achievement, because few women from South America at that time spoke in the United Nations – about world hunger and poverty and getting children off the streets and building beautiful farms where they could be educated, fed and clothed. She divorced, which was unheard of at that time, and yet she educated her children in such a way that they all had perfect marriages.

Heather Brigstocke: My mother was by far the more dominant, but I loved my father too. There were only two girls. I was the elder one, and my father was very sad he didn't have a son, so he treated me as one and said I must never rely on anybody else, and must always rely on myself. My mother influenced me because she made me work, and he made me do things for myself, so they were both quite strong. They were both Scots, and of course the Scots worship education. My mother had taught for ten years before she was married. She taught boys in Glasgow – her forty backward boys she called them – and she was a first-class teacher. My mother was a graduate, she'd been at Glasgow University; this was before the First World War. But my father had left school at about twelve or thirteen, I think, to go down the mines. Then, under age, he joined the Royal Flying Corps in the First World War.

Suzanne Brøgger: I was influenced by my grandmother and my mother with sadness and my father with happiness. My mother was very ambitious. I suppose she wanted me to lead the life she had not, so she read Freud and Neill (the man from Summerhill) about modern liberal upbringing so as to free the child, to let all the faculties bloom and the talents develop. I was ten when my brothers were born, and I never had the impression that boys had more freedom, more power. I was brought up for part of the time in South-East Asia, where I met people who thought of the universe in a very feminine way; they were not interested in traditional male power but thought very much of the female potential, and they sowed that in me and stimulated and inspired me. It was only later as an adult, as an accomplished writer, that I discovered how male-orientated the world is. All its structures are really made by and for men.

Janet Brown: In a way I was a kind of rebel. The life I watched in my home – we lived in a tenement building in Rutherglen, outside Glasgow – was of girls growing up and going to school, coming away from school, eventually becoming engaged, married, having children, staying right there in Rutherglen, pushing that pram up and down the main street. It was a picture I just couldn't cope with and, at a very early age, I said very strongly, none of this for me.

Tina Brown: My mother was the biggest influence because she was at home all the time. She made bringing me up her career. She was a glamorous figure who looked marvellous – like an opera singer, rather like Callas – and everybody always thought she was a model or a movie star. In fact she just brought us up. She was so enormously entertaining that she was quite a hard act to follow, and I think a lot of my life has in some ways been trying to equal her lustre. In other ways, though, I wanted to be my father, because my father was a film producer and seemed to be always doing exciting things. He came home with all his outside stories of going on location and film stars. I could see what an enormous effect he had on my mother, and I was so attracted to my mother that, in a funny way, I wanted to be my father so I could attract her admiration. My mother was incredibly protective, too protective. She was obsessed with the idea that any harm should come to me. We lived in the country, so I never did anything particularly. There wasn't much chance to go out and take drugs and so on, but she was extraordinarily protective while, at the same time, nurturing great ambitions in me. She was a mother who wanted everything for me and encouraged me to get it.

Somehow it was born in me that I must try to go to Oxford or Cambridge. And then I would be a writer or a dramatist or whatever. I was never encouraged just to get married. No one in my household ever thought that that would be a role for me. I was a very timorous child. In many ways, all my career exploits are about going against the grain. I think it's true that people who achieve quite a lot in their lives are often people who are shy and timid and trying to prove to themselves that they are not. My mother could never leave me at a party. She always had to sit in the car and hope I was all right before she drove away, because I was so anti-social. I was always crying for my mother. I was a tremendously timid little girl, and I have remained quite timid inside. It's just that I've always dared myself to do things, and in that sense I was influenced by my father, because he was the daring one.

Joan Juliet Buck: I remember this kind of dim, awful feeling when I turned about sixteen or seventeen and began having a social life, and meeting a lot of girls who had been to Heathfield, and they'd received no education. And meeting young men who seemed to have received no education either, and who naturally assumed that I hadn't read a book and only wanted to get married. That was the one time I started to feel constricted. When my parents wanted me to meet the sons of rich friends, I refused, I never went. It was much more interesting hanging out at the corner with some tortured poet or a journalist who was a friend of a friend from Paris. That was much more exciting than those people with sports cars and futures and businesses.

Averil Burgess: My grandfather was the greatest influence. Chiefly in establishing values which I held for a long time, though, to some extent, I have now moved away from them. He was a headmaster of a school in a very deprived area of Liverpool. And he retired the year I was born. His elder daughter had died of diphtheria when she was ten and he gave to me all the loving and caring educational influence he'd like to have given his elder daughter. I think, to some extent, he even thought I was some sort of reincarnation, because, although a Presbyterian, he was highly unorthodox and believed in reincarnation. He was an old man who was in many ways – I knew even at the time – rather intolerant and narrow-minded. But he valued intelligence highly, above almost everything else. Again, that's something which influenced me for a long time and which doesn't now quite so much. But he turned me towards reading things at an early age which I wouldn't otherwise have done. He gave me things which were far too old for me, and I used to struggle through those books in an effort to discuss them with him because I admired him so much. And I could express myself to him far more than to my parents because he had time and we were intellectually more on a par. I sent all my youthful poetry to him. He took everything that I said and did seriously, and he believed in me. He thought there were only three worthwhile professions: healing, teaching and preaching. That, too, perhaps, I don't believe quite so much, because I try to influence girls to go into productive professions and so generate more wealth. Paradoxically, I have now rejected quite a lot of his values. Nevertheless, when I was young, he influenced me more than anyone. He wasn't ambitious for me in a materialistic sense. He wanted me to achieve intellectually more than socially. I don't think he was really conscious of the conflicts, the difficulties which could arise for a woman in combining success in one field with success in another, although he was very keen on my succeeding. He died when I was seventeen, and strangely enough, when I got my headship here, when I was thirty-five, the first thing my mother said was, I wish Taid – that's my grandfather, Taid's a Welsh name – was still alive. He would have been so proud.

Liz Calder: Although there was encouragement at home, I didn't really perceive myself in terms of a career for a long time, and I suppose that was partly due to the time in which I grew up and also the place – New Zealand in the 1950s. The thing to do was get married, and I accepted this, and although my mother always said, think of your life in terms of what you're going to do as well as part of a partnership in marriage, it was so much the mood of the times that I was anxious to be first down the aisle, just as later I was anxious to be the first where possible in other fields of endeavour. And so I really did, when I married at twenty, envisage that this was it – what I was going to do. Just be married to the man I was in love with.

Carmen Callil: Women were not important in my family. They're never important in Arab families. They have power, but they're not important. I think the person who had the most effect on me in my life was my cousin. She died a long time ago. She was the one who changed my life most.

Angela Carter: I had a straightforward English professional-class childhood. I was supposed to go to university, but didn't get sufficient A-Levels, and so my father apprenticed me to a newspaper as a reporter. It's fairly unusual for a father to persuade his daughter that journalism is a fine career for a woman, but certainly my father was convinced that it was a fine career, and he was right. Perhaps I was particularly susceptible to advertising or women's magazines, because I worried a lot you know, about what in America they call popularity. How dumb can you be? My parents certainly disapproved of me worrying about it, and that was when I began to feel boys had a better time, they didn't have that worry.

Barbara Cartland: My brother was a great influence. He was the first Member of Parliament to be killed in the Second World War, and was a great visionary and an idealist. He would undoubtedly have been Prime Minister if he had lived. He was a great friend of Winston Churchill and was the first Member of Parliament to ask, in 1935, for holidays with pay – nobody ever had holidays with pay in those days. He asked for holidays with pay, and for family allowances, which they said at the time would bankrupt the country, and for planning for industry; and he asked that every workman should have a stake and say in that in which he had contributed his capital, which was himself. In other words, you should have shares in the company in which you are working. All of those things have been achieved, except for shares in the company, which is now coming along.

Luciana Castellina: My mother influenced me very much, not from a cultural point of view but because she was a vital person and very active. She loved to talk to people, to be sociable. One's relationship with other people and the world is probably more important in life than a specific ideology or a specific religion. I wouldn't say she was ambitious for me. She had a relaxed way of looking at the world. When you are ambitious, you think you have to succeed, because otherwise it will be a disaster, but she was optimistic. So she never thought that if I didn't do this or that, it would be a disaster or a catastrophe, or I would be unhappy. This was not a problem. My mother came from Trieste, and so I had what you might call a Middle European education, which was far more free than the rigid Italian education at the time. So I was used to being free, but nevertheless I was not as free as men, of course. And so I tried to do whatever I could not to follow the rules, but sometimes found myself embarrassed.

Tina Chow: When I was growing up, I thought my mother was very strict. We were the only Orientals in Cleveland, and I wanted to be like everyone else. I thought my mother was saying you cannot buy an ice cream and walk down the street eating it, because it's a different sort of etiquette, and this and that. We were very sheltered and very protected by my parents. I always worried about being half-Japanese, half-American, so I never felt there was a problem in not being a boy.

Felicity Waley-Cohen: I would say I had in many ways a very relaxed, very happy childhood. My sister had cancer and died when she was fourteen and I was thirteen, which obviously had a very major effect on my life. And because I was at school abroad, that also had an enormous effect, because even if you are in boarding school in England, you're quite close to your parents, you feel that there is some contact. When it's actually a plane flight away, when the letter you send about the drama takes four or five days to have a reply, you become very self-reliant. I became more and more independent because I had no contact. One had nothing in common with anybody other than one's age, one's sex, one's school. And those are obviously very important things.

Shirley Conran: I loved my mother, and I did not love my father. I was frightened of him. But the biggest influence on me was undoubtedly my school. I was very lucky. I went to St Paul's. We had wonderful teachers and those good, clear-headed, clever women taught us to think for ourselves. Also at St Paul's we were brought up regardless of colour, creed or nationality. I never knew what racialism was, or snobbery, until I left school at fifteen, and then it came as a terrible shock.

We were all treated as individuals by our parents, but it was certainly never expected that I would work. Nothing could have been further from their minds or my mind. It was expected that I would grow up, get married, have four children, and that would be that. As it is, I have a very absorbing job, writing books. I think of my mother at my age, when she had just been widowed, and I know that her life somehow came to an end. It makes me think I'm very lucky.

Genevieve Cooper: I think, like most women, I have an ambivalent feeling and attitude towards my mother. I hate her and admire her as well. She was much stronger than my father. She was quite free. She was very liberal, very advanced, sexy and ostentatious, very visible and very beautiful, and quite demanding and manipulative. She did not believe in education, she didn't believe in school, she didn't like sending me or my brother or sister to school. She wanted us to be original rather than educated. She was rather superficial in a way; she wanted flamboyance and sexiness. I think she would have liked me to be notorious rather than famous. She would probably have been quite pleased if I had been Christine Keeler. She was a very strange woman, a great character. She used to dye her hair purple, used to have green fingernails. She always liked to be noticed, which was very good in some ways and quite bad in others, because you can't live up to that sort of expectation. You can't be as outrageous yourself, if you're the daughter of somebody like that. I still feel that she's not really very proud of me because I'm not as beautiful as she would want me to be, or not as famous as she would want me to be. I feel she wants something more than I can give her. My father worked for Marks & Spencer, which he left quite early on, and he also used to buy property and run farms. He used to buy very big houses, wonderful houses, usually old schools – castles, some of them – and run farms from them, in Cornwall and Sussex and so on. They were places for my mother to play out a sort of fantasy. I think he loved her very much and they had a sort of fantasy life of being rich. He wasn't rich at all, but he lived as if he was. He had big cars, big Buicks and a Rolls-Royce at one time, and a Lagonda. Everything was very flashy, and the houses were visually stunning. It was lovely except, within the houses, we had no money, so we were sharing a banana between five, six people, and all that kind of business. Crazy.

I'm quite unshockable. Nothing shocks me much. And I'm sensitive to pretentiousness. I hate pretentiousness. I think my mother's strong preoccupation with appearance was bad for me. It made me too self-conscious as a woman, as a person. As a woman, you've already got that pressure anyway. It was a bad start which made me insecure.

Michelle Coquillat: My mother is a professional woman, a professor. I am from a family of women. I have two sisters and my mother never considered that I was not going to be a professional woman. She influenced me tremendously, I think, going her way, leaving me alone. I was a very independent child and adored having a very busy mother who didn't take care of me, who only had intellectual conversations with me when I was twelve or thirteen and probably gave me enough tenderness when I was very small but not too much presence. In a way, I had a strict upbringing, because I come from a bourgeois environment where the idea of being well brought up and having a certain attitude as a young girl was something very important. The relationship with men was something codified, very stereotyped, and it took me a while to understand that I could have other kinds of relationships with men.

Susan Crosland: I was brought up in a close family – a very close extended family – and loved both my parents and was a much-loved youngest child of a youngest child of a youngest child. So I was very much a pet. At certain ages, my mother influenced me more; at other ages my father did, and it went on like that throughout my adulthood until they died. It shifted back and forth. My father was probably the greater influence in terms of tolerance. My mother was much more prejudiced, but I loved her.

Mary Crowther: I think my father probably had the greatest influence. I saw him rather as a soured figure. Both my parents had grown up during the Depression, and that was a very strong influence in the sense that it taught me the virtues of saving money, working hard, always worrying about the next disaster around the corner. But the other thing was trust. I saw the sadness in their lives that the Depression had left with them. Both my parents had had aspirations to do certain things with their lives, and all those dreams were destroyed by circumstances far beyond their control. So they channelled those aspirations into their two children. My father was the stronger personality, because I think he was the sadder of the two, and perhaps my mother, like most women, could fulfil herself in other ways, but it's more difficult for men, when they have an abstract dream and it's not fulfilled in their lives.

Alma Daniel: My mother, at a very early age, tried, I think, to overcome her natural sense of possessiveness and over-protectiveness and put me out into the world very quickly. She took me to school on the first day, and after that I went to school by myself. And when I was six and a half, we used to travel from one county to another, from Queens to Brooklyn, to visit her mother on Sundays. She sent me on the subway by myself when I was six years old. It was an hour's trip. It was her way of saying, you see, you can be on your own, you can be independent.

Sister Camille D'Arienzo: My mother died when I was eight years old, but my memories of her are strong. One memory is of the first day that I went to school into the first grade. I was, I suppose, six years old, and she gave me a lunchbox. It was a public school, and we would eat on benches in a basement room. And she said to me, now, you have a sandwich in there, and when you sit down and you look around, if the person next to you doesn't have any food, you have two options: you can either share your sandwich with the person next to you, or you can keep it closed in your lunchbox until you come home. That made a profound impression on me. Another time I overheard an argument between her and my father, who was also very generous, and warm, and loving, and good. This was during the Depression in the 1930s. It wasn't easy for any of us. We had many beggars coming to our doors, not that we were rich; we were middle to lower class in terms of finances. There was an old woman in the neighbourhood whom I always considered to be some sort of a witch, because she dressed in black, with a veil over her head, and sold paper flowers, not particularly attractive, made out of crêpe paper. My mother would buy a few when she came to the door, and then she would have to hide them from my father because money was so precious. One day my father discovered them and they argued. He said to her, Ray, you fall for every phoney that comes to the door. And she said, Lou, if they are phoney, it is on their conscience. If they are hungry and I send them away, it's on mine. Now those are very small snippets of life, but I remember them and really think that they influenced my concern for the poor throughout a lifetime. My father, who was both mother and father to me for many years after my mother's death, also influenced me in many ways. When I was eighteen, I told him I was thinking of going into the convent. My father was not a religious man, and I expected tremendous opposition. He was very quiet and his eyes filled with tears and he said, that is not what I had planned for you. I wanted you to marry somebody rich who would take care of you, I wanted to send you to Europe, I wanted to give you a car. But if that is your devotion, I won't stand in your way. And he never did.

After my mother died and my father remarried, it was decided that I would go to a Catholic boarding school. I was almost twelve, and it was my first real exposure to sisters. I had never gone to a Catholic school; there were none in our parish, none in our neighbourhood. I really and truly admired the sisters. I thought they were generous, wonderful women. I suppose, because of their trappings and their habits and so on, there was a sense of mystery about them that intrigued me. But more and more, as I came to read the Gospels and understand who this man called Jesus was, I really and truly loved that person of the scriptures. I couldn't find anybody that I would rather spend my life working with, being with, being like, than Jesus. So the attraction was certainly Jesus Christ, if I had to say why. I don't know when the fascination began, but by the time I was seventeen I had decided I would like to enter the convent and be a sister. Actually, I wanted to be a missionary sister and go to far-off places and do dangerous but dramatic work. The reason I did not follow that option was because I thought it would break my father's heart. So I joined the Sisters of Mercy.

Dr Mary Jordan-DeLaurenti: My sisters and I were all encouraged to become nuns. My mother encouraged that. It was, to her, the epitome of success, to have a daugher a nun or a son a priest, and I guess that if your behaviour is geared or guided towards that, then that's probably what you'll become.

Kay Dick: I think I influenced myself. I'm illegitimate, but didn't know this until I was seventeen. I have a mother whom I absolutely adored, and a stepfather who was a German Swiss, and I was sent abroad to be educated in Switzerland and then at a French lycée. My mother was one of the most feminine women ever – beautiful, adored people, a great flirt, absolutely droves of men about her life. I remember that, as a kid, I loved the men, because, in getting in good with my mother, they bought me presents.

My mother came of frightfully good family but because of the accident of me she was chucked out, so she reluctantly became a sort of kept woman until made respectable by my stepfather. But she adopted the point of view that women were made for love, beauty and romance. Of course, when I got to sixteen and seventeen I was intellectually priggish and thought she was terribly stupid. You know: women never understood money, women were there to be cosseted and courted and taken out to balls and to *thés dansants* and given chocolates and Parma violets and so on. So I suppose that by deciding at the age of twenty to go out to work, I was revolting against her chocolate-box attitude.

Dame Jean Conan Doyle: Undoubtedly my father had the greatest influence. He was a man with such personality, and both my brothers and I looked up to him. He spent so much of any free time he had entertaining us, playing games and being interested in us. My father was a man who was larger than life. I grew up much influenced by men, because all my cousins were male cousins and I had my brothers. I was the youngest, and I wasn't going to be left out of anything. My father was extremely kind and understanding. I had extremely bad eyesight and he knew this would be a handicap. He wanted me to have a career, and he thought I would be best with people and in a leading capacity, which was funny because I am a very shy person and had no wish to lead anyone. Women were always on a pedestal as far as my father was concerned. He looked up to women, he thought they were by far the greater sex, but that they should be kept out of the trouble and the worry of this world. He admired their brains. If my eyesight had been better, he would have liked me to go to university. But I couldn't take exams. I think he'd have been surprised to know I joined the Air Force.

Margaret Drabble: My mother was a frustrated woman and she put a lot of ambition into making us ambitious. She herself hadn't found an outlet for her undeniable intelligence, and therefore she wanted us all to be high achievers. I'm one of three sisters, and we were all made to feel we had to achieve intellectually from a very early age. I think that's quite bad, really, to be made so competitive. We were made to set our sights wholly on intellectual achievement which is not wholly bad. At the same time, it made us, I think, unhappy at times, lacking in social pleasures, because we weren't allowed to go to parties or encouraged to have friends in the home at all. I think I would have been happier as a child if I'd been allowed a slightly more normal home life. It was a fairly strict upbringing, and it was directed towards the exact paths that my mother was interested in: reading and literature. She never said she wanted me to be a writer, but it was quite obvious she wanted us to do well in school and university. My father, who was equally interested in reading, was a more relaxing influence. His role was to comfort us and make us feel that it didn't matter if we weren't wholly successful. My father was a very strong man, but he was away during the war when I was small – I was born in 1939. He came back and settled down in 1946, but by that time my character was formed. I'm still trying to work out the influence my mother had on me.

I had plenty of confidence. I was brought up to believe I could be top of the class all the way through, and that was partly my mother, but I do also remember my father saying to me when I asked at about twelve or thirteen, could I be anything I wanted in life – he said, well, if you say you want to be prime minister, I think you probably couldn't. If you say you want to be the principal of a women's college in a university, of course you could. And that now seems to me a very realistic assessment of my chances. He was encouraging, but my mother's influence was much more diffused. It was simply that her children were best. And that was that.

Sally Emerson: My mother studied English at Cambridge, and always encouraged me with my writing. She was very much the person who helped me. My father and brother were both what you imagine men to be: very rational, very sensible about everything, whereas I was dreamy and could never find my way anywhere, and sat reading books. My brother would do things like reorganize my whole library, all my books, so that a book on cameras would be under C, whatever the title was. I knew exactly where they were in terms of the first letter of the title of the book, under H if it was *How to Use a Camera*. My parents certainly treated me the same as my brother. My mother came from a fairly unconventional background – her father was a left-wing potter in the potteries in the Midlands, and she had been brought up (and this was unusual at that time) not to cook or clean or to do any female tasks. My grandfather was very emancipated – he'd never let their children call his wife – my grandmother – mother, and never let her use the name Mrs, although she was quite a conventional woman. So she was known as Nelly and he was known as Jack, and in the little village where they lived people were shocked by this kind of behaviour and thought that they weren't married. In fact, they were married, but all the villagers thought that they were outrageous. I think that came through to me. The idea of having children, or getting married, seemed a completely shocking, extraordinary idea. All the games I used to play, complicated imaginative games, concerned women on their own, without men. The women in one game used to live up on the window ledge: about six dolls dressed up in bits of cloth and a rubber band around them. I pretended they lived in caves in mountains, and used to come down to the little town below and sell the produce they got up in the mountains. A kind of alternative society before its time, because this was in the 1950s. They also used to steal from men, I'm ashamed to say, and used to spend the night with men sometimes. I didn't have any idea of what happened, but I knew they came off richer. I'd obviously seen things on television. There was a whole complicated story about them, but essentially it was that the women were always very independent, getting on with things; men weren't incorporated at all.

I don't think there was any one mentor. My best friend was Tina Brown, and it was the first time I found somebody like me. I didn't like going out much. My first instinct was always to stay in. To find somebody who was quite pretty and good fun and who also used to hide away and lock the door to make sure nobody came to visit in the evening, who enjoyed working and writing and was obsessed by writing in the same way I was, was a great relief to me. I had always thought I was rather peculiar.

Marcia Falkender: I was the third child and therefore a little lonely, because there was a gap between my elder sister and my brother, and myself. I felt a bit out of everything in that my sister was made a great fuss of because she was the first child and my brother was the son and therefore special. But my father was wonderful with me. He went to great lengths to make sure I didn't feel like that, and so I became very attached to him and he always had the greatest influence. My mother and I didn't get on very well. In later life, we learned to get on better and to understand why we were made as we were, but she was very religious and quite a strait-laced lady. My father, on the other hand, was much more tolerant and it was therefore easier for me to be good friends with him.

My parents belonged to that age when girls just got married and had children. They were ahead of their time in believing we should have a good education and stay on at school until we were eighteen. It was not the norm for working-class parents to feel like that, about girls in particular. They had a very low income. It was a strain to get three children through high school. It was quite a grind for them. So in that respect I suppose they were liberated, but they would not have minded if it had ended with getting your A-Levels, then going straight on to get married. The idea of going to university, which I did, was mine not theirs. They accepted it because I was the youngest one who had always been a bit unorthodox. They accepted I was going to do something different. But I was, I think, motivated by this desire to prove that I could also have as special a place in their eyes as the other two had: one for being beautiful, the other for being male.

Esther B. Ferguson: I was born very poor in the south of our country, and only my basic needs were covered. I had quite a tragic background. My mother killed herself, and my father was unfortunately an alcoholic all of his life. So it was particularly devastating. And I had great difficulty working, because I was unable to get an education in the beginning, so could barely make any money to live.

Christina Foyle: I adored my father. He was always so full of fun, and he was so clever. I learned more from him than from anybody else in the world. The day I left school I joined him at Foyle's. I was seventeen, and I was with him from that day on. We got on so well, and I think I was helpful to him because, in those days, things were difficult in the book trade. Everybody was hard up in the 1930s, and nobody had any money. I used to help him with his creditors. I used to go to see bank

109

managers and persuade them to hold, to give us big overdrafts, and I used to persuade the publishers not to press us for payment. My father found me useful as a very young girl. I learnt a lot that way.

My father was really rather a gambler. He was always up to something. Once, coming back from America, he kept playing cards with some rather sharp people. First of all, he won quite a lot, about a thousand pounds a day – this was in the 1930s – and then he lost it all and a lot more besides. He told these men – they were real sharpers – that he couldn't pay, but they accepted a cheque. Then I had to get off the boat very quickly at Southampton to stop the cheque. He used to give me all those sorts of things to do. And then there was a lot of money owing to him from the Soviet Union, with all kinds of bad debts, and he sent me over there to collect them. I went to Russia, by myself, when I was twenty-one. I went all over Russia, but most of the people who owed us money had either been executed or gone to Siberia. I didn't have much luck.

Rebecca Fraser: My mother decided what books we would read, although my father would, from time to time, appear and suggest we go to the library. But my mother was at home the whole time, and inevitably I think you're very influenced by your mother if you're a female child. We were only allowed to watch an hour's television a day, which I think is probably a good thing. And we had quite rigid rules of behaviour. My mother was very ambitious for us all to write. And so there were endless competitions to write diaries in the holidays and to write stories, to imitate poetry and to imitate novels.

Gisèle Galante: I was never brought up by my mother. She used to work a lot and travel a lot, so I don't have too many early memories of my mother. I don't have too many early memories of my father either, I must say. The only memories I have are of my nannies. I was brought up here in Paris in this house, and I stayed here until about the age of twelve. Then my brother got very sick with Hodgkin's disease. I was a healthy little girl, but just the same I had sore throats and colds, and my brother's white cells were very low, and, because he would catch anything I had, I had to move from the house, to a small flat my father rented near-by. So from the age of twelve till the age of eighteen, I was extremely close to my father, and the situation was not easy for either of us. He had no social life, nothing. He gave everything up for me. Like a mother, he would wake up in the morning and get my breakfast ready and I would go to school. Then, at night, he would prepare my dinner.

He was my mother. He was a big influence. For all those years, I was not close to my mother because I did not have much time to see her. After I was eighteen, she thought it would be a good idea for me to come back to the house. My brother was much better, and now is totally fine. So I've lived here from the age of eighteen until now, which is thirty. I don't know if I'm right, but I have a feeling my mother is doing all the things now that she was unable to do when I was younger because she was busy with her own work and with my brother. I feel she is trying to give me all the things she was unable to give me before, which is a little late.

Teri Garr: My father was a kind of failed actor who drank a lot and was a romantic, singing, wonderful joke-telling guy. He died when I was eleven, and I must have felt that I had to finish what he started because I went and studied acting and dancing and singing. I made it my business to finish off what he didn't get. I don't think I thought it consciously but maybe unconsciously.

When my father died, my mother had to take care of three kids. She put us through college, and she had no education, so she lived on her wits and invented things to do. She taught dancing and she instructed knitting and ended up seamstressing and going to work in the studios. She worked very hard, but was a competent mother and determined to get us through school. I used to go to work with her because she worked on TV shows where you work all night, and I would go and wait with her. In fact, I'd go into the big wardrobe rooms and try on all the clothes, and this is how I first started thinking I wanted to be an actress.

Pamela Gems: My grandmother was a great influence. I spent a lot of time with her. She was widowed in the First World War. My mother was also widowed very young, but I spent a lot of time with my grandmother. She was a witch really. You imprint at a very deep level, and I imprinted from her. My mother was, still is, a melancholic from the loss of her lover husband. But my grandmother was very strong, very wise, very tough and unmalicious. She was a little bit frightening, and I don't know why, because she was very benign. We were, in a way, sisters. Just before she died, she used to come to me and say things like, look after Else, Pam. Else is my mother, whom I neglect. My grandmother was a very important woman, but quite uneducated and very funny. She had three sons and three daughters, no money, lived by poaching – all that kind of thing. But she was formidable.

I had two younger brothers, but one had a heart defect and the other was severely asthmatic so missed most of his schooling. I was the eldest of the three. And we were told that neither of them would survive, Once, when we all had measles, they told us to lay my baby brother on the bed, because he was going to die. In fact they are both alive and well. My mother was told, when she was widowed, to put two of us in a home. And she refused. She was very beautiful, still is, in her seventies. She looks like Garbo, and I'm still frightened of her. I'm a plain daughter of a beautiful woman. I am in love with my mother – we all three were – but we had to placate her constantly. She sang contralto beautifully. In fact she was taken up by the local gentry. We had no middle class where we lived, only ourselves and people with titles and huge houses and thirty servants. So I grew up knowing the difference between an Aubusson and a Chinese carpet, for example. I saw the end of the feudal life. You see all this and yet you are not part of it. Of course, you are full of hatred, really. You're full of resentment, because it's so unfair. We lived, seven of us, in a coach-house. Next door lived an old lady with, I guess, seven or eight servants, counting the outdoor – one woman in a house with fifteen bedrooms. It was a house where Scott had written some of his books. So this collision was very dramatic; it was a dramatic childhood. In fact I didn't know that the middle class existed until I grew up and went into the WRNS, when I realized that there were gradations rather than the nobs and slobs. I was a terrible snob myself, and still am a bit, because of that early hierarchy and knowing how to behave. My uncle was an under-gardener who got the sack because he refused to bow when Queen Mary went by. The servants had to line up and bow, and he said, I can't do that, and they said, well, I'm sorry, but you must. But when she came he hid behind a bush. He voted Labour, secretly. It had to be secretly in those days, or you lost your job. But he was seen and he lost his job.

Victoria Glendinning: I was brought up in Yorkshire and my parents' life seemed very far away from me. The people who seemed to me to be really exciting were the boys I was not meant to play with in the village, the rough boys; I would escape from my house at all times, and I would do anything to be allowed to play with them. They would say, if you want to play with us, you'll have to eat a worm, you'll have to eat a snail, climb the water tower, jump off it. I would do all these things, because the important thing was to be allowed to play with them. I remember driving in a coach from my school through Oxford and the French teacher saying: you will be here, you will go here, you will come to Oxford; and me saying in my head: I will not, I do not want to, I will not; but I did. So it was despite all that, that I did all those things. I

112

remember not wanting to be clever at school. There is a poem by Andrew Marvell about a garden and there is a line in it: annihilating all that's made/to a green thought in a green shade. The English mistress said, what does annihilating mean, and how do you spell it? I knew and put up my hand and everybody turned round and said Brainy – and made hissing noises. From that moment I knew you weren't popular if you were clever, so I wasted a great many years concealing the fact that I knew everything, because I thought people would slight me. I had to learn gradually that it could be quite interesting and profitable to show what you knew.

Lady Annabel Goldsmith: My father was a dominant figure, brilliant in his early days, very well-read, very amusing. I think he was the kind of father who really did try and mould you. He was quite frightening but very lovable, strict but not nastily so. As children, we also spent a great deal of time in Ireland with my paternal grandmother, the famous old Lady Londonderry. She was a dominant lady, a very fascinating lady. A great hostess. She had strong ideas, but she was also rather fey and made one believe Irish folklore, fairies, all that sort of thing. All the Londonderry women have always been strong characters, Londonderry men slightly weaker. My father was quite strong with us as children, but basically he was quite a weak character; the strength came from her. She was definitely an influence. She always joked with me. She was absolutely convinced I was going to be prime minister, which was unthinkable in those days and I would have been a hopeless prime minister. My father always thought I'd write. He wanted me to go into journalism, to have a career. He was very against getting married early. It was a most unpopular move and he was furious when I did it. I'd had my interview with Frank Hain and I was going to start on the *Daily Mail*, which was lucky for me because I could have started on a provincial paper. But then I met Mark and that was it. Eighteen is very young. After that I did charity work.

Isabel Goldsmith: I was brought up by my father, who's been the main influence along with my maternal grandmother. My grandmother's Spanish, highly Catholic, keen on religion, formal in her views on education. And my father is Jewish, atheist, against religious education, not particularly formal when it comes to education and feels it's appalling to be over-educated. So I was there, in between, trying to do what each wanted without the other one knowing, because they had opposite views. All of my mother's family, being particularly Spanish, were keen on when I was going to get married. But I had no direction at all from my father, and no particular leadership in that way, none at all. At eighteen he just said, now, you're grown up, and you're your own responsibility – which wasn't much help. The few things I wanted to do were always criticized and so I got discouraged quite quickly.

Felicity Green: I was an only child. My parents didn't like each other at all. Their relationship was fraught and fairly unhappy. Each looked to me for their happiness, which is quite a burden for an only child. They had very different ideas about what they wanted from me and for me. My father wanted me to be happy, my mother wanted me to be something. Both my parents were Jewish: my father came from an immigrant family from Poland, my mother came from Russia and her grandfather was a rabbi. Hers was an educated immigrant family, and the one thing she wanted for me was that I should have an education, though she had very limited views of what an education ought to be. I don't think she saw me as a don. She saw me as a very successful shorthand typist. But at least she wanted me to be able to earn a living. My father had absolutely no capacity for earning a living, and we never had any money. Because we lived in a very rough neighbourhood – very much a dormitory neighbourhood – my mother wanted me to go to a better school, so instead of going to the local state school when I was very young, I went to a private school, where I probably had the worst education available at that time, but at least she felt it might rub the rough edges off. My father kept a shoe shop, and my mother made sure that, out of the takings each week, she had enough to pay my school fees. And when she didn't, I have vivid recollections of her pawning her wedding ring to pay the school fees. If this is a bit hearts and flowers, and comes out sounding a bit sentimental, it is my background. My mother was stone deaf from the time I was born, and the only person she could ever communicate with, other than her sisters, was me. And I learned to lip-read just as she learned to lip-read. My father had a very short fuse. He was a man who got very angry, very quickly. A lot of my recollections as a child were of my father getting desperately impatient with my mother because she couldn't hear him, and being quite cruel, quite cruel. He was an emotional man, a sentimental man, an incredibly generous man who, the moment he had £5 in the till, felt obliged to give £4 away, which made for a great deal of bad feeling between him and my mother, who had better things to do with the £4. She was worried I would grow up outside the Jewish religion, although she herself was not particularly Orthodox, but more Orthodox than my father. She used to send me, every weekend, to stay with my grandfather so I wouldn't have a Cockney accent, though my grandfather had such a Russian accent I don't know what she thought

114

this would achieve. Anyway, off I used to go to Stamford Hill to stay with my grandfather, and try and get some kind of religious education. I never did, and I can't say that any of it has stayed with me. My mother died about ten years ago; she had been ill for quite some time and it was sad at the end because she didn't know me and it went on longer than one would have wished.

People always say only children are spoiled. I think, to spoil a child, you have to ruin their character, and I hope my character wasn't ruined. I think they gave me whatever they had, but since whatever they had was very little it didn't disturb my values.

Katya Grenfell: Franco Zeffirelli had a lot of influence on me, because I worked with him when I was quite young and he's my godfather. I used to see him a lot actually, especially when I was between eighteen and twenty-one. We used to go every year and stay with him in his villa in Positano, and I worked on films with him when I was twenty as an assistant. He started off the whole photography – a crazy thing, I think, probably.

Baroness Grimond: Oddly enough, I think my childhood was dominated by three women who all had very strong characters, and these three, in order of importance, were first our nanny, who was a most remarkable woman who today of course would certainly have had higher education and would never have looked after children; secondly, my mother; and thirdly, my stepgrandmother, Margot. But of the three, of course, our nanny was the one we lived with all the time, and she was certainly the dominant person. She had a typical puritanical working-class outlook but she was a highly original woman who made her own decisions. At quite an early stage in her life, she decided to leave the Church of England, which she was brought up in, and become a Non-conformist. She also went her own way in politics. She was a Liberal, and was always careful to say that she was not a Liberal because of us, but that she came to us because she was a Liberal. So she instilled this kind of radical outlook, but combined it with a strong dose of puritanism, and honesty, and a belief that you must speak the truth and own up if you had done anything bad. My mother provided enormous stimulation and fun. In those days, one saw one's mother mainly for an hour after tea. You would be changed to the skin, and have your best clothes put on to come down to the drawing room and have a great time. But she also used to do things like read aloud to us a lot, and come and tell us stories before we went to bed at night. So did my father, whom we absolutely adored.

My mother contributed the love of literature and poetry and that kind of thing and also made life great fun. In other ways, it was quite difficult to live up to what she expected of us. But then that was much more social than moral. Nanny represented the sort of moral imperatives, and my mother the social ones. Margot, when we were very young, was rather disconcerting, because she was an extraordinary character and one who pitchforked us into tremendous social pressures at the age of about five. We used to go and stay with our grandparents during holidays at Christmas, and also in the summer. Margot had huge lunch parties with all these Bloomsbury figures, and at the age of five one was expected to go round the table shaking hands with people who then asked terrifying questions; and whatever one answered would be greeted with peals of laughter. Children don't like being laughed at, and the people who are good with children are those who take them completely seriously, treat them like another grown-up person, which is what simple people usually do. So that took a bit of withstanding. And then one was often asked to perform, to sing or recite poetry or something of the kind. I think this has given me a certain resilience in the face of social ordeals.

I think it's always hardest for the first child, so my sister certainly had the most daunting task, which was to wear down the parents a little. They are learner drivers with the first one, and the second one is therefore always slightly more irresponsible. But I'm afraid my mother expected my elder brother to be the fulfilment of all her own ambitions. She had been a brilliant performer in politics but had never stood for Parliament, and indeed didn't want to until the end of her life, but she very much belonged to the generation which looked to their sons to embody whatever ambition they had. And so she put an enormous pressure on him which she didn't put on us. Oddly enough, she was not at all a feminist. My sister would have liked to have been educated and to have gone to university, but my mother wouldn't have it. I had no ambitions of that kind, so it didn't frustrate me in any way. She was only ambitious socially for the girls. My father wasn't ambitious at all. He put pressure on none of us, and was the supportive element in our life, and also had a vein of rather charming irresponsibility himself. My mother wanted us to be rather *dans le monde* and to shine and be attractive, amusing and successful, and here she was influenced by her own stepmother, who also wanted that. She was haunted by the fear that we might not get married, my sister and I. I don't mean that in any serious way, but she would have been horrified if we hadn't. I had a facility for painting and drawing and she longed for me to be an art student and to paint, because that was all right. Had we had literary gifts, that would also have been all right, but going to university would have meant you were a bluestocking, and to be a bluestocking was not at all all right. In

116

her world, it was considered to be very gloomy and boring. Not acceptable.

Amy Gross: The older I get the more I realize how much my father influenced me to work, to be independent. My mother didn't work. My father pushed her to work, but she liked being a lady who went to do volunteer work, went to the theatre, went to art galleries, took painting lessons. And the older I get, the more I see that my father's judgement that a woman has every capacity and should work was right. And he made no distinctions between what men can do and what women can do. My brother is the youngest, and the minute he was born, I saw the difference. My father's a doctor, and in my family that was considered, you know, a step slightly under God. And I remember my brother at a year and a half, not able to speak yet, being held up and my grandparents' friends saying to him, so you are going to be a doctor, too? Now nobody ever said that to me. That has frozen in my mind, become a snapshot. And I was even pre-med when I went to college, though as circumstances worked out I dropped out and became the editor of the newspaper.

Miriam Gross: I was an only child and I had an extremely strict mother. I was born, in fact, in what was then Palestine, and my mother was half-Russian, half-German; but she was Prussian in her attitudes – not at all like a Jewish mother. She was the opposite of a Jewish mother. I had to have books under my arms so I didn't stick out my elbows when I ate. I was terribly alone, as an only child is, so I had no sense of perspective. I didn't have other children around to tell me my mother was actually overbearing, very strict. For instance, although I went to Hebrew school, I had to learn German every evening after school – and I had to learn extra maths, and I had to learn English. I was brought up like a Victorian German child, as it were – strict in every way.

I went to boarding school very young, first in Switzerland when I was eight for a year and a half. I was completely alone there because I didn't see my parents for about a year, and I had to learn a new language – Swiss German. Then I was brought to England to a progressive school – Dartington Hall – now a laughing stock because silly things have happened there, but it was a famous progressive school: Bertrand Russell had sent his children there – that kind of school. I went there when I was about ten and a half, and again had to learn a completely new language, and had no contacts in this country at all. My mother came and visited me sometimes, and I was absolutely miserable, and

117

used to go off and cry in a big gym every evening. I said to my mother: I can't stand it, you must take me away. She said: I'll leave you here for three months. If you're still unhappy, I'll take you. After three months I was still unhappy and she didn't take me. I've never forgiven her, but it was the right decision – ruthless though it was – because after a year I was extremely happy. Once no one knew I wasn't English I was perfectly happy.

Flora Groult: My parents were artists. They were friendly with all the artists of their time. All those people came into our home – Picasso, and Cocteau – all that was my background. I didn't even know they were special people. I was astonished sometimes later in life to find people could be boring because I always saw sparkling people as a child.

Georgina Hale: My mother came from a poor working-class family of twelve. My parents were publicans, so they worked seven days and seven nights a week. And even though my brother and I were never locked up or beaten or anything like that, we were deprived of other things because I didn't know them. It was always: run along, do what you like, eat what you like, keep out of the way, go where you want, just keep out of the way, keep out of the way. I would never bring anyone home because I was so embarrassed that I lived in a pub. I didn't understand why I couldn't live in a council flat like everybody else. My father was a very strict man because he had been in the Navy and everything really had to be shipshape. And my mother – I loved my mother but I didn't know her because she was always busy working. When my mother died, my father remarried a girl younger than me, which was a strange experience. So I guess, as a kid, I used to daydream an awful lot and live in a bit of a fantasy world. But I was mostly a loner, mostly a loner.

My environment was going from pub to pub; we were always on the move. Most of the young people I knew were thieves, and the girls were prostitutes, also thieves. Nobody had a proper job, nobody did anything. And if I hadn't had an ambition, I would have ended up being married to some small gangster. As a kid, I always had to tell myself, I am going to have better than this; I don't want to be a housewife and have a load of screaming kids and worry about where the food is coming from.

Jerry Hall: In my family I have a twin sister and three other sisters –

118

five girls and my mother – and I had eight aunts and my grandmother lived with us a lot. My father travelled. He drove explosive chemicals across the country, and he'd be gone most of the week, so our house was definitely a totally female house and my mother and grandmother were always teaching us to cook and sew and this and that. My grandmother said I had to learn all these things to get a man. My mother had different ideas. She always said, you can be anything you want in the world, you just have to think positive; any goal you want you can have if you believe in yourself. So she was always telling us, especially around twelve years of age, now is the time you have to start thinking what you want to be, and you can be anything, so don't stop yourself just because you're a woman. You can do anything now, because it's a great age. She read a lot of Norman Vincent Peel – she totally believed in that. So, in our house, all the girls were walking with books on their heads. We had to learn all the social graces and manners, plus the cooking and the sewing.

Mira Hamermesh: My father was my greatest influence. I'm a daddy's girl. I've observed that there are some women who are daddy's girls, and these have received from their fathers a kind of tacit permission to function and go out into the world. I use the parallel with the story of Athena who sprang fully armed from Zeus's head and became the goddess of war and of many important functions usually regarded as masculine. My father was the one who encouraged me, and delighted in the talents I showed as a child, spinning stories, drawing and so on. Mother was remote. Maybe she was already tired of having children, or maybe she never knew how to relate to children. Whatever it was, father is the one whose spirit moved me.

When the first bomb dropped during the invasion of Poland, I knew I had a destiny. There was something about the war which mobilized in me a burst of energy, a burst of consciousness, awareness and curiosity. I wanted to see the world. I knew I'd have to write about the war, and I'd have to see and observe everything. When I looked in the faces of the first Germans who entered – when I saw those handsome, triumphant faces of victors – my rage at belonging to the conquered people was so intense that, from the first day, I invented resistance, without knowing what it was. Progressively, each day, there were new prohibitions: what the Poles could do, what the Jews must not do – you mustn't use trams, you mustn't go to cinemas. Every new order, I would disobey. My mother didn't know, my father didn't know, but I would vanish from home and spend a whole day with a gang of friends, hopping on and off trams and staring into the faces of Germans. No cinemas? I must have seen the Nazi propaganda film *Jud Süss*, the anti-Jewish classic, a hundred times. I saw all the war newsreels, so the spirit of resistance came to me and I kept plotting to get away. I became an early resister in spirit. I couldn't bear the idea of being prohibited, of having no entry anywhere; even today, if I go to a club and hear women aren't admitted, I feel I want to explode.

Romaine Hart: My father was definitely the person behind who I am today. He very much wanted me to join the family business, and I fought against it for a long time, but eventually I did it. We had a company owning small cinemas all round London, going right back to the turn of the century – my grandfather, my father, it was a three-generation thing. So he very much wanted me to join the family business. Unfortunately, he died well before he saw the success I made. It was only after he died, that my career started. It was interesting, that, all the time he was alive, although he made me what I am today, I never blossomed. I only started to blossom and become what I have, and achieve what I've achieved after he died.

Olivia de Havilland: My mother had a sense of responsibility towards both her children, and I think she rather thought they would accomplish something, and she was rather for that. She was a kind of adventurous person herself, though very conventional in many ways. None the less, she won two musical scholarships to Reading College, the first when she was fifteen. It's only in thinking about my mother now she is gone, and thinking about her in the terms of the period in which she lived, that I see she was quite unusual and had lots of initiative and was quite wonderful. After she won the second musical scholarship, at twenty-one, they wanted her to stay on at Reading College as a teacher, but she decided the academic life was rather narrow and got on a ship and went out to Japan to be with her brother, who was a brilliant young man, a lot older than my mother, who had married a Japanese, and they had a child, and that in 1907. She loved the life in Japan and joined the Tokyo Amateur Theatrical Society, who apparently put on very good productions. One day, when she was singing in church, a lady came up and said, may I write a musical play for you? My mother thought, well, I am trained as a musician, but I had better find out something about acting if people are going to write musical plays for me. So off she went, back to London. Then the First World War broke out. My father, whom she had known for seven years in Tokyo, came to London and persuaded her to marry him and so she went the second time to Tokyo. I was born two years later, my dear sister a year and three months after me. And

120

again my mother did something unusual – separation and divorce weren't all that common then. Off she went with me and my sister, to take us back to England. The war was just over. We had to stop in San Francisco. I had a fever and the doctor said, you cannot cross the country with a child with tonsils like these; they have to come out. So she stayed on in San Francisco and then moved again, down to a better climate south of San Francisco, to a lovely village she found, and decided to change her mind yet again and live in another foreign country. Then she went back to Japan to arrange the divorce from my father. She had technically abandoned him by not living where he lived and where his business was conducted. But she made these decisions, and though I don't think she thought of herself as a courageous and enterprising person, she really was.

Brooke Hayward: Both my mother and father were very educated people, even though they were in the theatre. We lived in Los Angeles, which was considered fairly barbaric. My mother believed in education and took me out of kindergarten when I was about three or four because she didn't appreciate the way we were being taught to count, which was with piles of lima beans, and she hired a tutor. So, from the time I was about four until I was twelve, I was tutored instead of going to school. And so were my brother and sister. From nine to twelve every morning, when everybody else was in school, we were being tutored at home, and we never, therefore, had any sense of rivalry or competition with other children. We flourished in this way, I must say. By the time I was twelve, and my sister was ten, we had to go to school, because mother decided that we had to make some nod towards conformity. It was quite traumatic at first. Among other things, we were better educated than anybody else in the school, and we were much more sensitive. My mother and father, being in the theatre, were both involved with art, and I was brought up in a house with beautiful paintings: Impressionists, Picassos, Monets and so on. As small children, we were always squabbling about the paintings – who would get what when mother and father died. These paintings were very important; they really had a profound effect. Also because they were in the theatre, mother and father led flamboyant lives. Their lifestyle was extraordinary. We had houses in California and New York and Connecticut, and we travelled a great deal. Looking back, I realize that at no point in my childhood, not even when I was eighteen, nineteen, twenty, was there the slightest intimation that it would be harder for me, as a woman, to get a job in this country than it would be for a man. I was treated as an absolute equal by both my parents, no matter what I did. Great premium was placed on accomplishment on every level, particularly at school. When we finally did adjust to going to school with other children, we did very well, except for my brother. He went to school in England for a year but he was very sickly so, although he did brilliantly, he was sent home by the school because the winters were so hard in England and I guess there was no central heating. After that, he was never able to readapt to American schools, and I think it's probably because he was too bright. He would have done better if he could have been educated totally in England.

There were very strict laws about meals in our house. We were not allowed to eat with our parents when we were very young, which was fine with us. But when we got to be a little older, and a little more articulate, we were weaned into the grown-up world at the dining-room table. And there were strict laws, one of which was that conversation, good conversation, was imperative. There was no newspaper reading allowed at breakfast or anything like that. It was all about what had happened the night before, what theatre had been seen, and vast tracts of conversation about books and so on. And father had a kind of rod that he kept by his chair. It was a joke, but it wasn't a joke. If we misbehaved or spoke out of turn, he would sort of rap us on the knuckles. It was amusing, but it very much defined a kind of discipline that was important in our house. Which I must say, looking back, I am grateful for. I certainly don't see this going on in anybody's house today.

My mother's authority had one kind of meaning to me, my father's another. In fact, my mother probably had much more of an influence, and what pleased her probably meant more to me. She was a tough task-master, much tougher than my father. Her expectations and ideals were huge and monumental. She died when I was about twenty-two, and I know that I would not have taken certain steps in my life had she remained alive, because she wouldn't have approved of them. There were steps that my father didn't approve of either – for instance, a certain marriage. Had he gone so far as to say he would disinherit me, I probably wouldn't have taken the step, but he never went quite that far. My mother would have talked me out of it. She would have definitely talked me out of it. I would have listened to her.

Cynthia Heimel: My mother was very fearful, very conventional, very frightened of anything strange, anything new, anything different from the small world she came from – her relatives were in concentration camps in Russia during the war. So, by the time I was born, I was never allowed to do anything. If my feet looked slightly askew, she'd take me to a doctor because she was afraid. She was afraid of everything.

Marie Helvin: I was brought up by a very strict atheist, my dad, and was not allowed to have anything to do with the Church in any way whatsoever. I could have girlfriends that went to the Catholic church, but I wasn't allowed to have anything else. I never went into a church until I was nineteen. I was fascinated by the nuns and would sneak down after school to the Star of the Sea, the Catholic school, and ask to carry their books for them to their dorms. I did this for several years and my father never found out. I think I did it first because he always said I couldn't have anything to do with the Church, and that's why I wanted to; and secondly because there was something about them that I just thought so beautiful. And after the nuns it was actresses who played saintly women, like Gina Lollobrigida in *Hunchback of Notre Dame*. Oh, she was such a heroine of mine. Bernadette of Lourdes, the one played by Jennifer Jones – all these kind of women, to me they were so perfect. It's not so much that they were good, it was more they were so beautiful. That's what I thought – physically beautiful. And I couldn't understand why my dad was so against me having anything to do with people like this.

Margaux Hemingway: My father influenced me most, because I think I was basically the boy that he didn't have. We are three girls, Muffet, myself and Rea. I'm the middle kid, and I was the one who went on all the fishing trips, the hunting trips, and so I was like a whipping boy, I think. And I'm absolutely in love with my dad. I could pretty much do what I wanted to do. I grew up as a tomboy. Maybe it's being a Hemingway or something, it was sort of a charmed life, but I never even thought about disadvantages in being a girl. Because I was always a cowboy, one of the boys, in the bar drinking tequila, driving my own truck – I had my own '57 Ford pick-up truck – and I was on the ski team and so I was pretty go, go, go. My father was really the driving influence in my life, and still is. I love my mother, but my dad is the best. He wanted me to do more than just marry. As it turned out, I did get married twice.

Val Hennessy: I was influenced mainly by literature. It sounds terribly pretentious to say this, but I had read the whole of Dickens by the time I was about fourteen. And Charlotte Brontë. I think of myself as a romantic and I'd like to say that, from a very early age, I've been aware that Mr Rochester would never ever have fallen for Jane Eyre.

Dr Leah Hertz: There were three daughters in the family, and I was the eldest. I was born in 1937, and my youngest sister ten years later, and when she was born people came from the neighbourhood and patted my mother on the shoulder and said, don't worry, the fourth will be a son. And my mother stood and looked them straight in the face and said, but I don't want sons, my daughters are going to be better than sons. When you hear that about twice a week for twenty years, you start believing it. So my mother was a great influence.

Elizabeth Hess: I'm a child of the 1960s, so I was influenced by what was going on in the world – the Vietnam War, the civil rights movement in this country, and the second wave of the women's movement. I grew up in a very conservative Republican household at a time when there was tremendous turmoil and political upheaval. I went to private schools and wore uniform every morning from kindergarten to twelfth grade. My mother had tremendous influence over me. I think there was always a bit of a power struggle in the family, in that my mother was a real liberal and my father very conservative, and I was witness to a lot of their debate and a lot of their troubles. I think, in some ways, I'm a real product of my time, a real product of the baby-boom generation, growing up in the 1960s and becoming independent in the 1970s. Certainly, in America, this was a time when young women were struggling for and given a tremendous amount of freedom and independence. I read Simone de Beauvoir's books and they changed my life and really created what I am today.

Arianna Stassinopoulos Huffington: My mother is the ultimate earth mother. She was not just a mother to myself and my sister, but to everybody who touched her life. She is still alive and is still very much an influence. She always made me feel, not so much by what she said, but often just by her attitudes, that there was nothing that was impossible, that whatever I set my eye on I could do, so she never limited my vision. Even though I was brought up in Greece and most of my friends were getting married at eighteen, and it was still rare for a woman to have a career – all that has changed dramatically in the last twenty years, but I was born in 1950 – as far as she was concerned it was always taken for granted that my sister and I would go to university and that we would have our careers. As to which university, for some reason I decided to go to Cambridge in England, and everybody was saying, oh she'll never get in, it's hard for an English girl, but my mother was always absolutely certain that I would. It was that kind of unconditional confidence that she had in me, as well as the unconditional loving which went hand in hand. Very often mothers who feel their children can do anything withdraw their love if they don't, but she wasn't like that at all. When I failed my driving test, or when I failed whatever it was at different moments in my life, her love was always there and always unconditional, and hand in hand with that was that amazing sense that the sky was the limit and there was nothing I could not achieve if I really wanted it. My mother and father separated when I was ten, so it was very much a matriarchal household – just my mother, my sister and I, although my father was very close to us and still is.

Isabelle Huppert: I was the youngest of my family, so I guess my older sisters and my brother and parents influenced me, because I was raised as the baby, and that lingered for quite a long time. From my father, I learnt integrity and a sense of certain values and morality, and from my mother, will and energy and a lot of positiveness. I don't know if we were brought up to be independent. We were brought up to be curious of everything very early; we travelled, we went to foreign countries when we were very young, and I never felt any big pressure on me. I always felt that I was going to be free to do whatever I wanted.

Angela Huth: My father was a remarkable and talented and clever man, and I absolutely adored him. My mother, in fact, wasn't there for most of my childhood. She went off. So I was actually left alone with my sister and my father in a very large house with some servants. I had a lonely childhood really, and I think that is why I started writing because I didn't like reality too much, so I went off into my fantasy world whenever I could. I started writing at about five, and my father was a most wonderful judge always of what I did. He always talked to me as if I was a grown up, and I can remember at about five, I suppose when I was writing one of my first plays, about elves, I wanted to know what he thought the elves should wear. I sat on the edge of the bath while he was shaving and he discussed with me, in all solemnity, whether they should wear green, or brown or whatever it was, and I found this terribly touching from a very young age that, whatever I put to him, he would take completely seriously and discuss on a sort of grown-up level. I think really I owe an enormous amount to him in everything I have ever done. He was an example of somebody who worked terribly hard all his life, and I admired that. I always thought that I should like to work just as hard one day. My only regret is that he died before even my first book was published, because he would have been terribly pleased. He said, I know you will always be a writer, but unfortunately he never lived to see it.

It was a very conventional sort of upper-middle-class upbringing of those days, I suppose. I was sent to boarding school at eight. My mother had an absolute obsession about people being able to speak languages, and so she sent me off, at the age of nine, all by myself, to Switzerland, to a town, to a convent, where nobody spoke English at all. I was totally miserable there, but she didn't seem to mind. She just said, well, you will come back speaking French. Which, indeed, I did. I think it was there, when I was nine, that I wrote my first book for my sister. I was so unhappy, and so cold in the evenings, sitting in this horrible house *en famille*, that I started writing just to forget reality. Looking back on it, I was always writing to forget reality.

Angela Janklow: I am very antagonistic, very forward, very bumptious, very difficult. I am very provocative, basically. My brother is kinder than I am. He's much easier to get along with. Because of that, my parents found it much easier to cope with my brother than to cope with me. I am very anti-authoritarian, almost to a ridiculous degree. My brother had much more freedom, in part because I was the eldest. I broke the ground about every single thing – late nights, music, parties, general behaviour, or whatever. My mother was over-protective with my brother, but he got out from under her wing and grew into his own when he was about fifteen or sixteen and started playing electric guitar and hanging out in clubs and with rock stars. My mother was worried, because I was so mean to him, so consequently she over-compensated. Because my brother was too nice, I saw him as a target and pounced on him. But that was long ago, and now we are the best of friends. Now he is independent, but not in a ferocious way, the way I am. I am staunchly and vehemently independent.

Dr Lukrezia Jochimsen: I grew up during difficult times and dangerous years. I was born in 1936, and what influenced me a lot was that my father was in opposition to the politics and the life in Germany. In school, I was taught about the victories of Fascism and Hitler. Teachers taught children what would happen when, one day, Russian hordes, as they called them, came into Germany, what would happen to us children and what would happen to our mothers, and I went home crying and upset. When I told my father, he took me into his study and showed me the map of the world. He pointed out America and Great Britain, and Russia and France, and all their colonies around the world, and said, they are at war with us, and here we are, and here is Japan, and we have to think about the idea that, sooner or later, we will be defeated and the defeat will not be what they teach you in school. This

126

was very courageous of my father because I was nine years old, eight and a half even, and in times like that children were under pressure outside their home. He even risked my going right back to the teacher and saying, my father sees the situation quite differently. But he told me this was a secret between him and myself and that I should keep it, which I did. So this, of course, was a very strong influence. And unlike other children of my age, in 1945 my world did not break down, did not change. It was something that was going to happen and we looked forward to it, and it was something we lived through and experienced together.

Sally Jones: My grandmother was the one I always wanted to be most like, because she had been an excellent tennis player and an excellent hockey player. She is somebody who's got a determination of spirit, and I think it was that indomitable will that I most admired, whether in games or in ordinary life. I've also got one spinster aunt, who's also my godmother, who'd been a great rat-catcher during the Second World War. She's always been a maiden lady, and she used to go off with her dogs, her traps and her poison. There is a wonderful picture of her with a pile of several hundred rats that she had killed at one particular barn. It always struck me that becoming a rat-catcher or something unusual and not particularly girlie, was rather a fine thing to do. I think it was that kind of role model that really led me into things like sport and into a world that is not particularly feminine.

Rana Kabbani: My grandmother was a most incredible woman who worked for women's suffrage in Syria. Her brother was Prime Minister, and therefore she had a great deal of political power and entertained all the statesmen of the period. She was the one who taught me how to get out of the bed, and it's helped me most of my life I think. She believed that if one had strength, and if one had some cleverness, then one would be all right.

Tessa Kennedy: We were babies when we arrived in the States: twin girls, always dressed alike, and so prettily dressed that everybody would stop and turn. People just stopped and talked to us, with the nanny, when we were in a pram. I have very early memories of that. We raised such attention in Central Park in New York, so I hear, that my grandmother, who was terrified by the Lindbergh kidnapping, which had happened a few years before, decided we would always wear trousers if we ever went out in public. We only wore dresses at home.

My grandmother had always been very very liberal with us and spoiled us like crazy, but when we came back to England after the war my mother was running a large house in the country, practically on her own, with two smaller children and us and rationing – clothes rationing, food rationing, all that kind of thing – which we had no idea about, nor wanted to know about. My nanny used to cry when we cried; she was so upset for us that they got rid of her very quickly. They realized we would never toe the line if we stayed with her, so she had to go. We ran to the nanny every time they said no, you can't do this. I remember very strict years after that, especially once my parents divorced when I was ten. Divorce was absolutely unheard of in those days. Nowadays there are few children at school who don't have divorced parents, but we were looked on with awe. I think people at school thought, how fantastic, to have two homes to go to, two families to play against each other, and that kind of thing. My father did seem unbelievably strict. I ran away from home and left him when I was sixteen, to my mother, who had spoiled us like mad during the few weeks she had with us each year. My father had got care, control and custody of us four children when they got divorced, so she spoiled us a lot. So when I ran away I thought it was going to be fantastic. I'd wear nylons and lipstick and make-up, which I had been doing with her at the age of fourteen. But she suddenly realized that she had these two young sixteen-year-olds to look after, and she couldn't be so lenient as she had been. So she then was very strict, and I ran away from that. I was constantly running away from anything that was authority. I have done all my life. I've always rebelled. At school, they finally made me a prefect; they thought I would conform if I were in a position where I had to make other people conform as well. But that was out. I have always run from authority.

Patsy Kensit: I've had a very open upbringing. There's nothing we can't discuss in my house. I mean, my mother – even when I lost my virginity, I could talk to my mum about it. I wasn't hiding it from her. I've had a brilliant upbringing.

Princess Yasmin Aga Khan: My mother's influence was strong in terms of discipline and values, what is right and what is wrong. I think I was born fairly enlightened and aware and knew, at an early age, that she was a fragile person. But she had incredible discipline and was able to teach me that. The influence of my father was one of love; he showed me, he gave me that love. The love of both my parents influenced me into being concerned about people in general, and caring for them. I am involved with Alzheimer's disease because my mother is a sufferer. I've always felt, since I was very small, that I was a helper.

My mother wanted me to be an actress. I wouldn't even consider it. I saw Hollywood, and I saw the struggles she was going through, and I didn't enjoy it. It wasn't fantasy for me. It was struggle and unhappiness. I could see through all the glitter and the lights, and the make-up and the costumes; I could see through to the sadness. Of course, my mother had a wonderful career, and then difficulties developed in her life. But I really didn't want any part of Hollywood and I had no interest in it. My interest was music. I was interested in composition and in voice. I had a four-octave voice, and I practised and sang in small concerts. I continued until my mother took ill, and that's when I decided I could be more useful in reaching people who have similar problems to that of my mother.*

Soraya Khashoggi: My mother was a single parent. My father was a prisoner of war when I was born, so she had to raise me alone. My grandfather was very Victorian and hated children. I had to be sent away out of the house because my grandfather couldn't stand any sign of a child or toys or a child's friend. He was very strict. At the table, for instance, he would hit me with his fork if I was eating incorrectly. My mother loved me and tried to protect me, so eventually she sent me to boarding school. She was very poor but she worked hard to send me to a good school and give me a good education. The school was a Catholic convent, which was like going from the frying pan into the fire.

I never really met any boys. The only man in the school was the priest. We only met him at confession, and my sole contact with him was trying to invent a list of sins for myself and the whole class. When I came home from school, my mother would still be working, so I had to be farmed out to friends' homes for the vacation because my mum couldn't look after me. There were also times my grandfather was meant to be looking after me, and I had a strange education during these periods since he was a gambler and an alcoholic. When he was supposed to be baby-sitting while my mother was working to support the two of us, he would take me to the racetrack, the Leicester racecourse, and he'd put me on his shoulder so he would only have to pay for one – he was very mean – to go through the turnstyle. He would sit me on the ground with some crisps and lemonade all day while he went betting on the horses. And then he would teach me how to read form. So my education in learning how to gamble started early. I hate gambling now. I can't stand gambling. Of course, he would tell me not to tell my mother where we had been all day. I had to tell her we had been to the park, having a walk. She wasn't stupid, she found out. Then, being an alcoholic, when the races finished he would take me to the pub, and I would sit on the steps because I wasn't allowed in. So, as soon as my mother found out, it was back to school. My grandfather hated me so much, probably because I was a liability to him. I stopped him gambling and I stopped him drinking to a certain extent, because he had to look after me. So then it was back to school. Even during the times when there was no school, I would be in school, alone, the only girl.

Lesley Kingcome: My grandfather influenced me most. He was a Scot; he was absolutely wonderful. I respected him totally. He was a naughty old man. He always made absolutely sure he married millionairesses. He married three of them, including Edith Gould. My mother was splendid, tall, beautiful, an identical twin, very wealthy in her time, brought up as a spoiled brat, as I was. She had all the advantages, all the wonderful things, and much too late in life she became, unfortunately, not so wealthy. Never, ever, start in this life by having lots of money and then losing it. A really terrible, terrible way around to do it.

Irma Kurtz: My mother told me marriage was hell, so I was influenced against ever getting married. There was evidence of it in front of my eyes anyway. My mother set me free. She was not a possessive, loving woman; she was an open-handed woman. I think if it hadn't been for that I'd be a neurotic lady, on my third husband. If I'm thankful for life, which I am, then I am thankful to my mother.

My brother went to a better school and I was taken out of it because my father didn't think that sort of education was necessary for a woman. Of course, I went to a university, and it all evened out in the end, but I resented being taken out of the school I loved, where I was doing well, and put into a place where I was bored for four years. My mother tried to resist and failed. Maturity begins with an act of forgiveness. You forgive your parents for everything, and now I can understand what my father was saying. He honestly felt I was going to outclass myself in the marriage market. I am fifty now, so we are talking about quite some time ago. But he felt that if I was too educated and made too much money, no man would want me. I think he really felt he was doing it for my own good. He felt that the sort of education my brother was having, learning Latin and Greek, was not good for a girl like me because a man would not want to protect me. And he was a very protective and loving man. That's how he saw the relationship of men and women: that the man was the protector.

Marghanita Laski: I was brought up in the home of my grandparents in London to start with, who had thirteen children, and was the first grandchild and virtually the youngest child of the family. I was adored. I couldn't have been more cherished.

Two people influenced me: an aunt who introduced me to literature and a good-looking friend who introduced me to sophistication. My recollections of my parents are much more of revolting against them than of being influenced by them, although later on I came to realize how much my mother had influenced me in an appreciation of domestic matters, of luxury, of decent living, good living. My father had come back from the First World War shell-shocked and was, in any case, so desperately busy as a young barrister trying to make his name, that we children unhappily saw little of him in our early days.

There were so many disadvantages to being a Jew that being a girl really didn't matter. In Manchester, where I was mostly brought up, Jews were still right on the outskirts of society; also my family was extremely Orthodox, which meant I wasn't able to mix fully with schoolmates and friends. And when I came to London I was so strictly brought up by my mother, for fear, I think, that I should either lose my virginity or marry a Christian, that Judaism was a fence, a horrible fence, all my life, until I broke free from it. University was my breakthrough to freedom. And at university being a girl had enormous advantages. I was a very good-looking girl, I had a wonderful time.

Sara Leighton: From a career point of view, I think I inherited a grasp of business from my father. I was close to my mother. My mother used to appear in my nursery when I was about five or six and I used to think that she was a cross between the Archangel Gloria and the Blue Fairy from *Pinocchio*. She was a magical, beautiful, blonde creature, which I suppose I have idealized in a lot of my women in paintings ever since.

Catherine Leroy: Jazz musicians influenced me more than anyone and I wanted to become a blues singer. When I told my mother she said, very shocked, oh yes, you want to sing in a brothel, so I closed my piano. I wanted to become a blues singer or nothing at all, and since my mother told me I was probably going to end up in a brothel, I decided that I would never play the piano again. My parents were my parents, but they were not a great influence.

Lady Lothian: My father and mother were divorced. Perhaps the person who influenced me most was the Italian housekeeper, in Tuscany, who took me over. I spent two years with her in a smallholding above Florence where I discovered the real necessities of life and the real happiness – spaghetti, sunshine, truth, great dignity. No refrigerators and not much (in fact hardly any) money by standards today. She had such a careful, wise assessment of what people should be like if they were going to be worth living with. She made me look for it everywhere, and I've looked for it ever since. This sounds trite, but I've looked to see whether people were true to their friends when their friends were failures. That is one of the things that mattered on the Italian mountainsides. Or whether they looked after old people, or whether they liked babies, or whether they were kind to people who got ill. Above all, these were the qualities that enabled people to live in what's now known as a collective. And I've looked for them ever since. She influenced me most. I think my father, who was a Yorkshire administrator, also influenced me because he was straight and dependable. He amused me because I once asked him if he thought God was an Englishman, and he had a long think and said, I wouldn't be surprised. My mother fascinated me because she was Italian, small and unbelievably brave. She didn't know what fear was. She was also outrageous, and taught me that one didn't have to be conventional, one could actually get by on one's own personality, one's own character, whether it was in a slum or wherever. My father wanted a son, so he was very pleased when I behaved like a tomboy, which I did. My mother was extremely beautiful and made great use of her beauty. So she thought it wonderful to be a woman. Because she was beautiful, she'd get away with murder in a market place in Greece or wherever, so I think, as I grew up, I thought it was better to be a woman than a man.

Blanche Lucas: My mother influenced me in every way. Tremendously. My father didn't think it necessary for women to be educated at all. I sometimes think he wanted to be a woman himself because he used to say: the best thing is to get married. I think he felt it would be nice to be dependent. But those are only later thoughts. In any case, he had absolutely no interest in my education or the education of my sister, or anything, nor did he pay for it. My parents were very unalike. My father was a soldier and my mother was the daughter of quite a well-known statesman. They came from totally different backgrounds. Her father was at one time chancellor of a university, and my father was the son of a landowner in Hungary. No one in my family ever married anyone of the same nationality. For generations. So I just feel that I belong everywhere and nowhere.

Gillian Lynne: I lost my mother very early on in a car crash. She was killed when I was nine. But I loved my father, and in the end my father became my closest friend and was until he died. I was an only child. But the things I remember about childhood are my mother – my mother making me practise dancing, my mother having little surprises for me when I came home from school. She'd always find a tomato with a funny shape, or the biggest tomato on the block. She knew I loved tomatoes with brown bread and butter for tea. There was always something different, always a surprise. She was a great friend. And she made me have my passion for work from the age of about five. She wasn't a theatre mother at all, but she recognized something in me and she brought it out.

Sheena McDonald: I could not say that either my father or my mother had a greater influence over me than the other. They both influenced me in different ways. I'm close to both my parents, and we're good friends, but what I share with my mother is probably an easier relationship. I don't really like to use comparatives, because I don't want to suggest that one is better than the other, but probably because, in a way, we're still shy of each other after thirty-one years – my father's probably had the greater influence, and he's as shy of me as I am of him. We get on terribly well on certain levels – he has a great sense of humour. We enjoy the same things, although sometimes I think I enjoy these things because I want to please him, so I enjoy the books he enjoys, those he recommends. But I suppose the ultimate influence he's had is that I'm very protective of other people. What I learned early on, and probably it's because he is a minister – because a minister spends his life looking after other people's problems and is accessible twenty-four hours a day and duty-bound to listen to everybody, no matter how terrible their problems, and has to come up with some kind of comforting words – when he comes home the last thing he wants is somebody's problems. It's hard on my mother, I think. At least it has been. But ministers' children learn fast that their problems are not very interesting and they can cope with them themselves, and you grow up protecting your parents from your problems. And so my relationship with my parents depends on my telling them the things that I know they would like to hear. They want to know that I'm happy and healthy, and prosperous and successful, and basically doing all right, and so that's what I tell them.

Susan McHenry: The women in my childhood were Southern black schoolteachers, that's what the women in my family did. So there was my mother and her sister, who had both been born in Selby County, Tennessee in the 1920s. They had been born to a woman who was a schoolteacher as well, until she married and was basically a farmer's wife, and her work was bringing up her ten children and doing the things she had to do to keep the inner parts of the farm going. My mother, was widowed when her five children were between the ages of five and fifteen. Her sister, my aunt, had one child and her husband left when he was about six, so my mother and her sister raised their children together, so we were a combined family of six. There were a couple of things I learned from growing up in that household. First of all that women needed to be able to make their own way in the world. I saw that we lost my father, my grandmother also lost her husband at that time and had to take over the running of the farm, so I saw very clearly from them that you had to prepare yourself to work in the world and earn money. Of course there was the importance of education, that was built in with the fact that they were all schoolteachers. Education was your way of carving your niche in the world and making sure that you had skills that people would pay for. So earning your own living was important. The other thing is that you don't have children unless you're prepared to rear them on your own.

My mother believed that we should be capable of operating in all areas. We lived in the city, but every summer we would go back to my grandmother's farm and we lived essentially a country life. The kind of jobs that the boys had were the outside jobs and we had the jobs inside the house, so there was that division of labour. Also there were definite rules about where girls could go and where they couldn't go and what time they had to be home and all of that sort of stuff. My mother, when I talk to her about that now, says, I had to raise you to live in the world that I knew then, and hopefully I gave you enough sense to be able to adjust to the world as it is coming. She acknowledges that there were some sort of sexual divisions and some prescriptions that she put on the girls that she didn't put on the boys, because that was what she thought was best at the time.

Deirdre McSharry: My father died when I was six. My mother was a journalist, and my earliest image is of my mother with her long red painted nails and her hat, a very smart hat, and fox furs, going out the door to work, and I always thought that's what women did. It wasn't until I was about twelve that I discovered that other people's mothers didn't work. She was very ambitious. She wanted me to be beautiful, successful, and if that included marriage, that was fine. She had been very happily married, and married again when I was sixteen, so she believed that one should go on marrying, that one shouldn't give up on marriage. But because she was a successful journalist and an editor herself, I think she realized that the best way women can express themselves is in some form of work, in some kind of career which gives them an enormous self-esteem. She had a strong sense of self-esteem, and I think I learned that from her.

Norris Church Mailer: I grew up in Arkansas, in a working-class environment. My father ran heavy bulldozing equipment. He built roads and dams and that sort of thing. My mother was a hairdresser, and still is. I was a much-beloved only child. So the early influences, I guess, were my parents. We were very strict Baptists, a very religious family. I guess I was always interested in art, and when I went to college I became an art major. I worked and put myself through college, as most of us in that area did. It's hard to make a living painting in my part of the country. So I taught high school and I got married in my sophomore year in college and had a child, two years later, who is now fifteen. But ambitions were not large then – a nice house, a nice job and a nice car. That was it.

Kate Millett: I grew up in a small Irish town which was originally French, St Paul, on the Mississippi. There was a left-over French tradition which mixed with a strong Irish nationalism, and a sense of exile from Ireland which my family encouraged and kept up. They also kept up with Irish politics: the struggle for the freedom of Ireland from England. I grew up also with Catholicism. So those together were the larger social features of my upbringing. My mother, my aunt, my sisters and my father were the biggest influences in my life. I've written a book about my aunt, which is not yet published. It will be called *A.D.* which is a pun on Anno Domini; her name was Dorothy, so we called her A.D. for Aunt Dorothy. She was very rich, very beautiful, very intelligent, probably very spoiled, very domineering and absolutely fascinating. My father was her brother. He was an engineer who worked hard and finally succeeded in breaking away from working for the Highway Department and founded his own company. For a while he lived in glory, and then he went bankrupt. He was supposed to be also an alcoholic, which I think is probably my mother's opinion. She was a different class and type from the Milletts. She was what we call Irish Irish, peasant Irish from Galway, very strong and very determined. The Milletts were Norman Irish, very ancient, very difficult, very obscure people, but wonderful, fascinating, extremely delightful, very brilliant, always sophisticated. They had an endless sense of gentry which could be irritating and which was also very captivating to a child. I ended up growing up with my mother, who had majored in English at the university and therefore pushed me full of literature. My aunt did as well. I had two great teachers in my aunt and my mother, but my mother somehow made a much deeper impression, and I guess that I ended up throwing in my lot with my mother and her people and with their point of view. But it was always very ambivalent, because I also very much identified with the Milletts. It was a kind of schizophrenic childhood in a sense, always very divided loyalties, at any rate. I had two wonderful, brilliant sisters. One is an actress and one an attorney and also a banker, and my mother gave all three of us a great deal of encouragement and strength. We were, in many senses, her surrogates: we did all the things she was never permitted to do because she was raising three children and her life to some extent stopped when ours began.

Cristina Monet: Probably my mother influenced me most. She just is very well read. She is very off the wall. She's always raised me up on candlewick mats and said there was nothing that cannot be transcended by scorn.

Bel Mooney: My mother had to get married. She got pregnant when she was eighteen, with my brother, and she had me when she was twenty. My parents were quite poor – lived really very simply in Liverpool – and I think my mother always made up her mind that my life was going to be very different. When she had a daughter, she was very ambitious for me, and when I was a little girl, I had to do my homework. I remember my father saying: she ought to be doing some housework, and my mother saying (they were always quarrelling): I'd rather she did her homework. And that formed me, because when I got a degree – I got a first – when I got the news, though I was already married, I didn't think of telling my husband. I picked up the phone to my mother. It's always, always my mother. We don't have that much in common, but she made me realize that to be somebody, to succeed, you have to work very hard and go out and prove yourself. She always used to say: you're as good as them. And them were rich people, people with private education and money – because we never had any of that.

I used to want to rebel. I remember when I was fifteen I went through a stage of wearing a leather jacket and smoking Woodbines and wanting to go out with boys and saying I wanted to leave school. And she said: what do you want to go to work for? And I said: I want money to buy clothes. She said: you stay at school, I'll buy the clothes.

Lynn Nesbit: It is important that everyone learns to take responsibility, and I was taught that at a very early age. Like many girls, I wanted to please my father and I felt the way to please him was to become independent, and responsible, and tremendously efficient. Those were all virtues my father preached constantly. They didn't fall along gender lines. Now, the interesting thing, of course, is that my father was married to a woman who never worked a day in her life. But if you ask me what he thinks of me today, I would think he is enormously proud of me.

Emma Nicholson: We were a very female household. We lived in the country. It was in the war and after the war, so we didn't meet boys very much at all. In my nursery school, which I stayed in until I was seven, there were boys in the early years, but then they went quite rapidly off to school. Certainly boys were a different species, they had a completely different lifestyle. They were something to be respected, but not necessarily something to be made friends of. They weren't really there, apart from anything else.

In many ways, my mother really couldn't see the point of sending us to school at all. I think she would rather we had been educated at home. My father automatically sent us to school. He was well educated himself. He went to Winchester and on to Oxford, and almost straight from there he went on into the House of Commons when he was a very young man, and at the same time he went into the family business. I don't believe he thought a great deal about our education. I have three sisters. The first three of us went to the same very good prep school in Sussex, and all four of us went on to the nearest public school to home, which was a Church of England convent school called St Mary's, Wantage. Unusual people, Anglican nuns – very intelligent, very élite in the real sense of the word, and remarkable women. Nobody planned for what we were going to do when we left. I'm sure my mother felt that girls got married, and were happy getting married, and then had children, and I don't think my father thought that women would necessarily have a career. He certainly didn't think it through or discuss it. So it was very much left to us to decide what one wanted to do or what one could do.

Mavis Nicholson: Both my mother and father were an influence because I loved them dearly and they loved me dearly. It was very uncomplicated; I just felt secure with them. They were poor, very poor, and we were very overcrowded in our house. We lived with my grandmother and grandfather and so I had to share a bed with my grandmother until I was seventeen and went to university. And so, in another way, my grandmother was a great influence until I learned to think for myself, and then I began to work out that she was quite a frustrated, angry woman with a disappointed life and a drunken husband, which had also been hidden from me although we were living in the same house. She influenced me in that she taught me early on – and I don't how she did it – that I would work people out. She used to tell me odd stories at night in bed, about a little girl with black hair, and it would be me, I knew, but she would never name me; and I worked out her psychology through these stories. She somehow made me quite aware, early on, that I was terribly interested in people – not interested in judging them but in assessing them. And that's kept me nicely in work all these years as an interviewer.

Jane O'Grady: When I was small I really was clever and very good at writing things like poetry, plays and short stories, and at school they often used to let me do things by myself. And I was allowed to be in a room and write, or something like that, but I then went to this crappy convent – plenty of people managed to come out of it all right, but it wasn't good academically. I got a terrible depression when I was about fifteen and none of the nuns said anything. Years later, passing by the school, I dropped in and said to the one of the nuns I liked, look, couldn't you see that I was in this terrible suicidal state? And, you know, I teach, and if a child was like that in a comprehensive, they would immediately be picked out and sent to a psychiatrist or a doctor, or given anti-depressants. This nun had the gall to say to me, well, we did see you were in an odd state, but we didn't want to interfere. Why not, when they interfered in every other province? They were always telling us extraordinary things about what we shouldn't be doing, mostly to do with sex.

Fifi Oscard: My mother was a remarkable influence on me. She was an adorable woman who never, in ninety-three years, ever became less adorable. She was the soul of kindness and love and gave me lovely confidence. My mother was a product of her times. She wanted me to have as much education as was available, to have a wonderful life and to marry a very successful man. She respected diamonds and the things that people in those times respected – servants and big houses. She herself had dreams of becoming an opera singer. She sang charmingly, but not very well, and she always beat her wings against the constrictions of her life in the hope that maybe something would happen. She wanted to be of some use and accomplishment in the world, and somehow I acquired that impulse.

Edna O'Shaughnessy: I still remember, when I was about fifteen or sixteen, coming across a book of Freud's belonging to my father, opening it, reading about the Oedipus complex, and suddenly thinking this is right, this is me, this is not arbitrary. One reads about the inside of a radio – four valves, six wires, and two nodes; it could instead be seven valves, three wires and five nodes. But the Oedipus complex struck home as true, and I knew at once, although it was a long time before I became a psychoanalyst, that there was a truth that met something in myself.

Clare Park: I had a pleasant childhood. My memories are always warm and affectionate, not demanding. It's like recalling how summers used to be always warm, or much hotter than they are now. That's how I remember my childhood.

Diana Parker: My father died when I was nine, and I suspect that he influenced me most, not so much in his presence, but by his absence during my formative years. I was very conscious of the fact that he was not there and that I, as the eldest of the three children, had to live up to what I imagined were the ideals he would be setting for me.

I always understood that it was my mother's wish that I should have a degree of independence, perhaps not so much financially as emotionally, because I think she felt that she had suffered through not having any kind of outlet other than the home, particularly after my father died. As the eldest, I was really looking after the family to a great extent, because my mother suffered a nervous breakdown after my father's death and I was quite used to being fearfully independent.

Molly Parkin: When I was seven I was evacuated down to Wales, to my grandmother in the valley I was born in. My parents moved up to the seedy suburbs of London, like Willesden and Kilburn, that sort of place. Up until then, I had been in hospital because I was a very sickly child –

undernourished – for nearly a year, as we didn't have much money, so that seemed to wipe out the memory of my parents in a sense. My grandparents were very old, because my grandmother was forty when she had my mother. She'd had twelve children, and they'd all died in that valley, and my mother was the last and the only one to survive. I was particularly influenced by my grandparents' physical presence, because I actually did sleep between my aged grandmother and my aged grandfather. Strangely enough, that gave me a fixation on much older men because my grandfather was always there as a warm presence on the side of me in this huge feather bed. I used to watch him when he woke at half past five in the morning. He was a miner, of course, and I used to watch him, fascinated, while my grandmother slept beside me. He would get up early to light the fires in order to have hot water in the house, but he used to relieve himself in the chamber pot which was underneath the bed because we didn't have an inside lavatory, and then used to swill his face in his own urine. Of course, that was the only hot water in the house at that time in the morning. I used to watch this procedure every single morning. Then he used to make the fire, make the porridge, make the tea, and then we would go down, and he had done all that ready for us to start the day.

The upbringing was deeply religious and my grandmother, having lost all these children, turned immediately to God. We went to chapel on Sunday morning, Sunday evening and Monday night, and Sunday school on Sunday afternoon. There was a lot of reading of the Bible, which, of course, was a strong influence on me because later in life, in my writing – comic-erotica – and my mode of living, I obviously reacted against the strictness of that background. But I see it as valuable now.

Penny Perrick: I think I differ from a great many women in careers, because most career women say: it's terrible, I can't talk to my mother, I love her very much but she just doesn't understand the demands of my job, and the family and how my life is. My mother, as a successful journalist, would have understood perfectly well, but, of course, because I chose to despise the life she led – which was being successful and famous and hard working – it was always hard for me to talk to her. I wonder whether every woman looks at her mother's life and says: no, I don't want that. Most women of my generation looked at their mothers' lives and said: I don't want to be a housewife, I don't want to be always a servant to somebody else, I don't want to have no life of my own. But I looked at my mother's life and said: all I want to be is a housewife. My career has all been in spite of myself, which is very ironic. I did everything I had dreamed of doing. I married at twenty, I had two children by the age of twenty-four, I had eleven years of running a big house, entertaining, doing all the things I wanted to do, and then my husband's business collapsed at the same time as our marriage, and so, at the age of thirty-one, I had to start work. If you have to work, you might as well work successfully. So I did.

Lorie Scott Peters: I think it was to do with the lack of love from my parents that I felt I was very self-contained and had to play in my own little sandbox, create my own little world and teach myself how to get along in the world and be happy. Obviously I couldn't have taught myself everything, but I feel that my father always wanted too much and my mother probably never really wanted a whole lot. I was the second child, so I felt there wasn't a whole lot of love there. I was constantly trying to prove myself to them, and never could really succeed because I was never going to be the apple of their eye. They were always going to have this first daughter that they had spent six years trying to have, who was their pride and joy. When they got to me, you know, I was doing everything a bit late and it was, stop going through this phase, your older sister went through it. So I just pretty much tried to content myself in my own world and do my own thing. I felt very unloved and very unhappy as a child.

Davina Phillips: I had a very varied upbringing. My father was killed a week before I was born. My mother was terribly young and couldn't handle it. It was such a shock to her, she completely broke down and passed me over to my grandmother. I didn't see my mother for the first six years of my life. Basically, I was brought up by my grandmother in the larger part, and my grandfather. My mother had a sister, younger than herself, who was still living at home, so I saw quite a lot of her. My grandmother became ill and subsequently died, and my aunt oversaw me somewhat, but she, by then, had married, so I didn't see a great deal of her either. Still to this day, at my ripe old age of forty-five, I miss the idea of having mummies and daddies. I particularly miss the influence of a father, because I think girls always like that. But, at the same time, having had to struggle from a very young age to find my own identity has made me experiment with different things. And it made me, in a way, much more domestically independent.

Lynn Phillips: I can't think of a person I can name who influenced me most. One of the biggest errors in maternal thinking I've run into is to imagine that people, individual people, bring up a child. For me, the most important experiences have always been the interstices between influences, where one thing I've embraced bangs up against another I've embraced. I would have to say that the most important influences in my life have been contradiction and accident. My real upbringing wasn't the upbringing I was given by my parents, but the tension between that and everything else. My mother was a lawyer and my father was a high-school drop-out, and in that era it was quite remarkable, so that, for example, the contrast between my parents' role choices and the television-, media-defined norm was always shocking. I never knew how to react to the media's injunction to tell my mother when she went to the store to buy such and such, because it was my dad who went to the store, and I never knew whether to be proud or embarrassed, and so I'd alternate constantly between the two. My mother was an impressive woman with a high, rather self-righteous moral sense, and my dad was a much more live-and-let-live humorous sort of fellow, and I think they've both been influential. On the upstairs, there was a woman who was an artist, who never painted her nails and who was married to a heart surgeon. They fascinated me. I couldn't stand the husband, but she had something, a kind of sober sense of self-defined clarity that attracted me. She didn't seem connected to the world in the normal way, and I didn't quite understand what that meant, but that was interesting. The other person who completely fascinated me was my first piano teacher, a man called Israel Sidkovitz who had an apartment in Carnegie Hall. I never knew anyone lived in Carnegie Hall, and when I first was dragged up to visit him, he did not have any shoes on – the first grown up I'd ever met who walked around barefoot. He hadn't washed his sink in a few days and he had laundry hanging around, and as a child I thought this was an ultimate dream: not to be forced to tidy up and not to have been disciplined in any way. He had a Cézanne water-colour, an empty refrigerator, and I thought he was the strangest, most curious character. He turned out to be a very lovely man, knew that I didn't like the piano and taught me chess. We had long talks and he became, in some ways, a friend, and then he married a terribly wealthy woman, moved off to a castle and I never saw him again.

Sarah Fox-Pitt: A certain amount of my childhood was spent alone in the sense that I was born during the war in 1941. My brothers were in America, my father was at war, so in fact I was surrounded by three women – my mother, my nanny, my nanny's mother. Certainly until we were taken to the South of France, the influence of women was paramount. I then went to my first school in France, so I began mixing with everybody in another language, a language I didn't know. I was at convent schools throughout, a Roman Catholic convent, and then an Anglican convent, so there, again, I was entirely surrounded by women. Nevertheless, I think that my interests were very conventional in terms of a country life, a sporting life, directed most probably by my father, whose interests, following his retirement from a military career, aided and abetted us in our enjoyment of horses and dogs and all those sort of things.

I think there was a conflict between the influences of my parents, my mother obviously aiming towards a certain kind of intellectual understanding of the arts. My father pursued a more regularly maintained, landed-gentry sort of life. He came from a big property and had always led a life furnished with all that goes with living on 2,000 or 3,000 acres, but after the war that property was sold and we moved to a house with only 100 acres, so the social infrastructure changed. In that sense, we didn't have a freedom we might have had if we'd lived in the remote areas of Wales, where we might have grown up much wilder, much more closely associated with real nature in the way he was. For example, he knew about all the movements of migrating birds. In a sense, I think we missed out on the real understanding of nature and man's relationship with the land, its flora and fauna. There was no demand to explore these things intellectually.

Having been virtually an only child for the first three or four years of my life, with the intermittent companionship of my nanny's nephew, who was exactly my age and no rival for my parents' attention, I was suddenly faced with the return of two elder siblings who had been absent in the United States during the war. So I was suddenly overwhelmed by two cuckoos in my nest. And there was I, a cuckoo in their nest. So we existed on a curious mixture of affection and competition, with a strong element of teasing and provoking. I did not want to be left out, but by virtue of the fact that I was six or nine years younger, I couldn't do all the things they did. They were both my heroes and my rivals, and then they were sent off to boarding school so I had long periods of reasserting my 'rights', only to find that, during the holidays, it all became topsy-turvy again.

It was never suggested that I should go to university, but that was perhaps partly because I fell out with the nuns at school. A bargain was struck, and I was told that if I got six O-Levels I could leave. I did. I think they were longing to get rid of me. I was sent to Paris, where I spent a year 'messing about' with other girls of the same age, between sixteen and seventeen, but it wasn't an intellectual pursuit. Living in Paris for that year, and working at another convent, at an annexe of

143

the Couvent de l'Assomption, I was shown the marvellous art works of Paris. We followed a series of well-organized classes, visits and discussions covering topics from *savoir vivre* to Romanesque architecture and back. *Savoir vivre* was, as far as I recollect, about being careful not to be picked up because there was a wicked white-slave trade. The other cultural classes on European literature, history and history of art were well presented, but the environment and the girls were there more for social reasons than for intellectual ones. However, the experience of living in Paris with a delightful and kind French family gave one an extraordinary sense of well-being and an ability to travel and live in other countries without fear or feelings of isolation. It introduced me to the broad world of culture – as a spectator, I have to say, rather than as a participator. I became a participator much later on. It was a wonderful opportunity, but with hindsight one which I did not know how to exploit because I wasn't somehow aware of the people who were there creating the culture of the moment. We were mostly interested in going to parties in our free time. They were beautiful parties, but based mostly on the culture of the past and not on the creative present. But all that was accumulating inside me and forming an interest, although, at home, we didn't collect works of art. You might have your portrait painted, or your children painted, but it didn't go beyond that. My mother had a certain style, which was pleasant enough, but there wasn't anything tremendously personalized about it. It had a period flavour within certain restrained conventions.

I don't think I had a very clear focus on anything except the steady social round of parties, prolonged visits to stay with friends and getting to know a great many people both here and abroad in a relatively short time. However, my parents definitely wanted me to get married, although mother saw to it that I did a secretarial training. I obviously had a superficial interest in the arts, but it did not become crystallized until I was in my mid to late twenties. The idea of a career as such was never discussed, although subconsciously I had a need for a focus other than a family life. I never had the great urge that some women have to bear children. While I was interested in status, I didn't really know how to achieve it except by marriage. My parents wanted me to marry into the local aristocracy but there were all sorts of nuances I didn't understand. My mother comes from a Scottish Presbyterian background, which has a rigid system of morality: you don't play mistress to people and you probably don't even like your body. My parents' idea that they would like their children to marry 'well' was based on breeding rather than intellect. From my mother's middle-class professional background, it was most important to her, and from my father's background, it was natural for him to want one to marry into his own status. To take a particular example of the conflicts of understanding that I tried to cope with and failed at the time, I had a great admirer, a nobly born and wealthy neighbour. He was always generous and kind, and he asked me to stay in his chalet in Switzerland for as long as I wanted. I was perhaps nineteen or twenty. I accepted and was his guest for at least a month, and he was kind and generous as always. Towards the end of the stay, his stepfather asked me why I did not respond to him and love him the way he wanted me to. I was amazed. During the whole time X had spent most evenings and nights with his local girlfriends, and to me it had been an indication that I was not really part of his life. At home we had never discussed the nuances and social *moeurs* of this kind of relationship. I didn't know what I was attempting to deal with, and couldn't easily talk about it. I was perplexed. I had not been brought up to understand and accept *les petites flutes* as an adjunct to the central core of married life. I only came to understand that later on. The Presbyterian/puritan ethic had somehow had a powerful influence. Although its higher ideals had never been a forum for discussion, an understanding had been implicitly absorbed and I didn't know how to match a different set of ground rules with my own muddled ones.

Eve Pollard: My mother was a wonderful woman. She was very clever, and very kind. She was not English, neither of my parents was English. She was a mixture of Viennese and French, and was very *simpatico*, and everybody loved her. And she always worked, always, with my father. He was a mad sort of inventor: Hungarian, lunatic. She really kept his business going. He would blow up, and everybody would walk out and my mother would say, he doesn't really mean it. And so I learned a lot because my mother was brilliant at what women do best – she juggled. She had three children, a house, a social life, entertaining and work. And I watched her juggle. She said, always have an account at Selfridges because, even if you haven't any time, you can always get food from them quickly, nobody will starve, nobody will know you're disorganized. And she was very organized. My father influenced me a lot too, in that he thought women were there to be decorative objects and did everything he could to stop me continuing studying. He thought I should just marry somebody rich and look after them and him in that order. I did the Royal Wedding on the BBC, and talked all about the fashion, and people made a terrific fuss. Everybody I knew rang up afterwards – except my father. In his eyes I was a failure. I was still working. However successful I got to be, he thought it was a mistake because I was too busy to run him to his card parties, to live my life through him. And, in a way, I always almost feel that I do all this to show him I can do it and will do it, that I was right and he was wrong, that women shouldn't just sit there and look pretty.

Diana Potter: I absolutely don't know who influenced me as a child. I had a very funny childhood. I was adopted when I was about two months, and my adopted father's first wife died at the beginning of the war when I was seven. He was so desperate with grief, he went off and left me with various aunts and uncles. An uncle and aunt looked after me for about two years, before my father came back from the war with a new wife when I was about eleven. After that, I had rather a bad childhood and didn't really meet my uncle and aunt again until I was about nineteen. Theirs had been one of these influences where you knew you were loved and looked after and cared for, and if you were naughty, you weren't slapped or screamed at. There was a sort of strength there, and they were the only members of the family who thought I was all right. And then my father came back with the most monstrous woman, who was my stepmother. We didn't get on at all. She was so jealous.

Usha Prashar: The person who influenced me most was my father. He was in some ways a very exceptional person, because, given the fact of our Indian background, he was not orthodox and always believed in women being educated, in encouraging us to do things not normally done by women. The other person who I think had an influence on me was my eldest sister, who is a short-story writer and in her own way quite a feminist; she used to express herself in writing about the position of women. My eldest brother, I think, was slightly orthodox; he would say, women don't do this or do that, but that was very much counter-balanced by my father's broadmindedness, so I never in myself felt inhibited. For example, I was sent to England to study at the age of fourteen. There was no restriction in that way.

Marjorie Proops: My grandmother, my mother's mother, was a remarkable old lady. I didn't know her until she was bedridden and came to live with us. She was very beautiful and vain. She used to lie in bed in pretty bedjackets with lots of fancy embroidered pillows behind her white hair. She was stout but elegant. And she was a gambler. My sister and I used to go after school straight to my grandmother's room, and she'd listen carefully to make sure my mother was out of the way, and then, from under the bedclothes, would extract her pack of cards. And, at the age of nine or ten, I was a great poker player. She also

146

taught us lots of bawdy songs. She knew all the Edwardian music-hall bawdy songs. She talked to us frankly about everything, and I think it was mainly her influence and partly the fact that I was brought up in a pub in the City of London that I developed quite young into the person into whom I matured. I think because of this very positive childhood, both my sister and I were quite self-assured children, quite confident children. We grew up feeling we were loved and belonged, and I don't think we had any feelings of repression, about boys or about anything.

My grandmother was very much a let's-have-fun-today old lady. And when she heard my mother tapping along the passage outside her bedroom door, the cards and the money (we played for money) were pushed under the bedcovers and she would start telling us the story of the three bears or something. So my mother never knew. My grandmother was a great character. Wonderful.

Andrée Putman: I had a relationship with my mother which was very extreme. To me she was a person out of a fairytale. She had so much magic in her approach to reality and life that she almost took me through a dream, I would ,say. She made my life rather unreal by avoiding reality. She was a wonderful artist, a famous private interpreter, and played the piano like few people do. She could never be a professional because her family wouldn't let her have a career. She married early, and her husband died, and she remarried much much later, with my father. She never concentrated on a career because she knew in advance it would not be accepted, so she kept that unbelievable talent for our private life and it became almost overwhelming to her, I think; it was too much to be so near perfection, to be such a great performer, and not give it to the world. She was more ambitious for me. I was born exactly after a little boy died from pneumonia, and was somehow to replace the little boy. I was given a boy's name, which is quite agreeable for a woman. In Greek, Andrée means courage. I was timid in some ways because I had a strict education, but I was extremely wild and liked to shock. I was totally independent. My mother always escaped my criticism, but quite early on I was the most cruel critic of the rest of my social environment.

Charlotte Rampling: My father was a powerful man, and he had a charismatic personality. He was somebody who was immensely severe and had a sense of justice and goodness which was illustrated in everything he did. He was somebody I always wanted to please, but he was a man I was frightened of because he had enormous complexes which I understood only later. He was a perfectionist, an Olympic runner, and everything he did had to be perfect. And so, as that can't happen in life, he was a very disturbed man. It's only now, at the age of seventy-six, that he has come to terms with it. His life was a constant emotional and psychological jigsaw. But he was basically a good and just man. My mother was besotted with my older sister, who was very fragile and died when I was twenty-one. She was constantly ill and constantly having problems, so my mother spent all her time with her. My sister was very ill when I was born so I was put into the nanny's hands and always had the feeling I was unwanted. I resented my mother a lot for that. I always wanted to be a boy and I wanted brothers. I used to lie to people and say I had three brothers at home. Or I invented a fantasy world inhabited by men.

Esther Rantzen: Both my father and mother influenced me in quite different ways. I think my mother provided for me a model of family life, a model of relationships. She was insistent that there was no rivalry between my sister and myself, that we grow up friends. She enjoyed our company. We were, quite clearly, the priority in our parents' lives. Emotional relationships were always considered more important than physical materialism of any kind. We were never particularly proud of the things we owned. But we saw our family all the time. In fact I still do. My mother was the main emotional influence, but my father really steered my life. I remember very clearly asking him what my ambition should be. He said, well, if you turn out to be on the arts side, you ought to go to Oxford, and if you turn out on the scientific side, you ought to go to Cambridge. I think he told me that when I was about seven and it stuck in my head. As I turned out to be on the arts side, I went to Oxford. He was at the BBC, so I grew up to believe that the BBC was a great patron of the arts, which I still think. And so it was my ambition to join the BBC which one can blame my father for, because he was head of engineering designs there. He worked for Lord Reith, and believes it's a great institution. One of the things I am extremely grateful for is that neither parent ever saw my life in terms of marriage and babies and the female lot. Both of them regarded education as the top priority of my life, and they were gender-blind.

Mirella Ricciardi: My mother influenced me most. I would say she was one of the first rebels. She was born into a very closed family in Paris, and when I talked to her about the evolution of women, she would often tell me how difficult it was for her to live her early years because she could not accept the restrictions of womanhood – this was in the period

1910 to 1914. She was one of the first people who broke away from her family and her environment. And for a woman of her milieu, in 1920, having been married twice, to have gone away with her lover to Africa, was something that had never been heard of. She just did it. She then married my father, who was Neapolitan and believed women should stay at home and go to church: women were there to breed, to look after the home and suffer in silence. That's the man she married. So obviously I must have inherited a lot of her genes, because when the time came for me to decide in which direction I would go, there was no way I was going to be subjected to becoming a breeder of other people and someone who stays in the kitchen.

Nancy Richardson: I grew up mostly in Greenwich, Connecticut, and early on, like Madame Bovary, I knew not so much that I wanted to get out of the country as that it was sort of boring. It was as though I were gaining strength for something. There wasn't enough to do that really interested me. Thereafter we moved a lot, and my mother and father were separating and coming back together again. I was always an outsider in the various communities because I arrived in the middle of school years and things like that and so I spent a lot of time reading. Books were always my best friends. When I was about nine or ten, I found something called *Over Sixteen* behind the bookcase. It was a collection of faintly ribald little stories about sex life in the upper middle class: those Greenwich Connecticut couples where the husband was commuting to New York and, on his way home, he'd stop at a station which wasn't where he lived, spend an hour or two with a woman he knew, and get back on the train and come home. That's what my father was doing. I didn't realize then that they really weren't happily married. I had so much privacy and so much isolation that I knew the whole of English literature. I lived through books and had amazing dreams as a result, and in my dreams I imagined that surely I would be President. Then life proceeded to beat the ideal out of me.

Stella Richman: My mother was a first-generation immigrant from Middle Europe, from Poland, via Germany, via France, where my brother was born, and she always wanted to better herself. My father came of a generation of men who played cards all day and worked as little as they could, and women did the work. So I think my mother was my greatest influence. She wanted me to learn there was a world outside the self-imposed ghetto and that one should go out and find it – that's all. She didn't care what I did.

What I thought was that I'd got to get out of the enclosed atmosphere, I'd got to get beyond the limited horizon. It wasn't to do with being a girl at all. To be honest it never crossed my mind that it was going to be difficult. My father was terribly conventional, a Talmud-bred Jew from Poland who stuck to certain rules out of habit but not out of true feeling. I recognized that very early. About the age of eight, I thought, he's only saying all this because that's the way he was brought up; he doesn't believe in one thing he's saying to me – like: you must never leave home because only bad girls leave home. I wanted to be an actress from the age of about ten, and he thought that was like being a whore. And those were the words he knew, so he used them, but it wasn't to do with being a girl. It was: your place is home, a son or daughter stays at home until they get married, that's all. It wasn't any deeper.

Angela Rippon: I'm an only child. I was born when my father was away in the Royal Marines during the war, and apart from one instance when I was very tiny, just a few months old, he didn't see me until I was almost three. And it's interesting that he always carries my photograph with him, taken when I was six months. I asked him once why he did this, and he said because I've got a photograph of you all the time, as you are now, but I never saw you as a baby. I have a feeling that, because he missed out on the first three years of my life, my father and I did spend a lot of time together through my early years and my teens. I suspect therefore that a lot of the attitudes that I have come from spending a lot of time with a man who, while he obviously took great delight in having a daughter, passed on a lot of masculine influences to me in the way he might have done with a son. It was my father who gave me a great interest in the countryside, because he was born in County Down and as a young boy spent a great deal of time in what was then open countryside around the village he lived in. My mother was also an incredible influence, perhaps in a way she was never aware of and I don't think intended. My mother has always worked. Before I was born, she was a trained seamstress. When I was born, money was short because my father was in the services and servicemen were paid very little. So I was looked after by my grandmother, who was my kind of nanny during the day, while my mother went out to work. So I grew up in an atmosphere where it is quite normal for a woman to go out to work, normal for a woman to have a career, to fit her husband and her family into a regime that meant she was one of the breadwinners. My mother was a breadwinner out of necessity, which gave her a certain down-to-earth way of thinking about life. But it meant that I grew up finding nothing unusual about women making their contribution to the family pot.

Anita Roddick: I had two mentors who were teachers. To this day I am only trying to please them. I don't try to please my children, or my husband, or the press. I constantly have these teachers as my guardian angels. I don't know why, but they channelled me. The thing that those two had in common with my father was that they made me feel special. My father always made me feel special. And when you are told you are going to be special often enough, you wear that specialness around you with ease, like a cloak. My mother was always in the role of provider because my father died when I was ten, so she had to run the restaurant: Italians either have a restaurant or they have an ice-cream factory. We were the original latchkey kids; we used to arrive home from school, and she'd be in the café working. My father was the artist. He played the violin, he was the first person to take me to the theatre. I am sure he would have smacked me or beaten me up during my teenage years, but he never had to go through that, so he remained a fantasy person. I love my mother because she loved my father, and because he loved her. She was a hard person for me, because she had to work. She had to bring up three girls and a boy – four kids on her own. She was not so much fun because having four wilful children and running a café was difficult. It was always confrontation. But looking back on her, she is very important to me. She had a sense of fun, she broke rules, she did things in her life that I am immensely proud of. She's very much like me, and I see, as I enter my middle age, that I am becoming everything I promised myself I would never become. I'm following my mother.

Deborah Rogers: My father was a great believer in femininity. He wanted one to be wonderfully educated, but never a bluestocking. He had a generation thing, I suppose, about being old-fashioned about women who were militant. He was more quickly bored by somebody who wasn't well educated, so it's not that he wanted a mindlessness but that he was rather intolerant of or didn't really understand women in more aggressive or forceful roles. I don't think that had any great effect on me, because I think I went my own way anyhow.

Selwa Roosevelt: I absolutely adored my mother. I do adore her, and yet she let me loose, she never tried to overwhelm me. She is a tiny little woman, but a very strong personality. I came into my own as a mature woman, but as a young girl I was not attractive. I grew up in east Tennessee, in a community where everybody had blue eyes and blonde hair. And I was a scrawny little pale thing, and my mother was so wonderful because she kept me focused on what was important in life: not whether one was popular with one's peers, and things of that sort, but whether one had integrity, a sense of honour, a sense of truth, and these are the things that she taught me. And scholarship. One wanted to learn and wanted to pursue. And so she said to me, and quite rightly, one day young men will be part of your life, but what you really must focus on now is developing yourself, and your character and your brain. So she encouraged me to be a good student. She herself is a brilliant woman. She went to college after my father died, and got her Bachelor's, her Master's and her PhD, in her forties. My father was not a big influence on my life. I loved him, but it was a woman professor at Vassar, Evelyn Clark, who was a terrific intellectual influence on me because I went to college a big liberal and I left a conservative, and that's why I am today a conservative appointed by Ronald Reagan. And that lady is the woman who, I think, formed my intellectual approach more than any other single person – my philosophical approach. She made me go to the source material, and she made me learn to analyse it, so that I wasn't duped by propaganda, so that, I asked: who is saying this and why is he or she saying it. This was an enormous intellectual experience, and I was not like my peers who came to school conservative from their parents, and left liberal, having been brainwashed by very left-wing professors.

Juliet Mitchell-Rossdale: The physical environment of the first three years of my life in New Zealand had a terrific influence on me in terms of the sheer beauty of the country. I never realized, until I went back in my late thirties, what this terrific nostalgia I had had was until I went back and saw the light, and the mountains, and the sea. That was very important. Also I was born into a Jewish refugee community. My family weren't Jewish, but we lived among a Jewish refugee community which was a very interesting environment. My godparents, who were young Jewish refugees, a philosopher and his wife who was a sculptor, were a terrific influence on me. I adored them.

Joan Ruddock: My father had the loudest voice in the house, and, as men do, was always instructing us to pay attention to what he had to say. I suppose he provided a kind of negative influence in that he set out truths as he saw them. In my youth, he became very conservative. He was a working-class shop-floor manager in a factory, always having disputes with the trade union, and so he was a great political influence on me because he said, you should believe all of this, you should accept my position, this is how things are. Fortunately I had somehow acquired a questioning mind, and I wanted to know what the other side thought. I was able to question and form ideas of my own. But if I look at my

152

values, what really matters to me and perhaps what has been most enduring, then I suspect the greatest influence was my mother. She was a considerable naturalist, taken from education by her father when she was twelve years old, but they lived in the country and she knew all about natural things. What she used to do throughout the whole of our childhood, was take us out into the field and woods, which in those days were not destroyed by pesticides. She gave me wonderful insight into the value of nature and how extraordinary the universe is. And perhaps that has been the most lasting thing. I was the elder child, the elder of two daughters. My father, of course, would have preferred sons, but not having any sons, he brought us up as though we might have been boys. He didn't pander to the fact that we were girls. We were talked at and talked to as though we had the minds of boys, and as though there was absolutely no reason why we shouldn't engage in the kind of discussions he wanted us to engage in. The important thing about my parents is that they were both working-class people and they were both denied education. My mother was taken out of school at twelve to work for her father. My father had gone to a secondary school, and then his father died, and his mother was pregnant at the time with the fourth child. This was in the Depression in South Wales. So my father couldn't stay in school. So the motivation for both my parents was really about the present: their children were not be be denied education. They were highly motivated to have us educated. I don't think they ever thought where the education might lead. It was simply that we should not be denied what they had been denied.

Melissa Sadoff: My grandmother and mother probably showed me what the feminine woman is. They delighted in being lovely women and emphasized making a man's life very pleasant and very charming.

I thought carefully about what I wanted even as a very young girl, and would simply ask for things and get them. Our family was a male-dominated family, but I had an equal voice. I was single-minded and determined, very. I always knew I was going to be a writer, and started reading when I was five. I was writing little pieces of prose when I was nine or ten, and always wrote my own cards at Christmas and birthdays, and particularly for Mother's Day and Father's Day, and when I was thirteen I had already started writing philosophical essays. I always wanted to be famous, not for the sake of being famous, but for the sake of leaving something to humanity after I died. If I had been a man, I probably would have been some kind of crazy general or war leader, even though war is not in my heart at all. But I think I would have been quite a determined man.

Naomi E. Sargant: My mother was extremely unusual. She was the daughter of a shoemaker in a village in Czechoslovakia, the only girl in her village to be allowed to go to the grammar school. My grandfather had to get special permission from the Austro-Hungarian authorities to allow her to sit at the back of class and listen in to the lessons; she wasn't actually taught. Then she won a scholarship to Prague University and later on went to study in France and met my English father-to-be. The marriage didn't last long, and my father left when I was three or so. When I was four and a half, she took my sister and me back to Czechoslovakia in the hope we would live there. Of course, at that point the Germans invaded and we were encouraged very rapidly to leave and to return to England through Poland. This was September 1938, so it was after Munich and there wasn't a father around, there wasn't anywhere to live. I suspect that if we had not been English we would have landed up in some of the camps. Of course, we were English, not Jewish. We came out, as it were, for other reasons. I can't remember at what time life became stable. I know I was boarding at that point, and that one spent weekends in YWCAs and different places. We went to a boarding school called St George's in Harpenden, and then my mother moved us to a Quaker boarding school, and that's where I first remember a longer period of stability. She got a job with the Czech government-in-exile, travelling around the country as liaison with all the women's organizations, so we might see her only in holidays, or we would stay with friends in school holidays. There's not much stability in this story. Certainly no men around, except a negative man.

Dame Cicely Saunders: I wasn't a very happy child. I absolutely hated school, but there were two or three teachers who were important to me. My father, who was the seventeenth child, left school quite early and couldn't go to university, was determinedly ambitious and built into me the idea that I had to be top, I had to work, I had to succeed. Certainly my father had a powerful effect on how I felt I had to do things afterwards. He was very critical and used to tease me, which I found hurtful. He tried to help me and give me confidence, but didn't always succeed. He wanted us all to succeed. My second brother happened to succeed at games and my younger brother succeeded academically. He had a great need for us to do well. He was very Victorian in his will, but he wasn't particularly Victorian in his attitude, he was moderate liberal. We were given a fairly free time with our friends. My feeling about my father was that you would be encouraged and encouraged and allowed to do initially anything, then suddenly the skies would fall and he'd say, now you've gone too far. You never quite knew what was going to happen.

154

I was pushed off to Roedean, which I very much disliked, but they certainly didn't believe girls were inferior there, or could do less than boys, even in the 1930s.

Sylvia Scafardi: The people who influenced me most in childhood were my mother and my black nurse. My mother was the nicest woman I ever met. She was warm, unselfish, completely unpossessive, and she loved all her children. She muddled up all our names – when she called us she would say, Bea, no, I mean Sylvia, no Lydia. She was the type of woman who had her own life and her own ideas, but she had absolute confidence in her children. She knew that in the tropics we could run barefoot and wouldn't be bitten by snakes. This was in Brazil. I was born in São Paulo. My father, who was a clergyman's son, had come out to earn his living, to make his way in Brazil, and my mother was Brazilian. My black nurse was the daughter of a slave born on my grandfather's sugar and coffee plantation. I think her mother was a domestic there, and so she belonged to the family and came to grandfather's daughter, Otelia, my mother, when she was married, to look after her eldest child. I was the second one, and we were all her children. She was just like a second mother, a warm black presence I knew from birth, the beam of her eye and her plummy cheeks. She never smacked us. We were never stood in the corner. I was never punished. There was no need. If you were deprived of that glow, it was punishment enough. I remember once – I don't know what I'd done – she said, Sylvia, you haven't got a heart. And, of course, that cut me to the quick and I knew how terrible I'd been. Those were the influences in the home – my mother and my second mother. And my Brazilian grandmother who was born at the time of Darwin, 1851, and lived to a hundred and one. When my mother was engaged to my father, they used to argue about the Boer War, and my grandmother, of course, took the side of the Boers, as did the progressives in England, and he used to fight with her. But when she was in her eighties, she wrote a history of Brazil, and when she was in her nineties she wrote the story of her youth in Brazil, which was then cobblestones and candlelit, and she lived on until it was skyscrapers and planes. My youth, my childhood in Brazil was a paradise. When I put my head on the pillow, I could have torn up the night to start into the next day of sunshine and happiness. We had the garden, our bicycles, our bull terrier. We had a huge make-up trunk with ostrich feathers and silks and satins. We had paint-boxes and books, and the day was too short for everything.

In our family, before we came into the cruel world, I had no idea that boys were preferred to girls, no idea. Disillusionment came when we came to be educated. My father wanted to do the best with his children, and we were sent to boarding school at Eastbourne, we three girls, and the boys went to public school at Haileybury. That was the step out of paradise. We were dying to go, we had been reading about it with excitement, the midnight feasts and everything. However, the head-mistress used to send us to church twice on Sunday and once each day in Lent, and I began to realize that the grown-up world I'd been excited about and dying to get into was a flop. Religion that promised everything meant nothing. And, of course, the world I was growing up into was a grey world. I went to boarding school in the summer of 1914, and so we were caught up in the war. And at the beginning it was all patriotism and flags and lovely, but then, of course, it got greyer and greyer with the appalling casualties. When the end finally came, and we went to church, the clergyman did a sort of Jeremiah from the pulpit: the England you have known is finished for ever, and now you're growing up in a different world, and this that and the other, and how it was going to be terrible.

Jenny Seagrove: When I was very very small, my mother was seriously ill and nearly died, and so there were all sorts of psychological things that were bred into me before I was old enough to realize them. I think it was the same for my brother. I remember her telling me of when she came home from hospital – I was too young to remember – and my brother jumped up and down, hugging himself, but was unable to go and hug her. I never really saw my parents giving each other much affection. There was no physical affection at all in my family. And that's something I've always greatly missed. At a girls' boarding school, you don't get physical affection either, so I grew up without it and I grew up a person unable to express it. I suppose, in a way, that's what's led me to become an actress in that I felt that, as an actress playing people, one would be able to express it without fear. And also the acting would teach me, as a human being, to express it. So it was a kind of therapy for life.

Emma Sergeant: I had two very strong parents. My mother's a painter, and helped me a lot and always took me to galleries and was always discussing painting. My father was just completely and utterly proud of anything I did. So that was the best advantage and the best beginning you could think of. Also I had as many art materials as I ever wanted, and so I happily started painting and drawing from when I can remember.

156

Delphine Seyrig: My mother was very independent, and she was hoping I would grow up to be independent, but she was not competitive. In fact she hated competitiveness. She hoped I would not be a passive, feminine little girl. She was hoping I would have scope and would be physically strong and independent. She herself led a very independent youth. She was a sailor, and she sailed with another girl of her age at a time when women did not do those things. She lived on a boat and went all round the Mediterranean when she was twenty.

Hanan Al-Shaykh: I grew up in an Islamic atmosphere. My father was very pious. He wanted me to cover my head, and to pray, but he wasn't against me and my sister going to college and to the best schools.

I thought there was another world in reading books, and in writing books, and I started feeling somehow very interested in women writers and writing about women in Lebanon. I saw my grandmother and the older women, and how genuine they were. I found myself drifting to the woman's cause. My grandmother wasn't educated. She didn't know anything about books, about television. She would see a woman on television – a girl – and she would think that I was on television. She was illiterate. But I was influenced by her, by the way she looked at life, the way she'd think about women, about children, about adults, about men. She used to talk as if she was a prophet or a philosopher.

Clare Short: My father was an Irish teacher who came to Birmingham, met my mum, and had seven kids. It was a very happy, warm, loving kind of a family. It was a very political family too. My father comes from Northern Ireland, from a Republican village on the border where there has been lots of conflict over the years, and he took a general view of opposition to British imperialism and colonialism all round the world. He was a teacher in a poor school in Birmingham, and I think we all admired and respected him. He led on the political values of the family, and then my mum was a loving, kind mother. Looking back on it, of course, it's a bad stereotype: she always there when you were ill or needed anything, but my father the one you looked to for ideas and so on. It changed a bit as my dad became sicker, and my mum more liberated, when my little sister was quite young, and she went back to work and got active in the Labour Party.

My father was actually a member of the National Association of Schoolmasters, which traditionally had been separated from the National Union of Teachers by its opposition to equal pay for women, so I'm not sure that he was properly sorted out on the question of men and women. But in the family, the aspiration for us to succeed educationally and the sharing out of the domestic tasks, looking after the baby, doing the washing up, trying to get on at school, was very equal. It might have been partly that there were so many girls around. I don't know, but my brothers feel it strongly. They are the generation of men who meet women who are part of the women's movement and who shout at men for oppressing women, and they say, but we grew up with all these strong women all round us, we don't know what you're talking about. I was a very strong child. I swam, I fought the kids in the street, I did everything everybody did. It wasn't an issue when I was little.

Rosemary Anne Sisson: My father was a scholar, a philosopher, and even when we were little, he would talk to us if we were at table. Our opinions were welcome so long as they were sensibly held, and then he would challenge our opinion. So every opinion we held we had to be prepared to defend. That was a great intellectual exercise for little children. It was a strict upbringing though it was so full of love that we didn't realize it, but my parents set very high standards and if we came home and said: I was second in my class, they always said, who was top? I don't think I ever wanted to be competitive. I don't think my sister did, but our parents were competitive on our behalf, and my mother still is. I suppose I am competitive, but not against other people. I always want to be perfect, which is a terrible thing to try to be all the time, but that was really what was asked of us. That we should always do the very best we could whatever we were doing. My sister and I always took it for granted that we would go to a good school and go to a university, and then marry. In fact I always planned to be married. The only thing I wanted was to be married and to go on the stage. I wanted to have children. And it was my sister who married and had five children; and I never went on the stage. Yet I'm a remarkably happy woman, so it's a good example of not getting what you want but getting what, in the end, is best for you.

Ginette Spanier: My two sisters and I were born in Paris. My mother was French, my father English, and while we were in Paris they got over an Irish girl to look after us. She influenced me enormously, because she was completely different from any of the bourgeois people I knew. She would say, if you do this it will make me sad, because I will have to punish you. Later on we came to live in England, and I went to school in England. We had a strict upbringing. It's far off – I'm eighty-two – and most children were brought up strictly in those days. I think it was easier for them in the days when they were strictly brought up than in the permissive society where, even if they don't want to lead a very sexy life, they feel ashamed not to. I always wanted freedom, but I didn't know what it was.

Gloria Steinem: Books influenced me most, and movies. I still remember movies, even before I could read, as being a very important influence. I didn't go to school very regularly, and we travelled around a great deal, so the usual kind of community influences were not there for me. No one gave me instructions or was ambitious on my behalf, except to go to college. My mother wanted very much to have both of her daughters go to college. She came from a working-class family, and she and her sister had been put through college by her mother. So she was doing the same thing for her two daughters. That was very important, a big part of her dream. She thought that would help to get us out of the poor neighbourhood where we lived and into a better kind of life. But what we were going to do with our college education was never discussed – perhaps just marry a better-quality husband, perhaps work at something we enjoyed part of the time. I certainly wasn't urged to have any ambition.

Andrea von Stumm: My mother was very tender, and she was there. My father travelled a lot. But as it is, one is rather ungrateful for mothers, and I had, like many daughters, a great adoration for my father, who always came back like Father Christmas. The usual story.

Janet Suzman: I plagued my elder brother. I made his life a misery. I wanted to do everything he did and was a bit of a tomboy. But I was always relegated to the outfield in cricket. I had to field, I was never allowed to bat.

Lisa St Aubin de Terán: I was always very close to my mother, very influenced by her. She always tried to put me into a position of being exceptional, so when I was a child I'd learned to read by the time I was two, and by the time I was four I could read Jane Austen. And this was my mother's doing. By the time I was five, I was very into the *Dandy* and the *Beano*, but I never dared admit it, so I had to keep going with the Victorian novels, the classics, so my mother could say, brilliant! It was a kind of vicarious ambition with her. I think she was ambitious on her own behalf, and had reached a point in life when she couldn't really achieve this, and so she wanted me to have a more interesting life than she had. We were an all-female household. My parents divorced when I was one and my mother had been married four times previously. My father was her last marriage, as it were, so from then on we were just all women in the house: she, my three sisters and myself. I was brought up to believe that this was a fantastic advantage.

I'm the second generation of an all-female household. My mother was brought up by her mother and her grandmother, no father. Her parents divorced before she was born. Also she had some pretty disastrous marriages, and so she had a rather low opinion of men and thought we'd all be better off if we didn't let them have too much of a grip on our lives. It's not advice that any of my sisters or myself have followed.

Fiona Thyssen: A negative influence, but also a very positive one, was my father, an admiral in the Navy, who started off by saying that women were not intelligent enough, indeed that none of his children was intelligent enough – and that included two boys and two girls – and he would not speak to any of us until we were thirty. This offended us all, especially me, being the oldest daughter. I took it as a great put-down on being a female – that I wasn't, as a female, intelligent enough to discuss anything with my father. He was so intelligent himself that he had problems relating to anybody who couldn't communicate on the same level, which meant that a lot of people shuffled out of his life, including his four children. But it is interesting – he did have a very positive influence. I spent my entire adult life trying to educate myself so I would be intelligent enough one day to speak to my father. He unfortunately died, but not before I had time to have him listen to me with some degree of respect or understanding or caring, but it took a long time, so although it was hurtful and an unpleasant thing to live with, it had in the end a positive result.

The background, the family upbringing, the moral values, the ethics were certainly much more from my mother than my father. But, as I grew older, I found a lot of them unacceptable, merely because they were constraining and I didn't wish to be constrained. If I'd lived in this generation, I would have left home at an early age, had my own flat, got my own job and been totally independent. In the days when I grew up, the end of the 1940s and the 1950s, when I left school, it was socially unacceptable not to live at home, so I lived at home and found it very constrictive.

Claire Tomalin: I was born into a family where there were only girls, and so all the ambitions were placed on my sister and me. There was no brother to deflect them. My mother was a composer and, on my father's side, my grandmother had been a schoolmistress, and my French aunt was also in teacher training. So there was a tradition that women worked established in the family. My father had come to the Ecole Normale from the provinces of France and my mother had come to London from the North of England, both with scholarships. They both saw life in terms of education leading to achievement. I was brought up with that assumption. My mother loved me very much. That sounds like a truism, but now I look back it was of great importance. She believed in me strongly, she believed I had some special quality, which I don't think I had, but I had in her eyes. If you grow up with that feeling, it gives you great strength. Somehow I took it for granted that I would be able to do certain things. As a small girl, I wanted to become the first woman prime minister, which was not, of course, the path I followed. I suppose I was more interested in writing, but I also wanted to be like my mother. I wanted to be married and I wanted to have children. I wanted both.

My mother was fairly strict in the sense that I had to be at home at certain times. One's mother in those days always had some terrible fear lurking that one knew mothers had. I suppose it was a fear left over from her upbringing (she was born in 1897) that you would somehow sink into some terrible abyss through sexual misbehaviour, but I didn't worry about that. I had a very good elder sister who was an excellent girl guide and was also adventurous. I think my sister fought a lot of battles about strict upbringing ahead of me and so cleared the way. She wasn't exactly rebellious – she was very good, was head girl, did everything correctly, but used to fight the battles with my mother. When I left my mother, my father became my guardian, and he was extremely liberal and not at all strict.

Polly Toynbee: My parents were divorced when I was three. My mother remarried, and my stepfather was an influential figure but very much the friend in the distance who wasn't trying to be a surrogate father. But I saw my father a great deal. My parents went on getting on. But my mother was absolutely the dominating influence and, looking back through my family, I can see that the women were always really the most powerful. Even in my father's family, where, after all, my father was a quite distinguished writer and reviewer, and my grandfather a distinguished historian, the women in their lives – their mothers, their wives – were the most powerful people in many ways.

I've always thought that I come from a very matrilineal sort of culture. It's hard to say just how my mother influenced me, but I always knew that getting her approval was the most important thing and that if she said something was all right and good, then that was terrific. Her praise was what really mattered. I think she led me, and when I started to write, and in what I did at school, it was always her approval I sought. She was quite a stern critic, and still is. She never said to her children, that was lovely, dear, if it was something that wasn't worth doing or you hadn't tried hard. In some ways, I think we children used to resent that and feel, why doesn't she praise us all automatically the way other people's parents do. In other ways, it always gave you something to aim for that was a bit further ahead from where you were. She herself never worked and never had any intention of doing so. She came from a rather well-off upper-middle-class family, where she was a débutante, and she went to Paris for a year, came out and then married. Though, of course, marrying my father was an entirely unconventional thing to do, because that wasn't his world at all. She was entirely sef-educated. She went to absurd schools and had ludicrous governesses. But, out of her own intelligence, she educated herself, read an enormous amount of French and German literature. She's much better read than I am. She was always an intellectual by instinct if not by background. And she married two extremely intellectual men, so I always felt it was this intellectual quality I was living up to more than any other. Also, she's a stern moralist. She was a Labour Party supporter, and is now an SDP supporter, which, for a person with a certain amount of money, is a moral stand not a stand of self-interest. We always judged ourselves not only by intellectual excellence but also by her rather stern moral eye on us. I don't mean moral in the sense of relationships, or sex, about which she was very liberal, but certainly in the sense of one's views and attitudes. She certainly shaped me in that way. I don't think any of my political views are entirely my own, but very much out of my background.

Kathleen Turner: We had four children in our family – two girls and two boys – and although my mother was certainly the one most around, my father was the last word, the law, and the model in that it was made clear early on that we were expected to earn our own livings and make our own way. The oldest child, my sister, was a good scholar. Education was intensely important to my father, and I did not prove to be the best student. So I think my parents were not so ambitious for me; they felt I would probably marry well, but they didn't see the professional future I think they hoped for in the others.

Jill Tweedie: My father was the one who was the outside world, and I quickly learned that he would be the one who would know its standards. So, when he judged me, I always felt that was the outside world, and that when I left school, and left home, it would be his judgement I would be getting. He was a ruthless judge, and so, although it was a strong influence, it wasn't necessarily a good one. It made the outside world seem frightening and competitive. If I brought home a prize for some essay or other, he used to say, yes, this is not bad. He was like the mother of Louis B. Mayer. Louis B. Mayer bought a yacht and got the hat and the jacket, and he came to his mother and said, mother, I am a captain now, and his mother said, to me, Louis, you are always a captain, but to a captain are you a captain? That's my father. He was always doing that.

I led the kind of life that was rather segregated from young men. We had an occasional school dance where we'd find men, but they were rare. I knew that the lack of expectation was peculiar. It was odd that nobody seemed to think I was going to go beyond school, and that everybody thought I would get married. Also I remember the odd things like cleanliness. Now, that was a very strong impression as a child, because my brother would go out and play rounders and all sorts of sports, and would come back and I'd say, God, you stink, oh, the smell, the sweat and everything. Yet nobody, to my child's view, said anything to him. And, of course, he would have a shower. But my mother was always saying to me, you must be very clean. I know now – I could analyse what it all means – but at the time I remember getting an impression that, in some extraordinary way, girls seemed to have to have baths many more times than boys, even though boys were quite obviously dirtier.

Sara Vass: I was an only child for seven years, but when my brother was born, I noticed immediately that he had a great deal more privilege than I did, that my mother gave him more leeway than she had given me. Now, I suppose I rationalize that by thinking she had already gone through one child and had learned that you didn't have to be quite as strict and quite as hard. But he was a boy, and she liked that about him a bit more than she liked it about me that I was a girl.

Tracy Ward: Tony Lambton influenced me most. He was very close to my mother and therefore saw us being brought up and liked us and wanted us to blossom in this world to the best possible advantage. But because he wasn't my real father, he didn't worry that he would be directly responsible for making sure we were married, making sure we had enough money, making sure we were not going to be hanging on to his purse strings for the rest of our lives. He had none of the sort of worries fathers usually have, of how to get rid of the women neatly. He wanted us to be strong, independent, confident and outgoing so that we could enjoy as much of life as possible, and also not let people who were boring and narrow-minded have any influence on us at all. Men who would come and take us out, we would say what we thought of them, whether they just wanted to go to bed with us, and he would make us excuses to get rid of them or tell us how to deal with them if we did not like them. It was a totally impartial, loving relationship. He wanted the best for Rachel and me. He is definitely quite a snobbish man, though only because he thinks it would be less of a fight for us if we stayed in our certain class, which any parent would advise a child. But he gave us the confidence and the encouragement as far as our intelligence was concerned, unlike most fathers, who basically think you are supposed to be a wife. Unless you are very brilliant, you are just a wife, and you are just a cook, and arrange flowers and have babies. He made us stand up on our own feet.

Marina Warner: I think, in a way, that my father and mother were such a complete contrast that I reacted across the sexes. Probably I was influenced more by my father through rebellion, through wishing to react against his prescription of what my life should be like. My father was a regular upper-middle-class man; he had been to Eton and Oxford and was a colonel in the Army. He met my mother, who came from a very, very poor Italian family, during the war. My father was a plain-looking man, my mother a very beautiful woman. She had a complete background in Catholic service. She had been brought up happily entirely by women because her father died when she was a child, and there was a sort of sweetness in her life. She was lively and vivacious, but she is somebody who can yield, and my father had, in a way, the kind of authority of his class. He had that English mentality and he was very tyrannical. So, in a way, he influenced me more, not to conform but to fight against him. But I also didn't want to be like my mother. There were terrible rows, for instance, about her clothes. She had never had any money to buy her own clothes, which seems an absolutely ludicrous detail, but I remember that I was determined I would always have my own money, that I would not be in the position of having to ask a man if I could have a coat for the winter.

My father was very ambitious for me and my sister. He didn't have any sons and always joked that, if he had sons, he would have forgotten about us. But we were his substitute sons and he had high intellectual ambitions. He became quite a famous bookseller. He was Bowes & Bowes in Cambridge, and they had a little chain of bookshops that were the serious side of Smith's in those days. It's a while ago now; he was quite old when we were born, and he's dead now. There were always books around. Any time we showed any interest in any subject, heaps of books would be brought back from the shop for us to read. So we were very very fostered. My sister was good at Latin and Greek, and she got all the dictionaries and everything, immediately, which were very expensive, so there was constantly that kind of input.

My religious upbringing was quite intensely Catholic, not because my mother is a devout Catholic, which she is, but she wouldn't have imposed that on us except that she liked us to be Catholics. My father imposed it because he thought it was a very good religion for a girl, which is terribly interesting. He was a Protestant – an Anglican. He brought us up as Catholics for the morality of it, sent us to convents because he thought this would make us proper young women. The Catholic religion is disciplined in a particular way for women, disciplined to self-sacrifice and sexual purity. At the same time, he wasn't an austere man. He was very genial, loved company and good wine and grew roses beautifully. He had a lot of facets to his character, and not in a boring tight-arsed British way; but he was very, very dominant. And I probably caused him a lot of grief, because I was anxious to get away from that, I did want to pursue my own lines. And a lot of my attitudes were not formed by reflective consideration over books, but were immediate reactions. My politics at first were formed entirely by the flip side of his politics. He hated the trade unions, so I liked the trade unions. But then I developed a more considered view, though I still have strong visceral antagonism to certain aspects of conservatism because I didn't like them at the dinner table at home. I didn't like the *Daily Telegraph* talk which was part of a world I didn't want to enter. He wanted me to marry a stockbroker. Even though he wanted me to have a good education, he never wanted me to be a writer. He said it was a very bad sort of income, it would never be reliable. He would have liked me to be somebody like a diplomat, and he would have liked me to do the Foreign Office, or something like it. I did languages. In that sense, he was a conventional man. He was very, very proud of me when I became a writer. He would laugh in a sort of ironical way about the things I wrote. He was touchingly proud and his interest in me, even his antagonistic interest, was very strong and strengthening. There have been some psychological studies in which cross-identification of children apparently is a source of high motivation. Girls who identify with their fathers in some way, even as rebels, and boys who identify with their

165

mothers can actually become more motivated, more able to express themselves, and this was true in my case, I think.

Felicity White: I can see it now. I looked at my parents, and at their marriage, and this tremendous vitality my mother had that became very subdued whenever my father was around – well, we must do what he wants. He was not a demanding man, but that's the way it was, the way she was brought up. And something in me then said I am not going to let this happen to me. I am not ever going to be subdued by a man. I thought, I am going to have a career, I want to prove I can be who I feel inside I am.

My mother was quite strong and, looking back now, quite oppressive. She desperately wanted children. She got them and she put her whole life and soul into them. And she was around the whole time – no nannies or anything like that. And I grew up with everything she told me in me, which inevitably causes problems in later life. My father was a shadowy figure. He was out at work twelve hours a day, he'd come home, go to bed – father's tired et cetera. And that, again, is a problem because I didn't actually start communicating with him until I was about sixteen. He is not a great communicator, anyway.

My mother wanted a daughter to be a mirror image of her. The woman who marries well, sets up a home, sits down and has children and doesn't have a career. So the fact that I went into a career has been difficult for her and quite difficult for me. I've gone into a male-dominated career as well. She would see it as that. She sees it as a man's world.

Katharine Whitehorn: At the time, it certainly seemed as if my mother influenced me most, but with hindsight over the years, I would say very much my father. My mother had got into university, but had never been able to go because she nearly died of an illness when she was sixteen. My father was a schoolmaster, and very remote, and like many schoolmaster fathers had great difficulty in being sufficiently matey with his own small children. I remember my mother telling me she heard me, when I was about six, saying here comes the old grump, and she didn't know whether to be more pleased that I felt I could say it, or sorry I wanted to say it. I don't think I really came to terms with my father till I was about fifteen, but he was a guy whose way of thinking was incredibly important to me and a whole generation of his pupils. It never occurred to him not to take me seriously or not to demand that I did as well as my brother or anybody else.

166

Shelley Vaughan Williams: Both my parents had enormous influence. The most important thing about my parents was that they adored each other. I think I was twenty-three before I realized that mothers and fathers could actually be unhappy. I think to be loved, and be loved by two people who adored each other, gave me the springboard to cope with all the terrible things that happen to any human being in life, and that's something I'm grateful for. I don't think many people have that.

My father wanted me to be, if anything, better educated than my brother, because he thought girls should have a much better education, if possible, than a boy. Because if anything happened to them, they had to have many more resources than men, who find it much easier.

Jeanette Winterson: I was brought up by my mother and a group of Pentecostal ladies – they were evangelical Pentecostalists, which is a very charismatic and outgoing branch of the evangelical Church. It's really like an extended family, which, in Britain, is quite unusual. Instead of being brought up simply by one's parents, I was brought up by a whole string of women, which actually worked very well, because I felt as though I had a huge family. It was the women who did all the organizing in the Church and who were very strong, and so it was with them I identified. It was a very strict upbringing, but it also had an unusual freedom in that they believed that they were all God's chosen people, which means that you're taught to respect your own instincts and your own ideas because they're God's ideas. So, in a sense, I didn't have any crises of confidence that children usually have. Indeed, I was preaching from a very early age, and let loose. I wasn't restricted at all.

Despite the conservatism of my town, which is in the north of Lancashire, and the conservatism of the Church itself, there was this flip-side, which was an unusual freedom because you were doing God's work and you had to be let loose to do it. So that was a great bonus. I gained enormously from it, even though I look back on the time as in many ways rather terrible in the sense that it was so totally rigid. If I did anything they didn't approve of, they would immediately assume I was demon-possessed, which meant having to be exorcized by the priests, which was quite a traumatic experience for a child. And it was very much that you were always living in a world of spirits and demons, and they were just as real as people you might meet. So it was quite bizarre and fantastical in many ways. I know that a lot of people who have been brought up like this don't fit in terribly well with society, and are not perhaps as well-balanced as they might be, but I was lucky.

167

The novel I wrote that won the Whitbread First Novel in 1985, *Oranges are Not the Only Fruit*, was really the story of my upbringing because I was so completely innocent in all senses that, when I fell in love with a woman, as many girls do at fourteen or fifteen, I just went round and told everybody because I thought it was wonderful. I didn't think to hide it, because I'd never had to hide anything. Of course, that was completely traumatic from their point of view, and from mine, so they said, you have to leave – by this time I was sixteen – so I left home and then went to live with a woman teacher and got a job in an ice-cream parlour in the evenings to support myself, and carried on at school.

I was so desperate not to go crazy, having been thrown out of home and having suddenly to fend for myself. I didn't think of anything except surviving. Gender problems didn't even arise for me at that time. I just thought, I have to work and I have to pull myself out of this. And it was that drive, which was almost an obsession, that carried me through.

Anna Wintour: My father was very much the leader. My mother was great too, but everything revolved around my father, about his world and his schedule. When I was growing up, he was working on the *Daily Express*, so he kept the most bizarre hours and we didn't see him that much, but the whole household was somehow directed about him. One was brought up to feel that publishing a newspaper was a very exciting, very glamorous, interesting world. I was very close to my father and I think that my whole career and way of thinking evolved from him.

Enid Wistrich: My father was quite influential because he had a very definite idea that girls should not marry until they had established some kind of job or career pattern. He greatly admired his sister, who had become a doctor and a dentist, and he used to say to me, you shouldn't marry until you're about twenty-seven, you should work, you should establish yourself and study before you marry. He wanted me to be either a doctor or a lawyer, and I know he had his sister in mind, whom he much admired. My mother, on the other hand, ran her own business, and she would say, well, I don't mind what you do, the important thing is that you should be happy and be good and all that kind of thing. But clearly she would not, I think, have expected me to be a completely domesticated woman. Both my parents were the same in that respect. They didn't see women as in the home with children. They would have accepted that, but they were happy to see if I developed further.

Boys were rather strange territory for me, because I had no brothers, and although I went to a mixed school until I was about ten, after that I was in a girls' school, so I found boys very strange. I never really had much to do with them, and I can only remember one moment when I really felt envy of a boy, and that was when I was about fifteen and I went with a friend to watch a football match where her brother was playing. At the end of the match this boy came off the field covered in mud and very pleased with himself, and I felt highly envious because I thought that would be a wonderful thing to do: to be a strong boy and play football and be covered with glory and mud.

---

*Princess Yasmin Aga Khan's mother, Rita Hayworth, died shortly after this interview.

2
Advantages and Disadvantages

'*The history of men's opposition to women's emancipation is more interesting perhaps than the story of that emancipation itself*'
– Virginia Woolf, *A Room of One's Own* (1929)

'*It is delightful to be a woman; but every man thanks the Lord devoutly that he isn't one*'
– Olive Schreiner, *The Story of an African Farm* (1883)

'*Men made the moral code and they expect women to accept it*'
– Emmeline Pankhurst, Speech: 'When Civil War is Waged by Women', November 1913, quoted in *My Own Story* (1914)

'*We are still the property of men, the spoils today of warriors who pretend to be our comrades in the struggle, but who merely seek to mount us…*'
– Maria Isabel Barreno, *New Portuguese Letters* (1972)

'*Whatever women do they must do twice as well as men to be thought half as good. Luckily, this is not difficult*'
– Charlotte Whitton, quoted in *Canada Month* (June 1963)

'*Beauty endures only for as long as it can be seen; goodness, beautiful today, will remain so tomorrow*'
– Sappho

Jenny Agutter: I didn't feel the disadvantages at all until much later, when I became aware of them in other people. My life was magical growing up, because I got a lot of opportunities that no other children had. I got a chance to go into the film world when I was eleven, and I travelled to Denmark and Berlin, then went to Yugoslavia and made a film. I had all of these opportunities and didn't think about whether or not they mightn't be possible. It hit me very late because, you know, by the time I came out of school I had established my work. I never had to battle for a place in the drama school, a place in university, or for a job. What I had was a different sort of battle because the work I did early made me more prominent, so there was the constant fight to maintain it.

You suddenly find yourself realizing, talking with people, that you are an alien animal. You are not being talked to as any sort of equal. You are patronized, and you are something strange. Sometimes you feel there is this wonderful respect; actually it's not respect. It's just enjoyment of something, that you are terrific, but you're still an alien animal. Which is odd, because one lives in the same world, with the same problems, the same education, the same background, the same information coming. Yet somehow one is meant to have deciphered all that in a completely different way. I mean, where some men get the idea I don't know. I was having a conversation the other day with a gentleman in business, who admitted indeed that the person in charge of the entire company was a woman, a very distinguished and very well-thought-of woman. However, in talking about the women he worked with, he couldn't admit to enjoying working with them. He said, well, there are problems. Say they want to go away and have a child. And I said, well, say a woman has come to the age of thirty and has made all those choices. She has either decided she's not having a family or she's had her family and has a set-up where either the husband or a nanny or someone is taking care of that. She is able to get on with her job.

173

There's not going to be any interference. And I could see the whole idea was difficult for him to accept. Having made up his mind that there was that difference, he would rather women just took care of certain things and men took care of others. A man would say, I have this home, I can give you this, I'm going to be out at work and you have these attributes. That's wonderful. We can work that out. But there's a terrible threat in it, because whereas women have always lived with being taken care of, and don't worry about it, a man has not lived with being taken care of. He finds it extremely difficult to cope with. I mean, what I could do with is a man who could be like a wife: the person who could be at home and would take care of things, who would let me carry on with the work and encourage me. And that's hard to find. Women are, a lot of the time, ego boosters. They spend much of their time building up their men.

One wants to see more respect. The girlie magazines and the particular use of women in an obvious sexual way came, I think, as a result of men feeling: OK, so women can do the jobs and everything, but we will put them in a particular place. And it was humiliating. I do think that most of the glossy girlie magazines are extremely humiliating to women because it's got nothing to do with anything other than whether they've got big breasts. So I think it's rather awful; it's literally putting women down.

I realize that it's rather dull to worry about ageing, because every period you go through has its benefits. You might not have a youthful complexion, but the lines only show what you have been through, which is a good illustration of who you are and where you have been. In fact, it worries me enormously, the exaltation that is given to youth, because beauty is inside somebody and to do with their feelings. And the more people worry about plastic surgery and changing their faces, the worse off they are. If somebody is fifty, why should they look twenty-five? If they're fifty, they should look fifty.

Lolicia Aitken: I was never a great beauty. I was more on the ugly side, but I became better looking with the years, because I was wise enough to brainwash myself that I was wonderful. I think the secret of beauty is what you project. That's ultimately what men sense.

I was patronized by a professor who said, why are you studying economics? You'll only get married, and you should go and cook. You're wasting your time studying economics. Go and get married. You're a pretty girl, go and find yourself a husband. That's the ultimate in patronizing.

I think the injustice is the self-image women are educated to have. That's why I think I was very lucky to have a father who never made any difference of sex, and therefore I always thought I was as good as any men around. I don't think, quality-wise, there is any difference. I think the difference is that women today are brought up to say, well, you are a girl, therefore you cannot do this, you cannot do that. My mother-in-law, for instance, said, well, girls can be nurses when they grow up. And I said, if they want to be in the medical profession, they can jolly well be heart surgeons. But women don't go for top jobs because they don't think they're capable. It's a deep-rooted image that they won't be accepted, and therefore they don't go for it. And if you don't go for it, you don't get it.

Maria Aitken: I did notice it was very much harder for me to get into Oxford; my brother simply sailed in. I passionately wanted to go, but there was a real worry I might not get there because of the pressure for places. And I thought, for the first time, that was monstrously unfair. I was relieved when I did get in, when I realized the odds were colossal compared to what boys faced. Just having A-Levels, you have to take special entrance exams for girls' colleges, or you used to need to. The whole system was much more stringent and tougher than for men. And, of course, we all knew that there were some men who merely wielded the cricket bat well and got in. That was impossible for women. It was the first time I became aware that there were difficulties for women in the competitive outside world. However, I have noticed that I have always chosen for myself meritocracies where sex doesn't matter. Once I got into Oxford, there was no problem in being a woman among men. In the theatre, there is no problem. As a writer, there is no problem. I am aware of it for other people, but for myself I have chosen fields, perhaps deliberately, where it is not difficult.

There are hardly any women directors in the theatre. The whole authoritarian structure in the theatre is masculine at the moment, and few actresses have made the transition to directors.

At the moment, we are in a kind of peak era of guilt, so you do sometimes, if you are articulate and relatively successful in your field, get given more opportunities because you are a woman than you might otherwise. This is only this decade. It probably won't last.

I am never patronized by men in the circles I move in. Occasionally, when I go to fund-raising dinners, beyond the world of the arts, I do encounter it, and then I find it is rather embarrassing. You have to

175

produce your credentials to get rated, as it were, otherwise you are just a little thing. I am a fiscal moron, and if I am mixing with financiers, I must seem a great idiot. And it's rather hard to say, but, actually, I do something else and I do it rather well. One wouldn't want to be that pushy.

I hate to admit this, but I do think that there is a glandular changeability about women which has always given men the advantage. Menstruation does mess us up – we do become rather irrational. Our temperaments change within a month, and although one can control it and be aware of it, it is extremely unfair that it happens. And we make rather bad decisions or fly off the handle more easily because of it. I don't see the same changeability in men.

I don't think you get very far if you begin with a grievance. I think you have to ignore the problem until it absolutely confronts you. The only time I felt humiliated – and I felt desperately humiliated – was when I was in a series with Jill Bennett. We had thought of the idea ourselves, and we had got a writer, a very good writer to write it, but Granada were absolutely contemptuous of the notion that having the idea was a contribution. In the end, the only way we got paid for the idea was by taking a percentage of the author's fee, which was monstrous, because the author got so little. I felt sure that, if it had been a couple of men bringing in an idea, bringing in a writer, it would have been different. It wouldn't happen to me now, because I know what to do, but that was the first time, and we were certainly ripped off. We squawked about it, but nothing happened. One of the dreadful things about performing is that you often swallow your pride in order not to lose the opportunity.

I'm afraid good appearance is a horribly strong advantage. One reason I know so much about that is because I had an eye disease which made me extremely unattractive for two or three years, and because you communicate everything with the eyes, you are tremendously aware when it goes wrong. Even buying a newspaper, taking a taxi, simple activities with men, I found horrendously changed, humiliatingly changed. And if it hadn't been that I lived with a man who simply would not allow me to give in and become a hermit, the sort of reaction I got (never from colleagues, but from employers and strangers) made me realize that the whole thing pivots on your appearance. Not as you get older, once you have some achievement, but initially.

I used to think I wished I was a man, but again it's back to motherhood. There's no fun being a man at all, I think. You miss out on almost everything, and you have to work very hard for the little fun you have.

Ageing is, in fact, not nearly as traumatic as this business of having an eye disease for so long. I had to have quite a long look into the abyss of being altered, and I didn't like it much. I don't like the fact that my face is changing with age. On the other hand, I care so little now about what people think of me compared to what I used to think. It seems to me that nature takes care of it in that way: by the time one becomes less attractive, one doesn't mind. Anyway, is it less attractive? It's different. This must sound egomanic, but as I get older, I find it harder to think that men would find young girls attractive, or seriously attractive. Stirring to the blood, of course, but how can they relate if they are themselves older, how can they? I used to have affairs with men in their fifties when I was in my early twenties, and I must have been so arse-paralysingly dull.

Lady Penelope Aitken: When I was young, there were great taboos and one had to be careful. I don't think I really missed out on anything, when I look at the next generation, but one had to be much more careful. It wasn't an accepted thing, for instance, to make one's friends and move about on one's own. It was not the accepted rule by any manner of means. I would have loved to have a career, but once one started to think about that, the war came. I was in the Red Cross on the river boats here on the Thames, which was really quite fun, because we were trained up and the moment war was declared we had to report. I had to report at Chelsea Bridge, and we got on our boats and went along the river to lie in the docks because that's where they thought the bombs would fall. So our little teams with eight VADs, a trained nurse and a doctor on board, would go out along the Thames at six in the evening, and sit among the ships, waiting for the bombs to drop. And, of course, nothing happened. We bandaged the people who cut off their fingers at Billingsgate and places, but that was about all. Finally we got bored, put hot potatoes to cook in the boilers, and blew the ship's boilers up. So it went into dry-dock and I left it at that stage and went into a hospital, where I was very lucky and did mostly theatre and casualty work.

I didn't feel disadvantaged in any way. I don't know what the difference would have been between me and girls today, except that the men respected you much more and didn't expect to get into bed with you the moment they saw you. Or they might have had that in view, but they didn't expect that to happen at the end of every evening, as they do now. My father was very fond of me, and he disliked the fact that the members of his staff would fall in love with me. One of the orders in the Sudan was, on pain of death, not to fall in love with the governor-general's daughter. My father hated this disruption. He couldn't bear to see this emotional upset in his staff, and there were some terrible scenes in which he sacked men. It was one of those things that happened. I think he was over-protective. He was a very loving father.

I would have loved to have been a professional woman, for I have great admiration for women who hold down big jobs. There was just not the opportunity in my life to do things professionally. When the war came, it meant that I went into jobs, and from that time I've never stopped working, but I haven't had paid jobs. I couldn't possibly be here at my age if I wasn't going out almost every day into a job. I've always run things, organized things, and I couldn't bear not to. But I think I'd have been much happier had I been able to put all this energy into something more lucrative. But I couldn't not have worked.

When I was, I think, about nineteen, I was painted by Simon Elwes, and there was a man next door who was a sculptor. Simon said, you must be sculpted by him, he keeps on begging. His studio was round the corner, so I went, and he did a nude of me. And that was fine – it was terribly boring – all in clay. Six months later, they rang me and said, it's in the Royal Academy in bronze. I said, what! God, you must get it out at once. (It was really like me. It had my head on it.) My father's Head of the Colonial Office here, I shall be absolutely killed, you've got to get it out. But there was no way of getting it out. So I told a friend, who later on became Minister of Works, and he bought it. Even worse, he put it in the window of his house in Palace Street for the rest of his life. And, of course, people who saw it did say something, but eventually I didn't mind in the least. By that time I didn't look like that any more. But that was a very advanced, naughty sort of thing to do. And my father never knew.

I wouldn't have been a man for anything. I think my sex is a tremendous sex. I think we've got practically everything, almost more than we want.

Life is very good, that's all I can say. I've had a perfectly wonderful life. I maybe have not had to struggle as much as a man would have had to struggle. I haven't had to earn my own living, which a lot of women have to do, and I have benefited enormously by the fruits of other people's hard work.

Shirin Akiner: I've never seen myself as a woman. I've seen myself as a person. Anything I've wanted to do, I've done. As a human being, one has the right to try and do what one can. It never occurred to me to think of myself as a woman.

There are, of course, disadvantages or problems inherent in the situation. As a woman, one has the possibility of being a mother, which I am, and that is a very serious responsibility. And so whatever one does in one's life for at least twenty years is going to be very much influenced by the fact of having had a child. In a sense, you could say that is a disadvantage. One's timing is very circumscribed. On the other hand, it's a God-given gift. So I don't think that one either complains about it or especially rejoices in it. One can rejoice in the child but one is neither pleased nor sad to have one's time circumscribed. It's just a fact, like being born.

I think I've been fortunate. I have earned my living, but money has never been particularly important to me; I've always been interested in doing what I wanted to do. For example, I was widowed many years ago, just before my son was born, and I came to this country with no money, about to be a mother, and decided I wanted to go to university and send my son to a private school. I put his name down on the waiting list immediately he was born. It was £20, which was an enormous sum, and I had no qualifications at all, because I'd been a music student and hadn't really been to school properly. I did all my exams – A-Levels and so on – in less than six months. I entered university, not knowing at all how I'd ever pay for my son's fees. But I worked hard at university. I loved my time there enormously. My son was at a day nursery the council provided, and I'd take my son to nursery in the morning and, as soon as I finished my classes, I'd rush back and take him home. Then it so happened that I got a reasonably good degree, and as a result won a scholarship. So just when he began at school, I had the money. Afterwards I remarried, and again there was enough money for me to pursue the work I was involved in, but it never occurred to me I should not do that because there wasn't the money. Maybe if things had worked out differently and there had been a long period when I had no money at all, maybe I would have felt differently, but when I came to this England I can honestly say that it never occurred to me for a moment not to go to university because of money, not to put my son's name down for a school I thought was a good school because of money.

I'm sure there are professions in which women have to behave very differently. I'm sure there are situations in which women are discriminated against. But that's never been my experience. I have no idea how one would be aggressive like a man. It's not a thing that has occurred to me. In the fields that I have been interested and active in, I've never had to be anything but myself. It's difficult being oneself, it's difficult doing one's work as well as possible, and that is enough of a challenge.

179

Baria Alamuddin: Sometimes I feel emotionally disadvantaged because I feel things differently from the way a man does. Sometimes I lie awake all night because of one word that's been said to me, and the man doesn't even notice what he's said.

I always tell my two daughters to enjoy their souls and their bodies, because I think at the base of all this repression of women in the Middle East are a lot of sexual and soul problems. The women in the Middle East are not sure of what they want to give, and what they have to give. Many people of my age who went to university with me wanted to have lovers, to have sex, yet inside was this tremendous struggle: what would society say, what would my aunties say, what would the man I love and marry say? There is a very strong struggle, and not everybody in the end wins, and this is why you see lots of complexes in our society. In the West, I see this to a great extent, too, because women are basically the same all over the world.

Madeleine L. H. Alatas: I think real women are much more self-confident than men. They don't compete against men because they haven't been trained to compete against men. They are scared of it because they haven't had the education, the psychology that says do it. I think competition is the wrong word. If you want something when you're a man or a woman, you get it, period. It's irrelevant whether you're a man or a woman. It's like people, children, who have come from divorced families, who turn around and blame everything on the divorce. Anything is an excuse. If you really want something, you get it. Look at Elizabeth Arden, Coco Chanel, all these women – determination, guts, drive, they started off from nothing. Nobody told them they couldn't build an empire, and they did. As a matter of fact it became more competitive, more efficient. Diana Vreeland, Tina Merrill, all these people – each one of them has overcome something, some event, that has made them extremely effective, but not competitive.

To a certain extent, women are permitted a tremendous leeway. I feel that if you set yourself up as a victim, you will be treated as one. I never considered myself a victim.

Women are, for some reason, expected to fulfil certain roles all the time. I can give you a perfect example. I have a child and my child expects 100 per cent of me when he does see me. He accepts that I work somewhere, but when he's back, he expects me to be 100 per cent there. When I'm at work, people expect me to be 100 per cent on that. When I'm with my ex-husband, speaking to him as a friend and as father of my child, he expects 100 per cent attention at that. When I'm with men who are friends of mine or I have a relationship with, they expect me to be 100 per cent into that role. When I go out socially, as sometimes I have to, 80 per cent isn't good enough. So if I was to give one thing to women, it would be somehow an understanding of how the various bodies pull on them and that maybe 80 per cent is not bad considering they're doing eight different things at the same time, playing eight differing roles, or ten, or fifteen.

Jan Amory: I much prefer men to women. I have quite a close group of women friends, but small. I've never felt inadequate, or that men are luckier. I've always felt that I could get away with more being a woman. Had I been a man, I wouldn't have been able to do half the things I do as a woman.

Adèle Anderson: I enjoy being what I am so much that any disadvantages I come across are nothing compared to the disadvantages I would have felt remaining the way I was. When you're making the transition and you know people are going to point at you in the street for a long time, you close your mind to it, you only want to know about the good things. And I find that habit hard to break. Even in a working situation with tensions going on around, I don't notice it; it's not that I'm deliberately not noticing it, I simply don't notice it. So maybe we do get discrimination and I'm simply not aware of it.

I have a very peculiar legal status in this country. I have certain rights but not total rights. I'm on a par with mental defectives, I think, in the fact that I don't have the right to marry (which is actually against the European Convention) and I don't have the right to adopt any children. Trans-sexuals who have been married and fathered children and then become women, normally get denied access to their children by the courts. We can't change the birth certificate, so we're constantly open to discovery when we go for jobs. And so it goes on. We're not accepted by the women's movement. I actually got attacked by a black lesbian feminist one night, who said, if you wore brown make-up you wouldn't know what it's like to be black, so just because you're wearing a bit of mascara, don't think you know what it's like to be a woman. The women's movement feel we are not real women, and all I can say is that I don't want to spend my life analysing and comparing myself to other women. I can only be who I am. People either accept that or they don't. I'm certainly not a man. When I decided to become a woman, I had to go to a psychiatrist first to check that I knew exactly what I was doing, and then after that there was a series of operations. I spent my twenties changing – I'd say it took me a good ten years to get from one end to the other. The sex-change surgery is only one operation, but then there are other bits of plastic surgery that one undergoes to refine the features et cetera. The first five years I was living as a woman, to prove I could be one, in order to get the surgery; then I had the surgery and everything fell into place, everything changed. But, in law, my status must remain what it was when I was born, because the law is an ass, as you know. There are certain countries where, once you have the operation, you get the full rights of womanhood, but Britain is not one of them. We've just taken a case to the Court of Human Rights in Strasbourg saying we must have the right to change our birth certificate, and we must have the right to get married, and it's been thrown out because there are countries like Greece and Spain in the EEC who won't wear it. I don't need to get married, because I'm not going to have any children, which is normally the reason why people get married, but that's not to say that I shouldn't be able to get married if I wanted. I might be a very religious person and feel it was very important. The Church doesn't accept me as a woman either, although I'm not a member of the Church. I believe that we're put on earth to find our own way through it, and I'm making my way as best I can, and I can't believe that God would condemn me for what I've done. I don't really acknowledge the presence of God, but I do believe there is some sort of power, I don't know what. If there is anything to draw nearer to, I have certainly been able to draw nearer to it, because I'm happy being now what I wanted to be. When I wasn't, when I was a boy and wanted to be a female, I raged against God, whoever it may be. Now I'm at peace with myself so I'm able to look outwards. The thing about not wanting to be something is that you turn totally inwards. It's all me, me, me, everything centres on me. Once you're happy being yourself – they say nobody can love you until you love yourself – once that happens, then you can look out at the world and begin to make your way in it. The transition wasn't as traumatic for me as it's been for many others, because I knew exactly what to do. I had total conviction, and I knew where to go. I didn't spend my time, like a lot of people, going to their GPs, who said, forget it, go away and join the Territorial Army or whatever. So I knew exactly what I had to do. I knew it was going to take a long time, and I had total conviction that at the end it would be all right. And I was right.

I don't think the feminist idea that we're actually identical except that we've got slightly different bodies, is true at all. I was reading this research article yesterday that said men's brains and women's brains are different, and I say *vive la différence*. I believe you can both achieve the same end by a different route. It is extremely unfair that women have been discriminated against, but it seems mostly due to the child-bearing aspect and the fact that they have to make a choice between having and not having children. I've got a friend, and she and her husband have been actively involved in politics ever since I've known them. They had consciously decided they weren't going to have any children, and they were just getting to the goal they'd been after for a long time. She became heavily involved in union politics and was about to take over a high-up position, when suddenly she found herself pregnant. And that's it, you know. Her career has come to a full stop, and it seems terribly unjust. I don't know what I'd feel in that situation. I know there are people who can't have children for whatever reason, who have a terrible longing which eats away at their life. I've never had any desire to have them. I think it's very nice for other people to have them. I've nothing against children *per se*. Perhaps because I didn't enjoy being a child much, I couldn't wait to be a grown-up.

I have suddenly become so conservative with a small c. I was a real tearaway when I was young. Fifteen was a great age, because everything was illegal, but you looked old enough to do it all and could get away with it. Now, suddenly, I've got friends who have got sons and daughters of twenty. If I walk into my friend's room, and her son's got his friends there, yes, I'm a completely different generation. I haven't got a great desire to be noticed any more, either. When I was young, I wanted the whole world to know I was there. Maybe I've assumed the world will notice I am here now without me having to yell, because they can read about me in the newspapers. I am aware of ageing, but I don't fear it; I look forward to it. I'll have had a pretty good run by that time, I think, and I figure if, at the age of thirty-four, I'm attractive to men of twenty, when I get to sixty-four I'll probably be attractive to men of thirty.

Dr Swee Chai Ang: We lived in a world where women have just begun to try to compete and work and go into occupations which in the past were not available. If I'd been born in China a hundred years ago, being the first, I'd probably have been drowned, because nobody wanted a daughter as a first child. We've come a long way. It is a continual process, a gradual fight for equality, for recognition, for being able to do the things you want to do, to develop your talents and potential. You see, I feel a woman and a man are very much the same. There are certain differences in the sense that we can have babies and men can't, but I know of a lot of women who have to give up what they are capable of doing because they're women. In many Chinese families, the boy can go to medical school or college and the girls have to work in a factory.

183

When you get married, if your husband is a very understanding person, he will help you develop, but if your husband is what standard husbands are like, you wash his socks, make his dinner, have his babies and that is the end of one's life. Even nowadays I think women have this concept of childbirth, housework, cooking being part of fulfilment and development. But certainly, in most parts of Asia, you don't see it like that at all. It's just chores, it's just hard work. You don't like being pregnant, but you'd better have a child, otherwise your mother-in-law will say you're not productive. That is the status of women in many many developing countries. And it is the hope of many of us that girls will be able to go to school and find a future for themselves and relate to their husbands and to society as equals, as somebody important, and not as somebody who is a kind of accessory. We can't just say we'll fight for equal status without educating women, without helping them to grow. Without educating men for a start, because I think most men would never never think that they are treating their wives as inferior. My husband will let me go to Beirut, because he's not an orthopaedic surgeon. If he were a surgeon, he'd go, but because he is not a surgeon and I am one, I can go. I can help, therefore I go. I think that should be the kind of relationship between a husband and wife.

The needs of women are so different in different parts of the world. In most Asian countries I would, if I could, give them education and a job. Not because it is the be-all and end-all, but it is the beginning. It is a key which unlocks the door into a world they can enter. After that, it is their own fight. And in this country, where women have already got jobs and education, I would probably have women learn to understand more and stop hating men.

The advantages are that it is very difficult for a woman not to be understanding. I'm a woman doctor and a fellow of the Royal College of Surgeons, and it's one constant tough fight. I have to fight the male establishment, the nursing hierarchy who cannot accept a woman doctor, least of all a woman surgeon, and even the prejudice of patients. It can either make you very bitter, very careless, very bossy, or it can have a very positive effect in the sense that you understand what pressures women are under. Most people say women are gentle. I don't think we choose to be gentle and I don't think we are born kind, but because women as a whole have suffered so much, we have no choice but to be kind and understanding. We sympathize with people who suffer, because we ourselves have suffered. I hate people being kicked around, being oppressed, not because I'm born to hate oppression, but because I've suffered it as a woman. I hate seeing weaker people being bullied by stronger people because, as a woman, I'm naturally weak and

184

smaller than men. I can't walk in the street at 2 a.m. without fear of being mugged or raped, so I cannot help but be understanding.

I have seen the ugliness of power, I really have. Power has always worked against me, against my mother, who was in prison. My grandfather had all the power in the world, and what had he got? Four wives, nothing much. The Singapore government has power, and what they did was to arrest my husband at 3 a.m. for defending a student. When I came to England, all I could see was the power of the English male doctors trying to prevent women and coloured doctors from promoting their careers. I went to Lebanon. I have seen the ugliness of Israeli power. That is where I really saw power in its cruellest and ugliest form, and I hate it. So power never appeals.

Lady Elizabeth Anson: I had a brief career as the first female receptionist at the Hyde Park Hotel, which was a job standing up all day. We were allowed to show clients up to their bedrooms by the lift, but had to come down by the stairs, and only the first floor of the stairs at the Hyde Park Hotel is carpeted, and we used to wear very long dresses and very high heels, and I caught my foot in the back of my dress and came tumbling down on my spine. I went off to the back doctor in my lunch hour, and this was the end of my career as a receptionist. I then had to have traction every day, and had a very painful time with my back, and it was difficult to know what to do as a career because I couldn't sit down all day and couldn't stand up all day. Anyway, a friend was going off to Australia to be ADC to the governor-general at very short notice, and he rang me and said, you're doing nothing and I'm going off to Australia in ten days' time, and I want to give a farewell party. Will you arrange it? So I did this, and I thought to myself, if my own generation wants a service like that, there must be room for it with other people.

I couldn't get far because I was very young and people didn't start businesses at nineteen. So I spent my first two years of business trying to make myself look older. I borrowed my mother's hats when I had meetings with hoteliers to get commission off them if I brought parties, and I spent my time trying to be older than my years, but not trying to be a woman.

I have three very weak areas. One is anything to do with law, the second is accountancy, the third is stockbroking – actually basically money. And therefore I really trust the people I employ. I have an enormous trust in my solicitor, my stockbroker and my accountant, and I let them get on with it. I say, listen, don't treat me like a child, but you know this is not my strong point, so you do actually have to spell it out rather more than you may think. Because people think that since you are fairly successful as a businesswoman you have all that absolutely there.

One is actually respected for being able to be – I hate the term – a career woman. I have always dreaded the fact that I would be labelled a career woman, but can't pretend I am not.

I find it difficult to walk into a room by myself. I always make my husband go before me. I gave up smoking through hypnosis, and my hypnotist said, have you got anything else? I said, I have this terrible thing that I cannot walk through a door first, I have to push the man through first. I remember once, the late King of Denmark saying, when I was hanging back, don't you know what sex you are?

I would hate to be a man. I think we do get away with murder as women. You are excused things for being a woman, whereas men are expected to be brave and courageous. For a man to lose his job, for instance, is desperate. For me, if I decided to give up Party Planners tomorrow, nobody is going to worry.

What would I give women? Total logic, I think.

I don't think men like serious statements coming from women, and I think it is something that perhaps makes the male ego suffer a bit. I am a very unpolitical animal myself, probably because my stepfather never stopped talking about politics to me. It's rather like I can't take a photograph except with an idiot camera because I've got a husband who is a photographer and a brother who is a photographer. You switch off at certain things. Certainly, in particular, politicians don't want to hear the voice of a serious, forthright, outgoing woman.

Beatrice Aristimuno: If a woman is really worth her salt, she is taken seriously today. If she's not good, she will be less helped than a man, but if she really is somebody, she will come through. I think today the world is for women.

Pamela Armstrong: When you talk about the media, it's no good thinking the media are some kind of strange aberrant growth outside of society. The media, in many ways, reflect the attitudes of an entire society. So it's no good saying Fleet Street gave me a raw deal over this issue, or Fleet Street were really good about this issue. What we are

186

really talking about is people's attitudes constellated in one area and given a form of expression that, in this case, happens to be through newspapers. When I became a newscaster, it seemed to me that the newscasters in the position before me had, to a certain extent, been exploited by Fleet Street. They had been used to fill column inches in a way that, in a sense, proved to be a disservice. They'd been focused on as some kind of novelty item, and if you focus on someone as a novelty item, you're actually disregarding what they're doing in their work on the daily responsible basis. You're marginalizing them, turning them into a sideshow, not allowing them to get on and do the job they're there to do. You're shaping people's perceptions about them in a way that negates their professionalism. I didn't want that to happen to me, and I thought it was time for it all to stop, so when I became a newscaster – and this is all on the question of discrimination – I was very resistant to having that done to me, and I was very picky and choosy about the kind of interviews I did and the amount of time I talked to the press. I think that attitudes have changed in Fleet Street in the time I've been a newscaster because there are so many women in television and because that particular job is no longer the sole high-profile job it used to be for women. Women in television aren't treated in quite the same way as they used to be, and I think that is a very tiny but a very positive step forward.

Women find it difficult if they have to go into a situation where the working set-up involves unsociable hours and they can't look after their families. Women are still doing two jobs. If you look at the statistics, women still do more housework than men – and that is among women who work. Women still earn a third less than men. Their average, nationally, across the board, is a third less, which I think speaks volumes. Because it means women do not have the same amount of choice. Most of those women are in ghetto industries – in the service industries, in textiles, in food industries. They're teachers, they're nurses. Again we get back to this thing that they go into industries where it is conventional for a woman to operate and where women's talents have historically been encouraged. Now it's changing. I'm saying it's changing, but it's changing very slowly.

It has always been men who have given me my biggest breaks in my careers, and it's always been men who've nurtured me and allowed me to develop whatever potential I had in whatever field I was in at any one time. But then, of course, it has to be said that it's always men who are in those positions of power, and maybe if women were in those positions, they would be doing the same thing.

The grand and venerable men in television, they have been doing their jobs for thirty years, which is why they are where they are. They have a mammoth amount of experience behind them. We simply don't have the equivalent women to draw on in television, because the women who would be their equivalents in their day stayed at home and looked after the babies. Until we have a generation that has grown up and lived and can put exactly the same amount of experience on the table and say: this is my working experience, this is what I have to offer – we are going to be in a slightly invidious position. I think the kind of change we're talking about will actually take thirty years. It's a very long change.

Debbie Arnold: Women do use their femininity to gain an advantage, and I think, if they don't, they're wasting it.

I like being able to make myself pretty and attractive. I wouldn't like to be a man. I'd probably be gay, because I like men too much.

I feel that an attractive woman has a disadvantage because men look at her differently. The first thing they do is give her a look they would never give an unattractive woman or a businessman who is an associate. That sort of hello, I fancy you, look, which immediately takes a few women off their guard, especially if it's a very powerful man – he can make you shrivel with one look. Even if you're a very powerful woman coming in to do real heavy business, and he looks at you as if to say, oh, I really fancy you, it makes you feel slightly inhibited. So I think a lot of very powerful women have got to go against how they want to look: wear their hair back, wear glasses, so they're treated more seriously.

Leslie Ash: I was always the tomboy of the family. I used to play with boys, climbing trees and running around, but I felt that, because I was a girl, they would never ever let me play football, or never let me play cricket, or if we had three guns and we were playing cowboys and Indians, I was always the Indian because they wanted the guns. I always had to be the Indian, and I always had to die.

There are so many advantages of being a woman. I think it's just fantastic. When you're driving and you get stopped by the police, the first advantage is being a woman, and the way you talk and the way you can flirt. I think the greatest advantage of being a woman is that you can flirt.

I hate it, actually, when women try and put down a man for being strong – I actually enjoy it when a man is very gallant and does something. He may cock it up, but I would never ever laugh. I think it's exactly the same thing for a woman if she wants to use her femininity, and it's awful when a man turns round and says, stop fishing or something like that. I think a woman should be able to use it.

The only thing I find quite difficult, the more successful I get, and the more independent I get, is to have a relationship with a man. Because a man always tends to feel that a woman is relying on him in certain ways. I'm taken out to dinner and I try to pay, and sometimes it's outrageous. You know – put that away, put that away! It's embarrassing. That's where I find it quite difficult.

I'd let a man experience period pains every month, I really would. We women have periods once a month, and they hurt, they bloody hurt, and I think men do not ever understand what pain it is.

Diana Athill: I came into the market for jobs as the war was beginning, and there were very few men about, so automatically one ended up head of the department of the little thing I was in at the BBC. There weren't any men around to be head of it. So there wasn't the competition.

I think that the basic things were achieved before I was grown up. We had got the vote, and we had got permission, as it were, from society to earn our own livings. Those were the two vitally important things, and they'd been done for me before I started. Having those, it was up to us to manoeuvre our way through. Of course, there is prejudice against women: not exactly a thought-out prejudice most of the time, but simply an attitude, a solidarity of men that certain things belong to them – unthinking, unquestioning. And, of course, women are supposed to be second in command if they get anywhere up at all, and their job is largely supporting their men. You see it all the time. We're just going to publish a book called *Reflecting Men to Twice Their Natural Size*, and any woman will agree that is what she is mostly doing when she is with men. And it's very annoying that one's fallen into that trap, one can't avoid it. It's not a deliberate political kind of persecution; it is conditioning, I think.

If you are in strong disagreement with a man and you argue as emphatically as you really feel, you cannot help getting (this is conditioning) the feeling that he is thinking you are a termagant, he will put you down as strident or whatever. And you see yourself a little with those eyes, which is very annoying indeed. Because if you were completely confident, obviously you would say pooh to that. It gets

189

easier as you get older. You become much more confident. At some level, you are sacrificing your sexual appeal by coming up against him as though you were two men arguing, and there is something that makes you flinch from doing that. Whether it's conditioning, or whether it's a sort of instinct, I don't know.

I think in England, you always come up against other things as well as sex or gender. You're going to come up against class and the way you're brought up. I was brought up in a puritanical way. For instance, I was always told that men don't like women who wear a lot of make-up. Well, not being a fool, I could perfectly clearly see that the girl who was wearing her lipstick put on well, got off much better than the one who didn't, so I didn't pay any attention. But there was the feeling that you mustn't be affected, mustn't be seen to be trying to attract the other sex, because it was common, vulgar. Of course, you wanted to – everybody wanted to. Your grandmother or your mother, who was telling you this, wanted you to get married, but they wanted you to do it in a curiously hygienic and scrubbed English way, and that went rather deeper than one thought. I always felt that girls who evidently manipulated men by their charm or beauty were doing something rather wrong. Of course, men do it too. It puts me off a man at once if he puts on his charm too much: the sort of man who, when he comes into a room, is clearly always going to come on like that. I've always had a hostility towards that sort of thing.

I really can't imagine being a man – I really can't. I like being a woman, and I always have. I think there are certain tedious responsibilities that men have, like looking after the money, and if you hear someone creeping about downstairs, it's the man who is the one who has to get up and go downstairs with a poker and hit him on the head, which I don't want to do. But seriously, I just feel very comfortable being a woman.

Leila Badawi: Being a woman is a disadvantage because one doesn't put oneself first, one is not encouraged to put oneself first, even if one is encouraged to be ambitious and intellectually striving. One has to make other people feel at home, feel comfortable with themselves.

In some respects, Arab women are certainly much more discriminated against, legally and socially. On the other hand, I think in particular families, and in certain respects because of the separation of the sexes, Arab women have a big advantage. I have a feeling that because the women tend to spend more time with other women and are interested in other women and compare themselves as women, they tend to have a

190

more positive self-image. It's only a small élite, perhaps, but they seem more concerned with themselves as human beings, and their relationship to men is much more limited: it doesn't constitute the whole of their interest.

Joan Bakewell: I think tradition, and the overlap of tradition, does make women rather emotional simply because they haven't got their bearings about what to do with their lives as they grow up. My father did well in life, but he didn't want my mother to have a job. My grandparents were all working people, and my mother was told that she should be the decoration, should stay at home and look after the children. She made the home very beautiful – a tiny home – none the less she did it every day: cleaned it herself, and made lovely meals, and was completely bored and quite unhappy. A book which was very important in my life was *The Feminine Mystique* by Betty Friedan, which actually ripped that veil apart. I saw it suddenly so clearly: that women had been told that they will find fulfilment in that kind of life, but then they say, I'm unhappy. And their husband says look, you have everything you want, you have a beautiful home, you have this, that and the other. Your being unhappy shows how irrational you are. The analysis of what makes for irrationality is very often a male logic.

I do not think the analysis has gone far enough into understanding the resistance of women to the structures that exist. I think women are quite right to resist the urge to belong in a male hierarchy, where the premium is on aggression and achievement and winning the race, being top dog, getting the best job, getting the most money. These are male-established priorities, simply because the ruling hierarchy is male, and I think women are shrewd to turn that option down. Women are familiar with what it's like to be at the top by living with the men who are at the top, and the record is not a pretty sight. Men are not blissfully happy, balanced individuals. They are often driven by aggression, and need, and wish-fulfilment that they can't quite reach. They're yearning and striving, which clearly very often makes for quite neurotic marriages, unhappy individuals. Women have perceived this and have stood back from it, and I think women don't want to enter that set-up on those terms.

As feminism gets older, women will be proud to be grey-haired and wrinkled, and it will become clear that it doesn't mean you've lost out. That's the next move. It's ageism: what will happen to women in their fifties and sixties. Will they still be proud and strong, the newly liberated women? That will be a wonderful testing time, because, of course, you are in your prime. I never felt more in control of my intelligence, and my ability to operate, and more secure in my life than I do now. It is a marvellous era, but women are taught to fear it.

Jennifer Bartlett: I don't think there is any question but that women are taken less seriously than men. I made a decision quite some time ago never to talk about these things. It's just a fact. It's there, and I'm not interested in participating in colloquiums about it. It isn't so apparent as the colour of your tie, but if you go to a dinner party and there aren't any servants, the other wives always help the wife to serve the meal, and the men just sit. I don't think that there is any mystery about it: it's the way it is, and I think we all know how it got that way.

When you're not supported at your job, when you're criticized and ridiculed, you'll be less likely to work well and happily. I was told, and am still told, that there have been no great women artists, that women are not capable of making good artists, that women are capable only of writing insubstantial and silly domestic novels, that they certainly could never compose a piece of music or conduct an orchestra. I've heard that all of my life. I chose not to believe it. Also, on a simpler level, it is always a double bind for a woman. I remember my mother telling me in school, Jennifer, don't always answer the questions in class because the boys won't like you. Or, don't talk so much. Or, later, I'm afraid your marriage is splitting up because your husband thinks you're smarter than he is. Don't show it, learn to ski.

Nathalie Baye: Femininity can open doors, but will the doors stay open? Femininity can be simply a varnish, and, of course, it can be used to obtain things, but the most feminine and attractive women don't get things because of that, but because there is also something else. If it weren't so, then any pretty woman would have the most marvellous career. It's the same for a man. A handsome man may be able to do anything, but you need charm and intelligence because good looks in themselves are only of short-term value.

I think that a woman bases her appeal on the art of pleasing, and a young woman, a girl, is considered a woman, whereas a boy of seventeen or eighteen is still regarded as a baby. On the other hand, a woman who is much older comes into the category of one who no longer gives pleasure. When you are fifty or so, that must be extremely painful, because to be able to please at seventeen is normal, but to want to do so at fifty must be even more normal.

Gilberte A. Y. Beaux: I began my career just after the war. Therefore conditions were nothing like today. At that time, a lot of people were looking for young staff to replace those killed during the war, and that probably helped. Also, my first real job was in a Jewish bank with a small but bright staff, and it was a very good company to start off with, first because when there are not so many of you, it is easier to get promotion, and secondly, because I think Jewish people are more prepared to accept people who want to do something – male or female, it doesn't matter. That was what I experienced, at least.

I don't think it is difficult for women to reach the top. I would think that it is more because, in spite of what they say, women are more confident if they are No 2 rather than No 1. It is more natural, let us say, to have a male leader, a chief, to discuss things with. I think it is a natural tendency of women, and I wonder if they are completely fair in saying it is a discrimination. If a woman is No 2 in the company, and does not like that, she can create her own company. If she stays in the company, it's because she wants to.

Rotraut Lisa Ursula Beiny: I was the first woman to be a dental student at the London Hospital, so, in that way, it was something completely unheard of. The professors were ill at ease teaching a woman. If you want to get ahead in dentistry, there is tremendous prejudice. If two people of the opposite sex go for a job, and they have more or less the same qualifications, the woman won't get the job. My very closest friend, who is also a dentist and doubly qualified as a doctor, had the same qualifications, exactly the same as her husband. Whereas her husband became professor of oral surgery, she never could get any decent job.

American women are very different from English women, or Italian women. Women in America do feel they are equal to men, and that they can compete, whereas I think women in this country don't really feel that. The people in the City are men, the managing directors of most of the companies are men. There are all the clubs, just for men, so it is a man's world here. There is discrimination in this country against women, you see it everywhere. So women don't feel that they can achieve the same. I'm not surprised that they don't have the same chance in an organization to reach the top. A man, I think, feels he can, a woman here feels she can't.

Jeanne-Louise Bieler: My experience tells me that women generally

193

work hard and work well, but is it to compete with men? Maybe. I don't have the answer for that. I see that there are disadvantages in society in general, but I think all those disadvantages very often come from the woman herself. It's probably the way she has been brought up, the environment in which she has grown. It may sound pretentious, but frankly I never really consciously felt any major disadvantage.

I am not looking forward to getting old, but so far it doesn't frighten me. I know that my hair is becoming a bit grey, but by the time it's really grey, I will have even more in myself to counter-balance it. You can train and keep as nice as you can for quite a long time, but one should not cheat. If you start to try to act something you are not, then you're not credible, and I hope I will always be credible. A woman of sixty is not attractive any more in the physical sense, so I hope, by then, I will be attractive in a different way. What I really hope for when I'm old is that young people will still like me. And for that, I must be authentic. You can't cheat with young people. It's a period of your life which should bring something to you and to others. You can't bring beauty, so you have to offer something else, which means that you have to work on it all your life, because it will not suddenly be there one morning when you're sixty.

Christine Bogdanowicz-Bindert: I think I was discriminated against in a concrete way only once. When I was at the IMF, I challenged my salary increase and the director of the department said, I don't know what you're talking about. Your husband is a banker, your salary is not a big issue in your life. And I thought, how can you say that? That's nothing to do with what we are discussing. I am talking about my evaluation and what the salary increase should be, not what my personal life is all about. The discrimination is quite subtle; it's basically that it's a man's world, especially the one I am in.

The advantage is that, as a woman in the business of investment banking, you are noticed. To give an example, I have been speaking at a lot of conferences where sometimes I am the only woman. I will be noticed, not because of what I say but because I am different from everybody else. It has an advantage in that, if you say something good, it's going to be magnified one way or another. And in some ways, it's the same thing at work. A lot of people know me, even though they have never worked with me. Whereas the male colleague who sits next to me will not be as well known because of the number of people who look just like him.

In America, a woman like me doesn't have any discrimination in the sense of you cannot do this or that. However, if you want to have children, there is no help with my job. Maternity leave is ridiculously short, and there is no crèche or kindergarten. Society is organized for a man, not for a woman, and I think, incidentally, that's where the feminist movement in America went completely wrong. The feminist movement in America wanted equality, and wanted women to be like men in many ways. The early feminists in the 1960s and 1970s were women who were against men. But the majority of women are not against men. The majority of women just want to have their own lives, which means to be able to choose the same way men do. If you want to be a housewife, there's nothing wrong with that. If you want to be a banker, that's fine. Unfortunately, we've reached a point in America now where a housewife is basically discriminated against: she's the dumb blonde sitting in the suburbs. And the professional woman is basically trapped, very often without a husband, and without children, because the infrastructure is such that it's very hard to combine all three.

Rebecca Blake: I didn't think of myself as being a female photographer, I just thought of myself as being an artist, period. Initially, I had more support from men. Then, as I started to get into my career, halfway through I started to get a lot of support from women and, in some respects, less support from men. It was ironic. I didn't understand why it happened, but through that period of time I became aware I was fighting battles. Sometimes they were very specific, and sometimes they were amorphous. But I was fighting battles that specifically had to do with the fact that I was in a basically male industry and competing with men and that I was a powerful individual and had a certain vision that I really didn't want to compromise. I started to have difficulty, maybe from just expressing that strength in a working environment with men. Whereas I think, had I been a man expressing the same energy, motivation, directedness, it would have been easier. It became apparent, at a certain point, that I was being misjudged or judged because I was, in a sense, behaving in a way that men are programmed to behave; and men did not find that appropriate, coming from a woman.

I always thought that, if a man were in my shoes, he would have to be good, but me, in my shoes, would have to be perfect. I don't feel bitter about it in any way. I just recognize it as a reality and I think that sometimes the wars we go through in our lives pave the way for other people so that they can then direct themselves towards other

195

evolutionary problems. I think it is a question of evolution, of consciousness. It's very fashionable at this point in time to succeed as a female photographer or director. There's a need and a desire and support for it within the industry. So I think if the talent's there, at this point in time, you're given as much prominence as a man. Maybe that's to do with history, maybe this is where we have come to at this point. But I find enthusiasm and a lot of support right now.

Emily Bolton: Being pretty has a lot of disadvantages as well. People have actually put a label on you before you walk in, before you open your mouth even, because of what you look like. And mostly people think that beautiful women are dumb. If you happen to be blonde as well, you've no chance. If you're too intelligent, then you're a threat to men. Men don't really like women to be more intelligent than they are.

If a man is in a room and there are ten women to one man, he'll think twice before he gives his opinion. I speak from experience. It was quite extraordinary, doing *Tenko*, when there were more women than men. We had a director, who will remain nameless, but I remember him walking into rehearsals and not being comfortable. He never said anything, you could feel it. We thought, perhaps he doesn't like us, but then why would he take the job, he knew what it entailed? Later, after we'd worked with him, it all came out. One day he confessed that he felt terrible having to walk into that room with all those women and being the only man. Now that was extraordinary. I always thought that men were so confident they wouldn't mind walking into a room with women; and he liked women, he didn't dislike women. My comment was, well, now you know how women feel when they have to walk into a room with men.

Betty E. Box: I'd grown up in a background where sex didn't matter, where boys and girls were treated the same, and it never occurred to me that anyone would discriminate against me. I can remember Micky Balcon, Sir Michael Balcon as he became, at one of the board meetings, being very angry because I was being allowed to produce, and I thought it was because he didn't like me. But I've discovered it wasn't. He didn't like women at all, didn't think women should be doing it. But, at the time, it didn't occur to me that he was discriminating against me because I was a woman. I just thought he didn't like my character or personality.

I think a young woman has a lot of advantages if she has the courage to do what she wants to do and isn't ugly. I think a woman is very lucky. I would rather be a woman until I'm fifty, and then I'd like to be a man. After fifty, I think men have the better time.

Liz Brewer: Being a woman was an advantage, because I went to a country which didn't recognize women at all. Women didn't work in Portugal in the early 1960s, or, if they did, they were prostitutes. Women didn't work, they got married or they sat at home. So what I did was fairly outrageous to begin with, and in a country like Portugal I had, even in those days, an enormous amount of publicity, not just in the Portuguese press, but in the English press. Therefore a lot of English people came out and bought houses and started to live there, a lot of showbusiness people. But I actually did find that being a girl was an advantage because I got away with a lot more, and people were fascinated. They couldn't believe I was capable of doing what I was doing. To be honest, I was capable of doing it because I had no experience. I didn't know what the problems were. Now I know what they are, and I don't think I could do it. In those days, it was so new and life was so wonderful, and it appeared so easy. I had tremendous enthusiasm.

Heather Brigstocke: I think if I'd been a man I would have considered a much wider range of careers after I got my degree. Nowadays, most of our girls become bankers or lawyers or doctors, but those jobs weren't open to women then. Even medicine wasn't something a woman could go into in my day – not that I would have considered it as I can't stand the sight of blood! But I might have chosen law or banking. I was very limited. I saw myself going on the stage, or becoming a model, and apart from that I couldn't think of anything much except teaching. At Cambridge, I acted the whole time. In fact, I seriously considered going on the stage, but I was far too tall. In the event, when I left Cambridge, I went into Selfridges for eight months as a graduate trainee. I got into a lot of trouble there because I was always ticking off the customers – telling them not to buy a dress or hat because it didn't suit them! I had a very funny time, but it was also a good nine months for me because it was very tough. And then I went into teaching.

I had a hysterectomy last year. I had an operation on both my knees this year. I feel I'm falling apart. I went to Sicily, and one of my teeth fell out. However, I look at photographs of myself when I was younger and I think I've got a more interesting face than I had then. When I was very young I got fed up with people saying how pretty I was, I hated being pretty. I wondered if anyone took any notice of me for myself.

197

Dianne Brill: As feminine as I appear, I think very much like a man because of the heavy masculine images and mood that I was raised with, so I can tune into the way a man's looking at me, and then, once I understand what he is seeing, I can change it.

I believe in working as a woman, working with my sexiness or sexuality, instead of working against it. I'm not trying to be an equal.

If you work against your femininity, then there will be disadvantages. But you can work with your femininity and use something people consider a disadvantage to your advantage. For instance, that's why I am doing menswear. A woman doing menswear, a woman adoring men, celebrating men, appreciating men. From that point of view, it's worked to my advantage.

Suzanne Brøgger: I have published eight books and there has always been a tendency in the media to play my books up as some kind of easy left-wing writing and to make me, as the cliché goes, into a sexual object and refuse to see the serious impact of my books. I am made into a kind of clown. That has been the overall reaction I have had from the media.

When a woman succeeds in our society, she is not on her own premises really, she is going into a territory that is alien to her. So she has to make an extra effort to make an impact on those who are in power and those who define what is successful and what is not. She has to make herself intelligible and work twice as hard to be taken seriously.

If a woman can only succeed by emulating men, I think it is a great loss and not a success. The aim is not only for a woman to succeed, but to keep her womanhood and let her womanhood influence society. Otherwise we just become a completely sexless society, we become robots.

Discrimination is a very subtle thing. Like racism, we have laws against it. But it is what people feel in their hearts – their hatred and fear and all these irrational things – that also makes discrimination against women possible and which makes their own self-hatred and their own insecurities persist. That is as problematic as it was, and I still feel strongly about it. Legally, there is nothing to prevent a woman reaching whatever position she aspires to. But emotionally, irrationally, there may be inhibitions, which need not come from the parents or her friends; she may just feel inside that, if she becomes a success, she is less attractive as a woman. Successful women are not *per se* attractive, and women know it.

It is difficult to be a whole woman in our society because, if you go into a career, it is difficult to include having children and a husband; and if, on the other hand, you put your priorities on your family and children, then it is difficult to make a career. No man is really confronted with that option, with having to split himself in half. Men can have both, but it is a very difficult thing to be a whole woman. And women seem to refrain from aspiring to higher positions because they still feel that their responsibility is at home. Most women are split. If they don't want a husband and children, then the world is theirs. I don't say that every woman should have a husband and children, not at all, but I don't believe that any woman can just easily say, never mind, that is not important, I don't want that. If a woman chooses not to have a family she has to go through a lot of grief, I believe.

I become happier and happier the older I get, because I feel I develop my inner potential more and more. It is a kind of liberation not to be so dependent on one's appearance and to feel more secure inside. I thought it was a tremendous problem to be young and pretty. It was very disturbing and very hard work. I think it is a relief to go beyond that.

Tina Brown: I am absolutely shocked at how passive and unencouraged English women are. They have very low aspirations. They never think of themselves as running anything. They always imagine that they will be playing a role doing little 'jobs' somewhere. At the time I was at Oxford, there were eight men to one woman. The women were so, so grateful to be at Oxford that they didn't really bother to shine much, except for a handful who then did go on to do wonderful things afterwards. For me it was the most fantastic opportunity, which I exploited. I never felt it was a handicap to be a woman, because I was so ambitious in the sense that I wanted to live life to the full. I don't mean that I was sitting there thinking desperately about my next career move, because I've never thought like that. But I did have to think big. I wanted to get a good degree and be a great writer and go to America and travel.

I was always very attracted to America, I think because I felt it was a land of great freedom. I've always found England a very constricted place in a funny way. There are pros and cons, and when you live in both places, you are obsessed with whichever one you are not in. But, I must say, what amazes me about living here in the States is that the women are so much more ambitious for themselves. They imagine themselves as running the Met., being the big power at the Museum of

Modern Art, or the big wheel at Carnegie Hall; the women expect to have these positions of power, and they go after them and get them. But you can't imagine a female head of the British Museum. You can't imagine a woman running the Tate. Whereas here the women are formidable in a way that I don't think is bad. Many of them have had wonderful educations because they have gone to Harvard and Yale and all these places, and they are really involved with the moving and the shaking. American women have much more confidence, and the confidence is born out of their expectations. They have not been told from the year dot that, even if they do go to Oxford, they'll still dribble on into some very low-paid job somewhere and be grateful to have it, and then, when they get married, they'll slip from view. Here I think women regard their lives in a much more positive way; they really want to make something of them. And they don't regard what they do as a little job to tide them over.

I don't think women have to become aggressive and horrible, I really don't. I think that for them to have higher aspirations is just healthier, that's all. Recently I went to Cleveland to talk to 120 women in a luncheon club, and I imagined that these women would be blue-rinsed ladies who didn't know very much. I couldn't have been more wrong. They were the wives of the Cleveland establishment, and even though they weren't doing glamorous things like Gloria Steinem, they were women who were organizing their community in a very high-powered way. They had got together and organized a big Dali exhibition to go to the museum; they were fund-raising; they were making sure that the head of the Met. was coming to talk to them next week. The same sort of women, a group of housewives in Henley-on-Thames say, what do they ever do? Nothing. I know. I grew up in that environment. They never did anything like that. They just sat around and had coffee mornings and talked about their children and didn't do a damn thing. It's true in England still: if you go to Gloucestershire nobody's particularly got any intellectual curiosity or cultural interest. They just do their country pursuits. I don't knock country pursuits; it's all very nice, but I don't see why you have to be in such an intellectual vacuum. I prefer the atmosphere here.

The great downside of the American women's achievement is the problem they have with men. There's no doubt it's much sexier to be in a relationship where the man is stronger; so what, of course, women want here is men who are so strong that they dominate these very strong women. They are looking for such a high-powered man to counter-balance their own quite high-poweredness that they don't find anybody and turn them all into homosexuals. The men are so utterly stricken by

200

the necessity to be so dynamic that they just decide, I can't cope with this, I'm opting out, and become gay. I am sure that the women have made the men gay. And it's sad. A lot of men are terrified, threatened, by these bright, committed women who come along. I don't think the answer is to slip back into women trying to pretend they are not like that. Strong women have been unhappy and desperate in situations where they didn't have an arena or scope. I don't quite know what the answer is. I think things will evolve, and I think perhaps women will realize they have to give something up.

There comes a time when women can feel very left on the shelf, very useless to society. Their looks have gone, and their children have fled the nest, and what is there in life for them? I've seen it happen, and I think these women are very, very unhappy. One of the nicest things about being a career woman is that, as I get older, it's not going to matter half as much. I'll be an older woman who is doing a job like this, and it won't matter so hugely.

I wouldn't be a man for anything. I think, particularly now, it's a woman's period. I think this is the time to be a woman, particularly in America. Even in England, it's better than being a man.

Victoria Brynner: I fear ageing very much, because I am basing a lot of my life today on my youth and looks. The more I age, the less I'm going to be able to seduce, and seduction has a great importance in my life right now. I hope eventually to have enough things to think about and to do professionally, with my hands and my mind, so as not to suffer from not having so many men court me, not to feel bad about it.

Joan Juliet Buck: When I married John Halpern, who was a journalist on the *Observer*, I had gone from *Vogue* to the *Observer* and was associate editor of the magazine. And there was a Christmas party at the *Observer*, and John and I were dancing around and I was wearing red corduroy jodhpurs, red boots and a red blouse. And I saw someone I was in the habit of seeing every day at the *Observer*, and was introduced as John's wife and he didn't recognize me. He said, what do you do? I said, what do you think I do? And he said, well, you're a dancer aren't you or something like that? In England, this is very strong. I am separate from those kind of stockbrokerish types, that sort of Englishman with a pheasant on the front of his Aston Martin.

The moment I started writing fiction when I was twenty-six years old, I

201

felt I was fifty-three. I aged from that moment. Everybody, all the people in the street, they say Madame and not Mademoiselle, and it pisses me off. I lived in California when I was twenty-six, and at twenty-six I was old, because I wasn't blonde, because I'd never had a nose job and because I was a writer. That made me old according to that society. And I felt fine. I thought, I don't need you fuckers anyway. I think the collective of each country is a great big pain in the arse. Ageing in Paris is supposed to be better for a woman, because men appreciate women. Except that the way Frenchmen appreciate women is that he stays married and you are the person he'll take to St Moritz for the weekend.

Averil Burgess: There were social disadvantages, more so when I was younger than now. When I was a young woman, I would have felt it almost impossible to consider not being married, and I was married for fourteen years. Now I think a young woman leaving school might consider marriage as an option which she could take or reject. When I was leaving school, if you were not linked up with a man socially, you were bereft. To that extent, men had more freedom – more freedom to be independent. In a social sense, yes, being a woman was a disadvantage.

In the selection to parliamentary candidature, I think that in constituency after constituency good women come up before selection committees and are rejected because they are women, not because of any deficiency. They are seen as being less acceptable to the electorate. In business and the professions, there are often practical reasons why men can appear more attractive candidates. In many cases, they've acquired more qualifications, they've almost certainly acquired more experience. The woman has been hampered either directly by time out having children or, if she has not actually had time from her job, she's had to look after them, she's not been free to travel, to acquire further qualifications. So I think that many people appointing to managerial posts, looking at the *curricula vitae* of a man and a woman, could actually find a man a better bet. His career has been more progressive and he has had the support systems at home, which enable him to go out and do more things, sit on more boards, do more courses and so on.

I do think a woman has to work harder. Partly because she faces prejudice and discrimination, she's got to prove herself; partly because she just takes on more. Women generally take on far more social and domestic responsibilities than men. Even if the men are very good at home, the one who looks after the relatives and writes the letters and buys the Christmas presents is usually the woman. So a woman devotes a lot more time to fringe activities, and generally has far more of what I heard somebody once call a portfolio life, a lot of different commitments. Whereas a man tends to focus more, is far more ruthless in excluding the other commitments, and can focus his efforts more.

I was at the HMC in September, the Headmasters' Conference. The headmasters were very welcoming, very pleasant, but one of the very tiny group of women who were there as invited guests was an ex-president of the Girls' Schools Association, an attractive and charming woman and a leader in her field. And she got her bottom pinched for a bet, during the pre-dinner drinks. She was very taken aback, didn't know what to do, didn't make a fuss because she didn't want to break up the party. We were appalled. Not because we are totally lacking a sense of humour, but because if an eminent woman guest at a male gathering can actually get her bottom pinched for a £5 bet, and they're boasting about it afterwards, and she's in her fifties and a woman of some dignity, where do you start? I mean, it's incredible. There's no female equivalent of pinching the bottom, you know. Women aren't like that. Or to joke about it afterwards. It was just like a boys' boarding school.

I think that the advantages of being older far outweigh the disadvantages. One cares much less about the impact one is making on other people. One is far less self-conscious, much more self-confident, more at peace with one's self. And I would have this in preference to the unlined skin of twenty years ago. I don't miss that at all.

Liz Calder: Becoming a fashion model gave me confidence and also an entry into a whole world which was nothing to do with my husband's world; and an independence. One has also to recognize that, in a way, it caused the break-up of our marriage. Having married very young, having actually not really known other men very intimately, it did open an opportunity for almost a double life. Brazil did represent, in a way, the other party in our marriage, and when we left at the end of the 1960s and came back to London, I knew I had to do something on my own. I'd got confidence that I could at least do something, but I also felt very insecure and uncertain. I just happened to have the sort of face which, at the time, could be sold, which was not something I could depend on for ever. I felt insecure because I wanted to take the children, go and live on my own, get a job and support us, and my husband said: you'll never do it, you'll be a lonely old woman. And I actually believed him. I thought: well, it seems to me there's a good chance of this – I've got no proof to show I can do it. I spent a long time believing that I actually needed this prop to my life, but when it came to getting a job, I found no disadvantages, no inhibitions at all.

Women can often work against themselves. You can be sitting in a meeting with twelve men around a table and you say something, and nobody takes any notice, so you say it again. It's intimidating, and it's demoralizing. You think, what the hell, and let it go, and then afterwards you're mad with yourself and everybody else because you did.

Angela Carter: There is only one thing I would say about suffering, which is that women have more experience of it.

The way in which a white middle-class woman is disadvantaged is actually very subtle. I'm obviously and always have been, more advantaged than an unemployed black kid in Brixton, or somebody working in the lower echelons of the Health Service, but it's a question of respect; of people not taking you seriously. It's quite a shock. You go around all the time thinking you're perfectly normal and that you have some weight in the world, and then you find yourself suddenly in a situation where you realize that a statistically significant percentage of the world doesn't feel like that about you. Because you are a woman.

Childbirth was a great revelation to me. I hadn't realized that masochism could be so useful. It's quite painful having children, and there are all kinds of other things, like menstruation, which aren't necessarily a breeze.

I worry about ageing, but I think everybody does. I worry about my teeth much more. There's nothing you can do about it. It's a natural process. One is lucky to have lived so long. I regret I didn't make more use of it.

Anna Carteret: In a practical sense, I often feel at a disadvantage. I have a fear of any kind of machinery, including my car. I feel ashamed that I don't understand how the engine works. I was never any good at maths or science, and in fact I gave it up when I was twelve, so I feel very feminine in the derogatory sense about anything to do with machinery, from mending plugs to mowing the lawn. I'm irritated by myself. But I don't feel, in terms of opportunity, that I have suffered, because in the acting profession you don't have that same kind of bias. Obviously it's dependent on the play that you're doing and how many men there are in it, and I suppose you could say that, until about ten years ago, most of the accepted writers, or successful writers, were male, and so maybe they wrote better parts for men than they did for women, but I don't think that argument really holds in the long term. Of course, television has influenced people's view of women, and I think there's a great responsibility among writers and makers of both drama and documentary television programmes for the way women are represented. I actually wrote an article about this for *Cosmopolitan*, because it's a subject which is very important. It's insidious rather than obvious. You'd think it would be obvious, but people watch television in a kind of uncritical way and the way they see women represented, be it Princess Di or Joan Collins or Anna Raeburn, is going to influence their thinking about women. So any one of us who is in a position to make their thoughts felt, as I was lucky enough to be with *Juliet Bravo* when I played Inspector Kate Longton, should do so. I only agreed to doing the last year on condition I had what they call a script consultation, and this meant that I was allowed to suggest ideas and storylines. I couldn't write it myself, but I could certainly disagree with things, which is a power that actors don't often have. I enjoyed that process very much, and it's led on to a certain amount of public speaking, both on and off the screen, at schools and universities. In that way, one is able to put forward ideas, whereas in the old days, when I was at the National Theatre, although I was playing much better parts, nobody took any notice of me as a person. I was completely anonymous, and nobody had ever heard of me, because I wasn't on television. The power of televison is extraordinary – 14 million people a week watching you, right in their homes. I sometimes feel that some of these very popular series don't have a sense of responsibility about what they could say. It's such an opportunity, and they seem to waste it some of the time on rather banal things, or preserving the status quo, whereas they could actually try to make people see things differently.

Interestingly, as soon as you become a public figure, suddenly doors are open and you get a kind of respect simply by being a recognizable person. I believe that, if you establish a confident image from the word go, then people respond to that. I personally am guilty of having apologized for myself for too many years. One day I counted how many times I said sorry, and it was something astonishing – like a hundred. I'm sure that a lot of women suffer from this automatic assumption that what they have to say is not worth much. So I think one of the things one ought to try and do is to have confidence (it's one of the easiest things to say, one of the hardest to do) so that when you meet people you are not afraid to be yourself. You don't try to be something you think you ought to be, or apologize for what you're not.

It's taken me forty years actually to have the confidence to say what I think. Men don't have that problem generally. They're brought up to feel that they are special and should be given more consideration than women.

Barbara Cartland: I think women are absolute idiots in the way they've discriminated against themselves. Women have ruled the world very successfully since the beginning of time, from the pillow, by being women, and now women are so busy being pseudo-men they have forgotten to be feminine. Princess Diana is the first feminine woman for a very long time, and she has swept the world – she has changed the thinking of the world. For about ten years, we have had nothing but women dressing up as men, being pseudo-men and demasculinizing men. It's very very serious. We've got to the stage when men don't revere women, don't find women attractive. It's entirely the women's fault, because they're not attractive as women. I've always had a wonderful time being a woman. Being a pretty woman is very helpful, but, at the same time, I think a woman can have far more power in many ways than a man. You don't go out fighting and shooting, as women want to do today. Why do women want to be footballers – why do they want to run trains – which is their new scheme – why do they want to do all those men's jobs? Why not do all the women's jobs which you can do very successfully and get your own way that way if you want to? Women were worshipped originally as goddesses because they were women and they could conceive – which men still can't do. They can do everything else, but they can't conceive. They had the wonderful position of being able to influence the world from the shadow of the throne. Because they were greedy, they wished to sit on the throne and push the man off it. What have they achieved? Absolutely nothing, except that they have debased themselves. They've gone down-market. A woman hasn't improved her position, she's worsened it. When I was young, there was an enormous gap between the prostitute and the lady. Now there's no gap. I'd had forty-nine proposals before I got married. Everybody wanted to marry you. No man ever suggested anything improper to a lady, but now of course, the girls are taken out to the cinema and the man says, will you, won't you? And if she says no, he says, well, I'll take somebody else. If you're selling yourself for a cinema seat, you're going very, very, low. To me, it's debasing women. It's not the men who are doing it, it's the women themselves. And these young women go away on a holiday alone with a man. What do they expect to happen? I would be very surprised if I went away with a man and it didn't. I'd think there was something wrong with him, and something wrong with me. The thing is ridiculous. Women have inspired all the great things. There's never been a woman painter who could paint like Botticelli – I'm talking about the romantic ones; there's never been a woman composer who could compose as well as Chopin and Strauss; only one woman could write wonderful love poems, Elizabeth Barrett Browning. Nobody else could write as well as Lord Byron, Shelley, all that lot. Instead of concentrating on that, women are concentrating on doing down the man. What's the point? In America, you find it tremendously. The women have those hard nasal voices, pushing the men out of the way. They've demasculinized the men; then they're complaining the men don't make love to them. Are you surprised? They don't want to.

I was offered three safe Conservative seats when my brother was killed. I had a husband and young children. I had a choice between losing my husband, because no Englishman ever wants to have dinner alone, and never seeing my children because the only time you see your children is when you say good night to them and you hear their prayers. So I refused. I became a county councillor instead, which isn't the same thing. Otherwise I could have been a Member of Parliament. It's impossible to be a good Member of Parliament, and a good mother, and a good wife.

Luciana Castellina: I remember that when I entered the Communist Party at seventeen or eighteen, I thought that the party would be the place where all those rules and conditions wouldn't apply because they were enlightened people. Of course, I was totally wrong, because those rules applied totally, in an even stricter way. Somehow the behaviour was more free in the bourgeoisie than in the party, and so I was very disappointed. Then, of course, I had all the disadvantages of a woman in politics, because if you are a woman, you have to work much more than if you were a man, to prevent people saying, of course she can't do it because she is a woman. Then I was, for a long time, responsible for the Communist students, and men don't like to be led by a woman. They react bitterly, they don't like it. So that was an additional problem. One might think if a woman is acceptably pretty, it is easier, but that is totally wrong because the tendency is to imagine that someone acceptably pretty can't be serious. What you do is never regarded for the contents of what you do, but just in a different way. So being pretty opens doors, but it also closes them.

The whole problem is that all the values of society are established on the grounds of men's perceptions, and this is the reason why women are unhappy. The world is uni-dimensional, and the point is to make it

207

bi-dimensional. Even beauty has been defined as perceived by men; women have conformed to a model of beauty which is a model established by men.

Discrimination in the traditional sense isn't the only problem. The other problem – and this is the negative aspect of the women's process of liberation – is that in this rediscovery of their own female values, women sometimes tend to consider, as their own, values that are not their own at all, but have been imposed on them and are in fact the values of the slave. Women have been slaves, and when they try to say, I want to be myself and not like a man, they tend to rediscover the behaviour and the values of slaves, which is not their behaviour, not their values. I remember always a beautiful sentence of Virginia Woolf's in *Orlando*, when she says, God, what history has made of women; what she meant is that women have all the scars of history on them, and the scars are the scars of slaves, and it is very difficult to free yourself. This is the much deeper discrimination. Less obvious, but very deep. And liberation is not just the revolt of the slaves, it is the attempt to achieve freedom, which is more complex.

I suffered being a woman, and I wanted to be a man for a very long time. Now I am happier to be a woman, because I think it is much more interesting. There are a lot of things which can be discovered now, and women are today a much more mobile section of society than men.

Charlotte Chandler: I feel discriminated for. I feel like I have special privileges. I'm treated better, not worse.

My first book was *Hello, I Must Be Going*, about Groucho Marx, and the way I met Groucho was, I called him on the phone, and told him what I wanted to do, which was an interview for *Playboy*. And it was the interview Hugh Heffner most wanted to have. He'd always wanted to do Judy Garland and Groucho and it was too late for Judy Garland. So when I was in California, I called Groucho and told him what it was I wanted to do and he said to me: *Life* magazine has just offered me $10,000 to do an interview and I told them I wouldn't do it with them for $20,000 and I wouldn't do it with you for $30,000. And then he said, where are you? And I told him. It was a few blocks from where he lived, and he said, why don't you come over and I'll tell you now in person? I went right over. I didn't waste any time. And he invited me in and he showed me his collection of all his souvenirs and memorabilia and invited me to stay and have dinner, and he showed me *Duck Soup*. And at about eleven o'clock at night, because I hadn't gone anywhere – I was going to stay there until he indicated he wished me to go – he looked at me a little bit sharply and said, why aren't you writing? I think if I had been a man and called him, he wouldn't have invited me over. With Juan Perón, I went to bring him a note. I brought a letter I was going to deliver. I didn't know I was going to give it to him. I thought I was going to leave it at his house. When I arrived, he was standing outside at the gate playing with his dogs and talking to his sentry. I gave him my note and he told me he couldn't do an interview with me because it was a condition of exile, that he was going back to Argentina, but until he left Spain he couldn't do an interview. I was going to leave, and then he said, why don't you stay and have tea, and my wife and I will drive you back into Madrid? I think there's an excellent chance that, had I been a man and delivered the note, he would not have done that. I also met Tennessee Williams at a party, and spent twenty minutes talking with him before I knew who he was. We talked about sunsets and he said he would invite me to have dinner but he was going back to Key West the next night. Would I like to go to Key West the next night, to go back with him and have dinner? Even though he was homosexual, it was an advantage being a woman.

I think it's a man's world, but that there are many women who live a life better than men do, in a man's world, and that the important thing is that there should be equal opportunity and there isn't. But there's a great deal more every year. And many more women have a chance to do things. I think some women even get a chance to do things who aren't fully qualified, just because they are women.

Alexandra Chapman: I have the feeling of being patronized if I deal with electricians or plumbers who assume, quite correctly, that I know nothing about it; or sometimes I think the bill has been higher because I am just a stupid lady. I have not felt it professionally. If men are patronizing to me, I am patronizing back. If they don't take me seriously, then I don't take them seriously. I ignore them. And while it certainly limits the number of men that one sees either professionally or personally or both, it makes life a lot simpler.

I don't think very much about ageing because it seems to me that, the more you think about ageing, the more worried you get, so the more wrinkles you get, and you get older faster. I feel older in my head. I don't have the innocence any more that I had at twenty, the illusions. I did things that I can no longer do, such as stay up all night, carry heavy suitcases. But I don't perceive of myself as old or even middle-aged, which I am. And I intend to be attractive to men until I am at least sixty.

I like being a woman. I've always liked being a woman. I think being a man must be so difficult, so difficult. You have to go to war and fight, you are never allowed to cry if you're upset, you always have to be the strong one, you always have to have an erection. Ooh, la, la. No, oh no. Despite the problems of being a woman, I accept these gladly and nothing would make me want to be a man.

Felicity Waley-Cohen: This is going to sound immensely arrogant, but I think I can succeed in whatever I set out to achieve. I actually feel that, and, because I feel that, it makes it possible. I have a conviction that I can get things done. I mean, at a huge cost, because you have to be completely blinkered and you suffer tremendously from having to fight every inch of the way. I think I could have achieved success but I think at a cost that no man would have had to pay. Women have to work much harder. And if they marry, it is harder still.

The women who succeed are very confident, more confident than men. They have to be. I think there is an immense number of women who don't succeed who are as able if not more able than the second rank of men, but it's not only because they lack confidence, but because they lack will-power and drive, and those who do succeed are, if anything, superior to the men because they need to be fighters, whereas, as a man, you can cruise along. I've always found it an advantage to be a woman. I would not be a man, and I don't want to be a man. However, I am very much aware that, had I been a man, my life would have been extremely different because I would have been very ambitious, whereas I was not brought up to work, and the job I had was completely of my own making. I mean, my parents were delighted, they were proud, but they were sort of amazed. I think if I had been a man I would have gone into business, and I suspect that I would have been very successful. So I suppose in some ways I think, if only I had been a man. I love business, I enjoy it, and if I go to lunch where there are high-powered businessmen, there's that sense of power. I can feel a thrill, and I think, why did I ever stop? The reasons I stopped the gallery were not really to do with the family, although that certainly affected it, but with the fact that I felt I no longer had what it took to run a gallery of avant-garde art and had lost track, I was out of sync. with what was going on. Then the Tate asked me to help them start something which would encourage interest in contemporary art, so I'm chairman of the Patrons of New Art at the Tate, and more recently I'm on the development committee of the Tate, and they've just set up a foundation with which I'm involved, so I still am very occupied, but it's not business. It's much looser, and it doesn't have the same excitement, the same fears. I can go home and sleep easy at night. There's always somebody else. I'm not responsible ultimately. If I chose to get out, I could get out. Before I couldn't. However, I have a daughter who's seven, and I worry very much about the way in which we bring up girls. You see, I wouldn't *not* have my family. I'm very happily married. I love my children, and my life at the moment is ideal, and yet, if I'd been brought up to work, I suspect I would never have married because I would have worked.

I've been able to use the fact that I'm a woman and allow the man to be protective, which, by and large, men still tend to be under most circumstances. They will help you, they want to be the shining white knight, and by and large I've been lucky enough to judge it so that they've been delighted to help at moments when I've been alarmed they might see it as a sign of weakness. I feel that certainly can be an advantage. I think that what would be regarded as an intolerable weakness or failing in a man is not as serious in a woman and can be extremely useful. I can get information out of men that I don't believe any man could.

I've always thought that women who are privileged, like me, who have either money or great intelligence or great ability, are in a perfect position. But the women who are not privileged are in the worst possible position because they have two jobs. They look after their husbands, their children, and they go out to work. It's the ultimate nightmare life.

Shirley Conran: All my life I've always had absolutely wonderful bosses, whether men or women, who have encouraged me and egged me on and pushed me into things. I never have felt any sort of drawback because I was a woman. On the other hand, I think I suffered from being a woman in the way that most women of my age suffer. We were always taught to hide behind some man. One of the things I'm very careful about is to give generous tips, because most women are considered to undertip. The reason is very simple. Few women have any money. All my books are about self-confidence in women. In every single one, that has been the main thing, even the gardening book, but in *Lace* I did digress a bit and talked quite a lot about women and money and the importance of money to women. Women are taught to regard money in a different way from men. They're taught that it's rather nasty stuff, vulgar, and that a nice woman doesn't think about it and doesn't talk about it. All she does is spend it. I'm much criticized for saying things like that, but I think a lot of the criticism stems from envy and a lot comes from people who really know that I've just hit them between the third and fourth rib with

211

my sharp little dagger. I want people to notice things about themselves that they don't want to notice.

Terence and I were both discriminated against when we started out in business. I can still remember wearing a bun, wearing spectacles, wearing a very severe grey dress, trying to look older. I can remember my assistant was a man called Jeremy Smith, and I made him grow a beard which he still has to this day, and trying to make him wear spectacles with just plain glass in them – he very sensibly refused. But Terence had a terrible time with bank managers who were not fair with him. They would say they would do something, and then they would draw back and not do it. We were terribly disadvantaged because we were young.

I think periods are, if I might coin a phrase, a bloody nuisance. Some people suffer from PMT, certainly I did. Other people are really really ill, desperately ill when it's going on; some people get bloated, put on ten pounds once a month, and have to have separate sets of clothes. We're all influenced to a great degree by that. You can't get round it, you can't avoid the fact that it happens, but you can cope with it. I think that's the only real basic disadvantage we have.

Everybody knows that Felicity Green should have been the first woman editor in Fleet Street, and everybody knows that she was not allowed to be because she was a woman and they would not have a woman as an editor on the *Daily Mirror*.

Who wants to be editor of a colour supplement? We're not talking about being editor of a colour supplement, we're talking about being editor of a newspaper. I would be very interested if the *Economist* was ever run by a woman.

Genevieve Cooper: I think I'm lucky, because I work in a world of intelligent people, and intelligent people are not as likely to be as stupid towards each other because of sex or any other reason as less educated people. I'm surrounded by people with university educations who treat me equally, whereas, before I went into journalism, I did a long spell in temporary jobs and offices so I could earn enough money, and was staggered at how old-fashioned some offices – City offices or boring companies, insurance companies – were in their behaviour to women. I'm sure they're still like that. My sort of world is obviously a more sophisticated one. In the less sophisticated areas I'm sure there's a hell of a lot of discrimination towards women. There are a lot of very stupid men.

I talk to someone, and they don't know what job I do, they can be very uninterested, and then, when I tell them, they are suddenly extremely interested and listen to my every word. That does happen, but whether that's because I'm a woman I don't know. I think they're like that with everybody. Everybody's impressed by status, and you can be talking to a man and think he was the local milkman and not be very attentive, but if he told you he was the head of Coutts Bank, you are suddenly much more interested. I don't think that's necessarily a matter of sex.

My boyfriend is quite young. He's younger than I am, and most of the people I know are younger than I am, and I think that within that generation, late twenties, early thirties, there is quite a good acceptance of women. But when I see girlfriends who are married to men who are older, I see a difference. Their husbands are inclined to say stupid things, like, oh, let the women go and talk about shopping. I had forgotten that went on.

Being a woman is very interesting, because how you appear and how you are is very bewildering to men. Men, in general, are very straightforward in that they are what they seem to be, and they expect that. So they don't quite know how to cope with people who are not what they seem to be, and women often aren't what they seem. Women can use that to their advantage – and do. It's a bad side of being a woman, because you can exploit men easily, and manipulate easily, if you're that sort of woman. I think that's an advantage over men.

Michelle Coquillat: Most of the time the men with whom you try to work try to put the relationship immediately on to a private level, and they know that, on the private level, they are the winners. So it is very difficult. They will try to have some kind of friendship with you, invite you out to dinner, because you are a woman. And if you make the mistake of playing the game, and you make it all the time because it is so nice, then it's over, because immediately they know that in the private relationship their strength and so on is going to play against you as a woman. Therefore I think that you have to be very strong if you want to make it on a professional level: strong and hard.

Fleur Cowles: A man who did a lot for me – who was very sweet and good about me, and who in his official autobiography describes me as one of his daughters – is Bernard Baruch, America's famous elder statesman. Now Bernard Baruch made my mind, I'm sure of it, first of all by having such belief in me. I had to live up to it. Secondly, by a habit

213

which I would have loved to pass on to a child. He used to call me up every morning at nine o'clock and ask my view on the leading question of that day. It could be the stock market, it could be the war in some remote place. I got up at seven every day – read every paper – read every book. I was most anxious to give him the right answers. And he created my brain. I'd love to have done that for a child.

I have never felt discriminated against because everything I have achieved I have achieved because I am a woman. Every important assignment, every professional success I've had, was because a woman was needed for a particular project. This includes White House assignments, half the editorship of one of the biggest magazines in the world, all the philanthropic things I do to raise money. They choose me because I can tell them how women think. I'm the woman in each instance. As associate editor, I brought the woman's readership to *Look* magazine (which went from one million readers to seven million before it died). And I brought to it a pattern of editorial content that brought women into the magazine as readers, which made it possible to sell the magazine to important advertisers, making the magazine more popular and helping it rise to even larger circulations in America. I never felt discriminated against. It was the other way round. I was sought after because I was a woman, because a woman's talent was needed – a woman's view. I didn't step in to a man's job. I did what needed the mind of a woman.

Women, are, I suspect, kept out of many things because they've never been there before – a lack of judgement by some men. Prejudice cannot be overlooked, and some of it is inescapable. Women are not considered long-range investments because of the threat of childbirth and the absenteeism which ensues. Often this is the biggest hurdle in casting jobs: choosing between a young man and a young woman. In the worlds that men occupy and dominate, a clever woman's place can often be as part of a team which is foolishly ignored. A woman can make the most natural companion to a man in many jobs and projects. Sometimes women don't make the attempt because they can't ignore the fear that women can't be as successful as men in a competitive situation; while other women, with the knowledge of the scope and size of their skills and brains, the variety of their talents, the value of their curiosity which is more definite in a woman than in a man, push on in a low-key and successful way.

America is in the forefront in giving women the big chance in life. What I was able to achieve thirty years ago in America could not have happened here. Never, never. Can you imagine being allowed to co-edit one of the biggest magazines in the world – in 1948? You can't see me being asked by a prime minister to carry secret, serious, delicate messages to heads of state, but they did in the United States. It's not a long hard battle to have people recognize what you are in America. It's pretty instantaneous – not here. Here it takes for ever to realize what the potential of a woman happens to be. She has very often to fight for that recognition.

Being a woman was an enormous asset because heads of state would talk frankly to me; perhaps they didn't worry too much about a woman. I, in turn, talked frankly to them. Men cannot so easily because men don't like such frankness from other men. Sometimes it erects a wall between them. A male ambassador, talking to a head of state, has to watch his prerogatives. He might even be *persona non grata* (as one I knew was) for asking the sort of questions I could ask, or commenting on their attitudes and views. I could ask them in the simple and sympathetic way that men find unacceptable to each other.

There are very few Margaret Thatchers in this world. And many women who achieved her kind of importance were not good women. For me, Mrs Ghandi was a vindictive, difficult, unpleasant woman. This is my own personal judgement. Perhaps the one great woman other than Mrs Thatcher who achieved particular success as a woman was Golda Meir – Israel's greatest man, not at all feminine. Great, distinguished, brave, she had many things in common with Mrs Thatcher. And there are others: Mrs Bandaranaike was a despot. And equally so, in her frustrated angry way, Mme Chiang Kai-shek in Taipei, whom I also knew. I stayed with her in Taiwan many years ago, but this genuinely Iron Lady really was one and revealed it on that visit: tough, cruel, devastatingly angry at her fate. She actually asked me why the United States was foolish and fearful enough not to do what they should – why don't they drop the Bomb on China? She didn't mind the idea of such destruction of her own people if it would give her the regal dynastic role she enjoyed in China when her husband was alive and they both ruled (and robbed) China. After they fled to Taipei, even her husband took her power away. No matter what side of politics one is on, no one could ever call Mrs Thatcher cruel and despotic. Evita Perón, about whom I wrote the book, *Bloody Precedent*, was equally harsh, cruel – much tougher than Juan Perón, for whom she performed with such brilliant but terrifying vengeance against the rich who rejected her. It was she who held the reins of the people – power over the Descamisados, the poor and helpless Argentinians – but under painfully false pretences. The rich (good or bad) disappeared, their money confiscated. She sold herself to the workers as a saint, but after getting to know her (the

215

musical *Evita* to the contrary) I came to realize her as one of the most evil women in the world – and one of the most brilliant. We were together in Buenos Aires at the height of her power. She was, in my view, the most corrupt woman in modern history, not excluding such a minor copy as Emelda Marcos. Every worker in the Argentine had to give one day's wages every month to her so-called mandated charities – which ended up in her pocket. Millions of dollars of jewellery and money in foreign banks. She was a consummate propagandist. Visitors were always shown the façades of big homes for unmarried mothers. No one actually lived in them. I saw children's homes (usually confiscated mansions) where expensive luxurious clothes (which were commandeered from shops but never paid for) hung in endless closets. Poor children were dressed in them for a hurried display for visitors like me. She was so devastatingly dishonest and politically frightening (a female Hitler) that she was fascinating and was loved by the poor who believed her. I went with her to one rally where thousands of women stood and cheered her as she pointed at her Paris outfits and her enormous diamond orchid pin, huge earrings and bracelets, and ranted at a high pitch at them: see how I'm covered in jewels today. I started life with nothing. My mother struggled – she was poor as you are. She ran a brothel. But it is all for you. I'm gathering everything from the rich just to collect and give to you, my people. They mean nothing to me, nothing. I went to her famous court of appeals, which was actually set up to punish the rich. An apartment-house owner was brought before her as she sat at a Napoleonic desk. He was accused of expecting his tenants to pay rent. No one needs to pay *you* rent, she hissed at him. You're too rich already. You will be sentenced to twenty days in jail! What she did to muffle the press was just as desperate. I dedicated my book to a heroic gentleman who struggled for so long to keep his fine newspaper the only anti-Perónista in print despite jail sentences and confiscated newsprint. The Argentine, before the Peróns, was the largest beef and wheat exporter in the world. Evita put an end to that. When I was there, they went ahead importing both for their own food supplies because she exhorted the workers to stop working on farms. Her story, in an ironic way, may be an example of woman's stupidity. The society of Buenos Aires totally snubbed the president's wife, wouldn't welcome her or invite her to be a member of the snobbish Jockey Club. Another instance of how cheap, small *feminine* bitchiness may have affected history.

In many ways, my life has been unique. Not that I have gone further than other women. But it's covered more territories. I've done so many different kinds of things – I've lived so many different lives. I'm sorry now there are no children because I would have loved to see how they grew up and what they'd be. I'd like to try to influence them the way other people have influenced me.

Susan Crosland: Child-rearing is where I would redress the balance. Largely because I think when the woman gets stuck with an atrocious husband – perhaps he isn't even atrocious, probably just boring – but when she gets stuck and can't get out of this marriage, and goes on running the household for a man she doesn't love, who doesn't appreciate her, she's usually stuck because of children. She can't leave the children, and she has no way to support them. If you could somehow put that right, give her help in child-rearing, I think a lot of things would flow from it. She'd be free to develop other sides of her character, and if she didn't, that would be her problem.

Mary Crowther: There is a sexual disadvantage to being a woman in that you get pregnant. Men don't get pregnant. As a child, there was no distinction made between my brother and myself because their ambition for both of us, again because of the Depression, was that we should have a professional life, get a job that was safe and secure. For example, medicine was good, but wanting to be an actress or a pianist or a painter, that wasn't good, because they were risky things in one's life. So, growing up, the emphasis was always on studying and books. There mightn't be enough money for clothes or toys or those sort of things, but there was always money for books. Then, during my teenage years, I think I became aware of the sort of disadvantages that women have, simply because of the warnings that they gave me, as I think most parents give to their daughters, about social interactions between men and women. They were always much more sinister than the ones they gave to my brother. You had to be careful with men, men would seduce you and take advantage of you. It wasn't spelt out like that, but you were aware of that fear.

There are clearly economic disadvantages, and there are cultural disadvantages in some cultures, particularly in peasant cultures, but those things have never, rightly or wrongly, bothered me that much. I think one major thing that women suffer from is partly cultural in that, in bad times, they may not have the means to provide for themselves. They are always brought up to be dependent on men. Men provide money, men provide a home, men provide protection for families – that's a very primitive sort of thing, but it still works for entire societies. I'm not sure that there are educational disadvantages as the education system stands. Where the disadvantage lies is that men may be pushed

217

and women not by their families, but again that's a cultural thing. It's not that the things provided by society are less for women than for men. It's that women are not pushed into them enough. But the main disadvantage is the biological one, and pregnancy. I'm not sure it's a disadvantage, but it alters women's lives in a way different from men, so that they are brought up with a greater sense of responsibility for their sexual actions certainly. But women are also brought up to be disappointed somehow. That sounds funny, but your whole life is painted by your parents as, at times, having great areas of sadness in it simply because you are a woman. For instance, if children die, or if pregnancies end unhappily, or if you are seduced and left abandoned. I think that's the difference.

There are 50 per cent of women entrants into medical school, yet very few, perhaps 2 per cent, less than that, go into surgery. And the reason, I think, is not so much stamina, but the demands it makes on one's personal life. If you go into general practice, dermatology or radiology, you can more or less count on a nine-to-five Monday-to-Friday job with occasional night duty, but there is room to have your family around you. It's not that easy with surgery. You have to be up in the middle of the night, emergencies are always unexpected and come at any time, and I think the physical demands on one's life are greater. The other thing is – and I think conditioning may have something to do with this – that women interested in anatomy and surgery in medical school gradually lose that interest somehow. It may be lack of confidence that they don't think they will ever be good enough to be surgeons. As small children, before ever going to medical school, I think people interested in that sort of thing very often plan to become nurses rather than doctors. I think that's because parents don't push them enough and don't think they can ever do those awful things that one always has the idea that male doctors are doing. The public has a very odd idea of doctors. Until the M★A★S★H series, I'm sure they thought of doctors – surgeons in particular – as being very distant people, very much on pedestals. M★A★S★H has in a way humanized the whole thing and, as more people have experience of hospitals, they realize that M★A★S★H isn't very far from the truth. A lot of hospital life is just getting by with a lot of luck.

I worked in a laboratory for a while when I was doing a thesis, and one of the laboratory technicians, who was male, and I would each wear a white coat; and if we ever went anywhere together we'd just say, we're from the laboratory, and he would always be called doctor and I would be called love, miss, nurse, dear, or whatever. But that doesn't make me angry. I laugh about it. I wouldn't get up and carry a banner and say this proves that feminism has to march forward. It's just their perception.

I hope, when I'm in my fifties and sixties, I won't try to look like someone in their thirties. I hope that I age gracefully, and I hope I'm proud of my lines, and my arthritic joints and so on. I don't fear getting old. I'm rather looking forward to it. I hope there will be some little old man who will still want me, even if it's only once a month. I think growing old can be lovely. It's unkind to say it, but I think that women who are unhappy when they're old have, if the truth were known, been unhappy when they were younger. They are the sort of women who have never really established solid relationships with men. Loving – not necessarily a man, loving anybody – is not all fun. There is a lot of pain in it, and sometimes you grow through it and sometimes you don't. If you can never accept the pain in relationships, then you will never ever have good, strong and lasting relationships.

Jennifer D'Abo: I've always been happier with older people. I've always pretended I was older than I was. I couldn't be less worried about age. My father said to me, when I was quite young, darling, your face is never going to be your fortune, so you'd better work on the charm. He was right. I couldn't care less. I'm not the least bit vain. I wouldn't have a face-lift if I had a thousand wrinkles. Men are much more vain than women about age.

I've been irrational since the day I was born, I have to say. You see, I don't run anything. The secret of my success is that I know what I can do. I can't run a business, add up, write letters. The answer is that I go out and buy the best. I have intuition and I have vision. I'm a designer of products. I also happen to be a deal-doer. I love seeing deals and I can see potential in companies that other people possibly can't. Therefore I get up and say, I've now decided I'm going to buy the boom. I have the nose. I cannot see secrets in balance sheets, I'm not clever enough for that, but I can understand the rudiments of it, and it's instinct. Then I get someone else to take it apart for me.

I've always stuck to the fact that I'm not ashamed of what I am, or who I am, and they either accept me or not, even though I don't look right, I don't sound right, but I do my job and I have spent night-shifts in factories. I am fascinated by production, by production lines, by conditions, by machinery. I will go off round the world by myself with my notebook looking at machinery, and people don't understand that. They think because I don't look the part and don't sound the part, that I don't know what I'm talking about, but I actually do care passionately about machinery. You see, having no training, I am an entrepreneur as opposed to a big company woman. Now it's probably much more

219

difficult to succeed as a woman working your way up through a tree when you're having to fight men all the way up the line. Remember that my business career has always been me deciding what I wanted to do, and then putting the mechanics in place. When I started with a grocery shop I had three part-time women: I found the women, I did the books, I cleaned the freezers, I worked on Saturdays, but the fact is that I organized it. Again, when I then went off and bought a bankrupt department store, I raised money, I designed it, I put the people in place. So I've never been through disciplines of having to go up through a man's world on an equal footing.

On some occasions, I'm expected to be sensible and just talk facts and figures; and on other occasions there are certain men who prefer to think they're backing something slightly different and they expect a bit of sparkle and a bit of entertainment; and there are occasions when I've walked into a room full of analysts and I absolutely know when I walk through the door that it's just not going to work. I consider that if the country is run by a woman, then the bank and institutions ought to consider that women are good enough to run businesses.

The attitude of Barclays Bank towards women is totally, absolutely disgraceful. I think they put what I call a statutory woman on the board because they felt obliged to, but they have nothing higher than managers; they don't have any executive women directors because, they said to me, women get to a certain stage, they don't move as easily as men. That's rubbish. If the husband moves, the wife moves, so it's a whole load of nonsense. They say they get to a certain age and can't take the responsibility, don't take strain very well, et cetera. I don't believe that. I think it's a way of thinking. I actually think that this Big Bang is going to do the City no end of good, because people are going to get judged on their merits, not on their names.

I've never been motivated by money. I've never been very clever at making money for myself. I think – touching wood – I've been quite good at making it for other people, but my accountant has a heart attack each month about the fact that I have no off-shore funds, no tax havens; that I pay the maximum amount of tax. I couldn't care less about my pension. And they scream because I haven't done the right thing. I'm not interested. I seriously am not interested. I do it because I love it, because it fascinates me, and I like creating things. This to me is magic.

I would use absolutely anything, almost anything, to get what I wanted if I thought it was going to help. But I'm not sure that it always does

220

help; I think that, in business again, a lot of men would react in the opposite way if one tried to use one's femininity. Some men feel threatened. There's a book just published in America about successful women and the effect that has on men. Men don't like successful women. They feel threatened by them, and they feel maybe they don't want to take me out to dinner if I have a bigger car.

None of my husbands has ever done anything at home. There's no way any of them would have expected other than their shirts washed and ironed in their cupboards, somebody in to clean and polish their shoes and press their suits; they would expect to have dinner for them at eight or eight thirty, they would expect to have their invitations answered, they would expect you to go to Ascot with the right clothes on, to entertain for them, go grouse-shooting with them, travel with them, blah, blah, blah. So there's no quarter, in that respect in my life, for having a job. That was Jennifer being Jennifer, but the fact remains, when I got home, I was expected to behave like a normal wife, and it killed me. You've been running round the world in seven days, and you've been to Lusaka and Taipei and Singapore, and you get back, and you're worn out, and your husband turns around and says, you've got twenty people for dinner.

Maryam D'Abo: England is much more of a man's country than, for example, France, where, because it's a Latin country, there's more interest in women in business positions. In the film business you will get women editors, you will get plays, scripts, films that are written for women, but in England it's much more of a man's country. Which I don't mind at all, but I suppose there's more of a fight. The approach to a woman is totally different in France. In England, I feel totally asexual, I could be a man or a woman. Which is nice, in a way, because sometimes in Italy you get fed up with being whistled at the whole time. But then, when I stay too long in England, I miss that Latinness I get when I go to Paris, see all my men friends, and feel a woman desired.

Béatrice Dalle: To begin with, I was sometimes treated as an object. I may not be very beautiful, but I have fantastic success with men. I'm not tall, blonde, thin and blue-eyed, and it's true that I had to please people physically to begin with. Now I'm treated much more seriously.

I'm terribly pleased to be a woman because people take care of me, people are nice to me. I'm protected, that's terribly nice.

221

I know that I am young, but I won't stay that way for long. I think about dying, it's frightful. It's awful to think you will die and the world will go on after you. There will be millions of things happening, so what's it all for? It's horrible, horrible.

What would I do for women? I would kill them all. Like that I would be the only woman on the earth and I would be loved.

Alma Daniel: I never felt there was a gender differentiation until I got into the business world. When I was seventeen, I went to work for a newspaper and was put on the women's pages, which indicated that they had less importance, less significance than sports or news. It was there that I first encountered the difference between being a woman and a man, when they needed to send me out on a story because they didn't have a male reporter. They would not normally have sent me, because I was just in what they called the social department. So I got to do something I wouldn't normally have had an opportunity to do. But throughout my business career, I would say, I never felt that being a woman was a handicap, truly. I knew that men were perhaps paid more for the same job, but it never bothered me that much.

Now, it is an advantage to be a woman, because there are many more opportunities being given to women in the name of equality, and in the name of women's lib. and of non-discriminatory policies and so forth. I know there's a difference between what is being said and what is being done, but the general climate is much more conducive. I think the person most likely to be given the opportunity to get ahead now is a black woman – from the standpoint that blacks have been militating and agitating for equality and women have as well. There are, I feel, an enormous number of black women rising very rapidly in business and other fields of endeavour.

In this world, money is power. Money is basically a facility, a basic of exchange. So if you are dependent upon another for that, you can never totally be your own person. Whose bread I eat, his song I sing. You are always in a position of needing to answer to the other to get what you need. That's why I think it is important for people to be economically independent. Or to adjust their style of living so that they have what they basically need; maybe not always what they want, but what they need. I think the tendency in this country to buy on credit and extend oneself is another way of disempowering people. It puts them in bondage to creditors; it doesn't free them for enjoyment. It gives them a momentary gratification, but often they are paying off the car, paying off the house, paying off the vacation. Economic independence is very important.

I'm blessed not to have been subjected to the kind of sexual pressure and prejudice that many women receive in business. And where they are in situations where men make passes and they can't refuse them, it's most unpleasant, and most difficult. Well, in some instances they refuse and then they are fired, I've heard. I am a therapist, and I have dealt with many women, and I know what the stories are out there. I know I haven't borne the brunt of this, haven't had the aggravation of it, I haven't been subject to it. I don't know why. I just wasn't.

A woman I knew once said that to succeed a woman has to think like a man and work like a dog. She went on to say that women have much to overcome. They have to work much, much harder. Maybe so. Perhaps, out in the community, where there are traditional ways, women do need to work harder. And maybe they need to emulate men in the sense of dropping their emotional considerations. The thing about emulating men is not to act like a man so much as to take a clue from the way men act in business, which is to separate themselves from their emotional responses. They can keep their emotions to themselves and act out of their programme, out of their agenda. Women tend much more to get caught up in the emotional side of their responses so they can't always move towards a solution. That's my understanding. I've seen these women who try to be just like men and look just like a man; they've got a suit except the suit has a skirt instead of pants. And they are very abrupt, very hard in their behaviour. Someone once said to me, when a woman is powerful she must also be charming, and the more powerful she is, the more charming she needs to be. And I think this was very good advice, because a woman of power can utilize her feminine aspect to encourage all around her and get everything done. She doesn't need to come on like gangbusters. She can exert her influence through, let us say, a feminine aspect which has to do with encouraging, cultivating and nourishing. I don't think that women who do become men-like in that way really succeed, because what they are doing is cutting themselves off from their own femininity. I went through a period of my life when I thought, well, it would be better to be a man, men have more advantages, but I wouldn't be a man now; I have all of the smarts that I need, but I've got a feminine body. And much more can be accomplished in this guise than any other. So, it seems to me, women are in a very advantageous position today.

The older I get, the better I feel, the happier I am, the more energy I've got, the more excitement there is in my life. I would never go back. My mother asked me once, about twenty years ago, what was my favourite age. I was in my thirties and I said, right now, this minute. And she said, oh, she wished she was eighteen. I said, I've never wanted to go back. And I'm not living in the future either, wanting to look forward. Each day is wonderful.

Self-love. That's what I would give to women. When I say self-love, I don't mean a narcissistic self-indulgent thing. I mean unconditional acceptance of self as an aspect of God. That's what I would give.

I know that my beauty is within. I know that my beauty is my love. And age can't wither my love. It can only increase my love, because the older I get the more understanding and compassionate I become. So it's my heart that grows and ages, becomes more mature, ripens.

Sister Camille D'Arienzo: The patriarchy within the Church has had a profound influence. We have said the Church is one, holy, catholic and apostolic, yet what we see in the holy and the apostolic is male dominance. The holiness, from Pope to parish priest, through altar service, must be male. What does that say about the women who cannot be in leadership positions in the Church? That there is something intrinsically evil in them, or in some way lacking, so that they cannot join into equal holiness? So I think the modelling of the Churches has profoundly influenced the sexism that permeates society. I would like to see that women who feel themselves called to priesthood have their gift and their call tested in the same way men do. I would like to see them ordained on the basis of their love of the law of God, their desire to be pastoral servants, their ability to express, through sacraments, their own love of the Lord; women would have their gifts and their call to the priesthood tested in the same way, in terms of ministry, of cultural concern, of education, of intelligence, of love of the Lord. I see, in that, a possibility for a renewed priesthood. Because the gifts of women would somehow temper the limitations of the men who have been brought up in what many of us have come to call the old boys' network. They listen only to their male counterparts, from the bishop down, and are not open to the intuition, the inspiration, the advice, the counsel of women in any formal sense – certainly not as a body of people struggling together to bring about the reign of God. There is a tremendous fear of relinquishing the authority and the power entrenched in the male-dominated hierarchy of the Church.

If women were ordained and retained the mentality that some men have, they would be clones, female clones, of what is already there.

That would not improve things very much. If women want to be priests to exercise power, then we are just substituting one inefficient and weak image of the Gospel for another. But if women are more focused through their own sufferings and the injustices meted out to them in the name of God, if they are more focused on the needs of the Church and willing to sacrifice themselves for it, I think they would bring new, creative ways to translate the Gospel. Certainly, I do think there are differences between men and women. Whether they are culturally conditioned or whether they are chemical I don't really care. In my lifetime, I have evidence that there are differences, that the kind of socialization that men and women can share with one another enriches both, and I have no reason to think that this would not apply in the Roman Catholic Church. The thing I would hope that women would do is not simply close the gate behind them if they join the clerical ranks. I would hope that they would take up the challenge of the Second Vatican Council, and that is to embrace the laity, to encourage their gifts, to offer them possibilities of education and service, and to work, not ahead of lay people, but with them, married and single, male and female. I think women are better at this for a lot of reasons.

I can't preach in a pulpit. I can stand before an auditorium of 1,000 people and know that I can move some hearts in that group. I can be on television and reach millions. Yet I cannot stand in my parish church and preach for seven minutes on the Scriptures I love. I don't know that I would do it now, even if it were an option. But there are many women younger than myself who have been directed towards this goal for years now, and who believe it to be a possibility, who have the proper theological and scriptural training. Some of them studied in seminaries, some are writers, researchers, scripture scholars or spiritual directors. I would hope that these women will not be denied the opportunity to do what they and I believe the Lord Jesus is calling them to do.

Régine Deforges: When I was a child, I wanted to be a boy, because I realized that boys had more freedom than girls. They could fight, they could run, they could tear their clothes, but girls had to be quiet, play with dolls. But I wanted to play war games. I was brought up during the war, so afterwards we wanted to pretend to be in the Resistance and fight Germans, so for a while I was a *garçon manqué*. At that age, I only saw the disadvantages of being a girl. Up to the age of eighteen or twenty, being a woman didn't seem very interesting, as the only way for a girl to get her freedom was in marriage, and that was another kind of prison. But now I am happy to be a woman, because I think that imagination, poetry, artistic creativity and the taste for life, the whole mixture of life and work, is going to be on the women's side. Women are going to be able to use all that they have accumulated during the centuries to do something positive and creative.

When I started my first publishing house, the first book I published was *Irène* attributed to Aragon. This was in 1968. The whole of the edition was confiscated within forty-eight hours. In French law, a book has to be published with the author's name, the publisher's name and what is called *dépôt légal* inside. I had written to Aragon several times, but he never answered my letters; the book had been circulating clandestinely since 1928. So I had to publish it without the author's name. It was confiscated for that technical reason, even though other books have been published without the name of the author. Really it was because it was thought to be pornographic, and when I was questioned by the police, and on other occasions for other books, the presiding judge or magistrate would say, how can a young woman like you publish such books? It was the fact that I was a woman which made it seem wickeder. My publishing colleagues used to say that, when I appeared before the judge, all I had to do was show my legs and everything would be all right. There was always something sexist and pejorative. The fact that I was publishing erotic books, whether by Apollinaire or Aragon or anyone else, made me appear a sex maniac. For a man it would have been regarded as normal.

There are disadvantages because, despite the law, we are not paid the same for the same job, and not enough women in France are yet given positions of high responsibility. Why not? I have asked feminists and others that question, and, first and foremost, it is because nothing is given in this world, it is taken. If women wanted to take active power in their lives, there would be more of them in those positions. We live, however, with ready-made ideas and are afraid of losing our femininity. This exasperates me.

I am one of those people who act first and think afterwards. If I want to do something, then I will do it.

Dr Mary Jordan-DeLaurenti: There are so many signs to a woman in our society of what to do and not to do, and she has to break all these rules to be like a man sexually, as a man might behave sexually.

I always felt inhibited. As a matter of fact, one of my models is probably my older brother. I wanted to be like him because I wanted to do what he wanted to do and I couldn't. There are choices in life: you could be a nun, a nurse, a teacher, but would it be acceptable for you to be an engineer or a medical doctor? Well, you could, but it would not be encouraged, and that was probably my biggest resentment, that the world was not open to me at that point to do things my brothers could choose to do. My brothers did very well. One is a lawyer. Another is a business manager for a hospital – his choices were clearly his own choices, he did not go to college until later in life, but he had that choice, and he could make some money until he did. Whereas girls, when they didn't go to college, were probably not going to make very much money at all. The choice was get married, or get a job for a year or two until they married. My older brother went into the priesthood.

I was looking for status. And a nun had status at that time, quite a bit of status in our family environment, in the town environment. There was a lot of adulation. I don't think it's any longer true in the United States but this was 1955. During the 1950s and early 1960s, prior to the Vatican Council, this was the strongest period in Roman Catholic history for numbers joining the religious orders. If you were accepted, then that was quite an honour. I felt I had a vocation, but there was also a bit of what I call today brainwashing, and it's a necessary brainwashing if people are going to be converted to an entirely different form of life: the discipline, necessary for a life of prayer, the spirituality that needs to be developed. They required a very certain way of life, and a certain belief system. The belief system was not contrary to what I was brought up to, so that was easy to accept until I started talking to people and going to university outside the system. That's when I began to question, and what really influenced my decision to leave the convent was the fact that I was no longer in that environment, I was outside for the first time in ten years. I saw things, met people, asked questions, had questions answered, saw other people like me asking questions, and found that very exciting.

Women should be able to become priests. They should have choices. The entire Church system is built on the male hierarchy. They'll say, if she were married, she'd have a family and her time would be used up in her family and not given to the people of the Church. There's no physical or mental argument that justifies the Church in this, nothing except an antediluvian mentality that says women can't be priests. It's Neanderthal.

I was seventeen when I went into the convent and thirty-one when I left. I was not afraid of the outside world, but it was strange in that I had to start with nothing. I had no money, no clothes, no place to live, no experience of the outside world at all, no experience with men. It was a

227

challenge, more than anything, to see what all of this was about. I got a job as associate provost at Lewis College, and I had no money to put down for an apartment. They had to give me an advance on my salary before I started so I could go work for them. Luckily I knew someone at the college, who recommended me to them, so they took care of that. But that was my entry. I stayed in a college dorm for about six weeks until I was able to accumulate enough money to survive on my own.

When I became the associate provost of an all-male university, there were clear distinctions between the lady dean of the nursing school, me, and the rest of the administration, which was male. The academic deanship – there was a move made for reorganization the year after I was there – was not given to me because I was a woman, and they told me that. It made me look elsewhere, out of Academia, when that happened. I thought, how could they possibly do that to me when there was no doubt I was more qualified? I had a PhD; the person who got it did not have a PhD, and my PhD is in the administration of higher education. I learned how to be a dean and a president. That was my goal, and the man they appointed did not have any of that background. He had studied for his PhD but did not complete it. I used the next year to look for another job, and I took one with General Motors as a project administrator.

I agreed to take less money so I could get into industry. I would say General Motors was more an entry into the world for me than going to university, because the university was a Catholic university, and I still had some of that knowledge of how it operated, even though they were all lay people. One of the reasons I wanted to go to industry was to have a change, to find out how it was as a woman; also to see whether the principles I learned in education could be applied or I could learn something new from industry or education. General Motors, I think, opened me up again just as Notre Dame did. I met dear friends, I found out how the corporation worked. But I got to General Motors through the influence of the president. One of my dear friends was his medical doctor, and she asked him if there were any jobs for me in General Motors, so he really got me the job, and I wanted to make that point, because if I hadn't known someone, I would not have gotten that job.

There were only five women out of a hundred on the staff when I went to General Motors. There were no women managers at General Motors' institute at that time. Women did not generally take the class by themselves. They always had to have a male partner. They would never let two women do the teaching together, even though they were certainly not against two men doing it together. There were a lot of protectionist moves, and events that happened under the guise of protection but really put the women in a lesser position. I was the last of ten people hired by General Motors that year. A year later, which was 1974, and we had the energy crisis, General Motors had its first major lay-off, and I was the first laid off because I was the last hired. They practically levelled all of their women who were in the organization because they dismissed absolutely by seniority, and a year after that they had only one woman left. And there are still disadvantages. I know, because I sued the federal Government on a sex-discrimination case and won.

A certain amount of attractiveness will certainly influence people to be on your side, but also generally makes men want to conquer you. It's a challenge to them to get you sexually rather than to treat you as an equal. The sexual thing is rarely too far behind, it's usually quite up front. And it's also a challenge to other men in the organization, not just the managers and the leaders. If they can meet you or defeat you on a sexual ground, then they have defeated you; you are no longer their equal in their minds. That's not talking about wholesome relationships which do, of course, exist.

I have had the opportunity to train over 5,000 women, and in that training I have met some of them in their personal lives. Both personally and in the way they are in organizations, they don't have the confidence. That is something that is learned, not a matter of biology, and I think it can be learned in spite of the fact that they didn't have it in their upbringing. Many of them had an upbringing that worked against it, but success, seeing that you can accomplish some things in an environment that supports you, can give you that confidence. I think there's another reason why women don't succeed. Many of them are not willing to pay the price, and the price is greater for a woman, especially if she chooses a family – much greater. The price is long workdays, fourteen to sixteen hours a day, whether you're male or female, if you are going to succeed in an organization in the United States. If you are going to succeed, you have to be dedicated to that company. How can you give fourteen to sixteen hours a day and raise your family? And women today are still responsible for the family.

I do not now have as many experiences of being patronized, and I think one of the reasons is that I'm older. I also think men have changed in general. I had a wonderful experience last year. I was nominated and elected to an all-male Chief Executive Officers group – they all own their companies, or are presidents of a public company – and my reception in that group has been extremely warm. As a matter of fact, it's the first public group I told that I had been a nun. In fourteen years, I had never said that to any public group. Only dear friends had had that piece of information. Their response was so warm and so complete, I was overwhelmed. I've been a member of the group now for a year, and I'm still overwhelmed by some of the affection. There was an article in the paper on me with my picture, and when one of the gentlemen saw the article, he had it emblazoned on marble and sent to me – a huge piece – on a gold-plated frame or stand, and it came in the mail. This is what I call acceptance. That would not have happened ten years ago.

I was never unhappy in those fourteen years as a nun. Never. How many people have asked me that question! I wasn't even unhappy when I left. The thought of going back after I had experienced a whole new life was something I couldn't accept, but while I was there, I didn't know any better and I was perfectly happy. When I got new information and met new people and asked questions and found out there was a whole world out there and that you were not going to go to Hell if you entered that world. One of the things I was brought up to believe, and many women who joined the convent were brought up to believe (and priests), was that if you were given a vocation and you did not follow that vocation, when you died you would go to Hell. I found out that was a myth. That was to keep you there. That was part of the brainwashing. You can have permission to leave, and I got permission.

Lady Camilla Dempster: I don't think femininity either a plus or a minus. It hardly ever arises.

I don't think the English upper classes have ever been macho. I think they're still dreadfully chauvinistic, which is largely the fault of the women they're with. I'm talking about the unenlightened upper classes – the ones who don't read too much, who aren't aware. It's not unknown for the husband to travel first-class going on holiday, and for the wife and children to travel tourist. I have heard that: the wife, children and nanny travel in the back. Unbelievable. If that happened to me, I would either not go or I would pay for it myself. And I would make a terrible fuss. I certainly would not be handed a second-class ticket by my husband.

Anne Dickson: If you use the woman's body to sell a car, or to sell motor oil or an ice-cream or a chocolate bar, it just makes a woman's body seem so utterly trivial. I think men have lost their sense of beauty.

Woman's identity depends on being desirable, acceptable, as a partner. And that is the fundamental nub. Women do not believe that, if there isn't a man there, they exist sexually. Their sexual identity comes with the presence of a man. Therefore, if you are threatened by this woman taking away your man, it's not just a friend, it's your absolute identity this other woman is taking away. You are threatened in your core, and that's it, because everything depends on how you are and behave, and how acceptable, how desirable you are to this man, which is a dreadful state of affairs. And this is brought out by sexism; it's nothing to do with feminism.

Dame Jean Conan Doyle: In the Air Force at the very beginning of the war there were certain prejudices against women which came from an older generation who were really shocked, and at first women were segregated. There were separate messes for women, and we were only allowed in the men's mess at certain times. And although we worked side by side, we didn't live side by side. And so one was conscious then that one wasn't accepted on the same terms. It was a feeling that it was a male service and the women were auxiliaries. In fact our name was Women's Auxiliary Air Force. There are one or two branches of the Air Force which are not open to women, like airfield construction, where you need to be very strong, and the RAF Regiment, which is a unit that can be sent anywhere with tents in an emergency and they would need to have separate tents for women. Certainly, up to now, women are not trained as pilots. To train a pilot costs a fortune. Women have this special clause in their contract of service, that if they marry they have the option to leave the service without any financial handicap. They can stay on in the service if they like, and more and more women do stay on, but they have this right to leave on marriage. It would obviously be sheer nonsense to spend hundreds of thousands of pounds on training a pilot who'd perhaps fall in love with another pilot, marry, and leave within a day or two of qualifying. So there you do have a case where it isn't sensible to treat a woman on the same terms as a man. There's no biological reason why she can't fly, but it is biological that a woman is a woman, and when she marries a man she may opt out of the service in order to bear his children.

I'd rather be a woman. I've had the career I wanted most in the world. I wouldn't have wanted to kill anybody, and I never wanted to be a pilot. I just wanted to be with the people of the services.

I've never had a hang-up about age, other people's ages or my own. I think it is very trivial to worry about age.

231

Margaret Drabble: I always felt that I was as good as any boys or young men I met at university. I knew I was. And, indeed, I was, intellectually. But I think that, through the emphasis on the intellect, I missed a lot of fun in those early years and I missed a lot of other things. But I've never had any doubt about my ability, and I suppose my mother is to thank for that.

In my early years, people did take what I said seriously. At Cambridge I was considered quite an intellectual star of the scene and people were interested in what I had to say. I never felt that the particular people with whom I mixed were ignoring or neglecting me because I was a woman. I was one of a group, and we talked equally. It was only much later that I came across that, when I was in my late twenties and thirties, when I was going to more sophisticated parties where there would be politicians or businessmen, and, of course, by that time I just thought what boring people and walked away.

In my chosen career, which was to go to university to study English literature, there were no obstacles. It was easy. Everything was laid open. It was only after I left university that I realized there were difficulties ahead: the difficulties of reconciling being a woman and a mother with having a career. That was thrust upon me very suddenly and abruptly. I simply hadn't foreseen it. I now can't understand why I hadn't foreseen it, but I married the week I left Cambridge and had a baby nine months and two days later, and I just hadn't realized what I was taking on. I had had no idea that my husband would be competitive with me, that my baby would take up so much time, that I would love my baby to such an extent that I didn't want to leave him with a nanny. All these problems suddenly became real and nobody had ever mentioned them to me. It was difficult to swallow the fact that I couldn't have the career I had chosen because I'd got a baby. It was very difficult to understand my husband's jealousy when I became a novelist and was doing things he couldn't take part in. I couldn't understand the balance in our relationship at all. I thought the reason why he liked me was because I was an intellectual who wanted to write novels, and when I started to write them, I couldn't understand why he didn't like it. Of course, it's now all terribly clear, but at that age it wasn't. It was a difficult period with, mixed up in all that, my very strong attachment to my little children, who demanded a great deal of my physical and mental energy.

I started writing novels in the early 1960s at exactly the period when, in the *Guardian*, Mary Stott was running the women's page, and there was some really serious women's journalism coming out for the first time. They were treating serious issues and there were some very good writers. Jill Tweedie's articles were excellent. They were tackling some big subjects, and I think this was a new thing. However, it's still true that you don't get so many women writing about economics or industrial affairs, or politics. I think the most lamentable figure is the number of women in the House of Commons. It's extraordinary how few women MPs there are after all these years.

Women can opt gracefully out of the competition. If you marry a rich husband and you don't want to work, you don't have to. And if you decide that you don't like your job very much and to stop doing it and do something else, no one is going to say, oh, what a terrible failure. They're just going to say, what an interesting woman, whereas, with a man, there's much more pressure.

I think that possibly the greatest disadvantage is this sense of inferiority and an expectation of under-achievement that women tend to suffer from. I didn't, in fact, suffer from this very much for reasons I've explained, and also I wasn't setting myself to be prime minister or even the principal of a women's college at a university. I wasn't aiming at a public life. If I had been, I think I would have found the decisions almost impossible, and now I realize that what I did was to construct for myself a career that neatly avoided all the usual obstacles. I discovered a career which meant I could work at home, and if a child was ill I could take time off. I could manipulate all these little bits of the jigsaw without suffering, whereas, if I'd adopted a more conventional career, if I'd gone into medicine, politics, the law or business, I'd have had to make much more brutal decisions about bringing up the children and about my working hours.

I've moved mainly in artistic, literary, theatrical circles. In theatre circles, there is a great deal of equality. You can't imagine a theatre evening without women there. I haven't really moved in the kind of clubland of men who go off to the club or who will have an evening talking to one another. They're not the kind of people I know. I now feel slightly left out by it. Just out of curiosity, I'd like to know what's going on, and I do get irritated when I try to make an overture to somebody. For instance, I was writing an article for *The Times* recently about unemployment in Sheffield, and I wanted to talk to the president of the Chamber of Commerce in Rotherham, and I got a very dismal response to begin with – oh, he hadn't got time, he couldn't help. When I actually saw him, he was extremely pleasant. By then he'd worked out who I was. His father knew my father, everything was fine. But his initial response was, no, he didn't want to waste his time. And I can see that that must be a very usual response.

I certainly feel I'm getting old, and I also feel, thank God, it doesn't matter in my job. I'm glad I'm not the kind of woman who has to live off her looks. I think that some women do feel that, if they have lived off their looks, if that has been their great passport to human society, then to lose them is terrible, and I've known people who suffered terribly from that. Nobody likes getting old and grey and fat, but, at the same time, I realize that it isn't terribly interesting and I look at this generation of women who are slightly older than myself, for instance, Doris Lessing and Iris Murdoch, and I think, well, they're jolly nice-looking. They may not be beautiful young women, but they're delightful people, they're made in the image of the life they have led. They're both charming, interesting, quick-witted, they have all the qualities that are enduringly attractive. I think the worst thing must be to have been a famous beauty who has lived entirely for seduction and then had to shore up the ruin. I think that is quite dreadful.

Maureen Duffy: I married while I was still a student, largely out of ignorance. And, in fact, neither the person I married nor I believed in marriage as an institution. But we did it for a very particular reason, and we eventually set up house together, though it wasn't in any sense a home. I taught and he taught, and in a sense the main restriction was that, although we were both working, I was the one who was doing most of the shopping and cooking and cleaning. He was willing to help, but because he had been brought up in a family where boys didn't do anything, where the women of the family did all the housework, he was actually much less competent at it than I was, although not at all chauvinist in the sense of expecting women to do it all necessarily, especially if they had a job. There was also some degree of friction in that, because I had ended up with a slightly better degree, I was paid more for the teaching I did. Several such things, I think, helped to contribute towards our relationship not working. Also, I'd always known that the teaching was a sort of filling-in period to be able to make enough to keep going while I became a writer. I was very anxious to give it up and get on with what I had always wanted to do. So, as soon as I felt I could, which was when I sold my first television play, I gave up teaching and concentrated on writing. And, at that point, our relationship broke up, so I was then entirely free and, in a sense, moved out of the female world into a male world, in that I became like any male writer, because I no longer had to look after and, in a sense, play the female role to somebody else. I had total freedom and a career in which women, in this country anyway, have long been the equals of men.

234

Unless women are, for whatever reason, made confident, they don't succeed. I was made confident by my mother, by her expectations and her belief that I could succeed. It was inculcated in me from the very beginning that I could succeed in the external world. But this is not true for a lot of women. A lot of women, the older women, still believe that home, marriage and children are the important things. And they still inculcate this in their daughters. The daughters have to be strong, or very obsessed by some career that they wish to follow, in order to overcome this, even now.

One of the things they try and do in these self-defence classes, is to get girls to overcome the point at which normally society and all their training and so on expects them to draw back. The old-style East End mums, for instance – women prize-fighters – had overcome this point. OK, there were a lot of women who were beaten up in my childhood. My family comes from the East End, and I grew up in pretty rough conditions, but there were also a lot of strong big women with quite small husbands and, if the husbands came home pissed on Friday night, they'd give them a really good clout. Women can be very strong indeed in defence of their children. But this is not what society projects for them. It projects in absolutely everything, in women's magazines and advertising all over the place, the soft woman. OK, she can be bright and she can be sharp, but in the end she has to be soft. And everything inclines her to accept this role. There is a myth of the sort of swinging Amazon, but on the whole this is not actually what men want, because it is quite frightening: you have to deal with someone as an equal, on their own terms, and there will be days when they win and you lose. I am not saying that men are great boots and women are always beaten to the ground or anything like that, because I happen to think that many women are very strong indeed. But often she will get her own way by playing softly, and a lot of women will even do this in their careers, by disguising their abilities in a sense, by slipping through rather than punching through.

There are some occasions when it is actually easier to be a woman. I was much involved with Bridget Brophy and the Public Lending Right campaign, and I remember her saying to me on one occasion, we are actually doing better because we are women. There are certain spheres, and I think, curiously enough, politics is one of them, where the ambitious and aggressive woman can get right to the top. And, of course, we have a long tradition in this country of queens. It is not unheard of for this country to be led by a woman. And tradition is extremely important.

I would rather have been a man. Physically, I would much prefer to be a man.

Princess Elizabeth of Yugoslavia: I think men do respect me now. I have certain unorthodox views which they find intriguing. I mean, I am not a traditionally educated person, because I never went to college, and I went to a gulag school in England which was awful, so I have my own ideas, and I have come to my own conclusions. I think, in a way, I can have the best of both worlds being a woman. I continue to learn and to grow. I'm sure if I were a man, at my age, I would be stuck in one direction only, and like this I can keep on branching out.

I feel very free to express myself as a human being in America. You don't have either the class hang-ups or the sex hang-ups you do in this country. In England, after dinner, the men will sit and smoke cigars and drink port, and the women are supposed to go upstairs and talk about nappies and hysterectomies. I hate that sort of conversation. The educational system for women in this country is so abysmally low. You know, the daughter of a friend of mine, a very well-known man, is packing boxes in one of the big stores in London. She can't speak languages, she can't type, she can't work a computer, she can't get a decent job. She is nineteen and she's been brought up to get married to the right man. I think that's appalling in 1986. This girl should at least have been given the opportunities that my son has in school in England: to learn a range of subjects, to study all sorts of wonderful skills and languages and get ahead. Girls are not educated in this country. I find it tragic.

In my second marriage, I started to study acting in New York – it must be about twelve, fourteen years ago – and I was offered a good opening role, doing a very good commercial with one of my children; and my husband said, please don't do it, it will be bad for my career. I stepped down, I did not do it; and I resented that because I was being the good girl and the good wife, doing something for her husband. Now I don't have to do that for anyone. I feel I can now do whatever I want, because I don't 'belong' to someone, and that is what I don't like about marriage: that you have to subordinate yourself.

I would have preferred to have been a man many times, because I have a rather analytical mind. I think I have often frightened men away that I would like to have as friends. I find it difficult to play the mousy role of a woman who wants to be the seductress. This is not my aim at all. I like being on an equal footing with a man, and if I want to debate something,

I want to feel free to say exactly what I mean. And often men find that threatening.

Sally Emerson: You can go to a big party, dinner party, political dinner, and you can say things, or hear a very bright woman saying something, and nobody takes any notice. And a man will make the same point, and suddenly everybody will listen. It's to do with being a woman, and it's to do with the way it's said. Women tend to talk without the same confidence. It comes from years of not being listened to. I think we aren't just women standing here with however many years we personally have behind us. We have decades of women being quiet behind us, and I think it's that we're fighting against.

I think women are discriminated against, but I think quite rightly in many ways. Discrimination immediately suggests that it isn't right, but there are real problems about women being equal in our society. Once you have a child, if you have strong maternal feelings, or even normal maternal feelings, it's jolly difficult going on doing your job as well as you did before, unless you're willing to neglect your children to some extent, unless you're willing to hand your baby over to some other person. I would have to say, if I was an employer, I'd be a little bit nervous. I'd end up probably employing a man rather than a woman, because I think a really strong-minded woman, a whole woman, would very often be nervous of leaving her children, and would not just leave them like that and be able to hand them over and handle it terribly competently. I think that would be more of a deficiency if they could, and I think this is the essential problem with women at the moment: you're torn apart because, on the one hand, you're trying to do the male role you've been brought up to do, as I was, during my twenties – not so much a male role, but just do well in your job, and don't think anything of it. Then, all of a sudden, there's this other very strong, important job that you have which tears you in two because you try to do one job properly and you're not doing the other. You try to do the mothering properly, and you're torn because you want to be doing the work. I don't see that there's a solution.

I've never worked in big business, but if you went and you started flirting with everyone, I don't think people would take you seriously. I think it takes a very exceptional woman to be able to manage to keep her femininity, her gentleness, and take these difficult decisions and deal with her staff in an effective way and be tough. It's difficult because I do think that women's natures are softer, and all those feminine things – softness, warmth and sympathy – if you're bringing those into a workplace, you might completely fail at what you're doing. I imagine people have got to be much tougher, and I think they do probably have to lose quite a lot of their femininity to be taken seriously by men. If you're being a lovely charming woman – not necessarily flirting, but just being warm – there is genuinely the attitude that, unless you've proved yourself brilliant, you're only a woman. I think if you've proved yourself, if you've made a million or you're head of the company, you might be all right, but while you're moving up there, it's very much more difficult for men to take you seriously. I have a two-and-a-half-year-old girl, and when I look after her, all those female qualities come out, and I'm very aware of what they are: a softness, a compassion, an ability to be able to listen and take it quietly. Yet, when I used to go out to work as opposed to writing, which I find more conducive to looking after the child, I used to come back and be quite tense. I'd been dealing with people on the phone all day and would feel quite masculine. I was just somebody who got things done, and it would take me about a hour to get back into the female mould of looking after the child. Similarly, that would be the case with my being female and flirtatious, I think. I would need to have a drink or a bath just to bring me back to my other self. It was as if these two worlds were apart. I never really thought about being a woman. It wasn't that I would be meaning to be tough or anything. I'd be perfectly pleasant, but I was just somebody who did the job.

I mustn't be rude about my husband's paper, but whenever I see the newspapers with nudes in them, I have this sense of how can people treat women with respect in their work if, on the other hand, they're looking at these pictures in the morning, in the newspaper, women in this strutting position, showing off their breasts to men for money? I think that not the most intelligent men, but a lot of men, do see them as sex objects. If women are willing to be portrayed merely as sex objects, obviously they are seen as that, and it's difficult for men to take them seriously. Somebody was saying to me that, in one newspaper where they have nudes or bare breasts or whatever, the men who are very keen on them, who actually work for the newspaper, and who thought these were a good idea, had great difficulty in dealing with the women executives. They found it difficult to tally the two: the idea of women in a bikini and women wearing executive suits and doing very well.

Now we have control over whether we have a baby or not, whether we do a job or not, and if we want to keep our bodies and our faces looking good. And there are lots of things that can be done. Jane Fonda, Joan Collins – they look marvellous for their age because they've actually taken a positive attitude. Instead of thinking, oh, I'm getting older, they've taken a positive, faintly aggressive approach and just got on with doing it. My mother's getting on for sixty – she looks absolutely marvellous, she gets whistled at in the street and people turn to look at her. She looks beautiful because her personality comes out of her. She takes trouble over her face, her hair and her clothes, but her personality is charming and it comes out: her warmth and femininity and those things that you don't lose if you're a strong female, interesting, intelligent.

Shirley Eskapa: I feel that men are used to women deferring to them. For example, when I have been to meetings with my husband's lawyers, even QCs, because I was a woman and they were all men, it was hard to convince them, including my husband. He was much more influenced by the men in the picture, because men are supposed to know more about these things. So although events proved I was absolutely right, I wasn't taken seriously because I was a woman. I was being humoured. I'm sure if I had been another man, they would have followed my advice – which, incidentally, would have saved my husband many thousands of pounds.

I work in an isolated world. I haven't been in the business world, so I don't know what it means to be a career woman mounting the corporate ladder: if being a woman can help you, or if your sexuality can get you to the top quicker. I don't know about that. I think, if you are a plain woman – I'm going to sound modest here – you have a much harder time. If you are an attractive woman and charming you can get away with things you couldn't otherwise – traffic offences, police and so on. You can use your femininity.

Even in today's world, I know of women – very intelligent women, wives of ambassadors – who, when their husbands come home, quickly hide books they are reading under the cushions. If they read, they are not doing their household duties. Not only are they not expected to read, but they are expected not to default in the home.

I think to be honest, if I had been born a male my life would have been very different – I would have achieved much more, though I'm not crying about what I have achieved. I am very pleased – I'm even amazed and delighted by it. So this is not sour grapes. But I'll tell you the reason. I remember one day my mother coming and telling me that I had the highest IQ in the class, so they thought, even though they were remarkably wonderful parents, maybe there was something wrong with the test. Then I went on, and when I got four distinctions – four out of six – two were the highest in the country. It was a kind of fluke, they thought. Shirley was lucky: she had spotted the right questions. And then I went to university. If I had been a boy, their whole attitude would have changed. I would have gone to a university abroad – to Oxford maybe – to a real university. I would have taken my career much more seriously. Instead, as a girl, it was always secondary because ultimately my destiny was to be a wife and mother, which was what I wanted, which is what every woman wants. Now they've got the freedom to pursue their careers before they are wives and mothers – and the tragedy is that they find too often that when they are ready to be wives and mothers, they can't find the partners, because the men of their age still prefer younger women. For men, it's a renewal of love. It gives them an illusion of their own youth – an appendage on their arm – you know. Women's liberation has meant that for women like me and younger – over thirty-five – it's much harder for them to keep their man than ever it was before.

Kathryn Falk: It would be very hard to get ahead if you're not attractive when you're young. Not that you should depend on that, but certainly it opens doors, and it helps. I was from Grospoint, Michigan, and it helped, I'd be the first to say it. My mother was right, you know, she was right. Certain social class advantages put you in a different league than if you were from some little town in Milwaukee.

I don't really belong to a particular group. Even when I went to college, I was asked but I never joined a sorority, so I've never felt any restrictions on what I could do, except my own. I never worked for anyone, I've always had my own business. I couldn't function very well in a corporate ladder structure. I've never had to ask somebody what to do, I've only had to ask myself what to do. I have never felt discriminated against.

Being in publishing in New York, it's quite a man's world. Even though all the editors are women, the presidents and the owners of the companies are 100 per cent men. The women do the work, but they don't own. I'm the only one who owns anything as a woman. All the other owners, from Matt Wattel to Crown to Walter Zacharias to Zebra, are men. Bantam's is owned by the Germans – men. Not that I'm necessarily in the same league as they are, but when I have been with them, they treat me differently.

Marcia Falkender: I find being a woman is a total disadvantage. I can't think I've ever met a woman who has achieved anything who hasn't had a terrific struggle and doesn't regard it as a great handicap at all levels. It's a handicap on an ordinary day-to-day level, the mechanics of life. If you are a woman trying to get something done in your house, you would get it done faster when a workman comes if you were not a woman. You'll be ripped off more likely if you are a woman. It's a struggle at every point. The attitude is very different once you say, well, I'll ask my husband, or will you ring my home, and if I'm not there, my husband will take a message, from the attitude you get if it's just you and it's going to be one to one. Men do take advantage of that, or try to. What you have to do is be particularly tough, and sometimes you really have to be quite nasty. You have to act out of character. That, I think, is regrettable, and after years of doing it, it tends to have an eroding effect.

For a long time, I didn't realize there was hostility to women. I can't ever remember it at No 10 when I was working there, and certainly not before when I first went to work for the Labour Party straight from university at party headquarters to learn about how the party worked, nor, after that, when I went to work for Harold Wilson when he was in Opposition. All those years, I don't think I ever had any consciousness that doing that job was necessarily something that women didn't do or couldn't be expected to do. When I was just his secretary, at the beginning, working my way up, or when I was in the secretarial capacity at party headquarters, obviously it wouldn't be unusual to have a woman. But once I became head of his political office and was actually running the political end of his life and his political campaign selections, it never occurred to me that, because I was a woman, I shouldn't really be doing it and that people were looking at me in that light. No, I think it's only after I came away, when I had a lot of aggravation and people said, you know, it's because you are a woman, that I suddenly stopped and said, oh well, I suppose they might be right. But that hadn't occurred to me before. I just thought that they didn't like the Labour Party, after thirteen years of Conservative government, which is what it was in 1964 when he first won. I just thought that the hostility was related to having Labour people coming into No 10 Downing Street after thirteen years, and having to allow a political secretary to have as much power within the Prime Minister's office as the Civil Service had. I attributed it to that rather than to being a woman.

A woman has to work much harder. If you go to a committee, you have to read every single paper there is to be read, either put to you for that month's meeting or put to you earlier. You've got to know every single thing about that subject before you sit down. The man doesn't, and at

241

most committee meetings I attend, or have attended, I find that they often have not bothered. They read, say, the minutes of the last meeting, and they know that one issue is particularly important, so they read around that. But the rest of the stuff they don't bother to read. But if you are there and one question comes up and you just happen not to have read that, if you are a woman, they turn and look at you as much as to say, one would expect that, she wouldn't be quite up to it. The general level of criticism is the innuendo that, if you're a woman, you're either diverted by home events or by the fact that you're really not up to doing the job. I don't think I've ever been anywhere where that isn't the case.

I think you meet patronizing men every day in your life, in every walk of life. It comes with 'dear' said to you from the front of the lorry driver's cab, or a taxi driver, or a bus driver, up to the very top, in the City of London, Lloyd's or whatever, or the Law Courts. That is something you have to put up with, and you have to learn to live with. In fact it's one of the bad habits of the leader of the Labour Party today. He likes to say 'love' to you as he goes by. It's irritating when you have that, 'Hello, love'. It's meant in a very warm-hearted way, but it's slightly patronizing without the man realizing he is doing it. That's a run-of-the-mill thing women put up with every day.

I don't fear ageing. I've always had a great fantasy that I would be a wonderful old lady in a wheelchair, when I would be able to say all the things I haven't been able to say before. And you can do it, because you can sound as if you are going a bit senile, and you shout at the top of your voice. And you wave a stick and all that. I have a sort of fantasy about the comfort and, touch wood, fairly good health of old age. I look forward to what it can offer. I've been happier with every decade. As soon as it gets to the round figure, I adjust myself. There's no way back. You've got to go forward. And I find that life is so exciting. I am not frightened. I'm very regretful that I can't live on to see some of the exciting things I think are going to happen. That I do regret. I'd love to be in there, see travelling into space, watch the world becoming, I think, a friendlier place eventually, when the barriers are down and you can communicate across the world by satellite.

I think I'd rather have been a man, because I would have liked to have got things done in my own right rather than have been mainly the staff officer who helped to get things right, or get them wrong. I think it's been a man's world. I don't think it necessarily always will be, but yes, I think I'd like to have been a man.

Esther B. Ferguson: I have never been aware of one day in my life, of one major meeting, before this particular marriage to Jim Ferguson, where I ever felt for a minute that if I could be kicked out of the world, that life and the issues would become stronger. It is almost annihilating. It is so devastating if you happen to be a woman alive today who happens to be issue-orientated and caring. You are never not aware of where you really are not wanted. Ever.

We now know that most women work in this country, and for that matter in the rest of the world, because they have to work, not for the chic of it. What I intuitively discovered in my early twenties was that women in the traditional system never make it – not in banking, not in business, not in publishing, not in art. There are few exceptions. In fact, the only way women can create a power base and survive and be able to become leaders is outside of the traditional power base. Some of the most famous leaders have all come from outside the traditional power bases, meaning they never worked for industry. If you look at the first woman vice-presidential candidate here, Geraldine Ferraro, she came from Academia; if you look at Jeane Kirkpatrick, she was a professor in college, she never worked in the traditional sense. If you look at Maggie Thatcher, and you look at Golda Meir, and you look at Indira Ghandi, they never made it in the traditional sense. By the miracle of me instinctively knowing that, I made sure that, even when I came to New York and had nothing jobs, I always volunteered my time when I was in those nothing jobs, and I took on the major issues of the day. When I was in my twenties in New York, I took on the issue of preventive as opposed to crisis medicine. As an example, all doctors are trained to treat the disease when you have it, when in fact that health-care system has almost brought this nation to its knees, as well as England and the rest of the world. If you don't look at it from the prevention stance, you're not going to be around. So I helped form the first preventive medical institute in American history, the American Health Foundation. I also, in my early twenties, put together the first major consortium: HMO – Health Maintenance Organization. I was twenty-something years old. I was never thinking of history or what I was doing. My sense had always been that private industry is the way for nations to grow in the wholesome sense, not through socialistic trends.

What a nation can do for itself is better than what governments can do for it. With that sense of inner being, and a struggle for survival, I started forming a network of friends and I became more interested in the people who were giving more of themselves to humanity. Because I knew the way I was put down and treated was because I am small and diminutive and bubbly and outgoing. All the traits that you put on a

man, 'follow through', 'vivacious', 'intense', 'interested', for women
are: 'come on too strong', 'don't pay enough attention', 'flighty', 'full of
fluff', 'more feminine than they are brains'. Yet here I am, head of one
of the largest organizations in this nation, and I'm the only American
woman, get the odds of this, who has ever married two Fortune 500
chairmen. Think of the odds – most people don't *meet* one, far less
marry two. And I look back and realize that the reason why I was
attracted to that group of inordinately conservative brains was that they
are the most, probably as a total package, conservative individuals in
the world. It's because they were consistently ethically powerful. They
never lost their sense of what's right and what's wrong, and never
deviated from that. And because that to me was where real power came
from, I was attracted to that kind of person, as they were to me. And
when I look back over that, it's just staggering. You also learn in this
country, you can be married to the most powerful people in the world
yet you do not share that power. It is never translated. You look at
every wife of every past president of this nation, you look at every wife
of every United States senator, you look at every wife of the Fortune
500, and you find me five, much less fifty, in the last fifty years who've
ever been able to go on in any unique, I mean powerful way. You won't
find them. Of that, I'm sure. Because I know the world of Fortune 500
and I know industry and I know politics, and I know where the wives of
most past presidents are today. Because no matter what the evolution of
women has been, it has been very noticeable in history that the male and
female together have never shared it, nor been a part of it together. In
my case, I accidentally found a man who then allowed me for the first
time in my life to bloom and become the best of what I could become,
and very quickly. Because now, in the last four years, I'm on six boards
and I'm getting ready to start one of the largest public campaigns in
American history on this issue of the drop-out. Here I am, lucky, living
in New York, owning a Fleur Cowles painting – from my sterling friend
Fleur – and a Picasso in the same room, when six years ago I couldn't
eat. I have now the strength and the friendship of the extraordinary
globe, like the Fleurs of this world and a staggering group of influential
Americans who are backing me to become the national spokesperson
for one of the largest educational social issues ever to have affected this
nation in this decade. But, in many ways, from nothing to here has been
hard.

Annie Flanders: There's good and bad in everything, and they balance,
and if you use your advantages as a woman and let your femininity come
out, you've got an advantage over a man every time.

When I left college, I went for a job on Wall Street. There were 150 applicants. I was the only woman. I got the job because I was the only one they could remember. There were 149 men and one woman, and they decided for the first time to give the job to a woman. I was a stock analyst and they'd never had a woman before, and it was in a very conservative Wall Street firm and I was the first woman stock analyst they ever hired. So it was definitely an advantage.

I wouldn't be in business today if it weren't for my banker, and it's truly because he thinks I'm a gorgeous woman and has a mad crush on me and went out of his brains and did illegal things to keep us in business in the early days when we had no money.

I wouldn't want to be a man. Men have a really rotten time. I feel sorry for men. Men seem to have all the disadvantages. Men have had instilled in them this responsibility, this need to have to grow up to amount to something, to have a career, to be able to take care of a family, to be the one who is very practical, to have to be the one to come on to a woman. They have to be trained to be the aggressor when they could be sensitive and not want to be that way. Men have a much harder time. I've never ever in my entire life even for one second wanted to be a man.

Lorraine Stanley-Ford: I find men less patronizing now. Much less than when I was flying, for example, because there you are a permanently sun-tanned vegetable handing out trays; nobody requires anything of you other than that you turn up on time. Passengers treat you patronizingly, the flight-deck technical crews tend to treat stewardesses as little sort of flibbertigibbets, not worth much, and if you sit and actually talk about serious subjects with the air crew, they don't want to listen because it's all too terribly difficult. All they want to do is sit with a beer, relax and talk about who did what in Bahrain or Singapore or wherever it happens to be. They don't like serious subjects. If you bring one up, they say, oh my God, Lorraine's trying to be highbrow again. It's a very shallow kind of environment.

Christina Foyle: I always most wanted to be in the book trade. I really liked it and I don't care for family life. I like being among books, and I've liked doing everything I do at Foyle's, and I love the country, but I wouldn't care to have a family or be a housewife. I'm not suited to it, because I've never cooked or done any kind of housework.

I could always persuade people. I was young and quite pretty, so I could get away with murder for years and years. Especially in the war. It was a great benefit being a woman. I didn't have to go into the Army. I think most men are very nice to women. I've always found them helpful. Also, running the business, we employ a lot of men. I find I work perfectly well with men. I've never had any problems at all. I think you're much better as a woman, you have a much better time. You're not so plagued by officials. I think men have a much rougher time than women. People give way to you, they don't worry you. I mean, I've been lucky in every conceivable way. I've never regretted being a woman.

When I first came to Foyle's, it was a wonderful time. There were very many great writers about: Bernard Shaw and Wells and Kipling, Conan Doyle. They all used to come into the shop, and they were charming to me. That's why I started my luncheons, because customers used to say, you're so lucky, you meet all these great people, I wish I had your opportunities. So I said to my father, we ought to give a luncheon and let our customers come and meet these writers. So my father said, well, you've nothing much to do, why don't you arrange it? That's how our luncheons came about. But I found that, although I was so young, they never patronized me or talked down to me at all. I used to go round and call on all these people, asking them to come and speak, and they always said yes. And we've had them from that day to this. The first lunch we gave was for Lord Darling, the famous Lord Chief Justice, and Lord Alfred Douglas came, who had been sent to prison over the Wilde affair years before; and then our most recent lunch was for Jeffrey Archer, who wasn't born when we started them. So it's been marvellous, and I can hardly think of a time when I've had any unpleasant experiences.

Lynne Franks: I like being a woman, in everything I like being a woman. I don't even mind the boring things like getting fat and having periods.

My biggest fear is old age, not just from the point of view of getting ugly, but death. As a Buddhist, of course, one believes in everlasting life, so I have this slight conflict inside where I accept that life is everlasting, that it goes on, that we come back, that we should make the most of this life and accept there is a further life and so on. But I also have tremendous fear. I'm thirty-eight years old, my friends are all about thirty-five to forty, and we sit round discussing our lines, horrible, horrible, watching the body go, especially when you are like me and you don't do anything about it. I sit there saying, oh my God, and do nothing about it, absolutely nothing.

Rebecca Fraser: I don't think we were in any way brought up to consider ourselves anything but rather superior to men. The idea of feminism has, in a way, come to me very late, because I assumed women were absolutely equal to men, so it's only when you go to the market place that you realize women are very much discriminated against.

I think you have to work twice as hard if you're a woman to get yourself taken seriously. I think being a woman is a sort of first layer that makes people assume you're not serious. I think eventually you can get heard, but it's a battle.

Gisèle Galante: As a journalist, for example, I know I'm not treated the way I should be, definitely not. I know that the men working as journalists for *Paris-Match* are paid much more. And they're more respected. But to be a woman is sometimes an advantage. For example, they gave me an interview with Jacques Chaban-Delmas, a former prime minister of France, because he likes a pretty woman. And a lot of assignments they give me are assignments with men not women. I would say 70 or 80 per cent of people I interview are men. For instance, I did an interview with Kashoggi. If I had been a man, it would have been extremely difficult.

To be able to love someone and be loved, I would say that's No 1. That's maybe because I lacked that when I was a child, and so I'm looking for it. I'm looking for some kind of recognition in that way.

Teri Garr: In show business and the movie business, not so much the theatre but films, it's the most attractive who gets the chance. It doesn't even matter if you can't act or have no talent at all. If you are attractive and sexy, you get a chance, where someone who's plain, ordinary, can be just as talented or smart, but she don't get a chance. I don't think this applies to men.

Women don't have the tenacity, or they are not taught you can fight for this money. In the old days, it was unheard of for a woman to even go and say I want equal pay. I think this influenced me a great deal, and later in life, during my salad days as an actress, I worked on Sonny and Cher shows, and there were five guys and me. The guys made $600 a week and I made $280. And every week I went to the producer, and he'd put his feet up on the desk and say, what can I do for you? I'd say, I want a raise, I want to get the same money as the other guys, I want at least half as much as they are getting, what the hell's going on here? But

I would never get the raise. And he would kind of placate me and patronize me and laugh me out of the door, and I would leave thinking, I guess I'm lucky to have this job, I guess I could be a waitress, I guess I could be a file clerk some place. But inside it was making me so angry. It's a strong motivator. One of these days, I'm going to show this guy.

Men automatically get more money. The top men actors get more than the women actors. It's just an automatic thing when you get to the top of the heap, whatever that is. Women will get $750,000 for a movie, men will get a million. Even when Meryl Streep was a star, and she got an unknown actor like Jeremy Irons to play opposite her, he got more money than she got. When my mother was struggling to bring up three children on her own, I would see her pulling huge racks of clothes back and forth, and she worked with this very good friend of hers, and she told me one time that he made more money than she did. I must have been twelve years old, but I said, mum, how come he makes more money than you do when you do the same job that he does? And she said, well, his wife is sick and he has a son to take care of. I said, but mum, you have no husband and you have three children and you do the same job as he's doing, and he makes more money than you, I don't understand.

If women are, in fact, equal to men intellectually and emotionally, then the only reason they are not succeeding in certain areas and certain fields is because they don't have the confidence, they are afraid and intimidated by men. I know I am. But I've also seen certain people who go *punch* through this. Women that come from poor black families become doctors, brilliant people make something of their lives against all odds. So it's possible to do it. I think it's important to have some kind of a little steel girder inside you that doesn't let you be knocked down or shattered because of certain things people say to you. I'd like to be out there in society, achieving and winning and playing the big game with the boys.

I have relatives in my family who are very very smart women, college degrees, PhDs, and married, and they spend their day making centre-pieces out of logs, and I would kill for this education. I couldn't afford it or I couldn't do it, and I think what a waste this is. But they are taught, through society, that the best thing to do is go to college and get an MRS degree. Better yet, an MRSDR degree. What kind of goal is that for a woman? To live through a man.

It's a subliminal idea that women have one purpose, and that is to have children, raise children, and run a house. If they do have a serious thing to say, or some point of view, they are really not listened to, or they are listened to on a certain level and then patronized. Women are not taught how to compete. Men are taught, as young boys, football, baseball, things where they compete. There are rules, and they win and they lose. Football is about territory, it's war on one level, it's just give me this land, I'll fight for this land, and it's physical. And women are never taught a thing that's competitive. So they grow up unable to fight back, so when a man patronizes them and says, yes, and pats them on the head, they don't know how to come back. You're put down faster and you shut up instinctively.

I think it's easier to be a man in this world if you want to do anything. I haven't been able to relax into this thing of just shut up, do the dishes, have babies. I'll get to it eventually. But it hasn't been an easy thing for me to accept.

I couldn't name an advantage. I find it very hard to be a woman. I wouldn't rather be a man, men have to go to war, always be macho and fighting and they can't cry. But what are the advantages of being a woman? You've got me there.

Pamela Gems: I think, for a long time, I thought I was a boy. We lived on a marsh during those years, and I was very wild, I was just like a boy. It's hard to imagine now I am old and fat. But I fought as a boy, and I always had a stick. When you are the lowest, you are despised in the social hierarchy in a small town, so I was always very aggressive. As my brothers grew older, they became stronger than me because of the sex difference, and there came a day when I couldn't beat up my brothers if they misbehaved, so that was a rather bad day. I'm not so much motherly as older-sisterly; that is, that has always been my attitude to men: protective and bullying. You find it hard to lose those patterns.

I didn't really find disadvantages in being a woman. You have only your own life to go by. I am a feminist by condition and through politics, but war came when I was fifteen. Now, during wartime, men and women suddenly have amazing equality. Suddenly women are quite capable of ferrying large Liberator aeroplanes and becoming spies, or being dropped by parachute, and the camaraderie between the classes and between the sexes is amazing and wonderful. Of course, we all thought, after the war we'd have to get rid of the public schools and everything else. We didn't expect to revert. At that time, I didn't come across discrimination, and I was happy to be a woman in that I didn't have to fight and actually kill someone, though I guess I would have done it

249

then. I couldn't have done it after having children; then you change. It takes too much of your life to produce a human being; the sin of killing becomes total.

The first thing I learned when I came into the theatre was that, if you open the *Radio Times* or the *TV Times*, there's twice as much work offered to an actor as an actress, week by week, year by year. That means, five years out of drama school, the boy is twice as experienced therefore twice as good as his sister. The parts offered to women are written by men mostly, and they always are of an object, a sexual object – what I call the girl in the front seat of a car. I watch it like a hawk every time. She has no lines, she's not a protagonist. It's the man who has the action, who has the challenge, who is changed by his experience, who wins or loses. The girl is there to smile and be there and greet him, to be saved by him. I don't mind that, I quite like being saved. I don't want to throw the baby out with the bathwater. But when I came into the theatre, the lack of opportunity for actresses absolutely astonished me.

I have a young woman friend who is black, a very bright girl, got all her exams and wanted to be a vet. The most right-wing group of surgeons you can imagine is in the veterinary school. They tried very hard to discourage her; she had to get very, very good marks. When she applied, her marks were so much better than the boys' that they had to say yes. The day she went to register, the woman at the desk looked up, saw she was female and black and said, my dear, wouldn't you be happier doing secretarial work? Can you believe it? Now that's an extreme example. Some women are lucky. Some women are foxy, they will succeed on a man's back, or become his mistress and get a job that way. I worked in the BBC and I've seen that happen. Sometimes the man gets drunk so the woman does the job, the woman does the job again, and suddenly she has the job. But there aren't enough jobs to go round. We have such a problem to get women directors into theatre; we need them for various reasons, to explore certain kinds of work. But how can the men move over? I can't say to Ron Daniels, do you mind giving up your job because, fair dos, you don't have any women working there? Men say, we're glad to have a woman if she's good enough, we're not chauvinist, she just has to be good enough. But she can't be good enough until she's done the number of productions that men have done, with the privileges they have for production. It's impossible. In the theatre, it is really impossible. I see no sign of it changing. I'm very depressed about it, actually.

There is no doubt that, if you are to succeed in anything, you must be persistent and dedicated. And a lot of that is to do with whether you are lucky with energy, whether you have a good adrenalin, a supersonic system. I don't. I think there is a way and I think a lot of women haven't found it. I have just been in America, and women there do it at great cost, the ones who become mock men, the ones who become strident. Almost worse are the women who go, as it were, into drag. They become super-female, you know. They're very honeychile about everything, and their urine would etch glass. That is really frightening to live with, and men and women are, I think, repelled.

I couldn't dream of being a man, because of having a child, because it is such an ecstatic experience. On the other hand, I do believe in reincarnation and I would like to be a man next time to experience that.

Susan George: I think I'm treated very much as an equal by just about every man I know. I don't think there's a man I know who would overrule me on a decision. And that includes my husband.

Alexandra M. Giurgiu: My upbringing was totally sexist, but I myself made a distinction. For example, when I first started college, I transferred to engineering school after my first semester. I didn't tell my parents until afterwards, and my grandmother, who is really from another century, was appalled I had entered the sciences because it was a man's field. I felt that if you paid too much attention to the issue, then it got to you. That is, if you were conscious of the fact you were a woman as opposed to a man, your psychology or psyche was influenced and you could be intimidated. Obviously professors who had been there for years, and who did not like the concept of having women in engineering school, would try to intimidate me. There were definite disadvantages. However, I never really paid much attention to them.

A woman definitely has to do more than a man to prove herself, to establish credibility. But I think that's a fact we should live with because it's only very recently that women were educated. The modern woman has more of a choice. Now, what the choice is, is irrelevant. I walked into the elevator one day and heard a woman saying, can you believe she decided to give up trading Eurobonds to have babies? It made me angry, because this woman missed the whole point. What is wonderful is that we are now free to do either. It's much more difficult to balance the two, and there's a lot more pressure put on a woman who tries to combine both. In the interim, the man is going through a parallel crisis,

251

because he's no longer a pillar of the castle, he is co-operating. There's much more of a co-operation spirit in relations between man and woman now.

Victoria Glendinning: I think both my husbands – I've been married twice – have invented me and reinvented me, because they believed I could do what I didn't or hadn't thought of. My first husband was my professor at Oxford, and my second husband is a distinguished Irish literary man whom I met later. They both saw something in me which I didn't know was there. Other important people were John Gross, whom I worked for at *The Times Literary Supplement*, who also invented me. He used me in a way that I did not know I could be used, and because it happened, you then respond and you do it; and Claire Tomalin, whom I first worked for in the *New Statesman*. She gave me quite difficult things to do, and because she gave them to me, I did them. I think all these people had an idea of me which I had not perceived, and therefore they furthered me.

In the 1960s, it was accepted that my husband's career came first. There were various occasions when I made little bids to get out of that and could not do so. Looking back, I find it strange that I submitted. But that is partly history. I think journalism and writing, which are the things I have done, are professions where what you produce is what matters. I don't think anybody gives a shoot what sex you are, and latterly I think being a woman is almost an advantage. I had one publisher say to me, nothing sells now, except by women for women – in an almost angry way.

I like my double life. That suits me. I like my secret domestic life, and I like sallying forth to be a public person. To have all one and all the other would be a maiming, and I think that the dual life is really perfect for anybody. Most men don't have that, because they don't have the secret domestic life in which they know every corner of their house, and exactly what needs washing, and exactly what needs painting and the children. So I think women who can manage – and it's a question of energy – have everything the world has to offer.

I practise being a very old lady, stopping being sexually attractive and that sort of thing. I think about it in terms of just how eccentric I am going to be. I think the freedom of being old is that you no longer have to pretend to be as nice as you seem, or as ordinary as you seem, or as amiable and helpful as you seem. I see myself getting rather stroppy and difficult and odd. And I think it's going to be wonderful. I think it will

252

be very sad when the party's over, but I don't have *angst* about men not looking at me on the tube any more.

Lady Annabel Goldsmith: When I first got married, I never thought about discrimination. I was a woman, and if people didn't take me seriously, I didn't think anything very odd about it, because that's how it was. I didn't resent it, I was no different from any other woman, and I was perfectly happy. I did what I wanted to do. My life had changed. I wasn't writing for the *Daily Mail*, but I was married and having a baby. The die was cast in a way. Maybe, if I had gone to work on the *Daily Mail*, I would have been more aware. In a sense, what I did was to go from one rather protected environment into another one. In other words, I didn't stand on my own. I went into marriage as a baby, and was then protected by Mark, so I never stood on my own feet at that stage.

I have heard – I'm obviously going to be slightly influenced here by Jimmy – that women think with their ovaries, not counting Mrs Thatcher, who he thinks is wonderful. He says that women, on the whole, aren't really capable of taking a detached view because they think with their bodies rather than with their minds. That's his view, it's not particularly mine. But it may just be that it's difficult for a woman to make a snap decision in business because, maybe, she can't detach her mind from her body.

I like being a woman. Please God, don't let me ever be reincarnated as a man. I think men have an awful life. I would hate to be a man, I really would.

Isabel Goldsmith: You have more freedom as a woman. There are no restrictions, no rules around you. You are not expected to be a provider, you're not expected to be in a career, you're not expected to be chairman at forty or whatever. There are no set paths, no rigid sets of rules as there are for men. Women are not threatened by the sense of failure which men have like a sword of Damocles over their heads.

A woman has to smile to the waiter; why should she smile to the waiter? A man does not smile to the waiter; he has authority immediately. The woman has always to be in a seducing position. And, in fact, why should she? But a woman who doesn't do it is just told, oh God, what a tough bitch. It's unfair, but that's the way it is.

Ever since I was twenty-one, I've felt too old. I find ageing so worrying. Less attractive to men is the first bad news. The second bad news is that you are so much closer to death, and it would be so much nicer to die looking young.

Angela Gordon: Biologically, women go through a period of becoming more emotional. I used to hate it when my mother would say, are you having a period, Angela? And I was so angry and I would say, no, I'm not, I'm just reacting in the normal way. I'm thumping the table and then, next day, of course it would happen. Dammit, I hated that, but she was right, and you learn to accept it. I mean, don't resign this week, because you're probably just rather emotionally fraught. This happens to your body, it's something you can't control.

Even supposing you combine brains, looks, energy, softness, and supposing you get there, you're still going to find enormous resistance because that spells success, hard work and so on. And there are people that actually quite happily put all their energy into seeing that you fall. A successful man wouldn't be resented in the same way. Especially if he was rather fat and sweaty and wore an eyeshade and looked the image, looked the stereotype. I find people are so terribly bound up by stereotypes, so they won't give you a chance. But you've got to give yourself a chance. You've got to take them on head-on, and you end up regarded as a sort of aggressive harridan.

I'm discovering now, almost at the age of thirty, that there obviously are disadvantages, because, first of all, I'm finding it slightly a strain that I'm not married. It's a self-imposed strain, not a strain from my mother or anything else, but I'm finding that quite difficult to cope with because I think, Goddammit, I'm going to have to have children. Why am I going to have children? Because I am going to reach the stage when I'm forty-eight where I'll feel I've lost out. I think I'm approaching a crisis. I'm beginning to feel I've lost out in that I've pursued a career, and although I've a lot of good friends, I'd quite like, at this stage, to have a sort of mad passion.

When you're old, you can be as flirtatious as you like and no one will find you attractive any more. I'm frightened of that. I thought the other day, God, I've got lines on my face; and I thought, I'm going to have to rely on my personality suddenly – you know, hoping that one's got a personality, because I thought for a long time I'd probably relied a bit on being, I can't say a pretty face (because a lot of people would say, Christ, she's not at all pretty), but being presentable. The only reason for all this bloody soul-searching is because I haven't got a lover at the moment, I suppose. I want someone to tell me, don't worry, kid, you're OK. I split up with my boyfriend last June and I haven't had anyone since who'll send me flowers and things. I suppose women need this, and it must really make girls quite tetchy. Anyway, that presumably accounts for one's soul-searching, and a lot of the views I'm expressing now perhaps I wouldn't express in six months.

Felicity Green: I don't think there are any inherent disadvantages in being a woman. The disadvantages tend to be material ones. Until very recently, you couldn't have a bank account, you couldn't buy anything on hire purchase. If you were an entrepreneur, you had difficulty in persuading a bank manager that, as a female, you were a responsible person. You come up against patronage, you come up against condescension, you are discounted by insensitive men in areas where you have a contribution to make. This is sounding like a diatribe against men. Unfortunately, this has been the sum total of my experience. In one of my incarnations, I was publicity director of a newspaper group. I had to reprimand a sales manager of a television company, whom I had never met, and invited him to see me in my office. And he came in and put his arms around me and said, now luvvy, what is all this nonsense? Now that is extremely difficult to deal with for about ten seconds, and then you assert yourself. And then you get a reputation for being assertive.

It is well known that women have a terrible time getting into politics. We have no more women in the House of Commons now in 1987, than we had in 1927. I think we have two fewer, as far as I can remember – twenty-five instead of twenty-seven. The prejudice there is dangerous and dreadful, and although the Labour Party make great noises about being the party that is caring, and the party that is concerned with women, they have in their organization the most sexist body in the country – the TUC. The TUC have been anti-women to an absolutely disgraceful extent, not in what they say, but in what they do. They pay lip-service to women. And as for Mrs Thatcher, it is my deep belief that she is really a man. It is patently obvious that Mrs Thatcher doesn't like women and women feel this. Recently with a run-up to an election she realized the importance of wooing women and took two more women into her Cabinet. But Mrs Thatcher is not a woman who warms to women, and therefore women do not warm to Mrs Thatcher.

I am afraid there are many women who are incapable of realizing their potential because they do not get themselves into an environment of sensitivity where they are acknowledged. Ultimately, there will be a woman editor of a national newspaper. I think, in the past, there have been women capable of doing this job, but they have never been in a position where this was acceptable. It is becoming marginally more acceptable, month by month, week by week, day by day. The person who actually takes over will be an exceptional woman, but she will be the last in a line of exceptional women who were not in the right place at the right time or sitting in front of the right man. Because women are still in a position where favour has to be bestowed upon them by a man.

It is difficult to discriminate now in any visible way because, as we all know, it is illegal. I think the discrimination is still there, and I think it will be still there while there are so few women. After all, we are getting only the first waves now of competent, educated, trained, skilled women. I think we have entered into a funny, probably transitional phase. It is the smart thing, it is the progressive thing, it is the thing that gives the man conversational grist when he is out at dinner – I employ women, I am pro-women, I have made a woman my personal assistant, I have made a woman head of my sales department. I think men are pre-occupied with doing the right thing for the wrong reason, but it doesn't frankly matter as long as they are doing it. However, they are still bestowing patronage, and it shouldn't be seen as anything else. There are very few men able to take the next step, which says, I am looking for a partner in my business, I am going to get a woman because I think she will contribute something. They will say, I am going to look for an accountant, I think maybe I'll look for a woman. But it is always, in my experience, in a slightly or substantially subservient role. And I think it is going to take a long time to eliminate that from the male psyche.

One of the most beautiful women I ever worked for, my first boss, who was divine looking and very intelligent and very funny, I remember looking in the mirror when she must have been sixty-five and saying, don't let anybody ever kid you that growing old is fun, it's hell. That stuck in my mind. It's not hell yet, but it might well be. And it's much more of a disadvantage to women than to men, of course, because men judge women by how they look and women do not judge men by how they look.

Laura Gregory: I have been lucky in that I was a pretty young girl. I think pretty women have an advantage over women that perhaps aren't quite as pretty; and men – their first opinion of a woman is unfortunately her looks. So, as a young girl, I was always taken out, always asked to parties, always the one people wanted to have around as a bit of decoration. So I had a lot of fun as a woman, and therefore nothing seemed to be a disadvantage about being female until I first started my company and I was treated with suspicion by bank managers and people I needed.

It is easy, as a woman, to get to see people. If you are female and you have a nice voice on the phone and you talk genially without belching and screeching, I find it very easy to see people. I also find that women are very intuitive about people, moods, feelings. That's the reason I employ more women than men for jobs where dealing with people is something important, and producing is primarily dealing with people, your clients or your suppliers.

I pity men enormously that they have to be seen to be supporting the family if they are married whereas, if the wife doesn't want to work, she doesn't have to work. The pressure on them must be enormous because they have to go out and they have to earn a living for their wives and children. Women do not have that pressure. If a man fails in his career, it may mean bankruptcy or a heart attack. For a woman, if means that you go home and your husband is there to look after you – unless you are a woman alone, and then you start again. And it is very easy for a woman to start again.

A woman can achieve a top job in any field nowadays. Maybe ten years ago, the story was different. But for my generation, there's no target one can't set oneself and hope to achieve.

I've just gone for it, just gone and steamed ahead, and if I've been knocked down I've jumped back up again. Somebody won't see me one day, I'll make sure they see me another day. It is just an attitude, and my attitude is, nobody's going to stop me.

Katya Grenfell: All the girls I've photographed recently, they've always said that if I had been a man they would never have done it.

Elsa Gress: I consider myself an example of fulfilled humanhood rather than fulfilled womanhood, which is not to say that I have not, apart from a few years as a child and adolescent, felt perfectly comfortable, indeed happy, to be a woman and possess the ultimate power: that of bearing children. I have three of those, now grown, and am happy about them, as well as about a good, long-standing marriage. I have a fine education (doctorate in comparative literature) and have had a fruitful artistic and intellectual career in addition to as many lovers and friends as a person could hope for. Of course, there have been long periods of despondency about work and life, and losses, and pain, and sacrifices. And there have been instances of discrimination, but of a superficial kind, easily dealt with – actually more easily dealt with than the discrimination exercised by certain 'sisters'.

Baroness Grimond: I wanted to be a boy from the first moment I could think of. In fact, one of my dreams was that a miracle would take place and I would turn into a boy.

It's only since I became involved in public life to a limited extent that I have been conscious that women are discriminated against. My mother is a good example. I was very conscious of the fact she was herself a frustrated woman and that accounted for a great many of the difficult sides of her character. The reason she was unreasonable and made life difficult for lots of people was because she was a frustrated person of great ability who would have felt fulfilled if she'd had an opportunity to administer or get into public life. When she was made a governor of the BBC, which is only rather a minor activity, I can't tell you how she enjoyed it. It was almost pathetic. This was the first opportunity she had ever had to do something of this kind, where she could make a difference, take decisions, and make an impact on a large organization. Now that didn't happen until about 1947, and by that time she would have been nearly sixty. So I certainly think, looking at her life, that she would have been much happier, and probably everyone else near her would have been happier, if she had had the opportunity to do something. Women are discriminated against by people's attitudes. It is a psychological thing to a certain extent. It's the same as the social discrimination that used to be practised in England, but less now, by people who had been educated in a certain way, who had been to public school. I well remember when you couldn't be captain of a cricket eleven if you were a professional, if you were a paid cricketer. It was said, and people believed it, that unless you were an amateur, which usually meant that you had been to Oxford or Cambridge or a public school and spoke in a special kind of way, you couldn't exercise this kind of authority. It's rather like that, being a woman. The governing classes in this country find it easier to work with people out of the same drawer as themselves. It means making less effort. You are less likely to be misunderstood. Well, in working with women, men feel they have to make a special kind of effort, that they mustn't be rude, and the whole thing becomes slightly more of a strain. So if you are a woman pitchforked into sharing responsibility, or, worse still, exercising responsibility over men, you begin with all the men feeling they are going to have to make a special effort and so would rather not have you on their committee.

When I first started having to do with politics, and having to go and make speeches, very often it was assumed as a matter of course that my husband had written my speech for me. Because I, for some reason, would be unable to string two words together. Certainly, you do find those sort of attitudes.

If you're a woman, you feel you can't make a mistake; if you make a mistake, it's because you are a woman. Can you imagine a woman making the mistakes President Reagan has made? And getting away with them? It wouldn't be allowed. After once or twice making a mistake, you're for the chopper.

People like Mrs Edwina Currie and Mrs Margaret Thatcher are people who have cast-iron self-confidence, and it is rare when a woman gets right to the top without having this quality, though it does happen. Mrs Aquino doesn't have that quality at all. She's a very feminine woman who does things, as far as I can see, from a rather ignorant standpoint, but in a rather feminine way. She somehow muddles rather successfully. But I think the sort of woman who disarms everybody is someone like Mrs Golda Meir, because she was a sort of universal mother figure. Those are the sort of women who break down prejudices, but you don't really achieve those positions until you've been in public life a long time. Mrs Thatcher doesn't have that Mother Earth quality at all, and I think successful women need to have that quality if they're going to have an easy ride, otherwise you need the brazenness of Edwina Currie and Mrs Thatcher, who obviously don't question themselves at any stage.

When I was very young, I thought it would be the most terrible thing to be grey-haired, but when it happens, there are so many compensations. I think one is free from a great many self-questionings and fears, and indeed one's confidence is so much greater than when one is young and not really quite sure what one's there for. I think getting old, alas, one enjoys more and more.

Amy Gross: I agree with those who say that intuition is what the underdog, the slave class develops out of necessity. I see women reading men's faces as slaves must read their master's face. Is he in a good mood, is he hungry, what does he want? I believe it's for self-protection.

Also, just in nurturing a baby who can't express him- or herself verbally, you do develop those intuitive skills.

Women go to shrinks because the men don't talk to them. We all do. I know I do. I think it's to do with loneliness in America. A friend can sympathize with you, but a shrink can give you the words that knock you out of the orbit you have been circling in. A shrink can produce change. A friend is good for sympathy. That's the difference, for me. I think there is tremendous loneliness. We all live away from our families, with men who don't talk to us. American women are very introspective. We want to know how things work, how we work; we want to develop. We have this idea of development, of growing up, growing up right.

There's a phrase that has come into vogue now: the glass ceiling. It is said that in corporations these go-getter women get up to middle management and then they hit the glass ceiling. You can't see it, but they can't go any further. I would think it's more prejudice than the woman's own reluctance to go further, although I do think that women are more likely to think at a certain point about what makes a good life. Is the hundred-hour week what I want for myself, is that a good life? What about marriage, what about love, what about children, what about friends, what about, you know, the time necessary to pull myself back together? I think they're more likely to think about that, because of their training. Women are basically raised with the idea that human relations are what life is about.

Miriam Gross: I think it's very rare for girls to be trained to have confidence, whereas, even unconsciously, I think parents and teachers train boys to have confidence in innumerable little ways that one can't remember, that one doesn't notice at the time. No one does it for girls, at least in my generation. I think the assumption was that one was going to get married and it was pointless to teach one to stand up and say something or apply for something. For instance, at Oxford, I would never in a thousand years have tried to be president of any club or the Union or anything. It was miles from anything anyone had ever told me was in my reach. It was something just not on. I think you have to be, genetically or by fluke, very confident. A girl has got to be terrifically pushed by someone or other to get anywhere.

When I worked at the *Observer*, which I did for many years, if anything interesting happened, something political or they were making big decisions, they would go into little groups, the men, and ignore the women, which was very annoying. Even when I was one of the chief editors there – I was editor of one of the sections and three pages, which is a lot, were under my control – even then, whether it was internal or external politics or big decisions, the men would be unaware of doing it, but they would ignore the women.

For seventeen years, I was deputy to Terence Kilmartin, who is literary editor, and that was a nice job and it went nicely with having children. Nevertheless, I was useful to Terry Kilmartin, and when he was away, sometimes for six weeks, I did his job perfectly well on my own without my own deputy. Yet (I don't want to say anything against him or anyone) he would never have thought of promoting me. I was too useful to him, and I was too unassertive ever to push. It also did suit me quite well, I won't say it didn't. But there came a point, after about ten years of those seventeen, when I finally got another job on the *Observer*, as woman's editor, but there had been quite a number of years when I felt very undermined. I felt people wanted me to be where I was because I was so useful there. Also, I was not taken into the central part of the paper. I'm interested in politics and so on, and was never allowed to take part. The men involved would deny it. They would say, of course you could have, but actually I couldn't without being more assertive, which I hadn't been trained to be.

I think there's almost now a kind of lean-over-backwards to employ token women. I think if I'd been born fifteen years later it would have been very different, right from the beginning.

I very much enjoy being a woman, and I would be frightened of being a man, because I would fear failure as a man. I would fear failure in all sorts of ways, and I can disguise it as a woman. I can be successful in a way I couldn't get away with as a man.

Sometimes I fear ageing more than at other times. Sometimes I think, what a relief, when one doesn't have to go around being frightened of being rejected and all those things. At other times, I do fear it because I don't quite know what my life will be like. One is so habituated to being, as it were, in the sexual arena, that suddenly not to be in it any longer is sort of frightening.

Pamela Gross: I felt disadvantaged at Harvard, very much so. Everything was male. Even the closets didn't hold dresses well: they were short and the bar across came down so low you could only really hang a suit, never really a dress. And all the clubs were for men, there were no sororities, and the girls' club was three miles up the road. It's very much a man's school and it will always be a man's school.

Flora Groult: When I started writing books, I realized that men had a certain contempt for the work of women. One remained a feminine animal. Even if one thought in a strict, tough, strong way, like Simone de Beauvoir, men can never forget you are a woman. When you say you are working, they think you are doing embroidery or knitting. And I didn't know that, because I lived in a world where my mother was *una conquistadora* and I thought women were strong. And that men didn't mind. I think, emotionally and sexually, men are possessors, it's part of their nature.

Everything is possible now. Women have a choice and they mustn't feel ashamed if they just want to be a little woman at home, doing the soup and saying, don't do that, Jimmy. All that is good. We are diverse, we must express our diversities. What is important is that women who want to do something can do it. And now, if we want something and we are determined, we get it. Perhaps it's a bit more determination we need. Often, when I speak with men they say, woman is privileged, she can make a child. Some men want to be pregnant but they couldn't stand it half an hour – perhaps for half an hour, but not nine months. But they dream about it, like not exactly the lost paradise, but a lost feeling, a lost impression. So I think women have this privilege and must think of it as a privilege and every privilege is expensive. I think women belong to the earth, because of their biological destiny and because of something in their nature. The woman is the mother goddess. That doesn't stop her from being the tycoon, or a remarkable person, or a film star, but there is something of that in her nature. I think we have a larger range of possibilities.

Valerie Grove: Men who don't take women seriously don't interest me or influence me and tend not to be either my friends or my colleagues.

The best jobs are not the editors' jobs, sitting behind a desk, or all those terrible jobs of subbing and being executive, those nightmare executive roles and dealing with management and advertising. The best jobs are the jobs which involve going out and talking to people, that's the first fun; and then sitting quietly in solitude and writing it, which is the secondary fun, not quite as much fun as the first. And they are the nicest jobs in journalism, and all the women in journalism who have done well all do that. They might not even go out and talk to people, they may just sit and write, but it's the writing that's the fun, not the editing.

In my book, I say at one point that, if a woman is a driving force in an organization, she is regarded as bossy, pushy, but if a man is a driving force, he is a great guy, ambitious, and good for him. And Carmen Callil underlined this in the manuscript and wrote 'Yes' in the margin. Carmen is regarded, especially outside publishing by those who don't know her but who know of her, as a virago, and they assume she is this terrifying person. I've never found her to be like this, but you can't become someone in her position without getting that kind of reputation, and, of course, who wants that reputation? Not many women. We would like to be described as Gloria Steinem: soft and feminine, nice and warm and gentle.

The disadvantage of being a woman is being a mother. It's also a privilege, of course, but it circumscribes one's life for a time and there is no question about it; even if you say at the beginning, having a family is not going to change my life, I'm going to do the same as I did when I was single and fancy free, you don't. Geographically, you don't. You stay in one place and you do the safest job.

I've always felt enormously confident, but also very conscious of my limitations. What I think women do have is appreciation of whatever is given them in life: a high salary or a nice job. They appreciate it terribly and regard it as their good fortune. I think men tend to think of it as being their just desserts.

The cruellest thing that has ruled women's lives is the biological clock, because when you want children, you can't have them, and when you have children, you don't want them. It doesn't work out at all well for women, and the time when you are most needed by your family is the time when women are most liable to get the opportunity to forge ahead. When your opportunities arrive between thirty and forty, that is the time you have the children and stay at home with the nappies. The husbands can always go off at fifty and start a new life with a new woman. That is terribly unfair, the greatest unfairness of all.

I absolutely love being a woman. But the one dismal sentence in Anna Ford's book on men was this: that not a single man she talked to ever wished that he was a woman or envied the female role. Imagine what it feels like to be the completely unenvied figure, that loathed specimen, woman. But I think they're wrong, these men, they don't realize how much fun it is. However, I quite like the idea of being a man

263

for a while, a day at a time. What I'd hate, of course, is having to deal with women.

Except for certain batty old women who are very visible, most women become invisible. It's grotesque when women age. It's very sad. I will fight it in every possible way. I'm certainly not intending to go grey. I think you have to keep slim and remain as alive as possible, and if necessary go completely batty and wear mad hats, anything to be noticeable.

Georgina Hale: When I was a young girl, they hadn't invented the pill and I was constantly pregnant, so I had many, many abortions. I used to think that was terribly unfair. When I was twenty-three or twenty-two, the pill was discovered. Then I think I became a bit like a man, especially where sex was concerned. If I wanted somebody I'd have them and not really bother to talk to them, and then just get rid of them in the morning.

Jerry Hall: I always feel that men are very patronizing. But I feel that I have an advantage in a way. I can smile sweetly and things. I know that they're being patronizing, but I don't mind, because I usually get my way. I always say to myself, beneath this peroxide lies a smart brunette.

I've never been to a shrink. I think it's disgusting, I hate psychiatrists, with a passion. I think it's ego-masturbation, I really do. All these people talking about their childhood, their this and that and all the problems; their mother did this, their father did that, as if it was some important key to unlock why you're messed up. It's too much self-involvement. I think people should wipe the slate clean – every day is a new day, think positive, what do you want to do today? – and go and do it. There's no reason to think something is holding you back. That's all in your mind. If you go to any of these doctors they encourage you more and more to think about yourself and then you pay a fortune to spend all your afternoon with some boring old guy in his office. It's the worst, it's the most boring. I know so many girls, their day in New York is the hairdresser's, shopping at Bloomingdales and the psychiatrist in the afternoon. That is such a sick life. I think I'd rather not be alive than have to live like that. It's horrible. I get really upset about it. Every time I hear of anybody who's going to one, I stop them.

When I was sixteen I thought, when you're twenty-one you're old. Then I was afraid, but not any more. Now I'm very in love with Mick, we're

264

very happy, we have two beautiful babies, I feel so fulfilled. I've been modelling now for sixteen years, and I think, oh God, I've had all that time that I didn't think I was going to have; so I felt that was an extra bonus, and I'm still working, and I just don't worry any more. I think a lot of women have a real sickness. They go around doing all those weird things to themselves: they change their eyes, they change their nose, they get silicone breasts, they scrape their thighs, and they have all those horrific operations and I think it's like Frankenstein, it's horrible. I do. I can understand if you have something really wrong with you and you want to fix it. I know so many models, beautiful girls, who have been modelling for years; all of a sudden they start doing these things to themselves and then they are very depressed afterwards because when they did it they thought it was going to make them so much better that every problem would disappear. It's just like psychiatry. You can't count on anything but yourself. If you think, this is going to solve all my problems, when it doesn't then you're ten times more depressed. It's like taking cocaine. You get up then you crash further. All those things are just escapism, and they make you worse off than you were before. People should be more relaxed and comfortable with themselves. Everyone would like them better, and life would be easier. I want to live to be as old as I can. I'd like to be old and eccentric, and have lots of young friends call up.

Lucy Hughes-Hallett: I think one loses a lot by having a segregated education, and I would rather have grown up feeling more at ease with the opposite sex. But it is certainly true that, because I was never competing with boys, I never felt inferior to them. I was taught by women, then later I read English at university which certainly in those days, in the early 1970s, was considered a girl's subject. Then I worked on *Vogue* for five years, edited by Beatrix Miller, and all the people in power there were women. So, throughout all that first part of my life, I took it for granted that women could do everything, could teach, could study, could work, could be bosses. When I first started being aware of the women's movement in the early 1970s, when it became the thing, I was not very interested. I felt, perhaps rather arrogantly, that a lot of people were struggling hard to reach the position I had already reached by assuming I could do as much as I wanted – as much as I was personally capable of. Then, when I started working as a freelance journalist I suppose I had more direct experience of sexual discrimination. But, again, it was never very extreme. Quite often I would ring up an arts editor or features editor and suggest an idea for an article and he – often it would be he – would say, oh well, we're a bit busy at the moment, I've got rather a lot of stuff on the files, I'm not sure I could use anything, I'll pass you on to the women's editor – which is annoying. It's not terribly important, and I'm happy to write features for women and women's pages, but I didn't like the assumption that the women's editor is the person to whom I should be talking.

When women complain about men treating them as sex objects, they're not complaining about men being attracted to them, they're complaining about the difficulty of dropping that subject for a while. I've had times when I've been trying to discuss a perfectly straightforward, business matter with a man who has suddenly made little flirtatious jokes, and it is his way of putting me down and reminding me I'm just a girl. He probably doesn't even know he's doing it, but it immediately downgrades the woman.

I don't feel I can travel in a lot of parts of the world as freely as a man, and I resent that. I have sometimes travelled on my own and I don't terribly want to do it again. The hustling, the intense feeling of self-consciousness you get when you walk down the street in certain countries, when everyone is staring, I find not worth it, and that makes me angry. I understand the reasons, and I can't really blame anyone, but I do think it's bad luck on women. I've had very unpleasant experiences, particularly one night walking home in Italy. I was in Florence to research an article and didn't want to eat dinner in the hotel and went out to a restaurant by myself. I was followed back to the hotel by eight men. It was very frightening and unpleasant, and that can happen. Actually, it can happen in England. I've been bothered in English pubs if I have been sitting down for half an hour waiting for an appointment.

There have been times when I've envied men, and there have been times when I've come up against sexual discrimination, and my first reaction is to feel angry and to think, well, if that person is going to look at me that way, I don't want to have anything more to do with him. But then, sometimes, you do want to have more to do with him, you want to get that job, or you want just to be allowed to put your point of view.

Mira Hamermesh: All men patronize women. I curse the day I made the film *Two Women* because, since then, the rug has been pulled out from under my feet. Suddenly something was ripped from my eyes. I saw the world in which women live, and I'm part of it. It was a shock. A parallel would be if a member of the royal family was suddenly to live incognito and go to the office and be a temp. I was in a state of shock for years. I had almost a quiet breakdown, I think, because I couldn't adjust to the shock.

I once sat in an aeroplane between two men; we had conversation, we told each other the sort of things people on journeys tell each other – married, four children. Then I fell asleep, but I didn't sleep, and those two men had a conversation about me. One of them said, how do you think she makes out in the world? She travels, and does films, and, you know, she's not so young any more. And the other said, she hasn't got much time now, really, she won't do much now. Must have been fun when she was younger. Women suffer a great deal from this idea of what men expect of them. Fashion and the whole consumer economy profit from this female insecurity, which, as I understand it, is conditioned by the male assessment of what is feminine and what is not. There's a transaction whereby any man can tell me whether I'm a woman in his eyes or not. This is not something I'm born with biologically, it's not my birthright, it's something only on loan to me. And a man can say, you're not really a woman, or you're not a proper woman, or this is not how a woman acts. So it is conditioned. My sense of being a woman is forever in suspense, and needs affirmation from him, and him, and him, and him. Now that I'm aware of it, it's not very comfortable.

I have to work harder than men. I have to cover up more. I often have to make a conscious effort not to show myself as I really am. I'll give you an example. You are in the middle of a shoot. You have a male crew. (It is just beginning to be possible to assemble a woman crew, but it's very rare.) And it's a male director. He's temperamental, but he's good. Everyone will say, he's a bitch, he's a real son of a bitch, but it's a pleasure to work with him; he shouts, he bullies, but when you see the film it's worth it. If I were to shout, if I were to explode, they'd say, the bitch, she's frustrated, she has no lover. So I can't afford to be myself. First of all, I am considerate, I look at people. I have a child and learned how to look people in their eyes and immediately gauge where they are: if they're all right. Men don't have to make this effort. Another thing, whenever I voice any ideas which are censorious of the male system, of the patriarchal system, you're likely to have people say, she hates men. Nobody says Marx hated humanity because he was so critical and had ideas about about how people ruin each other within particular economic systems. But it is inevitable that people will say to me, or if not to me, then to others, what an aggressive woman. If you are competent, in control, they will accuse you of not having any feelings. When people say, oh you're so competent, I find myself reacting, saying, actually I'm not, I am terribly careless; I find I defend myself, instead of saying, yes, of course I'm competent, or even, I have a reputation for being competent. And apart from having to try twice as hard, you have to be on your toes. It's the story of the Jewish minority in the Diaspora: they tell you they are clever and do well because they have to – right? This is unfortunately the principle under which the majority of women function. We are not a minority, but we are outsiders, outside of the cultural norm, and therefore a woman out there in the world, mixing with men on so-called terms of equality, will do so on terms of suffering from men.

At home, there is an awful lot of work, women work as hard as donkeys, but they can break off when they want and they can have a think, a dream; they can have a read, they can rock something, they can think of somebody. What women lament is that men have separated themselves from those values. I don't think women really believe that men are devoid of them, because, after all, we bring up the children, and our boys are as soft and as tender and emotional, as dependent as our daughters, needing everything our daughters do, until at a particular age, those creatures suddenly become aliens. The values of the culture they stepped into take over and knock out everything they have learned from mummy's lips. The rewards are immense, the punishment immense. The reward is: you rule the world, you conquer, you go to the moon; the punishment is: you made yourself the sole controller of the world and you die for it. On the battlefield, you die. And if I am the one who is going to die, I want privileges, I want more money, more women, more speed, more adventure, I want more and more, more, more, more of everything. Because I am going to die, not you. You give birth, you give life. I'll create wonders, I'll create miracles, I'll dazzle you, I'll take you to the moon, but I also am the one who goes out on the battlefield and sorts it out for you. You must trust me. I'll sort it out for you, I'll fight wars for you, I'll conquer land for you. I may lose it for you, but it's me. So I should have privileges.

Do I enjoy being a woman? I can't say. All I know is that as a woman I have managed to live a life without killing another human being. At my age, if I had been a man, I doubt if I could have lunch without being able to declare that, in one war or another, I had a good few corpses on my conscience.

Katharine Hamnett: I remember once trying to pee standing up in the bath, aiming it and failing miserably. But, apart from that, I never felt any need to be a boy.

When I ran my first company, I wanted to go for an overdraft at the bank, and I had to fill in things saying, although I am a woman I don't need my husband's permission to sign this document; or although I'm a woman, I'm fully aware of what I'm doing. That shocked me. But then I was quite pretty and I had big tits, so I suppose that was a help also.

In my business, I didn't think it was who you knew but what you could do. And that's hard work, but then it's hard work for anybody. I don't think I had to work harder than a man, but as hard, as hard as anybody who's going to get it right. I didn't have problems in the workroom. When I did the magazine, then I had problems. I had to work much harder to be a successful woman in the printed word than in the fashion business, because even in the nineteenth century there were women heads of French Paris fashion houses – and all those people in the 1920s and 1930s; there have always been women bosses. It's quite a liberated business, the clothing business.

If I'm going into the City, I take two very sharp guys with me, killers, because I know if I went in there by myself I wouldn't be taken seriously. So I go with these real Munsters and send them in, and watch, and they don't know it's being done to them, they take it all terribly seriously.

Claire Harrison: I think you can still have a little bit of the best of both worlds, being a woman. You can no longer lie on a chaise longue with one indolent hand draping across the carpet. I don't think that's really going down very well any more, unless you've really made something of yourself and can afford to be very eccentric.

Nicky Hart: In some ways, there are big arguments for girls having separate schools still, because the only reason I feel now that I have confidence enough to talk and formulate views is because I was involved with other women. In mixed schools, boys do better than girls, even if girls start off seeming as bright.

There is discrimination all the way along the line. When I was at university, it was all the more apparent because I was studying feminism and art history, so it came out more. But in every other way – the way the government is run, the economics of the world, the distribution of wealth – there is discrimination.

Obviously I am judged more on my looks than on my brain, which is a disadvantage. Sometimes you want people to take you seriously, but because I am a woman, men in business talk to me in different ways. They patronize me.

Being an agent is a bit of a martyrish role because I would, as a man, instantly be given more respect by both my clients and by producers. As a woman, because I look young, I have to appear terribly professional, simply because I'm not a man. American male Hollywood agents, who are on a par with studio heads and executives, are in a much more powerful position where they can command lots of respect. Being a woman agent, especially in England, you are weak and you're in the middle; you're the one that both the clients and producers shit on.

Romaine Hart: I think the advantage of being a woman is that you are probably more able to be more direct, your ego does not come in the way of you making relationships. You can be more easy with people and you don't feel you have to make an effort.

I've found it easy to get media publicity as a woman doing this job, whereas it might not have been so easy had I been a man doing the same job. So I think, from that point of view, I have to say not necessarily having to show any femininity, but just being a woman, can be an advantage.

Occasionally, if I'm invited out and I take with me a male friend who is perhaps not quite as successful as me, but fairly on a par, we'll go somewhere and he is patronizing me, and I'm back to being the little woman while he is chatting up all the big boys. That I find insufferable to a degree that it's out of sight. I think, being a woman, when people ask you what does your husband do, it is an impossible situation. And I don't move a great deal in society, probably for that reason.

In *Time* magazine they said recently that a woman over thirty-five has more chance of being attacked by terrorists than of getting married. By comparison with an American woman doing the same job, I'm sweet, feminine, I'm a babe-in-arms, because they are out of sight on the whole and they're just too much. But American men are less frightened, on the whole, by women than Englishmen. They haven't been to public school.

Bettina von Hase: There are disadvantages, probably in the sense that you always have to do better than a man to get something or get somewhere. In all my job interviews, from Oxford to the first jobs that I did, I always felt there was a sort of discrimination, that basically, if I'd been a man, it just would have been easier, particularly in England, which has a sort of old boys' network system.

I have observed in England, and particularly in New York, that most of the women who are seemingly the most incredibly successful also seem the most insecure. Even if they have had a wonderful private life, children and everything. I think a lot of women, when they become successful, feel guilt, a feeling that, I've got to compensate if I am in the office thirteen hours a day and my child is being brought up by the nanny. That's a guilt trip, you know. And it's that sort of division of one's life which a man just takes for granted.

I think lots of women have to sacrifice enormous amounts to hold down a career and have a family, or have a marriage, or have a good relationship. I think, in a way, it requires more energy than on a man's side. They still have to do all the other chores as well. Really, the balance isn't perfect yet. And a lot of women are quite insecure, I suppose, about getting ahead, so they neglect the personal areas in their life, and that maybe makes them even more insecure. Therefore they lose their femininity, they feel the only way they can prove themselves in the office is by being efficient, by being very strong. Whereas, in a way, femininity can be a real weapon, just as effective in business as anything else. I think women should use it as much as possible.

Nikki Haskell: Women don't delve into their own qualities for the things they could do, or end up doing, as a career. For instance, I was an art major, I was under scholarship to the Chicago Art Institute when I was nine years old. But my father was an artist and he always pushed me into doing things and trying new things. When I moved to Beverly Hills, none of my girlfriends – and I love all of them – has ever worked a day in her life. They've never done anything. They all got married and divorced and that was it.

Compared to men at the top, there are very few women in business. The only woman who's a self-made millionaire is Estée Lauder, and she started with nothing and she's the only woman who is in the Fortune 400. All the rest have either inherited it or married it, which is the easy way out. It's very tough for a woman to go from nothing, as she did, to being the multi-multi-millionaire. You have a lot of obstacles to overcome. You have to be unique.

If a man gave me $10,000 to invest, he'd have given a man $100,000;

once I'd proved myself, I always got more, but I had to prove myself a lot more than a man would.

It's hard, as a woman, to start in a top position. I never had that problem. I just somehow always started at the top; I found it was easier to do. And it's given me a lot more creative ability to do the things I want to do. When I wanted to do my own television show, nobody stopped me. I went out and produced it and edited it myself and it became a very creative thing for me, beside the fact it was a lot of fun to do. But most women don't take that chance, they don't get that far. They've been married twenty-five years, their children are grown, and now they want to do something with themselves and they're completely incompetent. They don't have a career to fall back on. So what do they do? They find another husband and get married. It's hard for a thirty-five to forty-year-old woman to go to work, unless she's very well educated. It's really who you know, and I think that's one of the problems.

I had a lot of problems with relationships because people were intimidated by the fact that I was in a man's world. But they were always very weak men. A strong man never has a problem with that. A weak man feels very threatened by me, but there again, I don't want to be with anybody who's threatened by me anyway.

As power-oriented as I am, and achievement-oriented, if I were in a situation where I was madly in love with someone and it was between being with that person or working, I'd give up working in a second. But the emotional trip I'm on is because I'm alone, because I'm not married. If I were married, I'm not saying I would stop doing what I do, but I wouldn't do it the way I do it. I'm like a chameleon.

A fancy dress and a little perfume behind the ears open a lot more doors than a very fat unattractive woman. Most people look at you, and the first thing they think about is, am I going to be saddled with this person, or am I going to want to do business with this person? And it is really your appearance that people buy first.

The truth of the matter is that I look better than I did ten years ago. I never looked bad, I looked great ten years ago, but for me it's lucky, because I'm petite, and I'm small and I look young. But there's going to be a point in my life when I'm not going to be married and I'm going to be very upset about that because I don't want to spend the rest of my life alone. So there is that break-point. Every year you get older. For instance, I'm attracted to a lot of very attractive younger men who are not really attracted to me. They want somebody who's younger. I don't really have a problem with it, but I notice it more now.

Olivia de Havilland: I don't think I've ever felt a real sort of imprisonment in the feminine role. I love being a woman, I love being female. The motion-picture industry was dominated by males, of course. But I rather liked working with them. Most of the administrative positions were held by men. Sometimes I thought their opinions unreasonable, but I have since discovered, as women grow into positions of authority, that they lack practical common sense and good judgement. I found it more frustrating dealing with women in administrative positions than dealing with men in administrative positions. Men are more reasonable, I think, and they have a sense of the architecture of a situation; they understand its structure and elements involved and what has to be respected to have things go well and an objective achieved. I find women thick-headed, muddy-minded, if not bloody-minded. It's very surprising. I don't know how to deal with women yet, and I am going to have to do it because I have got to keep them from making their mistakes. I mustn't be so compliant and so polite.

Sometimes men would not trust my judgement because I was a woman. Another thing in the film business was the enraging attitude that, if she is pretty, she has to be stupid. But much worse was to be thought an intellectual, because an intellectual woman obviously was sexless, and to be sexless was fatal in the film industry. That was what you had to put up with and that was maddening, absolutely infuriating. I had to go to London recently for some fittings for films for television, and the travel arrangements were being made by a company apparently run by women. Three of them met me at the airport, and one of them said, oh, you know Miss de Havilland has written a book, to which the second woman remarked, she's written a book? Really? There are actresses that are intelligent? I've never gotten over this, especially because it came from a woman. It's unbelievable, that women suffer from that prejudice, too.

Kitty Hawks: Women have to work at their jobs as hard as a man, and then they have to do the rest as well, like run the house, raise the children, entertain, and all of that that men don't do. I think most men, faced with the responsibilities that women with well-rounded lives have, would completely go to pieces. I'm amazed that women can do it, and I think a lot of women, now that we're reading, are beginning to question the validity of having everything, because you can't be a full-time career

273

woman and have a baby and get as much satisfaction from either as you would like. Something has to be sacrificed. Even in marriages, working women come home as tired as men, and yet they get dressed, they have to look pretty, go out to dinner at night, maintain it all, go home, collapse, get up at seven in the morning and show up in the office. I can't think of any profession where a woman can get away without working as hard as a man, no matter how smart. Men are looking for the chinks in the armour much more than they are with other men. I mean, you certainly hear that men don't like the emotionality of women. A woman's impulse, if she gets some bad news or if she is chewed out by her boss, is to burst into tears, and she's not allowed to do it. I think she does have to work very hard at convincing the men she's adequate, if not more so; that she's just as good as a man.

When I see women who work in legal positions, or executive positions in big firms, I sense there are certain compromises they are making, that there are adjustments because they are dealing in a male world. And certainly one feels that men are often uncomfortable with women in those positions. I think women in those positions sometimes have a harder time gaining the respect of their peers. Because they don't hang out, they don't play squash, and they don't do all the stuff men can do together without a sexual charge to it. The minute that becomes part of it, something is added to the recipe. You are either overcoming it or ignoring it, but it's there. I think I was brought up with the impression that women pursuing a career were tough and that it wasn't becoming to a woman, to say nothing of not being as lucrative as marrying a rich man. But this isn't who I turned out to be, so I had to make my own way and try to overcome those guidelines.

Youth and beauty are more of a commodity here than anywhere else I've ever been. I think it is very damaging to the psyches of women that there is no value placed on just personality, certainly in advertising. You are not going to sell a product on an interesting, unbeautiful woman. The way things are sold in this country seems to be getting worse if anything – the minute you are over thirty years old, you are useless.

I love being a woman. I wish I had known twenty years ago what I know now, and I would have done certain things differently. But I think being a woman is a gas.

Brooke Hayward: When I went into the world at large, I went in with the great blessings of both parents. Whatever I did, I was encouraged. Even though at one point I decided to be an actress, and my mother was disappointed, because she thought it was going to be a difficult life, in the end she supported it. And if you go into a profession such as acting, or even writing, you don't see all this sort of discrimination you read about against women in the market place. I had – I have no concept of what that is.

I think that women play a defensive game, even in this age of liberation. To achieve something in this world, you have to do it in a subtle, sinuous way. You can't come at something in a headstrong way to get what you want because men don't like women like that. There's a certain way you can talk to men that is going to get you what you want. Women can get things from men that men can't get from men. A woman who knows how to go about it is a powerful creature indeed. My stepmother, for example, Pamela Churchill Hayward Harriman, has just been left her husband's entire fortune. I don't believe his children were even mentioned in his will. So there are people who are very accomplished in getting what they want from men.

My life, I must say, is a rarefied life. I have never had the slightest problem with being a woman. Except with various husbands. I think that there are men – and unfortunately I was married to two of them – who don't really like women at all. That, to me, is very surprising. But they are the only really close relationships I've had where I've seen this to be the case. I don't see it across the board. I've never seen it in my workplace, in the theatre or the literary world.

I enjoy being a woman, but if I had had my druthers I would have been born a man. If I'd had any choice, I certainly would have been born a man. Because I think that even now, men can be more effective. They have more power, there is no question.

Cynthia Heimel: When I was growing up, I noticed that the women never got to put the record on the turntable when there was a group around, never got to decide what TV show anybody would watch, and never got to plan for the group. A woman would never be the leader of a group of people. When I worked as a secretary, I was patronized incessantly, even by Germaine Greer, who would walk in, see me working as a secretary, and not talk to me.

I fear being raped. I guess that's the obvious fear. People are raped, and this is not Utopia out there, it happens. I think one can safeguard oneself, but it's a real fear.

Now that we've all had the feminist movement for ten years, the discrimination is much more subtle. People are much more careful to be overtly non-discriminatory. I think we collude. I think men are in a position of power and always have been, so it is to their advantage to try and keep that power. It's rare to find a man so altruistic that he will give it up in any real way. He'll say the right things, but he wants to hold on to as much power as he can.

I am going to try to be philosophical about the time when I'm no longer attractive to men. I don't fear it so much as I'm depressed about it. I think it's inevitable. I think a woman is more attractive when she is able to bear children, and that's biology, that's Nature. I just wrote a poem about this for *Playboy*. It gives me pain to know that, at some point, men will look at me and not wonder what it would be like to go to bed with me. That could happen next year.

Marie Helvin: It is a kind of game, in a way, to be able to use your looks or whatever, to get the man to do exactly as you want, and I like doing it. Maybe that's bad, but I do do it.

Women take a very patronizing attitude to another woman if she is pretty and if she is in a field of work where she is using her physical looks. I feel that I am much more patronized by intelligent women than I am by men, to tell the truth.

Being a foreigner here, I find Englishwomen difficult to become friendly with, and I've always thought that's probably because of their education. The way they go to school with other women, boys go to school with other boys, they are always separated. I've been living here for over ten years, but I don't have that many English friends. They are not so approachable. Englishmen are much more of the – oh come on boys, let's go down to the pub type, they have that kind of mentality. But, again, I must say that Englishwomen have it as well.

I married very young, and I married a strong man, Bailey, and I was a kind of child-bride that grew up within the marriage. All of my friends therefore were Bailey's friends. It's not harmful. It's just I feel now it was degrading because it was a patronizing attitude. He doesn't mean to have it, but he has it, and he always says himself that it is something from the East End.

I can tell someone, whether they're a man or a woman, to piss off if I want to. But, in general, women are most definitely discriminated against. But I think any woman – whether or not a feminist – every woman has the right to say no. And I think all women feel that today, and that power alone is more than anything we have had in the past. Now I say no whenever I feel like it. Ten years ago, fifteen years ago, I would have been terrified to.

Margaux Hemingway: The advantages of being a woman are a mile long. I don't know where to begin. I don't think there is a single disadvantage.

Anouska Hempel: I left Australia when I was seventeen, and came to London. I never felt it was a disadvantage to be a woman. Hardly ever. I don't think I ever had the ambition to be anybody other than myself, or any sex other than the one I am. It didn't really bother me. Whatever the disadvantages, you can make up in another area with the advantages, so you balance it out. It's no good ever thinking that you want to be anything other than what you are. Use your head and don't be discriminated against in the life or the role you've chosen. Maybe my life is much more of an artistic, strange, closed environment, chosen for myself and worked from the inside out in my own way, weaving my own thing. I never regarded any man doing the things I am doing as competition, or any avenues or areas as closed to women, because I've never thought like that. I've never really felt at a disadvantage. And I've been so busy doing my own thing, whatever it is in my own eccentric, strange sort of way, that I've never belonged to a group where women have to compete against larger numbers of men for jobs. Maybe I just wasn't conscious of it. Maybe I worked a little bit harder, but it's a woman's role to work a little bit harder sometimes and go round the corner and bring it all together in different sorts of ways from a man.

I don't regard my work as hard work, I regard it as doing the things I particularly love to do, with an awful lot of luck thrown in the middle. Before I established myself, when I went to the bank manager, I was a little Australian from the bush with no real qualifications, except I had a lot to say for myself. A little bit of manoeuvring and chatting, and getting your point across, and making somebody believe you and trust you, was just as good in those days for me as it was for some young man who had stepped straight out of university, with his degree, his little grey suit and his hat, who gave a waffling story of no consequence whatsoever. I didn't regard it as more difficult for me to get that first £1,000 from the bank manager than for the chap down the road. I was doing what I believed in. I was doing what I wanted to do.

277

Certain things are unseemly. It's not seemly to be a clever business-woman; you play it down. You either read a book or you do tatting or you help out in charities. Men don't want competition, and you are regarded as being hard, difficult, and awkward or whatever in coming into their world. They don't want you in their world, either. They don't really want you to bring the gossip from their world back to the other world, which is really where women belong in their eyes. I think that's been a problem, especially for the English girl.

Part of the fun of being a woman is being able to cope and being given the chance to cope with a multitude of things. And it's fun to be differ-ent, it's fun to be able to see it from a different point of view and do different things all in one go, listen to fifty different telephone calls and three other conversations going on at the other end of the room because your conversation with the person you are sitting next to is boring. It's great to have that ability, and to have the sense to take advantage of it.

Beth Henley: I fear ageing and dying and everything like that. My mother says she looks at her face and she can't believe it's her face. It's weird, this uncontrollable thing, this ageing process that takes over your body. It scares me. I think it's spooky. Some people look pretty terrible when they're old. Some people look interesting, and it is in the eyes, but personally I just love my health and being able to run and skip and everything. Even now, I feel bad that I can't climb trees like I used to.

Val Henessy: There's one disadvantage I've noticed. In my job as a journalist, I've been on a couple of fairly dangerous assignments. Nothing really dangerous, to war zones or anything, but, for example, last year I was sent to do a story in Milwaukee, Wisconsin. I was pleased to be sent, and it involved going into the ghetto area of Wisconsin, which is very rough, and predominantly black – all black, in fact – and doing interviews. I was working with a male photographer and we got into a cab and the cab driver, who was black, said, I ain't taking you into that part – even the black cab drivers don't go into that part. Where-upon the male photographer said, bugger this, I'm not going in there, you've had that, I'm not risking my neck. In fact I did go in, because I thought, if I phone back to the office and say, look, there's no way I'm going in to do this story, I'm frightened because I'm a woman and I might get raped, they're never going to send me on an interesting investigative story again. And if I want to imagine that I'm equal to men, I've got to be prepared to take these risks. What is unjust in the point I am making, is that it is far more dangerous for a woman.

Walking down those streets at night was a very frightening experience. I was hassled, I was harassed, and all the time I was thinking, I've got to go through this. It would be so pathetic if I ring back to the office and say, I'm scared, I'm scared to go into the ghetto, because to me it was a great honour and privilege to be sent on this story.

Anna Ford would never had got her job if she had had acne, fat legs and a moustache. You have to be pretty good-looking to get jobs on television. If you think, for an instant, about some of the male presenters – big bags under their eyes, dropped jaws. Think of Alistair Burnett's complexion for a start. Any woman with a complexion like Alistair Burnett's would never get anywhere near a TV screen, even though she might be brilliant at interviewing people, at doing newsreading and so forth. I became very aware of this shortly after I began journalism, when I was asked to interview for a job with *Magpie,* which is a children's show, and it actually said in the letter please wear for this audition a mini-skirt. And I thought, I don't believe this. So I rang up and said, what do you mean, please wear a mini-skirt? When Michael Fish went for his job as weather man, did you tell Michael Fish to wear a pair of short trousers? What the hell have my legs got to do with it? I would have thought children watching this programme might not be bothered whether their presenter's got shapely legs. That was something that maddened me, and when I went for the audition, I wore a pair of trousers, I believe. But as soon as I got there, they bunged me in this make-up room, they put Carmen hair rollers in my hair (I had long straight hair at the time), they slapped make-up all over my face, they even put fakey eyelashes on, and the image that appeared on the screen was simply not me, it was some sort of glamorized, idealized, young, bright, glamorous woman. It happened again. I did a series for ATV in investigative journalism and interviewed people and so forth, and after, I was called up to the top floor of ATV by somebody in control – I can't remember who – and he said, I've got some good news for you, lass, we're thinking of offering you a contract to do a late-night chat show with politicians and so forth. I thought, hmm, this is very complimentary, you know, they've obviously taken me seriously. And he said, what we're actually looking for Val, is a dolly bird to appeal to the dads after the *Ten O'Clock News.* I said, excuse me, but I don't simply see myself in terms of a dolly bird. I'm thirty-two for a start, my dolly bird days are very distant. I was really very angry. We had a bit of a ding-dong and naturally, I didn't get the contract. These are the areas where I do think you are treated differently from how they would treat men. There's no way they would get a man up there and say, we want some kind of toy-boy Warren Beatty glam figure to appeal to the mums after the *Ten O'Clock News.* This is an area of inequality in my view.

My husband and I went to a bank to get a mortgage, and we had to take along our receipts for our earnings for the previous year. My earnings happened to have been three times my husband's, and the bank manager looked at both lots of earnings, turned to my husband and said, oh, this is a handy little hobby your wife has – referring to my job as journalist, for which I had earned three times as much. And I just thought it was hilarious to say it was a handy little hobby. That's completely true.

I always take a book if I go into a pub on my own, so it looks as if I'm reading and I won't be hassled. If you're a woman sitting in a pub on your own, within five minutes some chap will come up and say, do you mind if I join you? If you say, I really would rather you didn't join me, thank you, because I want to sit on my own, the man will then say, oh, anyone would think I was trying to chat you up, I wouldn't chat an ugly old bag like you up, ugh, don't you kid yourself. Or if, because you know that's going to happen, and you can't face it, you say, yes, by all means, join me, then the man will immediately start chatting you up. So you can't win either way. I do find it very difficult, or I did when I was younger. As you get older, you get far more capable of handling these things. I would have found it very difficult to say, please will you go away, I find you very boring. But now, as I've got older, if I'm at a party or gathering, when I get some boring old drunk come up and start wittering on about his boring self, I have actually said, look chum, you are boring me to death, I simply can't stand here talking to you.

I don't see myself as attractive. I look in the mirror and think, Christ, you ugly old bag, look at your dropped jaw. I was never led to believe as a child that I was particularly attractive; my mother was highly critical of my looks, and she would say, you ugly bitch, she would actually say, ugly bitch. I used to have to wear glasses from an early age, and my mother used to say, oh, fish-face, look at you. I'm terribly self-conscious about my glasses, and I've always been terribly self-conscious about not being particularly attractive. I'm not fishing for compliments, that's how I see myself, so I've never been able to walk into a room and think, oh, I will use my devastating glamour to knock these people dead, because I'm not aware of having any devastating glamour.

What would be a brilliant idea in this life is not to have marriage as your goal, or even living with a person, a man, as your goal. The great thing is to leave school, get a job, be utterly independent, to have your own place and just know what it's like to be your own boss and not to think about somebody else the whole time – just get to know yourself first. I think that's quite an important thing. What happened in the past,

280

certainly for me, was we left school, we got our qualifications, went on to university or whatever and then we got married. I have never ever, to be perfectly honest, had a room of my own. I sometimes think now, in my forties, what a wonderful thing it would be to have my own place, my own stuff about the place, my own friends, to come back at what time you liked. To be utterly independent. I've always thought in terms of the man in my life, and I'm not sure that's a good thing.

Carolina Herrera: I don't think I would like to be a man. I don't want the boredom of all the responsibilities men have to take. Regardless of what women's liberation say, men still have more responsibility than women.

Dr Leah Hertz: I came to England when I was twenty-three and met my husband. I stayed here, and I found myself a bloody foreigner. In Israel, I was definitely going to be at least a minister, I was organizing and doing things from the day I was born, and here I was a bloody foreigner. It was difficult to get into the system, so what attitude does one take? It's the same thing as being a woman. You are at a certain disadvantage, so you become aggressive. If someone told me I was a bloody foreigner, I would say, you're lucky a bloody foreigner like me wants to come to your shitty country and help out. That was the way I looked at it, I felt I was doing them a favour. I used the same attitude as a woman: I have disadvantages, but then I immediately make sure I twist them into advantages. They're not really advantages.

Mrs Thatcher got through with a few other women, the way I got through, because we had the right conditions. I had the right husband with a certain amount of money, the right children in the sense that none of them is retarded, none of them is an invalid, because the minute you have one invalid child you've had it; you can be a genius, ten Margaret Thatchers rolled into one, but you'll get nowhere. If she had had a husband who ran around with other women, if she had had a child who was seriously sick, it would have been a different story. So I would say, I was fortunate, she was fortunate, but we have to help those who are not fortunate. Now, she doesn't say that. She says, I've done it, why can't you do it? That's why there is a very strong reaction against her.

If I could do something for women, I would take away their guilt complex. It's always so sad. They feel guilty about everything, every-thing, and I don't understand why. When we came to my mother, like most children do – well, as vociferous Israeli children do – and complained that we didn't do this right, we didn't do that right, my mother used to say, look, kids, three of you I brought to the world, three of you have hands, legs and everything, you are not abnormal, you are healthy, you have education, you have husbands, you have children – what do you want from a mother, a golden tombstone you will not put on my grave? Women feel guilty about children, and there's no reason to feel guilty, they are doing more than enough. And now, especially in America, career women are going back and playing the motherly game all over again; they are stopping careers just to be the whole day with the washing up.

I don't fear ageing, I feel like good wine. I'm better today than I was ten years ago. It's a matter of confidence. I warn my husband, look after yourself, because if you go, the next one will be fifteen years younger.

Elizabeth Hess: I think women continually have to prove themselves in ways that men don't have to simply because of the fact that they are men. I think women have to work twice as hard to stay on top. A woman makes a mistake, and it's fatal; a man makes a mistake, and it's simply a mistake, it's human.

I don't think menstruation is a great disadvantage. I think that menstruation is something that's historically been used against women for years and years. I think men are as vulnerable as women and often as much in pain over other issues.

Min Hogg: I have a brother I worshipped, but so did my mother, even more than I did, and I realized I was a second-class citizen in my mother's eyes. I may add that my mother and I are the best of friends, she'd far rather have me than my brother any day now, but it was a most awful shock, I do remember, and I couldn't come to terms with it at all.

You can circumnavigate a mountain of argument if you're a woman. A lot of women have frightfully clear minds. If you're a woman, you can think it out, present it somehow or other, change the entire system and smile so prettily. And, indeed, sex is the most useful thing, of course it is.

I don't fear ageing. I'm forever hearing these days about eighty-four-year-olds leaping into bed with each other and having a lovely time. One used to think of one's parents doing it, and think, *yukh*. Now I am reaching the age, or have reached it, when I don't mind a bit.

Marie-Hélène du Chastel de la Howarderie: I'm sure that disadvantages exist, but it's just that I never noticed them, because when something didn't go right, I would never feel it was because I was a woman, it was because I felt I hadn't tried well enough. And when something went right, it was because I wanted it to go right, that's all.

Jeny Howorth: You can get away with a lot more things being a woman. You can play little games, be girly if you want, and get away with things with men, because men are very susceptible to women in that way.

Arianna Stassinopoulos Huffington: I wouldn't say that women generally lack the confidence of men. I think that in certain areas, because there aren't so many role models, there aren't as many women who have succeeded. It takes a more pioneering woman to set forth and do it, like a woman politician, or a woman scientist, but I don't think that generically women have less confidence than men. In fact, if you think of it, childbirth requires a lot of courage and confidence, and a lot of the primal, primitive roles that women, by virtue of who they are and by virtue of their sex, are thrown into, require a lot of courage, strength and confidence. I think it's just a question of where they choose to channel it. It is often true that daughters are brought up to have less confidence than sons, and if a woman is brought up in that restrictive environment, then it takes somebody more exceptional to overcome this obstacle. But you see it happening all the time.

Thank God, I don't fear ageing, and I always mention my age to everybody. It's always been on the covers of my books, because when my first book was published I was twenty-one, so my publisher thought they should put it on the cover. I think the reason I don't fear ageing is because I love seeing transformations in me as I grow older. There is no part of my life that I would like to go back to, which doesn't mean I didn't love them, but I see how much wiser I am now, and I know that, in ten years, I will think I was very foolish the way I am now. So I love the process of wisdom and ripening that comes with age. I suppose it must be a lot harder for women who are making their living through their looks, but that has never been the case with me fortunately. Those will probably have a harder time ageing, although those of them who have developed their own identity will surely be able to cope. I have met women who are older who are so attractive to men it is devastating, who are so sensual and all-enveloping and also who have that wonderful relaxation that comes with ageing. They don't have to prove anything, and there is nothing more attractive, even sexually attractive, than a·

human being that doesn't have to prove a thing. They have that sense of themselves – what the French call being well in your skin. That feeling is so attractive, and you can't fake it, it's as though you smell it in another human being, like an animal can smell it. With age comes serenity, and also that feeling that you can say and do anything and you don't have to behave according to certain prescribed rules. I wrote an article for *Town and Country* called 'The Eternal Feminine', about what I find attractive in women, and I mention some of the older women I have met, like Rebecca West, who have that quality. It is not a function of looks, it is a function of personality, and that, if anything, gets bigger with age.

Caroline Huppert: It is still more difficult for an actress to become famous. The French public still prefers male roles. It's a question of supply and demand: if the public wants heroes then that's what it gets. I tend to think that there is no difference between a man and a woman, because that is how I was brought up, but, for example, I am about to do a TV film in a series of detective stories, the *Série noire*, which is very popular in France; they are violent films and I have wanted to do one for a long time. I had enormous difficulty in convincing the producer of the series that I could do one. It took two years before he would agree, and it was because I was a woman. He said I would not be able to respect the format, even though he knows my TV films and reputation, so it wasn't as if I was going to impose my own way of working. So, after two and a half years, I'm going to direct an episode, and I will be the first woman to do so.

When I make a film, there are enormous financial and artistic responsibilities, but I am always brought back to everyday problems: a child has to go to school and must be registered on a particular day, or I have to go to the doctor's on a particular day. Men do not have these problems as they can always say they can't, or find someone, their wife, to go to the appointment for them. Whatever important work has been planned for that particular day, I might not be able to do for a reason that is relatively trivial. So I am caught between two things, both of which have to be done, but of unequal value.

I'm not in the kind of profession where I will think that life stops overnight because I have three extra lines on my face. I can continue to do what I want, I don't see any problems, and I think that's partly the reason I love children, because your connection with them projects you into the future. A mother of seventy still has pleasure in her children and her grandchildren, and I need that strongly, it's my protection for the future. I can see myself with my jams and my grandchildren, and I'm not afraid of that. There will be some things I will miss, of course, but there will be a large slice of life which I will still have.

Isabelle Huppert: America is a very hard country. I can imagine how much you have to fight, and it's probably difficult to fight so much and be feminine at the same time. Probably the French are better at this little game. In America, I think a lot of women become threatening for men, although I think both sides are rather traumatized. There is much loneliness in the United States, and it's so competitive you have to make money. Here, in the Old World, there is still more sensuality, and, you know, we let it go. In America, you can't let it go.

Angela Huth: In the days when I first started, it was much harder to do the things I wanted to do than it is now. For instance, in about 1965, I decided, having been in Fleet Street, that I would like to get into television. For those days, it was an unheard-of thing for women to be serious in television. There was Joan Bakewell doing *Late Night Line-up*, and I think there might have been one more reporter, and I had literally about a hundred auditions. And then I was lucky enough to meet Desmond Wilcox who was a man – I have met a few of them in my life, thank God – who gives someone a chance. He said, go out and make a programme, I can't audition you. So I went out and made a programme, and then I was signed up by the BBC. But they were all very nervous about it. I mean, when it was decided that I should go to America to make a film about middle-class Negroes, there was a man who said, will she be safe, can we send a white blonde girl aged twenty-three to America to interview what was called a Negro in those days? Can you imagine that sort of discussion going on now? So it has always seemed to me that it is just a bit more difficult if you are a woman – especially now I'm a married woman – because you have to deal with two lives: the professional and the domestic. And the domestic life ultimately is your responsibility no matter how much the feminists say men are going to share in it – and I am very lucky to be married to a husband who does share a lot of things. None the less, it is ultimately my responsibility to deal with that side of life, and I want to have another side, so I have two jobs, and I think that's the case with a lot of women. And, too bad really, there isn't time to sit and grumble about it too much.

I suppose the advantages are what they have always been, in that women are, well, a more attractive lot than men on the whole. Heavens, if I was a single woman now and wanted to get married, which I am quite sure I wouldn't, what on earth would I do? I know an awful lot of women of my age and indeed much younger, who are wonderful, marvellous women, attractive, intelligent, hard-working, bright, and the only thing they are lacking is an equivalent man. I really do think there seems to be some kind of imbalance in the sexes. I don't know that it has always been like that. And the best men all seem to be married, or taken up, and there are a lot more attractive, wonderful, single women around than there are men. It can't be anything to do with the war any more, and men getting killed. I think that attractive men are probably snapped up quite early and married quite young, and remain married for a long time, the ones who aren't divorced. I think it is a problem with my daughter, among her generation. She's twenty-two, and she is in a group of about twenty absolutely enchanting, bright, attractive, wonderful, intelligent young girls. And they all go out together. They've got men friends, but very, very few of them have got a whole-time boyfriend because there just isn't the sort of calibre of men around.

Women's bodies are such frail, hopeless things compared with men's. A woman in her mid-forties who has had four children is a great deal more tired, more exhausted, than a man in his forties who has had four children. Because she – I am talking about the average woman – has to deal with the children, the whole thing, and there is probably no more exhausting work in the world than dealing with the moods and ups and downs and wants and all the rest of it of four children. It is totally exhausting, let alone the child-bearing, particularly if you go on having children late in life. The whole monthly frailty, the pre-menstrual bit and all the rest of it, actually affects women deeply, if not physically then psychologically. There really is a shift in the veins, as it were, with the moon, and you can actually feel these hormones or whatever they are, you can feel waves of ups and downs in mood and everything. And, you know, it is actually physical, something to do with just the rhythms of your body. I really don't think men experience anything like it. And that is a terrible disadvantage for women. And, try though we might, I don't see how we are ever going to overcome it, because it is just that we are made like that.

I think, for a woman to succeed, she must have double the energy of men, because she has got to do twice the amount. She's got this split mind all the time, unless she's a very rich woman who can have all that side of life taken care of, and there aren't many of those. But for a woman to succeed in a tough man's world, she has got to have an enormous organizing ability, she's got to be mentally clear and well-organized in a way a man doesn't have to be, because all he has to think about is his work. He comes back in the evening and there's his dinner.

He can concentrate wholly on his work, and that's the only reason I would like to be a man. I'd love – and I've heard a lot of women writers saying this – to have a wife to take care of that side of my life. On the other hand, I wouldn't miss the good bits which men do miss – I wouldn't miss bringing up the children, the closeness to the children, for anything in the world.

I live in Oxford and I go to Cambridge a lot, because my husband's step-father is head of a college there. You sit next to these wonderful, famous, intelligent, brilliant brains of England at dinner, and they always say to you, what does your husband do? In the eight years I have been at Oxford, I have never once been asked by any fellow of any college what I do, and as I know very little about what my husband does, which happens to be Byzantine history, the conversation slightly closes there.

I think men have got the good sense to look at women and realize which ones are going to be complete idiots and which ones are worth listening to. My theory is – and I think one has to be quite skilful about this – most men, the sort of men I meet in the sort of world I live in (not necessarily writers or academics), are superior intellectually to me; I mean, they are better educated on the whole, and superior beings. And I feel that they are probably more interested in talking to me about something they want to talk about than something I want to talk about. So as long as I am a good and encouraging listener with an intelligent interest and ask them intelligent questions, they will be OK. I suppose, in that way, I feel rather inferior and have no confidence that I am going to be as interesting to them as they could possibly be to me.

There are so many people fighting for women to give them the confidence they have always lacked. In the old days, they didn't have any support, they were just fighting as individuals, and they're now all banded together, all on the same side. It has to be a pretty feeble woman now who lacks all confidence. There are so many people ready to push her from behind and support her in whatever job or whichever world she is going to land in. And she ought to feel much more confident now than she did even ten or fifteen years ago.

Sheila Innes: I think you are only just now, with greater education, getting an awareness among women that they have been made into second-class citizens. When you look at what's happening in the Church of England, how can we get away from an absolutely, fundamentally patronizing and disdainful attitude on the part of some men who think that man was created in God's image?

I didn't know about real prejudice until I started my working career. And even then, in the BBC, there is at least equality of pay. But you can have equality of pay without true equality of opportunity. You have only to look at the number of talented women now coming into broadcasting, and consider the fact that, when I left the BBC recently, I was the senior woman in the corporation. That seems to me to be ridiculous. I got my first promotion to a producer in radio after I had been in the BBC for about just over a year. And then it turned out that I had a good recording voice, so I became an announcer. I didn't notice any disadvantages until I went into television in the mid 1960s, and first took out a film crew, and found with film cameramen, electricians and so on, until they got to know you, it was much more difficult being a woman. I happen to think that a woman has to be three times as good at the job as a man. You don't find many lazy women in business.

The greatest barrier to women's progress is their lack of confidence, not of innate ability, which is partly why I am in this job, because I think we can do things for women, get women into more management posts and so on. The sort of management I think you need is a real caring for staff, which, you could say, is a maternal quality. A woman's place is to run a man discreetly. He doesn't know he is being run but, by golly, my father has been run for years by my mother. And it's true in most instances. Now women are beginning to come out of their starting-blocks and they can see, by golly, I'm not just going to be the great and exhausted woman behind a succeeding man.

There is quite a lot in a true story that happened in connection with a course I was once loosely involved with about making decisions. It was called 'Living Decisions', and a woman was asked, who makes the real decisions in your family? She said, you mean important decisions? The teacher said, yes. And she said, well, I suppose it's my husband, I mean, I decide on which school the kids are going to go to, and whether we can afford to have a new car next year, and whether or not we ought to increase the mortgage for tax reasons, and where we are going to go on holiday, but my husband decides on whether we ought to withdraw from the Common Market.

The worrying thing for men with this awakening of women's realization that they have potential and they can do things is that you are finding more able women than men. It is very interesting to me that now, when we recruit young people (and I was on the BBC's board right across radio and television for recruiting young staff), you can't find as many able young men as you can able young women. So this revolution is well

288

on its way. I think it's difficult for men to take, impossible for older men to understand, but very exhilarating for women. It's good to be a woman now, much better than it was when I started in life. There is this new kind of freedom, and one fascinating result, I think, is that men are now quite unsure of their roles.

I think the fact that men's sexual organs are external gives them an enormous preoccupation with sex. I also think it must be a problem for men to be dependent on having an erection before they can have intercourse. I think it's very freeing not to have that problem.

Angela Janklow: In the Deep South – take a trip down there – you wouldn't believe it. Women are at their husbands' feet putting on slippers every evening at six. In the Bible Belt – you know, Arkansas, Louisiana, Georgia, Kentucky, the whole Deep South, Iowa – the women are just breeders. Women are breeders in certain areas of the Midwest and many areas of the Deep South. Not so much on the coasts, because the coasts are always the most progressive. In a city on the coast, women move at a faster rate. But stuck in the middle of a farm with nothing for hundreds and thousands of miles except for a television set, and your living is your husband, your sustenance is your husband, and your children are from your husband, then of course life revolves around him. There are many famous stories about wife-beating, things that never go reported, because the women have no way out. They are not well-educated women, not women of good families. Mostly they are women stuck in very bad situations and unable to extricate themselves.

I think that America as a nation is far more aggressive than any other nation on earth. I'm a zealous patriot and I think we deserve to be. We have worked for it, we have earned it. We were nothing, we were just shucked off, were outcasts. And we've built it, in the shortest time ever, into the greatest nation in the world. The greatest humanitarian nation. That's something to be very proud of. And I think that, since we are younger than everybody else, there's less tradition and less custom, and consequently we don't compute the way that a woman would who lived in a society that didn't change for hundreds of years. In America, especially in New York, which is a very new city, we are less hindered by tradition. That is very crucial. It makes us more open to change and more crusading for freedom. Our starting-point to a greater good for women means a shorter distance than that of a country steeped in tradition and custom where the man is the all-supreme being.

I think boys do have more freedom. I think that basically, as with animals, the stronger physically will always be the more dominant. Intellectual equals are one thing, but war is the base of civilization. There will never be a woman President of the United States of America. Women were only granted voting rights in 1922. Maybe hundreds of years will have to pass to erase what's gone.

Men get more attractive as the days go by. And women decline. There is no way around that. It's a fact. It's very very detrimental to women because it makes them completely insecure; the older they get, the less secure. Their bodies don't react like they used to. An older woman is not going to be as attractive as an older man. Older men, I love them. I'm not talking now like wheelchair-bound, but silver-grey hair. The older man is much more attractive than he probably was when he was twenty, when he was stupid and easy to manipulate.

Tama Janowitz: I think that if I was a man writing, I would have been getting the kind of attention I'm getting now long ago. I wrote my first book when I was twenty-three and I wrote some really good books after that nobody wanted to publish. I'm taking a tremendous amount of negative reviews and criticism now, but men get negative reviews and criticism too. I feel that it's more discrimination in different ways from just writing – that whole business world. I think, in our society, white men are rated first, then black men, then white women, then black women, who are probably the bottom of our society in terms of the respect, attention and power they get.

Margaret Jay: In my profession, women have not done as well as they might have done because of the prejudices, but that is true in so many professions. I think those prejudices are mainly to do with people feeling that women are unreliable. In the world I have worked in, that has been the thing always said. If the child is ill, if the husband wants to work abroad, if there's some crisis in their lives of a personal kind, then they won't put the work first, whereas a lot of men will, so male employers will say women are unreliable. I think it's because women are trying to carry so many burdens that sometimes they try to fiddle the priorities in a way which may not suit the employers. The employers should be more flexible, because if they want to have very good women, they'll have to acknowledge the fact that they often have responsibilities domestically.

It's much more difficult for a woman to function on her own, and that goes for everything from getting a mortgage to going to a dinner party.

A woman must be escorted, there should be some partner in the background, and if there isn't, then it's assumed there is something strange, a peculiarity about this person. I think it's still ingrained in all of us that we are in some way a failure unless we have a partner, which I'm sure in men is not quite so true.

Dr Lukrezia Jochimsen: In my experience, the disadvantages at first were coping with the feeling that, in the university, in journalism, you were the one young girl amid a crowd of men, so that you were treated differently, although this didn't always mean that you were treated negatively or to your disadvantage. It started with where to sit, where to go, how to stand, how to be judged on the way you talked, the way you were dressed. Always at university, there was this experience of being alone among the other sex, but there were no actual disadvantages because you took your examinations and you got your degree. The real disadvantages started the moment decisions were taken about entering a profession. I started as a member of a television network. I entered the *Panorama* crew, which is a similar thing to the *Panorama* of British television. I was the first and only female member of this staff, and, of course, they always thought I should deal with female, social and education topics, and that hard politics and really important topics had to be dealt with by men.

Every woman is asked by her surrounding world if she's going to marry and what is going to happen afterwards. Nobody ever asks a man that question. Men grow up with the idea that they are going to marry one day, but this marriage is never anything that will change their way of life.

Twenty years ago, it was difficult for women to deal with each other at anything other than a rivalry level. One of the wonderful things today is that you can be together with women without those emotional barriers, although I still observe that if women are talking to each other, let's say at a cocktail party, and a man comes towards them, women immediately are tempted to stop their conversation and wait to question the man. He can easily interrupt women's talk because he attracts more attention.

It is one of the biggest unfairnesses that women at a certain age cease to be sexually attractive. About ten years ago, I got a written agreement from a lover of mine at that time, that when I am sixty-four – it was connected with one of those Beatles songs, 'When I'm Sixty-Four' – he would love me and go to bed with me if I wanted. So he wrote an agreement: 'I hereby assure you that when you are sixty-four, if you would like to sleep with me and I am still alive and around, I'll come immediately.'

Sally Jones: When I started in my first reporting job, with Westward Television in Plymouth, I found a tendency for people to send you out on stories about the fattest cat in Cornwall or the talking mongoose, little frothy animal stories. I found I had to work quite hard to get accepted. One great step forward came when I was working for ITN as a freelance reporter and I was in there the night the criminal, David Martin, was recaptured. Police had picked him up in the tube, in the underground tunnel between Hampstead and Belsize Park, and I was sent out to cover the recapture. I then did a reconstruction next day of what had been a fairly hard, brutal sort of recapture, and that was a turning point because there was a lot of praise for it and people started taking me more seriously as a journalist from then on. Subsequently I covered things like the Handsworth riots and a number of quite heavy, hard, industrial stories. In fact, I deliberately steered clear of sport in my early days because I knew, from the amount of sport I had done, that I was going to find it difficult to break out to do anything else, that sport could easily become a sort of cul-de-sac. And so I very deliberately aimed towards hard news and the fire-engine chase. I made sure that I was always there, that I was always around if there was a tough story to do. I tried not to do it by being unpleasant to people, treading on heads, but by making it entirely clear to the men I was working with that I was there, that I was competent, that I wanted to do the story as much as anybody else.

One aspect of confidence, which I have found increasingly useful as I have got older, is the readiness to complain if I don't think I am being paid enough and to be confident also to dismiss a freelance job. If somebody is offering me a freelance job at less than I think I am worth, I now don't have this dreadful confidence barrier of, God, I'll never work again if I don't accept. I now say, look, that's simply not enough money, either you pay me X or get somebody else. A lot of women still think that pay is one of the four things you don't talk about at dinner – you know, money, sex, religion and politics; four things you don't touch. A lot of women look upon actually facing up to an employer with some sort of confrontation and saying, look, I don't think I am being paid enough for the job I'm doing, or look, there's a man in that department on a comparable job being paid £2,000 more than me, why aren't I paid that much, as Americanized and aggressive. And there's always the thing that women are there because they like the work, like the fulfilment of the job, and are simply doing it to get themselves out of the house rather than for money like a man. A lot of women's work is downgraded for that reason. When the woman works outside the home, it is simply for pin-money, to keep her occupied until her husband gets back, and therefore she shouldn't expect comparable pay for comparable work. In my own sphere, it's not bad. I am probably paid comparably with men for what I do.

The people who perhaps have the most trouble being taken seriously are the exquisitely doll-like pretty girls. There are quite a lot in television who are good, hard-news reporters, and yet, because they look so much like everybody's image of a Barbie doll, they have enormous trouble being taken seriously. I think I am healthy-looking rather than beautiful, perhaps more serious-looking, more ordinary, more like the girl-next-door than some beauty queen. So people don't say, well, she's got where she has because of her looks. They will say, well, she's obviously got an interest in it, or, she's not just there for the sake of being a pretty girl on the box, or, she's not just an empty-headed little plum dolly. The people I feel sorry for are the ones who look like a Barbie doll but have actually got a very sharp brain in there. If you look at a lot of the people who make the most authoritative television performers, people like Sue Lawley, Kate Adie, they are easy on the eye but not raving beauties. They are not people who, you'd say, cor, what a stunner, not many of those to a pound, or anything like that. They are people who have an air of authority and are often slightly more mature.

In my job, as I'm the first woman sports presenter, if I make a Horlicks of it, everybody is going to say, no women are any good at sports presenting. They'll say, that girl's no good, therefore no women are any good. If some man had my job, and he was no good at it, they'd just say, well, he's useless because he's not much good. They wouldn't say, all men are useless at sports presenting.

I've unashamedly got to say that to an extent, apart from my interest in sport and my sporting background, I am very much cashing in on my gender.

Rana Kabbani: I find it more difficult to be a woman in the West than to be a woman in the East. In the East, if you are an educated woman and an ambitious woman, doors open more quickly and you can get ahead more quickly. And you don't find the kind of sneering contempt from Arab men that you do from Western men, I think, if they feel you are as good as they are. That's not saying that Arab men don't discriminate against women or aren't guilty of a lot of sexism, of course they are. The whole system in the West is geared to male advancement and the graduations in that hierarchy are so subtle and so difficult to break out of that, if you are a woman, you are already at a tremendous disadvantage not being in the slot men fill. You have to create your own network and rise in it.

Every time I was sexually harassed, I always tried to fight it by bringing it out into the open, by either reporting it to whatever authority there was or by denouncing it in a way that would make the person harassing me embarrassed. And that happened to me many times. The most notable was when I was at Cambridge and a professor there said that, if I didn't sleep with him, he would not recommend me for a PhD. He thought I would be so terrified that I would. So I went to the highest authority I could find in the university and reported it. And I was given a different supervisor the next day and asked to keep it quiet. So I think women have to learn not to be cowed by this sort of treatment. On the contrary, they should make a great big fuss about it.

I've felt the patronizing attitude less, but I have seen my British women friends feel it. I was always treated with a great deal of curiosity. Men didn't immediately have the response to me that they had to British women, and so I didn't suffer as much from their patronizing, because they were unnerved by the fact that I came from a so-called exotic background. The way I see men, educated men, talking to women in this country really appals me.

Women's lack of confidence is something quite remarkable. I'm struck by the fact that the friends I've made in the West, women either of my generation or of a slightly older generation, who are beautiful, capable, intelligent, who have everything to make them feel confident, are extremely unconfident and extremely insecure. It amazes me. I don't understand it. I don't know why they have this handicap, and it is a handicap. It must be something to do with the way they perceive themselves as females in a society that doesn't digest women easily.

I think we have come so far from the animal world that we've probably broken our link with it completely. And therefore the urges we have, for example, men raping women, that's not something natural. That's something to do with conditioning. That's something to do with a great feeling of suppressed hatred and fear of women that comes out in that way. And I think these things are to do with the way society brings up men and shows them how to behave to women rather than any natural urge. Animals don't rape each other.

Why do men treat women badly? Because they get away with it. From the time they are small, they are told it is possible to treat women badly and get away with it, so they do it. And if you can get away with something, you go on doing it.

If women were independently wealthy, if each woman had enough income from the day she was born till the day she died, to live her life the way she chose and to function as a social being the way she chose, nothing men could do would ever impede her progress. Every seemingly happily married woman I have ever asked, if you had a million dollars right now, would you stay married, have all said, no. I haven't met a woman who didn't. Even very wealthy women.

God, what a relief it is to be a woman and not a man, under that kind of terrible physical strain. It must be awful. I think, if I were a man, I'd be impotent most of the time. The idea of being at the mercy of one's body is so abhorrent to me.

Elaine Kaufman: Going to a bank to borrow money is still just a disaster as a woman. You have to fight your way every inch, and when you're an established businessperson, you have no credibility. For instance, I've finished paying off major loans, and when I went to borrow money again, they made me go through a three-month waiting period.

I have a good time being a woman. I always wanted to be Ruth in the Bible when I was a child. A lot of people come to me and talk to me about things, and I'm logical. You know, if you throw the dice, you get a pick, you might as well have mine as anybody else's. It's worked out all right.

Dillie Keane: Once when we were making a record I felt very much that the boss men were patting us on the head and saying, now now little girls, we're the men and we know best. I felt very angry about that. But I haven't come across a great deal of discrimination. What I have come across is an attitude to female comedy. A lot of men don't like a woman to be blue or be rude. And that's where I find difficulty. And a lot of women don't like women who are rude on stage, so while one part of the audience would be wildly appreciating it if I was talking about my tits or something, there would be people in the audience who would think, that's not nice for a woman.

As a woman who is beginning to have success, I can say it takes a longer time for women to have success, because there is always that thing that you think, well, I don't know if it's worth working hard, really hard, to try and achieve success, because I might stop and have babies. I think for me and other women there's this almost fallow period when you're getting on with things, but you are thinking it's marking time until such time as, well, here's my mate, I'll go off and have children with him. And for me, it took me a long time to get out of that. What I was thirty I suddenly thought, I'm thirty, I'm not married, I haven't jumped at any of these proposals, I actually do want to be single, I do want to work. It wasn't until then that I went at it hammer and tongs.

A good example of women being discriminated against, and discriminating against themselves, is the university graduates who come out. There's more pressure on the women in a way because men will hang about for the right job. Women panic and do a typing course, then they go to the BBC or into publishing and are a secretary for a while. And it is very hard then to break that mould, although they have just as good degrees as men. Men don't do that. Men hang about. Men are never going to be employed as secretaries. You wouldn't employ a young male graduate aged twenty-one or twenty-two to come and sit and make coffee and type and answer the phone and be extremely efficient but very much lower in the pecking order. Women panic, they get themselves into a menial situation. And they accept it there.

Caroline Kellett: I fear age perhaps more because of what I'll learn, because of disillusionment. I'm terribly idealistic. I think I will always be the object of men's attention. I am a romantic, and I think beauty is from within.

Tessa Kennedy: I think, on the whole, that the more you have to do, the more time you have to do it in. I seem to be living three lives at the same time, and enjoying them all: the wife, the mother and the career woman. I'm stretched like a bit of thin chewing gum at times, but I wouldn't have done it any other way. I was forced to start working to support my three older boys, and I wouldn't have changed it for the world now. In retrospect, I think it's the best thing that could have happened.

I suppose one inevitably thinks about agony, and probably the earlier one dies the better, but I saw Barbara Cartland on television the other night – she's unbelievable. What an incredible vitality, and Claudette Colbert – those kind of women absolutely inspire one to old age.

296

Claudette Colbert looks the same as she did when she was twenty. She has such an interest in life, which I think is probably 'interest in' as opposed to 'interest-ing', although interesting as well. I think that's what keeps you young. Children keep you young. I'm always saying that to people. And I think the more interest and the more love you have for life, the less you age.

I think it's fortunate to be a woman. In this day and age, in my generation, we have everything made for us, absolutely couldn't be better, and I've been lucky to have been born in this age. I used to dream about being a courtesan of Louis Quatorze, because he is the kind of person I would really admire. He created a palace in the swamp, at Versailles, and lived so grandly and on a scale that I adore, and I think that if I had been living at that time, I would like to have been one of his mistresses. But when you read in depth into that part of history, there are so many things I would have hated. They never brushed their teeth, they didn't use lavatories. I don't think that's for me.

Mary Kenny: I have been in all ways enormously advanced in my work by men – always terrifically encouraged by men. Even when I was absolutely at my most rebellious feminist phase, I was always being egged on by men.

When you're young, femininity is a great advantage. I don't think femininity is such a strong card when you're middle-aged. When you're middle-aged, experience is a stronger card.

I think Simone de Beauvoir has been totally over-praised as a role model for women. She was a big failure as a woman, I think. She refused marriage, deliberately and in a silly way – to the point where it would have been more convenient for them to get married because they could have got teaching jobs together in a town in France. She refused motherhood. She chose abortion rather than having children, which again seems rather sad when you think of these two extremely clever human beings. And, at the end of her life, there she was, having refused marriage, but with all the disadvantages of marriage, still having to look after Sartre when he was old and very senile. She had all the disadvantages of a wife, without the dignity of a wife, and she didn't have the fulfilment of motherhood, and I think her writing shows it.

Perhaps somebody like de Beauvoir would see a married woman or mother as being in subjection, whereas there would be many married women and mothers who would think they are actually in power. There is no greater power you can have than the power you have over children.

You really mustn't compete with men too much on their own terms. I feel, instinctively, that if ever I say or interject something, it must be a contribution which is perfectly sensible, but not too aggressive. I think men are quite sensitive about being respected, and you do have to show them respect and not threaten them too much.

Sometimes in a man there is a kind of residual gallantry – he feels protective about not sending a woman right into the front. That's a sort of old-fashioned chivalry, and I don't think it's such a bad thing. If you're going to talk about discrimination or being victimized or compromised, I could argue that it is as hard being Irish as it is being a woman. And if I think in terms of my brothers, I don't think I've had a worse time. Sometimes I've had a better time.

Patsy Kensit: If someone would like to think I'm a bit dim, which I'm not, well, I let them think that, but I'll be so charming, sweet and nice that I'll work them round to saying, let her do it. I will manipulate people that way, because sometimes it's the only way. It's a conditioned response to think I'm a bit dense, especially being a blonde girl, so I just let it work round to my way and eventually people will realize I'm not that stupid when I've done everything I wasn't meant to do. I'm quite clever in that respect, I think.

If there was something bitchy in the paper, I used to cry, it used to really upset me. One week someone would say I was too fat, the other week someone would say I was ugly, and the next week they'd be saying I was one of the most beautiful women in the world. And one minute I felt so great, and the next minute I felt suicidal. I just overcome it all now. It's done me so much good, this past year, all the shit that's been written about me and everything, it's made me so thick-skinned and tough that I just believe what I want to believe about myself.

Griselda Kerr: Because one is a woman, one can sometimes get away with being innocent and making innocent remarks that one couldn't as a man. You can send poisoned darts or an arrow carrying a message that nobody else has dared fire, very much more easily if you start off from a kind of innocent (ha-ha) background. You're able to say things which perhaps a roomful of men wouldn't have dared to say. And I find this happens again and again in my life. And that's a clear advantage of being a girl, and I use it absolutely all the time, I know, in my negotiations. I'm not saying I do it consciously, I do it totally unself-consciously, but I adopt a degree of innocence or naïveté or a kind of ease of manner which a woman can have and a man can't, a kind of informality, which I know works.

I remember one male member of staff here screaming at me down the passage, you slimy bitch (in fact he's a great friend of mine) and I was terribly upset and angry and cussed him and stormed out and said, either he's going to work here or I am, one of us must leave – and we're both here ten years later. But he was summarizing what really aggravated him in the way I dealt with people. I don't think I'm slimy, I think quite a lot of PR people do that sometimes. But it's a kind of – coyness. It's to get under his skin. It's to make him feel he's making the decisions and you're suggesting them to him, but never that you're making the decisions. I never set the running. I make a point of not presuming he's going to say yes, so that his pride is never overtaken. It all sounds very devious, but it isn't at all, it's not something I've even thought about much. But it works all the time. It's actually using one's role as a female to get something.

The problem I can see with women, in all the arguments for emancipation, is the problem of having children and maternity leave. It must be said, when I'm interviewing new people to work for me, I'm always wary of the fact that, if they're married and haven't yet had children, and they're at an age when they might start wanting to have children, they might be going to be trained up and then lost. I haven't actually ever employed a man, but that's because I think that women are better at PR. Their mothers taught them to smile genuinely. But I completely sympathize with those people who don't choose women in jobs where that might be a danger.

I actually enjoy the role of a wife, though I appreciate that two fantastic careers might easily not make for a happy marriage. But I have, all my life, longed for that role. Even when I first came here, I came to fill time until I got married, and then I came into this career and had these fantastic fifteen years, and now I still want to be a fulfilled wife; and so one is having to balance being a wife and doing a job. It's made me use my time at work much more constructively, and it's made me able to delegate better, to calm down and see what is most important and what in fact can wait.

Soraya Khashoggi: From the moment the doctor says it's a girl, the

299

discrimination starts. As you know, we have come through a revolution and an evolution of women. However, I think it's just political. I think it's all manipulated by men. It is a hypocritical, political move by men, for their own purposes. Women are put in positions and jobs as tokens. Let's give a job to a black this week, let's give a job to a Jew, let's give a job to a woman; we have to, the law says so. They don't give us a job on merit, they give it to us because they have to. So we are discriminated against totally by men. Men rule the world and they use us. I don't believe in equal rights. I don't think we are equal in any way, legally, politically, and certainly not biologically or physically.

An average dinner party where there's six men and six women: OK the polite gentlemen will let the lady talk. However, it normally winds up with the men controlling which way the conversation goes. But an intelligent woman, or a woman who know the subject about which she is talking, as long as she knows how to project herself can silence the table and make them listen to her. I can do this.

If I could do something for women, I would banish periods. I would make it that no woman ever had to have a period. It would make life easier. I was talking to Shirley Bassey, and I said, if someone asked you, would you prefer to be a man? She said, well there would be one advantage, no more periods, because it interferes with sex life for five days of the month.

I feel I will always be attractive to the opposite sex. I don't ever see that day coming when I won't be, when a man that I couldn't have could walk through that door.

Lesley Kingcome: I think men take me quite seriously as a business-woman. I never talk women's prattle. I find men totally fascinating and interesting anyway, businesswise. If they don't have a business, I'm not particularly interested in them. In fact, I think I've always been able to talk to men. I never felt patronized.

If anybody says they don't mind growing old, they are talking out of the back end of their heads. Everybody minds it, and it's rotten, absolutely rotten. Disintegrating flesh, wrinkles and the whole caboodle is really boring, and anybody who says it's really not important is talking twaddle. In general, it's worse for women. Mind you, I think it's rotten for men, too. They wouldn't have to rush off and prove themselves otherwise, would they? I mean, just growing old, finding a wrinkle, having a saggy tum, whatever, is deeply boring. Avoid the subject if you can. Look at the beautiful Fiona Thyssen, magnificent, and now she's going to start getting old, because that's a fact of life. She was head girl at my school, so I have known her that long, and she was the most beautiful thing. I remember, aged sixteen or whatever, looking at Fiona Campbell-Walker as she was, thinking, how can anything be so beautiful? She was an amazingly good-looking girl, and was a marvellous-looking woman, she had immense style, and in the next five years she is going to start looking older, and it's rotten, it's not fair, as simple as that.

Rhoda Koenig: The main disadvantage of being a woman is that a woman's span of attractiveness to the opposite six is so much shorter than that of a man. A man's attractive to women till he's dead.

Women have much better clothes. I don't see how men can always bear to go round always wearing dark blue and black and brown and grey. That would depress me tremendously.

Irma Kurtz: When I first went to university, you were supposed to put your hair in curlers, and everybody wore girdles, all these skinny little girls, struggling in and out of awful clothes, everything restrictive. A few of us just stopped. We said, no, we are not going to do this. We went in with a rather raffish group of artists, homosexuals some of them. All us eccentrics tended to gather into a group, and as we were top of our class, we were left alone. If I'd had to have gone on with the curlers, and the girdle, I think it would have driven me insane. But as it was, I was like an existentialist moll – the black pullovers and the long hair. So I had a good time being a girl, it was quite fun.

I have no bitterness, and no anger the way a lot of women do. I would say none whatsoever, to be quite honest. Because I think being a man would have been a terrible disadvantage. People would have been too interested in what I did; my family would have been too concerned to let me go. I see what happened to my brother, who wanted to be a sailor or an historian; he's a doctor because he was forced to do things. Nobody thought it was serious for me. They thought Irma will fall in love, she'll get married, it doesn't matter if she has a little fling. And they left me alone. They didn't know that little fling was going to last decades. I think I was lucky to be a woman. I think I had more freedom because I was a woman, because there was no ambition invested in me except for the man I was going to marry. I was a waitress after university for a year, to earn money, to save money. We were all women in that restaurant,

301

we were badly underpaid, we lived on our tips, and they depended on how charming we were, how we charmed the diners. I found that perfectly understandable. I earned lots of money. I mean, to be paid for one's charm is an awfully easy way to earn money. Physically, it was hard work. I got on terribly well with the other women. I began to respect women, by meeting those waitresses, in a way I had never really done at university, where I looked at them all dying to get engaged and wearing their hair in little ringlets. Suddenly I was with tough, hard-working, struggling women, and they were wonderful. It was a real sisterhood. I wouldn't have missed it for anything.

The joy of life is so often missing in New York. I love New York because it's got the energy, the vitality, the buzz, but God, it's good to leave because it lacks joy. When I go to New York dinner parties, those are joyless people. They are witty, that cracking wit of theirs, and I do enjoy two weeks of it, but they are not joyous people. They're fiercely trying to live for ever, to be correct about everything, and they are not laid back at all. I feel women, especially New York women, are fiercely intent. It is a town of lonely women.

I don't mind being less attractive to men. It's served its purpose. I had a ball with men, I've had a good time. I had a nice sex life, I have a lovely kid, I got what I needed from men in that way. I don't even think about it. I have a lot of men friends. A man is as likely to come over for a drink as a woman in the evenings if I want to see a friend. But I don't require sex from men any more. I'm not saying all women are like this, but for me my sex life served its purpose, gave me pleasure, gave me a child, and I don't see what else I need from men in that area. So it doesn't bother me to be less attractive, because I am less attracted to them as sex objects, though I find it much easier to get on with them and much easier to talk to them. When I was young and juicy, I used to go to *Punch* lunches and it was all men and me, and it was quite a traumatic, frightening experience sometimes because, like it or not, I would be looking around at them with what I called the sexual surmise. Now I can go to a *Punch* lunch and have a ball. I can have so much fun, I say what I think and we like each other more and I am not afraid to dislike a man. I think ageing is, in some way, worse for men, because they lose their power in lots of ways. They can go on doing it, but not with vigorous youth. And also, hell, they've got young men behind them coming up in an area where they are also competing. A woman may have young women coming up behind her, but they are competing for the men out there, they are not at her back. There's no young woman who wants my flat, my kid, my anything. Not even my job. A young woman couldn't do it. Men have that threat: the young stag.

Verity Lambert: I come from a Jewish family where it was traditional for girls to grow up and get married and be looked after. The fact that I didn't do that really caused some distress to my mother particularly; my father not so much, because he did believe that I had a brain and should use it. And I know that girls I grew up with who were very bright and intelligent were swamped by that. They were perhaps not as obstinate as I was. My mother hated the idea that I worked in television.

Marghanita Laski: I think one has to distinguish between work and social life. In social life, I like the women's role and would not wish to see it eroded. In work, I'm fortunate in that I've always been in a profession where there are few disadvantages to being a woman. There is the disadvantage of not having capital as a whole, which makes it much more difficult to be independent, or to set up a publishing firm, or to do any of the things for which capital is needed; or, indeed, to be invited to become a partner in a firm – one hasn't got the industrial clout, the economic clout that men respect in each other. That apart, no, I see no disadvantage in work from being a woman.

I would say that if you want to work in a career, you have got to have all the equipment to work in that career, and one of the equipments may well be confidence. To complain of not succeeding because of discrimination, as I've heard women and blacks and all kinds of people complain, I think is weakness. To be able to stand up against discrimination, if indeed it's there, is one of the necessary equipments for the job, as important as being able to count words in my job, or use a typewriter. I'm not excellent. I know I'm less than first-class. I accept that. But that's not because I'm a woman, it's because I'm less than first-class.

Women can be very cruel indeed. I was reading a book this morning about Alison Uttley – the woman who wrote the sweet little children's books about Little Grey Rabbit – she drove her husband to suicide. I met Mrs Gandhi. I didn't know her, but thought she was a cruel, cold fish.

I can see no compensations to growing old whatsoever. Men hate ageing too. Look at them, as soon as they get to their fifties, off they go with little girls. They need to prove their virility. And also they get bored.

Frances Lear: It is very hard to get what is your due if you are a woman, and I've worked ever since I was seventeen, so I know a good deal about the workplace, and it's difficult to be a voice in this society if you are a woman, unless you excel. For the first time in my life, I have real credibility because I'm not with a man who has more.

I've always wanted to be a man, and I think the reason is because, as a woman, I have often felt a powerlessness which I don't think I would have done if I were a man, and maybe that's just a dream and a fantasy, but I've always wanted to have the power of men.

There are social inhibitions because I'm a woman. There is a stigma for women who are alone, for women who are above thirty-five, in most social situations. Women who are alone are not asked to dinner parties. Women above thirty-five are not as desirable as younger women. There is as much ageism as there is sexism in America.

The reason that ageing is so severe for women is that it's a combination of losing sexual viability and coping with mortality. Men just cope with mortality. We cope with the two things at the same time.

Sara Leighton: When I was twenty-one, I was the managing director of my own puppet film company, and I was obviously very young and very inexperienced. I was appointed because I had done some drawings that somebody had decided should be made into films, and I'd written a children's book. The whole board was men, my former husband was also producer on this, and I sat down at a board meeting and they were all discussing everything, nobody was taking any notice of me at all. They said, well, we'll incorporate the merchandizing rights for this, that and the other; and they took a vote and they turned to me, and they all said: yes? And I said, no. And they said, what do you mean, no? And I said, because you can't give away merchandizing rights; and I started telling them why, and the whole thing turned around. I was amazed that they hadn't seen this particular loophole and how much money the company could lose if they didn't tie up the merchandizing. And that made a difference. I don't think they were pleased that I'd pointed this out to them. If I had been a young boy – if I'd been the son of one of them – they would have said, well, you know, isn't that great, my boy spotted that. But they didn't. They were all rather embarrassed and got the whole thing out of the way quickly.

People often say to me, oh, your pictures are so delicate and so feminine. Now they wouldn't say Arthur Rackham is feminine, yet his work is far more feminine than mine; because he's a man, they don't take any notice. But if they can hit a woman and be slightly denigrating about it, they will.

I have noticed for a long time something I have called man's inhumanity to woman – right from the beginning of time, right from blaming Eve for the downfall of Adam, the downfall of the Bible, through to female circumcision, to stripping their heads right down the centre of their hair in Borneo, where they not only shave their women's heads once they are married, they take the woman round behind the hut and they pull out all her teeth, because they don't want anybody else to look at her. And so it goes on. You can find tremendous cases. And to me it seems to be a fear, and I don't know why men have this fear, that women will be unfaithful to them and make them look fools. Man does not want to be made to look a fool. At any price.

Catherine Leroy: It's a man's world, absolutely a man's world, but I think to be a woman with the right qualifications, purpose and state of mind has 100 per cent personal advantage. In my own field as a photo-journalist, travelling a lot and covering violent situations, men fighting each other and dying, I've always felt that being a woman was a great advantage, that I was accepted much more, that I was tolerated much more. I think it's a Japanese philosophical thing; being a woman is such a great disadvantage that you work your disadvantage into an advantage. It's a Zen thing. If you are so weak, you work your weakness into strength.

I have always been very feminine, even when I was sleeping in shit-holes and being bitten by rats in Kesan. I've always been a woman. I don't think I have ever tried to be like a man. I was dressed like a man, I probably swore like a man, but I was very feminine in many ways.

Doris Lessing: When I was bringing up a child, I never dreamt of trying to write when he was around. I couldn't. He had to be somewhere else. If he had gone away for the weekend, or was staying with somebody, I used to write in short sharp periods. This is my training, which now does me a disservice because it would suit me to write differently – not to write in short, very tense periods. A man writer has a wife who looks after all the uncomfortable things in life, including the children, which is why you find men writers locking themselves up and writing from nine till five. No women writer I know can do this. She's always having to deal with the roof, or the plumber or something.

I'm well past the menopause. Now I look back at the period from fourteen to the mid forties and I think that I was perpetually in the grip of biological necessity one way or another, not to mention menstruation. Nature wants us to have children – this is what Nature wants us to do. She doesn't care if we're happy or unhappy, if we get on with someone or don't. Nature doesn't care if half the children die. Nature just wants women to have a baby once a year for X years, and looking back I see an enormous amount of my energy went into either being in love or deciding not to be in love, or deciding to have children or deciding not to have children – being preoccupied all the time with it. What a relief, no longer to be possessed by this thing.

Maureen Lipman: I was in a youth club, and my brother was president of this youth club when I first joined. And as a teenager, or just turning into a teenager, he was the guy who had the men round. Our house was the focal point. It was the time of coffee bars and innocence, but it seemed very glamorous and sophisticated. I had a set of braces from practically the time the first teeth came through. Consequently, when I had my first boyfriend, I had a huge perspex brace and couldn't speak at all. When he came home from university, I remember I flew and embraced him, and my God, the fact that that boy still was remotely interested in me after that was enough to have made me marry him. But what I was saying was there were the boys, the men, every night. We had an extension built on to the house with yellow plastic strong furniture, bucket chairs, palette-shaped tables. Every night the boys came round, all the young men about town. And they sat and they talked about life. And they said, you know, I mean, let's be totally basic about this, I mean, let's face facts, man. A lot of that went on, and I would not be allowed in. But my thing was to come down and ask if anyone wanted coffee. This took an hour and a half's preparation. I didn't have any make-up, but I used to pinch my cheeks for about an hour beforehand, take the braces off, because you could in those days. I had glasses as well, and a terrible perm. And so all this preparation would go on. Socks stuffed down the bra, everything. Then I'd go into this room and say very casually, I'm making a cup of coffee, does anyone want one? There was all the careful preparation and knowing what everybody took, and then going in and angling to stay for maybe ten minutes, without looking as if I was remotely interested, and to sit listening to these gods. The first time one of these boys asked me out, my brother was furious for his sister to be regarded as anything other than someone who made the coffee, a terribly inferior being. In fact it has taken about thirty-eight years for Geoff, my brother, to come round to the fact (a) that I exist and (b) he likes me.

When my brother was president of the youth club, he was elected to go to America, and this was the cause for jubilation. He went away a little, callow youth, and he came back a Californian. He'd obviously had his first sexual experiences, he was totally his own man. When he came home, he rejected everything. He rejected the family, he rejected what he was going to do, he rejected Judaism for the rest of his life. The following year, I was elected sister president, which meant I made a hat and made very emotional speeches about how this year had been the most important of my life and I will treasure it always. And I was elected to go to this convention in America, but I wasn't allowed to because a fourteen-year-old girl is very different from a fourteen-year-old boy. My parents didn't allow me to go, and I remember having fourteen-year-old hysterics in the bathroom; this was the ruination of my life. Because I knew, somehow, that if I did go my life would take a different course. Well, of course, my parents knew that too, but you don't want a fourteen-year-old girl to go and have sexual experiences and grow up. But you do want it for a boy. In fact, you actively promote it, as in all the royal families. You send Andrew into the Navy in the hope that Leading/Able Seaman Coppit will teach him how to do it. You don't do that with a girl. So I didn't go. So my life took a very different course. I stayed at home and didn't reject anything. It took me, I suppose, another twenty years before I rejected things, and then I rejected things in a big, sort of teenage way, which I might have got out of my system had I been allowed to go. Now, as a parent, I can totally understand why they didn't want me to go, and I would be paranoid if a daughter of mine wanted to go, and my explanation to myself is, well, it's a very different world now, there's a lot of lunatics around. But that's not the reason. It's the same thing really.

I think there is a blind eye turned to a boy getting very early sexual experience. It's good for him, he'll make a better husband. There is a great deal of religious and social prejudice against a woman doing the same thing. A girl allows herself. You never hear that she wanted it as much as he did. The girl allows herself to become impregnated, and she's in disgrace or she's just foolish.

As a girl, you are taught very early on you must never get angry, it's very unfeminine to get angry. You can cry, you can needle, you can whinge, you can cajole, but don't say what you want and get angry, it's not nice coming from a girl. And this is one of the problems that we find now in business of one kind or another. When it comes to the point of saying to a superior, or even an inferior, you are an absolute dumb bugger, you have done this and I told you to do that, and if I'd been doing it I'd have done it that way, why do you never think, why don't you learn the part before you come into rehearsals, why do you call yourself a director when you are patently someone who has drifted into it from a secretariat? – we can't do that as women.

I belong to a body of people who have a theatre company, and I said something to the press about the leader of this company, and he was very hurt, very upset, but I believed that what I'd said was fair, and I believed, at the time, that I was not the only person saying it. As it happened, I was the only person who was named. The three men there immediately took not only a punitive stance against me, but a very patronizing stance, that I was personally a daft woman, for having done this. In the end, what they did was say, you are personally inadequate in some way. And then I could feel the emotion and tears about to come and I thought, I'm buggered if I'm going to let these men see me cry. I'd defended myself calmly and quietly for an hour and ten minutes, and in the end the only way they could break me was on a personal level. You are a manipulating woman, was what they said. And they won, because in the end what happened was that one of the actors there who was on my side, but hadn't said anything, started to say, now look, Maureen cares about this organization, you only have to read her book to see what she says about it. And that was the worst thing. That did it. I had to go to the toilet and cry. Because sympathy, on top of being patronized, somebody being kind to me, that was it, I lost. I lost at that moment I was patronized and sympathized with. And that is infuriating as a woman. Because it means you can only ever go so far. When women start to be successful, everyone says, isn't this fabulous, a woman who thinks like a man? Suddenly that woman becomes higher than you are or on an equal footing, and you don't like it. You don't like her cracking jokes in the boardroom, and you don't like her coming in looking stunning and then putting you down. It's primeval, it goes back to every conditioning you have had in your life.

You can be pliable or a monster. There is no in between. This is the thing about being a woman. You can be malleable and a bimbo, or you can be a monster. But a man who's a monster is not a monster, there's another word for it, it's a different thing. People don't call Aristotle Onassis a monster, though maybe Jacqueline Kennedy does, I don't know. If you crack jokes about men, you are a bitch. If you crack jokes about women and you are a man, you are simply following an age-long tradition of seaside-postcard humour. It's expected. Men are not regarded as being bitchy. It's only applied to women. We are paid less unless we behave very badly and demand or have charge of the production ourselves.

My notices throughout twenty years always, no matter what I'm playing, describe me as goofy, gawky, angular, plain, or else in terms of a lot of bird analogies, you know, that I look like a stork carrying a tea chest or an oil derrick on wobbly legs. All funny, all nice, you know. Now, if I was really ugly, like certain actresses who shall be nameless, they wouldn't mention it. If you are gorgeous, it's almost impossible that you could have any talent. It's miraculous. In fact, it's worthy of two columns of drool because not only can you act but you're pretty. I'm somewhere in the middle, and I've got gawky, goofy, glasses – nose cartoons of me that make me look like Marjorie Proops's grandfather. It's all to do with how you look. Now nobody went out and wrote Colin Blakely with his balding head looked like a rhinoceros, Michael Gambon looks like an unmade bed. It doesn't matter with men.

Lady Lothian: There is a secret discrimination against women which is difficult to define. Black people find it. I found it, first, as a half Italian, and then as a Roman Catholic. People won't say to you that you are not part of their tribe, or their club, as they prefer to put it in England, because you are a woman. You just find you aren't. Men are more comfortable without you, or perhaps more selfishly wish to retain positions of influence for themselves. Enormous change has come in this country with the woman Prime Minister. A woman Queen and a woman Prime Minister combined produces a most changed chemistry.

A man can have a child when he's eighty, a woman must stop when she's about forty-five. Sexually, I think there is no question, a man is infinitely less disadvantaged than a woman as he gets older, and I think it is very important to his self-respect, his happiness, that he can have joys which a woman perhaps can't have.

Cecilie Løveid: I think, as a modern woman, I want to have it all: I want to have sex, I want to have children, I want to have a job, I want to earn money, I want a career, I want everything. And that makes me more than double. Sometimes I feel I am wearing a mask. It's difficult to come home, it's difficult to go out, and I change all the time, but I think I can work it out better now than when I was twenty-five. When I was twenty-five, I had large problems with myself. As a professional woman you have to go to bed with all the men, and I did.

Woman can give birth, or she can have an abortion, she is the centre of a family and she can choose to be lazy and not use her gifts in a career and nobody will ask her why. She can use her slave role to avoid responsibility. And men are so romantic about women that they have great power over a man, especially when a man is in love.

When I was young, I looked older than I was, and now I'm very happy when people say I look younger than I am. So it must be important to me to be young, or to look fresh. However, sometimes I long for the peace of being past this very hot area of sexual potency. But I can already feel the old woman inside me. It isn't that I like sex less. It isn't about sex; it's about all the struggle in life.

Blanche Lucas: Women's capacity to concentrate on a particular thing is greatly eroded by occupation. When you are a mother, you can't be single-minded. You've got to be terribly flexible. Here comes a child wanting that, here comes a child wanting this; you've got to get five different children off to five different places, you've got to look after their clothes. There are endless things, and then the husband wants food, and everybody comes in. All the time you're waiting on other people. And then so many women are secretaries, or go into jobs very like family jobs – being a man's secretary is very much like being his wife, except there are no children around to distract you. It's the same thing: he buzzes the bell, up you get; he wants this, he wants that, up you get. In the middle of typing you have to stop, you have to do something else for him. I think that is a danger for women. One always comes back to the society in which one lives. If, in polite society, the admirable thing is to put your nose on the chalk line and keep it there until you've got to the top of the tree, then those who do that will be considered much better, they'll be more respected; the fruits of the world will land in their laps rather than those who are madly scratching around doing this, that and the other. I think the feelings of value that people have about themselves are very much decided by the society in which they grow up. I always get quite cross when I hear a woman say, I'm only a housewife, when I ask, what do you do? Which is a stupid question in the first place, but sometimes one can't think of anything better to say. Why *only*? It is because the job of being a housewife is not well considered in our society, which is why, when there is a divorce, the wife's contribution to the marriage is always, in my opinion, grossly undervalued. And yet it is a remarkable thing that one human being is prepared to do so much for other human beings, without any visible reward.

Recently I had to go to hospital, and my feeling was that the doctors, the surgeons, were somehow patronizing. It was rather, don't bother your little head about it, sort of thing. I felt that if I'd been a man, they would have been much more forthcoming. I can't prove it, it was just that feeling. And I've had that feeling with bank managers, and also socially. For instance, for a long time I've gone to legal conferences and, particularly abroad, I have felt that I'm of no interest at all on social occasions because I'm not a nubile woman. The only thing that might interest men in me would be if I were very important, or very rich – more likely if I were very important, if I was able to fix things or get them to meet someone.

Sex is a great advantage. But it can also be a disadvantage. It can take your mind off what you're doing, it can corrupt you. To be a beautiful young woman – not that I've ever been that – is a very corrupting thing; it's too easy then, and it makes it too difficult later on. You don't even have to be beautiful; it's enough to be young and beddable. Of course, the disadvantage of that is that you're not taken seriously, or weren't. I think all this has improved, but to what extent I don't really know.

I still don't think women get a fair deal in divorce situations. They get a much fairer deal now than ever they did before, that is, since 1970, when the law was changed. The judges became more and more willing to interpret the law in a way to the advantage of women – and when I say 'to the advantage' what I'm really saying is 'not to the disadvantage'. And then, just as it seemed to be going forward in a sensible way, a fairer way than before, there seemed to be a great public opposition and so we had the 1984 Act which I think made things worse for married women. Until 1970, divorce was not possible unless there was a matrimonial fault, and then that was done away with, the quid pro quo being that the financial side was improved. Well, because everybody could get a divorce after five years' separation, it completely changed the whole scene, and of course you had a lot of new marriages and second marriages and so on, and in the second marriages wives and husbands were dissatisfied because, of course, there wasn't enough money to go round. So you got quite a lot of movement against the first wife, hence the 1984 law.

Thank God, I'm not a man. I've always thought that, actually, because of all the awful things men have to do. You see, I wouldn't like to be a soldier, I wouldn't like to have to go round killing people. I wouldn't like to maintain wives and children. There are all sorts of things that men do without ever questioning them, which I think, in a sense, puts them almost among the angels. The things they take on! They've got to keep these wretched people – all these children they're encouraged to have. I mean, they can't have sex unless they've got a wife. When

311

they've got a wife, then, of course, she becomes pregnant, and then they've got this awful business about coming second, where up till then they were first, and then the children come in between, and then all those wretched children keep them awake all night and make it almost impossible for them to work. Each little mouth means they've got to work longer and longer, and I think, in the end, many of them feel they've fallen into a trap. So I'm very glad not to be a man.

Jenny Lumet: I'm nineteen, I'm a cute girl, and it's hard for some people to understand that cute girls have brains. It's just harder for people to be maybe a little bit louder or a little bit pushier, because a lot of people just don't take you seriously, and I'm in the publishing business – I work for *Detail* magazine – which is very competitive and very nasty. Women are just as bad. I think there is a general prejudice against women who are attractive. I find I don't take them seriously either. The beautiful woman says, yes, I'm an artist, right, give me a break; and she may be wonderful for all I know, but I tend to write her off, so I'm guilty just like the next person.

My stepfather, who is a wonderful man, says a woman, especially an attractive woman, is the kiss of death in the business world and in the literary world, and definitely I think that in the art scene of New York, they eat women for lunch. There are no women in the New York art scene, and yet there are wonderful women artists in New York. I think that, in the creative scene, there may be a tendency to think of women as dilettantes.

The whole structure of our society was designed by men, it was built by men. Men basically rule the world. Men and women think differently, and the whole societal system, since it was built by men, is more appropriate for the way men think. It's not going to change just because the girls are here now. We have to adjust to it, it's not going to adjust to us.

America is completely shrink-happy. Some of the shrinks are mad themselves, completely mad. America is completely devoted to the individual, which is a good and bad thing. It's raised a nation of self-obsessed people. I think some people think that going to a shrink validates their own existence. I am fucked up, therefore I exist. I was sent to a shrink by my parents.

I think that some people think it makes them more valid to have these problems and have their neuroses. Every single member of my family

312

has been in therapy, and they live for their shrinks. Europe is completely different. First of all, if you go to a shrink, which you don't, you don't talk about it. Here, it's like a cocktail party. You invite your shrink to your kid's bar mitzvah.

Gillian Lynne: Once I started to get powerful in this job, I felt there were sometimes disadvantages. Because women do slavishly call a spade a spade, and sometimes men don't like it. Of all the women I have come up against who are in a position of some kind of power in their particular job, over a cup of coffee or a glass of wine, I have never met one who didn't admit just now and again there is a stupidity attributed to us. That still somebody suddenly will look at you, or make a remark when you become a leader on an issue because either your train got there quicker or you have the guts to speak up. You feel they don't quite like it.

When I'm directing television, which I do from time to time, and I want something out of one of my cameramen on the floor, I am quite shameless about it. I put my arm around him and I say, now, if you could bring your camera just that little bit more. And I think that is more effective than if I were a man doing it through the tannoy and looking through the monitor. Certainly. And even as to speaking out, I can sometimes say, that's a load of balls and ba – ba – ba, and I'll be furious, but then I can turn on a bit of charm and shamelessly use a little bit of sex – I don't mean overt – and perhaps get away with it.

I think in some strange way men think we won't have the generalship, that's it. But I think we are wonderful at it. Men find it difficult to think of two things at once. We can think of five at once because it's part of our equipment. We're a lover, and a mistress, and a mother, and everything for a man in one, and cradling one minute and urging the next, and at the same time having a look at the oven. We are geared to think of many things at once, which is being a general.

Anna McCurley: A woman is expected to take on a variety of roles, all at once, and keep them going, all at once. You don't expect a man to think about bringing home the shopping or doing the cooking when he comes home, but you do expect him to have time to himself to think, time to withdraw. These are things which I actively now do myself, and although I haven't attained the kind of state I would like, I get a little flash of it, little tiny flashes, of what it would be like if I was able to do it all the time. I know I could be anything were I given that kind of condition, that climate to work in.

I can talk about things in a very expansive way, and I don't feel the slightest bit aggressive, and yet the automatic result is that people say I'm aggressive. By God, I can never think of myself as aggressive. By God, I can turn it on, I can be fierce as anything, and in some situations something will trigger me off and I will get very angry. Discourtesy, bad manners, cheating, that kind of thing, I hate, but generally, if it's just an interesting political point or, you know, just an argument, I can argue away perfectly happily. I don't think I'm strident, but I give the impression to men of being strident or aggressive. I don't feel it.

The rugby club syndrome is where it's a man's world and you're not there by right. It's a privilege to be there. And when you are there, they are inclined to treat you as a second-rate citizen. If you're there to butter the sandwiches fine; if you're there to act as a decoration, fine; but don't tread on it.

Sheena McDonald: I suppose, on the lowest level, being a woman inhibits you from walking round the streets at night, from going into certain public places. These are all things I do because I'm defiant about it, and I've been fortunate because nothing terrible has happened to me when I've done things it is sensible not do do, like walking home alone at night through the streets of Edinburgh across the Meadows, which I do regularly, because I don't see any reason why I shouldn't. But it would just take one bad experience to stop me doing that. On a grander scale, I don't think it has ever inhibited me, partly because I went to an all-girls school (and I would send my daughters if I had them) because you have no idea at a girls' school that women are discriminated against until you're old enough to be able to cope with it. In fact, after school, I did an arts degree at university, in English, where the women out-numbered the men seven to one, so I wasn't aware that the world seemed slightly tipped in favour of men until I left university, and by that time it struck me as so absurd that I never stopped to think about whether I should or shouldn't do something.

I'm in a job where I'm actually paid more than a lot of men in my business. And I'm in serious discussions about what I'm worth and what I should be doing, and what, professionally, I'm worth to the people I work for. But I'm always debating that with men, not with women. And I think (I don't know how you get round it) the basic difficulty is that women have children and that's the ultimate choice you have to make: whether you pursue a career, or whether you stop and have children. If you stop and have children, it interrupts everything, but then there is

314

great joy in having children. I know, because plenty of my friends have children and I can see it. But you give up the fight.

It's trendy to have women because everyone is supposed to be feminist nowadays, and if you can be more than a pretty face – if you can construct an argument and follow the theme and generally use your mind and articulate as you go – that's a bonus. Then they stop thinking of you as a woman. I'm sure I've been hired for superficial reasons and got on for real reasons, because I can do the job. But they didn't hire me because they thought I could do the job.

Journalism and broadcasting are areas where women have got on better than in other areas, because there is a false impression of liberalism and equality, which is to say, women are allowed in, most often obviously, at secretarial level. Most television companies still employ an exotic bunch of women as secretaries and production assistants, who dress competitively and behave in a traditionally female way. And, poor souls – I couldn't do that job at all – they get very badly paid. Women do get in as journalists and presenters, but where they're discriminated against is that they're not encouraged to progress beyond a certain level and not encouraged to go to the pub afterwards – they don't particularly want to go to the pub afterwards. One of the things that is very annoying about working in all businesses is the amount that goes on after hours in the pub, in the wine bar, on the golf course. That's where decisions are made and a lot of relationships (good old buddies) and friendships are established.

I've always been extremely fortunate and well favoured and successful and therefore interesting. I mean, I've always been healthy, attractive and generally fortunate. It is much harder for a woman who's been 'hauden doon' for years and years to break out at twenty-nine to do an Open University course, or get a job and join a trade union. That's much harder, because she's demanding that everybody change their perception of the way she is. I'm incredibly fortunate, I always have been – and I really have no reason to feel anything but cheerful and optimistic because I've never had a bad time. Somebody who has made a break from being an unqualified mother of three into becoming a professional woman will be able to explain in a very practical way the differences and what she had to fight against, but I've led a charmed and easy life.

I think if liberation means giving up the common courtesy, that is no liberation at all. The liberation of men is a different thing altogether. I think men have to be liberated from feeling they have to behave such and such a way, and amass a certain quantity of things which have to be this colour and that shirt stripe and that tie. I think the burden on men is immense at the moment. They are materialistic and they are sex-orientated. Women sneak through very well, but it is much harder for men to sneak through and be different.

Susan McHenry: There's a saying I grew up with as a black woman, that you had to work twice as hard to get half as far, and I think that's true for women in general. You're going to need to make as few mistakes as possible. Men have the latitude to make certain mistakes and recover well. The old-boy network often helps you recover if you make a serious mistake in public or in the workplace. Even, say, if you made a mistake that caused you to lose your job, you have a network that other opportunities come from. Women don't have that latitude.

There's a certain kind of taking seriously that happens when you are contributing to the funds, when you bring home a pay cheque. But later, when you are at home with young children doing that unpaid labour, very often your husband doesn't take you quite as seriously as when you're getting up in the morning and going out, just like he is, with a briefcase. So there's a tendency to patronize women who are in the home as just home-makers or mothers or housewives or whatever. Then, in public life, there's a presumption that our private lives are going to encroach upon our ability to perform. Certainly, women are more aware of basic priorities: like, are the children safe and all the things that go into making sure that the children are well and where they're supposed to be. We pick that off with the other things we have to do, but that's often used against us. We're thought not to be taking our public roles quite as seriously because we're intermingling them with our private responsibility.

I'm someone who suffers from a moderate amount of pre-menstrual syndrome and menstrual discomfort, and I suppose, when I was younger, I was annoyed by that. But you learn to work around it just like you learn to work around anything. I hate to compare our normal physical cycles to illnesses, but the truth is that we are temporarily indisposed very often. I was talking about this with a friend recently, discussing her menstrual discomfort with her gynaecologist, and what her doctor was saying was essentially that, if you could find the time or flexibility to lie there and take care of yourself, the discomfort doesn't last. For those of us who don't work in environments where that's possible or where people allow for taking an afternoon off and hindrance, I suppose it would be a great annoyance, but since I work in

316

a women's magazine where everyone knows about and understands that kind of thing, it doesn't present a problem to me. The same thing with pregnancy. I work in an environment where it's part of our experience, we know how to deal with it. We've just had a round of maternity leaves here. It's a hard-working time for those of us who have to fill in, but it's a joyful time, too, and also we share in the joy of the children because they are free to be here with us in our work environment. If I were working in a more typical American corporation, these would be big problems. In a workaholic, corporate environment, the job takes precedence over everything, and that's not healthy for anyone, male or female. We have to recognize that people need restoration time, that people need to spend time with their families and that, in fact, taking over an employee's every waking moment is actually not the way to get the best work out of that individual. Workplaces are beginning to acknowledge that, but it's very, very slow.

Donna McKechnie: In dancing, you just have to work hard, there's no discrimination.

I used my dancing so I could avoid discrimination. I was very shy and misunderstood much in school because of my aloofness. Dancing was the one thing that gave me a sense of freedom because I could do it well. And later on, as I grew up, I realized that no man could replace me. The women's movement was happening and I was very much aware of discrimination against women, but I wasn't experiencing it in the same way in my workplace. Because I could make as much as any man and I couldn't be replaced because of the specific requirements for female dancers.

I think successful women still run the risk of being saddled as masculine. And they get these very unattractive names hurled at them – men haters, whatever – and I think that a lot of women are afraid of that. And a lot of women friends that I have feel they are going to be alone if they really succeed, because they won't have the feminine allure and appeal that is going to be attractive to a man. They're achieving and they feel proud of their achievement, but at the same time there's a lot of fear that they are going to be very isolated, very alone. I make jokes with my women friends – we are in and out of our relationships with men, all of us trying to find the big relationship which I think is impossible. But I can see us travelling together in our sixties and seventies around the world on cruise ships. We joke about it, but I think there's a real fear that, if you become that independent, and that successful, you're going to be alone.

317

Deirdre McSharry: In journalism, the influences in my life were very strong men, because there weren't too many women at the top, but I've always admired women. When I worked in Fleet Street, the most disillusioning thing for me was the pettiness of so many men. I'm not talking about editors, though even they could be very petty, but the people down the firing line on newspapers were enormously bitchy. They seemed to suffer all things that one thinks women suffer from: they were neurotic and they never trusted one another. This was the No 1 influence I picked up when I went to the *Daily Express*, and this was when the *Daily Express* was selling a million copies. Bob Edwards was the editor, and he was lovely to me, but the people who worked there were very unhappy. It was already a very unhappy newspaper. I remember coming home in the evenings thinking, if I'm ever organizing something my way, if I'm ever running an office or a newspaper or a magazine, I will abandon these appalling tactics of distrust and dislike and stabbing in the back, and I will operate on an area of trust.

I never knew what discrimination was until I worked in Fleet Street. I was thirty-two, and I was women's editor, and it was a big job for quite a young woman. Absurd things were put to me about what you couldn't write about, or parts of the newspaper you couldn't influence. You did the women's pages, and you got on with that, and if you had a good story – their idea of a good story was something about hemlines – it could go on the front page, but if you said anything about what was happening to women, that was of no interest to anybody.

It seems to me that in businesses where a lot of women work together, the fact that their responses are very often emotional is to the general benefit, because we don't live in a rational world (we like to think we do) and we impose rationality in the shape of architecture and computers. In fact, it is a very emotional world. We're all living inside our heads; there is this other thing happening outside, but really what is happening is inside our heads. The world has to be a better place when these emotions are recognized in politics. In many ways, Thatchers's so-called Iron Lady stance is not a male stance. People say she's a kind of pretend man. In fact, her reactions are often quite emotional, including her impassivity apparent from time to time, and her incredible inflexibility. I think that's often quite a female thing, although we are more flexible.

I'm very irrational, and sometimes it bothers me and I get upset, but then I think, out of this comes good. I can say, OK, that's all terrible, we'll start again; and everybody gets very upset and mutters in the corner, she's making an irrational decision. But it doesn't matter. I once

318

said to my shrink, who is a woman, what do you do when you work from instinct? She said, what do you think instinct is? It's based on years and years of, as it were, computer studies; its based on years and years and years of your thinking your way through life, so when you come to a point and you say, I'll make a decision instinctively – that's as logical or has as much validity as saying, I'm a very logical person.

In the end, business problems are based on people, and women are, on the whole, better at dealing with other people.

Norris Church Mailer: I've always considered myself a liberated woman; I've always supported myself and taken care of myself. I have no illusions that I need someone to take care of me. That's just not the case. I was married early and divorced early, at age twenty-two. I had a teaching job, and all the things that a man would have, but when I went to buy a house, they wouldn't let me have a loan unless my father co-signed, although I was over twenty-one and had a good job. That was my first brush, I guess, with how women are treated in society. I couldn't get a credit card on my name without my father co-signing, although I had good credit rating. Because I was a woman, they wouldn't give it to me.

I like everything about being a woman. There are so many advantages, I just don't know how to go into them. I'm happy being a woman, happy being a mother and a wife, and I also am happy with my career. I don't have to go to an office from nine to five every day. I can bend my work hours around my family, as my husband does. We have a nice loose family life because one or the other of us is always around and we can make plans, go off somewhere else and take our work with us, which we do, like in summer time. I'm very fortunate and I'm so happy about that aspect of my life as a woman. I don't have any complaints.

I like doing housework; I'm an obsessive housekeeper. I like everything shined and spotless and polished and in place. Fortunately my kids are pretty neat children, I guess from being hit over the head so many years about putting things away. I really have to live in an orderly house. It sounds a little crazy, but one of the ways I relax is to clean out closets and that sort of thing.

I think one of the most important things is to give women a hand as far as childcare goes. One of the upsetting things about the Reagan administration and the new policies are the cutbacks on childcare and finances for children's food. I think every big employer should have a

319

nursery so women can bring their children to be taken care of properly, and not have to leave them in the hands of people who run day-care centres. It's hard for women to get quality care for their children and still have a chance to have a career and make a living. So if women are going to compete with men and raise children at the same time, they really have to have some help.

I think that successful women in America should retain their femininity as well. I really hate these skirt suits like the men wear. You can dress nicely and attractively, and femininely and conservatively, without having to wear a cardboard shoulder and lapel suit. And those awful running shoes they wear when they walk to work to get their exercise. That's one of my pet peeves.

It's so unfair. My own husband is sixty-three. If I was sixty-three, I doubt I'd be married to a thirty-seven-year-old man, let's face it. And as I get older I probably will do all the things women do to stay looking young, have face-lifts and all of that stuff. But I think that's good; women should use whatever is available to look as attractive as they can.

I've never for one minute wanted to be a man, never.

Alice Mason: I didn't come to New York until I was twenty years old. I didn't know what career I wanted. I met a woman who was in real estate, and she said it's a good career for a woman, so why don't you come and work for me? So I worked in her office and decided that I liked real estate and was going to become the best, the top real-estate broker. So I really set out to do things that almost no one did. At the time, in the 1950s it was difficult, because New York had six or seven managing agents and they only hired women in the *Social Register*, which is like *Burke's Peerage* in England. This woman I worked for dealt mainly in rentals and houses, but I decided I wanted to do everything. I was always a little politically minded, not political Democrat or Republican, but in terms of judging people, whether they were right wing, or left wing, liberal or reactionary. I always reacted to what type of mentality people had. I saw that the left-wing people lived together and the right-wing lived together. The people who were liberals all lived in the same buildings, so I decided to try to get people into those building that were liberal, and that if I presented all the credentials and they didn't have strong prejudices, I could get them in. Because at that time they had no Jews, no Irish, no Scandinavians, and no one with no vowels in their name. It was really the White Anglo-Saxon Protestant descent and the Eastern Establishment – they couldn't be from Texas or California either. So I said, I am going to be the broker for everyone who is not in the *Social Register*. And I filled the void. That's how, four years later, I became the top. In other words, I recognized the void, and I just said I was going to be that person to deal with all those people. Imagine all the rich and successful New Yorkers who didn't have a broker because they weren't in the *Social Register*.

The men in my business tend to be homosexual types. It's really a female occupation, so I went into a field that's largely female. Not that there were not men, regular men in it. But most women who went into it, and were in the *Social Register*, went into it when they were either widowed or when their children had grown, and they were all over fifty-five, so everyone I met in the business was between fifty-five and eighty. I was the only young person I ever knew. I was the first young women ever to get into this business.

I think economic independence means a lot, but I think that also women are just not liberated in their souls. Even if they had total economic independence, I think most women really can't understand how they can survive without a man to go to a restaurant with, go to the theatre with, or do anything with. I don't know when that will ever change, I really don't. I think there will be individual women, but I don't think women in general will change.

Margaret Matheson: I went to a private school with little in the way of academic ambition. It was once claimed, at one of our annual prize-givings, that the school existed to produce women who would be good members of committees and make good wives for diplomats.

There is absolutely no question that there are hundreds of men around in London, in my industry, and related industries, who are enormously patronizing towards women – often not really consciously. They may think themselves tremendously progressive and open-minded, but in fact there is just an absolutely innate tendency to assume that because she's a woman, she's not actually taking everything out of the meeting that the men are taking. Consequently you get those wonderfully amusing occasions where women just clean up because men think they aren't listening, and they actually have a better grip. All of those traditions that we've all lived with, that secretaries are women, that we are all going out of our way to turn the other way up – it takes a long time for that to correct itself, but I think the drift is right. There is no doubt that, just as it used to be perfectly acceptable to refer to black people as niggers, it isn't any more. Even in fairly right-wing unpleasant company, it isn't thought to be acceptable any more to refer to nignogs. Just so, with Western women, there is now a clear understanding, a general acceptance, that women ought to have an equal opportunity, that women are equally bright. Except for a few lunatics, there is a general acceptance that we're biologically different, that as far as relationships go, we're complementary. But as far as achieving in careers and business and the arts and so on, I would suggest that society now believes that men and women are equal. They just aren't yet, because we haven't worked through all that, and most jobs are held by men, in the film industry, just as in television.

I think that the way that some families bring their children up, and the way certainly British education, both state and private, approaches children, is calculated to reduce their confidence. That is to say, I think the most important thing when you're bringing up children, if you're trying to help them have a broad and enjoyable life, is to make them believe – not in an arrogant or selfish way – that they're really valuable, that they're important people. And I think in that sense that my own upbringing was very *laissez faire*, very much you live your life and here we all are living in this place together, but we're all doing what's interesting. If you want to go off and sit watching rabbits in a field for a week on end, that's great, do that; if you want to go and sell the milk, then go and sell the milk. That's a good attitude to take to children. I'm grateful my upbringing was not directed, except in a sense that it followed what were, for my background, the conventions. They sent me away to boarding, single-sex school and so on, but aside from the fact that it ran along those tram-lines, it was very free. I think that's a good way to let people develop their own interests and develop their own confidence. Confidence is to do with having a view about what you're interested in and what you do, and having the courage to express it, for which you need tools. You need to be articulate through talking to others who are articulate, and maybe knowing about others' experiences. I most definitely don't think that women have more or less confidence than men. I think the somewhat over-directed childhood that a lot of Western children have reduces their confidence because it's very ordered and their schooling tends to be rather competitive, so if you happen to be in the bottom and not the top half, you've already branded yourself as a failure. That's hard to get over.

Homayoun Mazandi: Women don't cry so easily any longer. My mother cried more than me, And my daughters cry less than me. My grandmother cried more than any of us, and I think she was happier, too. She

322

was treated as not equal, she was treated as a fragile, important belonging. That was why she was crying: she couldn't face reality. She never went through anything I went through and my daughter is going through in life. She was treated something like a flower. I am not treated like a flower at all. Here I am, treated like a big tree, something to punch, having punches here and there, and I have to punch back. I'm not going to cry; I punch back.

I find I am becoming better with age. I am like a good wine and an old carpet. I find myself happier and I know what I want. I don't want to go back to eighteen. With age, I find I am becoming more attractive to myself. That's why I don't try to hide my age. I even try not to tint my hair. I think you have to live with reality – reality is beauty. I don't want to be without the things I've learned. An older woman can have a young lover. I went through that relationship, was loved by a young man, and when you go through that sort of relationship, you really build up the confidence I have now.

Lady Menuhin: In the ballet, it was not equal, and I fought for equality. It was absolutely absurd. I'm talking about the war years, and just before, when I was young and dancing. The men got paid almost twice as much, and they danced half as much, because there was no such thing as the male *corps de ballet*. The girls had to find their own shoes – they were given one pair of point shoes – the men didn't have to buy their point shoes. There was tremendous inequality, and I was always known as the battling Diana, the wild half-caste, by my family.

The kind of life I led was not really an ordinary woman's life. The ballet is a stevedore's life: seventeen hours a day of the most gruelling work in the world. Harrowing, gruelling, ghastly – bleeding feet, everything. It was a vocation.

The tasks that lie automatically in a woman's field are mostly what the Germans would call *Nichtigkeiten* – nothingnesses. Is there enough linen? Has this come back from the cleaners? Is Yehudi's picnic basket ready? All the things that add up to devotion, and one gives willingly, but they are not terribly interesting. I'm a more than willing adjunct to Yehudi. I'm terribly lucky that I should find a man to serve, because all my life I have felt that love was service. I could never marry a man I couldn't serve.

The irritating thing is that people think that to be Yehudi's wife means I go to Elizabeth Arden every Monday, I choose a new dress from wherever, usually at least every ten days, that I have a pedicure instead of scrubbing my own feet with pumice stone, that it is a glamorous life. It isn't in the least. It's one of the hardest working lives in the world, if one wants to do the job properly.

There are women who are intelligent and funny and manage cleverly to keep their superior intelligence under wraps. They know they must never degrade their man, because that spoils the balance. A woman has to be a sort of giro-compass in a rough sea and know how to keep the balance of the ship going all the time. I always think, about my life, that Yehudi is on the bridge looking at the view and the vision and everything he wants to do, and I'm the poor old stoker in the boiler-room, stoking away, keeping the good ship Menuhin going, not so much important as fundamentally necessary. I think women who don't recognize priorities cannot make a success of their lives or their marriages.

It's a biological fact that the woman is in a nervous state – I'm talking pre-pill – if one is going to be absolutely crude. In a way, I envy all these young people. Not the ones who just do it for the sake of it, but when I was young and very much in love, I was far too terrified. And there was this feeling of the awful disgrace of abortion, which I've always had. I'm not a prude, but the thought of killing something is awful. I do think, again, that's why women have to be much more subtle, so much more self-controlled and self-denying.

Kate Millett: It was very much a turning-point for me that, in my own country, I couldn't make a living, although I had a very wonderful education and gained an Oxford Master's degree. It was about that time I began to hear about the women's movement, so I joined it, but it was a call that I had been waiting for all my life. From the time I was a child, I was aware of how unfair things were between men and women and how entirely masculine control of society was – the Pope, the President, the whole business; the family structure which I saw doing so much to suffocate my mother.

Women artists are not even represented in museums. We have to fight back this absurd misrepresentation of women through art history. Much as we were discriminated against, we did actually paint pictures and make sculptures, but I never heard of it when I was a young artist. We have virtually no sense of our past in the visual arts at all. The work of our predecessors is not exhibited; we ourselves, in my generation, do not really have access to the museums. Of course, it's all a stacked deck, all of it, everywhere. Publishing is the same. I'm always paid less than men. I'm always treated like a child, I have to be a good little girl. Agents think so, publishers think so, editors think so. I'm infantilized, even in my own profession, but it's typical. Popular literature is often written by women, and some of it makes a lot of money, not only in these times but in the nineteenth century as well. I think, however, when you are talking about serious writing and fine arts, you really are up against an enormous wall of prejudice and discrimination, and it is spelled out in reality in the number of exhibitions, the number of museum entries, the collections, the way dealers and collectors feel about you, the way editors, publishers and agents feel about you. It's not only a matter of money, it's a matter of prestige, encouragement, sense of identity, all of it, and this is someone speaking who has probably had a lot of privilege and a lot of good luck. About 80 per cent of people who go to art school in this country are women. About 10 per cent of people who exhibit in the museums are women. This is a man's world. And what we're trying to do is to make it a different one, one of people.

If we started from the base of equality, I think people would be startled to see how unequal things are in America. Start with the Congress. We have virtually no representation at all, and certainly less than any other country. It's not because women don't want to go into politics, it's because this is a patriarchy and it hasn't changed much. It had two big waves of organized feminist political agitation, but it hasn't changed. It didn't pass the Equal Rights Amendment, and we are now in a very dreadful period of reaction to Reagan's regime. All progressive forces in this country are virtually at a standstill. The women's movement is holding its own, but it's not making any great progress. Blacks aren't making any progress and we don't have a left. These are really bad times.

There has been a remarkable and wonderful little bit of progress on the part of gay people in view of the fact that you couldn't even say lesbian or homosexual fifteen years ago. The fact the gay people can identify themselves as gay, organize as gay, run for office, demand their rights, it's fantastic. Historically speaking, it is an amazing amount of progress in a short span. But you still have enormous prejudice as well, enormous contempt and hatred. And it's gotten much worse in this country under the present reactionary climate of the Reagan regime and the right-wing screaming about Aids being the scourge of God and so on. It's a dreadful, dreadful disease, but it is not the scourge of God.

Cristina Monet: For every discrimination, there's a pay-off like protectiveness, and in forgoing all that discrimination, women have also forgone the paternalism, the seats for pregnant women in buses. It's loaded: you give up one, you lose the other. I guess a lot of women don't want the other. I'm not a feminist. I think I'm quite a wet sort of woman, not very aggressive, and so in areas where I should be aggressive and furthering myself, intellectually, the great rationale is for me to see my femininity as a reason for passivity, to feel feminine instead of wet. If I were someone who was aggressive and prepared to fight tooth and claw to get where I wanted in some sphere, and was continually kept back because I was female, I might feel very differently. If there's a man in a position to give me something professionally he didn't give me because I was a woman, I'd be livid. But I've never suffered that. That would be a pain in the arse.

I feel very frightened of letting the sand run out of the hourglass since I'm still such an intrinsic believer in women as items in the market place where being very bright is an extra bonus to prettiness. One day the prettiness has gone and you're bright and you haven't done enough with it. I think I have to carve an identity for myself intellectually, undistracted by being pretty and being a mother, before my child grows up and my looks fade.

Bel Mooney: Men's attitudes are to do with their own limited view of what being a woman is, which is handed on to them. We are talking about thousands of years of conditioning. And so they do see women in certain roles – they prefer women to be passive. Very few men don't. Very few men want their wives to go out and work and be equal. Even men whose wives do work – as soon as they have children, they assume that their wives should be with the children. And that is the second thing which is the main cause of inequality. It's biological. Many women will have a baby, or two babies, and want desperately to be with them – even if they thought, at first, they were going to take six months' maternity leave and go back to work. Mother love is a very real thing. I certainly have it. I hate leaving my children. My husband can leave his children – our children – much more easily. Why? It must be innate. And that is an inequality which is biological, which all the legislation in the world won't do anything about. So I'm not a militant feminist in the sense that I say, even if you have twenty-four-hour day care, it wouldn't stop women actually wanting to be with their babies, then feeling frustrated and bored, then resenting the fact that their husbands don't do more to help. I see it as a sort of cycle.

326

A woman can be a totally independent, achieving human being in public, and can be, as I am, a loving romantic person privately. And they are not mutually incompatible. On the contrary. You have to have a lot of confidence to be a romantic. It's nothing to do with being passive. It's being able to show that you love somebody and to know that your love is valuable. That's confidence, you know. My love is worth giving – I know that.

I'm not cynical about most things, but I'll use anything. I use my brain, I use my appearance, I use charm, I'll use bossiness, I'll use anything to get myself an advantage in the market place, because I am a freelance person and I need to earn a living.

I like to look quite sexy. And men can't put that together in their minds with the rather terrible book review or essay. They can't actually put the two together. I've had said to me, with surprise, well, your second novel was really very serious, as if this woman couldn't be expected to produce something serious. So if they could categorize me: this person could be a *Daily Mirror* journalist, could be a chat-show hostess. They find it hard to get their masculine minds around the complexity, especially if you like to wear sexy dresses and Janet Reger underwear. I also write books about suicide, and essays about the miners' strike, and they can't get their minds round that and find it intimidating. I think it's a pity. My husband doesn't find me intimidating, but some men do. They get the intellectual equivalent of brewer's droop – they can't actually get an intellectual erection because they find it so scary.

I wish I had the strength not to care what men think about me, but I do care. And therefore I always try and play down the serious side of me in public – always, always. I drive my husband mad. He thinks I shouldn't do it. But I do. And I think it's because of wanting to make things easy. I don't argue. I hate arguing with men – seriously arguing – so I will turn it aside and compromise. I suppose that must be linked with something in women which goes back centuries, which is the desire to please. I think I'm a throwback to a woman in the thirteenth, fourteenth or nineteenth century whose one asset was her marriageability, and you had to be pleasing to men; and in order to be pleasing, you were compliant, you agreed, you were charming, you were pretty, you were all those things: passive, submissive.

I would rather have been born a man. I would. It's very difficult. I love being a woman, I love my life, but I think it would be easier for me to do all the things I want to, be all the things I want to be, if I were a man. Because I feel like a bird whose feet are stuck in the mud. That's the image which comes to my mind: the feet are in mud – all soft, sticky lovely, emotional oozing mud – and I can't quite get off the ground. And I think, if I were a man, I'd be flying.

Sara Morrison: I remember resenting being female because it was taken for granted exactly what my life would be like. There was a bit of me that rather resented that in a sort of laid-back way, because how did anybody know? My very Edwardian grandmother, who was an extremely intelligent woman, half-knew that life wasn't that simple, and so, in a way, she was something of a pilot light as I got older, because she appeared not to disapprove of the fact that I didn't take for granted that pattern of British life which really stopped before the war. It was of a privileged kind which one shouldn't knock at all, but I knew perfectly well it didn't exist in a real way by the time I grew up. I can remember thinking, when I first married, what's so dreadful about this is not that there's anything dreadful about it, but that I have begun the rest of my life. Nothing much else is going to happen. The nearest I am going to get to a drama is the dog being sick on the carpet or making the Sunday joint.

It is lonely at the top. I'm not much given to introspection; all that does is send one nearly round the bend with dissatisfaction with oneself and everything else. But if one does try and have a sort of cool moment of honesty, I sometimes think I'd be deeply lonely even if I hadn't been an only child anyway, and born lonely, and brought up to think and honestly believe that I am only not alone if my dog's with me. It sounds crazy, but it's true. And therefore it makes you not worry about being largely excluded from some of the ordinary vibrations and grapevines of working in a man's world. Because you start off with a sort of lonely capsule round you, so you don't mind. But if you are a woman who was extremely gregarious in a large family, who has brought up her own family, why take that step to the summit of whatever it is? It's very easy to be there or thereabouts; quite different to be at the top.

Truthfully, I am rather pro-men, and I can say that I have not been patronized or condescended to on the whole. I may have been deplored, but not condescended to.

I would rather have been a man, but that's purely for some things which would really have required a male physique to do. But I haven't not enjoyed being a woman.

Kathy Myers: There's a sense in which women learn to be deferential. Part of the way they are brought up is to admit the mistake. You discover that conceding ground very early in the confrontation gives you a form of power, and that's a useful thing to learn. I think women are good tacticians, in meetings and so on. One thing that girls are brought up to, even as children, is that boys do the talking, girls listen. One of the things about listening is that you watch very closely. I must have spent the first fifteen years of my life at my parents' dinner parties and business meetings, just watching how people manoeuvred round each other. Seeing who likes who, who's got the power. You learn a lot that way.

The good thing Cambridge did was teach me that women friends are important.That's when I started to have female friends. It was one of the pay-offs of the system. After I graduated from Clare College, I got a PhD scholarship to Downing College, also at Cambridge, and they only had a few women there and they were all over fifty. And the first time I was there, they actually sent round a memo saying they found it disruptive to have a young woman in the academic establishment, that it interfered with the academic process. I lasted four or five months with nobody speaking to me, and then they had their big commemoration dinner, to celebrate the founding of the college, a hundred years earlier. I had come up from London, and arrived late because there was a lot of snow on the railway line. And the bursar, who is basically one of the administrators of the college, as I came through the college door came rushing up and said, thank God you've arrived, we've laid all the places, we thought you would never get here. I thought, that's really nice, he's actually acknowledged the only female student they've got, because everybody else ignores me. He said, you must come this way, and whisked me through all the back passages of the college and we ended up in the kitchen, where he flung this little white apron at me. I thought the commemoration dinner must be a bit like the masons, you have to wear some very unusual clothing, so I put this apron on. Then he handed me a dish, and it suddenly occurred to me that there was something a bit odd, and I said, who do you think I am? He said, well, you are the new supply waitress, aren't you? And that was it, you know. I discovered by accident that they hadn't laid me a place at the meal either. It was, oh, appalling, and I left the college next day. I thought, right, I've had enough of Cambridge. I went to London after that.

One of the things I realized going through Cambridge was that, if you want to be considered attractive to men, then to show you are clever is a dumb thing to do. In a sense, the very bright girls played at being dumb. I learnt that if I wanted to be socially acceptable, to speak too much was a very stupid thing to do, because you posed a threat to a lot of men. Now, if you're used to displaying your intelligence in such subversive moves, keep quiet and not threaten, there's a very narrow boundary between that and starting to lose confidence because you don't practise any more. It can be very undermining if you try, and then are rejected because you tried and succeeded. That is an amazing blow. That would never happen to a man. Men do not get rejected for succeeding, women do. If you're unconfident, at least you'll keep your man, even if you don't keep your job, which justifies in a way that lack of confidence.

Whereas a lot of ambitious women are inspired by ambitious men, a lot of ambitious men are deeply threatened by ambitious women. That is a problem. It is also a problem that what you might say may not carry the same weight as if a man said it. Often that might push you to the point of an hysterical outburst, which confirms the opinion they had in the first place, which is that you are not competent. And whereas if a man is firm with somebody, it's a sign of masculinity and strength and integrity, in a woman it's a sign of a complete harridan. So what women have to learn to do is be charmingly smiling while telling somebody off. Women learn to operate in quite sophisticated ways to get through that.

The fact that women have to move on several fronts at once means that you stay in more control in a sense, you're better at surviving emotionally while physically doing your job, while caring for other people. To be goal-directed is quite a dangerous thing. Men die earlier. That's no accident. They die early because they lead a tougher life. Not because they work harder, but because they live it in a more stupid fashion.

It can get very annoying if you're trying to write something in a pub, and you've got five minutes, and somebody thinks, oh, this poor girl, she's only writing because she's been stood up, and comes and talks to you. I find wine bars better than pubs. You get left alone in wine bars. You don't get left alone in pubs.

I spent the first twenty years of my life as a boy as far as I am concerned, so maybe I've had a sex change somewhere along the line. I think the best place to inhabit is the middle ground, and then take the best from both. The boyish side of my nature is something I value very much. I've abandoned that at a high cost.

Lynda Myles: As a child, I grew up in a block of six apartments which my father had designed. There were six young professional families in the apartment block, and all the other families had boys, so I grew up with boys effectively until I went to school, and was a complete tomboy. The first crisis came when I was about five and couldn't become a wolf-cub, which they had all done. That was the first time I realized there was a difference. I began to realize I wasn't going to have the kind of freedom they had. I had no interest in dolls. I had train sets and guns and no desire to play with little girls, and I found it very bizarre when I went to school and always felt I wanted to be with the boys because they seemed to have more fun.

I had a rather charmed time, in a way, because I read philosophy at Edinburgh University – which was a spectacularly civilized department, a department with rather a lot of teachers and comparatively few students, and the teachers tended to be dramatists in their spare time, or write poetry. So it was a tremendously civilized environment and there was no sense of any kind of sexism there. When I was about nineteen, I started working for the Edinburgh Film Festival as deputy director. When I was twenty-five I became director of the Film Festival, which I thought quite interesting, because Scotland tends to be rather backward in terms of that kind of social development, and it seemed extraordinary that no one seemed to worry about my becoming director, even though I was twenty-five and female. I worked for the BBC as a radio producer in between university and taking over the festival full time. The only time I ran into problems there was when I moved from radio to television and got married in the summer, and that was the first time I thought seriously about discrimination, because I knew they would be reluctant to give me the job had they known I was married. The assumption is that a female, once married, will not make the same commitment to the job. So, for the first six months or so in BBC Television, I didn't wear my wedding ring and didn't let anyone know I was married, because I wanted them to be confident I could do the job. But the rest of my professional life I've been very lucky. I've been helped at odd points in my career, always by men by definition, because men have been in the positions of power where they could help. All the men who have helped me in any way professionally have been men who have very easy relationships with brighter women. They all tend to be married to more intelligent women than the norm, and I've always been extremely suspicious of any man who seems intelligent and capable yet who is married to an idiot, a glamorous idiot.

What is most unfair at the moment is, I think, that more women do still have to choose between a career – a serious career – and a family. Ten years ago, I would probably have argued that a woman should have a child and get a nanny and get back to work in six months. The trouble is, I've now seen friends with children at close quarters, and they're

331

perpetually exhausted for the first year or so. I also am now not so sure it's good for the children. A nanny is one thing, but the idea of children being dumped with child-minders is a bit problematic. But that's something one can't solve by legislation.

The sort of sacrifices one has to make to have a major job, like running a studio, negate the possibility of any kind of normal life, and sometimes I think it's not that women can't do these jobs, it's that a lot of women are actually sane enough to reject it and say, we want a life, a life outside work. I sometimes envy the men who have the back-up of a family, the wife who does the packing so they can leave for a trip at ten minutes' notice. Somehow men are allowed to have the surroundings done, to have all the comforts, but these top jobs do demand incredible sacrifices, and I think a lot of women basically have a much better balance than men. There's something rather crazy about the sort of drive that takes people on these very high-flown jobs, and a lot of women just don't want it. That's probably a sign of sanity.

There are still a lot of men who feel it's not worth having a serious talk with women, that somehow women aren't likely to generate the same kind of ideas. For intellectual companionship, they'd rather stick to men. I rather share the William Boyd view of public schools. My ex-husband was a product of a Scottish public school, and I think the damage they do to men is unspeakable. I don't think they ever quite recover from it.

I did a documentary in the summer with a Scottish television crew, and the director failed to take notice of anything I said. If it were repeated by a male, he would listen. One thing that now would come under the Sexual Discrimination Act happened years ago, just before I went into films full time. I had an interview with Scottish Television for a job as a TV director, and when they heard I was married they said, what about the children, what about the 'weans'?

I've led a charmed existence because I've always been able to run the organizations I've been involved with, but I notice – for example, on a film shoot – the way women are treated, the way women are talked about. The assumption is that women are pretty nightmarish. The first day on *Defence of the Realm*, a film I produced in 1985, I met the heads of department I hadn't met, people like the electricians, and one of them came up and said, are you hairdressing? I said, no. Ah, he said, you must be make-up. I said, no. I thought, I'll let him wriggle a little bit more. He said, continuity? And I said, no. And then I thought this is enough. I said, actually I'm the producer. It's this same boring

332

assumption that, if one is female around the film, one is one of these three jobs, or the producer's secretary.

The thing I love above everything which I fear I will never achieve, is serenity. I've known one or two older people who have this quality. One was my first analyst, a wonderful woman in Edinburgh called Dr Winifred Rushforth, who was practising at ninety-eight when she died. She was quite amazing, but she had this quality of serenity which I thought the most enviable single quality I'd ever seen.

Lynn Nesbit: I've had children, and if you're a working mother you have to be better at your job than any man because people are too ready to spring on you and suspect, well, she's doing this and that, she's not working as hard as she should be. Another problem for a woman is how to be taken seriously professionally and remain a woman in her psycho-sexual life. To hold both those things together is much more difficult for a woman than it is for a man. If a male executive is having an affair with somebody in his office, there would not be nearly the amount of criticism there would be if a woman was doing it. There is that sexual fear about women on the part of men. The presence of women in the workplace is a very potent thing for men. If we don't acknowledge it, then we can't deal with it, so I think it's best to acknowledge it.

I am very comfortable with my female identity. I like the whole physical sense of being a woman. I like the fact that women in many ways are allowed more emotional range than men. Also, women are often free to choose whether they work or not, and I think that's an extreme advantage, although it's not relevant to my life. I always was the wage-earner in the family in terms of the person who made the most income, and since I've been divorced I totally support my children. I'm in the position of having had to pay a settlement to my ex-husband, so I am not in any kind of traditional female role. In the United States, we have divorce laws that have gender neutrality. There is something called the equitable distribution of assets, and therefore the person who has the most money has to pay the other partner, regardless of sex.

Julia Neuberger: The advantages of being a woman, certainly if you're a professional woman, are that you are still relatively unusual if you reach the top of your profession. Quite clearly, I get asked to do television, radio because there I am. I fit any number of the general bills you could possibly want: I'm female – that's not a minority, but, you know, we're rarer; I'm Jewish; I'm a rabbi; I'm SDP. I've got a lot of good labels. I protect gay rights, that sort of thing. So to that extent it's an advantage: one has a scarcity value at the top of a professional tree. One works with men who actually like the company of women; I often work with men I like and admire enormously, and the working relationship is lovely. That's a tremendous asset.

In the Jewish community, in the more traditional side than that I belong to, women are at a profound disadvantage. In Orthodox Judaism, women are second-class citizens, as they are in Islam and, indeed, as one could argue they are to some extent in Christianity, although the reasons are different. One of the things I'm going to do one day is write a book about the contrast between Judaism and Islam on the one side and Christianity on the other, because I think the attitudes are very different. But they are second-class citizens. Their testimony is not considered as weighty as that of men; they're not considered teachers beyond a certain stage; their intellectual value is not considered as great. Now, that's enormous prejudice.

Despite being SDP politically, I'm seen as the hard left of Judaism. I'm seen as being very extreme, very liberal, and rather odd. And, therefore, to what extent the attitude of others is because of my own personal views and to what extent it's because I'm female is very hard to judge. Various colleagues and friends would say that, however much I'm respected in the non-Jewish world, my own intimate Jewish world will never take me entirely seriously. They take me more seriously now because the non-Jews take me seriously, but they will never take me entirely seriously.

I've been a rabbi for nine years. It's a long time. I was treated entirely equally by my colleagues when I was one of them. From 1983 until 1985, I actually chaired the liberal rabbis, and what my colleagues found difficult was my being in a senior position to them. Only temporarily – we elect a chairman, and the chairman only lasts for two years – but for two years I was basically their senior. They found that terribly difficult to take. Equal, yes. Senior, that's too much.

Nanette Newman: By nature, I'm a sort of dilettante. I love going off in different directions. And I hate not doing *something*. So, to me, the worst thing that could happen would be to have nothing to do, although when I got married, I loved being married and I was fortunate to fall in love with somebody I am still in love with. That's wonderful. I had children I adored, but I always knew I wanted to keep just one toe in the water so I could, any time I wanted, resume some sort of career. And all the time I was married, I always worked a bit just to keep things bubbling over – bubbling along, rather.

Women are made to feel insecure in lots of ways because of the constant accent on youth, or the obsession with some people to remain young, particularly in America, where you see women who are lifted sky-high with every known invention in order to remain on the outside young, and it's a very spooky thing. I can understand women wanting to remain as young as they can within reason, but there is a kind of obsessive desperation that sets in. It's frightening. I think it must sometimes be like going to bed with a sort of female Frankenstein's monster. But I think women do that out of a feeling of fear of getting old and being unattractive, and sometimes I think women who are born unattractive have an advantage, because no way is a man going to fall in love with them for their beauty. So the man that falls in love with them loves them for something very special, which they are always going to have.

Emma Nicholson: I have never felt that men patronize me. Nor would I tolerate it. People have always taken me seriously, sometimes too seriously.

I had been in computers for six or seven years without ever bumping into judging people by sex, and then I became the computer consultant of a prestigious consultancy firm. They actually had to have a board meeting to decide whether they could take a woman consultant on, and I was so astounded I thought they must be joking. That was the first time, apart from two very odd happenings, but they were burned into my mind because they were so rare. When I wanted to join our family firm, a private gin-distilling company founded in about 1780, my older cousins wouldn't let my father bring me in because I was a girl. That astounded me. Then, when I was looking for a career, my father suggested stockbroking, and I got right the way through all the interviews before discovering that girls couldn't be proper stockbrokers, so I dropped that like a hot potato. These were almost the only times I recall realizing that doors were shut against me because of gender rather than in terms of what I did. I judge human beings by the quality of their output, not by what they are, what colour they are, what creed they are, where they come from, which is all fascinating. It's all a blend, everybody's a blend, but I judge them by what they achieve.

Women can get to the top, certainly in Western society. Where the law is on your side, there is no real barrier, and British women have had equal treatment in law in almost every sphere since 1924 when most of the laws of equal opportunity came in. My grandfather was in the Cabinet at the time. I suppose I was brought up in the knowledge that I'm as good as anybody, man or woman, but none the less I must recognize that there are areas of residual prejudice where women have a tougher battle than is necessary to get through to the levels of achievement they can make.

The reason which makes many women not take chances and opportunities open to them is, first, the great biological pull of having children. It's enormous, it's Mother Nature, it's the biggest pull of all, for all humans, to reproduce, and that overwhelms many women who want to be successful, who want to be a chairman of ICI.

I do not for one moment say there are still not walks of life in which women are rejected on grounds of their sex. There are. For example, in medicine only 11 per cent of consultants are women, and yet more and more young women doctors are coming up trying to become consultants. It's taking a long time to break down the archaic views of the British Medical Society. They will be broken down, but it's still very tough for women to get on in medicine. It's the old-fashioned professions where tradition reigns supreme. In the law, there aren't enough women judges or enough women barristers yet, but they're coming on. There are lots of women solicitors; it appears to be easier. In accountancy, there are many many more women chartered accountants now, but it has been traditionally very difficult. An old and respected senior member of one of the oldest chartered accountancy firms in the City said the other day that, although over 50 per cent of proposed new entrants were women, he was only taking 20 per cent of women because he didn't want to upset the balance of the offices even though the women were better qualified than the men. So I would never deny that there are areas of lingering prejudice. And where you find prejudice, it is not a question of working fifty times harder. You've got to do something very clever to get round the prejudice. But in normal circumstances, of course, a woman doesn't have to work twice as hard as a man. That's ridiculous.

I have never thought of myself as attractive. I had three very pretty sisters. I remember my mother, whom I love dearly, saying, don't worry about not being pretty, darling, you've got a brain. And I suppose that's how I see myself. Real quality enlarges with age, whether you are a man or a woman. To worry about losing your looks betrays a shallow mind. Some of the most wonderful women I've known have been eighty, full of spiritual beauty that shines through their faces. Do things for other

336

people, and beauty will shine out of your face regardless of age. If you're selfish, self-centred, buttoned up with yourself, worried about what you look like, the quality of your skin, then at the end of the day it's irrelevant, you will get ugly.

Mavis Nicholson: When I got into television, I found my niche in afternoon telly. At that time Jeremy Isaacs was trying to redress the balance of only men on in the evening in the important jobs, and we women jolly well knew that in one way it was a little back part of telly we were in. A lot of people thought, oh, it's only television in the afternoon, it's only for women, and they'd leave us alone, so we got away with blue murder. We used to do advanced subjects quietly in the afternoon. But I like that little niche where you talk directly to people and they listen, because they are at home in the afternoon, usually uninterrupted. Young mums would write to us: you are a lifeline, when I hear you talking about the things you do, it gives me heart and I know I can perhaps be out there one day again with all of you. It was really quite a moving experience.

I must be the oldest woman presenting on British television. But I've just got to grin and bear it, and grinning and bearing it makes you much more attractive, I think. I don't like the idea of my life shortening; I haven't lost my zeal for it, so therefore I'd hate to die. I think growing old is just sadder. You don't feel wiser, necessarily.

There is one characteristic of women which I know I possess: I do not wish to be disliked. I quite like being admired, but more than that, I want to be liked. Now, if you want to push in a job, you probably have to risk being disliked. A head of a company may be disliked by a lot of people. He's got to make decisions to sack people, or change people, or promote or not to promote people. I think quite a lot of women don't want to face up to that particular responsibility because they don't want to be disliked.

I wouldn't have minded being a man. But I've never had penis-envy – Simone de Beauvoir's famous penis-envy. I wanted to be a boy when I was a young girl because I just thought, somehow, it was more useful to be a boy. But no, on the whole I'd come back as a woman.

Béatrice Nivois: I agreed to pose for *Playboy* to give a different image of a journalist. You normally see a journalist sitting in an office looking very classical and serious. So why not present a different image, and undress? In any case, the photos were very soft. The miracle is that I am the first journalist to have done it; I'm very glad to have done it because I was the first. I'm not unusual. I have a normal destiny, but ever since the day I posed for *Playboy* people have been talking about me. It only embarrasses me if someone comes up in the street and pesters me and says vulgar things. But I think they do that because they're frustrated, because they can't find elsewhere what they think they can find in me. It goes back to the idea that, if you can appear in the nude in a men's magazine, you must therefore be an easy lay. I thought about reactions like that before I did it, but the thought didn't torture me.

Men can't hide their excitement. Our advantage over them is that we can conceal ours. In that respect, we equal out. We may lose blood every month and become ill with it, because it does hurt sometimes, but we have compensations because, when we are excited, when we fancy a man, we can easily conceal it. And a man can never hide it.

Christine Ockrent: When I started producing the news, people would say, oh, she's so dry and harsh. The stereotype of a woman, especially on the air, is someone who must have her hair done properly. In the case of a man nobody minds. She mustn't have pimples on her face, and she must change her shirt every day. Whereas if a man wears the same tie twice, people will giggle, and say, well, he didn't go home last night. A woman is also expected to smile, but often you don't necessarily feel like smiling, so in the beginning it was a little difficult. But after a while, people become accustomed, and even men, I think, agree now that a woman can be as serious as a man and that, even if she doesn't smile when she talks about five people being killed in a bomb outrage, she can still be a woman.

I think that every age has its rewards, and its wrinkles. Old age is not a major problem.

Jane O'Grady: I feel I have been born at the wrong time. If I was a bit older, I could have been very promiscuous. In the 1960s, everyone was promiscuous, but maybe then it wouldn't have been much fun. But now I feel it's impossible to be.

Women can't be disgusting and dirty and farty and so on. Men can be like that. Men can somehow be in many different sort of phases, but a woman has a much more limited way of behaving, and that's why she can let her hair down among women and really talk disgustingly and be disgusting. That sounds awful, but there is that sense of freedom because men are somehow so easily offended, so fastidious.

Talking to a transvestite made me realize how private and different each person's sexual thing is. He said, well, after all, women shouldn't be passive all the time. I mean, there's no reason why they shouldn't put their tongues into a man's mouth, and after all, they never do that. I was really amazed. What an extraordinary thing to say. What sort of women does he know? Somehow women have always had the worst of both worlds. They're supposed to be above sex, on this sort of pedestal; they are somehow asking for it if they are in any way provocatively dressed. Also, it's their fault if they get pregnant because they're the ones that give in to men.

I would much rather be a man than a woman, but I do mostly feel like a woman, except that I often feel much too exuberant, excitable and aggressively sexual for very straight men to cope with. Somehow, therefore, I have to seek out alternative types, who are usually rather unintelligent, and I do think that intelligence is very attractive, especially in men.

If I'd been born a man, I feel I could have let myself go more, I could have done a lot more of the things I wanted. I would have had a better education, I would therefore not maybe have had a terrible depression in which I was turning everything in on myself, and binge-eating. If I had been a man, maybe I would have been more aggressive and outward in my unhappiness, and maybe it would have dissipated more quickly. Also, I would be less emotional. I would much prefer not to be governed by the emotions and my body. I would like to be single-minded, get on with things, write a lot more. Also, I would like to be a woman in a different world. And a woman with a different upbringing, not having had such a bastard of a father – and not bringing the disparagement in on myself.

Most women feel terrified of age. I feel I've used that female side of being a woman, that sexy side, little enough, and it's going to pass me by, and that irritates me: the fact that a woman is disparaged so much. How dare men disparage women who are really quite attractive, but flawed in some way? Men are themselves grotesquely flawed.

Kitty O'Hagan: I was very clever at school and I didn't understand why the boys could be top of the class and popular and the girls couldn't. I was very competitive. I wanted to win, and I remember being first in a lot of things and not understanding why people, or the boys, didn't particularly approve of a clever girl. I can remember feeling that there was a rule I was not aware of.

I've spent twenty years doing research with women, with good discussions with women all over the country, and I think British women particularly have tended to hold back, not to fight, because there is an attitude among them that they do want male approval and the British male doesn't tend to dish out approval for somebody who is confronting him.

Women have an instinct, and it's quite difficult for me to rationalize my decisions. I will make a judgement about particular commercials, and people have to rely on my judgement and my instincts, and yet they don't have them because they are all men, so they look at me as though I have three heads. That's difficult for them. It's easier for me with clients. Clients are surprised by having a woman in an advertising agency, so often I get my way in a way that men can't, and men resent it.

I work in the area of communication which is dominated by men. Television advertising is insidious. All those images and stereotypes of submissive housewives and all the rest that women see every twenty minutes are out of line with reality and certainly out of line with the way women want to be seen. It's a male-dominated environment, so if I want to shift the image of women portrayed in advertising, then I have to keep at it, I have to keep saying it. I start off trying to be reasonable, trying to explain, making them realize that women actually identify better with this image of women or whatever. If that doesn't work, I shift up a gear, get my arguments in place, really work it out. And if that doesn't work, I throw a tantrum and walk away.

I'm annoyed by ageing because it's not particularly attractive, certainly not within the convention of today, and so I think I might well consider plastic surgery at some point or other. And I don't think it's just that other people will think I look better. I think it's actually so, that I will think I look better too. The reality of it is that men do not find women who look old attractive. That's why they like the current phenomenon of Joan Collins and all the rest, because she is fifty-five and doesn't look it. If she looked fifty-five years old, they wouldn't find her attractive.

I wish that I was living fifty years on. I don't really like being a little ahead of the times. It's lonely. Extremely exciting, but also lonely, if you're a feminist, if you're moving ahead.

Fifi Oscard: In general, women have a harder time, especially women in corporate America. Mostly, men in America think that a typewriter and a typist are the same thing: they are both machines.

I found being a woman a disadvantage when I got married in my second year at Barnard College. I had a very strong, very conventional husband: a smart man whom I stayed married to for forty-five years until he died a year and a half ago. So I started life as a young married woman in 1940, and marriage at that time in America was designed to turn women into nothing. It was really terrible. Wives did nothing except discuss children, domestic help and prices of meat. I had a hard ten years. I felt like I was in a box, and if I suffered from being a woman, that was when it was. Women were nowhere then. We would have Saturday-night parties, and somebody would be sure to give you a little rap on the fanny, or a tweak here and there, and there was a lot of flirtation going on with other people's husbands, and it was really kind of dumb.

I'm sixty-five or sixty-six. I would say that in the years from sixteen to fifty, maybe fifty-five, biology makes it hard for a woman because with trying to make a decent life, or trying to make a decent career, or trying to bring up decent kids, we are beset by this business of, is this man attractive and is he going to come after me, and shall I have an affair or shall I not have an affair, and if I'm having an affair should I have two affairs, or if I'm having an affair should I stop it? That's not so much part of my life as it was, but it is very important, because everybody is a victim of his and her sexual drives. I am sure that I have made determinations based on sexuality very often.

I don't believe people should worry about ageing. If you're a forty-five-year-old woman and trying to be a thirty-year-old woman, you fail. If you're a fifty-five-year-old woman, and you try to be a forty-five-year-old woman, you fail. Just go with it. That's what I believe. I feel very strongly that older women should not be dependent on their children or anybody. I have discussed this with many friends, and we are going to have a great big lovely house and all of us old folks are going to come together and live in it, and we are going to be so charming and have such a lovely life that all the young people will be pounding on the doors because they want to be part of it.

Edna O'Shaughnessy: I am a South African by birth, and there discrimination is chiefly on the hideous basis of colour. It was a country I was glad to leave for that reason, and I looked forward to coming to

Europe, and especially to England, where my mother had been born. I had won a government scholarship to Oxford to study philosophy, and in philosophy, as I believe was the case in all fields of study, I met no discrimination between men and women. Oxford colleges in those days were, of course, hugely sexist and separatist. I found these traditional arrangements fascinating and strange rather than a cause for indignation. I do think of myself as one of the fortunate women, because equality, even nowadays, doesn't hold everywhere for all women. I have been lucky.

It's an interesting fact that psychoanalysis, though it filtered its findings about the psychology of women through nineteenth-century prejudices in its early days (mind you, it had the grace, even then, to be perplexed about women), never discriminated between men and women as scientific colleagues. From the first, psychoanalysis welcomed women as analysts. Women like Lou Andreas-Salomé, a famous beauty and intellect, approached Freud and his early colleagues in Vienna. There's a record of a discussion in 1910 on whether women should be admitted to scientific meetings. Eight voted for, and three voted against, and Freud himself criticized the three for their irrationality and prejudice. In psychoanalysis, women have always been welcomed on a par with men.

Kathy O'Shaughnessy: I think instinctively a woman can be less urgently ambitious. You can have deep ambitions that you want to realize, but you have less of the impetus to prove yourself. I also think that, as you get to the end of your twenties, you can feel quite bored with the idea of climbing up some power structure. I think that family can seem a very important thing to do with your life, but as something you would ideally want to combine with work; certainly I would. I wouldn't want to be a mother or a housewife only. I'd never want to be a housewife, ever. No way, José.

Change is a very chicken-and-egg matter. As more women become successful, and are seen to be successful, and seen still to be women and not ogres or bullying machines of ambition, and it's seen that they can even be mothers as well, then gradually the perspective for younger women growing up changes and their expectations gradually shift. And, given that expectation is so much the premise of achievement (I really think it is), a lot of things slowly become positive that weren't so before.

Clare Park: I can see very clearly the stages of my life and what I've inflicted upon myself, and how I've developed from there and how I've changed my attitudes, particularly towards men. I'm much more open towards people, whereas before I had a terrible reputation. I was aloof to everybody, particularly men. But that all stemmed from a certain time in my life when I was ill. Between seventeen and twenty I had anorexia. For three years, I didn't eat very much, and it took five years to recover physically and psychologically. This is why a lot of it is very biological, I believe. Having that completely altered my relationship with men.

Everybody has an incredibly distorted view of themselves and nobody's very honest. I didn't see myself for what I was. One could say it's to do with age; I was very young. It wasn't that anything particularly traumatic happened in my life, it was more of a character trait. I'm very obsessive, and if I do something, I want to do it very well. It's not because I want particular recognition. I've already avoided a public way of life. I don't like glamour particularly, I don't spend fortunes on what I look like, or go to places to be seen, but I love quality, and if I do something I will try to do it as well if not better than other people.

I was numb, I was numb, and I can hardly recall how I thought. I was incredibly depressed, but I didn't know how to get out of it. It was triggered when I first went to ballet school. I got into a world where people were questioning and looking at themselves, and criticizing themselves, so I started to do the same. I didn't realize that maybe people say things but don't really carry them out. But I do, and I did, and I got trapped in it, because it's a whole mental state, like being hooked on drugs. It had severe effects on how I related to other people. I was very insular and very separate, and after getting back to dating normally, and my weight returning to normal, it was like I had been reborn almost.

I've been training my body for my whole life. So I'm terribly aware of my body, and it's something which is very important to me. Those five years of anorexia were connected to my body – really abusing my body very very badly.

I've been involved with quite a lot of women body-builders recently, and I find it interesting that their obsession with diet and the way they live is similar to that of an anorexic ballet dancer. I think a lot of anorexics could be treated by introducing them to weight-lifting. That might sound ridiculous, because if you put a weight-lifter and an anorexic next to each other, the difference is unbelievable. But it's that type of obsession, and if you could lead an anorexic into thinking they would only be making their body more muscular, it would be a way to start to get them to eat.

There are a lot of pressures on women, because if you're much concerned with business and you marry late and have a family late, people are always asking when you're going to do these things, and isn't it about time you had children? Likewise, in the reverse situation. If you're just a mother or just a wife, then nowadays people are thinking that maybe you're not doing enough, maybe you should be working as well. So, in a way, women are expected to be doing both things.

Diana Parker: The disadvantages in this day and age are that everybody expects you to do everything. You're expected to be a Shirley Conran Superwoman, and it's an expectation which has become rather insidious in the same way as the expectation that was there thirty years ago, that you would either have a career or a family. I think women are under a lot of pressure to combine running a home, having Cordon Bleu dinner parties on Friday nights, managing the children and ensuring they're always neat and tidy and ever so polite, plus having a very demanding job and at the same time managing to be extremely attractive sexually, both to their husbands and to the world at large. I think that is a tall order.

I feel discriminated against professionally whenever I come across a male solicitor who is patronizing and who adopts the attitude, well, there, there, you needn't trouble yourself about this that I'm telling you; or somehow adopts an old-school-tie mentality indicating that one is very firmly outside the club doors and one really is not expected to be able to pull one's weight fully. Outside the profession, very rarely indeed – almost never, I would say.

It's splendid being a woman. I've never wanted to be a man. I think we've got all the advantages. And a very great number of choices. We must be grateful for that and stop griping.

Molly Parkin: I think women are conceivably more irrational, especially since scientific fuck-ups like the pill. But I think that those swings in women to do with the moon and their bodily functions are a bonus. I believe that people benefit from swings in fortunes and emotions – if you have the lows you're necessarily going to have the highs. And that is an advantage, it gives a woman's life a different perspective, whereas men may be simply travelling along the same railway track without

344

deviating. People think of women's cycles as a disadvantage, because they're not reliable in their response to situations, but I would think that the very variance in a woman's psyche, to do with the cycle, gives them a greater reaction, a great range of reactions, which is good.

Judith De Paul: I'm known as a tough lady in business. I'm known as a tough deal-maker, a lady who drives a hard bargain and someone who has achieved a great deal. And there are just some times when the deal is harder to close because I am a woman. There are others when there's a problem in the deal, and some guy is really going to show me he can squeeze me, or that he is the boss, and it can get very aggressive and very nasty. I am as tough a fighter as the rest of them. They go for the jugular, I go for the jugular. But there have been a couple of times when men have been so unnecessarily aggressive that it had nothing to do with anything other than emotions. Little by little, that is changing. But men do feel threatened by women, they do; not all men, but some of them.

Penny Perrick: It is impossible to be a woman without suffering an advanced state of schizophrenia. A man never has to ask himself how he is doing as a man as he goes about his business. A woman always has to ask herself how she is doing as a woman as she goes about hers. And I can't see any solution.

I work in an area where it is absolutely no disadvantage to be a woman. Journalism has always had equal pay. It has always had equal opportunity. People always ask, well, how come there is no woman editor of a national paper? And I reply, because no woman has ever been prepared to devote the hours necessary to be the editor of a national paper, and as soon as women show they are willing, there will be one.

A very interesting theory is that women's intuition comes about because women know that, if they get things wrong, they are going to lose out. Therefore they are always on the qui vive to what things really mean, to what someone really means when she says something, what a certain gesture really means, and they interpret it because, if they get it wrong, they could find themselves in a lot of trouble.

The grass is always greener on the other side of the fence. I think, as I trudge along Smithfield towards the picket line every morning, that it would be nice to be at home, going to Sainsbury's, washing the windows, but perhaps not. I think the life that one doesn't have has a mystique. Betty Friedan, who wrote *The Feminine Mystique*, now talks about the 'career mystique', women now becoming disappointed in what their careers offer. Especially as so many have sacrificed other areas of their life to fulfil a dream of a career which is often as unsatisfying as the life of a housewife.

Just as my youth and my early middle age have been better than that of preceding generations of women, I trust that my old age will be better than my grandmother's old age too. It is something I fear, but I would fear it equally if I were a man. I think when one divorces earlier, one is used to being alone, and one is used to many things that, a generation ago, perhaps only happened to older women.

Lorie Scott Peters: Women have a certain edge in terms of the fact that they are not driven by their sexuality.

I was raped. The first time I was fifteen, and because of that I learned how to talk myself out of the second rape. I think it's a terrible thing for women, and I guess I've been very lucky to have survived it. I've had some subliminal problems because of that, but I feel I'm a better person because I've gone through it. It's like training a puppy dog not to go on the street, and the most you can hope for a dog is maybe it gets skimmed by a car and the rest of its life it will be afraid of cars and will learn to look properly when it crosses the street. I got skimmed, I got beat up a little bit, and I had an unfortunate experience, but I survived, and I feel that because of that I know how to look before I cross the street, so I'm more able to live in society.

I didn't know what rape was when I was raped. I didn't know it was a word, I didn't know it existed. I was very protected, a little Jewish girl brought up in the suburbs. It took me ten years to talk about it and face it. I went through some therapy ten years later, but I never really told my parents. It happened when I was travelling through Europe. The people I was with never really understood. They thought, here was this girl, and she walked off at four o'clock in the afternoon and didn't get back till two in the morning, a bit battered. They didn't know what had happened, and I wouldn't talk about it. I just said, don't ask me any questions, I don't want to talk about it, and basically blocked it out of my head. All I wanted to do was get home. A lot of the rest of my trip through Europe I don't remember. I really kind of lived in a vacuum. People travelling with me said, what's your problem? They thought I really must have been a screwy kid. But after I had gone through a little bit of psychotherapy, I realized what had happened to me. I don't regret

346

anything I've ever done in my life. I don't regret my marriage or my divorce, I don't regret being raped, I really think I've learned from everything.

All too many men expect women to go out and have a job, and take care of the children and come home and take care of cooking meals. My sister's a diligent worker, she's very successful, she makes as much money as her husband and yet she comes home and makes the meals and takes care of the household. They don't have kids yet, but I imagine she will be expected to do that as well. I was expected to do all that in my marriage. It was exhausting. I worked till ten o'clock at night and my husband worked at home and he expected me to come home and make the meals. Why wasn't it waiting for me? That's the reason why I got out of my marriage, becauseI think that women have too much of a boulder to carry up the hill. I feel that what my life is about is bringing that rock up the hill. It keeps falling down, and I keep bringing it up, and no matter what women achieve, they're expected to do that much more. Maybe women today are questioning why they're bringing this boulder up and down the hill. You go out there and you build a career, you build your self-worth, then, when you meet some man and decide you want to have children, you're faced with, will I continue my career or do I have the children? Do I have to give up one for the other? I feel like Eve being tempted with the apple, the apple being what I was brought up to be, a child-bearer. I want to have children, but I'm afraid, if I bite the apple and have children, everything I've built up over the last sixteen years to be a career woman will be destroyed, because my idea of a woman and a mother is 100 per cent. I don't go into anything 50 or 80 per cent, I go 100 per cent.

Davina Phillips: Everything is made up of the yin and yang, the positive and the negative. As much as there were negative sides to being a woman, there were always the positive sides. For example, if you get a group of men together who are all clever businessmen, however much they may be discussing business, they are always aware that they are competing with one another and they tend therefore to be rather guarded in what they say. They'll never sit down and give another businessman, who is perhaps going to be their competitor, good advice. Whereas, because I was a girl on a sort of social level, an awful lot of men would give me good pointers and tips. I don't think that other businessmen feel threatened by me in any way. Of course, I started fifteen years ago when there weren't that many 'businesswomen' around. Now there are a lot more, and much more successful than myself, and so the whole thing has changed. But, in those days, if I was running late or I needed to confirm an appointment time, whereas a man would ask his secretary to do that for him, and everybody would accept that as perfectly normal, if I asked my secretary to do it, they thought it was rather snotty. People were a bit funny about my using a secretary in the way that other people would use a secretary. Banks, I think, were also a bit peculiar with me. I once went to the bank and applied for a loan to buy a rather substantial house, and they agreed to it, in writing, of course. And on that basis I went ahead and exchanged contracts. Then I got engaged. I went to see my bank manager (a) to give him the good news I'd got engaged and (b) to tell him that, of course, I would finish the project I had undertaken, and although I had got engaged I wasn't going to be married for some months. I thought he'd be terribly excited, but it was incredible, he retracted completely and said, no, we can't go ahead, if you're getting married you'll be thinking about your marriage, you won't be concentrating on things. And they actually withdrew and gave me a terrible problem because I had to complete the purchase. I went to see my solicitor, who was horrified, and we had to threaten to take them to court and go to other banks – all the sort of tough-man things you do. In the end, they capitulated on the basis that they had written this undertaking to complete for me. But it was a nasty moment.

Men think you are going to be more distracted by your children and your home life, and they're right. If a woman is still a woman, she can't cut herself off from that. I work from home, I have my office at home, specifically so I could be there for the children. Even if the children knew that I was working, I was at home, so there was an availability that they felt. Very few men work from home, and when they do, the office is just not interruptable. The wife keeps the children away and he's protected. Whereas my children could walk in in the middle of dictation or whatever. It's a heck of a strain, and I think there's no question about it, it reduces your efficiency. It reduced my efficiency certainly.

I think that where success brings tension is that one just doesn't have the time to be available to cater to the man in a way a woman does who is not so busy. I am not Superwoman, I am a long way from being that. I'm totally self-educated because I left school at fifteen because of family circumstances, and there is still masses I don't know. I've done it very much by trial and error. I don't think there's a woman born who doesn't stand in the middle of the room and scream sometimes when the kids are all driving her mad and the dog forgets to go out and does something on the carpet, and the phones are going, and you are giving a dinner party. What happens, unlike the woman who's got more time and greets her man at the door looking wonderful and ready to go out on time to the theatre, is I would be late because obviously the children and business had to come first and the social thing third. So I did somewhat get the reputation for being late for social things, because there was such a lot to pack into a day. I am basically, I hope, a loving mother, and therefore it was hard for me to get ready to go to the theatre if John or Paul, or Lisa or Tania or Melody was having a bad dream or worrying about her friend teasing her at school or about exams, or not feeling well. You stop getting ready and you deal with the child because children are little human beings and need you. The combination of children and business would strain me to breaking-point at times. And men feel that.

I think that ageing is the hardest thing for women to do. Men, God bless them, get better and better. If you look at somebody like Robert Redford, in his middle fifties, and you take most women in the middle fifties, even the gorgeous, glamorous ones like Joan Collins, and you put the two of them in a room, the pulling power, to be frank, is totally different. Getting old is the hardest thing in the world for a woman, it's not just a question about being conceited about one's looks. It's also very hard to come to terms with the fact that your children are growing up and leaving you. Men see children growing up and leaving the nest as a positive act, and so do sensible women. But there's a side of us totally lacking in sensibleness.

I basically enjoy being a woman, but I must say there are times when I'd have loved to have been a man. That's usually when I'm hoping that the man I'm rather keen on will phone me, and if I were a man I could phone him.

Lynn Phillips: I knew that men had more freedom, but not from looking around my family. In my family, the woman was the professional and the man was the professional by marriage, though they both had careers, and my mother even went out of her way to let my father out-earn her, she told me. So I was aware that men were given advantage one way or the other, that it was somehow a conspiracy, a rather arbitrary conspiracy, on everyone's part. But I didn't think of it as something natural or inevitable.

Urination has always been the first disadvantage. You just can't whip it out. Obviously the disadvantages of being a woman now are of growing up at what, hopefully, is the tail end of hundreds of centuries of totally pervasive male-dominated culture (culture with a small c). As Nancy Chudwell points out in her essay, 'Women, Culture and Society', even in a matriarchy, where the economy is controlled by women and descent is matrilineal, you still find that whatever men do is considered special. This is the conspiracy that I found in my own family. So if what men do in a culture is put on make-up all day, that's considered the road to God, whereas when women do it, it's considered vanity and frivolity. And this language – the structure of assigning positive and negative, or powerful and impotent, or yin and yang in all world cultures now – does favour men. And that will get you, no matter what you try to do. There's always a negative vision, a negative term barking at your heels.

Women are discriminated against, but even worse, the feminine is discriminated against, so that even if a woman does succeed, it's often because she has been able to adopt, lock, stock and barrel, what I call male culture. That means rejecting the maternal, rejecting a sense of process. It means the de-individualization of perception for the sake of the rule of law. And it often means an assignment of aesthetics to secondary or tertiary status, or a contempt for aesthetics which is unnecessary and destructive.

Any kind of bigotry and prejudice will produce two standards. If a woman does something simple, clear, above-board, practical, straight-forward and effective, she is seen as not necessarily being like a woman, whereas if a woman is catty, spiteful, vain, she'll still be seen by many people as 'like a woman', so that the negative traits in the group are used to define the group as a whole.

Bearing live young has always been the great advantage and great disadvantage of women. But now is also a very remarkable point in history, because production is shifting from a biological to a techno-logical event. I think that is a most profound change in our culture, period. I think it's bigger than the moon, bigger than the bomb. Women still have to carry the child, but I think that the end of that is almost imaginable, and it's the first time in history it has been.

I feel my market is shrinking, but improving, improving. I've been able to enjoy my own version of a good time so much with so much less guilt and confusion.

Sarah Fox-Pitt: There are many advantages in being a woman, not least that the tradition still holds that the majority of men enjoy the presence of an attractive and entertaining woman. However, there are fewer men who enjoy the company of an intelligent woman and enjoy the dissemination and dissection of ideas. Many men prefer to have their ideas confirmed rather than altered.

There have been disadvantages in being a woman, stemming from largely patriarchal family attitudes. There is no doubt that I am the daughter or the sister, and while there is an undoubted affection, the men in the family have never shown anything beyond a superficial interest in what I do now, or have been doing for the last twenty years. My father, while he is supportive in many ways, does not really accept that what I do is serious and has obligations that could be more demanding than those of the family, while my brothers get all the privileges of that sort of understanding. For instance, I still get quite upset by a lack of response and interest from my brothers on the few occasions when I, probably rather feebly, attempt to gain their response to something I am involved with and that appears to be of interest to quite a wide section of both my intelligent friends and the general public. The result is that one attempts to distance oneself from those encounters. I have never managed to convince my father that what I'm doing is actually quite interesting and can contribute generally to the world, because it's not a world which he understands and it's out of his orbit. I possibly went into that orbit because it was out of his.

I think there are times when men do not take women seriously. Again, I find that when it happens to me it is usually the case that it happens with the people I have known longest, because they take you for granted and only consider you on the one level, the level at which your friendship coincided. Therefore the longer you have known someone in a non-professional capacity, the more likely they are to know only the less serious and therefore the 'un-professional' part of your life. It is quite perturbing when you discover your closest friends are myopic. Certain types of men do patronize women, but now I just dismiss it as moronic and uninteresting, and it doesn't terribly bother me any more.

I don't actually fear old age while I'm physically able. I do fear a time when one will become unable to deal with the daily chores of living. I will be happy with my garden or my books, or the animals. We have a curious characteristic in our family, which was described to me in a letter by one of my cousins the other day: that while we have passions and enjoy people very much, we actually don't need people all the time, in the sense that there are lots of things going on in the mind and in the life without having to be surrounded by people.

Baroness Plowden: I was slightly peculiar when I grew up in that I

351

wanted to earn my living, which, on the whole, people with my kind of family background didn't want to do. I earned my living until I was married. I became a secretary in a boot factory. I think if you'd been able to have women teachers, then I'd have probably have become a teacher. But you couldn't have married women teachers. I therefore involved myself in the kind of things one gets involved in. I started sitting on school boards, and I have gone on from there. When I got to sitting on school boards and being a magistrate, there was certainly no disadvantage in being a woman at all. And when I went on the board of Trust Houses, there wasn't a disadvantage, except I wasn't well versed financially and I got more interested in staff conditions in Trust Houses. I didn't have a financial knowledge until I started looking at charities for the BBC and started learning to read balance sheets. And so it just went on like that. Once I'd got to the broadcasting, it didn't make any difference at all.

Most women, I believe, want to have children, but they're pulled between wanting children and the future of their careers, and it's obvious to them that if, at a crucial moment of their careers, they say, I am going away for a year to have a child, it's difficult for their employers to feel they are as valuable an employee as a young man who would be prepared to work from half past seven in the morning till eight o'clock at night. I think this is the real problem. And what seems to be happening now, particularly with young women who want to have careers, is that they are postponing having children until they think they are firmly established in their jobs, till they are thirty, and then they're thirty-one, and then they find they are longer as fertile as they hoped to be, and they don't have children. Now, this is a terrible heartache for them. It's also a problem for society, because it means intelligent and educated young women, who want to be having children and bringing them up in a liberal, intelligent way, are denied the opportunity, and therefore we are being denied that source of intelligent, educated people. And I don't see a solution to it, until it can be accepted by men, as employers, that they have a contribution to make by accepting the important role of the educated woman in having children.

In the media, women remain as assistants, and they don't get through. I don't think they are quite as pushing. And even if they are pushing, you've got to be slightly better as a woman to get the same job as a man. I think you've got to differentiate between women with children and women without children. Women with children will, for a large portion of their life, find it difficult to abandon their children like a man can abandon his child and leave the home at half past eight and never come back till half past nine at night. If I look at women in broadcasting whom

I know, who have reached the top, none of them has married or had children. It does make a whole difference to one's life, because one just isn't a free agent once one's given hostages to fortune, which one has by having children.

The lack of confidence, I think, comes very much more with women with household responsibilities. They get stuck in their homes, and the moment they have children they get no stimulus unless they are careful to do things. This is the whole problem of child-bearing: women moulder; they get isolated and trapped at home with the company of small children. They get physically tired, and when their husband comes home, he tells them what he's been doing and isn't at all interested that they've been having a very dull day. And this makes them lose confidence, unless they can take steps to keep up their interests and do things, which is difficult because of physical exhaustion.

One of the interesting things that's happened has been the miners' strike and what the women did then. The women who had been used to sitting at home and looking after the children suddenly took on a new purpose by running food kitchens and doing all kinds of things. And the result was that they have confidence in themselves and are more accepted by the men than they were before. What they had lacked before was confidence to move outside their home and play a complete role in a man's world.

I would impress on women the necessity for them to gain confidence and experience in living in a world outside their home. I started by being a member of my local Women's Institute. And I was so unsure of myself at that stage, that I blushed every time I talked and couldn't open my mouth without turning dark red. But gradually I learnt to sit on the Women's Institute committee and become chairman and then do various things. It's really doing things while you are having children which is important. They should still keep some outside interest so they remain people in their own right with their own interests, and don't lose confidence thinking they can only talk about the washing machine having gone wrong or their children having been sick. It's the process of keeping confidence, of learning to move in the outside world, which is the important thing.

There is a story my mother used to tell me of how the reigning beauty of one generation was taken to see Lillie Langtry when Lillie Langtry was very old, and the girl burst into tears, because she saw what she was going to be like in fifty years.

It would be nice to have been beautiful, but I never have been, so I don't mind as much getting slightly older, it isn't a terrible shock. But I think, for the very beautiful, when your face and body have been your greatest asset it must be disconcerting. It must be very awful if it's taken away from you if you haven't put anything else in its place.

Eve Pollard: When I went to school, I felt very aware that my parents were foreign though I always felt British. I can remember saying to my father, when you take me to school, please don't speak. He had this wild Hungarian accent, and you know how one wants to conform. My father thought that girls should just be decorative objects and, of course, that men should be the aggressors, the successful ones, so I always felt girls were inhibited. I had twin brothers younger than me – so all of the pressure was placed on them. I was just there to look pretty, behave nicely and bring him cups of tea. I always felt it was terribly unfair.

When I worked on newspapers as head of a department – and I was a very young woman editor, in my early twenties – I knew that I was not being paid as much as other male heads of departments. In fact, I proved I wasn't and went to see the editor and got a bit more money. When a job came up as features editor, I knew they automatically looked round for the men and didn't look in my direction. I knew that men thought women were allowed to go as far as being a woman's editor, but that was it. There were even certain meetings at the beginning where you felt that women were interlopers and you weren't really welcome.

Even at somewhere like the *Observer*, where I was woman's editor on the colour magazine, men were in charge and women were allowed to do the attractive bits, the frilly bits, the frippery bits. Whenever you wanted to do something really serious, they looked at you with great suspicion.

I don't think women do have the same confidence as men. In my own sphere of work, but also socially, men whose views you really wouldn't listen to necessarily will stand up and pontificate and women who may be much cleverer are hesitant. You know the surprise when you go into the kitchen of the house and you talk to the woman, and you discover she is really quite clever. But you've never really been allowed to hear this cleverness, partly perhaps because she's kept it hidden because the husband doesn't quite like it and partly out of habit. You are not listened to, so why make waves, why make a fuss?

We discriminate against ourselves. We don't network the way men do.

My male friends, my husband, they still see people they were at school with, they see people they were at university with. We change our names, we move away, we don't keep up with old friends. So we don't have this useful network: you scratch my back, I'll scratch yours. Most women don't go off to the golf club where deals are done, don't go off and play squash where deals are done. So we women don't help ourselves. Men are in some ways supposedly more finely tuned in to politics, and the fact that we have a woman Prime Minister hasn't stopped that. So you will find, for example, if, at a dinner party, a woman comes out with a strong political view, she is still looked upon as a sort of *arriviste* – how does she think she knows? Whereas a man can be much more stupid, but he'll be listened to because he is a man. Women are not taken as seriously, and we are not as good at speaking. It has been proved that women smile more than men because we are trying to please more. We are not used to being listened to either. If you are used to being listened to, you get more mellifluous, fluent, better at explaining your argument. As a woman, you almost feel that you have always got to say something very quickly and get your point out because men's attention will wander. It has happened so many times before.

There is this terrible problem of attractiveness. Women are conditioned to feel they are failures if they cannot attract men. You have to be a very strong, very self-possessed woman, or perhaps a woman who is not interested in men, before you can say this doesn't matter. And we are so conditioned to think that we must be attractive to men, that often that influences us mentally too; you think, do I really want to override this man who I would like to be attracted to me, by saying this is absolute tosh, you don't know what you are saying? In fact, if you ever fantasized about him, you won't, because any time you find a man's stupid, you go off him faster than anything.

I was assistant editor when I left the *Sunday People*, and after I'd made my speech I said, now I want to turn to the man whom I have been nicer to than either of my husbands and any of my boyfriends. And I went on about how supplicatory and charming and delightful I had been to him, and everybody at this grand lunch wondered who on earth it was. Of course, it turned out to be the head printer, because in the old days of Fleet Street, he was the man I had to be charming to to get the issue out. In fact, we had improved print times while I was there. If we were late, if we wanted to change anything, I was the one sent down and told go and ask Len. There was no doubt about it, I fluttered my eyelashes, and said, could you possibly change this paragraph, this picture, this caption? I had no pride in the way a man might have had. And he did it for me, and he might well not have done it for a man.

There are double standards. It's still true that if a man has romances and affairs all over his workplace, he is regarded as a bit of a twit, but a Casanova is something to be admired. A woman is regarded as a slut. A man who comes back slightly inebriated after lunch is regarded as, well, there's old Bill, he's had a big business lunch. A woman who comes back slightly inebriated after lunch is not on. Also, this new generation of women who have succeeded in business feel all the time that we are special, we are pioneers. We feel it very keenly that society doesn't help us, certainly in this country. Nothing could be harder than trying to juggle your job, your children, your career; nothing is made easy. Secondly, you feel very keenly that only one woman has to let the side down and they'll say, oh, we'll never have another woman. And thirdly, you feel that you've got to be better and smarter. And again, this candour we have means we give ourselves away. A lot of men are very practised at explaining where they were at four o'clock if they weren't in the office. I'm quite sure I would just look totally guilty if I wasn't somewhere I was supposed to be. I think we are new to the game, and like all newcomers we have to try harder. We have to struggle, we are the first in the fight. After another two or three generations, that may not happen, but when a woman makes a mistake, it's because she is too soft, or doesn't know how to play the game, or, worst of all, well, she hasn't been doing it for long, she doesn't know the ropes. Whereas, of course, a man can get away with it: there was a decision made, not perhaps the best, but it worked last time, and so he did the right thing; it will turn out all right. Their mistakes are not analysed in the same way. We stand out too much; there are not enough of us.

Most of us are much too attached to our children. The umbilical cord is not cut. We can't say, right, you found this wonderful little bimbo, terrific, you have her and take the three children and I'll stay in a flat on my own. We can't do that. Women do worry about that. Of course, in many ways we have painted ourselves into a corner. You are a successful career woman, and you have three wonderful sons, and then your husband meets the bimbo and, instead of his keeping you, he says, well, you earn almost as much as me, you carry on working and I'll pay a bit towards the kids, and, you know, thank you very much, I'm off. There is always that vulnerability, a biological vulnerability, so it isn't even of our own making. When my child cries in the night, it's for me he cries, his mother. This is Nature and you can't change it.

At Christmas, which I think is a nightmare time for women because all the responsibility of everybody having a wonderful few days is put on the woman, I always say (as a joke) in my next life I am coming back as a man. I suppose the wonderful thing about being a woman is actually

having those children. But then the terrible thing about having been a woman is that you have the responsibility of them for ever in a way men don't. It's great being a woman. But I think it will be nicer for the ones being born now.

Antonia de Portago: The music business is the business of men, and all the top positions are held by men. I've been here eight years. They really don't take even a woman artist seriously, let alone a woman producer or a woman record company executive. They keep women at a certain level and that's it. It's much better for a woman artist, song-writer as I am, and singer, to come to a record company with a male lawyer or a male producer. If she comes alone with the same material, they will not take her seriously. That's absolutely the way it is.

Men don't trust women. Even the fact that women have pre-menstrual syndrome – that's a put-off. Oh, my God, we're not going to use a woman if she has PMS, my goodness. Everything is against women.

Barbara de Portago: I use the fact that I'm feminine, and when I do come across a man who thinks, well, perhaps she is a little dumb, you know, in finances, I use my charm or my feminine attributes to act more helpless. It doesn't offend me to be taken for a woman at all, in whatever derogatory sense that person might think. And anyway, I've always functioned under the aegis that it's better to be underestimated. I function better.

I enjoy being a woman and I would not want to be a man. My heart goes out to men when I see them in the street with their little briefcases, coming home from their offices to their families. What an enormous responsibility.

I think the only thing I fear is being a fool in love. I might not have thought it out before I take action, or acted it out before I've thought. I might miss an extraordinary man.

Diana Potter: I've never wanted to be a man, except when I'm in the middle of a loch fishing and have to row to the side every time I want to go to the loo. Sometimes, biologically, it would be quite nice to be a man, but otherwise not.

The normal pattern is for women to marry and to have children, and you must be with your children when they are young, we all know. And that's where the career pattern breaks down. Some women go on working and neglect their children slightly and then feel frightfully guilty about it. It's very difficult for women, because we are not structured to be able to take four or five years off and look after our children and see them into primary school and then go back to work. We've got a woman at work who went on maternity leave, a black woman, a Nigerian, and when she came back her job had gone. Everybody is so frightened, because in that time the men catch up and take your job and go on. Nobody's going to keep your job open for that amount of time. I think it is a conscious choice for a lot of women, and I think that if only companies were more lateral thinking, they could solve this problem and women could go back to where they were. It's fine if you are a writer or something like it, but if you're working in television or radio, or in a bank or a City firm, you've more or less had it.

If I were omnipotent, I would put proper nurseries into every single street so women could take their children to work and see them at lunchtime. And I would spend a lot of money on highly paid staff so that the women were reassured their children were being looked after up to the age of five. That's what I would do. And I would make all the firms pay for it, so that it didn't come out of women's pockets.

I think the treatment of rape cases is discriminatory. I don't like the way rape victims are treated. I don't like that whole masculine attitude to rape, which is, of course, she enjoyed it really, you know. They would consider it much worse if their house was burgled and their study torn apart. They can't possibly conceive what it's like for a woman to be thrown into the bushes by somebody she doesn't know, and raped.

I've never thought about ageing really. I was never beautiful, so I didn't fear losing the looks. I fear old age and lacking faculties and being ill, but everybody does that. I have found each decade nicer than the last.

Emily Prager: Aggression comes across much worse in a woman than it does in a man. It's not acceptable, especially on television. You can never look angry if you're a woman, never. I used to do a little tiny talk show, and once had terrible jet lag and one person on the show made me angry. When I watched it, it was horrible. I just looked bad. People hate aggressive women, they hate them. I don't care, though.

Usha Prashar: Women don't have to become like men. I think I'm more conscious of that, because it is something I've had to look at not just as a woman but, if I may draw a parallel, as a black person in a predominantly white society, where the same applies. I have always felt that you have to be very sure of your own culture, your own identity before you can make a success elsewhere, and to me you get the best of both worlds in that way. To some extent, that applies to moving in a man's world: we have a different perspective which we bring to bear. Now, if we try to emulate men, to become like them, we are defeating the purpose of the exercise. We may have to do that in the short term, but if it becomes a habit, then we have lost the battle.

People have doubts about whether women have the ability or the stamina and all the qualities needed for the job. Comments were made in jobs I have held about whether the organization was ready for a woman director, or a black director. There is a kind of double jeopardy in my case. I am first not English, and secondly a woman, so that is always at the back of people's minds, and you always feel you've got to prove yourself before you are accepted. Once you've proved yourself in one setting, it may present itself in different ways in another setting.

I hope, when I come back in the next life, I am a woman. I like the sensitivity of women, the caring side of women, and also the ability to do a whole range of things. I could have been a mother and had children, I had the choice. But if I were a man, I couldn't have had that choice. I also quite enjoy challenges, and I think the whole challenge of fighting the kind of battle on equality and the battle on the cultural side and carving out a life for myself has been a very exciting privilege.

Judith Price: There are a lot of things in my career that I could get away with. I think it's been a great advantage for me that I am a woman, and I have played it to the hilt. I can be really crazy, I can jump up and down in an office, I can bark like a dog, *urf-urf*, but have you ever heard a man bark?

When I first started the magazine, I was more like a woman. I was advised to call a man – a well-known man – from one of the biggest agencies in the United States. I was very polite and explained I was the publisher of a new magazine, and asked for a few moments of his time. He said to me, I don't see any f-ing sales people and they are all just dumb c-s – four-letter word. Why, that word to me, I didn't even know what the word was, and he told me I could take my f-ing magazine and shove it up my f-ing you-know-what. I said, well, thank you, sir. You

359

certainly explained it to me. I put down the phone and started crying. I was hysterical. I didn't even know what the word meant. So I called my husband up right away. I was crying, and he said to me something very clever, very smart. He said, you have a choice in life, you can either continue crying and go back home to Park Avenue and everything will be OK because you don't have to work; or you can decide to stop crying, and you will hear this talk again and again, but you make that decision and you'll have a magazine.

I think it's very hard to run a company today with women. Gloria Steinem used to tell this joke: if the man got his period, he would say, it's a sign of strength or virility. Women take a day, two days off before they're going to get their period, and they take off when they've got their period. So, I'm smart. We now have a rule. If you don't take any sick days you get paid an extra week.

I fear getting older and not being beautiful. I don't think men fear not being beautiful. I have this preoccupation with being beautiful. I think, as a woman, you can't just be smart, you can't just be clever (and I'm clever), you've got to be beautiful.

Colombe Pringle: My mother was a feminist, my aunt is the best-known feminist in France after Simone de Beauvoir, my grandmother had always worked, and all the women on my mother's side had always worked. So I never thought I had to fight. I had to fight to make it, but it was never against men. Since I did not have qualifications, I went off, trembling and blushing, to see Daisy Galard, who had a well-known TV show. She needed only an unpaid help for six months, but I took it as a job. After a while, I got a pedometer and showed her that I had walked eighty kilometres in connection with one of her shows, so she gave me 800 francs, and that was my first salary. Afterwards I learned something of the fashion trade, and after I'd had a few jobs I went off to the People's Republic of China for a month and a half as a buyer for a French company. It was just after the death of Mao, and it was very exciting. We found all sorts of splendid materials in warehouses. I tried to teach the Chinese something about style, telling them that, above all, they ought to preserve their own native style and not lessen its beauty by compromising with Western modes. It was when I got back from China that I decided to give up fashion and become a journalist, and I got a job with *Elle*.

It's difficult to have two lives; it's difficult to be good at the office, and good at home in the evenings; it's difficult to cook and to do your telephone calls, to travel away for four days or twenty-four hours, to arrive in Bombay alone and come back; all that, it's difficult. At the same time, you have your child, you want to talk to your child. I see all these businessmen in an aeroplane, and think, they don't care the same way. I think we are vulnerable there. But I don't think it will be true of the generation who are twenty today.

I've just come back from India, and I met a woman who is a maharani, a daughter of a maharajah, very rich and intelligent, and she said, I never call my husband by his name because he is higher than I am. I said, what do you mean, what about all you've done in your life? She said, yes, but he is higher than I am. That's culture. That girl goes round the world, she does incredible things, she's a princess, she has a thing in the nose, and she still thinks the man is better than her.

I fear age because I think about death, but not because I'm going to lose my power, I'm going to have wrinkles. No, what bores me is to die. That's the problem with age. Apart from that, it doesn't annoy me. I'd still be attractive. Lovers at eighty, I'm not worried about that. Some men of eighty are irresistible, and some stupid young cunt of twenty-five is a horrible bore.

Marjorie Proops: I didn't discover the disadvantages of being a woman until I went to art school. I realized then, for the first time, that I had physical disadvantages – the girls who were blonde and short and rounded and pretty, and didn't wear glasses and have funny teeth, they got boyfriends and dates and things I didn't get. And that was when I first began to realize that, if you were a boy, it didn't matter what you looked like or who you were. If you were a girl and you were a gawky, plain kid, then your chances of having a relationship were remote. The first boy I ever really loved was a very kind art student, a Polish boy. I was trudging along the street with my large portfolio, and he said he would carry it for me and walk me home. He was the first male who actually acknowledged me as a female. And although I was probably about two feet taller and much stronger and bigger in every way, and more capable of carrying the portfolio than he was, nevertheless he made me feel attractive and feminine.

What I'd like to do for all women is make them financially independent so that they had enough money to live on. When I say live on, enough money for dignified existence, not dependent on anybody else. The lack of resources makes people slaves, puts them in a position where other people have power over them, makes them dependent and therefore

361

forces wrong decisions about themselves and their lives, and their children, and their men.

I have never seen myself other than in an absolutely realistic light. I am no feminine charmer. I've always been a plain woman physically. I think that the beautiful women have a weapon, and I've seen them using it. Everybody, I suppose, uses whatever advantages they've got. What you haven't got you can't use. The fact that I respect people, whoever they are, whatever they do, and that I want them to like me, despite the fact that I don't have these strong feminine assets, makes me perhaps put myself out more to be useful, to be empathetic, to try to help people, which is after all the basis of my work. My life really has been built on that realization.

Andrée Putman: I am courageous by nature and strong about my ideas and point of view, so I didn't accept that anything would be different for a young girl or a young woman. That helped me not to become a victim, except for a period of my life where I was too stupidly impatient in a dead marriage. This is maybe the only regret of my life: I should have gone much earlier, but I did divorce in the end.

I think ageing is a drama for everyone: for men, for women. If you look at it in a negative way, it can be an absolute catastrophe. But I never live or act in agreement with my age. I feel I'm so young in my mind, and I have so many intense relationships with very young people who come to me and get a lot of fun out of me, that I've never yet thought it was too late for me. It's a miracle, it's something that was given to me by my mother.

Mary Quant: Men are frightened of women's abilities and successes at work. I notice that certain sorts of success are acceptable to men, but if you add another which is more historically masculine, such as an ability to make money, that would be unacceptable. I think it's only nervous- ness that makes men react like that. They can accept that a woman is successful in one area, but if it spreads out into others, it may become too threatening.

The whole advantage of having a child is the biggest and most exciting experience of all, and men are completely left out of that. I can only imagine being very envious of that, and I think men often are. It does make everything else seem tame in comparison, and it does seem that everything else takes such a ridiculous length of time for what is really very simple when something so amazing and complex is achieved in such a relatively short time.

Charlotte Rampling: Having the advantages of a woman – that is to say, I was pretty, had a good body, wasn't rejected as a woman by society, I always told myself that this had nothing to do with the person that I am, it was an advantage I was born with. So I had to use it to compensate for the things I couldn't do because I was not a man. That's how I worked it out at a very young age. I would never use my looks gratuitously. I would never use them for the wrong reasons.

A woman has to work harder, but nobody should know about it, nobody has to know about it. Because, for a woman to be a real woman, to be able to hold a very successful career and do all the things that are supposed to fulfil a woman – to have children and love a man and protect him and bring up his babies – you have to make enormous personal sacrifices. It's to do with biological feelings that you have if you want to be a mother and a successful career woman. There are certain things which you have to do, but you don't complain about them, you don't let anybody know about them. But you work twenty-four hours a day. And the man doesn't. He doesn't have to come home and clean, look after the children or do their homework. He doesn't have the kind of feeling that he must do that. And if a woman doesn't do that, then her children are not going to grow up healthy human beings. Her relationship with her man is probably going to go on the rocks, and she'll take lovers because it's easier and less responsibility, just having a few quick bangs here, there and everywhere. You can get high on having a relationship and being secretive about it, but for a woman who really thinks about what she is doing, it is not very rewarding. Because the reward of a woman is to make a success not only of her career but of seeing her children grow up strong plants and making a man happy.

I fear ageing because I don't know what it will bring. I am going to actually decompose, I am going to change physically. I'll look at myself in the mirror, see myself in the mirror, see myself starting to get lines. It's going to be slow and gradual – after thirty-five, thirty-six you start to see changes. You don't know how you are going to accept it, because your power of seduction is probably going to go. Men aren't going to follow you panting down the street with their car horns honking.

Esther Rantzen: When I graduated at twenty-three or twenty-four, the first thing I did, which no man would have done, was to take a secretarial course, so I can touch-type, which is jolly useful. But none of my male contemporaries did a secretarial course. Then I went to the BBC, and eventually found myself in television, where I was made a filing clerk. I filed 22,000 photographs while my Oxford contemporaries, friends working on the same programme, were being film directors and trainee producers, and they used to come in and sympathize. It rapidly dawned on me that women were useful in the jobs they did conscientiously and well at the BBC, but they weren't going to be promoted. And in those days, that was true. Now, looking round at the BBC, I am still in the same department, and what I see is that women are promoted, and promoted all the way up to producer. But not beyond. You do not see them as heads of departments, or even as assistant heads of departments, except in, so to speak, specialist departments to do with women, or families, or education. You certainly don't see them as senior controllers, senior administrators. Never would you get a woman director general. When I say never, never's a long time, but there's nobody in training, there's no one on the way up. Perhaps this is the self-limiting factor that women impose on themselves, because actually programme-making is much more fun than power, so a lot of women make the choice that they are not going beyond producer.

I have been in television since 1968, which is nearly twenty years. I no longer feel, when I make a mistake, which I frequently do, that people are going to blame my gender for it. I think I have been there so long that they'll blame me for it, quite rightly, and not really care whether I'm female or male. But for a new reporter, and for myself when I was new, it was desperately important to survive those first two or three years. Because if I didn't, not only would I have lost my job but the next three women applying would be turfed out and not considered. It would have been a precedent. My mother had a friend who got a terrifically important scientific scholarship in acute competition with a lot of men. But she got engaged and went to the trustees and said, I am sorry, I am not going to be able to take this up. And they wrote into their constitution that it was never to be awarded to a woman, because they were so angry at the waste of time and at the number of other candidates who would have loved the scholarship. So one can see that, if a woman wastes an opportunity, she does a great disservice to other women. But I think I am past that stage.

I had one boss whose only conversation with the women in the office was, take your knickers off. That's all he ever said. Extraordinary really. I think he was brought up in Ireland where he had never met a woman until he was about twenty. If you are a glamorous, dizzy blonde, you are likely to be patronized. But I was never a glamorous, dizzy

364

blonde. I was a brunette until I was about twenty-eight, never glamorous and certainly not dizzy. So people used to treat me, not patronizingly; but they'd ignore me, and certainly not promote me. I really do think that was because I was a woman.

Most little girls are trained to be prim and pretty and quiet. So that when failure comes along, you fall in an unlovely way on to a cow pat and then crawl away and think, I'm not doing that again. I must say, that's never been my attitude. I've always thought to hell with it, it's worth having a go. I've never felt it a problem to fail, provided the thing was worth attempting. I have made failure programmes. Who hasn't? So I know what it's like to open a newspaper and read that you are the stupidest, ugliest, most pathetic creature that ever ought to be booted off the television screen. And it hurts. But my lovely husband – we've been together something like twenty years – says, for God's sake get on with it, what does it matter? Do you really respect that, is that what you feel about what you have just done? I think, this is my great advantage, to have somebody there who has been through enough of the same kind of ordeal by fire and who can restore my self-respect.

We have got to sort out what we want as women. At the moment, my life is very unsatisfactory because I spend too little time with my family. In the production rhythm of a weekly programme, it's only six months a year, but during these six months, I spend six days a week working on the programme. I have to force the time with my children into my schedule if I am to get it at all. I'm going to take Wednesday afternoon off this week. I know it's going to cost me blood in the cutting room because I should be watching films. But I have to do it. I take them to school every morning I can. I am at such a conflict in my life, and there is no way, for example, that I'd want any further promotion of any kind. I don't want the hiring and firing power. I don't want any of those things. Even as it is, I feel I should pull back from my work commitments. My husband actually shares a lot of the parenting, a lot of the house management, because while *That's Life* is on the air, I can't force extra hours into the day. When *That's Life* is not on the air, he makes documentaries and does his filming abroad, and I take over the lion's share of those responsibilities. Fortunately for me, he is a partner.

Barbara Chase-Riboud: There are disadvantages in being a woman, there were also disadvantages in being black and in being American. As a woman, first of all you weren't taken very seriously. Whatever you did you were not taken seriously, and the same thing happened because I was black. I had to be ten times as good as the men to get any recognition whatsoever. But I went to Yale, where the ratio at the time was something like six hundred boys to one girl. So I got used to being in competition with men very early, and lost this inhibiting factor. I came out quite an arrogant little girl.

Women earn less, they work harder. It's harder for them to get credit, to get loans, to start a business, to get on to a board of directors. There's still this sort of old-boy system that works quite well to keep women in their place. I know it, because Yale is part of it. Women reach a certain level and, unless they become really superstars, they are stopped quite effectively by men.

It's absolutely impossible for a woman who is married, or at least happily married, to have that single-mindedness that she has when she is single or unhappily married. It's impossible. And I don't see any remedies for it. I think that European women manage well because they do have the advantage of having more help at home, of having good schools for their children, of being able to send them away to school, which American women rarely have.

Mirella Ricciardi: I was born in Africa and there was no difference between the boys and girls. I very early on in life felt myself equal to a man. In my potential. I never thought that, because a man was a man, he was stronger than me, apart from physically. There was no reason why I couldn't do certain things he did, and little by little, quite naturally, I slipped into a world of men. But I always desperately tried to remember that I was a woman and I never ever wanted to become a man. I was very jealous of my femininity, and I'd try desperately to keep it, although lots of people say I have lost it. If people say I've lost it, it's probably the biggest insult they can give me. When people really want to hurt me, they tell me I am not feminine.

I never found being a woman a disadvantage. I found, if anything, it was an advantage. I don't know why – maybe I was lucky – but wherever I went, being a woman certainly allowed me to do certain things which maybe a man wouldn't have done. And if I wasn't allowed to do it because I was a woman, then, since I had a sort of man's attitude, I did it all the same. I can't say that being a woman ever hampered me at all.

I have never never been patronized by men. On the contrary, lots of men have been intimidated by me, and I don't know what it is or why, but maybe it is this strange mixture of remaining feminine yet having the force of the male. My poor husband is the one who has suffered the most. He cannot, he just cannot understand me; he says, you are a dual person. One side you are a woman, and the other side you are a man, and I never know when you are one or the other, so I never know how to deal with you, because if I try to deal with you as a woman, you react like a man; when I treat you like a man, you react like a woman. So it is very off-putting. But no, I have never felt that men have been patronizing to me. When I look back at my life, the only time they tried to stop me was when I went on to the front in the Eritrean War, and men tried to stop me by saying they couldn't take a woman into the trenches. That was the only time I realized that, had I been a man, I maybe would have got in more easily, but anyway I got in, so what did it matter?

Ageing bothers me, it definitely bothers me. But not because of the need to attract men, because there comes a time in life when you don't even want the men that much any more. Other things take their place and fucking takes second place. It is for your own ego. When you get up in the morning, get dressed to go out, look good, you feel good. When you get up in the morning and look haggard or get tired very quickly, or people say, wouldn't you like to go home, you look so tired, that's very demoralizing. However, I deal with it, because Nature is such a wonderful machine, and when it takes something away it gives you something else. And very often what it gives you in return for your youth is really much better, because the stuff that goes with looks and youth is very effervescent and doesn't mean anything. When Nature takes your youth and looks away from you, then gives you something else which is more quiet and more deep, your relationships are better actually. Relationships you form in later years are much better than they are when you are young and beautiful and effervescent and you don't give a shit.

Nancy Richardson: Women in publishing get along very well. It's the ideal profession for us. Condé Nast is a very special thing, but when you are in a huge bureaucratic publishing thing, it's just like being in an insurance company. Tina Brown, out of any woman in that organization for the last forty years, has done the biggest thing: she got rid of Alex Liberman. Her magazine goes to the printers without any reference to him.

Financial independence is the most important thing. Forget about sexual liberation, that's nothing. I have achieved in twenty years of professional life a certain national reputation, but the real struggle is to take it further to the level men set for themselves – autonomy and the freedom to be constructive. Will I have that opportunity? Tune in next week. I don't know. I am not willing to do the things that the women on their own do to get to the top, because I see it as wrong. My moral structure sees it as wrong. I won't lie, I won't steal other people's ideas, I won't manipulate people. If I want them to do something, I say to them look, I want you to do it for this reason, I can only tell you that I hope you will do it my way. I cannot be devious.

I have just finished five years of out-performing certain homosexual male art critics, and I've worked triply as hard as any man. I've worked every weekend, I'm in a state of exhaustion. But men in my business don't have to work as hard, they spend most of their energy not in their work. I knew the only thing that would float me free was not my influence at the magazine, not my influence outside the magazine, it was the work itself. Because they couldn't say I was a woman with children, therefore it's only to be expected that it's inferior. They could only judge it on the printed page, by the quality of the ideas, how they were put together. Did it take us in a new direction, was it clean, was it based on personality or was it based on a principle or an exploration of a field in a new way? And finally, from around the country, I got letters. The editor-in-chief goes and lectures, and at the end of the lecture he says to the people who come to speak to him, what do you like best about the magazine? And they all say, Nancy Richardson single-handedly in her column has changed the way we think about these subjects. And he had the honesty to come back and tell me. So I was able to do all that, but at great personal cost. The men who are against me are the kind of art critics who are very well linked with, say, Alexander Liberman, the editorial director, and they didn't earn their way into their position, they didn't write their way into it; it's like lord and vassal. I had no alliances. Men operate on these alliances where the stronger ally themselves with the weaker and they proceed as a group. The woman is always alone, pitted against the universe. That's my feeling.

If Frank Richardson isn't really behind me if we start up a magazine in New York, then I'd be a lunatic. I would have a magazine maybe, and then I would have to reinvent the wheel. My husband is rich now, but I am not in control. But it is a benign influence for the most part. The men often think, well, I have a benign influence, so what's so bad about that? So what if I control you? It's benign, I am taking care of you, you'll never starve. That's their argument.

Sexually, a man of sixty is going like crazy and a woman is really not. All the more reason to start a magazine. Women for the second part of their lives, if they have something to do – the word career sounds so ugly, somehow it sounds so wilful and self-important – but some legitimate activity I think is the antidote. It's true that women are not attractive sexually at sixty, they're just not, it's even unbecoming. If she's within an existing marriage, I'm sure her husband will make use of her. I hope to be made use of at that point. But it's true that a man can have a sex life right to the end. Look at Arthur Miller, Charlie Chaplin.

We used to think that women were threatened by straight men, but perhaps the secret threat these days, and far greater in my world in New York, is the homosexual, because on the one hand he is undervaluing the family, and on the other he is undermining women if they are straight. He likes irregular forms of beauty and goodness, and values the bizarre and witty over the genuine achievement.

If I could do something for women, I'd make fantastic day care. I could have conquered the universe by the time I was forty if there had been good day care. I was sabotaged constantly by the other women working for me at home, their bad habits, their lack of any standards, their lack of discipline, their lack of reliability. There are some people who don't feel well and still go to work, and there are some people who stay home all the time. I can't tell you how unreliable many women are who take care of children and work in a house, and the sinking feeling when you are ready to go and you can't. The day-care system didn't even exist in a private way that was good enough to let my children be a part of when that was important to me. I still had to hire people at home, but they were terrible. I don't know if our society would be capable of doing good day care. Apparently the Chinese do it very well. But they are very orientated towards the family. I'm not sure that the Americans could even staff it.

I think a lot of men don't take women seriously. But society offers you your first chances. In Western society, if you want an education, you can get it; if you want a job, you can get it; if you want to get out there and do something, you can even get a loan. We women are in the same position as the blacks maybe, and many of the people who think about how much the blacks have gained since Martin Luther King have come back to say the reason blacks haven't got any further is maybe they haven't worked at it enough. You can only give so many programmes and so many incentives and force so many companies to hire them, but unless they do a good job when they get there, they won't get any further. Your greatest defence is if you are given a first chance, and if you make good. I have already passed the point of making a good living, and if my husband left me I might be able to support my children if I didn't have them living in New York City. That is what you want in society, that, if a woman has to work and support her children, she is capable of doing it. But what you have to work twice as hard for, and what you may never get, is the top job, the influence, the control of the organization.

Stella Richman: The only person who didn't take notice because I was a woman was Rupert Murdoch, and therefore doesn't count! I'm extremely fond of Rupert at a distance, I hasten to add. I would never wish to work with Rupert, but at a distance I have a great deal of respect for him. He's the only man I ever met who can walk into a boardroom, pick up the papers – first board meeting – and simply say things like, you've got a £10 million discrepancy, where is the money coming from? Which people more gentlemanly than Rupert wouldn't perhaps say quite in those terms. He was always right. He gallantly apologized to me a year after he fired me, but in fact it was the greatest favour anybody could ever have done, because I couldn't stand that world of the top hierarchy and being away from programmes. Rupert did me a great service, because I'd offered to leave for nothing and go into hiding or whatever, and, of course, because I was fired, I got them to pay me the full whack of two years' money. A year later, when I went to interview him, he apologized. He said if we'd only known each other better, he wouldn't have fired me. I said, please don't apologize, you gave me my freedom.

I think women have this terrible sense of duty which they let keep them imprisoned. The man will wake with an erection, the woman too, though she doesn't show, but there may be a kid crying, two kids to get to school, the husband having to get to work. I think it's only rich people that can afford the luxury of paying attention to their sexual needs before the needs of the day.

Angela Rippon: One of the saddest things that has happened is that when you are trying to define the role of a successful woman, you tend automatically to assume that the successful woman is the woman who has a career and a job in the market place, but, very often, equally successful women are the ones who never go out to work but work at home as mothers, wives and, to use a modern term, house technicians. Because a lot of women don't like being called housewives. If you are going to try to say, if you are successful it is because you have a career, whether you are a man or a woman, you immediately alienate all those women whose real skills are being good wives and mothers and home-makers. Because I get involved with various charities that deal with deprived and badly treated children, I have seen the end results of bad mothers, bad home-makers. I've also seen the end result of women who take their role as good mothers, good home-makers and good wives seriously. They are the women who spend a lot of time with their children when they are very young, ensuring that they learn how to eat properly, to read, learn how to write. They take a genuine interest in what their children are doing at school, they join the PTA, are supportive of children on sports days, are supportive of them with their homework. They may not have two ha'pennies to rub together, but the house is always clean, the laundry always done, they give their children the best food that's possible, they make a warm and comfortable and loving home for them, and they do the same for their husbands.

What I find incredibly hypocritical is a certain kind of man, who doesn't perhaps have a very good education, who will decry women's role in society when women, perhaps, are doctors and looking after that man's children, or teachers teaching that man's children, or lawyers representing him or his family in a court of law. And yet, still he says, no, women shouldn't have equal rights. Perhaps we are never going to overcome that kind of entrenched chauvinism. But eventually I think that simply by being there and doing their jobs, women will prove they have earned the right to be given that kind of equality.

One of the most spurious arguments you hear thrown up about women having responsible jobs in business is, well, suppose the children are taken ill, is there a need to get time off from work? That presupposes that, if a child is very ill, or has an accident, and you go to the factory or the office and you say to the father, I'm afraid your child has been knocked down, he'll say, oh, really, well I knock off at five, I'll come and see then. Men are just as emotionally involved with their children. And if their child is dangerously ill, or suddenly involved in an accident, they are going to down tools and go home as well.

We women cannot rid ourselves of guilt. I can't think of a single man (say, a man working in a bank), who, if the bank came to him and said, you have worked for three years in Plymouth, we are going to move you to Aberdeen, wouldn't go. If you are a serviceman, and the army says, you've been in Germany three years, we are going to send you to Aldershot, you go, and you take your family with you. But if an employer says to a woman, you've been really successful, we are now going to move you, and she goes home and says right, John, we are off, John is likely to say, oh no we're not. This is what women have to contend with now. Do they go? Do they put their career before their marriage? It's overcoming that hurdle, that final hurdle of releasing all guilt from the woman in that situation.

Age is something I am aware of because of my profession, which is highly visual, and the way we look is terribly important. It's very interesting that there are no sixty-year-old women working on television. People like myself and Sue Lawley, Joan Bakewell and Esther Rantzen, all came into television at round about the same time, and we are gradually working our way through the system. It will be interesting to see, in twenty years' time, whether or not there are any sixty-year-old women. You have forty-, fifty- and sixty-year-old men working on television. You have the Sir Robin Days, the Sir Alistair Burnetts, the Parkinsons and the Wogans and the Aspels. All men in their late forties, fifties, sixties – totally acceptable. I am now forty-two, Esther is in her mid forties, Jan Leeming is in her forties, so is Sue Lawley. We are all pushing back the age barrier the longer we stay in television. So it will be interesting to see, in ten years' time, if all of us are still acceptable as faces on television.

Shirley Ritchie: When I went to the Bar in 1966, women were not being taken on in chambers because of a quite legitimately held view that, once they had reached a certain rung on the ladder within a set of chambers, they would almost inevitably take off to have their children, and that would leave a gaping hole in a set of chambers that required to have a continuous ladder growing in seniority and experience. I don't think that sort of so-called prejudice is prejudice; it is plain practical recognition of what is good for a set of chambers and what is good for the Bar as a whole. Now, that meant that the women who came to the Bar at that time had to undertake that, if they did get married and if they did have children, they would take off the minimum amount of time to have the children, and that is precisely what I did. I worked until the Friday and gave birth on the Sunday in the case of each of my two children. I had six weeks off, and then I was back. Six weeks is the sort of time that anybody might take for a holiday. So one had to be determined to do that. These things have eased considerably – women are taking six months off – but I'm not sure that is necessarily a good thing. They are finding it very difficult to come back and adjust to being back at the Bar when they have had as long as six months away.

I have now reached the position where men recognize that, having had twenty years at the bar, I must mean business, so on the whole I'm taken seriously these days, but certainly I wasn't to start off with.

At the very first trial that I did at Assizes in the old days, before the new Crown Court, I was defending a bugger. Two charges of buggery to a real old lag who had done it lots of times before, and we were in front of Mr Justice Park who was very much of the old school. For the whole of the first morning, I could do absolutely nothing right. He made it perfectly plain that he thought this was some sort of cheap trick. At lunchtime, by pure chance, my clerk telephoned his clerk about the arrangement for some further case in the list at a later day, and said, oh by the way, how is such and such a case going in your judge's court? The judge's clerk said, oh, you're the bastard that sent a woman to defend a bugger. My clerk said, I beg your pardon, I don't have men and women in my chambers, I have barristers, and I sent a competent barrister. From two o'clock on, I could do nothing wrong. The judge was sweetness and light from start to finish, once he had been satisfied that it wasn't a cheap trick on the part of my client.

A woman has absolutely everything she wants. She has a choice whether she wants to have a career or whether she wants not to. She doesn't have to go out to work. She can choose to make her career at home, she can choose to mix and muddle the two, she can do as she jolly well pleases, and it's not open to most men to have that choice.

I've always seen to it that I've had superb nannies and a good housekeeper, and I've taken the view that the whole thing runs far better if I'm not there, putting my oar in, than if I am. When I'm at home my time is to enjoy with my husband and my children, and frankly, I think that I've seen more of them and been able to give them more fully of my time than I could have done if I had been a full-time housewife without the sort of help I'm able to afford.

It still remains a woman's privilege to be waited on at times, and it suits me down to the ground.

Hélène Rochas: The day my husband died, people in the society (House of Rochas) came to see me and said, what are we going to do now? I said, well, I'm going to work, and they said, you don't really need an office, and I said, yes, I do need an office. They said, we have meetings very early in the morning, at 8.30, and I said, I will be there. So it was all a bit like that, just look good and be quiet, be the ambassadress – because my appearance wasn't bad. But nothing was based on will-power or the willingness to make a choice. Nowadays I don't think that anything like that has to be proved any longer.

373

There are still privileges that women have over men, all the things we include in the term 'gallantry'. And we still flirt. When I meet someone at the office, there is still the idea of seduction, which is an additional plus and a card everyone plays.

Men quite early on have a problem with their virility. It's quite a deep problem, and they have fewer escape routes than women. Women can have themselves looked after, they can buy a dress if they are worried, or a piece of jewellery. They struggle, but with a certain kind of frivolity. A man can't. What does he do? He starts to run after much younger women as soon as he's forty. Women can pretend in life, men can't.

Anita Roddick: There can be no worse example of discrimination than living in an Italian family where there is a total dual morality code *vis-à-vis* boys and girls. My brother used to bring home his girlfriends at eighteen and take them up to the bedroom, and my mother would pat him up, my son, my son, Rudolph Valentino. She was so glad he wasn't gay. He was her son, the hero, and she would bring up bloody cups of tea in bed to him. The girls had to be home by nine. I must have been twenty-one or twenty-two when I lost my virginity, and she said, my daughter's a whore. Even now she worships my husband and says to me constantly how wonderfully lucky I am to have met him, how wonderful he is, and I should be so grateful, and I should get on my knees and subjugate myself to his desires. It's typical Italian duality. The man is almost like the Christ figure, and the woman – forget it. Yet she was a strong woman, she ran her own family, she ran her own business, she was successful. But every time my brother came home, she'd bake him a bloody cake full of fruit. And we would have the crumbs.

A successful woman doesn't have to emulate men, for God's sake; that's too aggressive. The aggressive principles of business, where you see men and their corporate trading and their soullessness, are so out-moded. A woman has got to adopt feminine principles, which I believe to be the most exciting new approach to business. These principles involve encouraging innovation, encouraging gut feelings, encouraging a sort of putting love where your labour is, talking in terms of passion, using a different vocabulary, talking about love, talking about human potential, being everything that is positive and feminine and rounded, and thereby making the aggressive principles outmoded.

I actually think a woman can be more eccentric than a man. I play on eccentricity. It's easy for me because I'm an Italian immigrant, so I cut through the class barrier in this country. My passion is acceptable because I am Italian, my flair is acceptable. I stress those because I can cut through the garbage so quickly. I can go to meetings in the City and say, come one, speed it up, speed it up, and they think, oh yes, Italian nature coming through.

The policy-makers are men, usually in their sixties, whose wives don't work. Certainly with men, the majority I've spoken to, because I'm considered a major success in what I do, the relationship they have with me is quite bizarre. They know how to talk to their wives, or their lovers, or their mistresses, but they don't quite know the vocabulary for business. When they are dealing with a female in a male situation, there is constant discrimination in the semantics, the words used. The attitude is, why should I employ a woman when she is only going to leave if she gets pregnant? Well, I know a million reasons why men leave a job, and it's not necessarily pregnancy. I also think men have this wonderful ability to endorse their career structure themselves, and so much business is done on the polo field, in the Rotary Club, in their Lions' Club, and every goddammed club in the world. The women don't forge business deals that way. Women haven't got their act together to do that, or they're not even interested. They have to come another way; they've got to ring up and say, can you help me with this?

You have to work damned hard to get to the top, irrespective of whether you're a man or a woman. But I think it is harder for a woman in one respect: getting the money is harder to set up your job. You have to deal with the most boring of people, the bank managers, who don't have a creative idea in their heads. What they actually want is a male clone. An example of what happened to me: I went in to ask the bank for £4,000 to set up my company, but I did it wrongly. I did it with enthusiasm and a sense of verve and joy; I had my kids on my back and in a pushchair, and I wore a Bob Dylan teeshirt. I said, I have got an amazing idea. Well, you never say that to a bank manager. You have to have a profit-and-loss sheet, a feasibility report. And so I was not given the money. I realized very quickly what I did wrong, and so I changed, I bought a suit, I got my husband to come along, we had a profit-and-loss sheet which was garbage and gobbledegook, but it looked terrific and we got our £4,000. Bank managers will lend women money for bloody deep freezers, for a kitchen, but never setting-up money for a business. However, once you get to the top, God, is life easy for you, because you are the token woman. Then they start to listen. And it's a rotten fake situation to be in, because you are unwittingly supporting a concept which is slightly immoral, the concept of the token woman.

375

When I'm saying things which I think are serious and intelligent and should be listened to about the role of business in the community, about the responsibility of profit, about what we have to do to stop the division between the haves and the have-nots, what successful business can do – every goddammed time I say anything serious, nobody wants to listen. They want to trivialize everything I have done. Ah, you're worth £89 million? OK, how do you manage a company and a relationship with your husband at the same time? How do you keep two teenage kids happy? They aren't interested that we employ 1,500 people, that we are international, that we have done a lot for British business in terms of endorsing a British concept; none of that interests them. Everything is trivialization. It's this absolute hellbent need to be mediocre in this country that I find obsessive. They don't even take you seriously when you've made it, and to make it in this country you have to be a financial success – that's something I have learned in the last three years. I have been doing what I have been doing for ten years, but suddenly, having a full listing, being quoted, being terrific with the shares, suddenly I have made it. Even so, it is still difficult to be taken seriously. When I won the Businesswoman of the Year Award – this is a great example of how crummy the whole thing is – it was the first time I had the luxury of sitting down and thinking about what I had achieved. I went up on to the rostrum and there was the TV, radio and a multitude of press. Two things were referred to first of all. One was my small stature and two was my bubbly hair. And I thought, if Terence Conran were up here, they wouldn't say, Terence, you've got a receding hairline and a big fat stomach.

I see lack of confidence in my own staff. They have no vocabulary for challenging, they have a respect for authority, and the authority is usually a male authority. They are basically better mannered, and they are basically not career-orientated. Now a man is territorial, he is protecting his patch, and God help anybody who gets on to it. Certainly, with my own staff, I have encouraged them on a vocabulary for challenging hierarchy, being a little bit more anarchic, making them challenge established rules. We've done that brilliantly with my top management team of women who have effectively ousted a director because they didn't think he was the right person. They have every right to do that.

It's actually quite bizarre that men are running an industry for a product that 98 per cent of women are buying. Basically their axiom is: what women want is hope and promise. Bullshit. Women do not buy a cream for hope and promise. They buy a cream because their skin is dry and it makes the skin feel better. These men haven't got out of their ivory

376

towers or huge great Mercedes to go into the shop floor, to get to know the new woman, the woman of the 1980s who feels that she can effect changes, who is more cynical, who wants information and education. She doesn't give a toss about the toilet-paper brand, she knows every damned cream cheese going on the market. She's a different woman. But they're still thinking of that type of irrelevant, Dallas-imagery woman. They are not addressing themselves to the fact that there are women out there who are from one-parent families, who are choosing to live with women, who are choosing to live on their own, who are choosing career rather than marriage. They are not addressing this multitude of different minority groups.

I worry about ageing all the time. If I don't say, oh, God, I've got another line, my kids say it. Ageing worries me because death worries me. It's not the fact that you're not perceived to be a twenty-year-old nubile woman, God help me. But you are walking down such an inevitable road; there is no option, absobloodylutely no option. You're just walking this pathway to the ultimate experience. It's not the aesthetic, or, am I looking forty-five? It's that I haven't lived enough, I want another fifty years. What's going to happen in the next fifty years? How will I know what's going on? It's that constant reminder of your mortality, the constant reminder to pack every goddammed day with something. So it's not an aesthetic feeling of lack of confidence, it's, oh shit, I'm dying. That's what it is.

Deborah Rogers: I'm very truthful about myself. I think it's always been to my advantage being a woman doing the work I do as an agent, because literary agencies are a newer form of business, much less hierarchical than publishing houses, for instance. I think it's just much easier for a woman to progress without going through all of the various levels. I think what somebody like Carmen Callil has done is infinitely more impressive and much more of an achievement, because it really does mean taking people on on their own terms, whereas, as an agent, you take on the work but you do it in your own way. What makes an agent is your own tone of voice, your own way of doing things.

An enormous number of professional women I know – of course, their emotional side may be in their personal lives – conduct their professional lives without the sort of overriding emotional kind of charge that people think dominates their judgement. A lot of women are infinitely more rational than they are given credit for.

377

Selwa Roosevelt: Men are more afraid to bring bad news than women, and they're more afraid to take a strong stand. But women can get away with it. Let's say I have to go and tell a man he's done something wrong. I can do it in a way that the man doesn't feel threatened and his machismo isn't involved. A man cannot go to another man and say, hey, you're all wrong, this is not something you should have done, you're going to reap some bad results and so on. That would be bitterly resented. Whereas a woman can do it, and I have done it. I can get away with murder.

I know that, as I grow older, my choices in life, should I be widowed or anything like that, would be limited. But I'm not afraid. I don't mind being by myself. I've thought about it, but I'm a writer, and writing is a great solace. And also I love people. I'll always be surrounded by people. So I'm not afraid of being alone, though I'm afraid of the loneliness: I've been married all my life, since I was twenty-one. I got out of Vassar, and I got married three months later and I'm used to being married and like being married. It would be very sad not to be; not to have someone who cares about you more than anything in the world and to know you're No 1 with that person, no matter what.

Kimberly Du Ross: It took me a long time to get used to the fact that there was this other tribe who think they might be superior. But they were only a small minority. Things have changed, we have evolved a great deal, but one does seems to encounter these people from time to time who still were brought up to think they were the superior race.

A woman can really do anything, it's just that you're going to have to put up with a whole lot more misery than a man, because nobody will bother a man. You can do anything you want just as long as you can deal with the people who are going inevitably to be harassing you. It takes a stiff upper lip, but you can basically go anywhere, do anything – I went off to India by myself and heard endless questions, why aren't you married, what are you doing travelling alone? It didn't bother me.

A man is a real go-getter, but a woman is aggressive. A woman, if she has a lot of money, is very eccentric if she sleeps around; a woman, if she has no money and sleeps around, is a slut. This is the old double system we've had to live by.

Women really have to live by their wits, and if their wits happen to include charm and being pretty, and being capable and self-sufficient, then by all means use it – it's Darwinism.

Juliet Mitchell-Rossdale: My mother was a sort of proto-feminist, I think. Before there was feminism, she was an individual feminist herself, and very politically involved in modern peace movements at the end of the war. She married my stepfather when I was about eleven, and they'd met through the International Friendship Society. She was an active sort of woman, and I think it just didn't occur to me that there would be any discrimination. It really hit me late that there was discrimination against women. When I went to university, to Oxford, men students were meant to get either firsts or thirds, and women students were meant to get seconds and work steadily and not to have that erratic genius men were allowed to have. So that was one introduction to discrimination via a very dubious privileged position.

Yvette Roudy: Freud at the end of his life said that women were *also* human beings after all, and during his whole life he hadn't seen that. He had seen female sexuality as something incomprehensible. He'd never understood them. Women have always had capacities and potential, but it has been muzzled.

The legal inhibiting factors have gone. In many countries, there is now equality in law between the sexes. For some time I was in charge of this type of legislation, which unhappily now seems about to go into reverse, but nevertheless, if women want to and are determined, they can do just about anything.

For five years there was a leap forward politically, because the President appointed women to be bank directors, but now the new government has replaced them, not specifically because they were women, but because they had been appointed by the old government. They were told, thank you, and are being replaced by men. There are also fewer women in government. Before, when the President made important appointments, he would ask, are there any women? So he was supporting my political position. For five years, women were pushed and encouraged; there were honours like the Légion d'Honneur and important nominations. This has now stopped because we have a conservative government which prefers to favour the family, the role of woman as mother – a much more traditional concept.

I promulgated a law about professional equality (the *Loi Roudy*), and because I didn't only want it to be about principles, I included the means of reaching equality, rather as in America under Carter and the laws for minorities. I said that, every year, businesses should provide a report showing the relevant statistics about men and women in their businesses, and that they should make plans and provide measures to enable women to emerge, to take top positions, and so I was able to nurture about twenty such plans. Some worked very well and after about three years I went to a firm – directed by a woman – she's no longer there since she has been replaced – and saw the results of one of these plans. There were about twenty women who had become directors, but although they had the same work and responsibilities as directors, they had neither the title nor the salary of one. I asked why they hadn't protested, and they said it wasn't worth it.

Joan Ruddock: I was educated in an all-girls school and so didn't have to compete. I was educated by women who today would be recognized as feminists, although they certainly weren't recognized as such in South Wales. I suspect that what I enjoyed in my school was what has now been discovered in research in the United States: that, not having to compete, you actually are valued for yourself and educated as an individual and there is no question of feeling inferior to boys because the boys aren't there. I didn't realize for quite some time that there were disadvantages. I chose to do science, won a state scholarship to a science college, and in the science college there were 100 women and 3,000 men. But I did a very unusual thing. From an early age I had acquired a boyfriend, and after one year at university, and this was in the early 1960s, I got married. So, again, it was an unusual situation because I was taken out of the competitive environment. I had a secure emotional life, I wasn't constantly competing for male attention or whatever, although I'm not saying I didn't enjoy it when it was available. But I was a very serious scientist, and at that stage it didn't occur to me, I have to say, that I was any less a scientist or less able than the boys in my year.

When I was an undergraduate, I do think, because of the subject I studied, I held my own and don't think I felt inferior. However, I would say ever since I have not necessarily felt inferior, but constantly been aware of the fact that I have been disadvantaged as a woman, starting with job interviews through to being considered less important in jobs by the director of the organization or whatever, even though it was absolutely clear that I was carrying a load of responsibility equivalent to any man, possibly at times having better ideas than my male colleagues. Certainly, at a fairly early stage, when I was involved in competing for a particularly big job, I had no doubts whatsoever that the only reason I didn't get the job for which I had a proven ability was because I was a woman. The law doesn't discriminate, but all culture and all practice in Britain does discriminate.

Women are not seen to be of equal status, not seen to be of equal potential. Most positions of power are already held by men, so those who determine your fate in general tend to be men, and they are always looking to put people like themselves into positions of authority. I think, for many men, it's habit, part of their culture, part of their upbringing, entirely their experience. They're conditioned and not able to move outside that conditioning. I would think that is probably true of most men to a certain degree. But there are now many men who (a) know that the law suggests that things should be different, and (b) will have had experience of women who are extremely capable. I can think of examples in the university environment where a woman will compete for an academic post, her scientific record be very well known, and she will not be appointed to a senior position, and the male colleague, who is no better and perhaps often inferior, will be. So I think there are occasions when it becomes, who will we, as a group, be comfortable with? And the answer is, with our mates. I would really want to see some objective studies on this to be convinced I am right in my thinking, but it certainly is my feeling that most men want to have male colleagues and are most comfortable with men and don't want to work with women on a professional basis. They want to compartmentalize women into a role which is, of course, to do with sexuality, and which means that they are something else, not individuals, not human beings on quite the same level.

I have been a manager in a number of circumstances in which I have employed men and women, and the turnover of men, especially high-flying men, is actually quite rapid. Men these days, especially if they are ambitious and want to get on, tend to move about; they don't stay in a job for fifty years or whatever. So, I am not sure that, if you want a certain job done and the woman has the ability equal to a man, these prejudices about women not staying in jobs are borne out in practice. Many people remain in jobs two or three years and expect to move on to something else. So many women would be able to say, with very real expectations, that they were intending to work two, three or four years and then they might have a family or they might not. And anyway, there are laws about maternity provision, and women who are sufficiently highly motivated, given the possibility of having proper help, are perfectly capable of holding down jobs and having children. But what our society doesn't recognize is that children should be the responsibility of both parents. You don't discriminate against men who have children, because they don't physically give birth, but they are still their children. That is the major problem: that men are not seen as having responsibility for children. It seems to me that is more where the problem lies, than saying that women are seen to be the people who are taking care of the children. So it is a change that doesn't just involve women and attitudes to women, it involves men and men's attitude to other men and men's attitude to children.

I don't think there is any doubt about the fact that women have to work harder to be successful, because, as a woman, you are conscious of the fact that (a) you may not be taken seriously anyway, or your boss has got reservations about you; or (b) your boss may well have some sexual interest in you and may expect some kind of response, albeit on a fairly superficial level. So there are obstacles for most women from the very start, and you are constantly having to overcome those things, so you endeavour to do better, to prove yourself more conscientious, more hard working, more reliable et cetera. The man doing the same job may well feel that he can take a three-hour lunch and come back and laugh it off. The woman doesn't do that.

I have been recruiting women constantly for the advice agency I have been working for, and these women are in the main young graduates who have children and feel unable to pursue full-time careers. They are provided with training and they work for expenses only. Now, almost every single one of those women that comes to me to be interviewed to seek the opportunity to do this work, is a frustrated woman; they have men who are successful partners or husbands, and they don't accept that they have an inferior role, and that, because they are the mothers of children, because they are financially secure in middle-class homes in general, things are actually OK. Maybe this is not voiced in the household, maybe the husband is not even aware of it but every one of these women – and I've seen hundreds over the years – resents the domination of their menfolk at home.

I don't fear ageing, because it is an inevitable fact and I don't fear things that are inevitable and you can't do anything about. I'm actually not given to many kinds of fears at all. The things I'm afraid of are on quite a different plane.

Eve Ruggieri: In my business, there are more men than women. When we are on tour, for example, making programmes in several different towns, my male colleagues have their bags packed by their wives, the tickets and hotel reservations are done by their secretaries and everything runs smoothly. Before I leave, I have to make sure there is food for the cat and the birds, because neither my daughter nor my husband will think about it. I see there is enough yoghurt and so on in the fridge, and it's only at the last moment that I can take care of myself. When I do leave, it is with an enormous feeling of guilt because my daughter will say I am leaving in the middle of something important for her, but she would never say that to her father, as it is traditional for fathers to be away, for their work. Even in our milieu, people will phone and say, your wife is away? How awful!

When I left a programme called *Les Rendezvous du dimanche*, a popular variety programme in which we had variety artists, cinema artists, in order to go to a classical music programme, there was a sort of raising of shields on the part of my colleagues, who didn't quite go so far as to ask to see the certificate of my first year's studies at the conservatoire, but near enough. I have several examples of men who have arrived suddenly in the world of serious musical programmes without my qualifications. My parents were both professional musicians, I studied music and had a first prize for piano and afterwards went into the channel *France musique*, I can read the scores of contemporary music, I still play the piano not too badly, so the move was well within my possibilities. Even so, it was difficult because I was asked, how was it, what right have you, how can it happen that you, et cetera? But around me were proliferating examples of men who were going into the field of classical music programmes, for whom it was simply a change in career, a move forwards, and no one asked them a single question.

Femininity opens doors that lead nowhere. If you use your femininity to force open a door, then one day it will be slammed in your face. Either it will be slammed because you will be asked, are you free this evening? and you say no. Or if you say yes, then six months later someone else will come along and take your place and you will have the door shut in your face just the same. To try to use femininity in this way is what is called a short-term investment.

Women have been taught to play trump cards which are not the right ones. It's a game that has been fixed. They have been told that they have the assets of charm and attractiveness which have nothing to do with the job; they waste time, or put them on a track which is very difficult to follow. They are put in a false position and afterwards the damage is irreparable.

The great revolution in our century is not having reached the moon, though that is breathtaking; it is contraception. Our century will remain the century of contraception, by X, Y or Z method, or the pill, but as soon as women can plan their children, and therefore their careers, then everything is in the melting-pot, and differences, if not quashed – they never will be – are softened. Then the cards will not be handed out in the same way. I think that the differences *are* biological, but on that essential difference we have superimposed *idées reçues* and culturally acquired ideas.

Contraception has considerably modified the sexual behaviour of women. If a woman is not attached to one man in particular and she wants to make love to men then she will. When I was eighteen, to make love was to rethink your whole life because there was the possibility of becoming pregnant. There is that frightful expression in French, 'to fall pregnant', which implies a metaphorical slap in the face and being outside society. Phrases like that stigmatize the position of an unmarried mother. Happily, I think we have got over that these days. But, at the same time, a woman's behaviour emotionally is diametrically opposed to a man's. The progress that has been made in the field of female sexuality is that a woman can say to herself, I want pleasure, too.

A French writer, Henri de Montherlant, committed suicide not because he was afraid of old age, but at the idea of being diminished. He had poor sight and was going blind and he decided to end it. When I was thirty, I could envisage myself going from the stage of a mature, attractive woman directly to the stage of an old woman loved by her grandchildren with a totally different status. The difficulty for me is not seeing myself as an old woman, touch wood, but the intermediate stage of watching my physical disintegration. I have never been particularly pretty, so I have never played on that; on being amusing and energetic, yes, they are my assets, not my appearance. I did my studies at Nice at the time when so many were coming from Algeria, and we were drowned in a sea of women all prettier than the next, so I realized my forte wasn't there! But now I realize that that is really a good thing, because I know lots of women who are worried about their appearance, who have plastic surgery done, who have a whole strategy for slowing down the process of ageing – the eyelids done first, then a face-lift, then goodness knows what. I can't say it leaves me indifferent because women in this state wring my heart.

Carol Rumens: When I went to secondary school, I went to an ordinary girls' grammar school which was very much geared to taking exams, and I became a bit less creative. When I wrote, I wrote essays, and poetry tended to get squeezed into diary writing. It became something you did privately, on your own. It took me a long time to get back to the sense of myself as having something to say as a poet.

384

Most women want to have children, yet I think you have children at a time when you need to develop as a person, and if you've got a career, you need to build that. So you either find you have to do all the things simultaneously, which is what I tried to do – having young children and having a job and writing – or you have to decide to do one thing at a time.

I think at the back of my mind was the attitude that I was carrying on with some tradition that was male, and though I didn't do it consciously, I think I adopted mental attitudes that I would now think of as being more masculine than feminine. For instance, I would have found it very hard to write a love poem to a man, which I can do now, but for a long time I found that impossible. I think that's because there is very little tradition. Most love poems are to women written by men. It's only fairly recently that I've felt at ease writing that sort of poetry.

I fear the lack of my health and loss of my ability to think. I think I can face the idea of just not looking good. I suppose it's hard for people who are very beautiful, but I've never felt particularly good-looking, so I don't mind that I'm going to lose what looks I've got. But the idea of just not being able to get on a bus, just not being able to go out for a run easily, or go swimming or do the things you take for granted when you're younger, that frightens me. I think, then, you must develop a philosophical outlook and build up your intellectual interests. If your mind goes, if you become senile, that's horrible. I'd be on to Exit, the society for voluntary euthanasia, because I saw my father – he lost his ability to speak, and he died quite young, but it was very unpleasant for him, I think. He knew that he couldn't communicate any more, and it was very degrading. I think old age is very unpleasant, actually.

I wouldn't have liked to be a woman in any other century. Or many other societies today. I think I'm very privileged to be born in a Western democracy in the second half of the twentieth century. I think women have got the best chance they've ever had. So, I'll settle for it.

Doris Saatchi: I think I was competitive from early on, but it certainly didn't come from my mother, and I don't know whether that came directly from my father. He had always said to me, from as long ago as I can remember, you should always pay your own way in life. He had also said there was no such thing as a free lunch. And those two notions were applied to me as a female equally. I grew up with the idea that I was an independent unit, and my sex had nothing to do with whether I could expect favours or privileges I hadn't earned myself.

385

I've never felt any inhibitions about doing what I wanted to do, whatever that might be. When I went to work after university, I often travelled alone on business, and while I was invited to dinner with some of the men I met in the course of the day, and sometimes I think rather improperly invited to dinner, I certainly never got involved in any of that. I've always enjoyed, to a certain extent, being a man. Yes, being a man. I have no problems, and didn't then, about going into a restaurant and dining alone. The only disadvantage I think I've ever felt is a certain frustration because I have felt from time to time that I would like to really settle the situation by punching somebody on the nose, and I'm not physically strong enough to get away with it.

In the very first job I had when I left school – I was a young trainee copywriter, and very excited about my job, and pleased to be in the firm where I was working – I was actually threatened, straight out of a B movie. I was threatened with getting fired from my job if I would not co-operate over a certain issue – not a sexual one – with an accounts supervisor. I couldn't believe what was happening; he actually leaned across his desk, having called me into his office, and said, now Doris, you do like your job here, don't you? And I said, yes, I do very much. And he said, you would like to stay here, wouldn't you? And I said, yes. And he said, well, then I think you should learn that you have to get along with people and co-operate when they ask you to do something – meaning co-operate with him. Well, what he was asking was an issue I didn't agree with and I had to take a stand on it.

I have been fortunate in being in the advertising business, which, I think, was and still is one of the most democratic businesses there are, and I feel that if you do the job like a professional, it doesn't matter whether you are a male or a female.

Talent always finds its way to the top. You see, women have certain advantages. And a woman who is good at what she's doing, who loves what she is doing, can use what has been given to her in her genes, given to her biologically, to manipulate the situation to her advantage. Women are manipulative, they are more devious than men. They can use all sorts of tools to achieve what they want, that men don't have at their disposal. It all balances out.

I am very sensitive about aggressiveness, for two reasons. One is that there is an image, put about by men, of course, that a successful woman is aggressive, that that is one of the necessary qualities or traits of a successful woman. The other is that Americans, *vis-à-vis* the British, are aggressive. So, when I came to England, because I chose to, because there were things about the British society, the British culture I felt I preferred to America, I had those two notions in my head. So, if anything, I have tried to cover up my competitive instinct, and tried not to speak in a loud voice and to scream and shout at people when I was angry. Aggression is spoken of so often as being bad. Aggression is terrific. There is nothing wrong with aggression, but aggression carried to the point of belligerence is bad.

I've never been concerned with my femininity, or my softness or my charm. Whether I'm more or less charming does not, will never affect my attractiveness to other people, whether they're male or female. Certain people will find me attractive for what I am, certain people won't.

Altaf Al-Sabah: In Kuwait, our culture is conditioned by the desert, tribalism and the sea. The women of the desert tribes, the Bedouin women, are emancipated in the sense that they were quite strong in asserting their ideas. If a woman wanted something, the men around in the tribes would stand aside and allow her to get it. They were married three or four times – divorce was never looked on as it was in the cities later on. So I certainly think it was the Ottoman Empire that conditioned these women to be more submissive. Women in the desert played such a strong role, and still play it, but the West had this idea of a harem we didn't have – the idea that women were submissive, subservient to men. But Bedouin women were really amazing. They say still now, in Kuwait, that a woman of the desert is much more outspoken and stronger than a woman of the city.

I love what I am, I'd never like to be a man. Women are much more pampered in our part of the world, and they are admired for what they really are.

Melissa Sadoff: The more I've read history, the more I've read literature, the more I've felt that a determined woman, in all cultures, through all history, could achieve what she wanted. Even in Roman history, you had women leaders, women queens. There were quite well-known priestesses in Greek society. We know that Egypt had queens, Cleopatra and Nefertiti. It's not just the social position they were born in, but a woman who was determined could always achieve what she wanted – for example, Joan of Arc. Which woman, even today, would lead an army dressed as a man, and there she was, she did it, she was a friend of kings. So I never felt that a woman as an individual was

387

restricted, although I would say that rules, regulations and laws in certain cultures didn't allow the mass of women their freedom.

In some societies, maybe many societies, women are still discriminated against *en masse*, but that is changing. It has been changing for a long while. It is a slow evolution, but it is getting up speed and it's getting more and more straightened out. I personally have not suffered discrimination, but not because I had any advantages. When I was about five years old, we were thrown out of one home, in Hungary. When I was seven years old, we were thrown out of Yugoslavia. We did not have a chance to take even the little dolls – at that time probably the most important thing to me. When you couldn't take sentimental possessions, never mind material possessions, that should create a tremendous complex in a human being. When you are seven years old and you see a dead body hanging off a tree, with all the insides out, that is not an advantage, that should create a tremendous disadvantage. When I realized at about thirteen or fourteen that, due to different political philosophies, people mistreat each other very badly, I was shaken into reality from my romantic, idealistic world. It should have left me cynical, it should have left me bitter, and quite insecure. I had the same ability or inability to cope with my problems as all of us do. The difference is that many of us do not think about our lives. We do not realize how long we live, we don't ask ourselves what we want to achieve in that life, we don't ask ourselves how we can cope with our own problems without going to psychiatrists, without asking for all sorts of help, without becoming alcoholics or drug addicts. We don't ask ourselves whether we can solve our own problems. And very often we can.

I still say that, as long as a woman is very feminine and knows what she wants, and tells it honestly, she is going to get everything she wants, whether it is a career or children or whatever.

Women may have problems with their cycles, things like that, but even though there are times and reasons and physical causes for a woman to react that way, it annoys me when you hear women saying, oh dear, I can't get up in the morning too early, and if I do I have to have a cup of coffee immediately, and my cigarette, and I can't talk to anybody before noon. I could say the same thing. But I wouldn't, it's a waste of time. I would say that is a negative approach. If I have to get up very early in the morning, I do. I am going to be pleasant, and I'm going to speak to people before noon. Why not? We are sophisticated human beings. We are no longer animals, to react in such natural ways and say we cannot cope with this, that or the other. We have a brain in our head and we should use it.

Ghida Salaam: Fatima Mernissi makes the point that, in Islamic societies, a woman is viewed as a potential threat to the social order because of her power, and that is why she is tamed and kept, whereas in Western society a woman is viewed as inferior, and that is why she is not given a job as deserving as a man. I hadn't given it much thought, but it struck me as an idea that is maybe true; that in Islamic societies the woman is not allowed to express herself because she is viewed as a force to reckon with, a force which could destabilize the social order, and that is why she is put behind closed doors and tamed, whereas in America we see how extremely intelligent women university graduates are not even able to break into the Senate.

Khairat Al-Saleh: At school, I was always top of my class, and then I had a scholarship and left when I was eighteen for Cairo. So I was virtually free at eighteen, mistress of my own fate, and that was something I planned all the way through: I wanted to be the one who ruled my destiny. But I don't think it was that I was exceptional; it was because I was gifted and because my mother was an educated lady and because of a certain social standing that I got something that other girls would not have, or that they would have to fight a long time to achieve. But I also had a very independent mind and a great deal of determination. I never really regarded myself as a woman, I always regarded myself as a person, a human being. Sometimes, when people refer to me as a woman, I am bewildered because it's not how I look at myself.

I don't think that any human being on this earth is as free as some Arab women. I suppose because their freedom was won after a very hard struggle, because they paid for it in flesh and blood, they are perhaps among the very few free people in the world. I've met some Arab women who are totally free – spiritually, mentally, emotionally free in the most beautiful way you can think of.

Many people regard me as gifted, as a person of quality. Since, as a human being, I have enough qualities to attract attention, why debase myself and try to use what men expect me to use? I wouldn't use my femininity with a woman, so why use it with a man?

Bushra Salha: I am not inhibited by nature. I am probably inhibited compared to the Western woman, but I don't feel inhibited because I am a woman.

Generally speaking, women are repressed in Saudi Arabia and the Gulf

389

States because they are there primarily to breed and be the object of desire. But if we take Jordan, Lebanon and Syria, it is much less evident. In a very cultured Arab society, women are very much the equals of men. In Lebanon and in the Arab community here, you can see that they play an equal role. Of course, you have cases of domination, either by a woman or by a man. But, on the whole, they go parallel.

Naomi E. Sargant: Inevitably there are all sorts of jobs which seem to be buttoned up by men. But I started work in a company which, although it was a man's world, already had quite a number of women in it. The difficulties aren't really insurmountable, and one chooses a number of strategies to deal with them. I don't particularly like trading on being female, though a lot of men at work trade on being male. When I was a pretty twenty-one-year-old senior market-research executive dealing with people from advertising agencies, men either wanted to get into bed with me or they wouldn't take me seriously. I remember going and getting some black-rimmed spectacles in order that they would stop making passes and begin to treat me seriously. My first job was with an appallingly badly run market-research company, and I decided to leave. My boss-to-be, Henry Durant, had written to me saying could he poach me, so I went and told them I was leaving and why. And a week afterwards it was put about that I had been sacked because a male client had complained about the quality of my work. In actual fact, first, I'd simply shown that he'd been doing his work wrong for the last eighteen months and didn't like to admit it, and secondly, he was doing his very best to get into bed with me. He went on doing that for five years. Quite amazing.

Women lack confidence and courage. It is to do with conditioning and environment; the expectations are laid on boys and not on girls. The only piece of research I ever saw that made sense was that the small number of women that had gone on working in the same way I have, and had got to the sort of levels I had, in principle had grown up either without brothers or without fathers. That is a piece of American research, the first about women that made sense to me in relation to my own situation. Because, if you think of the mother and two sisters managing in wartime, and the mother a distinct foreigner, you actually simply had to go on and survive, you had to do everything, and there wasn't anyone else to do it for you. Both my sister and I had to survive, and nobody ever told us there was anything different, nobody ever told us we shouldn't be doing those things because they were for boys. It was only later on, when we met up with these stereotypes, that we realized these barriers had been set up in other people's worlds.

I think I've succeeded without copying men. I've got one advantage: I do not know whether it's instinctive or not, but I have a very strong analytical mind. It's not a sex-related characteristic, but loads of people haven't analytical minds. I'm not talking about creative areas, I'm talking about management. And, also, I like people. I derive a lot of pleasure both from making people happier and giving them more space to do what they are good at. If you put all of those things together, the bundle works. Nobody told me that when I was younger, I only learned it as I've gone on. My elder sister was the clever one, and I was the stupid younger sister. I married young, I broke a first marriage, it was all disastrous – a sort of outcome of all this emotional misery. I came back, married again, gradually worked my way up, but it took me a long time to get any confidence back. I kept on thinking everyone out there was brilliant. Every time I was asked to do something new, I thought they were all brilliant. And when I got there, and started working with them, and listening to them, I discovered they weren't. Sometimes the emperor had no clothes at all. So it is very painful building one's confidence back up, but now 98 per cent of the time I know I'm as good as all the rest, in fact am probably better than most. I don't feel it is male/female, I feel that working my way up was not difficult because I was a girl, but because I had that appalling and difficult childhood.

I take for granted that I've got to be better than a man at the same job, that I've got to work harder. I take that as a fact of life. It doesn't mean I want it to go on in perpetuity, but it does mean I try, for the next set of women coming after me, to help reduce the barriers I have had to go through. I take all those things for granted, because that's been the evidence of my life. I've got absolutely used to being the only woman on every committee. The Local Government Training Board seemed to think I was the coffee girl. I went to the Committee of Vice-Chancellors to stand in for the Vice-Chancellor of the Open University. There'd never been a woman there, and I was pouring out my own coffee when an old man came up and took it from me and said, thank you, miss. And I thought, no, this is my first time at the Committee of Vice-Chancellors, I'm not going to let him get away with it. So I looked at him and said, I'm sorry, that's my coffee.

I know it's happening, but I'm trying to ensure that it's not going to happen to many more people. It's within the upbringing and institutions of generations and generations of men who've made the rules to fit their own predilections. You've only got to look at the Catholic Church setting up rules by men which are going to be suffered by women. Why does it go on? Because these institutions are reinforced by men, and it's much more comfortable for men not to accept that women have the same ability.

I think that it's been quite threatening for men to have to admit that a number of women can do their jobs just as well. But the problem is not with men who are good, the problem is with second-rate men. Second-rate men are extremely threatened by intelligent women. Not first-rate men, not the Jeremy Isaacs, but the second-rate men. They have a variety of strategies to deal with the threat, the most obvious one of which is to try to get you into bed because that puts you back in your proper place. I find that category of man very difficult to deal with, because if you have to go on working with them, you have to find a way in which you are non-threatening to them without giving up your possibility of doing your own job. I have no solutions, other than to try very gently to understand that person and stop threatening him. There are so many more men around in boss jobs, hundreds of them, and the high-class ones are only a small minority. It is the second-rate men who frequently are sitting just above you, and you have to find ways of getting at them. I've got one at the moment. I can't possibly name him, but he is a trial. He is in a position of responsibility and none of us can get rid of him. We have to work with him, so we have to make a way in which we don't show him up all the time, because our competence threatens him. It's extremely difficult.

Of course, having children restricts you. But with birth control, unless you are a Catholic, one's life is restricted for not more than about ten or fifteen years. It's idle to go on arguing that it's worse than that, and idle to pretend that that has prevented you. A lot of people have used that as an excuse. That it is something that somehow overwhelmingly affects and changes the whole of one's life. I simply cannot agree. OK, some women go broody. I was going to say, more fool them. It will not take the whole of their lives. If, as in my grandmother's times, they had had ten or twelve pregnancies and then died early, that would have been different. But life is not like that now.

I thoroughly enjoy being a woman. My mother always says my father left us because I wasn't a boy. She blamed me for years. But now I thoroughly enjoy being a woman. The combination of being able to do all this and do it with grace, I think is marvellous.

Dame Cicely Saunders: I have been able to listen to dying people so they could teach me, and I could then show what their teaching was to other people. I think that's a feminine characteristic rather than a male, and when a man has it, it is the feminine side of his nature. Why St Christopher's and the whole hospice movement eventually got off the ground is that I was able to allow patients to speak for themselves, which meant I had to listen first. Women are better at that, because they tend to do the nurturing. But to get the hospice accepted in a fairly male-dominated medical world, I had to show that it was medically respectable as well as compassionate.

If there was patronage, which I did meet from time to time, I didn't feel it was because I was a woman. It was because I was caring for dying people. It was the dying they were patronizing. I had to fight for them.

Nursing is a woman's world and the move into medical school via social work, which was also at that time certainly very much a woman's world, wasn't particularly difficult. My problems in medical school were that I was so many years older than everybody else, and I had not done science before. My problems were not anything to do with being a woman. I only did medicine to get to care for dying people, and nobody else particularly wanted to go and do that, so there was no competition anyway. I didn't particularly feel I had opposition, I just felt it was indifference; you can cope with that. I had a privileged background because my parents were pretty wealthy. We had a lovely home, and we had a good time, although we weren't a particularly happy family and my parents finally separated. I've never gone around feeling discriminated against. I've much more gone around feeling I wasn't necessarily particularly lucky in my own accomplishments. But I was lucky in opportunities, and when I was setting out to do St Christopher's, which, of course, didn't even have the name to begin with, that was very much in response to what I believed was a call from God. I believed He would give me opportunities and I would have to wring every last drop out of the opportunity I was given, and that if He wanted a hospice of the kind that was gradually building up in my mind out of experience, reading, and so on, He would see it would happen, as long as I worked hard. I didn't feel discriminated against, but I suppose, having had advantages myself, I should be more concerned about people who don't have advantages. There can be discrimination in medicine because so many of the good women doctors do move out to have their families and it is then difficult to get back on the ladder. That wasn't my problem. I wasn't married, which I didn't find easy, but it certainly gave me opportunities. Yes, there is discrimination, but it didn't impinge on what I wanted to do.

I'm sixty-eight now, and I have gone on being happier year by year

393

through my life. I am happier now than ever I was. I wouldn't go back to being young for anything.

Sylvia Scafardi: At that time, in 1914, England was philistine, insular and completely male-dominated. It was the public-school tradition that boys were segregated from tender years and their loyalty was all masculine loyalty and they belonged to the club, as it were. Girls and women were just to play a supportive subsidiary role, and they could only come into the picture if they made the pace, if they passed muster. They had to be pretty, but not too much to rouse a man's lower nature. They had to fit into the scheme and well, be complementary, and play the game and be sporty. My sister knew a young lad at Cambridge. When he wrote to her – I saw all his letters – he used to refer to her occasionally as old chap (this was a beautiful girl) and ask her for another photograph showing her eyes – like a theatrical agent, rather than a prospective lover. That was the kind of background, and I realized at boarding school that I could never ever fit into that picture. I was quite outside the pale, and therefore I'd have to paddle my own canoe and take another line. I had to, and I have.

I do remember, when I was young, there were some wonderful golden youths in khaki who gave me a cold look because I wasn't sufficiently in their class, and one had the feeling one was less than the dust beneath thy chariot wheels, but as I was cheeky and young and quite pleased with myself, it didn't hurt or crush me, it just brought out a little pugnacity.

I think the difference between men and women today is levelling out. In my girlhood, the word sex didn't exist, but men were known to have a lower nature. Therefore, in a marriage, there were things that had to happen just because of the man's lower nature. There was something low about the quite natural curiosity about growing up, about feelings which are natural in adolescence, and I had the feeling I was an outsider because, naturally, I had feelings that shouldn't exist. From the point of view in those days, female love was masochistic. You accepted, rather than felt anything. That was what it was supposed to be. Of course, when I grew up I realized I would never fit into that pattern, it was nonsense. I knew I could never get married, but, of course, I wanted to have love and adventure.

Going on the stage was a reaction against the excruciating boredom of the higher life, the life in college. I escaped, as it were, into life on the stage. My father, very generously, paid the premium for me to be a pupil at the Lena Ashwell Players. Lena Ashwell was a West End actress, and she got the OBE and had concert parties in the 1914 war for the men at the Front, shows and so on. She was a respectable woman and her little theatre in Notting Hill Gate was supposed to shed theatrical enlightenment to deprived areas – this was before films.

I think today it's appalling, the way commerce and men in commerce have exploited the female form to sell things in the most brutal, vulgar and, I can almost say, sadistic way. Of course, you get women to co-operate: you get a daft little girl who's got an over-developed bust who will talk about it, and when she comes on the television, men and even women will say to her, when did you begin? when did they develop? as though she were growing a fruit farm or something – which I think is pathetic. I think it is disgusting, revolting. I call that absolute discrimination and exploitation of women's sex. It doesn't matter if a girl is silly enough, if her father co-operates, that doesn't seem to me to excuse it at all. And there are still women prostitutes. It's no good saying there always have been. Perhaps there have always been boys who tout their poor little bodies, but I think it is an outrage that it should happen.

I think of the women who, because of the slaughter of my generation in the 1914 war, never married, never had children, and who hadn't got the kind of feeling I had of escaping into life and doing their own thing, and who withered away. And before that in Victorian times, there were women who were made a butt of in the Gilbert and Sullivan jokes about being on the shelf. When I think what they had to endure from girlhood, never ever having a sexual contact. It was a form of torture, I have no doubt about it. There is no doubt the situation today is much much easier for women.

I am surprised, with so much freedom and so much opportunity today, when I read about adolescent girls and hear them talk sometimes, to find that the same problems come to their minds as when I was a girl – the same feelings of inadequacy. And they must have this or that to make themselves attractive, and all kinds of ephemeral things which don't matter a ha'pworth really, like make-up and just the right clothes. They're tying themselves into knots just as much as we were in the old dead world.

I was never afraid of getting old, but when Ronald died and I was forty, and I had resigned from the post in the council in that summer – not because I was disenchanted, but because they were cutting staff and I didn't want a very good woman to be lost, and because my mother was dying of cancer and so I wanted to be with her (she died in October 1941 and Ronald died in May 1942) – everything had gone really, and then, for a while, when I was in that state of nothingness, I did have neurotic feelings about getting old. I would see, on the bus perhaps, a plain, horrible woman with a wedding ring on, and would feel the awful feeling that my life was ended and this ugly horrible woman had something that I was being deprived of, but it was a neurotic state and it was foreign to my nature. Time and the hour run through the roughest days, days came and went, came and went; you live through it, you get your sense back and I became myself again. It was the only time I remember thinking like that, and of course, I've never felt old, because I got married when I was fifty-four and that kept me young, because I was very happy.

Alexandra Schlesinger: I went to Radcliffe, and they did a study, I don't know how many years ago, about women who graduated. When they came, they did terribly well, and by the time they graduated, they were already doing less well. And they didn't want to succeed. They did a study on why women don't want to succeed. And I suppose, if you figured that out, you'd know everything about human nature. Was it the society that made them think they had to be second best? Was it because they didn't like to compete? Whatever it was, it happened. Terribly smart people would graduate, and then they wouldn't want to compete with men.

I think, when women started, they thought, well, we'd better copy men as much as we can so that we will melt into the landscape and they won't notice we are women. But it doesn't turn out to work that well. I think it's going against what you can do best. So you end up not doing the other thing very well because you are copying something you are not.

There's a whole group of men who never take women seriously. It's a defensive thing. If you don't understand someone, you don't have as much to do with them. You don't confide in them, you don't trust them and so you'd rather deal with someone you understand. So that sort of man would deal with another man. I don't think it's because women aren't as bright. I don't think it's because they think women are more stupid. I think it's because they think women are fearsome in a way. Men sometimes can't understand and therefore are in awe of us, are slightly derisive.

Anne Seagrim: It was absolutely accepted that there were only sufficient funds for the boys to be fully educated, and they were sent to public school in England. My sister and I went, for such schooling as we had, to the Free French School. I didn't stay there long, partly because my mother got ill when I was fifteen and I left to run the house, so my formal education spanned only about three years.

My mother was the first woman secretary at the Cheltenham Ladies' College; they'd never had a woman before. So I don't think I had a chip on my shoulder, or a feeling that women had a bad deal. I just felt that I had got to make my way as best I could as myself, with the limitations I had.

Confidence is what women need so that they don't get chips on their shoulders, so they don't see things with little, personal, channelled vision. Tunnel vision, that's their greatest defect. But whether it's innate or whether it's because of history, I don't know.

I suppose I have felt I was paid less than a man. But I have been in jobs which were primarily women's jobs. I was always a secretary until I became the adminstrator of the Churchill Trust, which was a pure fluke, just fell into my lap – as all my jobs did. I competed for the one with the Windsors. I answered an advertisement in *The Times*. It was as simple as that. It didn't say it was for the Windsors, and I was sworn to secrecy. But there were fifty other interviewed candidates.

Jenny Seagrove: I remember making a film in New Zealand, and I was having dinner with the director and the first assistant director. They were talking about Hitler and Mussolini. I know very little about these subjects, but I have an opinion, and they made me feel like a little stupid girl who had no right to her opinions and should listen to these gems of gold coming from these people who, when I think back on it, were talking absolute bigoted rubbish and really did make me feel very inadequate. I'm sure it was because both of them were male chauvinist pigs, to use a well-coined and overworked phrase, but, I mean, they really had an attitude towards women that I couldn't put up with now.

Susan Seidelman: The way I did it was I didn't wait for an opportunity to happen, I made my own opportunity. Let's face it, even now, in terms of directors, I can think of maybe ten women, American women, who are directing films and there's probably hundreds of men. I knew that, but I am an impatient person, so I didn't want to wait for something to happen and I knew the chances of Hollywood, or anybody making a movie, knocking on my door and saying, will you direct it? were rather slim. So I decided to go out and put together my first movie on my own, to raise the financing, produce it. So *Smithereens* was essentially a project that I put together and raised the money for, to give myself a shot to direct it, and it worked out pretty well because it was made for less than $1 million and was in the official collection at Cannes. As a result of that, it got distributed all around the world and had a pretty good run here in New York. And that's what brought me to the attention of the studios. Then they came to me after seeing *Smithereens*, and that's how *Desperately Seeking Susan* came about. In other words, I had to make it happen to myself, and after that they came to me. But it was also interesting because the person who put *Desperately Seeking Susan* together happened to be woman also, so it was a kind of rare group of people who got together. The producers were women, the director was a woman, and the studio executive in charge of the project, who gave us the OK, was a woman.

Emma Sergeant: I was very isolated from boys because I went to an all-girls school and then my cousins were a rude shock to me whenever I did come across them. We had a very loving relationship, my sister and all our boy cousins. I do remember thinking, as all girls think at a very very young age, how convenient is the way boys go to the loo, and being absolutely furious that I couldn't do the same. But otherwise it really didn't occur to me that boys had an advantage in any way at all and I don't believe today they do.

The rudest shock I had of the wider world was going to art school, Camberwell, which is a very good art school. Not only was I discriminated against as a girl, but also as a girl with some kind of a background because you were mixing either with people who were inverted snobs and busily disguising the fact they came from decrepit aristocratic families, or with people who genuinely had to struggle – sons of miners or whatever – and it was a very difficult thing for them to be there. So everybody was looking for me, who had obviously had things soft and easy and come from a loving family, to prove myself. I felt far more under pressure at art school than I've ever felt before or afterwards in the so-called big wide world.

Being an artist, I like myself the best when I'm looking my most exhausted and most haggard, because I am somebody who functions on adrenalin. I hate to be plump and happy, I like to be really pushing myself to the limit, so if I can see a couple of extra lines by the end of the week, I'm happy, and I feel with my work that getting old will be an exciting thing, it will be interesting to see what happens to my painting as I grow older. I keep throwing myself down fresh challenges. I'm really not afraid of growing old.

Delphine Seyrig: I couldn't as a child think in terms of advantages and disadvantages in an objective way. I could see what my advantages would be, very early, before I knew how to speak. I think one begins to face life in babyhood. We're not allowed as children to consider that we have a hard life to face. We're told we're going to face a hard life when we are not with our parents any more, but they don't tell us that our life is hard when we are children, and I think it is. I do think I had to face life extremely early. This is a very important point for me. Life was never as hard for me as an adult as it was as a little child, because, as an adult, when life is hard, I can say, my life is hard, but when I was a child I was not able to say that, I was supposed to be a happy little girl and materially everything was provided for me. I was not able to say, my life is tough, I was not even able to think it.

Women have not been encouraged to make a living, they have been encouraged to work free at home. Women asking to be paid to work is still a novelty.

I'm trying to work day by day. I'm president of an association of a women's centre which is called Le Centre Audiovisuel Simone de Beauvoir. This centre is trying to create a memory of women of our time through audiovisual documents, film and documents about women or by women. Sometimes they are films by men, but they are about women. It's trying to bring these things together, to create a memory of women of our times, of their work, of their thoughts, of their visions.

Hanan Al-Shaykh: When women have achieved a great deal, they are treated seriously to a certain extent, but when a man sees that a woman cares about her looks only, and about jewellery and money, he doesn't treat her as an equal and I can see his reasons.

Woman is stronger because nobody really knows what is in her mind or in her body. Is she happy, is she satisfied? This is a mystery. This is her power, I think – the mystery.

Clare Short: I suppose when sex and men rear their ugly heads when you're sixteen, seventeen, immediately there are all the questions of getting pregnant and contraception and what's going to happen to you in life. I didn't articulate this sort of thing much for myself at the time, but I connected youth with a lot of freedom and I thought that I inevitably would end up married with some children and stuck at home, and in a way my resistance to it was to enjoy my youth. And then, of course, as time goes on, it gets more complicated.

Lack of confidence is a deep part of what you imbibe as a child and the culture you live in. The hardest thing I did in the process of getting elected to the House of Commons was to say to anyone that I wanted to do it. I felt ashamed. I'd worked in the Civil Service, I'd worked in the House of Commons, I'd seen it all, I knew I could do it, I knew I was at least as good as most of them, but I was so ashamed to say to people I'd like to try. Then, when I did try, people voted for me and I was selected quite quickly and fought the first election in a safe Labour seat. For women to put themselves forward, to say, I'm going to be chair of this, I want to be that, I think I'm good at that – it's very difficult. It's somehow part of the condition of womankind that you don't do things like that.

I experience patronizing attitudes in the House of Commons. But I am quite a strong person and there are a lot of silly men in the world. The kind of men who are crudely patronizing tend to be very silly, and it's usually fairly easy to put them down.

Objectively, it's obvious that women are discriminated against. If you look around, the overwhelming majority of low-paid workers are women. In a profession where women do succeed, teaching, the overwhelming majority of teachers are women, but only a small minority of heads of schools are women. There are hardly any women judges, senior lawyers, consultants in hospitals. Wherever you look, it's obvious that women aren't in equal numbers through all the different ranks of society, which is a pretty clear indication that something's wrong, especially when you look at the educational attainments of girls, which are as good, in fact a little better than boys', throughout the system. So objective evidence is clear and overwhelming. How far individual women are conscious of these forces that discriminate against them acting on them at any crucial point in their life varies from woman to woman. A lot of things that hold women back are internalized in women's conceptions of how you have to behave to be a proper woman. So we oppress ourselves to a large degree, only because we're given all that with the kind of culture we imbibe, which tells us how we have to be. The biggest factor is the way in which, as a culture, we distribute responsibility for childcare. The average family size now is 2.4 and the physical time it takes to produce that number of children is very small.

400

No one could seriously argue that that would necessarily transform their life or opportunities in the sense of career, employment, political involvement or whatever. So it's not the fact that women have this beautiful capacity to give birth to new life, it's that society expects women to take the leading role in the caring and nurturing, to give up the job opportunities, to stay at home, to be the one who takes the time off when the children are sick. They're expected to dedicate the major part of sixteen to twenty years of their life, depending on how many children they have, to their main priority of caring for the children, and that's an enormous chunk of a life.

I think all women are superwomen. I don't accept the categorization of super- and non-superwomen. Some of the women who are ambitious and successful come from privileged backgrounds and are able to have a well-paid job and afford full-time childcare. Certainly the women I grew up with, we'd never heard of anything like that. We wouldn't even think of it. Everyone would probably disapprove if you did. If you look at eminent women and their backgrounds, few came from fairly poor backgrounds where they had traditional mothers who stayed at home and looked after the kids. Lots of superwomen are women who have had a hard time and still struggled on and are still themselves, and they're out there somewhere, looking after their kids, keeping their house going, and are some kind of character in their local community. And there is a real sense in which being responsible for a home and childcare is a massively complex, variable, continuing task.

Women are entitled to enjoy having children and being mothers just as men are entitled to enjoy having children and being fathers. But men are allowed to have everything: they are allowed to have that deep, important pleasure, to be active politically and to rise in their careers. And I'm saying it is a distortion that women can't have both. If you went back to kind of slavery, there would be some people who would say, I don't mind being a slave, you moan a bit, but other things are worse. Similarly, women who say I'm happy with my condition have never had the other option, have not actually freely chosen it. If we had a society where men, as a matter of cultural norm, shared much more, and that was expected in the workplace, and they were given time off; and where we had massively more childcare provided at work, in neighbourhoods, at meetings, wherever, then I'd be interested to see how many women would not say, of course I want to be a mother, but I also want to use my brain, to be physically active and keep myself fit and healthy, to be creative artistically, or whatever it is. Just because some women say, it's OK what I've got, I don't think that's really necessarily true until we've built a society where women can choose, then we'll see how many reject everything other than childcare for 99 per cent of their time for twenty years.

In lots of ways, women are treated as sex objects. And then they treat themselves as sex objects. It's this muddle that says you're not a real woman unless you dress like this and make yourself available; and lots of men put women down with comments about how they fancy or don't fancy them, or comments about their bodies, even in totally inappropriate situations. Our society is so littered with images of women as desirable and available sex objects that it's deeply ingrained in our sexual culture. What's being said over and over again to young women is: this is what you've got to be like if you want to be a real woman. And what's being said to men is: that's how you should treat women, that's what they are, that's what they're there for. It's not that they're occasionally treated as sex objects, it's deeply embedded in the whole outlook.

I enjoy being a woman. I think it's a better condition to be in. Despite the fact that most women have been subject to injustices, I think they are bigger people than most men.

Alexandra Shulman: I'm most privileged in that I was brought up where I was brought up, had the education I had. Most girls are put into a class with boys and the boys are the ones expected to succeed, the girls are not. Therefore from an early age there is an ingrained lack of desire to succeed, or only to succeed within certain spheres. But I never had that.

I think, for a woman to succeed, it has to cease being a question as to whether she's a woman or not. If she's thinking of the fact that she's a woman, then she's not going to succeed. It doesn't mean, however, that she can't be quite feminine, but the thought should not be there about whether she's a woman or she's a man.

Rosemary Anne Sisson: I went to Cheltenham Ladies' College, which is, of course, a girls' school that believed in intelligence in women, so all my friends were delightful and intelligent girls. I was happy there, and at home we were treated with great respect – our minds, as well as our personalities, so I never felt the slightest inhibition and we had a lot of pleasant friends. Those were the days when the boys who were your neighbours were also your friends, and you played golf and tennis together, and you went exploring the fields together, and sex didn't enter into it. They were your friends, different, more interesting friends, but still just your friends, so I never felt any inhibitions because I was a girl.

Once I started writing, then I did feel that women writers were not treated with the respect men writers were. Certainly, when I wrote my first play after the war, it was much harder to break into the world of the theatre and critics tended not to treat you with the same respect. My first play was an historical play. The men took it for granted it was a woman's play, and the fact that it was a very funny play and the audience adored it, and it was very exciting – none of that made any difference. I was a woman writer and therefore they judged it. It's a very subjective, difficult thing to put your finger on, but this – Miss Sisson's play – somehow the attitude to it was different.

Certainly in my world it was very hard to get to the top, much harder to get to the top for a woman, but once you get to the top, there are only about half a dozen of us, so it's an enormous advantage, because everyone knows my name in the business. If they're looking for a woman writer, I'm one of the first names they try.

There is no discrimination moneywise at all, partly because of the Writers' Guild. I'm one of the highest-paid writers in the television business; I am in the very top bracket.

I did find when I was chairman of the Writers' Guild that I had to be aggressive, but that was because they were a rowdy lot round the table and, unfortunately, if you were going to keep control, like Mrs Thatcher in Parliament, you had to shout a bit and be rather ferocious. And the men didn't like it; they would have accepted it from a man, but didn't like it from a woman. That's the only time I've had to behave like a man. I'm glad I'm not in politics.

I use every advantage a woman has. For example, very often it was difficult to get to rehearsals in the early days. Directors didn't like you there. So, instead of saying, as perhaps a man would, listen, I'd like to come to rehearsals if I may, I would always say, would you mind very much if I came to rehearsals? I'll sit very quietly. So I'd use my woman's charm. It was a great advantage – I didn't threaten them in that way.

No one could have had more encouragement than I had in my private life, in our family life, and among my friends; no one could have been more lovingly encouraged and praised, and yet, still, one bad notice or

adverse comment and I am knocked off my perch and have to struggle
back on to it again. I find it hard to disregard.

Lady Anne Somerset: After I left university, I became a research
assistant, which isn't particularly well paid, and it didn't have obvious
prospects – and my parents were delighted, they thought it was
wonderful. But possibly, if I had been a boy, they wouldn't have stood
in my way but they would have been concerned that I was embarking on
something that was obviously not going to be lucrative.

I think if women happen to be very maternal and like devoting
themselves to being a housewife, that's fine, if that's what they want.
But I think it's appalling if that's the only option available to them.

Ginette Spanier: I never felt anything wrong about being a woman. My
father's business went awry and so my two sisters and I decided to earn
our livings. I don't like draughts, I like bright lights, and I love luxury,
so I shopped around for a job and I found the perfect thing in the gift
department of Fortnum & Mason. I had never done any work before, I
had been a girl of leisure, and I had a wonderful time at Fortnum &
Mason. It was my favourite job, it was absolutely lovely. Then I went as
a sales manager to a firm that used to sell to Fortnum & Mason, then
backwards and forwards from Paris to London with a firm in Grosvenor
Street which sold dresses ready-made in America. That was the first
time I had to do with clothes. There they made me directrice, and I had
very serious problems with the staff, but I didn't feel it was because I
was a woman. We realized somebody was stealing, and if I had been a
man it wouldn't have been any different. Then I came back to England,
fell in love with this Frenchman I had met in Paris, married him in 1939,
and had a horrible war. For five years, we were hunted like animals. I
fainted from hunger in the street, I almost went blind from malnutrition.
But I don't see that being a girl made it any different.

During the war it was hell, but it was less hell for a woman than for a
man. After the war, we bicycled through the German lines into
liberty. That morning in September 1944, I realized that by night I would
either be dead or free. We were free. And then I worked for the
Americans. They sent me to the Nuremberg Trials because I was
bilingual and they needed simultaneous translation, and they decorated
me with the Medal of Freedom. Then, when the war was over, it was
time to earn my living because we had borrowed money to live during
the war. My husband and I are Jewish – were Jewish, my husband is

404

dead – and I didn't know what job I was going to do because nobody knew me in Paris. My husband was a doctor and went back to his practice at once. A friend of mine sent her daughter of eighteen to stay with me, and to make her first trip to Paris exciting we went to the new wonderful couturier Pierre Balmain to buy her two dresses. The salon was five minutes from my flat. I had never heard of Balmain. After five years of being hunted, my frivolous instincts were a little quashed, and suddenly I saw luxury and beauty and handwork and everything was lovely. The girls walked very slowly up and down the catwalk, the whole thing was beautiful and very dignified. We went into the fitting room to choose the two famous dresses, and the child – it shows how life has changed – wanted to look like her mother, and wanted a sophisticated black velvet dress trimmed with jet. At that moment, a lady came into the fitting room and I thought she was going to say *oui, madame*, what can I do for you? But she just looked me straight in the eye and said, it's a woman like you we need in this firm. She was Pierre Balmain's mother; I was interviewed by her son next day, and I worked for him for twenty-nine years.

Life in America is so very different. These assertive women could put on a little charm and have the same result. They don't have to be so assertive. Mind you, when I was the boss at Balmain for twenty-nine years and we had forty, fifty people working for us and I was responsible for organizing the firm, I wasn't kind. I was assertive there. People had to behave. Authority doesn't make you nicer. I used to tell everyone, I used to be a nice woman till I came there. But whether it's a man or a woman, I don't think you have to be so terribly assertive as the Americans, and work morning, noon and night. I know so many people who work in America, and they are wrecks, absolute wrecks.

My mother was a very shy woman, and when we were children she said to us, if you're shy, hide it, it's not going to help anybody, it's certainly not going to help you. Shyness is not a quality. There must have been many occasions on which I've been shy. The first time I met Laurence Olivier I was shy. I've just had lunch with him. He's one of my greatest friends now.

I think men take fewer responsibilities than women. Women have so many responsibilities, they have to run the home, they have to do all those boring things. I can't grumble about being a woman, but I think I would prefer to have been a man.

Koo Stark: I liked being a girl. I still like being a girl. If I had to come back and do it all over again, I think I'd like to be a girl. I never felt I had the raw end of the deal. I always felt that boys rather had the worse end of it because they had to be responsible, they had to be very grown-up about things.

I didn't have the same kind of pressures to perform as well at school. If I wanted to go off and pursue acting or the arts, it was all right, it wasn't too serious, whereas if my brother had wanted to go off and pursue something artistic, everybody would have been much more concerned – how are you going to make a living out of it?

Men don't tend to look upon you as competition. It's much easier for a woman to walk in and meet the most influential man in the company. Obviously, once you've met him, you do then have to make your impression – but there is a curiosity value. Men would more easily see in a Miss Smith perhaps than a Mr Smith, so there's an advantage.

If you want to be truly independent, then it's harder as a woman because, so far in my life, men are in control of the companies you're dealing with, and generally your bankers are men, the people you have to go to for financing, the people you have to approach to be independently set up, are men. They will tend to pat you on the head, be a bit patronizing, and it's very difficult. And then, if you have a good idea and it's a serious good idea, you tend to get taken advantage of. They'll either want to become involved in it themselves and take a controlling interest, or just take it away from you without fear of repercussions, because they think, oh, well, at the end of the day, who's going to listen to a girl?

My natural inclination is to trust people, I'm a very trusting and honest person, but I keep thinking to myself, I mustn't, I mustn't, not everybody is nice. It took me ages to be able to be photographed. I thought I'd never be able to be photographed again because I had so many people taking pictures of me, that I thought that I could not face a camera, let alone take my clothes off in front of a camera. I got over that. But if you do something in all innocence and naïveté and you've been encouraged to do it, largely by men you trust, and then suddenly something happens and your situation is turned round and you're exploited, you're on your own, nobody's there to protect you. It's an awful experience for anybody to go through.

I have been grossly exploited as a sex object – when I was working as an actress, of course. It's very shocking to find other people's reactions, because you might not have any idea of what you're doing. You're an actress, and you're playing a role and you're performing a job, and suddenly somebody will pick up a photograph that you appeared in, or stop a frame of a film, or start writing stories around a role you played. They'll build up this whole image, and you just can't believe it. I really couldn't believe it.

I look forward to being an old lady, because old ladies get away with an enormous amount. They can be totally outrageous with dignity, whereas younger women can't. I think it's middle age which is probably the most awful. Old age is great; middle age is the real rocky road, particularly for women. You're neither one thing nor the other, your face is sagging, and your body's not quite coming together as it used to. You might be going through the change of life, you might be having other traumas, like financial crises, or crises in your marriage, or your children are reaching adolescence. All of these life crises seem to happen in middle age. I'm not looking forward to it.

Gloria Steinem: I always realized boys had more freedom, but I just accepted it. It was all right for boys to be in the street, all right for boys to sit in the movies and put their feet up over the chair in front of them. Boys threw snowballs at you when you weren't supposed to tell on them or fight back. In almost every way, boys had more power, but I accepted it. I assumed that that's the way it had to be. It took a long time for me to realize that perhaps that wasn't the way it had to be – probably when I was well past thirty years old. There were always certain rules of the game that I assumed were immutable. I assumed I would become who and what I married, that my identity would come from a man, because that's what I saw around me. Aside from actresses, I didn't see any women who had their own identity, and even in the movies the story usually ended with her marrying someone. I read very young. I don't remember learning to read, I just remember knowing how to read. I was reading books like *Little Women* and *Gone with the Wind* before I was nine, I think. Louisa May Alcott was, of course, a feminist from the first suffragist wave of feminism in this country. Her books have a very strong thrust of independence, and morality, and autonomy for women, and I absorbed that. But I also assumed it was impossible to achieve. The only woman I saw who was doing anything admirable was Eleanor Roosevelt, and she was only able to do that because she had been married to Franklin Roosevelt. So you still had to have the luck to marry a President or you couldn't do anything. I just didn't see any women whose power was their own.

A woman is not equal under the Constitution of the United States. She doesn't control her own body to the same degree that men do, legally or medically. If you are a poor woman in this country, you can still be denied an abortion. It's a sexual caste system; a racial caste system. Both. There are something like 8,000 federal laws that discriminate, based on nothing but gender, and no one knows how many state laws, but possibly many more. If you are a woman in the United States, and in most countries of the world, you can get an abortion under some circumstances. But, in many cases, you may still have to have your husband's permission or you may have to provide or fabricate medical excuses. You are still a supplicant, you still have to ask someone else to allow you to do this. Conversely, there are still many circumstances under which you can be coerced into being sterilized. Some states here want to pass legislation so that, if a woman is on welfare and has four children, they can say, we won't feed your existing children any more unless you have an abortion.

We are raised to believe that taking responsibility isn't feminine. If you are aggressive enough to be ambitious, to do the job well and have a career, you are not feminine. So you are not a real woman. And if you decide you want to be called a real woman, then you can't be ambitious. The culture gives you a double message.

If women could have slept their way to power, there would have been many more women in power by now. Using your femininity is a double-edged sword. You can use it and get noticed, but the notice you get is not serious; it isn't as if it's a great thing.

Lack of confidence, lack of self-esteem, is the single greatest affliction of any discriminated-against group. It happens to Jews, it happens to blacks, it happens to poor people, and it happens to women. We absorb society's assessments of our group: society says that we are inferior and we come to believe it ourselves. So it erodes our self-confidence. It doesn't spell it out in the same way that it did a hundred years ago when women could be owned like furniture can be owned, when women had no legal citizenship, no legal identity. Clearly, we've moved forward from that point. Women are citizens now; but we are not equal citizens.

Economic power has been defined in male terms. Women still suffer from a kind of semantic slavery in that those who work at home are called women who don't work, which is ridiculous. They work harder than any other class of workers in the United States, and deserve all the kinds of protections that workers, in general, should have. A woman who works outside the home has two jobs because one of her jobs is not counted.

I feel that we have to take whatever is given to us and use it. When I turned forty, I turned forty publicly at a press conference, because I realize that women have a problem at that age. When I became fifty, I had a big dinner party, I became fifty publicly. So I try to use this to make change, because it is true that women are still more penalized for ageing than men are. This is because women are supposed to be valuable for child-bearing, so as soon as our child-bearing years are over, we are less valuable, whereas men are powerful in the world so they can be quite old and funny-looking and still be thought attractive.

I would always rather be the victim than the victimizer. Because I don't want to grow callous. If you victimize other people, then you grow callous and your feelings become deadened. You use whatever is available to you to survive, of course. But the point is to equalize the powers so we can be friends. A room with the door locked is a prison, but the same room with the door open is a nice room. What matters is choice and the power to make the choice.

Pamela Stephenson: In my profession I've got to be extra good, I've got to prove myself twice as much. I try to be twice as funny as a man.

In Britain, and that goes for Europe generally, there is a difficulty with a woman doing comedy. It's got slightly better as my career has progressed, but I'm not sure that women are supposed to be funny according to a lot of people's views. It is considered threatening to be funny a lot of the time. Very early in my career, when I first did *Not the Nine O'Clock News,* was when I came to public attention. It was myself and a team of three men, and the men were asked just the normal questions people ask, but people just always immediately said to me, but can a woman really be funny?

I sense that a man in conversation is talking me down through sheer volume, sheer loudness. He shouts me down and talks through me, and I think there's a way of handling that. I just let him finish and then come back and exhaust him. Women have to learn tactics. At the end of the day, I don't actually want to compete with men in that way. There's no point to it.

If a man is at a party and has a few drinks too many, or even if he doesn't, but just starts letting himself go, clowning around, doing something outrageous, telling dirty stories, he's the life and soul of the party basically, and people think that's great. If he's a family man, they say, oh, Bill was in great form last night. But if a woman does it, and she is a mother and gets a bit drunk and relaxes and tells dirty stories, that's not the same thing at all. People might enjoy it at the time, but they will probably say things like, oh well, of course, I don't think things are all right at home, or maybe she's a nymphomaniac, maybe she's unhappy, she really should behave a bit more discreetly.

Lady Arabella Stuart: My father died when I was nine, and until I was sixteen I was really unhappy. If I had been a boy, I would have inherited the place where we lived, we'd have stayed in Scotland, my life would have been totally different. And if I'd been aware of that, if I'd been conscious of it then, I think I would have resented it very much. But I wasn't. My elder sister always was conscious of this and always resented deeply that, because we had no brother, we had to leave and go and live in London. It completely altered our lives. We lost our roots, everything. But it wasn't till I was completely grown up that I became aware of that.

I don't think during the war years parents like my parents had ambitions for their children, particularly if they were girls. They just wanted them to be happy. I had a funny letter from my mother about ten years ago, when I'd published several books that had been successful. She wrote me a very sweet letter congratulating me for what I'd done despite the drawbacks of my upbringing. She saw that it was a sort of a disadvantage for the life I later had to lead, making my living, getting on with it in London.

I had nobody I needed to compete with. My sisters were away at school, so I was the only child. I was the opposite of competitive in fact, that's what I found very difficult in life because I think you have to learn to be competitive and stick up for yourself when you're very small, and if you don't, you never do, it's too late. I was watching some little children playing the other day in the park; they were about three or four and they were fighting with each other quite nicely, just sticking up for themselves, and that never happened to me. All I had to do was be polite and everything was given to me and I had to say thank you.

Married women have a terrible time in England; they're much better off living alone. Either they are happily married, when they are ignored by other men, or they are neglected by their husbands, when they're shunned by other men. (Stretcher cases aren't attractive, as a man said to me about a mutual friend who was unhappy because her husband was in love with another woman. We were wondering why she didn't have admirers of her own, as she was very pretty.) Or they are married to very successful and/or attractive men, when they are humiliated and patronized by people in general, who can't wait to talk to their husbands. I remember Cynthia Kee telling me how, a few days after her marriage to Robert, he took her to a party of Annie Fleming's. Mrs Fleming swept Robert away as soon as they arrived, leaving Cynthia alone in the hall. She found herself standing next to Peter Quennell and Cyril Connolly, who were talking about Robert in flattering terms. I'm married to him, she said proudly. I know, said Peter Quennell, turning his back.

I felt that men tended to patronize me terrifically when I was married to Mark, particularly in the early years. But that's not so much to do with being a woman, it's this terrible problem that I and quite a lot of my friends have had who married people who became stars in their own right. The wives are just treated so badly – they're ignored, patronized, humiliated.

I think I'm an odd person that doesn't quite fit into categories, and it's my own nature that's rather a disadvantage in some ways in a modern world. I sometimes feel I'm a bit like an oriental person living in an occidental world because I just don't think I have the same standards most other people have. As you get older, that gets easier, because people get to know you and they get to know in the end what you expect, and people I work with become fond of one, like one, because one has good manners, however unusual it may be. So I don't think just being a woman or not being a man has really had much effect on me. I should say less than most people. I know some women use their femininity. I have friends who used to say, oh Arabella, if only you knew how to manage your life better, and I know that they're right. As I say, I haven't really benefited because I've never somehow chosen to.

Imogen Stubbs: I had very pretty blonde hair when I was little, and everybody thought I was splendid. I was horribly cute, I expect, and I was led to believe I was God's gift to four-year-old children. I also looked like the girl in *The Sound of Music*, which meant people used to come up to me in the street and ask for my autograph. All that built up my confidence from an early age, and also my parents encouraged me enormously, they never put me down. I was brought up to think that if you really want something you can get it without having to be obnoxious.

I don't think I'm quite the type to be treated as a sex object, mainly because I tend to come across as very tomboyish. I've learned, ever since I went to Westminster, that if you're lucky enough to be confident, you can give off signs, like an insect, to indicate to people before they approach you how you should be treated. Maybe it is a privilege to have the confidence to do that.

I'm sure I have used my femininity. Hitch-hiking with boys, they always shoved me forward and hid in a bush. As a waitress, I exploited my charm ruthlessly to get tips. There's absolutely no denying it. Maybe it is unwitting now, but I'm sure I still do. My brother's always making signs, throwing up in the background when I'm trying to be charming to people. I suppose it depends on the kind of girl you are as to what you can exploit. Being sweet and innocent is probably what I've exploited most.

I think I tend to exploit being a feeble woman and looking hopeless, and that's when I exasperate people to the point where they say, oh look, I'll do it, I'll do it. Men do that likewise over washing up or cooking.

In my life, the disadvantages have never been associated with being a woman, they are just situations. In acting, it's a disadvantage being a woman because there are far fewer parts for women. If you go to RADA, there are eight girls and fifteen boys, so it's harder to get in because you're a woman. But then there just aren't the parts, so it's not fair on actors and actresses in general if you have too many women. Even at drama school, there are ten boys in every play to two girls. I've played men's parts at drama school, and I remember thinking, God, I wish I was a man then I could play this part for real.

Definitely the worst side of sexism comes from stereotyping. If you have blonde hair and blue eyes, then a lot of people treat you like their idea of a fairly typical blonde. What's worse is if you show you are more intelligent than they anticipated, and they suddenly shift gear. They say, oh, I see you are a person and not a kind of pet. I hate that, I hate it when people suddenly change. You say, oh yes, I went to Oxford, and suddenly there's a complete shift in gear from the way someone talks to you because they'd assumed that you were just a silly girl. When I was a waitress, quite a long time ago, at Coconut Grove, and at Brown's at Oxford, when I was a student, I came across appalling sexism. Even from people who actually were students with me and just didn't recognize me. It was snobbism, people just being very rude to me as a waitress because they're used to treating waitresses very badly, as servants.

I think, whatever everyone says, that it's all right to be a bachelor, there's a lot of bravura about being a bachelor, but a spinster is a cold, horrible word. In this society, when you're young, everything goes swimmingly, but as you get older into middle age, there's no denying women are really at a disadvantage to men, because, for men, somehow age doesn't matter enormously. They don't say, oh, he's gone a bit ugly, or his hair is falling out. Men have a constant value in society's eyes, and they don't have the same worries as women as they get older. When women lose their looks, lose their hair, lose their teeth, they plummet in value in men's eyes, except for your nearest and dearest. That will never change. There's nothing you can do about it. The advantages you have as a woman when you're young and pretty will go, whereas if you're a young and talented man, you're likely, as you get older, to get more desirable.

I'm very romantic. I wish I had been born in another era, I would love to have been courted, to have had beaux and go out walking. I find discos and things completely unattractive because there's no romance. Jiggling opposite someone else jiggling doesn't do wonders for me. The wonderful thing about being an actress is you get to do things like wearing fabulous dresses and waltzing with people. You get to live in different eras, even if it's just three hours a night, and you do all the research and get to know the period well. There are eras where the woman's situation was very different. I played Sally Bowles in *Cabaret*, who dominates the thing completely, wacky and extraordinary power, and I've played pathetic women in Galsworthy who had no power at all and were trampled upon, silly women.

Andrea von Stumm: I'm not ugly, I'm not old, and perhaps, if I was a little older and uglier, I wouldn't find it so pleasant to be a woman. I can imagine then everything changes, because you have fewer weapons in your hands: perhaps only charm and an appearance of softness, of helplessness. Women who are clever elicit protectiveness, with a man in particular and the world in general.

To love is something active, and there is a recipient, and the recipient is obviously talked about and often treated as an object. It is the most normal thing in the world. Men do it, women do it. From the moment you say 'my husband' or 'my boyfriend', you are already talking about a possession, and there's a connotation of being like an object. However, there are objects and objects. If you are an object that is treated well and cherished and polished and cared for, that's fine. There is nothing wrong with being an object, unless you are put in a box or a cage and you can't go out. Of course, if you're an object that is kicked

413

around and neglected, then it's certainly very painful. I think there's something very nice about being an object. It is a prolongation of childhood. I think women are privileged in that they remain children, in a way, for longer.

Christine Sutherland: It is almost biologically impossible for a woman to compartmentalize her emotions, I am sure of it. If a woman is very much in love, and is physically and emotionally involved with a man, it is like a blanket that comes over her completely. It obscures her judgement and vitiates it, and dries out her forces of energy. She is almost incapable – depending on how strongly she feels – of carrying on her normal job.

I think men pay far more attention to women's intelligence in America than they do here. In England, men tend to be patronizing. Not on the Continent. Frenchmen, for example, like intelligent women. When you show a Frenchman a photograph of a beautiful woman, he says, *attendez qu'elle ouvre sa bouche*. No Englishman would ever say that.

I loved the old days when men brought you flowers and took you to lovely places to dance and got up to give you the seat. I think women had a far better deal. If we could combine the two, it would be the ideal world. But you can't have your cake and eat it.

Janet Suzman: I grew up in the 1960s, so I am a product of that so-called permissive age, and I'm not too damned sure it is a very good thing. I now feel the lack of those stringent moralistic stances which made you fight against them, but being aware of them gave a structure to society which I see crumbling all around me now. And I think I actually have to admit I disapprove. I disapprove because it's leading us down some awful chasm and we don't know what the end of it is. There are too many single parents, there are too many discarded people, there are too many children growing up without any real structure in their home. And it seems to me a sort of greyish, porridgy mess at the moment, and it will probably get worse. Maybe society will save itself from total chaos. But I feel terrible dangers, and that's because I am bringing up a young child, so my antennae are out for structures to help him.

I have recently had the ghastly experience of having to go to lawyers for the first time in my life. And I am now with a woman lawyer. Why? Because it became absolutely apparent that the male lawyer belonged to a sort of club which I didn't and said, oh, don't worry about a thing, I'll take care of it, that sort of attitude. I began to see there's a glass wall. I could see through it very clearly, and on the other side was this male lawyer who was going to take care of me. My apprehension of that sort of diddums attitude to women became very clear. And, of course, in this instance my life was involved, my living, the quality of my life – to do with children and all that sort of thing. So I changed. I felt that out of a woman there would be a greater frankness, a greater understanding, a greater ease of talking.

If you set your cap at somebody, if you want them for whatever reason, the sacrifices you might have to make might be enormous. You might have to pretend to be not as clever as you are, you might have to pretend to be poorer, you might have to pretend to be weaker or more malleable. Men are often, it would appear, a bit wary of intellect in women. By intellect, I don't mean clever, clever; I mean a woman who has been somewhat educated and has a few opinions, who is able to hold a conversation. So I think women on the whole know that a game is to be played.

Conny Templeman: I think that men have made a mystery about making films – the technique, everything. Women are slowly taking up positions of responsibility within the film industry, but there is still an awful lot of mystery. I'm not saying I'm a good director and I know what I'm talking about, but from my small experience, a lot of people could have done what I can do. Maybe one can see this as my own lack of confidence, but if you find a woman who at least is not afraid of talking in front of twenty people, just telling them what she wants, and if she's observed life a bit, and learned a little about where you put the camera, but only a little, I think you can direct a film. The whole perception of achievement is a male perception. I can't see that I've achieved anything. If someone says, do you feel a sense of achievement, I say no, I don't. It's because we have these role models that are male, and values that are male. Who says I've achieved something? Men say it.

I don't feel at ease in the company of men in the film business. In general, I find the company of women more interesting, because you don't feel in any way less of a person. I don't think of men as a possible sexual threat at all. I think only of the way, if you have a group of men, chartered accountants, bankers or whatever – they can be from any walk of life – they will still think they have the more important things to say because they're men. It might be true, but it might not be true. With women, that assumption is never there.

415

I want to run a goat farm. You don't have to kill the animals, and it's an honest way of life. I don't have very much experience, but I suppose I'm looking for more wholeness and harmony and getting away from the urban way of life which is quite pressurized and rather snobbish, particularly in my job. And there's an awful lot of bullshit around. Women, on the whole, don't care for so much bullshit.

Lisa St Aubin de Terán: I've always found it an advantage to be a girl. I think girls, at least good-looking girls, get away with murder, and I came from a good-looking family. I was always aware that one could do the most blatant arm-twisting, and do what one wanted in the world, because people would allow it. I left school at fifteen and never went to university. Then I saw there could be disadvantages, but I always actually found advantages. I found, time and again, by merely being winsome or smiling or dropping a tear I could get what I wanted in life, in the world in general; I was very manipulative and I think I was lucky in having this certain amount of confidence and at the same time being able to ride on the fact that a pretty girl can do what she likes. And I do believe that. I see it with my own daughters.

In my life in England, I have never come across discrimination, but I can see that if I were in business or the medical profession, or teaching, or in the stock market, I would be in trouble. It's a mixture of social pressures and habit. People accept what they believe to be the position of all the different people within a society. It's interesting when one goes to the Caribbean, for instance, and observes matriarchal societies where women wield a tremendous power within the family in a way I have never seen anywhere else. The woman is in charge. People accept in certain parts of the Caribbean that it is the woman who can beat up her husband, just as people accept in England or Italy that a husband can beat up his wife. And I think children then grow up and imprint what they see, and so their expectations are either raised or lowered.

Women in Venezuela are fifth-rate citizens really, they have very few rights. When my daughter was born, if I travelled to a neighbouring town to do shopping, I had to have a permit from my husband to say I could travel with my own child through the road block. There was tremendous prejudice against women, yet I took over the entire management and running of the plantation I lived on, and was in charge and not just equal with the other men who were running haciendas in that area. I was way above them, since I had such a large hacienda. I think that would have been more difficult in a society where there was less prejudice, because they were so astonished, their reaction was one

416

of incredulity. I had fifty-two men working for me round the year, and I could manipulate them all to get everything working well without feuding and fighting or squabbling and being upset. I never had problems because I was able to deal with them all in a very feminine way, which meant actually understanding a little more than just the situation as it cropped up – seeing all sides of what was happening and actually soothing people. I think that is something women can do: they can actually soothe and calm people if they follow a sort of intuition. Intuition is another big advantage that male competitors don't have, and so they can't compete at that level.

It is difficult for a woman writing in English to be taken seriously as a poet. There are tremendous advantages as a novelist in being a woman, and I come across them time and again. There is an unfair advantage in that I, as a woman, am actually favoured over very talented men who should have equal opportunities and don't. But I think, as a poet, there is a definite disadvantage, probably because there is no great woman poet in the English language, so people think you aren't or won't be one either. In Spanish, there are a great number of women poets and a tradition of women's poetry, but here, in England, female poets have always been minor poets.

Fiona Thyssen: I had an asset which was a very unfair one: I had amazing beauty, and that beauty was a passport into a way of life or situations which normally I might not have expected to have had available. I was totally unaware of it, which made the whole thing bearable.

Looking back, I find it was a terrible burden because, like all beautiful women, I think it is an accident of birth which you may or may not be aware of, and it's difficult to live up to people's expectations. People seem to expect more of you perhaps, because you are always in the public eye. Everybody can see you, people are attracted to you, people run after you and you seem to have been given a whole way of life which may not actually be very compatible for you. I think I would have been a very happy person if I'd married a delightful farmer, somebody who loved the land (because I love the land), and lived a very passive, peaceful life somewhere in the country. Because of the accident of birth, I was projected, to put it mildly, into a way of life which for the most part I found difficult to handle. I was not equipped, I wasn't trained for it. It meant that I grew up inside, as a woman, very slowly. My values took a long time coming. It was a long, slow birth process.

417

Getting older has released me from a lot of burdens. I don't have to be glamorous any more. I don't have to go out to parties I don't want to go to and drink, which I don't do any more. For what? To try to attract some ravishing man? I need it like a hole in the head.

Although I haven't had to earn my living with men, I have had to deal with men. I modelled, yes, but I was the valuable commodity, not the man, in the modelling world. I could name my own price. With great respect to the famous photographers with whom I worked, I was the commodity.

I made the disastrous mistake of divorcing when the children were very young, and I see the impact on those children growing up without the presence of their father. For instance, my daughter, Chessie, will not be told anything by a man because she has never heard the voice of male authority in the house. It's made things very difficult with the men in her life. She is not prepared to accept orders or suggestions. She'll do something because she chooses to do it. I, on the contrary, was trained to accept orders. I find it totally natural and totally acceptable.

I spent my married life living up to the expectations of my husband, and then, when I divorced, living up to the expectations of my social environment. It was only much later on that I started to suss out that I didn't need to do that, that I could perfectly well be myself, that I didn't need to prove anything to anybody. But, first of all, I obviously had to lose that barrier of beauty. It was a barrier between me and people's understanding, a barrier specifically through which it was difficult to project myself as a reasonably intelligent human being.

Now, I'm battling for my inside life, battling to reassess my values and find a way to be the sort of productive person I could have been years ago if I hadn't been so damned beautiful.

There's a boring cliché: if it's a woman who says it, she is opinionated, and if it's a man who says it, it is a good idea, it's wisdom. I think the injustice will be prolonged probably for centuries because obviously men feel threatened by any impingement on their domain.

Martha Tiller: I felt no disadvantages at school, but the moment I finished it was a different story. The world was filled with limits for a female, particularly a young female. I was a broadcasting/journalism graduate, finishing in three years, *cum laude*. I had produced pro-grammes in Spanish for 'The Voice of America' professionally while I was a student in school. I had also produced television programmes in German and a television series on science. When I came to New York to look for a job, nobody believed I had done all of these things, and during interview after interview they would pat me on the head, offer me a Coke and suggest I go back home to Texas. Although I had a production degree, I was not allowed to join a union. I couldn't belong to the union because I was female.

The only reason I have my own business is because no Dallas company would make me vice-president of public relations. They'll allow women to middle management level, and that's it. There is a way to be firm, to be exact, to be decisive, to make decisions, to move ahead, and be thoroughly feminine. This is why the successful women who know how to apply these skills can be more successful than a man. It's the old iron hand and the velvet glove, the steel-magnolia syndrome.

I need to take advantage of every opportunity because, as a woman, I have started two steps behind. What man has ever walked in a pair of women's shoes? They are designed by men to keep women in their place, two steps behind. They are impossible to walk in.

Claire Tomalin: Clearly, to some extent, women were still strongly discriminated against when I was young in the sense that when I went to Cambridge there were ten men to every woman. That was obviously discrimination, and I suppose I was mean and proud enough to feel it was rather fun to be one of the few women who got there, which was probably the wrong attitude.

I moved into a world in which women are somehow given licence, and I didn't even think of trying to succeed in areas where they're not. I've always thought life was harder for women, because if you want the traditional feminine side of life, which I did, and you want to succeed to some degree in what is traditionally a man's world, you have to work twice as hard. And I felt that I did work very hard, but I also felt that I expected a lot, and I suppose, looking back, in one way I probably gave too much of my life to having children.

I've been a widow for a long time, and widows are somehow given some kind of magic thing. They are allowed authority, or are allowed respect, that perhaps divorced women or unmarried women are quite unfairly denied.

I can't remember in my life ever wanting to be a man. I don't think the traumas I have been through have been because I was a woman. I think life can be cruelly hard for men, and painful and traumatic, and they can't have babies. I'm very lucky, I gave birth quite easily, and I remember the births of all my children with really intense pleasure.

Lili Townsend: I was much involved in horses and running around outside as a girl, and I really didn't feel any restrictions until the teen years, when the opposite sex started looking pretty interesting, and then it was interest rather than envy.

In spite of the fact that I've been able to succeed in my life's goals, I have certainly been impeded and injured by men. I've been involved with very strong men, and I've been injured very strongly by them, and I've learned a great deal about the nature of action and reaction. I don't believe we really learn until we are in pain. Not until we've reached the bottom of an area that is difficult do we finally push off from that bottom so we can burst into the light of the truth. And I think that in this evolved state of being in which I am now, I cherish those relationships, because they taught me a great deal.

Women have a great fear – at least I do – of appearing frivolous, particularly now, because the kind of work I do is hard to describe and doesn't have the kind of titles that are acceptable in the world today. Before, in my very concrete life in New York, I was director of this and vice-president of that, and those credentials were obvious. Now it is harder to establish my credentials, because I'm in a place where those titles are meaningless. So, from that point of view, it is essential to have some kind of an establishable background to be accepted as an equal. And yet one has the feeling with certain men that they have what I refer to as the grey-flannel mentality, and women are never equal to them in any way. There's still the kind of old-boy backroom attitude: fine, you handle the cosmetics and we'll take care of the deeper realities. When what is evolving now – why women are so fascinating to everyone now – is that we are beginning to understand that we're at the centre of those issues. The new way of thinking and being in the new age is that we are sharing the concept of feeling one's way to a decision by trusting the intuition, and that's what women can teach, because that's what we know how to do.

It is the purpose of women to spread the gospel of love, to instruct and teach how to feel emotions. We're not trained in societies to feel, we're trained to think. Basically all the problems in the world right now have come from total-mind thinking. The holistic point of view is that decisions about life and love and the pursuit of happiness are made with the entire being. The being is the will, and as the will of the individual evolves it becomes more in line with the will of God.

I used to worry about ageing. I don't any more. I have the example of a mother, perfectly ravishingly beautiful at eighty, who can still knock people's socks off. It's the light within, and she takes very good care of herself. In the world I'm involved in, the world of personal transformation, it's a lot easier to believe in someone who looks wonderful, who looks as though their lives are working for them. You can't really believe me if I don't look well. You can see the truth, because I look healthy, because I am attractive. I don't worry about the signs of age in a paranoid way, although I believe that we need to do everything we can to feel healthy and look the best we can. I think women can do anything they need to make themselves be well: we can use surgery, health techniques, diet, nutrition. I have a holistic view about the sacred temple which our body is, because I really believe that, if God is dwelling in each one of us, the more we are aware of that the more we want to keep a clean and pure temple for that spirit.

Polly Toynbee: I felt I could do anything I wanted. Later I came to look back on it rather differently, but I was brought up with the idea that girls were going to go out and do something. So the environment I was brought up in – I went to a girls' boarding school, intellectual rather than social – suggested that everything I might want to do was available. Later, looking back, perhaps through slightly more feminist eyes, perhaps knowing a little bit more about the world and seeing the way things map out for women and men, I realized I had never once wanted to do anything that wasn't to some extent a traditional women's thing. I wanted to be a novelist and a writer, and there are plenty of role models for novelists and writers. It may not be easy to achieve, but at least nobody says that a woman can't be a writer. I wanted to be a journalist, and there have always been quite a lot of journalists. I never wanted to be a scientist. I came from an entirely unscientific background. I never wanted to do anything but what women, or reasonably intellectual women, might want to do. And I'm so thoroughly conditioned by that, I just don't know if I might have had it in myself to do any of those other things. I'm not good at science. I don't read it or understand it, and I'm not a natural mathematician. I suspect that, like most other women, I've been strongly programmed to want what other women have already got.

In going into journalism, you were quickly channelled, rather as in

421

politics, into what women always do. You write about social policy and housing and sub-stories, and you write about exactly the same sort of issues as women in politics tend to be given – minister of education, minister of health, that kind of thing. In journalism, it's very seductive, because there is a sort of star role available to women: you can become a star columnist, and once you're there you have tremendous freedom. If I were starting again, I might want to become a political correspondent. I'd start by being a labour-relations correspondent, and I'd try to have more understanding of economics, and perhaps one would have to have training. Certainly, if one wanted to be an editor of a serious newspaper or magazine, one would need to have come from that side of journalism, and that's one reason why women don't become editors, because they've not done the heavy jobs, been defence correspondents or war correspondents. I didn't positively want it at the time when I could have made a decision to fight for it and say, right, what I want to be is a political writer, because it looked much harder work and the rewards were slower. You can be a star feature writer quite young by not doing the hard work, by not becoming a trades-union correspondent and sitting outside TUC headquarters waiting for meetings to end night after night. You can do it the easy way, and that is very much true in lots of women's lives. There is a sort of red carpet laid out for you, and if you do well in those traditional roles, it's all easy and nice, and if you succeed, men don't feel resentful. And I don't feel resentful, because I've done tremendously well, and I have a job I love, but I wonder if I might have done even better if I had done something more challenging.

There is always a tendency to push girls towards what they won't have to fight for very hard. It's done subtly and not on purpose. They do it in the girl's best interests. They might be women or they might be men who look at any individual girl, and they don't say, I'll take this girl and force her to go through all sorts of battles; they say, what can I offer this person that will keep her reasonably happy? I often long to go and teach in a school for a while – girls of fourteen to sixteen – and make them realize that that's going to happen to them and they've actually got to decide very positively to seek a non-traditional occupation. But then, of course, it is true that if you do try to get a job in Marconi or somewhere like that, the interviewer says, well, we're going to give you six years of intensive and very expensive training, you're going to go off and have children; you might not come back again. There is a strong feeling of that throughout industry and the more male-dominated occupations. They make the fact that they think women are going to get married and have children their excuse for preferring men. It's not economic considerations, it's an excuse. Because the statistics show that, in industry, women are far more reliable. They move jobs much less often than men, and they stay for longer, and perhaps because they're uncertain of their own roles, they don't shop about for promotion the way men do. You can train a man and be absolutely certain that, every two years, he will go off and get interviews and try to move on, whereas women, once they do well in a company, tend to have more of a Japanese attitude and stick with it and work for promotion within the company. This has been shown statistically. So it isn't the evidence of their own eyes that makes them think women are a bad bet – mostly they're a good bet. Professional women now take off very little time to have children, really very little: six months to a year out of a forty-year working life.

Women simply don't seek out promotion, they don't expect to be promoted, don't expect to get this or that job. They underestimate themselves all the time, because they are used to being underestimated. If you have a group of men and women standing around talking, the men do all the talking, and unless there's an incredibly forceful woman, the women are quiet. In the company of men, women are not assertive, and over the years women have assumed a natural inferiority. And even if they wouldn't admit it, even if they say, I think women are just as good, or, I think women are better, when it comes down to it they're quite frightened by men. They're used to being intimidated, in conversation, in attitudes, in men tending to be more forceful in the expression of their views.

I am constantly, constantly patronized by men, and never more than in the field of politics. Since the formation of the SDP and getting involved in politics, all this has come to the fore far more in my mind. The way male politicians behave is unbelievable. They treat all women as if they were absolute idiots, and it's taken incredibly hard fighting by myself and a number of others to be treated as equals, and as just as intelligent. In fact, some of the women on the National Committee of the SDP are considerably more intelligent than some of our MPs who behave in this extraordinarily lordly fashion, who dismiss what women say because they're women. It happens in committee after committee all the time. If you challenged them on it, they would retreat, but, among themselves, it's those women getting in the way of the general progress of male business. Some men are not like that. I live in a protected world of rather liberal decent people who at least think in terms of equality and of respecting women, and I forget that, out there, are a lot of worlds that aren't like that at all. Politics is one of them, and I dare say the world of business is another. On the whole, it's fairly exceptional for people genuinely to regard women as being of equal potential.

423

For a woman to succeed, she's got to look reasonably feminine, she's got to be very intelligent, a lot more so than most of the men she's competing against, and she's got actually to surprise people. Sometimes it works the other way. When I was a reporter and features writer on the *Observer*, the fact that I tackled a serious subject made everybody sit up and say, wow, that's a good piece. It might only be comparable to a piece written by a man, but the fact that I am a woman would make them notice it twice as much. The implication being, well, who'd have thought a woman could do that? So sometimes it works in your favour, because people's expectations of women are so low, but mostly it works the other way, where you really have to be twice as good and knock men into a cocked hat before they notice.

The powerlessness of women and their lack of money is probably the most important factor in how they're seen. Once women can and actually do earn as much as men, and own as much as men, then you begin to see a real shift. Only in those families where that is the case, do you find that men and women seem at all equal. You find families where men are nice to their wives, but the only ones who seem equal are families where a woman has a job which is just as important, has as much status attached, and she's getting as much money. They're very rare. Obviously a lot of women go out to work and do quite important jobs, but their husbands have a much more important job and the mortgage is really paid by him, and her wage just covers having somebody to look after the children. That's true in working-class households; and in a lot of middle-class households where they've got a nanny and the mother only gets paid a bit more than the nanny when she goes out to work. The state can't decree real economic equality, but it can influence and it can push towards it. Then I think we could begin to answer some of the questions about what was nature and what was nurture.

Society divides up roles between women and men in a very rigid way. It's still the case. It happens with children at the youngest age. Men are the outgoing, tough, aggressive, hardened characters who have to fight out there in the jungle, earn their living and be tough. They mustn't admit to any vulnerability, they mustn't admit to any weakness. Women are given the entire caring, gentle, nurturing and communicative sides where they talk about and investigate their feelings and are the carriers of all of that in society. This is, of course, absurd, because there are many women who are not instinctively like that and many men who are, but the line comes down and it's very hard for either side to cross it. But it seems to me that, in terms of human values, women ultimately have the better deal, because that's what matters most.

I don't think I mind ageing as much as I thought I would. I used to think, I'll kill myself at thirty, that's the end. It may be that I'm very lucky that my life has been as good and I am so essentially contented, that I have a husband I love, children I love, a wonderful standard of living, a job that fascinates me, a lot of friends. It couldn't be better. I get up almost every morning and thank my lucky stars. When people say, wouldn't you like to start all over again, I think, no, I might not be so lucky next time. I look in the mirror and see I'm getting older, and it doesn't worry me much because I don't honestly think my looks were ever an asset. I've looked all right, but I was never going to be a great beauty and never expected to be. There were times, as a teenager, when I minded desperately, sucking in my teeth and doing things to my face, but even then I knew in my head that my relationships would be about what people were like, not with people who were going to expect me to be the most beautiful woman on earth.

Abir Dajani Tuqan: An Arab woman has a lot of influence over the children. If the man is understanding and she has a strong personality, then she can also influence her husband. That's very important if she's emancipated, if she wants to look ahead, if she wants to learn. But some women just accept. In certain Arab countries, the grandmothers were more emancipated than this generation, which is rather sad. They were less inhibited and more emancipated, and their granddaughters admit it.

If you're economically independent, you can do a lot, you can do your own thing. But if you have to answer to someone, for money for instance, then you are tied. The countries in the Arab world which have come into a lot of money, obviously because of the oil, were much more emancipated before the oil. You notice it when you sit and talk with some of the older women. They are very outspoken, very powerful. They used to get some of the men and thrash them, and they had more influence than the women have today.

Kathleen Turner: When I lived in Venezuela – I was there from nine to fourteen – then I felt intensely restricted, but that was very much to do with being a blonde, blue-eyed American in Latin America. As a young woman, it would have been impossible to go anywhere on my own because that would have been a statement that I was not a good young woman. No one would even have thought to take me out without some adult over-watching us. When I got to London, I was feeling so headbound, so tied up, that the first day I got on a subway and just rode around for three or four hours and called home from different stations, I'm at Hammersmith, at Kensington. My parents felt I was safe in

London. In South America, they did not feel I was. We stayed three and a half years in London, until our father died. I was at the American School, and trying to study acting, but with my father's death we lost our diplomatic status and it was necessary to return immediately to the United States.

As an actor, I don't have the difficulty of competition with men simply because, quite honestly, no man could do what I do. I didn't encounter the lack of credibility that comes with being a woman until I really started to become successful and was going to Hollywood with ideas about a script or wanting to meet a director before I agreed to work on a project. Then, suddenly, I realized I was running up against it: well, we think you are very pretty and there's no doubt we think you are talented, honey, but your opinion really is not so valid. I never felt slapped in the face until I began to attain some success.

I was with an actor in my first film, *Body Heat*, and by his third film he had a million-dollar price tag. It took me five or six to get to that price level. I really don't know why. Certainly if you look at the record of commercial successes, my record is almost incomparable right now in terms of audience appeal, and the actor in question has never had a success. So I find it a great mystery. Perhaps it's because we had a period of very strong women in films in the 1950s, with Bette Davis, Joan Crawford, Lauren Bacall, those women. And then, in the 1960s and 1970s, we lost a lot of impetus and it became very much male-orientated with Dustin Hoffman and people. And it has taken until now, until the 1980s, for women to win back full-time on screen. I think they are starting to command comparable salaries, but Hollywood is always five years behind the public, and they are still coasting on the concept of male stars.

The greatest sexual oppression has been in a lack of encouraging development of individuality in women. The goal is not to become some form of a woman, it is to become an individual, to be encouraged to develop oneself to the extent that men are encouraged to develop themselves. That is what we lack, and that is what I resent.

A woman not only has to work harder usually, but if she wishes to have a so-called normal life, then she has got to have enough money to hire herself a wife. A man can marry and have so much responsibility taken off his shoulders: the essential running of a house, the raising of a child, getting the laundry done, having food in the refrigerator – all this is taken very much for granted. A professional woman, at a certain income level, is certainly expected to achieve all these things as well as carry on her job. And, in fact, I think we expect that of ourselves also. About two or three years ago, I hired someone to help out, to do shopping, clean the house. And I felt terribly guilty. It took me years to be able to do that without feeling I had failed somehow in not providing the full home as well, which I felt was my job too, even though I don't know anybody who works harder than me, I swear to God. I mean, a film is fourteen-hour days, in theatre it's ten to twelve. The physical drain is immense. Where the heck I get off thinking I can do it all, I don't know. Now I am getting past that. But you have to make a certain amount of money to hire a wife. And this is not true necessarily of men. They don't have to hire a wife. She's there already.

I look better now than I ever looked. When I was eighteen I had baby fat everywhere. I find the wrinkles that are coming exciting, my face is more mobile, I have more expression than I ever had. I think that this will continue to be true. I'll mind, probably, when I'm fifty looking at *Body Heat* when I was twenty-five. I'm going to have to be a *grande dame*, I'm going to have to be eccentric and wonderful, and commanding and commandeering. It's going to be a question of personality. They are not going to look at the face and say, what a beautiful woman, they are going to say, oh my god, *what* a woman. That's fine.

Jill Tweedie: I knew from the first moment, I should think, that there were disadvantages. I knew that the world outside my parents' house did not belong to me. I realized very clearly it belonged to men. And I noticed, as I got a little older and began to have ideas, that wherever I went there would be men and they would be nice to you and want to go out with you, but they didn't want to listen to you. I learned that your role was to be attractive. You were allowed to go as far as being unpredictable and flirtatious, but you couldn't be funny, you weren't allowed to be funny. You could see the distress that caused. They might laugh, but it caused a certain distress. And you couldn't talk seriously. I learned that when I went out with a particular man friend to a party, and heard the men discussing something that interested me, I had to feed my idea about it through the man. I would say, I think this and this and he would say, well, of course, what I feel is ... And that is the way it would enter the conversation. But I couldn't do it directly. I minded very much about that.

I came out of school extremely confident among girls. But then I found the terrible split that happens to women, not men: that if I wanted to lead a working life or intellectual life in the world, but also wanted to be attractive to men, I had to choose. Men don't have to choose. And that

427

comes as a great shock. Of course, you don't suddenly become aware of it. It's something quite secret that seeps into you where you pick up little signs and realize that you want, of course, to make men like you and to be popular among men. I think that's a little less so today, but in my childhood and young girlhood, your status was men. And you wouldn't get men friends from men listening to your ideas or talking to you as a equal, it would be from putting forward your feminine attractions. I think that has changed.

I'm very puritan to say so, but I think women have, in general, a harder life. If you take any level of society, whether very poor or poor or whatever until you get to the rich, the woman is likely to have a harder time. But she is also in charge of lives in many ways. She has children. She has to make relationships. She is always at an emotional level with people. That leads to great strength. And I think women have much more strength in adversity than men.

I don't think I would have lived half the life I've lived if I were a man. In and out.

Marie-Claire Valène: I don't really see that there are disadvantages, only additional difficulties. In France, we have an extremely macho society where, if a woman wants to occupy a position of responsibility, she has twice the work and twice the problems of a man.

A woman doesn't necessarily have to want to work, to fight with this century. She can remain protected by a man. But men who want someone else to earn their living for them are rather despised by society and called pimps. Women are not so despised when they want that. On the contrary, they are admired and regarded as being in their rightful social position.

Joan Vass: The women in the South in the United States are painfully discriminated against. Men are just awful down there. They treat women in such a way that it makes my flesh creep.

Sara Vass: There's a lot of excess baggage that is thrown in the path of doing anything if you are a woman. I don't find myself complaining a lot about it, because it's just part of one's life. One tries to get rid of bits of that baggage if one can.

You can't take a walk in New York City alone at night if you're a woman. It's hot, I've eaten a lot, I think I'll walk home – you can't do that.

I am a woman, and my sex is part of what I am, and I think we have all used what we are and what we've got to whatever advantage. Hopefully not to my moral detriment or as in a grade-C spy movie, but there are ways of behaving, a coquettishness that comes to me naturally that certainly I have used. I would be a liar if I said I hadn't.

There are a lot of advantages that I simply don't choose to play. A woman can say, I don't want to work, I want to stay at home and have children and be taken care of. That can be an advantage. I would not want to live that kind of life, because I am someone who works very hard and I take care of myself. I don't take money from my family, I struggle along on my own, I am not married, I don't have a man in my life to cushion me, to say, yes dear, go ahead and work. I know a lot of women who have a certain freedom in their work because they don't really have to win the bacon.

Women are now expected to work, to have it all, to do it all and come home and do the cleaning and have the babies, because that is what, biologically, you do. But men expect to be applauded because they've tried to help – they did the dishes sometimes.

Diana Vreeland: I would never like to be a man because the average man's responsibilities are of no interest to me.

Virginia Wade: Definitely, for most women, there are huge disadvantages. One thing my mother always said was women don't ever really have their freedom. I think by that she meant that, whatever you do, as far as sexual freedom or even having children is concerned, you are always locked in. Maybe that's why I avoided the particular restraint of marriage, because I think I was probably brought up still to expect to play a role if I had married, to be looking after the man and be the secondary person. I never really felt I could come through in that position. I would be too independent and wanting to do too many things. Things are different now. I think you can marry as an equal now. Whereas fifteen years ago, when I probably should have been getting married, I was still thinking of marriage as a secondary role for the woman.

429

Michaela Walsh: I think I recognized that women are disadvantaged almost from the beginning of my career on Wall Street. The firm I worked for had a training programme for men which was not offered to women. My training consisted of going to night-school, to the New York Institute of Finance, paying for it myself, and becoming a registered representative of the New York Stock Exchange. This was done out of sheer determination. When I returned to the United States in 1965 and wanted to go into sales, I was told that they didn't have women in sales and there was no position. So I left the firm and went to another firm and began to double my salary and create opportunities based on what I had done. A year and a half later, the firm I had worked for was sued for $12 million by a class action suit brought by a group of women who were discriminated against in joining the firm as sales persons. But, in those days, I regarded myself as just lucky for having an opportunity to learn and travel and take more and more responsibility in a profession. It wasn't until I went into that career that I realized, because I was a woman, I'd had to leave a firm in order to further my career. I think the issue is quite different now. The issue is to ensure that all people have access to the benefits of our society, and not to discriminate by saying whether it's a woman or a man. My own view is that much of the discrimination is brought about by our own lack of experience and our lack of access to utilize the system. Where women are still discriminated against is in the market place. I do believe women more and more recognize that we can compete with men for limited resources. And it's our responsibility to fight for that access, to take responsibility for it, and then help to open it up for a larger number of people.

Part of the discrimination comes about through women's own perception of themselves. There are now some women role models, and there are opportunities for women to begin to understand what creates the discrimination. I believe also that, in the large institutions of society, most women will never be in the top leadership role. So it behoves us to create alternative lateral accesses for institutional development. With that belief in mind, I've helped to establish Women's World Banking, which is not a competing institution, it is designed to create an environment for women to gain access to the traditional banking institutions, the traditional institutions for management, information and technology transfer in the markets. And to run it as a professional business, but one which focuses on the access of women to all those benefits. It is clear that the venture capital available does not go to women on an equal basis, nor do the top management positions go to women on an equal basis. But there are many more women in middle management than there were when I began my career. Part of the problem is the process of time in terms of the experience that women

430

need to be able to acquire the skills and psychological capacity to manage those positions. I know many women who are choosing not to go that route. Many women are choosing to divide their time between their career and their family or other activities that interest them. There is a very high price paid by anyone who is president of a company or a chairman of a board. You're finding more and more women wanting to be involved, but also wanting time to do other things and willing to make the compromise. I think, in another few years, you will see some women making it to the top, but it will be a very small percentage. Where women really function, as equitable members of society, is much more at a community, middle-management, small-business level, and I think the economy is beginning to structure itself that way, so we will see more and more women taking economic control.

There was, for a long period following the Industrial Revolution, an understanding that industry was going to promote the stability of family society, where the man worked and the woman stayed home with children. That has shifted. I don't know any young educated woman today who is not struggling to balance her time now that she has a choice of whether she wants to marry and have children and stay home and take care of those children, or have a job and career, or balance the two. It complicates life, but it is now a choice, she has the option. Twenty years ago, most women did not have that option. Everyone should have the option of having or not having a job, not just women, and most people in society don't have it. So, my feeling about the role of women is that we need to keep pushing to ensure that there are more women involved in the institutions that provide them with the option. And that begins with the attitude and role of parents, the role of girls in a family, the educational opportunities, all the way through society. It's a very complex issue, and the more we study it, the more complex we realize it is.

I think that women generally work harder because there are fewer of them, because they are newer to the game. When I started working, I was the only woman doing what I was doing. When I took the exam to become a partner of a Wall Street firm, I was the fifth woman who had ever sat for the exam. Now there are many women who have been made partners of firms. The process is going on.

I would say about 90 per cent of the men I know patronize women. Where I see a big change coming is in those men and their relationships with their daughters. For instance, I know a couple of men who are judges who became furious when they discovered their daughters could not be the clerks of a judge. Then *they* tried to do something about it.

431

But it wasn't until their own daughters were denied something they wanted. The fathers knew that they were intellectually capable of doing it but because of the system were excluded.

No matter at what economic level you are, if you have a sense of confidence that you can be economically independent, then you don't have a false dependency. You are not dependent on a mother-in-law, you are not dependent upon a husband who beats you. That's not to say that many single heads of households – women raising children and working too – don't have it hard.

Life's been very good to me, as a woman. It's given me a lot of opportunities and challenges. And, at a particular time in history, it has given me a sense of freedom, a sense of liberation, that I think I have had long before a lot of men I know.

Tracy Ward: I remember when I was young thinking, thank God I am a woman because I don't have to have this complex, which I am sure men do, to get out there and earn enough money to live the lifestyle they were brought up to lead. Because of the taboos and the conventions, there is a certain stigma of failure in not having lived up to that. And, as a woman, I have felt much freer in that, if I want to be a housewife and have children, I can. But if I want to have a job as an actress and risk failure, it doesn't matter because there is no big taboo.

Boys were definitely a class above girls, and I always felt that when I was younger. When I was a teenager, I wanted to fight it and to prove I was as good or better. I wanted to be clever, but I was told by my family I was not clever. So I wanted somehow to get independence, and get equality with men. Going to live in America gave me that feeling of equality. I felt totally free, I felt that earning money was my own thing.

In America, they were prepared to give you that chance. By finding the work I enjoy, finding a job where women are equal to men – acting, because we are equally in demand – I've been totally liberated. Actually, I won't go to a film unless there's a woman in it.

Recently I've been asking myself what do I really want? When you are acting you self-analyse quite a lot and I realized it is easier (and maybe it's a lazy way out and maybe I'll regret it) not to have this big stand that I want to work, that I'm going to be the breadwinner, be equal to men. I now realize that basically I want to have children, to have time to do things which women have time to do, like reading, studying politics or anything. So, in a way I've slightly compromised now and I'm prepared to sacrifice parts of my job – acting – for a family and leisure time.

Being attractive is definitely an advantage in that I feel I have things going for me even from the moment I walk into a room. People in galleries were always interested in me because I was attractive and sexy. They used to come up to me when I was at Christie's looking at the paintings and ask, what are you doing here? Come on, you're not an art dealer and you are not a secretary, what are you doing here? Therefore I realized that I shouldn't go against the grain of what I was born with. I mean, I am very tall, not bad-looking, big bosom, sexy. I can't go against that.

There is a certain act which I think women are very clever at, which is to feign the weak one but actually to have the balls underneath to follow through with what they want.

Marina Warner: I had tremendously split fantasies. I did want to be a very girlish and perfect girl. I longed to be beautiful and spent a lot of time in front of the mirror dressing up in my mother's clothes, attempting to look like a sophisticated and beautiful woman. At the same time, all my night-time reveries before I went to sleep were of being an incredibly active and effective young man. Which really took the form, not of an intellectual thing, not of being influential or a writer (I was about ten), but of being somehow physically free, of being able to move. I imagined adventures, and when I was in these adventures, which would be in rivers and mountains, I would be a young man. My body would not somehow be this body, which was going to be one that meant that I would marry and be confined. One of the things that possibly has happened historically is that, when women are confined and attend to these private ceremonies of upbringing and meals, it actually fosters the best in human nature. We think of the feminine, in a way, as a better order, and I think it is, because it is to do with rituals of preserving, and growth and love, and cherishing and nurturing. I'm one of the feminists who doesn't believe that this is intrinsic to the female soul. I think it is the possibility of all humanity. When we say that Mrs Thatcher is masculine, it is more that what she is required to do has belonged traditionally to the masculine order. What we haven't solved is how you set up a society and run it, how you don't have an anarchic system in which there are no rulers, and yet avoid falling into this masculine way which is all to do with oppressions and cruelties.

Different expectations of women do limit their chances, there's no doubt about it. I was lucky, I went to a convent school, and I never would have had a scientific or an engineering bent. So humanities, which were offered at the school, suited me, but certainly they didn't offer the girls anything on the scientific side. I wouldn't have flourished if I had been an engineer by inclination.

Women are in an acute phase in England. The difficulty now, of course, with massive unemployment, is that the expectations of women have been reduced even further and the birthrate has risen terrifically among young, very young women. I don't want to give the impression that having a baby isn't a great pleasure and a great experience, but it worries me. I feel that these young women are entering into the difficult occupation of caring for a child in very reduced circumstances, and this is partly because their expectations have been cut, have been limited; they don't see their lives as offering other possibilities. That relates to some of the mythology that is becoming ever more current. One is the myth of the Royal Family, and I may be quite wrong about this, and it obviously is harmless compared to some other political systems and political ideologies, but what we see is a continual adulation of young women who arrive to greatness through chance. I think this underlines the idea that women don't take their destinies into their own hands, but, with a modicum of looks or grace and a charming way, something wonderful might happen to you. This is terribly determinist. It's not saying who am I, what am I capable of, it's floating, and it's asked of women and not of men. It is interesting that, within the Royal Family, the men are trained to do lots of things, however poorly or adequately they function at them. But the young women who now enter this family and become heroines of the entire world (there is nothing in the popular press except Fergie, Diana, Caroline Monaco, Stephanie Monaco), have initially, as far as I can make out, nothing more asked of them but that they be images, something to look at. Beauty, of course, has its place in the world, and beauty can be life-enhancing. The body is a place to start from, but it mustn't be the place where you end.

Even to a woman like me, and I have every sort of advantage, there are little things that happen constantly. I get Johnnie to do things for me sometimes, because I won't get a hearing on the telephone, they won't listen to me. The police can be very nice and they can try, but they are more likely to listen to a complaint from a man.

In England, class systems patronize one another. That's still the major source of discrimination, and it's still visible in England and absolutely isn't in America. Except that poverty now is very visible in America,

434

but, above the poverty lines, it then becomes much more open. Within the class systems, there are the sub-set of sexual systems and there is a kind of, let her have a go. I'm afraid even in places where you think it wouldn't happen, like the BBC, it happens a bit.

There is still a feeling – for instance, if women get very agitated – that this is not a genuine concern, just something to do with temperament; that they are not really agitated, it's just the wrong time of the month. It's very interesting that woman is often constructed by voices outside herself. There is a tendency for men to say: we all know women, we don't have to listen to what they have to say or tell us about themselves. I feel that it's possible that, when there is more listening to what women have to say about all areas of their experience, the construct woman will start fragmenting and we will find there isn't such a well-defined entity as a woman in the way we have inherited the idea. In the same way, the construct man is so generic that we don't really know what we mean by a man. It is capable of so many different manifestations because all the complications of humanity are there. It will cease to be possible in historical books to index women; if you buy a book on the Middle Ages, agrarian movements or something or other, in 1200–1250, the index will have women: pages 88 to 90, because they are seen as particular as ants or primroses that could be indexed in such a way, whereas, of course, they are not, they permeate every aspect, every structure.

Heather Watts: As a ballet dancer, it is a huge advantage to be a woman. We dance and the men carry us around. The whole focus, the spotlight, is on us. The man is frequently a sort of porter, or just a consort.

As a woman, you have to be willing not to play games, you have to show your intelligence, show your mind to people. Otherwise you can be seen as just a little dumb dancer. There are dumb dancers and there are smart dancers, you know.

I do think there is a real problem with the menstrual cycle and mood swings. I can feel them very strongly in myself, especially as I'm getting older. Men don't have these really radical mood swings that we have. It's not made up, it really happens. You find you get upset about things that any other time of the month you wouldn't be so upset about. I don't like to see that part of myself. I feel, because I know that's what it is, I should be able to control it, but I can't always. I find myself watching television and crying over some dumb show. Now, I know it's just before my period, I know I should be able to say, that's why you're crying, but I can't always get a grip on it. That's a little scary.

I enjoy being a woman, and I think in today's world it is very hard to be a man. I don't think they know how they're supposed to act. They don't know if they're supposed to open the door or not open the door, they don't know whether to carry your bag or if they shouldn't. And then, if he's polite, he's a wimp, and if he's not, he's a male chauvinist.

Arabella Weir: The hard-line feminists would not like what I say, and I do think of myself as a feminist, but men are easily manipulated, which means that you can get what you want in the end by playing the game up to a point.

The other day, I stopped myself getting clamped by pretending I was a dizzy, stupid girl. As I walked towards the guys who were clamping my car, I thought, I've got two choices: say, please don't, in a straight-forward manner, or be silly and girly and giggly. I was ashamed, but they bought it. It was like fishing, they just bit the line: oh, you're silly, it would have been £70, and naughty little you. And: I'm really sorry, I won't do it again. Just nonsense, but they bought it, so I fed them it.

Speaking in general, the disadvantages of being a woman are menstru-ating and the emotional gamut that a woman experiences, which, I would say, is impossible to make someone who doesn't have them understand. Within the sphere of male experience, a woman can identify with almost everything, and if not identify, she can sympathize. The area in which women suffer is much greater and the difficulty for men is not that they're insensitive necessarily, but that it's impossible, literally impossible, for them to understand things like pre-menstrual tension, which is appalling. The other disadvantage for me, being a woman, is the fear of being attacked. The constant, not necessarily fear, but awareness of not going out late, of not wearing high-heeled shoes if you're going to be on your own because you wouldn't be able to run if you don't have your car. It's only recently that I've had a car, but that doesn't make a difference, because two of my friends have been raped getting out of their cars. The man has made them get back into the car.

I have been aware of people wanting to employ me because they want to sleep with me. In one particular case, I went out for a secretarial job to a writer, and he made it absolutely blatant. He's a well-known writer. I didn't know who he was until I got there, and then I realized by the nature of the books that were there. I don't know whether he's active, because I didn't stay to find out, but he made it clear that he wanted me to be his secretary but that wouldn't be where the job ended. That was the most blatant advance I've ever had.

Some of the best directors I've worked with, and that includes highly intelligent, educated directors, not men who would consider themselves feminists, but men who would consider themselves socialists, ask you to play the game of flattering their egos, especially on a set where a director will get a lot of kudos if the leading or prettiest actress is spending a lot of time with him. I can think of one guy in particular who is a real socialist, but he, without knowing it, was playing the game of wanting the crew to think he was sleeping with me, because this would enhance his image with them. Much as he would intellectually have despised what he was doing, he was playing the game, no doubt just as I was playing the game of being the one preferred above anybody else by the director.

Felicity White: I was conditioned that I must be a wife and mother, and yet there was this tremendous forceful feeling inside me that, no, there is more to life, I've got to explore it. I found that quite difficult. I sometimes wonder if I went into the law because it was so male-dominated at that stage, just to prove it could be done, and that this was the most male, and the most difficult, and the most extraneous thing I could think of. It wasn't quite like that, but I sometimes wonder. When I went into articles, I had already decided that the one thing I was not going to do was to learn to type because, I thought, that's the road downhill. And the first day I was in articles I was in this chap's office. I was going to be working with him for six months – and he said, oh, sorry, I haven't really much for you to do. I sort of scratched around the whole day and then right at the end of the day, he said, oh, would you just do these three envelopes for me? And I looked at him and I said, well, is it all right just to write them? And he said, but can't you type? Absolutely astonished. I said, no I can't, and I'm not going to either. I'm an articled clerk, not a secretary. And I think, oddly enough, that that attitude on the first day absolutely set the scale for the rest of my life.

If you are married, you are certainly not taken seriously. If you have a child, you may also not be taken seriously, although I am new to that one. I kept my own name when I married, because I knew that career-wise people are very slow to accept you as a female. If you are a Miss they think, oh well, that's all right, I suppose; but if you are a Mrs, you have only got half your mind on the job – the other half of your mind is making up shopping lists or deciding what you are going to have for dinner et cetera.

I could never afford to make a mistake, and I still can't. And that is a tremendous strain. It's also an extremely good discipline because it means that, whatever you do, you have to do it absolutely perfectly, or as perfectly as you can. That's a good thing generally, but it is incredibly stressful, and I think that once that's come into your professional life it seeps right the way through into the rest. So sometimes one can be extremely manic about things, like how one gives a dinner party. The whole thing has to be perfect.

Katharine Whitehorn: I remember one or two instances of feeling disadvantaged, but it was far more a personal thing. I was deeply jealous of my brother because he was older, and also a boy, and could do things like hitch-hike, which I couldn't. I did in the end, but I couldn't at the same age. But it was much more that John was the eldest and always could do things. I think I could honestly say that, until the end of the 1950s, I can't think of anything that I was ever prevented from doing being because I was a girl. When Marilyn French, who wrote *The Women's Room*, came over here, she was talking about what women had to put up with in the 1950s, and I tried very hard to persuade her that I hadn't had to put up with all this. She simply wouldn't believe me. What I was trying to persuade her was that, in Europe, middle-class educated women had a very good shake after the war. We had a far longer mating season than the Americans. I remember being horrified when I went to America in the mid 1950s to discover that people thought they were unmarriageable if they hadn't made it by the time they were twenty-two. So for those of us whose mothers wanted us to do other things besides get married, there was no particular pressure to get married. You might have wanted to marry a particular guy, but there was no feeling that you must be married.

I was allowed to do a lot of things, which I imagined girls couldn't be allowed to do. For example, I went youth hostelling by myself on a bicycle in 1945, and I went hitch-hiking around France in 1950 by myself. I hadn't planned to go by myself, but the girl I was going with got a job and my parents – it was funny – wrote to my brother and said, we don't know, you're a contemporary young man, do you think this is safe or not? My brother wrote back and said, the trouble she might get into with a lorry driver is as nothing to the trouble you'll be in if you try and stop her. My grandparents' generation did not necessarily believe, as a matter of principle, in people making their own decisions and having their own freedom, but by the time we got to my parents, it was an article of faith with them that their children must be allowed to run their own lives. A hundred years ago, people would not have thought that was the best way to run their families, but they did. I don't

438

know what had happened to thinking in the 1920s to make them think that way, but I was obviously the beneficiary, and my husband, whose parents are Quakers, also very strongly felt that people have to run their own lives. Quakers have had this quaint belief that women were in charge of their souls since the seventeenth century and I think the way my husband regards me owes a great deal to that tradition. I think I've had a lot easier time because he is more likely to say, you're letting yourself down, you're not doing your work properly, than, never mind your work, that's not important, do what you have to do for me.

By the time I began to realize how many disadvantages women do suffer – that was about the mid 1960s, I suppose, when the women's movement was starting in the States – it didn't apply to me. I have been exceptionally lucky, because I know of so many other people who have had the choice to make between being personally happy and being able to do whatever they thought their job was, and it's never actually presented itself to me as a choice in that form.

The whole world is designed for men to work and be fathers and not for women to work and be mothers. Take parliamentary hours, afternoon and evening. Now, in Canada, they got a woman Speaker of the House, and the first thing she managed to do was get the thing to end at six o'clock. It immediately opens the door to four times the number of women if you get predictable hours.

When I say to my building society, why don't you have more women branch managers, they say, well, you see, they can't move around. This is always the mobility argument. Then you go to Wales and you find that half of them have never worked more than twenty miles from Cardiff in their lives. You go to South London, and there are a lot of building societies in London, so they can take their step up by simply moving within the area. So I was having this discussion in a quite friendly way in the Midlands with somebody, and he said, oh, well, yes, it's all right in South London because the distances are so small. So I said, how long does it take you to drive from Derby to Nottingham? He said, twenty-five minutes. And I said, well, in London that would be considered an amazingly short commuting journey. And then I realized that when he was thinking of women, he was thinking of public transport, because most of them are secretaries or sales cashiers who can't afford anything more. And I was absolutely delighted that when we drove into the parking lot of the building-society branch we went to, there was a bright yellow sports car blocking the space he wanted, and it belonged to his female chief clerk/cashier.

The *Observer* is currently having a very stormy time because, by a series of accidents, it has a woman news editor and a woman colour-magazine editor, and there's a lot of to-do about that. About a year and a half ago, they did reader traffic figures to show exactly who reads what, and they found that women weren't reading the newspaper very much. At that particular point, they had one or two women specialists, lots on the women's pages, and some on the business news, but they didn't have any women as regular reporters to be sent out on any old job. The education correspondent and I, when we were told these figures, said, well what do you expect if you have no women reporters? The chaps got very huffed and said, are you trying to tell us that men can't write for women? And we said, of course we're not, but consider the process by which stories get in the newspaper. This is a Sunday paper, the time schedule is like this: news conference on Tuesday, certain stories are suggested by certain people, you follow up half of them. By Thursday you say, well, these ones are not going to make, we'll go harder on this one and that one. On Friday, new stories come in, so you have to say, well, sorry, you'd better drop that and take something else. And finally on Saturday they're chosen. If everybody in that process is male, inevitably the stories that interest men are going to win out over the stories that interest women, and we'd like there to be a lot of women around the place because their view is different, not because they can do the job just as well as the man.

Supposing you had a blight that wiped out nine tenths of the males, as in that John Wyndham story, and women had to run everything because there were only about four or five men left who had to be kept for stud purposes. Then you would organize it quite differently. You would maybe devote ages twenty to thirty-five to having babies, and then you would do enormous quantities of training programmes from thirty-five to forty-five, then you'd let them go on working until seventy because that is their area of major productivity. But because the thing is predicated on male life structure, you train, and you're then supposed to be trained for life, which is increasingly idiotic with technology what it is. When the women come back into the workforce at thirty-five, you say, oh, sorry, you missed all these absolutely vital years. You only have to watch what happens to a man who is made redundant at forty-five to see that their perception of their life is only helpful in the particular structure we have at the moment.

The expectation of fathers is extremely important, and I have never been able to understand why the average businessman, who is greatly given to seducing his secretary and ignoring his wife, none the less sees no other future for his daughter but to do some not very important job until she gets married. So not enough tends to be expected of women. Including by themselves. They don't necessarily think of a lifetime of work, and when they do, they don't really envisage it. Secondly, they encounter expectations of limited goals from people who hire them. They're constantly being asked, what about the children, and so on, and they very often quite consciously choose to put their private life first. Yeats's phrase, the intellect of man is forced to choose perfection of the life or of the work, also applies to the intellect of women, and more women would choose happiness, I think. Probably because they've got a better idea of what they think they mean by it.

I think I probably have been a woman at the luckiest moment in the world's history to be one. I regard myself as exceptionally lucky, historically and personally. But, in the Middle Ages or the middle of the Victorian era, I might have said something very different.

Shelley Vaughan Williams: I think I've earned my lines. If I am ever loved again, and I ever love anybody again, I don't think age will have anything to do with it at all.

Jeanette Winterson: I think the main disadvantage is that men assume certain things about you because of your gender. It's not such a clear meritocracy for women: they can't prove themselves in various ways and be taken on those grounds; they can't make their own rules, the rules are already there. Before you can start achieving anything, you have to knock something down, you have to persuade quite a lot of men, first, that that doesn't mean you're any less a woman, second, that you can do it, third, that you still might want to have children, whatever. There are all kinds of hidden assumptions that get in the way.

I'm worried that many of those women who are pioneering new places are having to give up so much that is traditional to a woman, that perhaps the compromise is sometimes too great. That worries me enormously, because it means you might be able to break down a certain attitude towards women in the minds of men in power. They may think, well, perhaps they can come out of the home, perhaps they can do these jobs – but they won't think in a quantum leap, they won't think, well, we must somehow make these jobs more woman-orientated. Instead, the woman has to come straight into the male framework and put up with it. And it's very hard for her to change it once she's in, because there are plenty more who will take her place.

441

We have an inherited cunning from our past when all we could do was manipulate men. There's a great juggling sense that means we can take on lots of projects and somehow manage to keep them all separate and keep them all going, which is, I think, what makes women very good to work with and to employ.

There are so many men who still call you dear, which is terrible. Even in casual encounters, if you want something in a shop, or if you're ringing somebody on the telephone. I think it's an easy way of putting women in their place, if you like, of saying, well, you know, this is you and you're a bit of a frivolous creature and I will call you these names to make you feel better. In fact they make you feel worse.

Anna Wintour: Alex Liberman was the reason I went to work at American *Vogue* five years ago, I guess. I took the job because I wanted to work for him, because he was a myth in terms of American publishing, in terms of any kind of publishing. I think he is the great art director, creative genius, for magazines today. He's shaped magazines today, and I was very lucky in working for him every day for three years. He taught me more than anybody and he's the person I certainly miss the most in my working career now I've moved back to London.

Alex always said he gave me my job because of my legs.

When you see a woman walking down Madison Avenue, she looks very confident and strong and she strides along. I see so many Englishwomen here shuffling along, a bit hunched, and they don't have that confident appearance you find in America. It's very different, very different. I think it's absolutely to do with confidence and attitudes, and just a sense of yourself.

Enid Wistrich: The main advantage of being a woman is the ability to bear children, there's no doubt about that, which is a marvellous experience, a wonderful experience denied to men.

Women don't push themselves as much as men in jobs, and that's an instinctive holding back because of feelings women have, which I shared for a long time, that they are not really for the top jobs, only for the second or third ones. So I felt some disadvantage there, but I think it's one which, as they say in the books, has been internalized. It's rather that women see they are not in the top jobs and therefore don't think of themselves in the top jobs and don't aim as high, and that's something which I, like everyone else, suffer from. It was only when I was about forty that I started looking round and saw the people I knew in the senior positions, and perhaps a little bit more senior than mine, and thought to myself, you fool, Enid, you're more competent than them.

Priscilla Woolworth: I see a lot of women who are obviously treated like sexual objects because they behave like that. Or they're very aggressive, or they try to be over-sexy and a bit sleazy, which is unattractive. You have to be in the middle. I can understand that they're easy, and if they give in to a man, then they should be treated as sexual objects, because that's what they want to be seen as. But if you project yourself in a way that you're not a sexual object and are also a person, then it's very different. It really all depends on how you behave.

I've talked myself out of so many situations just being charming to a man, and he will forgive you. That is the natural weakness of the man. If you have to deal with another woman, if you have a problem, it doesn't always work out, because women can be tough with other women. But I don't use my femininity consciously. I do it because that's the way I am.

3
Feminism

Lolicia Aitken: It's much more confusing to be a woman nowadays. They have all this publicity going on to say that you have actually to be independent and career-making and intelligent, and a lot of women are screwed up by this because they really don't know what they want. They marry, and suddenly they have this brainwashing: I have to do something, be successful, be independent and have my own life. I had my own life, my own career, I know I can have it. Basically, the difference is with self-confidence. If you know you can, you don't have to prove it. I choose to be a mother and a wife, and I'm very happy in the role. Maybe I'm naïve, but I consider I have as much power through my husband, whom I think I influence a lot. So I don't feel I have wasted my life, I don't think I'm somebody stupid who has no influence. I have my influence in an indirect way. For the moment, I'm much happier being a mother and a wife. I'm not saying that in ten years I might not go and do something else, but I think you can do it if you know that you can do something else. What happens to a lot of women is that they have to prove something and they become aggressive.

God no, I'm no feminist. I like being a woman. I'm a strong woman, and therefore I don't need to prove anything, and therefore I can be a totally humble woman. I can go on my knees if I feel like begging my husband to do something. It doesn't worry me being weak, because I don't think I am. The feminist is aggressive because she has got things to prove. If you're at peace with yourself, there's no point in being nasty and aggressive.

Maria Aitken: Something horrifying seems to be happening to Mrs Thatcher. She's achieving a sort of dragon-woman myth status moment by moment. I used to rather admire her. I am absolutely allergic to her now. I find her insensitive, alarming, almost cruel.

447

Lady Penelope Aitken: I think Mrs Thatcher is an absolutely amazing woman. She's done a great deal for this country and what she has managed to achieve won't be fully realized probably in this century. I admire her enormously. I can see how difficult it is for clever, brilliant men round her to have to be second to a woman and to continue year in and year out and not get a chance themselves as leader. Men don't like that, they don't fully accept a woman, and she is very often abrasive with them. When the time comes to look back on it all, all the frictions will be forgotten in her achievements.

Where we have failed most, but it's not just with women, is in the educational field. I think the education of the past twenty years has been simply dreadful in the state schools and everywhere else. The kind of women they have been turning out are pretty frightful. The whole of women's education needs to be looked at again, and decent training, which we used to have, has gone out of the window now with militants and the outrageous subjects they teach. Even the little nurses in the hospitals have bad manners; the shop assistants are rotten and don't have any regard for anybody. Women are going to lose if they don't keep a degree of gentle femininity with all their intelligence, because it's a great weapon. The young women I see turned out today have such bad manners. They don't know how to behave. They shout, they yell. Something has gone of what we used to be taught. Manners maketh man. Manners perhaps maketh woman as well. And you see it in really good headmasters, headmistresses, the leaders who give us back old values. I sound like Mrs Thatcher.

I think women must remain women. I don't like to see women who aren't what I call wholly feminine and wholly women. In fact, I had a shock this summer. I drove an old friend up St James's Street across Piccadilly and on to where he lives, and there was a demonstration in Piccadilly which we couldn't cross, and I had to drive alongside it. To my utter amazement, it was a demonstration for lesbians. And they were there by the thousand: mile after mile of these terrible-looking people. I cannot understand this, I cannot. If it has got anything to do with feminism, it is dreadful. I'm sure it is probably very silly of me not to understand it more, but I think if you are very feminine, as I am, you find that something you can't swallow.

Shirin Akiner: Men and women are different, but they are equal human beings. Equality is such a difficult concept. I would never, for example, expect my husband to clean the house, it's not a job I see as suitable for a man. It's not that he feels it is not suitable for him, it is that I don't think it suitable. However, equally I don't like looking after my money, so I'm happy for him to do that for me. In other words, it's not that I think we should both do the housework, both do the bank statements, both do the cooking, both plan the holidays. I think we are equal in the sense that we can decide between ourselves who does what, and I am perfectly happy to abide by that. Husbands and wives often seem to have battles over who should control this, who shall take that decision. Among educated, reasonably intelligent people, I really don't see how that can be.

I am not a feminist. I would say I am an individualist. I think many feminists fight the wrong issues. They are concerned with the confrontation between men and women, and also with the sort of rights and wrongs only people of my type of education might have to face. They are not concerned with the vast majority of women, who really see themselves as entirely dependent on a man and choose a husband according to the lifestyle they're hoping for. Later, when they are unhappy in marriage, they think how will I live alone, how will I survive, will I have enough money? The one thing I could wish for women, though I see no sign of it happening for most people, is that they should worry about themselves not as men or women, but simply as individuals, doing what they want to do and having the confidence to follow their own lives. If they meet someone who is going to help them and with whom they are going to be happy, that's tremendous, but to live your life thinking another person will provide you with all the good things you want, and then blaming him perhaps when it doesn't turn out, is to me illogical. You must take responsibility for your own life. The battle feminists should concern themselves with is the image women have of themselves: not the disadvantages they have in relationship to men, but the disadvantages they impose on themselves simply by not seeing themselves as able to follow their own lives.

Baria Alamuddin: I am not a feminist. I don't want a woman to be a fighter, or to rule the life of a man. I would still like the man to ask the woman to marry him, not the woman to ask the man to marry her. I still would like him to buy her a rose and call her and tell her I love you. I don't like the roles to be switched. In general, I think a woman is much more emotional, she is a softer person, she can live her emotions and her feelings a lot deeper, by the nature of her own being. Why do we want two creatures exactly the same? The world would be a very boring place to live in. But, to have a productive society, we should have equality between men and women. You cannot run the world with half its powers. In the West, I think it is slowly improving, although

449

sometimes in the wrong direction, but in the Middle East, it's taking longer because of different factors, basically the wars. People are not busy educating women at the moment. In Lebanon now, there is a whole new generation of boys and girls who have nothing to do with education and refinement or culture, and the same is true in many other Arab countries.

I think a liberated Western woman is a woman who can easily shed all the social factors and just walk away from them and go towards whatever she wants as a completely liberated individual, regardless of tradition. This is something that people in our part of the world can never do. I have often felt I am a pioneer of this in my society, because, even as a child, I always wanted to do things differently. I remember wanting to hurt society, to attack society and do things just to spite society because I felt it interfered in every single detail in my life. My God, society in our countries can even marry you off! There will always be a difference between the woman in the West and the woman in the East. A woman in the East has femininity which the women in the West never had maybe, and will never have. Basically, I like the evolution in the Middle East, in the Arab countries, better than in the West.

Jan Amory: I think women should be discriminated against to a certain degree. I am not a believer that a woman can walk into a brokerage house and do as good a job as a man. Men should be doing it, the stockbrokerage and the banking. I am not a believer in crossing over the line. Women are put on the earth to be feminine and satisfy men, and be intelligent, have intelligent conversations. I don't think they are moronic in any way, but I think women have their place and the minute they try not to have their place, then they cross over the Maginot Line and might as well have a trans-sexual operation and become a man. I don't understand why women have this desire to take over companies. I'm very happy bringing up my little boy and having my husband work. I was forced to have a job when I was young and work at *Vogue*. I worked for one year, and I found it an interesting experience. But frankly I have no desire to really work.

The feminist movement is not one I would back. I think it's wonderful that you can get a female senator, I think it's terrific that women can succeed in men's jobs, but I don't think the feminist movement has basically helped. The more intelligent man is happy to have a girl give her opinion, but he wants her to look up to him. But what happens is that some women put men down in public and try to castrate them. That's my opinion.

Lady Elizabeth Anson: I was once actually told by a fortune teller, a gipsy, never to employ a man. So I actually am very much pro employing women.

On certain levels I am a feminist, but not terribly strongly. I still respect the male for being the stronger person. I don't want to go out and fight a war. I would loathe to be living in Israel and be part of the army. I just know that I would be perfectly hopeless. On the other hand, the only place I find it quite difficult to work is Jordan because they don't like women working. I find that very difficult to cope with. I took a whole team out to do a wedding, and there were barely two women out of twenty-three people, and if I asked a question, it was usually answered back by one of the men. I found that absolutely infuriating.

I can understand that women would loathe Mrs Thatcher. It's also very interesting how strong the views of the male politicians are. Either they love her or they loathe her. I can remember when the first woman newscaster came on the wireless and I thought, this is desperate, it is terrible to hear a woman reading the news, a woman can't read the news. Then, when they came on television, I felt the same thing, but it didn't last very long. Certainly, I felt the same thing about Mrs Thatcher. But I now feel strongly that I would prefer the speaking clock on the telephone to go back to the woman now it's a man. Part of it is just change, not sex discrimination. I must say, I do have an enormous admiration for Mrs Thatcher, enormous. I work really quite long hours, and she works much longer hours on a much more serious subject than mine and survives on the minimal amount of sleep, yet never ever falters with anything that she says, never goes back on what she has said. I admire that quite fantastically.

Beatrice Aristimuno: I'm not a feminist, because I think the main job of a woman is *faire les enfants*, which is really why we are here. Today women work, women write, they do anything, and that is considered more important than having children, raising children and making a family, but that's what we are really here for.

Pamela Armstrong: If you look at the spiritual history of Western Europe, it has for the last 2,000 years been riven with charismatic movements that have all appeared extremely fringe to mainstream theology. I think it quite important that there have been and always will be communities that cut themselves off from the mainstream, because the mainstream of society simply doesn't provide what's needed for the people in that community. I think radical feminists are just one example – as the Shakers were, as the Methodists were when they first started out, as whoever was. Something in the mainstream community is not providing what these people need and they have to go elsewhere and find it and create for themselves what's meaningful for them. That's realistic and shouldn't be jibed at.

Men are complementary in my life, that's how it works for me, but I have great sympathy with the radical separatists. Like all pioneers, they're pushing the frontiers into areas the rest of us aren't bothering to explore, because it's either too threatening or we're not interested, or we know that we want to get on with a more normal existence, to stay more in the middle lane rather than going to either extreme. I think what radical separatists are saying is that they're very angry with the status quo. That may be a status quo the rest of us accept, but we are all questioning it, even as we accept it and even as we live with it. Probably we're questioning it no more and no less than the radical separatists, they're just coming up with their particular kind of answer. Also, if you look at the statistics of incest and rape within the family as we come to the end of the century, it's as if that's one of the bogies that's beginning to come out of the closet. And when you think of the amount there must have been in the past. These women might consider this absolutely libellous and slanderous, but one presumes they have had very bad experiences at the hands of men and simply don't trust men or men's bodies, don't find them pleasurable and don't want to have anything to do with them, negotiate with them or have any kind of politicking with them. And why shouldn't they absent themselves from men? Or a man's world? They live in a world they create – very safe. Some of them live in communities of only women, and in some communities, when a woman gets pregnant and has a male child, they have to leave because even a male baby cannot be tolerated. It appears very extreme, but I think you have absolutely to respect that that is the way these women choose to live. There aren't that many of them. It's not as if it was a plague sweeping across the entire world and all women are becoming radical separatists. We have to look at it in perspective. They may appear extreme to us, but why not allow them?

Debbie Arnold: A lot of American women will try very hard to be ball-breakers, they want to run all the companies, they want to do everything, they want to be so powerful. They lose their femininity. They're trying to be men.

If you look at the Prime Minister, I think she is one of the most feminine women I've ever seen. I really do. I was very surprised when I met her, how gentle and caring she was, and how she looked you deep in the eyes. She was just a nice person, a very nice human being. I don't even vote Conservative, and I was won over by her, so that's really quite a surprising thing to say, but I felt she was a woman first, and then a mother, and then the ruler of the nation. I didn't feel she was masculine at all. I don't think she's a particularly good Prime Minister, but I think she's a very nice lady. Very feminine.

I think feminists are rather militant people. I agree that a woman should get paid the same amount if she's doing the same job as a man, but I don't agree that women are totally equal to men. I don't think it's possible. There are certain things a man can do that a woman can't. I also feel that the femininity of a woman, and to be treated as someone gentle, someone to be treasured, to be looked after and loved, is most important. If I was a feminist I'd say, no darling, I don't want that, I can go out to work, I can lift the bricks up, I can do this, I can do that, I don't need a man, men are just there for sex or whatever. I feel feminists think like that. I also feel that they're just too liberated, and I don't think life is supposed to be like that. I don't think God would have made us so different if we were supposed to be completely equal. He'd make us all six foot tall and exactly the same, and he would make men able to have babies if we were totally equal. There is a total difference between man and woman. It was the caveman who went out hunting and the woman stayed at home and looked after the children. Obviously women want to go out and do other things, sure, but basically the only reason we're here is to produce more people.

Leslie Ash: I do agree with certain of the political things when it comes to feminism – equal pay and things like that; but they've sorted all that out mainly. If a woman's going to do the same job as a man, there should be equal pay, but I love femininity, I love being a woman. I find lots of feminists have lost that sort of perfume around them. They lose something. They became ethnic in a way, rolling up their own cigarettes and wearing these rather large woollen jumpers.

Josephine Barstow: The women I admire are the ones who succeed while retaining their femininity. A lot of Frenchwomen have this capacity, and a lot of American women have forgotten how to be women. I find it tremendously sad when you see the brashness it puts on to these women. And they all look the same – they make up their faces the same, they dress the same. You see business ladies in places like Chicago and they all have their suit and their blouse, just like the men – a skirt instead of a pair of dark trousers. That turns me off completely. On the other hand, when you go to France, you see the wonderful way Frenchwomen get their way, and have always known how to get their way, using their femininity. But they still are achievers.

I don't think Mrs Thatcher has succeeded. She's succeeded in an obvious sense of becoming Prime Minister, but as a Prime Minister she hasn't succeeded, in my view. She's made a mess of it. The country is less happy, and a less successful place to be in now, than when she came into power. I think she has set herself up as being the efficient lady who is going to make the economy efficient, and in fact it is now running less efficiently. That's what I can't forgive her for: selling off assets and using North Sea oil and all this stuff to keep people doing nothing. I don't consider that is efficiency, and I can't see where it's leading. I can't see what she expects to achieve.

Gilberte A.Y. Beaux: If feminism means that women must have the same possibility to realize their lives as men, then I am a feminist. If we have to be considered the same as men, then no. I consider we are very different. We are complementary, but certainly not equal in the sense of the same.

Rotraut Lisa Ursula Beiny: I am not really a feminist. Women should, in some ways, have equal opportunities, and for doing the same job they should be paid the same money. But this big thing about Ms and people demonstrating because we have beauty contests, all that's ridiculous. If women are appreciated for their beautiful bodies, well, that's very good, what's wrong about that? But women seem to object and pull off their bras or something, and I think that is ridiculous.

Christine Bogdanowicz-Bindert: I don't have that much respect for the feminist movement, especially in America, and that's where I live. The feminist movement in America is not geared towards average women, but women who are in many ways privileged. A lot of issues don't have the right focus. Lesbianism is not the most important thing in terms of issues facing women. The most important issue is how do you manage to give women the opportunity to manage a family, with or without children, with whatever else she wishes to do. Society is not geared to that, and the feminist woman is not really interested. They haven't been fighting for women to get longer maternity leave, to get more support in terms of federal government subsidies for crèche and kindergarten arrangements. So what happens is that a very privileged woman pays somebody to take care of the children and the other women are basically stuck in a bind. I guess that's why I don't have much admiration for the feminist movement.

Rebecca Blake: Feminism to me is to be able to create my own definition of my identity, not one that's been prescribed to me because I'm a woman. I want the right to live as I choose and be able to behave or perform, to live, really, according to truths as I experience them, not because I am told I have to be a certain way.

Betty E. Box: I'm not a feminist. I believe in equal opportunity, but I think the so-called feminists carry it much too far. Even Germaine Greer agrees she didn't make a lot of sense early on. I feel that if a woman wants to have children, then she should look after them. And I'm very unpopular. The feminists say, no, a woman should be free to do what she wants and children should be looked after by the state. I don't agree. If I had children, I think I would want to look after them as I was looked after as a child. But so many women don't feel that. They think they should be free to do what they want. What they want comes before the wants of their child, and I think that's wrong.

Francesca Braschi: In some ways, the Europeans, the French and Italians, are much more liberated than the American women. They're just starting now, the American women, to be liberated. They're very puritanical. Look at the way Europeans dress. It's very outgoing. A lot of mischief goes on around there. I mean, you can be seventy and you're still in mischief with a young boy of twenty or something like that. American women have no elegance.

I am not a feminist in the sense of being in a campaign and walking up the street with big signboards. I do believe that a woman should have her voice heard, that we should have positions open to us, but I'm a traditionalist and do believe in the way we were. In our old guard. The basis of society was what your grandmother taught you, was what her grandmother taught her. We have to preserve this beautiful vision or else, God forbid, our children and our grandchildren will never even conceive of it.

455

Heather Brigstocke: Mrs Thatcher has been enormously supportive to me. The power and support, the total commitment she gave to this school as a school of excellence for girls, was something I shall never forget. She can't dilute herself all over the place. And if she seems to be not tremendously helpful to women, I can see what is in the back of her mind. She is through and through a professional, and I admire her enormously for that. She, like me, has had a great fear of the women who say they want to get ahead but who give up the minute they come to a hurdle.

Dianne Brill: American women are not crafty, generally speaking. They try to over-compensate because they feel they are weak. I've been in situations with women in business where they're completely over the top, more aggressive than any man. You know: they act like a disgusting man. But I think that's individual too. You have to have these extremists, because it was so disgusting for so long, so extremely the other way, that now, and for the last twenty years, whatever you have – you have people.

What I really hate is when my friends that are newly liberated types, who're trying to cover up the hurt, say, ah, I don't need men, I might date him for a while, but I don't care about him. I know what they are really saying is that they really want to be treated well, they want to be with one man, but since it isn't possible, they fight against it, and they talk this feminist stuff. It frightens me, because then men get scared.

Suzanne Brøgger: I've changed tremendously. As a young person, one is questioning, revolting, in order to find one's own place and to make room to grow. I think I grew from the process of wanting freedom by revolution, by wanting to change society, to finding freedom within myself, so that now I can live in society and with a husband without projecting all my limitations on to him.

Lack of confidence is inherited downwards through the female line in families. It is not necessarily the fathers or grandfathers who say to daughters that they can't do this and that. The insecurity of the mother, the feeling of failure, of a wasted life, is passed on to the daughter very often. Woman's life has been reduced, reduced and reduced through history. It seems now that we have a lot of possibilities, but when we go back before industrialization, woman's contribution to society was equal to man's. There were two different worlds, but they were equally important and equally respected. But when the importance of the family is reduced, the role of the woman becomes more and more reduced. When she loses her platform – the family, the household – which used to be a little factory in a way; when the power and influence of woman is reduced to one and a half rooms in the suburbs, and maybe going to a factory or an office, maybe her expectations became more humble. And humbler, humbler, throughout history, until at last the women's movement – first the suffragettes and then the second wave of the new feminist movement – stood up and said, no, this can't go on. All movements as such tend to stagnate, to wither, and nothing is constant. If you keep on saying the same things, you are dead, but I think the processes set about by the feminist movement are still with us and influencing all our lives daily.

Janet Brown: Women can achieve a great deal because of their femininity, but in a truly lovely feminine way. I don't like the idea of the belligerent thing of saying we are feminists and burning bras and all that kind of nonsense; I never have. Sometimes, when I've listened to comments from women who have stood out strongly with views that they felt so powerfully about, and you see their marriage go and their children, the breaking up of everything because of their feelings for a cause, I wonder where's the woman, the feminine thing in all that. They've lost something terribly precious for another person's life, for the children who've got to grow up with that, and for a home that's gone. I don't think that's at all good.

Victoria Brynner: I don't feel the need to go on about women. I think I'm part of a modern generation of women, but not of feminists. Feminists are at least fifteen years older than I am. The inequalities between men and women I take advantage of, so they are useful to me, they don't disturb me at all. If a man is stupid enough to consider me inferior to him, I am going to turn that against him some way or another. I'm going to get what I want anyway.

Averil Burgess: Men need to take women more seriously in their homes, in work and in every possible way. And we are not entirely helped here by the activities of the most radical feminists, who are in danger of bringing about antipathy. They are not going to solve the problem. No, what I would do if I could do one thing for women is make men, all men, take their wives, daughters, female bank managers, everybody, as seriously as they take themselves.

Carmen Callil: My view of feminism is based much more on individual people and what they need. Social feminism I agree with in some degree, and I certainly vote Labour, though more and more unwillingly, but I don't believe the state is ever going to change the way women live or the way men and women live. If you take radical feminism, which is living without men, I have no time for that at all, but I have a great deal of time for the discrimination against lesbians if that is taking place. I'm sure it has taken place, because homosexuals are discriminated against. I don't care about anybody's sexuality, that's not my problem, that's why I never could take radical feminism seriously. I'm just not terribly interested. I couldn't care less if somebody is homosexual. It doesn't worry me, I can't give it any thought. My view of feminism would be an emotional one, because I think discrimination against women damages humanity.

What I really hate about Mrs Thatcher is her obsession with her point of view. The thing I hate most about her after her obsession with her point of view, is her obsession with the thought that anybody can do anything. Because, you see, I don't think we are born equal. I think we're born unequal, irrespective of sex. Certain people are born with the capacity to get on in our society and people think they're successful, as they think I'm successful, but there are some capacities I don't have. And therefore someone like Margaret Thatcher thinks that, in principle, I'm a good thing: I can work for myself, I can pull myself up by my bootlaces and all that kind of stuff that she thinks people should be able to do. A lot of people can't do that, but they can do other things which are not valued in our society, and that is what I most hate her for, because she thinks we are all capable of doing what she's done. I don't think she's done anything for women. She is actually a very unspeakable human being; it's a shame she's a woman. I'd hate her if she was a man. I hate her attitude to the human race.

Angela Carter: I think Mrs Thatcher stayed with the system. It seems obvious to me that the first woman Prime Minister would be a Tory, just because it's obvious that the first woman President of the States is going to be a Democrat. There's something about that which I know intuitively.

I would ban women's magazines if I could. Garbage. Garbage about shaving your armpits, being nice to people, all that garbage. Let it go!

Anna Carteret: I don't like labels very much. I suppose you could say that the work I do and the things I say make me a feminist, but I prefer not to be put into a slot. I'd like feminism to give women the opportunity to be heard, to be listened to, to be credited. You have to be a successful woman for anyone to take any notice of you. What about all the other women who are doing very good and worthwhile jobs, those who haven't even got a job, those who are bringing up the children – which is, after all, the next generation? Isn't that one of the most important jobs there could possibly be? Yet they are not really recognized because they don't earn a salary, so they're not worth counting when doing surveys or asking people their opinions; they don't carry any weight because they're not earners. I would like feminism to give women credibility in work and in their communities and in everything they do.

Mrs Thatcher denies her female qualities. She has extended her male qualities, the qualities usually associated with men – ambition, power and so on. I don't say insensitivity is a male quality, but she is certainly insensitive to human feelings. The way she dealt with the miners' strike was a prime example of total insensitivity to the feelings of those miners and their families, and what was happening, their whole villages being shut down. She has no concept of what that's like. I'll never forget when she ordered Trident II. At the same time, her son was lost in the desert and there were photographs of her in the papers crying. I thought, here is a mother crying for her son lost in the desert; at the same time, with her other hat on, she is ordering this weapon of total destruction, and she's able to do it. I understand *why* she's doing it, I understand all the arguments for defence, but I find it very disappointing in her.

Barbara Cartland: Princess Diana has now come along, she looks lovely, is charming, feminine, talks in a soft sweet voice. She's completely altered the thinking of the world. She's very feminine, terribly feminine. She thinks it's a miracle to have a child. She adores children, she thinks everything about having children and looking after them and being with your husband is wonderful. What more do you want? Why shouldn't women go back to being women?

The law's gone mad. I mean, this ridiculous thing now that if you're married to a woman, if you leave her, you have to pay her, but if she leaves you and goes off with somebody else, you still have to pay her. Why? I've never heard such rubbish in my life.

Women today are so strident. I asked a very attractive man why his marriage broke up. As he walked down the aisle, he said to her, you

459

must do so and so; and she said, I damn well won't – in that hard American voice. And so he had a divorce and lives with a man friend. Men are much more feminine than the women; the women are so hard, so aggressive, pushing them out of the way. In New York particularly, they absolutely connive to get the man out of a job so they can take it. They've got far too many women at the top of everything; they never last very long and they're very difficult to deal with. It makes business very difficult. I was talking to a welfare officer the other day. He said, I am so sorry for the men. I said, why? He said, well, these women come along with their sex manuals and they say, I'm entitled to this. But, you see, you're only entitled to what the man can desire. If a man doesn't desire you, you can be entitled to anything you like, but you're not going to get it. The first thing you've got to do is make yourself desirable. If you're not desirable as a woman, then a man isn't interested. He can't turn it on like a tap. A woman can pretend, a man can't. That's another tremendous difference between the sexes, and they don't seem to understand that. It's no good to say I want to do this, that or the other if he doesn't desire you. I mean, it's just too bad, isn't it? And that's half the trouble. They're brought up, these young women, on this rubbish: do it fifty-five times a day, which is quite immoral, and the men can't – they're frightened. I see the psychiatrists, the scientists in America, have said that owing to the women being so hard and making so many demands on men, a great many men have gone homosexual simply because they're frightened, they feel they can't compete. And a great number have gone impotent.

I don't believe in equal opportunity. I think it's terribly tiresome. The whole thing is absolutely terrible now because we've got vast unemployment. It's still a stigma for a man to be unemployed, and to be kept by a woman. It's not a stigma for the woman to be kept by a man. We should try to make people realize that, where your father's rich and can keep you, you can work, of course you can work, but not at a paid job. There are millions of jobs – like St John Ambulance Brigade – where nobody's paid. It's a wonderful, wonderful organization and it's a working-class organization. They're not rich people, they're working-class people who work all day and do their St John's stuff all night. None of them are paid – nobody at all – they pay for their own uniform, they pay for their own bandages, they do everything for free. There are masses of organizations like that. Now, if the father who could afford to keep his daughter said, yes, go and join the St John's, go and work if you like for a political organization, go and work for the old people, but don't take a salary because I can afford to keep you, then that would put other men back into jobs. Exactly the same with the husband who is rich enough to keep his wife; what does the wife want to have a paid job for?

Of course, you want a job – I quite agree you want to work, because women want to work now, but they shouldn't take a paid job while there's vast unemployment. You put a man into the job, because it humiliates a man to be out of work; it doesn't humiliate a woman to be out of work.

Luciana Castellina: I belong to a pre-feminist generation. Our problem was to try to be as similar as possible to men. The feminists discovered that the point was not to be similar but to be themselves. That's a great difference. For us, the problem was to try and hide our personality and our feminine nature; you would hide all female characteristics, physical or emotional, the way you thought, the way you acted, everything. I remember, all my life, struggling to hide being a woman, so that I could be taken seriously. When feminism arrived, all this was finished. It was a real revolution, because I had experienced what it was like before, and then suddenly feminism arrived and kicked me in the face when I was already forty-five. Later on, it was my daughter who taught me more, or my comrades, and then I started rethinking and said, God, how stupid I have been.

Professions have been shaped for men and not for women. All the professions have been made on masculine models. The woman doesn't only have to become an engineer, but to become an engineer in the way being an engineer has been thought out for a man. All our professions, the whole society, has been shaped on the model of their intelligence which is not the same sort of intelligence as women's, the model of their body, their feelings, their personalities. So women have to fit into a cage not theirs. It is quite natural that they are not as successful. Even the way to conduct politics is male-orientated, male-dominated, and women, if they are involved in politics, have to follow patterns invented by men, which is not their own way. It's much more complex than equal opportunity; equal opportunity is a claim of the past. What does it mean, equal opportunity? It means you can have the right to become a judge or a lawyer, or a president of a republic, or prime minister, like a man; you will have equal opportunity to become as a man, you will be paid as much as a man. You don't speak about the equal opportunity of men to become like women; it's vice versa. So, OK, it's all right to fight for equal opportunity, but one has to know that it is a very dubious claim.

One of the main tasks of the feminist movement has been to establish that even the sex-partnership models were imposed by men, not by women, so that women have always been passive objects in sexual

461

relations, because they did not invent sexual enjoyment. Sexual enjoyment was the man's enjoyment. Even the statistics found out by the women's movement are very impressive: an enormous number of women don't enjoy sexual relations at all.

One should consider lesbianism for what it is. There was a long period in which the culture, especially in this country, was the culture of being among men, pubs only for men, clubs for men, social life for men, colleges, schools, friends, and sexual relations with men. So it's very natural that women, when they finally freed themselves, went through this. I think lesbianism is part of a stage of the development of women who have finally found each other and started having relations among themselves – no longer through men, but directly. They started having a social life together. And then, of course, some of them decided they would reject men. In my pre-feminist generation, we never met women in social life. You met women with men, or family, but it never occurred to me to say, well, I am going to have dinner tonight with a woman friend, or I'm going on a journey with a woman. Never. That is something again that feminists have taught us. I remember my daughter once said, for God's sake, why are you so stupid, you never go out with women. So again, this is a discovery of women's community, of women's social relations, a great discovery. Whether or not women are aggressive partly depends, I think, on the society. American society, as such, is more aggressive than European society. It's such a meritocratic society, everybody has to fight so hard to succeed, and it's so easy to be a drop-out. I think there is a difference between American feminism and European feminism, even if it is difficult to generalize. American feminists concluded at a certain point that they had to organize themselves like a trade union and operate in society as a trade union; they established women lawyers, health care for women, and women in all sorts of professions, and all to strengthen each other. This probably makes them somehow more aggressive. Whereas the feminist movement in Europe has been much more cultural and less trade unionist, and they have gone on reasoning and reasoning about what a woman's nature really is, what motherhood is, what it means and so on.

In China, immediately after the revolution, they gave many more rights to the women in the constitution than to men, because they had so much historical discrimination to cancel. In a way, it was the same concept as the proletarian dictatorship: that, to really cancel all the rule that has oppressed the proletariat, you must have a temporary, provisional stage in which you cannot have a formal equality, since this would never be a real equality, because you have so much that comes from history. And this is what you should do with women. I would like to have 75 per cent of women in parliament and in power, not 50–50, because they have to redeem the past. I want many more rights, and much more power for women, in order to readjust the balance.

Alexandra Chapman: I don't like groups, I don't like joining. I don't like slogans or ideologies of whatever kind, they scare me. What I do like, what I try to do in my personal life, is to be supportive to women, also to men of course, but particularly to women who may be in a crisis or who may not have the insight I have; in my own sphere, to be as loving as possible to other women. It's not easy every day. And I don't think all women are necessarily my sisters. Some of the nasty ones I have eliminated, because they are nasty. But it's somehow feminism on an everyday level. You can be a feminist without belonging to any group, and men will still hold the door open for you. They are not going to say, you are a feminist, you can open the door yourself.

The feminist movement is on the wane, certainly in France. I don't think it was ever as strong here as it was in England or America, perhaps because Frenchwomen perceive themselves on the whole as being less oppressed, rightly or wrongly. I think also that there are so many conflicts of all sorts on the horizon that men and women are maybe, I hope, starting to think about joining each other instead of fighting so that we don't risk nuclear war, so that we don't risk local wars. This student march here in France was wonderful, because there the girls were in with the boys, they were students together, there was no sex discrimination at all.

What struck me recently in America is that all my women friends, whether younger or older, were all complaining that there were no more men around and they were all having man problems. And all the men were complaining that they were having woman problems. That seems to be a problem specific to America. I think the American feminists went too far too quickly. They didn't proceed by steps. A lot of the men were already frightened because of the way they were brought up by their mothers, because in American society the mother's power is in the home, not in the outside world. So there is a certain degree of momma-ism already, and then this rush of feminism. It must have overpowered and frightened many men.

Tina Chow: I think that America is much more of a mess than England. The men are a mess there, so are the women. Even though women are allowed to succeed in business in certain areas, they are so unpleasant.

It's a superficial liberation. Women in America who are successful with a career sacrifice family or children. A lot of gains are not real gains. Maybe they will become real in time.

Felicity Waley-Cohen: I'm absolutely not a feminist, and feminists bore me to death. I think they are a miserable sort of breed who wish to be totally different. To me, we are human beings and we should be getting on with it.

Shirley Conran: The first time I went to America in about 1960, I went to San Francisco and was asked to leave a restaurant because I was a woman; and then I went to another restaurant and again I got asked to leave because I was a woman. I was wearing a navy-blue suit, a sort of interview suit, low-heeled shoes, very respectable. I ended up with eating room service most of the time in the Hilton. Then the City Fathers gave a little luncheon for men and I was able to tell them how glad I was to be seen in public. I said they ought to be able to tell the journalists from the whores because the journalists had biro marks on their fingers. Well, that sort of thing doesn't happen today. I remember the time when you were not allowed in a restaurant if you were wearing trousers. This is all loony rubbish – those days are over. I'm sure there's a different sort of loony rubbish going on at the moment, but it's really not worth worrying about, you just have to brush it aside and charge on. We Conrans are very keen on that, on not allowing things to get in your way – just keep on with your eye on the target. I think that perhaps not enough women do that.

Women lack guts – take it from me. It's not considered polite to say this. I think men have had a very bad press for the last fifteen years. Women have had equal opportunity in Britain for fifteen years. I was part of the movement, I was with Women in Media, I was involved in all that in 1970. Now, why haven't women got further? The answer lies with women themselves. They just don't want to take the responsibility, that's what it boils down to. They want to scuttle off and skive, and hide behind their daddy, or their husband, or some man. If they do take responsibility, it's generally by accident. They suddenly find themselves holding the baby, and look how women squawk when they do find themselves in that position. If their husband leaves them and they're left with the baby, all you hear is bitter complaints. These days, if you have a baby, a woman should right at the beginning take responsibility for it and realize that the father might not always be there for one reason or another. You can't be certain the father will always be there,

464

or even that he will be a good father. She should take that into account.

I feel very strongly that, when women are working professionally, they should not bring their private life into it. They shouldn't say, well, I can't make it on Tuesday, because I have to take my little girl to the dentist. They should say, well, I cannot make it on Tuesday, can we make it on Wednesday? Right? They should shut up about it and get on with the job.

I met the Russian astronaut, Valentina Tereshkova, and was introduced to her by Lynda Chalker, our Minister of Transport, as the woman who has had more influence on the liberation of British women than anyone else. I was deeply embarrassed and Valentina immediately asked me, what did I do? I said, well, I wrote a book about housework and how to avoid it. But she immediately thought that was terribly important, she immediately saw the point of reducing housework to a minimum so you could get on with other things. A lot of women hide behind housework. You can reduce it to a very little if you set your mind on it. Even now, I don't have servants. I have a cleaner here every morning, that's all.

Of course, if somebody opens a door for me, I smile and say thank you, but when nobody's around to do it, then I open it myself, and if I see somebody, man or woman, with his hands full of parcels, or her hands full of parcels, then I open the door. I really think that these things are very old-fashioned and trivial. We were talking about that fifteen years ago, and anybody who is still talking about it deserves to be in *Private Eye's* loony female rubbish column.

Michelle Coquillat: I am definitely a feminist. I am not a radical, not a separatist. The ideal for a feminist is to have the vision of a mixed society where men and women would be all together and where chances would be equal, that's all. The essential is to stop defining the individual according to a sexual standard. That's the great point. That roles should be given to and taken by the people they suit. I don't see why I should pretend that I love cooking if I hate cooking. But if it is considered that it is a sexual role for me, then I refuse it. As a matter of fact, I love cooking, but I don't feel degraded by the fact that I love cooking because I don't define this activity as a sexual role. I think the essential problem is that we live in a very sexualized society where not only the roles but all the signs and the symbols are most of the time defined in terms of sexuality.

Fleur Cowles: I am definitely not a feminist, probably as I've never had to fight for my place in a man's world. But I do support half of the hopes and dreams of the feminist movement to have equal opportunities and equal pay – which too many do not have. I want to see this achieved, though without claiming themselves the same as men. This is unnecessary, if not foolhardy. Women have their own important places.

Women have to go without that clenched fist to get there. And I always say it is so simple, it is the easy way to get a message across. To my girl godchildren, I would say, remember, never mentally put on a man's trousers to get there – keep your skirt.

Susan Crosland: To my surprise, I find I have become a feminist. I thought I was born and bred a feminist because my mother had a job. Most of my married life I worked and I used to be rather complacent about feminists and think, why do they have to go on so about it, why don't they just do something? All this going on and on about it. But that drip, drip, drip process of theirs has had some effect on me and I have come to feel that I was lucky, and I could fight my battles, such as they were, combine them with marriage quite happily, but most people can't. By that process, I became rather a feminist out of compassion for women who hadn't had my good luck and opportunities and can't do it for themselves, and are trapped in poverty (money's a big factor) or trapped in a marriage (a hollow relationship).

Middle-class women are trying to persuade the working-class women and the working-class women are on the whole content with the set-up as it is. Mind you, a hell of a lot of working-class women have jobs outside the home and, again, don't quite know what all this talk is about because they have part-time jobs at Birds-Eye factories and talk to their women friends and are tough. But I think single-minded career women are probably thin on the ground still. One of the great advantages we have over men – and we have a lot of psychological advantages over men – is that we are not single-minded like Mrs Thatcher on the whole. We have families as well, so if something happens to the job, all our eggs aren't in that single basket. We can be at home and lead a creative life, a full life, whereas the man, if he's over forty and not very good at being at home – he's underfoot and miserable. What I don't like – it irritates me – is the married woman who beefs away about feminism and nags at her husband about the fact that he has the job and she doesn't earn outside the family. Frequently she has help, frequently – we're talking about the middle classes – the children are away at school. She beefs away about buying the groceries and this and that.

Why doesn't she get out – why doesn't she get a job? Or if it's that bad, why doesn't she separate? And she doesn't. Despite all these divorces, very few women pack in an empty marriage unless they have a replacement. And that gives me a pain.

Mary Crowther: I don't know what feminism means any more. When I was at university, the feminist movement was just starting. I thought that was something to be involved in and I horrified all my medical colleagues by joining the women's liberation group, and after about nine months or a year I became very worried about what was going on. It seemed to me that I had a very naïve view that we were going to help working-class women for economic reasons, or if they were beaten up by their husbands, had nowhere to go and so on, and pregnancy after pregnancy. But two things happened. First, I realized that many working-class women didn't want to be helped, they were quite happy being beaten up from time to time. There was something that kept them to their husbands, whether it was love or psychopathology doesn't matter, but they were prepared to stay in spite of the other things, and it was really very patronizing of us to go along and think we could change it. The second thing was, I worried very much about the sort of women that went into this group. Increasingly it became very politicized, terribly left-wing. You had to be a Marxist and then a Communist, and so on. And then there was this idea that all of life's problems directly related to sex and the sexual power men have over women, and so one solution was to become a lesbian, which was most offensive. These women were physically ugly, they were dirty, they smelt, and all of this was meant to be part of their own liberation. They didn't have to worry about the normal constraints, like having a bath or just being polite to people. Yet that makes the difference between a peasant society and a civilized society. So, in fact, I became terribly disillusioned and left, and I'm sad to say that I've never followed the more abstract points of feminist thought since. I've never bothered to read any of the feminist literature. I'm not really interested. There are wonderful things about men, there are bad things about all people, male and female. But you can't actually say that all men are evil and our destiny lies with us and us alone.

Jennifer D'Abo: There are men and women in my life everywhere I go, and I don't think about feminism that much. I don't expect my driver to open car doors for me; when it's easy for him to do it, that's fine. For instance, if we draw up in a crowded street, I would never sit in the car until he gets out and walks round and opens the car door for me.

467

Normally, my office door is open and everyone wanders in and out. I don't expect men in here to stand up when I stand up because it's a waste of time and energy. It's very nice if you go out socially for a man to hold the door open, open your car door for you and all the rest, but I don't really think about it. I think there are certain women who want to be independent, and certain women, like my sister, who would die rather than be independent. She likes living the way she lives. Her husband provides her with everything, pays all the bills, runs the house, tells her what he wants done, and she does it, and that's the way she likes living. Sometimes I think I'd like that too, but on the other hand, I don't seem to be able to provide the other side of that coin. I'm not there a lot of the time, I have to keep rather strange hours. In the old days, I used to get asked out to dinners in the evening that my husband wasn't invited to, and there were other endless problems – that I hadn't finished on Friday night when he wanted to go home, away for the weekend, or something of the kind. You can't have everything.

Maryam D'Abo: I find feminism ridiculous. I don't find those women interesting at all. Because I don't believe in fanaticism, I believe in individuality. As soon as you get into these sort of extreme systems, it becomes fanatical and stupid.

Béatrice Dalle: Women aren't superior or inferior. What would women do without men, or men without women? Nothing. Life would stop. Women couldn't live alone without men. What would happen to the children? Feminists are bloody stupid. There are things that men can do that women can't, and the other way round. It's fine the way it is.

Alma Daniel: It's a much greater problem when a man cannot perform sexually than when a woman can't. When a woman can't, she can fake it, but when a man can't, he can't. In fact, is this not an analagous situation where, if the man can't make it in business, his lack of performance shows, whereas if a woman doesn't, who cares, what difference does it make? Why should men be under the bondage of such considerations? It's just as incorrect as the stigma applied to women. Chinese girl babies were left in the river to die. The same with Negro babies. These are old, outmoded ways, and I think it is important that we examine them and look at them and that you talk to people about it. Because we are in the process of a tremendous transformation on the planet. Consciousness is being transformed. And that means that old ideas can be released and let go. We don't need them any more, they are not productive, they are not useful and they are not going to create the kind of society we want to live in.

Sister Camille D'Arienzo: One of the roots of discrimination is within the Church. And it's damnable because the Church equates it with holiness. Look at the traditional image of Our Blessed Mother, holy, submissive, hands folded on a pedestal. It would be wonderful if we could all be like that. We could all be turned into statues and put on pedestals and not cause anybody any trouble. Neither would we be able to convey in our own person the power or the love of the Lord. Certainly in service, yes, and we've done that for ever. Women have always served, we've always cared about the poor, we've always clothed the naked and visited the sick, we've always done all those things. But let me give this example. Some years ago, a newspaper reporter from the metropolitan area asked me what I thought about Mother Theresa. And I said, I think Mother Theresa is a wonderful, holy and compassionate woman. But I think a great disservice is done to the women of the world, particularly the *religieuses* of the world, when she is upheld as the only model for religious action. Certainly there will always be need for people to take care of the dying in the streets, symbolically or actually. But you also need other women whose education and call is to go to the systemic structures and find out why people are dying in the streets. That charge I made drew more negative publicity than anything I have ever said. I must have received over 500 letters from as far away as Australia and Scotland condemning me for being jealous of the saint and putting her down. I never did that and I never would. So editorially I was blasted across the United States in the Catholic press, articles ran in the *Washington Post*, it was incredible. The image of woman as servant is so associated with holiness that they cannot understand there are other ways.

They say women cannot be ordained because Jesus did not ordain a woman. That's one of the arguments, and it comes in two parts. One is that He didn't do it, though, given the cultural differences of His own time and place, He couldn't have done it. We know that He involved women in ways that no man of His time did, in discussion out in the streets with the Samaritan women, after His crucifixion and resurrection sending Mary Magdalen to go and proclaim the news of His resurrection. In the case of Martha and Mary – the Bethany story – He said very clearly that Mary had chosen the better part and it would not be taken from her. He means that Mary had listened to Him. The other argument is the *imago dei* argument, that to be ordained a priest, you must be made in the image of God, and since Jesus was male, to be in the image of God you must be, as Jesus was, a male. That's nonsense. And yet that was the argument in the Vatican declaration against the ordination of women that was produced by Paul VI in 1976 or 1977. That argument simply doesn't wash, because God, the image of God, is not a physical image; God is spirit. The major theologians, even those put to work by the bishops, have rejected those two arguments. And the contemporary feminist theology debunks that to the satisfaction of respected theologians and not a few bishops. I think the struggle is much more a matter of power. I think a lot of that struggle for power was a natural, or maybe an unnatural, alliance with national powers. Look at the vestments of the priests, or the bishops. Where did that come from? That didn't come from the Carpenter of Nazareth who went around in a seamless robe and sandals, it came from the association with monarchy, a lot of it from the Roman Empire. We had kings talking about the divine right of kings. So that there is, unmistakably, power. But the power is to preach God's love, that's what the power should be. In fact it is not. The power is used to control. If we look at the current situation in the Vatican, we see a tremendous concerted effort to suppress theological investigation because the theological investigation is done as much publicly today as it is privately. So we say that those whose theological findings differ from the established teaching of the Church may not publish, may not teach in a university. The women who have been involved in social programmes, who have been involved politically, have been punished, have been forced to leave their communities in order to do the work with the Sisters of Mercy. I see in this the abuse of power. I could talk this right down to the parish level. Why can't little girls stand by their brothers in the sanctuary? Why are boys, seven years old, taught at the altar of the Lord that they are somehow better than their sisters who can't stand with them? I think that power is ingrained from when they're young children – the sense of male power. And I think it is evident in Cardinal Rattzinger and the Pope, John Paul II, of our own age.

I don't want to present an impression of the Church as completely divided. There have always been, within the Church, men as well as women who have understood that the call of Jesus is not an élitist or sexist call, and that the possibilities of it need not be restricted to males in terms of power. When I say power, I don't mean power to control other people's lives, but power to better proclaim the Good News of the Lord in ways that are effective, in ways that are more holy. But there are men today, laymen as well as priests, who understand very well what the sin of sexism is; men who have become feminists and who try to advance the cause and the positions of women, both on a parish level in their teaching and in their reading and exchanges with women with whom they work. We have over 2,000 priests for equality, ordained men around the world, who are trying to promote equal rights for women and men. So I don't want it to seem that I am indicting all men; I am not. My closest friends include priests who share my vision and share the pain of limitation and who, in their own lifetime, are doing what they can to change that around.

Mandy Rice Davies: When I came back to England and my daughter was not automatically British because her father was Israeli, I had a small fight about that. The law was in the process of partly being changed. But it really made me angry that the child was not automatically given citizenship – which actually makes far more sense because you always know who your mother is. So, on things like that, on legal issues, I am 100 per cent behind women and any women's movement to redress the balance. On broader issues, for example, separate feminist libraries, then it begins to annoy me a little, because then you are being pushed into gender ghettoes and I don't think that's the way the world should work. It would be a lousy world without any men in it. I wouldn't want to live in it. I'd go to Mars.

Régine Deforges: Françoise Giroud says that the day we have equality will be the day when a woman minister can be as stupid as a male minister.

In the morning, I make my husband's breakfast and my daughter's hot chocolate, and I don't feel my stature is in the least diminished. It relaxes me and it pleases them. In Norway and Sweden, when I say that's what I do, they look at me as if I were backward.

Lady Camilla Dempster: I believe in independence, and I mean by that that I think it helps enormously if they can have even a tiny income of their own. That's the most important thing. I'm not talking about extreme feminism. I'm just talking about having independence so that you can say to whoever you are living with or married to, I don't want to do that, I don't want to come on holiday to Spain to play golf; I would rather go to Venice with a friend. That sort of independence. Enough to give you an edge.

Kay Dick: I've never felt discriminated against. Because I don't allow anyone to discriminate against me, ever. I can't stand bad manners and it would be bad manners on a man's part to discriminate against me, as it

471

were. I do realize that I have been underpaid in jobs and so on, but this is being righted. I don't feel I have to parade through the streets with a banner about anything, about sex, or about equality – about anything.

I know that there are things like inequality of pay in certain industries, so obviously they are not equal in that sense, but they've got to press a bit harder and they'll get it. It'll all come out fine in the end. You don't have to go and cut anyone's throat.

In the days of the suffragettes, I would obviously have gone to prison, and I would fight for my own rights today if anybody tried to take them away, but my rights as a human being rather than as a woman. I would fight for everyone's right, man, woman, whatever race, whatever religion. There's too much image-making, whether it's women's rights, gay rights, these rights, those rights. Fine, it amuses them, gives them something to do in life, but I have other things to do instead of marching up and down with a banner. When one was young, from the age of twenty to thirty, one marched, of course – Suez and all that sort of thing. One did, but one grows up. I think it's all right for the twenty-year-olds to go on; this is part of growing up. If it's not women's rights it would have been something else.

All my life up to now I've voted Labour; whether I shall next time, I don't know at the moment. Mrs Thatcher, abominable woman really, and yet so right in so many ways. One has to admire the way she's, let's say, made herself. As somebody once said, she says everything one doesn't agree with. She's terribly efficient, I think. I don't like her, but I have to hand it to her. I see characteristics in her that are a question of her class, frankly. You know, this English girl, daughter of a grocer, who managed to make it to the top, and aren't we proud? She's not my favourite woman. Thatcher has become her own caricature, really.

Anne Dickson: Given that the roles of men and the roles of women are changing, it is much more difficult for me to relate to men as equals now than it would have been at some other time, or may be in the future. I think women can go it alone now, and because of the women's move-ment, there is a lot more thought about being a woman. I do actually believe that a lot of changes can take place in the world if women change themselves and disrupt the whole stereotyping, but I don't think you can say that women and men are dependent on each other as people. You have a certain biological dependence for conception, but apart from that, I don't think there has to be a dependence. I think there's an exchange. That's what I'd like to see: an exchange of energies. And I do think there are differences, I don't think everyone is basically andro-gynous. There's a male way of looking, and a female way of looking, for both men and women. The Chinese are much better at thinking of it than we are in the West – thinking of it as a universal, of the way we identify with it, of the connection between us, between individuals and the universe – there you have the female principle. The male principle is much more discerning and individualistic. But you have to have the two, so, yes, there is a dependence. I don't think there's a dependence between men and women, but there's a dependence between what men can offer, if you like, or a male kind of energy and a female energy, yet it is much more contained within each individual. I don't think we've been separated out of existence – it's only that men have been able to feel male things only, women female things only. And I think there's a lot of anger because of that.

I wouldn't have considered myself as a feminist some years ago, because of the associations with the word. It is seen by a majority of women as being anti-men, and because of that I had to go through my own little process of not being seen as a feminist. I wanted to reach women who were in their own homes who, if they saw something feminist, would regard it with great suspicion, and feminism for me is a political viewpoint and applies to men as well. A lot of people disagree with this, but I think men can be feminist. It is a way of seeing people in their lives and behaviour without stereotyping them, without restricting them to a particular way simply because they happen to be born either female or male. It allows people the full range of characteristics, of appearance, of nature, of gifts, of qualities. It's allowing men and women a full range of being human – and that's what I think of as feminist.

People think of feminism as equal opportunities for pay or something of the kind. That's the very superficial layer. Lower down, for me, is much more how women behave with one another, our attitudes towards one another, our assumptions, our expectations, and the way that we punish ourselves for being a particular way. You know, I work an awful lot with women, and they punish themselves often for having feelings they don't feel they should have as women, for wishes that they shouldn't have as women, and it's all that kind of thing that I'm very much against.

So much of what women do is feminist. Refusing to be sat on, refusing to fit into a mould – it's feminist with a little f. But feminism is something you are accused of. It's not a compliment. Because of the connotations. Because of the media. Feminism equals man-hater, equals lesbianism, equals extreme, equals Greenham Common protester, equals ugly. You can't be feminist and attractive, because anything feminine is bad – like wearing a skirt, wearing make-up. It's a real dilemma for women. A lot of women who embrace the feminist ideal worry about whether they should put make-up on or not, because maybe that's letting down the cause. Or whether they should be having a relationship with a woman, because maybe that's what would be more ideologically sound. On the other hand, you can see the point of it. After all, I shouldn't have to make myself pretty in order to be taken seriously.

It's a pity to me that the feminist rhetoric is so vehement, that they lose some of the impact of what they say, because I do think there is a lot of sense in it. There is a lot of anger about the invasion by men of women, and I couldn't dismiss it out of hand. I couldn't say, well, it's symbolism. I use symbolism like that. I can think of things that happen to the earth as a rape of the earth. I was thinking that while looking at the rockets last night. All the male achievements, all the achievements of the West, are very phallic. This is where all the money goes – the guns, the whole thing. All phallic. I couldn't just dismiss this as symbolism.

If the woman says, well, I'm not going to look after my child, I want to go out to work, I don't think that's anything to do with feminism. I think that's to do with greed. I think that's to do with capitalism. It's pushing people to earn more, buy more; it's pushing people towards activity, towards goals, rather than saying, now I have a child. And I believe this as strongly as anything: if you have a child, there has to be some time for looking after that child, rather than immediately thinking, OK, I've had the child – tick – which is what people do now. Tick – done that. It doesn't mean total self-sacrifice, but you have to give something up. I think the reason people have children now is very suspect and has nothing to do with feminism. It has little to do with love, it has a lot to do with social expectations, with possessions. You know – well, I now have my children. It's to do with tremendous conditioning and tremendous pressure, and also the feeling of some people – I'm talking about the young and teenagers – that this is their only identity. It's something else to be done – everybody's doing it. More money, more things, and they are presented with a child, and they don't want to give the time up. They don't actually want to give the love that this child is going to need, and they need such an enormous amount of love. It's such a shitty world in many ways. And if you can't give your children that, then I don't think you should have them. I don't think it has anything to do with feminism; I think it is the way the world is – just going after more and more, and more and more, and not taking time to sit and be.

Dame Jean Conan Doyle: Many of the feminists have alienated other women. I think it is absolutely absurd to worry about whether you are called a chairman or not. I mean, how petty can you be?

Margaret Drabble: It's sad when one looks at the history of the suffrage movement, to see the very high expectations women had of the vote and how little use they've made of it, what a slow business it is.

I am a feminist, yes. I'm a moderate feminist. I believe in equal opportunity, in equal pay. I don't think we have either. Women are exploited at the lower end of the workforce by part-time work and once a job becomes a woman's job people tend to pay slightly worse rates for it. An interesting example is word processing and the new technology: once women master it, the rate for the job goes down slightly. When it is still a masculine preserve, as in computer science, it is well paid and highly regarded. But women are very bad at fighting for their rates of pay and also, because of the nature of their lives, they tend to go in for part-time work, right through from the lowest to the highest, and that, of course, leads to unfairness.

I don't like Mrs Thatcher, but I think that's because of her politics and her personality. I still admire the way she's got to where she has. I don't find that she has exploited her sexuality for good or bad, I think she has been very clever at being absolutely neutral. I rather admire her for that. I was watching her, with the Prime Minister of Norway – two very different women – but both of them seemed to be perfectly all right; they weren't being feminine, they weren't being masculine, they were just being reasonably well-dressed, ordinary women, and I thought that was quite good. Mrs Thatcher doesn't have a very feminine image, but nor does she have an aggressively masculine image. I'm talking purely about dress and manner and so on. And she never really refers to herself as being a woman, or pulls the emotional heartstrings. The only time I've ever really seen her upset was when her son was lost, and that was very human and perfectly acceptable that she should have looked slightly upset for a moment. I think that she has really not discredited the job. From that point of view, from the women's cause point of view (I'm not talking about her politics, about women in the Cabinet and so on), her own personal behaviour has been perfectly straight. It could have been a lot more worrying.

Maureen Duffy: One of the sad things about this whole debate, which becomes men *versus* women, is that both men and women are forced to

475

play a particular role. Men are often much softer than they are allowed to be without becoming, in the world's eyes, effeminate. And I think that if women were not forced to use their femininity to achieve all sorts of ends, they would be able to be more free and equal without going to the other extreme and becoming masculine. At the moment, either course is open to them: they can either become very masculine or they can remain feminine, but in neither course are they, in a sense, truly equal. They are still not quite people. They are playing roles. Perhaps true equality is impossible, but it is something we have to strive towards. If we don't strive, then we accept the inequalities and build them into our society and reinforce them. Unless you have an ideal of equality, however you are going to define it, you have nothing to move towards. You remain static, thereby reinforcing the roles and positions you are born into. So if you're poor, you've got to stay poor, and if you're ugly, you should not attempt to make yourself more attractive.

Princess Elizabeth of Yugoslavia: I think to be a feminist is necessary – just as I think the suffragettes were necessary at the beginning to get women votes. But they have fought as much as is necessary and they have now proved that women are capable and are intelligent and should be given a break. I don't like the idea of the very rough type of feminist who is bordering on being a lesbian because she wants to be known or noticed. I don't think that is necessary. I don't think women should rush out and decide to drive trucks and lorries because they want to compete with men, because on that level it's stupid, but equally, if they want to work in a factory, they should not be discriminated against and have ridiculous men insult them and throw things at them. That is monstrous.

Sally Emerson: I'm probably a feminist, as long as one can define one's own form of feminism. I have enormous respect for women and think they should be given more opportunities and allowed to do more what they want. You can't return to what it used to be like, and now, if they want to have jobs, they need every opportunity to do so, but they ought to bring their feminism, their sense of themselves and their respect for women into ordinary life so that the respect is for babies, for having a good family life as well as the other. Instead, what the 1960s and women's liberation seem to have done is to say, right, we're all going to do our jobs, men are a nuisance and babies are a terrible nuisance; and in denying that, they are having no respect for women. It isn't feminism. They're just saying, let's all be like men and do all these things that men do; and neglecting the extraordinary gift that women have, and the skill and talent involved in bringing up children.

Shirley Eskapa: Feminists downgrade mothering, they downgrade all the skills of home-making. And nothing is more important than that. Nothing.

From childhood, women are taught to serve. You see, they have to serve men if they want to keep the family unit going. They have to. When a man is not being served, or feels he is not being served, there is a greater chance that this biological family unit will be dissolved. And, of course, this is where the feminists part company with me. I firmly believe that the maintenance of the family, the continuation of the family, the responsibility for the family, rests with women and not with men.

Marcia Falkender: Am I a feminist? Yes and no. The feminists have been very brave, they started off this debate, they fought a very brave action on our behalf, right out in front, taking all the flak that was going. Without them it woudn't have been possible for women to have made the gains they have. But they are too strident, they are now in danger of doing a lot of harm if they keep it up. Because there is, in my view, some swing-back. Men are gaining a certain amount of strength from all of this in-fighting. And so I think there are dangers with the feminist movement. They can do a great deal of harm. But no one should decry what they did.

Esther B. Ferguson: I swear to God I am trying to stop this drop-out rate. We are 52 per cent of the population, so we are a major part of that issue, and if we are going to have to work, as it appears we are in this country, because we have to eat, then we need as much information as possible. How you interpret it, how you behave, are other issues. My issue is you don't have a chance if you don't know. And to be enlightened and be educated is the issue.

Annie Flanders: I was never part of the women's movement because I always believed in being myself and I'm fairly feminine. That's why I always think it's been an advantage to be a woman. I haven't ever tried to act like a man, I've always tried to act like a woman, and I always feel that it's gotten me further.

Lorraine Stanley-Ford: I admire what women have achieved in the last ten years for themselves. I'm not the sort of feminist who will put on

477

dungarees and go and scream at Greenham Common, although I am anti-nuclear. I am against violence and any kind of cruelty to animals, humans, children, anything at all. I'm not what I would call a raving feminist, the traditional stereotype: dungarees, short hair, no make-up, living in tents. I admire what they do, I admire the principles, but it's not for me. I'm not a separatist at all. I really think that in society the only way you can possibly get on is if everybody can live together as amicably as possible. And I don't agree God is a female and women are this, that and the other. In fact, all that almost undermines what women have achieved in certain respects, because they become a laughing-stock publicly with those kinds of attitudes.

Lynne Franks: I think Mrs Thatcher's public relations are appalling, absolutely appalling. She is very clever, no question of it, but her image just doesn't handle that. It's not to do with her hairstyle and her frock, and the way she modulates her voice, it's to do with her as a real person, because she's everything that most of us would like not to be – all that coldness and remoteness. At least, when you talk to the Kinnocks, both of them, you feel they are talking to you and there's a caring there. I don't know why Mrs Thatcher fills me and many other people with anger, but I do feel anger. We may even be supportive of her politics, but there is something very irritating and annoying about her.

Rebecca Fraser: I dislike the idea that feminism prevents natural relations, that it sets up barriers between men and women. In an ideal world, I would like feminism not to be seen as threatening to men, which it really is I think, but I think that is very unfortunate.

Susan George: I hate women's lib. I'm not aggressive at all. And that would probably be my downfall in America. To win in America, you actually have to go and tread all over everyone's head, and I'm not capable of doing that. I'm a much gentler, more soft person, so when I talk about my attitudes and my positiveness and my drive, I'm still a very very sensitive person; I think anyone who knows me well would agree. Even though I'm a decision-maker, I'm very much bound by my femininity and by being a woman.

Alexandra M. Giurgiu: To a certain extent, women probably are disadvantaged, but I think that it's a social phenomenon and I strongly believe that the whole women's issue, because of its political accent, has magnified the problem as opposed to solving it. I usually don't consider women/men an issue, especially in professional things, because once you've established credibility, it doesn't make any difference whether you are a woman or a man.

To emulate men is the biggest mistake women make. That goes counter to women establishing their credibility in society as professionals or as mothers. Why should they emulate men? They're women.

To deny you're a woman is absolutely ridiculous. Just walk down Park Avenue around lunchtime and you'd think you were in China – everyone dressed alike, all these clones. It is ridiculous as far as I'm concerned. Do they think they're going to succeed because they act and look like men?

I'm of the philosophy that, if you're intelligent, if you have drive, if you believe in excellence, if you have pride in your work, you'll succeed, irrespective of whether you're a man or a woman. I don't like the feminist label. It has too many political connotations, and I don't think it is a political issue. You can look at all these statistics about men earning more than women, and I don't deny all those facts. However, the law of large numbers has it that you're talking about an average, and in some cases it's definitely true and in others it isn't. The most important thing that women have to learn to do is to be very adaptable and be very smart – you cannot go against certain facts of life and you have to use finesse to get yourself through, you have to really use your brains. I'm not saying it's easy. I could have stayed home and had a very lovely life as opposed to going out and travelling on my own to all these very strange countries from the age of twenty when I graduated from college. I've been in the Far East, Africa, India, Eastern Europe, Central America; I've been in places where there is no water, no food, and I know that there are a lot of people who would not have put up with that because there is no glamour attached. But I think women have to realize there's a time that we have to all roll up our sleeves if we're going to learn and get ahead.

Victoria Glendinning: Antonia Fraser said to me, which was something I adopted, every intelligent woman must be a feminist. That I agree with. Of course I'm a feminist. How could one be a woman and not be? How could one say, I do not want the furtherance of my sex and not do what is best for women? Personally, I would survive without a man perfectly well if I were widowed tomorrow, but I certainly don't reject men totally like the most radical feminists.

479

Lady Annabel Goldsmith: I have never challenged any man's role.

I find American women rather aggressive, terribly unfeminine. If you go to a restaurant you see these women sitting together and their voices are so loud; they talk like men and drink like fish. American women have slightly lost their femininity, I really do think so, and I have noticed this for some time now. If you listen to them travelling on a plane, they will be swigging down Martinis and their voices are so loud, so abrasive, so frightening, so unfeminine. They are the opposite to how I would like to be myself.

I'm sure there are a lot of American feminine women, but I haven't met them. They started this whole thing of women's lib. All these ridiculous things about not having Father Christmas, it should be Mother Christmas; all those absurdities. They really have gone too far. I think the English are next in line. They're not as bad as the Americans, but whereas the Frenchwomen continue to achieve whatever they want to achieve while retaining their femininity, Englishwomen do only up to a point. They don't become so abrasive, but they are slightly more influenced by the Americans than the French. The Latins tend to keep their femininity.

I'm the most unliberated woman that's ever been. That doesn't mean to say I want to be a slave, but I'm definitely not a liberated woman. I'm very independent now, because I'm a loner. I like being by myself. I'm genuinely not afraid of being by myself, I love it. I don't get that chance very often, but I actually like it. I don't depend on, or have to have, a man for company. I'm perfectly happy by myself. If he's there, it's wonderful, if he's not, I'm quite happy. But I don't consider myself Jimmy's equal, or Mark's equal, or any man's equal.

Francine Gomez: Feminists are not real women. The ones who fought society got freedom for the others, but they are not real women. I don't consider myself a feminist.

Menie Grégoire: I was an extremely active feminist for twenty years until the moment when Frenchwomen were given, by law, everything I had been campaigning for. Then I stopped being a militant, and I am no longer in any way a feminist. I don't deny that I was one, and I would start again if I had to, but I don't see that there is anything to complain about now, nor that there is anything else to ask for. We must make use of what we have been given and it's up to us to fight to be able to profit

480

from it. I often say that women have nothing to ask from anyone except themselves.

For a month at RTL, I did a series of programmes on feminism – it's the most listened-to programme in France. I went over the history of feminism, the condition of women and what the present state of feminism was, with all that Mme Roudy was demanding and so on, and everyone laughed. Everyone who phoned or wrote in said, they're mad! Everyone made fun of Mme Roudy, who made pronouncements about pretty legs in advertising dishonouring women. When she was Minister for Women she forbade women to appear in advertising so that they would not become advertising objects themselves. Everyone just laughed!

Laura Gregory: I think women fight for themselves. No movement is going to make a woman's job easier. Only that woman herself can make her life any easier. I've never subscribed to any feminist movement to help me achieve what I have. In fact, I feel sometimes feminists can be a little bit bitter about their lot. Well, I am not bitter about being a woman. I wouldn't have it any other way. I love being a woman. And being a woman hasn't hindered me. Being myself is what is important.

Elsa Gress: Both sexes have, from the start, shown a genius for collaboration and a tolerance of variants, without which the race would not have survived. These positive traits and the glorious unused possibilities of both sexes have been counteracted through history by religious beliefs in man's basic wickedness, and recently by scientific beliefs in his basic aggressiveness. Sociologists thus labour to prove that traits like altruism and peaceful collaboration are merely 'the selfish gene' in disguise. Women, including neo-feminists, have swallowed this whole, though with the reservation that men are wickeder, that is, more aggressive. There is nothing to prove this is so. So instead of competing with men as humans in imaginative, creative ways, they spend energies and the capital of the future combating men in negative ways, imitating the worst features, flaunting the very aggressiveness and acquiring the very attitudes that should be counteracted in the interests of both sexes and their offspring.

Abstract 'sisterhood' is no solution to the troubles and tragedies arising from myths and misapprehensions about the sexes, and the very idea of our common heritage and a more humane future are sacrificed to yet another set of the old prejudices turned inside out.

There is a hell of a lot of difference between being a woman with a boring husband she can get rid of in the Western world, and being a maltreated wife in Calcutta. A well-pampered Western woman cannot begin to understand the terrible condition of women and men in less privileged circumstances.

The current liberation/sex revolution is backfiring because it is basically off target. Being of one sex or the other is not a cause, neither is having a little or a lot of sex. What can be, and have to be, fought for politically are certain rights, not privileged positions. The sex revolution is a male invention and not a new one. There have been earlier sexually liberated periods – Ancient Rome, pre-revolutionary France, the Restoration, the Weimar Republic – all disastrous, culturally and politically.

The very fact that, within one generation, women have become so masculinized and men so feminized is proof that the basic 'material' of the sexes, intellectually and emotionally, is not that different, and that the eternal battle of the sexes is socially conditioned rather than natural.

Baroness Grimond: The only thing I deplore about the feminist movement is that it forces women into behaving like men, on the grounds that, unless they behave like men, they can't get into the position where they can alter society. But if, in doing this, they destroy the gifts they have to give, then society as a whole is not going to be any better off.

Amy Gross: I've never felt professionally hampered. I am a feminist. I was in that first wave of journalists covering it and, as I once wrote in an article, I went in as a spy to find what these crazy women were up to and came out a convert. I have been a feminist since 1967. I basically work with women, I always have. I like men, and I like talking to them, but I find most men less interested in the things I am interested in. I am interested in very female concerns. I'm interested in emotions, relationships, women's politics. The only interests of mine that I share with men are peace and writing. I feel, for the most part, men and women want to talk in totally different languages.

Miriam Gross: I'm against all dogma. You can't live life by dogma. It always ends up by simplification and falsification. If you do things according to formulae, there are always faults because things are too complicated and there's too much variety in life. So in that sense, I'm not a feminist. And if everything feminists want to happen happened,

482

life would become intolerable. Also, in some sense, they go against biology. I'm afraid I think that having children is such an important part of women's life and that some feminists, most feminists, just ignore that factor. In a way, it is *the* important thing in any woman's life.

I'm always surprised that the women's movement and so on don't somehow think it wonderful that Mrs Thatcher is Prime Minister. I don't know why, but they hate her. I admire her enormously. Not particularly for her politics, but for her achievement in being a woman and being so powerful. I think it's a tremendous act of will and character. And I think it's absolutely extraordinary, when I listen to Question Time in Parliament, the way she answers questions in this roomful of men. It's absolutely astonishing, and I find it hard to analyse the hatred of her, particularly by women. I think it's partly because her object hasn't been to be a liberated woman; her object has been to be Prime Minister and she doesn't actually make a thing of women's liberation.

Pamela Gross: Why deny our feminine traits? It's sad to me. I went to school at Sarah Lawrence for two years, and a lot of women there were very involved in political ways; a lot of them were lesbians, and they cut off all their hair and dressed very boyishly and walked very macho, and no make-up, and sort of angry and bitter. Now, if we're advocating women, let's be women, let's still be feminine. I don't think it's unnatural for a woman to be a woman, and I don't think it's a disadvantage for a woman to be feminine. Yet all those words have become negative, as if men have made us, or conditioned us to behave in this way. I don't believe it. I feel comfortable behaving in a feminine way, it's my nature and I felt very attacked by those political lesbians at Sarah Lawrence who told me that what I was doing was wrong when it felt right to me.

I'm not a feminist. I think it's frightening what Gloria Steinem has done to us women. The feminists turned me off, and I'm a woman, so I don't know what men must think. I think a lot of men are confused. I have grown up with the boys who are the products of this thinking, and many of them don't know how to treat us, don't understand what we want from them, don't know if they should open the door, not open the door. They're confused, they don't know, and I don't know if we know. I really feel for a lot of the women who today are waking up alone. They live in their own homes that they've bought for themselves in the country. They're depressed, they don't have families, they want families. If they didn't want families, I would say, fine, they've got what they wanted. But a lot of them have wanted to marry all their lives, and now, here they are, with their china set and their silver, and they don't have a husband and children and they're scared.

Flora Groult: My mother was a feminist without knowing the word existed. She had children very late in life, she had already achieved and worked, at a time when women didn't work. She'd say, never depend on a man. I believe very much in feminism. I think you must be excessive and the feminists were excessive, brandishing their bras and their anger. That doesn't matter. The first soldiers always are in the front line and will be killed, but they are useful. Feminism has been very useful to women, and it's not finished, and we all have to be very much on the alert, all us women. I am a feminist as long as women need help. Feminist is a bad word in a way, because we don't say masculinist. We say feminist because there are some things that need to be done. When women have real equality of rights, there will be no need for the word. When women have the same rights as men, the feminist movement won't exist any more. You don't need central heating if you have it.

Georgina Hale: I'm not into any women's movements, haven't been on any women's marches or anything. I could find that pretty heavy. I do love women and I think they are great, but, equally, to be in a room with fifty women that look more like men, rolling up their Woodbines – no thank you.

Jerry Hall: Before I had the children I used to think women's lib such a bunch of bull: all these women going on about all this stuff, yet there are still all these girls who live with a guy for two years and get millions of dollars alimony and then there's secretaries who want to be executives and if they don't get their way in the office they burst into tears. I thought, women wanted to be liberated, but they're still using their old tricks; the whole women's lib campaign is too anti-men, so many things you read are so anti-men, and so aggressive; I don't think women should be like that. But when I got pregnant, then I started seeing the unfairness of being a woman, because your body gets deformed, it gets huge, and the man stays perfectly normal, and that's so unfair that one sex gets deformed for the benefit of both sexes. That made me think more about women, that maybe they've got a point. Then you have to look after the children, they're your responsibility, you have to be the perfect mother, you have to be the perfect wife, you have to run the

484

house. And to be important in our society, you have to have a career – you have to be this sort of superwoman, and it's very difficult.

Lucy Hughes-Hallett: What I mean by saying I'm a feminist is that I think the topic of relationships between the sexes and definitions of gender is an immensely important area of inquiry. It matters, and it hasn't been fully understood, and there's a lot of work to be done and changes to be made. I don't mean I have a set of answers to those questions. The sexes are interdependent. It's actually a pity that this movement has been called feminism because I think it is actually just as important to men, and men can contribute as much to it as women, because what we're talking about is a relationship, not about women on their own.

Katharine Hamnett: Women are different from men. I don't see that one is better. Both are necessary for the race to continue. They're equal, but different, and each should treat the other with total respect. I'm not a separatist. That's rubbish, it's ridiculous – some of my best friends are men. That whole thing really annoyed me: you shouldn't wear pretty clothes, you shouldn't use your body to attract. Why not? It's beautiful. God gave it to you, it's part of the magic of existence. It's an insult to creation to say you shouldn't celebrate everything.

Mrs Thatcher's a very aggressive woman, she's very good at arguing, she's quick, she's ferocious, she's ferociously haughty in a way. Nobody's prepared to stand up to her. I mean – Westland or Oman – everybody's scared. She's done nothing for women. I think Aquino has done more for women. OK, it's interesting to have a woman Prime Minister, but Mrs Thatcher's been so dreadful that I think it's unlikely we'll get another one in a hurry. I don't think that what she's done would have been tolerated from a man.

Claire Harrison: I grew up in an era when we haven't had to worry about whether we were liberated. I was born in 1962, so the fight was already fought by the time I became conscious of my position or standing in the world. But I think that, from the feminist point of view, we're going backwards, because everyone is going out and trying to get their job, and we're having a remake of the 1950s in a way, at least in the United States, where everybody is just thinking about their own lives and their own thing and not worrying about political issues whatsoever. I am not in any way anti-feminist. I wanted to get involved

485

in it, because I realized that I was born into advantages that I take for granted, as do many of my peers, but I think that feminism the way it is now, the movement, the people who live and work for that, are very messed up.

Nicky Hart: I am happy to associate myself with feminism. My feminism doesn't exclude men, but I can understand women wanting to be alone. Women have to be able to be separate from men in some ways, to organize their views and structure some kind of approach and give them self-confidence, so I can understand women that want to live their lives without men. I can't live without men myself, but separatists presumably have had a much harder time with men, or haven't felt as attracted to them, or as intrigued. I like men, because I like challenges. Because I'm a masochist probably, as well. I wouldn't allow a man to dominate me. I think that's why men always disappoint me, because each time I naïvely believe that I will find an intelligent man who is actually just like me except he happens to be a man with all the other parts. And then I get disappointed when I realize he's not in fact.

Romaine Hart: In the working classes, men and women go out to work, and the wife comes home and still cooks the dinner. And in the upper classes, the man goes out to work, and I don't know what the wife does all day, but she certainly isn't a feminist. All this is also influenced by the whole attitude, the whole political outlook of the men, the newspapers they take in the house, the whole rigidity of the English upper-class system. I have lived part of my life within that system, because I lived for nine years in Cheshire. During that time, my husband belonged to the Territorial Army, and so I lived with army people, with the kind of upper-class army people that are now commanding regiments all round the world. We read *The Times* and I was Conservative and I was part of that whole thing because that was my husband's view and I took it on. When I came back to London, I became emancipated, I ran my own business, I was much more capable than my husband, and there was no more need for my husband. My views totally changed, and I could see things very clearly about the world, about politics, about everything.

Women will not stand still, they will move, but not that far. Mrs Thatcher may be Prime Minister, but Mrs Thatcher is not a woman. Mrs Thatcher is in no way a woman. She has no intuition, she has no understanding, she has nothing of a woman in her, she has no intelligence. Mrs Thatcher is a machine.

Kitty Hawks: I believe in women having the same opportunities as men. I don't think there is any reason that they shouldn't. And if that's a feminist, then I am one. Certainly, if I were asked to campaign against a law that discriminated against women, I would. Because I don't think it's fair. We should be allowed to try to do whatever we want. If we fail, we fail. Even now, when I walk down the street, past a construction site, unless I am dressed deliberately to distract their attention away from me instead of to me, men are going to whistle. And that is, in its way, a form of discrimination. We have to endure certain humiliations that men don't have to endure. And one is told there are companies where women sue because they are fired because they have pre-menstrual syndrome or because the boss wants to sleep with them and they say, no. That is a form of discrimination which men do not have to endure.

I think conditioning is going to be less rigid, probably. But the chances are that the mother is still not going to encourage her daughter to play football, that she is still not going to encourage her son to be a ballerina. I think there is a price to pay for going against that thing that the biology makes easy. We don't live in a society any more where it's about hunting and gathering and cooking and raising children. Those societies exist, and it's interesting how they just keep going, and how the more primitive the tribe, the more clear those rules are, and I can't help but think that the people who live in them are happier. Because the confusion that goes on here is devastating. Men are confused beyond belief. I don't think they like it when a woman orders herself a drink in a restaurant. It's very weird being a woman when you begin to be aware of this. You think, why should this matter? Why should a man's masculinity or sense of himself be bound up in some gesture that small, like opening the door? But they still want a vestige of the representation of their strength and their authority. And women, in trying to establish their own territory, have taken a lot of that away and men really haven't had time to adjust to it. So a lot of them are confused.

Brooke Hayward: The question finally is this: if men and women are brought up to expect equal lives and equal opportunities on both the family level and on the earning-power level, what is going to happen to the family? Who is going to raise the children? We see in this country already a large portion of high achievers in the women's workforce completely and absolutely ambivalent now about whether they should go back and raise these children. They are not juggling it so well. They don't have the time. Let's say these young women of thirty-five, thirty-six suddenly decide they want to have a family. They are, let's say, the editor of *Vogue* magazine, and now they've got a tiny child at home, and although they thought they could juggle it nicely, they can't. My impression is we are going to see more and more of this, and I'd like to know what is going to happen to the children.

Cynthia Heimel: I don't understand the word liberated. I've never been able to feel liberated. I don't know anybody, especially in 1986 in New York City, who feels liberated.

Marie Helvin: I wouldn't say I am a feminist, but I would say I am definitely a woman of the 1980s, and I am in my thirties, so I am a product of all those years that saw the rise of feminism.

Margaux Hemingway: I'm not a gung-ho feminist, but I do think that things should be equal.

Anouska Hempel: I am not really a feminist. I don't mind the imbalance, long may it live. If we all had the equal opportunities they are all screaming out about, I think we'd find an awful lot of women wouldn't be doing an awful lot of things at all. Because they wouldn't be able to. But you can take advantage of the imbalance to be able to do whatever it is that you have to do.

Women have been out there expressing their desire to be equal, to be this, to be that and the other, but I wouldn't say they've done an awful lot with it. They've overdone it, they've overplayed their hand. It works much better to take a step back or to the side and reassess the situation and come back as it really ought to be. It's safer. It's safety. It's safety because of the sexual problems we have now. It's safety emotionally, and I think one really ought to face up to the fact that women need to be safe, to be loved and wanted. And they need to have a chap. And that's that. You can go on and do anything else you want with your life after that, but you do need that basic structure.

This battle of equal opportunities and things being open to women is something I wish women simply wouldn't keep banging on about. It's not really how they want it at all. They don't want the opportunities. They prefer to stay at home and not be a success and not to have had the opportunity and always give you, give themselves a reason for staying there, for not being able to take up the challenge, for not being able to do it. Because a lot of women can't do it. They haven't got the ingredients on the total level. They've got an ingredient academically, intellectually, but they haven't got the rest of whatever it is – the energy or the pragmatic approach – to push those things right to the foreground. Life isn't equal. Life isn't fair. Some women are short, some women are tall, some are fat, some are thin. They're all different. It depends what you do with it.

Val Hennessy: When I first began to think about the concept of feminism, I was perhaps in my late twenties, I'd got two children, and I hadn't really given it all that much thought. Then I began to read all this stuff in the magazines and I thought, yes, yes, I must give this some thought. I was living in Brighton and I went along to the Brighton Women's Group consciousness-raising session, and I was dead nervous because I was very new to all this and I felt I might not fit in because actually I was very happily married, loved my husband, loved my children. At the first session I nearly died. An American woman lay on a table, took off her knickers, lay on her back with her legs stretched out and said, sisters, the first process in getting to know ourselves as women is to get to know our vaginas. I nearly died. I thought, I am going to pass out with embarrassment. I can't believe this is happening. But because I didn't want not to look like one of the sisters, I stood there, I stuck it out, and she said we had all got to look at her vagina. And then she said, once we had all looked at her vagina, each of us in turn was to sit with our legs spread for all the other women, and we must say, this is my vagina, I am a woman and I am proud of my vagina. Well, I watched the first woman do it, and I thought, Jesus, I *am* going to die, I am actually going to *die*. I just said, I'm sorry, I am finding this very embarrassing, I really don't want to stay, can I go? She said, ah, that is because you've been so hung up by the paternalistic, the patriarchal society, you have been made to think your vagina is disgusting and revolting. And I said, I haven't at all, I actually don't give it all that much thought, and I certainly don't find it disgusting or revolting, but I would find it disgusting and revolting to lie here with my legs spread open with all these totally strange women looking up it. Furthermore, I would question *you*. I think you're the female equivalent of a male flasher, lying there displaying yourself in this manner. Then she got this thing called a speculum and put it up herself and said we all had to look up, at which point I simply couldn't handle it – handle it is rather an unfortunate expression – couldn't join in. I thought it was rather perverse and bizarre and terribly pathetic. That actually completely put me off the radical women's movement. I'm sure they're not all like that, and obviously I wasn't tuned in in some way, but that really put me off it.

Carolina Herrera: I'm not a feminist. For equal work women should have equal pay, but I don't agree that women are self-sufficient. I think women need men around. That's why you don't find many women wanting to live alone. Some pretend, but they always end up looking around for a man. And they always end up getting married. The ideal of a woman is to be married. It is also very flattering to have a man around, next to you when you go out, when you go to a restaurant, get into a car; they open the door and all that. I'm very feminine – I love it.

Elizabeth Hess: I'm a feminist who simply believes in equality of women and men. I don't hate men; I love men, and I'm fascinated by men. But I have certainly gone through periods of my life where I have had more of the separatist politics than I have now. I think that was a necessary transitional stage for many feminists; they had to back away from men and really unite with each other to figure out who they were and what they thought. But the women's movement has grown up, and most women in that movement are now working with men.

Most men now are coming up against women in all aspects of their lives, women who are very powerful and as articulate as they are. Women are not willing to simply nurture them, and feed them, and pretend they are not equal. Many women are so unsatisfied by patronizing relationships that they simply abandon them. They've realized they don't need them. I think it's terrifying for men to realize they are no longer needed by women, and I think it's creating a tremendous amount of antagonism. The illusion of the knight in shining armour, the romance that if you are a woman you will end up, at some point in your life, happily married with a two-car garage and somebody who will support you for the rest of your life – women don't grow up thinking that any more. Men don't support women financially for the rest of their lives any more; most women, if they have children, support them themselves at one point or another.

Min Hogg: I'm not militant because I've never felt the need. I wouldn't join any of them, for all the tea in China, and march and shout and spit and stuff. All that stupid business. We aren't going to be men. Why don't they do it by looking clean and pretty? Dreadful hags, making themselves worse than they are. I can't see the point in anyone making themselves look and appear worse than they really are. Why not everybody look better than God made them? What is make-up for? I'd die if I couldn't wear some make-up.

Arianna Stassinopoulos Huffington: I never felt inhibited. In fact, that was the reason I wrote my first book, *The Female Woman*. When I was at Cambridge, the women's liberation movement was at its height and I organized my farewell debate at the Cambridge Union on that subject. My theme was that women could have all the equal opportunities and equal pay they wanted and deserved, but didn't have to deny or negate the fact they were women; that that was really an incredible gift and it could go hand in hand with whatever other career opportunities, pay, equality we wanted. That was so natural for me, because that was how I was brought up. Even though I was surrounded by women's inequality in our own household, I was brought up with a feeling that women could do absolutely anything and there was nothing men could do that women couldn't.

There are disadvantages, but I am very concerned about the tendency to present women as victims. I always feel that this is not a very fruitful way to look at a problem. If we look at ourselves as being able to overcome any disadvantages – socially, by changing legislation, by changing conventions and rules, but also by overcoming them as individuals – we are if anything much more likely to see more women in positions of responsibility; rather than by taking the alternative approach, which is that women are still victimized by society, still victimized by the conventions into which they are brought up. This I find an ultimately very destructive way to look at the world. A lot of women sometimes talk in terms of being victimized by their men, their husbands or their fathers, and I always feel, as I felt when I was writing the biography of Maria Callas, because she had that tendency too, that victims never change anything. If you look at yourself as a victim, the chances are that you will remain in that position, because, by virtue of the way you look at yourself, you have taken away your power to act and change your condition. There are many facts that can be brought forward to show that women are still discriminated against. All I'm saying is that's not the way to approach the problem. What we want to see is women achieving results in any area of life, with equal advantage on an equal basis. That's what everybody agrees on, so to go on harping on women being discriminated against, women being victimized and downtrodden, isn't the way to go about it. It would be much more productive to go about it with the realization that women can do anything and it is up to us to change whatever conditions don't work, rather than to feel we are actually oppressed and thrown into extremely difficult situations.

Caroline Huppert: I don't like women to use their femininity as an alibi to hide behind, to say I can't do that because of the problems of being a woman. Men have problems, too. They could say, I couldn't do that because I am a man. So I don't like that argument. But I have great sympathy for what you could call social feminism. It worries me that the government is overwhelmingly male, because it is true that a woman's life is more complicated than a man's and it is only changing very slowly. As an artist, I am not a feminist, I think we should get on with what we've got. But it is a scandal that there aren't more crèches, nursery schools, and that everyday life should be so complicated for a woman. The traditional housewife and mother – that idea still exists, and it makes life impossible. Things should be changing much faster. There are little details: to meet your child's teacher, you have to go during school hours, and that's impossible for a working woman; 70 per cent of women in Paris work, yet the whole educational system is still based on the idea of the mother at home. It's lamentable. So my feminism is more concerned with the woman in the street than with intellectual abstractions.

Angela Huth: There are an awful lot of earnest women around today. It comes with feminism, I think, and this great grinding desire women have to be equal and not discriminated against, and to be sure of getting their rights. And all this pushiness on the part of women has made them horribly earnest, which I think is a pity.

Feminist women care about conditioning and everything, and are trying very hard not to mind if little boys want to play with girls' toys and get all the gender things muddled up in childhood. But in the end, you know, boys will out and do whatever is in their nature, and girls will do the same. I don't think you can push too far in all this conditioning. It irritates me intensely to see children's books with pictures of fathers washing up. They go mad in this great struggle to have everyone equal, and the fact is we are in no way equal with men and never will be, thank God. How boring it would be if we were.

I am a feminist, wholly feminist, I suppose, in that I think we should all have equal opportunities, equal wages and the rest. But it has to be said against women that, given the equal opportunities in large companies, for instance, they are very rarely equal. The only large company I have really worked for for any length of time has been the BBC, which employs a lot of women. And it is always the women who take time off, it is always the women who are ill, who are having babies, who have to deal with the domestic things. I know that is bad luck, but they are getting the same wages in some departments as men and they aren't there as much. I am not saying it is their fault, but because of their nature – we are the frailer sex, I suppose, and we have the domestic responsibilities – they are not able to be there and be quite as reliable in some ways as men. That will make women furious, but I really do believe it. I am rather against women. I think they are a whingeing lot at the moment.

Angela Janklow: I would never want to be considered feminist. I wouldn't want a woman running this country. I just think they are more unpredictable. I think that men are more immature. Men are largely not what they appear to be, and not what they want to be; they are much weaker than they think they are. But that doesn't mean they are weaker than women. Women are chemically imbalanced at least 7 days $\times$ 12 = 84 days. I know that to be true, because personally, I have very bad experience with that. In England now you can get off a murder charge by invoking pre-menstrual syndrome. Your period does affect your personality, there's no getting around it.

We have to co-exist. I do not think women are superior. Absolutely not, and I'm probably anti-ERA – Equal Rights Amendment. Women deserve a place intellectually, but I think the feminist movement is somewhat responsible for the death of femininity. It has changed the opinions of many people, both positively, in that they see women more for intellectual beings, but also in that it's caused a lot of backlash against women. There was always a suppression of women, but women coming into their own and exerting themselves has caused a backlash. So it is sort of a no-win situation for us, which is very unfortunate. But if we just sit and shut up, we are ignored and insulted, and if we rise up, we are being downed.

In some ways, I am aggressive, but I am very secure in my femininity. I can speak directly and strongly, but just as easily I can wear pink and lace. Career, ambition is not my highest goal. I hate to see what is happening to women with their fitted tailored outfits and briefcases, defeminizing themselves in order to be taken seriously. For instance, when I was interviewing for jobs, in September 1985, I went to Murdoch, and I went to see one of his men, John Evans, who runs many of the magazines. And the first thing he said was, you should wear your hair pulled back to an interview. Now if there's one thing I like about myself it is that I have long curly hair; I am complimented on it all the time. I was wearing a perfectly tailored suit, I was very well-dressed, I wasn't wearing 8,000 different colour eyeshadows and lots of foundation, I looked nothing like a tart at all. I wasn't wearing black, I wasn't wearing seamed stockings, and for him to make a comment like that, I almost spat on him and left. That made me sick, physically sick. How dare he? What does he want me to do? Pull my hair back so I look like a skull, so that I look like a eunuch? That's not me. I wouldn't work for him if he offered me the editor-in-chief of any of his publications.

Margaret Jay: The whole thing about being a feminist with a capital F is that it implies a number of rather extreme attitudes which often verge on hostility to men, which I certainly don't share. I don't feel hostility to men at all, and therefore I don't have any sympathy with that. On the other hand, I can feel a sense of solidarity with a lot of women, but not women *per se*, any more than I feel a hostility to men *per se*. I may feel that in a particular relationship a woman has been treated badly by a man and feel sympathy for the woman and very negative towards the man. On the other hand, in another relationship, I may feel that the woman has behaved badly. If you look at an employer, I may feel the woman has been discriminated against; in another situation I might feel that the woman wasn't good enough for that job. So I don't see myself as being a waver of a woman's banner at all.

Rana Kabbani: I am not a separatist. But I would say that I believe that men and women are completely equal, and that women should struggle every day of their lives to enforce that. Because it's not taken for granted by a long shot. It's something that has to be worked for, and struggled for, and one has to be militant without shunning men totally and without perceiving them as the enemy. But one has to work within the framework of society to change it. I think I do feel a lot of hostility to men, but that is probably repressed in me. Sometimes my reactions to men are so violent. Why do I have hostility towards men? I think because of the way women are treated in the world men have created. I perceive men as people with power who abuse it.

Elaine Kaufman: The Jewish momma has real power, she runs everything. And reaffirms the husband's position. These women's libbers don't understand this.

I've just always gone on and done what I wanted. I didn't need anybody to tell me that I had to move one way or another because there's a new social group that says so. I think the feminist movement is great for equal pay, which is a more natural thing. From there in, I don't know what the other benefits are. I think it's disturbed the whole family structure, made women feel worthless in basic needs, in having families, made bringing up children less important, when it is all-important. It's as much a job, and an interesting job, as it ever was, and just because a group of women got together and said, no, it's not, doesn't make it correct. They've destroyed more than they've helped. And they're only interested in the major achievers. You watch how they all group together. It's a clique and it has nothing to do with the average woman, it has to do with over-achievers. The working class can't afford to be feminist, and it's not very amusing. To be socially accepted in the working class is still to be accepted by the male.

I don't think men have it so wonderful. They have a lot of trouble with the image, because a man wants to prove himself macho all the time, because of this performance business: modern society expects him to perform, not only in commerce, but sexually, emotionally and everywhere. He's got to perform. Let me tell you something. The women's rights have fucked themselves, royally. Now let them go play with it. There's no way for anybody to get married any more. Forget it.

Dillie Keane: I am a feminist by virtue of the fact I live the life I do. However, it's a very pejorative word now. Feminism has come to mean something it didn't ten years ago. Feminists you associate with dungarees and hairy armpits now. That's not me, I wear make-up and I take care of my appearance. I am a feminist with a small f, yes. I want to go on working till the day I drop. And I am very proud that I don't live off anybody, with anybody else's money supporting me. And I shall go on doing that, God willing. I don't think the sexes can survive without each other. That's foolish. That's why I dislike the feminist movement. I feel that sort of lesbian feminist separatist movement is as irrelevant as the typical bachelor club. It is just as divisive. We've got to get on with one another to reproduce, so we might as well try and like one another.

Caroline Kellett: There are too many women working too hard at being equal, and they are making men frightened, which is why there are so many men who are gay now. Particularly in America, women are so much more up front and aggressive and forthright, that men feel so threatened they don't want involvement. Those women are, in a way, making life harder for intelligent women who appreciate being feminine but who are also ambitious. In the next ten or twenty years, there'll be a swing back to the more maternal, elemental earth-mother woman, the figurehead who doesn't feel second rate or supercilious simply because she is very good at being a mother and wife. I think that's what women

495

were biologically intended to be. It's a great gift to be feminine, and amusing, and intelligent without presenting a threat or a challenge to a man. Women who, as perhaps I did at sixteen, feel they have to be equal, to be a challenge, independent and as good, if not better, make more problems for themselves than they need to.

In America, men are being hounded emotionally and physically, and in the work context. They are actually being put off, they are retreating. The women have over-compensated to such an extent that they are actually becoming tiresome, or are just becoming stereotypes. The whole idea of women trying to dress like men in the workplace, which is far more apparent in America, is ludicrous. Obviously you are not going to tart into the office in a lace dress, but this business of the black ties, the flowing cravat, the dark suit, the trainers, the short haircut, the harsh make-up – all this movement towards too little definition between the sexes, which is very, very typical of this age – is ludicrous.

Mary Kenny: Some of the feminist aspirations are very anti-female, and they are very hard and insensitive to women's caring nature. In a book that Emma Cross wrote, called *Male Secrets*, she said, women will mother. The mothering instinct will come out, no matter what you do to it. If it's not children, it's animals, it's plants, it's gardens, it's the most idiotic things. This is the maternal instinct.

Some of the things that the middle class or the rich find in liberation turn out to be a tyranny for poorer people. For example, it's obvious that easier divorce is fine if you can afford it. That's really what it comes down to: if you can afford a good nanny, if you can afford the alimony, if you can afford to support two families. But when it comes to poorer people, it often just means that the woman is not provided for.

Griselda Kerr: I think the difference in the sexes is something to be protected. That difference will need a cataclysmic event to wipe it out, thank goodness. One is always told that women can get into colder seas, women can bear various degrees of pain more easily than men. I earnestly doubt that they are physically a weaker sex. The women in politics seem to show that women can stand up to the rigours of political life just as well as men, though I couldn't be a politician in a million years, I couldn't work on four hours' sleep a night. I certainly need all the physical and moral support my husband can give me. And I constantly wonder whether I'm giving him support. He says I am. I get much tireder than he does. I love being treated as a woman. It's so silly to talk about such mundane things, but I love dressing up, making myself look pretty for people, car doors being opened for me, being brought flowers. I like people standing up when I come into the room. They very seldom do, but I notice it and I love it.

Princess Yasmin Aga Khan: I wouldn't become a feminist. I wouldn't categorize myself. I think that what makes men and women so wonderful is that they are very different.

Soraya Khashoggi: The laws are so ridiculous now. We've taken fifty years to become liberated, and now we don't know what to do with it. We are going to take another fifty years to undo all the damage half those women have done.

All women, just by being women, can influence the man in their life, be he husband or the father. Take the example of one's own daughters. The father is usually completely wrapped around the daughter's little finger. Without realizing it, she's using her sex. I think you can get whatever you want out of a man, either by being a dumb or an intelligent woman. You don't have to burn your bra and stand on soap boxes and chain yourself to the fence.

Lesley Kingcome: I don't think I am a feminist at all. I'm certainly not a Ms. I believe in equal opportunities, but the feminists are boring women on the whole; the ones that I can think of, on the whole, are very dreary.

Irma Kurtz: We women have reached a point where we must say we are partly responsible for this situation and we are the ones who have got to change. It is my theory, my firm belief, that nobody else can be depended upon to change when a situation is not good. You've got to change yourself. The other person cannot be bullied, coerced, threatened. There is no way to change another person's mind, you can only change your own. Women have to see the situation as it exists, and adapt, thereby changing it slowly, slowly, slowly, slowly. It has changed enormously in the past fifteen/twenty years.

Some of the girls who write to me, twenty-three and already married two or three times, are still looking for Mr Wonderful. They still think that romance should continue after marriage. We are the most unrealistic romantics. A lot of the girls who write to me, certainly in the

United States (and I get letters from Japan, Australia, South Africa), see this women's liberation that all supposedly struggle so hard for – and we did work pretty hard in lots of ways to get certain laws changed – as liberating them into a Mills & Boon novel.

My job is to talk to women. Men are nice people, some of my best friends are men, but my actual job is to address myself to women. And it's no good for me to say, come on, women, get angry, get out there, fight the men. All I can say is, understand and take responsibility for yourself. Women, since the beginning of time, have been responsible for everybody else, but not responsible for themselves. What we really have to learn is to be responsible for ourselves. And whenever I start getting into the argument of men *versus* women, my mind blanks, because I don't see it in those terms. I don't see it as a conflict. I see the problem is there, but I see only that the solutions lie with us.

Verity Lambert: I don't believe that, if a woman makes a choice to marry, have a family, she cannot be a feminist. Women should have that choice. I also believe that the role of a mother and looking after a family is very important, and that a woman should be allowed to have some sense of pride in it. But if a woman does decide to work, there should be a career structure in the same way as there is for men: they should have the same opportunities, and they should be thought of as equal when they go into areas where they are working alongside men.

I don't think Mrs Thatcher understands working women's problems at all. I think she feels that she is a working woman, that she has managed to do all these things that women complain about, and she forgets she's had a lot of help. I wouldn't expect her to take on women's rights as part of her brief, because she is PM and she has to deal with things fairly and in a decent fashion, but she has actively said that women should go back to the home, that they are taking men's jobs away from them. She is very unsympathetic to women in working roles. I don't know whether she sets out to bully men, or whether she simply is an intransigent person. What I do think is that she has done nothing for women while she's been Prime Minister, and in fact I think she has done the reverse. I think she has actually set women's liberation back.

Women don't dress for men. Women dress for themselves. And other women, actually. I don't go out when I buy a dress and say, gosh, well, what effect is it going to have on a man? I just look at it and say, does this make me look fat, thin, tall, short? I'm only interested in how I perceive myself.

Marghanita Laski: This anger of women against their situation is very similar to the suffragette anger in the early 1900s, and, indeed, to similar angers earlier, and it makes me rather angry because it seems to me that there are so many causes, if people want to take up causes, so much more important. Just as the suffragettes started agitating for themselves and were mostly middle-class women and privileged in a time when a third of the population of England was living below the poverty line, so women are still agitating for themselves, and the agitation is all an agitation of middle-class women, not an agitation of working-class women, and a fifth of England is living below the poverty line. Most of the revolutions, most of the creative work happened in the middle classes, but this particular movement does annoy me. I'm afraid it will erode the sexual delights between men and women.

Someone once said, only my enemies can make me a Jew, and I feel only my enemies can make me a woman, or a black, or a cripple.

I'd like to like Mrs Thatcher. She was at my college, I was very proud that we have the first woman Prime Minister. But I think simply Mrs Thatcher is felt by everyone now to be a dislikable woman. Perhaps one sees in her the kind of schoolteacher who was most unsympathetic and most dislikable, who didn't enter into anybody's sympathies, who simply despised and patronized people.

A great deal has been said, without much historical knowledge, about the position of women, particularly about the position of women in the last century, and I think women were, if they wished to be, a very great deal freer than it's normally supposed they were. Certainly, in a family relationship, whether the man or woman was dominant has always depended on the nature of the man and the woman and not in the least on anything to do with society. And I think that is equally so in, say, Chinese societies, Arab societies, where the dominance of the male is far more obvious than it is here.

I don't believe that the past is relevant. Everybody lives in their own generation, not their mother's.

Frances Lear: I am a profound feminist.

My mother, whose own life made me a feminist, was married to two men. The first one failed her in the most profound way; the second one abused her. There was nothing she could do with either, because she had no means of support for herself or for me. At one point, when there

499

was a conflict between my stepfather and me, she chose to remain with my stepfather and I had to leave the house, because she could not survive without him. When I was a child, I heard the expression a great deal, oh, what a good marriage she made. He's worth *blah*, *blah*, his father has so much. And then I heard in more secret conversations, she married for money, she married for money. Now, that's one of the taboos of our society, like incest. The fact that women marry for money is a taboo. You don't say it. But it's true.

Economics to me is the ability of a woman to earn a living. It would be true if you substituted the word man. And that is hindered and lessened by many forces, but it's the crux of the war between men and women. Because if a woman has no means to earn a living, she is dependent upon a man. When she is dependent upon a man, she is not free. She also doesn't trust him, because if you're dependent, you can't trust. There cannot be a healthy relationship if you're dependent upon somebody else for survival. By keeping women dependent, men really are very self-destructive. They think that they're doing something which is good for them by keeping the woman with them, but what they are really doing is keeping somebody with them who wishes to be without them – very often. There is a survey which has just been taken by one of the women's magazines, which shows that 38 per cent of the women who had married men in the past would not have married them if they had to do it now, they would not have married their husbands; 85 per cent of the men said that they would marry their wives again.

Many of the women who began the American feminist revolution were lesbians. They were women who had been abused by men, who hated men, so this flaw, this crack that runs down the centre of feminism keeps coming out in every area. You have to examine those areas each time and say, is this the sensibility that hates men, or is this the good feminist? I call them the good feminists and the bad feminists. It's that simple. The good feminist believes in women's rights, the bad feminist believes in women's rights because she hates men.

Women need to understand that they are separate human beings, and that whatever life affords them – their mortality, their ageing, loss, abandonment, abuse – they will meet it by themselves, even though they use things from other people. If women could consider themselves separate, I think a lot would happen in the relationship between men and women. It's that women consider themselves attached to things, to people, to their jobs, to their children. If they would just stand in their centre of their universe...

Sara Leighton: I've always felt that feminists do more to destroy their cause than to help it. Feminism, to me, is equal rights for women and men, to be treated as an equal human being and not as an inferior sex. That to me is feminism, and if it's more complicated than that, then I don't understand it.

Doris Lessing: I don't agree with the feminists most of the time. I do think they tend to be very fanatical. I understand why they think like that, I understand how they've reached this frame of mind. It's just that I don't agree with it. They didn't invent friendship between women; they seem to talk as if friendship between women was invented in the 1960s, which is a very extraordinary thing. They seem not to take into account the history, the long history of women's friendships, which has always existed, side by side with their relationships with men.

I don't agree with the feminists when they say men are responsible for wars, that if women ran the world there would be no wars. The behaviour of the feminist movement proves it. They tend to be tremendously violent to their opponents, and unkind, and I think this is just historical nonsense that women are kind and full of generous emotions and men are not. I don't agree with it. Nor even necessarily more compassionate. I always come back to the individual. There are always individuals – men and women – who have got these qualities.

There is no good telling a woman that she's free if she has to ask her husband for money to buy something. It's all right if it's a good marriage, and there are many of them, but they are not all good marriages, and this whole revolution, the women's revolution, hasn't touched the working women in any country.

Maureen Lipman: There has to be a way of not becoming a man in order just to have men work for you, without then going to the other extreme and doing what Mrs Thatcher does – you know, totally feminine and sincere, softly spoken, with a heart of solid aluminium.

Women have built-in shit detectors. If there's one thing we do have which is different from the majority of men, it's that we can sniff a phoney out at a distance of twenty yards. And I think that's probably because we have had to suffer all these patronizing years of being patted and told to do things in certain ways, and you must be nice, and so on. A bunch of girls at school is not a pretty sight I can promise you. A bunch of girls of about twelve to thirteen in a classroom can be very cruel, very

501

cliquish, very difficult, always ganging up one against the other with, you know, we don't like her, we'll set on her. But it trains you early on to spot a phoney, and we are very observant of people's lack of sincerity, of people putting on acts, because we have to put on so many ourselves. The truly good agony aunt is someone who has every neurosis she's prescribing against. Anna Raeburn, I would imagine, makes a good agony aunt because she is totally jam-packed with every neurosis in the book. So you learn early on to spot an act, and if there's one thing that a woman can't stand it's a bad act that succeeds. And, in Mrs Thatcher, you have the most patently insincere, manipulated, built image – the voice, the hair. I've nothing against plastic surgery, but somebody has packaged that particular person into an image that has so many holes in it, for me personally, that I can't believe they have a percentage lead.

Mrs Thatcher's completely against everything that women, over the last few years, have striven for. That's why intelligent women hate her. Everything we've worked towards. She wants women back in the home. The only person she is giving half a chance to is Mrs Currie, who makes Thatcher look positively genial. She doesn't want women to succeed in the way she has. She's not like anything we have set out to accomplish. She's not sincere, she's bullying, she's heckling, she's a very bad judge of character. I mean what minister, what person in any high-ranking job, could have chosen such appalling people, such a ghouls' gallery? The sort of men she surrounds herself with are the sort of men women have been desperate to avoid: smoothies, terrible smoothies. Jeffrey Archer – you spend two minutes in a room with Jeffrey Archer, or on a platform, as I have, and you see an ego the Albert Hall could not contain.

Lady Lothian: It's totally part of my being, of my selfhood, part of my religion even, that I love justice, love lack of hypocrisy, love equality. And just as I am a feminist, I am also a paid-up member of the anti-apartheid movement. I am a feminist because I think women were so discriminated against – equal pay, equal opportunity, and in terms of the family. If a relative got ill, it was never the son who had to come home and look after the relative. I remember an aunt who was an almoner at St Thomas's Hospital, a brilliant almoner. When her mother got ill, she was the one who had to go home and look after her. It's these sort of injustices that I couldn't bear, and so definitely I became a feminist. But I am a feminist in the same way as I am anti-racist.

I think that what my feminist friends and colleagues would say of Mrs

Thatcher is that she is not a sister. That's quite an emotional term. She's not a sister, I don't think. She's someone who believes in the imperative claims of merit. If she found that she couldn't do without a woman for a Cabinet post, she would put a woman in. But I do not think that she would ever stop to think it would be fair, or just progressive to choose a woman instead of a man. Why I oppose her is that I think she is hard-hearted about the unemployment of youth. She's maybe actually turning a blind eye on a lost generation. But I don't think that is a problem to do with her being a woman. She would have been the same if she had been a man, which is an odd thing to say. She is just not a sister. By sister, I mean somebody who is worried about discrimination, the dictionary definition of which is distinguishing unfavourably. And I am a natural for that: I can't bear discrimination against skin, or religion, or children, or old people. I long for a society – here I go, back to my Italian farmstead – where everybody has equal dignity, the old grandmother, everybody.

I think it isn't only men and women that complement each other. I love Germaine Greer's idea of persons rather than gender. That is my dream, that is what I think we are looking for: we are looking for complementary personalities.

I'm a real Germaine Greer person, but I would want to give women what I would want to give men. Three things are essential: one, that you should be able to fulfil your talent in life; two, that you should be able to love somebody – a lot of people are prevented from exercising their power of love for another person; and three is that you should have a financial security which is not dependent always on another person. But that would apply to men as well. The way my mind is working, I see it less and less a clear-cut issue between men and women, more as a clear-cut issue for human beings. Where are we all going? Are we progressing or regressing? Are we going back to a capitalist society which is very cruel, with the rich very rich and the poor very poor? Are we doing to the Third World what men did to women in the nineteenth century? Mrs Pankhurst said something which was rather beautiful. She said she wanted to free half of the human race, women, so that that half could help to free the other half. And I think I would come back to her. I would like these three essentials to be everybody's rights. Perhaps I've got past my feminism, I don't know.

Cecilie Løveid: I was very interested in the sex roles when I was very young. I had a daughter when I was seventeen. And I didn't want my girl to wear a dress, she should never have a dress on, I said. That didn't last long, but for a period I was very strong on sex roles. I believed that an emancipated woman should be like a man, that the sexes should be like each other. I don't believe that any more. I want to be feminine, and not stupid, and I want a man to look upon me on the same level, but I want him to have this manly charm and I don't want him to be soft.

Blanche Lucas: I understand feminist as being a derogatory word, a derogatory description for someone you don't particularly care for. It's supposed to mean a lot of strident unpleasantness, burning bras and so forth. But the word has been over-used, and so has lost its original meaning. But, to me, feminism really means being fair to women – that is to say, giving them the same place in society as men.

Jenny Lumet: Feminism has made some people think that being female is a burden and a hassle, when it's so wonderful. They've made motherhood seem insignificant. There's nothing wrong with a woman who does not want to work, who wants to have children and stay home and raise her children. What could be more honourable? What could be tougher? Raising a kid is so much more relevant than raising a company any day of the week. Women have such gifts, and they get it backwards sometimes.

The ultimate feminism would be for a woman to succeed by thinking intuitively.

Gillian Lynne: I'm certainly not a woman's libber at all. I'm an old-fashioned woman when it comes to love. My husband rules the roost in our house, and he is many years younger than I am. He's thirty-three and I'm fifty-seven. He rules the roost, and I wouldn't have it any other way. Because if it was any other way, I would behave badly probably – I don't mean with other men, but I need to be ruled, and I like it. So I am not a feminist, I suppose. I am very strong at work, but when I get home I quite like to be thrown on the bed and held, cuddled, and I quite like to sit at his feet with a cup of tea, and I mean sit at his feet. I once said on American television, and it practically stopped the channel – this very brassy woman was chewing away, and Peter and I were sitting hand in hand, and we are quite well-known because of the age difference between us, and its being a wonderful marriage, and she said, look here, she said, now c'mon, who wears the pants in this family? And with one accord and instantaneously, he said I do and I said he does. And her mouth dropped. And I said, I am an old-fashioned woman, I

504

like to be discovered, and she said, what do you mean by that? I said, well, I like to walk a pace behind him. Why would you do that? I said, because he will turn round and see me there and he'll say, who's that dear little thing and put his arm round me and I shall feel fabulous. Well, they had hundreds of letters. Because it's not the American outlook at all. But I think it is right.

Anna McCurley: Sometimes the division of labour in society is not demeaning. I am still perfectly happy to do housework, and to do all the things that I feel are better done by me. I don't think there is anything wrong with that. I don't expect to carry weapons and go to war. I don't expect to bear entirely (although possibly I do now, but I didn't) the family finance and the strain of home and business. I think women get off extremely lightly in society in many instances. I am talking about middle-class women now, and they're the ones that bleat most.

Sheena McDonald: I think you have to be feminist, because, since time immemorial, as far back as history records, there has been systematic prejudice against women in all areas of power and influence. Individually, there are women who have fought through in an eccentric kind of way at the expense of various things, like happiness and family, to find great personal satisfaction. But, on the whole, it is no less true today than it was. In fact it is probably more true today than it was two hundred years ago, particularly in Scotland, where, at a certain level of society, women have a good deal of independence. I think the fact that I am able to say this now is a credit to women of twenty years ago, who did a lot of fighting.

A lot of feminists are motivated to become feminists because they've been so disappointed by their personal lives. They are terribly angry and they take it beyond that reasonable humanist standpoint to a political point where they are anti-men at every level. The lesbian feminist movement is an extreme, ultimate expression of feminism – which, personally, I don't agree with. I don't know who to blame really, but I don't want to blame men. Men are trammelled and really degraded by the stereotype society has set up for them. I don't think all men want to be bot-bollocking beasts, I don't think they want to go around chalking up as many women as possible, I don't think they are lacking in compassion and tenderness. But, yes, there has been a systematic oppression of women, and it's women who will be the moving force in the liberation of both sexes.

505

I'm not against eroticism, but I'm deeply against the breakfast-time portrayal of women as sex objects, the Page Three girls, which I think is an abomination. It has a terribly bad effect on young boys who grow up to be young men. I think, initially, everybody is embarrassed by it, boys and girls, but that boys get in the grip of it because they feel this is the way the world is – you know – and that's how women are. Girls never really come to terms with it, so they kind of blank it off and don't object to it. They just don't think about it any more. But I find it deeply, deeply offensive, and I am a great supporter of Clare Short. I was woebegone by the response she got in the House of Commons to her Bill, which I don't think has anything to do with censorship or freedom of speech or freedom of image. It was against a very simple and effective putting down of women.

Mary McFadden: I'm not into the women's causes. I have no interest in them whatsoever. I think they're going to get there – it's going to take another ten generations, but they're going to get there.

I'm told about discrimination. I read about it in the newspapers constantly. Those women that it happens to are not operating off a power base. They come here from the Middle West, and they have no money and no power and they're maybe not very bright. And therefore they get discriminated against. Maybe they get sexually abused, or maybe they use their sex, I don't know.

Susan McHenry: My brand of feminism is not just the gender thing, it's also race, class, caste, all those things that we use, as human beings, to divide ourselves from each other. I stand against those things. Human beings shouldn't be categorized in any of these ways. I also stand against those institutions that have helped perpetuate the systematic dividing of ourselves from one another, so I'm always looking for change, for egalitarian, democratic change, in all of the institutions of public life. I think women and men have different experiences and, as a result, different needs. What I don't like to see is our differences being used against us, being used to keep us out of certain situations: oh, a woman can't be involved in this because we need a long-term commitment and surely she will have children and leave us for a while or whatever. I don't like that.

There are still those age-old notions about what women do, and what they don't do, and how much women should be in control of the situation or have power and influence – principally, I guess, in how men relate to us in public life; and in private, actually, if I really think about it. We're still working on that. We had thousands of years living under patriarchy, and it's going to be thousands of years until we evolve into the kind of society where we are free as individuals and not proscribed by gender. Not only gender, but by class and caste, all the other ways we divide up ourselves as human beings. There's still a reluctance, I think, for men to be 100 per cent partners in raising the family and doing the work inside the home. Then, in the public world, any time they perceive that they're going to have to give up something in order for women to have their rightful place, it's a very difficult situation. There's hostility and there's challenge. But it's up to us, as individuals, to work them through, tired as it may make us.

In the 1970s, it looked like everything was conspiring to make us all act like men. I'm happy to say, in the late 1980s, most of us are still women who have been out there living our lives. If you talk to women in business, they constantly have to be aware of whether men are responding to them positively or negatively out of a sense of, well, this is a woman, she can get away with that, I can get away with this. What you have to do is find your own personal style, and it's going to be made up of a whole array of behaviours that are just natural to you.

Donna McKechnie: Now I have an overview of the last maybe ten/twenty years, I feel it has been a very exciting time. I think that, personally, I have lived through a very exciting time and seen the emergence of women. I think the men right now have a real hard time.

Deirdre McSharry: Every woman is a feminist. I don't see how you can not be. When women come up to me at parties and say, of course, I'm not a feminist, but I believe in equal opportunities or equal pay, I say, well, what else is a feminist? You used to be suffragettes or whatever. It's not important what we call ourselves, but all women are feminists in the sense that anyone who thinks anything of herself wishes to stagger through life with some kind of self-respect, and really that's what feminism is. It's about determining who you are.

I was often attacked in the mid-1970s, for pushing women too far, because they said I was giving women an unrealistic goal. I said, there may be some truth in what you say, but I have seen so many women of my generation (not me – I was very lucky, I was very privileged and very separate in that sense) who were brought up not to tell the truth, not to trust one another, not to have a good education, not to know how to cope, so I always felt my role, once I had some power, was to promote the idea that women must rise above this discrimination and help one another and generally make a climate where that kind of discrimination is impossible.

Quite recently I've been doing the salary reviews for my own staff and some come to me and say, I really need some more money because I'm buying a house. I say, don't ever say that to me again. You don't ask for more money because you need it, which is the old-fashioned woman's thing of begging. You should say, I'm very good at my job, therefore I need some more money. Women are so brought up to that that it's difficult to lose those tricks, and they are tricks. Women smile more than men – all of this is historically checked out. We have to ingratiate ourselves, so we walk into a room and we think it's lovely if everybody smiles. But we shouldn't have to rely on those things.

It would be wonderful if we could live alone, but the point is, we can't. I don't mind if the person you're dependent on is another woman or a dog or a cat, that's not the point. When it comes to the sexes, we need each other, and we must love one another or die. I'd hate to live in a world where there were no men, although I'm very fond of women.

Norris Church Mailer: I don't like the word feminist. I don't like some of the people associated with the feminist movement, because I think they don't like men. I like men very much. I am a feminist in that I think it is terribly important for women to be treated equally with men in all aspects of wage-earning, and laws, and discrimination. But I don't want to be a man. I do think there are important differences between men and women. I don't dislike men; I love men. And I really don't like some of the things the feminist movement stands for. Women need men and men need women; it goes both ways. I don't think one can move off to an island and be the Amazon woman without any need of men. On the other hand, a lot of women are very capable of living alone, as I have done. I was a single mother for three years before I met my husband and did very well. So I don't know whether I would necessarily have to have a man in the house all the time, but I think it would be a much sadder place without men.

Alice Mason: Women are really the victims of their emotions. Even big achievers are victims of their emotions. I am lucky that since I became forty I have not been a victim of my emotions at all. I don't know any other woman who feels like I do, not one. All the achievers I know are

508

always surprised when I talk like this. As a matter of fact, I went to a dinner once with about eighteen achievers, all women. There was Gloria Steinem and Marlo Thomas and Mary Tyler Moore and so on. Each woman was to get up and say what women meant to her and how they had helped them in their lives. I got up and said, well, I have to say I am not a feminist, even though you are all feminists here, but as far as I am concerned, I am the only liberated woman in this room. I say this because all of you women depend upon men. You, Marlo, are married to Phil Donaghue; you, Gloria, have always had a man in your life. I am the only one who ever made the decision that I wasn't emotionally going to depend upon a man in any way and that I was going to be a person on my own, and I decided that at forty. And all these achievers were all in shock. I went on to say I could never be a feminist, because, in my business, in twenty-five years I have had two hundred women go in and out of my office, and they are most undependable; they don't come in if they have had a date the night before, or if they have their period, or if they have this, or if they have that. Women, especially in my genera-tion, are raised to think they really have to get married and have a child, and that they are identified through the man they marry. And if he is a prominent man, then they become a prominent woman. We are raised to think all our identity is going to be through a man. So that, even if you have a career, it is just to help the financial aspect of the family, not because you are going to become great in that career. I think a handful of women become great because they decide they are going to become the best. When I was in my early twenties, I decided I was going to be the best one in this business. And I did; I became the best. In my field, I am No1. When I was emotionally involved, before I was forty, it didn't affect my real-estate work or my child, but it affected other things that I didn't do because I spent that energy in men. In other words, I had three things. I had a man in my life, I had a career, and my child. However, once I decided to give up my emotional life, I was successful in a lot of other areas. In other words, I had a lot of energy to give in other areas, and also I could think clearly and I was more of a person. I was really what I set out to be, what I originally wanted to be.

Homayoun Mazandi: Rights are something you create for yourself; nobody can give you rights or tell you what your rights are. What you create, that is your right, that is your power. It comes from you. You can't go to Downing Street and get it, and you cannot buy it.

Sonia Melchett: Women are getting more and more involved in admini-stration, in politics and the running of the country, and I think it's a very good thing. I'm not one of these people who think that men and women think alike, and should be more alike; I think they are very complementary to each other. I'm not a feminist in that way. I'm on the Women's Playhouse Trust, which is a feminist group, which wants to create theatre just for women. They want women writers, women directors, plays for women; even technicians should be women. Well, although I've helped them, been a spearhead, I don't really feel like that. I think the mixture is good, to have men and women working together.

The fact that the feminists have worked for equal pay and equal retirement age and equal rights generally has been a very good thing, and getting women into trades-union movements, which would never have happened ten years ago. All that has been excellent, because it has been a humanizing thing right through the country. I think, taken too far, it has become ridiculous. When boys and girls set up house together, whether they believe in marriage or not, this feeling that they must share everything – one must do the cooking one night, one must do the cooking the other night, they share the responsibility of washing the nappies – I think that can all be a bit too extreme. It's putting down rules, and I don't believe in too many rules in life. I believe in being much more pliable, adaptable, and I really do think it is a natural thing for a woman on the whole to spend more time with the children than it is for the father. She actually has given birth to the child, and it comes more naturally to her than it does to the father. Feminism has taken that to a slightly ridiculous conclusion. I'm afraid I'm a very boring liberal kind of a person. That is why I am a member of the Alliance Party – I always take the middle road. I really don't feel aggressively female.

Lady Menuhin: I don't like the word feminist. It's been traduced; it doesn't mean anything any more. I like to think of women and men, and I like to think of them as something that should be dovetailed, complementary entirely, which is what happens in sex.

I don't believe there is such a thing as an egalitarian society, and I think it would be most frightfully dull. I do believe in egality of opportunity, that you should be able to sign your exam papers in a way that nobody knows what sex you are, and therefore one inborn endemic prejudice, the man against the woman, can play no part. Man's sovereignty is very important to him; men are fundamentally vain and women only superficially vain. And the feeling that the man has to struggle against, I'm convinced, is that he's going to be overpowered. I don't know why.

Kate Millett: You don't have any oppressive system without its continuance being assured by members of the oppressed group. That's true of all oppressed people. Therefore, if the feminist movement is to succeed, it must start at home with women and with the conditioning of children: to decondition them, in fact, so that they have a fuller sense of themselves as little people, and not little males, little females, horrid little stereotypes that they have to live out. I taught kindergarten once, and at about five years old my kindergarteners were already so stereotyped that it was almost funny, but tremendously sad. They had so accepted the silly sex roles of their culture, they were like little caricatures of masculine and feminine behaviour in some respects. It was interesting to try to talk them out of some of that rigidity. And not easy.

A little token woman here or there doesn't really change anything that much. It doesn't approximate equality; it's the index of some change, but the change has not been accomplished. The process is long and tortuous, slow and tedious and silly. It consumes years of many women's lives, just burned up in trying to achieve an equalization between the sexes. And all unnecessary, a great waste of human spirit, a great waste of lives. I mean, they accomplish something wonderful – all people who work for liberation do – but we didn't need to have the oppression situation at the beginning.

Mrs Thatcher is a bad excuse for a woman in power. She is a deplorable reactionary, and the fact that she is in power is hardly an example of women's progress. Throughout history, there have been cases of these dreadful reactionaries who happen to be females being given a break. It is not an example of female equality any more than Elizabeth I was.

I see patriarchy increasing its colonial oppression of other peoples. I'm an American. I watch my government commit atrocity after atrocity upon people in South America, for example, or throughout the world, through the CIA, its support of dictatorships, and torture. I'm watching torture resurrect itself in the twentieth century and become one of the ways in which governments govern. One of the things I'm doing during this period of my life is writing a very long book about torture and its re-emergence. I see patriarchy as grotesque, increasingly militaristic, increasingly greedy, colonialistic, imperialistic, brutal, with a terrible disregard of civil liberties, of democratic forms. This late-stage patriarchy is a tremendous threat to all citizens. The state's invasion of private life is absolutely terrifying. Ultimately, patriarchy is about the continuation of male power as we have known it through history, but the means it is using now are very grotesque and very frightening.

It's a really exciting time to be a women. We are on the move, and we are making history. It is an exciting time to be one of us.

Cristina Monet: Every new movement has been rooted in the middle classes. The middle classes are the only ones discontented enough and yet, at the same time, leisured enough to be obsessed with new ideas and to create change. They're not in the state of contentment and complacency and holding on to an old order that the upper classes traditionally are, nor are they preoccupied with more tangible worries, like the working classes are. So everything, not just feminism, seems always to begin with the middle classes.

I would say I'm absolutely not a feminist, but I have an aversion to -ists anyway. As soon as things become radical movements, the seeds of their own corruption are evident, but, of course, unless there are radical movements, they can't change anything. That's the paradox. But feminists tend to become so bombastic, humourless and unobjective. Every revolution starts in the hands of thoughtful intellectuals who usually have the best ideas about necessary things, and they can only move mountains when they reach a level of hysteria and mass emotion, only then are they a force. But as soon as that happens, they tend to go to extremes. I mean, the whole pregnancy issue they're having here now, about how it shouldn't specifically be called maternity leave because it's degrading to women. It's split the feminists down the middle in America. Some of them say it shouldn't be called maternity leave, it should be just the same for measles, or an ankle. It's absolutely not true. Obviously a good father is better than a lousy mother for a child, but given half a chance, biologically a child needs its mother. Till it's three years old, it has to have its mother first and foremost. All the feminism in the world won't make the men the ones that have the babies. So where feminism enters into messing around with psycho-sexual roles, I think it's ludicrous.

Bel Mooney: If anybody asks me are you a feminist, I say there is nothing else to be. Every intelligent woman in the 1980s must be a feminist. It grieves me bitterly that so many women dismiss feminism. The reason they dismiss it is because of a bad name feminism got from radical extremists, not just the lesbians, but other women who have said it was wrong for women to want to look pretty and all that sort of thing. But ordinary women (not that I think of myself as *not* an ordinary woman) started to think this meant a dour rejection of love, of marriage, of children, or beauty – all the things that make life rich and attractive.

The women's liberation movement needed the radicals. If any movement in society is to change it, it always needs extremists, and in the 1960s and 1970s, the women's liberation movement needed women who were going to burn their bras – not that they ever did, but that kind of extreme. I regard feminism as simply the philosophical not the political belief in every single woman's power to realize the best of herself for herself. It is nothing to do with the children, nothing to do with men, nothing to do with anything other than an inner confidence, knowing who you are, knowing you're a woman and celebrating the wholeness of yourself – and you cannot do that without assuming you're equal to men.

Sara Morrison: In the early days of the wilder fringes of women's lib, none of which I ever joined in any way and was probably considered traitor to my kind for it, I used to try and implore the women, if nothing else, just to be the best version of themselves. Because any woman who tries to be a pseudo-man, whatever that means, is bound to be a failure. She is conceding the wrong point. But persuading some of the super-educated, brilliantly intelligent, highly specialized but often rather narrow-visioned or narrowly focused women to be themselves is much more difficult than persuading them to be good professionals. That they are. But to handle that professionalism well, as women in a team, is rather more difficult because it sounds as though you are making a point about them being women. You're not, you're making the absolute opposite point: you're making a point about them being themselves quite regardless of whether they are women. It's necessary with some men, too. The stupid thing of aping men, whether it's in silly ways like playing golf or drinking beer or whatever, has nothing to do with it. I don't know why women get it so wrong, I truly don't. Now and again, when I have five minutes to spare, or while I'm lying in the bath, I puzzle as to why so many women get it wrong. I peel the onion down to the fact that women's sense of humour sometimes becomes rather fragile, or even gets left behind, the more senior and successful they become, and that's when they start being pseudo-men.

The Americans make the stupid mistake of counting heads in political places as though that was a measure of the progress of women. But it's no measure at all, or it's not the right measure for the United Kingdom, in my view. I'm not at all sure that Mrs Thatcher won't have put the cause of women back about thirty years. She hasn't put the cause of women forward.

Kathy Myers: There was a time in the feminist movement when it was definitely thought to be the case that, to get on in a man's world, you had to deny your sexuality and femininity. And actually, on one level, it does make it easier, because men are not threatened because then they can write women off who behave in quite a masculine way as non-sexual or bluestocking or a bit fuddy-duddy. And they just treat them like one of the boys. One of the reasons *Dallas* and *Dynasty* and the glamour soaps have caught on is that they centre on that very delicate area of women who are pushing their sexuality to full tilt and also being quite ambitious and ruthless, which is actually a threatening and dangerous combination. It's bad if you use it to alienate other women, because powerful women are completely dependent on their female friends. If you start playing women off against each other, then you lose all the way down the line.

Middle-class women have the time to be liberated. Liberation is a luxury. And that's one of the reasons why, in Britain, working-class women have never identified with feminism. Because they don't have the time. And, in a way, because they already practise it on a daily level because their lives are so hard, they have to be strong.

America is a very goal-orientated society. Feminism in America is less to do with women liking each other than women getting on, women succeeding in a man's world. You push yourself to the limits, whether it's jogging or becoming the head of a multi-national, or getting as many orgasms as possible.

Lynda Myles: I absolutely detest Mrs Thatcher. I think there are different kinds of women who make it. There are some women who make it who are very open, and keen to help other women. There are other women who make it, and it's as if, once they get up, they want to pull the ladder up behind them to ensure other women don't follow. It's been very clear to me, certainly in showbusiness, that there are the women who are keen to help others and those who love their position of being one among the boys. I can understand the appeal of that, but I think one also has a commitment to try and bring on other women, and Thatcher has done virtually nothing for women. She's made the condition of women much worse.

Lynn Nesbit: I believe in equal rights, equal pay. But I also believe in two very different genders. I am a firm believer in heterosexuality. If I was told that I was going to be in the company of women from now on

514

and never going to see another man, I'd be extremely disturbed. I like men. I feel sorry for them; I mean, I have some compassion for them in this new world we are all grappling with in terms of sexual identity and gender and women in the workplace. I don't regard men as my enemy.

I can't emphasize enough that an ability to bear children makes an enormous difference between men and women. We all tend to pass over that little fact. But you can't pass over it. It's such a crucial difference. There are certain feminists who have never had children, and they are often addressing themselves to women's issues. And if they've never had a child, it makes me a bit uneasy that they are telling women – and mostly women who have low-level jobs – how they should conduct their lives. Are those women really better off working as charwomen or slinging hash in a diner than staying home and having a family? Now they are trying to do both. They need the income, that's why they are doing it. Very few people, men or women, have work that is really meaningful. That's why America has spawned the women's movement, because we have the largest middle class.

Julia Neuberger: I'm not a radical feminist, but I'm a feminist. I'm concerned about the welfare of women and about how the world can give equal opportunities to men and to women, and how women in a sense can get what I regard as their fair rights within a society. For me, in Britain, in 1986, that means looking at equal opportunities for education for girls, at equal pay for women, at fair tax arrangements for women, at benefit arrangements for women. It does not seem to me that the main concern is about the use of language in the liturgy or anywhere else, or, indeed, to a very large extent, actually worrying about women's therapy groups, encounter groups.

I chair the liturgy committee of the Liberal Synagogue, and the classic issue is whether we use sexist language in the prayer book. I really couldn't care whether we use sexist language in the prayer book. I'd rather worry about whether women are actually going to get equal educational opportunities. It seems to me that it is so back to front, and so crazy, and not where the real work is at – an utterly middle-class, very narrow interest group concern. Yet there's a whole world of very underprivileged women out there, particularly in the North and the Midlands, which the women's movement has not given any attention to. The extremes of feminism of the late 1960s and early 1970s led to a polarization of the sexes, and there are certain moments when I find myself quite automatically talking about something, and my husband

515

says, but you're really excluding men, you're really not interested in what we think. I'm aware of that – I *am* aware of that. If I'm honest about it, of course any kind of real progress has to happen through interdependence of the sexes. To what extent women are ready for that is a separate issue; I think a lot of women aren't ready to be interdependent with men because they haven't been away from men, taking their own decisions, for long enough.

A lot of the women who've worked best for women's issues and women's rights have been those who've used the present system, and also used men to argue their case. A classic example was quite a recent one in this country with the case of equal pay for work of equal value. The women who spotted just how important the European Court's decision was as far as Britain was concerned used men to back the cause.

The real concerns of the women's movement in this country have essentially been very middle-class concerns. The concerns about how you manage to have children and go back to work (i.e. buy a nanny) are entirely middle class. The working class has never stopped working – they always had to find a child-minder or whatever to look after their children.

Working-class women reckon that the option in life is not to take a job, but to get married. The boys get jobs, the girls get married. Their expectation tends to be rather rosy: they think they're going to get married and live happily ever after and have 2.4 children. The reality is that they're going to live in appalling housing, going to be short of money and going to get divorced (because one in three still get divorced), and they're financially going to be at the bottom of the pile. And if you're a feminist and really concerned about the welfare of women and the future generations of women – in other words, the children of these women – then that's where you've got to start. You've got to look at what happens in ordinary schools, in ordinary housing estates, ordinary GP surgeries, hospitals and the tax system. I think it's an extraordinarily small proportion of working-class women who have broken out of that. The majority of women who hit the headlines in the 1970s and 1980s have, in fact, been middle-class women. They may not have middle-class voices, but they are actually middle-class women with middle-class aspirations, with parents who have pushed them. The majority of working-class women have parents who don't push them, who aren't interested in the welfare of girls, who go to schools where the teachers are more interested in the welfare of boys than of girls, and they just lag behind.

Nanette Newman: I think a woman should not be tied to the kitchen sink, should not be tied to all those things which have always been allotted her as her job to do and the thing expected of her. It is right that she should be liberated and allowed to choose, but the pendulum has now swung in a very curious way and you have a whole lot of women who quite rightly want to get married, live at home, not have a career, bring up their children and be totally home-orientated, and they are being made to feel guilty by the very liberated women. And I think that's very wrong. There is no harder career in the world than being a housewife and a mother. And I don't think those women should be made to feel they are missing out on something, or that they're not fulfilling themselves, or not progressing.

I am obviously speaking from a rather privileged point of view because I could have the money to employ somebody to take care of my children or my home, but the great problem is in certain areas where a woman would like to do something but just doesn't have the financial ability to employ somebody at home while she gets some freedom. That must be very frustrating. That's why you find a number of women who resent the fact that they are the ones who are tied at home, and perhaps got married and had children. Obviously, today, you can't help but be aware of women's liberation, because it's being pushed at you from every magazine and endless television programmes. You would have to be blind or deaf not to be at least conscious of it. Of course, it still has a long way to go, but that lies in our hands as much as men's.

Very often people equate liberation with toughness, a masculine approach. That is so stupid. One will always be a woman. There will always be, thank God, this enormous difference. Why would one ever want to change that? Liberation is much more of the mind than anything else – and to be really liberated is to be able to do things and use your mind and go into areas of your choice, but never be anything other than a woman and never be anything other than feminine. I don't like aggressive women who feel they have almost to become men to be accepted in a man's world. The really liberated woman isn't like that.

The one thing we mustn't lose as women is our sense of humour, because the liberation movement can become so humourless – all that boring period of burning bras and frightening, grotesque women running around. That did nothing for the liberation of women other than make them into a joke. Some people find it offensive that there are always mother-in-law jokes, and jokes about women drivers, but you can't be too gritty about it all. You have to balance that up with some of

517

the rather nicer things we all hang on to. If you're really clever as a woman, you can have your cake and eat it.

Emma Nicholson: It matters very much indeed that women should have a maximum amount of choice, to choose to marry, to choose not to marry, to choose to stay at home, to choose to go out to work, to choose to have children, to choose not to have children, to choose part-time work, to choose full-time work. All those are choices that the modern woman has, and the important thing is to keep those choices open. Where I would disagree with some women is that, if you're not going to make the choice to be successful, don't complain. It's not because your sex is against you, it's because you haven't tried. It may be that you don't have the fire, the drive, the energy, the vision, the guts or the determination. Or it may be that you actually want something quite different, which is to stay at home. And, lucky woman, she has the choice: men don't. I think women today are much luckier than men.

I think that what some women say about Mrs Thatcher is that she has succeeded in a male-dominated world in a way they could not succeed themselves, and they turn against Mrs Thatcher by saying she's not a woman. Well, *a priori*, Mrs Thatcher is all woman; she is a mother, she is a wife, she's feminine, nobody can say she's not a woman. She *is* a woman – biologically, but also spiritually and as a human being. Some critics go on to say she doesn't care. I would say to you that many men care, and caring is not the prerogative of the female half of society. Care is something built into all of us in different measures, whether we are men or women. The level of Mrs Thatcher's caring doesn't determine the level of her femininity. As a matter of fact, Mrs Thatcher does care, and she does a mass of things like hospital visiting unknown to anybody. She works very hard and always has done for the NSPCC, for example. I have known her visit great friends in hospital who have been desperately ill, and she's asked for no publicity. I've seen her myself at Brighton, immediately following the bomb, where she and I were both in the same hotel. I was a few doors down from her on her floor. Mrs Thatcher cares deeply and perhaps, in many ways, she cares so deeply about things that she doesn't show it.

Mavis Nicholson: I don't have a strong feeling of gender. Everybody has such a mixture of it in them that I prefer people whose gender comes out if it wants to and is not suppressed by foolishness. I am who I am. I've never had a muddle about gender.

I'm not separatist. I don't want Home Rule for Wales either. I think the nearer you get to people the better, therefore the nearer women get to men the better it is for their cause. I'm not saying that I wouldn't want to influence men a lot to change, because I think if men change, women will get a better time of it, but I'm not a separatist. I'm certainly fiercely for women's rights though, because they've been so slaughtered in the past. You can usually equate black and woman in people's prejudices. In fact, you scratch a prejudice on anybody and you find all the rest there. If somebody says, I hate blacks, I'm sorry but I do, they usually hate women, too, I find. I'm savagely against the way in which women have been put down. And for what reason? Because men probably wanted wives who were dutiful and mothers who looked after their children and cleaned their home. It must have been for a very selfish reason they put women down, because women wouldn't have put themselves down. They are perfectly capable of doing most of the things men can do. So I am a strong feminist that way. No question.

Béatrice Nivois: I think if I had been born a lot earlier, I would have been a feminist. I know feminism has done a lot for us. I think, for example, we have feminists to thank for the fact that we have abortion in France. Nearly all the major problems women had before the feminist movement have been resolved. There are still a few things to do, but yes, I am grateful to the women who did the fighting.

If you end up hating men, it's because they've done something really awful. They've driven women beyond their endurance. If women have a grudge against men, they have reasons for it. I'm independent financially and intellectually, otherwise I would never have posed in *Playboy* – my boyfriend might have told me not to. I refuse to live with anyone who prevents me from doing what I want.

Christine Ockrent: I am a feminist because I'm a woman, but I'm certainly no crusader for the extinction of the sexes. And it's very old-fashioned now; you would hardly find, in a country like this one at least, the kind of feminist you had ten or, indeed, fifteen years ago, when abortion was a very important fight. A lot of things have been accomplished in the past ten or fifteen years, so I think there are fewer grounds now for the crusader type.

Jane O'Grady: I don't really see how any sensible woman couldn't be a feminist in some way. I can't unfortunately categorize myself as one of these socialist radical feminists, but I know that what women need – and gradually they're rectifying that – is to be no longer seen by men as a sub-species, something somehow not quite human. People say all that stuff about changing language isn't important. It is very important because the next generation might not perceive it quite like that. With all those experiments they've done about man, and how he uses language, women have the odd feeling they are not quite included in it. You would never say, man is a creature who suckles his young and menstruates monthly, but you would say man is a creature that requires food, shelter and access to females. That just shows women are somehow outside. I would just like to be able to have the same sort of freedoms as men, to be able to be dignified while being undignified. I always feel in the position that I have to make a fool of myself in order to be honest. It's easy to make a fool of yourself as a woman, but on the other hand, why should women look nice, why should they bloody well make-up, why should they et cetera? I find all that very pathetic to have to do and narcissistic; I find it very irritating that it's required of me.

Kitty O'Hagan: I guess I see feminists as a fairly radical group and not really representative of most women, in that I feel they are the more intelligent women and do also tend to be the women who are not terribly pretty, and therefore can't use that as the way of getting their own way and are understandably sore. So they find other ground, find something else to fight on. I've done it myself. I also feel they are terribly brave. They have done things I don't think I would do, and I'm very grateful to them. How I operate within it has changed. I used to use skills other than the ones I have now to get my own way. I used not to want to confront, because it took longer, and it does take longer if you confront the issue. Somehow there is an impatience in me there, and I just will confront it now.

Fifi Oscard: There were feminists when I was young, and when they started inventing things like the National Organization of Women I did not participate because I was already emancipated. In 1949, I started to work, by 1969 I owned my own business. By the 1970s my children were grown up and I was just enjoying it. So I never had to be a feminist.

Edna O'Shaughnessy: The sexes are interdependent, and one cannot understand a man without looking at a woman, nor woman without looking at a man. I think it sad that the feminist movement, like almost every good movement, has its fringes and its distortions, so that some

520

feminists have become female chauvinists. I wish it hadn't happened. It confuses important issues.

Kathy O'Shaughnessy: People find it quite difficult to reconcile the idea of success in a woman with her femininity, but I don't see that we all need to converge into a neutral gender for women to succeed freely. I think it's important that women can keep their femininity and be ambitious and succeed. But you walk into a mire of complexity there, because there are so many things bound up with femininity, not least of which is being an object of desire to men.

Diana Parker: Most people would consider I'm not a feminist, because I'm not particularly in favour of women being given any kind of preferential treatment or positive discrimination. I accept that women have been discriminated against in the past, very badly, and continue to be discriminated against even now. It's usual for women to be asked at a job interview whether they're married, whether they have children, how they tend to cope with having children and so on. I would also make a point of asking men the same questions, but I would expect the men would have much more pat answers than the women. The point of asking those questions as much as anything is to bring it to the potential employee's notice that they have a responsibility to their employment, and the important point is to be guided by their responses to ensure you accept that person as a potential employee not as a man or a woman. Therefore, if they say they reckon that they can cope with having children and the job, I think there is an obligation on the employer to take that answer at face value until disproved. A lot of women feel that, in many situations, a man would be preferred. Now, whether or not that is the case, the fact it is so commonly felt itself operates in a discriminatory fashion.

The issues of both divorce and abortion have to be regarded as capable of transition, so they must reflect whatever is demanded by the particular society at any time. I believe in the democratic way of life, and as a consequence I have to believe that it is a democratic right and responsibility for the people to choose what laws they want to have concerning what really are moral issues, even though it's an impossible task for the law-makers in a morally and culturally diverse society.

Molly Parkin: Feminism is a very humane movement; it's the female trades union, and I'm much in favour of trades unions.

521

One of the earliest and most laudable feminists was Mae West, somebody who was utterly feminine, utterly charming, totally sensual, but competed and did even better in men's terms: she rescued a whole studio from bankruptcy by her films and the directness of her approach and what some would call her single-minded aggression.

Judith De Paul: I've always been an entrepreneur and an independent, and therefore I've always worked personally on achievement and success. The term feminist is so negative, and has such unfortunate connotations, be they right or wrong, that I wouldn't want to be associated with it. I would want to be associated with the woman who has been helpful to other women and who has been able to become a role model. I never had a female role model in business, but I had my mother as a role model. And she always taught me never to lose my femininity: that was the most important tool of all.

All this business about karate classes is bullshit. Women need the psychology of being successful in society, the psychology of being at peace with themselves and their own abilities to succeed.

I believe that a woman like myself has been trained to win. I am a survivor and a winner. I will not accept anything else. That's a very male-orientated type of viewpoint, and few women are trained to think that way. Therefore, psychologically, I am extremely secure, and when a problem occurs, I don't take it personally, I just figure it out. Do I knock the person out, do I go sideways, do I go through another door, do I regroup, do I move on to a slightly different psychological position or business position? In other words, I use a business strategy to overcome a situation. Most women, unfortunately, take a situation personally, number one, and number two, are not trained to be as aggressive in business as men. They tend to be more sensitive to problems, and if it's the difference of kill that guy so you can get the job or back off in order to be nice, they back off. And I don't do that.

I've just come back from India, where I spent a lot of time doing business. Obviously the men basically run the businesses in India, but the women are the power behind the men. And I, as a woman, am achieving more in India than most men. That is because of my entire mentality. I, as a woman, accept that I have to work harder. It doesn't bother me, because in the end I get the golden apple, and it would seem to me, as long as you know that, you have a very good chance to grab that golden ring, you do whatever you have to do to get it. My view is

522

rather radical, but then, again, I have achieved a degree of success, so perhaps the attitude works.

Penny Perrick: My idea of feminism is that anyone, regardless of their sex, should have equal opportunities in every area of life: which means that men should, if that is what they want, and if circumstances permit, be allowed to stay at home and look after the children if their domestic circumstances are such that they're able to do that without losing face in society. If that is an acceptable definition of feminism, then I am a feminist. If being a feminist means man-hating, bearing a grudge, looking backward at women's history instead of looking forward at women's opportunities, then I'm not.

Radical feminism, a total rejection of the male, could mean the end of mankind, of course, but I think that era has gone. That was in the forefront of feminism in the 1960s, when there were organizations called SCUM, which was the Society for Cutting Up Men. We've now reached a second stage. It might be that, to get a movement off the ground, people have to over-react and say outrageous things which they don't necessarily live with afterwards. I think there's very little of that kind of radical feminism around now.

Lorie Scott Peters: I am a feminist in that I believe in the cause and want to work for my equality. I'm tired of being judged for something I'm not because I'm a woman. On the other hand, I'm not aggressive, actively aggressive, about feminism and women having their rights. I'm very much a loner. I believe in the cause, but I won't go out and rally for it, hold up any signs for it, picket anybody for it. I like to survive and win or lose on my own merits, so I'm a feminist for myself, I believe in my own rights. Maybe that's terribly selfish. I do believe in the other women. I will try and help women and if a woman's doing the same job I would ask a man to do, I will give her the same wage, because I believe she's equal. But I will judge that on her capabilities or whatever. As far as helping the movement goes, well, I am my own movement.

Lynn Phillips: The language of generality is so confusing that I find a lot of the arguments that go on, even between men and women, about the nature of the sexes and what should be and what is, are confused by vagueness of terms. I get dizzy when I try to sort my way through the language to the meaning. I think when you reach the level of meaning, there is much less disagreement than people choose to think. A lot of people use the word feminist in a media-defined way. Most women in America use the word to mean a certain kind of feminism that the media have promoted, which stands for bra-burning, which nobody understood, and various other symbolic actions that are ineffective and vague; and also hostility towards men and towards eroticism, and most women logically choose not to identify themselves with that image of feminism. I also have problems identifying myself with feminism because the women's movement has been politically quite self-destructive and ineffective in this country, for reasons I understand and forgive but don't go on to identify myself with. I can have a conversation about feminism with several of my friends, and none of us will have been talking about the same thing or for the same reason. I've had heated arguments go on for a really long time, and they mean absolutely nothing, have no content whatsoever. When you talk about what men can do, what women can do, you're talking about biologically determined necessity from which there is no escape – a biological predisposition which can be overcome by cultural reconditioning but only at such a great expense it probably never will be. I'm talking, in other words, about something essential or something accidental or something *de facto*. A lot of the time, when people talk about men and women, they're talking about what they observe in their life, and there's nothing essential about that. It's a result of culture and particular biological and cultural factors. You don't have to be governed by that, yet our sense of reality is.

One of my big disappointments with the women's movement is that it never developed a sense of process. I thought that the women's movement was going to have a spectacular sense of history and individual process and change, because women do bring up children and anybody who has brought up children sees each one is different and each one keeps going through stages, and these stages are part of a search rather than the conclusion. So, for women to be looking at each other's lives as a series of final statements rather than as a searching in good faith, seems to me criminal, and this, I think, has come a lot out of the lesbian movement, because it isn't maternal. One of the consequences – not that I think it's bad in itself – but one of the consequences for the women's movement of loving women and withdrawing from the heterosexual world has been that it has tended to undercut the lessons you can learn as a mother. Some of the lesbian women are mothers, so the failure to learn from motherhood or apply the maternal rules to the world of politics has been universal, not simply the fault of gay women or straight women. I think all women have thrown the baby out with the bath water when it comes to maternal lessons, maternal perception. Even our successes in the political arean have been, in many ways, vitiated and undercut by that failure. But the hatred and fear of men is a stage that many women brought up in a culture which values men so highly have to go through. In our culture, you're brought up virtually to worship the batter, not the pitcher.

Eve Pollard: Often the most feminist women are the ones who have the most spoilt, brattish, macho-nonsense as sons.

You cannot change the years and years that women have felt the inferior sex in a generation. Which is, of course, what feminists would like to do. It is going to take a lot longer. We have to be careful how we bring up our sons, we have to watch how our grandsons are brought up, to change that. You can't just change hundreds and thousands of years by saying, we are here, now open the floodgates.

I'm not sure what feminist means any more. Do I believe women are as good as men? Yes. Do I believe women are as clever as men? Yes. Do I believe that the way to achieve this is to be aggressive towards men? I think not. The best way you can succeed is just by going there and doing it. Whatever one may think about Mrs Thatcher's politics, it is great that my teenage daughter thinks she could become Prime Minister. She is the first generation to think this is an option open to her. There's no point in fighting men. It would be far easier to infiltrate by becoming successful in their world, and that's what I think feminism should be all about. I also think we should help one another more. And we are a long way from learning how to do it.

Mrs Thatcher's job is not to worry about women, her job is to worry about Great Britain. You cannot expect her to help the rest of us because of our sex. She has just made an announcement that more women should join the boards of the great and the good. She has put Sally Oppenheim, Edwina Currie, in the Cabinet. But the point is that we have got to be good enough to get there. Supposing a woman becomes editor of a Fleet Street newspaper – something that hasn't happened up until now, and it would be wonderful if it did – you can't expect, because of that, she is going to elevate women into a successful role on the newspaper. She has just got to take the best people who are there at the time. I think women expect Mrs Thatcher to do too much. The fact, the very fact, she's there will serve as a beacon for future generations.

Antonia de Portago: The Frenchwoman is also very assertive and liberated, but in a different way. It's a question of manners. They're more feminine and, I think, more sexual. I would say that women here are more obsessed with money and their position in work, where women in France are more obsessed with their beauty, their femininity and their sex life.

Barbara de Portago: I'm not a feminist in modern terms. I've always understood one thing: throughout history, as long as you were an exceptional and intelligent and sensitive woman, you could do and be whatever you wanted. There's Catherine the Great, there's Eleanor of Aquitaine, there's Elizabeth I – it's never been a problem to me. It has never entered my mind to think that I couldn't do something because I'm a woman. I've done everything I've wanted to do. I will continue to do it and I will probably find a few men along the way too.

Diana Potter: I am not a feminist in the terms of the feminist movement as it is now. I feel the word feminist now connotes lesbianism, lack of humour, stridency and finally boredom. I think they do more harm for the cause of women than intelligent people, sisters helping each other.

Emily Prager: When the feminist movement started, it was news to me that women weren't equal to men, it was something I had never considered. My father had brought me up to believe that women were not only equal but possibly superior.

I've never met a man who did not believe that men were better than women simply because he was one. That's the way I feel, too. I am a woman, therefore I feel that women are superior to men, because I'm not a man, I'm a woman. Women can do anything men can do and men can't bring children into the world.

Sexuality in women, especially in America, is an ugly problem. It's people who call themselves feminists who contribute to it. The idea that any woman who is in pornography is a victim is anathema to me. It's so condescending. It shows so little knowledge about these people and who they are. It shows no understanding. When I was doing my piece, I met prostitutes who were much better adjusted to what they did than girl-friends of mine who were angry and twisted about the jobs they're doing and whether they're getting enough recognition. They weren't all twisted, victimized human beings by any means. They just worked. But people don't want to accept the fact that women can be what they want to be. Who does it hurt?

When these idiot women go on about pornography making men rapists, it makes me crazy, because it's so clearly not a possibility. It may be true that the average rapist likes pornography, I'm not going to dispute that, but the average man likes it, too. Another thing about pornography is that it is sexist and there is no pornography for women, because, of course, the main thing that might turn a woman on is considered obscene, and that, of course, is a man with an erection. You can't have that in a magazine, so they'll have a thing like *Playgirl*, which is basically a lot of pouty-mouthed homosexual guys with limp dicks, and this is supposed to be the turn-on for women. But what would turn a woman on, what does turn a woman on, is considered obscene.

Usha Prashar: I believe in genuine equality of opportunity for all, and I believe the work of women should be recognized. I would think hard how you go about doing it; I wouldn't want just symbolic gestures. I want recognition of the worth of what you're doing, whether that's a career or bringing up children. And if you are liberating women, if you are changing the whole ethos of society where the role of women, whether as mothers, as people who run homes, or as women who go out to work, is recognized as worthwhile, I feel you are also liberating men. People think that liberating women is a one-sided game, but I feel that men should also have the choice. If a man wants to be the domestic person and the woman wants to go out to work, it should be an acceptable thing.

The point I am making is that it was previously thought that the whole of life was organized round the man: the man was the breadwinner and the woman ran round him to organize the domestic life, so she was always the weaker partner in the game. Now things are changing. The woman is saying, I have the choice, and, in that context, the way you have your domestic arrangements and how they relate to your working arrangements are on an equal footing. To me, that is working towards real equality. Equality in terms of going up the career levels, like men, is not what I call progress. To me, equality is actually changing the base of society and how it organizes itself, and how people are conditioned. That way you liberate men in the process of liberating women.

Judith Price: What's happened, at least in this country, is that the feminist has become, in other words, a lesbian.

527

I think what counts for a woman is not to be brilliant, but to be beautiful.

Colombe Pringle: Each time I go to the States, I am amazed, even at parties, by the relations between men and women. I think women have gone very far. They were right to go far, but were they right to go that far? I'm not sure. Women were terrible here, also, during the feminist movement, really tough, really boring. Women hated men, and got very aggressive, and ugly and unconcerned. I was already married and had children, so it was different for me. But if I had been alone, maybe I would have been tough and grumpy and avant-garde, as well.

Marjorie Proops: I am not really a feminist. I consider myself a personist, a humanist, in fact. There's an awful lot of inequality and injustice in this world of ours, for both men and women, and a lot of people need help and support, not just women.

If a woman, a competent and experienced journalist who happened to be a woman, were obviously the best choice at any given time, then I see no reason why there shouldn't be a woman editing a national newspaper.

Andrée Putman: I think if women didn't accept sexual discrimination, it wouldn't happen. In other words, instead of blaming the men, I would blame the women.

I am a feminist. Of course I believe in equal opportunities. More than that, I admire women beyond words, when they get rid of their problems. But I have a humorous vision of what I would call the bad feminists who, in the end, did hurt women enormously, because they became men. I don't think it's a good idea to become a man when you are a woman. It's not the way to protect women.

Mary Quant: Economic independence is vital, and it started being possible when women also became physically independent, in that they had the pill. One was necessary to achieve the other. The pill was the major and absolutely vital step. Without an efficient and general form of contraception, economic independence was impossible, because if you never knew when you were going to be pregnant, you couldn't be economically independent. That is the process we've been through since, roughly, the 1960s. What is surprising is how little upheaval this caused, rather than how much.

Charlotte Rampling: I agree entirely with feminism, if it's equal opportunity. All the other stuff is shit. If you want to become the other sort of feminist, it means that, biologically, you are imbalanced. You don't have the basic normal urges, to procreate, to have a family, to want to protect and bring up your children, to want to have that responsibility in this world which is full of bombs, is full of this, full of that, as it always has been. If you don't want that kind of responsibility, it's fuck all that, it's all shit anyway. It becomes, I want to go and do this and do that, I want to live my life and not have all that responsibility. Believe me, in a certain sense it is much easier to do that, much easier. But you will not have the same kind of fulfilment and reward, of that I am 100 per cent sure. You won't be a whole woman. They're all going to scream at me if this is printed. But the sexes complement each other. Of course they do. That's the wonderful thing about man and woman, that's what's so exciting, that man can love all those things that are feminine, which are difficult, moody, lunatic, cyclic, intuitive, instinctive – all those things which perhaps feminists would say, oh, that's stuff and nonsense. That's all part of the woman, and that's what man loves, because it's so different and mysterious, and it's exciting. You never know how your wife's going to wake up in the morning. You know she's had a period, or she's overworked – most women, especially women who have careers, are exhausted a lot of the time. The mystery of woman is something man is always after. That's what makes men fall in love with women. It's not the model in the magazine, it's not the film star. It's the woman in bed in the morning in all her states.

American women have an enormous chip on their shoulders about their femininity and women's rights and all that. They are very ball-breaking people, the Americans.

There is always a time in a woman's life when she has to decide between being feminine and desirable to men and leading a feminine life, which is marriage, children and maybe a career, but nothing too overwhelmingly time-consuming; or breaking through that barrier of femininity and really going into the world of men where she's competing with men and usually has to lose a certain amount of femininity. There are very few powerful women in history who have remained extremely feminine and desirable, because that needs a terrific kind of woman, and there aren't many of them. The ones that do succeed in big businesses or big careers are very tough ladies, and they therefore lose a lot of their feminine weapons in terms of charm, in terms of their relationships with men.

I'd make women recognize the power they have over men without threatening men with it. She doesn't have to be beautiful, but she should recognize the powers she is born with in terms of her potential of seduction over men. If you threaten them, you will have more and more homosexuals in the world. I am convinced that it's the woman that seduces, that the woman has the power in seduction, that it's the woman that plays the game. If she could only recognize it without threatening men.

Very early on, I realized I am not a man, so I must just get along with my lot and make my life as a woman work. And now I enjoy it enormously. And I say to women, enjoy being a woman. The power of a woman is there, don't abuse it, use it. But use it for goodness, don't use it to castrate.

Barbara Chase-Riboud: No one who holds absolute power over anyone else is going to give it up willingly.

I've never in my life met so many beautiful, young, intelligent, well-educated, sexy women in New York in my life, never. And they seem to cause a terrible threat to men. There seems to be a backlash, a male reaction, of simply ignoring these women, and either seeking the company of men exclusively or seeking the company of much younger women whom they can dominate.

Mirella Ricciardi: I am absolutely not a feminist, because I do not like people who go against their natural role in life. Although I understand the feminist cause, I don't think it brings happiness and I think women who say they can live without men are talking bullshit. Because every female needs a male.

Nancy Richardson: I am sure feminists wouldn't think I was a feminist, but I certainly am a woman facing the problems that feminists discuss all the time, and with a great deal of anger – the problems of inadequate day-care, working in a corporation, having a baby and then being forced back on the job too soon, perhaps. I always went back soon, mind you, and I always wrote columns right through my pregnancies, and even in the first months after I had a child, when I wasn't back at the office, I was still under deadlines. I sympathize deeply with the problems of women, but there is not a feminist in the world today who appeals to me as a human being.

Stella Richman: I've never been somebody who is going to get up and wave a banner for my rights, or other people's rights, because I think you are born free. If you then let yourself be trampled all over, you've got to suffer the consequences; or equally, if you rush to break through imaginary chains, you have to suffer the consequences. I never saw the point in fighting to be treated as an equal when I'm the first person to want somebody to give up their place for me on a bus or open a door for me, or help carry a bag for me. I wouldn't mind who helped me, but I don't want to exclude myself from being on the helping list. I would equally help an old lady across the street, or an old man across the street – it's only a matter of courtesy. I hope that's a tradition that never dies. I know a lot of young men think well, I'm not giving up my place to you on the bus because you're fighting for equality. I didn't ask for it, so be equal, stand up. I think all these things are ridiculous, to be honest.

This word emancipated is very dangerous, because a lot of women equate that with going from bed to bed. That's a very poor use of the word emancipated. It means you can be free to go where you like, do what you like, pick up a phone to whom you like, write a letter to whom you like, have an affair with whom you like. That's OK, but a lot of young girls made the mistake about ten years ago of thinking emancipated means, I can smoke hash, take heroin and sleep with whom I like. That's a fairly miserable sort of existence. If that's all emancipation means, you're putting yourself into another prison.

Angela Rippon: I've got a theory that, if we were not put into a position where we were forced to have an opinion on women's role in society, evolution would ensure that women would take their rightful place, because they would turn out to be brilliant doctors, or engineers, or lawyers, or teachers, and one would accept them on merit and ability. But, because so much has been written and shouted – shouted, rather than discussed logically and rationally – about how unfair the system is to women, and how terrible it is, that immediately sets up entrenched attitudes. Suddenly something that could have happened normally, perhaps without a great deal of attention being brought to it, becomes a matter that has to be taken issue with. You get women who say the woman's role is in the home and set against the career woman, which means that women who do want to achieve need to be more strident and dogmatic. And immediately, instead of nice calm waters in which everything should go along fairly naturally, you suddenly have raging torrents with one fighting against another. And as soon as that happens and people feel they have to have opinions on it, those opinions become very dogmatic and very hard line. I fear that saying, we must have the token woman, has made men resentful. They feel as if they are under siege.

Shirley Ritchie: The feminist movement did a great deal of damage in that it put up the backs of men who had decided that, if this was the way women were going to behave, they didn't want any part of it. The individuals who embraced it enthusiastically and rushed around burning their bras and being Ms instead of Miss or Mrs, killed a great deal of their own warmth and personality and, I think, were the ones who lost out. Nobody enjoyed them, they didn't enjoy it, and the results weren't very dramatic. Any woman who puts her mind to something will do it; the opportunities are there. Even if they are iron ladies, they still look and behave like women.

There are one or two small areas – certainly one – where men are discriminated against, and that's in the domestic violence situation. Frequently these days a woman gets an injunction to turn the husband out of the house on the basis that he is being violent. Now, I've seen many a case where the woman has been just as violent, but it is jolly rare that a husband gets a woman turned out because she's throwing plates at him, jolly rare. So, in that sense, the men are discriminated against.

I'm a great fan of Mrs Thatcher. I think she is terrific. She is a shining example of someone who has used her intelligence, her personality, and indeed her femininity to get herself to the top of the tree she chose. I don't know on what possible basis anyone can say she is not interested in women. She has brought, as far as I know, as much pressure as she could bring to bear on people like, for instance, the Lord Chancellor, to appoint more women. You can't just rush around indiscriminately appointing women because they're women; they've got to be appointed because they are right for the job. That has happened with our judges. Admittedly we have only three high court judges out of about eighty, but that's because only three should be high court judges.

Deborah Rogers: I can scarcely bring myself to talk about Mrs Thatcher. Her great gift, if you can call it that, or her great strength or whatever, is not so much confidence as an absolute conviction she is right. There doesn't seem to be any part of her that really questions herself. And you don't even feel that, at the end of the day, when she goes home, puts her feet up and thinks about the result, there is a part of her that asks, should I have done that, was that right? Maybe that is confidence, but I think it's something more overbearing. And all that she's done for women is to make people realize that it is possible for a woman to do that job.

Selwa Roosevelt: I am not a feminist. Not at all. I believe women have the best of all worlds. I love being a woman, and I think we are luckier than men. I really believe that women have it made, particularly if they're bright and if they can use their femininity and, at the same time, be responsible about it.

I think very little of feminists. Where the feminists have obviously made a contribution is in the practical matters of legislation – all of the things that are there to be done to make life better for any minority, for women and others. Where I don't like them, and where I disapprove of them, is this attitude that somehow there is an adversarial relationship between men and women. This I can't accept. You see, I think a woman's role is to love and give, and not to worry what she does and what she gives, and therefore she'll get a great deal of love and affection in return. By giving love, you get it, but you don't get it on the cheap. There's a price to pay for everything in life. And you must be generous-spirited. And these women are not generous-spirited. Any woman who tells you that man is your natural enemy is, for me, not a person I can admire. Women who try to make their sisters feel that men somehow are to be despised, are adversaries, ought to be put down. I have nothing but contempt for this kind of feminism. I think it's so unhealthy.

I think there would be a lot of resistance to any woman who wants to be President, and I certainly have no ambitions of that sort – Vice-Presidents or Presidents. Even though they ran last time, I don't think the country was ready for it. They'll get ready, it's going to happen, and I think a woman would be excellent as President or Vice-President.

Women shouldn't want to change the world too much, because they'll upset their advantages. Everybody has some advantages in life. I'm just a realist. I think that whatever you've got as an advantage, you should grab on to it, use it. Each of us is dealt a hand in this game of life, and each of us has some high cards, and you can take it any way you want. If you want to interpret being a woman as a deuce as opposed to an ace – fine. But I see it as being an ace.

Kimberly Du Ross: I'm the generation coming after the feminists, and thank God they were there, because to make any sort of progress one has to go to extremes, and they went to extremes for me, so now I can sit back. We're already one peg up without having to be as aggressive because they already did the work for me.

Juliet Mitchell-Rossdale: You don't legislate against attitudes that have lasted aeons. You can't will people to change their ways of feeling, just say, well, now we are changing this law, this practice, would you please feel differently? Feelings take a lot longer to change than that. And the reasons for those feelings aren't simply that, historically, there's been domination by men. It's also because there's been domination by women in men's very early childhood, and therefore a need for some compensation. So it's a complex pattern of dominations rather than a simple one. And if you were to have the mother figure of early childhood continue dominance throughout life, you would have a very unbalanced society.

Yvette Roudy: It is marvellous to be able to participate in a period of transition, of course. I envy the early American pioneers marching westwards, discovering, creating. Every period of new creativity for the human species is fascinating. Women are in such a period now. They suffer less than in the last century, when they didn't have the right to vote, couldn't cross a border into a foreign country without their husband's authority; and when they worked it was the husband who received the salary. Our grandmothers suffered a great deal, treated rather like blacks in the United States at the beginning. That is a question I have studied a lot and from which I borrowed the idea of quotas for women, for example. In law, now, we have equality, so it is a question of personal battles. They are both psychological and political and therefore fascinating; when there's little left to win, one must get very bored. A lot depends on women now, and it's their responsibility, but they also have to know what they want themselves.

Joan Ruddock: There are studies which have demonstrated that girls are physically handled differently by their mothers, and that their mothers will soothe and nurture girl children and will rough up boy children and actually contribute to the boys acquiring a certain kind of behaviour. But, equally, where mothers try to bring up their children in an absolutely identical fashion, the mothers say that boys behave differently from the girls. My scientific research was in the field of genetics, and I think it is impossible, to the extent of my own knowledge at least, to say what factors are truly environmental and what factors are genetic. But whatever the case in terms of upbringing and conditioning, I don't accept that society cannot proceed on a basis of real equality. I believe that real equality can be established, and I believe that, whatever their early years bring to them and whatever conditioning there is for them, it is possible for women to become sufficiently confident to compete and to live with and alongside men on equal terms.

Carol Rumens: I am a feminist in that I believe in equal rights, equal social justice for women, absolutely. But I'm not a separatist. I don't like hate movements, I don't like divisions between people. I think it's important to try and find points of unity, and so a movement that wants women to develop away from men and use women's insights only to plough back into women's lives is completely wrong. Women do, perhaps, have special things to offer men in how to behave, more because of background than temperament, but the dialogue has got to go on. It's a horrible idea that the sexes are split off from each other, that they can't imagine each other's experiences.

It would be good to think that people could get to the top without huge struggles and having to put each other down, but I think, once you're aiming for success, you are in a power struggle, and, in our society, women have to behave like men to get anywhere. We should be assertive, but not aggressive. Most women are not sufficiently assertive, and I don't like aggression in either men or women. That's where women can perhaps influence men: in being less aggressive. A womanly society would be a less aggressive one.

Ghida Salaam: I might be considered a feminist in the Arab world – in the sense that I'm a step further from the condition of women in the Arab world and I believe in equal opportunities for women. I believe in woman's independence and her right to self-determination, to assert herself. However, I would not go so far as to condone what the liberation movement for women in America stands for. That goes back to the question of whether I think I belong, whether I'm Western or whether I'm more Eastern. I think it depends on the set of values you cherish, and in that sense I believe I am more Arab, because my priorities are my home and I don't believe that stops me from pursuing a career at the same time, but I still believe that, in the East, our priorities are collective rather than individual, as most of the liberated and feminist women call for. We still place very high values on family, on friendship, on collective ideas, as against individual pursuits or individual achievement.

Khairat Al-Saleh: I wouldn't label myself a feminist, but I would agree that women are in a state of bondage all over the world and that this state of bondage is relative. I do believe, very strongly, that they should break out of their prison and come into their own. But then, if men were in this position, I would also fight for them. The problem is that not only women are not liberated; it's men too. The men who oppress women are also lacking in true freedom.

Bushra Salha: I'm not a feminist. The problem in this day and age is that everybody tries to take on the role of somebody else. Women are trying to be too much like men, which we cannot be. We have to be what we are. But, at the same time, we have to be equal, we have to have equal opportunities. We can have as intelligent women as men, we can have as capable women as men. But we shouldn't try to change our roles, to take on a man's role.

Dame Cicely Saunders: I'm not a feminist. I've been fighting all my life for dying people, not for women. And dying people, men and women, are equally needy, and equally capable of achievement, right up to the very last minute.

The women who really stir my concern are the women of the Third World, much more than the women of this, where I think you can get on with it. OK, we may be a bit disadvantaged, but most people ought to be able to handle it. But the Third World women – the toils they have, the disadvantages they labour under, physical as well as emotional, and the way they are considered – that moves me much more.

Sylvia Scafardi: I've fought for civil rights. I think I would much prefer something to be done for the human race rather than for women as such, because I think, in many ways, men may be disadvantaged from childhood. They're supposed, to a certain extent, to be macho and be good providers and so on. Some want to do that, and some don't. Some love being regimented and some have very many female traits, and I therefore think men and women are both disadvantaged. Not equally, because women are more so, but what I would do would be for people in general. Of course, I'm a socialist, but today the fight between left and right seems to be at an impasse in democracy. One follows the other and cancels out and we don't seem to get anywhere. I'm a member of the Green Party and CND, and the key issue, I think, is the way we are living today, the wilful and aggressive way we conduct trade and business and the ruthless and aggressive way we are devastating the planet we live in, fouling the sea, and every now and then letting off these ghastly risks into the air we breathe. Doing something about that is what matters more than anything.

Mrs Thatcher is a remarkably able woman. Of course, she was lucky enough to have money behind her, but she had the will and she did it. Personally, I think she is an absolute disaster, a horror. She stands for everything I think appalling. I mean, who is her God really? It isn't St Francis of Assisi, it's money. If the till is ringing, if orders are coming in, that's OK by her. What has she done for this country? What about the miners? The miners and the unemployed today, many of them, their fathers, their grandfathers and their great-grandfathers, produced the wealth of this country. Those marvellous men worked in the industries which made Britain, helped the Empire. Mrs Thatcher permitted the police to have battles with these men and women who were the stock, the very value of England. These are English, British men, who are worthwhile, and their womenfolk, and we had battles in which both the police and the miners got mucked about. But the police had their protection and their helmets, and the miners just had their ordinary clothes and were bashed up. There was a war. She set one class, one lot of British people against another. What for? Because she wanted to break the miners. It's an outrage. She's done nothing for women at all. I'm not up in the details, but a lot of her privatizing has been extremely damaging to women.

Alexandra Schlesinger: I think the feminists express the anger a lot of women feel, but I don't think anger is that positive a force, and I don't think it leads to a solution.

Anne Seagrim: I haven't at all agreed with this women's lib. business, I've just thought it was a ridiculous thing. If women are going to make their mark, they make it without all that bra business. What's happened is that, in about fifty years, women have tried to reverse what has been the situation for thousands of years; they've tried to do it very fast and it's made them harsh, ruthless and cruel in lots of cases.

Women complain about being treated as sexual objects and then wear outrageous clothes which are designed to attract sexual attention. That really does annoy me. And I think it's absurd, getting all hot and bothered about, say, beauty queen contests being degrading.

Emma Sergeant: The word feminist repels me. I really don't think there's any excuse to bandy it around nowadays in England and America. One should talk about being feminist in the places I've been, where it is really needed, where women's rights are abandoned, but here there really is no struggle to do what you want. And women so often hide behind these feminist movements to cover up the fact that they're not particularly talented and not particularly efficient.

An emancipated woman in America – she'll be streetwise, she'll be aggressive, she'll be efficient, but she's lost something, whereas a very successful woman who has made it out of an Islamic society, or even a backward Latin society, has everything – she has her background, she knows where she's going, she has her culture, she has total roots of strength. At the same time, she's made it as a woman and is respected as a woman still.

A businessman can train a woman, give her top opportunities, top priority, and then she can turn round with a silly expression on her face and say, oh, sorry, I've just got engaged, I'm getting married, I'm having a baby, tatty bye-bye. Meanwhile this businessman has invested a lot of money and time into her. So when women come out with this strident feminist talk, if they don't come up with the goods, it is most aggravating for men to listen to, and it aggravates me as well. I like a girl who just gets on with her work and does it well and with enthusiasm, and there is nothing more annoying than somebody who becomes fanatical and who is not actually producing the goods.

Delphine Seyrig: We're not at home on this planet. All the institutions are male institutions, so we have to adapt to them, that's all, and we don't. That is why there are so many women in mental institutions, so many more than men. Women do not have power. Even if they have a little more power in New York than in other places, and if they have taken responsibilities for certain things, American women are just as oppressed as European women. There is no question but that money is in the hands of men, everybody knows it. What is in the hands of women is infinitesimal. Money is in the hands of nations which are led and lawed by man. It is a male-run planet. I'm talking about reality, not about how I feel. Reality is that economy is in the hands of men, law is in the hands of men, dissent and aggression are in the hands of men. And politics is entirely in the hands of men. It is not just a theory. It is already a big step forward to say we are aware at this time that the power is not in the hands of women and all in the hands of men. I think this is already important and very shocking. I have been doing what I can to become aware of it myself, and read what other women have written on that subject, meeting women who are questioning this power. This is what I have been doing for the past twenty years. I don't have any hopes for the future, but I think that, even when there is no hope for the future, being a human being and being a female human being, you have at least to say what you see and how you feel about it and what can be changed in your own small realm.

The fact that you have a woman Prime Minister, that's nothing, that's of no consequence, that's not interesting to me. Women always show up somewhere in places of power, but they apply the men's laws and they are men in their profession. They have to abide with all the male structures of society. They can't change that, there's no question of that.

There is now a big issue in France about incest – one out of five families has an incestuous relationship. That's 20 per cent. You have this problem everywhere, of course, because of the male structures of the society. So those are things where women can speak out and act to stop certain things, or at least to make things evolve.

There are a million things men could do to improve harmony between men and women, but they don't do them. The women's movement has not at all encouraged men to think for themselves. It's extraordinary that men do not bring up certain subjects among themselves, such as rape, violence, sexual violence. It is only women who discuss it. Men don't, but they want to listen when women are talking about it. Why don't men who do not rape organize a convention about it? Why do they not discuss it? It's strange, but they don't. How come men are not interested in discussing the subject? They say, I'm not a rapist, therefore I'm not interested, therefore I don't have to discuss this. All right, who is going to discuss it, the rapists? Are you going to leave it in the hands of the judges, and the repression by jail and punishment, and is it not a subject that should interest men? It's very strange to me, this.

I consider myself a woman who has adapted very successfully to a patriarchal society. And within that successful adaptation, I feel extremely rebellious. I can see, within my life, what has happened, and I can question this adaptation. I consider myself in pretty good shape considering what it is to adapt to this society. I could have gone crazy.

Hanan Al-Shaykh: Women in Europe and America are still arguing that they want to be equal, and they have their own reasons, but they don't know how lucky they are. When you are determined to reach a goal, wherever you come from, of course you reach for it and give to other women the incentive; you open doors for other women.

You don't think of liberating yourself when you are thinking about getting food or managing your daily life, the necessities. You don't think about it at all. The middle classes who are a little bit comfortable – they think of it.

Clare Short: Most women who call themselves feminists have reached towards other women and joined groups where there were discussions and a great closeness and an honesty and a beginning of self-revelation about the status of women generally and individual women. I haven't been through that. I think it's partly because I've got all these real sisters of my own and partly because I've been busy in other things. So I was a belated feminist almost. Politically, I'm a socialist, from Irish Republican roots; I'm an anti-racist and my constituency has a lot of poverty. These are my top issues, but since I came into the House of Commons I've found, more and more, how women look at me as being there for them just because I've said things about low pay or whatever. I'm a member of the National Union of Public Employees. It's overwhelmingly a women's union, very low-paid part-time women, cleaners, caterers in hospitals, schools, dinner ladies, and I'm conscious of their demands, which are all to do with objective things about low pay, about employment protection and the suggestion they shouldn't have proper maternity rights and shouldn't have rights against unfair dismissal. So, as I grow older and more experienced, the feminist is growing more and more strongly in me, but it has to be part of socialism.

Mrs Thatcher is an odd woman in that she is a perfectly attractive reasonable-looking woman, but in no sense politically does she stand there as a woman; she has never sought once to advance any cause to benefit women. On the contrary, she has done a number of things that have put back life opportunities and improvements in the status of women. So nothing has flowed from her being a woman, which is odd, because a lot of the argument is that women need to be seen in positions of leadership in order for young girls to think, yes, I could be anything. She's cut back on childcare, health care, all the kind of public services that women need to have better care for the people they care for, and she's deliberately working a policy that encourages an increase in the number of people who are low-paid, and these are predominantly women. She's never identified with the cause for improved cervical cancer screening or anything.

The sexes sometimes complement each other, but sometimes they're brutal and vile to each other. Sometimes it's good for women or any group that lacks power to be together, or like each other and support each other. But I'm not against men or against men and women becoming entangled with each other in the way we always have and always will. I think for lots of women, somehow subconsciously, the thing was to get along with men, to spend time with men, to be attractive to men. Hence, I suppose, the tradition of women being catty about each other, about their clothes, their looks, about who fancied whom. But the women's movement has said it is a good thing that women like each other and are nice to each other, and I'm part of that. I feel that I can have an easy, instant and uncomplicated relationship with women. If you take the Parliamentary Labour Party, there are right-wing women who would be opposed to my position within the Labour Party for whom I have a warmth and fondness, whereas most of the men who parallel them would tend not to spend time in my company because they see me as a politically labelled creature. There is some bond and warmth there just because we're women, which is very enjoyable, and it's warm and friendly.

It will actually be liberating for men when they don't have to keep playing those macho games and are allowed to be worried and weak, and sensitive to other human beings, and express their emotions and don't have to go round pretending to be in charge of everything. There will be more space for women, and I think it will be a world that will allow men to be more complete.

Every girl is her mother's daughter. But that's the cycle the women's movement has tried to break out of, and when women become clear about all this there will be quite a change. There are a lot of mothers today, who would either call themselves feminists or are influenced by that ethos, who are going to produce massively different daughters. It's an up-and-down society, and it will be interesting to see what those girls are like in twenty years' time.

Alexandra Shulman: As far as I'm concerned, the battles were fought before I had to fight them and won before I had to think about them, and I'm just a recipient of those victories. I'm not a conscious feminist. I think what we're doing is right. It's like colour prejudice or racial prejudice, prejudice of any sort; it's always difficult to redress the balance because, if you start inverting the prejudice, you then, in a way, reinforce the prejudice already there.

It is at the schooling stage that the work needs to be done. There should be instilled into all children the same expectations from life. And from that point, they can make their own way. Over a period of decades you will then get to a point where it works itself out. It's not likely to be within the next ten years, but in the next thirty years, when you start having people in powerful positions who were educated in that way, it should all be even.

It's very nice being a woman and having all the advantages that it brings. I don't wish to see a society where men and women are totally unisex. I don't wish to wear boilersuits. I don't wish to go out to work and have my husband sitting at home and darning my socks.

Rosemary Anne Sisson: I'm definitely not a feminist in the sense of thinking there is no difference between men and women. I love being a woman, and I wouldn't be anything but a woman for all the world. I'm only a feminist when my professional standing is not treated with the respect it deserves because I'm a woman. Women should get respect for being what they are. When they do work equal to men, they should get equal pay. But also they should accept their responsibilities as mother of the family and expect the father to accept his responsibilities as father of the family. Some feminists would claim that is an old-fashioned view, but I think it's the natural view, and when you depart from Nature you get into terrible trouble, physical, moral and spiritual. And I'm also a Christian, so that conditions me to some extent. I do think the last shall be first and the first shall be last. I think the more you try to assert yourself and be aggressive as a woman, the less respect you will get.

Mrs Thatcher expects women to get on with it, which is certainly what would have been said in our household. You know, if you can't manage children and a job, then don't have children or don't have a job, otherwise get on with it and find a way. It's very hard, but it's realistic. They're asking now for nursery schools from the age of three – well, that is exactly what used to happen: people used to have nannies. So the very people who say, what a shocking thing to put your child into the care of a nanny, still want to have the child and have the job, not because they need the money, but because they want to have both. Nothing is for nothing in this hard world, I think Mrs Thatcher has said, and those of us who were brought up in that same hard school know that's true.

Lady Anne Somerset: I completely disagree with the feminists who see it as a struggle against men. You've got to make yourself accepted as a person who, in her own right, has a career, but not to pose a threat to men, because a liberated woman shouldn't be a threat to men.

Maybe women who are firmly anchored in the world in terms of having a very successful career are too busy to necessarily want to change the world for other women. They just think people should get on with it, like Mrs Thatcher – she is obviously not interested in the women's question as such. Like Elizabeth I – I don't think she was interested in feminism at all, because she benefited, for instance, from the fact that Henry VIII encouraged female education at his court, but she never did that at her court. She was quite pleased to be an exception to the rule. And I think very successful women often are like that. One of the things that feminism has suffered from is that it is too often seen to be espoused by women who are failures and whining on about what a hard deal they have had.

The attention feminists pay to trying to get women called Ms really seems so disproportionate, and anyway, in the seventeenth century, when women were at their most unliberated, or comparatively unliberated – unmarried girls were all called Mrs – short for mistress – and it didn't really help very much, so I think it shows an inability to concentrate on priorities.

It would be quite depressing if you got a world where women were made to feel failures because they didn't have a job and they were running a house.

Gloria Steinem: Part of the antagonism towards Mrs Thatcher may be because, in a deep sense, we fear women having power in the world because we associate that with childhood. That's maybe an underlying reason. But it's also that she's not there representing women as a constituency. The first Jewish person in power is usually anti-Semitic; it's the same phenomenon. In societies that have a strong class or caste system, you may get a woman in the top job first, like Indira Gandhi. If Indira Gandhi had had a brother, she never would have been chief of state, but she didn't and the patriarchal family name was even more powerful than the anti-female bias, so she became chief of state. Thatcher represents class and political interest. So even though she was a woman, she was allowed to become chief of state. In the United States, we are much slower in getting women in those top jobs, but when we actually get one, she usually represents women, she represents sexual equality. As Geraldine Ferraro did.

Pamela Stephenson: I do think the women's movement has made tremendous progress, but where it has yet to make progress is in the situation of the lot of women who don't have careers. The major issue is how do you manage to have a career and have children at the same time? It just hasn't been solved. I think if you really scratch the surface of any career woman who has children, you will find that it's a painful issue.

Women are beginning to get the message that they can support each other. One of the greatest disadvantages the women's movement has had is female chauvinism. You see it everywhere. Look at Mrs Thatcher. I'm sure that she could have encouraged more women in her particular field, and I don't think she's done that at all.

Lady Arabella Stuart: I'm sympathetic towards a lot of the feminists' views, and I think feminism needed to happen, even if it becomes ridiculous, as it often does. Eventually the balance will have been righted by it, and then we can relax and forget about it.

I went and visited Greenham Common a year or two ago, and I was quite impressed and moved by the women there, despite everything that was written about them. On the whole, the press was so incredibly unfair, always making fun of them, mocking them, and I was very impressed, though I've no wish to go and join them. Although I don't like its militant side, I do think it's had one good effect in that it's made women supportive of other women.

Andrea von Stumm: One thing that disturbs me about feminists is that they want equal opportunities, but very often don't want equal duties. I've never seen a feminist group campaigning to be in the army or, in the case of divorce, for paying if she earns more. You find all those feminists wanting to share all the privileges of man but not the duties and hardships. And that I find disturbing.

If there's anything good about the feminist movement, it's that those mores which were limiting for both sexes have become more elastic, more flexible.

Christine Sutherland: The term feminist conjures up to me a woman with greasy hair who carries banners.

The so-called working-class women are liberated, but, as a result, they seem to be shedding tasks rather than acquiring new ones. The average working women – miners' wives or wives of working people – seem to spend a lot of time in front of the television and feed their husbands pies from travelling shops. Many of them don't even clean their houses. The progression has come at the cost of old-fashioned virtues, sadly.

Conny Templeman: I don't believe women should complain; they shouldn't whinge about not getting enough. It's true that maybe one doesn't, but I don't think one should ever say it. One should just get on and do the job as best you can and not complain about being treated differently. Of course, one is treated differently, but then we have advantages as well.

Mrs Thatcher doesn't do anything for women. Having got there, you'd think she could lend a helping hand, she could set up female organizations, but there's nothing, nothing.

Martha Tiller: I may not be a card-carrying, bra-burning feminist, but I am a feminist, and I never fail to seize the opportunity at the appropriate time in the appropriate way to enlighten someone, to help broaden their horizons. I think we had to have the likes of a Gloria Steinem and a Betty Friedan; I'm so glad we had them although I'm not like that at all. We had to have somebody make noise very loud and perhaps a little bit obnoxiously to create a general awareness. I've had men say to me, in some conversation about architecture, because that's a man's field, I have had them say, my God, my wife can't talk about anything like this, I wish my wife was not so stupid. Whereupon I want to kick them under the table. What they should do is help their wives expand their horizons.

The Equal Rights Amendment did not pass, because of people like Mirabelle Morgan, the antithesis of Gloria Steinem. She really did marshal public opinion to such an extent that the Equal Rights Amendment did not pass. She said, I'm not denied anything, I have everything I want, I have a lovely husband, a lovely home, lovely children, I don't have to work to be fulfilled. She was travelling the country making speeches, receiving fees for her speeches; she had hired a secretary to keep up with her schedule and she jetted around in her own aeroplane; but she was totally happy as a subservient woman.

Claire Tomalin: I am a totally engaged feminist and always have been in the sense that I think there should be equal educational opportunity and equal job opportunity, and it's obvious that there's a very long way to go before this really pervades the whole of our society. You get curious effects there. I'm very keen to see more women in politics but I'm a bit dismayed to see more women in prison, and to have to accept that, if women are going to do everything men do, they're going to do a lot of bad things as well as good things. This is something that feminism is having to think about and tackle now.

I suspect that the sort of ruthlessness Mrs Thatcher shows is very much modelled on male ruthlessness. In her way of running her Cabinet and her general style in politics, I would say she is behaving like a very despotic man.

Lili Townsend: In most ways, I certainly think I am a feminist. I've never been at the leading edge of feminism, because I don't have that edge of rage to fuel me, but I support my sisters that do. I've been able to use my femininity to advantage and I haven't felt it necessary to engage in a pitched battle. When the pitched battle gets to a high intensity and those ladies are in the front lines of fighting for equality of another sort, I'm still back in the nursing area and a caretaker and a healer. So I support those front lines, but it's not my way to be there.

We can influence without having to control. I think one of the great issues we're all facing now in personal life is that of control and how important it is for us to strangle, to dominate, rather than dance with. But the female mystique is to create that dance and that element of flexibility in relationships.

The innate wisdom of women is there, lying dormant. The only thing we need now is to drop the fear of communicating the truth.

Polly Toynbee: Feminist is a word that frightens people because they always imagine the most extreme and lunatic things. I think feminist means believing that women have a hard time; believing that the apportionment of roles between men and women is unfair and damaging – particularly to women but also damaging to men; believing that something's got to be done about it; believing it permeates every aspect of our life, from cradle to grave; and believing that, as a result, society doesn't have a wholeness and a unity, doesn't achieve the potential of each individual. Each individual is damaged by this forced role-playing, prevented from fulfilling all sorts of sides of their character because they're only allowed to acknowledge half. Of course, some people do cross over, and people will always point to the exceptions like Margaret Thatcher, but the exceptions don't prove anything.

Mrs Thatcher is one of those women who has come up fighting tooth and claw through an entirely male environment, where the only hope of success is to pretend you're not a woman and go about actually complaining about other women, saying, I'm not one of those feminists, in order to establish quite how masculine you are; and that you're one of the boys and you're in there and you're serious. All right, she looks feminine, she wants to be thought a woman in some ways, but it's important to detach yourself from being a woman in politics, because you get made irrelevant. You've got to show that your views on the economy are as important as a man's, and as a result you've got to trample on other women, or on the ideals supporting other women. You can't afford to say, yes, I'm going to spend time going to meetings or encourage other women, I'm going to be identified with women, because they'll say, oh, that terrible feminist who is always going on about women. So when she got there, it's not surprising that she was the first Prime Minister not to appoint a woman to her Cabinet since the war.

Mothers are themselves conditioned by how they related to men, to their fathers, their brothers, and also how they relate to their sons. And even if you have a mother who is an extremely intelligent mother, who maybe has a job of her own, the son still sees the mother basically in relation to what she does for him when she is there, which is, of course, the washing and cooking and everything else. Even if you have a husband who does some of these things, it still basically falls back on the mother every time, and maybe that conditions the son. None of this produces any answers as to how you're going to change things, except very gradually, and I've never said as a feminist, right, we'll pass this law, we'll write this book, we'll make this statement, and the world will change. It's always seemed to me to be a very long-term project: to get men to change basically.

Kathleen Turner: Feminists have brought a great deal of attention to the inequality that has existed, that still exists. In the last fifteen years, the redress has been tremendous. I think they have done a great job. I think the United States has the greatest level of feminine freedom in the world.

Jill Tweedie: I can't imagine any woman who is intelligent, with a feeling for equality, democracy, self-respect and pride as a human being, who isn't a feminist. Because, if you are not a feminist, what does that imply? It means you do not consider you require the same opportunities, the same dignity in the outside and the domestic world, as a man. I had three years at the beginning of the 1970s when I really found men intolerable. I could not talk to men at all. It was a bad time, because it's not a nice feeling. I don't like that feeling of being alienated from other human beings. I've got over that, but certainly then I did feel that men were the enemy. Consciously or unconsciously, they had certain attitudes so deeply inside them that I felt they constituted, to some extent, a threat, either to women's position, women's opportunities, or women's physical well-being. And I'm not really far away from that today. It's easier today, because I know enough feminist men whom I have learned to trust, and I know underneath the layers I am not going to find something frightening; they are not suddenly going to make some awful remark that makes me feel, my God, they are like that after all. But when I look, for instance, at the crime figures, I have to say that there seems to be something in many men which is unacceptable and which constitutes a threat to other human beings: children and women. I remember writing about it once, and James Cameron wrote to me and asked, how could you say that? And I wrote back and said, look, you are a wonderful man, but open your newspaper day after day and tell me who commits the crimes, who kills the children, who kills the women or other men or old people – it is men, one after the other. It is always men. *Your* sex. You do something about your sex.

Women are not yet fitted for the Western world, and it is not yet fitted to women. I used to campaign a lot about the fact of women entering every single profession, politics, newsreading, everything. Now when I see, for instance, people saying that women have not got into politics, there's still only a comparatively small number of women MPs, I think to myself, well, perhaps women have more sense, they don't want to enter those fields. Because the whole impetus of life in the outside world is contrary to all the things women have learned. Whether women will continue to be like that if and when they enter public life in great numbers I don't know, but at the moment it is competitive and aggressive, it is difficult to be honest and many of the things that women are, and you have to give up those things consciously in order to

548

succeed. A lot of women are not prepared to do that, they feel the price is too high. Until that changes, there will be discrimination. I believe you can have success without speaking a male language. But you have to have a lot of women with you. You've got to change the balance.

I would have said that something went very wrong a long time ago emotionally with Mrs Thatcher, so that she became a man. She succeeds because she has all the male qualities. When I say 'male', I'm not discriminating against men, but the male needs to succeed. She also has some of the female things which I consider very dangerous: emotional convictions which are not open to rational discussion. One of the things women have from years and years of oppression is irrational convictions, and they are quite dangerous sometimes. One of the things we don't learn in school or in our lives is the analysis of emotion. Mrs Thatcher has all the male strengths and drives, but she also has the ability of the woman just to believe, and has the strength of that kind of conviction; which many a matriarch has in a family and ruins the family through having it.

Marie-Claire Valène: My basic principles in life are feminist ones. I believe that men and women in life are equal, even if not the same: equal in both rights and duties. In France, there is theoretical equality, but not always in practice, and even that famous law about equal work and equal pay is less respected in France than elsewhere. Perhaps that's true of the Latin countries in general.

Joan Vass: Thinking is not sexual. And what we all have to learn to do is think, and if everybody learnt to think, there probably wouldn't even be a war, we'd all be pacifists, and we'd all understand things. What has happened with people who are put down, whether they are black or white, or men or women, is that they have not learnt to think.

Sara Vass: I'm not a separatist. I think that people can survive without people if they have to. But it's not a very happy situation for people to survive alone. I'm a heterosexual woman and would like to have a man, men in my life. But I believe in equality. I don't like inequality wherever I see it, and I don't understand it. And so I am a feminist because one has to be, because things are not equal and not fair.

Virginia Wade: In the heat of the feminist movement ten years ago, I would probably have said I was not a feminist, because I hated that butch feeling feminism was associated with. I thought they were trying to be second-rate men. Things have progressed a lot over the last ten years. Now all that has calmed down and it isn't so aggressive, I think I am probably more of a feminist, because I believe there's a lot of work that could be done in equalizing things and getting people to understand each other better.

Michaela Walsh: I really don't associate with anyone who is not a feminist. By feminism, I don't mean the traditional concept of the political feminist movement. I believe that, in terms of preserving life on the planet, the world has to be based on a feminist set of values. But I'm not a separatist. I like men very much, and I don't think you can have a successful or healthy institution if you have separate institutions and separate values. It's true of political values, too. We are in a global society, and we have to learn to create what I would call a feminist environment for all of us, and stop this competition for the wrong reasons. Competition in the market place is one thing, competition for control of people and destructive power is not feminist and not life-preserving, that's for sure.

There is a very strong movement in the world today of women bonding together, for the first time, I think, in history. Women who don't know each other, and who have never been out of Latin America, go to Africa and try to get to know African women as people. And African women try to get to understand Western women as people, or as individuals. That's never happened before. That's a new phenomenon which I think will strengthen the self-confidence of individuals: knowing they are not alone, that they are not isolated; that there are women everywhere in the world who have a common bond. That also came out of the 1960s and the trip to the moon, when we shifted from 5 per cent of the world's population knowing there were people on the other side of the world to only about 5 per cent who don't know that today. My interest is in making sure that women gain the confidence to realize they have an equal opportunity and equal responsibility to make decisions about investments of their own.

It is as much the responsibility of women to make the demands on society and keep the pressure on to bring about change as it is the responsibility of males to recognize that their business can be run far better if they involve diversity of talent and tap the largest pool of talent and resources instead of just people with an Eton or a Harvard tie.

550

Tracy Ward: I am very much in support of feminist views, but I happen, at the moment, to feel that I want the man I love to make the decisions now. If I have to give up some of my acting for my love, I will. Maybe it's because I want to be with somebody I mentally admire. I don't mentally admire men who are just successful and who just want to be successful, because there is something aggressive and selfish about that. You don't have to be wonderful to be successful. You can be wonderful and quite laid-back about work. I'm not so aggressive any more.

I have heard people say that the reason there is so much appalling unemployment at the moment is because women want jobs and women shouldn't have jobs. Well, that's bullshit. Men and women have got to have equal opportunities, because we have both got the same amount of energy, determination.

Marina Warner: I think Mrs Thatcher is an individual who is detested, I don't think she is a type. I don't think the people are just reacting against a woman in power. I think we could have a woman in power who we would love or like. She is bossy without, very often, giving a good reason for it. She represents a kind of thumbs-down consul and we are all the gladiators. We are the poor people who are wheeled out to do the work, and she is the ruler who sits in the imperial purple box and does the thumbs-down to this frantic piteous humanity. That's how I feel about her. I hate the way she is all so collected in her appearance. But I try not to hate her because I think hate is a very confusing emotion; you tend to stop seeing clearly. At times I try and understand what she does. I met her once; I interviewed her for *Vogue* when she was made leader of the Conservative Party, a long time ago. It's not my party, but I was overjoyed that the Conservatives unprecedentedly, incredibly and surprisingly had elected a woman – and she was horrible. She was so supercilious and defensive, and almost rude and angry. Then her PR people told her she must behave better with journalists and she became better. She just has a very unfortunate way of managing to behave as if everybody else is somehow inferior and short on all the funds of energy and ideas she has.

Heather Watts: I feel I've been born late enough to reap the rewards everyone else has worked for. I don't feel I have to fight for it, they already fought for it. I do believe in the equality of women. And I do believe that female children should be encouraged to get educated and go out and work. I don't think it's enough for anyone to run a house for ever, I really don't. I live my life independently, I'm single, I own my own apartment, I have friends I like, and if I marry I'll keep my own name and my children will have my name and my husband's name. But I don't feel submissive, and I don't feel dominated. I feel like I live my own life.

Felicity White: I am a great believer in women being given the opportunity to show what they can do. I don't believe that concessions should be made for them, I don't think there should be positive discrimination. But I feel women are very strong, I feel they have a tremendous amount to offer. And that they haven't been able, and still are not able, to fully give everything they've got. I'm not a feminist in the sense that I think men should be put on a desert island and left to rot. It is terribly important that there are both men and women. Men have a lot to offer women, as well as women men. I couldn't live without a man. I require the balance very, very strongly.

Katharine Whitehorn: There are two separate types of feminism: one which says women are essentially very much like men and could do all the jobs men can do if they weren't conditioned from babyhood, if they didn't have the wrong education; and another, which is closer to my own view, which is that women have a different point of view, different sets of priorities, different views on what is important. But that is exactly why there ought to be enormous numbers of women at the levels where any important decisions are made.

Jeanette Winterson: For me, feminism is giving women an equal chance to live as they please in all senses – in the home, at work and as individuals – to let them start from the same starting-block as men, without being hindered in the first instance. Because that's not possible, maybe one has to be more militant or more determined than otherwise. Not many men really care that much about what happens to women. Until they start doing the work as well, there are always going to be fringe groups, off-centre groups of women who have to carry the feminist cause on. Clearly, it's a pity radical separatists have to exist, but they have to because they're saying that things are still really wrong. They're a voice crying in the wilderness, but there's no need to have off-centre radical groups when things are going well in the centre. That's obviously a political metaphor as much as a feminist metaphor. It seems to me that, as long as these groups have to go on existing, things are not right. It's not enough for just a few white well-educated middle-class women to have got on. There are a great many bitter women who could

552

perhaps do better for themselves if they were able to put aside that bitterness, but women do suffer more in the sense that our economic power is usually less to start with, so it's quite hard even to buy your way out of it, even to get yourself small comforts to make life a bit easier. Poverty is so grinding.

Anna Wintour: Feminist is a word which was coined at a time when it was needed, and that battle is won as far as I'm concerned.

Women going around in men's suits and trying to efface their femininity in the City is crazy. That's changing in New York, now, I think. There are more women working in America than there are men, and that sort of anonymity women were looking for in the late 1970s and early 1980s is changing. Women are becoming much more aggressive and proud of their femininity. It's changing a lot in America, and I think that it will change here afterwards.

In the 1970s all the fragrances that sold were these very light things, like Crystal, and denying the fact you're a woman. Now all the fragrances selling the best have names like Opium, Poison and Diva and these are very strong things. Women are rejecting the anti-woman kind of perfume and are going for the very sexy feminine perfume again. I know that's a light-hearted example, but I think it has to represent a change of attitude in women.

Enid Wistrich: My definition of feminist is a person who is interested in women developing to the full in society and not having their potential moulded and suppressed by the dominant group, who are still men.

4
Sexuality

'When modern woman discovered the orgasm it was (combined with modern birth control) perhaps the biggest single nail in the coffin of male dominance'
– Eva Figes, quoted in Elaine Morgan, *The Descent of Woman* (1972)

'I find it absurd to assume that all coitus is rape. By saying that, one agrees to the masculine myth that a man's sex is a sword, a weapon'
– Simone de Beauvoir, quoted in Alice Schwarzer, 'The Radicalization of Simone de Beauvoir', in Francine Klagsbrun (ed.), *The First Ms. Reader* (1972)

'Women complain about sex more often than men. Their gripes fall into two major categories: (1) Not enough (2) Too much'
– Ann Landers, *Ann Landers Says Truth Is Stranger* ... (1968)

'I love my past. I love my present. I'm not ashamed of what I've had, and I'm not sad because I have it no longer'
– Colette, *The Last of Chéri* (1927)

Lolicia Aitken: I was never seduced. I always seduced everybody. Nobody ever seduced me.

Maria Aitken: It's been so convenient to equate our experience, to find that there is a female orgasm, that we have it too. In fact, it's often much nicer without it. It just depends. It isn't a definition of it, anyway, for the woman.

Lady Penelope Aitken: A woman has to be very careful about her husband's indiscretions. She may be very hurt. Some women find it impossible not to tear their husbands apart because they are so hurt. But it's not wise, because men do have a constant need. A woman equates sex with love. In loving somebody, you feel betrayed, and it is difficult to take a man back if he's been in someone else's arms, although you don't understand that it probably hasn't meant anything to him. You've got to grow up and accept that very quickly if you want to keep your man.

Shirin Akiner: Some men are extremely devoted to their wives, some women are very devoted to their husbands. Others, both men and women, need, like, want to have affairs, and do. I really don't think it's an inborn thing for men to have affairs and women not to. This is playing into the feminist camp, making a social judgement on a biological basis. I can well believe that this would upset the feminists, but I simply disagree with it.

Baria Alamuddin: Needs are basically the same in men and women, and

557

sex is a matter of education and culture, upbringing and training. In our society, a man is brought up to be aggressive, to look for it, to go and get it; whereas a girl is not. She also has the need, but the application is different. Application is a very individualistic thing. I don't think any two people can make love like any two other people. I always have the feeling that there is a misconception about sex in the world, both in the East and the West. I have personally interviewed people about marriage, and to some women it is just a means to get children. I interviewed one woman who had never even been kissed. I know women in the Middle East who hate sex, who think sex is dirty and not something you talk about. I am sure in the West, too, if you have a father attacking a daughter, then this girl's perception of sex will never be the same. There are many elements involved in the application of sex. To me, sexual relations only make sense in the context of love. Any other time it is just like eating; you can go and get it in this restaurant or another restaurant. And I don't believe a man can make love to another woman if he loves his wife.

Madeleine L. H. Alatas: Certain men, the minute you meet them, undress you with their eyes. You can feel it and you know it. Some women are attracted by it. I'm not. I find it an invasion of privacy.

A woman requires much more affection, much more foreplay, much more ambience, much more skill – skill in the sense of a skilled lover. Whereas, to a man, it makes little difference if the woman is skilled or not. If he just wanted to get somebody into bed and screw them, he wouldn't care if they were competent.

I would say that men are more dependent on women, than women are on men. On a purely sexual basis, a man needs to ask, how was it? Whether he's using you or not, he needs to ask, how was I, in comparison? There's always the need to make sure that the person is on line with him, whereas a woman can keep absolutely quiet all the way through. Women can fake orgasm, they can do whatever they damn well please. A woman has more power sexually than a man. A woman can come many times, a man can't in one act. He is not as strong sexually. I would say a woman is much more sexual than a man.

Jan Amory: I don't think sex is vital at all. I think it's over-exaggerated by the media, definitely.

Women can do it for passion, I am sure, but I don't think that's the normal woman. That's the woman that wants to beat the man in the marathon race and everything else. I don't think that's the feminine normal woman.

Adèle Anderson: There wouldn't be any point in me falling for gay men, because gay men only want men; they don't want women, they want to go to bed with somebody who has a penis.

Men see sex as power. They want to dominate, I feel, and so the more they have, the more conquest. I have spoken to so many men who say, I wouldn't have a vasectomy because when the nuclear bomb comes I want to be the one who propagates the new generation. I haven't met any women who feel they want to be the mother of the new world. Women can use sex as a weapon, but I think in general they don't.

When I was a boy, before puberty, I didn't really acknowledge sex. I knew I wasn't a girl, because I'm an intelligent person, I could see I wasn't. But I knew somehow there must be a solution, there must be something that could be done, so I held on to that and filed it away. Then, when I reached puberty, I suppose I would say I was gay. I certainly led a gay existence in the fact that I had sex with boys, men, whatever. I was a member of the Gay Liberation Movement, because it all started about that time, and there were plenty of others around me who were all perfectly happy to carry on being gay. For about a year, I'd thought maybe that was what I was feeling, that I desired other men, therefore I must be gay. But then, much to my surprise, I discovered that wasn't it. I didn't actually enjoy having a gay relationship. Then I had a double battle to fight, because, being a member of the Gay Liberation Movement, I announced to them, no, I wasn't gay, I was trans-sexual. And I got shit from them as well as everybody else. They said, you're selling out, there's no need, you're reinforcing sexual stereotypes. In the end I said, well, I can't live my life for a political cause, I have to live my life for me. If I had listened to them, I'd have been thoroughly miserable and ten years behind.

I did find it difficult to find a partner at first, yes. It's getting better now for two reasons: (a) I'm more at home with myself and (b) I refuse to take any shit. I used often to sleep with totally unsuitable men who only wanted to sleep with me to find out what it was like, who really had no respect for me whatsoever. That's completely out now, because I'm proud of who I am and I measure myself against any other woman. But if a man was trying to choose between me and another woman, I would back off. I would think, really, it should be her. My first boyfriend said to me, I love you, and I love going out with you, but I won't be able to stay with you because I have a long-term plan too, and that involves getting married, being respectable and having children, and you don't fit any of the criteria. So I tend to go out with men who are younger than I am. I'm thirty-four and go out with men who are probably five to ten years younger, and that's because I feel I didn't really have a sex life until I was twenty-six. I sometimes get very sad, just a personal sadness, when I see teenagers (and they start very young now, fourteen or fifteen) desperately in love, and I think I missed all that. I'm really terribly romantic.

I know men who don't get orgasm. It's not nearly as common, but I do know men who can screw and screw and never come. At least, not when they're with a woman. They might be able to in private. It seems you stroke one way, and it can be the most divine sensation; stroke it the other way, and it can be nothing at all. What I find is that, if I'm going along and somebody does something that isn't quite right, instead of just going back that far and building up again, I shoot right back. It's like one of those pinball machines, and I have to start again.

I can still have sex and not be in love, but I find it more difficult; and I can sometimes be in love with people and not have sex. The hardest thing has been to get the two to go together. I'm gradually getting there now. When I was in Australia, I met somebody and we went swimming in the river, and he swam across the river with this wine cooler and opened it up and there was a bottle of champagne and two glasses. I was a total goner after that. I thought this has never ever happened to me before and probably never will again. It was like one of those glossy adverts you see in the cinema. I just adored it. I love romantic things, and what is most important to me, what I like about my present boy, is that he is really proud to be going out with me and very affectionate in public. For a long time, I was like the mistress kept in the back room, or the hotel room, and I got fed up with that. There was also a time when I went out with people who didn't know. I went out with somebody for months before they found out I'd had a sex change, and they were really disturbed, they felt their whole world had been turned topsy-turvy. Not all men are intimately acquainted with the sexual organs. Mine are as near as dammit the same, though a gynaecologist would know immediately. But a man can penetrate me, and I can bring him to orgasm and have orgasms myself. It's much more difficult for me to have an orgasm now, but when they do come, they are ten times better than they were. A male orgasm to me was very much centred in the crotch. Naturally. Female orgasm is not centred there, it infuses the whole body and lasts much longer, and it really does come in waves. But I have to be desperately in love with somebody now for it to happen, because I have to be totally relaxed.

Dr Swee Chai Ang: Sexual behaviour is such a complicated thing. I come from a very Asian, East Asian, Japanese, Chinese, Mongol kind of background, and women were taught traditionally never to enjoy sex. If you did there was something wrong with you – I'm talking about the older generations – and so if women enjoyed sex, they would not tell anybody. The younger generation of Chinese women are quite different.

Speaking as a doctor, I don't think men's sexual drive is stronger. I know of a lot of men who are frigid, who have sexual problems, impotency and so on. Now, women have a potential sex drive which is, I think, very great. A lot of the sex drive, sex need is stifled and most girls are brought up with: don't sleep with a man unless he's going to marry you. So there is this kind of conscious inhibition of your desire to go to bed with anybody, because, No 1, you might get pregnant; No 2, if the neighbours hear, you are cheap. There's all this psycho-social thing that inhibits a woman so much that, in the end, when a woman goes to bed with a man she has got to justify it by saying I love him, which I think need not be the case. I have no hang-ups on this. Basically, sex between two persons is a development of affection. Certainly nobody wants to go to bed with a person they don't like. Even a man will refuse to sleep with a woman he can't stand. But, if it is someone he or she likes – I don't want it to be reduced to a state of playing squash or that kind of thing – but certainly I don't think it should be a situation where a woman, when she goes to bed, feels she is giving him everything, and a man, when he goes to bed with a girl, feels wow, he is God.

Lady Elizabeth Anson: Sex is over-discussed. I think it is very important, but there are too many books, too many shops. In a way, to me, it slightly loses the whole magic that it is so open.

I can't find the male in me. I haven't found the male in me. I have read endless articles saying that the ratio of women who have lesbian tendencies is as high, if not higher, than men with homosexual tendencies. I haven't come across it, except twice in my life. Once was my typing mistress, and once was a client; and I am absolutely allergic to lesbians, I have to say. I haven't met many, I don't think, or if I have I haven't known they were, and that's perhaps because I don't recognize them. But I can't imagine myself having a great lesbian friend. I would be frightened of it.

I have very strong moral views, and I always accepted that a man doesn't have to have them but a woman should. Yes, I do think men have to spread their seed and that probably sometimes they get more joy out of the fact that they have made somebody pregnant than the woman, depending on the situation, naturally. I think there is this tremendous feeling of reproduction in a man: he must reproduce. And I've always felt that a man can sleep with somebody and forget about it the next day and a woman can't. A woman remembers it, and it's difficult for a woman to understand when her husband's been totally unfaithful to her that it really didn't matter or mean very much to him at all. I think, for some of us, it is very difficult to understand that. It's something innate in men, I don't think it is conditioned by society. Society has changed a lot in the last twenty years, thirty years; it was a terrible stigma if somebody found out a girl had got pregnant before she was married. It was a disgrace. When I was eighteen, and when I came out, it was considered the most dreadful sin you could imagine. In fact, she would have had to have an abortion.

Beatrice Aristimuno: There are two kinds of women. A normal woman has her sex life in her head, and for that she needs to be with someone she is happy with, but their sex doesn't have to be fantastic at the beginning. It's never fantastic at the beginning when you're normal; it's completely cerebral at first. But if a woman continues to fantasize, it means she is not well suited sexually with her partner and she needs many of them. If she enjoys doing it, just for fun, she is a sick woman. It's normal that we fantasize, it's necessary up to a certain point, because fantasy is mystery and mystery makes it interesting. But there are limits. And the people that don't have limits are never happy with what they have.

We exaggerate the importance of sex because you can live with someone and go two weeks without having sex. There are certain women who, if they don't have sex every day, get hysterical because they think they are treated like shit, and that's not true, not true. You can have a very normal life with a man and not have sex for ten days. That doesn't mean anything. People don't have normal relationships any more. People are so disgusting, they really have disgusting relationships, especially in our rich world of money and jet-setting and going out. People's relationships are rotten.

I thought it could never happen to me that I could be with someone for one night, enjoy it and just forget about it. Well, it did happen, and I didn't feel a shit, I didn't feel a whore, I didn't feel anything. I just felt great.

Pamela Armstrong: I would like to see what would happen if women were conditioned to explore their sexuality. I would love to see what would happen if someone set up a brothel full of glorious, wonderful men. I think both sexes are able to feel and explore and exploit their sexuality in all areas, in all manners. You can have all kinds of different experiences within one relationship, or you can have all these different experiences with lots of other different relationships. And it can happen for men and for women. Sexual needs are the same for men and women. The pursuit is pleasure. The pleasure, as far as I can understand it, is equal for both. What's really important is the fact of birth control. There has always been birth control; it's a question of who had access to it. But, for the first time in history, millions and millions of women are freed of the threat of pregnancy, which changes the way you express yourself sexually. And that's what we're all coming to terms with really.

Debbie Arnold: I was talking to my grandmother about orgasms, and it was very interesting. She was reading *Cosmopolitan* and she asked, what is an organism? I said, an organism? And she said, yes, everyone's having organisms. I read it through, saw it was an orgasm, and I said, that's what happens when you sleep with someone, you have an orgasm. She said, do you? And I said, well, didn't you have them? She said, I don't think so, would I have remembered? I said, yes, you probably would have done. And she said, well, I didn't have one. And then I thought, how ridiculous it is to talk to your grandmother about sex. My grandma had been married to the same man for sixty years, and that was obviously the last thing women thought about in her day, or her group of women: upper-middle-class Jewish ladies in their twenties and thirties. They just got married, they had their babies, and very few of them went on to have fulfilling sex lives. It was in the separate-bed era. Now women have come to the forefront, especially ladies in their forties; they are still regarded as very very attractive. That's only happened recently.

The orgasm comes with everything else that goes with it. Just to go out and screw somebody is, to me, the most unsatisfying thing. Initially, it's want: you want, yes, yes, this is great, and all of a sudden, you think, oh, what am I doing here. I usually get to that point before it's past the kissing stage and I run away. That's how I've always been. Most of my girlfriends are like that. It's very unfulfilling. So I don't believe those women when they say they're all crazy about sex, I just don't believe they want to screw all day long and have orgasms here, there and everywhere, because I can't believe they can be that fulfilled. The most fulfilling form is to feel 100 per cent loved.

Leslie Ash: Sexual needs must be parallel. I know, in a lot of my relationships, the other person has wanted it more sometimes, and it's awful. You just feel like you're being used as a sex object. You've got to both want it at the same time. So those relationships haven't worked. I think everyone's got to find a compatible person to be with. It's actually finding one. I don't actually enjoy going to bed with someone for the sake of going to bed with them, although a man can do that, so I think their sexual needs are probably a lot more than a woman's. I suppose I act like a man in a lot of ways. If I had a relationship with someone who was married, and I was quite happy with that relationship, seeing that person whenever I could, I'd be quite happy. A lot of women wouldn't be able to cope with that, they'd want to be the only woman in that man's life, and probably want them to leave their wives. You play men at their own game sometimes. There was one man I used to see who I knew had another girlfriend, and it was a great relationship. We just saw each other when we could, and he was a man who adored her and me too. That really opened my eyes to thinking you can have that sort of relationship with someone. I had a relationship before like that, and I knew he had four or five other girlfriends, and I was quite happy to be part of that as long as I knew. But I can't understand women who actually want to be the only person or not at all. I mean, I do enjoy being the only one, but I find it very difficult sometimes to be faithful to one person, so a lot of women have said I am playing the man's game. I don't know why. I suppose, again, it's just working, and I love being a woman. I'm not saying I sleep around with a hell of a lot of people, but I just enjoy it. If then I was to see the other person, the married person and his wife, I would behave impeccably. I could be that person's best friend. You've only got one life and you might as well live it.

Diana Athill: The idea, that absolutely Victorian idea which went back further, that women didn't really need sex but put up with it because men had to have it, already has changed so much. It goes back to the primitive thing, that even in the age of the pill, which is after all a totally artificial thing, each time a woman copulates with a man she could be landing herself with this completely new development: her whole life could change. Lo and behold, she can have this responsibility of the child growing and having to deal with it, whereas the man can come and go. Because of that I don't think you can help making a slight difference in your attitude to sex.

The misapprehensions about sex are not just Victorian and English. I republished once a little Chinese erotic book in which it was widely supposed that what women desperately wanted was an enormous organ in the man – a huge penis – and she was going to have a lovely time. Absolute nonsense, of course. Any woman could have told any man who asked. But the Chinese firmly believed that, way back, God knows when; and most English people, most men, still do believe it. Nobody ever asked women, or women were too inhibited to say what they liked. They went on like this, generation after generation.

When I was young, we were all quite sure we were soon going to go to bed with a man, but it had to be a man you were going to be in love with. We took completely for granted that we couldn't really, we didn't want to go to bed with anyone unless we were in love. I am beginning to think now that that was a cultural thing. Basically there is something in a young woman who could conceive that makes her want to find someone who will be there, looking after her if it happens, which will give her a slight wish to be more involved. But as one gets older, one ends up being quite masculine about such things. I know an awful lot of women who, if they want a man, they want a man. And I've known women – I wouldn't do this because I'm so old-fashioned – who say to a man, I want to go to bed with you, quite cheerfully. On the other hand, I always, right from the beginning, recognized two possibilities for sexual involvement with a man. One was that one was going to love him and this was going to be the big thing, and the other was an authentic sexual flash – you know how it is sometimes. If that happened, that happened, and it didn't matter whether I loved him or not; that was equally a good reason for going to bed with him. I thought that from about the age of eighteen and I found it was true. I was quite promiscuous when I was young, but as long as it was authentic, it worked. I hated getting into the position when one is doing something silly, like going to bed with a man to be polite to him or something. If you really wanted to, it was all right, I reckoned. I didn't have to be in love. If the authentic attraction was there, it could be just friendly, nice, enjoyable.

Leila Badawi: Sexiness may lead to sex, but to travel is better than to arrive in many instances.

The few I've known who will sleep around and be promiscuous won't feel it as a conquest so much as an exploration, perhaps, which is a completely different game. I don't think women feel the need to go out to prove themselves sexually in this way, or to stake a claim, or constantly to prove they're in charge and capable of dominating. Seduction has other roles for women. It can have other uses.

Dame Josephine Barnes: Speaking as a gynaecologist, I do think promiscuity among girls is a very bad thing. A lot of partners is a bad thing, and we're beginning to know this now: that the girl who has many partners or starts sex early is at greater risk of getting certain forms of cancer, for example. And the more partners she has, the more risk she has of getting some kind of unpleasant condition. So that's a bad thing. Morally, I think it depends on the girl. But as far as the teenagers go, the pressure mostly comes on the girls from the boys, because, remember, the boys are most sexually active between the ages of about sixteen and twenty. Sex is different for a woman, because, after all, sex for a man means a certain amount of gratification. Sex for a woman means the possibility, on each occasion, that she might conceive a child.

A lot of women never have orgasm, even now, but how important that is is another matter. A man can't get sexual satisfaction (or very few – some can) without orgasm, but a woman can feel perfectly sexually satisfied without having had a complete orgasm; or she may have many orgasms and the man only has one. It varies so much I don't think it matters. This obsession is quite ridiculous. Interestingly enough, it was started in this country by Marie Stopes. Of course, her first marriage was a disaster, I think it was never consummated – in fact there was an annulment suit. But the idea that a woman is deprived if she doesn't have orgasm is complete nonsense.

Josephine Barstow: Some women decide they can't go to bed with a man unless they love him, some women decide they'd rather go to bed with a woman anyway. A lot of these feminist types say they function the same as a man, but I don't believe that. I really don't believe that that's true. I believe that they are conditioning themselves to believe it's true as far as they are concerned, but I don't believe it's fundamentally, physically, biologically true. I've seen too many women suffer from this thing that tortures women: this instinct that they have to garner the man to them. I suppose it's an instinct to garner the father of the child towards the child.

Jennifer Bartlett: I think sexuality is very personal to each individual. I think perhaps some people want to have sex once every three months, some people want to have it every night, some use it to get power, others don't like it at all, some enjoy it once a week, some only want to do it to have children. You find so many different attitudes and I couldn't say that one was masculine, one feminine. Of course, in the act between men and women, or even between gay people, there seems to

566

be one who gives and one who receives, but there's all sorts of ways of getting around that, too. I can be in love with somebody and feel quite a strong desire for someone else, but I would be very reluctant to act on it because you have to lie, and once you start to lie in a relationship you set up a climate of mistrust.

Jeanne-Louise Bieler: Everybody is told they should have orgasms all the time. I'm sure before television there must have been a lot of women who didn't even know what they were, so could live very happily without. And now that they know they should be having them, it's a problem.

Christine Bogdanowicz-Bindert: Part of the reason why men are promiscuous is because they can go and talk to their colleagues and friends about how successful they are and how many conquests they've made. In Latin America, where I travelled a lot, the man is valued by how many mistresses he has; that's part of his status, his macho. I always tease my American friends and tell them that their wives must be doing the same thing, because there are just not enough women to go around. Of course, they think their wives stay home and take care of the kids, but my guess is that's not the case. In Africa, interestingly enough, the women go around as much as the men. In a lot of societies, it is quite taken for granted.

Rebecca Blake: In general, women are more interested in monogamy and security, and what is romantically described as love. That's not to say that men don't want love as well, but I think men are not necessarily programmed to be monogamous. It is encouraged by our society, in some way, that men aren't monogamous, because for men it's considered a certain kind of triumph to have varied sexual experiences. And it encourages their sense of their own virility. Some women are more like this today. It depends on who the woman is, on awareness and how much deprogramming there's been. I couldn't sleep with a man, then forget it. I'd get involved.

Francesca Braschi: For the man, it's a sense of conquering. It's a machismo type of thing. Even if he hates her and he'll never see her ever again, he'll use her and throw her off. Because he's proved to himself that he could conquer, that he could get anybody he wants. A woman doesn't have to prove that, because a woman is always beautiful in a way. She can always conquer a man, she can always play around with a man, she can always play her games and a man will always fall for them. She doesn't have to prove herself by going to bed, here and there, all over the world. I think she respects her body more than a man. She respects her body and she thinks twice. She's much more selective and she knows what she wants. A man, after doing it, realizes the next day: oh boy, was she trashy! But women know from the beginning, by talking to you. She'll see through you.

Dianne Brill: With sex, for a man, there's a beginning, a middle and an end. But with a woman it's more like a circle.

When men are married and sexually active with another woman, it takes away from the relationship, the centre of a marriage, because they're spreading their seed everywhere else. And when it comes down to the woman they love, the drive, the centre isn't there, they're spread out, and eventually it breaks up the relationship.

It amazes me, the ability of men to have relations with a woman sexually and, after the act is done, feel free of it. Cherish the memory, think fondly of the woman you met in Santa Fe, but actually have no attachment to that person. That, to me, is something that, as a woman, I can't relate to, even in these liberated times. I'm receiving something, so to receive that and have someone inside of me, and then for me to remain emotionally uninvolved, is unimaginable.

Tina Brown: I think we do exaggerate the importance of sex. The old cliché is true: sex isn't important until you are in a relationship where it is going wrong. I underestimate its importance perhaps, because I am actually very happy. Long periods of chastity are perfectly OK, particularly when you are working hard. I think that gay men are better off in the closet, actually, most of the time. It's fine to have the occasional relationships, but this pressure to be promiscuous, as a homosexual, has turned out to be medically very unwise. I also think a promiscuous woman is very unlikely to be a happy woman. She is usually a woman who is desperately looking for something. Women, of course, are much more aware of their sexuality now and can enjoy being single and having flings and get a lot out of it. But rabid promiscuity in a woman usually means she is desperate about something.

Victoria Brynner: There are women who are sexual maniacs and don't give a damn who it happens with as long as it happens. However, I think men can have sex more easily and forget about it more easily, definitely. I tried it one day, you know. One day I said to myself, well, men go out, pick up a girl, spend the night with a girl and forget about her, why shouldn't I do the same with a man? It was a disaster. It was awful. But it was an interesting experience, and I'm glad I did it. I think we have to know about everything and can't judge things without having done them. Now I know the way it is. I really hated it.

I am not the type of woman to have a man just to have a man. I have one man if I feel like it. Not having feelings towards a man is a very sad thing for a woman. Very. There's a certain need which I can't disassociate from emotions, so even if the need, the urge, is there, if there's no emotion at all, I just can't. It doesn't interest me. I know so much of the disappointment of sex without emotional involvement that I don't even consider it now.

Sex is important in one's life. We do have to prove something. I think a lot of men are out for women who are good at performing sex. It's not just fucking a woman any more. I think sex is important for our mental stability, very. It's very healthy to have a man and to have sex, much better than not having it. You see women who don't have it, and it's frightening. Their whole perception of everything changes completely.

Joan Juliet Buck: Women probably used to fuck a lot more, but it's also a case of form defining function. A woman receives as a vessel. How much different stuff do you want to carry around as a reservoir? I also think people's behaviour is either decided in advance or entirely open to whim. Every time a man fucks, he doesn't think, oh gosh I'm sure she's a wonderful cook, and her house is just great, and she'll give wonderful parties and have great conversation, and we'll go on great journeys to far-away places. A man doesn't fantasize about every woman he sleeps with. I think he fantasizes about the physical thing before it happens, and then it happens and it's over. The woman is prone to fantasize about every fucking thing she runs across. Women have been commodities, objects, fungible goods, for so long. The clever ones, the cunning ones, would market themselves carefully to get the best deal, and certainly that must have involved a lot of going to bed with people they didn't love. Then, for a while, we had women trying to act like men. The 1960s ethos was you had to fuck everybody, and that's still in people's heads. But now, because of Aids, everyone is going to be pulling back.

Averil Burgess: This is a platitude, but I think it's absolutely true that, in my own generation and experience, sex has been indistinguishable from a relationship. I have never been aware of any woman who simply needs sex and will have it with anyone. This may be changing now. We have a far more promiscuous generation, and it may be that today's young women are interpreting a sexual relationship as a simple thing on its own, not as part of a long-term relationship, which could have been our social conditioning. But these are differences in perception. Women are rarely sadistic, they are rarely violent. The male is the criminal sex, and I see this not as conditioning but as an innate difference. Oh, yes, our sexual natures are different. But less so perhaps than they used to be, and less than the stereotypes indicate. The males are encouraged by their peer group into sexual boasting and obscenity, which seems to indicate that they are insensitive to the more spiritual aspect of sex; and girls are conditioned by their peer group into romantic fantasizings and so on which seems to indicate that they're less concerned with the physical aspect. In fact, I think they are, perhaps, nearer together than the stereotypes indicate. But the one-night stand is much more a male thing. If a woman does the same, she is going to be racked with guilt.

A lot of parents with girls at my school, while quite progressive, are worried about the effects of promiscuity, and so on. But I think the more usual pattern for a girl is not wholesale promiscuity and experimentation but establishing a sexual relationship with a serious boyfriend which is likely to lead to marriage. It may not, but she believes, at the time, that it may. This is a more likely pattern.

Carmen Callil: Probably, in a perfect world, brothels wouldn't exist. I think men can put up with a lot more than people expect them to. They moan and groan, I must have a fuck, but that's only because it's culturally acceptable for them to say it. They can put up without it for years, just like a woman. I think women are just as sexual as men, and I think sometimes women like it more. It's always been my experience. But circumstances circumscribe it.

Angela Carter: One of the big reports from Marsters and Johnson said it is just as well that women have never culturally realized their full sexual potential, because men would never be able to cope, and I'm sure it's true.

Anna Carteret: In my experience, men seem to need the physical act irrespective of who they do it with, whereas my desire for somebody is very much tied up with that person in particular and usually associated with something beyond just the sexual urge. It's either that I love them or that they stimulate some primeval thing inside me; it's never just casual. I have felt lust, I'm not devoid of lust, but it's never been as important to me as love. I suppose now, since I've had children, everything I do reflects on them, and therefore I can't lead a promiscuous life, even if I wanted, and therefore my sex is very much tied up with my marriage and has grown better and better. Like anything, if you get to know it really well and cherish it and practise it, and you get time, it gets better and better, whereas casual relationships, by virtue of the fact that you don't know the person well, can't possibly be as satisfying.

Barbara Cartland: In life, one always has to have a pupil and a teacher. You can't have two pupils together, you always have a pupil and a teacher – right from the Ancient Greeks, and therefore the happiest marriage is where the man is three or five years older than his wife, and he is the teacher, he teaches her about love. But you don't want him particularly as the virgin, because there's something strange if a man is a virgin when he gets to that age.

Sex is important to everybody, but I think it's been blown up into a thing that you must have and must do, and what we're talking about as sexuality today is lust – it's not love. People are told they must rush into bed and do peculiar things off the chandelier, which is a lot of rubbish. The whole thing has been blown up. I was the bestselling author in America when the romantic era came in. I sold something like two million copies of every book I wrote. There was no competition. Then along came these romantic authors who were told to write like Barbara Cartland with pornography. I know them well, they're very sweet to me. They're middle-class, middle-aged women. Half of them have never been kissed, let alone done those filthy things off the chandelier, but they're told it's what sells. That's just nonsense. I sell more than any of them. None of my books are dirty, none of my books are immoral, I don't have any pornography in them, and mine sell. If you read the books in the bookshops, they make you sick anyway, they're quite revolting. And if you watch television, half the time people are rolling around naked. People don't go about rolling naked on beds unless they've seen the television and think they ought to. It's been blown up, the whole thing, into a sort of sex bonanza. Half the time the men are incapable of doing all the things they're expected to do, and it's made everybody miserable.

571

I'm winning my battle. I'm the bestseller in the world and my heroine is never allowed to go to bed until the ring's on her finger. They've now got a cult in Los Angeles just started, in which the women say they will be virgins until they marry. Because of me. And in the Philippines, the girls are only allowed to read Barbara Cartland. Women have thrown away something very precious. Things are getting slightly better. *Cosmopolitan*, which is the young person's magazine in America, carried out a survey (which is why I went out, just last year) asking, do you believe in sex before marriage? And every girl said, only with my steady and the man I'm going to marry. That was an enormous advance on four years ago when they said, anything in trousers. The editor, whom I met afterwards, a woman, said, I think we ought to get together with Barbara Cartland. Gradually, gradually, people are beginning to see what fools they are. Now, look at the case I had the other day: someone I knew very well was working for me, and her daughter, aged just eighteen and a half, was going away on a holiday with her boyfriend. I said, goodness me, you're not allowing that? She said, well, everybody does it. Which is a rotten answer. And they went away on holiday. The girl was devirginized, she came back and the boy dropped her. She then went off with somebody else and had an illegitimate baby, and her mother's dropped her. Is that very desirable? The whole thing would have been stopped at the very beginning if she hadn't been allowed to be promiscuous.

One of the things which shocks me tremendously, which is entirely new, is this ghastly robbery, and robbery with violence. They knock about an old woman of ninety, then they get a sexual urge. This is something quite new. It's never happened before in my lifetime. Pretty girls have been raped since the beginning of time, there's nothing new in that – that's gone right back to Adam and Eve. But the idea of old people being knocked about and a man, a young man, being excited by blood and a piece knocked out of a very old body is something very unpleasant. I think television and radio have harped on sex until they've invented perversions of their own. People say, oh, well, putting that on television, you can turn it off; but once you've seen it, you've seen it. I read by mistake a book of Harold Robbins's and it was absolutely revolting. I only read half of it, I felt sick, and Gloria Hunnicutt said exactly the same. But, you see, I can't forget it, you can't, it's in your mind, your mind's an encyclopedia. I think about it sometimes, and I think how awful it is, but that's the beginning of perversion – you think about it, and it becomes the thing. Because you keep on saying how awful and wicked it is to carry on with young children, more and more people want to carry on with young children, though they've never thought of it before. Very young children – three, four and five –

being raped is something entirely new, entirely worked up because they're always talking about it on television. The more you say don't do a thing, the more it goes into your mind that that might be worth doing. If people keep saying to you that you ought not to eat raspberries in January, sooner or later you'll think you'd rather like to try raspberries in January. That's exactly what happens with all these things. There's so much talk about it, children think, well, I'll just try it, I'm sure I shan't be hooked – and they are hooked. It's exactly the same with sex. You hear of something, of doing something revolting, and sooner or later you think you might try it yourself.

Alexandra Chapman: The male is penetrating and the woman is receiving, which does not necessarily make it a passive act, of course, but that must be part of the difference in the perception. And men may not take the act as seriously, but they certainly take their penises seriously. The penis is part of man's self-image. Perhaps there is an element of Don Juan in many men. I used to know one man, however, who was afraid of spilling his seed because it would keep him from being creative. If he had an orgasm, he was very nervous that the next day he would not be able to write. He was an exception.

Shirley Conran: Women go to bed with men for very much the same reasons as men go to bed with women, including boredom – I mean, if you're stuck in Chicago, my goodness.

I would love to go to a brothel. I would like to *in theory*, but actually I wouldn't much care to be touched by somebody I didn't know. But the next time I go to Hollywood, I'm going to ask to be taken to Chippendale's, the male strip club. My son assures me that everybody that strips is gay. I think it sounds tremendously interesting, but the people I shall be looking at are not the strippers, I shall be looking at the other women looking.

Genevieve Cooper: Women are more easily distracted from wanting sex by everything else that's going on around them, by life in general. Women have a wider field of interest than men. They have too many other things going on for them to be as obsessive about it. Women are curious, curious about what goes on in the house, about this, about that, whereas men are interested in women. I mean, they're interested in sex, and think about it, and they might go out and buy a dirty magazine and think about sex, and they're not really very distracted by anything else.

Though women might be quite obsessed by it for a period, they can be quite happy without. Women love to read about it. They love it, and they're turned on by it. I think it's fascinating that men can look at photographs that seem absolutely hideous and be turned on by them.

The problem with sex is that it is a power game, and that's one of the reasons men like to do it – go around and fuck everyone, I mean. It's conquering people all the time, and women in general have never really seen it as a power game. They've seen it as an expression of commitment, an excuse to get close to somebody – most women. Now I think they might change. If they get more confident, I can see them becoming like men in that way. I think we're getting closer.

Michelle Coquillat: There's a lot of romantic convention in women, but undoubtedly women feel a great deal of lust.

I don't think it is very good for a girl to have sex too early, too young. I don't like to see little girls become the field of experiment for young boys. It can break something in them, in all senses of the term. And I have seen a lot of young girls feel bad because they have had no sex and feel they should. It's most unfortunate that there are all these girls having children at thirteen or fourteen. If I had girls, I would try to make them understand that it is better to wait a little bit longer, until eighteen or nineteen, when you are emotionally capable of dealing with the situation.

Susan Crosland: I've never wanted to be a man. I've never had penis-envy. I've always felt, even if I had understood it, the last thing I wanted was a penis, and now that I've come to understand it, I still think the last thing I want is a penis. Because of the anxiety. I suppose there are some women who get in that state of mind now over the great orgasm, but on the whole women don't, and can have pleasure and satisfaction in different aspects of sexuality. Even the most tender relationship must have a tiny bit of anxiety in it for a man. The woman can do what she likes – she can have an orgasm or not have an orgasm – she doesn't have that anxiety.

My feeling is that the orgasm is overrated – that it's lovely, and it's important to have had the experience. What is most important, I think, is that the man wants the woman to have the experience, and then, if the woman doesn't have an orgasm every time, it doesn't matter. There are other pleasures in sexuality – many – besides the

574

big O. The key thing is that the man cares about the woman having this experience. And then, whether she actually has it time after time, is to me less important.

Mary Crowther: In initial sexual exploration, when people have their first sexual experience, for men it's very much a physical thing. They simply want to lose their virginity, and society allows that and that's OK. For women it's different. Part of it is the Christian or not necessarily just the Christian ethic that sex is something sacred and tied in with procreation and a gift from God. There's the other thing that virginity is a commodity: the girl who has her virginity is a nice girl and the girl who doesn't is a bad girl, and one's worth more than the other, in pure commodity terms. I think probably in our society initial sex for women is usually pretty unexciting. It's something they're led into and something they do because the man wants them to do it. But it's not something they actually want to discover, and probably it's only after months or perhaps after years that women begin to understand the real joy and the real gifts of a sexual life. It takes a lot longer for women than for men.

I think sexual drive is as strong in women as it is in men, but there are more social constraints against them expressing it. Men can find sexual outlets, if you like, far quicker. A man can go to a business lunch or something, and if he's actually attracted by a woman there, and if he wants to, they can indulge themselves very quickly and that's fine. It would be unusual for a woman to initiate that. I mean, she would go along with that, and it would be very flattering that somebody would be giving her the eye across the table at a business lunch, but it would be unusual for her to initiate that. So, in that sense, there are more social constraints on women to control their sexual urges. But when it comes to frequency or whatever – national average – I think women probably have an equally strong sexual drive as men.

Women, for example, can fake orgasm. You know, it might be the most boring thing in the world, but if it makes him happy, you fake it, fine. And it's not that possible for men to do it. But two things have made me curious. One is that, in one of the investigations of infertility, there is a particular awful test called a post-coital test. Basically at the time of ovulation in the woman, she has to get her husband to make love to her, then not wash and come to the hospital. We then do bits and pieces, find out if there's sperm in the uterus and so on. Now, occasionally, you will get women where there is no sperm anywhere to be seen, and you say, did your husband ejaculate? Yes, yes, yes. I don't know, I've never read this anywhere, but I think that what happens is either these men fake ejaculation for their wives, they have an erection but that's all, or else the women are lying, they never made love at all. That intrigues me. The other thing is that I recently saw a patient in her fifties who had had a very sad life, had married many years before, and the marriage had never been consummated. Her husband was very eccentric, and in her fifties, after twenty-five or thirty years with this man, she decided she couldn't stand it any more, and met somebody who initiated her into a sexual life. She said that this man, who was in his late fifties and married, and only saw her two nights or so a week, would actually make love to her five or six times a night. She said he was terribly highly sexed. That rather surprised me for a man in his late fifties. But presumably it can occur.

There is no woman who biologically can't have an orgasm. Either the man's sexual technique is so poor that she doesn't know what's going on, or it's in the mind. Every time men make love, they have to have an orgasm, it's the natural completion of the process. It's not the same for women. There are times when you're really not interested: you're thinking about something cooking, or the kids or whatever, and it's nice and it's comforting. Sex is comforting sometimes – it doesn't always have to be the great arousal. But if you're just not interested in having an orgasm, that's perfectly OK. You can either fake it or not, as the case may be. But I think there is no reason, no biological reason, why women shouldn't have an orgasm.

Maryam D'Abo: I don't enjoy sex just for pure sex. There has got to be some magic in it, some poetry.

Béatrice Dalle: Among young people, the kind I go around with, a bloke can get a girl for the evening, but a girl won't. If she spends the evening with a bloke, it's because she likes him, there's something. A bloke doesn't care if a girl's stupid or as ugly as sin as long as he gets her. Women are more sentimental.

Alma Daniel: People eat much more than they need to. They eat more frequently than they need to. And I think the same thing is true for sex. Sex to me is no different from other aspects of our natures, in that it is part of who we are, and how we are.

Men's sexual needs and women's sexual needs are different. Because of the nature of sex for a man, he needs to have it more often. He shoots his load, he is done, he has to do it again to get that same sense of satisfaction or gratification. A woman in sex is on the receiving end, so she has much more of a sense of completion or fullness. She is not emptied out, he is. Women can go for much longer without thinking about sex, without having sex, without having problems about it. But men, particularly young men – men up until about thirty-five or thirty-six according to some so-called experts, think about sex every seventeen seconds. There's a difference in men and women's responses, and I think it has to do with the nature of the physical organism. Men's biology, men's chemistry, is different from women's, and therefore they have much more of a preoccupation with it. To them it is much more a mystery. Women are a mystery. How does this baby grow in there? What happens? You mean, if I do that, that's going to happen? As a woman, you have much more of an understanding of the nature of the universe, of the nature of the earth. And you've got the menstrual flow, you have a body that changes very noticeably from pre-adolescence into adolescence, and the changes girls go through are far more educational than anything a man can learn by reading books. Men's bodies don't undergo those changes. Women have menopause. That's a whole other trip.

Men enjoy spreading their seed. And I think women like to collect the seed. That's why they tend to be monogamous; that's why they tend to be possessive. It has to do with holding, and containing, and nurturing, and nourishing, and it's different.

Women act out sexually as much as men, in different ways. I have known women who would be the counterpart of Don Juan, who sleep with hundreds of men. And basically it all goes back to daddy: not having received the acknowledgement or recognition or love from the father. So each time they get a man, they are gathering that to them. But it never lasts. It's like a fix, it never lasts, and they've got to go back for another. But, again, this is very specific to certain kinds of women who have never resolved their relationships with their fathers.

Sister Camille D'Arienzo: Sex is not a subject to which I have devoted a lot of personal intellectual energy since I am a celibate woman. I certainly suspect that many of our attitudes are attributable to conditioning. Why is it that the kids who run around Brooklyn where I live – it doesn't matter whether we are talking about the little Italian stallions, or the Puerto Rican fellows with black eyes or whatever – think that they achieve their manhood when they score with a girl? If

577

they have sex they prove their manhood. And why is it that, for the young man, it is a triumph, a kind of conquering that is to be celebrated, and when a girl engages in sexual intimacy it is part of an emotion which generally is motivated by what she believes to be affection and love? What happens in the end is that she has the guilt, possibly the baby. There seems to be little in our society that has said to the young men, generation after generation, that sexual relations are not a game, you don't have the right to go around having sex with anybody, that doesn't make you a man. That makes you something less than a man. It may put you on the same level with the animals, but it doesn't define you as a man. A man who cares is responsible. Men, I believe, on the sexual level alone, learn the lesson that they don't have to live with the consequences of their choices, that they don't have to be responsible for their actions, that somebody else will carry the guilt, and the burden, and the disappointment, and possibly the child.

Mandy Rice Davies: In my twenties, I had very very little sexual urge. In my early thirties, it was a little more interesting, and from the age of about thirty-four, much more – funnily enough, in what people would term a more masculine way. I mean, I never used to walk along the street and suddenly think about something sexual from the night before or whatever. But as I get older, that happens to me quite frequently. I enjoy it more, much much more. It might be something to do with relaxing. As you get older, you're becoming happier with yourself, there's less pressure.

If women could have orgasms as easily as a man has an orgasm, then, what a world we'd be in! I suppose women can have multiple orgasms every now and again, but what really turns a woman on is love rather than lust. That is the major difference. A man can be almost instantly turned on by flashing a pair of breasts, or a bit of leg, or something like that. A woman is much more difficult. I think when you are really turned on by love, then you have a most incredibly sexual relationship. If it's pure lust, you're just left in the desert again at the end.

Régine Deforges: Women can have a desire, to put it vulgarly, to have it off, just as men can when they meet a pretty woman in the street, prostitute or not. A sudden desire. My husband says women are different, but I say, how do you know? There is a whole archaic terminology. I think both feminists and what one calls traditional women are right: one lot can have sex without any feeling for the man, the other can't. But I know that a woman can have a sudden desire for a man because he is handsome or she is in the mood and doesn't want anything else. I tell my husband that men talk too much, they want to tell their whole life story to a woman before making love to her, and a woman couldn't care less about all that. I'm talking about a casual encounter. Men think that, without the talk, a woman would feel she was a pro or an object; whereas I think that a mutual desire is fine and love doesn't come into it.

Dr Mary Jordan-DeLaurenti: The sexual drive varies in both men and women. I know some friends who have lost their husbands, who did have a lot of boyfriends and who slept around, but that was for a whole other reason – mostly to get rid of their grieving. I know many men who have a commitment to one person and keep it, and I know many men who don't. I don't think it has to do with being male, it has to do with being conditioned. It's either OK or not OK, or your own masculinity has not been fulfilled in some way, either intellectually or psychologically. I just don't believe that most men necessarily have to have more sexual encounters, even with one person, than women. I'm not taking away the fact that their drive is stronger, but there are many men who have a value system that says, I may or may not sleep with some people. It may not be the same as women, because we have a different conditioning, but if they have made a commitment to a person, oftentimes they'll keep it.

Men feel that their masculinity is affirmed in the sexual act. I don't think that women feel their femininity is affirmed in the sexual act. Women feel sensual and good and complete in the sexual act, but I don't think it has to do with their identity, with who they are. This has to do with the male's identity, and the need is even greater if a male is trying to prove his identity to himself rather than to someone else.

Sylvia Deutsch: A man has a very animal instinct in that he has to inseminate. Perhaps a woman's sexual needs have increased these last few years, taking into account new contraception and so on, but there are still more men interested in the question than women. Any woman who acts like a Don Juan is still a rather marginal character, controversial even, but for a man it's something that glorifies him, often makes him attractive. I don't think a Don Juan would attract me, but it arouses more admiration than contempt, whereas in a woman it shocks. In addition, men grow weary more easily with one partner. They need multiple sexual encounters; there is a taste for adventure and seduction, which in part is to reassure himself, prove himself, dispel those doubts

579

he has about his virility and sexual performance. A man is sexually much more fragile than a woman. A woman needs to prove her sex appeal to herself as well, but it can be done without the sex act.

Women can be of two kinds: those who hope to find something solid in the sex act and those who behave much more like men, and they aren't all feminists. These women will find a man attractive, want him and that's that. It happens more and more frequently. Whenever I have a sexual fling, I don't expect to be provided with a home, children and so on. It can be brief, last a month or two, but it leaves a pleasant memory. I can have an affair knowing perfectly well that it will lead me nowhere and I will expect nothing from it but I will do it simply for the pleasure.

Kay Dick: Sexually, a heterosexual woman would want to be dominated more than anything else. And she wants to be given pleasure. Now, in the past, that wasn't so. It's a very good thing that women at long last have decided that sexually they are entitled to pleasure as well as men. I'm sure my mother's generation didn't like sex. They liked all the courtship, but not the actual sex, which is why men probably went to more experienced courtesans, shall we say, or Continental women who were much more sophisticated in these matters. I mean, the English are so unsophisticated.

Gratification with men is purely sexual, whereas with women it's also emotional, it's romantic. I'd have to like the man, we'd be friends, mates, nothing in the memory. Afterwards we'd go out and have a bloody good meal and talk about politics. But I think that with any good sexual relationship there should be romance, because there would be more fulfilment. People talk about sex, they forget to talk about being in love. That's what most people want, really.

I don't like the butch woman. That's out totally. I like a sophistication, elegance. And a brain and a wit, and, of course, a nice body. But, again, you can often be attracted to somebody totally different from all the other people you've been attracted to. So there's always the exception to the general rule. I suppose what I really like about women in this sense is the skin. The softness. With all due respect, men are not so attractive in their skin and, of course, I suppose there's the fact that women have breasts.

Two women making love is basically the same as a man and woman. I know the physical details are different, but to my mind the feeling, the sensuality, the orgasm, is the same. Someone once said, two women together, all that is lacking is a penis, and what's that? If you see what I mean.

To say the penis is important is to be awfully masculine. I suppose, in some places, the penis might be important, and in others it probably isn't at all. From what I've heard, and what women confide in other women, not so many women like penetration in that sense. They would rather have all the other things. I suppose basically, if we really analysed this, way back it's the total invasion: the weapon, the kill. So the man has to be a good lover to avoid bringing back that primitive reaction of fear. Only a man who is really sexually sophisticated would manage not to imprint even very faintly that old primitive image of invasion and absolute annihilation.

Margaret Drabble: In a society where the economic basis is very different, you might find the sexual basis very different. I'm sure a lot of women would have liked to have had a much more emancipated sexual life if they hadn't been frightened of criticism or worried about the effect on their health, or worried about the economic implications of going off the rails and finding their husband expected them to be on the rails. It's a terribly complicated area. Some women enjoy the feeling that they've got men running around after them. Some women find their greatest gratification, not necessarily from seduction, but from having men paying court to them, which is really a kind of parallel to seduction.

The emphasis on orgasm is something to do with technology, it's to do with the contraceptive pill. Women discovered, or thought they had discovered, that they could have sex safely without producing a baby a year and then dying at the age of forty. They then discovered that sex could be pleasurable. Maybe they'd always wanted it to be, but had been too frightened. I do think that, even now, women spend a lot of time worrying about the physical consequences of sex in a way men possibly don't: the fear of pregnancy and the fear of bodily decay. If you have four or five or six or seven babies, then you begin to feel a bit worn out, whereas a man doesn't. He may feel the financial burden, but he doesn't feel quite the physical burden, so women have been more wary about their physical commitment, and this has certainly restrained their sexuality to a degree where a lot of Victorian women genuinely were frigid. They just couldn't face having sexual intercourse because they didn't want to get pregnant again.

There are some very promiscuous women and some very promiscuous men; there are some timid men who never have any sex life whatsoever and some women who are very frigid; and if one was to take a map of the whole of Britain and people were ready to tell the truth, one might find there wasn't all that much difference.

Maureen Duffy: Some women have what could be identified as a traditional male attitude, and response, and need. But a great number of women require much more: affection, support, kindliness, love as distinct from passion, and so on. It is no good pretending they don't. Now I would have said OK, a lot of men require a rather aggressive, energetic and athletic sex. But I am quite sure that there are a lot of men who don't, who require what seem to be more feminine experiences of tenderness and togetherness. I think the biological, the evolutionary drive is for male creatures to spread the seed. For the woman, for the female creature, technically speaking, any mate, any seed will do. But what in evolutionary terms she requires is the best, in order to produce the best offspring. Once she has the offspring, she then has to make sure it is supported and fed, warmed and looked after, and if she is part of a society, a grouping, a tribe that requires two people to do this, she will want to make sure she maintains a permanent relationship, at least as far as her children are concerned. This, we see, is now changing because our society is changing in this respect. It is easier for a woman to find another kind of support for her children, and so you have many more unmarried mothers who are much less concerned about it than women used to be. On the whole, it seems true that men tend to be more promiscuous, but it is reinforced by society. In time of war, when the social structures break down, women also become, as we would say, promiscuous. Men look for spreading their seed still, women look for comfort, for relationships, even if those have to be constantly shifting ones, because people are on the move all the time. You get a great deal of female sexual activity in wartime. And you also, of course, now get a great deal more female sexual activity than when I was young, quite simply because there was no contraception then. Women from our grandmothers' generation to our generation have stopped having fourteen children and now have two or three. So what they want to do is one or two jobs properly and nurture those children and build a structure round them which will enable them to grow up best. So, in a sense, they are taking over the role of Nature, of the survival of the fittest, in that instead of having fourteen of whom two or three will survive and succeed, they have two or three and make sure they survive and succeed as far as possible. Humankind always does this, it takes over the evolutionary role.

There are all gradations of sexuality from exclusively heterosexual to exclusively homosexual, and people go in and out of different phases at different times in their lives. The Greeks knew this, and in a sense brought it into their society. Some are able to love both sexes. I don't think I could. I certainly can't at the same time. I can't, I think, love men sexually since I discovered homosexuality. I was brought up in a level of society where such things simply were not known about. Love between women is something wonderful, though I'm sure it's perfectly possible for the love of a woman to a man or a man to a woman to be equally wonderful.

I think men become more exclusively homosexual, but I think there are a lot of women who are able to marry and have children and maintain homosexual feelings which may never find a physical expression. People write to me and say I have been married for twenty years and I suddenly find myself in love with my next-door neighbour, what is happening? Sometimes, after a long repression, feelings will emerge and find a physical outlet. But, in many cases, women maintain a very high level of affection, of, indeed, adoration, for one or two women throughout their lives, but never actually go to bed with them, often because, I think, the idea never occurs to them. There is still less education about female homosexuality than about male homosexuality.

Princess Elizabeth of Yugoslavia: A man needs the sexual conquest to prove he can still do it, that he can still get it up. It's like having a duel with himself. He has to prove it all the time. We don't have to prove it. And very often we'll sleep with someone, not so much because we're turned on, but because we really want companionship, or we want the feeling of someone in bed with us.

Shirley Eskapa: Many men have told me that they can come away from a night with a woman – a day, an afternoon – sated with several orgasms. Going home, weary, exhausted, they see coming along the street a woman in tight jeans – a sexy woman. And this is how they put it to me: they find, to their utter dismay, that there is still lead in their pencil. They still can feel this attraction even for an anonymous woman. Show me a woman who can come away from a night of satiety and feel the same.

Marcia Falkender: The media hype sex and make it nasty. They do it a disservice, because it is a grotesque caricature of reality. The reality is that sex is the most dominant feature in human life, the great motivating factor, whether we like it or not. We might not like it, but the repression of it motivates us as much as the expression. And for some people to say, oh, well, it doesn't worry me, maybe it doesn't, but is there a reason why it doesn't worry them? Sex is the great motivator, and because it is, you have to learn to come to terms with it and to know your own sexuality and how you can deal with it as much as you have to know your own character.

I was always being told when I was in No 10, you know, darling, this is the aphrodisiac of power. Well, I could never see it like that because I knew the people. I'd known them very well all my working life, and to me they were the same old boring people that they were anyway. I didn't see it with politicians, because it's difficult if you work with them for a long time to find any aphrodisiac there at all. I can understand there is a seductiveness about them, because of the sheer strength of their convictions and the way they want things their way. Taking it back to the cave, the caveman who stomps around and has the strength, he's in the equivalent top bracket of the men who make things happen because they have the strength of their positions. It's admiring the man who's got authority and can make things happen for you. I'd be dishonest if I didn't say that there isn't a great attraction about men who have the authority and the power in any walk of life they are in. But then, I have to confess, it's not only to do with top people, I also sometimes get that when I'm watching a very skilled plumber or bricklayer doing his job. Or when a working man is in charge and making a building come up, or making something happen physically. I'm as attracted to them as I am to someone who is running a country or running GEC or something.

I don't frankly believe in those women who claim that lots of one-night stands and casual affairs are as much a woman's domain as a man's. I don't believe women are like that, I never have believed it, and nothing will persuade me. I think, for some women, for one or two, it may well be true, because none of us are total in one way or the other. We have a bit of everything in us, we are part masculine, part feminine, whether we like it or not. On the whole, men are more tuned in to the casual relationship and the need for a casual relationship. I don't think women need sex in quite that way. For a man, it is a release. For a woman, it's a form of expression solely. A woman might find it a release, but it isn't the overwhelming need it is for a man. Women who pretend it is otherwise are deluding themselves and making life unhappy for themselves too. Because eventually they are probably going to fall in love with the one man who has a great need to have lots of casual relationships, but who could make them the happiest of women if they could turn a blind eye. I come across them all the time. You know, they would have a wonderful thing going there, if only they could turn away from what is for a man nothing. A man doesn't go into casual love affairs with the same sense that this woman is going to mean something to him. It's very much a physical thing. He likes the look of the woman, and he would like to have a nice time, and that's the end of it. Tomorrow, he's forgotten it totally.

Esther B. Ferguson: Society does a lot to condition what's allowed sexually. Look how different it all is as society changes. Now you see a conservative swing in this country, bigger than ever. Let me tell you one thing: you've got to be a pisser to be out there in the field now, because of the horror of gonorrhoea – forget Aids. I mean, it's a nightmare Society has already put a damper on it. You've got to be out of your mind to be out there now, with all the horror stories around.

Annie Flanders: They make a big thing if a man can't get it up. It's no different from a woman who can't have an orgasm. She can have sex, but if she's not having an orgasm, she's not having a good time.

Women fake orgasm if they really care about the man because they don't want him to feel a sense of failure. I think it's a really kind thing that women do. But they're doing themselves an injustice, because probably, if they could get over it, if they didn't fake it, and they learned how to relax, they would probably have their orgasm. Some men aren't good enough to give it to you.

All the modern women I know have more sex drive than men. In fact, the women I know are more aggressive in a sexual way; men seem shyer. Women now are looking for the same things men had all their lives. We're looking for male whorehouses, for safe sex. We can buy it, we have busy lives and we just want to get laid. One-night stands are no problem at all. We just want to get fucked. The modern women I know, myself included, my friends, we talk about this openly. You like sex for the moment and you can have one night with someone and not have any emotional involvement, have a good orgasm and maybe some laughs and that's it. There doesn't have to be carry-over, especially with married women or women in long relationships, because we know sex goes in a long-term relationship or a marriage, and they want the sex, but they have very good partners they want to stay with and have a relationship with, and one thing has nothing to do with the other. Men

585

told that to women for years, and now women will tell the same thing back to men, there is no difference. We love sex. When I was young, my mother said, don't give it away for free. And I said, what are you talking about, giving it away? I want it as much as the guy wants it. I'm getting as much from it as he is.

Lorraine Stanley-Ford: I think the double standard is still there, that men don't want a woman who is tarnished, who has got a lot of mileage on her, but it's still OK for them to talk in the pub about the number of women they've screwed. Only they know how much of that bullshitting is true.

I'm talking purely from a stewardess's point of view, but when you've been away two and half weeks from your boyfriend, even the room-boys start looking good. You go through the same frustrations as the stewards. It would be wonderful to be able to go somewhere and have a nice uncomplicated hour, pay for it, have a good time, have somebody massage you, do the biz.

I have experienced a relationship which was totally open in that we used to go to sexual parties together – not orgies exactly, but multiple sex partners – but it was totally open in that if we went out together, and picked up somebody, be it male or female, they would come back with us and we would have a threesome. That kind of open relationship. It wasn't really based on trust, it was just that if we were going to sleep with other people, it was going to be in front of each other. It didn't work. In the end, I found I was having a better time with the people I didn't know than I was with him. And I think he was, too.

The majority of men don't take the time to get to know properly how a woman really responds. It's all very much, well, let's get at it. I read recently, in one of the tabloids, thirty-eight facts you never really wanted to know about lesbians, but you were going to hear them anyway. It said that, in surveys, a man took thirty seconds to touch a woman's breasts, whereas between two women it could take anything up to about two to three minutes before that kind of contact is made; that there is much more a sensual response between the two women, that they don't want to be rushed. Women don't respond as quickly, and the guy is doing all he can to hold off because he's at the point of climax much quicker usually than a woman, and the woman is doing all she can trying to catch up. There's a terrific imbalance in sexual responses and needs, but I wouldn't say a man has a greater sex drive or a greater need for sex. It's a very individual thing. People have very different libidos. I think women tend to be a bit more discriminating in their sexual partners. But they don't need to be involved. I can have a one-night stand like any man.

Christina Foyle: Men's sexual appetites are, I think, much stronger than women's. I know that when I was a girl in my father's shop, I'd get all these men always pestering me. I used to get awfully sick of it. I wasn't interested. I don't think a lot of women are. It's very nice if you fall in love with somebody, but I think women have other things they'd rather do.

Lynne Franks: I can see men that I think are physically attractive, but I don't get overwhelmed by lust. If I start talking to them and find I really get on with them and click and connect on another level, then I could go to bed with them five minutes after – that would be something else. But just purely on a physical level, no, I might think them very attractive, but there has to be more. I was talking to a girlfriend in Paris this week, and we were saying, to be kissed properly is more than going to bed with fifty men. You know, just to be kissed and held. And we both were saying, how sad it is that in marriage you stop kissing, and how lovely it would be just to have somebody to kiss. Perhaps, if one started kissing one's husband, they would think the same thing. But I think most women go through a promiscuous phase. I certainly did when I was in my early twenties; it was quite fun and I enjoyed it. But even if I picked up somebody in a club and went to bed with him the same night, it would turn into a relationship; it always turned into a relationship with me, which was the way I was, and most of the women I knew were the same.

It is rubbish, total rubbish, to say the female orgasm depends on emotional involvement. Women's bodies are made in such a way that orgasm is achieved mainly through clitoral stimulus. You don't have to be in love with a man, but you do have to feel fairly relaxed. Enough stimulation at the right point on a woman's body would, inevitably, ultimately produce orgasm. Most men don't seem to understand much about women's bodies, which I always find interesting. Perhaps we have only just discovered our own bodies. I certainly remember when I was twenty and we were all very worried about why we didn't have orgasms.

Gisèle Galante: It is very difficult to separate sex from emotion. We have tried. The feminists maintain they can; but I don't think you can, probably not. There is something kind of empty in their quest. For me, sex is love. For a man, it can also be conquest. I think, if a woman is fulfilled on every level by a man, why should she go elsewhere? Men do because the woman loses her appeal much faster than do men.

Teri Garr: Sex is a basic motivator for men and women. That's what it all started with. Men rape, they are the predators. For men to be powerful on top of the corporate ladder, it is almost like great sex. Whereas, for women, great sex is great sex. We've always been told, honey, for men it's different, they can do it with anyone, it doesn't matter to them. Sometimes I find this to be very true. For me, if I have sex with someone, it's a serious thing, an important thing. I can't imagine someone will just leave next day and never call me again. Because it is an intimate personal thing. But, for a man, it's not so much. They can have sex with a wall, I think.

Orgasm is completely about *Cosmopolitan* magazine. Somebody got this brainstorm that publicized this a lot. I mean, to me and my group of friends that are a little more intelligent, we looked at this and laughed. It's bullshit. The G-spot and other stuff. Women have always got pleasure from sex, just as men have. But suddenly to throw this idea out: are you getting enough orgasms? I mean, it's a joke, a joke. I also read women are responsible for their own orgasm, and I said this is the saddest thing I ever read. This is what the feminist movement is about? Get out of here.

Pamela Gems: There is a very wide sexual spectrum. My doctor friends tell me people still come into the surgery and say, we've been married six months and haven't got a baby yet; and it turns out they haven't been doing it. Amazing. On the other hand, there are people who are the opposite, and it's just as difficult for them. I've known men whose desires have been uncontainable. A dog's life. What do you do? Such a man has to find an answer. And I've known women like that. So we have this very wide spectrum. I have often thought, because I myself never had a lot of energy, and it happens I have a husband with very high energy, that some of the rules about marriage are silly. I mean, some men should definitely have three or four wives. It would really be kinder for the woman, too; occasionally, not so often I don't think, the other way round. It is a problem. In America, they have serial marriage. They are a high-consumer country: every five years you have another hat and a wedding, and a new deal, and lawyers have been paid off, and you have a new one. Liz Taylor is the arch example. It's romantic, and

588

very immature. In France, it's the *ménage à trois*, which is a very good system, a very good system. Of course, the French do everything best. But we'll never do that here because we are Anglo-Saxon and we're puritans, you know. England, I think, has always been a mess sexually. We send our boys away to school, and all that.

Susan George: Sex is very much a romantic thing. When one is away on holiday, it's part of the holiday attraction, but in an everyday working environment, I would never like anything to be routine. I've never been routine. I live from day to day, I'm very impulsive, so anything that's routine I couldn't be doing with, and if love-making became routine, I would become unsatisfied and it would become unpleasurable. Love-making to me is all part of a romantic surge of lust and energy for somebody when you want them, when they want you.

Sarah Giles: Men have this sort of incredible, very strong, overriding need to prove themselves sexually. They have this psychological need, which is not to do with their being weak, it's just born into them. To be absolutely crude about this, they need to show they can make their cock stand up. I'm sure that's just biological, and that half of sex for them is therefore proving something, whereas a woman isn't proving anything when she has sex. She's either enjoying it or she's not.

Believe it or not, although it is the man that has to perform sexually, women feel very frightened of sex. They feel threatened. The first time a woman goes to bed with a man – and the man will never believe this – the woman is terrified. It's a terrifying experience. And therefore she might fake an orgasm to show she's capable of having one. The woman hopes the man thinks she is a fully developed, sexually aware female.

Alexandra M. Guirgiu: I cannot take sex out of the context of love. And I don't understand how someone can. I don't judge someone if they can, but it's something I can't relate to at all. Sex is always being taken out of context, and this is something that never ceases to revolt me.

Victoria Glendinning: A woman's sexuality is mixed up in what she's doing in the house and what she's doing in the garden. It's the same bits of her she's using for all of these things. She's more diffuse and more unified in that way, whereas a man can be talking to you about Proust one minute and raping you the next. A woman can't do that.

I think that women are not constant in that there are times in a woman's life when it wouldn't matter to her if she was never made love to again; there are times in a woman's life when that is the only thing she wants. I dare say it depends on a surplus of hormones flooding around, on what else she's interested in at the moment, on a great many things. I always imagine men more like railway trains chugging along, just wanting to go bang-bang-bang when they can. I think women are far more variable. When they're feeling desirous, I think they're probably even more desirous than men. The only other thing I've seen about women is that women want sex with a particular man – him, him, him, him. Somebody else wouldn't do. Whereas it is possible, to my mind, that somebody else would do with a man when he is in that condition, because it's the act he wants rather than the person. Even if he's in love with somebody, he can displace the drive, whereas I think that's harder for a woman. I'm sure there are lots of women who don't need an emotional involvement, and I'm not sure the emotional involvement is cultural, but I think that for a great many women it is there. I think what a great many women want is some sort of huge love, of which the sexual act may sometimes be the price they have to pay. The sexual act may occasionally seem to her like a huge sudden hockey match when she's been in heaven before that.

Lady Annabel Goldsmith: A woman likes to be looked at, likes to be admired. All men are natural voyeurs, and the woman should be excited by the idea he wants to look at her. I'm sure that's how it should work. Men are titillated by the visual, but women are bored stiff by the idea. Men like the erotic pictures that women find quite revolting – I certainly find them quite revolting. On the other hand, there is no question about it, women are awfully titillated by the idea of showing themselves to men.

Women may have those same very strong sexual urges as men, but I'm sure there is a difference between the two, I'm certain there is. I think the man does feel this urge to go out and conquer. I can never understand the wives who really mind, the wives who set such store by fidelity. How extraordinary, and how mad they are. Because, surely, if the man goes out and he comes back, it's not actually doing any harm. I can't see why there is such an enormous fuss. It's a very oriental way of thinking, but it is one I really do believe and have felt strongly since I was very young. I can't see any harm in the man going out, going to bed with a few women, coming back. It's not going to make a difference. It might make it better. There's a risk he may fall in love, but if he's going to fall in love with someone else, he's going to do that anyway. I think, if more women could understand that, there would be fewer divorces. I am married to somebody who does this, but this isn't why I'm saying it.

Angela Gordon: I could never go to bed with a man if I wasn't going to perform myself.

Felicity Green: Sexually, men and women are very different. I don't believe that every man is that easily aroused and can satisfy himself with whatever woman happens to be passing. I believe there are many, many men who don't have that kind of indiscriminate sexuality. But I think there are very, very few women with it, very few indeed. And I think it is true that women – whether you call it romantic or emotional or whatever – certainly have to feel something for a man before they put themselves into a position physically, as well as emotionally, of total vulnerability. It doesn't have to be a lifelong thing any more, it doesn't have to be an emotional commitment for any length of time. But there has to be, however ephemeral, some kind of feeling a woman has for a man if she is going to have sexual intercourse with him. Another thing which I think has been very misleading and has led to a great deal of unhappiness and dissatisfaction, is that before the advent of television and X-rated films the physical act went on in people's minds, or in their bedrooms, or behind the haystack. But now every child, from the age of whatever, sees people copulating on the screen in their living room. And very rarely is it anything other than an indefinitely prolonged orgasm of extreme, exquisite ecstasy. Now anybody who has any kind of ongoing sex life knows that is not true. Sometimes it's wonderful, sometimes it's OK, sometimes you can't be bothered, sometimes it's unbelievably good, sometimes you wish he would go away. The expectation that people were given by these soft-focus scenes up there of Richard Gere humping about on top of Kathleen Turner or whatever, were such that sex has been a disappointment for a lot of people – unjustifiably. But this is inevitable. If you are educated to expect, if you are shown with visible evidence that every time a couple copulate the earth moves, you are set for a life-long disappointment.

Sex is a problem for women who do not wish to become pregnant. It's as simple as that. And therefore sex for women has always had in-built inhibitions. I don't believe men will ever have a pill in the way that women have a pill, because I don't believe men could be trusted ever to take it, I have to say. Why should they? They are not going to have the baby. All the medical evidence is now suggesting to women that, along

591

with the choice, go certain health hazards, therefore that is going to affect their attitude to sex all over again.

If a man can't get an erection, he can't get an orgasm, and it is sad for him. It is quite possible for a man to give a woman an orgasm without his having an erection. There are other ways, and in a well-adjusted relationship a couple will work out methods and practices so that each manages to reach some kind of pinnacle of satisfaction. The great quality in the sex act has to be sexual generosity. Once you have established that, many things become possible. It isn't always a man getting an erection and putting it inside a woman and they come together; sometimes it happens one way, sometimes another, as long as people don't go into the sex act with a textbook in one hand saying, this is the way to do it, and if we are not doing it that way, all is lost.

Men react much more quickly to visual stimuli. I think men are much more overtly sexual. We have lived through the sexual revolution and have come out the other side, and women have had their whole sexual balance, their whole perception of sexuality, thrown up in the air, destroyed, re-embraced, and are now having to rethink the thing all over. The 1960s were an amazing era for women to live through. They had to go through a whole lot of quite false assumptions that were thrust upon them by the media, by the new thinkers. We went ten steps, I won't say forward, but ten steps in a different direction about sexual freedoms and total liberty and lack of restraint. And, having trodden that path, not only women but men, too, have drawn back and are now, in the late 1980s, rethinking the whole of the sexual role in relation to life. In the 1960s, sex was absolutely everything and everything revolved around sex and one's sexual attitudes and performance, prowess and conquests. There is now a very funny surge, almost of celibacy, which I think is as unreal as total libertarianism. Somewhere along the way, we will re-adjust. We won't go back to where we were pre-1960s, but there will be a readjustment, and sexuality is going to find its proper place in the human profile, in the human psyche.

Menie Grégoire: A woman in love doesn't want another man. If a woman is not in love, then she can change partners as much as she wants, but if she is, she won't. If a woman wants to ask herself whether she is in love, she only needs to wonder whether she would go with another man. A woman in love is fulfilled, she doesn't need anyone else. A man feels the need for change because his pleasure is exteriorized. Female pleasure is interiorized, it goes right to the guts, to the

592

heart. It's too difficult to explain to a man the kind of pleasure a woman gets; it goes all through her.

A man or a woman who is not fulfilled sexually is handicapped. A frigid woman or an impotent man is ill, deformed. I'm an analyst and I know that anyone who has a block sexually is lacking something, going round with a crutch; a fulfilled sex life is very important. I created the first programme on sex, even before there were any in the States, and it created a scandal even though I was careful not to allow any words which might offend and tried not to shock too much. I did this programme for five years, and discovered men and women everywhere who wrote in with enormous problems, and these problems coloured their whole lives.

If women want love, then their sexual needs are greater. Pleasure for a man and a woman cannot be compared. Everyone has thought about it, and even the Ancient Greeks said that goddesses had more pleasure than the gods. The intensity of female pleasure surpasses masculine pleasure. I can't compare it, I'm a woman. But the intensity of a woman's pleasure is something extraordinary.

Laura Gregory: When you were younger, you tended to sleep with more people because sex was something that was fun and was new. Now sex is something special. It is very exciting. Your tastes change and your expectations are far greater, your desire is more choosy. So you find you're desperately, desperately horny and you just can't go to bed with anyone because you know it will be a disaster. And after you have slept with them and they come and you come, you just look and think, oh, God, what am I doing here, get out of bed. You stop doing that and you become very selective in who you choose to partner. If that partner isn't available, then masturbation is the best answer because it is far more enjoyable than choosing a partner that is going to be a disaster. Obviously, this is before I was married.

I think women are beautiful, beautiful creatures. I think most young girls at school have been attracted to women. And I certainly was, with a young girl my own age, and with an older woman. And I still find women extremely attractive, sexually and otherwise.

I have made love to women in the past. It's different, but equally satisfying. A woman knows how to touch you because she knows how to touch herself. And sometimes men are a bit clumsy. The same way as we must be clumsy to them. When a man touches himself, he has then to teach a woman how to touch him in the same pleasing way. And it is up to a woman to show a man how to touch her the way she touches herself. Women are halfway to understanding that because they touch themselves.

Women are very good at masturbating, better than men. There isn't that need to prove oneself sexually that men have. Women are powerful, peaceful with themselves. I am quite happy to masturbate and have a fantasy rather than go and find a man in a bar that isn't going to be very important. That's quite satisfying enough for me, if I need to have an orgasm to go to sleep, or for whatever reason. But, for a man, it is more difficult, because they have to prove themselves. They have to be seen with the girl on their arm and so on. Women don't have that, women are much more private.

I think masturbation is wonderful, sometimes greater than having a man. I mean, sometimes the enjoyment from a man is greater, sometimes you might be thinking about a fantasy and everything is right, the atmosphere, the mood, your feeling, and wow, that all goes and it is amazing. I have the ability to orgasm maybe ten/twenty times in a night, but they don't trip on, trip on, trip on. I must be stimulated each time.

Some women have never had an orgasm. I know lots of women that pretend, that have always pretended. Some women can't ever masturbate and achieve orgasm, they are too afraid to do so. Or they don't want to touch themselves, or some reason. Whereas men – little boys always masturbated round the back of the shed at school, it was normal, they played with their willies. You know, they stick out and they play with them. Little girls tended not to, or were told it was naughty. But that is changing.

I fantasize about being tied up. I fantasize about being told what to do, probably because I tell everybody else what to do all day long. I fantasize about being whipped. I fantasize about enormous penises which couldn't possibly go inside me. They are just enormous, frightening and terrifying. Oh, I fantasize about all sorts of things. Romantic strangers in robes, flowing robes. I have one fantasy, which is to be led blindfold into a room, a vast room, with a feeling of space. I just know it is enormous, and nothing – no furniture, no nothing – bare floorboards, with a wonderful piece of opera playing; and then to have the person that led me there make love to me quite violently and then take me home and leave me, and I'll never know who it was. That's quite a good fantasy. I like to find clubs all over the world where people are there exhibiting themselves. And there is one in London called the

Maitresse Club; it's a place where the strict dress code is leather, pvc or rubber. And down there you find men in sou'westers with long raincoats and wellingtons, with nothing on underneath – just dancing naked with the raincoat flapping open. Young women in antique lace and stockings and suspenders. Men in kind of restricted garments with colours with spikes on and funny corsets. And there, they say, the code is anything goes. If you want to whip someone, you can. And I go down there dressed in my leathers and chains and things, and there is one man there who always asks me to whip him as soon as I walk in the door. And I do. I make him kiss my feet, lick my shoes, and then I whip him. It's a feeling of power I think, really. It's amazing. He is not the master. He is doing what I tell him to do, and I dismiss him, I give him back his whip and tell him to leave. I have no feelings for him. I can only whip the unknown. Somebody I don't know. I think it's an aggressive thing for me, it's taking my aggression out. I want to hang a punchbag up in our new office so everybody in the office can hit it if they feel angry. It is very important that you allow your emotions to escape. After it, I feel marvellous, I feel wonderful. And I've also given somebody pleasure, somebody's enjoyed me whipping them. A lot of people do the same thing. And some of the people that go to the clubs are quite the straightest: lawyers, geologists from BP, strange people. It's obviously some way-back fantasy where, maybe, he's been whipped by a nanny or his mother.

An orgasm a day keeps the doctor away, I say. It's important for me because I find it a great physical release. Probably the same as the whipping.

Katya Grenfell: I would certainly discourage my daughter from casual sex, strongly actually, because I never have had casual sex and I've been very happy, and so I think she will probably find that she's much happier that way too. Also, I think it means more if you don't sleep with lots of different people all the time. In the end, it just becomes a physical thing and it's much more difficult to really give all the emotion it needs.

Elsa Gress: That women have recently tried to emulate men in liberated sex is hardly progress. There are sexually voracious members of both sexes, but they are hardly the norm or ideal. The more sex of all kinds the merrier, is an idea now being killed off by Aids and common sense. It is bound to recur in periods of extreme stress as a red herring, distracting people from essential issues, but it has nothing to do with human freedom or progress.

595

Amy Gross: I believe that it is certainly possible to have a very satisfying evening with a man you didn't know ten minutes before, and won't want to know tomorrow. It's not my idea of satisfying, but I believe that it's totally within women's capacity to have that experience and just to have a wonderful evening. It has never worked for me.

Pamela Gross: I think, for women, sex is a very intimate thing. It's an acceptance, it's a vulnerability that men will never understand. You're literally allowing something inside of yourself – how much more vulnerable can one be? For men, I think it is a very aggressive act, by the mere nature of what happens, of the physicality of the whole thing. It's a penetration, an attack, it's a release out of himself, and a woman is taking into herself, so it is a much more intimate act for her.

Women don't go into sex thinking about orgasm. When I go into making love, it's to love. I don't think about orgasm. It doesn't occur to me, it's not a thing I think about. I don't think orgasm is the answer to gratification. It's two seconds, it's over. You don't have to make love to make love. You can get an orgasm and not feel gratified. You can masturbate. Does that make one feel gratified? A lot of women who are feminists feel that wanting to please a man is not right, and maybe it's not right, but I don't want it to be an issue. I certainly don't want my sex life to be the issue Gloria Steinem is talking about. I don't want to get into bed at night with my husband someday, or my boyfriend or whatever, and think he is worried about what Gloria Steinem is going to think about our love-making. I don't want him to worry that it is an issue whether or not he makes me have orgasm or I make me have it, or whoever is responsible for the damn thing. I don't want that to be an issue. It's none of her business, quite honestly. I don't want those feelings to make me uptight and worried about it.

Valerie Grove: A friend of mine, a writer, sees her husband's attitude to sex as being the same as his attitude to food. Her husband will eat anything if hungry – whatever's there, a grape, a banana. Food is a permanent need, and he'll grab what's going. She is a very good cook and will always wait until a meal is perfectly prepared. She'd rather have the gourmet meal once in a while than a banana any time. I agree with her. I think the sex urge which was so rampant and extreme at the age of sixteen or seventeen doesn't actually lessen, because the desire is as strong as ever, but in women (in me anyway) it's a desire for perfection; everything has to be just wonderful. Men, on the other hand, don't seem to mind quickies. I'm still surprised by how many men play around. However, I do know a caucus of men who simply don't and never would under any circumstances. They are as faithful as a woman would be, and for the same reason, because they regard the commitment of marriage as a privilege, not an imposition.

Georgina Hale: When I was young, I was so miserable. I was constantly being pregnant, and constantly having abortions. I hated sex because I didn't know about it. I just thought, oh, well, the fellow came along, shoved it inside you, and you made a few noises. I actually used to lie there vomiting all these noises, because I thought that was how you did it.

I'm very old-fashioned and very basic, and if I am having a relationship with somebody, then I am very loyal and faithful, that's me. The men I have been involved with, when I've found out that they've been with somebody else, it's usually the same old shit: oh, but I didn't mean it, it didn't mean anything to me. And you think, well, why the fuck did you do it if it doesn't mean anything? But then, there we are. A man is made differently, I suppose. They say, oh, I didn't know what I was doing, or it was just a fuck, you know. I am sure that's true, and there are a few women like that too. For a while, I became like a fellow, like a machine. I was very young then, and that made me feel quite tough. But then, also, because I had been pregnant so many times and had so many abortions and gone through horrific pain, I did become rather hard, I suppose, and rather cold.

Jerry Hall: I don't think you have any control over what your children do about sex. I think they do what they want to do. I mean, my mother always told me, your virginity is very special, and you must save it for Mr Right, the man you love and will marry, but none of us did. And very few girls do now.

I think men can have sex with anyone, with all sorts of girls, anyone. For them it's like changing the TV, like a toy, something to pass the afternoon. For them, it's very light-hearted. I'm not saying love – I'm saying sex. But women have to be in love to enjoy sex with a man. They have to be in love, otherwise it's a bit revolting, I think. Sure there's a lot of girls who fuck people all the time, but I don't think they enjoy it as much as they could if they were in love. That's the big difference. It makes women feel sick and dirty. Women feel dirty, men don't.

I can't understand what's wrong with all these women who don't have orgasms. Maybe they're thinking about it too much. To me, sex has always been very easy, very normal and uncomplicated. I suppose some people aren't lucky and have all sorts of problems, so that's why they get obsessed. But there are so many women who don't have orgasms. Maybe it's because they're not in love, maybe it's too much promiscuity. And it's been encouraged, all along, in all the magazines: how to get a man, this and that, first night, forms of contraception, comparing men sexually. All that is very unhealthy and very bad. I think sex is private and I don't think you have to get so complicated. But I've always been very lucky and never had problems with orgasms.

Lucy Hughes-Hallett: Freud had this idea that we'll all go crazy if we don't have sex. Yet I do know people who are celibate and they're not going mad. Sometimes they have a kind of serenity others don't.

It seems to me that, for a man to find sex endlessly interesting and new, he needs a new partner, whereas women perhaps experience sex more subtly somehow; it's more a question of a different mood; they will make it completely different even with the same partner. Women don't always need to have an orgasm. A lot of them will feign one, often to protect men's self-esteem; also perhaps to protect themselves. Men do attach more importance to orgasm. Perhaps it's difficult for a man to enjoy sex without coming, whereas a woman can actually enjoy the foreplay as much as the climax, and sometimes she doesn't want to go on all night just to reach climax: it's been very nice, but now let's go to sleep.

There's a lot of confusion about orgasm. I was reading a book by Doris Lessing not very long ago that she wrote twenty years ago, I think. And in it she was arguing against orgasm of the clitoris and saying that the vaginal orgasm was the only one that really mattered, which is the reverse of what feminists now say. They claim that the vaginal orgasm is an invention of a masculine myth, and I don't really see how you can tell the difference. It's a very fine distinction, but of course it matters, and people are concerned. If a lot of people are talking about orgasm and you've never had one, you're cross, you want to do something about it.

Mira Hamermesh: Men culturally have a licence to goggle at women, universally. Even with the lowest of low, the street-cleaner, if a woman passes who has shapely legs, it is his duty to look. Any female is fair game. To eat up with your eyes, or to screw, or to murder if you want. I don't live in that culture. The maleness I was used to as a child was that little boys peed and we showed each other our genitals. As an adult woman, you give birth to a male, you bathe him, you nurse him and you get used to the human body, the totality. The genitals are something to be gentle with and taken care of. Nobody is making fortunes out of pornographic magazines for my eyes only to gratify and make sure I get wet between my legs in the middle of the day when I don't know what to do with myself. Nobody has devalued the male sex for my benefit to such an extent that I can walk out of this house to find a male ready with his sexual organ to gratify me if I fancy. So women don't look universally at men with that eye which devours, mutilates or conquers. Any more than Palestinian young men look at the young Israelis armed to the teeth. By which I mean that they are two different worlds. One knows they have the power; the others have been rendered powerless.

The men I have met were people who matched me, who were, in other words, as emotionally linked to their sexuality as I was. And I'm very selective, I'm a poet. If you are a poet, you are sentimental, you are emotional, and you are actually very passionate about it. It is not just an Anglo-Saxon business for a few hours and forget it. In our Western societies, the fact is that woman's worth is so low, prostitution is the share that anyone can pick up for a penny. The fact that you can buy female sex, and could throughout history, is a patriarchal arrangement, so any male can have a system of access to any amount of females at any time on convenient economic terms. I had a husband and he was English. I don't think he was undersexed, but I would sometimes think, oh, gosh, another day like all the others, and I'd call him and say, what about going for a walk and then making love? But, in the world of men, you make love only when they finish business.

Katharine Hamnett: My generation of mothers let their daughters masturbate, but I know that my mother's and my father's generation were horrified. When my father saw my two-year-old brother on a potty, playing with his willie, he smacked him, poor little thing, he smacked him across the balls. The potty had pooh in it which went all over the carpet, so the child had not only been punished for this moment of pleasure, but he had also got his shit over the Persian carpet. And there was such family consternation at this shit. But now my girlfriends come round with their beautiful babies and say, oh, yes, she's really masturbating, she sits in the bath doing it, it's great. I'm sure if you're allowed to masturbate, then you have orgasm just like a man.

Everybody goes to bed for lust, but lust is love too. What's interesting is that women are afraid to admit it. I think women lust for somebody, but they don't get it over with after one fuck. That's rubbish. Everybody gets involved. If you fuck somebody, you can hardly be more involved than that, can you?

Nicky Hart: Women have as much of a sexual drive, but don't know how to bring it out. Because of the sexual rituals, women aren't encouraged to take initiatives. So maybe they dissipate their sexual desires into other things. The fact that orgasm is easier for a man is nothing to do with sexual drive; orgasm and sexual drive are two different issues. I think men who are bad in bed don't know what to do. Men don't need the same kind of stimulation as women because of the purely biological nature of how men and women have orgasms. A woman doesn't necessarily need to be emotionally involved to have orgasms. She needs a good lover.

Bettina von Hase: New York is the most asexual city I have ever lived in. London is positively sensual by comparison.

Nikki Haskell: I used to think that men needed sex a lot more than women do. I think that a lot of the gay community thrives on this abnormal desire for sex, and I think it's obsessive with them. It's all they think about. A woman is always under the gun, as far as not being promiscuous and not being this and that. But there are a lot of very over-sexed women, very over-sexed. A lot of it doesn't really come out till their thirties or forties. Because they got married, and they married a man who was the first lover, and all of a sudden they conjure up all these fantasies, and now they're divorced and they're sleeping with everyone. I'm not into orgies. I'm very strait-laced, but you'd be surprised the people that are, and it *blows* me. I really love romance, and I'm not in the least bit inhibited in bed with someone I'm in love with. But I'm not into casual sex, I never have been. My girlfriends are not abnormally over-sexed, but there are quite a few I know who are.

I always have a house rule – and there is no exception to the rule. I never sleep with anybody the first time I go out with them. That's the law of the land. And I have girlfriends who say, gee, I don't understand, I went out with this one and I slept with him, and I haven't heard from him, and it's the pattern that always happens. Then I say, well, it's none of my business, but did you sleep with him the first time you went out with him? And she says, yes. I say, well, it goes back to the old standards: men don't respect a woman that's easy. You know, sex is really overrated. People look into each other's eyes and can't wait to get into bed, and the minute they get into bed, they're ready to leave.

All of a sudden everyone is realizing: what have I been missing? I myself have orgasms all the time, and it's natural. But it became such a topic of conversation. It was a real sign of the times. For instance, I would always end up meeting a man just getting divorced. In fact, one time the phone rang and this man said, hello, my name is so and so. I said, let me guess, you're either in the real-estate business or you're a stockbroker. He said, yes. You're between the ages of forty and sixty. He said, yes. And you have between two and four children, you have a dog. He said, yes. I said, and your wife left you – she ran off with the postman, the garbage man, the milkman, somebody twelve years younger than you, and you are all alone looking for a date. And that's exactly what had happened. All of those women went through this sexual social revolution and dumped their husbands and families and ran off to have orgasms, and that was it.

Olivia de Havilland: Sex is one of the most wonderful means of communicating with a man. It is glorious when it is part of a really responsive relationship. Nothing can touch that.

Promiscuity is absolutely bad form. It's unattractive, it's wasteful, it's wasteful of life, and it's unaesthetic.

I was just talking to a man down in Vienna, and he told me he had been faithful to his wife for ten years. Women were always after him, he was a terribly attractive young man, but he resisted them. And he did that because he knew his wife was faithful. He expected that, of course. He would have been destroyed if she weren't, psychologically destroyed; men do expect that of their women. But, finally, when the marriage apparently was over, he became very promiscuous for five years. Then the next five years he was promiscuous but more selective. He asked more of this sexual experience than he had before. And finally, and this is really terribly sad, he became disgusted with it all and has given it up. That tells you something. I don't think promiscuity suits men. It is just as tatty for a man to be promiscuous as for a woman. And it's terribly irresponsible, because there he is, spreading his seed, and that is a terribly negligent thing to do. Terribly irresponsible towards himself and his possible children. Dreadful, dreadful. It is criminally irresponsible, when you really think it through. Women are supposed to be more selective. Whether they are today or not, I don't know. I don't know what moves them, I don't understand them.

Kitty Hawks: I've seen photographs of breathtaking boys. I think of Calvin's advertising before anything else, which is very titillating. It wouldn't make me go out and hire somebody to sleep with, but I'd certainly look at those boys and think, if one of them walks through the door right now and says, how would you like to spend the afternoon together, it wouldn't be a bad idea.

I can imagine having sex for sheer lust, but I would literally not want to speak to him. I would see somebody, say, that's physically attractive, and I wouldn't want to know anything about him. I certainly would not go through the ritual a man will: the taking her to dinner, having cocktails and going through the charade of getting to know her, when the next day they are never going to see her again. I'd rather just go to the bottom line, have the sex, and have them be gone.

Brooke Hayward: I preferred sex in the 1950s when there was still a sense of mystery about it. And it was forbidden.

I think women can go to bed for lust. And I think they do it to be defiant and prove a point. But I don't think it's naturally what they want. I don't think they can do it night after night and get pleasure from it, no. On isolated occasions, yes, absolutely. Again, because it's sort of forbidden and naughty. I think what's sexy really is basically what's forbidden, what's illicit. So the minute you open it up and make it available to everybody at any time under the cold scrutiny of day, I don't think it is nearly as attractive. For instance, I've just see this movie called *Blue Velvet*, and the girl Isabella Rossellini looks a whole lot sexier when she has her clothes on than when she takes them off. I mean, I don't particularly ever want to see her nude again. And as for Dennis Hopper – that's one of my husbands – why do I need to pay $6 to see him acting as he acted with me every night for seven years? I mean, he's just nuts. He's playing himself, definitely.

Cynthia Heimel: It would be very frightening to be a man and have to get an erection, to be forced to perform.

I think a man would sleep with every woman he could, except that his girlfriend or wife would kill him. I think men have a much more visual pattern of arousal. They can look at a picture of a woman, will look at a woman walking down the street, not know anything about her, look at *Playboy* centrefolds, and want to make love to her. Women are not – I

602

don't know if it's cultural or biological, I think it's partially both – women are not visibly excited by men.

Margaux Hemingway: Sex is most important for a union, for two people to be together, whether married or not. It is everything at once. Sometimes the need for sex goes through cycles. I know I need to have it when the moon is less full. I think it's all gravitational pull.

Anouska Hempel: The fascination and the challenge, and the idea of conquest, and the hunt, and the nonsense and everything that goes with it, are there with a man for very much longer. It's very convenient for men to have been brought up to sow their wild oats. It's a wonderful attitude for a man to think that's his job in life and what the hell, and why not? But I don't know that all men think like that. There's an awful area of insecurity in men where they probably need the same sort of love as an insecure woman. But there are always those who whizz off out there into the world and don't give a damn. I think sometimes he thinks he's in love with a woman, but doesn't know what love's all about. It's all just wonderful and too much; it might be love, or might not be, but it's all delicious and wonderful at the time. There's a great area of confusion in loving and the whole blooming thing, much more for a man than for a woman.

Val Hennessy: There was a survey done recently in which people in New York were asked which they would prefer, a fancy meal in a 4-star hotel or a good night's sex, and 95 per cent who responded said they'd go and have the meal at the 4-star hotel. Probably what I would have said was, I'll go to the meal at the 4-star hotel and have some good sex afterwards, but eating is just as important as sex. Everybody loves having a good meal, or getting off on a wonderful book, or going to a wonderful concert which leaves you in a state of immense elation. These are all very valid, important experiences, and I don't think you can say one is any more important than the other. People are far too obsessive about sex.

In my experience, people who have difficulty in having orgasms are the ones who talk about it all the time. The others just have them, get on with it, and it's very nice but they're not really particularly obsessed about it. It's a bit like people who talk about sex all the time. They're the people who actually aren't getting very satisfactory sex in my experience. The only time you start thinking about sex obsessively is if you aren't actually having it.

Carolina Herrera: Men have more responsibility in the sex act than women, therefore a woman can fantasize but a man has to be thinking about what he's doing. He doesn't have time to fantasize. If he fantasizes, his performance is over.

Elizabeth Hess: I think, for both sexes, relationships where there is a certain amount of emotional involvement are probably preferable. But if you have to make a choice between no sex at all or having an experience with a man where there is good sex, a woman will choose the latter, whether they are in a monogamous relationship or not. For women, there is no longer a stigma. Statistically, married women and single women are both having more casual sex, one-night stands, than they have ever had before. And it's out of a positive desire for this kind of sexual relationship, it's not necessarily because it's the only thing out there that they can get. There is a certain amount of pleasure in having a sexual relationship divorced from all of the trappings of various other relationships that you get involved with. Men have always had the liberty to have as much sex as they wanted in marriage, and to fool around outside, and have enjoyed that as a privilege. There is nothing implicitly wrong with that, and I think women have realized that too. There's a certain amount of pleasure in the idea of conquest, a certain amount of power in that. Sex can be a very empowering experience when it's good. But I don't see it has to be a battleground. I think we view sex as traditionally a power struggle, one person dominant, the other submissive. We view it as a conquest of sorts. I don't think it has to be that way. But I think that is often a drama people enjoy.

Sex used to be a very male-centred experience for women. Women, until the last two decades, were essentially not having orgasms. It used to be they were called frigid. Sex was something defined as a little foreplay and a lot of intercourse. It was an act geared to male pleasure. The obsession with female orgasm was healthy at a certain point because women had to be made aware of their own potential, to educate themselves in how to have orgasms, and they had to retrain men into having sex with them. Now, if you read all of the studies that have been done, the majority are having orgasms and the culture itself has become obsessed with them. Every month there is a new orgasm discovered; there is a G-spot or a Z-spot, a this or a that. That, again, is the market place toying with our fantasies: always the promise of novelty and always the lure of a new orgasm. It is fairly evident now that an orgasm is an orgasm, and most women are having them and most men know about them. The sex manuals all used to be written by men who

604

assumed that women were not orgasmic. We have come a long way since then.

I think pornography serves a real function. I think fantasies are healthy and visual images stimulate people's fantasies. There are a lot of people who are simply starved for sex and don't have people with whom to talk about it. They need to nurture their fantasies.

Min Hogg: Gratification is the word I would use for a man, but a woman needs it to be much much nicer than that. I think a man couldn't care less half the time. Oh, let's have sex, yes, let's have sex. And the woman thinks, oh God, was that it?

Arianna Stassinopoulos Huffington: Men's sexuality has an urgency which women's sexuality doesn't have as much. The essential woman has her sensuality – and I prefer that word to sexuality – as a constant presence in her life, and I think the men who are really sensual are sensual throughout their lives, not just when they are in bed and having sex. That, for me, is what our culture is gradually beginning to realize after the whole permissiveness and sexual revolution, when sex was reduced to statistics and multiple orgasms and the sex act itself. We are now realizing that the great sexual experiences are those that are deeply sensual. For me, the real question is whether sensuality informs our whole life or just the X number of hours you are in bed with somebody.

A woman receives a man, and therefore she is left with part of him. The man can go on and it's over, he's released himself and he's off to another thing, and the woman can't really do that. She's the one who pays the price. That's why, in my experience, a woman needs to feel the man is still there with her in some way. Sex within a relationship is so different from casual sex because, in a relationship, a woman can surrender, and I don't believe sex means anything without surrendering. If you don't trust enough to surrender, it's so mechanical.

Caroline Huppert: Women can divorce sex from love, like men. Even if lots of women don't at the moment, it's in the air and will come. I see it with the young women I work with: the more freedom one has, the more difficult it is not to separate the two. They don't want to renounce their freedom, but that can't be reconciled with a desire to have a home, a place where they can feel safe with one friend or lover.

Angela Huth: There are these women who want to associate orgasm with all these stars in the head and wonderful feelings of romance and love and all the rest. It comes on different levels all the time, different nights of the week, different years and different months. It is always changing. That I think is, on the whole, the best thing about sex: that, unless you're terribly unlucky in your husband or lover, it's never the same. It can never ever be the same from one night to another. People say it gets dull with familiarity, but I think it breeds a different kind of closeness. People who worry about orgasms are absolutely nutty; there are many more serious things to worry about. Why should there be orgasms all the time? There are lots of other pleasurable bits of it. I don't think it is anything you should get too preoccupied by, and if you do there must be something wrong. Perhaps I speak from the superior position of having a wonderful sex life. But OK, a man has an orgasm every single time and a woman doesn't. So what? It doesn't matter. It only matters if you start getting worried about it.

Sheila Innes: It is possible to learn lust, there is no doubt about that. And, therefore, if the custom of the day is to have it off with everybody and anybody, I don't think it will be very difficult. It just happens that I am much more selective than that, and I like to think it matters. You've also got to think of what you consider to be both the dignity and the self-respect of a person. It wouldn't do anything for my self-respect to knock around and have it off with anybody I fancied, even if that happened to turn them on. I don't think it's too difficult to do it, I just happen to think it's diminishing.

Angela Janklow: For men, sex is really more of a conquest than it is for women. It is now becoming more of a conquest for women. My friends and I talk really graphically now, whereas before 1965, even when women talked about their men in the parlour, they were knitting and they spoke in generalities; it was not the carnality we speak of now. Of course, there were orgies around. The Victorians were banging at every turn, behind closed doors, but they kept up appearances. I think now that wall has been broken down. But men want women as a notch on their belts far more than women want a notch on their lipstick case, to quote Miss Pat Benatar. For a man, it will always be far more a sign of his own greatness. Men are hunters. They always have been and always will be. That's one of the things which distinguishes them from women. Women are out to preserve, men are out to kill. And I love men. I am anything but a man-hater. I have men around me all the time. It was men who originated the Olympics. Women had weaving competitions, they weren't throwing javelins and doing all these incredibly phallic things to prove themselves. Man and woman are different sexually. The male sex drive is not stronger but more focused. Many men don't even know how to have sex. For many men, it is just orgasm – come, come, you know, that's all they want to do. Now there is a movement away from that, which is good. And there have been many things in recent years which are good. But men never cared, never even thought about it. They were like, yea, yea, you're a receptacle for our seed, that's it. That didn't mean they didn't love; many of them did. Women would not go in and storm and loot cities and rape the men. Men will always come into the cities and rape the women. Always. It's a way of control, a way of power.

Tama Janowitz: A lot of men seem able to have casual sex without feeling any kind of bonding with the other person. And many women say they can also have sex purely for the pleasure of having it, but I do find that my women friends, when they have casual sex, are very unhappy later and wonder why they didn't hear from the guy again; or if they called him, why he wasn't interested. So most women I know, at a certain point, don't experiment with casual sex. It seems to be a college-age phenomenon.

Margaret Jay: What is interesting is that when you get one of these serious scares, whether it's Aids or whether it was herpes – Aids is obviously much more serious – you see people change their social and sexual behaviour in a way that, if it was all completely instinctive, they wouldn't. But they do. Look at the extraordinary growth of celibacy in America. Those things are much more socially determined. Men have been for generations brought up to think they could be more promiscuous, and it's probably become like one of those learned responses, almost instinctive.

Dr Lukrezia Jochimsen: I think I am always more reactive than active. In my first marriage, I regarded myself as a very fulfilled sexual partner in reacting towards the desires my first husband had. Then, after getting dissatisfied with the whole situation, being divorced, and having other love affairs, I found my desires changed with each lover. It was very funny. I found out there was, each time, something completely new and wonderful, more wonderful than the experience before. And then, in my second marriage, love was again completely different. The astonishing thing is that those new approaches, those new desires did not come from me, they were responses to a new attitude coming towards me from the new sexual partner. Like men, I think I can divorce sex from love. I can have nice experiences and leave the town and fly to another country and think, it was wonderful, but that's it over. Afterwards, I'd forget it.

Sally Jones: Although there are quite a few lesbian relationships on the sports circuit, I don't think it is nearly as widespread as people would make out. One reason for the number of lesbian attachments, which I think is probably higher than in the rest of the population, even though it's not that widespread, is probably that the women have been highly trained from a young age to be extremely tough, self-sufficient and competitive. They are also going around on an all-women circuit, so there aren't the opportunities to mix, week-in, week-out, with men that there would have been in the old days when all the great tournaments were played together and the various circuits would have included a lot of men on the team as well. These days, the women are thrown together very much, and it can be a lonely, tough, gruelling sort of business, and it's natural that your closest attachments should be with the other women you are with because there simply aren't any men around regularly. Just as many prisoners thrown together in a jail will have homosexual relationships, even though probably they didn't go in there as homosexuals, I think it is slightly the same with women.

To many men, sex is almost like a form of gymnastics, or like a good game of squash. You do come upon women, particularly younger women these days, perhaps because they've become sexually active very young, to whom it is a very mechanical act. Somebody at work the other day was talking rather casually about whether she should go to bed with somebody after three nights or four. It seemed to me extraordinary, to have such a mechanistic and clinical approach, almost like a game of chess, or the changes on a map of a battlefield with pin and line. She was just marking out her campaign as she went along. In general the average, not particularly feminist, woman might find that a rather reductive, debasing way. I know a number of men who would find that attitude in men very debasing: that going around for conquests, the idea of notches on the bedpost. And I know lots of men who almost get more worked up about sex than women, who see sex as a great symbol of closeness. A lot of women see it as equated with love, but if, for instance, it breaks down, or if they can see they have been used by somebody who wasn't really in love with them at all, they can very often accept it pragmatically and say, oh well, I just picked a wrong'un, far more easily than a man can who thinks he has had the love of his life and her having sex with him proved it. If she says, oh well, I was only sleeping with you because I felt like it rather than because I love you, often men get much more hurt by that because they are not conditioned to expect it from women. Women, on the other hand, always think at the back of their minds, well, one reason he is so fond of me, or one reason he goes round with me, is because of sex.

One of the feminist comics once said stick your hand up if you have never faked an orgasm, and not a hand moved in the entire audience, and there were terrible conspiratorial giggles. People naturally want to please. This business of some man saying to a woman, well, how was it for you? I'm sure that either man or woman, when asked that question, if they are fond of the person, would consider it rather bad form to say, well, actually, I was bored sick and I was just looking at the ceiling waiting for you to finish. They are going to say, well, it was wonderful darling, how was it for you? Well, it was wonderful for me, too – whatever they feel like.

Dillie Keane: Statistics overwhelmingly prove again and again that men are unfaithful outside marriage and women tend not to be. God knows who they are unfaithful with. The 15 per cent of women who aren't faithful must be kept very busy, I think. Or else somebody's lying. I do think there are different needs. The act of penetration is so much more personal for a woman, the man is putting himself inside her, it's immensely private. Whereas a lot of men might as well stick their finger in a jam jar. I don't know whether their needs are different. I think they think they are different. I have this argument with my boyfriend. It's much more impersonal for men, men can be more impersonal about sex.

Sex is conquest, definitely. I myself don't have to to feel anything. I would have made a wonderful prostitute. Unfortunately, I balked at that. Some women do feel it is necessary, and some men. Years and years ago, I went out with a bloke who just couldn't touch a woman unless he really liked her; he just wasn't interested. But I think that's rare. And I think women are under the impression that they have to like somebody, feel an attraction, love. You'd mistake it for love, whatever. And women fall in love very quickly once they've been to bed with somebody. It's that thing of, oh, I've let him be so private with me, it must be love. I think it's a fallacy.

The idea now is that the *Cosmopolitan* woman must be having great sex and five orgasms a night, several affairs, preferably with a married man,

609

to increase her credibility, and one with a black man, for super-credibility. And then, and only then, will she become a full woman, as long as she's orgasming at the drop of a hat, or hemline. That's a pain in the neck, I think. It drives me crackers. If you are not seen to be fucking, you are a failure. And the emphasis in sex is that you can't possibly have a good time without orgasm, without doing the full athletic works like fellatio or cunnilingus et cetera; that you're really not hip with just cuddling, which is just as nice at times, just saying, night, night, and feeling the warmth of somebody. There's much too much emphasis on sex, I think.

I can quite happily live without sex, and have done for years. I'm very dispassionate about sex. I think one of the differences I detected earliest between men and women, was that men were much more detached and seemed a lot happier being detached. So I thought, right, why get involved? Why break your heart? And I sort of adapted.

Caroline Kellett: A woman can function, more or less, even when she is being raped. I maintain, and always will, however many people argue against it, that you cannot rape a man. It isn't possible for a man to perform if he is not aroused. The whole thing becomes a farce and doesn't work. That, I would imagine, must be one of the most chastening experiences ever for a man. It can happen when they are so in love, they want to perform so much, they are so turned on, that they are absolutely overpowered and intimidated, and the whole thing turns into a farce and they are mortified beyond belief. I should think, psychologically, that could do a lot of damage, not just in the short term to that particular relationship, but in the long term, because they have a lower self-esteem and a lower self-respect. I think, probably, three quarters of women fake orgasm because the male ego is that much more fragile.

I've always believed that there's something about that English upper-class lack of affection that makes for a lot of latent and sometimes expressed homosexuality at school. It has one advantage in that in a man who is only very sightly ambivalent, with perhaps 5 per cent, 10 per cent of his nature potentially homosexual, he actually gets it out of his system. In someone who perhaps is 40 per cent or borderline, it might encourage it and, particularly in the climate before Aids, it might well have chucked him over the edge. As I get older, I also now notice a lot more dykes; I know the signs, the odd things. You walk into a room and there's a certain type of woman who's middle-aged, well-preserved, attractive, normally wealthy, bored, worldly-wise, and there's a strange eye contact you get. I don't know whether it's because I am more sensitive or more attuned, but certainly, working in the fashion business, I am more aware of it. It is much easier for women to be bisexual than for men, because it's essentially a passive and sensual act, whereas for men it has an aggressive, active connotation. At the very bottom line, we are talking about penetration, physical penetration, which is much more of a mental commitment, I think, if that doesn't sound too absurd. It's very easy for a woman to be sensually aroused by caressing, by touching, by kissing, whereas, for a man, it is much more of a physical need, an urge. It has a beginning, a middle and an end. Women can prolong pleasure without a climax, whereas men have to have that. And therefore, if a man gets involved with another man and that type of physical contact is made, the end result is much more finite and definite and draining. It takes something away from them. I don't think a woman necessarily loses anything of her own nature, her real nature, by having a relationship with another woman.

Mary Kenny: It's true that the sex act may mean more to a woman, but there could be a biological basis, because, after all, once the man's seed is discharged, it's finished with, but, for a woman, the act of love may last nine months – there may be a consequence. Therefore her investment in this act is much higher.

Patsy Kensit: I would never ever sleep around, but if I was so attracted to someone, I would definitely do it. I mean, I have done. And without getting involved.

Princess Yasmin Aga Khan: There's passion and there's love, and I think love is different, love is much deeper. You can have passion and think you love, but you don't love really.

Soraya Khashoggi: Sex is first of all a very visual thing. A man walks through the door, and I think, yes I would, no I wouldn't. And any woman who says she doesn't think that way, at least for a second, is a liar.

Rhoda Koenig: Any girl or woman who has achieved a marriageable age and has not had sex is showing a deplorable lack of maturity and curiosity and courage.

Men's biological urge is, probably, to propagate, but I wouldn't take it so far as Norman Mailer, who says that any sexual encounter that doesn't have the risk of pregnancy is worthless. That's taking all the biblical seed stuff to masochistic extremes.

Women have probably a more active fantasy life than men. Women can imagine things more, or can get more pleasure from reading rather than having to look at pictures. You know, women looking at pictures, it's too blatant. When I was in London, I saw that famous exhibition of erotic drawings and paintings, and I thought it might be amusing, but I was put off by most of it because the emphasis was so much on the genitals, not on the person as a whole, that I found those pictures ludicrous and vulgar for the most part. And also, because they want to show you the genitals of both people, the people are contorted into unusual positions and look uncomfortable.

Irma Kurtz: The perfect sexual act for a woman ends in conception, pregnancy, delivery, lactation. It goes on and on, one sexual act. Theoretically, it can go on for the woman for a year or more. For a man, it's over. Very soon after a sex act is over, he is ready for it again. For a woman, it's different, because it's involved with love, and the love has a maternal drive to it, I'm sure it does. For the man, it's different, it's sex. Men rarely say sex is love. Women think sex is love. Men see it as another thing altogether. You get the fear of failure among men. Every once in a while, a man has just got to know that he can still make it. I once interviewed Norman Mailer, and he said, you know the big difference between the sexes? I said, what's the big difference between the sexes, Norm? And he said, a man has to get it up. A woman can lie there and think of the Queen, she can be thinking of tomorrow's menu, she doesn't even have to enjoy the act. One of the reasons women are combining sex and love so much now, much more than they used to, is because of contraception. Now that sex very rarely is used to make a baby, how can you make it resonant again? It's only sex really, it's just a thrill for a certain length of time, then it's over, it's like eating a sweet. So what can we do to give it back the significance it had when it made babies? So we now make it connected to love. Now we come to something even more complicated, because if the wife is thinking that sex is love and if he loves me he won't do it with anybody else, so is the woman he is doing it with, she is making demands on him too as a wife. She also thinks sex is love. Well, she may think it's money if it's the kind of man who pays, that's OK, that's his business. You know, if he pays a woman, sets her up, or pays the occasional prostitute, that's his business. But if it's a secretary who has gone off on a weekend, I promise you she thinks that's love too.

I had two letters from women on the same day telling me they couldn't have orgasm, and they both came from the same town, and it was called Climax, Georgia. That's an agony aunt's joke of a high calibre. Just recently, we don't hear so much about orgasm. It was a fashion to discuss orgasms, having them, a simultaneous orgasm, that great pie in the sky, you know, wow, gotta have. For a little while, the woman was always wrong, we had the frigid woman. Then we learned that maybe it was the man's fault that she was frigid, and then the man was always wrong. And the poor bloke was being dragged to a shrink, or a sex therapist. People have come to terms with the fact the female orgasm is an elusive and interesting thing, and it happens to different women at different times in different ways. It is not an arrow hitting a bullseye. It's not as straightforward as men's orgasm. Mind you, you don't even think of a man's orgasm in quite that way, do you? We say ejaculation. It doesn't sound the same, does it? Orgasm has almost become a feminine word. But a man's orgasm, too, is a little more complex maybe than we thought. I don't know if the men always get so much joy out of sex, actually. I think women get more pleasure out of sex than men, I really do. They are much more sensual. It's a harem thing. This is another theory of mine, it's very unpopular. The women who write to me and say, they want cuddling, to be touched gently, they want soft touches, stroking, all this stuff – well, that's what eunuchs in harems used to do, or the women could do it to each other when the man was away. It kept them happy when they were pregnant and when he was doing other things. I'm not sure that the female's way of sex is any less normal than the male's – the male's being wham, bam, virtually. I think a couple work out a happy medium themselves and decide the best way they like to make love together. If they can't decide, then they are not compatible in bed.

I think bisexuality is a myth, to tell you the truth. When you make love with your own sex, you are homosexual. Bisexuality is just a cover. I've never known a gay man who couldn't make love with a woman if he had to. But they're not bisexual. If you desire your own sex, it's homosexual, that's all. And maybe we all have the homosexual strain and they are simply giving vent to it, but to call it bisexual is to give it grandeur. To hell with that. Sex is not love. To say I love my own sex, and therefore must go to bed with my own sex, what utter nonsense. Sex is not love, sex is war. We can't have sex without a difference. Sex is purposeful, it's only fun by accident – to make us do it, to make babies, like any other animal. Their argument's wrong, that's what I'm saying. I think it's absurd.

You can whisper in a woman's ear and have her. A friend of mine, an amazingly nice man, says there isn't a woman you can't have if you ask nicely. And he's absolutely correct. A woman is susceptible to the word. It's a turn-on. It's sexy if you say certain things to a woman and in certain ways. They don't have to be dirty. Some women like it dirty, some don't. But you just talk softly to a woman and it's a turn-on.

Verity Lambert: I have to say that, as a woman, if you go to bed with a man and continually he can't get it up, you begin to feel it could be to do with you.

Marghanita Laski: There is a confusion between love and infatuation, between infatuation and sexual need. If you need a man, you need a man. Women who say they must be in love and so on really find the idea of sex rather disgusting and only when roused are prepared to have it and don't recognize that they have these needs, and so, when they are aroused, they think this must be love.

The morality of our society needs thinking about a great deal so that young people have its protection. I think of this a great deal in relation to my grandchildren: they have no moral protection at all. It's all attenuated and weakened by the number of generations it's passed through without being reformulated. I don't know what it should be, but I do know the one thing the BBC will never talk about in any sensible way is morality, and they have the greatest influence of any organization or group in the country: more, I should think, than parents, more, I should think, than teachers. Schools never give lessons on morality. Yet morality is really important. I don't know the new generation except for my own grandchildren, and they seem to be sensible and level-headed, but you never know what will happen in peer rivalry or falling in love. I don't know if they have enough precepts to make decisions against. I don't know how they will make important decisions when the time comes. In many ways, they're very much more grown-up than we were at their age, but with quite astonishing gaps in knowledge because of the way they're taught. With virtually no historical perspective for instance. It's all very patchy knowledge.*

There's been so much nonsense talked about orgasm. Some people say you can only have a clitoral orgasm, and so on. I think it's simply a fashion, like Freudian psychology; once people heard of orgasm, they could think of nothing else. I think people confuse orgasm, which is sexual satisfaction, and sexual ecstasy, which is very rare. It happens two or three times in a life, just as ecstasy from music or anything else. I've written a book on this, by the way. You know the phrase people use nowadays, the earth moved. This is not something that happens every day of the week.

Sara Leighton: I don't think there are any frigid women, I think there are only bad lovers. Women take it more seriously, because that's their stronghold. That's the thing they've always held over men: that they could deny it and reduce a man to his knees. They know the power of saying no. Nowadays, women are afraid to say no, because they think he will just go out and find somebody else who will say yes.

I'm all for prostitution. If we didn't have controlled prostitution, and if we didn't have girlie magazines, a lot more innocent ladies would get themselves killed in rather nasty ways. It's a way a lot of not very well-adjusted men can get rid of their problems, if you like. There are an awful lot of normal men that like these things, too. But, again, men like the fantasy world – it's their sort of sexual fairy stories, and I don't see anything wrong with that.

Catherine Leroy: Germaine Greer would say, no sex any more, you can live without it. But what if you're hungry? It's supposed to be in man's nature to try to lay every woman he meets, but I've known men who don't do those things at all. And I've known men who are mentally and intellectually faithful to one person; who might lay someone once in a while, but the woman doesn't count. And I've known women who are very faithful, mentally, intellectually and emotionally, to a man, and might get laid and it doesn't count. There is far less difference than there used to be, because now a woman is more liberated, she is working in a man's world more, she will have more possibility of meeting men and maybe, once in a while, has a fancy for someone. It can happen.

Lady Lothian: A woman's whole physical make-up is maternal. A woman can love a man in a sort of torrid physical way, but at the back of it there is always a protective instinct towards the man in the woman. I think a man can have twenty women he loves equally, whereas in a harem, presumably, they all are orientated towards one man. I feel very strongly the woman has not achieved sexual freedom. We think we have. We take the pill, we get blood clots. We get the pill wrong, we have abortions, our stomachs are torn apart. Our feminist friends wouldn't agree with this, but they are coming round: Germaine Greer and Jill Tweedie and all. If you wear the cap, you get cancer. I think the woman also gets cancer from the condom, from the friction of the rubber. The woman is at a great disadvantage from the physical act, and she wants freedom. God, how she wants freedom – equal to man's, but I don't think she can get it. She is stuck with either being a spinster or being a receptacle of a man's fertility or sperm or whatever you call it. I suppose intercourse can be totally sterile, in the sense that it need not come to any form of creation. Still, to make it sterile, she has to take measures which hurt her body. The difference between a man and a woman sexually is a deep dividing frontier. The physical act is made out to be totally disproportionate in importance. We have lived in a century where orgasm was the only thing that mattered. I know a brilliant Jewish psychologist who said, it's only a convulsion of the pelvic wall. He was tired of having to spend hours and hours with women who hadn't got it, and, he said, let's just face up to what it is.

Maybe it's because I am old, but I do think the sex act has got terribly out of proportion, terribly. But I certainly was never a refrigerator.

Cecilie Løveid: I think women never forget sex. They want – I want – it to be there always.

I fantasize a lot about women. I have tried to sleep with women. It has happened sometimes. It wasn't very interesting, so I stopped.

Jenny Lumet: A woman would rather go home by herself than go home with someone she wouldn't want to wake up next to, whereas there are many men who have no qualms about waking up next to somebody they felt no more than a passing sexual affection for. I just don't think women go home with bimbos. A woman can go to bed with a man for sheer lust, but personally speaking, it's a waste of time; I'd rather be asleep.

Women have no problem any more with thinking of sex as a conquest, and no problem any more being sexually aggressive. They enjoy the power game as much as anybody else, the ego flattery, the ego lift. It's very nice to know that that man right there is absolutely yours for the evening. And you have him, you nail him, he's yours, you've gotten him.

616

There are weird things going on in this country. It's very Orwellian, that's the word, with the sex police. Sodomy is illegal in certain states. Oral sex, any way it's performed between any two people, is illegal in certain states. My family's politically pretty left wing, yet my whole family has joined in this whole fucking witch-hunt and Aids paranoia. It's mind-blowing how medieval this supposedly, apparently progressive nation is. It's actually weirdly, terrifyingly conservative. Of course, everybody is scared of Aids, but the kind of sex one indulges in is up to the individual. I don't want the police coming to my house and saying, you can't do that because you might get Aids.

Gillian Lynne: A man's is an aggressive shape, ours is a receiving vessel. The difference might be as deep and as simple and intrinsic as that. And whereas we all know that, when we are making love, it doesn't matter who is the leader, and it's essential that each one is from time to time, in the final analysis in the normal act of love – and we all know there are many ways to make love – in the normal act the man is going to push his point home, isn't he? And I think it really may come from such a basic thing.

I am basically an old-fashioned woman and I have been through my times when I have enjoyed leaping into bed for the sake of it, and always felt naughty about it. I was, I knew, doing it because I hadn't found the right person. I would find that totally impossible now. It wouldn't matter if the best-looking film star in the world was working with me and I really felt, oh, what a dish you are. If he tried to get at me at all now – because I have given my loyalty to somebody – I would be sick, I couldn't bear it. But then I'm old-fashioned in my outlook on life. But it's innate, because it all goes back to the biological thing. It stays with us, it's gone with him, it's in us. So, if it isn't something you really wanted, or if it was fabulous at the moment but after it you say, Christ, I've got to wash it out, still it's entered; with him it's just, exit.

Nowadays there is so much choice. People are spoilt for choice, and they keep looking elsewhere, and in the end it is only the new fuck that's exciting. It seems absolutely vital that you make the constant fuck wonderful all the time, and that's possible, you know. But then it's not often you meet someone whom you find delicious constantly. I took years to find that person, years – and I wasn't even looking, I'd given up. Totally given up.

Sheena McDonald: Women's sexuality is very complicated. It's a very hard thing to describe. I think men who are good lovers are rather unusual. But I don't know – it makes me sound like Catherine the Great, which I'm not. Men's sexuality is much easier to perceive. You know where it begins and ends.

A lot of women's thinking on sex is governed by the physical risks, and women are worried about (a) getting pregnant, and (b) catching a disease. I really don't want to go into the nitty-gritty of this, but there are a lot of odd little diseases that women get – not gonorrhoea or any of the big ones, but lots of itchy, rotten, smelly, little diseases that women want to avoid. The older you get, the more you think it's really not worth it. I'm being very prosaic and down to earth about this, but women are.

Women's fantasies are so dirty that they wouldn't do anything about them. It would be impossible. They are probably much more exotic, multi-racial than men's.

Mary McFadden: You can't over-emphasize the importance of sex. It's too important. It should and does only bring happiness. Of course, with Aids and so on, everyone is into a new kind of sex now. That's all you can do. Otherwise you're going to die.

I love looking at *Gentlemen's Quarterly*. All the time. And so does everyone else in my office. The most beautiful men in the world are in *GQ*.

Apparently all the orgasms you have in the world equal about five minutes, so people spend a lot of time talking about something that's stupid. Anyone can have an orgasm, it's just a matter of concentration. If your head is so screwed up you can't have an orgasm, you'd better go to a shrink.

Any woman can have as many men as men can have women today.

Susan McHenry: The things I have experienced about male sexuality are very frightening to me because of the aggressiveness and the hostility that are sometimes inseparable from it. But also, I think that kind of thing is culturally based, and that, as we modify the sexual images available in a culture – maybe not modify, but diversify, make a full range available to men – then maybe men will drift away from the more aggressive forms of sexual expression.

618

Donna McKechnie: It takes women a little longer for the nervous system to respond to the genitalia. For a man, it's like you push the button and it's there. So he has got to find a way to slow down to please a woman, and this is where it takes a very generous grown-up man. A lot of men really enjoy pleasing a woman, so they will find a way. A lot of men don't really care. Not because they don't like women, but because they are so preoccupied with, can I do it? Women don't have this problem.

I can't just get into bed with someone I don't know, it doesn't appeal to me. I would not, I could not fantasize someone else. My fantasies have to do with that person. It has to have more significance. Maybe I could do it, but not easily.

I certainly fantasize a lot. But women generally need the spoken word. You know, they need the connection. Men can maybe go off more on their own. It sounds like a general thing to say, but in bed, during the sexual act, the sounds are very important to women. The sounds, the words, are like a physical connection.

Deirdre McSharry: The great thing about sex for women is, first of all, they don't have to perform. This is the most terrifying burden for every, any man.

Norris Church Mailer: Women take sex more seriously than men. I definitely equate sex with love. Men don't. Men equate sex with sex usually, not always. I don't think every woman necessarily equates sex with love; I am not going to say I always have either over the years. But generally it means more to women. It's a sharing of oneself, in a way. Men maybe don't look at it that way. Generally a woman needs to be in love and a man sometimes just needs to have a good work-out.

Speaking from my own point of view, sex is very important in my marriage and my life, but it's really overdone as far as selling toothpaste goes.

Alice Mason: I don't have any sexual feelings any more because I put all that energy into other things. What is sex? It lasts what – an hour or whatever? You pay hours for it because there are all those other things that you have to put up with. It doesn't interest me whatsoever, it really doesn't. I was never really that sexually interested in any men. I don't mean that there wasn't sex in my life, but I was much more interested in life on a higher level. I was always metaphysical. For years. Even when I was pregnant with my daughter, I was very metaphysical and thinking, what is life about, what does it mean, what is this, what is that? I have all these metaphysical books, and in metaphysics sex is always a lower level of yourself, so I was always attaining the higher level of myself.

Margaret Matheson: The most worried-about thing in life is sex, and society is riven with pornography – distorted sex. There is a whole lot of spurious sex out there in urban life today, and it's revolting and has nothing to do with people leading happy, healthy lives. It's about money and power, and is absolutely nothing to do with gender differences. It's entirely to do with society.

I think men and women equally have a physical sexual need. I don't think there's any question that, if somebody's life, somebody's body is altogether lacking sexual activity, it produces a less healthy mind and body. I am absolutely certain of that. Everybody's body needs sex.

I'm fairly body-conscious. It's good to use your body, use your mind, use your sexuality, use your limbs. That's what bodies are for. Of course, modern living isn't terribly well geared to using bodies, and I loathe jogging and gyms, but there is some sense in jogging and gyms because it's good to use your body. Also, whether it be monogamous or not, loving but not necessarily lasting relationships are sacred and wonderful and equally important to men and women. Either you believe that sexual relationships are fun and healthy or you don't. And if you do, then it's a joint enterprise, so it's equally available to men and women. There are human relationships that involve sex, there are no two alike, and of course there is often a situation where you have longing on the part of the man and no interest on the part of the woman, whether or not there may have been a sexual relationship, and vice versa. Life isn't full of perfectly matched couples meeting, it's full of disappointments and fear and desire, and that's half the fun of life.

Homayoun Mazandi: Love starts for a woman because of sex. Women are more discreet about it. That's why there's less scandal about women's sex because they don't let anybody see it. Men are more open.

Sex is like having food if you're hungry, you will eat whatever is there. Some women are just as capable of lust as men.

Cristina Monet: Men can respond in masturbation or erotic fantasy to visual images. Most women either can't or don't, they respond to stories, fantasies, situations, they don't look at a picture. I've known men who have looked at a picture and masturbated. So there must be a difference there. From what I can see, women elaborate. They talk to their girlfriends: he did this and I said that, what do you think that means? Men don't talk to one another in the same way about their private lives, their lives with women, unless they're buffoons: oh, I had a lovely little blonde last night and all that sort of rubbish. That's not what I'm talking about. I, for one, would be much more aroused by having my knees squeezed under a table in a certain way, with the mood, with a certain something, a certain expression or whatever, than by a blatantly obvious sexual approach. Obviously, if you were terribly aroused, it would be lovely to do it five times, but the sheer gymnastic feat of five times might not be as much for a girl as having subtle creation of mood and so on. I can't explain it. For a woman, a lot of arousing is more in an old-world context of mood, fancy, situation, and something in the air, and what he said, and this and that. For a man, a lot of the time, it seems to be more purely physical.

A sexual need, if you scrape the surface, might often be something else. You're depressed, you're lonely, you don't want to go home, so someone bites your ear in a certain fashion, you're impressed and you think, oh, what the hell, because you can't face the night alone. That's not quite the same as animal need. It's some other kind of need that translates itself sexually. But I don't think it means that they get really horny. Maybe they do, but probably not to quite the same degree. If she doesn't feel anything for the man and thinks he's just a hunk and what the hell, I really need sex, I haven't had sex in ages, or I'm going to have this little adventure in a train or wherever, I would think that nine women out of ten will not succeed in keeping to their game plan. After they've had the little adventure, it's either a disaster and they want to forget it, in which case they'll feel degraded or depressed, or if it's any good, it won't be quite the unconnected physical whatsit they decided they ought to have. They'll think about it, and upset the pattern and wonder about it, and maybe wish it could have been a relationship and who knows what else. Probably sex does mean more to a woman. It's probably difficult for women to have a good time sexually. The way they're built is such that greater subtleties are required, both physically and mentally, to make them enjoy themselves.

You don't hear about too many men being impotent. Do you know how many women don't really have orgasms? How many of us fake it nine times of ten? It doesn't mean they don't enjoy themselves, but maybe things would have to be done a bit differently actually to bring them to exactly the right point. They almost get there, they're grateful for having got that far, they don't know the man well enough, they're not going to show him how, or inform him it didn't quite happen, so they make the right noises to be polite and leave it at that. And they've had a lovely time, but maybe only two seconds more and they would really have made it, but they're not going to start being games mistresses. Maybe it would take two months before they're comfortable enough with their lover to have an orgasm or tell him they didn't. Women's bodies have got to be known more by men for men to really give them pleasure.

Bel Mooney: Men would be shocked if they knew how women really talk and feel about sex. If you go to a factory – that play *Steaming* by Nell Dunn was about this – you'll find that women have a highly developed sexuality and quite a raunchy attitude to sex – not nearly so emotional as a lot of men would have it be. But I think all women just want a really good screw and then they can forget it the next day.

I have absolutely no qualms in admitting publicly that I have all kinds of fantasies, and I think they are healthy and there's nothing wrong with them and I see nothing wrong with occasionally putting them into prac- tice, just as men do. It doesn't impinge on your real love at all. But most women are so dishonest. It's not the done thing for women to say that.

Most women want orgasm, because it's otherwise very frustrating. A lot of women don't experience it and always feel: what was that all about? The thing about now is that we know so much about sex. In the Victorian age, it would be a pleasant surprise, they wouldn't expect it. Now, because of the whole sex industry, everybody is expecting the earth to move, in Hemingway's phrase, and of course a lot of the time it doesn't. A lot of women who are never awakened in that way feel very frustrated.

Kathy Myers: The last hundred years or whatever have been spent under patriarchy. It is only recently that certain things have been challenged about power-sharing. Men are very much told to expect power and to share friendships – although of course they don't really – with men, to trust other men. Yet somehow to sexually desire women. So women are very other. They are very outside the culture, in a sense. They are there for reproduction, for a romantic fix, a kind of obsession, but in a way they shouldn't really be a part of your traditional man's working life in Britain, they are separate. On the one hand, that creates the potential for a kind of romance, but on the other, it creates, in a lot of British men, a deep insecurity. As I saw in Cambridge, women are literally alien. And if the thing you are supposed to love is alien to you, then it's very cherished but it's also very frightening. So a lot of men are obsessed with the most bizarre things – for instance, with sexual performance – because they all feel they are on show in some sense. Sexual insecurity is the preserve of men. Men have to be dealt with like babies in terms of sex. Women are much stronger, and it's much easier to shatter a man's ego than it is a woman's ego, because of all those things that are expected. On a physical level, what is needed maybe is quite similar in the sense that both men and women love to be touched and cuddled and hugged. I don't think men like that any less, but they're brought up not to show it.

There's a friend of mine who went to Eton – he's now a merchant banker – who can't bear to be kissed or touched or cuddled in public. He has to be in control in public and he is in a suit, that's his work environment. Anything to do with physical affection is to do with the home and private where nobody can see. Now, there are very few women who wouldn't mind being given a kiss or a hug in public. The British education system has played havoc with people's sexuality and I think men are the victims of that. A lot of rape and sexual crimes have to do with that paranoia and that fear and resentment of the power they think women have. It's bitterness, it's nothing to do with sexual desire. Rape is a crime of fear.

Physical contact is very, very, very important. And I think a lot of people have sex because, once you pass the age of twelve or thirteen, there is nobody who can legitimately touch you any more. You have had all that physical cherishing from your parents, then suddenly you can't share beds with your brothers and sisters and you don't get as many hugs and kisses. And I think a lot of people strain relationships, not because they have a massive libido drive but because of the amazing physical, emotional and mental importance of just having somebody physically close. Where sex stops and affection starts, I don't know.

I haven't any concept of lust in the sense that what I find sexually attractive about somebody is usually their brain and whether they're humorous and interesting. So it's not necessarily a physical thing, not necessarily, oh, this person looks like Adonis, I'll go and jump on them. The erotic side of my nature is dependent on whether or not I find somebody mentally interesting. It's also that I don't want a complete stranger crawling all over my body. And also it's an arrogant thing – I

623

don't regard it as an amazing success or challenge to get somebody into bed – that's easy. Making the right decision is probably less easy. I'd rather read a book than have some complete stranger prancing around my flat. That's a horrible idea.

I'm like Pavlov's dog. My desire for sex is stimulated by finding somebody attractive, so if there's nobody around, then I'm like a hibernating hamster. I don't have these great needs, I don't have this overwhelming urge to satisfy, which is probably why I don't end up in bed with completely unsuitable people. That probably is quite different from a lot of men, who seem to have an urge independently of whether anybody's about. My urge is completely object-orientated, it's to do with desiring somebody. If I don't, then I go off and write on my typewriter or do something else.

Lynda Myles: I hate to come back to all the old positions. I thought, like most people in the 1960s, the whole system was going to change, but reluctant as I am to say it, most women I know are more naturally monogamous than the men. It's a fact I resist, I wish it were less so, but it certainly seems to be the case. I think male sexual identity is much more tied up with the apparatus. I see this a lot, because of the nature of making films. In films, sex is readily available, there are always girls throwing themselves at actors, directors. But what I find interesting is that the men find it so hard to resist. It's as if, once it's offered, they can't refuse, whereas if the reverse situation happened, women are just so uninterested. They don't feel that their sexual identity is on the line or that they have to prove anything. Having come through the promiscuous 1970s, I think for most women of my age there is a general lack of interest in that kind of hydraulic; I mean sex as hydraulics rather than sex in a context of some sort of relationship.

I hate this notion of sex being reduced to a question of hydraulics. It's of little interest. I'd rather read a novel.

Through the 1970s there was a sense of general promiscuity and it was almost *de rigueur*. It was terribly hard to find reasons not to go to bed with people: one was regarded as some kind of bizarre puritan, but that's changed a lot. I think it would have changed anyway, but the epidemic of sexual diseases has shifted it as well.

Lynn Nesbit: People are talking about sex more and doing it less. That is what I think.

Julia Neuberger: I'm fascinated by very early rabbinic law that argues that one reason a woman can ask a man to divorce her, although she can't divorce the man, is that he's not fulfilling her sexually, not satisfying her sexual needs. That must be second or third century: a very early recognition of women's sexual needs. I think women do have strong sexual needs and desires, but that they manifest themselves differently from men's, although I know a lot of men who are not highly sexed, for whom the experimentation is not part of their need, and I know a lot of women equally who want to experiment, who want to mess about, because they feel they never quite had the chance before.

I don't like promiscuity, because it seems to me devaluing for everybody concerned. A huge amount of sex with a lot of different partners: you may learn a lot about sex, you don't learn a lot about the relationships that make the sex worthwhile.

It would be a very rare couple, male or female, whether it was the man or the woman, for whom getting married both as virgins would be a satisfactory way of going about it. I can't imagine myself having wanted to marry without actually knowing what sex was going to be like with my husband-to-be, and I would have thought that was quite important, that to be a total sexual innocent at the point of marriage would be a dangerous thing. One wouldn't actually have any idea of what it was going to feel like, be like, how important it was going to be to one.

People don't talk sufficiently often about women's sexual difficulties. For instance, many women find sexual intercourse painful – and that's not really talked about. People are so concerned about men who simply can't get an erection, who are temporarily or permanently impotent, that they tend not to think of the women who find sex painful, constantly unpleasurable, who don't reach orgasm, don't know what orgasm is. I think, on the whole, because it is so much more physically apparent with men, that's where the concern has been. I suspect that if one actually examined it closely, one would find as many women as men who somehow, in some way, simply participate, can't join in, can't enjoy.

Nanette Newman: Women are not necessarily turned on by centrefolds of naked men. It's a more directly physical thing with men. I once knew a man who was hysterically funny – he had great success with women – and I think he laughed them into bed. Perhaps the women fantasized that he was a serious sometime lover. I don't know.

Perhaps all sex is a private fantasy.

Jane O'Grady: Maybe if we were in a different culture, where sex was underplayed, we wouldn't be in this state of torment about sex.

I think that once women experience sex, they can long for it all the time, but if ever they betray that need, it's totally condemned. It's unattractive in men as well, but it's doubly castigated in women. Obviously women are very sexy. They must be, because they realized they were going to have terrible pain in childbirth, and culturally they had that terrible stigma about having illegitimate babies, yet the risks they put up with through time to have sex, outside or inside marriage, it's obvious they really wanted it. Many of them were pressured into it as well, but some of them went to extraordinary lengths despite tremendous difficulties and obstacles. And hearing a lot of women I know talking about sex – admittedly many of them lesbians – they obviously have a tremendously powerful need. But somehow, if ever that need is displayed, they are much denigrated and despised. I think we need it equally. It's the application that's different.

I have an odd sexual history in that it took me years and years to begin, although I think I was always very sexual. But I always had this idea that it wasn't necessary, and until it was absolutely inevitable I mustn't succumb. I used to get into tremendous ecstasies over music, nature – this was even starting at school – having extraordinary feelings, and I didn't know whether or not this was sexual. I'd sometimes comment to my mother – this is how naïve I was – about odd physiological things that were happening to me (I don't mean menstruation). She'd look very embarrassed and say, oh, that's quite normal. And so these things would go on and I would insist that I had to be a virgin, although I got more and more a demivierge, and it was all excruciatingly frustrating and annoying, and I used to dance for hours and hours and hours.

It is often very unintelligent men who are very good at sex but very boring to talk to afterwards. There's that sort of liveness and sensuality and something more sporty about them – not sporty in an upper-class public-school way, but something more sort of virile.

I know that I wouldn't be totally fulfilled by childbirth. I often feel very sort of cranky and weird. I felt much better when I was having a solid and permanent sexual relationship. Even then, I didn't get enough sex, because I wanted it all the time. And there isn't enough time. But it kept me steadier.

I find in periods of celibacy, first of all, there's that sort of edginess and all the time thinking about sex and longing for it. Then the wound closes over and you think, oh well, how funny, I just feel completely sexless. Then suddenly, I don't know what it is, whether it's menstrual, though it doesn't come at any specified time, it comes back again: lots of erotic dreams, and feeling attracted to some of the most inappropriate people. A very attractive woman once sold me some ginseng, but when she came to sell it to me, she started somehow pinching my arm, and I suddenly realized it was so long since anyone had touched me. And I bought the ginseng simply because I was pleased to be touched again. Obviously there were people I could have slept with but none I wanted to sleep with, people like old friends – it's very embarrassing some- times to sleep with old friends – and I needed to meet somebody new. The trouble is, I find that I get into one of these terrible sexual states. I'm in one at the moment, that's why I'm talking so fast. I get very wrought up, and it's such a nuisance, it would be nice to get it over with. If I was a man, I could go to a prostitute.

I do feel it's so easy to use men sexually, but I've always felt guilty about it until recently, and then I thought, well, fuck it, you know, if women are used like that, why can't we use men like that? Sometimes you just want to sleep with someone, and if there's someone you find burningly attractive at that moment, they can be used; forget about it the next day. The difference with women, the trouble with women, and I know this from a boyfriend I had recently until Christmas, is that they sometimes think they're in love as a result. I loved sleeping with him, and once I started, after a bit I really got addicted to it, and so I would keep persuading myself, well, you know, I am in love with him, and I probably was in some way. I also realized, in the end, that he could manipulate me in a lot of ways, though so long as I could get him into bed it would be all right. But that was awful.

The first woman I slept with, most men think she's terribly unattractive, but she really has something about her which is very attractive to women. I don't know what it is. She has slept with so many women, she definitely has that sense of conquest. She's very like a man in her sexuality, not in the way of being aggressive necessarily, but in the way she somehow tires of people quickly, which I always associate with men.

Some men are sensitive, but sometimes women are much better at absolute, sheer sensuality. There was a woman in Austria who was more sensual than anybody I've slept with. She was very beautiful and tall with bee-stung lips, and I could only sleep with her one night, because I was going away the next day. In fact, it was only an hour, because it was most unfortunate that we didn't seduce each other until we went swimming in this Austrian lake at about five o' clock in the morning, and I had to catch a train at seven which I missed because of her, so we obviously exceeded the hour. I don't know what it was, but every touch was almost open dimples of orgasms, everywhere, back or anything, and it wasn't that she was thinking about it particularly, it just seemed something very spontaneous.

I never fantasize during sex just like I don't need to fantasize about a meal when I'm having it, because I'm being satisfied. If I fantasize because I'm celibate, the feeling I'm trying to get is rapture and excitement, that state of being carried away, and therefore I don't need to think of weird and kinky things, I simply have to think of some sort of scenario by which I'm in the position where it's what I call broom-cupboard sex – where I'm so excited I have to run down a passage with someone and find the nearest broom cupboard. That's what I want out of sex: that feeling of being swept away and not something weird and cerebral and sort of mechanical.

Kitty O'Hagan: I feel that men are looking for a home sexually, physically. There's this little thing searching for something, it's probing. It's a very outward-going experience for them, and sometimes, if it's aggressive, it becomes thrusting, and I'm not sure that it doesn't start off like that. Women have the power base, women have what it is men want, and men have to go and get it. That's something else I sometimes don't like about women. Why can't we make the move towards men, why can't we do it at the same time? Why do we just have to be waiting for them to take the decisions?

A sexual experience – it's always intimate on one dimension or another, but it doesn't always have to do with love or having a continual feeling of caring. You can have different levels of sexual longing, different sexual experiences. I've had about three or four main relationships in my life, and they're all very different. I have an ex-husband – golly, the idea of planting his seed, or being aggressive sexually, would just not occur to Philip. He's much softer than I am, much more tender, much more in need of reassurance, all sorts of things. Equally, I've had relationships where I do seem more submissive, so they vary. I seem to change with them too, it's not as though I'm always constantly in the same sexual relationship with someone. My sexual relationship changes depending on who my partner is and how I feel at the time.

Fifi Oscard: There was a year or two in my life when it was kind of a game to see how many men I could have, but in my day that was a very secret and very complicated thing to do. And not anything that anybody

628

would find satisfactory. I knew it was a terrible thing I was doing, but I did have about a year of high adventure and investigating everything about everybody and taking advantage of all the opportunities. Now sex is the same as having a dance with somebody.

Fantasy is part of a woman at every moment. I have had some extraordinary fantasies about men I've known, and they are very satisfying.

Edna O'Shaughnessy: Sex is very important to women for sensual gratification and a confirmation of their femininity. When one says this, one always has to allow for those women who have neurotic problems, just as one has to allow for men who do, but if we're talking in general, sex is very important to women for the pleasure it gives in itself.

Kathy O'Shaughnessy: Promiscuity is a risky thing for both sexes, and I'm not talking in terms of Aids. I hate the idea of separating myself from my body, as it were. I think it's to do with immaturity, I really do. Men who have to go and sleep with X, Y or Z to prove their masculinity, and can't love and stay faithful, are tragic. They're self-defeating in the end; they deplete themselves as people. Their own self-image becomes tarnished. That sounds quite moral, and I'm not anti-promiscuity; as far as I am concerned, everyone can do what they like. But I feel it's detrimental towards oneself. In the past, it's always been thought women can handle it less, they get branded as tarts. And I think on one level, that's true. Language spells out those differences: Don Juan and stud *versus* whore and tart. But I don't actually think men come off very well in themselves either. They have a sort of thinner conception of themselves and their own needs, and that's quite dangerous, that separation of your body and yourself.

The kind of eroticism pornography offers is absolutely depersonalized and dehumanized. That's its appeal. Everybody has sexual fantasies, because sexuality is an incredibly amorphous, complex, diffused phenomenon in each person rather than a homogeneous thing, and it takes all kinds of forms. Everybody is capable of dehumanized sexuality, but women less so than men.

Clare Park: When you first meet somebody, even if you get on, you don't really know each other that well. You just know you have similar interests, so if you sleep with them, usually, particularly the first time, a lot of that is lust. It's an incredible experience, because it's the first time and it's all sorts of things, but basically it's craving for this person who is new to you. I've been in two professions where people are quite promiscuous and I've seen men and women, quite at random and out of control, sleep with lots of different people, and I've spoken to people who are what we call promiscuous, and some of them actually reach the point when they seem incapable of ever being able to love somebody, just one person, because it's a complete obsession with having a first time all the time, this incredible heightened lust.

Diana Parker: There seems a great consensus of opinion that women are more concerned with the atmosphere in which sex takes place than with the act itself, and that, to a man, if you talk about sex, what he immediately thinks of is basically intercourse.

Molly Parkin: I was brought up to believe you shouldn't give your body to anybody until you were married, whereas the boys that one knocked around with were brought up to believe they must sow as many wild oats as possible, lay as many girls as possible, before they were married. In those days, marriage was meant to be for ever, as it were. Of course, that has all changed now, and certainly what girls demand or expect from sex is different from what they were aware they required from sex say twenty or thirty years ago. I had certainly not heard of the orgasm.

I didn't understand that you could enjoy sex until my time between marriages, when you can have as many partners as you like.

If you think of the body as a door, and there is a person entering the door, which is the stronger, the door or the person who's entering it? Many people can enter it, but there's only one door, and it can be either locked or left ajar or completely open. Everything depends on whether you welcome the intruder. I myself have always welcomed the intruder.

It must be pretty daunting for men at the moment to understand that women, girls, females, understand their bodies very much more and are disappointed if there isn't a certain amount of arousing, foreplay, before actual penetration. A man – I'm talking about years ago – didn't go in so much for foreplay. I don't think that he quite understood that it existed, that you should perhaps play around with breasts before you shoved it in, as it were. People are much better lovers now than they were in the past, simply because there isn't so much ignorance. I think

630

men were very selfish. I know an instance – well, they're divorced now, and I'm not surprised – where a wife said to me that sex between her and her husband had become absolutely awful: he popped it in when he felt like it and he just turned over and went to sleep and she was still awake, ravening for something more.

There's a certain amount of pressure on the woman – well, a likable pressure, a pleasurable pressure – to arouse the man enough to get an erection and then coax them to orgasm, or lead them to orgasm. Not just once, but, four, five, six times, if that's what she requires from the night. We mustn't underrate the tenderness that lack of ignorance brings to relationships. There is a lot of tenderness and understanding on the part of women; they understand now that sometimes a man or a boy, for different emotional reasons, or simply total fatigue, cannot get an erection, and they're perfectly content to hold that man and to stroke each other and fall into sleep together. Women now are not absolutely voracious beasts, as the media would have you believe.

The attitude to sex that I and my friends have is very open, and you talk about it or you don't talk about it, so in that way it doesn't assume great importance. It's just a fact of life, like good food or reading or music, or anything else.

In that moment of joyful coition there is a great deal of tenderness as well, and anybody who suggests that one-night stands are devoid of tenderness, fun and emotion don't really know what they're talking about. They think that one-night stands are cheapening. I understand from many girls, and from women such as myself, that the difference between marital intercourse, for instance, or intercourse in relationships on a long-term standing, and one-night stands, is that you don't always feel like a four-course meal. You sometimes feel, in terms of food, like a quick sandwich or a quick snack, which is no less nourishing emotionally or physically than the four-course meal, and that is the difference between the one-night stand and intercourse which has to do with marriage. Marriage is a four-course meal; a snack, a solid snack is like an affair; but a quick sandwich or a bag of crisps is like a one-night stand. And there's space for everything.

I am seduced by a sense of humour first. Then, size of the equipment, though that's fairly low down. I have had wonderful lovers with very small apparatus which didn't make very much difference because they knew what they were doing with it. I've also had persons with members like elephants' trunks who were so insensitive they didn't make great lovers. But that can be rather disappointing, if somebody comes on as a macho stud and you find the equipment is less than average, which quite often happens.

I think political affiliations are very important. I never really would like to go to bed with a rank-and-file Tory, for instance, because we would be in basic disagreement about life and people and values. Age is immaterial because you can have great lovers in their seventies, or even one I had who was in his eighties – I was twenty-one at the time, so I didn't have much experience. But he was a wonderful lover, he had a very active tongue. I don't say that his member was great, but it didn't seem to matter at that time. He was a man of huge, of vast experience, and great wisdom. I went back again and again. Thought he was wonderful.

I've had very young lovers. I suppose my youngest lover – well, I'd best say he was sixteen, because otherwise it's seduction of a minor. If you're sexually orientated, your sexual life can go on for ever, but I must say that, since the menopause – because I'm post-menopause now – sexual activity for me has lost the overwhelming pull it had before. I do find other things taking its place. My sexuality seemed to reach its peak at forty, and I was married to a younger man and that was a wonderful sexual time, and also after the divorce. But at fifty, things seemed to open up in a strange way: all different kinds of opportunities present themselves; to do with working, I mean. And I do think that's to do with the ceasing of menstruation.

Judith De Paul: I think sex is like business, the stakes are very high. Just like somebody will go for the kill to get the business deal, I guess people will go for the kill in the sexual conquest. I, as a woman, have tried to be respectful of other women's position with men, mainly because, when I was running around a bit more than I do now, I was always the other woman. And it got to a point where I heard the same story from these guys all the time: my wife doesn't understand me, or she doesn't really know what I do and she doesn't this, she doesn't that. And they never ever accepted any responsibility for either a lack of communication in the relationship or the fact that, at the mature age of anywhere from fifty to sixty-five, they felt they could recapture their youth by screwing an eighteen-year-old or a twenty-five-year-old.

Men do have a different kind of physical need. In particular, until they reach a certain age, they need some kind of physical release, either in sexual copulation or however they achieve it. It doesn't necessarily mean that they need a lot of sex. It's also been proven with women that, if they have regular sexual relations, their menstrual cycles tend to be very consistent. One of the differences is that men have been taught to feel that the sexual act itself is necessary, as opposed to thinking that an orgasm is a requirement a certain number of times a year in order to release this physical hormone. And therefore men tend to come across as sexual animals as opposed to being emotionally sensitive. Women tend to feel that the sexual act is secondary to how you feel emotionally. But, realistically, the two do have to work side by side, because if a woman doesn't seem to have a sexual drive, it's not very stimulating to a man. If you just sit and talk about it, it is a bore. Women need to be open about this sexual drive, coupled with their sensitivity, and men need to take that sexual drive, which I think is a little stronger than in women, and couple it with caresses and understanding. Men like the power of the conquest, but there are women like that as well. It makes you feel good. I've been like that. I have come to terms with a form of self-morality and with standards that are very important to me. I have rules and regulations that I have created for myself, standards I've set for myself. In my twenties and thirties, sure, it was a degree of power. Just like the guy likes to be able to seize the moment and, quote, conquer the woman, I think the woman can do the same thing. It depends on whether or not you look at life that way. There's nothing to say that the woman who sees the man and wants to conquer him should have to feel badly about that. Baloney. Sometimes you don't remember his name either.

Sex is a biological drive that is normal and it plays certain roles in our lives depending on social standards of the moment. The kind of sexual permissiveness we've had has been a disaster for society, for family life, for children. It's been a tragedy, it's been really wrong. I'm terribly sorry about this Aids disease, which is terribly frightening. But people have got to get their act together. They have been running wild like badly behaved children with no direction, and I think it's damaged the social fibre, in particular in the West.

Lorie Scott Peters: Enjoying sex is something that women still have to learn. I was never brought up to just like a man, go out there and enjoy sex, one, two, three, four, five, six, bang and you come and it's over. Women have to be there mentally and physically in order to come, I think. Some of them go out there and have a quick orgasm – and all the more power to them. But my brain has to be there, my mind, my emotions, everything.

I don't need men to make love to me. I don't need women either. I can

633

go months on end without having sex. That's not what drives me. What makes me happy on a daily basis is my own creativity. That's what I did as a child. I learned to be happy on my own, I played in my own sandbox. I built my sandcastles and I destroyed them.

A lot of women are still trying to go out and prove their sexuality, and I think if they stopped trying to prove it, it would just happen. The reason it doesn't is that there is a lack of intelligence about what women's sexuality is all about. They still don't know that a lot of women out there aren't just having orgasms left and right. There's a lot of locker-room talk about women, how they're portrayed in movies. There's this constant thing that women make a lot of noise when they're coming, to show they're coming. A man's penis gets erect and then it ejaculates and then it becomes flaccid. That doesn't happen with women, so they have to show that verbally and physically in some way. So women think that if, in fact, they don't get screaming, yelling fits and heaving, that's it: they're not coming. Women feel they have to fake it to let men know that they're coming, and that's not what it's all about. I still don't know the answer. Talking to women is so hard because they're so afraid to open up and say, well, I haven't really had an orgasm. It took me a long time to find out what my sexuality was about, and I can only say that I'm lucky, because I've actually been able to talk about it.

Davina Phillips: Generally speaking, for women to fulfil themselves sexually, they have to feel very relaxed. They have to feel that the man is there to make them as happy as he is himself, not just there for self-gratification. Therefore, for a woman, there is a risk factor. She won't necessarily leap into bed with somebody she doesn't know very well because she's afraid it will all be over in ten minutes and she's going to feel ghastly. Very few women, if they are honest, enjoy it that much the first time. They tend to enjoy their relationship with a man physically as they get to know him. It isn't something that just happens automatically. It's not like the movies. I wish they'd stop showing it on the movies, because I think it's giving people an inflated expectation, and far from making people more relaxed with one another, it actually makes people more uncomfortable. They feel they should perform the way they see it on the screen. Making love is nothing to do with the orgasm. That's a very, very small part of it. It's all to do with being able to laugh, just to chatter through it sometimes. If you're really relaxed with somebody, it's a comforting thing. It should be so many different dimensional things, and you can't gain that overnight. There's a sort of thrill with the first experience, but that's a different thing. It's not real love-making, that's really screwing, to use a crude word. It's doing it to each other for the sake of it.

There are some men and some women who are not that sexy. But if you are a sexual animal, now, because the taboos are down, you can meet a man at a party, and you get that skin feeling and you fancy him like mad, and you can go off and go to bed with him, and it has nothing to do with the intellectual relationship you have with your partner in life. But the difference is that a woman would choose not to deal, whereas a man will see somebody's attractive and he'll go ahead and do it. A woman might want to desperately, and know she could do it, but decline, hold herself back. Because what she can't cope with is the morning after. The man accepts it was just an experience, and he doesn't feel guilty about it, doesn't feel he's lost anything, doesn't feel he's given anything away. On the contrary, he mostly feels quite pleased with himself, because it is a bit of a feather in his cap. Women don't really feel they've gained anything. It's not something you go and brag to your friends about. The next day you feel, oh dear, why did I do it? You know it was lovely, it was wonderful while it lasted, but why, what was the point? Women do feel differently afterwards. They regret it. Not seriously, not, I'm going to cut my throat; but they just think, oh, did I really? I shouldn't have done.

Lynn Phillips: It's hard to tell what is sex drive and what is the drive for conquest. I've had periods in my life when I just wanted to score men. My girlfriends didn't like it, but it was a lot of fun and really interesting. I put myself in what is traditionally called a masculine mind, very objectifying, very instrumental. There was always a motivated reason for everything I did. I was very manipulative, and I found it quite a lot of fun and interesting as an experience to have, but not a life. I felt I understood men better. I certainly began to be able to understand and forgive men for running off with younger women, because I discovered I really liked young boys. I explored some of the interest of sexual objectification which I found can be extremely pleasurable and self-restorative. To keep this sexual experience in oneself, rather than allow that confusing female blending and mutuality to take place, did feel strengthening in a certain way, but not on a lifetime basis, not on a long-term basis. And I was also very rigorously responsible in that I would never confuse somebody about my intentions, or involve myself in any problematic marital structures, or undercut.

A lot of what I had always called love, had disguised to myself as love, was just a kind of insect-eyed fascination. I realized that men fascinate

me, they fascinate me like insects fascinate me. I found it really
interesting to go into insect-mode, or lizard-mode: that detached,
traditionally masculine sexual motive. A lot of men adore women in a
completely objectified way, and I was able to understand what that felt
like. To be looking at a completely beautiful young man, and to feel, oh,
this is magnificent, he is magnificent, I adore this, when it is really
beauty you're in love with.

My fantasies are almost exclusively masochistic, sometimes entertaining, sometimes monotonous. I've always found it fascinating that I've
had to reconcile this passionate masochism with a very adamant love of
freedom and feminism. I don't think feminism has ever dealt with the
question of female masochism clearly, or masculine masochism, and I
have never entirely sorted it out. To me, it looks like childhood.
Hierarchical power impulses and sexual impulses are located in the
same part of the brain, and it's a common crossed metaphor: sex and
power. If you think about sex and love the way most women choose to,
you don't make that confusion, but once you are in a sex and power
mode, you do, and this happened very clearly in my life. I don't think it
was a result of cultural conditioning, I really think it was something that
happened because of familial relationships, my reactions to power, my
reactions to infantile impotence, to not being able to get my way when I
was a baby. For me, its origin is in confused feelings about wanting to be
protected and hating to be dependent. I think men live in a world of
fantasy. I don't think men make contact with other human beings very
often, at all. Most men I meet, their entire social life is a fantasy.

I like to be dominated by men in bed. I also like to dominate men in
bed. I also like to have sex in the arena where neither of these things
happens. I just like sex – I like all that stuff – but orgasmically I'm
hooked to masochistic fantasies. It has nothing to do with a live man. I
think, sexually, people get themselves off, that it's your own vision, it's
all in your head. I think orgasmic sex – for women anyway – is a
completely self-enclosed activity. But I don't think orgasmic sex and sex
is the same thing. I don't think there's a better kind of orgasm. I just
think there's a better kind of sex. I think it's religious, I think it's ritual,
I'm using these words loosely, but to mean a certain level and quality of
experience. It's a profound and important experience and doesn't
necessarily have anything to do with orgasm. For some women it does,
but I'm not one of them. I can have my orgasms, I can have sex, I can
have them in the same location with the same person, but they're not
the same.

The female orgasm has become something of a fixation on the part of women, and I'm not sure that orgasm necessarily means the same thing to women that it does to men. But, in a more direct way, yes, men seem to be much more easily excited and brought to a climax, and once they climax, it's over and they seem to be sleepier than women. All of which sounds simple, easy and fun, until you start to put it into something like a marriage where it has to be repeated over and over for a lifetime. For a night, these things aren't a problem, but when two people live together for a long, long time, I can see where the predictability of difference becomes exhausting on both sides and the need to accommodate each other becomes obligatory rather than exploratory. So, in my mind, the biggest consequence of sexual difference is the way it affects monogamy and the desirability of permanent monogamy as an institution. Because I think people need to change their problems from time to time. Problems are exciting when they're changing, and oppressive when they're predictable.

It is much easier to get an orgasm without a man, but you can't have sex without one. I really like sex. And I don't think it's about having an orgasm. I think it's a religious rite, a profound exploration of identity and of boundary, of the contradiction of the individual and the social. It is a profound and fabulous religious rite.

Sarah Fox-Pitt: Traditionally, men have had more freedom to indulge their sexual needs, stemming from the days of hunters and warriors when their lives were continuously at risk. The male needed to procreate in the short time available. At the same time, a man has a physical need to rid himself of the build-up of semen and release tension, although there is a difference in thinking between East and West on that. In the West, I would say that the male has generally a greater sexual need than the woman. I think women certainly have the physical urge, too, but women are perhaps more self-contained and can masturbate on their own more easily. Men are, I think, more satisfied by having a partner to do it with. Of course, they can masturbate, but on the whole men prefer not to do it alone, apart from the fact that probably they enjoy a certain tactile quality more than women. But I don't know, as I have never slept with a woman.

Women may and can fake an orgasm, but it hasn't released in them what they needed to release if they do fake it, so, in a sense, there is pressure that builds up by only being able to fake it. Certainly, for a man, it's much worse to be impotent. It's a real problem. It's much harder for a man to deal with. There isn't such a thing for a woman really, except that she may not be able to have children, but that is another thing. I think if more men could be more considerate or more thoughtful, more women would get more pleasure. I know of certain apparently very sensitive men who can't get over what is not a very difficult hurdle: to assist a woman to orgasm. It's a question of time and understanding. And I think that's a disadvantage men have: that they miss out on learning more about people in a more intimate way. Possibly men are less good at wanting to understand people below a certain surface than women.

Baroness Plowden: Women on the whole, I think, don't want to sleep with a man without love. Men will sleep with a woman for sex. Women want love and affection, and women get much more hurt as a result. Because men will leave them; they have done what they wanted to do. And women are left with their hearts broken because they thought there was something more than that.

There have always been people sleeping with each other outside as well as inside marriage. At the moment it's gone absolutely lunatic. It's seen as the be-all and end-all of everything: you simply have to have a satisfactory sex life. One wonders whether God hasn't sent Aids to make us pull ourselves together after what has happened in this country. In this country and in America, you get this belief now among the young that sex is something which you can have with anybody you want, and it's your right to have it. It's a sleeping act which has no relation to communities' interests or to respect for each other. It's actually body to body, and I think this is degrading; particularly degrading to women. They're more likely to suffer, but they do it as well. They want to be slept with as well.

Eve Pollard: Of course we over-exaggerate the importance of sex. We write about it all the time, we read about it all the time. On the other hand, *au fond*, why do you stay with somebody and why does a marriage work, and why do we see extraordinary marriages that look as if they have nothing in common? Because, in the final analysis, they work in bed. And however much we want to say to ourselves, we are intellectual, intelligent beings, we are also animals. The danger about women is that some are so determined to be successful that sex becomes somewhere down about No 10 in the list of priorities in their life. I don't think any man feels that. And I think it is very important that women think, I have got to keep attractive, I have got not to let my work grind me down, so that every night I get into bed, plastered with cream, and I'm shattered. Tiredness is the great thing you have to fight. And it is very important that women realize that, however important men think their new careers and their new lives are, they still give sex I should think No 1 or No 2 priority.

Antonia de Portago: It's very healthy to fantasize, because then you don't have to do the real thing in your life.

I don't think there's any sex life in New York. Why do people talk about orgasm so much? Because there's nothing going on. People who talk about it so much are covering up the lack of it. In France, everyone is having love affairs: men, women, everyone.

Women need sexual fulfilment just as much as men, but they are not liberated enough to realize it and act upon it. I think many women would do the same as men, sleep with someone, just because they want to sleep with someone. That would be real liberation for women. That would put everything in perspective. But my own feelings, anyway, are tainted with society's dos and don'ts. Everyone is conditioned by it. Anybody who tells you, no, I am not conditioned by society, I think my own thoughts in my own mind, would be at once stupid and Utopian.

Barbara de Portago: Certainly you can have just an incredible chemical reaction to someone for a night or a few hours. Wonderful. But I'd rather be involved.

Diana Potter: Women like to have one man who is theirs, to set up a house and have a family and so on. Unless their marriages are unsatisfactory, women don't really want to take lovers. Most of my friends have been to bed with, say, five or ten people, but I know very few women who have been to bed with more than fifty men. Very few. It's the nurturing thing: they want to protect their families, their nest, their home. That's innate, it's sensible, it's common sense.

Emily Prager: A man I know said to me he thinks that men want to fuck every woman on earth, and the only reason he doesn't is because he'll have a big scene at home if he's found out. Certainly I don't think that's true of women. I don't think women want to sleep with every man they see. I think women are less lustful in general. But I don't think this is biological. I think it is cultural. Women in most societies are culturally constrained not to be sexual because they're supposed to bear the children and so forth, and therefore we don't have any society where women have sexual equality. There isn't a society on earth where women could go out and pick up, let's say, two men in a night and wouldn't be considered ready for the loony bin. Whereas a man could do that and get away with it. It would be kind of, oh, he's a dog, but he wouldn't be considered insane. There's a boundary, like outside the tribal village, and if you go beyond it you're in no man's land as a woman. Once you hit that boundary, you're never allowed back.

I recommend sex before marriage to everybody. I'm a big sexual pioneer. To a large extent I've written about sex and humour all my life; this is my subject, although I've branched out into politics. I was a big crusader for freedom of sexuality, because I grew up in the late 1950s and early 1960s when repression was so thick it threatened to strangle you. When I was in high school, I didn't know how I was going to live. I thought I would have to have three lives, because socially you could not have sex and a career. If you were a career woman, you could never have a husband, so basically you couldn't have sex. All the sex had to be underground anyway. The twist of rules that involved sex was unbelievable, so for me the whole thing was to let go of it. I can understand that, once you get free, you get extremes of freedom and people go wild, and so you get bondage magazines on the rack. Well, fine, but freedom is freedom and people who can't remember or who weren't alive at the time should know that this is so much better than that repression, so much healthier.

I did a big piece on prostitution and I used to say to them look, I understand what you do is a job, but you have to explain for people who don't understand how you have taken yourself outside the legitimate boundary. Now anyone can throw a stone at you and anybody can hurt you that wants to. Why do you want to do it? The prostitutes, the girls in porno and things like that – I don't care what they do. It doesn't mean they're subhuman beings to me. To a lot of women it does. These Women Against Pornography think these girls must be out of their minds. What I'm trying to say is there is an outcast population of women in society, in American society especially, on whom everybody can heap their disgust and spit. These are the women who have gone beyond the tribal boundary, and to me, as long as there is this outcast population of women, outcast by everybody, men and women, you'll never have any kind of equality, and certainly not sexual equality.

Judith Price: I think it's easy to say sex is more important to men than it is to women, but on the other hand, I just came from a ladies' lunch where the women were talking for an hour and a half about how good these guys were in bed. And I don't think, at a men's lunch, they'd be talking for an hour and a half about, or be obsessed with, how good a woman was in bed.

Americans are very uncomfortable about sex. They're so uncomfortable, they're consumed by sex. They not only talk about orgasms, they talk about size of penis, size of breasts, length of sexual union, if they have made it two or three times during the night. I mean, I know more about someone's penis than I know about how his balance sheet is doing.

Marjorie Proops: With increased sexual education, and knowledge and freedom, and freedom to talk about it, women are now acknowledging their own sexual needs more than they did. When I first started my agony column, women used to write and say, my husband expects me to submit to him three times a week, or a month, or whatever. Now no woman would ever use that word submit. Ever. And in those early days, women never wrote and said, how can I get an orgasm? Now they write and say, I only get one orgasm a night, or a session, or whatever and I think I ought to be getting more, can you give me some advice? So women now perceive themselves as having a right to expect gratification where previously they didn't. If they had it, it was a bonus, a kind of secret delight that they probably didn't talk to anybody about, including their nearest and dearest, who was perhaps providing this pleasure. But now they do write about it.

Women do fantasize, probably more than men. I don't know. I haven't done any research into these things. I simply gain an impression from what people write to me, and quite a lot of women write about fantasies. They fantasize about pop stars, or some bloke who reads the news on television, or Wogan or whatever. I don't know whether men fantasize about Samantha Fox, but certainly women do see themselves as sort of Mills & Boon heroines of erotic situations.

Quite a lot of women do masturbate, and it's easier, I think, for a woman. If she's lying alongside a man in bed and he's gone off to sleep, she could quietly masturbate and fulfil herself. Whereas, if he does it, then it's not such a private thing. And so I think they are more self-sufficient sexually.

Andrée Putman: Sex is like the weather forecast – always there, but

641

normally not the only thing in your life, and then at times in your life it becomes like an obsession. How could it be that great, that obsessive, from sixteen to sixty-six? It cannot be seen as food or oxygen or sleep, without which you die. And yet, when it becomes like an obsession, you feel you'll die without it.

Fewer women can experience a very intense sex life without any love or admiration. An incredible amount of men, wonderful men, can adore their wives or their lovers and still have a lot of other sex perhaps with no meaning. I think it is conditioned rather than biological, although the possibility of conception – let's forget about the pill – makes a difference in a woman's attitude to sex. They wouldn't want to be pregnant by a man they absolutely didn't like or respect, or by someone with just a beautiful smile or a beautiful sense of humour whom they wouldn't see more than four times.

Mary Quant: When one thinks about it, women's appetites must have been so terrifyingly huge, the risks they took were so amazing. With every pregnancy, they risked death until fairly recently, so, God, they must have been sexy.

I think historically, because the woman had to take the gamble every time – not only perhaps of her death, but also her vulnerability through pregnancy, her need to have help with the child afterwards – she had to be a bit more cautious, to remember who the hell it was and where he went. That seems to me perfectly straightforward and logical. And now that that isn't so, of course you get a rather different attitude from women. You do see some women with what would have been con-sidered a very masculine attitude to sex, because they don't have those risks any more. Other things are coming to take their place – Aids and various other sorts of terrifying diseases which are reversing everything back to the starting-point. People will have to go back to being very faithful to each other, and it's already happening. In such a short time we're back at square one again. Both sexes are capable of enjoying sex purely to satisfy lust, but both sexes are more and more aware of the disadvantages of that, and the advantages of long-term relationships.

The worrying thing about sex is that the design of it is disturbing. It does tend to encourage the male to overwhelm the female, and the female reaction tends to be to want that to happen. The actual design has a flaw in that it brings on, at its worst, violence – which is, of course, now one of the most difficult things about sex to deal with.

Charlotte Rampling: From the men I know, I think men are as sensitive about sex as women. Men seek much more warmth and tenderness, and love. The greatest reward for a man is to meet somebody who cares about him and can lie in bed with him, and if he can't get it up, it doesn't matter. I think a man must have many more complexes about sex. He has got to get it up, so he must be in a panic most of the time. Especially if he meets a radiant woman and she's attracted to him and then he's got to go to bed. Quite often he desires her, and has desired her for years, and he can't do it, and he is going to be judged. It's terrifying for a man, when you think of it. A woman just has to lie back, and she can moan and groan, and even if she is not enjoying it, she can always pretend, but a man can't. It needs an enormous amount of psychology from women not to judge, because a man is obviously absolutely mortified when he can't do it. But a woman doesn't have to go through that trip; she can be as promiscuous as she wants and cheat all the time. Whereas a man can't be promiscuous unless he has an erection permanently.

Sexual attitudes have changed enormously because of contraception and abortion. A woman doesn't have to be in danger any more. I believe she has the same desires. A woman can have a one-night stand; she can get pissed and see a man and have a relationship. OK, her husband is away for two weeks, she's a bit lonely. If she has the attitude in her mind, she can just have a wonderful romp, like having a fabulous meal, and forget it next day. She can still feel involved, for you can feel involvement for twenty-four hours. You *can* feel involvement with someone for twenty-four hours. It's quite diabolical, what I am saying, but it is true. Maybe it's because of the business I am in. I am somebody who sells my emotions on the screen, so I know how to sell them. I know the impact I can have. Possibly I've also lived a life playing games with emotions and pretending they are real, so I am perhaps slightly deformed in that judgement.

Barbara Chase-Riboud: Men need sex to affirm themselves. Women need it as a proof of their femininity, which is not the same thing. I would say the drive is the same but the needs different. Little girls have as much sexual drive as little boys; even though they don't have a penis they see go up and down, it's still there. And the sexual drive in women, although it may be sublimated in so many different ways, is just as strong as in men.

A man doesn't look upon the sexual act as expressive of his own personality. It seems to me that men separate this, and they separate it in a very childish way. This thing they have is for them altogether

643

different from what they are. It has its own life, its own personality, sometimes it has its own name, and it's completely separate. It's quite charming, but it's true.

Mirella Ricciardi: I have been living in a very high-sexed society with a highly sex-orientated man, so sex has always been a major issue in our lives. From my personal experience and observations of the male, be it animal or man, I find the famous drive is indeed a word one can use. If you look at it from the physiological make-up, the very fact of the penis being a thing which drives means the woman is always the receiver. A man goes forward, driving, and is driven by his sexual energies; his sexual energies make him go to war, write music, do great sculpture, painting. I have a theory that if you dig deep enough in anything you will touch a three-letter word called sex, however you want to masquerade it. Keep digging, and you will find something called sex which is affecting it. I once watched a small Shetland pony trying to copulate with a thoroughbred English mare. The Shetland was on one side of the wire, and the huge English mare was on the other. The driving force through that animal was like a locomotive. There was a barbed-wire fence between them, and he just went right through it with a thing as long as your arm, and he fucked her through the wire. I was watching that, and I said to myself, that is the sexual drive of the male. I'll never forget it. I have been brought up with animals, and it's much easier to understand men because I've seen what male animals do. Men are just evolved animals; there is not much difference. When you get down to the nitty-gritty, the sexual drive in the male is exactly the same as in the horse.

I find from my own experience and observation that, when a woman loves somebody, the ultimate proof she craves for is in the sexual act of love. A union of that intensity and intimacy is so strong that there is nothing else you can possibly do which can make the statement. That is as far as love is concerned, and when a woman feels she needs no roses, no money, no Rolls-Royces, no nothing, all she needs is that – that's the thing that reassures her. When she doesn't get it, or she gets it badly, she starts to shake. And when the man can't give it to her because he is thinking of someone else, or because he doesn't feel it, he starts to give her roses, he starts to give her diamonds. However, the fact that he feels it for her and gives it to her, doesn't stop him going and giving it to someone else – without the feeling. Believe me, I know an awful lot about what goes on in men's sex, because Lorenzo and I have had a very open relationship. We don't even talk about it any more, because we are bored with it, we have said everything that has to be said, but I have got

644

the full ration of the man's point of view from him. That's why I can speak the way I can; it's as if I was inside his body. I know it so well: all his hang-ups and problems, his this and his that. I was like his mirror to whom he talked it out, and although it was often painful to me and affected our relationship, it was very enriching. Now I have overcome it all, I am enriched because I know the point of view of the man. Therefore I am able to help and counsel people who haven't got to where I have in my evolution. I would be prepared even to go as far as experimenting at this point, now that I feel myself totally evolved. I would like to become a high priestess. I have got out of all the earthy things, I've entered into an area more of spiritualization. I would love to be able to make an experiment now of bringing in a woman to our family, a thirty-three-year-old, good-looking woman, who would also please me, not sexually, but whom I liked as a person, and have her become my husband's lover. Not because I want to share it, because I am not into those games, but because I really feel that would show I have understood and accepted. Lorenzo continues to say it's not going to work, but who knows, maybe the right person will come. Of course, everybody is terrified of doing it because they are so intimidated by men. Unfortunately, they all become my friends, and because they become my friends, and because they haven't evolved, they are afraid of letting go completely, so I don't know if it ever is going to happen. But it certainly is an experiment I wouldn't mind trying.

Nancy Richardson: Before, I could be attracted sexually just by someone in the nude in the street. I could have a kind of spontaneous reaction. But the sexual arousal now comes from a mental state of union. That is the pre-condition. My body won't behave for any other reason, it's not interested. My body announces it's not interested unless it's for a specific emotional state, which, in a frothy way, might have been described as love earlier, but now it is mutual understanding and it's become the finest thing to go for. And if I have to make all kinds of arrangements in our lives so I can have that with Frank Richardson, I am willing to do that, because that's a big priority. But it takes a lot to arrange it because he is so busy.

Angela Rippon: On the whole, women feel their bodies are rather different and inviolate, whereas men feel it is all right to sleep around. But, in the end, you come down to specifics, and individual people will feel quite differently, I am sure. There are many strident feminists who think that, yes, it's all right, anything the fellows can do we can do just as well, if not better. Sleeping around, fine. That is actually not the way

645

I personally feel. So, in the end, it comes down to what I as an individual feel, and that isn't something I have ever wanted or needed to do.

Shirley Ritchie: It's always been said that women didn't need sex and didn't necessarily enjoy it, and all this business of lie back and think of England. That was something that came in, certainly to our society, with Victorian times. You only have to go back to Nell Gwyn to be perfectly satisfied that she both needed and enjoyed it and was frank enough to say so. Even Charles II's court here – the court as opposed to the tarts – were tumbling in and out of each other's beds as happily as they chose. That wasn't one-sided. It couldn't have been.

I'm perfectly satisfied that businesswomen, running round the world in the company of a whole lot of businessmen and with the same opportunity to jump into bed with them on a one-night stand, are going to do it.

Deborah Rogers: For every man spreading his seed, there's a woman who's a receptacle for it. Women also can be immensely excited by the man's expression of desire for them. Not every woman who succumbs is necessarily a scarlet woman or a temptress. There are those who in their own way get great pleasure from more casual encounters.

Kimberly Du Ross: The media have spoon-fed us sex till it's coming out our ears, so people don't know whether they're normal and they go by what the media tell them.

I think there are very romantic men and very romantic women, then there are sportsmen and sportswomen, and it's hard to say that there is a major difference, as I have met both kinds. Some people think sex is discovering the myth of the world, and some people think it was good exercise, and why go to the exercise club today, I've already gotten it. It depends on the people and the mentality, and I don't differentiate between either sex. There are those who can live without it and those who can't. We're talking about libido. Some men are born with more of it and some women are born with more of it, and I hope they find each other!

Juliet Mitchell-Rossdale: There is much mystification about the sexual act. First of all, there is confusion between erection and orgasm in a man. A man may be able to have erection without orgasm, and that doesn't mean he can't have a release of semen, but he can have no really total physiological orgasmic experience. There's frigidity in men, which hasn't been recognized. Frigidity is different from potency. Frigidity in potent men is quite a possibility which people have not looked at and not talked about because of stereotypes of sexual behaviour. And there's much more vaginismus or impossibility of penetration in women than people have recognized, as well. If women can't do it, they really can't fake it.

There is profound bisexuality in all of us. We are absolutely more fundamentally the same than we are different, but we necessarily, in a sense, exploit differences between the sexes in order to have sexual relationships from points of difference. And where those differences are exploited in an entirely discriminatory way, I think the practice is as abhorrent as any form of oppression. Where those differences can be more playful, I see nothing wrong with them. If there are biological differences, we exploit them to produce a sexual social relationship of difference. There's no way that biology produces the particular stereotype that results – it's the other way round.

Yvette Roudy: Boys are taught to be conquerors and hunters in sexual matters. There is an old popular saying, beware for your daughters and chickens, I'm letting out my cocks. Boys are let out and girls have to be protected, to be removed from the hunting field. So any slightly simple boy can't control himself, he goes out on the hunt. Sometimes he goes out in groups and thinks it's normal. And hence this difference in education and upbringing, which is not a good thing and does not allow equal opportunities for girls. When a girl is liberated, she also finds pleasure in looking at a beautiful male body, and she will also have desires, which she won't express, but if she is honest with herself, she will have them nevertheless.

Recently there were interviews with politicians about their first sexual experiences, and one said, quite spontaneously, that it was a failure because, I didn't know I had to move! So although there has been the famous sexual revolution, we still haven't resolved the whole business and still haven't reached the serenity in relationships that is possible between the sexes. Too much has been explained to us about how we should behave. With liberated, spontaneous lovers, there is a realization that there is not one who directs the affair and another who is directed, not one who has to be on top and the other underneath, but an exchange, sometimes one, then the other. One day we will get to the stage when the two sexes bring equal amounts to the relationship.

Too many men are preoccupied with ejaculation, and too many women imagine it is the main element of a successful partnership. It's absurd. There are many other areas. Ejaculation is not the only important thing. We're not very civilized about it – hence violence, which can be seen in certain men because they do not master their sexuality. And some women cannot contain their sexuality either. They're neurotic and don't know how to behave. When we've learned how to cope with this, there will be less rape and violence, and more couples who are at ease with each other.

Some men confronted with very liberated women are *charged* with giving them an orgasm, the poor fellows, and, of course, it's not the right way. These are the negative aspects of something positive – the liberation movement – but it's done in a way that makes it seem a demand, a right. But in the end, it is an authentic demand, because we do have the right to pleasure. Men take women, women give. Nowadays, there is scientific research into orgasm, and it is realized that the whole body can be awakened and women brought to orgasm simply by the touch of arms and hands. Men, too.

Joan Ruddock: In the gay community, from what we know and from what I have observed, most men will have a very large number of partners, whereas most women in the gay community have much longer-term, more fulfilling, more secure relationships, where the sexual act in itself is only part of the much greater emotional involvement. And that must say something about sex and emotions.

Eve Ruggieri: I try to teach my daughter that pleasure is a rare thing, linked to feeling and emotion, and to try to multiply it in the way one repeats gymnastic exercises is to deprive oneself of that exceptional thing, love, for the sake of something mediocre. I think she understands that, and the girls of her generation seem to be profiting from the stupidities of the 1968 generation.

Doris Saatchi: A woman no longer has to justify a desire for sex by calling it love.

It's not that women in the past were ashamed to enjoy sex, but they felt embarrassed about admitting they enjoyed it. Now, of course, if you don't enjoy sex there is something wrong with you and you embark on a ten-year course of psychotherapy. The situation has gone totally mad the other way. It seems that not only are you supposed to enjoy sex, but you're supposed to talk about how much you enjoy it. And that I find tiresome, I must say.

America is Self-Help Country – it was bound to get on to sex eventually. Books sell like crazy – we had *How to Build a Shelf in Your Kitchen* and then we had *How to Have the Perfect Orgasm*, and it's absolutely no different. It's just a kind of focus on various subjects, and America is the generator of all those notions and ideas.

Melissa Sadoff: We're prompted to believe that, to have exciting sex, you have to make love all the time. First of all, much as we would want it, or our imagination would want it, you can't do it physically, simply because there are other things to do. By the time any man comes home at night, he is half-exhausted if not completely exhausted, he is not in a very good mood to perform. And if a woman has an ordinary or average life, she is not ready to hop into bed either. So if a woman is clever and creates romantic situations, such as a weekend away or visiting her husband in the office, if she can seduce her husband in different circumstances and situations, she can keep that going and really kindle his imagination.

Most men do not equate sex with love. Women do. But even a man can be a victim in a strong, clever woman's hands. Let us say it starts with a flirtation, then leads to an affair, then the woman, the other woman thinks, this could really become something of a much more permanent nature and she likes the whole idea. She can trap him without difficulty. I don't care who the man is, he will think this is the greatest love he ever had in his life. So it is possible for a clever woman to change men's minds and therefore, what was in the beginning just a flirtation, an affair, can become a love.

It is not the speed and quantity of sex that matters, it is the quality. Making love every ten days is much better than making love every day and not knowing what this is all about.

Khairat Al-Saleh: A woman can sleep with more than one man, and she can do it purely for the sexual urge, without love. And this is really proven, it happens. But I personally cannot do it and would not do it. I believe in the refinement of the urges.

We are despoiling sex in a way, we are doing something monstrous to

that extremely vital human relationship and experience. We are levelling it, exposing it, to the point that we can no longer see it. Things just
become objects in this life; women sometimes are objects and sex
becomes an object. You de-spiritualize it, you de-emotionalize it, you
kill it by too much exposure, too much emphasis. You sever its
emotional roots.

Bushra Salha: Women fantasize, and they have this fertile imagination
that helps them to see the naked man without him being naked, so to
speak.

Naomi E. Sargant: The nature of the sexual act for a man is much more
ephemeral, and much more rewarding, as it happens; therefore it is
much more tempting to do it a lot. I find it very difficult to come at all,
and the motive for having an affair is not actually a sort of instant, acute,
physical satisfaction; I mean, the odd affair I have had. I start by having
an affair of the mind, after which I get into bed with somebody if I like
them enough. I don't ever do it the other way round. It's not worth it.

It's just as possible for me, as it is for men, to go and spend a pleasant
night with somebody. I wouldn't do it with somebody I didn't know at
all, but in the sense of a one-night stand it sometimes puts the seal on a
good working relationship. I've known that happen. For my part, I
believe all of those statements about women not being able to have one-
night stands have much more to do with not being prepared to be
pregnant and the sort of risks one would take in one-night stands than
with any genuine difference. It depends. If you are a woman looking for
a perfectly friendly encounter, then you can be just as happy with a one-
night stand as many men. I also think the sexual act is far more
threatening for men. I mean (a) women don't have to have an erection,
and (b) they can always fake orgasm.

Sylvia Scafardi: I think the feeling is that the man must have his latchkey
and it's only natural and right for him to have sexual relations to a
certain age. However, for women, many highly sexed women, it's just
the same. Also, though I'm not that type of woman myself, there are
quite a number of women who take pleasure in it, like eating straw-
berries and cream.

Anne Seagrim: Some men can have totally disassociated sexual relationships with people, prostitutes and so on, apparently perfectly easily and without its interfering with their normal, loving relationships. I find that very difficult to understand. I would find it absolutely totally repugnant.

Jenny Seagrove: Sex is very important because through sex comes new life. It's also very important because, in its purest form, it is a sharing, an expression of extreme vulnerability and caring and openness and honesty. But I think it gets perverted, it gets blown up. The books and movies make it into something that people dream about and don't always achieve, and therefore they have great inadequacies, and this often interferes with their relationships.

Women feel an inadequacy if they don't reach orgasm. Sometimes they feel terrible because they feel they've let the man down. That's why they sometimes fake it, to make the guy feel good.

Women have erotic fantasies. It's generally not the look of a man that will excite you, it's something he does or the way he talks. It's his attitude, because it's mental. To be aroused is a mental procedure, and it generally comes from feeling wanted.

Susan Seidelman: There are certain times you just want to go to bed with someone. That doesn't mean you want to have a long-term relationship, but I think we're all animals inside. I don't think that's my primary thing, that I want to do that all the time. But occasionally there's somebody you just think, boy, that guy's really sexy, he'd be fun for the night. For me personally, it can't go on that long unless something else is there too. If it's just great sexually and that's it, it gets boring pretty quickly.

Emma Sergeant: I do believe in some form of mystery for women. I think it's important that you're not open about your love life. It's important that you are feminine, and to be feminine you have to remain somewhat aloof and be difficult to pin down. A man has always liked challenge, and if it takes a long time to get a woman, he values her more. The man never values what he gets easily, this is the law of nature.

The film *Nine Weeks* did nothing for me. I noticed a lot of women found it a huge turn-on, and I was quite curious about this, because for me it was just a rather cliché series of places to make love: one in the snow, one on the steps, one outside the fridge, one with food on her face. To me it did nothing, but obviously a lot of girls need that kind of set-up, that pantomime around the sex act, because maybe sex doesn't mean that much to them. It is not the climax, it's the whole act around it, and therefore they love a film which titillates the imagination, where they can imagine themselves in cami-knickers and various positions. For me, it doesn't mean anything, because sex is sex in the end when it comes down to it. It's not doing it on a pile of feathers.

Hanan Al-Shaykh: Women have a different constitution. They can wait if they don't have a partner, a husband or a lover. The urge is not like a man's. I think, in men, the urge is more physical. They just don't know what to do with their erections.

Failure for a man is dreadful – the end of the world. But even a woman, when she doesn't reach an orgasm, will feel the same. Within herself, she feels as if there is something very wrong. She does not feel happy, she feels as if she cannot control her body and thought.

Sometimes a woman, while she is asleep, feels the sex urge even in her dreams; and she is fulfilled.

Clare Short: I don't believe that men need sexual release, and if they don't get it, something happens. I believe they could be celibate or not celibate, or masturbate or whatever, just as women can be sexually active or not, or can feel equally aroused and not do anything about it. The sexuality is very similar, but the way men are conditioned and socialized into sex is not like that, and so there's ever such a lot of screwed-up men who can't perform very well, who are very insecure about sex and who go for a quick release because that's all they can do.

It is true women don't rape men and men do rape women, but I don't believe, for a minute, that is physical. I don't believe that if male sexuality doesn't get some sexual release it goes out and takes it by force, which is one of the explanations of rape put forward. When you discuss pornography, it's always defended with, if you don't give them that they'll rape people, as though male sexuality is there and has to have a release, otherwise it is such an overriding force it will use violence. I don't believe men's bodies work like that. I think that is all in the mind and in our sexual culture, and it's this distorted view of sexuality and of women and of who is in control that leads to rape and wife-battering. I don't think that is at all biological, I think we can construct a society where it won't happen.

Rosemary Anne Sisson: I was brought up to think that love and sex went together and I can't imagine anything else. I cannot imagine going to bed with a man I didn't love and want to spend my life with and have children with. I don't think it's conditioning, it is part of the feminine nature. It's Nature making sure that a lot of little animals are not scattered about the place with no father.

I've had a very long and happy life without sex. I know many women can live without it. Obviously some women can't. But this great need for sexual fulfilment is rather like compulsive over-eating or compulsive alcoholism. I wonder whether it's a compensation for a lack of love in their lives, whether it isn't, in a way, a sign of insecurity for a woman to need it so continually. As if she is always trying to prove she is immensely successful because she is successful in bed.

These programmes on *Woman's Hour* and television, discussing sex publicly and continually, I find very distasteful. I feel that I'm a voyeur when I'm invited to attend someone else's sexual experiences. I wouldn't stand on Wimbledon Common peering down at them, I don't really want to read about it unless it's wonderfully well done in novels, and I certainly don't want to see it on television or films.

Koo Stark: Men are probably much more vulnerable sexually than women. You have to be so careful as a woman not to damage a relationship, because it's such a fine balance. It's not a question of ego or anything as basic, it's a sensitive issue and you can really hurt somebody. I've come across men who, in every other way, they're together, very mature, very sophisticated. They've been able to deal with the most appalling crises and yet, somewhere along the line, some woman has damaged them or their own sexual image of themselves, and they can't recover. A man's sexuality is an incredibly fragile thing.

Within a marriage of long standing, I would imagine that at certain times sex is very important, and at other times isn't. I don't think you can put yourself on a sex diet, like you can on a vegetarian diet. The balance of each person's sexuality is organic, it's ever-changing, and therefore it must change within the relationship.

Gloria Steinem: I don't think there's really a big difference in men's and women's sexual needs. After all, the sex organs essentially come from the same cells; the clitoris and the penis come from exactly the same substance. I don't think there is a major difference. Men can experience orgasm without an erection; many men report having multiple orgasms without having an erection. They may do it by masturbation or some other way, but without a full erection, and they can still have an orgasm. If there's any difference, it is that women have more orgasms. If women don't have orgasm, it's because they have bad lovers or not enough knowledge of their own anatomy.

Sexual attitudes are changing now. For instance, some women go to male prostitutes. They are called escort services, and in some cities in the United States they are listed in the telephone directories. A man can get a female escort or another man, or a woman can get a male escort. There's discrimination even here, because it costs more to get a male escort than it does to get a female escort. If you look in the phone book in Miami, you'll find that. The woman prostitute has fewer alternatives economically, and the man prostitute has more, so he charges more and she charges less. But the fact is that some women do go to male prostitutes.

Pamela Stephenson: Because the actual physical experience of sex is different for men and women, that must have a bearing. There is something about the receptivity of women in the sexual act that must make a difference. I think it's silly to pretend otherwise.

When I was a teenager, having casual sex with somebody you hardly knew at worst meant syphilis or gonorrhoea. That was the worst you'd probably experience, but it's not the same as death. It's quite different now. I do feel very fearful.

Lady Arabella Stuart: The quality of a woman's sexual relationships is more important certainly than the quantity. I don't think she needs to prove herself in this rather frantic way that men sometimes feel they have to.

Andrea von Stumm: I think women ultimately don't need men sexually. If they do, it's very much emotional or perhaps it's in terms of reproduction and at a primitive level. But erotically, they are not dependent on men. Sexually, men are more dependent on women.

654

Women are self-sufficient in a way. Women tend to use a man to achieve sexual ecstasy or satisfaction. Let me put it this way: I can understand women's homosexuality better than men's; there is something about it that makes it more acceptable to me.

A woman is much much more dependent on the erotic component of sex. A man can have sex and sex and sex. A woman is, in my opinion, incredibly dependent upon what is called foreplay and the whole atmosphere. If a woman wears garters, it is perhaps more for herself than to please a man. All the accessories of seduction have perhaps more effect on the woman herself. That it might turn a man on is an extra bonus. A woman likes an undercurrent, ambiguity, an ambivalence, desire, the prolongation of desire.

Sex is important in my life, certainly. The necessity to seduce is vital, it makes you exist. And seducing is not necessarily conquering – another difference between men and women. A woman wants to seduce, but she doesn't want to conquer. She loves those games, but she loves to please, she needs to please much more. A man is perhaps more straightforward. If he wants to seduce, it is because he wants to conquer. Whereas it's a sort of nourishment for a woman, she needs to see desire in a man's eyes.

It is a good thing that men have come to realize that all women are different, that what they consider an orgasm doesn't necessarily provoke an orgasm in a woman. I think that 50 per cent are clitoral, which was always the case. In a way, they don't need a man, if you see what I mean. They get orgasm by touching or caressing, not necessarily by the act of sex. So that makes a man, at long last, perhaps more interested in the erotic.

Christine Sutherland: Girls have a very difficult time now because there is pressure on them to go to bed – with practically everybody – and it is very hard for them to say no. This is the price they pay for liberation.

Physically, a woman doesn't actually suffer if she hasn't had sex for two or three months, but men do.

Conny Templeman: Good sex is very important, and cheap sex is very unimportant, and there's a lot of cheap sex.

Women can find a man more easily than men can find a woman. I don't know if men want sex all the time, but because they don't get it all the time, they're always in a state of wanting. If a woman couldn't have a man very easily, then she would probably be in a state of wanting all the time as well.

I've been surprised about women who haven't had orgasms, or who haven't had good experiences, because I haven't known any difficulties. I hadn't realized other people had difficulties.

Fiona Thyssen: I don't think it's possible for women to be as promiscuous as men sexually, for the simple reason that, if a woman has an orgasm with a man one night, and then happens to have two or three, and they turn out to be sexually compatible, the odds are that, after two days, the woman falls in love with the man. Women tend to fall in love with men who give them orgasms, because it is difficult for a woman to find the ideal lover. I accept that, theoretically, the woman can be promiscuous and use sex merely as a lustful experience for one or two nights, but the reality is that she generally tends to fall in love with a man who is providing her with very good sexual satisfaction. So the whole thing becomes self-defeating. She does inevitably grow very attached to such a man. Whereas the man does not. A man can get sexual satisfaction with any amount of disparate females, which a woman can't do.

I've talked to women who have not had orgasms and were obviously not very concerned about it. But, of course, you never know whether it's a defensive mechanism. Maybe women who haven't had orgasms with men don't want to go through the whole hassle of male/female relationships. Maybe they have had them with women, or maybe they have had them through masturbation, but it becomes then very private and very individual.

Claire Tomalin: Sex is as important as bread and butter in life. If it's there and happy, it's absolutely basic, and if it's absent, it's a terrible lack; but all of us, at some moments in our lives, probably have to live with the lack.

It is more difficult for men to suppress their purely physical urges. Women who can't, tend to be rather unhappy. But that's a contentious statement. I am writing at the moment about Katherine Mansfield, who suffered such damage from her sexual adventures when she was young, such appalling damage. I can't help thinking that possibly I should have

656

been younger when I wrote about her, because I find it quite baffling now.

I don't want to sound too prim, because I can remember, when I was young, there were times when an adventure did seem just like an adventure, and that's part of growing up. It's like adolescent animals playing: you're testing out your sexual powers and what you can get away with, and young girls are testing out their ability to attract and charm. That's very much a part of youth, and quite a short part of youth. If people want to have purely lustful engagements, that's fine by me, that's entirely their own affair, but I would have thought it was a very grim way to live, and I can't see what's in it. I mean, a little physiological spasm.

The happiness of my life has been in sexual love and in my children, but the sexual part of one's life is entirely private. It will die with one, or if one dies before the person one loves, maybe it will last in his memory, and I think, in a sense, you can give to your children some sense of your own sexual fulfilment. My mother had a very unhappy sexual life, and she thought my sister and I would go rather wild when we were young. But she once said to me, although I don't really approve of the way you've lived, I have seen that you and Marguerite have both had a lot of happiness, and I'm glad of that. I thought that was a wonderful thing for her to say, and I always felt it very sad that she didn't have a sexually happy life and you could feel that in her, whereas, if you have a sexually happy life, or some part of your life is like that, it gives you something inside that can't be taken away, and it gives you a sort of confidence.

Lili Townsend: I married the first man I made love with. I held out for a long time, too. It wasn't a conscious decision: I will keep my virginity until I am married. It just seemed to happen that the circumstances weren't right, and I had a very high regard for my own intuition even then. I was simply not going to be seduced into a meaningless love situation. I had the Aphrodite view rather than the Hera view of the goddess in myself. We women must cherish the goddess in our nature, must recognize that this new woman has a new role: to bring out the best possible aspects of ourselves and the men we interact with.

Sex has to be much more focused towards the inner realms than simply a recreational physical act, which is more of a man's point of view. I remember one man saying, he absolutely had to have an orgasm at minimum every ten days. If he wasn't living with a woman, then he would have to organize a way to have that physical release. I don't think women have that particular biological need. Women, for instance, can find celibacy much easier. I don't think they have that strong sexual drive always. At times, when it's appropriate, that drive can be dormant. I'm speaking for myself, of course. Certainly I have experienced parts of my life where I was totally following my sexual instincts and went away from my own traditions and value systems to experiment. I lived a very free period of life where sex was totally at my whim, I didn't feel a relationship had to be involved. But really, for myself, it's always been essential to have a heart connection, it's just my nature. Now it's scaled up because I want to have a spiritual connection with a man, and I'm only interested in men who have come to explore the spiritual side of their own natures.

My attitude to sex now, since the process of discovering the inner nature of my being and recognizing the inner nature of men's beings, is that it's something sacred. It's a sacred participation in an intimate relationship that is essential.

Polly Toynbee: How people see sex is so much how they see life and relationships. I really don't think it's separate. You set your mind in that way. Men say, yes, I can do it anywhere, any time, it doesn't matter to me. That is what the culture tells him to think and say and be. A man who says, I'm afraid I can only do it with somebody I love, is pathetic, not taken seriously. The culture doesn't tell him that's an acceptable sexual model. He might say, I can, but of course I choose to remain faithful to my wife, but the attitude has to be there, whereas for women it is still the acceptable model to want and expect fidelity. A lot of men who are capable of being really honest with themselves, on the whole, particularly as they get a bit older, in their thirties, admit that sex is in fact pretty terrible unless the relationship is quite close and important, and admit they've destroyed a lot of years of their lives in promiscuity that does them as much harm as anybody else, and that they didn't get much out of it, and that there is something demented about a very promiscuous life. A lot of men do come to that, but it takes time for them to get over the ball-team view of sex.

Abir Dajani Tuqan: Normally a woman will only sleep with a man if she cares. While, for the man, it is important for half an hour, for one hour, then that's it, he can switch off and forget about it. The whole thing is more of a strain on the man, because a woman, in love matters, maintains her secrecy throughout, while a man is an open book. A woman can fake anything, she can feign anything. With a man there is no faking, it is either/or.

Kathleen Turner: Most people are seriously disappointed in sex. I would say good sex, meaningful sex, is vital; I would not say sex in itself is. Invested sex, that makes one feel cherished, important and the focus of attention, of energy, is absolutely vital to humankind. I would not say it's simply a matter of being admired, or being touched, or being screwed, or proving one's prowess. I can't believe that would leave anything but a feeling of being taken from.

I would say that many men feel they have a greater need for sexual satisfaction than women, the myth being that women can exist essentially without sex, if need be. A man thinks he must get his quota of sex every so often, whatever that may be, or else he is somehow constipated, you know. I think that's pretty stupid. I don't believe that.

Jill Tweedie: Visually, I think women are much more turned on by women. I don't think there are any women who are turned on by pictures of men, not one. There are plenty of women who are turned on by pictures of women, I think because they are identifying, they are putting themselves in the place of that woman, so that's a part of the fantasy.

Marie-Claire Valène: Women are more sensitive about love, and perhaps women invented love, or at least have transposed all the different factors, such as physical desire, and have subliminated them.

Joan Vass: Women were told that if they had sexual urges it was unseemly, it was improper, it was dreadful. Now it's a whole new attitude. Women are supposed to have orgasms. In the post-Second World War period, the orgasm became very important, and it was thought women had not been having them for centuries and they were there all the time just for the having; all you had to do was find them. And then there was the whole idea of how you could have orgasms, and multiple orgasms, and they talked about it a lot for fifteen to twenty years. But I don't think people are so crazy orgasm-mad now.

Popularization of a lot of things causes it to become full of error, and watered-down theories and anti-intellectual attitudes make people behave badly and get nervous. It's like examining our navels endlessly. Sex is just as important as eating, sleeping and breathing, but we don't discuss the fact of sleep. We have to sleep in order to go on. We can't survive without sleep. Occasionally, one reads an interesting article or book about sleep, but sex is like a commodity, a business. They've made it into money, and it's unfortunate that sex and violence, especially in this country, have become part of our economy.

Sara Vass: Sex is generally over-exaggerated. I mean, it's how you sell everything: you sell a car, a cigarette, a bottle of perfume, it's with sex. You buy a can of beer because it's going to make you have a happier sex life. The more clever Madison Avenue gets, the more that seems to take over, and then it becomes our conditioning and our expectations. Unfortunately, it also takes the goodness and reality out of our own sex lives because we have these expectations that can't be met. It's hard to find a man now who wants to settle down under a certain age, to be married and have a family. Because he can have everyone: why should I just settle for you, even if you're great, when I might find something better tomorrow? And everyone is so sexy and everyone is jogging and exercising and getting new noses and better breasts.

I think Annie Flanders is saying that women like to be fucked for effect. You know, we women like to be fucked all the time, we're all equal, we're all the same, I can be like you guys and that's what you guys like to say. I don't feel that way. I can't speak for all women, I'm not all women, I'm just one woman. I can tell you from reading, and from observing, that that seems to be a general trend. That could well be conditioning. To be perfectly honest, I don't want to be fucked all the time. I don't even really want to be fucked; I don't even want to fuck; I'd like to make love. You know, put the shoe on the other foot, as it were. And I'm not such a mild and meek human being and such a Pollyanna that the idea of being that aggressive frightens me. But I don't really want to be fucked. I don't want to be raped. The idea of a raping, or a pillaging, or a fucking, to me is repugnant.

Virginia Wade: So often there's the feeling that you get used in a sexual relationship. That, of course, is presumably the lack of skill on the male part, but not necessarily. On the other hand, there's a lot more pressure on the man. God forbid that he can't get an erection. If he can't perform, it's just terrible. There is an awful lot attached to that performance. A man is much more worried about that. I think promiscuity has also put a lot of pressure on everybody, because you have to go out and have sex or else there is something wrong with you. That's ridiculous, really. What's happening today will quieten it all down again. It is very interesting to think back to where Aids came from, and what happened thousands of years ago. I think it was true that the Romans, at one stage, were not allowed to kiss because there was an epidemic of herpes. Maybe the whole basis to religious morals is health and well-being, and that's where Christianity's gone wrong, because it says you will not commit this, you will not commit that, you will not have sex out of a relationship and all the rest of it, pointing a finger at everybody. Maybe if they'd made it clear that the reason was for cleanliness and survival of the race, then people would say, right. But people hate to be told, you will not, you will not.

Tracy Ward: Women need sex just as much as men need sex. Women enjoy sex just as much as men enjoy sex. And that's only been discovered, actually, since the 1960s. I am not even sure that women aren't more sexually demanding than men. It's probably easier for a man to get sexually fulfilled than it is for a woman. But the demands on a woman aren't nearly as strong as on a man, because if he can't get sexually aroused, then he's a failure. So the pressure on a man is very strong, and women are becoming more demanding. Maybe that's why men are not feeling so clever any more.

I have never been to bed with a man for purely sexual reasons, without wanting to see him again, to continue a friendship, to have a relationship. Maybe once. But it was sort of taboo, and I knew I was being bad. I would never do it now.

You love somebody and you want to be close to them. You can kiss them, you can hug them, you can talk to them. But I think the physical closeness of sex can release some of that love that you feel, which is actually quite destructive in the end if you just go on loving, loving. And an orgasm is quite important in that it is a climax but the whole thing of sex is an incredibly good feeling throughout, whether you have an orgasm or you don't. Maybe it's more important for a man to have an orgasm, maybe they need to feel it was done, it was completed. All the men in my books have always had orgasms, and that's what they seem to drive towards. Whereas, with me, either I have an orgasm or I don't. It doesn't matter.

I can demand sex with my boyfriend even when he doesn't want it, and I can succeed in getting what I want, so it's hardly an invasion of him into me then.

Marina Warner: One of the great improvements of the last twenty years, I'd say, is that women's sexual needs have been recognized in a way that in my childhood, thirty-five years ago, they were not. I was brought up in a creed, Catholicism, which denies sexual need. It believes in the sexual danger of women, but doesn't interiorize it; sexual danger exists because of how she is beheld by the desiring man. It's not so much female desire the nuns told me to watch out for, they told me to watch out for male desire. Female desire was something they wanted to pretend didn't exist, or they had successfully imagined it didn't. And that has changed, that has imperceptibly changed. Female desire is admitted and to some extent accepted without the sort of rancour it used to cause. The idea of female lasciviousness was absolutely abhorred, both in Protestantism and Catholicism, and indeed in the Greek plays. Female lust was really bad; male lust was something we could live with, that was human. I think the word lust is not used now in quite the way it used to be. I don't believe people ascribe quite the same negative quality to it.

It certainly used to be true that women felt they should legitimize their sexual urges by calling it love or hankering to some extent. People now rather deplore that there is a lot of sexual licence among the very young: one-night stands, people getting sexual release without caring much for one another. I know that people do worry about it. I'm not very keen on having one-night stands – I haven't done it for years. But I was very screwed up about sex because I was brought up to believe it was a terrible sin. With every Catholic, it goes very deep, and the spectre goes on haunting you that it is a sin and those feelings are sinful, come from a sort of diabolical part of you. That is something I have struggled with, and personally I have, I suppose, felt love when I probably haven't loved at all.

I am terribly against sex being used as an index of personality or sexual prowess or sexual achievement. Of course, it makes fascinating reading, but there has been rather a tendency in biographies to create characters through sexual inclination. One knows from friends that this isn't really the case. Very often their sexual life can't be divined from their characteristics. I don't have enough experience, but I have often imagined that you can have somebody who makes love in a very similar way to somebody else, yet they can be extremely different people.

Men, because of their power being identified with their physical potency, experience the poignancy of so many women they may never have. Now that I am about to be forty, I do look at young men in the street and suddenly understand what men feel when they say, so many women, so little time. I suddenly thought I saw these young men whom I would never know, whereas, when I was seventeen, I imagined I would have lots of experiences. Now I know I will never have all these experiences and I did feel that poignancy. So many men, so little time. Time has gone.

I'm sure that many women didn't have orgasms in the past and had satisfactory sex lives. A lot of pre-marital sex that didn't go the whole way, which used to happen more than it does now, probably didn't achieve orgasm for the women, but it was very satisfactory, all that teenage petting.

I have an anthropologist friend, and we had a long discussion about female circumcision because she worked in Africa close to people who did practise it, and I was impressed by her argument that we have given orgasm a very very high value in terms of happiness, whereas the African tribe she was talking about value something else very highly. These women haven't put orgasm in a privileged place in their ideals for themselves and their lives. She thought it was a Western discrimination to feel only *we* know what is important, and that tribes should be allowed to practise circumcision if that's what they felt like. I find this so deeply abhorrent, and such a denial of human rights, of sexual pleasure, that it upsets me terribly.

Heather Watts: To a certain degree, I fantasize. I don't find the sexual aspect of my life very important to me.

I feel that, if the rest of the world is really having as much sex as the impressions you get, then there's something wrong with me, but I suspect everybody feels that way. I don't think the whole world is turning round madly, having sex wildly five times a day, meeting in hotels. There are probably moments when sex takes on an enormous importance for a few months at different points in your life with different people or different situations. Maybe it's about yourself, or about a romantic fantasy of real love, or maybe it's just a biological urge at that time that is very much satisfied by some particular person. But, it seems to me, it's really in periods that it takes on a big importance, and that mostly the rest of the time it's not that big a deal.

Arabella Weir: There is no such thing as uncomplicated sex, unless you're in a foreign country and you're never going to see someone again.

Men's egos are so fragile that, if they are constantly screwing, then they know they're attractive, they're wanted and lovable and they're every-thing they think they are.

No sex has been considered complete unless a man has had an orgasm, but it's always been considered complete if a woman hasn't. I think it's terribly unfair that the male orgasm is essential for reproduction, whereas the woman's isn't.

I am really, as someone said, an Italian man trapped in a woman's body. Because I love conquering people. I love making people want me. I love all that much more than actually going to bed with them. The whole kind of thing of making somebody desperate for me, and really wanting me – not just to tease him, I'll usually come up with the goods – but I love the whole conquest.

Katharine Whitehorn: Sex is not as important as we're made to believe it is at the moment, because the thing has got completely out of hand. Our reproductive life is vital to us, but when you read that sex is the mainspring of people, and you look at a busload sitting there in their mackintoshes, you think, well, is it really possible that sex is the main thing in the lives of these people, it doesn't seem very likely. It is generally supposed that what men have is the norm and what the women have different is a disadvantage.

I think one of the most interesting things is the idea of what happened to female chastity over the years. Obviously there were lots of women who were very unchaste through the ages, because the men must have had somebody to be unchaste with, but the idea that you kept your daughter under lock and key until she was married, and she was monogamous from then on, is as old as civilization. We are now suddenly in a situation where girls of fourteen and fifteen are asking why are they still virgins. This is the most extraordinary change. I don't, as a matter of fact, think it particularly helps the girls. I think they find this very hard to handle, because the biological connections between sex and repro-duction, and therefore permanence, haven't gone away simply because somebody has discovered the pill.

Casual sex is very much a question of what the culture allows or suggests. I'm not saying it isn't true to an extent, but I'm saying there are cultures where a man going off the rails even once would be regarded as appalling. Graham Greene's *The Power and the Glory*, where the priest – he is a bad priest, a whisky priest – has an affair with his housekeeper and there is a child, has a marvellous phrase: it said, to her this was a matter of no great importance, a wound that heals in the healthy flesh, to him it was as if a whole world had ended. Now it depends on the culture whether or not the sacrament can be made to have that kind of force, and on the whole I think men tend to programme things so they get the best of both worlds where they can. And I don't doubt women would do exactly the same. I don't say they would programme it to have a variety of sexual encounters, no, but I think that anybody with power tries to work things the way they prefer it.

Shelley Vaughan Williams: Sex is the vital force of life, it's the whole process of the world. And it's our responsibility to use it in a wonderful way. Then you really have divine energy, because when a man and a woman are joined, they're just unbeatable, they have so much going for them and so much to give out, they radiate it. I mean, you see two people happy together, it's so enchanting, and it's not something that you can fool. You do see people putting on acts, but people who actually are wonderfully happy together, whether it's the wonderful happiness of new love or a couple who have been together a very long time and adore each other, you can't fake that, it's so great. It's what gives you the courage to go on when you're alone and lonely.

Jeanette Winterson: Women probably find it harder to have casual sex, very much harder, because their emotions are always involved, and I'm not sure, because I'm not a man, to what extent a man's emotions are always involved. In a sense, men sexually need women not just for sex but to make their appetites safe. I don't like gay men very much. I feel very uncomfortable with them, and much more comfortable with straight men. I think you can let any desire or any feeling go completely out of its natural bounds. I think, to an extent, gay men are a trap to themselves in this myth of needing to have constant sex. And, because I used to work with them, I know lots of them don't want it, but it becomes a mad merry-go-round that if you're not doing it, night after night, with somebody different, there's actually something wrong with you.

For me, it's more exciting with women, because although I like to live dangerously, I like to know I can get back. It's like going into the Minotaur's cave: it's OK if you've tied your string round a rock and you know you can get home, but if you're going somewhere and you're completely at sea, then maybe that's too frightening to be exciting. I've had exciting relationships with women, and there's also more tender-

665

ness, much more, because tenderness is not threat. The relationships I've had with men, even the nice ones, it has been a threat.

Anna Wintour: I think the sexual revolution came, and now it's going to end almost immediately, because people are going to be so frightened of what it means going to bed with someone they don't know.

Dr Enid Wistrich: Women's equality has meant that women expect to enjoy sex more than they used to in the old days. If people get obsessed by orgasm, it's as silly as if they get obsessed by anything else. It's an important part of sex, but if people are constantly talking about it and thinking about it – and how many did I have, and did I have it then, and didn't I have it then – it gets to be as silly as anything else.

Priscilla Woolworth: There are a few women who just can't have enough sex. But in general, women do not enjoy having sex regularly. And it all depends on how the man is with them. If it's something quick, with no feeling – just body, body – women don't like that. They love much more to be touched, to be hugged, to be loved, to have their hand held. They prefer tenderness so much more to lust.

That's all you hear about: orgasm, orgasm. There's an article on it every month. It's an obsession no one understands. Every woman, I think, is different, and with some women it happens frequently, with others it doesn't, but I don't think it should be such a concern. It can happen in all different ways, and if it doesn't happen, well, it doesn't happen, but you still felt great, didn't you? You were close to the person you love, or whatever? It's just an obsession: performance, performance, everything has to be perfect. This has to happen, if it doesn't happen, then I'm not normal, I'm not right, there's something wrong with me. And then they go to see a psychiatrist; then they get more and more messed up and can't make up their minds about anything; and then they're frigid, they're scared. They just have to relax. Well, it didn't happen this time, too bad – maybe in two weeks.

---

*Miss Laski wishes to make it clear that this interview was given before she had any real awareness of Aids.

5
Motherhood

'We bear the world, and we make it ... There was never a great man who had not a great mother – it is hardly an exaggeration'
– Olive Schreiner, *The Story of an African Farm* (1883)

'... mothers of the race, the most important actors in the grand drama of human progress ...'
– Elizabeth Cady Stanton, with Susan B. Anthony and Mathilda Gage, *History of Woman Suffrage*, vol. 1 (1881)

'For like as women take a greater pride in their beauty than pleasure or content in their virtue, so they take more pride in being with a child than in having a child'
– Margaret Cavendish, *Sociable Letters* (1660)

'She goes through the vale of death alone, each time a babe is born'
– Margaret Sanger, *Women and the New Race* (1920)

'It is misleading and unfair to imply that an intelligent woman must "rise above" her maternal instincts and return to work when many intelligent, sensitive women have found that the reverse is better for them'
– Sally E. Shaywitz, 'Catch 22 for Mothers', in the *New York Times Magazine* (4 March 1973)

Maria Aitken: There are three species: there are men, women and mothers, no question of that. I joined the mother species when I became a mother and was very aware of doing so. I don't mean that it makes you feel a lofty separate species, but the idea of sacrificing yourself unthinkingly on somebody else's behalf is quite new. I am a very selfish person, but there's no question but that I would hurl myself under the bus to save my son, there would be no quibble. But I don't believe that is necessarily always so with men and fathers. I think it is always true of mothers. The moment I had a child, I certainly understood what my relationship to my mother was. I thought, good heavens, this is what she thinks, feels about me, this is what a mother is. I had no idea before.

I think we have the biological edge because, if you have given birth, it gives you endless patience and what could be called kindness towards that creature. That is the only difference: if you carry a child, your attitude towards it is necessarily coloured for ever by that, and you have an infinite tolerance for it because of that, so actually it is a form of selfishness, perhaps, rather than the great virtue it is painted to be. But that is the only way I think we have the edge, and we don't have it in general; we are not tremendously patient with everybody.

Now that I have a child, I am absolutely horrified by the fact I've had an abortion, because, had I known what birth meant, whatever the circumstances, I could never have done that. And it was illegal in those days, so it was all very sordid. When I came round from the anaesthetic, there was a black nurse who spat at me and I was horrified, made miserable by it, but in retrospect I understand very well; she was probably a mother and probably found the entire thing incomprehensible, appalling, obscene. I did it because I was very young and didn't think I could manage. But I think about that child now. But you could never be expected to know this. So one should never blame men for

669

encouraging one to have an abortion, because they'll never know what birth means. If a woman doesn't know, then how can anybody else be expected to? It would be difficult to imagine any circumstances under which one would have an abortion again. Perhaps if there was gross physical deformity involved or something of the kind but not otherwise.

Lady Penelope Aitken: It seems to me, having gone through the business of birth which is so wonderful, that, whatever happens, these babies who grow up are so special that nothing in this life could make you dislike or hate them. You might be hurt by them, but you could never not love them. And that is a very maternal thing, I think. But then you see people who reject their young. Again, I am very lucky in my life in that Jonathan and Maria and I have a very good relationship.

I am not so different from the young of today. I had love affairs, and before I married I had an abortion. I had an enormous urge, at that stage, to keep the child, although I realized it would be terrible, particularly in view of what it would do to my parents if they ever knew such a thing. I think one has a very strong biological urge because, even then, when keeping it was something totally impossible to do, it was very hard to come to the decision of having to get rid of it, to have this abortion, which in my case was against the law.

Madeleine L. H. Alatas: I was absolutely terrified of having a child. I'm not a very maternal type. I was very independent, and three things happened simultaneously. At twenty-one I married, at twenty-two my father died and I had to take over all the trusts, and at twenty-three I had my son. So it was one, two, three, and I remember feeling very scared about the whole thing. But the minute he was born I realized, it's fantastic, I'm responsible for this creature that is mine, my flesh and blood, and he must be defended – not in the sense of putting walls around him, but being given every opportunity that I ever had and more. I will teach him every trick I've learned to be able to sustain and develop himself. Money is irrelevant, what's important is the ability, the skill to move in and out of life. I began to think of things in the long term which I had never thought before. As soon as I had my child, I began to think of things in a much different way. When I married, somebody said, oh yes, you'll have a child. I had said, no, I don't want a child, I'm scared of it, I don't want to have anything to do with children, I'm not maternal. I wanted to take care of myself. My mother said, uh, huh, we'll see. And when my son was born a little bit later, she said, you see, you're like some great cat, one of these tigers or lions; you lie next to it and you teach it how to hunt and how to think even at a very early age; God help anyone if they touch a hair of that child's head. It's very true. I'd sacrifice my life for my child.

Jan Amory: I've always wanted children. That's why I was very happy that, at thirty-four, I had a child, because I had already been married twice with no children. And I've always wanted the normal life of being married, bringing up children. I was never embittered against that, I always felt that's what a woman should do. When I had him, I felt I had produced something a lot more important than an interesting dinner party. I felt it was my best production. My life has changed; my values were totally different before. I was putting more superficial things first than I am now because of my child. I feel much more fulfilled. Also I feel it very easy to divide my love between my husband and my child, my husband being his stepfather. I find I am much more of a person now I have had a child. I was a little bit flippant and a little bit, you know, flakey before. It's made me realize the importance of life.

Dr Swee Chai Ang: I think abortion is a very touchy thing because it involves human lives. Personally I would never do one, or have one myself. Because, when the day comes, when I actually stand before God, I don't know how I can answer for it. I understand there are terrible circumstances; women get raped and get pregnant and they just can't have this baby. There are lots of these kinds of circumstances when you would justify an abortion. But I have been a coward on this issue because I would personally refuse to have anything to do with it. That doesn't mean I will go out and prevent other women having abortions, because I understand the conditions they are under, and I don't think it is funny at all when you cannot afford to be pregnant, and when you are going to lose your job, or your marriage is going to break up because you had an affair with someone else and the baby is going to come out looking different from your husband. Those kinds of problems are individual cases, and certainly I will not object to them having an abortion, but I will not personally get involved by doing them.

Beatrice Aristimuno: I haven't been married, but I really feel like having a child now. Absolutely. I feel that very strongly. If you can't do it, it's sad, and most women of my age who are not married are in that position.

Debbie Arnold: A woman is not fulfilled until she has a child; any woman who says different is lying. I don't believe women when they turn to me in their mid thirties and say they don't want children. I don't believe that's possible. It's a biological thing, and that is why sex is such a strong instinct. God says, we're going to give them something that they're going to want more and more of, to make sure the human race keeps on going. And therefore yearning to have a child is a must for women; it's just there, that's why we're different.

Now that I've reached thirty, I suddenly think I've got to have a child, I really want to do that. I don't know why I'm here, apart from that. I feel my career and everything else in my life are really insignificant, because it has nowhere to go, because when I go, that's the end of it.

Leslie Ash: I'm dying to have a child. I just have always thought of myself as a mother one day, apart from acting, which is my life, and which I look at like a job, a business, not really a career, you know, not glitter and things like that and wanting to go to Hollywood and be famous. I look at it as a business, it's my bread and butter. And I hope that whoever I have a child with will understand that I will want to work as well as being a mother.

If the woman falls pregnant, and the man turns round and says, of course you can't have it, you must get rid of it, I think a woman should be able to make up her mind whether she wants that child, because, after having one abortion, you may never be able to have another child. I have had an abortion and it's caused quite a few problems. There is a lot of speculation about whether I will ever be able to have a child. I can't believe it, and won't believe it. I know I'll fall pregnant, because I've been told in my fortune-telling I'm going to have a child, so I'm looking forward to it. I think it's the worst thing also for a man to say, that child in there is mine and I want you to have it. She should be able to choose whether she wants that child, and then turn round and say, look, I want nothing from you, all I want is this child. I wanted the child and I knew the man didn't. And I could very easily have had the child. I could afford it. But I wanted an abortion because I was in a relationship with that man and had no intention of leaving him. I was just sorry he didn't want it. If he didn't want it, then it wasn't the right thing. If he'd wanted the child, that would have been fantastic, but if there was any doubt at all, then I wasn't going to have it. But I was very sorry afterwards, because then the relationship did finish and it actually had a lot to do with the abortion. He was a million miles away when I had it, and afterwards a woman goes through this thing – I don't know what it is – but every time you turn on the TV it's this is what your baby looks

672

like at three months, and suddenly every commercial on TV has got a baby in it; and you pick up a magazine and the first thing you see is a baby. Everything goes through your mind and reminds you that you are taking away a life. Oh, God, it's so awful. It's a horrible feeling. It is traumatic to a lot of women who want to be mothers.

Diana Athill: I had abortions at a very early stage and no sense that what was being terminated was a person. It was an evolution of cells going on in my body that had reached only a very limited stage. I didn't, it didn't, yet know whether it was going to be male, female, what it was going to be. It didn't seem to be a life, and it still doesn't, strictly speaking. One could argue that, of course, it was, as a Catholic would, but I still think that's rather an absurd argument, really I do. It was better for that child not to have ever developed into a person rather than be an unwanted child, which seems to me to be a very bad thing. I've seen a great many unwanted children and what happens to them. It certainly was not at all a traumatic thing for me, I'm sorry to have to report. It was sensible, it seemed to me. It didn't distress me much at all.

Leila Badawi: Motherhood is a tremendously elating experience, it's exhilarating. It gives one added confidence in one's ability to withstand pain, for example, which is an important feature, because women are supposed to be more delicate and more sensitive, which is nonsense. But I wouldn't say it makes everything else pale into insignificance. It throws everything into sharper relief because it makes one organize priorities better.

Joan Bakewell: I do feel that the experience of bearing children is probably the most creative thing you can do. I cannot think that there is anything – a symphony or a great painting – which compares with a human being. Life before art. If you create life, you are master of something quite mystical and there's no comparison. A woman has a sense of her capacity to do that. Strangely enough, she doesn't strut around boasting of it or making men feel inferior, she just holds it within herself; it doesn't warrant a great display of bravado or ego. It is so complete in itself, it need not even be spoken of.

I rejoice in being a woman, I enjoy it greatly. I'm delighted to be able to have had children and have great bonds with them which are maternal; maternal bonds are so eternal. I feel that creating life and perpetuating the human race is the most important thing I've done, although, God knows, I worried. They cause one a hell of a lot of problems. They drain you, they are little sicky, sucky things, they latch on to you and bleed you for sympathy, love, understanding, money, God knows what. They're almost like mantises, they just devour you. I felt a huge drain on my resources, but I knew it was something very important to me, so in a sense I would have been desolate if I hadn't had children and I can't imagine my life as someone who hasn't.

Elisabeth Barillé: I have always had this conviction that I would write but never have children. I don't have any pride in this, nor any sadness, it's just a fact. I don't see my accomplishment as an old woman surrounded by children; mine will be in literature.

Dame Josephine Barnes: I have been accused of being an abortionist. This is not true. When I was working in hospitals I had to do abortions and always hated doing them. I looked at this from the point of view of the Anglican Church and came back with the idea, from a very distinguished theologian, of the doctrine of necessity. And if anybody asked, are you pro-abortion, I would say, no, I'm against abortion, but there are some circumstances in which abortion is necessary; that is what I would say. It is not desirable, and I would much prefer people to be responsible about their sexual behaviour and contraception than to have to come to me for an abortion. That would be my view.

Josephine Barstow: The way a women's body is designed to reproduce is one of the wonders of the world and a lot of men are incredibly jealous of that, of that capacity a woman has to create. That is the ultimate creation: to create, not re-create, but create a totally independent and wonderful human being. And grown inside a woman's body. I mean, a man could never even be sure it is his child. I don't have any children of my own, but I think it's incredibly sad when women try to deny there is this difference between us biologically, and just have a child and stick it on the conveyor belt. That syndrome saddens me enormously. I unfortunately left it too late and, as it's turned out, I haven't any live children. I hope my imagination is big enough to be able to imagine it, even though I haven't experienced it.

I've had an abortion and I would ultimately argue against it any time of the day. It's terrible. Dreadful. It's a violation of everything. It's not something that I think consciously, it's something that I know instinctively, that I know because it's happened to me.

674

Jennifer Bartlett: If you are born with two arms, you want to use them. We women use what we have. Women have the ability to have children, and I don't know what comes first, the ability or the urge.

I've had an abortion and I wouldn't want to have another. It is a very difficult thing to do. But I would certainly expect to have the right to do it if I wanted to. I don't want some ass-hole doctor telling me whether I should or not. Or giving me permission. If I'm not running amok and cutting people down in the street and poisoning large quantities of water or doing something really destructive, I expect to pay my taxes and be left alone.

Nathalie Baye: The day I had a child, I realized that the most marvellous things I could do, the most wonderful successes I could have, would never touch what I had just done. Nothing can equal the miracle of the birth of a child.

I am not against abortion for the simple reason that, if a woman does not want to have a child but gives birth to it, then there is much more likelihood that it will not be properly cared for. Childhood is very important, and if a child does not have the love of its mother, then its whole life will be influenced. Animals are much more natural about things like that: if a cat has a kitten it does not want, then it kills it. We do it before birth, that's all. If a woman is pregnant by a man she does not love, or if she doesn't have the resources, the strength or the desire to have a child, why should we throw a stone at her? You have to think about the child, too. It's awful when women have a child, then abandon it. There are so many who are sent off to be looked after by other people. What kind of a life is that? Far better not to have it in the first place.

Rotraut Lisa Ursula Beiny: It is the woman who bears the child, and if she doesn't want to have the child, who is going to look after this child afterwards? A child needs a mother. I don't think a father will take that place. Therefore it is much better if the woman doesn't feel she wants it, that she should not be forced to have it. It is her affair. If you want to have your appendix taken out, you have your appendix taken out. It is up to the woman to say whether she wants to have this child or not. It is she who bears it, carries it and goes through the process.

Christine Bogdanowicz-Bindert: I'm thirty-five years old and I've never

675

really thought very seriously about children. But now, given the fact that my biological clock is running out, I am seriously thinking about it. That said, I would not give up my job. So I would want to play the superwoman and manage everything – have the perfect kid and the perfect husband and the perfect job – which is going to be very hard.

Should a woman who is eighteen, who by accident goes to a drive-in movie and gets pregnant because she has not taken precautions, should she live for the rest of her life with those consequences? Apart from the woman, it's the child that comes unwanted into the world. The moral issue is a bunch of baloney. I'm a Catholic, but I think it's a bunch of baloney. It's an irresponsible position the Catholic Church is taking on the whole issue of abortion. Because in developing countries, where I have travelled widely, some women are really afraid of getting abortions because of the Church, and they have these twelve or fourteen kids who they watch become beggars.

Liz Brewer: Being pregnant was certainly not elating. I found it incredibly annoying when I discovered I was pregnant. That was one of the major reasons for getting married, because I wanted to have a baby. I'd left getting married quite late, and everybody said, if you don't do it now, you won't be able to have a baby. But having discovered I was pregnant, it really hit me and I was furious. I was in tears, and I remember saying to John, my husband, and my mother, everybody said I should have a baby, but nobody actually asked, did I want to? You don't feel particularly well in the third month when you're pregnant, and then I got into it with the clothes. That was quite fun, and it didn't worry me at all until the last three months. Then I thought it was an absolute bore. I was fed up with being that shape, loathed it. I got so fed up that the last month I packed my bags and caught a plane to the South of France, which was very dangerous, but I did, to join a girlfriend on her boat, and I just lay there in the sunshine and swam, getting nice and brown, because I was fed up with the situation. It didn't appeal to me at all. When I had the baby, I had an epidural, and I decided which day I was going to have it, and it was all very civilized, and I had a marvellous gynaecologist; we decided on that day because he was playing golf the following day. In I went, there was no pain at all, except the hunger. I was starving hungry, it was eight hours, and towards the end the epidural was wearing off, and I remember sitting up and saying, I'm never ever going through this again as long as I live, and I meant it. And, you know, they gave me the baby and I felt nothing; it was terrible, I felt no maternal instincts. They wanted me to hold the baby before they cleaned it, and I was absolutely freaked, it wasn't what I wanted. It took two months for me to have any actual feelings, and until then I went through all that emotional change: you know, you're in tears every minute. We went to Australia when the baby was two months old, and it was then that those feelings started with me, rushing to the cot every five minutes to see if it was still breathing. And then I discovered the most extraordinary feeling I've ever had: I actually felt that you could close the door, and there I was with this little baby, and I would never ever want anything else. I was totally contented just with that little baby. It is the most extraordinary feeling, and I couldn't believe I was feeling it. I didn't want to go out, didn't want to do anything, and that lasted a couple of months. Then everything started to rationalize. So the whole thing changed from having felt nothing and having thought what a nuisance, what have I done, now I've got myself this baby, to thinking it was absolutely fantastic. People say, oh well, it changes your life. It didn't change mine in the least after that. I got on working again, but what it did, it added a totally new dimension to my life, which was wonderful.

Heather Brigstocke: We have terrible choices nowadays that we never had before. I would say, on the whole, that abortion is a very sad thing, and I think it happens much too often. But there are cases when it *is* the right thing to do. I do find it shocking sometimes. I know one couple who were so proud that the woman was pregnant, but they were not married and it would have shocked his family, and so she had an abortion. And then, a year later, they got married and now she is pregnant again. I think that's an awful way to mess about with your body – just for temporary convenience.

Suzanne Brøgger: I think I always had the urge to have a child, but I had to stifle it because I couldn't see how I could combine my writing with raising a child. I was really terrified of the responsibility, and even though it is common in our day to be an unwed mother, a single parent, I really didn't want to make that choice, not for the child, not for myself. So it is a matter of luck that I met a man I respected and loved. I'll soon be forty-three, and I just had my baby last year, so, you see, I was really lucky.

Motherhood has changed me, I think, in the sense that I am more vulnerable and I have more anxiety. Before, when I was just on my own, I was stronger; I had no fears because I was only responsible for and to myself. But bringing such a little creature into the world and having all the fantasies of what can happen to that little girl, makes one,

677

as a mother, very vulnerable. I suppose that, with the child, fear came into the world. So, in that sense, I understand women who want to be successful in society and who refuse to have children, because it makes us more vulnerable. But it also makes us richer on the human level.

Janet Brown: I was married a long time before I had a child, and I was terribly off-hand over the whole business. I couldn't come to terms with it. We wanted a child, but I was so far removed from it, I found it embarrassing to mention prams, baby blankets, they were foreign words to me. I couldn't stand to look in baby shops and say, isn't that a pretty dress? I wasn't taken up with anything like that at all. I think I was really quite odd. And then, when the baby was born, I went completely into reverse in that I felt so elated: not the actual birth of the baby, because it was pretty tough for me, but at actually holding this baby in my arms. It was like falling in love all over again, the most wonderful feeling of being alive to everything around you. I thought that the skies, the trees, the grass – everything was so beautiful. Everything had a kind of magic for me when that baby was born. And I looked at myself after I had the baby and I thought, oh, my skin is so clear, my eyes are so clear, and I said to my husband, you must look at me, I won't stay like this. Because it was like losing some years. I was really quite knocked sideways. When I went out into the street, I saw women with children, and I'd never noticed them before, but suddenly I thought we are one of this marvellous thing. You are wonderful, you women. I thought they were terrific, they had produced a child. Because I then had learned what it was about. In that way, it changed my life immensely.

Tina Brown: Being a mother does change you enormously, and the whole nurturing side comes out. It's a wonderful, softening thing. It's the ideal thing to introduce into a successful woman's life, to restore that balance, because everything becomes nicer and you also become a more loving wife, because it softens you, in a way. And there's no doubt that, in a funny way, having the child hasn't changed me in a sense, because I always knew I'd be like that if I had a child. I will just cancel anything for the baby, you know. And I do all the time. But it's a constant pull now, and a constant conflict. I now have to get up at six o'clock in the morning, and I spend between six and eight with the baby always, and then I try to get out of the office at five, and not later, so that I can spend until bedtime with the baby. But if anything upsets that, then I've lost out on the baby for the day. Your life becomes very complicated with a child, and you think, well, maybe I'd better give up my job because I feel so terrible about walking out and leaving him during the day with the nanny. I always imagined I would give up my job when I had children, but now I understand myself better and know I can't be at home all day with the child because I do have a great driving flair and I'm a very good editor. I find it exhilarating to be an achiever in this world of competition. It does make me feel good about myself. I have to keep proving myself. For instance, when I was between *Tatler* and *Vanity Fair*, I was just a nothing. I wasn't happy just to bask on what I had done at *Tatler*, as it were, I was a big nothing, just a nobody. I went right back to zilch, which is my particular hang-up in life. But one has one's hang-ups, and they are what drive you on. That's my particular neurosis, so I may as well fulfil it doing what I am doing. Every weekend, I have the nanny go away and I spend weekends completely with the baby. And I turn down everything. I don't care what it is. Even if it's Barbara Walters's wedding party, it's too bad. The weekends are for the baby, and I am ruthless about that. I've offended a lot of people this year by saying I can't leave the baby. But I don't care.

The more I worked in New York with women who had decided against motherhood because they liked their careers so much, the more I realized I didn't want to be like those particular women. The clichés are true: they are harder, narrower, tougher, more self-absorbed. Obviously some women have tragedies and can't have children, but that's rather a different person from the person who has made a choice because they want to have more freedom to travel and all those things. And they usually regret it, I am sure; nine times out of ten they do regret it.

I never thought terribly hard about abortion until my baby was in an incubator in York Hospital; he was born at seven months, weighing 4 lb 8 oz, but there were many babies in there that had been born at four months' gestation who were 3 lb and 2 lb, and even 1 lb, and they were being nurtured back to life in an incubator with mothers weeping while they waited to see whether the child could make it or not. I felt, then, I could never have an abortion. If a three or four months' baby can live and grow into an adult, and at four months people are having abortions, then the fact is, it is a kind of murder. Of course, I understand there are tragic personal circumstances, and I wouldn't like to be forbidden to have an abortion if something terrible happened. If I was raped, or if I was unwell and was told it was dangerous to have another child, I would want to have an abortion. But to use abortion as another kind of birth control is criminal. I can't understand intelligent women who say they had an accident. They are taking the pill, what's the matter with them? Why did they have an accident? It's pathetic to say you have an accident if you've got a brain in your head. A middle-class woman, who has got a job, who has an accident, is criminal if she then has an abortion. It's madness. I know it happens, and I know lots of women, lots of my friends at home, who've had abortions. I personally couldn't because I find it too agonizing. The idea that my baby George could have been aborted is, to me, fearful.

Victoria Brynner: Today my career is 90 per cent of my life. Even a year ago I wasn't thinking that way. But I imagine that some day I will feel the biological urge to have a child. Right now, I am too busy. My mind's with my career and my work. I think I'll have to have a man in my life to inspire it. And, right now, I have a man in my life who I don't feel like having children with at all. So that doesn't preoccupy me right now.

Averil Burgess: I expected to have children when I got married. I was married at twenty-one, and I wasn't expecting to go on working. But we careered from debt to debt so I could never afford to stop. I found my husband unreliable, unwilling to face the challenges of responsibility for a family. Therefore it became clear, quite soon, that it wouldn't be a good idea for me to give up work and have a family. And I'm jolly glad I didn't. He has now married a second time. So, yes, I expected to have children, I was never opposed to the idea of children, though I am not a strongly maternal woman. I haven't regretted not having them. I thought I would, but I haven't.

Liz Calder: I was firmly rooted in the world, in the sense that I had extremely strong-minded parents who were socialists, pacifists, extra-ordinarily strong-minded people who gave me that great bedrock of love and support for a long time, for my whole childhood. But that didn't stop me trapping myself in a role expectation of something which actually didn't really suit me. I had those babies when I was twenty-one or thereabouts, and I was utterly miserable and didn't have the strong maternal instinct I was expecting to have, that my mother had always said was there. And my mother was always enormously keen on things like breastfeeding, and never had a bottle in the house, and because I was so far away from her, I tried to do things by her book, and I was miserable. It didn't work at all, and I was resentful and unhappy and didn't feel the great glow of motherhood that I thought it would bring, which was really quite a shock. And I think, in a way, I would perhaps have been more suited to it later in my life. I was too young and unsure, and green and unaware of myself and the world, and what I could and couldn't do.

Carmen Callil: When I was younger, I used to think it was just environment, but I now think it's much more complicated, because I've had women friends whose grief at not having children has been really intense. I've never felt any grief at all. I don't think all women are the same. Quite a lot of women will choose not to have children, but nevertheless, while women have children and men can't, then their life is always going to be different, there's no question about it.

Abortion is the one subject on which I would go to the stake. I feel very strongly about abortion. A woman must have a choice. Must. Absolutely. I accept the fact that you're killing a baby, and I would personally continue to do so. It's a ghastly experience, but it doesn't scar you for ever. I mean, I've had two. One was absolutely awful, but I survived and I'm OK. The other was nothing. If you haven't got the absolute right to choose what you do about having a baby or not having a baby, then there's no hope at all that women can ever do all those other things, because pregnancy can stop you doing anything. The capacity to be pregnant and not have an abortion is what makes you afraid to go out on your own in Bangkok because a man can just grab you and rape you.

Angela Carter: I don't see that abortion is a moral issue. I think banning women from obtaining a hygienic abortion is immoral. You are not legislating about a moral issue, you are legislating about whether women are going to have abortions safely and hygienically in hospital or whether they are going to be aborted with knitting needles on kitchen tables. As far as one can tell, abortionist is probably the first profession. I get so angry with women who come around saying how awful they feel about having had an abortion, and I feel like saying, cheer up, girlie, you might have murdered it. I really do, I get so angry. She might have battered it to death. A lot of women do batter the kids they don't want to bear.

Anna Carteret: This is a very corny image of women, but my mother is a perfect example. She's given her whole life to my father and us, and now that we've all left home, flown the nest, got our own careers and lives, and my brother lives abroad, my mother has nothing left. My father has hobbies, he goes sailing and so on, but she is absolutely dependent on him and on us for stimulation. So it's very important that women should continue to be stimulated and have a sense of their own validity beyond being somebody's wife and somebody's mother. It doesn't mean any thing grand or impossible to achieve, it could be very simple things like gardening or cooking. Sometimes you frighten women by talking about these things, because they think you mean them to become a top businesswoman, and that wouldn't suit every woman. I'm not suggesting for one minute that we should all be aspiring to that. I think women have many gifts, and they should explore them.

I say to people that having children is the best thing that's ever happened to me, and I utterly believe it. It's even better than marriage – it's like an extension of marriage. Just to look at your children, and to think you actually created them with your husband, is the most extraordinary feeling, and then to see bits of yourself emerge in them, and bits of him too, and to argue with them and realize that they're individuals, they are part of you and yet are absolutely separate – it's extraordinary.

If a woman's already got five children and she's exhausted and unable to look after the child, what kind of life is that child going to have? You've got to ask yourself what kind of life the child will have if it lives before you weigh up the merits of killing it. I did have an abortion before I was married, and it was because, at the time, I was in no position to bring up a child. I was unmarried, I didn't even love the person who made me pregnant, and there was no question that I could have brought up the child, economically, mentally or anything. I am pro-abortion if it means the quality of the child's life would have suffered if it had been allowed to survive.

Luciana Castellina: Men create a lot of things, but they don't produce children, and children are probably better than pictures. Again there are different (male) criteria in evaluating the two things. I have children. All women have a problem with motherhood, whether negative or positive. It is a dominant problem in their lives, and it is the truth that, once they have children, their lives tend to change. The problem is how children can become the children of men and women, when up to now, at least for part of their lives, they have been the children of their mothers, and only later on, when they socialize, become the children of their fathers. A process still has to be invented to make children become a shared task.

Charlotte Chandler: Abortion is to be regarded as a perfectly horrible thing, but absolutely available to people. I'm for it being available and people having the choice, but I do think they would be better to be careful and avoid that necessity. It's a terrible thing to have it become so easy, so available, and so taken for granted that it becomes birth control.

Alexandra Chapman: I had a child when I was very young. And merely because I had a child, I have never felt the urge since. For me, it was essentially a negative experience.

Not all women create life. There are many who either, for physiological reasons or by choice – for example, Simone de Beauvoir – do not have children. The thing about women who have children is that they are so busy raising them that they literally do not have the time for anything else. I think of Sylvia Plath, who had a hard time raising her two children and writing her poetry, and it ended very badly for her.

Felicity Waley-Cohen: The point of marriage in general is to raise a family, and I can see that, were I a man, I would be very alarmed about what would happen to this high-powered and beautiful tycoon I loved when she had children. The most difficult thing successful women have in life is coming to terms with having a family. It is immensely difficult. You feel quite differently. Having children is a very strongly emotional thing. You actually don't know until the point that you get there how you're going to react. There is an inner something that feels quite differently and simply won't be controlled by reason. Immediately after I had my first child, I longed to give up work passionately, and my husband kept saying, no, no, it's not a good idea, and thank God he did. It didn't last long, only two or three months. And basically it was because I just couldn't cope with the emotional tie of the baby. I always had a nanny, so it wasn't that I didn't have time for the business, it was that the two things were somehow too much.

There is probably a tremendous muddle educationally about women's role, and there are very few people who can really and truly successfully combine being a parent with working. I know that, if I had worked in the City, which probably I would have loved, I would not have been able to go home and be kind to the children. I think the children would have suffered most. You'd come home after a long day, very tired, and children – I've got four children – always demand a lot of you, and you wouldn't have what it takes. Even on the occasions when I stayed at home and looked after them when I had the gallery, when the nanny

683

had a day off, I'd always go absolutely mad. At the end of the day I would be in despair because I expected the children to behave in a way that I'd expect an adult to behave, and of course they don't, but I just didn't know that.

I love the family, but I would go absolutely mad if I had to look after them. I wouldn't be able to bear it. And there must be a great many people like me who can't, who are much less privileged and who have to because they don't have the money or luck to have an alternative situation. What is very lucky for children who have parents who work, providing they are doing interesting work, not doing a chore job like working in a factory but something they actually want to be doing and enjoy and love, something presumably rewarding on all levels, is that ultimately they have parents who are interesting to them. And, at the end of the day, you don't end up living your life through your children, which is another problem of women who do nothing but bring up their children. That must be a nightmare.

Genevieve Cooper: I didn't particularly want children when I was younger. Now that it's almost too late – if I don't do it tonight, it will be too late – then I think, perhaps, I would quite like to be a mother, yes. Lots of women say how elating it is. I wonder if it's another power thing, though, that those women have. There are some women who love having babies, who love that whole image of mother and baby. As soon as the babies begin to grow, they don't really want to associate with them. They almost see them as competition and reject them rather. They're the sort of women who go and have another baby because they want that feeling back again. They are the sort of women who very often have too many children, because they're always seeking the mother/ baby thing, but they can't cope with the child as it grows up. The roles are so clearly defined for a mother and baby. A lot of women want something which is totally dependent on them. God knows why, I never wanted it. The responsibility is horrendous to me. But they want the lovely idea of this little being that's totally dependent.

There are so many bad mothers around, so many screwed-up children because their mothers are not fit to be mothers. Not every woman is fit to be a mother. There are lots of them who make appalling mothers and should never have had children. And if abortion stops a little bit of that, then it is fine.

Michelle Coquillat: The relationship that a mother can have with her

684

children – and I have no children, but I have a mother – is the most incredible and tender and perfect kind of relationship one can imagine, apart from sexual passion.

Contraception is not 100 per cent safe, and abortion is essential for women. You are taking away a possible life, but not actually a life. Because, for me, life is consciousness. And no woman, I think, will make this decision easily. I personally don't think I would have had an abortion, because I wanted a child, but I can well admit and understand that it is essential for a woman if she's in a bad situation, if she is depressed, unhappy, has no financial means, if it's going to break her career, create problems with the man she lives with, with her environment. It's her right, and it is essential for her to keep it.

Fleur Cowles: I've never had a child (although I have nine godchildren and three stepchildren I love very much). I have to achieve my own sort of fulfilment in the work I do, the things I create – my kind of children. I can get joy from them. When I enter a room, my eye instantly locates my own book on a crowded bookshelf twelve feet away. I see my paintings hanging almost all over the world. I get fulfilment from the friendships I've made. Recently, in Texas, I was interviewed by a not-so-friendly woman journalist who asked a cryptic question: so you've done just about everything, what now? The same thing, I replied, but hopefully, better. OK, OK, she ended in an extraordinary way, suppose you're dead and buried, or cremated. What do you want on your tombstone? Not what you think, I replied. I'd like six little words: 'She made friends and kept them.' The answer literally fell out of my mind. (Naturally, this was a problem to which I'd never given any thought.) It made good reading and I was grateful for the chance to say what attribute I'd like most to be remembered for.

Mary Crowther: I work in a hospital in the East End of London which is tied in with St Bartholomew's, and it is in a very poor area, high immigrant population, very poor black population, poor white population. And one of the fascinating things about working-class women that strikes me over and over is that, in spite of contraception and family planning, they actually want to be pregnant year after year. There is some power about pregnancy and having children, even if half of them are in care, which makes these women feel worthwhile. They need to be pregnant, and I don't understand why. I've never really gone into it in enough depth, and if you spoke to these women, I'm sure they wouldn't be able to verbalize it, but there is something there.

As regards abortion, if you are prepared to take life in that situation, I don't think you can really argue and say it's unethical to take life in the case of the woman who just hasn't bothered to use contraception or suddenly decides she doesn't want a pregnancy. If you're prepared to abort one woman, you have to abort all women. Where I would draw the line is on the stage at which you do the abortion. I think at less than twelve weeks, statistically, it's safer to have an abortion than to use the pill if you're over the age of thirty-five. You have far more risk of dying from the pill than from an abortion. But after twelve weeks, statistically, it becomes increasingly difficult, and I think therefore the reasons for agreeing to abort somebody should be very strictly valid then. If the child is mongoloid, if there is a congenital abnormality, that cannot be decided until the woman is already sixteen, eighteen weeks. If it's simply for social reasons that she suddenly decides at sixteen weeks that she doesn't want to go on with this pregnancy, the risks outweigh the difficulties and I would encourage her if she really doesn't want the pregnancy to think about adoption. I won't abort over the age of twelve weeks unless there is a medical indication. After twelve weeks, the operation is more difficult and more dangerous for the mother. The mortality to the mother goes up quite substantially. Under twelve weeks, the foetus is really quite small. After twelve weeks, it has bones, a bony head, ribs, arms, legs, it's a life. I don't know if life begins at conception. Philosophers will say it doesn't, it begins at quickening. Traditionally, it used to be eighteen to twenty weeks, but now that we have ultrasound scans and can see what is going on, the heart starts beating by about five weeks, you can see movements from seven or eight weeks. And so I think, yes, there is life, you cannot deny there's life there.

Maryam D'Abo: I am now just twenty-six. I haven't got the maternal instinct at all, and I know it's going to develop very late if it ever does. I wouldn't be able to cope with the idea. I mean, I looked after a cat for a year and that was a great worry, and I thought, my God, I wouldn't be able to cope at this moment with having a child. But I know it will develop in a few years' time.

I think there should be restrictions about bad abortions, about cheap ways of doing abortions, because that can affect a woman's body and mind. They can be atrocious. But I believe very strongly that a woman's got to have a free will about abortion, definitely. If I was pregnant now, I would definitely abort.

686

Alma Daniel: Recently I was thinking, suppose I got pregnant? I'm fifty-one years of age and I could still get pregnant, I'm still menstruating. So would I have an abortion? Would I go through and have a baby? I don't know. I've had three babies. If I got pregnant now, it must be God's will, because I've never had a baby I didn't want to have. And yet, on the other hand, I don't want to be raising a baby at this age. But I don't know. I doubt very much, if I got pregnant now, that I would have an abortion. I don't think I could do that. On the other hand, if I knew my baby was going to be damaged, I might very well abort that baby. Because I know how difficult it is to be in the world when you are normal and well. And to bring a baby in with handicaps seems to me not very responsible. I don't think it's an easy question.

Sister Camille D'Arienzo: Abortion is the hardest question anyone can ever put to me. I may be wrong, but I will still be open about it. I really don't know about abortion. In my heart I feel that the greatest gift is life. And that to make any choice which demeans that gift, or denies that gift, must be evil. To say that abortion is evil is not to conclude that the person who chooses abortion is evil. There can be times when a woman asks for abortion, not out of malice, but out of extreme duress. I don't want to go into the consciences of every woman. I am sure there are times when a loving Lord will look at that choice and make a judgement about it. I do not uphold abortion as a form of birth control. If abortion is going to be acceptable, then it must be in special circumstances. I don't believe a woman has absolute control of her body. I think our bodies are gifts of the Lord. We exercise some authority over our bodies but we are responsible to the One who gave us life, and just as I would not harbour a nuclear weapon in my house, I wouldn't harbour an abortion in my body. But I've never been confronted personally with that choice.

I sincerely believe that, given my orientation and my perception of the meaning of life, even if I knew I were carrying within my body a child that was going to be malformed, I would still give birth to that child. Even a limited life, a defective life, is better than no life at all. And whatever sufferings we endure in this world, the end of all life is union with God; we are not terrestrially confined for eternity. Even a malformed child offers all of those who will meet him, in their lifetime, the opportunity to show the loving, feeling, tender, caring of God, or to show the brutal rejection of evil. The child represents another option in human life. I've seen enough families that have had children with disabilities, enough people who have been declared defective who have out-distanced people without physical or mental handicaps in their contributions. Look at Helen Keller as an example. So, no, I would say for myself it would be better for me to have that life than not to have it. And that if I were to destroy it, I would be destroying something of my potential to give to the world. I can't make that choice for other people, and I think it is dangerous to judge motives and declare condemnation, but for me, I don't think a defective child is the worst thing I could bring into the world. I think a defective heart in theory and a warped mind and misdirected energies are much worse. It is much worse to support capital punishment than to bring a defective child into the world.

Mandy Rice Davies: I grew up in an age where the abortion laws were not what they are today. In fact, there were no abortion laws, and I saw butchery, I saw real butchery. The poor will continue to have to have children. You can say there are many more options open to women, but that's not always true; accidents happen all the time. I think it's up to that woman to say if she wants a child. Abortion is probably far less traumatic than having a child you don't want, and then having to give it away for adoption. Far less traumatic. Carrying a child nine months, giving birth to it, feeding the child for the first week of its life, and then someone coming in and whisking the child away – that is something women never get over. Women get over abortion.

Régine Deforges: If I had not been able to have children, I would have suffered enormously because I would have felt it as a betrayal of my body. It is not that I am excessively maternal, but in the pleasure of carrying a child there is complete fulfilment. Men cannot grasp or understand that, but to feel life growing inside you is extraordinary, and afterwards to hold against you the baby you have carried has a physical fulfilment akin to the act of love itself.

Women should have the right to an abortion because it is their body. I just think it is sad that they should have to in these days when there is contraception. It's scandalous. To have to have an abortion means you have been a complete idiot. I've had abortions before the pill was available, and my memories are of traumatizing experiences. We feel instinctively that it is evil. Apart from cases of rape, there should not have to be abortions these days.

Dr Mary Jordan-DeLaurenti: In spite of having been a nun and coming from a Catholic background, I disagree with the Catholic Church's position on abortion completely. I disagree with the Catholic Church's position on most sexuality. For instance, on contraception. I believe that one of the major problems in the world today is over-population, and I think God gave us an intelligence to make those decisions. On abortion, I strongly believe that the woman has the choice and the woman has to make the decision. It is a moral decision as well as a physical decision; she makes it with all her value systems. I agree there are some people who have value systems that I may call immoral, but that's not my business, that's their business. They have to have that right. Some people feel that there's life at conception, some feel life does not take place until the foetus is able to function on its own outside. My own feeling is that there's enough life somewhere around twenty-four weeks that you could begin to say it would be difficult for you to abort. If it were a life, I would not advocate taking it, but I don't believe it is a life; or rather, it's a life, but not a human being, which is much more important. I really don't see it as much different from birth control. There's a big difference physically. Physically, the trauma to the woman's body is so much greater and birth control is certainly *the* way to go. I think we'd have a lot less problems with abortions if the Church would start talking about birth control *versus* abortion.

I have no children of my own, but my husband and I raised four of his in the last twelve years. No, I never wanted any children. Probably because when I left the convent there was so much I had to do and learn, that time passed me by before I really wanted them, and then, by the time I was thirty-seven, I just thought I was too old. If I had been twenty-one and not in the convent, I think I would have had them then, but I don't regret not having them.

Sylvia Deutsch: I have one daughter, and it completely changed my life. When you've had a child, you're never the same again. I'm not at all the mother-hen type. Some women need to prove themselves by having children and talking about them the whole time, but I had my daughter almost without noticing. My life was cataclysmic during my pregnancy: I seemed to spend the whole of it in hospital or the graveyard; the whole of my husband's family died. I suddenly found myself one day a mother. I wasn't prepared in any way, mentally, but I had to look after things, move house, have building work done, and I think, for eight months, I didn't give my daughter a single feed. Perhaps I had her in my arms three times. I didn't have the time, and, in any case, the feeling of dominating a tiny baby isn't my thing.

Dame Jean Conan Doyle: I've never had the biological urge to have a child. There must be something wrong with me, but it's very fortunate that I haven't. But, I may say, that neither of my brothers had children. Years ago, I would have liked to have had a child by a man I loved. Then my husband and I would have loved to have had a child, but both of us were much too old for children by the time we married. Earlier in my life, I would have liked to have a replica of the man I loved. That would have been my reason for having a child.

Margaret Drabble: To me, the tremendous elation of becoming a mother was totally unexpected, because I hadn't been brought up to expect it. My education had led me away from it, if anything – you know, you're wasting your time just being a *Hausfrau* – but in fact I thought it was absolutely wonderful, I felt fulfilled as a person. And I've known men who have been tremendously excited by the birth of a child. I've known one or two men who, it seemed to me, ought to be fathers and became fathers and were absolutely radiant about it. But for a woman that is a more common experience. It certainly changed my character completely.

I find abortion the most complex issue, because I know that I would have been personally incapable of having an abortion. I think that now I might, because it would be silly to have a child at my age, but when I was young I just had to have them, but for that very reason I was very keen to argue that people should have the right to choose. I've always argued that it's a woman's right to choose. But I do worry about this generation of young persons who've had every control, every way of choosing, how would they ever know if they want a baby or not? I feel very strongly that it's wrong to compel women to have babies they don't want to because they will be bad mothers, they will be unhappy and so on, but I also believe very much, in pragmatic terms, in the happy accident of the young girl who finds she's having a baby and decides to have it and then is so glad she did.

Sally Emerson: Motherhood came as a complete surprise to me, and I think it is to a lot of women. This is one of the things we've been losing: we've been so concerned with our careers that many people have actually forsaken this other way, and nobody seems to talk about it. People are rather shocked when you start talking about babies. No, the creation of life was much more elating than writing a book, although the book had been a high point in my life. Having a child continued to be elating. With the novel, I could look back at the novel and think: well, that was a good novel, I was pleased with that, but to see this human being growing up was quite different. It also taught me about every-thing. I just started looking at her and watching her closely, which you have to do, having a baby. I learned so much about the human race, more than I'd learned from books. I understood so much: things like sex differences, things as simple as that. I understood that the core of humanity was something very sweet and hopeful, powerful and strong and lovable, and yet somehow wicked at the same time, which was the soul of my child from the very beginning. Seeing that in that raw state, before she'd been conditioned and passed through society and had learned things, gave me more hope and respect for humanity than reading any great work of art, whether *War and Peace* or *Paradise Lost*. This was just watching it. One of the problems women have is that they don't respect this. They do themselves down all the time by not pointing out the very interesting things, intellectually interesting things, to put it in male terms. They always talk about how wonderful and lovable it is – and it is so wonderful, the love you have for the child – but there is also that other side, the intellectual interest, in just watching how a human being develops, how it first learns to use its hands and touch, its growing sense of itself looking around and seeing the world, and the way it uses language, the way the language expands. Men write whole intellectual treatises about all these things: women are watching day by day, watching and seeing it happen. Maybe that's why they don't do so much good intellectual work, because so many of the answers to the questions men raise you can see just watching a child. So many things have been answered that I've been puzzling about for years of my life, reading the various intellectual treatises, philosophical essays and books; they were just there.

Shirley Eskapa: Women's only true creativity is in giving birth. That, for a woman, is the ultimate creativity. I can only tell you it in this way. Everybody said to me, when you hold your first novel in your hand, it will be the most wonderful moment of your life. Now I saw nothing of that first novel – no proofs, no jacket – which meant it was even more exciting for me. I waited for that day to come, I cannot tell you with what anticipation. Six came, wrapped up beautifully. I opened it, held it. It was beautiful, much more beautiful even than I'd dared hope. It was the most disillusioning moment of my life, because people had said, you will feel the way you felt when you had a baby. Now I've had four children, I can honestly say there is nothing I have done that is comparable to the kind of elation, the kind of achievement I felt when I did the most mundane, the most ordinary of all things possible. Because every woman who has a normal reproductive system can produce a child. Nothing exceptional about it. But there is nothing I can ever do in my life that can come close in the same universe to that. That was the ultimate. If I had been a mother and had only experienced that, you could say, well you don't know what it means to create anything. I haven't created any great works, but I do know what it is like when you hold a book where there was nothing before. And it doesn't compare. Now, for men, I can't believe that becoming a father can transform a man the way becoming a mother can transform a woman. I'm watching it in my own daughter. I'm astonished to see her coming more and more withdrawn into her pregnancy and this developing child, which is really all there is in the universe. She no longer exists and she is quite irrational. It's not that she's neurotic, hysterical. She is a fully rational person, an educated person, involved in the arts. She has a double honours degree, she has done a year's course at Christie's. She has been good at her work, but she is totally possessed by her pregnancy. The problem with the women's situation (I see myself as a feminist) is that they have moved too far away from human biology. You can be what you like, rationally, I can argue with myself, but essentially I am a mother. Essentially, ask me whether I am a mother or a woman, or a writer, or even a wife, and the answer is: a mother. Most mothers are reluctant to admit to that, because our society has done mothers and mothering such an injustice.

I was much harder on my daughter than on my sons, because I didn't want my sons to feel their masculinity was being compromised by a woman. Because I was a woman, I was concerned not to emasculate them in any way, whereas I didn't have that fear with my daughter because there is no feminine linguistic equivalent for virility.

Marcia Falkender: There are women who just love to be having babies the whole time, the pumpkin-eaters who will go on having children for ever if you let them. But I don't think they are the norm, they're a very small percentage. Usually a woman will want a child because she wants to have a particular man's child.

I really feel people have to decide for themselves certain things that are very basic and very crucial to the way we see living. And abortion is one. I couldn't do it. I think it's a terrible thing to have to do, but there might be circumstances when I would, I don't know. I sit here saying this, but how do I know? How could any woman ever know? And so, to be arrogant enough to say there's no situation in which I could tolerate this, well, it's like saying there's no situation in which I'd commit murder or suicide. You hope they are things you won't do, but you don't know. You can't know. You can't say what other people have to

692

suffer or what other people have to do. So I am one of those characters whom many describe as wishy-washy, but I really do think it's something that you leave for others to decide for themselves. That's why the state has to have a role in the provision of the facilities if the person chooses to use the facilities, but not to the extent of encouragement.

Esther B. Ferguson: I'll tell you something. There is a whole bunch of white women in this country who are opting for no childbirth. I mean, millions. We are at zero population growth. When they became in control of their own lives, they opted no. We're not talking about a few thousand, we are talking about millions. Millions.

Annie Flanders: The physical experience of having a child is fulfilling for the moment because your belly is full. But even though I am a mother – I've had one child, I've lost one child, and I've had a fabulous career, and I love my child (we're best friends now) – I don't really believe a woman has to have a child to be fulfilled, any more than a man has to have a child to be fulfilled.

In my particular case, I didn't want a child, my husband wanted a child. He was the one that nurtured the child, a hell of a lot more than I did. I was out with my career and he was home taking care of the child. He did it better than I would have. He's a sensitive and beautiful man who really wanted a child, and he wasn't as nervous as I am, he wasn't as emotional, he could see things more clearly. I don't know if this is because he is a man, or just the man he is. He's a wonderful man with a great mind and a beautiful sensitivity. And he's a wonderful father. I don't think I was a good mother. I was the one who came home, played with the kid after work, and just had a good time. He was the one that got up in the morning and made her breakfast and put her to school and took care of her most of the time.

Lorraine Stanley-Ford: I'm nearly forty. I don't know that I would now be able to change my life to accommodate the demands of a child. Also, because I was an only child and hated it, I wouldn't like to have only one of my own. Because I know what it was like as I was growing up: it was awful. I resented very much not having brothers and sisters, and not having a nice sharing sort of family.

I've had two abortions. The first one I don't regret. I was nineteen when I got pregnant, and that was just the careless stupidity of a child. This was twenty years ago, so it was an illegal operation. I had to go up and down Harley Street, getting signatures, two from psychologists saying I was mentally unfit, the gynaecologist, the anaesthetist, £10 a go. Now, that gynaecologist, who has since been struck off for professional misconduct, actually assaulted me in the surgery about three months after he had done the abortion. I was going back for a check-up, and he actually assaulted me in the surgery, but because I was nineteen and had had an illegal operation and wasn't earning very much, there was nothing I could do. I didn't know where to go. I was facing away from him, I'd heard of the routine with the rubber gloves and all the rest of it. It's embarrassing to have this done to you, you try to think about other things, and I was thinking about God knows what, and suddenly my mind snapped back to reality and I realized he wasn't giving me an internal with his fingers. I really didn't know what to do. A year later, he had obviously done that to somebody else. She had taken it to court and he was struck off. The second abortion, I was actually going to be married three months later. He was a steward with the airline, and I got pregnant; I had a coil, so it was a total surprise, and probably that's the only time in my life I did meet a man whose child I wanted. He was somebody I was engaged to, we were very much in love, and it was a great relationship. We had been together for three years, and I couldn't see any reason why we could not get married, why we couldn't go on. The thing was that we had both recently started flying. We didn't have a house, we had no savings. He was starting his career, I had only been in the airline for about a year. We had no foundation, really, for that kind of responsibility at that point, and he said, no, we cannot do it, it is just impractical, I can't support you, I can hardly support myself, I can't support a family and a child. And we had a long battle about it, and eventually I said, all right, I will have an abortion.

Lynne Franks: Every time I got pregnant it was a wonderful feeling; my body felt alive and as though it was performing what it was put here to do. And giving birth is also a wonderful, wonderful experience. Having said all that, in retrospect I don't feel it was what I was put here to do. I felt it at the time, that's the way the body responds. I think I was put here to use my mind, use my potential in every area of life. Having children was part of it. It was a wonderful fulfilling experience I will never regret. I absolutely adore my children. They are the first thing in my life and I am thrilled I had them when I had them, and I would like to have some more at some point, but it's not my all. I don't think a woman who has not had that experience is as fulfilled. I don't mean that in a patronizing way, because I have a lot of women friends who are desperate to have children and who cannot conceive, which is a tremendous problem in the 1980s. It's a result of being on the pill for years. This is the first generation of women that have been on the pill. They go on the pill at eighteen, and when they get to be thirty-three, thirty-four, they want to have a baby and can't have one. And their husband has a low sperm count, which comes from drinking too much. It is actually a disease of our times. I suddenly know so many women who cannot conceive.

I feel incredibly lucky that I have never had to make a decision on abortion, because, for me, to kill life is against everything I believe in, as a Buddhist, as a person. Life is the most valuable thing we can give, so I am very anti-abortion for myself. But if there was a fourteen-year-old girl who had been raped by her uncle, who would I be to say don't have an abortion? It's a very big question, and I think until one is personally involved and has to make a personal decision, it is very difficult to make generalizations.

Teri Garr: I don't know if I want to get married, but I do want to have children. Very much. I stayed away from it all this time because I am afraid that's such a powerful thing. If I have a baby, forget the rest of my life, forget the world, forget my career. I mean, it will be pretty much like that. But I still want to do it nevertheless.

What's the difference between me having an abortion and me having sex with someone wearing a condom? We've still prevented a pregnancy. To me, abortion and contraception are the same. One is a little more difficult and one step further, but the intention is not to be pregnant. I am pro-choice. It can be the most traumatic experience or you can just accept it and think of it in terms of being OK.

Alexandra M. Giurgiu: I'm against abortion. If you're brought up a Catholic, the motivating factor of any of your acts is unfortunately guilt. In the case of a woman who has an abortion, it's like entering into a marriage with the idea, well, if it doesn't work, I'll get divorced. If you're a woman, you have certain responsibilities towards yourself. We're not in the Dark Ages any more. If you're decently informed, you don't take risks and put yourself in that situation. So, ultimately, the woman must take much more responsibility for herself and not shift her responsibility somewhere else. If you take the risk, it means you have to live with the consequences – it's part of being an adult.

Victoria Glendinning: I agree theoretically that a woman should be free to do what she wants with her body. She should never bear a child she cannot bear to bear. I also have a horror of unwanted children in the world which I think is sad and wicked. Yet, myself, I know I could never have an abortion. That's because I've had a lot of children and I know what it is for me, and therefore I would never want an abortion. But just because I would never want an abortion doesn't mean I must say that nobody else should have an abortion.

There are two sorts of women who have anything to do with men at all: one is the woman for the man, and one is the woman for the children. Although I'm a woman for the man in every ostensible and visible way, I know that the children are, secretly, the most important thing for me always. I can't see why that is, and obviously it's not true of all women. Having children is brilliant. It's the most brilliant thing you can do. It's the only miracle in the world, and one's damn lucky to have done it.

Lady Annabel Goldsmith: There are women who hate having babies. It's an art in itself to be able to carry the baby, to actually want to carry it and to enjoy it. I've loved every second of carrying the babies, having the babies, bringing them up. To have older ones, and then to have one little one aged five, it's wonderful. The house is alive, it remains alive. I'll be old by the time my youngest go out to the nursery, but that's marvellous. The whole art of having a child and the wonderful blossoming – no man can ever know what that's like.

I don't see how anybody can argue against abortion. It's your child, it's your life, and if you don't want to have it, I assume you've a very good reason for not wanting to produce that child, so you must obviously get rid of it. But I am terribly against abortion in the late stages. I think that is appalling. I can't see that you can really go that far and not know you're pregnant.

Isabel Goldsmith: I'm not keen on the idea of being pregnant. I just find that lawyers keep telling you to make your will, and I find it very annoying that I haven't any heirs. There's also a lack of continuity that I miss. I'd like to be able to think, well, if something happens to me, this all goes to my children. I don't feel this biological urge to reproduce, but it would be quite nice to have an obvious line of continuity, which gives you a kind of link to the future.

Francine Gomez: I have three grandchildren, and I am much happier with my grandchildren than with my daughters, because I have no ambition for them. With my daughters, I was very hard on them and anxious they would succeed, and they didn't, so I only had disappointments. But with my grandchildren, there is not the same need. They are as they are and I love them that way.

I had my first daughter when I was nineteen, so I didn't really wait until I was anxious to have children. In my generation, we didn't have any choice: we just had children, we didn't have to choose. I am sure that if I had had my daughters late, my own behaviour would have been different. We would have had a better relationship, I'm sure of it. Our relationship is not good, stressful all the time: one is jealous and the other is too much dominated by me.

Felicity Green: Abortions must be made easier. Offering choices to women in any area that excludes the choice of whether or not to have a baby is hypocrisy on a celestial level. It is my body, I should choose, and if I don't choose, to whom shall I delegate this choice? There isn't a person in the world. I should only make the choice with the father of my child, if he is available.

Menie Grégoire: When I was expecting my first child, I used to wake in the middle of the night with a feeling of great anguish and say to myself that I would never be myself, alone, ever again. I will always be me, *plus* another being I have made, until I die. I will never be alone, I will be me and this other. And I used to have shivers down my spine. And I was right. Each time it was wonderful, spectacular, a miracle. A baby is so soft, so gentle, every time I see a baby I want to melt. We women are so lucky to be able to produce babies. It's a wonderful experience.

Having children is the best thing I've done, the most important. If I were asked to give something up if I had to, I'd never give up my children. It's been my greatest success. It's given me the most. Of course, I've been lucky in my career, I've been unique, my name will remain, I'm one of the greatest names in the media, in opinion polls and so on. I was the most loved woman in France. But, for me, that's less important than having created three wonderful beings, my beautiful, intelligent daughters who have their own children, their own careers.

Laura Gregory: Having a child is like a job. If you are going to do it, you do it properly. This year I've already been away about a hundred days. How could I possibly have a child at home with a nanny when I am trying to achieve a certain stage in my career that is going to involve a lot more travelling at least for another three or four years? Maybe then I'd think about having a child.

Katya Grenfell: I'm not keen on abortion and never have been. I refused to have one, because I felt very strongly that I would be killing something and I'd have to live with that for the rest of my life. It would have been very traumatic and I just couldn't do it.

Baroness Grimond: Well, I'm rather in disagreement with a great many liberals (liberals with a small l) on abortion in that I do think an abortion should be an absolutely last resort. I do feel, if it is not murder, it is very near to murder. You are a partner with a man in producing a child. The fact you are the person who carries the child doesn't, to me, give you complete rights over that human being. It is quite wrong to get rid of a child unless you know there is something wrong with it. I once had a miscarriage, and I felt so awful after that, having not particularly wanted to have that baby. After that, I felt a feeling of almost physical revulsion towards abortion. Having said that, I would be very loath to say that every woman had to subscribe to my set of rules. I'm not sure that it would make for the happiest upbringing for children if women were forced to bring them into the world, hating the idea of bringing them up.

Amy Gross: I don't have a real strong maternal instinct. I satisfy my maternal instinct with people, my friends, especially now, when I have a generation of assistants who're almost young enough to be my children. I feel I have the instincts of an aunt rather than a mother. I did want a child, but I've only wanted children in a being-in-love state, to reproduce this man. I wanted a baby boy that looked just like him, that's all. And it worked out that my husband and I couldn't have children, so that resolved that. We chose not to adopt.

Pamela Gross: I believe abortion is death. There is life, and if you stop the natural course of that life, you kill. It's anti-procreative – it's anti-life. I've had lots of friends who have had abortions, and I've watched them suffer. I believe very much that people are helped by ceremony, that ceremony helps us to get through the day. Whether we smoke our cigarette or the way we pray in church, ceremony helps us to transcend in a funny way, but there is no accepted way in our society to mourn the death of an aborted pregnancy. I think, in the Far East, they have a god called the God of the Water Children where women can go and mourn the death of their aborted pregnancies. It helps them. But I've seen women here cry for nine months because they aborted their child.

Flora Groult: Once you have a child, you have a child for good, you are always the mother of the child. That makes life more diverse and complicated for a woman. But also more interesting. It is a privilege to have a contact with creation. Even a woman who is not otherwise a creator, is a creator if she has a child. She has a mysterious contact with what it is to create, to make. I think you are made for that in a way, but lots of women are not, and it is one of the marvels of the twentieth century that women who don't want to have children now needn't do so.

Pregnancy is a private affair, and if you know you are not going to love your child, that you're not going to want that child, that is to say, not know how to love it, then you should never have a child. It's too serious.

Georgina Hale: I think the idea of having a child is a bit of a fantasy with me. I get carried away and think, yes, I'd like to go into a shop and buy one. And then, three weeks later, I've forgotten about it. So whether that will ever happen I don't know. I don't have much time left, anyway.

Jerry Hall: I certainly can't say that being pregnant for nine months is fun. And having a baby is very painful. But when the baby comes out, the thrill of it is so fantastic, the adrenalin rushes through your body, it's like you took some amazing drug. It really is the most exciting moment I ever had in my life, and of course, the wonderful thing is that women immediately forget how much it hurt, and I'm sure God made us this way so we continue to have babies for the survival of the species. I had another one right away, one in 1984, one in 1985, and I forgot from the first to the second. And it's amazing how the body goes back. It's amazing, it's such a miracle.

I had two abortions before I had my children. I had to have them because I had the coil inside, and they were wrapped around the coil. If I'd had the babies they might have been deformed. The doctor said it was a miracle to get pregnant twice with the coil, but I did it. It was very, very sad, very sickening. I had the most horrible feeling, as if the spirit of this baby was screaming, no, no, no! I could hear it in my mind, screaming, don't! And then I felt so sick afterwards and I kept saying to this spirit, you'll come back another time, I promise I'll have you another time. It might be all fantasy and imagination, but I felt really terrible about it, terrible. But sometimes it's inevitable; you have to sometimes. I think most women have an abortion because they have to, not because they want to. It's important that you have the option, but I wouldn't do it again. I would never do it again.

Lucy Hughes-Hallett: The woman's role in bearing children has been perhaps over-stressed and over-glamorized somehow because it has suited the way society was previously constituted: that women should be persuaded that was what they are here for. And, of course, it is a very engrossing and fulfilling thing. I don't have children myself, but I know people who find it a sufficient reason for living and a sufficient life's work.

Mira Hamermesh: There is no literature from women about what actually happens in the act of birth, not only physically, medically or clinically, but also spiritually. I knew what should happen from what doctors said and from what literature told me: that I was going to be this blissful, Madonna-like character. Nothing of the sort, but lots of other things. I was never so fully anxious or fully mobilized in ways that made me feel closer to a goddess. I never had such a sense of power as when I was pregnant. I had two hearts in me. I was a human being walking around with two hearts beating. My God! This is a feeling that should have been picked up, but I've never read poetry or literature that mentions it. All I knew was what I knew from literature: that it's painful and a sin and a punishment, that women suffer in labour because they are punished for original sin. But, to me, it was a Nietzsche-like experience, Protean, Olympian. I was ashamed to talk because people would think I'd gone crazy.

Katharine Hamnett: Once I'd got a baby, I couldn't go out, I had to look after it. I went through hell suddenly realizing I had to look after the child and was not able to do all those things I'd done before. I think it happens to a lot of women. The easiest thing is to say, right, get a nanny, dump this baby as fast as possible, and get on with it. But I didn't want to do that because I thought there would be no point in having kids in the first place. So I had to learn to combine the children with everything else and throw away other things that were useless. My personality changed completely. It had to, because I was going off on a really stupid track at that stage. My kids really saved my life. I got very concerned about ecology and pollution and the nuclear issue, because, instead of just having to worry about myself, I had my kids to worry about. Suddenly you become terrified of everything. I'm a single parent. Of course I've got a crew, the cleaner, the nanny, the man at night, and now a boyfriend who helps out – great. But I have to be prepared to cope with it on my own.

Abortion is a terrible thing to do. I've had two abortions. You always regret it. It's like when you lose somebody, you feel grief. But I got pregnant by mistake by the wrong people, and I just thought the future of the child and myself would have been almost impossible. However, I do regret it. It's really such a terrible thing to do. I still think about it.

Claire Harrison: Abortion troubles me terribly. I think abolishing it, as some elements of the present American government are trying to do, is a terrible mistake, because there are cases where abortion is necessary. I don't believe in forcing a fourteen-year-old girl who goes out, gets drunk and whatever, to have a baby, because that's going to change her whole life. At the age of fourteen you're not even sure who you are yet, and even if you are going to put the baby up for adoption, to have to go through nine months of doing this very premature, deeply biological thing at that age, I don't think it's right. You are taking a life, but on the other hand, I am very ambivalent about abortion. It is still your body and it is your life, and you are taking the life, but it's the life that you made.

I do still believe in the rights of the individual to determine whether or not it's worth bringing a child into the world: this is a pretty crummy world, as it is. I don't believe in bringing babies into it when you haven't got it all fitted up for them.

Romaine Hart: I was a virgin when I married, and because I came from a whole stratum of society where virginity was everything, was incredibly important, and everyone got hysterical if there was any blemish or any thought that you might not be a virgin – I was probably much freer in my attitude to my daughters than I would have been today, with hindsight.

Bettina von Hase: Society perceives the mother in a totally different way from somebody who hasn't got children. In a way, a career woman who has children is a mother first and a career woman second. A woman who hasn't had children is just a career woman. Somehow, you are more complete if you have had children than if you haven't. Particularly at a certain age, which I am just beginning to realize now, being thirty and not yet married. I must have a child. That's a very selfish thing to say, but I would like nothing more than having a child. But I don't have a biological or compulsive need to have one, because I can't imagine it in my life now. Maybe I'm not ready for it, maybe I'm not grown up enough, I don't know. But it would certainly affect me in a very detrimental way if I knew I couldn't have one. I think it's one experience I can't miss in my life.

Olivia De Havilland: Nothing surpasses having a child.

I think abortion is murder. That's all there is to it. I'm absolutely against it.

Brooke Hayward: I would abort easily, without thinking twice. My view on abortion is that it's like having a tooth filled. What is life? You go out on the street and you see people who are very much alive lying down, homeless. Do we help them particularly? Do we hand them the contents of our purse? Life is a complex issue. I don't even understand why we talk about life like this. I mean, we send our boys off to war, we create all kinds of situations in which people are annihilated, we discuss chemical warfare, we discuss this nuclear business. I don't understand why there's all this fuss about little creatures that aren't even born yet. This business of a sacred thing called life which we have no right to destroy, yet once it is on earth we pay no attention to and do nothing about, I think it's ridiculous. We dispose of life easily enough at other times.

Cynthia Heimel: I love my child more deeply than I could ever love anyone. And what else is life for, what else is it about? It's important for every human to have a child if they can, if they want to. I mean, family is very important to me. And it's very humbling to care about someone else more than you care about yourself. You might do that with a lover, or a sister, or a brother, but you definitely feel that with your child: you care more about your child than you do about yourself.

I don't like abortions. I think it's an awful act to perpetrate on yourself. But if abortion is not legal, people will still go out and have abortions,

702

and they will hurt themselves. People have always had abortions. It is a grisly, horrible act, but I think it is necessary, necessary to have it available. It's even more or equally as horrible to bring an unwanted child into the world and brutalize it. The Right to Life people have done nothing to help retarded, abused, hopeless children. They say we must bring all these children into the world. What are we going to do with them once they're here? There is nothing sadder than a brutalized, abused child. It's just as bad to brutalize a child as it is to kill a foetus.

Marie Helvin: I would have loved to have had a child with Bailey, I loved the man. But it just wasn't right, then. I didn't want one then. And as we parted, I am glad I didn't have one. I would hate to be divorced and have this child between us, knowing there would be problems, custody and all that.

Margaux Hemingway: I'm going to have a child, that's for sure. I really look forward to it. It will probably be the best thing that ever happened to me. My mother thinks so. We had a long conversation. My mother says there is nothing like it. You can't explain it, it's absolutely indescribably delicious, it's the best thing you can go through. Absolutely. I said, boy, that's the nicest thing you ever said about me.

Anouska Hempel: I think children came from falling very deeply in love. That was the next stage of an emotion called love that went on to the reproduction side of life, and one was doing one's bit for the man one loved and for oneself as well. I suddenly woke up and there was a very small bundle there that was all sort of wiped off, looking rather wonderful, and I had a terrible pain in my tummy. But that small person there, that love for that very pink, horrible, porridge-looking creature, that was really your creation, is the most amazing feeling, and the most protective, and the most worthwhile, and the strongest bond anybody can ever have. I think as children grow up over the years, that bond goes, obviously, because you have to relinquish yourself from that initial, amazing love that you feel for a new-born child. As time passes, you've got to let that go, because it's not constructive. In fact, it's very destructive if you hang on, and hang on, and hang on. But having children meant the loss of my freedom for the rest of my life. I was a mother, that was that, and if nothing happened to them I was going to be a mother for ever. And that was an amazing change, because although I was married very young, I wanted to do a lot of things. And I did know that having that child could have been my excuse for not doing anything at all, if I needed an excuse. I chose not to have an excuse for not doing anything at all, and took them with me on whatever I was up to. They were part of my everyday life, and I was young enough not to know any better.

Beth Henley: I've been with the same guy for fourteen years and I don't, really, at this point want children. I feel guilty, in a way, for not wanting children; I do feel that: I feel I should want children, I should be the type, I should be writing plays, cooking big pots of spaghetti and having a bunch of kids hanging off me. But the fact is that I hate to cook and don't want children but love to work. It's a funny thing, because there's a real guilt in saying I don't want children or feel the need. It makes you kind of a freak, but that's how I feel right now.

I would definitely abort if I felt I needed to. I don't think anybody knows when a life starts. They say the foetus doesn't feel pain up until three or four months, something like that. I just think people have a right to choose, and society can't choose for them, they never have been able. People have always gotten abortions some way or another. And with ghastly consequences, if it's not legal. They're going to do it, if that's what they want to do, and it's irresponsible not to have that a legal option.

Val Hennessy: Personally, the thought of abortion is utterly repugnant. I can't bear it, and I know if, for instance, in my late forties, I suddenly found I was pregnant, I would find it very difficult because the mere thought of ripping out this little potential human being from my body, and flushing it down the lavatory or a sluice, is hideous. I know that, every year when it would have been born, I would have thought of it. But, having said that, I think every woman has to make up her own mind on this issue, and I would thoroughly understand any woman of forty-five who suddenly, to her horror, discovered she was pregnant and rushed in and had an abortion. It is her own decision, she has to make it. The thing I do find reprehensible is women I've met who will boastfully say, or casually mention, oh yes, I've had eleven abortions. I can understand someone having one abortion, perhaps two abortions, but by that time they ought to be sufficiently clued up to not make it necessary to have any more.

Dr Leah Hertz: Every woman should have an abortion is she wants. If it were me, I wouldn't think twice. If my daughters came to me tomorrow with a pregnancy – I've warned them already, I don't want to hear about it – they can have an abortion.

Elizabeth Hess: The truth is that being pregnant, having a baby, being a mother, is not a great, tremendous pleasure. There is a great myth that women have been so gratified by the fact they could give birth, have babies, be mothers, but the truth is it's a tremendous amount of work and women have felt and been told and taught it is their duty. It is not a tremendously blessed role in life. This tremendous mystification about women and birth is used as an excuse, usually by men. Men use the fact of motherhood, and the tremendous pleasure that comes from motherhood, to say that's what women do: they are mothers and that's enough for them. There are also a number of women who will tell you that having children is not enough. I want to have my daughter grow up, seeing me as a person who is out there in the world, participating in what's going on. I don't want her to learn that it's enough, that you don't have to be an informed person. You can't make choices if you are not informed. I don't want to undermine the fact of motherhood, because there is a tremendous pleasure in it, but I also think we are role models for our children, and that motherhood in this culture is still so mystified by men. I think women can feed it too, and I would argue with those women. There is tremendous pleasure in having children, and there is nothing wrong with being a full-time mother and having many children; but for many women it is not enough. And most women have to work. I mean, most women who have children no longer live with men, so they don't have a choice of just being mothers. Most women work and are mothers, too.

Abortion is one of the most important issues for women, and the right to have an abortion is crucial to the independence of women. Ideally, the father would be part of the decision-making process, but there is no question that the woman is pregnant, and the woman is pregnant alone, and in the end it is her decision. It's her body, and she is the one who is going to be left, chances are, to support that child. There is an obsession with the foetus in our culture, and people forget about the woman who is pregnant and whose life is going to be changed by the fact of the child.

Min Hogg: Mothers spoil sons. And the sons never get over it.

Abortion must be absolutely the easiest thing in the world, it must be. I have no feeling for the moral issues. There have to be medical cut-off points, of course, but anyone who doesn't want a baby should not have one. No question. I don't bring religion into it, and I do not believe an embryo is a human being: it's not.

Arianna Stassinopoulos Huffington: I've never had an abortion, and obviously I wouldn't have an abortion now, but looking back on my life I would always have been extremely reluctant. It is not an ideological thing. I would never say that women should not have abortions. I don't believe in that. It is an individual choice. But I do think women should know the price they are paying. It is absurd that there are so many abortions with contraception being as available as it is, and women knowing as much as they do about the risks of getting pregnant. I think we have so many abortions partly because we have not really stressed the psychological price a woman pays when she has an abortion.

Caroline Huppert: I am more sensitive now that I have children, and I find it much more difficult to accept violence around me. Previously, I was more indifferent to war, murder, and now I realize the truth about the mother of the soldier, and my son, who is growing (he's seven), keeps asking me questions about military service and war, and I am very worried about how to answer. I see violence in the world with a totally different eye. In my films, I find it difficult to introduce unjustifiable violence with respect to a certain morality. I couldn't have a brutal murder of a child in a film; I know such things happen, but I instinctively couldn't film it. As a director, one should be able to film everything without prejudice or preconceived ideas, so I realize I am closing certain doors for myself. On the other hand, I realize that certain sensitivities have deepened.

Isabelle Huppert: I always wanted a baby, from the age of eighteen or twenty, but for several reasons I had to delay. I thought I was not ready: physically and psychologically unable to have a baby. But I always wanted one. And it's very hard for me to figure out that it's possible not to want one. From a moral point of view, I perfectly understand: it is not a necessity. But, for me, it was. It was an obsession.

Motherhood has changed me. It's not that it changed, boom, in five seconds, right after the baby was born, but there was a mental change, and I can tell from how people view me now. It altered everything, my perception of life, my perception of being an actress. It's not that it solved an issue, that's not it. Before I had a child, I was very jealous of women who had children. Now that I have one, I am very jealous of all women who have another child; I am obsessed with having another child. There was an English film I loved, *The Pumpkin Eater* with Anne Bancroft and Peter Finch, directed by Jack Clayton, and made in 1964. It's a wonderful picture, because it's one of the only films I've seen dealing with that obsession. In the film, the woman keeps having children, one after another. She loves the children but it's anguishing because it's as if she constantly needed to be filled. The process of having a baby, certainly in my case, was the same process as doing a role. When you are an actress, you give life to a role; and when you are a woman, you give birth to a child. There are no words to describe how elated one feels when one gives birth. It's the oldest thing in the world, yet it's surreal. There are actually no words.

Angela Huth: I have had four children actually, though I've only got two, and several miscarriages, and I am very bad at being pregnant. And if you're very bad at being pregnant, that elation goes out of the window. If you are sick all the time, have to be in bed all the time, like I did, you don't feel much elation. When the child was actually born, my overwhelming feeling was one of relief, thank God that's over. I was too relieved to feel elation. And if you have had two babies who have not been all right then the feeling for the ones that are all right is something almost indescribable. The good thing that comes out of disasters in pregnancy is that the ones that do work you are grateful for for the rest of your life. I mean literally every single day, when I see my five-year-old daughter, whom I had a great struggle to have, and I was quite old when I had her, that is a sort of pleasure beyond anything I think a man could feel. Obviously your husband goes through it with you to a certain extent, and feels relief, and excitement and happiness. But he doesn't have the daily worry, night and day, for nine months: will this child be born or not, will it be all right or not? And so, when it actually is, that is a pleasure that remains with you for the rest of your life, every day. Certainly the best thing I have ever done in my life is to have two live children.

Abortion is such a huge subject. I did think about it a bit because when I was having my first child with my second husband, at the age of thirty-nine, which is a very dangerous age to have a baby, I was trying to decide whether or not to have an amniocentesis, which tells you if the child is not sound. And because I am so bad at being pregnant, I decided not to. It turned out that the baby was a Down's syndrome baby and had everything wrong with it you could think of. It had a hole in its heart, its lungs were wrong, everything. The poor little soul only lived nine months, having a terrible life. He had pneumonia five times; he was in

707

and out of hospital. I wouldn't have wished that life on any child. I often asked myself, had I had the amniocentesis and known Jedediah was going to be like that, would I have gone ahead with an abortion? And I think I would. I hate the idea of doing away with life, but it was just one, luckily short, terrible struggle for that baby, perhaps full of fear and pain, and no happiness. I couldn't tell. I wouldn't wish that on anybody, and if he could have been aborted and saved all that pain, then I think I would have gone through with it.

Abortion has to be for a deeply serious reason. One doesn't ever want to put oneself in a position of being mini-gods, which is what some people do. But if there is something really serious, and absolutely no hope for this child, and the parents feel they will never, in a million years, be able to deal with it, and it is going to have a very short, unhappy and painful life, and that is absolutely firmly established (I really do think that has to be established), then abortion must be possible. On the other hand, if I had gone through with an abortion, even knowing all that, I think I would have probably had an unquiet mind for the rest of my life.

Angela Janklow: Men never go through the birth process. I think giving birth is always what separates the sexes. A man does nothing that he doesn't do every single day of his life. Men just don't understand the maternal process. There's no way they could, they don't experience it, and much of life is experience. Ejaculation is all they do, period. The big boom, that's it. We women are reminded of this horrible thing twelve times a year until finally, when we have a baby, it pays off, supposedly. I just think that nurturing another human being within yourself, actually physically, not being responsible only emotionally or only financially or only philosophically, but actually responsible for the life of another human being, is something which separates the sexes, and always will. This is why men are the ones who make war, because they don't know what it is to produce life.

My life is more important than an unborn person's, and any woman old enough to get impregnated is more important than a non-existing piece of cells. I am pro-abortion. I would abort. First of all, if I had an amniocentesis and knew there was something wrong with the child, I would abort, period. Without a second thought. And I would abort probably today because I am not involved in serious relationships I want to devote my life to. I know plenty of women who've had abortions, a lot of my very good friends have, and it has affected them all very differently. Some it has affected very seriously, others not at all.

708

Tama Janowitz: We're making abortion more and more difficult. There seems to be no problem in going off and shooting a country of people, but there seems to be a problem with abortion, which is one person's body and an individual decision, not the government's.

Margaret Jay: Being a mother is absolutely fundamental, and I think what is much more important to most women is not so much whether they have a wobbly marriage, but whether or not they have children.

The thing I'm more grateful for than anything is the fact that I have my three children. I would hate to be the age I am now and not have had them.

I find myself very alarmed about abortion in a sense. I did a lot of television work about test-tube babies and the whole business of how early you could tell whether a child was viable, or whether or not you could do experiments. I was very sympathetic to the scientists who said it was ridiculous for people to throw up their hands in horror and say this is a tiny human being and we can't do experiments, because it seemed to me to be quite obvious that, although it had the potential to become a human being, it wasn't a human being at that moment. It was eight cells or four cells or whatever, and I'm not religious and therefore can't think that it had a soul. Yet, when I think about individual people having abortions, and talk to people who have had them and hear about the emotional impact, it seems to me to be very troubling. The impact it has on people emotionally is perhaps not as much understood as it should be. So I think there is a real intellectual and emotional difficulty. But obviously I'm in favour of people being able to choose whether they want to have abortions. I would never do anything which would make it difficult for them to do so.

Dr Lukrezia Jochimsen: Having a child was a wonderful experience, but I would not say it radically changed my attitudes. Of course, after you have a child, you can actually never say to yourself or to the child, it wasn't worth the experience; you can't say, well, OK, OK, my life wouldn't be that much poorer if I hadn't had this experience. There is another human being, another person, and it is dear to you. But I would say, having had the experience and being a mother, especially in a situation where other things are important and dear to me as a person, it makes me understand better my own mother, my mother-in-law, my neighbours, my friends, my colleagues.

I would never make abortion difficult. I would give the woman the absolute right to choose, because who else is able to decide in that situation? And I would always argue that, if the experience of abortion is traumatic, which obviously it is in very many cases, this is because, up to now, women have not been given this ultimate right to decide. Others have had the right, and so women have these traumatic experiences because they, of course, feel guilt.

Sally Jones: With a lot of my friends in their early thirties, from being very tough, very convinced career girls who never wanted a husband, never wanted a family, suddenly the urge to procreate has become absolutely paramount. Many of them don't appear to want a husband. They will go out and have a baby, often using somebody almost as a sperm donor, a kind of occasional boyfriend perhaps, but somebody they are really just using to father a child because they feel they must have that sort of fulfilment. However high-flying their job, however careerist and motivated they are, and however much they will continue with the job after they have had the child – and they will probably be well paid so that they can afford nannies and everything – that urge to have a baby suddenly becomes an almost irrational obsession that takes them over. It's not something that has, as yet, afflicted me, though for all I know it may do.

Abortion is one of the saddest acts there is, because it suggests there's been a mistake, that either a relationship or simply a method of contraception hasn't worked. And there are a lot of feckless people around who will simply use abortion as a form of contraception. I would certainly give the woman the choice. I would also try to make sure, before it got to that stage, that they had counselling and help with contraception. An awful lot of abortions are very young girls who are perhaps just rather fecklessly sleeping around and then get pregnant; therefore they have an abortion, they get pregnant again, they have another one and so on. You often meet people of twenty who have had perhaps two or three abortions and are using it very much as a form of contraception. Which suggests there should be a lot better sex education.

Rana Kabbani: A woman should be completely free to do what she wants with her body, because it's her body and nobody else's. The strain of having an abortion and the guilt and whatever residual feelings there are later, I think she bears herself. She may have an abortion, and then regret it deeply. But then she has to suffer that, and it's not for society to

710

tell her she made a mistake. She will know she made a mistake if she did. I had an abortion when I was nineteen and I still sometimes feel traumatized by it. But I believe that it was the right decision and I couldn't imagine not having the choice, not having the freedom of that choice.

Dillie Keane: I hate abortion. I was born a Catholic, my family are Catholic, and that stays with me. I find it horrendous. I wouldn't abort. I say that to my man: if I get pregnant, hard cheese, I'm staying pregnant. And luckily it's never been a decision I've had to make. However, if I was proved to be carrying a hydrocephalic child, I would abort that child, yes, because I wouldn't see any point in having that poor, unfortunate creature live in a hospital, take up a phenomenal amount of money, time, energy, when there was no life in it. But I wouldn't abort because pregnancy was inconvenient. And that's why people have abortions, because it is inconvenient.

Tessa Kennedy: I'm a Catholic, so I don't believe in abortion, but just as I believe in liberated women, I think if you are carrying a retarded child and can't cope with it – and they do have the medical science now to tell you you are – I think that you should do what you feel you have to do. I'm certainly not going to judge them. Thank God, all my children were healthy, nor did we ever have those tests in my day. I know that Down's syndrome children are supposed to be very lovable and wonderful and lots of things, but still, they don't have a long age-span and to know that you're bringing something into the world that can't live very long, and can't enjoy life to the full, must be tragic. I wouldn't judge anybody.

Griselda Kerr: My experience is that women are lucky, in a way, because they can have a child and turn off the course they're on; and it's a wonderful thing to be able to do that. It's a change. If you consider that your life is a treadmill – God forbid one does – or you are on a road going straight on and on for ever, like French roads with poplars either side (you know how they always seem to go on for ever), suddenly having a child leads you off on a completely different track, 100 per cent different, and that's very exciting to me and I can't think where it's going to end. I don't know what I shall feel like when I've had my baby. I've no idea. I don't know what I shall do about my work. All I know is that, at the moment, that absolute commitment has vanished. No, that's not true, the commitment hasn't vanished. I will come back because I

711

want to maintain and sustain what I've achieved, and I'm frightened it won't be maintained or sustained if I go. I also think that there's a great deal more to do. But the ambition for power, that's completely gone.

I never have felt sympathy with the anti-abortion movement at all. Even when I married a Catholic, I still didn't feel it. Then I had a miscarriage, which was bad, but one in five women have a miscarriage. Then I became pregnant again, and because one is thirty-five or thirty-six, it is always suggested that one has an amniocentesis, but actually the threat of having to abort the child because it wasn't right was too much, and I just couldn't get rid of a child I'd carried for seventeen weeks, and I'm astounded by myself, at my change of attitude. I always felt before it wasn't a human being until it was born, and therefore didn't somehow matter. I don't believe the child has a soul. I don't feel this way about it on religious grounds, I just feel it on my own selfish personal grounds that, for the rest of my life, I'd feel guilty that I'd ended a life. I'd just feel the sadness of losing something one had begun.

Soraya Khashoggi: Women, however high in the echelon of commerce, politics or wherever, do not put their job before their family. I defy anyone to show me a woman that puts her job before her child.

My husband stayed with me throughout the birth of all of our children. And, in those days, for an Arab man to do it was totally unheard of. For an Englishman, it was unheard of. Can you imagine, in 1961, a Saudi Arabian man, by choice, his choice, walking into the delivery room with me and staying with me while I had my first child? And, to this day, he talks about it as the greatest experience of his life. And then again, and again and again, with every child. He wouldn't dream of not being there at the moment of birth. In fact, he even goes around and boasts that he delivered the children himself. He enjoyed the delivery to such an extent that he feels, I think, almost impotent that he didn't actually give birth himself. And after we sadly had our divorce and he remarried, and I remarried, our daughter went to him to tell him I had another baby. And he turned round and said, what do you mean, she had a baby? She can't have a baby without me.

I'm anti-abortion. No one has the right to take away a life. And life, I believe, begins at the moment of conception. No one has yet been able to disprove that theory. With all of my nine pregnancies, I knew the moment I conceived. It sounds crazy, but other women will tell you the same thing. They knew they were pregnant before their doctors told them. I would never abort. I would never assist anyone to abort. I am totally anti-abortion. I wouldn't help a friend or a sister, a child or anyone, to abort, not under any circumstances.

Lesley Kingcome: When I found I was pregnant first time, and when I had my first child, it was absolutely fantastic. The other two were a bit of a bore. But the first one was fantastic. I found making a human being absolutely riveting, and you are a bit odd if you don't find that fairly fantastic. I can totally happily admit that I knew I was the only woman in the world who had ever had a baby. I mean, without any doubt, I was the only woman who had ever had a baby. Most women must feel like that. I knew I was cleverer than anybody else.

I don't approve of abortion at all. I don't like it, but I would rather have a child aborted than an unwanted child born. And all the ghastliness you see going on with unloved children. Having a sister-in-law who worked with unwanted and unloved children, I can tell you it's a terrifying thing.

Irma Kurtz: Women and children are a whole minefield area, children are a minefield in a woman's life. A lot of my friends now are menopausal women, many of them childless, and not one is what I would call without neuroses. They are all very strange and highly strung women, and I think that must be connected to the childless condition. Throughout your life, your body is doing something and you are resisting it. Men don't have this, it's very different. And that's part of why you find these New York women so aggressive: they have sublimated all their tenderness and are overreacting to their fear of not being loved. I've seen them do it, it's scary.

I see abortion as a very unhappy thing. It's unfortunate. Nobody wants to have an abortion. I've had one, most of the women I know have had one, and it's terrible, you don't like it at all. It's even worse when you've had a child afterwards and you remember the abortion. At the time for me, it wasn't so bad. I was glad to be rid of the burden I knew I couldn't carry, really glad. When my son was born, years later, and I felt the wonder of that, I didn't regret the abortion, but I felt differently about it; it had another dimension because I realized how wonderful it is to give birth. But that wouldn't have stopped me having the abortion. It had to be done at the time. So what I am saying is this: abortion is the extreme form of contraception, it really is. It's used that way in Japan, in Russia, in Israel, it's used that way in lots of other countries. It may be safer than the pill in the long run. It's a very unfortunate thing to have to do, but it is, and has been since the beginning of time, an extreme form of contraception. We use contraceptives in order not to have to have an abortion. An abortion is the failure of the other contraceptives, the ultimate contraception. It's unfortunate, but it's a fact, and it's always been a fact. We cannot make it illegal because women will find an abortion always. There's always been a way to have an abortion, in every society on earth, I think, including primitive African societies.

Marghanita Laski: Women should have total freedom to abort. There are too many people in the world anyway, and though a woman is likely to bond with a child once it's born, this bonding isn't necessarily healthy, it only helps the child through its early years, because no one would, after all, want to tend a dirty smelly idiot of a creature without some kind of bonding. Many don't, of course. Many children are neglected. So I certainly think that abortion should be at will.

Frances Lear: Abortion may be a moral issue for someone else, but not for me. For me, it's an economic issue.

Catherine Leroy: To me, being married is about having children, and I do not want children, so why would I get married? Women are supposed to want to have children, but mothers don't necessarily love their children. I'm absolutely convinced of that. I've seen it happen many times. A woman is supposed to have a child because she has the organs to reproduce. Does it make her a better woman to have a child? I don't think so. There is no great desire in me to have a child, to reproduce. It's nothing to do with work. If I found I did want a child, I'd have to think about it very seriously, but if that doesn't happen, I'm not going to make an effort to have a child just because I'm physically capable.

Cecilie Løveid: I feel that childbirth is something so natural that it isn't fantastic. It is so natural that it is almost an everyday thing. When it happens, I lose awareness of time, the clock isn't important any more. I'm into another world, another reality. But I don't want to be completely submerged, so I remember when I had the last one, I had a very different book on the table and I read and read to keep myself mentally alert so that I didn't sink into just sleeping, dreaming, the milk, the smells.

714

Jenny Lumet: I think abortion should be as easy as conceivably possible. If now I got pregnant, I would have an abortion. The government cannot force me to have a child that I could not raise properly. If I had it, I'd give it away. If I had it, and had to raise it by myself, it would be ridiculous. Abortion is important. People say the foetus has rights, but what about the mother? It's her body. What if you're sixteen and black, and your family's on welfare? The idea of forcing anybody to have a child is abominable.

Gillian Lynne: I have had an abortion, and I regret it with every fibre of my being. I think I would make the law stricter. Only based on my own regret. The person whose child I carried I knew would not marry me, and I wasn't even sure I wanted to marry. But I was thrilled. I've always wanted a child, but ambition got in the way. Always. I was always going to do a new role or dance a new something. So it's my own fault. And now that I have found the love of my life, I can't give him a child. That's bitterness beyond belief. And he is such a marvellously open person. If I had had the child I aborted, it would have been embraced in our whole set-up.

Sheena McDonald: Lots of women are fulfilled without having children. They must be. It isn't every woman's ability to have a child – it doesn't make your life less worthwhile not to have a child. And that's not me guarding my back in case I don't have children. I really believe it.

Mary McFadden: You have to have children. I think you miss a world experience if you don't have a child.

I gave my daughter complete freedom, which was a mistake. In retrospect, I would have brought her up much more conservatively.

I'm in favour of abortion. I think the moral issues are very salient and important, but I'd wipe them out of my mind. I had an abortion, and there's no question it's traumatic, but you forget about it.

Susan McHenry: I have the right to choose whether to abort, because I'm the one who is going to spend the nine months pregnant, and I'm going to spend all my time in the physical care of the child. I mean, theoretically I can say, yes, the father should have some say in what happens, but practically it doesn't work out that way, practically it's the

715

woman who is going to be physically involved with this child. Therefore a woman should have the right to decide whether she is going to be as physically involved as it takes to nurture a child. It's not an easy decision to make, to have an abortion. No, it's a really terrible decision. What I would want in the best of all possible worlds is for us to have access to birth control that works. Fortunately, I have never faced an unwanted pregnancy, I've never faced pregnancy, so I've never had to make that decision. I know it would be very hard. Sometimes I think I would like to have a child, but for the wrong reasons, for narcissistic reasons: somebody who would replace me in the next generation. That's not a good reason to have a child.

Donna McKechnie: One of the most discouraging and disappointing facts of my marriage and divorce was that I knew I was not going to have a family. Divorce in itself is very painful for anybody who believes in commitment. I so hoped to have a family, and that was a very difficult thing to resolve. Any woman who has a child: I see the change in their lives and the importance of the most beautiful, simple things in life, how they grow up because they have to. But there was a time when I obviously could have had a child in the marriage and I didn't, because I knew it wasn't going to be the right thing. And as soon as I was able to accept that for myself, I felt a little easier about it, and then I realized I probably would have had a child if I had really wanted one.

Deirdre McSharry: No man should ever utter on the subject of abortion, because no man has ever carried a child. The choice must be the woman's. She knows what her reasons are. Very few women abort a child lightly. It's one of the most horrendous experiences in life.

Norris Church Mailer: I was pregnant with my first child when I was twenty-one years old, so I was practically a child myself. I have two children, both boys, one now fifteen and one eight, and I wanted desperately to have both of them. The first one was welcome as was the second. I would be very unhappy if I didn't have children. They are such a delight. I have enjoyed both of them so much, every step of the way from babyhood to where they are now.

I am pro-choice; I'm not pro-abortion. I don't think abortion is a viable birth-control alternative or that it should be taken lightly. It is something that is very serious for a woman. On the other hand, I don't think it is something that can be delegated by the government; it's a woman's

716

choice and no one should be able to tell her she can or she cannot do it. And probably there are certain circumstances under which I would have it done myself. But I would not have been happy about it.

Alice Mason: Children should never be raised permissively. I decided in my mind I was going to divorce my daughter Dominique's father, when I was pregnant. When she was an infant, I left him. I didn't want anything – just $50 a month. I just wanted him to know that he had to send a cheque for his daughter, not because I wanted anything. I also said he could see her any time because I wanted her to have the benefit of a father she would never miss. And she has as strong a relationship with him as she has with me. She sees him all the time. He's French, but lives in New York, and she was always very close to him. Interestingly enough, because we were divorced when she was very young, she didn't even realize we were ever together. Once he was picking her up and the nurse was downstairs and she was just two and a half, and I came in and he was taking her out, and she said, oh mommy, I want you to meet my daddy. She never even knew we'd met. She was so young, but she was just as close to each of us. He never remarried. She's his sweetheart, the centre of his life. She had two parents. But we were both very strict with her, very. I think children don't even realize you love them if you just let them do anything, raise them haphazardly; it means you don't care much. The problem with raising children is that women spend more time on a man than on their child. There is so much anxiety about either losing or keeping that man that they don't spend that kind of energy with their child. It is very important to spend a lot of energy with your child, because that child you will always have.

Margaret Matheson: Being pregnant and giving birth and nurturing a child is – I don't like the idea of best and worst – but I'm forced to say I think it's the best thing in your life and it completely changes you. There is no question but that your view of the world is different after you've had children: it puts everything into perspective. The single most important thing to you is this fact which is physically glorious. Obviously you don't get pregnant without the sexual relationship, which is in itself glorious, but the act of being pregnant does correct any physical failings in the body, and your body is tremendously well, albeit rather odd, and the moment of birth, which is one of the most extremely painful things you will ever experience, is wonderful. After the pain there's the beauty, the relief and the achievement; and then the relationship with the child is in itself so wonderful, for all that it is probably fraught for all sorts of external reasons, but it is just one of such pride and wonder. It's wonderful that you can have created something with these beautiful, beautiful hands and so on, something that grows. It makes you more important and less important at the same time. You're just a piece of the world, and you have the pleasure of seeing this thing which is growing up. I long for that to be shared with men, but obviously it's a physical sensation that men can never have. I know men who sobbed in harmony with the mother of their child at the birth of their child. In fact, I don't know very many who haven't. There is no doubt that there is a tremendously powerful emotional experience for a man in the birth of his child, in particular if he's part of it, but it's plainly different.

My mind tells me that all women should be free to decide whether or not they should introduce into the world a child, and that, if they choose not to introduce that child into the world, society should arrange that that's possible. Personally, I think I would be incapable of having an abortion. I simply cannot imagine, knowing that I had this thing inside me, anything other than having it. But that goes back to the absolutely overwhelming joy and pride of birth. Obviously, it's easy for me to sit here in a comfortable warm room and say that, but when I was younger I, like lots of people, said I'll never have children, I wouldn't wish to bring a child into this world. Whether even then, in my early twenties, had I become pregnant, I would have got to the point that I thought it better to abort the child, I don't know. I doubt it very much. I think, if I had been pregnant even when I was going on about what a dreadful world it was, and we'd better get the world straight before we start having children, I couldn't personally have gone through with an abortion, but I firmly believe that in this country and everywhere else in the world, we should create the circumstances in which women choose whether or not they abort.

Homayoun Mazandi: There is a lot of satisfaction in childbirth; you suffer and you come out a real person. All this suffering is good for you.

Kate Millett: I find the maternal instinct is really the end product of a great deal of careful social conditioning. Lots of women don't have children. I've never had any children. It seems to me absurd that my life should be judged on whether or not I have children. Lots of men don't have children; their lives are not predicated on their paternity. To care for infants or any helpless vulnerable creature is a good and wonderful thing that anybody could experience probably, but I don't really believe in maternal instinct. I realize, too, that it's dinned into us all the time. Propaganda, propaganda, propaganda.

718

Kathy Myers: I take a basic medical view on abortion, and I do not believe that small embryos are human beings; the same way I don't feel I am committing mass slaughter each time I eat an egg. I really do feel that people who argue ardently against abortion should not eat eggs. There is a certain point where it is developed, and I'm prepared to take medical opinion on this. But I think for women not to be able to have abortions is criminal. And if you think of women who have been raped or who are going to give birth to damaged or malformed children, then it is criminal not to abort.

Lynda Myles: It's a romantic fantasy: the glories of birth and pregnancy. I see the reality of trying to pick them up from their music lessons and going to the school play, and I don't see any way that can be integrated into the sort of work I do. I don't really find them endlessly amusing. I quite like them once they're older, once they're sort of articulate. I suppose one's own are different.

Anything is better than having an unwanted child, and if a woman doesn't want to have a child, she has the right to dispose of it.

Lynn Nesbit: Abortion is a question I have managed to avoid. It's a very difficult issue. I feel extremely fortunate that I have never had to have an abortion. I had three miscarriages before my first child was born, and then I had to have major surgery on my uterus, and then two caesareans. So, you see, I really wanted children. Abortion must be very traumatic because miscarriage was very traumatic, very.

Julia Neuberger: Maternal love is the expression of concern by a mother for her children. She doesn't feel it for other people's children; she really doesn't. When I'm doing the school run and I'm taking these kids to school – mine and various other people's – I'm very conscious that I do actually mind much more what happens to mine. I'm more worried about my own running into the road than anybody else's. I would feel terrible if it was somebody else's child, but the gut feeling is for one's own, and I don't think that the maternal love thing extends beyond one's own children. And I think that, if fathers had more of a chance to express their paternal feelings for their children, it would be as strong and of a similar quality.

Nanette Newman: The only reason I've managed both a house and a

719

career is because I made a choice. I wanted to be with my children. I didn't want to wait nine months, have a baby and go out to work and never see that child grow up. I had a very selfish attitude to that. They would probably have been just as well brought up by being placed in the hands of a nanny, but I needed them, I desperately needed them – I'd had them. If I was faced with a decision between a job or being with my children, I would have died rather than have gone off for three months and not seen them.

I am one of those people who are for abortion. I think it's the worst thing you can do to bring an unwanted child into the world.

Emma Nicholson: I would have loved to have had children, and not just at one point in my life. But I have always seen children as being part of a happy marriage, and have never wanted to have children outside such a context, and that, so far, is not something I have ever achieved. I've never explored, I never got married, so, for me, babies cannot be part of my pattern. But I love people, I love children, and I should think I have done more work for children than many married people. For twelve years, I have worked lock, stock and barrel for the Save the Children Fund. I was their director of fund-raising for seven years. During my last five years of office, I think I raised about £100 million for deprived children, so, in a completely different way, I have done more for children than merely having a couple of children of my own.

The person who bears the child seems, by a quirk of Mother Nature, to have built in the obligation to care for the child. I don't think anything is ever going to change that. It is in the hormonal in-put into human beings, and it's very lucky that Mother Nature's done it so that the person who has the child actually looks after it, otherwise nobody else would. Clearly most men don't.

Mavis Nicholson: I doubt I could ever have gone through an abortion. But what a thing to say, because if I had been up against things, of course I would have had one. But I didn't. I would have been very bad at having an abortion. I would fight for abortion rights for women, but I'd also fight for the right of any woman to have her baby even if she's out of wedlock. If you make abortion easy, you should also make it easy for a woman to say, I don't want an abortion, I will have this baby; I'm not married, and it's nothing to be ashamed of.

Christine Ockrent: A woman is indeed entitled to her own body, and her own life, but I think more and more people realize that the harmony in a couple and the need to have children are primary impulses. You will often find that women who were crusading for abortion ten years ago are the ones who are having children now.

Fifi Oscard: My children were born when I was quite young, and I found it not a feeling of elation. I hadn't been yearning for them. I think it is when you yearn to have a child, and then the child comes, that your heart sings. My children came and I was fascinated and interested and a good mummy, but my elation comes now that they're older and accomplished and I'm proud of them. I was furious with my husband when I had the baby because I wondered how he'd got me into this. It was awkward and uncomfortable and I didn't like it. Then I looked at the baby and the baby was rather cute; we made friends, the baby and me. But I didn't have the intense God-like feeling that people talk about.

When you are a mother who is not home when the children come home from school, you have to cope with a certain amount of pain. That is something which relates only to women who work. It's very hard, because your children are angry at you a lot, and it took my children a long time finally to realize that maybe they were proud of me instead of angry at me. That is a terrible burden. Men don't have that burden. They're supposed to go out to work and be away all day. Mothers are supposed not to.

It would not occur to me to be in any way disapproving of an abortion. Were it a friend of mine, I might say think twice because you can have a baby and a baby is a wonderful thing to have, and your life will be enriched and different, and I know a lot of people whose lives are magnified and maximized by it, but I do think it's a woman's right to decide. When I was in danger of illicit pregnancy, of course, I would have aborted, I would have had to. Because there was no way for a married woman to have babies who looked like one of the neighbours.

Edna O'Shaughnessy: I would want abortion to be reasonably easy, but also to be a serious matter, which I think is how the law stands now. When you have an unwanted pregnancy, one needs, to my mind, to be clear there is no solution that can be free of guilt. It seems to me obvious that abortion is better than bearing a child who is really unwanted – which means prolonged torture by rejection – but an abortion will still cause deep guilt.

Kathy O'Shaughnessy: I love little children. I am so drawn to them. And I love the idea of having a family, and I'd die if I couldn't have a family. It's always been part of what I've expected. It sounds mad, but I can see, with my dog, I have a sort of broodiness. It's like I want to hug my dog. Seriously. I know it sounds mad. Not just to be with it, but I actually want to hug it. That, to me, is the first sign of being broody.

I know some women find it hell having babies. One friend of mine had an absolute nervous-breakdown hell. Some mothers don't find it easy to love their babies. I don't know why, but I feel ridiculously confident that I will definitely love having a baby. But I am just happy for it to remain still in abeyance, because I am too selfish at the moment. I want time to myself.

Molly Parkin: Although sex between men and women is absolutely glorious, I do think, speaking for myself and having spoken to many women about this, that there is something quite surreal about having given birth to a child and suckling that child. To hold your own child and breastfeed it is a very, very strong and sensual experience, which men, of course, don't have.

Judith De Paul: I never wanted to have children. I made a conscious choice. I never had a biological urge. Psychological, emotional, yes, absolutely, in particular when I was in my late thirties and I knew that was about it. In the end, in my particular case, I felt rightly or wrongly that I'm a little different, my attitudes are different. I've had a very unusual life and I'm grateful for it. I always felt that, as a different person, I had to leave a bit of a legacy. Partly that has been my films, *Mountbatten, The Last Viceroy, The Life of the Pope, The Nazi Hunter,* all the Gilbert and Sullivan operettas. Now I'm developing the Indira Gandhi story and I'm doing *The Life of Lenin.* These are very important. They mean I'm leaving something here to society, some kind of contribution. I did not feel that I would have the proper time to take care of a child, because I knew I would have to treat the child as my mother treated me: time, understanding, patience, but most of all time, and I had no time. I never felt the biological need. That's nonsense as far as I'm concerned. You either want to have a part of yourself remain in this world and/or you fall in love with a man whose child you would like to have in a sharing relationship, but there's no biological question as far as I'm concerned.

Penny Perrick: I think I wanted to have children from the time I was five. It meant a great deal, but I can see many areas of life which create a fantasy around them, which are written about in terms of romantic fantasy. Childbirth and the bringing up of young children are not what you expect them to be, and hence the post-natal depression, the child-battering, the cruelty, because the reality of having a child and bringing it up is not in the least the way it sounds in parents' magazines.

To bring an unwanted child into the world is too much to ask of anyone. In these days of almost foolproof contraception, to be in need of an abortion and, even worse, to use abortion as a means of contraception, is immoral, but I would never forbid it.

Lorie Scott Peters: You learn from your mistakes, and if we take away the possibility of women learning from their mistakes in getting pregnant, then what are we doing for women in society? It would be better that women didn't get pregnant – they don't have to. But it happens, and if we take away from women the option not to be burdened with something they don't want, then we're making for a lot of unhappy people in society, for a lot of homeless and fatherless children, for a lot of women who can't take care of an extra person in their lives.

I think it's terribly unfair. I am a very rare woman, one in a million: I have a double uterus. Because of that, I got very much caught up with getting pregnant. I've had several abortions in my life because I didn't know what my physical make-up was and neither did the doctors. I said OK, I'll have an IUD but I got pregnant because I had the double uterus and a double cervix and a Panama Canal, and the Panama Canal let everything through to the other side. And they said, well, it must have slipped. So it was put back in again and I got pregnant a second time. So I said, screw this. Then I married and I spent a year and a half trying to get pregnant with my husband and went through all the tests with my doctors. They basically said, his sperm count is so low, and the sperm have so few tails he just won't be able to get you pregnant. So we didn't pay attention to contraception. And then, on the night I left my husband I found I was pregnant again. So I've had some very unfortunate circumstances in my life, and God forbid there wasn't the option of abortion. I'd be stuck with a lot of kids right now, not because I was being stupid but because doctors didn't know what they were about.

Sarah Fox-Pitt: I guess I never had strong maternal instincts. I'm fond of children, I like them, but I never had that overwhelming desire.

Having had an abortion myself, I'm glad I was free and assisted by somebody who was very skilled and morally involved with the Abortion Act.

I wish I had been stronger than I was and had had the ability to have carried it through and continued to pursue my work, but it took place when I was about to take my finals at university and that was a threshold I did not want to jeopardize. It was a question of whether one was prepared to go it alone, and I guess I wasn't at that point. The person whose child it was is now dead, and could not have been the support I perhaps would have wished for. I think I was more interested in not having distractions to what I perceived then as vital steps in my career. But I did know also, and I was very influenced by that, that the man whose child it was would not have been much help. I wouldn't have been demanding, but I would have wanted that child to know its father. Anyway, he was told, but not consulted. I made the decision and didn't waver until I went into the operating theatre, where the female surgeon, seeing my distress, asked me if I still wanted to go through with it.

I'm not sure I look upon it as a moral issue. I think I look upon it as a loss. Perhaps that's a selfish way to look at it, because life is so precious and a good life gives so much that it is a great tragedy to lose a potentially good life. I'm not a Catholic, so I don't believe in the fundamental dogmas, but I'm not distressed by the idea of abortion, because I think, in many circumstances, women need to be protected from what in some countries is a continuous slavery to the sexual desires of the male and where birth control is desperately needed. But, in these days of Aids, such things may have to be considered. Perhaps if abortion hadn't been so readily available, we would not find ourselves at legal loggerheads over surrogate motherhood.

Baroness Plowden: Creating children has been women's fundamental purpose. Having a child is to a man merely a moment's exercise, whereas to a woman it is a major operation. This must confirm her, on the whole, in her biological function as a mother, which is a very large function. And that, I think, is different in men and women. I know women who would like to have children and can't. It's a permanent gap in their development, a permanent pain. It isn't just wanting to have children about you: there is the fact that you have been denied this fulfilment. You may get this fulfilment in other ways. I've always liked children, I've always been interested in children, I've always known that I wanted children. And then I had children, so that was all right. I didn't feel any compulsion. I just assumed, in my innocence, that when one

724

was married one had children. And I was married and I did have children. It didn't cross my mind then that people didn't have children. I only knew one elderly married couple among my mother's friends who hadn't had children. And I remember my mother saying what a blow it was. But I am aware, now, of a lot of women of thirty-five and forty who haven't had children and the terrible deprivation that they feel.

I think to have a child against your wishes would probably be wrong. If you feel, I don't want this child at any cost, then to be forced to have it is like being a cow or something. It just depends what causes the abortion. It's the woman's responsibility. If she doesn't wish to have the responsibility, and the discomfort and indignity of looking like that, all the things that go with having a child, then she shouldn't be forced to have it because society says abortion is wrong.

Eve Pollard: My view on abortion is that I don't think you can be against it and I don't think you can be for it. I think it should be available. It's too cruel to say to a woman, you are pregnant with a child you don't want, that you can't keep, that you can't love, that you can't care for, but you must have this baby and you must send him up for adoption perhaps. I think most women, or many women, could not give a baby up for adoption. And so they are stuck in this terrible situation where they have a child which, perhaps born at another time and another place, they would have loved, but they cannot care for it, cannot love it. I'm not just talking about finance, I'm talking about mental ability at certain times of your life to cope with a child. So I think you have to allow abortion on the statute books. What's great about the modern world is that more and more women feel they can have a baby on their own, and that there are women who are just close friends who will support other women in that way and help take care of this child; that there's a family unit you can grow without actually being married to someone. Women, financially, can support a child, have their own nanny and their own house, and do it without a husband. On the other hand, I have to say, though this is very traditional and old-fashioned, that most children want a mother and a father. It is sad that most children, one of mine included, have a mother who lives in one house and a father who lives in another. It has worked, I think as successfully as it can, that whatever disagreements I might have had with my first husband, he is still the father of my child. He is a very good father, and he must retain access to her at all times, as if he lived in the same house. Most children want a mother and a father, so to bring them into the world without that is not ideal.

725

Barbara de Portago: I never thought I wanted children. Ever, ever, ever. And now I have a thirteen-month-old child, I am a completely different person. I feel totally complete, with or without a Prince Charming.

I do not believe in making abortion legal, which has happened here in the United States. I believe that it ought to be made accessible to anyone who can pay for it, or even, quietly, under the table. I don't believe in making things like that legal. I really don't.

Diana Potter: I have never had a biological urge to have a child. All I want is a dog. I really do. I'm never going to baby-snatch. But then, again, let's look back. I'm illegitimate. I'm not married. I consider to have a child out of wedlock really a monstrous thing. It's bad enough bringing up a child with two of you, but to start a child with that sort of disadvantage is monstrous. I'm never conscious of a biological urge. Intellectually, I knew I should not have children without being married. In fact, I had two abortions. I've been with one man for thirty years who is married, and there's nobody else I wanted to marry. It never affected me at all. Never. I've got a cousin who, at forty-nine, was saying she thought she'd have a child, and I did tell her I thought it was a bit late. I know a lot of women do feel a need to have children. I'm afraid I'm very insensitive on that point. But what's the point of feeling it if you can't do anything about it? It's absolutely loony.

Emily Prager: I always say anyone who can murder an unborn foetus certainly shouldn't be forced to bring up a child. It doesn't make sense. If somebody would go that far, then why do you want them to bring up children?

Anybody who has had an abortion and turns against it is guilty, and they'd better wise up to it. There's nothing takes you over more than being pregnant. You can't escape that. And then your body feels a tremendous sense of loss, just as it does when you have your period – the same thing really. You can turn that into a vacuum tube of grief and emotion if you want to, or you can accept the fact that, for whatever reason, it couldn't happen this time round. People do things differently, depending on how they've been brought up or their religion, but of course you'd feel a sense of regret. Why shouldn't you? Your body does.

Usha Prashar: I am career-minded, and I have chosen not to have children, which is a very radical thing to do in my cultural background. It comes very near to sacrilege, but it is a choice I have made.

I have never felt a passionate need to have children. I am a very rational individual, my head rules my heart, and it was a choice I had made that a career is important. Life otherwise is very fulfilling.

I think that the woman should have the prime say in what happens to her. After all, if you conceive against your will and want to abort, that should be your choice, because ultimately you have to carry the responsibility. I don't see why you should be bound to do certain things because of the morality of other people. I am a great believer that you are guided, to some extent, by your own code of morality rather than other people's, so I would be opposed to anybody else saying what I should have done to my body.

Marjorie Proops: Women, because they are the ones who bear the children, are more tender, more tolerant, more patient, more loving. Any woman who has had a child knows that the first reaction when you have given birth (of most mothers, I am told, and certainly in my case) is, is it all right? This immediate anxiety about this little thing that is totally dependent upon you is followed immediately by the most massive sense of this little thing being in need of your care and protection. This is a fundamental feeling in all women, whether or not they have borne a child, because they have the potential for child-bearing and being mothers.

Women who have sons have to discipline themselves not to bring up their sons to believe they are young gods. From the time my son was very young, I used to think about the girl I hoped he would eventually marry, and I used to try very hard indeed to bring him up to be the sort of man who would be a great man for a girl to live with. And, in fact, my son is a very good cook. When he was a teenager, and he used to come home with a gang of friends, I used to say OK, you can empty the fridge and the freezer, do what you like, but you've got to do the washing up and the clearing up and all the cooking, because I'm tired after a hard day at the office. So he was not brought up to think that his exalted mother was going to slave for him any more than he was brought up to think that an exhausted wife's job was to slave for him.

I think it's unfortunate if a woman has to have an abortion, because there is a great trauma, an awful sense of loss and despair. On the other hand, there are lots of women and young girls, particularly, who, for

727

various social or physical reasons, need to have an abortion. I don't think they should be made to feel guilty. It's a decision each woman must take for herself. I get letters from fourteen-year-old girls who tell me they are pregnant by married men, and they ask, what am I to do? I say, tell your mother immediately and get her to take you to the doctor or to the Family Planning or National Guidance Council or some other agency where, I know, they will offer this girl an abortion. And with the support of her mother and her family, this pregnancy will be aborted, and hopefully the girl won't suffer too much trauma, though she will inevitably suffer some.

Andrée Putman: Having children is essential to my life. I think that, during the last minutes of life, many mothers remember that unbelievable something it brought to their lives, even if they have problems afterwards with their children. As a mother, you're needed indefinitely. I lost my mother two years ago, and the pain is growing, not diminishing. I need her. Until her last days, she gave me something nobody else could. And I have that with my own children. It's a miracle women experience that men don't. I don't see any miracle that men experience and women don't experience.

Mary Quant: I would like to have people made more aware of why abortion is a bad idea, but one has to see there are circumstances in which it would be the only thing to do. It would be very difficult to have a child by someone you loathed, because it would be very difficult not to loathe the child, and that would be an appalling start.

Charlotte Rampling: I didn't feel a biological urge to have children. It happened by accident. I wasn't thinking of having children until quite late, maybe in my late thirties. I became pregnant by chance and said, well, I'm not going to get rid of it. So I had the child and married the father. To marry him was really for my parents, because they preferred it. But the first child I had wasn't an urge-type child at all. Of course, I don't regret it. But it wasn't an urge. I'd had abortions before so I could have had another abortion, but I didn't. But I knew this wasn't the right man. I knew, in terms of the relationship, it was a mistake. So should I have had an abortion then or not? That's the kind of choice women have to face. I knew the marriage would break up, would be something that wouldn't work, because we were completely opposite. It was just on the rocks from the start. But I'd had three abortions and I was twenty-six. I decided to have

728

the child, and the marriage broke up three years later when the child was three.

I was thirty when I had the second child, and it was with a man I really loved. I knew I wanted to work at the relationship and be together with him, I went into it with that attitude, knowing that I wanted also to have a career, and knowing that the career I wanted was maybe not particularly compatible with children; knowing that it is a very egotistical, vain, difficult business to be in, where I would have all sorts of ups and downs and would hate to go back to my children bawling and screaming, and have to look after them after I had just been doing a difficult role. I knew that all that would take its toll. But at the end of the day – and I talk about the end of the day in terms of a lifetime – I couldn't not have had children. It would be something I know I would regret. So the dice was thrown. When the children were very small, I cut off my career for a little while, especially with the second child, because, with the first, I was working all the time. He came round on my back: it was like a gipsy life, living out of suitcases with babies under the arm, and I filmed and filmed in different countries. The child was becoming a nervous wreck and I was too. So when the second one was born I said OK, let's stop, otherwise we are all going to go mad. Because then I had a stepdaughter I had to look after: my husband's little girl. I had three children suddenly, all under five, so I stopped, for about a year and a half, two years, then made one or two films with big intervals between. And then I went through a very difficult time when the youngest was about five, when I knew I really wanted to get back to work seriously. That was a very, very difficult time. It was as if I had to cut an umbilical cord somewhere. Because I knew I had to go away, had to go off and had to do other things, but at the same time I had a very basic maternal instinct. I mean, they are all there, they are very real. I don't say necessarily I am a very good mother, but I think I give quite a lot to my children in a truthful way. But I am not a *mère poule*.

The woman has this very special relationship with a tiny baby. And for a woman not to make the man feel left out, she's got to do an awful lot of work. She is so proud of her baby, she loves her baby, and her baby wants her all the time. She breastfeeds, she changes it, she touches it. It's a whole love affair that comes. And the man is, in a sense, awfully excluded, and that's where a lot of trouble can begin in relationships. Because, if you don't include the man in that, he's going to be the loneliest man in the world.

When my sister had her first abortion, it was a long time ago. She was sixteen. I'd tried to squash it out, and we didn't know what to do, and then my parents found out. At that time, you had to see two psychiatrists before you could have it legally. You could still have it done in the back streets, but she then had a legal abortion. The psychiatry thing held fast for quite a long time, and possibly it's quite good to talk about it to people, because I have known a lot of women that have had abortions, myself included, and it's still a traumatic thing to go through.

Esther Rantzen: Interested as I am at the moment in child abuse, cruelty to children, it hasn't changed my view, it has intensified it, that children thrive and prosper on love, security and affection. It is dreadful to produce a child who is going to be scarred physically or emotionally. I would rather all the children born today were born into a family that could devote the care and love to that child that the child deserves. So I'm neither for abortion nor anti-abortion, except to say that I do believe it's an individual choice and women have the right to make that choice. I have the greatest respect for Mary Kenny, but I think she's done a conversion like Malcolm Muggeridge's and swung from far left to far right. I find myself still staggering along in the middle, maybe. I've never declared myself one way or the other on it theoretically. I suppose, in practice, I am saying: let a woman make up her mind whether that baby is going to be born into love, security and all the things that baby deserves.

Barbara Chase-Riboud: Women should have total control over their bodies and what they do with them. Men take life away every day. Disease, famine, all kinds of things take life away, not just women through abortions. I am more concerned with the quality of life itself. Life itself doesn't exist unless there is a quality of life. That's the difference between human beings and animals.

Mirella Ricciardi: I never felt the biological urge to have a child. But then I'm a rather unnatural mother. But the earth-pull, as I call it, does exist, there is no doubt. For me, it came very much later, but I have two daughters, and one of them has such a strong earth-pull now that, if I didn't make her put on the brakes, she would have already presented me with three grandchildren without thinking. But as I don't feel that one should just procreate without thought, I have told her, look, if you have a child you have to look after it, because you are not going to put it on my back; I had enough trouble raising you and I am not ready to start all over again with your kids. So she has put on the brakes, but her need to procreate, yes, it definitely exists. It exists between the ages of twenty-five and thirty-five; that is Nature's way of keeping the species going. Everybody produces children, whether they are married or not, between these ages.

I am an unnatural product of an unnatural world. I never wanted children. I had seven abortions before I had my two children. I was a very fertile person, born in the earth, grown from the earth; I come from the earth. And every time I looked at a pair of pants I got pregnant. In the beginning, it was illegal, it was very dangerous. I did it, though, and little by little it became legal. Seven of them. I would have had nine children by now. I had two. But I never felt any of the famous elation of childbirth. Bullshit. I hated the whole thing: being pregnant, the whole experience of having babies. I was alone, my husband was never there. One of them was a caesarean, the other, awful. I hated the whole thing of being a mother. At twenty-six, twenty-seven, twenty-eight, then I was at my worst as a mother, and my poor kids have suffered from it. I did my duty because I had to, but I would probably have been a much better mother at thirty-eight or forty. I am all for women having babies at thirty-eight and forty, because that is when the earth-pull is really at its highest. When you know you can't have something, then you want it.

Nancy Richardson: Before I married Frank I had an abortion and I was in uncontrollable tears for about a year afterwards; it was a terrible thing. So when I was pregnant with Isabel, having had that prior experience, and knowing Frank could afford to look after her, I couldn't possibly not have had her, even though I was then over forty. But I don't want a society that doesn't have abortions. Even though I consider it, and I use a value word to describe it – evil – it is a lesser evil than having fourteen children who turn out to be drug addicts or get killed or kill themselves before they are ten years old.

I wanted a child so much that I used to strap pillows over my stomach at night. It was the end of the 1960s and the beginning of the 1970s that my wild oats were sown, and at the end of that period I felt so much that the outcome of sex was children. I didn't come from a Catholic family, or even a religious background, that would emphasize that, but at a certain important moment in my life, before I got to be thirty-five, I knew I had to have my first child and I had to look at sex as something that would lead to children. Not so much that I needed to have a baby, but I felt that the race would die out if women lost touch with that. And it's the women who must lead the men to that. I don't know that men feel as strongly as women. And when I had a child, I felt infinitely, infinitely

731

different. I had a son first, and I was in Beverly Hills and I went down to try on a dress because I was getting my figure back. The milk was still coming through my front, and I didn't want to buy the dress, I just wanted to take those clothes off and get out of that shop and race home to the most wonderful thing that would never leave me. That was more satisfying than any dress, any restaurant, any whatever, this child. And the day that baby was born outclassed any experience in my entire life.

Shirley Ritchie: In Japan you can get abortion on request, but it's very difficult to get contraception, and that seems to me to be the wrong way round. I think we've achieved just about the right balance. I take the view that it is better to take life at that very early stage than to produce life that is going to cause misery probably to the child itself, and certainly to those surrounding it. It must be a traumatic experience for a woman, but is it any more traumatic than having a child and having to give it in adoption? Which is, perhaps, the only other solution, if you have an unwanted child and you're not in a position to look after it. It must be just as traumatic, if not worse.

Hélène Rochas: It wasn't really me who wanted the children, it was my husband. I was eighteen when I met my husband and he was forty. He'd already been married, and he took me in exactly the way you would take a mould, in the sense of saying this is the kind of woman I want to have my children. He warned me straight away: he wanted two children quickly, so the desire to have children was his. I adored my children and did my utmost to give them everything because I was widowed very young, so I had to take over the whole of their upbringing when they were still in the middle of their education. I also had the business to take care of, so it was a lot. But I think I was a good mother, particularly when I had them to myself. I felt then I had to be both father and mother to them.

A woman without children is rather sad, arid. It's the normal process of life, but I never had that feeling of bedazzlement about childbirth that other women have. I had the feeling of a she-wolf who has to take control of her weak babies, and that, for me, was a moving experience.

Anita Roddick: I can't accept that fourteen-year-old girls who are getting pregnant after a mistake or a faulty condom should have that baby. I have no qualms about that. I don't believe a foetus is a human

732

being. If my daughters were pregnant at the age they are, if they wanted an abortion, I'd have no qualms at all about it.

Deborah Rogers: I feel immeasurably grateful to have been able to adopt a child. It's true, if the natural mother had had an abortion, then we wouldn't have Jessica. And I shall always feel grateful that she didn't, but I still would support her right to choose.

Abortion is the result of all kinds of fears and the desire to conceal, and I don't think that society should put such weight on women that they're running behind a hedge to have an abortion, because it's going to be better than facing up to other consequences. But, equally, I think that if somebody feels she isn't in the right circumstances or whatever to provide a loving secure home for the baby she is having, and if she feels strongly that she is doing the right thing, then she should be allowed an abortion. There's a point beyond which one shouldn't abort – it's very hard if it should happen after three months or so. I certainly think that, before then, somebody should have the right to determine for herself.

Selwa Roosevelt: The anti-abortion movement is something I don't understand. I was brought up in a Protestant religion and it was not considered a taking of life, and I have always believed it should be legal. I don't believe people should be encouraged to have abortions – it shouldn't just be something like having a tooth pulled – but I believe it should be legal, and safe, and I think that's the only right thing in this day and age. In our country, they're trying to reverse it and make it unconstitutional, illegal, and that would be terrible.

Kimberly Du Ross: I want children. Becoming pregnant is this ultimate magical thing. It really makes life worth living: the fact that you can give birth to somebody else. God knows what they have to live through after us, but one doesn't really consider that.

A woman has her own body, she can do with it what she wants, but I personally wish she would only choose to have an abortion in extremely difficult situations where it would be better off dead; and that has to be really something extreme. My mother brought the two of us up all by herself – a nineteen-year-old with two children – so I've seen that under very difficult circumstances one can get through and have a really great life. I think a lot of these women should think twice before they go off and have an abortion.

Juliet Mitchell-Rossdale: I think small boys and girls have the same urges. A little boy says he is going to have babies like mummy just as frequently as a little girl, before a certain age, before there's an age of acknowledgement of sexual difference. Fantasies of giving birth are just as prevalent in men. The urge has been outgrown in infancy and only comes up through the unconscious, whereas it's allowed to be conscious in women.

Joan Ruddock: My husband and I together are unable to have children. The reason is biological; it's not a case of not wishing to have children. You reach the stage when your peers are all having children, and also your own mother has become of an age when she would very much want to have grandchildren, so there is not just the pressure of your own peers but also of the generation before, looking for a third generation to appear. The other thing I have felt is the sense that life is finite and that perhaps the only thing one could leave behind is another life. I am a biologist, and I think it totally logical in terms of species preservation that we should feel that. So I try to look at my feelings, not to deny my emotions, but also to say, well, this isn't a catastrophic situation, it isn't something devastating emotionally. This is something that is normal. What I need to do, if I am not going to perform biologically to the norm, is see what I can actually make out of that, see what is in life for me. Am I right, I ask myself, to think that the only thing I could leave behind of value is another human being? And the answer is, total nonsense. There are millions of human beings. I might have had a damaged human being, I might have had a human being whom I brought up to the very best of my ability but who turned out to be a mass murderer. It has to be thought through, and I had to think it through for myself, and the answer I came up with is that what is absolutely crucial is that life should continue; not a particular life, related to my biological life, but that life should continue and that, if I had something to contribute, then there was enormous scope for contributing to life being maintained. And that's really at the root of my politics.

I absolutely believe that a woman should have total freedom over her body. I can say that totally dispassionately because, first, I am an atheist, and secondly, I am a scientist. If you believe in spiritual life, then obviously it's different, but as far as I'm concerned, what you have biologically is not a self-sustaining human being. There is no way biologically at the very early stages of a foetus that it is anything other than, in my terms, a biological adjunct of the woman's body, and the woman whose mind is connected with that body has got an absolute right and ought to have an absolute choice about removing that portion of her body taking that particular form. But I acknowledge that that voice of certainty is one that is not in any way coloured by religious belief.

Eve Ruggieri: I had been told that childbirth was an overwhelming experience, but I didn't find it so; it was very natural and I had to get rid of the preconceived ideas. It wasn't as painful nor as joyful as I had been told; it was just something that slotted into my life, my work. I have been much more shattered by other events in my life. On the other hand, I was completely metamorphosed by the years which followed, because there was such a feeling of responsibility, and beyond that the recognition of being useful to someone. I can say to myself that I haven't written a novel which will influence generation after generation, I'm not another Mozart nor Victor Hugo nor Shakespeare, but for seven or eight years, perhaps thirteen years, if you are optimistic, I have been useful and necessary. That is an irreplaceable experience.

Carol Rumens: I don't consider I've created life. I don't think of it as creation. It's something my body did, from the point of conception. It was a wonderful moment, but I didn't feel as if I'd created the life. I don't feel as I feel when I write a poem; it's completely different. It's wonderful to see a live baby and see this little human being, but it's a gift. When you write a poem, you're working at it, and when it turns out well, there's a bit of luck involved, so there is a sense of surprise and you think, that's good, that's turned out right. But with a baby, it's somehow totally a gift. I found it so extraordinary: I had this live creature who could see and hear, but I didn't feel personally responsible. I don't believe in God, but that's the moment when you could think there's something divine which isn't to do with you. But it's Nature, you see. It isn't a miracle.

Altaf Al-Sabah: To have a child is an experience that is unequalled. Also, with time, children add to your knowledge of things, and when they grow up you don't feel you are alone. The idea of companionship with your children is very important. There are people who feel quite happy and content without having them, but in my part of the world, the woman is not looked on as a complete woman if she's not married and doesn't have children. She is stronger, she has more prestige if she's married, which you don't find in the West.

Melissa Sadoff: Rearing a child is probably the most important for a woman, but I would rather give that love to a man. I chose my vocation. I would be much more interested in making a man happy than a little child. Having said that, I have had happiness in children as well, but I did it because I love them, not because I really chose them.

Bushra Salha: I don't think we can maintain as strict standards with our children here as we would have in the East. We have to be malleable, we have to be flexible. Otherwise we will break these children. They've already been uprooted and thrown into a completely new society, and they feel the insecurity of it all. I'm not bringing up my daughters as my mother brought me up. I think there's a good middle road.

I am against abortion on the whole. I believe one has to have prevention rather than a cure later on. Later on, it's too late, the life has been conceived. Once the life has been formed, it should continue, it should be given a chance.

Naomi E. Sargant: I think women have a right to have control over their own bodies and that a drawing of lines at different points and saying one's all right and one's not is hypocritical. After all, having the coil in is, in effect, a mini-abortion every month. When I had the coil, I was absolutely aware that I was just scraping one out every month. There was nothing I could do about it. I was extremely fertile. I had a different type of period all the time I had a coil, and that must have been why. I do think it is up to women to determine. Moving between twenty-four and twenty-eight weeks doesn't seem to me at all helpful, and I don't approve of the violent lobbying of the Right to Life lot. If I am anything, I am a humanist, and I am quite strongly anti-Catholic. The Catholic Church has a lot to answer for in relation to women and women's rights and what's happened to women. The Pope has set the clock back for a woman by hundreds of years, and I personally think it's wicked. In those early stages, it is really the mother's choice to decide whether or not she wishes to go through with it. I know it's nice to have a father around, but loads of people don't, and whether a father has equal rights in those early stages seems to me not realistic. That's where I'd be a much stronger feminist than most of the feminists.

Dame Cicely Saunders: I didn't particularly want a family, I much more wanted a husband. I felt a great need to be married, but I didn't feel a need to have a child. St Christopher's is my child.

I'm basically against abortion because I don't think a woman has the right to do just anything. Having said that, I wouldn't judge. I don't like going round judging, I don't like telling people you mustn't do that, because I believe in freedom even more. But I don't believe in freedom that takes freedom away from another person, and therefore I think that makes abortion a very difficult issue.

Sylvia Scafardi: I went through a broody stage in my relations with Ronald at a point, but we were always so tied up in something else that it passed off. When I see a little baby, I don't want to hold it, I haven't got that physical maternal response. I appreciate and love their huge eyes, long lashes and silky hair, all those physical things in the young I find enchanting, but I haven't got that possessive physical urge to produce or have one of my own, except as a vague regret. I like more the spirit starting in the child, the dawning ideas and so on, but I don't want all the closeness of the physical thing, and nappies and so on. I don't feel I've missed anything in that way. I'm not that type of woman.

I don't think you can have strict laws today about abortion because there's so much promiscuity, and I don't think it's fair to a child to come into a situation that hasn't some security and serenity and attention. When that happens, the tragedies are appalling. Therefore if the only way to prevent it is abortion, then abortion is better.

Alexandra Schlesinger: Very few women I know don't have an absolutely basic, absolutely urgent desire to have a child. It's social conditioning or fear which sometimes makes them say they don't.

I have had an abortion. Most people I know have had an abortion. And I don't think it's a great solution to the problem of pregnancy. It's a godsend in a situation where you can't bring up a child, but I don't think it's fair for a woman to say I have total control when it's also the man, it's also his child. And then it's also the child itself.

Anne Seagrim: I am passionately fond of children. And it's one of the great regrets of my life that I haven't any. I would have had a wonderful time. I have masses of friends, children friends, baby friends, even now. Oh yes, that's a great, great deprivation.

On the whole, probably it's better not to have a child if you can't look after it properly. And it's a purely practical thing like that; not moral,

737

just practical. Of course, they should never get into the situation to start with. People who have two or three children by two or three different men are totally irresponsible.

Susan Seidelman: One of the reasons I want to have children is because I think it's important, for me, to think beyond myself. When you are involved in the arts, often you become obsessed with your own thoughts and work and sometimes it's good to get out of yourself a bit. And certainly, when you have a baby, its needs are so great that you have to stop thinking about yourself and have to give to somebody else in a totally unselfish way, which I think is healthy.

Abortion should be readily available. I think that, *because* I respect human life a lot, and because I think that the quality of one's life is important. I don't mean that in a superficial way, like you have to live in a certain kind of house, but if you are going to bring somebody into the world, it's important that you don't bring them into a miserable world. To me, that's tragic. And there are certain people, given the circumstances of their life, that would bring a child into a miserable world: maybe somebody who's too young to take care of that child, and the child's going to go off to live in an orphanage. Why should a child have to live like that? So I think it's better that that child is aborted. But I don't even consider it a child at that point; I consider it cells. The egg and the sperm and the cells: I don't think that's life yet. When you talk about aborting a child at a late stage, then that's another issue. I've had an abortion and I have friends who have had abortions, and yeah, it makes you think, but on the other hand I knew I wasn't ready to have a child at that point, I knew I wouldn't have been a good mother at that time and that the situation in my life wasn't right to bring a child into the world. And because I do respect life, I think that anyone who's born should have a good shot at having a good life. And the main thing, I think, is having someone who is going to take care of the baby well.

Emma Sergeant: An abortion is one of the most depressing things a woman can have. Having said that, I would not want a baby now under any circumstances, because I would not be able to be a mother, and I believe it's my choice whether I have that baby or not, whether I kill it or not. There is no good some man, some Roman Catholic priest, turning round to me and saying, this is disgraceful, you've killed a life. I would drive that child mad, I would not be able to look after it, and maybe I would kill it later mentally, in many ways, if I did bring it into life. Frankly, I believe it's got nothing to do with anybody else but the woman concerned: it's her child, her choice. It's upsetting enough for her anyway, without people interfering and saying you're being a criminal.

Delphine Seyrig: I think I was a conventional mother, with everything that implies. I'm not so proud of the way I educated my son. I did the only thing I knew how to do, and the only thing that was done around me. Now, when I think back, I feel I did what I could in those days. He is now an adult, but somehow I feel if I had to do it over again, I would do it differently.

I was in the struggle for abortion. I had abortions done right in this house when it was absolutely forbidden in France and they were arresting women who had abortions, and women who had performed abortions, and putting them in jail. So a number of us signed a manifesto, saying we had all had abortions, and we were not arrested. This was one way of showing the hypocrisy of the law, and we advanced to the point where abortion was admitted in France. I testified in abortion trials. Those are the kinds of struggles I was into, in other words; that's the realm of an individual's action in a group, but it does not change the world.

Clare Short: I absolutely assumed that I would have quite a few children, but I was scared of what it would do to me. I really love my mother, she lives with me still, but I think I was scared of being her. Because her life was so constrained. We're still a very close family, but most of the girls have delayed having children (it's starting to happen now), but the boys rushed off and had children quite young. And I think lots of women, certainly of my generation, who were suddenly given all those new options, were frightened of becoming their mothers. Although they loved their mothers, they knew that their mother's life and role in life were restricted and less valued and honoured and free than, say, their father's life. But it's an enormous sadness to me that I don't have my own children. Fortunately, I have lots of nieces and nephews, and there are lots of kids around, and I can love them and so on. I think that loving children is one of the things that makes humans into decent creatures.

I don't think women talk about the miracle of motherhood as much as they used to, partly because the women's movement has said they should be more honest about everything. So women are honest about how much they love having their children, but also admit how oppressive and awful it is at times, which people really weren't allowed to say in public before, because that sounds like being a bad mother. So there is a lot of falsity about that kind of romantic, perfect, maternal, satisfied dream-woman.

I'm very close to numbers of my friends who love their children passionately but also talk about the negative things and the times when they felt like squeezing them, throwing them back in the cot. That admission all women make: that they understand parents who batter their children, because there are moments when any child drives any adult to feel like battering them. That's a more complete picture.

I don't think the experience of birth itself is significant. What is significant about being a parent is the loving and nurturing, helping a child to grow and being there all the time. And men, if they engage in it closely, which a lot of men don't, can be as much part of motherhood as mothers.

Alexandra Shulman: Right now, I couldn't do my job if I had children. I could be married, but I couldn't have children, and it would be pointless for me to have done what I've done and stop at this point. I need to do a bit more, get a bit further, till it would make sense to be able to take a year out.

Everyone says it's absolutely wonderful having a child, and no matter what agonies they went through, they'd do it all again. But I don't get the feeling with most people that they're in a kind of fairytale land being pregnant. They feel like toads walking around like that, and they're dying to get back to not being pregnant.

I see myself being able to be a domesticated creature for a few years at some point. I don't see that I'm going to have to be in an office every single day of my life. If I can find a way to work it, there is that option open to me, but I don't see myself as being supported solely by a man, ever. I wouldn't ever be able to give up working, I shouldn't think, but I could slow down, I could earn just enough to pay for a nanny to help me at home.

If the circumstances were that I had to bring up a child on my own at this point, I would abort. Or if I knew that the child was going to be malformed in some way, I would abort. I don't have any moral scruples about it.

Rosemary Anne Sisson: I don't know what else you can call abortion but murder. It's a crime, it's murder. I really don't think that just because of my religious opinions, funnily enough, though obviously that would start me off from a certain position. Women have always been able to have contraceptives. Jane Austen said, why doesn't she practise the simple regimen of separate rooms? when a woman had another baby. But now, when contraception is so safe and so natural, to have an unwanted baby and murder it – I see it as infanticide. There is no other word – it's infanticide.

Ginette Spanier: I never wanted a child, I think because I made such a nuisance of myself as a child, and I didn't want to be bothered with somebody who would do the same.

Gloria Steinem: The first thing I would do if I were omnipotent is give women control over their own bodies, so that they, and they alone, made the decision whether they would have children, and where, and how many, and under what conditions, and with whom, and so on. That would be first. And I would be just as likely to fight for the right of a woman not to have an abortion as to have an abortion. But the point is that she makes the decision. If it's going to be traumatic for her, she shouldn't be forced, or encouraged, or pressured to have an abortion. I'm not saying that abortion is good; nobody wants to have an abortion, it's not a pleasurable experience. I'm just saying that women must have the power to make the decision to have children or not have children: reproductive freedom, as we would say. Because it is an event that takes place for nine months in her body and uses all of her blood vessels, and heart, liver and lungs, so naturally the decision has to lie with her. In terms of the law, if a woman had to get a man's permission to get an abortion, it would be the most intimate form of slavery. To be forced to be pregnant for nine months and risk your health because the law was forcing you to, that's not acceptable. The law has to give women the right to decide.

Pamela Stephenson: I'm against abortion. I wouldn't want to have one myself, but that doesn't mean I would dictate to other people. I feel very concerned about the taking of human life.

Lady Arabella Stuart: I don't think that young girls should be encouraged to feel they can have abortions on demand, because it is an incredibly destructive, awful thing to do to yourself and I don't think, when they're young girls, they understand that. I feel it should be possible but not too easily available.

Imogen Stubbs: Having got to the age I am, I really do feel broody about having children. I don't think it's fantasy. I do somehow feel naturally that somehow I ought and would like to have children. I don't imagine that men around the age of twenty-five biologically suddenly feel the need to have children. The whole business of children and family and of wanting a rootedness is something very animal in women, though I know a lot of men want that kind of security too. I feel it terribly strongly, which annoys me no end, because the last thing I want to do at the moment is to have children. But, biologically, I definitely feel that my body is trying. It's rather like when you've drunk a lot of alcohol; the next day your body is crying for vitamin C. At the moment, I have the same feeling about children; my body is trying to tell me that now is the moment it feels like having children. And that is something which makes us very different from men. So, at an age when most men are just building their careers, you have this sudden problem that your instinct is wanting you to be a home-maker, yet your imagination and your agent, if you're an actress, tell you that this is the moment to launch yourself on your career and go for it. But I can't see my life in terms of thinking that to be a successful actress would mean as much to me as having a nice family.

If I had the choice between being as well known as Meryl Streep and having a terribly successful career, or having children and a husband, I'd choose a family any day. When you die, just to leave behind some reviews where people say this is terrific, isn't like leaving behind people who will remember you and talk about you, and who have learned from you and been touched by you. I don't think there's any comparison. It's odd in acting, because you spend your whole time pretending to be in love, or acting as a mother, or in difficult situations, and you're not actually living all that. If I go on acting, and when I get a little older play a mother, I'm sure I would feel a total cheat if I'd never been a mother and think, well, really, what's the point of pretending to be a mother for a film at the expense of really being one? Acting is a lovely career. It's an enormous privilege being an actress, indulging a hobby and being paid for it, but I don't think it's a substitute for having a family.

I don't think anybody takes the idea of abortion lightly. When people who are anti- talk to me about abortion, they always talk about it as if women are going to totally abuse the idea and have abortions as if they

742

were just hot dinners. It's a horrible thing, abortion, and nobody wants to have one. But I don't believe people should have children when they don't want them. I really think there is nothing more unfair on society, on the child or the mother, than an unwanted child. It's the same with euthanasia. I mean, you shouldn't go bumping off old people, but just from my own experience of my own family, when people are really ill and in pain, everybody who has been close to someone dying must have thought, oh, why is it that we only put down animals when they are at the stage when they just want to die and are in pain? Why not people? Human life is worth living, it's not worth simply existing. Please let someone put me down if I get like a vegetable. I've seen so many of my relations like that, pleading to be put down, and it's sad we can't do it.

Janet Suzman: I now understand the Christian myth, I understand BC and AD. I now see that I cannot even remember life properly before the child. Something too different happens to you. You are like a glove. You are exactly the same number of fingers and thumbs, but you are turned inside out; now you can see the seams. It's the same shape, but it's completely inside out, something of that ilk. That's a bad analogy, but it is a complete display of your innards, I suppose. Probably the most perfect relationship in the world is between the mother and child.

Lisa St Aubin de Terán: I married at sixteen, and at sixteen I didn't particularly want to have a child, but I discovered by chance that I was unable to have children, I was sterile. From the time I was told I was sterile, I felt a great craving to have a child. I was quite obsessed; I didn't want not to be able to have a child. Because I was told I couldn't have a child, I felt a sense of incompleteness in myself and I tremendously wanted to have a child. When my daughter was born, when I was nineteen, I felt a tremendous sense of satisfaction. Even though I was only nineteen, and she obviously cut back my own freedom, it was what I wanted very much. I think I wanted to have my second child because my mother had died, and I felt a rather peculiar sense that somebody must be born into the family.

A woman should be free to choose whether she has an abortion or not, but I don't think society as a whole is free just to say, well, women are free to have abortions. Contraceptives should be pushed a lot harder, because it's very traumatic for a woman to have an abortion and unnecessary when contraception is available. I am sure that society puts a lot of pressure on people not to have an abortion, and to experience motherhood and have a baby. I think it puts on too much pressure.

The idea of having a baby is not the whole story, because a baby is a baby, and then it grows up and it's still there. A lot of girls have babies because they literally want to have a baby, and then they've got the baby and find their life is ruined, not to mention the child's life, because it has a very resentful mother. The whole syndrome of child abuse, baby battering, is very sad and could be avoided a lot more if there wasn't this idea of how wonderful it is have a baby, and also how awful it is not to keep a baby. When a girl or a woman, for whatever reason, has a baby she doesn't want, society puts a lot of pressure on that woman to keep her baby, and given there are so many women who are sterile – and having been in this position myself where I thought I wanted to adopt and really was unable to because there are very few babies for adoption – it seems rather sad that women are bringing up children they don't want, making the child's life hell and often actually killing the child by the time it is three or four years old, literally beating it to death, when there are people who would love to take the baby. The pressure now is that adoption is Victorian and Dickensian and a terrible thing to do, so that most girls, having a baby they didn't really want, wouldn't dare to put it up for adoption. All this talk of freedom and independence and doing your own thing has actually resulted in a whole generation of unwanted children who are being brought up in appalling conditions unnecessarily.

Fiona Thyssen: I think it's very damaging to have an abortion; the regret and the sadness stay with you for ever. The moral dilemma certainly marks you. But despite all that, and despite the cost to yourself you inevitably have to pay, I think it is a woman's right to decide. I'm for abortion.

Martha Tiller: I don't think the ability to have children is particularly an advantage. Bearing the child and raising the child are of equal import-ance. Of course, that may be easy for me to say, because I have never given birth, but I am sure our child has been cared for equally with total love, devotion and importance, and that is the way it should be. I think he is a much better person at thirteen because he has had considerable exposure to his father, which many children don't enjoy. I also think that many children would be better off not being exposed to their mother so much. His father has shared totally in the responsibilities of raising the child: chauffeuring to school, seeing that he gets to the dentist, buying clothes, even to the extent of packing the school lunch. We both have done all of these things; it's not that one has had the total responsibility for the child.

744

Claire Tomalin: Throughout the whole of human history, century after century, women have had abortions, have been forced to have abortions, and have borne their children, without the help of men. I think the idea of abortion is abhorrent, but I also think it's better to have legal abortion, to have abortion properly organized, than to have illegal abortion, which is what, all over the world, you inevitably get if you don't have legal abortion. I don't think abortion is nice, it's heartbreaking to think of the loss of a child, but if you think of the millions of spontaneous abortions that happen all the time, I feel that argument was over a long time ago. Mary Kenny's squeaks and squalls about it do not impress me.

Lili Townsend: I had an abortion in the days when it was illegal, and it was a very unpleasant and disgusting ordeal. I had to go to another city, to the black part of the city, to the poor part of the city. I was in a very hostile environment. It was horrendous, and that was due to an absurd legal system. First of all, on a spiritual level, I believe that an abortion is simply saying to a spirit waiting to be born in this womb, I'm sorry it's not now, don't take this personally. This soul may not enter through this portal at this time. I don't believe there is any moral judgement about that, I think that is a practical necessity. Animals know the correct herbs to take to abort if things aren't correct. It should be an inalienable right. I totally support women's individual decisions, and I deeply resent the idea that any law could have jurisdiction over a woman's trust and confidence in herself.

Polly Toynbee: I'm amazed that women don't all have twenty children, women who can afford to. I think pregnancy is terrific. I think giving birth is terrible. A lot of rubbish is talked about that, you know: all this romantic stuff about how it's the most elevating experience in your life. The Natural Childbirth lobby has a lot to answer for, putting women through a lot of unnecessary pain. And I don't hold with any of that sort of mystical communion with the earth, mother earth stuff. But I've always liked being pregnant. It always makes me feel very good. And having a small baby is wonderful. It's all so exhausting and terrible, but it's amazing. And, however good a father there might be around, there is absolutely no doubt that that baby is totally and utterly the mother's. It's actually very hard to imagine what on earth a father's supposed to be. That's partly because I never really had a father, I've never known what a father is supposed to be. I've been very puzzled, and as I see my children growing up very fond of their father, I still wonder quite why. I mean, he doesn't do very much for them. He loves them, he's around, but I don't quite know how, from such a young age, very small babies, they latch on to the father as being a pretty good thing too. I can't work out for myself what that role ought to be, or why it's important.

Abortion is a terrible thing. When we were campaigning for the Abortion Act, we used to go on these demonstrations and people would shout, what do we want? Abortion! When do we want it? Now! That's obviously absurd. Abortion is one of the worst things that can happen to a woman, and it's deeply upsetting. Even if you think it doesn't matter, it upsets most women profoundly. Some it sends into deep depressions, but then unwanted pregnancies send many more women into life-long depressions.

I'm in a situation where to have another child would not be the end of the world, but if I was alone and unsupported with very little money and few friends and without a supportive environment in which to bring up a child, then, yes, without a doubt I would have an abortion. I know that most of the women who do are in that situation. People don't do it casually, they don't do it as a form of contraception without thinking about it, because it's a traumatic experience. But so is birth for a large number of people. We now have one and three quarter million children being brought up in single families – mostly deserted wives – and they have a terrible struggle and a lonely life without enough money. It's very hard going. I said I don't really know what fathers are supposed to be, but I know what husbands are supposed to be. They're supposed to be your companions and keep you going and take over when you can't stand it any longer. You know how you feel about your children: they are just the very best things on earth, and you have to be very polite about them in front of other people and pretend they're really the same as everybody else's; but if there is one other person on earth who agrees with you and says, yes, without doubt this is the cleverest and most beautiful child there has ever been, things seem a lot better. If you're the only one, that feeling seems oppressive, you're terrified of something happening to you, you're afraid for the child. The child is so vulnerable if nobody on earth loves it as much as you do. What happens if something happened to you? I think that unwanted children are worse than abortion by far.

Kathleen Turner: I have always thought I would have children because I come from a good family and I love the feeling of family we had. I would like that in my life again. When I met and married my husband, it was the first time I felt that I had a family again. When you leave home and you go off to university, it's still your family, but you don't have a home any more. When I married, I felt that had happened again, that I had a home and he is my family. But then there was no thought of children for a while. Now I feel I have the time, the money, the power, none of which really was available before. It seems to me now that there is no reason not to have children.

If you have no money, if you have no home, if you have no commitment or resources, I cannot imagine a worse crime than inflicting this upon a child. A child does not deserve to be the victim, to be given nothing, to be unprepared, unsolicited, unloved, not to have the financial resources to be protected. I don't know when a child becomes an individual. I would think a foetus becomes an individual when it is wanted, when it's planned, when it's loved. I loathe the idea of making a woman bear an unwanted child, since the child is the one who suffers so greatly. I find that morally offensive, as great an offence as the taking of a so-called life.

Jill Tweedie: I had children too early ever to have the biological urge. I had them at eighteen. So there wasn't time to feel anything. In fact, I felt very much that I had only just put my nose outside the door and somebody was pushing me back and saying, back into the house, you've got children now. It was very alarming. I've always wondered about women who don't have children, because I think, fancy having all that apparatus going on year after year, year after year, and you don't use it. It's the best thing in the world, the best drug I ever, ever had. Immediately after giving birth is the most wonderful feeling, and I don't know if every woman has it, but I know a lot do. It is a wonderful feeling. I expect there's a kind of elation for men, too. I expect actors have it after a great triumph. But it's certainly the greatest feeling of euphoria I ever had. And unfailing; it always works.

In the end, the decision on abortion has to be left to the woman. Mainly because she must be happy with the fact of the child being born. The child needs her too badly to risk any element of reluctance on her part. To add to that is my knowledge that the drive for most women is towards having their child, so if it is not there is a good reason.

Joan Vass: I once met a woman who said the thought of carrying a living thing inside her made her ill. She couldn't imagine having a child, whereas I had children joyfully. She found the idea of having children very repulsive, and was fulfilled without them.

Virginia Wade: I always wanted to have children. Even when you realize that you don't want to bring them up and don't want to change your lifestyle that much, it still enters your mind constantly. Probably, even when you've passed the child-bearing age, you wonder whether you shouldn't have done it. But I am also a great believer in not having any regrets. I really don't think you can do everything, and therefore you have to do what you want to do, and it probably chooses itself for you. You can debate for ever whether you want to have children, but if you really wanted to have them, you'd have them, presuming you could.

Tracy Ward: It is incredibly important to procreate in this world. What's the point of living it, working at it, loving it, but dying and leaving nothing? You've got to leave a child. I think everybody feels that. If give your whole life to your career, you will always have a regret that you didn't have children. It's very, very rare not to regret it. I know I would always regret it, therefore I have to compromise some time in my life, and that time is pretty near for me now.

If I became pregnant with Harry now, I would beg him for us to have the baby, but if he refused, I wouldn't have it on my own. But that's weak of me because I would love to have his baby more than anything in the world, so I should have it on my own. In the past, I have never had an abortion, and I've never had to go through that, but if I was with a man and didn't want his child or to get married to him, I would abort. You only live once, and if it's my decision, then I'm going to make the decision that suits me. I know it's killing a life, but there are so many lives on this earth and, you know, it's just tough. I'm sorry.

Marina Warner: Abortion is a very bad remedy for unwanted children and it's absolutely essential for society to concentrate its attention on adequate contraception. This means that men should be educated in it, too. What has happened disastrously since the pill is that boys' education in contraception has been forgotten. They were terribly careful when I was young. They knew it was a risk and took it seriously.

Heather Watts: To me, if you have an egg and it's fertilized, and you have an egg that never got the chance to be fertilized, I don't see the difference until it's grown into a living thing. I don't consider it murder to kill something that hasn't been born.

Abortion for a woman is incredibly important. I've had abortions. If I

748

had been forced to have a child when I was nineteen, I know I would not have raised the child well. I didn't have very much money, I had no mental stability. I was living in New York, trying to have the career I needed to have to support the child, and emotionally I had gone through a lot of grief. It was nightmarish. It was horrifying, emotionally. I don't regret it intellectually, but emotionally on some levels, yes. But it wasn't possible. I had to grow up myself before I had a child.

Arabella Weir: I don't see myself having children with a person. I see myself having children on my own. I may be wrong, but that's how I see it. I see myself as having a relationship with someone, but not living with them, if I have children. I think that is something that happens from living on your own. You become quite inflexible and not willing to change.

A woman must be free to decide on abortion herself, irrespective of the moral issues and irrespective of the father. Because the bottom line is, if a marriage breaks up, a woman is left. A woman's life completely changes when she has children; a man's doesn't. A man's life is enriched in a delicious way, but if a couple breaks up, the woman is still the one whose life is still irrevocably changed. She still has the baby, still has to go on holiday with the child, still has to get a baby-sitter if she wants to go out with another man, but a man then becomes a visiting father. That's why the decision to have an abortion is a woman's and a woman's only.

Felicity White: The actual creation of life, what it does to you as a woman, was a tremendous shock to me at first: that this could happen, that a perfect little life could be created without one really noticing in those nine months. And there it suddenly is. When they put my daughter on my chest and said, here is your daughter, and she just looked at me with this piercing stare, I thought, gosh, this is frightening, this is another individual. And there was so much in that look, ages past and ages into the future.

I would be very, very against seeing abortion abolished here. I think it is very necessary, I really do. My child was a surprise, wasn't a planned pregnancy. Everything I'd built looked as if it was going to crash, and I felt, at the time, I can't cope with this. And although I never seriously considered aborting the child, I would have been horrified if that opportunity hadn't been available. And almost the fact that it was available actually allowed me to make the decision, and to make the choice. It is absolutely vital that a woman has the choice. A lot of women, professionally and in all senses of the word, have come a cropper because they have conceived a child, and if they can't do what they wish to do, and have to go on and have the child, it can totally change their lives. It can totally ruin everything, and it stops the life force. There can be nothing worse than having a child and the responsibility of that child you didn't want. It's a very destructive thing for that woman.

Jeanette Winterson: I'm an adopted child, and it's worked out for me – and honestly, I'm glad I'm here, very glad. But if the option was either to abort a baby or have it adopted, I'd have to think very carefully. In a sense, you will never know whether you made the right decision, you just have to take a gamble. Obviously, it wouldn't happen to me unless I was raped, because I would choose to have a baby, I wouldn't just have one.

Anna Wintour: I think that a woman who sacrifices, as they put it here, her home and her kids to go out to work, is still considered not quite the thing. Frankly, if I had to stay at home and take care of my baby, divine as he is, I'd go nuts. There's really not much you can say to a six-month-old baby.

Enid Wistrich: It is a terrible thing to be forced to bear a child you don't want. On the other hand, it's a wonderful thing to bear a child you do want. So I am in favour of women having that choice to make about themselves and their lives.

Priscilla Woolworth: A woman is created to give life, and that's the one thing women have to succeed in. That is the most important thing, to be a wife and be a mother. You're going against Nature to say anything else. If a woman has not been a good mother, and if her children haven't been brought up well, she has failed in her life. If the children end up being good people, successful in their own ways, then she has been a good mother.

I have dreams of having babies. For a man, it must be different because it's not possible for them to have children. But for a woman, to think that she can have a child, bring life, have her own child – it's incredible. A day of suffering, for giving life, for giving a whole life to someone. It's the most beautiful thing.

6
Creativity

'How idiotic, let it be said in passing, is the pose adopted by certain writers and poets who claim that they write "for themselves and for God"! That's the worst of it! One doesn't write for the reader; one writes because it gives life meaning, because it is the only source of joy, because one has to write; but one longs for a reader (as many of them as possible), one needs him in the way an actor needs an auditorium; the way a prisoner longs for fresh air and space to move about'
– Stanisława Przybyszewska, quoted in Jadwiga Kosicka and Daniel Gerould, *A Life of Solitude* (1986)

'I am so used to living for Lyovochka and the children rather than for myself that I feel empty and uneasy if a day passes when I do not do something for them. I have started copying out Lyovochka's diaries again. How I regret now that perpetual emotional dependence on the man I love has killed all my other talents – my energy too: and I had such a lot of that once'
– Sofia Tolstoy, diary entry for 31 December 1890, in *The Diaries of Sofia Tolstoy* (1985)

'In the nineteenth century the men when they were writing did invent all kinds and a great number of men. The women on the other hand never could invent women, they always made the women be themselves seen splendidly or sadly or heroically or beautifully or despairingly or gently, but they never could make any other kind of woman'
– Gertrude Stein, *Everybody's Autobiography* (1937)

'I hope another year will really make me something of an Analyst. The more I study the more irresistible do I feel my genius for it to be. I do not believe that my father was (or ever could have been) such a poet as I shall be an Analyst & Metaphysician, for with me the two go together indissolubly'
– Ada, Countess of Lovelace (the daughter of Lord Byron and a nineteenth-century mathematician), quoted in Margaret Alik, *Hypatia's Heritage* (1986)

Maria Aitken: Writing is a more solitary activity maybe: something that could be done without any hope of anybody ever reading it and still in itself a satisfying activity. Music requires a listener and musicians, painting requires somebody to look at the painting, the painting needs to be hung, perhaps to be sold, but writing is a satisfying activity on its own; and I wonder whether women have gone off and been able to practise this craft secretly for a very long time. It's not been frowned upon, to be going off to write, whereas to go off and write a symphony would have been laughed at. And to paint, apart from niminy-piminy water-colours, was also not encouraged particularly. It's an old argument, but I think that, rather cold-bloodedly, most art flowered through commission, the most obvious form of encouragement; and I think that, for women, only writing was encouraged. Until all art is encouraged, it would be foolish to make judgement, and I don't really see the difference between producing a book and producing a painting in terms of creativity. Both of them are very like having a child in terms of attention and focus.

Dr Swee Chai Ang: Childbirth is very, very consuming. I've seen a lot of my friends who are extremely gifted, extremely talented, but once they get a baby, that ties them up because the baby demands constant attention. At least one or two years of your life are written off. And you can't think, when you've got a baby. The child cries every five minutes, it wants to be fed. You just cannot function. I think to be productive, even in political fields, or to write, you have to have time to think and reflect. For instance, if you have a telephone next to you which rings every twenty minutes, and you are trying to write a song or compose a piece of music, it is almost impossible. A baby is like a telephone that rings every twenty minutes. Except you can afford not to answer the telephone, but once a baby starts to cry, you have to take

753

the baby out, breastfeed, something like that, so it's very disruptive.

Artists do not function in the abstract, because artists write about beauty or life or society. Tolstoy couldn't have been a woman, because he couldn't have travelled as he did, he couldn't have met as many people, and therefore he couldn't have written what he wrote. Now, if a woman historically has no place except the kitchen and the house, she has nothing to write about except the kitchen, the house and her own position. A lot of us wouldn't be where we are without the books and knowledge, medical discovery and so forth, the world has given us. It's just that 50 per cent of the world has not contributed their creative power, and I think that 50 per cent of creative power should be unleashed and allowed to develop so it can come into the possession of all of us, and the world will be a much richer and more pleasant place. We all adore Picasso and Renoir, but what is terrible is how many women artists who had so much talent during that time never had a chance to develop and we have lost them all. But this is something of the past. The present belongs to this generation and the next, and probably we will see women Picassos, women Renoirs, who paint just as beautifully, and who can share with us their beauty, their creation, their talent.

Diana Athill: Painting and music are both curious, because certainly I really cannot be persuaded that most of the women painters I know are as good as the men, although there have been perfectly good professional women painters. And music, certainly, equally not. I think with the word they're pretty well equal, but not in other ways. Whether that is conditioning (it may well be) or whether it is something more profound I don't know. On a simpler level, women have done extraordinary work in things like embroidery – artefacts which were taken for granted – absolutely wonderful stuff. In music, women were very good performers, from way back. Half Mozart's pupils were young women, and a lot of them he spoke of rather approvingly, they were obviously pretty good. And there have been wonderful singers, wonderful pianists, but they have not become great composers, as far as I can see. It is a curious thing, and I have no explanation. I know that, although I adore listening to music and listen to a lot, it is Greek to me how you set about composing. I couldn't begin to do it, so perhaps it's the mathematical faculty that is more common in men than women. And there's never been a case of that sort of extraordinary possession that clearly does happen to the great composer. He's a slightly mad being: someone whose head is completely full of it. You've only got to read Beethoven's letters and notes. There's never been a woman like that. Maybe women's creative ability is so focused on birth and nurturing. I suppose words are more connected with ordinary life. Writing is talking, which is something one does anyway. A lot of women adore decoration, design, they've got visual sense. But musical composition seems to me a much more mysterious thing than any of the other arts.

Leila Badawi: Femininity itself – to be very feminine – can lead to a dissipation of creative energy in a social way. Women socially are much more creative and imaginative than men, and there is a certain limited amount of energy each human being is given. A vast number of women are enormously creative as hostesses, as mothers, as friends, and just don't have enough creative energies to spare for other aspects, as writers, painters or musicians or whatever. A woman sees her creativity not exactly as a hobby, but as a complementary feature of herself; as an enriching feature rather than as the central feature of her life. It enriches her as a human being and as a woman, but it quite often is not seen to be central to her personality, whereas many men with equal gifts would withdraw a lot of other energy and put it towards this one concrete use. There's another thing: madness is much less tolerated in women. Slight eccentricities are severely discouraged in women and in girls, whereas a boy is allowed much more freedom to develop a particular interest, even if it means that, in other areas, he's a bit crazy or socially weird. The pressures on a girl to be socially acceptable are in some respects crippling, or at least debilitating, exhausting.

Elisabeth Barillé: Creativity in women is equal to man's, but on the other hand I don't think genius has yet been manifested in a woman. You have to distinguish genius from creativity, where someone will paint a pretty picture, but it's not going to be a work of art; someone can write something, but it's not yet art. With creativity there is no problem, it's the same for men and women. But when you reach the level of masterpieces, then, for symphonies or a novel like *War and Peace*, a woman has a handicap which she might be able to overcome but hasn't done so yet. I sometimes ask myself which women novelists can compare their work to *War and Peace* or other great novels which deal with metaphysics or a whole fresco of a century or society in the way Balzac or Tolstoy did. There are very few indeed. You can have a genius for form, like Virginia Woolf, that you may compare with Joyce, and then you get to Colette, who created a world but did not create *the* world in literature, if I can put it like that. Among philosophers, there is Simone Weil, but she didn't create a philosophical system like Spinoza. If I were God, I could say why it has not happened up till now.

Josephine Barstow: The male mind is able to reach out further into the unknown somehow. The flashes of inspiration that take mankind huge strides forward come, always, it seems to me, from men. I can't think of one that's come from a woman. Because they have this capacity to think beyond. Women, because they are tied up with their own instincts more, are less free to see beyond where we've got to. If you think of Wagner, of *The Ring*, as things are at the moment, it does seem it would be an impossibility for a woman to conceive of that gigantic work or have that level of conviction in her own genius. It's interesting that Mozart was a man. Of all the composers, it seems to me that the one the closest to whatever we might call God, whatever that ultimate inspiration is, was Mozart. He was like an open vessel, but he was a man. It's interesting that it was a male person that received all that. I say 'received all that' in a kind of silly mystical way, but somehow it's so sublime, what his brain produced, that one thinks in terms of inspiration from beyond.

Rebecca Blake: Probably, in the past, it would have been more difficult for women to come to the forefront as artists. It's interesting that there was more than one very great female portraitist in the French court, for instance, but we don't hear a lot about them. It was more difficult for women to achieve those kind of goals in the past. I think a definite evolution has taken place. I think it was lack of opportunity and encouragement. It's very difficult for any oppressed individual to develop a career or be creative while they're fighting whatever it is that's oppressing them.

Suzanne Brøgger: It is true that there are more male than women artists, but this is not because of ability, because the ability to go from A to B is not necessarily the basis of art. That's not what art is about really. You can create just as much from the cyclical conception of time, you can create a female rhythm. In a way, housekeeping and keeping a home is a kind of creative activity, but, of course, it has no status whatsoever in society. The reason there have been more male artists is because the structures of society are such that women do the dirty work, so men have had more free time to be creative. But it is true, having said what women are good at – that particular kind of female creativity which is not linked with going from A to B – we may also point to their weakness, and the weakness is probably that so many women refrain from searching into the unknown. They feel comfortable with the repetitious, which can also be creative, but they maybe don't have the tendency to want to break away from the known patterns and really throw themselves into the agonies of the void.

Joan Juliet Buck: There's a fear that, if you give in to your creativity you'll be unattractive, that if you really follow your unconscious drive – and I don't mean sexual drives towards another person, but your unconscious drives to express something you are not even sure of – you'll become a kind of monster. And I think monsters are a much more attractive role for a man than for a woman.

Everybody is creative, but few people have talent. I've felt it in myself about writing when good moments have come on, but I've left the typewriter and gone out and gone shopping because it was too scary. The strength of the certainty was like speed, amphetamines, just going fast. And I was scared of that. So I did stuff to avoid it, bought clothes, went to parties, went to the hairdresser's. But if you don't avoid that thing, your life is changed. It isn't made worse, but it's changed. The actual hard work demanded in doing real work scares everybody. I've seen men who were scared by it. And I think it's been easier for women not to answer that call, or to change the subject or put impediments in their way. Norman Mailer once said the first great book written by a woman would be one written by a totally honest whore with a gift for writing.

Liz Calder: I imagine that the kind of atmosphere where genius will flower is one which is very supportive, where there are other people looking after your meals and your laundry and the rest of your life while you get on with it. And this has not been offered to women. You could argue that, if they would seize it, they would make it happen, if they had the great creative drive. But it's much harder to flower when you don't get all the right seedbed fertilizers.

Carmen Callil: Women were forced to play the piano for so many years I wonder if that's why they hated it. I would. If you read Jane Austen and so on, think about their lives: they got up in the morning, did their toilet, did the flowers, went for a walk, came back and all they had to do was sew, paint or play the piano. It must have been murderously boring.

Anna Carteret: Composers live their music totally, they breathe, sleep and eat their music. I don't know whether you'd call it madness, or just that their minds are extended into an area which is so removed from life. In a way, that's a sort of privilege and luxury which men are able to have access to because, even though they might father a child, they don't have the same psychological feeling of commitment to that child as a mother does. I know that's rather a contentious statement, but I really do believe that, if you've physically given birth to a child, you feel it is part of you in a way a man can never feel. I know my husband loves my children very much, but he doesn't have that absolutely animal instinct. A few years ago, I was burgled, and I discovered two men in my daughter's bedroom with a carving knife and I nearly killed this man. I became a she-wolf. I don't know where it came from, but hellfire came out of me as I screamed and chased them. They must have been astonished to see this woman come screaming at them, because I was naked. They were terrified, they both were. Men don't have this kind of primeval quality that women have.

Luciana Castellina: I remember being very impressed in Venice about seven or eight years ago by an exhibition of embroidery. Embroidery, of course, was done by women, because they couldn't do anything else. They couldn't paint, they couldn't sculpt, they couldn't make music. A woman was kept at home, and the only thing she could do was embroidery. Now, those embroideries were absolutely wonderful, but embroidery is not part of recognized art. Most of these wonderful things which women made have never been considered as true art; they were considered as minor art, handicrafts. And why? Just because they were done by women. And women had no access, or only a minority had access, to music or painting, and we know that if only a minority can have access to music or painting, then fewer succeed. In fact, now, if you look at literature, which is something women have access to, you find more and more women writers. It's one of the phenomena of our contemporary society that writers are more and more women and less men. But who establishes what real art is? Not women. Women have to conform to criteria of genius which are male. So it's a very long process. It will take thousands of years.

Felicity Waley-Cohen: It's normally rather easy to tell a woman painter; there is something feminine within a work and, I think I use this pejoratively, it does tend to be a weakness.

Shirley Conran: There are two reasons why women haven't fared as well in the arts. Somebody like Jane Austen really didn't have many responsibilities because she was not married, and therefore she had no children. I think it was Mrs Gaskell who said the secret of writing was to put a casserole on in the morning. There are very real problems about how you get the time to write. In order to finish *Superwoman*, I had to go away. I went away to a little boarding house in Earl's Court and filled the deep-freeze with all the correct things and did all the organizing for the family, and before the first evening was up, there was howling, shrieking, problems. When I got back, it was all fine, they just didn't want me to go away. Men are very good at sabotaging women without women realizing it. They're very clever at it. Men like to have all the attention of a woman and do not like a woman's attention being distracted for any other reason, even if it is to make money. Basically, a man likes to have a woman's entire attention to himself, whether the man is forty or four. Any sort of creation, speaking as a writer, calls for an enormous effort of concentration that takes an enormous amount of time – with me it takes six months. I don't know how long it takes to write a symphony, but I know that composers have the same post-natal depression and exhaustion that people have when they first start writing books. And I just don't think women have the time for it. Mind you, I think that is a convenient excuse as well.

Béatrice Dalle: Men are creative because they waste less time on stupid things. Women spend their time bellyaching, wondering whether they are going to find the rent at the end of the month; the blokes go off and use their time for dreaming and creating things.

Régine Deforges: I don't see any biological or intellectual reason why there should not be equal creativity, though we have no composers and few painters who are women. But I feel instinctively that the act of creating is a virile and therefore a sexual thing in a work of art; and it will be obvious. In paintings by Rembrandt and others, there is a power which women do not have. A woman will express herself differently.

I think that what hinders or puts the brakes on creativity in a woman is the fact that she internalizes everything. When I wrote my trilogy *La Bicyclette bleue*, I think part of its success was that I lived it, it became a part of me, I cried, wept, was sick; awful for those around me, but through a sort of masochism which I cannot explain, I made it all come out, that violence.

Anne Dickson: If you, in your family, grow up to believe that your only purpose and sole identity is in being a mother, then it is into that you put all your creative energy. On top of that, to be creative – whether it's writing or painting, or following some kind of career – you've to make or be allowed a life of your own. Now, a lot of women are neither

759

financially nor emotionally in a position to do that. They don't have any lives of their own. I think they collude with that. And there's an enormous amount of very frustrated creativity in an awful lot of women. I'm not talking about the people who will excel and be recognized. There are a lot of women who would love to write, because it's about self-expression. That's what creativity is ultimately about. And if you don't believe it's there, if you believe that the only way you can express yourself is through your children and your husband, then that's what you do. People ask: what are you proud of in your life? I am proud of my children. And that is it. I am proud of that and that is how you get society's approval. And there are countless examples of women who haven't got any approval at all by being creative. OK, you may have a basically unfavourable personality, but it is difficult for women to focus and pursue a single object, and that is a feminine thing as opposed to a masculine thing. Men, on the whole, find it much easier to be single-minded and go after what they want. Women tend to look first at other possibilities, and in doing so lose out on focus, on intensity and opportunity. They think first, and that is largely conditioning.

Maureen Duffy: Sappho was a genius, an acknowledged genius of the whole world. As long as there is one, then genius cannot be biologically defined. She was certainly considered a genius by her contemporaries, and by later Greek civilization. There aren't all that many geniuses, Shakespeare, Dante, Sappho, Homer, Plato – as a philosopher, he's in a slightly different field – and a handful of agreed musical geniuses. A lot of people reach a top rank, but that we would nevertheless still argue about. I would say Purcell was a genius; others might say he was just a sort of overrated theatre writer. I mean, there is a great deal of the element of historical and personal taste involved in these things. Some people say Virginia Woolf was a genius, others say her work is miniaturist and second-rate. I see no reason why we shouldn't have more women geniuses now women are more liberated. In the visual arts, we have had some outstanding women in this century, and indeed in this country: for instance, Hepworth and Frink in a field which has traditionally been a masculine field and actually requires quite a bit of physical strength – sculpture. Now, once again, it becomes a matter of personal taste. We may or we may not care for their work. But we may or may not care for the work of Henry Moore or Epstein. They are nevertheless all of the top rank.

It is enough to look at Western society and its development to see that, for a woman to become a composer, has almost been impossible. The world of professional music has been entirely dominated by men.

What woman could have taken the job of *Kapellmeister* to become a Bach, or a Mozart, or a Purcell? What woman could have travelled by herself and lived alone in Vienna while going to concert halls and theatres and conducting all-male orchestras? It just was not socially possible. That's also the reason why women, until now, have done far less in the theatre since the seventeenth century. Since the theatre became a wicked place, women have not been able to use it and therefore the number of women dramatists, which was growing in the late seventeenth century, collapsed completely. The same is also true of artists. There's a painting by either Reynolds or Gainsborough to celebrate the opening of the Royal Academy, which shows all the academicians at a life class, and the model is a male nude. All the academicians are present but two, who are present only as their portraits hanging on the wall, and they are the two women academicians. They could not attend a life class. And certainly not with a male nude. They cannot even be in the commemorative painting. Now that is the degree of social difficulty that women have suffered under, and that is what has made it almost impossible for them, until the twentieth century, to become either visual artists or composers, or indeed playwrights. It is largely a romantic fallacy that genius is always recognized. I think the great periods of an art form are when it is practised by a whole mass of people, many of whom will never get to the top. If you take, for instance, the great periods of English theatre, there were hundreds of plays written and performed that have vanished from us, because they were trash. But out of that enormous ferment, like an iceberg, we got these tremendous peaks of Shakespeare, and Webster, and Marlowe and so on. The same thing happens with the British novel. In the nineteenth century, there were floods and floods of novels which have utterly vanished, and out of this great flood came the peaks. And because the novel is the form it is, it requires no co-operation and it can be exercised privately in the home, so women were able to take their part in it.

Victoria Glendinning: In my heart, I think women are quite satisfied with the world and what is in it. The fact that there have been no women philosophers or composers has nothing to do with women not being capable of abstract thought or one of those clichés. It's more to do with men being dissatisfied with the world as it is. I think men invent religions more than women do, and men want to transcend life as it is. I cannot think why, because life as it is is marvellous and quite heightened enough for anybody, but the wonderful thing about men not being satisfied with life is that it gives them this stellar aspiration which leads to music, and probably to physics and higher mathematics, which women don't seem to need in the same way. I don't mean that women don't listen to Mozart and Beethoven in exactly the same way and are grateful for it, but when a woman listens to it, it is reflecting what she feels about the real world. I think women are more satisfied with the material God gave. The whole thing seems so unbelievably fruitful that it blocks her from some sort of dissatisfied aspiration that makes these men write music and do mathematics.

Felicity Green: Mrs Bach, Mrs Wordsworth, Mrs Shakespeare, were running support systems for their husbands. Women have been the support cast of the world for the past 5,000 years.

It always comes back to the role women play in society. The Brontës, Mary Shelley Wollstonecraft, all of them were from middle-class families. There were no female Arnold Weskers or children of the streets coming up, simply because working-class women were drudges. They had a baby every ten months or a year, they died at thirty-two. It's not surprising that they didn't emerge into the artistic world. It is very difficult to be artistic when you have seven screaming children and all you can afford is a nip of gin.

Elsa Gress: So what, if there are more male geniuses than female ones? Men are the hybrid sex, and as such there are more extremes. There may be a handful more male geniuses, but there are three times as many male imbeciles as female ones. As for the normal wide range of faculties, the distribution is fair enough.

Flora Groult: A creator is sexless. One can't say, for instance, that a woman writes like a woman or a man writes like a man, or paints like a woman or paints like a man. I always find that extremely limited as a view. Does a poet have a sex? No. Great art is not determined by the party of the human race to which you belong.

Mira Hamermesh: Women can give birth to life, men can't, hence the stimulation and challenge. But creative people are a small minority. The majority of humanity are contented, don't need anything further. So if the frustration of not giving birth was a kind of inbuilt discontent, this would be universal, whereas it is only a rare individual that is uplifted to the heights of exceptional creativity. The rest: they plough, they feed families. All that prevents a future woman Beethoven is social conditioning. I, as a film director, will still go home and cook a meal and make sure my family are looked after, whereas my colleague, same age, same talent, comes home and is looked after by his wife, or in the office by his secretary. All male talent is serviced by female energies. There is no reverse transaction.

Creativity brings us back to the question of the gender of the muse. I've written an outline called *The Artist and the Naked Muse*. My father is my model, so my muse would be male, but the male is likely to rape me in the street, or if I am an elderly lady, knock me down and rob me of my purse. My male friend's muse is female, not likely to knock him down; she cooks him a meal, and when he is inspired, he can write poetry about the muse, paint the muse. Each art form has a muse. They are all females. Now, if the psychology of females is that they are in the service of male talent, how can I function? All the male muses I meet will either want to fuck me, or, if they want to punish me, say, you're too old, we don't want to screw you any more, you are no longer appetizing; they won't come and type my manuscript, they will not do my research, they will not go and negotiate for me. People have ignored this particular aspect. Reverse the roles, bring up a generation where men will be the muses to the talented females, when he will say, yes, darling, you are more talented than me, I'll look after the babies, I'll have the pleasure of basking in your talent and glory. But while our children are socialized that the male has the role he has, a woman like me wouldn't know how to break the cycle. The first attack of creativity, when I knew I was inspired, when I knew I was somewhere else, when I didn't hear people, when I could have walked through walls, was when I started menstruation. Every time I menstruate, I am charged. When I gave birth to my son, my creativity was recharged at the same time. I try to write about it, but it is so difficult and complex because it is outside what other women have said. I haven't yet managed even to talk to women about it.

Romaine Hart: You're either artistic and creative or you're not, as a person. I don't think there are any sexual limits to that, unless from education and the way you've been pushed. In the past, women haven't been allowed to be educated. There are people writing the history of women artists now that have never been mentioned before, and they are finding them, but still it was terribly hard, they were under-privileged. They weren't able to do that sort of thing. It's like saying all Jews are moneylenders – it's because they weren't able to do anything else. It's the same with women. They didn't get the chance. They certainly had the ability.

763

Bettina von Hase: Giving life and creating a family, creation within a completely different sense, blurs, or possibly diverts women from other areas. But I also think women should stop thinking all the time that they are being discriminated against. They have to come forward and come out, too, they have to start being more inquisitive about things. It works both ways. Women in history have been less creative, but it could very much be that the creativity of man was often assisted or helped, or women were instrumental in it. In fact, it has been so, it has been proven. But among women there's very often a certain reluctance to actually declare themselves, to come out and do something.

Kitty Hawks: Men are not able to have children. I've never had one, but I know what the impulse is, and I know from a lot of creative women with whom I have spoken at length that, once they have a child, there is a release of creativity. A man doesn't have that, so maybe the thing that drives him to be creative is stronger.

Dr Leah Hertz: The reason we don't have great women artists, or not as many as men, is basically because men have always been in the situation where they can dedicate themselves to art. They can say, the women, the children and everyone can wait, I am now doing my thing. The minute you have women who are able to say, I'm doing my tapestry, I'm doing my politics, I'm doing my writing, and all of you can go jump in the lake, you will have very creative women, so it's only a matter of being in a position to do it.

Min Hogg: If you are really, really a genius and great at it, you do in fact make your nearest and dearest suffer dreadfully for your talent and art. You do not consider them. What you're doing comes above God himself. Women find that very difficult. There is a sort of innate compassion in women which will say, the baby's crying, I'll put the paintbrush down. Or, they cannot actually leave and go away and be as selfish as a man can, even now. They can't, and they do consider other people, and I think men don't. Very often a man is able to go through life without really considering anybody because his mother didn't tell him to.

History is littered with the unhappy spouses of great men. There aren't a lot of them that say their lives were a bowl of cherries – they were absolutely ignored or worse, given the most terrible time while the creative process was going on inside the man. She's the battering ram

764

and he just sailed through. He may be having a difficult time, too, but she is the one who gets it in the neck when creativity is booming inside him. And she has to accept that they have to do what he says, they've got to live here, do that, he'll disappear, have mistresses, *blah*, *blah*, *blah*. Women find it much harder to bring themselves to do that. Indeed, I don't think women can bring themselves to, they're forever considering somebody else at the expense of their own potential talent. It will take a hell of a long time for women to be as selfish as that – by not having a husband perhaps. There are more and more women who don't want husbands. Possibly that would produce great talents within the arts or the sciences.

Marie-Hélène du Chastel de la Howarderie: A lot of women who are painters, musicians – people like my mother – once they've had a first child, they stop. That's been noticed time and time again.

Caroline Huppert: In France since the seventeenth century, men have had the major part in artistic creativity, but it is also true that women have lived since then in a stifling atmosphere and it has been more difficult for a woman to express herself. Last year I read the biography of Mme Vigée Lebrun, the official artist of Marie Antoinette, and she painted wonderful pictures which are now at Versailles and the Louvre, a famous artist of her day, and when you compare her paintings with others of the period, they are the equal of anything. Posterity wasn't so kind to her, perhaps in part because she was a woman; history is not on the whole kind to women, though women artists existed. She signed her paintings with her name, not Mme, she tried not to make the public aware that she was a woman. But when you look at her paintings, you know that they are by a woman, they are very feminine. Take the case of Mozart's sister, she was very gifted too, but the father concentrated on his son. Why did he differentiate? She could have gone far in music, but he was more interested in his son. It's a general phenomenon that is so heavy with significance that it is probably one of the reasons why there are few famous women artists.

There is certainly an affinity with maternity on one side and creativity on the other. I know women, me among them, who have a tendency to denigrate the pleasure of having children to begin with, but it is a trap because when the child is there, you have to take care of it. It gives you enormous pleasure and it occupies more and more an important place in your life. You worry about it growing up, and your mind has less time to wander.

765

Angela Huth: I think men do have a peculiarly deep madness when they are mad. When women are mad, it's shriller. There is a kind of magnitude on all levels about men, I think. I suppose it has to be said that women's creativity comes on a slightly smaller scale. And why not? It's nice that the human race has one lot of creatures looking at the huge issues and another lot looking through a slightly smaller pair of binoculars. Jane Austen was a genius, but she was writing about a really tiny world. Women are extraordinarily good on detail, they have this very detailed eye, whereas men have the grand sweep. Occasionally you get both. Chaucer has both the grand sweep and this extraordinary tapestry-like detail. Shakespeare, of course, had it but he is quite exceptional. Spenser, I suppose, had it. But, on the whole, women are not very good at combining the grand sweep with the tiny detail. I don't think there are any women Dostoyevskys either. Possibly, when the Lord was thinking up what to do with these men and women, he assigned us our own things to do to help the other side, to enlighten the other side. I don't see why we should sit around longing for wonderful women composers if we have got plenty of men. It doesn't matter, as long as somebody does it. The feminists don't agree at all, but I am not a feminist.

Angela Janklow: I would say men and women are equally creative. History doesn't bear this out because of suppression. When I say great women, only ten come to mind. When I say great men, thousands come to mind, and that is the fault of history, not the fault of women. It's because men have been educated, men have been sent round the world, shipped off to the army at eighteen, sent to sea where the most ruthless elements attack you, where you have to learn to deal with people, when you are removed from society. My favourite author is Joseph Conrad, whom many have accused of being a misogynist. I don't like to think of him that way. He was in a ship, he was sent out with men. How was he supposed to be able to understand women in a way that men do now who have been living with women on a daily basis, dealing with them in the office, dealing with them in bureaucratic affairs, as well as love affairs? But in 1900, people stayed put or they went to sea – and only the men went to sea. Great women – you think of Cleopatra, Joan of Arc – but these are like strange women that we don't really have a grasp on. They were perceived as complete anomalies, totally eccentric and weirdos. People think Cleopatra was a slut. Big deal – she had two love affairs. She is not a slut. Marilyn Monroe had twelve abortions. I don't consider her a slut either.

Rana Kabbani: Women, like other minorities or other groups that haven't had the chance to express themselves, are now coming into their own. And probably from now on we will see much more productivity from women than we have in the past. I don't think the urge to create life goes against the urge to create art. Antonia Fraser has produced six children but she still has produced very wonderful historical books as well.

Caroline Kellett: I have a theory about women and art which is why I think that, through the ages, the majority of artists, musicians, painters and writers have been men. It is that women leave something of themselves behind, they have the power to create, because, by giving birth, something is left behind them. Obviously men are part of the cycle, but for them death is perhaps that much more frightening, mysterious and final. They don't actually leave a part of themselves behind that they really constructed, or was a part of them, in the same way that a woman does going through pregnancy. All her life, she knows she is in a position to leave something of herself behind in a very much more substantial form. Art is perhaps a more masculine prerogative or domain, the desire to create a counter-balance to the female who can actually reproduce. And perhaps that's why greater art has been achieved by men.

Irma Kurtz: The evidence in front of my eyes, in spite of the apologists, is that some women have been very good, just good enough to make me wonder why one of them hasn't been transcendent. There's been a Beethoven, there's been a Bach, there's been a Mozart, there's been a Shakespeare, there's been a Milton, if you like that kind of thing. Why hasn't one woman reached that level? You cannot say it is the oppression of men; one would have slipped by, one woman genius. Look what Shakespeare overcame to become Shakespeare. These people were born into poverty, obscurity. Men, they struggled out of it and became geniuses in their field. Why not one woman? Lots of them were good, but I can't think of one on that level. So there is a difference in our genius. This isn't to say that we are not enormously gifted in our own way. But there is a difference, and we have got to face it. It's not an insult, it's not a bad thing, it's a fact. And until we look at it, we are not going to understand. There is some restriction on the female imagination, it seems to me. There is a ceiling on it. Women write very good novels, as we know, and there are some good poets, but there's not a transcendent one. I have theories about it that make me very unpopular. I think woman's imagination is fractured. It has to do with

767

child-bearing, or the potential to bear children. It has to do with the time and attention we give to finding a mate. It has to do with something else I have seen in women: the nesting instinct. I've seen women without children creating a nest with such an obsessive energy and attention to detail in their surroundings, as though they are making a beautiful palace. This is all distracting from greater issues, I think.

Sara Leighton: Chopin was right when he said that all creative energy is sexual. He was writing a letter and he said something like: and when I think, my darling, of how many sonatas I have poured into you. That's why I don't think there have been great women painters or recognized painters, because women pour that sexual energy into their husbands, their children; they dilute it all. I've spent about six celibate years, and they were the most creative in my life. It was when I came back from the Middle East, and they were the most creative years because I was determined to wait for the right man. I thought, I'm not going to waste my time, particularly with my children; I felt it was wrong to take lovers. I didn't want my children to get used to a lot of uncles, which would have been too easy. So I decided nothing until the right man walked in through the door, and when he did, it all changed. Until then, I did more work and better work than at any other time in my life.

Mary McFadden: The reason why there have been no great women artists is that women had to stay at home and sew and take care of the dishes. They couldn't concentrate eighteen hours a day on their canvases. That's the crux of the whole thing.

For the most part, I think men can design very well for women. They are masters of their craft when it comes to women's design, and we are slowly becoming masters of our craft, too. I think it will all be pretty even. It's a matter of who has the most talent. There are several American designers who design for men, and very successfully. I've been doing it for ten years. Jane Barnes has several Coty awards for doing it. She's very successful. It's just a matter of who has the most talent. It doesn't make any difference whether you're a man or a woman. It's who's got the talent.

Margaret Matheson: Much art is the result of an unstable mind, this is clearly my view, but I firmly think that women are just as creative as men and that the reason why there are fewer women painters, fewer women writers and fewer of everything is strictly to do with who has

768

done what traditionally, and the fact that, even now, women writers in the theatre are less readily performed than men. I hate saying all this, because I desperately don't want to believe it is so, but it is so. Most TV producers and executives are men, most artistic directors of theatres are men, and I don't doubt, for one moment, that they favour male writing. But I do think that the more that women are brought up or bring themselves up with the confidence, not even to bother with the debate, not to question it, just knowing that if they're writers or painters, then they are writers or painters, the better it will be.

Sonia Melchett: I have to say that men are possibly more creative than women. Most of the great artists have been men. There are always exceptions to the rule, but the contributions women make to the artistic developments of the world are not as creative. I think they are complementary to men. They have other qualities, possibly greater than men's, but I don't think creativity is one. Men are more poetic, more creative. Women are much more practical, more down to earth, because it is the way their bodies are made. They have to be, they have to cope with running so many different facets of life. Men usually can throw themselves much more into their work and leave the less creative side of life to be dealt with by somebody else, whereas women have to divide their lives into so many compartments and don't have so much time for the creative side. They are creative – but they are not quite so creative as men.

Kate Millett: Things were so arranged that women had babies instead of making symphonies. There are always enough women around who haven't got a baby this month who would have time to make a symphony if it was OK to make symphonies. But men said to us, you can't make symphonies, but you can make babies, and wow, that's wonderful. It is wonderful. To make a life is wonderful, absolutely marvellous. But it is also marvellous to make symphonies, and if you make lives because you have no other option, you are just a breeder and a slave. And most of history, what other option did we have? You can even poison maternity with this system. Just as you can poison sex with rape. You can ruin anything through invading it with power relationships. The history of men and women is a very sad disgrace.

Kitty O'Hagan: There's a dreadful sanity about women, a dreadful reality, a dreadful pulling down. It's hard. They're less excessive, full stop. And really great art comes out of terrific excess.

A woman's strength is focused, is narrower, one instrument not an orchestra. I feel it would be very difficult for her to create something, especially in the music world, because that's to do with outside your experience. It's very big. A woman, I would feel, would want something finer. Eventually you will see women grand masters of chess and you will see serious women composers, great women artists. But it will take a long time, because they are all very brave things to do.

Fifi Oscard: I think men have greater creative ability. I think women tend to have smaller talents and smaller areas in which to work. Generally, women see the world in specific and men see the world in gross, so the impractical, the visionary, the spiritual, the poet, all of these, tend to be more men than women, and from that comes the creative. I think the left side of the brain is freer in the man than in the woman. It may be bred in us because we have spent so much time organizing children, houses and families over the years, but breadth of vision and depth of creativity are provinces where the men have the advantage.

Diana Parker: One would need a great deal of self-confidence and perhaps self-importance to be prepared to envisage the prospect of a masterwork involving, let's say, a symphony orchestra. Probably it stems from conditioning, the fact that women really have been taught to have modest expectations. They've been taught that modesty is a feminine virtue. Women, historically, have really had very little choice about their creativity. They create perhaps the most important thing, life itself, but throughout the ages women haven't really had very much choice about that. They've become pregnant repeatedly throughout their adult lives, and quite frankly, if you're constantly either in a state of pregnancy or a state of post-natal exhaustion and looking after children all the time, there isn't a great deal of scope to be composing a major orchestral work and, at the same time, making sure you have your husband's supper ready.

Sarah Fox-Pitt: All people who are motivated towards being creative aren't equally creative. Some people are more creative than others. It's easier than it was twenty years ago, and the opportunity is there if a woman is prepared to make the sacrifices which involve sacrificing her family to a certain extent. But there's no question about it, I know the children of certain female artists who have suffered tremendously. I don't know that it's necessarily because the artist was female rather than male, but those children came second to the art.

770

I do not think of art being produced by men or women – I think of artists quite naturally as creators. For example, if you take the work of Henry Moore and Barbara Hepworth, how do you decide that the application of their art is different because one is male and the other female? In the early stages of their careers, they both drew the human form exquisitely, that was the tradition of the teaching of the day; they both explored the interest in ethnographic arts and the simplification of the human form, they both moved on to explore the interest of truth to materials and creating an abstract form out of the material they were carving. Then, as time went on, it was Barbara Hepworth whose work developed into the most extreme forms of abstraction imbued in nature, and it was Henry Moore who developed the female figure, the idea of family pairs and groups. There is no doubt about it, Barbara Hepworth had to overcome many prejudices against the female artist at that time between the wars. The feeling of intense competition to maintain her status at the forefront of the modern movement was always with her. There is a mask that sometimes shrouds her art. By looking at the work of those two artists, it is obvious that Henry Moore had the psychological freedom of the long-standing tradition of the male artist portraying the female figure. Although Barbara Hepworth had an equal technical ability, I don't think she had the same psychological freedom and chose, instead, to base her expression largely on concepts of natural phenomena. It may seem strange that such forces could come into play when one considers that they exhibited a certain restrained freedom in their enjoyment of the summer beaches by participating in naked bathing parties.

Charlotte Rampling: In terms of artistic creation, or even in business, men go further, deeper into the desire to create than women, because each time man creates it's as if he is trying to get as deep as he can to feel the pain of birth. He has to give birth, but he can't give birth, so he gives birth to his creation, which is either his painting, his music, his books or his business. Men have a biological desire, in a sense, to create as a woman creates, but they can't. The thing about women, too, is that they are given this gift of birth – most of them, God willing. A man is not given that kind of prize. He is dependent on women, he needs that companionship of women to make him feel those mysteries he will never feel.

Mirella Ricciardi: It's quite obvious that, in the past, even in the present, men have created many more extraordinary things than women ever have, but is that because they are more creative, or because the

771

poor woman has been so subject to other things that her creativity has not been allowed to develop? Since her creativity is allowed to develop because she is becoming somebody in her own right, then maybe in the next hundred years we are going to see female Beethovens and Picassos. I must say, I have a lot of wonderfully creative women friends, but when I compare them to my creative men friends, there are double the amount of creative men. I am sure that, because of the biological make-up of a woman, her energies go instinctively into the procreation process, which the man doesn't have, so, in him, that energy is available for something else. If he has any talent, that energy, instead of going to producing the child or keeping the home going, goes into his head and creates his genius. Women are very good with their hands, but they don't have any ideas. I haven't yet seen a great movie made by women. The great women movie directors, what have they done compared to the great movies made by men? Name me one.

Hélène Rochas: There are gifted women, good artists and writers, particularly Anglo-Saxon women writers, but there isn't the same strength or genius. The term *genius* doesn't exist for women. In fact, you never talk of a women as being a genius, so it's something lacking in us. We hear the words *talent* and *gifts*, but that's all. What women achieve in creative work is through application and instinct, but not that upper level of genius. It must be genetic, otherwise you couldn't explain it.

Anita Roddick: There is some extraordinary reaction to giving birth. The actual act of giving birth is so sublimely spiritual, and often has no boundaries, no parameters. When I was living in Paris, in the environment of artists, I used to think that men had this massive need to create, to find an alternative to giving birth. There is something about writing or painting that is the search for the birth experience which women have.

Kimberly Du Ross: I had a show in May, and there were three different people whose opinions I consider highly. One came up to me and said, you can really tell this work was done by a woman. The other one came up and said, you know, the amazing thing about your work is that you can't tell whether it was done by a woman or a man. And the third said, your work looks like it was done by a man, that's what's so amazing about it.

Joan Ruddock: Women's role historically in nurturing children and providing a home environment has, of course, been absolutely central to the maintenance of the species. Whether it's better to produce a symphony or raise the next generation is a debate one can't hold.

Eve Ruggieri: I think that in specifically female biology there is something less developed, because I cannot explain to myself why, since the beginning of time, there haven't been great sculptors, artists and composers and even writers who are women as compared to men. The percentage is miserably tiny, and the works of those few sculptors and so on are so modest compared to their male equivalents that you have to wonder whether there is a genetic difference. Perhaps women are not made to be creative, apart from that prodigious creativity of having children. I have asked myself that question often. In the 1960s, feminists would say that there is no reason why there should not be a female Mozart, but it seemed to me a specious argument. There have been so many male artists who have also been put down, but they still created works of art. In music, in particular, there have been no great women composers. People quote contemporary music at you, but even so, it's like a sapling in a huge, huge forest, and it's rather worrying.

Altaf Al-Sabah: In the past, women were creative in that they were very much in charge of creating the atmosphere for the creative men to excel.

Ghida Salaam: The gift of creation has been given to a woman; and it is the woman who creates the man who creates.

Sylvia Scafardi: It doesn't prove anything that, historically, men have been greater in the arts. You might as well say, do you think the educated classes are more productive than the working classes? Gray, in his country churchyard, answered that: how many mute inglorious Miltons, how many Cromwells, guiltless of their country's blood because they just didn't have the opportunities? They were harnessed to the earth and had to toil from childhood. In the same way, women, going further and further back, didn't have the opportunity.

Gwen John was a bigger artist than her brother, Augustus, who made all the noise and took all the acclaim. And when it comes to writing, I'm perfectly certain that women will be, are, as able and sensitive as great men writers. It's just a question of priorities and what they want to do.

Of course, in the genius, the creative ability is immensely strong, as in a Picasso, for instance, or even in Tolstoy. I don't think anything can stop it. But I think women will also climb to those heights. I don't see why not.

Jenny Seagrove: Creativity is a subjective thing. It comes and goes in both sexes, and it's to do with whether you're with people or in circumstances that make you think and want to express that, and whether you have the need. I think, in a way, that creativity comes out of a lack of something in your past which makes you want to express some pain which may come out in a nice way. Women didn't succeed in the arts before because of the whole thing of religion and the Church and what was done and not done. A woman couldn't go on the stage, she was considered a whore – all that sort of thing.

Hanan Al-Shaykh: A man can say, I'm a poet – and that's it. Women who have children and no help – they have to do everything on their own. A female writer – I forget her name – said one day that she could have produced more if she had not had plumbing difficulties. Because every day, when she used to sit and want to write, her bathroom or her kitchen sink overflowed and she had to chase the plumbers.

Rosemary Anne Sisson: If I had any kind of a musical ear, I can imagine my absolutely loving to compose a symphony, and I can't think why women don't. That is fascinating. It must be physiological; we don't hear as truly, obviously. What I find absolutely exhausting in writing, particularly with a novel, a complicated novel, is holding the whole thing, as if my hands weren't big enough. To hold this great big work, to keep all the characters and hold the whole thing together, that's the thing that exhausts me. Now, maybe, to write a symphony you have to have a great range of mind, and a woman's mind, I suspect, does tend to go for detail more than men. For men, it's the great sweep of a symphony.

Lady Anne Somerset: The fact that one week in every four women feel very ill obviously can't have been a great help to their creativity.

Pamela Stephenson: There's no doubt in my mind that sexuality is linked to creativity. So if you're in a situation where your sexual drive is stronger – and this applies to men and women (and they go through different stages of their life or different stages of a relationship in their life) – they will have a different kind of creative drive, a different power, a different direction in their creative drive, and it's sublimated in a different manner.

The act of creating life is an utterly selfless thing, and is therefore not tainted with any sense of taking. My greatest experience of creative work is actually to be on stage in front of an audience, really enjoying what I was doing: all those minds out there and mine just being joyful.

Andrea von Stumm: Women are less creative. Their act of creation is something more earthy. They are more subtle beings, and to be a real artist you have to be a little bit unstable and a little bit tormented. Quite a lot of irrationality comes into creation. Women, because they are perhaps more related to the earth and to material things, are too stable to develop this irrational instinctiveness.

Christine Sutherland: Women are meant to create, but to create other human beings, not works of art.

There are comparatively few great women painters. I once asked Kokoshka, whom I knew quite well, about that, and he said women didn't think in images, they think through their feelings.

Fiona Thyssen: Before I had the children, I used to play the piano a lot, paint a lot, write a lot, and then, when I had the children, it just wasn't there suddenly. There wasn't, in my case, the question of not having the time, because time is something the rich always have; you have the nannies and people to do all the work. It just wasn't there. I don't know if we don't actually have the same ability to be creative, or the ability is there but women choose to use their creative ability in a different way from men.

Claire Tomalin: So few members of the human race are creative at all, but obviously more men than women. You go back to Virginia Woolf and all the reasons there were in the past for women not to do things. Women were crushed by so many burdens, both physical and social, but I think that it has to be conceded that isn't the whole answer. Certainly none of the great composers were women. Clara Schumann composed, for instance, but not very well. But she did have seven babies and a mad husband. I think you have to be quite ruthless to be a composer, writer, painter; you have to really put aside other things, and put them aside from your heart and mind. It is more difficult for a woman to do that. We don't have the ruthlessness and the concentration.

Jill Tweedie: Fine arts, painting, is male, and handicraft is female and has a very low image. Yet, when you think of the beauty women have produced, co-operatively and anonymously, I can't see that it is less. Obviously, in a male world, things that require a strength will be valued more than things that require a delicacy. If women suffer from anything, it is from the early realization, which you have to fight, to some extent, that you can do one thing always. You don't have to ask why you are a woman, or what you are there for. It's taken for granted what you are there for: you carry on the race, you have children. How are men to assert what a man is? That is an eternal question. Art is shaping chaos, and men have a more chaotic element in their growth and psychology perhaps than women do. They have more incentive to shape it, outwardly in the world, than women.

Marina Warner: It used to worry me tremendously as a child and as a young woman. It really upset me and I was really anxious that misogynists who argued that women were inferior were right because of the historical record. It doesn't worry me any more because I think that, in the spheres women have entered, they have done as well. Writing is the main one; painting and sculpture, since the last century, are now very much practised by women. We wouldn't have had Michelangelo if that particular type of endeavour had not been privileged by the people who controlled money. I don't see genius as an unassailable demon that comes from the sky that you are born with, and you draw perfect circles and spout Greek in your cradle. I don't believe that. I believe there are exceptionally gifted people, of course, but I feel they could have disappeared if it hadn't been for their patrons. This is why I am a terrific believer in public patronage of the arts. I do believe in the fostering and sponsorship. The different things women have been good at probably reflect the pattern and experience of their lives: embroidery rather than monumental sculpture for many centuries, but embroidery of fantastic excellence and beauty. There is an interesting comment on French art, which said that our society has graded the arts according to how distant they are from the senses and that women's art traditionally has always been very close to the senses: food, embroidery. Architecture, music, although music is close to the senses in one sense, have been given a higher status, and this reflects both the Christian and slightly platonic idea that the further we are from being grounded in our bodies, the more spiritual and refined and immortal we become.

The musicality of women can't be questioned because of the performers, because of the singers, and also dance, which is related. I don't know how many women have tried to write symphonies. I don't think it is something women have wanted to do. But the context, the cradle of the symphony, is a great court and somebody who wishes to set the seal on their power and prestige with this piece of music. That was the beginning of the symphony. Then people did write symphonies without commissions. It's the equivalent of the official portrait in a way, and it requires an immense investment. You count on all these musicians that might come, copyists that copy the music, rehearsal time, many things that are in a high economic bracket. Jane Austen, writing on her blotter and hiding it under the blotter when her family came in: this is minimum economic creativity and that's where you'll find women's creativity. Women did not control money, even in quite enlightened societies, even in the Renaissance courts of Italy where they had a very high view of women and women's culture and women's poetry and so forth. There was no command of resources, of actual physical resources. As a young woman, say the twenty-two-year-old daughter of a *visconte* in Milan, even in that position (i.e. a millionairess), when you married, you couldn't go to your husband as you had to your father and say, here I am, I want to write for one hundred musicians and I want them to come here fifteen times at least and I want six copyists working. They didn't have command of money. That's why I now feel it probably will happen.

Arabella Weir: I won't accept that men are more creative than women. I accept that they've had the environment in which to be more creative. In other words, they don't have to bring up children, or clean the house or cook. It can't be generic, creativity. It just can't be.

Katharine Whitehorn: The reason I find it very hard to talk about creative people is that I think your genius people are so exceptional anyway that I don't know what rules apply to them. I think people pour their creativity into what they can, and there may well be a lot of people who have never been able to fulfil it, and social circumstances would obviously be relevant. Once you get up into the genius realms, I don't know what is the divine spark which actually inspires a genius, and I don't know whether there was some female Shakespeare who stuffed the whole thing under the mattress and it went up in flames.

I think you can get a situation when a woman painter is not admitted to a community of male painters, of which Gwen John is a classic case. Augustus John was insanely jealous of her painting, and one of these days that guy is going to be known as Gwen John's brother.

Jeanette Winterson: There are these little oases of creative women in the past that lead us to believe that, had conditions been different, they might have been able to produce more, or more women would have produced more. Because certainly, if you're denied access to education, or if you're doing all the work, or if you're having all the children, you're not going to have the leisure time to be creative. I think Virginia Woolf is quite right: you have to have a room of your own and your metaphorical £500 a year.

7
Relationships

'Marriage is slavery ... Human personality must develop quite freely. Marriage impedes this development; even more than that, it often drives one to "moral crimes", not only because forbidden fruit is sweet, but because the new love, which could be perfectly legitimate, becomes a crime'
– Nelly Ptaschkina, *The Diary of Nelly Ptaschkina* (1918)

'In my opinion, infidelity does not consist in action only; I consider it already accomplished by the sole fact of desire'
– Juliette Drouet, *Letters to Victor Hugo* (1847)

'I have come to the conclusion that the first great work to be accomplished for women is to revolutionize the dogma that sex is a crime, marriage a defilement and maternity a bane'
– Elizabeth Cady Stanton, diary entry (1881), in Theodore Stanton and Harriot Stanton Blatch (eds.), *Elizabeth Cady Stanton*

'Love between women is seen as a paradigm of love between equals, and that is perhaps its greatest attraction'
– Elizabeth Janeway, *Between Myth and Morning* (1974)

> *'Talk to me tenderly, tell me lies;*
> *I am a woman and time flies'*

– Vivian Yeiser Laramore, song: 'Talk to Me Tenderly'

'Boys don't make passes at female smart-asses'
– Letty Cottin Pogrebin, 'Down with Sexist Upbringing', in Francine Klagsbrun (ed.), *The First Ms Reader* (1972)

> *'By the time you swear you're his,*
> *Shivering and sighing,*
> *And he vows his passion is*
> *Infinite, undying –*
> *Lady, make a note of this:*
> *One of you is lying'*

– Dorothy Parker, 'Unfortunate Coincidence', in *The Best of Dorothy Parker* (1952)

Jenny Agutter: I got into a huge argument with an actor who came to see *The Taming of the Shrew*, a production which affected me very deeply, by the way, because it was Charles Merrit's and he was in fact using it as an illustration of relationships between men and women in the past and relationships today. If you take out a lot of the humour, what you are left with in *The Taming of the Shrew* is a very cruel relationship where it is clear that the woman is entirely put upon, and all she is doing is fighting, fighting, fighting for her independence. Well, this actor came to see it, and it was the first time I had heard laughter in the audience. It was, to me, derisive and very hostile and I got very upset and at the end couldn't really respond to the applause. Basically I just glared to where this laughter seemed to be coming from in the audience. Having dinner with the actor afterwards, I started to realize that it had actually come from him and the people he was with. And he then went on about how he saw it totally from Petrucchio's point of view. He totally understood Petrucchio, and as far as he was concerned women were chattel. He loved them, he adored them, but they were chattel. His wife was his wife and his property. He said, I know it's not the modern thing and people don't like that idea, and one shouldn't really express this. Then he discussed the fact that he also didn't think it was important to be faithful. As far as he was concerned, he adored women, and if he was away doing something, he could do whatever he wanted. I said, well, that's fine as long as your wife is aware. And he said, absolutely not, why should he have to explain that, that should be entirely separate. Then he said, if she did anything, it would infuriate him, there would be trouble. It seemed to me that he could see his wife as being this person whose life he owned in some way; he adored her but owned her, he was not at all honest with her, and she was not allowed that same response to her own life. It's always a big problem with men and women, how they face that, whether they are totally honest with each other. Whether they are saying what they are doing, what they are, and how they are responding to other people. I think it's terribly important. Women are much more honest than men. Men are very guarded about that; women will actually say what is going on in their lives.

I don't think we could survive on our own. It would be a horrible world without men. We joke about the battle of the sexes, but they have been a driving force for one another. Whether or not you lay down your life or do something extraordinary for the person you love, there is magic created in that combination of a man and a woman together. Most of the major love stories, and this is something in *Half Moon Street* which I don't think came across in the film, require that a courtship brings out how much the person loves you, whether you can actually take them to the point where they will almost destroy themselves. You can take them to the brink, and see whether they will endure. It's almost like a test, and a battle, and that's exciting. And that excitement shouldn't deplete the person, it actually should stimulate. If two human beings are just living a very even sort of existence – you know what was happening yesterday, what happens today and what will happen tomorrow – there becomes very little point to your life. The stimuli come from the strains and stresses, the possibilities, the newness, the changes.

You have to recognize the division between the way you feel emotionally and logically. I was not, in the past, settled down and that's terribly important if you want to have a family. If you are going to bring up children, you have at least to show that you can have a relationship with another person. That has never been a part of my life. I have not been able to settle down, partly because of going round the place, partly because I have been unsettled. It would be easier if I was able to marry someone and he could be my wife and get on with certain things and I could just travel about. But if I were expected to take care of the home and do things, I couldn't. A part of me is very much a home-maker: that's why I have been buying a house here, because I really enjoy making a home. More than ever now, if the right opportunity arose, I would feel I could settle, because I feel more settled in myself. But the unfortunate thing about having got to thirty-four without marrying and being that independent is that I will frighten off a lot of people. Literally, it becomes more difficult. And also, one is slightly set in one's ways. So it would take a very particular person to be able to settle down with. But I think, if I had ever married before, I would have been divorced, because I've changed a lot in the last ten years. Not that people don't change together. If you are there constantly with somebody, and you're not going off on separate ventures all the time and growing away, then I think you do have these wonderful marriages where people grow, change together, and that's their life, it's terrific.

But if you are taking off here, there and everywhere, and you're changing, then it's hard work to maintain the same relationship, and your partner might not enjoy the person you are becoming. I've never found a man comfortable with a woman earning more.

Lolicia Aitken: I'm an élitist: I like my men to be handsome and good-looking, intelligent, sexy and difficult, I like men to be difficult. I don't like boring men. I like men who are a challenge. I'd ten times rather ride a tiger and have a few bumps on the way, than ride a nice boring old donkey.

I feel more comfortable with men, because women don't understand what I'm saying. Most of my women friends are on the same base, most of my women friends are beautiful, successful, intelligent women – it sounds terribly élitist – but in order to be generous you have to be secure and if you're secure, then you can be giving and trustworthy. And therefore I like successful women.

A successful marriage is worth ten careers, and I think that's the ultimate feminism. Men and women are there to be loved, and we all would like to love and be loved. Ultimately that's what it's all about: a good relationship on a real base, on a complicity base. All the rest is trimmings. A lot of women don't see that, a lot of women are stupid about men. They see men not as enemies but adversaries; they want to catch them, impress them, seduce them. The ultimate relationship is complicity and deep-down friendship, and breaking those inhibitions and being really together and understanding and totally open and supportive.

Maria Aitken: I used not to be able to handle women at all. I used to have no women friends, not because I disliked them, but because I had eyes only for men as friends quite apart from as lovers. But now I enjoy the company of women inordinately and have some very good women friends. But only in the last eight years or so.

I rather like men who are sensitive and who are funny, who have nice eyes and not too big a bottom.

Shirin Akiner: I used to think that possibly I was happier with men, but then I realized it was mainly because I knew more men. Now that I have quite a few women friends, I'm equally at ease with them. I would say that women possibly have and expect to have closer friendships, and men tend to be colleagues or friends on a more intellectual level.

I think for a lot of people, myself included, there is a need for that completion of oneself by another human being. In my case, that has to be a man. Maybe for other people not necessarily, but for me, yes. Some men and some women are completely shattered by losing their partners, there are others who do recover. I would be totally lost without my husband, totally, to the point of not wanting to be in the house alone by myself. Not because I'm afraid to be in the house, but if he is away, there is such a sense of emptiness and loss and longing. It happens very rarely, but I dislike it intensely.

I find beauty of character attractive, and a sense of goodness. I have to be convinced of that more than anything. Good looks don't matter much, because a man can be extremely attractive whether he is conventionally beautiful or not. I wouldn't, I don't think, know how to judge conventional male beauty. Perhaps what I like is a spiritual quality which requires a certain moral conviction.

Marriage is the caviare of life, and I don't think it should be for everyone. It shouldn't be something you just go into. A good marriage is the most beautiful, important and rewarding relationship, and it's certainly not common, certainly not lying on every street corner. I would make marriage extremely difficult. I would always discourage people from marrying. I believe in marriage only as a public acknow-ledgement of a very strong private bond. I don't think there's any other reason for it. Of course, children do bring a different element into it, but then I wouldn't expect to have a child from a man to whom I didn't have a very strong commitment.

Baria Alamuddin: I feel most comfortable with men by far. There is no comparison. Most women actually bore me, and most women I find unsure of themselves, especially in the Arab countries, and that really upsets me. They are not in control of their destinies or lives, and I feel they are just souls floating around waiting for things to take them away, here or there, and I find it a waste of time.

Marriage has all the disadvantages the world has. It is a very difficult institution. I think most people are married because they are scared of society, because it is convenient and they have a car, and they carry a name and the children are there. I know of hardly any marriages that are there by virtue of love. I'm not talking about my marriage, because that is another story. I look at my marriage differently. I work very hard at it and yet I am always afraid. Not of losing the marriage, no, but of losing me in the marriage, or of losing the marriage to me. I am scared.

For the world to be straightened out and for us to be able to have a peaceful, strong, productive society, the woman has to change her attitude towards life, and the way she expects things from herself. I think she controls society since she brings up the child. For example, my husband has two boys from a previous marriage, and I brought them up. It was a beautiful experience as far as I am concerned, and I think for them, too. While they were growing up, they started coming and saying to me, today I kissed her, or I did this and that to her. I used to say to them, it takes two to kiss, it takes two to make love, it takes two to love, to build, to bring up a child. Anything not done together with the same intensity is not done properly. You can kiss a wall.

Madeleine L. H. Alatas: Englishmen just do not like women, period. They've been trained ever since knee-high to a duck not to. I wouldn't say that they prefer the company of other men, but they feel safer with it. They've been conditioned by their public school, or whatever it is that conditions them, that women are threatening, especially intelligent women, especially women who can take it or leave it.

I like good-looking men, or what I would call good-looking. What attract me about men are the extremes: what is apparently on the surface and what is really underneath. And I'm always pulled by the challenge of, like, opening an oyster. The only time I'm pulled is when I feel some sort of sensory perception or something that makes me feel there is the pearl in the oyster, that is, I see a heart of gold. If it's rotten underneath, you don't see me for dust. I'm not attracted to dangerous people. The more powerful they are, the more insecure and yet the more arrogant. That type of thing fascinates me, and, I suppose power does fascinate me, but it can be physical power, political power, mental power – I don't care – creative power. Power, yes. Perhaps because I love strength and am a woman and do want that. I want to be able to be independent from it. I can come back like a kitten, I can get into all types of trouble, as long as I can come back. I need that and I look to men to give it to me.

Jan Amory: I'm attracted to intelligence, honesty and decency. I don't think there are very many men around any more that would, if you asked them, be able to define the word decent. Whereas I do think there are many more decent women. I'm not talking about women's libbers. I am very lucky, I have met a decent man aged thirty-nine, who is kind to my son, who is decent in every way. I'm afraid, when you're too decent in America, and too honest, you can't really succeed and become the chairman of the board, the top of any company. And that's one of the reasons why I love my husband.

I was sure each time I married that it was going to be a commitment for ever. My marriage to my last husband, the Greek, the father of my child, was a commitment I had made which was going to be for ever. But he really didn't like living in America, he missed London. And he was Greek. And so there was a problem, because I am 110 per cent American, I wasn't happy living in London. We lived there seven months. My dog was put in quarantine and treated very badly; I took him out after four months, I couldn't stand it. I didn't find the life as stimulating as in America. I found it more of a routine kind of boredom, a nine-to-five job. I didn't find it interesting. There was no excitement, no adventure; just an existence, but not a life, in my opinion. Whereas New York: you can do what you want, you can have a wonderful exciting life, you can really exist, you can order in your food, you can go to the theatre. You can do anything and you don't have to do anything, it's both. But in London, there was a sort of a cloud over the adventure-some and exciting people. I don't know what happens to them; it's almost as if they are drugged. They have no enthusiasm.

Divorce is too easy. I think people drop out. They say, well, if the marriage doesn't work, I can always get a divorce. Years ago, divorce wasn't that easy and you had to make it work. Years ago, people had arranged marriages all over the place, and they worked. People don't work enough at a marriage. I've had three, so I know. The first one failed because I was young and made a mistake, a six-week bad mistake. The others failed because we didn't work hard enough, or one or both parties became disillusioned by the other, or there was a surprise, let's say, that you didn't expect. And then I think your choice is, am I going to stick with it despite what I know, or is it better to get out and be friends afterwards? That's how women think. The majority of marriages break up because the women leave more than the men. It's boredom. People expect the sexual passion to continue, and they don't understand it switches to another kind of passion, another kind of love.

I don't mind the ageing process. I turned forty last Friday, and I don't mind at all. When I was going out with men in between divorces, I was never nervous about the twenty-five-year-olds that were also going out with them. I knew when the man went home at night he had a better time with me. If we were having an affair, I knew it was better, because the mind and everything else were better. Whether her body was better, I don't know. But I know the whole thing worked better. I never had any jealousy or feelings about younger girls, ever, because I find I am more interesting than most of them anyway. So I couldn't care less. And most intelligent men would rather be with someone who is older, whom they have a good time with, whom they can talk to. One comment someone once made to me, talking about a model with nothing to say, was: by the time I'm out of the shower, I hope she's out of the house, because there's nothing to say afterwards, once it's done and the sex is over.

Adèle Anderson: When I was young, I definitely liked the macho man, the Burt Reynolds, the Sean Connery. It was always dark men as well, big and beefy. I'm still not averse to that, I've still been out with men like that, but I'm now going out with a tall skinny blonde who's got a baby face. I now like gentleness in men. I really wanted to be dominated by men to start with. Obviously my feelings have changed, my perception of womanhood has developed as I've lived it. I had only viewed it from outside before, and yes, I wanted a big strong man who'd come along and dominate me, and I don't want that any more. I don't want to dominate them, either. I want them to be my equal, and I look for gentleness in a man now. But I have to admit that I'm still the slave of good looks. I mean, if they're only good-looking and nothing else, that wouldn't be enough, but I'm a sucker for a pretty face, I must admit.

I've seen too many marriages in my family and around me break up. I've seen most of my friends only get married when they have children. I also feel that any man who is with me must have the freedom to walk away if he wants to. I'm a realist, and although obviously I regard myself as on a par with every other woman, that's me talking. But for somebody outside, somebody who is going to live with me, there are lots of things to put up with, like what do other people say, because people always ask the same question. They think that he must be gay if he's with me. Lots of people have said this. I wouldn't want my relationship to depend on a piece of paper. If I have a faith, it's a terribly personal faith, and it doesn't rely on what any priest might tell me to think or do. I'd be perfectly happy if I were living with somebody and we loved each other. Marriage to me isn't the height of being a woman by any means.

I am more monogamous now. If I'm going out with somebody, I'm quite happy to be with them, but then I never get a chance to get bored with them because I don't see them often enough. But once a relationship is over, then I probably would go from person to person. I don't see relationships as lasting for ever. I think I want to be with this man until such time as I don't want to be with him, or he doesn't want to be with me. I see myself actually going through life with a series of relationships, because I haven't yet met anybody I feel I could spend the rest of my life with. I'd be on a loser if I was going around looking: who is the person, are you the person I'm going to spend the rest of my life with? I think it has to creep up on you unawares. Suddenly you realize, yes, this is the person.

Dr Swee Chai Ang: In the past a woman was married to a man and he was not only her husband, he was her livelihood. You can't lose a livelihood. You might hate your husband, that is different. So a lot of marriages are hung on those kind of circumstances. Then, if you are stuck in a situation like that, you might hate your husband but you love your kids, so you make it work, you make it the home, develop in it and make compromises and adjust. Nowadays you càn go to W. H. Smith and get separation forms and just fill them in. If he's got a job and you've got a job and you don't like each other, then forget it. Let's find the forms and go separate ways. It's as easy as that.

Lady Elizabeth Anson: I came from a divorced childhood and I never knew my parents together, and I think it does have an effect on a child. At the same time if two people are not getting on, it probably has a worse effect on the child.

I am not somebody who is tremendously swayed by fantastic looks. I am just doing a party for Estée Lauder, where she is asking the hundred handsomest men. There was one in New York, and there is going to be one here, and I would have liked to have done it for the hundred most attractive men because that is quite a different thing. But the men on the board of Estée Lauder say, for the male ego, it ought to be the handsomest. But, in New York, Andy Warhol turned up and they had Henry Kissinger, and that's why I wanted attractive men because attraction to me comes through the mind, definitely the mind; an attractive man might have the ugliest face.

Beatrice Aristimuno: People get married too young and don't live first. People get bored, because habit dulls their relationship. People have so many temptations, there are so many nice things around to tempt a man or a woman. If you get married later, as I probably will, I think you will enjoy married life much better. You come to an age when you need calm, so you enjoy it. And even a man enjoys it. Lots of people get married lightly, and it's a mistake, because it is traumatic when it goes wrong. Of course, it is very easy to divorce. I mean, who doesn't divorce? Everybody divorces, but I have less chance of getting divorced if I get married late and have a child late than if I had done it ten years ago. I would have been wrong to marry ten years ago, and if I had, I would be divorced with a child today. My mother says it's better to be divorced than to be a libertarian, but I don't agree.

When you're older, you enjoy sex and you enjoy men, everything, much better than in your twenties. When you are twenty, you do it for the sake of doing it, you have to do it, and that's the way it is. I have friends of my age who have been married for seven, eight years, and they have children and some of them are very happy, but most of them are divorced.

Pamela Armstrong: In the past, people died, so you remarried, people married two or three times, four times. The first wife died in childbirth, the second in childbirth, the third of the plague; and the husband was taken off to sea, there were wars. Death was quick, fast and furious, and there were what we would now call serial marriages, but in those days it would appear to have been till death do us part because death literally did part them. There was also civil marriage. It's well known that there was an area in London, down by Tower Bridge, where working-class poor people would go, people who were outside the Church, who had absented themselves from the mainstream. They're not written about now, and historians didn't write about them, the historians wrote about the mainstream. These were people who didn't get married in church, but were married and lived with people, had serial relationships. People are much more demanding, now, in relationships, which is very important. I don't agree with this line, isn't it all terrible, and look how high the divorce rate is. I think that is a positively healthy sign. It means people are questioning marriage and are not prepared to stick in marriages that are bad.

Debbie Arnold: I don't like the company that much of strange men. But I like the company of men whom I know very well, and I like the company of women whom I know very well. I'm not very good with people I don't know, strangers. I like showing off in front of men. I feel like a female peacock sometimes, strutting around, and it's nice to feel attractive and you do glow, but I still think I feel most totally at ease with women.

I have been married. And I would have been married for ever. My husband's still my best friend in the whole world. Basically, we would still be together if we'd had children. But my husband couldn't have children, and that's what separated us in the end, because he felt I should have children, and he couldn't give them to me. Therefore he didn't want our relationship to carry on, and it broke his heart and it broke mine, too. I would have stayed with him. Now, that's a difference between men and women. My husband couldn't stand the fact that he couldn't give me a child. It made him feel inadequate; he didn't feel like a man. He felt that, because he couldn't have children, our relationship was over, but I didn't feel that way, which is interesting. My instinct is to have children, but I felt I wanted to be with him because I loved him. But he couldn't carry on like that.

I don't think I have that many close men friends, except for my ex-husband. All my very good friends are women.

I have a loyalty code with my girlfriends. If I fancy a girlfriend's boyfriend, I wouldn't go near him and probably wouldn't see her if they were always together. I couldn't do that to somebody else. My ex-husband and his girlfriend are great friends of mine, both of them. You see, she didn't take him away from me. We had already split up by the time they met, and the fact that he loves her must mean that I have to like her, because I love him and care about him and she loves him, so therefore I care about her.

Leslie Ash: I've never gone for looks. I'm actually quite amazed when I'm out with a very good-looking man. I find myself just staring at him and thinking, God, he's good-looking. I know people used to laugh at me when I went out with Rowan Atkinson – they used to call us Beauty and the Beast, which was totally unfair. Inside, he was the most beautiful man you could ever wish to meet.

The relationship always starts off with the man more giving than the woman, then, as soon as that man knows he's got that woman, if the woman says those immortal words, I love you, suddenly he switches off, unbelievable. I couldn't believe what happened to me in one relationship. He suddenly switched off. I felt I was following him around everywhere, that I was irritating him. And I was irritating him. And then what happened was that we would have arguments, and he would flirt with other women and I would get obsessed about it because he wasn't paying me the attention he was paying to me before. I would start looking in his diary, at his receipts and his Barclaycard to see if he was seeing someone else, and then I'd find out he was, and then we'd have another argument and then I'd get hit. But I couldn't leave him because I was obsessed with him. I wanted him to be back in love with me. I remember this man turning round to me and saying, I'm the one who says the relationship's finished, not you.

I think if I got involved with a man he would have to be somebody in the business, because I find that I don't have anything in common with people who aren't, like a banker or something. They just don't understand me or my life. I find it very difficult to get on with people who have no idea of the business, because you have to let people down at the last minute.

I got married four years ago, and as I was walking down the aisle, I thought, well, I can always get a divorce. I would love that commitment for life, but I was just too young. I think it's now starting within me, because of my real urge now to have a child, and I really do feel now I want to settle down with one person, and I want that one person to be like five affairs, all five affairs in one person. There's always something that you might find attractive in someone else, but there's nothing wrong with flirting, I think it's a wonderful thing. As long as you're with a partner who doesn't mind you flirting, as long as that's as far as it goes, then there's no reason why that relationship shouldn't work.

Energy is sexy. Energy is wonderful. For someone to have energy is the best thing. I remember a man saying to me towards the end of a relationship, actually, when you're not happy, you're ugly; I don't like to see you like this, because you look ugly; you've lost all your beauty, you're not happy in this relationship. You can always tell when a woman has met a new man. It's a delight, something in the face. I'm such a give-away. My make-up artist knows the next day when I've seen my boyfriend. Because there's a glow.

Diana Athill: I'm not at all sure that marriage ought not to be changed, that it ought not to be a renewable contract that you enter into for a period of, say, seven years, to be renewed at the end of that if you like, with built-in clauses for the care of the children. That would seem to me to be a much more realistic thing than going through the motions of this is for ever and ever. Again, it depends. I've known so many very good marriages, really happy marriages, but there, again, they would renew the contract, you see.

To most people, it's pretty climactic, breaking a marriage up, but even so it's no longer the unthinkable thing, no longer a stigma. It's no longer simply that you can't imagine doing it. You see it happening all round you. I've never known anyone who did it easily. Usually people have gone into marriage meaning to stay there, and very rarely does the marriage break up easily. There's usually one wanting to hold on while the other wants to go. That's why I think it is a good idea not to have it such a totally binding thing. I mean, have it absolutely binding in its duties to each other, to the children, but not so life-long. It would be much better.

When I was young, the thing that seduced me was not practical success. I didn't want him to be rich, but he had to be someone who was successful in that he was getting what he wanted out of life, that he was in control of life. And he had to give me the impression of being a rather happy person who could manage his own life. He could be a bit of a crook perhaps, but had to be on top, you know. I thought I couldn't ever possibly love anyone who wasn't like that. Then, as I got older, I began to be attracted by vulnerability and to fall for people who were obviously child substitutes to a certain extent. Then, thank God, I stopped falling in love, I began to dislike people. I think falling in love is a terrible business. It nearly always is slightly neurotic, something you are putting on to that person, not something the person has. A need of yours is embodied in that person, and what happens is that the person turns out to be himself or herself and you resent it because you want them to be that imaginary thing. But once you've managed not to fall in love any more, it's bliss. You just like people.

There's a certain comfortableness you feel with your own sex, old women friends. I remember Ruth Samson, poor woman, once saying to me, I believe that the people one will miss most when one dies are not going to be one's lovers at all, but one's own old women friends. I've thought about that, and I think that it may be true. I have one or two women in my life from way back whom I absolutely know as well as myself, and perhaps they are the people I am most easy with, far closer than the man I live with. I've got an old boyfriend I share my flat with. By now it's hardly a love affair, it's like family.

Leila Badawi: I do find that my friendships with other women have quite a different quality and are much more playful than the friendships I have with men. I'm completely at ease with another woman. Whereas, with a man, no matter how long I've known him, even to some extent with my brother, or even with my husband, there's still not so much a guarded-ness as an awareness that there are certain things where there is just no common ground – one's outlook, one's upbringing. Maybe that's one thing that makes marriage interesting – that there's always a dialogue, that no matter how long one spends in a man's company, there is always something else.

Beautiful men are not necessarily seductive. There's an extra spark some men have, and it's hard to say what exactly. It is compounded of exuberance, imagination and intelligence; not necessarily wit.

Joan Bakewell: I had a brief kind of passion for Galbraith, the economist, who is all elbows and long limbs, and I do remember sitting watching him doing a programme. He was holding forth and I remember saying, just look at that beautiful man, and I suppose I used the word beautiful and meant, really, fascinating, though I did think that in his exposition of his ideas, he became beautiful. I mean, the bronzed hunk is absolutely a turn-off. Personality isn't quite enough; personality – style, weight, confidence – someone who inhabits their life.

There are three parties to a marriage: him, her and the pair, the third. It's a romantic illusion to believe that, when you marry, you merge into one unit. It's not possible, it's not desirable, and the recognition that each individual's integrity and identity remain separate, even in marriage or in close bonding, is very important it seems to me.

Elisabeth Barillé: In my own life, I have more contact with men because there are more men writers, after all. I meet a lot of writers and journalists. It's quite different. When I am in the company of women, I become the novelist, I observe them; I don't feel superior, but I stand back a little. As my novels are about women, their life in contemporary society, I take them as such, like characters in my novels. When I am with men, I lose that distancing, perhaps because I want to please. I feel that I become an object, I lose control of the situation a bit. But I couldn't say that I feel better with either sex. It's just different.

I think friendship between a man and a woman – I'm talking for myself – can only come after a sexual relationship; that's to say, if you want a friendship without clashes or embarrassment. After sex, it sorts itself out. There is an additional factor, and it is more tenacious than friendship between women.

I have always sacrificed men to literature. I live quite alone. I'm twenty-six, and I might change, but I cannot conceive at the moment of having a relationship with someone. All my energy goes into literature. Do I need men? I need human contact, tenderness, of course, but not specifically men. I would rather read about a passionate life than have a lukewarm relationship. My passion is literature.

Dame Josephine Barnes: Many men get bored. They don't like to feel tied to the same woman, and they think, in twenty years' time the same woman will be facing me across the breakfast table, and they want a bit of novelty, a bit of new. Then a woman gets hold of them and says, wouldn't it be wonderful if we were married? And he's had it from then on; his wife has had it from then on. The other thing is, of course, that now, with many more women in professions and jobs, women have found they can do without men. And there is no doubt that there are many men who treat women very badly. Wife-beating has been a tradition in the working classes in this country for centuries, always has been, and very often a woman will feel that she's better off without a brutal man who beats her up and that she can stand on her own two feet, and that's it.

Josephine Barstow: We are all more concerned with our own happiness now. I don't know whether anyone ever achieves it. One achieves a feeling of contentment, and one achieves the feeling of happiness, of fulfilment, in one's success. But there's this odd thing that we all feel we are entitled to, and it's sold to us the entire time through sexual adverts, and holidays in the sun. We all feel that we have to achieve all these things, and then finally achieve this thing. I suspect it's probably impossible to achieve anyway. The people in a simpler age, looking after their one pig in a backyard and probably not getting enough to eat all through the year, had something we've lost.

I am more successful than my husband in our professional lives, and I don't think he would argue with that. But there are so many other areas in life in which one can be, relatively or not, successful. And I consider him, as a human being, immensely successful. Obviously, like most marriages I suspect, ours has had its problems, huge problems. We split up at one time, which was entirely my fault, and he, being a huge human being, accepted me back. But we are closer together than we have been before, and there's no way we could be prised apart now. And what's brought us together is our family. Though we don't have children, we have created a farm together – what we feel is a place where values are how we feel they should be. It's giving employment to quite a few people, and the struggle we've had creating this little life, this little place, has brought us incredibly close together. We are partners in that, absolutely equal. I obviously have put more money into it, but my husband has put in labour and love and thought, and it's drawn us wonderfully together.

Jennifer Bartlett: Marriages don't last for the same reason that we have so many magazines rather than books. I think people want things very quickly and really feel they can have what they want. We have such a lot of choices, and it's very difficult. A friend from England told me she went nuts when she first lived in the United States, because she got up in the morning and would go out to have breakfast, and they said, do you want your eggs soft boiled, hard boiled, two minutes, three minutes, scrambled, fried, sunny side up? She said, I just want an egg, and they said, do you want it scrambled, fried? And they would go through the whole list again. And then she would go to a store to buy some flowers, and when she said, well, I think I'll take some tulips, they said would you like the tulips partially open, long-stemmed, short-stemmed, completely closed, fully open? She said she would have one or two requirements that were very clear, but there would be a whole sequence of decisions she had to make on top of what she already had. It's the same with everything.

Gilberte A. Y. Beaux: The generation between the First and Second World Wars was attracted by a lot of different things and began to speak less with their children, to educate their children less. Partly because of the consequences of the two wars, we did not very often give our children the same image of a family, and it seemed more and more normal to get divorced. I think it is false, and absolutely abnormal, because if you don't marry, or if you get divorced, very often you are just creating problems for the weakest. You may effectively have a lot of love between a man and a woman without marriage, but marriage is a contract established by society to ensure that the weakest are better treated. What we have now is women of fifty without any job, without any husband, and with a lot of problems. We create a lot of problems with children through people saying they want freedom, not marriage; to be not married is not freedom. We have to show the persons who are not married and are having children without being married, that they are creating inequality, creating problems for the future. They are not people who love the other person; on the contrary, they are destroying more than they love. It is a complete change in thinking we have to bring about to restore the family, and I am very optimistic that we will manage, because young people now say what they want is a family. For the time being, we are on the road which was paved in the 1960s, 1970s, but we have to change completely, and little by little we will manage again to have a good strong family, which is where you learn to be educated, where you learn what you are to do in the future, where you have the traditional values of the country. That doesn't mean going backwards. If you respect your traditional values, you are in fact looking at the past to create the future.

Rotraut Lisa Ursula Beiny: Being more successful than your husband could cause tension, but of course I am married to somebody who has never resented it. Even before going into this business, I used to buy houses and convert them into flats. I was always doing something, and he always went along with it. But David is very, very easy-going, a very special kind of person. He is one of the nicest people you could meet, so he puts up with all my nonsense. My advice would be if you make more money, put it all together and never consider where the money comes from. I've never believed in separate accounts. We have joint accounts, we put it in, we take it out. I don't say this comes from me, this is mine. I think that you have to be very careful, if you maybe earn more, that you don't make anything of it, because that could cause great problems.

Christine Bogdanowicz-Bindert: It would be hard for men to patronize me because I would quickly straighten them out. The way I perceive it is different. For example, if we go to a social event where my husband is better known than I am, usually people say to me, oh, by the way, what do you do? They are just trying to be polite and make conversation, but when I say, I'm an investment banker, they suddenly think, she's not just the wife of so and so, my God, you know, how interesting! It also reflects on my husband, because they suddenly think, how is he putting up with that? He has his own career, and you know, she basically doesn't really cater to him. How do they manage?

Men make passes at me very often. I travel a lot with men and when we have dinner in the evening, the guy often has a little bit too much wine and starts saying how attractive I am and this and that. And I laugh and say, thank you very much. A lot of it is the way you respond. I mean, there is no doubt in my mind that I have had millions of opportunities. But I've never had an incident where I was really cornered, so to speak. If I had said the wrong thing at the wrong time, it would have become a very awkward situation. I'm very careful how much I drink, for example, so I am on top of things.

796

Nobody's perfect, and no relationship is perfect, so you have to understand what is the strength and the weakness of the relationship and come to grips with it. A lot of people don't do that. They blow the weaknesses out of proportion and forget about the strengths. People also get married for the wrong reasons. A lot of people get married for sexual reasons, for passion, and to have a lasting marriage, you have to have a lasting friendship. You have to have intellectual stimulation, you have to basically like the person. I cannot imagine any period in my life when I wouldn't want to have dinner or go to a movie with my husband. I just think he's a fascinating and interesting person. It just happens that, in addition, we have a wonderful relationship. Sex is very important, but in marriage, for a marriage to last, you have to have a little bit of everything. If I had to give up something, I would rather give up sex than the friendship and the kind of challenge and stimulation.

Rebecca Blake: When women have very strong careers and relationships, marriages, whatever, that's an area that I think is very difficult. A lot of men have difficulty coping with women who are that successful or that motivated. And, initially, what I found is that men sometimes say they are very attracted, but when they are in the reality of a relationship like that, they find it very difficult.

I have had this experience in advertising. Some men are so programmed they really have difficulty accepting anything coming from a woman – a point of view, anything. Sometimes they are not even aware of this because the programming is so total. I think changing social roles is a question of de-programming and exploring new ways of communicating; and also new ways of defining what our roles are as men and women.

Liz Brewer: A woman has to feel something emotional, otherwise it's a bit like rape. You have got to feel something for it to happen, some emotional feeling or desire to do it. Now, with some women, maybe they feel that desire more often. With other women, they never feel it, but they want to feel in love and that's enough. I don't think the majority of women have those strong physical yearnings. When they do, sometimes I think it happens later on in life. If they haven't been a right little raver when they were younger, then maybe with maturity it happens. With some people it develops. I know with myself, I had six fiancés, six men I wanted to be engaged to. I didn't necessarily want to spend the rest of my life with them, but I liked belonging to one particular man at a time.

Dianne Brill: I'm in menswear. I'm dealing with men all the time. I'm dealing with the most beautiful men in the world. These models are incredible, they're stunning, but being with all that experience, I have a different sense of beauty right now. I think I'm seduced by a connection that's made. I have to feel adored. I have to feel a man extremely driven for me. If I feel he's casual about his interest in me, I'm just not interested.

Suzanne Brøgger: Of course, we know all the superficial answers to why marriages don't last: we have so many options and so much freedom, and we don't know how to make priorities. But I suppose that one of the real reasons is that, for the first time in history, in the wealthier countries, people have the possibility of growing, of developing themselves. We are not toiling every day and dying at the age of forty, so that means that when two people are growing, going through the process of individuation, as Jung would call it – the process of becoming yourself, developing yourself, which can also be a painful process – then the chances that two persons grow and develop together are very slim. The risk is that they grow apart. The option is not to grow and just to sit and hold hands, but that is a very sad option. Of course, many people do grow and their marriages don't break. So it is a bit of a gamble. Sometimes I think that the Indian tradition, where the parents make the match based on good solid facts, is maybe wiser than the romantic marriage based on falling in love. It is historically a new construction, this romantic marriage based on falling in love; you could call it a historical experiment and maybe the experiment has proved a failure. Falling in love is a fragile basis for forming a family.

The difference between men and women in relation to being creative also applies to sexuality, because sexuality and creativity are in the end the same stream of consciousness, and so we are equally different in that respect. And, of course, seduction is a very masculine way of thinking, going from A to B, seeing the object, seducing it, and having seduced it, abandoning it – mission accomplished. Most women tend to want more and to have greater expectations from love relationships, and tend to be more disappointed when they are not fulfilled.

Janet Brown: I have women friends who adore men, who love men's company, who want to run and do things for them. Even in my girlhood days in Scotland, when we used to go to dances at the Plaza in Glasgow, my friends would all go dancing but I'd think it was demeaning that any man should decide whether he would come up and dance with me. I can

798

remember thinking this quite clearly, and saying to my girlfriends, I wouldn't talk to that person in the street, why should I think it would be very nice if he asked me to dance? I've always had strong feelings about things of that kind. Why should it have to be the man that would decide whether to pick you out or leave you sitting down? Of course, I know things are switching round and women will say to a man that they like him, would he like to go out with them? But that still, to me, sounds a bit shocking because of my background, my upbringing.

Women, for the most part, want to change somebody, or think they can do it. If they see someone who is a bit of a character, they're maybe drawn to him physically, but they also think they can make him stop drinking or stop taking drugs or stop doing something else. They will have that powerful urge within them to make that other person alter. It's very challenging. I think lots of women feel that.

Tina Brown: The fact is, it's not sexy to be with a man who is weaker than you are. In fact, it's very horrible. You can be as much women's lib. as you like and say these things don't matter, but the dynamics of bed are the same as they have always been. This is why the women are so unhappy, particularly in New York. We have got these wonderful, fulfilled, terrific, stylish women, but they can't find anybody to satisfy them sexually, not because they are ravening beasts, but because the dynamics of domination aren't there. So they become gay themselves, or they just forgo sex, or they have a wimpy husband. Very few have got husbands who dominate them sexually and make them feel really great. Of course, there are people who have that sort of marriage, and they are very happy marriages. Some women find, in the end, it's so important to have that that they are prepared to forgo their careers, but then they are not very happy either because they have lost something else that matters very much. The modern dilemma for a woman is very difficult.

I am more comfortable with women. I love having women around me, and most of my staff are women. I've got great belief in women, and I love my little guerrilla force of women. They work very, very hard, they are terribly committed, they love their jobs. And that exhilaration is very catching.

I am attracted to men who have great warmth and energy, and a great sense of humour. I suppose I like highly sexed men, full of instant energy. I quite like men who are extremely ugly, actually, but who, I think, are secretly very sexy. They turn out to be the best lovers of all. I like to have some sensitivity, tenderness there. If you are involved in the cut and thrust of competitive life, you really want the flowers and the candlelight.

There was a pernicious cult, which perhaps Gloria Steinem had something to do with, of making women feel they could have it all. And what no one really explained to women, as they went out on their feminist forays, was that they were giving up something. What is tragic to behold are women like Germaine Greer, who suddenly do a *volte face* at fifty and say, why didn't I have children? They become almost pathetic, because they are fifty, they are past the biological age for children, nor are they likely to marry anybody. I hate the sight of this pitiable regret for what they've missed. And I think the regret comes because they wanted everything. Sometimes you can have a combination for a time, then the combination changes, but you can't expect to have everything at once. That was the whole pernicious thing of the *Cosmopolitan* magazine philosophy, which made women feel they could have these torrid sex lives and great dazzling jobs *and* motherhood, and feel all these things at once. What's happened, particularly in America, is that people are too hasty to get divorced. Someone in my office, one minute she is married, then the next minute divorcing. I think she is insane. Why can't they just work it out? Many people who get divorced don't find anything better and really wish they hadn't. They could have rubbed along, they could have lowered their expectations perhaps, or introduced something else into the relationship. I'm not suggesting everybody compromises and takes third best, but I think this whole thing of racing off to get divorced at the first snag you hit seems pathetic.

Victoria Brynner: I am a charmer. Therefore I can charm men more easily than I can charm women. Furthermore, I find men's conversation more interesting than women's. I've learned to interest myself in women more now, but I have to make an effort. I am bored, I don't like hearing about the hairdresser, buying clothes, nail polish or make-up. I do it for three minutes, and after that I can't be bothered. I've not met that many women whose conversation has really interested me. I prefer talking with men.

I don't think fidelity exists. We travel too much, see too many people, live with too many people not to be at some point or another attracted by somebody else, by another mind, another body. I don't see how you can live with one man and look at one man for fifty years in your life. However, I think moral fidelity is very important. I find men who have mistresses terrible, but men who have adventures perfectly normal. As a woman, I wouldn't want to know about it, but it has to happen, and I would rather have a man having adventures than having a mistress. With a mistress, there would be a moral infidelity, because then it becomes lies, it becomes all wrong. I don't believe in sexual fidelity, either from men or from women. I think it's hypocrisy to say there's one man in my life and he's the only man. Even women who have lived in one apartment with their man eventually have some fantasy with the butcher, with the guy who sells the bread, with the man who goes by in the car. There's always something. But even when you are in love, saying you don't notice other men is bullshit. It's bullshit. Completely wrong.

Joan Juliet Buck: I feel horrible, let's say, around a lot of English businessmen. It makes me feel like shit. Or, in New York, that breed of rich New Yorker who will turn genial and say, don't you think your biological time-clock is running out? I'm now thirty-eight. It's an interesting age because one's no longer offering men a hell of a lot of free-floating potential of what one might be. With women, you share eye make-up, you cook together, you giggle and gossip and tell each other everything. I can do that with a few very special men friends, with whom it's gone on to a different plane from sexual attraction. For a long time now, there's been nothing any man could turn me into which would be satisfying. Somebody's wife, somebody's girlfriend, all of those roles are incredibly boring. I once went out with somebody very rich who has his private plane, and spent all my money on clothes so I would look wonderful every night when we went to the stupid parties. And it was an incredible waste of time and money. I didn't have a single good conversation for six months. It was perhaps the most glittering period of my life, but I can't sustain that. A friendship with a woman is so much nanana about this man or that, from the past or for the future, as a potential lover – there is always this thing of love. A friendship with a man is much more interesting because he can go on about somebody he is involved with and nanana about love and you can go on about that, but there will always be a bit of jealousy. A friendship with a man always has sexual tension, because either it's an affair that's turned into a friendship or it's something that keeps you a little bit on your toes. So if you stay with a girlfriend, you both put on your face-masks and are up half the night going *yak, yak, yak* about love. Whereas I can stay up a whole night talking with a man about love, but I wouldn't put a face-mask on.

Averil Burgess: I think charm is not something I possess, and therefore I never really try to deploy it. I may try to get people to see things my way, I may try to be persuasive, but I am just as likely to try that with a woman as with a man, because if I want people to see it my way, it doesn't matter who it is. It'll be one of my staff, be it male or female, or somebody else, be it male or female. I may well try to lay it on a bit with men. Consciously not.

Many men feel threatened by a woman who is intellectually their equal. I have certainly found this in my own life from time to time. This is a very great generalization, and it is perhaps disappearing, but many men do not wish to take women seriously in an intellectual sense. They don't want to be challenged, they need to feel that the woman is in some way dependent, or inferior, or naïve or what have you. For some men, their own self-esteem depends upon feeling that a woman is less worthy, is inferior.

I think the main reason why marriages are not lasting today is that the woman has an out. And there's no stigma to divorce. Most women now have a means of earning a living, and socially and financially they are able to make the choice. In my mother's generation, the choice really wasn't there. Divorce was the absolute end of the road, posing great financial and social problems. You undertook it only if things were absolutely intolerable. Whereas now the woman does have the choice. I think this is the major reason for the increase in the divorce rate. I don't think men have changed, I think women have changed. They are far more ready to get out of an unsatisfactory relationship, and far more able to get out of it, and this is borne out by the fact that two thirds of divorces are petitioned by women.

Carmen Callil: A good 70 per cent of my friends are married or live with somebody. For nearly all of them, it's the second time around, and the thing I notice about the ones who are happy is that they are unusual relationships in some way. I think that one of the reasons that marriages crack up a lot is that a lot of people make very conventional marriages. They marry because it's time to marry, because he's the boy-next-door, they marry because everybody's getting married, and I think those ones fail a lot these days.

I've never been married, but I'm not lonely. I have so many friends. There's a wonderful thing about my life actually, which is that, when you have so many friends, you're never going to be in the position that couples are in when a partner goes. That will never be something I have to put up with, because I'm divided all around the place. I think it's very interesting, being a single woman. People rely on me a lot.

Beige men have always been my downfall: soppy-looking Englishmen, weak-looking men. I go for sense of humour, I think, and in my youth, power. I'm much less interested in power now because I've got my own, but in my youth I was fascinated by power. Actually, I don't like powerful men now. All that egomania, I can't stand it – too much of my own. I've always liked weak men.

Angela Carter: The lesbian I know best is a young woman who is having a lot of fun, and the gay men I know best are all middle-aged and have settled down; so, my life being a self-selecting process, I have a completely different picture of what lesbian and gay society is like. Lesbians seem to party all the time, and gay men seem to sit at home and cuddle and watch television.

Anna Carteret: Men and women go into marriage with certain ideals they have received from conditioning. Women have been taught that marriage is this and you should expect that, and it's all going to be wonderful. Then they discover is isn't all going to be wonderful, and that in many cases their mothers had simply accepted certain standards, ways of life, patterns of behaviour which the daughter was expected also to accept. But, because of reading, education and meeting other women who were perhaps more advanced than themselves, they began to question their marriage and what it was doing for them, and the whole point of it. When you're young, you're not really taught about marriage, you're not really taught what happens. You're only taught the ideals, not the reality.

I used to think looks were important, but I married my husband when he was middle-aged with a pot belly and three children, which wasn't my idea of what I was going to marry, so there must be something beyond that – I think an ability to surprise. I don't like predictable men, and I certainly don't like men who worship me. I like people who are a challenge, and who are also vulnerable, because you will find the most challenging men are also the most vulnerable. The most secure men are often the most dull.

Barbara Cartland: I expect people to carry my parcels, open the door and say I'm lovely. I'd be extremely annoyed if they didn't. What are men there for, except to make themselves charming to me? But I have to be charming first.

Men like unpredictable women. Women have been unpredictable, and that's been half their charm. One moment they complain about it and the next minute they like it. If a woman is very predictable, they're bored with her. The trouble is, we're talking about women who are out to please men. Women are not out to please men now. When women come here and I say, you're here to amuse the men, they look at me as though I was something out of the ark. Of course women are there to amuse the men: they're the flowers in a man's life. Then you can get anything you want, and it all works beautifully. Women think that, by rushing and shouting at everybody and behaving like a man, they're going to get their own way. They don't, they're so stupid, they're not getting anything. Women today are more hostile, more aggressive and more difficult than they've ever been in the whole of time. And I'm eighty-five and I've known women always. It doesn't get you anywhere. I was brought up to get married – women didn't have a career in the First World War – you were brought up to get married. Therefore, when I came out in 1919, if you weren't charming to the men when they took you out for the first time, you sat at home and looked at the wallpaper. Which happens to a great many girls today. They're left at home to sit and look at the wallpaper. Entirely their own fault. Be charming, delightful, and listen, and make yourself charming to men, and why not? It's right for the sexes. Why should you want to be the top dog and aggressive, giving your orders?

I only like being with men. I don't like women very much. I've always had more men friends than women. I've got one or two special women friends who have been wonderful to me in my life, but on the whole I much prefer men in every way. They're much easier to get on with, much. Like boys, who are much easier to bring up than girls, far easier. That's why most English women only want sons. It's only American women who want their little girls.

They've just done a survey in America where they've proved that, where the woman is a virgin, the marriage lasts longer and is much happier. I've travelled all over the world, except China – which I am going to this year – and I've never met a man of any class, creed or nationality who wants to go into a room with a woman who is his wife and the mother of his children and wonder how many other men have been to bed with her. Of course they don't. The whole thing is so degrading to women today; they're degrading themselves. And all this fuss to make divorce easier. What was marriage for? Marriage was made to stop a man, when a woman is forty, throwing her on one side and taking a pretty go-go girl. Now, of course, women make the divorce so easy that the man can drop her at once. Marriage wasn't a religious ceremony to start with, it was a business arrangement, and the one thing you didn't want was the woman to be left without protection when she was no longer very attractive. Women have swept all that to one side. Women have done it – not men.

Women are very treacherous friends. A woman will be your friend, but she will always betray your innermost secrets to her lover on the pillow, and if there's a question of a man coming between you, she will always ditch the woman every time. That's the natural feminine way of behaving. If a woman falls in love with a man that you've got, she won't worry a bit about her friendship with you.

By and large, an Englishman is faithful because he is too lazy, he doesn't want to do anything. He's happy with his home, he doesn't want to be involved in love affairs. There are exceptions – the one or two you always see in the papers – but the average Englishman, once he's settled down, is perfectly happy and wants to come home to a nice dinner with his wife saying, darling, tell me about the office today. He wants to see his children go to a good school, and he doesn't think about love affairs. If his wife is awful to him, well then, when he gets older, he does perhaps think the young body of his secretary might make him feel young, which is a very different cup of tea, a different sort of slant on it, but he doesn't really want to give up his security of having his home and his wife and his children, and his position in the county, and all that sort of stuff.

In the Edwardian times, everybody strayed, and the only commandment was, thou shalt not be caught out. What is so appalling today is that people go to bed and then sell it to the papers. People have had love affairs since Adam and Eve, but you locked the door and kept your mouth shut, therefore nobody knew. What was the point? Any man who mentioned a woman's name when I was young was thrown out of his club.

Men always die quicker than women. Most men who were in love with me are all dead, which is terribly tiresome, but the point is that men are still charming to me as men. They look after me because I'm a woman, not because I'm rich or successful. You always have some – a certain amount of homosexuals – who surround you, if you are successful, but at least they pay you compliments and they're charming.

Luciana Castellina: I still feel more at ease with men because I am old, because I've grown up in a male environment, in male society. It's a bit schizophrenic. In a way, I feel more at ease with men because I am used to working with men more than with women, but, of course, you always resent them, you feel a certain distance, whereas with women I feel less distant because I know they can understand me better, but I lack experience in living and working with them.

Charlotte Chandler: Mae West told me I was a lost soul because I didn't have woman's wiles. And the thing is I'm not a very big enthusiast for pretending. I had a friend who liked a girl very much, and one of the things he liked was that he could take her out and she would eat half a chocolate cake with him. He'd never taken out girls who did that, they always picked at the food. He was very thrilled with her, but after he married her, she never ate another bite of chocolate cake again and he finally discovered – he didn't really care that much – that she had starved herself all day just to be able to eat the chocolate cake, and accommodate him and please him. Their marriage lasted a few years, and then there was a divorce. But I'm sure, along with the chocolate cake, women pretend a lot of other things, and I think men do it too. Especially in the time of dating. Everybody wants to please and be liked, but there's a point where if the pretence is great, you don't get what you want. So it's not just that, morally or ethically, I think pretending isn't a great idea, but if you pretend you get somebody you don't want; and they get you, they get somebody they don't want.

As a person who takes marriage seriously, I would feel that one has to think this could be a sixty-year marriage, and so will you like being with this person sixty years from now? You can't know the answer, but at least the thought would occur to me.

Alexandra Chapman: I think, between women, something can happen within five minutes of meeting. There is complicity. There is something I call the female Mafia. There is a connection. Or I feel hostility, in which case there is no dialogue. But more and more I notice there is complicity. Dealing with a man or a group of men in a business capacity, there is perhaps a more intellectual bonding, almost game playing. And if you realize that and play the game not their way but your way, then you win their respect.

It is Utopian to expect a man to be absolutely faithful. I also think it is Utopian for a woman to be faithful for thirty years without one little adventure. And it is not that serious. But I am also convinced that, if a woman is sufficiently diverting and has a sufficient number of personae to keep a man feeling it's not quite the same woman, then maybe he won't go elsewhere. It's really up to the woman, just as it is up to the man, to be sufficiently able always to discover something new to please, so that a partner doesn't stray.

I guess marriages fail because the expectations are too high. There are cases of people living very happily together for twenty years, and then they get married, and suddenly one is the property of the other and the wife can do no wrong and it becomes a question of clean sheets and toothpaste on the sink. High expectations and the wrong kind. Personally, I would only get married again if there were some legal necessity to do so, some really good, legal reason. Or if there was some enormous advantage in income tax or something like that. I would not do it just for sentimental reasons. No.

Tina Chow: I have so many gay friends. Until recently I preferred the company of men, but now more and more I like women. But I have more men friends that I trust and value than women friends.

Michael basically doesn't want me to do anything. I think he would prefer me not to. Even though he's quite proud of me when I do anything and he encourages me, he's very much afraid I'm going to leave him. He wants to be mothered, he wants me to be around, always. He's much more demanding than our children. It's difficult, because I'm in one way a late bloomer. Before, I was quite happy just to support him, his activities, and now I'm trying to do something apart from him, it's very difficult to gain that space. I never allowed that breathing space for myself. It's my own fault.

Felicity Waley-Cohen: Englishmen are rather bad at being friends with women. They're only used to being potential boyfriends or lovers or whatever, or superior. They're not used to women, and I think they feel uncomfortable with women as very good friends because they feel such a different lifestyle. Also, I think Englishmen feel rather beleaguered by the whole state of change that's going on with women at the moment, with women's position; they feel threatened. There are a great number of very pretty, very bright women who are unmarried, and men are simply absolutely terrified of them because they feel they are supposed to be the men, the superior beings, the strong, the invulnerable, and they see women who seem many of these things.

Probably friendship between women is a more rounded thing than

807

friendship between men, which is often based on one common interest, or one common thought, whereas with women it is the whole of their life and sharing the same lifestyle.

Looks are not important to me. Once, when I was walking down the street, I thought, what a wonderful-looking man. He was sitting in a car, and turned and waved to me, and it turned out to be somebody I knew. I thought, oh, so dull. So I knew looks meant nothing to me because I knew him, I didn't then even see him as good-looking because he was so dull. Another time, I sat next to a devastating man at dinner and thought, how wonderful; and after about five minutes I would have rather sat anywhere else. So I think looks are attractive initially, and I find it very nice that people are conventionally good-looking, but what really matters is what comes out of their eyes.

I find power very attractive. I love it absolutely. That sort of dynamism. I find people who are successful and dynamic more attractive, although in no way would it mean that I would necessarily want to go to bed with them, even if the situation was completely different. I'm attracted by energy, but not by ruthlessness, which is indifference to other people. In that sense, gentleness is very attractive. But I find unduly kind people, about whom everybody says, aren't they nice, very dull. I'm afraid I don't find it at all seductive.

Shirley Conran: I once went to a marriage bureau. I won't tell you the one it was, but the head of the marriage bureau knew it was me and I would be using an assumed name. She looked at my card and said, you have filled in your card totally differently from other women. I said, why? She said, well, it drives us crazy. They always want a tall man with blue eyes; they are even more insistent about the blue eyes than they are about being tall. And here you've written, I don't mind short, I don't mind fat, I don't mind bald, but I prefer millionaires. So I had this clutch of small, brown-eyed, bald millionaires, who were all very interesting. It was in the course of something I was researching, but I was also quite interested. I'm very interested in experimenting, and new methods and systems; I very much like evolving systems and improving systems. Querying existing systems is my favourite.

I like witty men, and I suppose I like achievers. I don't mean people who are famous, I mean people who do things. There's nothing good or bad about that, but I just happen to like doing things myself, so I would rather be doing something with somebody than going to a party and holding a drink in one hand and chatting and trying to hear what the other person is saying above the noise of the party for two hours.

Genevieve Cooper: I have friends who go for real shits. I think they're disturbed, women who are like that. It's women who actually don't like themselves who go for men like that. Why those women don't like themselves, I don't know, when they are so beautiful and appear to have everything. If I think of this woman I know who's like that, it's as if she feels she deserves to be punished. And I know that's the mentality, that's why those women go for those men. It is masochistic, that kind of feeling: that, if somebody likes me, he can't be very clever, because I'm not very clever; if somebody likes me, he can't be very bright not to see I'm not beautiful and not clever. So there's more credibility in somebody who is nasty to them. It confirms their own feelings about themselves. Why those women have those negative feelings about themselves, I don't know. Not simply because they're women. I think it's something that happened in their childhood, their parents who screwed them up. An analyst could explain all that more clearly. I've never had that trait in me, I know a lot of women do. I'm exactly the opposite. I would run a mile from anyone who looked as if he might not be wonderful to me. I can't bear that. I want somebody who is really going to be good to me and look after me and whom I can trust.

Michelle Coquillat: I have had at least three experiences close to marriage because of living for a long time with a man. And I think that the professional activity of the woman is certainly a big factor in the difficulty of marriage. My own experience, for instance, is that I had to go to another place for work and the geographical distance created the problem. It couldn't last that way. Also, the difficulty of living together now is very much linked to the feminist problem in that the males tend, after a while, to go back to feeling superior, to having superior behaviour, and the woman to feeling she is not treated properly because of this superiority. There is a difficulty in adjusting, it creates violence. I think that, when involved with a man, most women try very sincerely to make it work. But there is a great deal of violence in the relationship between men and women now, because a lot of men unconsciously do not admit that the woman will try and be equal, socially equal. And this creates a great many problems. I see among my friends – the friends I had when I was twelve, thirteen or fourteen – the ones who remained married to the same man are the ones who stopped working. They are not particularly happy, but they saved their marriage.

Susan Crosland: I don't want to be linked with another man. I've had that extraordinary relationship. I'm not going to have it again. I can't have it again; it's not going to happen again. It's me and my children and family. I have a number of men friends, and some very close men friends, but I don't want these men friends to move into my house and take me over, or me to take them over. I want them out there, separate.

Tony was a remarkable man who taught me so much. He liked the company of women, which no doubt was a help. Things are perfectly obvious to me now. They weren't then. I was very young when I met him. So, for instance, if I made some rather dismissive reference to homosexuals – I can't think why, but I did – Tony would say, well, if you find them so repellent, you are going to have to eliminate quite a few people from your life, because at some time or another they have probably been homosexuals too, certainly at school. And this was absolutely fascinating to me. It was the first time I had anyone to teach me that we all have everything in us – from sadism to masochism, to generosity to meanness, everything in some proportion or other. That we have everything – I did not know that. I learned it largely from Tony.

In the course of my thirteen-year marriage with Tony, it developed, as it wasn't a static relationship, and our, if you like, fantasy in part of our relationship, was always that he was the man, I was the woman, and the woman did for the man. And that kind of pleased me. I liked that, I liked that role. But it was pretend, a lot of it. We used to pretend we both enjoyed it. Then at some point, when the feminist thing was happening and began to be so drip, drip, drip, I began to think about certain things, such as why was I the one who always had to buy the petrol for the family car? It seemed frightfully important that I was the one who had to buy this petrol. This was saying that Tony's work was more important than my work. As, indeed, it was, as a Cabinet Minister and all that in this insane country, but it became a symbol for me so, out of character, I began going on about it and making this point. And he finally took to logic and said to me, you will have to be very careful or you are going to wreck this relationship. And what I said after I thought about it was, it isn't going to wreck the relationship, it's like two funnels. (That's how I visualized it – two funnels.) And one funnel has my emotional fantasy life in it with you, and the other funnel is my intellectual relationship with you, and one doesn't impinge on the other, there is no criss-cross between them. And he said, interesting concept, interesting concept – and that was the end. After that we shared buying the petrol. I didn't even care. It was just a symbol.

I haven't got any experience of a virgin marriage – I was never, have never been promiscuous, but neither was I a virgin when I married my first husband. Would it have been a better marriage? I doubt it makes a lot of difference. I know people who have entered marriage as virgins and have had a happy twenty-five years so far of marriage. I find it all remarkable.

Mary Crowther: Professionally, my whole life is spent among women, being a gynaecologist. Socially, if I went to a party, for example, and I didn't know anybody there, I would probably find it easier to talk to men than to women. In my personal life, I think the people to whom I would divulge my most intimate secrets would be women and not men. There is always the sexual element, whether we show it or not, and when I use the analogy of a party, I think part of that sexual attraction, which may be inhibited in fact, and rightly so, allows social interactions which are funnier really than the social interactions between women who don't know each other. Men and women can flirt, and that's allowed, so long as it's not too overt, and that can give rise to a lot of repartee. You don't get that between women who don't know each other. They talk about staid, solid sorts of things, and they really do just make polite conversation. On an intimate level, I think the friendship between women is very special. I don't know about the friendship between men. I'm sure that between certain men – perhaps priests, perhaps artists, perhaps the outsiders of the world – the friendships they have between each other are as deep and personal as the friendships women have. But on an overall level, women are brought up to look after each other and support each other, and that gives rise to a warmth you don't get between men.

Jennifer D'Abo: One of my weaknesses is that I'm totally not jealous. I've had three husbands, they're all great friends, and they will all tell you, I'm simply not jealous. If they wanted to go off and be naughty, as long as it didn't embarrass or hurt me or anything else, I didn't ask.

I believe that if the man, whether he's your husband or your lover, goes, then there's something wrong with you. I don't think any man will be stolen or poached if he's happy, because men basically are idle, they like comfortable lives. In emotional relationships, as long as they're happy and their shirts are ironed and everything's done for them, they don't like hassle, they don't want to move house. They'll go wandering a bit, but then that's again something men do that women don't, usually.

It's very much easier for people to get out and about and go their own ways. I also think that women have much more freedom, they have bank accounts of their own. My mother never ran her own bank account. She never ran anything. She just went to my father and said, I want a new dress. Actually, she wouldn't have said, I want ..., she would have said, please darling, can I have a new dress for ... or, do you think I can have the drawing room painted ... or, shall we have so-and-so to dinner on Saturday night ... or whatever it happened to be. She didn't have the kind of freedom that I have. I'm about to be divorced for the third time. I don't find that exciting at all. It's part of the price you have to pay. It's not easy to be a woman alone. I don't mind, because I'm spoilt. It depressed me to leave, because I think that separating from someone you've lived with for eleven years is desperately sad, but equally, I couldn't go on any more. So I'm realistic. When I say, I can't take any more, that's finished – bonk – I'm off.

I don't like the fact that I do an immense amount of travelling on my own; I hate staying in hotels by myself. There's nothing more depressing than me sitting in the Goya alone. I can't go to the bar – women don't. Then you go to airports, you have to change the currency, you get on the plane, and then it's late, and you go to see yet another ghastly place and have a long list of people to see all day and you long to go back to someone and say, oh darling, I had the most terrible day today, and I didn't buy anything, and the colours are all wrong. I find that very lonely. It doesn't matter how expensive the hotel is, it's soul-destroying. I stay in the Mayfair Regent, and they know me and they're nice to me and I don't have to worry; they never embarrass me about any money, they do my tickets, but it's still not the same.

Maryam D'Abo: Somehow I am not a man's woman, I'm very much a woman's woman. I've got very close girlfriends and I admire women. Some women I feel very uncomfortable with, but generally, if I like and admire a woman, I always feel more comfortable than I would with a man, and that's probably a result of my background and being brought up in boarding schools all my life. I haven't been brought up in a family where there were men – no brothers, no father and so on.

I can't stand losers. I always like successful men. That doesn't mean successful, powerful men but men who are fighters, who have charm and a strong personality.

I'm not ready for marriage. If my parents said, we want you to get married, I'd just freak out. It's not going to be easy to say I'll get married because I am very independent and I value my freedom very much at the moment. I think it's wonderful when you are young. I'd love to share my life with somebody one day, but not now. I still feel like a fifteen-year-old.

Béatrice Dalle: I like men who are physically handsome. I know that other women say they like inner qualities, but that's not enough for me. Not necessarily like a model, six foot tall and blue eyes, but he must have a good body. Take Marlon Brando. He's smallish, but he's frantically good-looking, ultra good-looking – a man must be physically good to be attractive. I can't fall in love with terribly ugly men, even if they have a heart of gold, are intelligent and everything else; it's not enough.

Alma Daniel: Women are afraid that if they become all-powerful they will not have a relationship, because for them a relationship is based on need. Now, a relationship based on need disempowers, but a relationship based on choice can not only empower but can help that person, and that relationship can flower. So it's very important that we see that we make choices and are not dependent on somebody else because we need that love. Women very often do not succeed, do not go as far as they can, because they are afraid they're not going to be loved if they do.

I know of relationships where the woman has made more money than the man and there is no problem *per se*. It isn't that the man has to go round feeling disempowered. In fact, the woman's financial security allows him the liberty to do many things that he would enjoy doing but he couldn't do if he had to be working for a living. So I think we are re-examining our values and re-examining our pictures of what a relationship is. The fact that a woman may make more money than her husband – and I've been in that situation – should not alter or make the relationship deteriorate.

I've never been able to be promiscuous. I'm not saying that I wouldn't out of some sort of moral prerogative. I'm just not drawn to that. What I'm drawn to is the connection that goes much beyond physiological responses of arousal. What arouses me are connections of the heart, connections of the mind, connections of shared sensibilities, not just lust.

I know my chemistry changes when my partner and I become close.

813

Sometimes I am in the middle of doing something, I am working on the computer, the telephone is ringing, there are people waiting for me, and he will come in and touch me and my chemistry changes. Something melts, I become all female. And yet there's another part, way, way distant, which says, wait a minute, wait a minute, you are in the middle of doing something. So what I've learned is to enjoy and savour that moment, and then return to my work. OK, I can have it all. It's not that I'm going to be turned into a jellyfish and won't be able to function any more. I can have those moments of contact, those sweet murmurings in my ear, and I can continue to do what I am doing. I don't have to give it all up. It's a question of balancing that I think we're learning about right now.

I have gone through periods of my life where I had no man, no companion, no sex, and I was fine, but there was a part of me that was not so, that didn't glow. My belief is that I, and therefore everyone, can have it all. I can have whatever it is I choose, with God's will, and that includes companionship, and relationship, and fun, and money, and work, and everything. There is no need to cut it off. I think when we say OK, I don't need this, and I don't need that, that's fine. The monks, who are totally abstinent, who eat once a week, who pray all the time, who don't talk at all, they are fine, too, but they are not fully functioning human beings. I am not saying that everyone has to have sex and everybody has to have a relationship. We all know about subli-mating energy, we know that if the sexual energy is not being used, that same area of the body is also the area of great creation, so we can move into more creative modes when we are not involved with putting our energies out sexually. But that doesn't mean that we can't do both. What I have observed in my own life, and in the life of women, is that women very often will put themselves, their work and their lives aside for a relationship, which is not what a man will do. A man will have a career, and he will have his lover; a woman will put her lover first, and then her career. Or, as I have examined in many cases, a woman will find that she can't be good in the boardroom and good in bed as well. She can be successful and powerful as a woman in business, but she has no love life at all. Now, I don't think we need to make those choices. We are coming to a time where, as I said, we can have it all. We can be full, flourishing women and businesswomen and creative and vocational people, and we can also have relationships. I think the challenge for me – and I can only speak for myself – is to maintain my sense of individuality, to maintain my identity while, at the same time, forming a second identity which is part of a relationship. They talk about the urge to merge, but it is not that I become faceless, nameless, without an identity in my relationship, it's that there is something about being in a pair, something about being in a two that I have discovered, very late in my life, has given much more energy to everything that I do. It doesn't take away from it. And yet I must sometimes say, no, I need to do my work now, you'll have to wait. And my lover, my partner, says, fine. He's got his life and he understands. Men understand that very well. They do what their heart calls them to do, whether it's their work, or their art or their music or their career, and then they also have women in their life, but it isn't as if they have to give one up or the other. Women very often have given up their career, their identity, just for having a relationship. I don't think that's necessary any longer.

Sister Camille D'Arienzo: I think it is unfair not to present virginity as an option. We now have young women, young teenage women, who have never even seriously heard of that as a possibility: that with discipline and self-control, and the very special nature of the sexual act, intimate relations could be refused to a man. I'm sure there are some parts of the New York area where no one ever says that, where it is taken for granted that a woman will be whatever vessel a man wants her to be. And so I think the Church has an obligation to talk about the sacredness of a person; it has an obligation to say that people are precious in God's sight, not only because of the combinations they form, but individually. In the Old Testament, we hear in Isaiah, I have loved you with an everlasting love, therefore have I drawn you, calling you by name, you are mine. There is something about presenting the relationship with God as the fateful relationship. I don't think it hurts to say that the Church believes, from its experience, teaching and understanding of what it means to be a whole person, that it is better for men and women not to have sexual relationships outside marriage. There are enough voices that will contradict that. I have been an educator now for over thirty years, in elementary schools through to colleges, and I know that children, students of any age, can only make choices from available options, available alternatives. If the Church does not present that alternative, who will present it? I don't tend to talk in terms of sin and Hell and damnation; that's the theology I relinquished many years ago. I don't think a person who is in love with, passionately involved with another human being and who has sex, is going to go to Hell, I really don't. First of all, a mortal sin has to be a serious matter. I am not sure that giving one's body, in a loving alliance, is the most terribly serious thing a person can do. It is worse to give one's mind to the creation of a nuclear weapon. I think that's a prostitution far beyond anything that two human beings, who are locked in love, can provide.

Mandy Rice Davies: I've always been very attracted to the opposite sex. I've always really liked men. All my really close friends are men.

Several things seduce me. Power. I like the glow of men with power, power which is brought partly by money, partly by position, status – the position that person has reached in the world. It certainly isn't looks. The other thing is that pure chemical reaction you get sometimes, nothing to do with looks, nothing to do with intellect particularly. It's just some strange chemistry that chops you at the kneecaps. I completely lose my taste for other men when I'm in love. Nobody can seduce me when I'm in love. I totally lose my taste for other bodies, other anything. After a while, perhaps ... That's not even saying that you've fallen out of love, but I might be tempted.

Régine Deforges: Sainte-Beuve said that there could only be friendship between a man and a woman if they had slept with each other at least once. He called that 'hammering in the golden nail'. I am not sure, though. It is difficult to spin stories to another woman, tell fibs; women are too alike and know how the other ticks. Two women together know very quickly what the other is like. Between a man and a woman, there is always a sexual element. Perhaps, when I am older, it will not be the same, but there is always this slight possibility that one day there will be a sexual relationship. My best friends are my former lovers with whom I have real friendships. With a woman, there is none of this (unless you are a lesbian, which I'm not), but it does not exclude attraction and sensuality. My women friends are people I can touch; I can't imagine having a friendly relationship with someone whose skin I didn't like, for example, because physical contact would be unpleasant. In the same way, I have never had a sexual relationship with a man who wasn't interested in literature.

There are some women whose femininity exasperates both men and women. If a woman is too beautiful or too feminine, then people say she's stupid. If she works in an office, then she disturbs the men and other women are jealous. As a woman, I cannot dissociate femininity and feminism; I have used my femininity in dealing with people. My husband says I have a South American attitude. That's to say, I like my cigarette to be lit for me, I expect a man to open the door for me if I am in a car, and to help me on with my coat and so on. These traditional gestures of courtesy between men and women seem to me to be charming and linked to the female sex – but I am in favour of equality, too. It is a great mistake for a woman to try to behave like a man. The interesting thing in life is that we are different. We should not try to be

816

the same, we are complimentary, which is in the interests of the planet after all, and women who try to behave like men often end up on the psychoanalyst's couch. One should be oneself and as close to one's own nature as possible.

I am sensitive to the way a man looks at me. I like to see a certain irony, teasing, intelligence and sensitivity: lots of things which can happen very quickly in a glance. An openness of mind. I like a man who has a calm exterior, but behind which you can sense some violence, a feeling he is ready to leap to your or his own defence. Almost a caveman spirit.

Dr Mary Jordan-DeLaurenti: I was not nervous with men. Most of the students at Notre Dame were males – there were very few of us females working for a doctorate at Notre Dame. So during that four-year period, I had dear friends who were males, non-priest males, who interacted with me and with whom I was very comfortable, so I never had that fear. The sexual encounter was the beginning of opening, more than anything I think. When you start saying, well now, this guy is asking me for a date, that's a whole different feeling of what one was going to do. I started to date a man who was eight years younger than I was; I went with him for three years, and almost married him several times, but we came up to the day and we didn't do it. My own analysis of that is that he took me very quickly through those years, and I think it was my growing-up period. I had to go through those same years that I missed in order to move into some kind of maturity, and it took some time. I did not marry until I was thirty-seven, so I was out a good six years before I met Robert and married him. Even though I had had several boy-friends over those six years, I didn't marry until then. I don't think I was ready until then. It probably took me that many years to catch up with the fourteen I'd missed.

I don't think platonic friendships are difficult. They exist all the time. And, for me personally, they are great supports. I have several good men friends that I've met in the business world that I could call on the telephone any moment and ask for a good favour, and I have, and they me; and there has never been any sexual encounter. It doesn't mean they're not attracted to me and I'm not attracted to them, and Robert and I tease about it a lot, but they are good, solid friendships. You have to get through that hump where your intelligence becomes more influential than your attractiveness. Your attractiveness is not a plus, your attractiveness becomes a disadvantage, until that happens, until people recognize you for your person.

Sylvia Deutsch: A friendship between women can also be fragile because men are not always pleased by it, they can be jealous, but it can be very solid. I don't have many women friends myself, but those I do have are important. I'm more at ease in the company of men because there comes a moment when women become a pain. The problem is that instead of blossoming, trying to find out different things, to have passionate interests, women tend to compartmentalize themselves, talking, for instance, only about their work or children, and they find it difficult to be critical. I like to talk about everything, different subjects, and I really am not capable of being satisfied in the company of women.

Power does attract me, but more the kind of power behind the throne. You can pay a very high price for power, and I prefer to have peace. I had a certain kind of power in the sense that I married very young a man from a well-known family. His father was famous, and after his parents died he inherited a lot of money, so I was thrown too quickly into a circle where I was well known and people were, well, foul. I've always tried to maintain my anonymity, not to be like those women who act like stars when they have a well-known husband. Despite this, I've still not had peace, and I sometimes ask myself what life must be like if you go looking for publicity.

I am in the process of getting a divorce and therefore live alone, am delighted to be alone, not to have someone complaining every five minutes. But I've noticed that some couples I'm friends with haven't exactly turned their back on me, but I feel that I represent a danger for married women, though never in my life would I dream of going for a married man, and never have. On principle. I feel nothing but contempt for women who do. So, for my friends, I am not a danger at all, their husbands do not interest me, and it's not only my friends' husbands but anyone's husband.

Kay Dick: I don't mind a simple fool, but I don't like a pretentious fool. It's as old-fashioned as my mother's attitude that men were put in the world solely to look after her and see she was happy and fêted and treated. When women say men don't take women seriously, in a sense they are saying precisely what my mother said. When you say a man is not taking me seriously, it's a peevish statement. If he's not taking a woman seriously, obviously she is not making herself interesting or she's talking to the wrong man.

I've known so many friends who lived together for a number of years and then eventually decided to get married because of the children.

Always they say they got married because of the children. Gives people security, doesn't it? I lived with someone for many many years, and I think it is very difficult. I think we need to be by ourselves, we need solitude. If you're living with someone, whatever the relationship, you're having to refer to someone about every bloody thing you do – you know, saying, I shall be late for dinner tonight, dear. If you live alone, you don't have to say that to anyone.

Anne Dickson: I understand women a lot more than I understand men. And a sadness to me is that I don't have more men as friends. I don't think men are very good at friendship. If there's no sexual element involved, I find – from my own and other people's experiences – that men are not that interested, they won't make that much of an effort to meet and go out or whatever. I regret that, because that makes for more distance.

Dame Jean Conan Doyle: People marry too young, and that is very extraordinary considering so many people live together before marriage nowadays. It's extraordinary that they still marry so young. There are a lot of advantages today, but I think our sense of values was far better and made for a happier life in the long run. I wouldn't wish to be young today. No. I'd rather be my own age. One could trust people far more in my time than you can today. I am very sorry for young people growing up in this world, with the state it's in and so much evil in it. It's a very difficult world indeed.

Margaret Drabble: I wasn't terribly happy when I was young at school. I got much happier when I was in my late teens. I did feel happier in the company of women at school age, and then, when I went to university, I was thrilled by this new world of men and couldn't see enough of them. I was just delighted with being in mixed society for the first time at the age of seventeen or eighteen. I thought it was wonderful.

I respond physically to certain people who are by no means convention-ally good-looking. Robert Redford, I couldn't care less. There are certain physical types I find attractive, and there are certain manners. I can't bear people who talk very slowly. I like people to exchange ideas, I find that attractive. I'm trying to work out whether all the people I find attractive are conventionally intelligent, and I think they probably are. Yes, I think they are. Perhaps I would call it quick-witted more than intelligent, because intelligence implies they are all Isaiah Berlins. I was

once seduced by power when I was nineteen and I was so bored once I'd
found myself in the orbit of this man who was powerful, I just couldn't
bear it. I was terribly bored. I kept saying, he's a very important person,
but I just couldn't wait to get away, because I was bored. But I was
certainly attracted by it, I got hooked with it, and it was very bad when it
was over. It's difficult to get away from, too, so I can understand women
being seduced by power.

The average marriage in the olden days only lasted ten years; death
ended it. Now, who wants to be married to the same person they were
married to when they were twenty, when they're seventy? I've been
married twice, and I see a lot of my first husband. My first husband and
my second husband get on very well. That's all very nice, you've gained
another friend. It seems to me perfectly natural that one shouldn't
remain in the same static situation all one's life. As one's children leave
home so, occasionally, one's husband leaves home.

Maureen Duffy: Many more people were widowed in the past. If you
look through parish registers, as I have done a lot, and if you look
through biographies, you will find that many women died in childbirth,
many men died of all sorts of diseases, and in war. So marriage was for
life, but the lives were often quite short. Quite often people would have
several partners, not through divorce, but simply through death. Also
there's no point in pretending that there wasn't a great deal of extra-
marital activity. But, of course, a divorce was not a thing that was
contemplated. It couldn't be got for most people, and so most people
soldiered on, often very unhappily.

Other feminists don't consider me a feminist. My philosophy is equality.
I don't believe in leaving boy babies to die. I don't believe that all men
are boots, and that men and women have nothing in common. In fact,
apart from my own sexual interest, I largely move in a masculine world.
Most of my friends happen to be men. I am much more comfortable
with men. I have nothing in common, really, with most women, because
my experiences have not been theirs. I like them, but as men like them,
not because I have a great deal in common with them. I like them as
beautiful objects, as soft, et cetera, all that sort of thing. Not because I
feel a great common spirit between them and me.

I'm attracted to women with a very strong maternal element. Obviously
I like there to be an intellect, otherwise there's not going to be much in
common. And I want, obviously, a well-defined personality. But I don't
necessarily require strength.

Sally Emerson: I've always felt very close to women friends. Certainly the very good friends I have I could say anything to, feel very comfortable with, and understand very well. Somebody like Tina Brown, or some other people; we have this deep friendship more so than there would be with men. I like women enormously. I actually tend not to like women who say they don't like women. I find, in my experience, that women who say they don't like women are often nasty bits of work because they don't actually like their own kind, they're in competition, they're jealous, and always trying to get one over on them. In a way, the males are the audience and you perform for the audience, so you're not really being quite yourself. It's a lack of respect for yourself to say you don't like women when you're a woman, but it's deeper than that. It's like a woman saying, well, I'm very attractive to men and men respond to me, that's when I'm most interesting; but you're seeing yourself only as a kind of mirror of somebody else. It's taking one part of you out and showing it to somebody and saying, that is the good part. Whereas you, as a woman, are all those different kinds of things that are inside you. One of the great problems women have, and one of the things we're growing out of, is this sense of competition which means women get isolated and don't join to do things together. Now we're beginning to have more respect for other women, there is more of a feeling that we are actually all in the same boat and banding together.

Shirley Eskapa: There is nothing more rewarding or elevating than pleasing a man. Now that, with women's liberation, they are free to participate in the wide world, much more is required of them because they have to balance so much more. They have to balance, but they still have to please a man if they want to be happy. I have talked to so many women who were at the tops of their careers who either didn't have a man and couldn't get a man because of (and this is very prevalent today) male homosexuality – because there are fewer men. People would be shocked if I were to tell them the numbers of beautiful and intelligent women in their twenties who have sat here and told me they can't find a man to take them to bed. That is what the shortage is like. In America, a book has been written – *Man-Sharing* – because there is a shortage of men. What I am trying to say is that even these women at the tops of their careers, who are liberated and who are succeeding, will do anything for a man. That's why they give up top jobs and move countries – to follow their man. You do not find men doing that. Because somehow – and I don't believe this is cultural only – women need a man in their lives.

Ten years ago, my daughter's friends felt free to flirt with my husband, and they did – and if he had gone off with one of them, who would society have condemned, him or me? Me. Because I couldn't keep my man. I've written about this extensively: what has happened is that it has become perfectly respectable for a liberated woman to go after and pursue any man – married or not. It happens every day; there is no stigma attached to it. I have to work a thousand times harder at being a wife than my mother did. I have to work much harder at keeping my family together than my mother had to. I would love to walk around the place not worrying about combing my hair and that sort of thing, sometimes. It's become much more burdensome, much more difficult, much more complicated. Look at Sara Keays and the Parkinson affair. He was condemned, he stayed with his family, he stayed with his existing children.

Kathryn Falk: I don't compete with men. Two gay men work for me. The rest of my office are women: two black women, a Brooklyn girl, and an Italian girl. We have an international group, which is the kind I like, but I have no man working for me. I'm very careful whom I work with. I've maybe ten employees and we all get along very harmoniously. I don't want any trouble and I learned from previous experiences. I've worked with men and didn't like it. I'd much rather have gay men work for me.

Marcia Falkender: I adore being with women because I love gossiping. I am a great gossip and I admit to it. I love women's gossip, the sort that's harmless. I don't like the harmful sort where you rip people's characters apart, because that I find very counter-productive. But I love to hear what everyone's been doing and whether somebody's getting married or who they are with or whatever. But I do like men's company because, on the whole, it tends to be more stimulating. Eventually, if you are in women's company alone, they'll reduce it back to the level of home and family. In a sense, I'm contradicting myself, because I think the fact that women live very much in the home and related to families, and the whole bit of creation, makes them special and different and, in my view, in many ways a lot better than men. On the other hand, when they're together in a whole crowd and it's reduced back to that level, you can find it very boring. Men tend to be more stimulating in the sense that they are roaming the world (in inverted commas) when you are with them. They like to talk about lots of different things. Unmarried women will be like that, or those who aren't in a relationship. But even so, it will come back to relationships at the end of the day, and to whether somebody is happy or unhappy. Whereas, with men, it will be a really stimulating conversation about whether we think the Russians are doing something they shouldn't be doing or will the Middle East ever have peace? I find that much more stimulating. But one gets something out of both.

Today, the stress of living is so great, and it's such a complicated world, and if you are doing a job as well as your husband, you won't look the other way, you won't turn a blind eye or a deaf ear to situations which, maybe before the war or years ago, you would take in a deep breath and forget about. Now it's all rush and pressure, and a lot of work and a lot of aggravation, so that if somebody does get up your nose too many times, you wonder why on earth you are locked into four walls with them. You just want to escape. I was married, and the reason I didn't stay married was because my husband wanted to live and work in America. And I was right in the middle of wanting to be involved in British politics and didn't want to go and live in America. And so the marriage came to an end. The one startling thing about that is – and I look back on it now quite in amazement – that we were very good friends, we'd got on very well. But maybe we didn't have the other sort of excitement. We were young, maybe the sex wasn't as good as it should have been, and the two should come together to make it worthwhile. I still envy people who have a happy marriage. But don't get me wrong, that doesn't mean I would want to lock myself up in a marriage for the sake of being married. There are many women still, in this day and age – I'd say a good 50 per cent of the female population – who are happy to opt for anything so long as they are in a marriage, even if it's not going to last. And they jump out of that one into another. Now, I admire and envy those who have a happy marriage and a lovely, friendly relationship, and if they also have a good sexual relationship, that's even better. I envy that, I think that's what Nature really intended us for. I think, if it hadn't, we wouldn't have been constructed as we are. I know that's a sort of cliché, but it has to be true. And I think it must be lovely. I envy that.

Annie Flanders: I've only ever been seduced by the mind. I've always been personally attracted from getting to know someone and talking to them, and I've been involved with a lot of very brilliant men.

I've been through two kinds of society. I grew up in the 1950s and totally understand the outlook and points of view and experiences of men and women in the old-fashioned sense. I also, because I've been very modern, am totally a part of today's culture, through the 1960s to the

1980s. And I think there is really a serious change, and one of the most serious changes is between women. There used to be a time, and I can say this specifically about the fashion business, when if two women went shopping together, one would never want her friend to look as nice as she could, because if they were out together, one would always want to look better than the other. Modern women, young women, help each other, because they understand that, if two or three women are out together, the better they look, the better it is for all of them, because they attract more attention. So it is a completely different attitude. I experienced the same thing when I first went into the work market in the earlier 1960s. Women who had worked in business then were tough, they were mean, they were hard. I hated working for them, but I understand, on looking back, it was because they were fighting in a man's world and had a really difficult time, and there was no other way they could conduct their lives. They had to fight one-to-one against men, and they got really hard-boiled. But younger women today in business are open, they're warmer, they're feminine, they don't have to feel like they're men, and they don't have to feel they're really competing with men. They can be who they are.

I don't think women need men to glow. Some women can get it from other women. I've seen a lesbian glow. It's the same kind of relationship. But I need a man to make me glow. I need a man to help me, I don't function well in a sensual way without a man. Maybe it's because I grew up at a time when men had their roles and women had their roles, and even though I've always been very secure in business, I've never really been adequate in taking care of myself in a personal way and at home. I like to have a man around to take care of me.

I don't believe in marriage. We've chosen to stay together for seventeen years, but I have no marriage certificate. I have a philosophy. When we're young, we're conditioned subconsciously, or we were, and many people still are, with the male role, with the female role, with what being a husband is, being a wife is, and once that ceremony takes place, you somehow become a husband, become a wife. You can live with someone and never have that ceremony and never have those titles, you can be two people, two individuals who love each other living under the same roof, but that subconscious role-playing does not enter into it. Because you haven't had any built-in subconscious roles about living together. That's why I'm against marriage.

Lorraine Stanley-Ford: If I am more successful than my male partner, then there are problems, whether it's a boyfriend, a live-in boyfriend, a

824

potential fiancé, a serious relationship. On two occasions, I have found they simply can't handle it, just can't cope with someone who is either away a lot of the time or who has an independent bank account.

I think, to a certain extent, a lot of women have felt threatened by me because I appear very confident. I appear not to need the security of a marriage. A lot of women who are married, who live at home: they've got children, they don't work any more, or perhaps they just do a job which just brings in a little bit of extra money, but they would not term themselves successful career women. And I think that they resent my freedom, my independence, my ability to say, come on, let's go out and have a meal, because the husband wouldn't like it if they're out with the girls. They feel perhaps a little in awe of successful women. A sort of jealousy. They would like to be free, they would like to be a bit more independent, they would like to be self-confident in any company, but perhaps they're not. I have certainly felt women in awe of me.

I'm more comfortable in the presence of men for the simple reason that, because I'm not married and do not have children and have never really had a family environment, I can't talk to women who have children and can only talk about children. I have nothing in common with babies, with knitting, I don't know how to thread a sewing machine. But put me with a spanner in the garden, and I'll fix the fence. I tend to be a more masculine-orientated person. I don't find housewives very interesting to talk to. I've never been a girl who will go out and have coffee with all her girlfriends and sit and chat about the husbands, boyfriends, sex lives, or medical problems. Generally, men seem to have a much wider-ranging conversation than women, who are perhaps so totally wrapped in their own environment at home that they don't get the chance to do very much in their lives. Probably because I travelled so much, and I've seen so many other places, I find people who have travelled very interesting. We have things in common.

What I would like, as I go into the latter half of my life, is an old-fashioned type of relationship which is one-to-one, where I'm secure, where I would like to know that what I feel for somebody is reciprocated fully, and I don't want to worry about the guy if he says, oh, I'm going out. I don't want to think he's going to pick up somebody and phone me up and say the car's broken down while he's in bed with somebody else. I've had all that. I've had people who lie to me, who profess total honesty, total fidelity, and they're out all over the place. That's awful if you trust somebody.

Christina Foyle: I don't like being with a lot of men. I don't like a lot of smoke and drink and noise, really; but I like men, I like women, too. I don't take much part in local women's things. I'm president of lots of things and I get on well with both sexes. I don't care much to be with women with children, though, because I've never had children and I've not much interest in that, really.

Lynne Franks: I think marriage is an unnatural state. It's very difficult for two people to live together. It's nice to bring up a family and so on, but certainly it is very difficult today for two people to live the whole of their two lives with and through each other in a world where people challenge the roles they used to accept.

Gisèle Galante: I don't have too many women friends. Up till now, I feel much better with male friends. About 80 per cent of my friends are men. I've been trying to have more women friends, but I scare them. They see me as a rival, as a threat. I've had that experience a number of times, in my work and elsewhere. In my work, I don't have any women friends at all. I could never live in an environment where there are only women or where there are more women than men. I could not.

When I was younger, I could only see the façade, and I would go out with an extremely handsome man. And recent boyfriends I have had, actually they were ugly, but they were very intellectual and obviously very charming and extremely bright, and now that's the only appeal I find in men.

I would like to live without men, yes, I'd like to be totally independent of men, emotionally and financially. I'd like to be all by myself. On every level. But I realize I probably never will be. Probably I will always live with a man, but I would like to be able to be happy on my own. Without depending on anyone. I expand probably in the presence of men, which I don't in the presence of women. My mother has always been extremely independent, never dependent, and she taught me quite a number of things. In her work, and in her public life, she has been very successful, obviously, but her private life is a total disaster. She has been married twice, the two marriages failed, she has tried to have a family, she did all she could to raise us, but I don't think she did it in the proper way, and I see the result. She's extremely powerful and extremely domineering.

I'm trying to struggle in the face of reality. I have a dream of marriage, of having a close family and working, of being able to combine all these things and doing it well. And the reality is that it's very very difficult to combine all these things. It takes a lot of courage, and a lot of self-confidence, to be able to sustain a good marriage. I'm not against divorce, but I would hope marriage was a commitment for ever. Otherwise there is no point in marriage.

I think I would rather be a man. I wouldn't have so many problems if I were a man. I used to have a boyfriend, and I was the one who was working at the time and he was putting me first and career second. I must say, I enjoyed the situation. I would come home to the apartment and he was the woman and I was the man.

Teri Garr: Years ago, Francis Coppola was in LA casting his movie *The Conversation* and he decided to have this cocktail party and invite all these girls and all these people, and they'd talk to him in a casual setting and he'd get to meet everyone. So I went and I saw what it was: all these women throwing themselves at him and talking to him, and flirting and getting drinks. I thought, I cannot play this game, this is not what I am here for, I can't do this. I talked to some friends, I had a drink and then I left. Well, a couple of days later, I was chosen as one of the three people to screen test for this movie. Not only that, but I got the part. So there I am, confirmed in my idea that, you see, I didn't have to play the game.

Someone who's making a lot of money or a huge success in something, usually they don't know how to plant a garden. And that kind of stuff is important to me because that's a very nurturing thing. What attracts me to men is not just physical. It's their sensitivity and intelligence, and wit and humour, and all kinds of things. I couldn't be attracted to someone just physically. I suppose everybody says that. Everybody says that, even men say that, and they're full of shit.

It's frightening, how I've gotten myself into being independent. I mean, it's almost a burden to have another person in my life. I am able to function very well on my own, and have friends when I want them, and have conversations with people when I want to, and pick different people. The minute you get a partner in your life, you have to start weighing different people: this one we can see, and that one we can't see. I am an independent person. I can see whoever I want whenever I want, it's easy living. But having that one connection, or that one person, makes things start to get complicated.

Pamela Gems: Discrimination is at a very deep level. There is an awful lot of lip-service paid to feminism, particularly if it sells newspapers or whatever you're involved in selling. We live in a buy-and-sell society. But the discrimination is there, and it is there *au fond*, because a man is stronger than a woman and in the end he can hit her. That is one of the major differences, and one men and women both find it difficult in different circumstances to deal with. The honour between men and women which began in the twelfth century – this code of I am stronger than you, therefore my role is to protect you – is an incredible code. This was fine when men and women were together in a static feudal society. Now we smash men to pieces and people are surprised at this venomous increase in rape. There is a terrible sex war going on. The hostility between men and women is dreadful. It's terribly difficult for men. I've spoken, and been regarded as reactionary, at many feminist meetings, because I've agreed it isn't in men's interests to give up being looked after, first by the mother and then by the wife, while they shoulder the responsibility for the family. You know, I have never seen a good production of *A Doll's House* because it is always played as though Nora is escaping from this silly husband. He is not a silly husband, he's a perfect husband. They are in the middle of their conjugality, they are in love. They have three beautiful children and he is doing his best. She gets into debt, she can ruin him, and if she ruins him how can he look after the three children? This is a wonderful sub-text in the play which is not ever dealt with. He is played as a wimp, and what woman wouldn't want to run out of that house from such a silly man? But all of those systems of protection started to go when the machines came in and muscles weren't necessary any more. Man is in a tragic state in the West because his heroic qualities are no longer needed and not revered.

The difficulty for a woman is the deception. You see, it's a moment's thought for a man. I know, because I was complaining to my son the other day about my husband, and my son said, surely now you can accept the fact that we are not like you; when we see it, we have to have it. He was actually talking about himself and his father. And I said, yes, but I still can't get over it. I've lived with this man forty years, I love him, he's the father of my children, and he comes in with a bland face and a bunch of flowers; and the bunch of flowers always gives him away. Why has he bought me those dreadful daffodils, which cost him 50p? I know why he bought them, and so they go in the bucket. He has no charm, no style. He's not going to buy a jewel, he's already got me. Anyway, I'm older. I used to say to him twenty years ago, can't you say, oh, Pammy I've met this wonderful woman and she's gorgeous, and you know you've never been good in the legs, and she's got wonderful legs. I wouldn't mind if he had the odd kid elsewhere, but he could never tell me. My son says, don't you understand, that's half the fun. But my husband is making me into his mother, and I don't want to be his mother. That's the dilemma. I see no way out of it, for men or women in the society structured as we are. I started to think in the 1960s, the communes are going to work it out – it's going to be an extended family, like a gipsy group, there's going to be little bits of love here, and maybe a kid, and then they're going to move on. But the shotgun comes out at some point. There is always one who breaks it up, not two. In any of the normal daily papers, there is always somebody who has shot himself or his wife because she has been having it off with the man at the pub.

I always fall in love with men who look like my Uncle Ted, who was not my favourite uncle, but he was the best cricketer in the village, and he had a very English face, and fair hair and blue eyes, and if anybody looked like that, I fell in love. But I never went near him, because I was too afraid of rejection. I tended to go with men whom I felt needed me. I guess it was maternal, though I was a bookish girl and hated to be thought of as that. You spend your twenties finding out about sex, being concerned about sex, but mostly getting it wrong, but when I came to maturity in my thirties, I found that my sexual taste was for rather repressed men, almost perverse. And I think it is something to do with the English, and something to do with being brought up in the kitchens of these very lah-di-dah men who were also terribly repressed because the only relations they knew were power relations. They had no relations with their parents, whom they rarely saw. They were brought up by nannies, nursery governesses, with whom they had relations of affection, but also they had power over them. I like that. I like men who are kind of spies, and I like moody men. I had a friend who, alas, lost her husband who died on the operating table. It was twenty years ago, and she went to a marriage bureau. You had to write down what kind of man you wanted and what sort of personality, and my friend Ann wrote, moody. She had had this lovely moody man, never boring. I think to be married to someone boring must be the worst thing.

Susan George: I really was terrified of losing my independence when I got married, and I found, in actual fact, that I gained every independence, all my independence, by being married. Because when there are two people, you create a rock, a place from which to venture from and something that's incredibly solid; and when you've got something that's incredibly solid and secure, you can then go out into the wide world as far afield as you want, and stretch your imagination, to do a million different things, because you know you can always come back to the rock and the solid place and security. When one doesn't have that basic security, one is always floundering.

I love power. I love assertiveness. I certainly don't find powerless people attractive. That's interesting, though. Often in my life I've actually fallen in love with somebody who didn't have power and wasn't the strength. And it's a mistake in me, because I am so strong, but there's something that's very attractive about it – it's like the little boy lost. I am attracted to that, too: somebody who can rule an office and rule people, and rule an empire and at the same time can cry when something goes wrong.

Sarah Giles: Englishmen are frightened of women, which is why they'd rather have other men or prostitutes. That is why an English upper-class man will always say to you, I expect you to be a lady when you're my wife and a prostitute in bed. It's something to do with their mothers or their nannies. The upper-class kids weren't brought up by their mothers, but by nannies who bossed them around and beat them when they were bad. They never knew any femininity around them when they were growing up very possibly, and then they went straight off to boarding school, where they were surrounded by boys who played around with them. That was their first sexuality. Otherwise it was a woman in a starched uniform with a starched everything, starched voice – the whole thing, starched. It's not basically feminine that, is it? Why do I have to do this? Because nanny says so. There's no kind of logic to it even, and I suppose the first softness and emotion they have is when it's another man giving it to them.

That is the disadvantage with women, you can't trust them – unless you've had a friend for a very long time.

Alexandra M. Giurgiu: I'm less tolerant of stupid women than I am of stupid men, the way I imagine that men are less tolerant of stupid men than they are of stupid women.

Marriages don't last because people don't understand that they have to give and take. They only want to take. It's the post-me society; jogging is the best example of the me society, in terms of sport. Everyone took up jogging because they didn't have the team spirit any more. All you had to do was to go out and run with and against yourself. Anxiety of choice is something that is opening up a can of worms. It's good, but it's

830

also bad, because without guidance and a lot of maturity one can get very confused and very disturbed.

Victoria Glendinning: When I was a teenager, which would have been in the late 1950s, if, at a party, you weren't talking to boys or men, somehow you had failed. Therefore I spent a lot of energy talking to men and to boys and did that quite effectively. It is only as I've got older that my relationship with women has become quite different. I think there is a lot of nonsense talked about women being antagonistic, jealous of each other, in competition with each other. In fact, if they'd only look sideways, horizontally, they'd see that is where the solidarity is, not outwards to the men. Now I find that my best conversations – and I don't just mean about houses, children and families – my best mental conversations are with other women, because men very often still want to talk in a faintly badinage kind of way, whereas, with women, you talk about really important things very often. I'm more interested to know what women think. I take great pleasure in the company of men – the opposite sex is somehow wonderful always – but I'm more interested in the opinions of women. I reckon them more than the opinions of men. It's not true in every case, but I think men feel more stereotyped, typecast, and with women you don't know what they're going to say.

Marriage should be made more difficult. People embark on it not realizing what it entails, because actually it's almost impossible. People go into it very blithely, without thinking about it, without knowing the least thing about each other. Perhaps less now. I see no reason for prolonging a marriage when it has ceased to function. I think that's a killer. That's a spiritual killer, a frightening spiritual killer to both people because neither of them is functioning as they should be, they've both been squashed in not being.

If I was God, I would make a rule that nobody should marry until they were about twenty-eight. I think a woman of twenty, she doesn't know who she is yet, she doesn't know what she's going to do, what her life's work is going to be. She will be a different person by the time she's thirty. I think women develop very late in that way. A girl of twenty is a very different person at thirty-five. A fault of women has been using men as stepping-stones, which maybe we'll grow out of. You know, at a certain time in your career you fall in love with a certain kind of man, because that's the kind of man who's going to teach you what it is you need to know or what's happening to you inside.

I do not like the sort of man whom all the women gather around, who's the raconteur, the one who's had an affair with everybody. What value is he? I like the one who is very lonely, in the corner of the room, rather anxious-looking, sort of Jewish and hollow cheeks – miserable. Then the fantasy, you see: I alone will be the one who will make him feel happy. It never works out like that; they're never the sort of men I get involved with, nervous, anxious, intellectual. He could be a garage man.

Lady Annabel Goldsmith: The woman has to be in love. If she is a real woman, she has got to be in love, or believe herself to be in love, with the man she is going to have as a lover that night. Surely she must. She can't just say, oh, that's a really attractive man, that's it for tonight. Whereas a man can see a really attractive woman, take her to bed that night and perhaps forget about it next day. It sounds very callous, but I think that is the difference. For me, it would be impossible. I can't think like that, I think that's terrible. You must believe yourself to be in love before you do something like that. That is the whole point of being a woman, I would have thought. It doesn't matter how many lovers you have, it is the manner in which you choose them, why you take them.

Any woman who has lived consistently with a man for a length of time is going to be lonely on her own. It's not going to happen to me. I've been married twice, both times to men who have actually been away some of the time. I've never been with them all the time, and I've got so used to that. If I summed myself up I would say I was an extremely good mother, a very bad wife, and an extremely amusing mistress. I don't really much believe in marriage. I don't see the point. I suppose one does it for the children, but you can live perfectly happily with somebody. Marriage is ridiculous.

Power is very seductive, yes. But I must say here that I haven't been seduced by power, because both my husbands became powerful after I married them. I've been with Jimmy a good twenty years, and he wasn't powerful when I met him, but he had the potential for being powerful. Power is a tremendous aphrodisiac.

One of the reasons why marriages don't last is this tremendous importance put on fidelity, which really should be irrelevant to the marriage. Sometimes, maybe not so much now, people marry too young. The way you think at eighteen and nineteen and the way you think in your mid twenties are completely different, a metamorphosis. I can understand now why there are fewer and fewer marriages and people are living together and not getting married, because, in a way, if it works, what is really the point?

If I could live my life again, I would have done something first, and then I would have married in my thirties. Most of the successful marriages I can see are people who have married late. I don't regret it now, because I've had six children and consider myself extremely lucky. I think I'm a truly contented woman. I mean, I've had a horrible summer because I've lost a child, but not forgetting about things like that, I think I'm extremely lucky, I've got everything I want. I don't want to be free, because I do want to feel that I belong to somebody in a way. I hate to live full-time with somebody, I couldn't do it. I'd go mad. If you had to live with Jimmy, day in and day out, I think you'd go mad, you couldn't do it. He's too energetic. I'd be a wreck, I'd be in the loony bin, he is so dynamic. Mark is very demanding, but also he's just a wonderful friend. I talk about Mark a lot because, although I'm not married to him now, he is my best friend and we're still together in a funny way.

Isabel Goldsmith: I prefer, and I am more amused in, the company of men, even if there is a majority of men, even if I am there practically unnoticed as a spectator. If I'm at a dinner party with my father and there is a very political conversation and I am a mere spectator, I will be much more fascinated by the conversation. I much prefer hearing about that than about somebody's children, or pets, or flowers, or cooking, or schools. I'm not very interested in those things. Intellectually, I find it totally unfulfilling.

What I don't like is the attitude of certain men, particularly in France. Now, I suppose, thank God for Aids, there won't be this any more: the kind of meat-market attitude and a feeling of being used. Men never get the feeling of being used as women do. And that is very disagreeable. I find it typically French, that's why I couldn't bear living in Paris after a while. The attitude of Frenchmen towards the women is quite ghastly. I always prefer Englishmen's company. Living in France for a period of ten years, if not more, I found Frenchmen were always interested in women as interchangeable objects. Frenchmen go out picking up girls as a hobby. Englishmen, as a group, go out drinking, and it would never occur to them to pick up girls. They much prefer riding or whatever.

I usually have stupid boyfriends. I've never ever noticed intellect in somebody I'm in love with. I've only ever noticed a lack of intellect in the effect my boyfriends have on my friends. I usually have intelligent friends. But I very seldom turn out to have intelligent boyfriends. I always think they're brilliant at the time. With hindsight, I realize that they're totally idiotic.

It's very stupid and sad when you see people who had a perfectly good relationship, particularly in America, where the husband goes off and has a fling with some tart who's forgotten the next day and the woman wants a divorce. It's totally irrelevant, and if she puts herself on the same level as a tart, she definitely has a problem. I think that's totally pathetic. If the husband is carrying it to extremes, it makes you feel there is something wrong with yourself, then it's no good. But one can't get too upset about the occasional fling. You never know, you might learn some good tricks.

If a man is going to be totally faithful, I don't really want to know. How boring. I would really hate to be able to rely totally on someone, not to be on my toes, not to think I've got to make an effort. If he expects it of me, that he could take me for granted, that he has to make no effort, I think it would be terrible. I don't want to feel threatened whenever I go out with somebody to a party that he is going to go home with somebody else and dump me there; I don't want to feel threatened, but there has to be a slight tension, a slight doubt, a slight excitement in the air. For everything to be routine, how boring, how boring.

Power is certainly fascinating. But I've always kept quite far away from it. Maybe it comes from having a powerful father. I know what it's like to live with, and I find it absolute hell.

I believe in the institution of marriage, but I hated being married. I fantasize now about being married. I like having somebody steady in my life, but I just don't like being married. I don't like being Mrs What-have-you. I don't like being somebody else's property. I hate this feeling of being stuck with a person. Everything becomes things that you have to do, should be doing, when before there would have been questions.

I will probably marry again, because I want children and I'd want them to feel secure. I had a very insecure childhood, and I'd never want my children to feel insecure, and in an ideal world, what could be nicer than two people who adore each other having children and everything, a wonderful home? When it really works out, it's fantastic, but one sees so few examples about.

Francine Gomez: For me, a couple, a real couple, is like an egg. It is intolerable for someone like me to think that even for one night I have not been preferred and the man I live with took the risk of falling in love with someone else. Because it is a risk: to make from one night a second one, there is always a risk. It's nothing to make the sacrifice of not following a girl, even if she has the legs of Betty Grable. Women refrain all the time, because they think that if they do it, they may be involved, they may fall in love, they may want to do it again, so it makes complications. If you have something good at home, you have to make the sacrifice and not follow a passion.

When I was thirty-four, I married Alain Gomez, who is President of Thomson, one of the biggest French companies. I was nothing then, just an old disturbed child, and for maybe ten years he dominated me strongly, playing Pygmalion. Then, one day, I woke up and I thought, it is finished; there is no more domination to receive. So one day, five or six years ago, I told him, now I am grown up and I can be myself, I don't need a judge at home, it's no longer possible for me to live like that. He was always having young women for his use, and I told him, I won't accept that one minute more, I'm leaving. He was very surprised and very affected. He thought I would never escape. But I escaped. I'm married now to a man who is fifteen years younger than I am. He doesn't want to dominate. Maybe I dominate him a little, maybe, but he is very nice to me, and kind. He is not at all jealous of my success because my success was already made when I met him. What I think is impossible is to build a career side by side, because there is competition. One day Alain Gomez told me, it is too much to have two crocodiles in the same creek. It worked for ten years only because I was happy to submit.

The great story of my life was with a man who was, I think, ugly. It was a great affair, but I was always afraid that he would leave me five minutes afterwards. I was so terrified that it occupied my life. I was in a terrible state of anxiety. It was horrible. I couldn't eat, I lost ten kilos. Now, when I see a man I fancy in the street, I say to myself, maybe two women are fighting at the same moment for this man, and he's not worth it anyway. It is impossible to say what qualities attract me. All my life, I loved men with blond hair and blue eyes, and almost never married one; I usually married black hair and black eyes. Curious. There was only one with those blue eyes and blond hair and he was a monster.

Angela Gordon: Needs can be an excuse for infidelity, I suppose: but darling, my needs, my needs. I've never been with anyone, or, at least, I've never knowingly been with anyone who's been unfaithful to me. I think, as soon as he's unfaithful to me, he'd be out, goodbye. I couldn't cope with infidelity. It's like work, I just want total commitment.

One of my boyfriends that I was actually just wild about said I was like cling-film because I obviously believe in too many hugs. And when he said I was like cling-film, that was it – I perished! It's a terrible thing to be told. They're not into physicals in Britain.

Felicity Green: I am comfortable in a mixed environment. I don't like working entirely with one sex. I think when women, all women, work together it can become slightly unbalanced. And if there is a rotten egg in that female barrel, it tends to rebound on women as a sex instead of the one person involved. Socially, I think the same goes. Hen-parties are boring. I think stag parties, not that I have ever been to one, must be an absolute punishment. The sexes are made to interact, to provoke each other, to blend with each other. I do have more women friends simply because they have mostly been gathered in my career, and my career has been in the company of women in that I have been pre-occupied with women's pages, women's journalism, women's publishing.

Menie Grégoire: Men are bad listeners. On the radio, my success was built on the fact that women (and 80 per cent of the participants on my programme were women) talked to me about their lives, what they were doing and living through, to ask my advice. I would tell them that they had a husband and families, but they said they couldn't talk to them.

Women can be best friends until there's a man they are fighting over. Then there's no more friendship: a man always takes priority. I don't know if it's the same between men over a woman, but for women, it's the subject which comes up the most in my programmes. They get indignant sometimes, saying that they believed the other woman to be their friend, but there's no friendship which can stand up to love.

Laura Gregory: I like a man whose face looks as though it has seen and done everything.

The love of a woman, as a friend, is far stronger than the love of a man to a woman – unless the man is very special, and a very special friend. Women have an inner strength which is exceptional. They have a single-mindedness, when they really feel something strongly, that no man has.

My first marriage unfortunately wasn't for ever, but perhaps because I was married very young, when my career was just beginning, and I changed so dramatically over the first five years of our marriage that we just grew apart, we both went in different directions. My husband found he didn't like a career woman. He would have preferred me to be at home, dabbling in my career, having babies and maybe doing a part-time job. He didn't want me to be so fiercely competitive in my field. It didn't help that we were both in the same area. He was also a producer. We failed there. But we are still good friends and that is important. So this one I hope – I married at twenty-nine – is going to be the right choice.

Katya Grenfell: If I dislike a woman for a reason, I think I could dislike a woman far more than I could ever dislike a man. Only because one can totally understand why they've done things. I dislike certain men, but my only real hate has been for two women.

People get married too quickly. Society still conditions a lot of women to feel that, by a certain age, they must get married and must have a family, and so young women aged twenty-eight now are getting desperate, and probably marry people just for the sake of marrying.

Baroness Grimond: Obviously men and women's sexual drive is of a different kind. It's much more mixed up with attachment to a person in the case of a woman, much less separated. Now that it is thought the usual thing for women to go into some kind of work, it may make them less interested in sexual relationships than they were in the past. In the past, they had so few other outlets that they were driven into this. Any sort of competitive urges they had were to shine, to perform in their particular area, which was that of being very successful with men. This was one of the very few areas where they were allowed to be competitive. Now that they have this other area, it may make them less interested. I know women now who don't particularly want to get married, who are completely satisfied with their professional career, who don't want to strike up a permanent relationship. They don't see their lives as ending up with a family, a long-term partner, a home. Their main ambition is centred on their work.

Intelligence certainly is important if you are thinking of somebody you would want to spend a lot of time with. There are stupid people that one likes, too, but there is a place in life for stupid people, and I don't think I would be specially seduced by stupidity in a man. Sense of humour is another attraction, though I know there is a type of superficially attractive man, the Mr D'Arcy, the David Owen type, who has no sense of humour, the proud strong silent man, but we all know we wouldn't want to spend too long with them. I really like men who are rather like women, men who have a certain amount of feminine quality.

I think marriages don't last because the iron conventions no longer exist. There is nothing more difficult than living with one other person, whether it is your sister, your brother, your mother, your father, your best friend. There comes a time, I imagine after so long, when it seems intolerable to go on living with this person. So unless you erect very strong barriers, which, in the past, have been partly convention, and partly, for women, the fact that economically it wasn't really possible to exist any other way, this thing flies apart. I think the centrifugal forces are stronger than the centripetal.

Amy Gross: Given a choice between Henry Kissinger and a poor, young but brilliant talented artist, I would go with the artist any time.

There is a very strong difference in the gay community between male style and female style, and I've always thought that the difference in those styles is the epitome of the difference in sex and desire between men and women. Men, for the most part, are unbelievably promiscuous. There are men who have just hundreds of thousands of sex encounters with different people, even when they are in long-term relationships. And the women, they pair up, joined at the hip.

Miriam Gross: I feel more comfortable in the presence of women. I can relax more, feel more myself and be more straight and honest. Perhaps women are a little bit more intuitive, whether it's through environment or biology, I don't know. I feel most comfortable with my husband, but apart from that, in a group, I feel much more comfortable with women. I'm more honest with women than I could ever be with men. I will tell them all my dishonesties, tell my ploys, my nastinesses or jealousies to women, which I don't think I would ever tell men. I would never tell a man quite how devious I could be, for instance. Not to say that I'm all that devious, but in so far as I am, I would never admit it to a man, but I would to a woman.

I've always been someone who actually has to fall in love practically to sleep with a man, but now I'm getting older, I can just about see myself really liking someone and going off having a one-night stand, it doesn't matter now. When I was younger, one would think that the person would think badly of one if it was known, everyone would. One had to play hard to get. Nowadays, one doesn't. But I can just about imagine seriously finding somebody attractive over a dinner party and going off. I've never done it, but I can easily imagine I might.

Pamela Gross: A lot of career women now are very frightened, and rightly so. An article in the *Wall Street Journal* showed that more than half of all the women over thirty today who are not married and have super-duper careers will never be married. Those over thirty who have been married and divorced have a better chance of being married again. It was a terrifying article, and it caused a bit of hysteria. A lot of women are very afraid that if they do stay in these high-powered jobs they will sacrifice any chance of getting married and having a family. Those statistics are starting to hit home, and I think they're the backlash of the Gloria Steinem days.

I don't think I could be seduced. I've never wanted to be, I'm not interested. Sex isn't such a big deal to me, unless I am in love. I have to be inspired. It just happens, it's a chemistry, I don't know exactly what it is. I don't like show-offs, and I don't like to hear how many Maseratis or what colour Porsche he has. We all have billions of dollars, or we don't, and our fathers do, or they don't. I don't want to hear about it. I'm getting bored with the son of the son of the son's, too, and my father is *blah, blah, blah*, who are you? I'm bored with all that stuff. I like men who are understated, who aren't show-offs, who are easier-going than that.

I don't think a marriage is an end, it's a means to an end. A healthy marriage has three entities in it: me, him and us. And there's no reason to stop being me because of him or us. I can't do that, and I don't think I'd want to marry a man who would want me to consider doing that.

I don't know about the old people who divorce. Maybe they think they've missed something. As for young people who are married and divorced, I honestly believe that we have all grown up in a sort of throw-away society, we've never had to work for anything very hard. We are hungry, we eat, we go to McDonald's and it's ready. We want to go to the bathroom and there it is. We want a mink coat and daddy buys one. I'm a part of all this, and we all are, we've grown up without really understanding values and without having to work for something.

Flora Groult: I think we will remain very different human beings, men and women, but men, perhaps because of the sexual facility of women today, have a different view. Perhaps they give more value to sentiment than they did, because before they could only go to bed with tarts or easy women. There was a certain lack of respect for women because of the type of women they could see to satisfy their sexual needs. The other sort was taboo, and you could marry or not touch. Now they can touch and not marry. And, on the other hand, women don't have to be so fascinated by men, because they know what men are. They are more cynical. Men have this instrument which lives its own life in them. It must be very interesting to be a man, but it is difficult to imagine. Sometimes one pities men if one is a woman, sometimes one envies.

I'm very susceptible to the charm of the way somebody speaks. Naturally, I like beauty, like everybody else, and I like people to be tall and so on. But I can be under the spell of a conversation. I like intellectuals on the whole. I like people with whom I can exchange ideas.

Marriages do not last because religion doesn't have the same importance and we don't have the same social mores. Before, divorce was a sin. We don't respect the same things, we've changed gods. And we want happiness. Before, we wanted stability. Now we are looking for this impossible word, and world, happiness. And perhaps the risky world in which we live makes us capricious in our feelings, we don't want eternity.

Valerie Grove: I would really hate to be married to most of the men I have ever met, who were impossible from the point of view of telling you what they really thought and felt. Trevor, I am glad to say, is extremely poetic and emotional in expressing what he feels, but he does feel differently, there's no doubt about it, from the way I feel.

What I went for, both when I got married and before, was a walk, a kind of way of walking, an attractive way of walking, a really good stride, straight-backed, nothing slouchy or apologetic about it.

Why don't marriages last? Because getting up every day in the same house, in the same room with everything the same, is extremely hard to live with for absolutely anybody. I think people do get really bored and irritated with each other, irritated with their mannerisms. It might be something silly: the way they drop litter about, their untidiness, absurd things. And when those things become irritating, then the boredom and the sameness of your everyday life is blameable on the other person. I had a six-year marriage before my present twelve-year marriage, which is my proper marriage; and what went wrong with the first marriage was that friendship went out of it. You're not unfaithful to your best friend, you don't want to go scampering off with somebody else, it would be a madness. The friendship thing is so marvellous and incredible, and so rare, and so shining. You can have such freedom in a marriage like that. You can say things without thinking about what you're going to say first. You don't have to think about anything, just say it, because you know that person will always understand and accept you. It's the greatest possible thing.

Georgina Hale: The few men in my life that have been extremely or reasonably wealthy, normally bored the arse off me. I'm not into all that.

Marriage sounds very romantic and wonderful. And being very working-class, that was the way one lived: you were going to meet somebody and marry and it would all be wonderful. But then marriage is a very difficult thing and you really do have to work at it. It must be great to have some roots, or to have another half of you somewhere, but I don't know if I could handle it seven days or seven nights a week. I've lived on my own for a long time and I get incredibly selfish. I don't know how you live with somebody because I haven't done it for about fourteen years.

Whether the majority of women like to admit it or not, most of us do dress up and make up to please men. Even if you are not doing it for a particular man at that time, you will still go out and buy clothes and make yourself up, hoping you may bump into somebody or that somebody is actually going to notice you. I don't do it all the time. I can, especially if I am working, not even think about it for months. And then, suddenly, I can be very aware that I don't have a man, or I'm not married and don't have any kids and have done it all wrong, and that somebody else has done it all right.

I have a lot of gay friends, I think because I am not married and don't have any children. The few women friends I did have are married and have families and are involved with their children growing up. I still have a few close women friends, but most of my friends are gay. There are an awful lot of gay guys in my profession.

Jerry Hall: Every time Mick buys me a present for no reason, I think, I'm sure he must have done something. I never say anything, but in the back of my mind, I think, umph, oh well, I didn't have any heartache, I didn't hear anything, I don't know anything, I'm not going to make a big fuss about it. But I always suspect that the reason I'm getting this present is because he's done something.

Lucy Hughes-Hallett: In previous eras, marriages lasted because they had to, because divorce was so difficult, because people believed they'd go to Hell if they broke their marriage vows. Obviously the climate, the religious motive, was very important. I don't think there are many people now in this society who really think it's morally wrong to end a marriage if both partners are very unhappy.

I slightly think of men as rather frivolous creatures with whom one flirts and giggles at parties. Men are for fun, because I have, for a lot of my life, done my work with other women. With other women, I will naturally fall into an unself-conscious conversation about things that matter to me, whereas with men – and this doesn't just come from me, it also comes from men's attitude towards me and other women – the conversation will tend to be more bantering, more self-conscious. People are anxious about being serious, I think, with members of the opposite sex. This is the well-established convention: the sexes will meet, say, at a formal dinner, they will have light and unimportant conversation while they eat, and after dinner the women will be sent out and the men will talk about what they really want to talk about. Traditionally, the women are supposed to go into the next room and talk about clothes and hair-dos, but the women will actually go into the next room and talk about what they are really interested in: their work, or the books they've been reading, and that goes very deep. People are inevitably self-conscious when they are in a situation potentially sexual, where they feel they have got to be attractive to the other person. It's difficult to relax. That's why it's a great pity so many people have had segregated education, because all that, I think, comes from being separated in early life.

There's always some kind of power relationship in marriage. Sometimes one person is dominant in one area, and the other is on the other sides of life, but it's a delicate balance. And every time that's altered there are storms. We have more choice, although we're still immensely limited and there are financial constraints. I know a lot of people who are still married because they can't afford not to be: women who can't afford to leave their husbands, wouldn't be able to support their children; there are always those limitations. And then, I think, there are all sorts of constraints we probably aren't aware of. The women's movement, feminism, have shown us the kinds of social conditioning that previous generations were not aware of, took for granted, and didn't see. And I'm sure there are other constraints, prejudices and preconceptions that we all carry around with us which we haven't yet seen because the next big intellectual shift hasn't yet happened.

Mira Hamermesh: I remember my mother (a very conventional old-fashioned lady) one day, in a crisis, sighing and saying, if it wasn't for you children I would have divorced your father a long time ago. My father was the most wonderful man to me – what did she know about my father that I as a child didn't know? She must have had reasons. But she wouldn't have divorced, because in those times you didn't. Today her daughter is divorced. Women are not contented with what men are prepared to give. The economy has made this transition: the fact that men are no longer the breadwinners.

I haven't been feminized in the sense that mothers break in girls. I remember once there was a dinner party and a few women were talking about the moment a mother pulled them down from the trees and said, girls don't climb trees. I couldn't think of anything comparable. I still can't. I only learned it through interest in families, after I made the film *Two Women*. Before that, I didn't know. And there's no doubt I am the sort of woman who loves men, not necessarily sexually, but loves being with them, because I feel comfortable, like with my father and my brother. But I don't feel comfortable with women, although I spend a great deal of time in their company. They make me anxious, they are a bit like my mother, a bit like my sister, I never know what they want of me. I never know whether they approve, disapprove, and I go crazy. A woman has only not to smile and I blow with anxiety: what have I done to offend? I haven't got any of these tensions of guilt and misery when I am in the company of men.

Katharine Hamnett: I've been very happy when I've been by myself without anybody, being celibate, really happy, perfectly happy. The first time it happened was after I got rid of a really horrible man, and I was two or three months just shaking, and then that calmed down. I went on a trip to Japan, and coming home I suddenly thought, right, that's it – I don't need anybody. It was one of the happiest times of my life, because it was when I had everything: kids, a happy job, everything except a man. But I decided I wasn't having any men, that was it finished. And I felt fine, so creative. I used to stay up until two in the morning, dancing round the kitchen by myself, pottering round, reading books, taking photographs, really getting on with it. Because if I've got a man I've got very little free time, a man will take that up, I won't be doing things only I care about. Sometimes it can be nice to be dominated. It's nice to be dragged off to bed if you feel like going – you know, that game – but I hate having anybody tell me what to do, ever. I'd hate to be dominated.

Claire Harrison: It's very rare that the man does not make a move, no matter what the circumstances. I have various friendships where, from time to time, there is definitely some little scintilla of bubbly undercurrent, but I've noticed that, with my closest friends, they will admit they feel that too, and they enjoy just the latent aspects. Or else the man makes the move because men are somehow trained to, at which point it's all exploded to hell because you can't do anything and the friendship changes.

Nicky Hart: I feel a natural affinity with women in some ways. If I'm with people I don't know, I will automatically feel close to the women and want to talk to the women more. There is an unspoken bond between women that comes through. I have closer friendships with women, but I do have very strong friendships with men. But they are always tainted with something. Most of my very close male friends are ex-lovers. One meets new women each day, and I'm attracted to them primarily physically because they look interesting, look strong and attractive and dynamic, and I would naturally forge a relationship with women like that. You meet and you are instantly connected and get on well, without the sexual tensions.

Romaine Hart: I went straight from home to a marriage without any time in between to be free myself, which was extremely bad for the marriage subsequently, and for myself. From one man to another.

I still look to men for a certain amount of interest and excitement and whatever. Maybe wrongly, maybe falsely and maybe disappointed at the end of the day, but one is still looking. That also is the fault of the media, the fault of the cinema, the fault of the fairy story we've all been brought up with: that the Prince is there. One looks to that to add spice to one's life. That is possibly a myth, and possibly isn't where the spice lies, but it's sad because one still expects it. I've lived without a man for sixteen years much more happily than I lived with a man for sixteen years, so I can't be sure we really need each other.

844

Women have more choice, and more expectations. They don't any longer have to stay at home and do the washing and the dishes; they don't want to. They want much more out of life. They don't just want to be the little woman waiting for the husband to come home and tell them what happened in the world. They want to be out in the world, doing it themselves. And they can, they can – much more probably than they ever could. We're talking about middle-class women again. We're not taking about the lower classes, and we're probably not talking about the upper classes; although they can do it, mostly they don't. The woman doesn't have to stay in a bad marriage, because she can go out and do her own thing. It's sad because, at the end of the day, you may have a very good career but not nearly enough of a good private life. I think sometimes one feels one sacrifices one's private life for one's career. I have done it. Because I'm so bossy, because I am dominating, because I am in power, I frighten the men I would wish not to frighten, and so they feel they couldn't, as they put it, handle me. And, of course, they couldn't handle me. Now it's probably to late for anyone to handle me, because men have a great sense of insecurity and they like very much to be in the top position. Most men, especially the kind of men I like, who are usually the vulnerable kind of sweet men, would be absolutely petrified by me. I can't help it.

Life has to be a constant disappointment, because however much a man loves you, especially if he is full of life and vulnerable and all those things, he has the same quality for other women, and then, when other women find him attractive too, he is not going to turn them down. That's the nature of the beast.

Bettina von Hase: When I started my first job, I didn't get a contract for the first eight weeks. All the other people who were trainees, who were men, did, putting one in an incredibly uncomfortable situation just because one was a woman. I have worked with men, or have tried to, and it has failed miserably, I think simply on account of the fact that I was a woman and they could not work for women or take women seriously. That's one of the great mistakes men make, because women are much better employers very often. Because they are incredibly loyal, very courageous.

We have too much choice for marriage to be stable. We live much more frenetically, much more energetically. We are a throw-away society now. Habit and tradition are not as important in a general sense. Maybe, within a small environment it is much easier to have harmonious lives than leading this crazy transatlantic existence, although that appeals to me too. I think we want too much, we want to have it all, and it's easier to get divorced than to give it another try. It is so easy. And there's not the social stigma. Not even when you have children.

I think most women actually just want a pretty ordinary man; I don't think they want a sort of super-achiever, but want someone who can handle the wife's or the lover's success as well as his own. But, somehow, relationships in New York (New York being of a rather peculiar nature) always end up more like mergers and acquisitions rather than true relationships.

A promiscuous woman is sort of an odd thing, because she looks, I think, for affection, and thinks she can get it through brief, intense encounters. Of course, she can't, and it becomes a vicious circle, whereas a man can just shut off areas more. Maybe this is terrible and old-fashioned, but I think a husband's infidelity is probably not as bad as a wife's infidelity.

I definitely think fidelity is unbelievably important. It's probably too important to me; I probably shouldn't be so dogmatic. But in this life one has to compromise so much anyway, and there are so many people all of the time that, if you don't have an area of trust, all sorts of other things break down somehow.

Nikki Haskell: When I was young, I always dated much older men. In fact, the men I dated when I was a kid are dead now. As I got older, I started dating younger men.

Out of all my girlfriends, there were several who had affairs with my husband. I would never do a thing like that. I'm from a completely different school of thought. I don't want anybody's husband, I don't go out with married men.

With women, it's really dog-eat-dog. They are out there hunting, and they know this is not a dress rehearsal. And if you've got something they want, they will go for it in one minute. I've seen girls do things before my very eyes that you would faint at; and never think twice about it. You know the old expression: no good deeds ever go unpunished. So I avoid them. You'd never find me out at night with four girls having dinner. I may have lunch with the women, but when I go out every night, I'm always with men, never women. It looks terrible to see two women having dinner alone. You think they're hookers, they're prostitutes, they're dykes, or no one wants to take them out. I'd as soon stay home than be seen out with a bunch of women.

Women are very vicious, very vindictive. I think they are pathological liars, they all have an axe to grind with you. You see, I live in a dream world. To me everything is terrific: I have a great time, a great family, a great life. I have no axe to grind with anyone. I'm not jealous of anything anyone has, I go where I want, do what I want, but it drives people crazy.

I guess that subconsciously I'm seduced by power, but overtly I'm seduced by looks. You can sell me a really mediocre act with a pair of gorgeous blue eyes.

Olivia de Havilland: I am much more comfortable in the company of men. Much more. I don't find women interesting, generally speaking. I have women friends, lots of them, but I don't have the tremendous need for female companionship many women do.

Sexual attraction can be very blinding. It has to be there, of course, but you can be attracted to someone who won't be good for you at all, not at all. Destructive even. And, in the long run, a deep and destructive disappointment.

I think you have to examine the marriages that endured but may not have lasted. The framework endured, but what about the relationship? In so many cases, it was because that was the convention and there was no other choice for most women. They had to stick with it for practical reasons, all sorts of reasons. They weren't permitted to work in a dignified and rewarding manner. Maybe the real truth about marriage is that many of them probably didn't work at all and were absolutely hollow and empty. Women have other alternatives today, they have more choice. We need education on what sort of person we will fulfil and what sort of person will fulfil us in a continuing relationship. Marriage is a very special, very extraordinary relationship. I don't think you can put just any two people together and have a good marriage result. It's like casting a film. You can miscast people and you are going to get a very bad film if you do, no matter how good the script may be.

Kitty Hawks: I was married once, for six years. And I think, if I had lived in a time when it was harder to get out of marriage, the problems would have been worked out. Because I still love my husband, and he still loves me. But it's so easy to undo it.

847

There are times when I sense that my audience may be more receptive if it's male, but I find it very easy to be with women, to talk to women, because the sexual element is not there. You can go right to the issue, and you're not flirting, or they're not flirting. I will go to a dinner party and end up spending just as much time sometimes with women who are fascinating to talk to. Women who have accomplished, or women who have certain interests and have learned certain things are just as interesting as men to talk to.

I am more prey to a man with a good sense of humour. I've been involved with men of every description: there have been beautiful ones, tall ones, funny-looking little ones. Physically, they are very different, but they all have a sense of humour and intelligence.

The older I've got, I won't even have dinner with somebody more than once if it's not somebody I really want to be with, let alone sleep with. It's a waste of time. If it's an effort and not going to reward me in that I can give and take with this person, then it's not worth it.

Brooke Hayward: My marriages didn't fail in the way most marriages fail. Most marriages fail, at least in this country, because people expect too much from marriage. They don't have a pragmatic enough view and they are looking for idealistic situations that they see in the movies or read about in novels where you go off into the sunset and raise a wonderful family, and there's no attrition whatsoever, it's all divine. But it's not all divine. It's like anything else, it's a business. Sometimes I think that probably the best marriages are arranged by parents. Because then there is a more *laissez-faire* attitude, there aren't these dreadful ideals that break. People get divorced all the time because they find their husband is having an affair with somebody else. That's an insane reason to get divorced. Why break up an arrangement that clearly might work on a lot of other levels? My mother certainly divorced my father for that reason. She was very ill-advised to do it, but she was jealous and felt hurt, she felt as if the world was laughing at her. I really couldn't imagine why she broke up that marriage simply because my father started having an affair here in America when she was away acting in London for six months. But she wanted a divorce, she was wronged, she was affronted. The great puritanical vision had failed. And you see this a lot. Mine failed, in the first place, because I had decided I wanted to become an actress, and this made my husband so furious, so enraged, so appalled. He had a vision of me being a socialite. But I had no interest whatsoever in going to charity balls, or running charity balls, or going to golf, or going to country clubs. I wanted to be an actress. And that was a terrible thing. The second husband quite simply was crazy and got involved with drugs and alcohol. It would have been self-destructive to have remained in either of those relationships. The first one is a good example, however, of what men in this country in the 1950s wanted from their women. They didn't want careers for their wives, and certainly not careers where other men were involved. There are many movies and plays in which you have to embrace, and my husband just couldn't bear the concept. He was enraged that he might have to go to a movie theatre and see me in the arms of somebody else.

Americans are very naïve about this business called marriage. Both men and women. If a man finds out that his wife is having an affair, he wants a divorce. But, in Europe, you don't see any of this; it is absolutely taken for granted that people are not going to be monogamous their entire life. It's absolutely ridiculous to assume they are, in my view. In fact, if it made my husband happy, I wouldn't care how many affairs he had, I just wouldn't want to know the names, the faces, the times, the positions, you know. I wouldn't want to be brought into close contact with it. But if it makes him happy and therefore keeps my life calm, makes him nice to me, I say it's a very valuable thing.

A good example of sexual conquest is Mercedes Kellogg's conquest of Sid Bass. I am sure that's a sexual conquest. She is exotic; she has a quality that attracts men and she's using it to great advantage. And I'm all on her side, because I think she came up against a tough Texas girl who doesn't have the slightest concept of how to attract or keep a man.

If marriage doesn't work out, well, to hell with it. I don't think you should suffer the agonies of the damned just because you are married. As you get older, it's interesting. I think the reason parents probably advise their children not to get married till they get older is because, when you get older, you automatically begin to know what you like and don't like a lot better. So your marriage is apt to work better. I was married when I was nineteen and when I was twenty-three. How did I know?

Cynthia Heimel: It's possible to have depth between men and women, but it's rarer. Women have already so much of a frame of reference together that we can skip through a lot of the layers one has to go through when talking to men. Women can talk in shorthand together. I'd say on the intimacy you could have with a man, if he's a lover, you can be even closer than you can with a woman, but as friends it's very rare to find that kind of depth and intimacy.

I'm seduced by loyalty; I don't know if I'm the only one, but I've had experiences with infidelities before and I find them too nerve-racking to put up with. Smell, looks, intellect, sense of humour – obviously sense of humour – all turn me on; and kindness. When I say loyalty, I mean kindness. Maybe even political leanings would influence me. I don't think I would like someone who was a real Ronald Reagan supporter.

Marie Helvin: I have more problems dealing with new women friends only because of my looks, or because of what I do, than with men. I think men have grown up a lot. Five years ago, I could go to a dinner party and be talking to somebody, whoever I admired at the time, and he would maybe hear what I had to say, but I'd know he wasn't listening. Now he listens.

Margaux Hemingway: There's nothing worse than a really competitive egoistic woman. They're very difficult to deal with. They can be really monsters if not handled in the correct way.

I remember, my parents, they almost broke up about four or five times, but they held it together, they just stuck with it. I have had two divorces, and I almost had a divorce once before, in the second marriage, but we kept it together. I think if I had had a child, we would have stayed together in the family unit. But there is a lot of stress on marriages. One has to be witty enough to be able to work for it. Everything is not just a perfect love affair, you go up and down like a roller-coaster. Sometimes sex is so much better than at other times. It's all to do with the stars, it's all where the stars are in your cycle and what sign you are.

I thought my second marriage was for life. The first one I did out of absolute boredom. Absolutely stupid! Boy! The second one, I thought, was an absolute commitment. But it wasn't. We were together about twelve years, which is a long time. And I really miss him, too, but he wasn't pulling his weight and he started to lean too much on me and wasn't equal any more, so I lost respect for him. That's where that went wrong.

Voice, serenity, good hands, a calmness within. I think being gentle. Gentleness is very seductive; it's the killer.

Money is also very attractive. I know of some very rich men who are not very good-looking, but they become very good-looking all of a sudden.

850

Anouska Hempel: I feel more comfortable in the presence of men when I like them. And when I don't like them, I'm very uncomfortable. I don't want to be judged, I don't want to have a conversation with somebody I don't particularly like. Men handle that much better than women. Often the hair will stand on end on the back of my head because I am so uncomfortable. But when I am comfortable, I am very comfortable. I have friendships with women, too. They are not necessarily deeper or more relaxed, but you can be open on certain things with women. Obviously you can talk about lots of things with girlfriends that you can't talk about with men. But even in the closest women's relationships, there are certain areas women don't discuss with each other. There's a safety something that's there, I guess, protecting one's own self against a female predator. Probably it's something as basic and as deep-rooted as that.

You have to have some area of vulnerability, otherwise you are just not attractive to a man. No matter how bright you are, no matter how you compare with them academically, no matter what you have done with your life on the same sort of level, whatever rat poison you have both been developing, one's got to slip and one's got to hold the other one up.

I'll always be attracted to the person who is rather quiet, over in the corner, rather than the person who is standing, making the most noise. I'll be attracted to the person who isn't such a flamboyant character, who isn't the life and soul of the party. I don't necessarily like men who are up front with all their regalia. I'm much more attracted to somebody who is much quieter. I've always been like that. My first boyfriend was a quiet, dark horse, extraordinarily beautiful, and wonderful kind eyes. I was much happier with him than with all the others who were the life and soul of the party. I could be the life and soul of the party myself. I did my bit and was an aggravating so and so for many years, I think. But I was always attracted to the person who was more of a dark horse. I didn't really think about being attracted to men who had power. I was too busy doing my own little power thing, creating a jet-propelled substance of some sort in me. But I wonder. If I'm honest and open now, if somebody does have a little bit of power, I will find that person attractive because there's obviously been some sort of a success story. I'm talking about men who have actually made it. I'm not talking about inherited wealth or any kind of power like that. I'm talking about an ability to have made one's way in life from nothing to something. I don't know if I would go as far as to say power is aphrodisiac, but I'm attracted, definitely, to the positive people in life, and the people who have done something with their lives, rather than the chap who hasn't.

Beth Henley: I don't believe in marriage for me. It seems like an archaic sort of ritual for people to sign legal papers that they belong to each other. If you're in love with someone, and you care for someone, why not just be with them? If you are no longer in love with them and no longer care for them, you shouldn't be with them. Why should you be bound, legally and publicly? It turns it into some sort of business deal. I think it's a very unromantic view.

Val Hennessy: One of my greatest sorrows in life is the very hopeless relationship I have with my mother. It is something I find very painful to discuss, but it has influenced me in so far as I've always had tremendous difficulty in making women friends. I can't trust women. I actually don't like women particularly, and I'm sure this is because I have no close relationship with my mother. It's a matter of deep regret for me, and one of the things that I can be reduced to tears about very easily.

I loved having boys as friends. And suddenly, at about the age of thirteen or fourteen, all that changed. Instead of being just mates and chums and rushing about on bomb sites, going on bike rides and doing all the things we did, it altered – the subtle alteration of when the sex thing starts to intrude. I remember experiencing a tremendous sense of loss when I lost my boys as friends and the sexual thing intruded. Something very sad to me.

If I was suddenly on my own and desperately wanted a lover or, you know, a romantic liaison, I personally, at the age of forty-three, would not have a clue how to go about pulling a man, to use the modern terminology. I don't know how to do it. When I was a teenager, I rather resented the attention I got from boys. I actually didn't want it, it was unsought attention. It staggered me because, there I was: this rather skinny figure with glasses. Actually, I didn't wear my glasses. I still don't. I hide my glasses. But I've always rather resented it, and always get very prickly if I think people are trying to get off with me, men trying to chat me up. I get very ill at ease about it. The sort of men whom I have found attractive are the men I've really had to go after in a big way, who weren't initially particularly interested in me and I've really had to work at it; I suppose you could say the men who are a bit of a challenge. Perhaps that's rather a masculine thing, a masculine attribute I've got, because they say men are the hunters. I think that is untrue. I think women like to hunt, too, and if a guy is a walkover, if he is flirting outrageously with you and it's quite obvious he fancies you like hell, I find that a bit of a turn-off.

852

I can't bear the feeling of being dominated by anybody. I have no rape fantasies. Obviously, if you're in love with somebody, he does in a sense dominate you, he dominates your thoughts, you can't think about anything else. Everything you buy in the shops to wear, you're actually buying it for him. So I think one is dominated by any man one is in love with. One is dominated intellectually, but by dominated I don't mean somebody who knocks me around, wallops me. I would absolutely despise any man who would wallop me around. I know some women do get off on that, but, again, I've never met anybody like this. I've read about it in women's magazines, but I'm not altogether sure it exists. I think probably the greatest turn-off in the world for me, apart from somebody who smells awful, is somebody who wallops you or uses physical violence on you. I just think it's pathetic.

To me, my marriage has been very, very important. Perhaps not the marriage; it's the person I'm married to. My relationship with him, much as it has altered over the years, is still crucial and important to me. Obviously my marriage hasn't been all plain sailing, but when I've gone through bad or miserable patches, I've always thought, well, I'm going to make the effort to keep this going, partly because we've got children and we both love our children; nobody else is going to love my children in the same way as their father does. So it's nice to be with him, and working together, and working to create a home for our children.

People think, oh well, this isn't working out, perhaps if I find somebody else it will be better. Of course, it never is, it's always exactly the same. The big romantic scene quickly wears off and the reality of living with somebody day to day, and seeing them padding around in their socks and being sick down the lav on a Saturday night, quickly destroys the illusions of romance, and this is going to happen with everybody you get involved with. But, to me it's been very important to have one stable figure in my life, somebody who's seen me at my utter worst. You know, all the awful aspects of me, sees me wearing my glasses and still loves me in spite of all this. That's very important to me.

Carolina Herrera: Now, if you see that your husband is having an affair with a very good friend of yours, you don't behave the way women used to behave. You don't stop her coming to the house because she's having an affair. She just becomes very good friends with you, and the man gets tired of seeing the woman, every day in the house, being very friendly with the wife.

Dr Leah Hertz: I don't have close relationships with women, but I don't have close relationships with men either, and this is an individual thing, because I am very happily married and I don't have any more close relationships. But I feel very much at ease with women. Most of my employees are women. I would say 95 per cent of them are women, and at the higher level, again 95 per cent of them are women, because I really am aggressive towards a man. I don't accept from men the same things I would from a woman. Let's say a young man comes to me and he says, I don't feel well, I say, what do you mean, you don't feel well? Is it your period? When they behave like women behave, I don't accept it from them. I don't accept from them when they make mistakes and try to cover up. When they try to persuade me not to do something, I'm really very aggressive with them. If I have any disagreement with women, I say, just bloody well shut up, we're doing it this way, it's finished; with a man, he becomes very uptight, extremely uptight. And once they're uptight, I become worse.

I've been married for twenty-five years, and I've never had any relationship outside marriage, never. Before I got married, I had many many men, many many men, and in those days it was very unusual, especially in Israel. So I had a tough time morally, and the only reason I got away with it was I was a very clever girl, a top student. I had a lot of fights with my mother because of my free attitude to sex before I married. Today she says, with her tongue in her cheek, no wonder you have a happy marriage, you chose from enough. So I don't think sex before marriage is a bad thing, I don't really. The fact is that, when I found the right person, there was no need to look further. And it's not only the right person, it's a state of mind. You're doing things you like, you're not frustrated, and sex is not the be-all and end-all of everything. I don't think one can generalize, but I was honestly a very promiscuous little girl, and I married the right man, and now I'm so square I feel ashamed.

Elizabeth Hess: My close friends are all women, and that didn't used to be the case. I have lived in apartments with men who were not lovers, and grown up and had close friends throughout college, but at this point I find my closest friends are women and that women are much better at talking to each other and much freer when they are with each other.

I don't really think anything is for life. When I married, I considered it a serious commitment, ideally for the rest of my life. Actually, I was very cynical about marriage, and for me the commitment was when I decided to live with Peter. That was a much harder decision for me than it was to

854

marry him. He was much more interested in marriage than I was. I didn't want marriage as a result of passion and love. I felt that was there in the relationship, and, if anything, I was scared marriage would ruin the relationship rather than enhance it. In the end, that's not what happened, but I think marriage has taken on a lot of ghoulish connotations and I have seen relationships destroyed simply by the fact of marriage. Now what I see is people getting married for economic reasons, and people getting married mostly to have children, because they don't want children born out of wedlock. Marriage is almost redefined as an ecomonic and social liaison. It's not a romantic one any more.

Min Hogg: I never got married. My mother said to me the other day, you know, I used to think about your wedding and all that business, but gosh, you were clever not to get married. At last she's admitted it. I have a brother and sister, both married with children, all conventional. I never did, I never could bring myself to. I always wanted to make my own decisions, and while it is wonderful to have somebody taking care of you, you sacrifice an awful lot in doing what they've got to do all the time. In any case, it's rather fun playing the field.

I think I'd make divorce easier. It might make marriage more difficult.

I have thousands of homosexual friends. I don't have very many close normal men friends. It's partly our age. They're married mostly. Therefore you can't monopolize a man and ring him up and go to the movies, you have his wife as well. And if you don't include her, there's going to be trouble probably. Women can be unbelievably marvellous friends. And are. I've got lots of long-term women friends. Not that they wouldn't go off with my man, they might easily.

If going off with somebody rears its head, it doesn't matter what sex you are, you actually do swallow all the things about how awful you're being, and do it. If you're going to, I mean. Or you cut off and don't do it. You've decided that long before you worry about how much you're hurting the other person.

Powerful men are often very amusing, so one is seduced by the amusing bit, and the other is sexy with it, it's not sexy on its own. Take Jimmy Goldsmith, the most entertaining man. I mean, you can't resist him. I refuse to meet any woman who could resist a man like that. You may absolutely loathe his ethics, his manias and his temper, but most of us aren't married to him, so we don't see that, we see the outward charm.

855

And, of course, it's sexy. Men are forgiven more for the rant and rave; women, oh, you know, she's hysterical. Hysterectomy, after all, applies only to women.

Jeny Howorth: I like to be liked by men, and most of my friends are men. I've always been with the boys, always, ever since I was at school.

I'd always have lots of friends who were boys, and it would never dawn on me that they'd want to be my boyfriend, and then it would always get to a sticky situation and I'd think, my God, I don't want to be sexually involved with you. I like you, and I like spending time with you, don't make it like this. It's taken me quite a while to realize that that does happen, and it does happen quite often actually, and I have a few problems with a few friends at the moment, but it's all being sorted out.

I don't like working with women photographers. I much prefer dealing with men. Women photographers seem like they're on another level completely. They take a long time to get themselves together. I find women not as direct, not as sure exactly what they want.

I once had a boyfriend and didn't see him very often because he was travelling all the time. I slept with somebody else, and after I'd done it, I knew I shouldn't have done it, I should have just dreamt about it. That's why I say if I walk into a room and see somebody, it's better to fantasize about it than actually do it, because sometimes, when you do it, it's not as good as the fantasy. Better to dream, better to dream.

I don't find sex that important. I think I'm much more a mental person. I can't just sleep with anybody. I have a boyfriend who lives in New York I've been seeing for two years – the longest I've ever had a boy-friend – and we have a perfect sexual relationship, but it's not the first thing in our relationship.

Arianna Stassinopoulos Huffington: I have a lot of very close men friends who are not lovers, who have never been lovers, and every man who has been involved in my life, every man with whom I have had an important relationship, is still a great friend, and I also have a lot of women friends. So, in my case, I would say that the only thing all my close friends have in common is not their sex but their ability to be intimate and to communicate in a deeper way and let the barriers and the masks down. Otherwise it's just a waste of time for me.

856

I've had long relationships with men which were very profound and very important, but something happens when you commit yourself to that one person for life, when you take those vows. It is mystical, it is not anything rational. For me, marriage is beyond anything else I've experienced.

I always knew that I would get married. I always had this longing to find my mate, a kind of underlying longing in my life, and to have that longing fulfilled has brought me an incredible peace and serenity. It's a very deep feeling of having arrived somewhere that I didn't know I was really going. I think it is a deep longing in everybody, and I had a very deep longing in me, to find that mate, that human being with whom I wanted to share everything, and sharing everything with somebody is something extraordinary. I feel that a marriage, when it works, is something truly cosmic, not just two people coming together. It's something which goes beyond anything which I have ever experienced. There is such a foundation of strength from which to approach the world, and such a self-contained nurturing. It's a not a question of being together all the time, because Michael works very hard and comes back very late, and I work particularly hard all day when I have a deadline looming. It's just knowing the other person is there. I just love being at a party with him, and even when we are at opposite ends of the room, there is this kind of cord that connects us, and the intuitive ways of knowing each other and knowing what the other person is thinking, of keeping discovering each other. I really think it's the greatest adventure anybody can embark on, and I feel like a child about it. There is something very sacred.

I feel that a lot of marital breakdown has to do with our expectations and the way, culturally, we've been brought up. We have a wonderful friend in Houston who is the Dean of Christchurch Cathedral there, who has written a book called *Becoming Married*, and he talks about the fact that marriage is not a process that ends when you get married in church, when you make those vows, but a process of becoming married. It goes on and on and on, it isn't a process of living happily ever after, which is where the mythology of marriage is so confusing and so misleading. I really think we need a new mythology, a new archetype around which to build our expectations of marriage and that, for me, would be what our friend calls becoming married. The day we take our vows is the day we commit ourselves to this adventure, and every day brings us closer to becoming married, but it's not achieved the day we get married. That way, all the downturns, the conflicts, the sand-papering that goes on in a relationship are included in our expectations. People are all looking for something, and we think we are going to find it through another human being, and for me the ultimate thing we're looking for is our relationship with God. I feel that when that third partner is there in the relationship, that's what gives you the strength that is able to withstand whatever problems and difficulties will inevitably result in any relationship. If I look back in my life, I have grown more through the painful experiences than the joyful ones. It's awful to say, and I wish it was different, but that's how it is. I know that Michael and I have found that, through adversity, the things we found most difficulty understanding about each other were the moments of growth in our intimacy. What I'm really saying is that, if we are looking to find that ultimate communion, ultimate union through another human being without the existence of God, the Divine Spirit, whatever you call it, we're going to keep looking. We'll keep getting divorced in the hope that the next person is going to bring it to us. I feel that every human being ultimately has what I will call in a book I want to write one day the fourth basic instinct: the instinct towards wholeness, completeness, communion with the Divine. I feel that it is a very deep instinct in each human being, whether we know it or not, that drives us to art, religion, altruism. So to fulfil that instinct, we often look for a mate, but that mate cannot fulfil that instinct, and that is the misconception. The mate can be a partner in that adventure.

There are certain men, and I'm lucky my husband is one, who can take you for a cappuccino in the local coffee shop and make it an adventure, who can make the commonplace and the everyday seem quite magical. That is a real gift, because there are men who can take you on a safari and make it as boring as going to the grocer's.

Caroline Huppert: When I was young, I automatically thought a man had to be intelligent for me to like him, but now I realize there are different kinds of intelligence: the way a man behaves, his philosophy on life and so on. I can be attracted to different kinds of intelligence which might have nothing to do with culture. I don't really find beauty in a man seductive, even to the extent that, when I am choosing an actor, I can have a reaction against too good-looking a one. When an agent shows me photos and says, so and so is superb, he's going to have a wonderful career, and I look at the eyes and see nothing there at all, a hole, I wonder how he is going to make a career with nothing between the ears.

There have been times when I preferred men friends, but at the moment I tend to prefer women. As I have been growing older, I have discovered the world of young women with children who work. I have come close to some of them; we have points in common. They are extremely concerned about their children, perhaps more so than their own mothers were.

Isabelle Huppert: I don't mind sometimes being an object woman; there is something passive in the way a woman has to be seductive and likable, and if you are not like this, then you miss a lot. It is a pleasure for a man to see a woman like this, and it is a pleasure for a woman to behave like this. It doesn't mean you have to be exploited. That's something I feel very much, being an actress. Professionally, I behave like a big girl, but artistically I know that deep down between a director and an actress there must be that strange relationship of being passive, and being led by the director, and if you are not like this, there can't be a relationship, you can't be an actress. Being an actress depends on this.

Angela Huth: I actually hate people who say I like men best or I like women best. You can't generalize.

Women are very good friends to each other. On the whole, it is quite hard to find such good friends in men. Obviously there are a few, and being friends with gays is quite a new sort of fashion for women at the moment, which they rather enjoy because there is no other complication. But usually, if you are friends with a man, you're always aware, without flattering yourself, of a bit of a twinkling in his eye because, in the end, you might end up together. Which, on the whole, a lot of women don't want to do, they generally just want to be friends and nothing else. So it is all much easier if you are just women together. I mean, I don't in any way like great groups of women, and I hate women who sit around discussing their problems and analysing themselves and talking about their roles and their grumbles. But actually, just being friends with women is much easier than being friends with men on the whole. They are the ones who appreciate what other people are doing. It is all my women friends who seem most interested in my work, in what I am doing, and vice versa.

I had eight years on my own, rather good times from thirty to thirty-eight, and I had various boyfriends obviously, though I didn't ever live with anyone. I always wanted to retain my independence. But since I have been married, very happily, a sort of polythene sheet comes down and the green light is off and I keep thinking I am deeply unattractive to all men now, which perhaps I am. But it might be also that they just see I am unavailable because I am happy and I am committed to somebody else; so there is no point in making one of those stupid passes because they won't get anywhere.

When one was younger, men were extremely attractive and the whole thing of flirtation and the game and all the rest of it was absolutely wonderful. Now there isn't time for any of that. Apart from anything else, the idea of adultery is just too laborious, too cumbersome. Who wants to get undressed in the middle of the afternoon, who wants to go to a hotel room or order a bottle up? What do you drink at three o'clock in the afternoon? You know, the man straightens his tie and goes off to a board meeting. I've written a play about all this. Adultery is just not practical on the whole, and I think it's corrosive. If you have any respect for your marriage at all, then you shouldn't indulge in adultery because, unless you are a very special kind of person, or two very special kinds of people, it doesn't work and it corrodes something so much more precious than a minor flirtation with a passing fancy.

I'm not remotely interested in power. It is a boring concept on the whole. It brings nothing but cliché attitudes. I know enormous amounts of women who are immensely turned on by really awful men, and because they are powerful and possibly famous, they have succumbed; they are intrigued by power. I can't see its fascination at all. I've never wanted to be powerful myself, I don't want to have any power over anybody. One would like to influence and help one's closest friends, but the idea of having wall-to-wall, ocean-to-ocean power doesn't interest me in the least.

Sheila Innes: Nobody, in my view, should ever marry without having a period not just of sex, but of actually living together for a time. People are so different when you live with them. I just think that's an insurance. You've got to make sure the sex part works, and works very well. A one-night stand couldn't be anything other than an act of lust. If you are actually after love, that actually comes by growing together and understanding each other and doing things together, because the whole thing is about sharing. And if you share properly, you share everything, and that includes sex.

Angela Janklow: My brother has had the same girlfriend since he was fifteen. I never ever do that. I am constantly with millions. I'm Gemini, very duplicitous and scatterbrained.

Some men appear swashbuckling on the outside, and inside it's just these quivering ninnies. You take the sword out of their hand and they don't even have one where it counts. I don't want someone who's going to drop all their defences, I really don't. I don't want someone who's going to cry openly, constantly, at the littlest thing. I don't like weak men. I hate it. I am a strong woman and I don't want to be around an indecisive man. I don't want to be a crutch.

Any woman who says she doesn't want a man is lying through her teeth. Unless she'd rather have a woman. But any heterosexual woman who says she doesn't want a man is bullshitting, period. I don't believe it for an instant.

I am seduced by the unknown. There has to be – I hate this word, but I am going to use it – an aura. There has to be something, some look in the eye. I love the veins in the hand, I love hands. There is this guy I see once in a while who has got a chipped front tooth, but that chipped tooth makes him. Because it makes him imperfect; that's really compelling. I hate plasticity. I hate plastic boys, I hate models. I think male models are the ugliest creatures ever concocted on the face of the earth. They are flimsy and pretty and I hate pretty like that.

The reason I jump around from man to man a lot, doesn't mean I sleep around. It just means I change dates frequently; it's because I find them all too malleable, and none strong enough and none in that position of authority. I'm twenty-two, and I don't know if this is what I'll be saying ten years or twenty years from now, but at the moment I want someone who would have more iron rule than I find now. Certainly people my age, it's just pathetic. I could reduce them to nothing in an instant. And I don't want 50/50. The man that I want, ideally, is going to have a fortitude unmatched by my own, much stronger, much more powerful than myself. It doesn't mean that he has to be a CEO (Chief Executive Officer), but it has to be someone who is a higher thinker in some way. And I am terribly intelligent. It has to be a different intellect from mine. I don't want match, match, match, all the time. I want someone who I feel is beyond me, but who can see something in me that he will want.

Tama Janowitz: I've always liked men, but I've had problems, difficulties with them, partly because my parents split up as I was entering my teen years. I felt, in some ways, that that was a rejection of me, and in some ways my father felt I was my mother and managed actually to reject me.

Relationships are just not very easy or simple, and to live with somebody, even a friend, is almost impossible. It's something that takes a lot of work.

I think we're all terribly disappointed in our relationships – not just women, but men, because it's never such a close connection as the one you had when you were a kid with your parents. It's just the way it is. You can be very close to somebody, but you're always struggling to reach that feeling of connection with another person. We're taught love is this wonderful, beautiful thing, but love is really not happiness, all kissing each other; everything's beautiful and a happy life together. Most of the time a relationship with another person is spent fighting about who left the top off the toothpaste, working out a living existence and wondering why you're losing interest in the other person; not this beautiful thing you see in the movies.

Margaret Jay: What I would hope is that, if young people are given more freedom to experiment, without hurting people – I don't mean they should be casual with other people or casual with their feelings – but if they do have a chance to at least know what the alternatives may be in different types of relationship, then marriages may become more stable again. I would like to have a stable marriage. I think it would be something everybody would want to have in the sense of giving a sense of security and a continuity and a framework for your life.

Dr Lukrezia Jochimsen: Men and women have the luxury to go on the priority of their feelings. If I look at the marriages of my parents and my grandparents, times were so difficult, the economic struggle and every-day-life struggle so great, it didn't even occur to them, I would say, to think of other partners. It probably didn't occur to my grandmother that, after ten years of marriage and eight children, she could have maybe had a rather more leisurely life with some other man. The luxury of hedonistic private possibilities didn't occur to her. And I think, for the first time in this society, people have the economic means to leave a marriage, women especially; it is not always the economic disaster it was.

Sally Jones: There's an enormous emphasis on the sexual side of relationships these days, and there's something terribly dreadful about confessing you're celibate. I feel very self-sufficient. I'm also very sociable, I love friends. I try to treat people well. A lot of people overlook a quality of *gentillesse* in a relationship that's far different from the love aspect. It's almost a form of good manners within a relationship that – whatever you are feeling like, or even if you are falling out of love with somebody, or even if a relationship is coming to an end – you still keep things happy, you consider them, you keep things on an even keel, and even if you eventually decide to part, you part on good terms. There's not a single person I've even been out with whom I am not still friends with, and that's the way I'd like to keep it. I hate this business of a relationship that's been a loving one disintegrating into absolute hate and loathing. You see it a lot with people's divorces. They have been so close during a marriage that it is easier for it to degenerate into real vitriol.

Power is not something that I find a turn-on, because many of the very powerful men I have met, and I have met a number with my job, have been virtually the next thing to psychopaths, very unpleasant characters. They've very often given me an impression of physical violence being extremely near the surface, and I think that's one reason why often powerful men are attracted to other men as well as to women. They've got this image of immense strength and ferocity, mentally and physically. I don't especially like that, because I feel confident enough in my own right not to need somebody who is going to try to trample over me or make me into something different. I feel I am my own person. And I don't want somebody trying to change me or force their own character upon mine.

Rana Kabbani: I've been married three times, but I don't believe in the institution, no. Some passions need marriage to anchor them a little, otherwise they are too impossible. Sometimes you fall in love so violently, and you feel that this man or this woman has to be contained somehow, and you have really to live out the experience with them. And you can only do that in marriage. Because marriage creates a sort of bond and an intimacy that an ordinary relationship does not. And I like that. I like that feeling of going to the end of a relationship.

My father used to have fits when I said I was in love, when I was going to get married. Every time I got married, which was quite often, he'd run away, he'd go to the farthest place he could. He'd get on the plane and just go.

Intelligence seduces me. Intelligence, creativity and generosity, these three things. I can fall in love with an extremely ugly or unattractive man if he is intelligent and creative. There is something very threatening

863

about a good-looking man, to a woman. I feel this. I have never been attracted to a man who is considered extremely handsome. For me, there is something slightly frivolous about male beauty that goes against the seriousness of intelligence. That's my own private perception. I don't think it applies to many people.

I relate more to women or gay men, because there is no physical tension at all and also because they are usually people who have been able to get out of that claustrophobic traditional male role and just be more feeling and frail, more fragile, more human, more like women.

Unless people are very lucky, they start boring each other after three or four years; they use up all there is to use in the other person. And unless they are very clever, or wealthy enough to have separate households, that is the normal way of things. The only way marriages last is if people can have separate rooms, separate houses, separate countries, separate friends. And then interest remains alive and you have that little bit of independence which is very important. The possibility of being alone, which you don't have in most marriages, is vital, because you need time to recover from togetherness. Marriages in the Middle East tend to last longer because the woman has a separate life from the man. They can see other women, and they can entertain themselves, and they have privacy, and they have an area in their lives which men cannot enter and are not allowed into. The men also have a life apart from the women, with other men. It creates an area of relaxation for both of them, so they are not so tense in their conflict. And also there are things expected of a man, and things expected of a woman, and they both live within these expectations and the marriage prospers. Whereas, in the West, where there are no set expectations any more, it is very difficult, very difficult. We are going through a period of transition in our ideas about the other sex so unnerving that the best marriages collapse under it.

Elaine Kaufman: Women go to psychiatrists today to find out how to keep a male interested. I think they go there to find out how to have the doorman. When the family structure broke down in America, which was in the 1950s, I think (more and more, after the Second World War), when that broke down, the psychiatrists came into more popularity. There is nobody to talk to. The priest doesn't make sense, the rabbi doesn't make sense, so you create another personage to talk to. There were no more wise men.

Dillie Keane: We've come to expect or demand a degree of comfort

864

which has nothing to do with real living. Also people don't work at marriage. One failure, and they're out. They give up too easily. You've lost your extended family, they are not round the corner, you haven't got them coming round to say, now, for goodness' sake, Edith, pull yourself together, it's not the end of the world. The support system has changed. It's not mother coming and saying, it happened to me too, your row is not the end of the world. It's your friends who say, oh, my God, Edith, for God's sake give him up, the man's a shit. You're being influenced by people who have no responsibility towards you, and therefore whose advice is actually much less valuable.

I'm extremely lucky because I am with a very non-competitive man who is just so delighted when I'm successful. For instance, we've played in the same theatre he has, and I've come back and said, we've sold out, when he hadn't. I'm much more competitive; I would loathe it if he were more successful than I am. He's much more generous-spirited. But I think he is a rarity.

Caroline Kellett: I feel more at ease with men. Women among women are far more competitive. This also illustrates the fact that the fundamental role inbred in them is to attract, to procreate, to find a mate, and that's very much more a solitary condition; they gravitate towards one mate. When they've found him, it's the business of making a home and the business of having children. The more intelligent women are, and the more broad-minded, then the more they understand and the more they want to know about life. And they are much more likely to get that sort of understanding and assimilate it from the company of men. Women are more enjoyable company for the bulk of women, perhaps. I don't want to bang a drum about intelligence, but when you put a group of girls together, the topics of conversation, according to their age group, are clothes, female biology, home-making, children, gossip. Men, of course, are actually underrated as gossips. Men are just as bad, and actually far more competitive – vindictive even. But the elementary topics of conversation among women are very, very narrow. I have a few close women friends, and they are worth their weight in gold; they are very much the same as they have been since I was eighteen. I make very few new girlfriends. I find I make a lot more men friends, men friends who are platonic friends. There's always the edge, an underlying flirtatious current. But that, in itself, adds spice to a relationship and friendship, because if you can get beyond that, it's a hell of a lot more stimulating, more rewarding. As a student, say between the ages of eighteen and twenty-two, I really enjoyed the company of gay men; I loved their flamboyance, their lack of threat, the fact that they were easy-going, amusing, entertaining, easy to be with and there wasn't any sexual undercurrent. But then, I think, that's a mark of naïveté and of youth and adolescence. It never ceases to amaze me, particularly within the arts and within fashion, that older women are still playing up to that type of man, still enjoying their company. I think it's something that's missing in them that needs reassurance, that lack of threat, that stability a homosexual man gives them. Certainly I am very tired of my gay friends. I've grown out of them, I like to think. Obviously, I've still got homosexual friends, but in the end, I think very, very many of them, deep down, loathe women, unfortunately. I think they are intensely misogynistic, much more so than even the most misogynistic of heterosexual men. In the heterosexual man, it's something thwarted, very often to do with childhood, mothers, sisters, some sort of oppressive feminine influence in their lives which made them mistrust women deeply. Homosexual men – this is the great thing – think every man's gay and every woman's a threat to converting men to being homosexual. And that's very tiresome, very sad and very wrong.

Women I found increasingly difficult as I grew older. I found they gave far less. It was easy to be on good terms with men, and to get closer to them, without any sexual threat. Women were always looking over your shoulder, always looking one further, very hard to get close to. I think that happens to all women, actually: you make fewer women friends when you get older.

There are still enormous numbers of men who see women as a perpetual challenge physically, sexually. And they want to dominate you, to overpower you, and very little else. There is a major distinction between two types of men: there are predatory men and there are sensitive men, and obviously, like a Venn diagram, there's a mean where there is a type of man who wants you but is also prepared to be open-minded. But the predators are the ones that are difficult. They make too many assumptions, they take too much for granted.

I can't bear being suffocated, I can't bear being pampered, over-powered. I like someone to be delicate, amusing. Perhaps, at the onset of a relationship or friendship, I like them to behave almost asexually so there isn't an enormous sexual come-on, a sort of oppressive sexuality. I find overt flirting and animal, carnal, basic emotive responses very unattractive. Equally, I just can't think of anything less attractive, less in my nature, than to pursue. I like to be pursued. I also like to leave things to chance, to instinct. I think it is totally ungratifying for a woman, so unfeminine, so totally without emotional strategy or sensitivity, to see men in terms of conquest. There is no reward in that, nothing at all. One becomes as a geisha, or a prostitute.

Tessa Kennedy: I despise women who think it's the end of the marriage, and how can she live with him when she finds out he's been unfaithful once. To a lot of men, it doesn't mean more than shaking hands, and women don't seem able to understand that. I don't see why, if a man has fallen by the wayside or whatever – which to him meant nothing more than a fling or he was lonely, and he's been alone a lot because of his work – a woman should make it the cause to disrupt a family union and the marriage. It seems ridiculous. Men feel definitely a two-standard thing, that they can fling around, but their wife must stay absolutely on a pedestal and mustn't be touched by anyone. I think that's unreasonable, too. People should really do what they want to do, but I do think the appetite of men is a different appetite, and what it means to them is completely different from what it means to a woman. A woman, on the whole, does it because that moment she feels deeply in love. Whether the next day she'll feel the same way, I don't know, but I would think so.

I have the children whom I absolutely adore. I live for them, completely live for them, my kids, and I wouldn't have it any other way. That's been fantastic. Even when I was divorced, and I had three little boys to look after, I found I had more men running after me than ever in my life: men with a paternal instinct who wanted to look after a pathetic-looking woman with three little boys. I don't think it ruined my life at all.

Patsy Kensit: I have loads of men just as platonic relationships, but my manager, Steve, he's very young, and recently we went on holiday to Antigua together and, I mean, every single newspaper was saying we were having an affair, and I swear to God, we weren't. He's really, really, really a good buddy, that's it. We're just brilliant friends, and we talk about things I talk about with my girlfriends, like periods, sex, and I tell him when I fancy a boy, and he tells me when he fancies a girl, and that's it. It's very sad when people, certain newspapers, are so small-minded that whenever things like that happen it's immediately a sexual relationship.

Griselda Kerr: I've got masses and masses of friends and only a few very close friends. And I think that's more because I spend an enormous amount of time at work, and actually you do need to look after your friends to have very close friends. You need to spend a lot of time with them, telephone them, talk to them, write to them, entertain them, be entertained by them, and for fifteen years, since I've been here, I've worked from perhaps nine in the morning till eight at night and gone home and gone out to a party, night after night after night. And if you go out to a party, you're not looking after your close friends, you're building up a huge circle of friends, and I did that, I'm sure, from 1975, when I became press officer here and began to work very hard, until now. People used to say, oh, Griselda never gives a party but that there aren't twenty-eight people at least there. I could never entertain small numbers. I found the discipline of having six people to a small and beautiful dinner party at the brilliantly beautifully laid table terribly difficult, and somehow my glasses were always a bit dirty and my plates never matching, and it was much easier to invite twenty-eight people and have an extraordinarily fun party. Now I'm married, it's quite different, because my husband likes small intimate groups.

What does one admire in one's husband? One admires his absolute integrity and loyalty and constancy; constancy is the most important word in my life, I think.

Princess Yasmin Aga Khan: I have men who are very close friends, very close friends, whom I would never think to have romantic involvement with. Perhaps there are certain things I would not discuss with my male friends; there is that difference.

I think it is possible to expect total fidelity in a man. Being the idealistic person I am, I believe it is possible. But it doesn't usually happen. I don't think a man has the discipline.

I don't think we over-exaggerate the importance of sex. That physical contact, and the unity and the sharing, is very important in a relationship. To keep it going for years and years – well, that's another story. There has to be a fair amount of independence, and freedom and space, to keep that little bit of tantalizing sexual thrill in a relationship over a period of years. But then I don't know, because I haven't had a relationship for ten years. My marriage lasted three months.

Why should relationships last for forty years? Don't we change as human beings? Don't we go through evolution? If we are really lucky and we have a partner whom we can communicate with and we can change with over ten, twenty, thirty years – that's incredible. But we develop, we evolve, and we don't always evolve in the same direction.

Why should people want to stay together for the sake of marriage for forty years if they are at two different ends of the pole? What does that prove?

Soraya Khashoggi: I have women friends that are with me through life, through thick and thin. I find, for instance, when times are bad, when things are really hard and tough, women stick with you. Men tend to go away, then, when things suddenly get good and you are on the up-swing again, they all come flocking back and think you are going to forget they deserted you when times were bad. Men waver in their loyalty. Women stick in there through thick and thin.

There is a lack of respect for the family structure, the family society. This is probably why I married an Arab. The respect for the family, the respect for the father, the mother, the grandmother, the parent, and everybody, still exists in the East. You don't find it at all in the West. People will risk a whole marriage for one night or one weekend going to bed with somebody else. It is such a shame. There is no longer this close family society, people don't make an effort. People go into marriages light-heartedly and go out of them light-heartedly. They go in making contracts: when I divorce you, you are going to get this or you are not going to get that. What kind of a way is that to go into a marriage? To go with the idea already that you are going to get divorced. It's disgusting. What's the point of getting married if you are going to go in with that attitude? You must enter marriage with the idea that this is going to be for ever. If it isn't, it's very sad.

Power is an aphrodisiac, absolutely. In fact, I would never go out with a man who wasn't the best at what he was doing. I've never been with a man in my life who isn't the best. If I was going to marry a man who sweeps the road, he would have to be the top, he would have to be the head of the union or something. Yes, definitely, power is an aphrodisiac. Political power, financial power, intellectual power, all levels.

Lesley Kingcombe: I hit London when I was seventeen and really had far too jolly a life too soon. Even grandad said to me, at the age of nineteen, watch it, you're getting stale. So Kingcombe married me, he did actually say he had to marry me for that, to save me from this wonderful life of unparalleled licentiousness, and he was absolutely right. I was jolly nearly promiscuous. I mean, I was really very naughty when I was little. So, having done it, I've never had to do it again.

I like women very much indeed, I always have stunning girlfriends. They are always bright, always good-looking. They can always sing for their supper.

Mothers can be awfully boring, let's face it. Married women with children and their coffee-type minds can really be very boring.

I find successful businessmen absolutely delicious. I find all sorts of men attractive. They don't have to look particularly good, they have just got to have charisma.

I still don't think it's a good enough excuse if a man goes off and has an affair round the corner and then says, oh, it's not important to me. Whichever way you look at it, a cheat is a cheat. But I do think chaps can jump into bed with a girl much more easily and jump out of the bed and forget about it. Whereas we have to be in a sort of state about the whole thing, and psych ourselves up: oh, my goodness, it's so romantic, oh, it's so wonderful. But it still doesn't alter the fact that he's cheating or she's cheating and cheats are bores. But emotionally I think it is harder for a woman to do that. If she's going to have an affair, she is going to get herself hyped up about it. If he's going to have an affair, he's had a jolly good lunch with a jolly nice girl and that's it. It actually doesn't fret him. He's not going to go and fall in love. And she, for some stupid reason, has to decide she's in love, even if it's only for three days. She's deeply in love, and the whole thing is all terribly roses and wonderful, and *bonk, bonk*.

I think you have to be totally committed to keep a marriage going, and it's bloody difficult. I think you should think long and hard before you get married in the first place. It's too easy to get in and too easy to get out and too easy to have an affair. It's too easy all round for everything.

Rhoda Koenig: I feel more comfortable with women because I can relax more and know that we have our experiences and attitudes in common, the way we look at the world. With men, there's always a sexual element. Even the absence of it is a fact that militates against perfect comfort and relaxation.

Irma Kurtz: In the love of a woman for a man, like it or not, there's an element of respect. Feminism has never quite explained what we do about this, because respect is a dangerous thing, it leads on to other things. You have to be careful where respect turns into something else.

But a woman does not stay in love with a man she doesn't respect. Women write to me who have been married for five years and say their sex lives are *kaput*, they like the fellow but are no longer in love, and it's because they have lost respect for the man. Now, when you get a woman of about forty, forty-five, who's got a high-powered job, who can buy herself the pretty rings, buy herself all that – what the hell kind of man is going to want her? A man in her position can afford to go home and relax with a nice little wife who's going to cook for him, who's pretty, who organizes his life. The high-powered woman needs a wife, too. She really does, more than she needs a husband. She needs company, she is lonely. A man in her own area is not going to enjoy the fact that he goes home to competition. A man in another area is not going to understand how she disposes of her time and how necessary it is for her to get up at dawn and go to meetings. There are exceptions, but this is a general rule. And a man who is superior to her, who has got lots of money and an even higher position, what the hell does he want with her? He can have at home the sweetest, most darling little wife to give him ease and comfort, who will never complain, raise no objections to anything he does. How can you blame a man if he prefers to have a sweet little blonde at home instead of a tough person? The best she can do is an absolutely inadequate man who needs her, who is grateful, whom she cannot respect but who is company. A lot of them do that.

Women are not so all-fired intelligent, not all women. I knew girls at school who would respect a man because of the car he drove. Now, is that sensible? What do you get into when that starts? There are women who write to me who respect a man because every once in a while he comes home and knocks the hell out of them. They think that's worthy of respect, that every once in a while he demonstrates the fact that he's stronger than they are. This is very dangerous country. This is where respect becomes diseased.

Romance worries me. Romance is deceptive, it's a terrible thing. God, I'm such a reactionary, they'd say, but I've thought this all my life: I don't think men are monogamous by nature, I really don't think so. I think they do a woman a courtesy, they stay with her, that's fine, and they may love her dearly. But I do believe that, sexually, they find it very easy, indeed almost necessary, to have partners outside a marriage. The happiest marriages are where women tolerate this, not only tolerate it but in a way understand it and don't worry about it too much. But the romance doesn't allow for it. The romance is creating a monogamous woman, a monogamous romance. It's so fierce that, the least transgression on the bloke's part, and she becomes that one in three with a divorce.

Women's demands are impossible. They want fidelity, absolute fidelity, because sex is love for them. And they often persuade a man, because men are so convinced that women know more about these things, that, yes, sex is love. Then he goes through traumatizing guilt when he finds he is attracted to, just attracted to another woman outside his marriage. So they want him to be fuck-faithful, then they want this peculiar thing called equality. Now what the hell is equality? I don't know what it means. I knew a feminist household: she wouldn't cook for him, he wouldn't cook for her. They'd stand side by side in the kitchen, each cooking a meal, his own meal, for himself. I call that selfishness. I know women who say equality means that he has to do the cleaning on Mondays, Wednesdays and Fridays, I do the shopping Tuesday, Thursday. That works for a while, but it doesn't go on working very well.

It's been so long since I've been seduced. First of all, I've always, in my past, liked good-looking men, which is a terrible weakness, shameful. I call that the male side of my nature. And if he makes me laugh, he's halfway home. And I am sure I am not the only woman who has said that. As a matter of fact, I forget about the looks if a man can make me laugh. A really witty man, I feel great, I'm comfortable and attracted. It's a voice I want to hear in the morning. I've never been seduced by men's fame, never, and fame is a kind of power. And never by money. On the contrary, I've often found very rich men unattractive. No, no. I'm afraid I've been an artist's sort of moll, you know. Originally, I suppose, I saw my destiny as in a parrot garret – spaghetti and red wine for the boys, you know. And then I found out that I had as much of it in me as they did themselves.

Verity Lambert: If I was honest about it, I would say I prefer working for men. Not because I don't like women, but because I think I can manipulate a man more than I could ever manipulate a woman. A woman would be absolutely on to another woman doing that.

Power in a man is a very attractive and sexual thing, I think. Power in a woman, I am not sure if it has the same effect on men. I think men, unless they are very confident, are nervous of women who are in positions of power.

Romance is transitory. It only lasts for two or three years. Maybe you can keep some of it going, but romance happens less when you get older.

Marghanita Laski: I think there is the misunderstanding between love and infatuation, and the belief – it arose in the Middle Ages with chivalry and the whole romance of love – that love has its rights, that nothing must stand in the way of love, the rules of love, as they were set up in the thirteenth century. And so people look across the room and catch the eye of someone of the other sex and feel a shiver. And instead of thinking, I'd like to go to bed with that person, they think, this is love, and once they think it's love, they think everything is justified. People, friends of mine, people all around us – and you must have seen it, too – have committed in the name of love cruelty they would have been sent to prison for if it had been physical. They've destroyed families, destroyed children.

Whomever you marry, after all, it comes to the same thing in a few years, unless they are particularly cruel or particularly nasty, or particularly nice or particularly one thing or the other. The thing is to make a right marriage. I'm all for arranged marriages myself. At least you worked at it. At least it's certain that all the basics on which a marriage is likely to founder – the similarity of belief, of tastes, of family, of money, all that kind of thing, which may well be the rocks on which a marriage founders – are overcome before the marriage takes place. An African chief once said to me, marriage is not an affair for individuals, it's an affair for families. I'm sure he was right.

I have to say, though, that my own marriage was a rebellious marriage, with both families disliking it intensely, and it worked out very well. I was Jewish and he wasn't. My father was then the secular head of the Jews in England, the president of the Board of Deputies, and it was a disgrace for him. My grandfather was the equivalent of the chief rabbi of the Sephardi community and he cut me off, it was a disgrace for him. My Manchester grandparents, who were Ashkenazis, cut me off, it was a disgrace for them.

If I had not lived the life I chose to live, I would have liked to have men constantly. Jack Priestley said once to me that the main reason for infidelity is naughtiness, and I agree with him, but one wants to be naughty. It was to do with men's need to be assured that the child was their own, that women were kept very much more strictly, but not all women were. It's just a belief that women were the faithful sex. They weren't, of course they weren't. But when divorce wasn't easy, things had to be covered up.

It's safer for a married woman to have more friendships with women than with men, and one of the dearest wishes of my life always has been

873

to preserve my marriage at a time when marriages are breaking all around me.

Why should I look for anything else except sexual potency if I was looking outside marriage? I sound very romantic, but though I slept with several people before I met my husband, I never fell in love except with my husband. I just looked across the room and we fell in love.

Frances Lear: I just adore women, and I don't want to talk about what's wrong with them. I want to talk about what's right with them.

A woman's comfort with men depends on her health within a man/woman relationship. I was a victim of abandonment very early by men, and I think it has scarred me for life. I love men – I find them very interesting and amusing – and I love sex, but I am more comfortable with women.

Sara Leighton: Women still love to be subjugated. A lawyer, whose opinion I respect – he's a divorce lawyer – said that the trouble was that most women have a strong masochistic streak, and I think this is very true. That's why they return time and time again to a man who treats them badly. And while that masochistic streak exists, they will become subjected to other people; they will be tyrannized, because if they take that attitude, their husbands are going to take a more dominant attitude. I've seen it time and time again. A woman will go back and back and back to a man who is physically violent with her. The same lawyer told me of a case he defended when he was a young lawyer – a murder trial. The husband used to come home drunk every Saturday night, in a working-class English family, and throw the wife downstairs. He had broken her arms, he'd broken various bones. Finally, the boy, the son, got to nineteen, and one night the man threw his wife downstairs. She was in a terrible state the next day, and the boy, when his father was shaving, went into the bathroom, took the cut-throat razor and cut his father's throat. The wife never spoke to the son after that. All she could say to him was, you killed the man I loved.

A woman likes to feel the dominance of a man. I'm sure, if she's truly feminine, she loves to feel that physical dominance; I don't mean mental dominance. I love it. And I'm the first to say that I love to feel physically in bed that the man I love is stronger than I am, and that he conducts the whole scene. I will do it, but I don't want to be the leader of the game. I want to feel that he is stronger than I am.

Catherine Leroy: I've never considered men as my enemies or competitors, because I've always been with men – always, all the time. They are my confidants, sometimes my lovers. They are very precious and important to me. I never had this kind of relationship with men being on the other side of the line, because I've always been with them in very normal relationships, always.

As one of the very few, very rare women news photographers, all my competitors are men; 99.99 per cent of the photographers and journalists I know are men. It's much more difficult to be competitive on the one hand and friendly on the other, because I'm a woman. I've found that most of the time they have good friends among themselves, but, with me, they worry, they are much more careful.

I have a few close women friends, of course, but I like men, I like to be around men. They are like my brothers. I think, in France, men and women like each other. Some of my best friends are men, and there is nothing sexual at all, and they are married or they have girlfriends, and the relationships I have with their wife or their girlfriend are also very close, but the woman can understand that her husband is also my friend. It's something typically French and not something you find in England or America. Men in France like women; in England they don't particularly, and not in America either, where men will stick together. In France, the relationship between men and women is very different. Maybe it goes back to the Revolution, where men and women were together on the barricades. I don't know. I think men and women in France like each other. They fuck each other too, but that's something else entirely. But basically they like each other. They like to be with each other. You know, I could call a man friend, and say, let's go out, and we would. It's a very unique relationship, I think, in France.

The man who seduces me – it's almost like the Humphrey Bogart cliché – is a man that is very tough on the outside, and very soft, very tender inside; and, to me, the best definition of a woman is exactly the opposite: very soft on the outside and very tough on the inside. Even though physically a woman may not be feminine, she must work at the femininity. I think it is the primary obligation of a woman to be feminine on the outside.

Being powerful is no substitute for being a tender and good lover to a woman.

Doris Lessing: There is a kind of understanding that women share and I

have often wondered about it. It's probably got something to do not
with anti-male feelings at all. It has something to do with the fact that we
are so rooted in our physical nature by the mere fact that we have to
have children, we have to menstruate.

I think men are in all sorts of cycles that may not be recognized yet. It's
very easy to see a woman's menstrual cycle, it's so obvious, but I don't
believe that men are cut off from Nature at all. The older I get the more
complicated everything seems to me, and if I make a statement, I can
instantly think of all kinds of facts that contradict it. It is said that
women are closer to the earth. Well, I wonder if we are. This kind of
understanding that women have, I value very much, but I don't think it
is necessarily the highest way of communicating. The fact that a couple
of women in a room will have a whole range of understanding – it's
very pleasant and a lazy kind of relationship, but it doesn't mean to say I
have the most interesting kind of relationship with them I could have. I
could have a much more interesting relationship with a woman who is
difficult, who hasn't got this quality of earthiness, and who is a different
kind of woman altogether.

Why do we women put up with men the way we do? There is always
somewhere in the back of our minds a, well, he-can't-really-help-it
attitude. It's true. When men behave abominably, you often find that
kind of humorous shrug as if you're describing something that can't be
helped.

Maureen Lipman: It seems to me that most of the nicest women I know
– and I mean really caring, decent, nice, funny, attractive women –
are with some of the most appalling men I have ever known in my life.
This is a syndrome. I can sit back and look at these women and think,
what does she see in him, why does she want to be pushed around by
this person? In every other part of life, she's a person who can
distinguish, but in the case of men, she can't. That has, in the end, to be
because we somehow feel we are not worthy of the love of a good man,
we are rotten some way inside. Eve was rotten in some way, and she
took the apple. And therefore, if the relationship is to be good sexually,
it has to be with someone who pushes you about, someone who is
basically using you or saying, you are only good for one thing.

I never ever managed to enjoy myself sexually with someone I wasn't
keen on. And the most rewarding times were when it was with someone
whom I didn't just want to have a relationship with, but was kind of in
awe of. I happen to think, personally, that falling in love is a very mean

876

trick on the part of God, or Charles Darwin, or whoever it is who thought it up. It is a chemical state induced by mental mania. It's nothing to do with life, and you can't lead a normal life in a state of advanced passion and love. And it's our nature to build this quest for love, this fantasy that all adds to our enjoyment of sexual relations. We've been trained to strive for that, and if you're lucky enough to get it, what happens is, it can't last. I don't believe it can last in a situation where you have to empty bins and go to Sainsbury's and skin fish and things. You can't be in that heightened stage all the time.

I have a penchant for lost men, for people who are going through bad times, who are a bit lost. It's probably the agony aunt in me. Men who are very English, slightly aristocratic, a bit down on their luck and lost and thin and pale and hopeless. Byron would have suited me down to the ground. That's not what I end up with. Because I'm a bright girl, and I know that that's not what's good for me in the end. But I have a hopeless fascination for men in trouble, because then I can put my arms around them and say, I can give you a bit of me and you will be so much better. I grew to about my twenty-seventh year before I realized it was a supreme act of egotism on my part.

When I look back reflectively, I can say that my husband and I very rarely argue and we have to manufacture arguments, which is not always the best, but that's the way it is. We both shy away from conflict, and that's undoubtedly because I was aware of so much conflict at home, and so was he. His parents were at each other with a meat cleaver. Mine were not quite that extreme, but there was certainly always a terrible tension in the air, and sulking, and you never quite knew what was going to happen. I must have been very much influenced by this to look for a man who would be very easy, no trouble.

Lady Lothian: When I got cancer and had to lose my eye, the kindest, most loving, most sensitive letters came from friends who were men. I hope that we are beginning to realize that it is personality that matters, that a man can be, if you like, what a woman would like to be at her best. A man can be a very good mother to his children. Equally, a lot of women, particularly in Italy, are actually fathers to their children, because the man is so lazy or doesn't want to work. There are a lot of women who are both man and woman in their families.

Marriages don't last because human beings are unruly. Hardly any of my friends are Catholics, very few are Christian. I've talked about this to them, and they say, you are very lucky. If you quarrel with Peter, if you walk out of the door saying you never want to see him again, to hell with it – then, next morning, regret having done it – you can say to Peter, without losing any face, if it wasn't for that bloody Pope I wouldn't have come back. The amount of men and women I've met who have regretted slamming the door, and there hasn't been any way in which, without losing face, they could pick up the pieces. I think it is that the law allows it, and unless you have very strong religion, like the Jews or the Asians or the Christians do (and it has to be very strong now), you part. And you may regret it, but there is very little to help you get together again. And that's why marriages don't last. If a married woman said to me, I've never had a cross word, or, I haven't kicked my husband, or I haven't shouted or had periods of total hatred for him, I would look at her very carefully.

If a man who is naturally faithful is unfaithful, the woman ought to think hard about what is happening to her relationship. I am a Christian believer and have come to think that the Bible, both the Old and the New Testaments, is extraordinarily and mysteriously wise. Very few Christians practise the Christian idea of the man and the woman being faithful to one another and not having sex outside marriage, but still I would have to be honest and say that, as a Christian, I think it is not only possible but desirable. But we often don't do what is possible and desirable. For instance, it's possible and desirable, fat as I am, that I shouldn't eat a box of chocolates at night. I'm going to probably, because I like it. That doesn't make me a lesser person. I think we have to be much much more forgiving to women. Why do men resent their wives or their girlfriends being promiscuous, but do not criticize themselves for the same sort of behaviour? It is a great puzzle. I think, if I had married a man who was naturally very attractive to women, didn't think very much of the physical act, loved me very deeply for certain things, was wonderfully kind, generous, supportive, I think I would have had to be forgiving. I didn't marry that sort of man, I married the opposite. If Peter were unfaithful, he would be untrue to his own character and his own personality. But if I had married a man with the other sort of personality, I would have loved him no less, I think. It is self-indulgence, and I don't think it is necessary. But then we all live by self-indulgences, whether it is food or warmth or whatever.

The Dennis Thatcher syndrome is a very important one: a man who accepts and is pleased and happy to help in his wife's career. I think Dennis Thatcher has made an enormous influence on the future, because he is a very likable person, people like him. He hasn't lost his sense of humour, he hasn't lost his sense of proportion. Very British, so the British like him. I think he represents a new form of husband. If he was totally negative as a person, never had a good job himself, he would be ridiculous. But he is a man who has managed big business. Judge Donaldson is married to the Lord Mayor or London, and he is terribly proud of her. They are equal, it's the companionhood again. I don't want to be boring, but I do think that this is where we ought to find Valhalla eventually, if only we could accept each other as companions.

Blanche Lucas: If you want children, then you must plan on the basis that, for at least twenty years, maybe more, you will do your utmost to stay together during the periods your children are growing up. I think that most people do try and many fail. They don't have divorces just for fun, but I don't think, on the whole, one thinks sufficiently seriously about what one is undertaking. If one undertook the having of children in the same way as one undertook a career, perhaps it might be better. In that event, of course, one would have to discourage romanticism. There's no good being romantic about marriage.

I have spotted envy in some men, and I think this must be much more general than one imagines: envy about women being able to have children. What has really happened in history is that women have had child after child after child. I shall never forget, going to India, and going to the Taj Mahal, because up till then, I was under the impression that this was a great expression of love by a man for a woman. You know – his building the Taj Mahal when his wife died. When I got there, I learned she had died in childbirth and that the child was, I think, her fourteenth. So my whole attitude to the Taj Mahal changed. I thought, if this man really loved this woman, he would have abstained from sexual intercourse. But no, he went on until she died, and then he built a temple. To me, the Taj Mahal is an expression of guilt, not of love at all.

Jenny Lumet: When I first meet a man, I can be really talkative and articulate. I know I can pull it off on a man like that. If I want to make him think I'm charming, it's easy as pie. With women, it takes me a lot longer, because women know women. So I have an easier time with men. Put it that way.

Gillian Lynne: I've worked with some incredible-looking men but it's always the mind and what it does and what it says that attracts me. Not power. Even Sam Spiegel. Sam Spiegel had a real go for me because I played Puck in a television production he saw, and I was very tiny with a little tight bottom and my hair was cut like a boy, and my bosom all bandaged; and he was totally besotted. His car used to follow my little Morris car, he tried to buy me things, and, I mean, there was no more powerful man. In the end I said to him, stop it. I remember saying, if you had just stayed talking about your knowledge of paintings, which was consummate, your knowledge of film-making, without all of the other, then I might have come round. But if you must do that with it, no. I don't think I ever will be seduced by power. I find it exciting, I like to be around it and be part of it, but I don't want to be made love to.

It is essential constantly to make romance, constantly, daily. It depends so much on the maturity of the person. People could be married twenty years and not have matured. You could have a man married for twenty years to a woman, love her, have children with her, but sexually he could be immature. Then suddenly he is thrown right off by something that gets to him sexually, and because he is not mature he can't control it. I think it is all to do with development and never to do with age. Otherwise my marriage certainly wouldn't work. But my man is infinitely more mature than I am in many, many ways. Yet he is all those years younger. I am still a child in many ways.

Anna McCurley: When my daughter was small and I was indulging in the coffee-morning set, I didn't really like it much. It always became competitive: whether your child was doing something before somebody else's child. There was always this element of competition. Discussing children always amounted to something that became personal. Everything was taken to oneself. You don't do that with men. They don't take things to themselves quite so easily. They will discuss in the abstract a good deal more. They will discuss in generalities.

I bet three-quarters of marriages, if not nine-tenths of them, break up because it's lousy sex. I think it would be absolutely disastrous to go into marriage a virgin. I wouldn't recommend it to anybody.

Sheena McDonald: When I was in my early twenties, I was alarmed when I had a party and had men and not women to invite – I knew more men than women. Latterly, it has balanced out and I enjoy the company of women very much indeed. Professionally, working with women I've more easily been able to do the things I would like to do, whereas, with men, I've done efficiently what they would like me to do, but I've worked in teams with women most happily and satisfactorily.

880

When I was very young, I met the man I wanted to marry when I was seventeen, and he didn't want to marry me. And, without going through the whole rigmarole, when I was nineteen, I thought that I'd experienced as much basic raw emotion as I could and had been as miserable as I possibly could, and until one of my parents dies, that will be the most miserable I have been in my life. Looking back, it was actually quite a useful experience, because what you learn from that is that being miserable is so uncomfortable and makes your stomach ache so much, makes you such an unhappy person, I would never let myself be that sad about a man again. So probably that one man has had more effect on me than anybody else. And ultimately it has been a good effect, I think – because I protect myself. I don't know whether – yes, I think it has been good for all the other men I've met subsequently.

Tough cookies. He ain't getting it. I'm a recidivist. I'm an elderly would-be virgin: all the courting and the flowers and the walking out together. The only relationships I have found to be satisfactory have involved long courtships.

Mary McFadden: My career was always the most important element of my life. Marriage was very secondary.

In my case, my husbands were very supportive of me. In all cases, my husband was more successful than I was. By miles. I don't think the fact that I'm independent has any importance at all in my relations with men.

The major dimension in life is that women be with men and vice versa: and the two, when together, create a greater product, because of the yin and the yang. A woman creates, a man adds a certain degree to a product, a woman adds another degree, and when the two are equal, it's a much more interesting product. I think we are completely complementary. That's when the great relationships occur, when people are complementary.

In the old days, everything was locked in, the Catholic Church was behind marriages. Once you've broken this sacred trust, which has been broken certainly in this country, no one takes anybody seriously any more. And it's very cheap to get divorced. In India, people don't get divorced, they have tradition behind them. Here, no effort is put into marriage. You don't have to work on anything, you can move on. I think it's got to be made for life. I married several times, but each time I considered them to be for life, with the exception of my first marriage, which was because I was pregnant.

One hundred things can seduce me in a man: his brains, his beauty, his athleticism, power. The stupider they are, the more illogical they become, and therefore the more fascinating, because they're then unpredictable.

Susan McHenry: I've met men who could not deal with me other than as a potential bed partner. The way I deal with that is by saying whatever is necessary to bring that person up, to make the person think. Not to clobber them over the head, but just to make them think and re-evaluate how they're treating me. Usually I do it with humour.

Both times when I married I thought I was marrying now and for ever more. Now I see how hard that is, I don't know whether it's realistic. I didn't marry people who had values consistent with my own. I think that's basically what happened. Also, in the first case, we were very young. I was nineteen years old, he was twenty, so that I think had a lot to do with it. I think for people to succeed in a long-term relationship, they have to be very parallel in terms of their basic values. In my case, I worked hard both times to try and make the marriage work. It was not easy in either situation to leave those marriages. I would tend to say, if anybody takes advantage of it being easy to get out of a marriage, then it's more men than women. I think, when women get married, it's a very serious matter to them. To men it's a little more capricious and they haven't really thought, maybe, as much as women have about the meaning and significance of it. There have been few women in my experience whose marriages didn't work because they weren't com-mitted, or they didn't really give it a good try or whatever.

I've been very intrigued by power. I have had to watch myself, because power is very seductive: what you can do with it, the kind of freedom it seems to offer, is very appealing. In New York, there are what we call power couples, where he does this, that and the other and she does this, that and the other, and the two of them together are just dynamite. And it's easy to get seduced into wanting to be part of that sort of couple, but that actually can be a very superficial way to be connected to someone, based on their matching set of credentials, professional credentials. My second marriage, for example, was a situation where I was joining myself less to a human being than to somebody with a specific set of credentials, options and opportunities in life. I can say that now, in retrospect.

Donna McKechnie: I believe marriage is the most adult thing one can do, the most mature thing one can do. It's like having a baby. It's the most simple but the most beautiful experience in a human's existence.

Because of the kind of work I do, if I meet a man, he is very intimidated because I am up on stage, thousands of people applauding me, people running after me asking for my autograph. It takes a particularly strong, independent male, someone with an identity, to deal with that, to approve of it, to appreciate me and not envy it.

Deirdre McSharry: I like working with women. I like very much the atmosphere of women working together, probably because I was brought up in a home with women and went to a convent at the age of seven and feel very comfortable with women. But I certainly find being with men, on the whole, more stimulating.

You look around the streets of London, and the boys look prettier all the time, and they can have mascara and scent, and if they feel like wearing frilly things, if they feel like wearing a skirt, they can do it. The girls are doing the other thing, and going to work in trousers. It doesn't always happen, but the great thing now is that you can choose your role, and you see them choosing their role every day. You watch them come through the door in the morning, and one day it's the tart – ruffles and lots of lipstick and too much hair; another day it's very Simone de Beauvoir – trousers, no make-up. I think the great thing now is it's not thrust upon you, you can decide for yourself. It's the whole business of bisexuality and androgynousness. Years ago, I interviewed Mick Jagger's wife, Bianca. It was a marvellous interview, sold all round the world. It was the one really good piece of journalism I ever did. But what was fascinating about Bianca was that she knew she was very bi- and she knew that was why Mick liked her. She understood men very well, and she understood this androgynous thing, long before anybody else got the message; she was wearing those kind of clothes, and she understood that was her attraction. She had the whole thing worked out, and it was very clever, very clever.

Norris Church Mailer: When I got married the first time, it was to a man I had been dating since I was sixteen years old. Neither of us really knew what we wanted to be when we grew up, but we married and he went off to be a nuclear engineer and I became a painter. And we just really found our interests had diverged to such a point that we had nothing much to say to each other. Although we are still very good friends, it just was not a marriage. I don't think marriages were necessarily that happy in the past. I think people have decided, these days, they want to be happy and don't have to live with someone for fifty years that they really don't like. And sometimes it takes that long to decide you don't like somebody.

The first time I married, I thought, maybe if this doesn't work, I'll get divorced. I was so young and so hesitant about it. It was a different era from today, even though it was not that many years ago. It was the time of Vietnam and my husband was obviously going to go to Vietnam because he was that age and had gone to college on an ROTC scholarship. So it was sort of, let's get married, man, because I'm going to Vietnam. I might never see you again. It was a changing world. It was a very different time. I think, if it had been today, I would not have gotten married while in college, I would have waited. But he was two years older and did indeed go to Vietnam. But even at the time we married, it never seemed a very permanent kind of thing. Whereas my second marriage, I hope, lasts for ever. I couldn't be happier. It's just a wonderful marriage. I love being married. We've been together twelve years, my second husband and I, and I just hope it goes on for ever.

I was always attracted by power. That's one ingredient in a man's attractiveness, part of his ambience. Some very stupid woman once said to me, would you be with Norman Mailer if he wasn't Norman Mailer? And I said, well, I know a lot of people who aren't Norman Mailer, and I'm not with any of them, so I guess I wouldn't. It's like saying, would you love me if I was 300 pounds? If you were, then you wouldn't be you, and I don't know if I would love you or not. Maybe not. Probably not. So if a man wasn't in a powerful position, probably I would not be attracted to him in the same way.

Alice Mason: I always felt I really didn't want marriage. I've been married three times, but only three and a half years, six months, and then two and a half years to my daughter's father. I really didn't want marriage. But it wasn't until about fifteen years ago that people decided that you didn't have to have marriage. In the 1960s I never wanted to be married, but then you really had to be married or you weren't a whole person.

The first time I thought about wanting to do something special was when I first saw New York and Broadway and the lights. I thought, this is what I'd like to do, conquer New York. What I really felt I didn't want, though, was a bourgeois marriage. I felt my parents had a very bourgeois marriage and I felt it would be boring to lead a married life like that. The main thing was I didn't want to be bored in life. When I turned forty, I decided I would never have another date because it just didn't interest me ever to be married again or to have a relationship. So I put my mind into many other things. I wrote down every single thing that I didn't like in life, and decided to do only the things I liked. That took about two or three pages, and most of the people I was seeing then I didn't see any more. Including my mother.

I think every woman should get married and have children. They certainly should get married to know they are not missing anything, and they should have a child, because that's, I think, the most important thing, and elemental for a woman. But then, I think, when she reaches young middle age preferably – because, in older middle age, they might give up a man because they have no choice – but when they have the choice and are still good-looking and men are seeking them and all, that they should make the choice that they do other things rather than give themselves emotionally to a man. This way, you have all this energy to do other things. And really, then they don't even miss sex once they decide and put energy in something else. They really don't, because, for a woman, everything is emotional anyway. And these relationships are so silly. I have a great friend, Helen Gurley Brown, and I said to Helen, when you think about it, women spend all this time laughing at the same jokes their husbands tell them six or eight times. And she said, well, how about thirty or forty times? If I was married to you, she said, I would have writers around the clock, I'd never give the same line to you. Every day, my writers would supply me with a different line.

I feel absolutely 1,000 per cent self-sufficient. I just went to this dinner that Ann Getty and Brooke Astor gave for Barbara Walters, which I attended alone. It was a large dinner at the Metropolitan Museum, but I was happy to be alone, I knew l looked good. I feel I always get a better seat than if I had a husband or a man along. I feel absolutely successful on my own, I love that. I don't want to share my life. I would have lunch with a man just like I have lunch with women, but I wouldn't have dinner with a man, because I don't want to hear what he has to say and I don't want to tell him what I have to say. It just doesn't interest me. I have escorts if I have to go to a big dinner dance or something, and I give dinners once a month for sixty people in my apartment, all achievers. And I have a list of maybe sixty single men I invite to dinner. Men call me all the time to get my advice, or about this or that. They know I am not a threat because I am not interested. And married women don't consider me a threat because they know I am not interested. But I think I am the only woman I know who is not interested. Everybody says I am unique in New York in that sense. I like men in general. I just don't want to put up with them. It doesn't interest me to give any of my energy to a man; I have other things, better things to do in life. It doesn't mean I don't like them. I am not willing to sacrifice my life. I think it's a tremendous sacrifice, except for women who don't have that much in their life, so that's an up-side for them, that a man gives them their apartment and supports them, and does this and does that. Or perhaps they are afraid to be alone. I love to be alone. There's nothing pleases me more than to know I have an evening alone, because I am a news freak, I love to watch the news. I love to have dinner on a tray. I love it.

I had three wonderful husbands. All those three husbands said that whatever I wanted, they would let me do. Dominique's father was wonderful. The last husband I had was a Dutch diplomat. The only reason I married him was because my daughter was only nine at the time, in 1959, so I couldn't have a romance in my home. I married him in three weeks, and divorced him in six months. I was ready for a divorce in two months, but everyone was giving me dinner, they were so thrilled that I got married, that I finally found the right person. So I had to wait a bit. But on my honeymoon, each honeymoon, I knew I had done the wrong thing. Because, I thought, here I am, I might as well be in jail, I have no options. Every day I wake up, it means I have to have dinner with this man. And then you have to see all these boring other couples because you are a couple. When you are alone, you can see who you want. But when you are married, you have all this bourgeois life, which drove me crazy because I hated being bored, ever. One husband, whichever, would say, you can have dinner on a tray, I will eat in the dining room. But I would say, I'll know you are in the house so I'll have to say hello. Another would say, you don't have to speak. They were wonderful husbands, whatever I wanted. But I just didn't want it. So, once I recognized that, I thought, why should I be like the world and be married? I am going to do what I want. And that's when I took that yellow pad and wrote down every single thing I didn't want. Every day, from then on, I only did what I liked.

I decided I wouldn't take a client out whose company I didn't enjoy. I enjoy lunch with an interesting person, I am booked for lunch always weeks in advance. I also like to have dinners where I only have achievers and the people I think are terrific. So I made this book. Every time I met a person I thought was terrific, I wrote it down so I would remember to invite them to dinner. And I decided never to invite anyone any more that I'd already known for ten years, or they were some part of my life. So, finally, those people stopped talking to me. All those people. So I love my life now. I get up at nine, I am on the phone till eleven, I never make an appointment before eleven to show an apartment. Every day I have lunch at twelve-thirty. Every afternoon I play cards. I work three or four hours a day, that's it. If I make an appointment to show an apartment after lunch, it's at two-thirty so I can play cards at three. In the evenings, I never go to dinner more than three times a week, and I only go to interesting dinners. Anyone who asks me for a dinner, and I know they don't have interesting dinners, I always say I have an engagement that night. And I have four nights a week to myself. I just love my life. I would never change it.

Anxiety is what deters you in a career. All these women, it's not lack of confidence, it's having all these anxieties. You know, even if they are married, they think, are they going to keep their husbands? Only *you* will never leave you. If you decide you really love your life and yourself and what you are doing, only you will never leave you, so you have no anxieties as such. Do you know, I rarely get depressed about something. I may get upset if I'm losing a deal, but I rarely get depressed. I don't think I get depressed even once a year now, and those years when I had romances I got depressed once a week. I don't mean if there were a tragedy in my life I wouldn't be, but there hasn't been, and hopefully won't be. But I think the tragedies in women's lives are men and all that energy they spend on them. I was madly in love three or four times, absolutely. But, you know, madly in love is really infatuation. No matter what it is, you get over it. The reason I decided not to marry again, and not to go out on a date, was, why should I fall in love with somebody? Because you do, you can fall in love, and it either works or it doesn't work. Let's say it works and you get married, and then there it starts again, where suddenly it's boring, always. So why start in the first place? So since it's not going to last anyway, no matter what, why should I waste that energy? To me that's negative energy, negative energy. So I decided never to do that again.

I am a very metaphysical person. I was always interested in why we are here and if we come back; I was always interested in astrology, numerology and all these various things. So I had metaphysical crushes instead, which were really love in the abstract. When I went to the UN, it was because I admired the foreign minister from China, and China was just coming into the UN, so I would write to him in China, and I would get messages back from him in the Delegates' Lounge. I went to all the UN things, because I liked and admired this man at that time and admired the People's Republic of China. Then I made a map, called the Alice Mason map of missions, showing where all the missions were located and all the flags in colour, so I would get to know every country and how many people. I got to know all the Third World countries, every one, so that if they were going to entertain the foreign minister of China, I would be invited. So I put all my energies into that, but that was totally metaphysical. It wasn't someone I was going to hold hands with or go out with; it was someone I admired. So I had things like that. It was very interesting, because then I knew every ambassador at the UN. And the Arabs were wonderful because they were very young Arab ambassadors, so they often would have a dinner with just the men diplomats and two or three women diplomats who were ambassadors, and they would invite me because they knew I liked the foreign minister and didn't stand on protocol like the Europeans did. And it was marvellous. I had a great time at the UN. For four years I did that, then I met Jimmy Carter and I thought, he's terrific and I am going to help elect him President. And I did. I never was interested in politics, I had never raised money before. But I raised more money than anyone in the country. Of course, I guided him to the Eastern Establishment because all these people were my clients. So he became one of my closest friends, and even today he and Rosalind come once a year, and I give a dinner for them. They sleep in my daughter's room, that's how close friends we are. In other words, I had all this energy to do other things, and there are men I might admire and like, but I am not going to hold their hands, that's the point. In other words, it's abstract. I like them because they are doing something I admire, so I can have a tender feeling for them, but it's love in the abstract, and that's very safe and very nice.

A man who doesn't want to marry you wouldn't even return a phone call. Though, as a matter of fact, those three husbands I married were because they were really dying to marry me. They begged me, so finally I married them. I met men whom I fell in love with, who I wanted to want to marry me, but that's not because I wanted to marry. They always mistook that; I always said, do you want to marry me, and that was very important to me, but not because I ever wanted to marry them. Once they understood that, they understood me. I felt they should respect me enough to want to marry me, but not because I wanted to marry them. I always explained, it's only because I wanted you to want to marry me, not because I wanted to marry you. So they were always shocked when I said, I don't want to marry you, I never wanted to marry you. My point was that I never wanted to be married basically, because I think marriage is very dull.

Homayoun Mazandi: I think marriage is the most unnatural thing. You bring people from two different societies, sometimes from two different environments, and you want them to stick together for ever because of their family, children, everything, and expect it to work. It won't work, but sadly we couldn't find anything instead of marriage. We cannot replace marriage with anything similar or better. We have to stick to this. That is why more interesting people, more exciting people, when you find them, have more marriages, because it doesn't satisfy their minds to stick to one marriage. Exciting people usually marry a few times.

For me, divorce is something totally romantic and emotional. Marriage is created for the family. Who cares if you don't want to sleep with your husband, or your husband doesn't want to sleep with you? That is a matter of personal taste.

Lady Menuhin: With women I always have to make an effort. There are exceptions; there are exceptional women like Fleur Cowles who is extraordinary, but I prefer the company of men because I like talking about the things that interest men and I'm not in the least interested in the things that women talk about. You know–children, groceries, hair-dos.

I am afraid it may sound very cynical, but how can it be possible for a man at the age of twenty-one to fall in love with the woman he is going to be faithful to physically until he's seventy? I don't think that's practicable. The French, of course, have a wonderful way out, a marvellous way out. You can keep *la petite maîtresse* at the end of the street somewhere, and the wife knows it. What was unfair – I don't think it happens now – was that the wife would be murdered if she dared have a boyfriend at a certain level of society. Lower down, it doesn't matter. I think, if it can be done with great tact and great sweetness, then it often refreshes a marriage when either one or the other has had some little affair and feels just enough guilt and shame to love the other even more. I really think that. What happens today is that the cork has been taken out of the wine bottle. So, what happens? The wine is undrinkable next day. The cork has been taken out of the scent bottle. You forget about it and next week the smell has gone. Idiots! They don't realize.

It's not just the sex, it's the living together. You don't know a person until you've seen the way they put the top back on the toothpaste. They irritate you, and you don't know whether you love them enough to overcome petty irritations, and life is full of petty irritations. I don't think you should marry too young. By the time we're older, we've each of us developed our own special idiosyncrasies, and they can be maddening to other people.

Kate Millett: I like men very much, but I live very much of my life with women. Once upon a time I didn't spend so much of my time with women. I knew more men, and I was married to a wonderful Japanese sculptor and lived in a heterosexual world, men and women. Of course, men dominated everything and talked all the time, and it was extremely frustrating in thousands of ways. But I had a greater sense of contact with the world than I do now, when I live mostly with women. Most of my friendships and contacts, and the work I do and the people I know and am close to, are women. If I'm likely to fall in love, I'm more likely to fall in love with a woman at this point, but that doesn't mean I couldn't fall in love with a man. I have. It seems to me that the natural state of human beings would be bisexuality. But, under certain social conditions, that would be less likely to happen, as, for example, in a very oppressive regime of heterosexuality. Or, in this case, where there is a kind of withdrawal from the male world to strengthen ourselves, and an enormous sense of solidarity, we would be more likely to form relationships with women.

There are some women who, for probably excellent reasons, choose to live in their own sphere, separately and so forth. Like any people who have been much aggressed upon, oppressed, so women can get a lot of strength from each other. That makes sense. That's a political event in a certain period of time. The degree of separatism that actually exists is very much exaggerated, but it frightens men a lot, so they fixate on it.

It seems to me that heterosexuality is also conditioned into us as a result of endless propaganda, because otherwise we would just love whomever we like, which makes sense. But we are very carefully conditioned into heterosexuality. It is all part of the same set-up: conditioning you for motherhood, for heterosexuality, for feminine acquiescence in a patriarchal society, those are the things that make it work. I've loved both men and women. It's sensible, I think. They were lovable people.

Sara Morrison: The men I am attracted by have got to be umpteen times sharper; I've got to be surprised. One of the very sad things about being middle-aged, like me, is how few people surprise me. My children are always saying to me I'm just getting sort of battle-soiled. I understand why men don't like me very much. I find it totally explicable that the young men of my generation think that one's just weird, tiresome, and either a bossy old cow or quite an amusing old thing, really. But they're a wee bit, just a little bit scared. Our tongues are a bit quick because we've been sticking up for ourselves. We are a bit crushing at times. We make the terrible mistake – which ought to be very flattering, but I

890

know it's annihilating – of treating everybody naturally as our equals, and of course nothing is more frightening. And we are a bit awe-inspiring. Therefore they trot off to their clubs or their lunchtimes at the White Elephant or whatever, and say we are tough or humourless because it's their defence·against this new creature which most of the time they can get rid of. They enjoy us in the workplace because we're useful. But when they have us round their dinner table, they'd rather we weren't there because we rather ruin their stories. And anyway, because we are much more self-denigrating, self-diminishing and laughing at ourselves than they are – the male ego doesn't allow for that – we tend to seem much more impressive than we are. It's a very British-man thing to prefer male company. The French enjoy women much more. I can understand that, because the French matriarch was a much more enjoyable sort of woman than the English cup-of-tea sort of woman.

On the whole, women know just what they are doing. Most prefer commitment, the risk, the one where they'll get hurt. There is a slight kamikaze in every woman, which I think will continue, however professional, however cool, however detached they become. She does not set herself up to be hurt, but will permit herself to the point where she knows rationally, and has observed it a thousand times, that she is very likely to be, but she prefers it that way because that way it is real. The other way is meaningless.

Kathy Myers: I was in the first year of women at a men's college at Cambridge, and I first realized I was a girl because of the horrendous reaction from the men there. Cambridge is a feudal institution, and the only women they'd ever seen in men's colleges were the dons' wives and the bedders, who are the cleaning ladies. All my relatives said, oh, you'll have an absolute field day, it will be wonderful, all these boys. But if a boy's managed to go all the way through Eton and never spoken to a girl, then you put him in the same class as one, it's about as emotionally satisfying for the girl as being classed as a wildebeest. I mean, they were horrified, absolutely petrified of us. I and thirty other girls were almost in solitary confinement. They certainly didn't chase us all the time, as my relatives said they would. Well, they did in a very perverted weird way, leaving little messages and following us. Breaking into a flat was the favourite thing, and leaving a message saying, I've been watching you for the last six weeks, I have brown eyes. I mean, there are 1,100 men in Cambridge, and 80 per cent of them have brown eyes. It was very nerve-racking, very frightening, like something out of *Psycho*.

I'm not married. I'd like to have children. I'm very lazy and I think, for me, marriage would be a disaster, because it would make me stop trying. Now, that doesn't mean I don't want to stay with somebody. But the point where I've got the piece of paper – it's like getting your O-Levels or your A-Levels or your driving licence – is the point where you start to mess about because you know you can take licence. I was a very naughty child, and you don't stop being naughty, and if I think I've got confines, then I'll push against all the boundaries. So I think actually to go through a wedding ceremony would be a disaster for me, because it wouldn't keep me on my toes. I'd think, well, I've got him, you know, that's it.

Partly because of the break-up of the whole extended family, a couple are thrown much more on to each other. Therefore you have to fulfil a much higher percentage of the other person's needs than maybe you did in the eighteenth century, when you had all your relatives around and your lifestyles were much more divided. Men and women had their own friendship groups, and their marriage was much more based on an economic reason and the caring of the family. I'm not sure that arranged marriages are so bad in that sense, actually. Because if you marry for a romantic ideal, you can only be disillusioned, and when you become disillusioned, you become bitter, and when you become bitter, you become dangerous. I would think the best thing women can do is marry their best friends. To marry for romance is to marry for all the things you don't see in yourself. You might be lucky, they could be good things, but they could also be disastrous things because you marry your own aspirations. And your aspirations may not suit you.

Lynda Myles: To achieve the kind of relationship ultimately worth having needs a long time and a lot of work and a lot of sacrifices on each side, and people give up too easily. What I don't like about a lot of marriages I know is that the women are still expected to give up more. I think there should be equal amounts of renunciation and sacrifice to make this thing work. I sound horribly Victorian, but I think marriage should be regarded as permanent.

Lynn Nesbit: I think there are many men who would resent my success, or even be frightened of it. But it doesn't really concern me, because I wouldn't be interested in them anyway.

I always related to my father a lot, so I feel extremely comfortable with men, I always have. But I wouldn't say I don't feel comfortable with women. I think there are certain women who have always preferred the company of men and they feel ill at ease with other women. I don't. And I have a client list which is pretty equally male and female. I've had clients who initially wanted to have male agents but they've chosen me instead. There are certain women writers who want a father-figure, so they may want to go to male agents. Or they are looking for a kind of flattery that they don't think another woman can supply. But there are always some modes of choosing in the world, and sometimes it's on the basis of one's sex. And I can't agonize over it. Certain people have chosen me because I am a woman.

There is no opprobrium about divorce. Divorce is now permissible, not a social scandal. And there is not a strong religious structure any more. It's one thing for men who divorce in their late forties and marry a younger woman and have another child, and quite another for women in their late forties or early fifties who perhaps don't have any career.

Julia Neuberger: I think that an awful lot of the Jewish-mother stuff is a myth, actually. There was, in Eastern Europe, the idea of this very concentrated, actually rather difficult Jewish family, who usually lived in fairly squalid circumstances, where the controlling factor would very often be the woman: the Jewish mother. I think that really existed. There's no question in my mind that, in the *stetl* in Eastern Europe, the Jewish mother reigned supreme. But that society has gone. It is a romanticism to say that the Jewish mother reigns supreme now. She doesn't, because that role has gone. There isn't that very tight community any more, thank God. I have to say that, with all the romanticization that goes on of what it was like in the *stetl* in Eastern Europe, I'm actually glad that's over. It was dirty, it was nasty, there was anti-Semitism. It was revolting, and one just wouldn't want to see that back again, and if you try to transfer that to Redbridge or Stanmore or wherever, it doesn't quite work, any more than it does if you transfer it to New York or New Jersey. Of course, the women can still see themselves as having that role, but it doesn't really exist. Most of the women either work at some kind of paid employment, or they're very bored. Because this whole thing of controlling the family and running the business or whatever else you had to do doesn't exist any more.

Because of the public perception of homosexual/lesbian relationships, they are more threatened, they feel more self-conscious, and that may in itself make the relationships more intense. If you're very worried, either because people are going to discover that you're gay if you haven't come out, or that you're just worried about the whole nature of the relationship, whether or not you are going to get Aids, I think that, in itself, makes the relationship more intense. You'll not relax into it, because it's not what society accepts even now. One of the terrible things about the 1980s is that homosexuality, which was just becoming accepted in this country – not very easily accepted, but just about becoming accepted – has a real backlash now. I think that the bulk of British society has now decided that in fact the best thing would be to make it illegal again. Which I think is terrible, really terrible. Nobody is as interested as that in lesbians. It's a prejudice against male homosexuality much more than against women, but the result is that the people in those relationships, whether male or female, have a very rough time, and that may intensify the good moments of their relationships. Most of us in our heterosexual relationships are quite relaxed. Nobody is going to argue that what we're doing is wrong.

Nanette Newman: My husband has been the greatest influence in my life. I met him when I was sixteen, which is a very impressionable age.

To treasure the more beautiful moments of your relationship with somebody, and to try to mark them and make them remembered, that is what I think being romantic is. There are some people who do that better than others. Also, true romantics know when they are deliriously happy at the moment they are happy. Therefore they make the most of it. People who aren't romantic, can only look back at life and say, oh, I was so happy in 1973, I didn't realize it, and now I'm so miserable. Whereas romantic people, because they are always looking out for it, will make it into something special. I don't mind that at all. I think there are so many awful things in life, it is nice to be able to do that. And I think women are drawn to that – even women who scoff at it. Some men can separate emotion and career. Women tend to colour everything with their emotional state.

Emma Nicholson: Today's lifestyle for women is so much better. When I was eighteen or twenty or twenty-two, with my background women didn't work. I'm forty-five, so that is not that long ago. Twenty-five years ago, women of my particular background didn't work. At the very most, they became secretaries to fill in time until they found a husband. I couldn't follow that pattern. I tried to, but I just couldn't cram myself into that narrow little channel, and so I thought to myself, I can't take this, I'm throwing all that aside. So I said no to everybody who asked me to marry them. There were an awful lot of them. There must have been well over a hundred people, I can't remember. People who were very kind, very nice, very sweet, and of course, in those days, you didn't have to have a close relationship with somebody before they asked you to marry them. Those were people I knew and met socially, and went to dances and parties with, nothing further than that. And doubtless they could have made good marriages, but I had not thought through how I myself could come to terms with marriage. I found it a very difficult problem. So I turned my back on it and did what I wanted to do, which was to use my mind in things completely alien to my background, and I loved it.

I have always distrusted marriage for the woman. I have always, from a very early age, felt that marriage was right for children. I think marriage is actually created as a safe mechanism for bringing up children, and I have always thought marriage was OK for men but rock bottom for women. I was born in 1941, so the women I saw were not perhaps typical, but all my life I remember seeing sad, unhappy mothers of my friends, isolated, unfulfilled, unhappy. When you're a child, you tend to pick up a lot of things. You pick up a lot of vibrations, you tend to see a lot, perhaps without the grown-ups realizing; and I remember over and over again (I think I was quite a bright little gel) seeing my friends' mothers unfulfilled and unhappy. And from an early age it was built into me quite solidly that marriage on the terms those women had taken it on was not conducive to a woman's happiness. Looking back on it, perhaps the post-war period wasn't much fun for anybody, for all I know. I wasn't really grown up enough to tell. I just recalled seeing so much middle-aged unhappiness for women. I don't recall the men looking frightfully happy either, but I remember thinking, I am not going to get into that muddle; it's clear that, once you're in it, you can't get out of it. I'm a great believer if you take up a cause, take up a person, you stick with them. You can't just pick things up and drop them. I remember thinking, I am not going to get caught in that trap, even at the expense of not having children, which is a sacrifice for me, as I am sure it is for every person. I wouldn't have been able to last in a trap if I were unhappy in it. I would break out and yet know that is not the right thing to do.

The marketing man takes sex as a way of marketing products because it is such a potent force, the life force, the trigger from Nature to us to re-create our species. I think it devalues, not sex in the way one tends to use it in the modern world, where it merely means two people making love, but human relationships. For surely the highest form of life is the achievement of happy and fulfilling human relationships. To me, that may be an aunt and niece, a girl and boyfriend, husband and wife. It can be a nun with God. The relationships are the pinnacle of most people's achievements in life. Few of us split the atom, few of us create the most compelling piece of music, very few of us paint the perfect picture, even fewer of us create the right piece of computer software. Most people's major achievement seems to be on the human level. So I dislike trivializing human relationships in the way that using sex to market a car does. It doesn't worry me, but I feel it devalues things.

The thing I find almost impossible to tolerate is intellectual boredom. Whatever the person is like, whether man or woman, I find it desperately difficult if they are dull, if they are not challenging and stimulating. The boot's on the other foot if I am there to help them; then it doesn't matter a scrap what they're like. But if I'm the taker, what I need is intellectual challenge.

The sort of men I enjoy talking to most have better minds than mine, therefore stimulate my thinking, my intelligence, make me want to think further and talk more. And I couldn't possibly be close to a man who didn't respect my mind, who didn't challenge my mind and didn't want to talk with me. I think you find that most women don't worry a scrap what men look like, they really don't.

I now have someone in my life who is very close to me, and if circumstances improve will marry me. I would marry him. And there is no tension at all, it's a question of $1 + 1 = 4$. So that is the perfect partnership. Of course, in another year, if we do get married, I might say something different.

Béatrice Nivois: I think real love can go very well with sexual relations. I'm living in a love story where everything is complete. But there are people who experience love solely through sex, people who can't abide the other person outside the sexual context.

Jane O'Grady: Because I was a Catholic, and because I was very intense about spiritual things, I thought I was a soul first and not particularly a girl or a boy. I suppose it was later that I began to feel this unease slightly as to what exactly I was. I felt this very much when, at one point, I was having lesbian affairs, and it really made me feel extraordinary because I thought, what am I then? That was when I was about twenty-nine.

I often feel attracted if a woman is so sweet and vulnerable and somehow needs to be protected. Not feminine in a narcissistic way, but something rather soft and vulnerable.

I suppose it would give a certain strength not to need men sexually. I sympathize with lesbian separatism, which is another form of celibacy from men but not from women, but there is something rather dreary somehow about old dykes. They're fine when they're young.

At one point I was having an affair with a man and an affair with a woman, separately but at the same time. And I slightly hero-worshipped her somehow, and also, she wanted it to be very magical. It *was* very magical, and therefore I felt more uncomfortable with her; and also she was very clean and tidy, very beautiful and immaculate and dressed very well, and she was rather horrified at the way I dressed and some of the ways I behaved. The man was much more laid-back in a way, and I remember turning up at his house after seeing her, I just somehow couldn't take the pace; his place was nice and untidy and I thought, oh God, I feel so at home. Also she was American, so there was that slight difference, but I really felt more at home with him. However, I suppose, in general, I feel more at home with women. There's that strange rapport: it can be in the street or with women who are strangers; you can smile and hug them, and you know exactly where you are, you can have that instant recognition and appreciation. But if you did that with a man, you would be on body ground, and they might be a bit nervous and neither would know what the other wanted.

Kitty O'Hagan: I don't like weak men. That's why I find myself very disappointing as a feminist, because a lot of men with characteristics that, in theory, are good from a feminist's viewpoint – men who are awfully fair – I don't really like. I don't find them very attractive.

The eyes seduce me. Always the eyes. Once you start on this eye contact, then it's there, you could do it. The eyes convince me that this person is sensitive, that they're hearing me, that they have souls, they're understanding, that they care a little, that they have aggression. It's a sensitivity and a sensibility, and an understanding of, do we share that? And if we share that, then that would be on.

Fifi Oscard: For a long time, I longed to be with men. I don't mean in a private situation, but in a general situation, because the women I knew didn't talk politics, didn't talk art or theatre, they just talked the small matters of householding. So, for the first fifteen or twenty years of marriage, I would find myself always with the men, because I found discussions of business interesting. Now, in my long life, I see that a kind of levelling out has taken place. The women I know, especially in

897

business, who live in New York, are very smart and just as interesting as men. But for a long time, I did like to be with men and spend a lot of time with men. I was compatible with men. Now I'm compatible with everybody.

I don't think aggressiveness is unfeminine. Look at *Dallas* and *Dynasty* – look at all those feminine ladies who do terrible things. Of course, it's very hard to be feminine when you're beating someone on the head.

It's the unusual man who is looking, in his middle years, for a real and lasting relationship, whether it be with a wife or a mistress, or with a girlfriend. My impression is that men have heightened demands which are easily sated, and the closeness a woman longs for is very often not a part of man's ambition. A woman never gets over the feeling that there is some dream prince out there who is going to want to do nothing in life but stay closely involved with her; and you're just going to talk for the rest of your lives about all the things you care about. That, I believe, is what I wanted: somebody who was extremely interested in me, and in whom I could be extremely interested, and whom I would love for the rest of my life. I never quite found that.

I always loved a large man – because I was always large. I appreciated it if he was strong, muscular and self-confident, but I loved a man who looked like that and also had a purple streak – if he was a poet, or also a great clarinettist, or also an amateur actor, or something very artistic. I tell you, if you get a big strong man who is also a poet, every woman will drop dead. That is my idea of the most seductive man. At this point in my life, I have different requirements. I'm a widow of a year and a half, two years, and I'm longing for a man of significant accomplishment. He doesn't have to be strong and tall any more.

Edna O'Shaughnessy: Between a man and a woman, sexuality can effloresce, while, if one is not a homosexual, sexual feelings will not arise between women. One of the pleasant liberating things about present times is that it is possible for a man and a woman to meet, to talk, to take a meal together, without the presumption that there is a bedroom at the end of it. When I was growing up, there was always that presumption. Now I think there can be an appreciation of sexual attractiveness, even on both sides, without either wishing to yield to it. Temptation is voluntary nowadays.

Possibly women do value continuity of sexual experience more than men. In regard to faithfulness, perhaps not everybody values a quality like fidelity. Yet one can't escape one's inner world. What one does in external reality deposits a sediment internally. All human beings are prone to being possessive, to being jealous, suffering the pains of jealousy. The husband who is continually unfaithful, or the wife who sleeps around, do actually affect their partner and their relationships. If it's concealed, there's deviousness; if it's open, there's usually a denial or a masochistic use of pain. People have conflicting wishes. They may wish to be faithful, but they may also have opposite and other desires.

Kathy O'Shaughnessy: I feel it quite a privilege to be a woman now. I feel that things have changed a lot. We've still got masses to do, but there's a particular pleasure to be got out of being a woman and succeeding because you know there are odds and prejudices against you and you are still doing it. I feel my female friends seem to have a vitality and recognition, an honesty and all sorts of things that I love. And although I've got some great male friends, they don't, with one or two exceptions, seem to have quite the openness. What I like is that there is usually an honesty and a realism nearer the surface with women, and an emotional realism that can prove great fun to communicate with. The question of what it is like being a woman is something that you think about quite a bit, so there's reams of stuff to talk about if you do find a woman you feel an affinity with.

No intimate female friend of mine I really trust would fall in love with a boyfriend of mine. If you trust someone, and if they merit that trust, they don't abuse it. And it doesn't start. I would not flirt with a friend's boyfriend or husband. I mean, if there's a sort of spark, it's there a tiny bit, but it's very muted. I'd never play it up, I'd leave it alone if it was a friend's boyfriend or husband. And I'd expect the same with my friends. I know women who are like that, and I don't like those women at all. I can't stand women who can't stand women, I hate them. It's like seeing life with one eye shut. They are people who have all male friends, who cannot be truly intimate and trusting with another woman, who only see you as sexual competition. I can't stand that, it's so paranoid. And usually those people are terribly neurotic, they can't cope with the idea of another woman being attractive. It's ridiculous. I must say, I have come across quite a few, and I sense it immediately. I sense a kind of hostile watchfulness towards me. I can't stand it.

Clare Park: I've always been wary of my obsessions. I do get obsessional, and there are times when I find people very attractive, but I will not do anything about it, even if it's there for me if I want, because I know they're wrong for me. I'm one of the very few people I know that have never taken any sort of drugs, because I know it's bad for me; I know I would become obsessional about it, and I have enough problems. It's the same with people who are promiscuous. I don't believe that it's spiritually good for you just to have a physical relationship with anything you find attractive. I just don't think it's right. I would become promiscuous, and I don't want to catch Aids, which is actually something one has to consider.

At this moment in time, I would like to be married and I would like to have a family. I feel I'm ready to be doing that, but the situation isn't right at the moment, so I get on with other things. If I had felt the way I do now several years ago, I probably would have met the right person several times over, but the combination wasn't right then, and I've certainly had a lot of things to battle with and get over before I could be mature enough to have a relationship and a family.

Diana Parker: Really, today, the only dependence there is in a marriage relationship is the emotional dependence. Historically, there's been an economic dependence in addition, and there's also been very much of a societal dependence: one has been expected to conform to society's expectations. Society no longer has a requirement that a couple, once married, will always remain indissolubly wed, and so there's been a great flattening of pressures and that has made divorce much more the easier option. It has also contributed to the sterility of a great many relationships, because once there is no longer an emotional interplay, then there is, really and truly, nothing left of the marriage. If there is no great economic dependence, if there are no very great societal expectations, and if you're no longer emotionally involved with your spouse, quite frankly, your marriage is dead. It might as well be buried. It does seem to me that there is a great deal to be said for the theory that divorce is often almost an escape from oneself, that it is a completely fated escape. If you are constantly living with someone else, then you're brought face to face not so much with that other person, but face to face with yourself. The hope is that, by getting rid of that other person, who, as it is thought, creates such unhappiness or gloom in oneself, then the unhappiness and gloom will be dispelled. But I consider that, very frequently, it is a flight from reality, and the reality is oneself, and there's the need to get to know oneself better.

The most lasting seduction is, I think, if a man can make me laugh without telling the same joke twice.

Molly Parkin: There is a particular type of man whom I do find more difficult to get on with, and that is the typical English public schoolboy, because of the repression they've suffered in the actual process of their upbringing, where they're confined in an all-male environment. Some of them go away to school at eight, and haven't had the benefit of the constant presence of their mother or sisters. They feel easier in the company of other men. I went to Henley Regatta recently for the first time, and the sexuality thrumming in that throng of men, the bonhomie and the camaraderie among them, with a very strong homosexual feeling, struck me most forcibly. Their wives, daughters or girl-friends, all a certain sort of Englishwoman, were there as well, and these men are not easy with the presence of women. They put their women on pedestals, because they don't know them, don't understand women. They've got a distance from their mothers or their grandmothers, and they've had to stifle all their growing adolescent emotions, and then, it's quite natural, they get fixations on other boys in that environment. And they've got this ridiculous aspect of the stiff upper lip, not only in matters of bravery, but also in that they find it very difficult to cry. I find most of them emotional underneath all that superficial stuff. I was married eleven years to a public schoolboy who was typical of that genre, and all his friends were. I find the upbringing and conditioning of men of that class horrifying, and they unfortunately are the ones who come to rule the country and the ones who become figures of industry, chairmen of the board.

Women don't see any earthly reason why they should remain with a man for the sake of the status of a wife. The word doesn't carry the same status it used to. The word spinster doesn't carry the same besmirched values it used to. There's no such thing now as being on the shelf. It used to be the horror of our time, to be considered an old maid. And I think possibly a union between male and female at an early age, as it usually is, in the early twenties, is unrealistic. Two people, given that they want to explore their own personalities, should not have to stay together when they've moved apart emotionally, intellectually. And there is no stigma now to children being from broken homes. People don't stay together now for the sake of the children, which is good, because those marriages were hell-holes of marriages.

Judith De Paul: I've never really felt men as friends, I've always had them as either business colleagues or lovers. I guess for what one calls friends, I have women. As I've gotten older I've become more generous with women. I've given them more opportunities in working with me, I've been very supportive with them, and I have found that they can be excellent friends in moments of need and trial, even in moments of great joy. Lately, they are not jealous any more. That's a combination of the times changing and my getting older. It was a little more difficult when I was younger and the glamour girl.

The social fibre is broken down. It is a terribly serious matter. The family unit has been given the right to split. It is allowed to part, to separate. People don't even bother to get married any more. The responsibility a man has towards raising the family and towards the woman he marries has changed so drastically in the last twenty-five years that I think a woman getting married now and wanting a family could be in a very vulnerable situation. The laws are too liberal, the sexual freedom is too overt. And they just don't give a crap about the kids' life, they only think about themselves. It's a me, me, me society. I do accept the blame myself for the failure of my marriage. I was travelling around the world, I was rather young, and I had a very glamorous life. And I think I didn't want to be married. What caused the tension was I was like a guy, I didn't like being tied down. I didn't want to live in Rome and have babies. I was off and running round the world and having the time of my life. I felt I was being held back. It's the same story I get from all these guys: I married her when I was very young, and I grew and I became successful, and she never grew along with me. My story is the same. I became successful, I was charging round the world, and he wanted me to stay home and have babies. And I said, my God, if I stay home and have babies they'll have your face and my brains.

Penny Perrick: Alas, now that I have a fairly well-paid and rather public career I find, not altogether happily, that I relate better to men.

I think, as women's lives get more difficult and more hassled and frenetic, and more complicated, laughter is the thing one craves more than anything. I would choose Woody Allen over Robert Redford any day of the week.

Even in this age when divorce is very easy, most marriages survive, and survive for a very long time. I don't think anyone would say, yes, I'm really in favour of divorce the way they would say, yes, I'm really in favour of adultery. It's not something people want, and people get married with the expectation that it will be for ever. Most people get married with stars in their eyes.

Lorie Scott Peters: I don't relate to women at all. There are a lot more women now in the working world, and I respect that, but a lot of them use their bodies to achieve what they want to achieve; and the ones who have got there on their own merit either become so cold and heartless that they don't recognize what is natural and feminine or else they're barracudas.

I've not made use of my sexuality as a woman. I don't believe in playing with people you work with. I've always kept the two apart, and I can't say it's helped me in my career. Maybe it's hindered me, because I've gone so far as to say I won't play that game.

Men feel they can't survive unless they have sex. It's this macho thing that they have to prove themselves by showing how many women they can have. Somehow they need this release. They've been conditioned, too, and I think they are an unfortunate product of their programming. That's what they're supposed to do: go out and drink beer, drive fast cars and drive cute women. They have been brought up that you have toy guns and toy trains and toy women. I've never understood all these heavy-duty businessmen. They work all day, and they have all these pressures all day, and come home to these bimbo wives. I wonder how they possibly can marry these idiots.

We don't have any great child-bearers in the masculine race. Why are men trying to get pregnant today? Is it because they think they have to get all these gay men pregnant, because they have all these long-standing gay relationships? Not at all. It's because men are threatened by the female race. Women can live without men, and men are afraid of that. Women can procreate without men now, because of artificial insemination. We can produce children, male and female, and we can choose to kill all the males, just as in ancient times the Chinese killed the females.

We don't fight wars with our fists any more. We fight wars with our intelligence. The next war will be male to female, it won't be nuclear war. We've outsmarted each other in terms of technology. It's not a matter of who can build a better machine or a bigger machine; it's our intelligence and our smarts.

Davina Phillips: After my father was killed, my mother married again and she had two children from the second marriage. That, tragically, was not a very happy liaison, I think because she did it in a very distressed state, reacting to her unhappiness. Then, quite a lot later, she

903

divorced and married again and had three more children. But, of course, she was never really very well, so I left school at fifteen and brought up the two children she'd had from the second marriage. With the money I earned, I subsidized them while they were building up their careers. My half-brother, who was the elder of the two, wanted to go into and eventually own a chain of hairdressing salons. I was very friendly with Vidal Sassoon at the time, and Vidal was wonderful. He gave Peter a chance and taught him, and then, at a tremendously young age, gave him the opportunity to open up in Canada for him. So that's what he did. And then my half-sister from that marriage wanted to go to Canada to join her brother, so I helped her on her way to that. When my mother became very, very ill, and the father, the third husband, died, those three children were taken into care. I couldn't bear that, so asked to adopt them, which was a strange thing for a half-sister to do, but effectively I did adopt them. It wasn't an adoption in the documented sense, but the county council, who were *in loco parentis*, put me on trial for two years to see if I could do the job properly. It worked very well. They came to live with me. I had by then married and had my own two children but I was in the process of getting divorced, which was the other problem in that I was now going to be a single parent taking on three extra children. But they finally allowed it, and I had five children living with me for two and a half years. The problem was that one of them, the youngest girl, was diabetic and it affected her emotionally. She felt resentful, which can happen, and understandably so. She wanted and demanded my total attention, and was rather jealous of the other children. In the end, it got to the point where, to get attention, she would refuse to take her insulin. It was hard enough to bring up five children, and work, on my own, but she was stretching me to the limit. In the end, we had a family meeting with the social workers and decided she would have to go to a foster family. Something had to give, clearly. I kept up with her, and she came and stayed for holidays. I then continued with the four children and brought them up. Now, of course, they're completely grown up, so I am looking forward to having a little more time to myself.

Generally speaking, it's much easier to go out with a girlfriend because you don't have to worry about what you're wearing, about what you say. I'm sure men feel the same when they go off and they play golf or squash or whatever it is and are very easy with each other. But I like men, I find them fun to be with. At the same time, if I'm late for a girlfriend I'm less worried about it than if I'm late for a man. If I've got a spot on my chin, I'm less worried about it than if I'm with a man, subliminally or consciously. But I do like men, I find them stimulating and amusing. I get a bit scared of them at times, because I think men tend to judge me more dramatically, more definitely. They form definite opinions, they don't give me much chance to be myself.

Each era has had its own emphasis. We are living in a very sexually-orientated era. The result is that people tend to put too much emphasis on being attracted to and having a successful sexual partner in their lives. There is no marriage born that just happens and is automatically happy. People have to work at it, they have to be tolerant with one another through all the ups and downs of the relationship. I saw a documentary on China the other day, and how they have mediators and all the family gather to try and get a couple together when they talk about divorce. And they are very successful. They have an 80 per cent success rate. Here parents are considered interfering if they try to stop a couple getting a divorce. We all go through arguments and misunderstandings, but where do you see people trying to encourage people to stay together if they are going through difficulties? They just aren't there. People don't go and talk to their priests any more, they go to psychiatrists. But psychiatrists don't have a particularly positive attitude towards marriage. You know, if this partner doesn't work, well, then, find another.

Lynn Phillips: What seduces me is my way of looking at a person, my way of opening myself to him. I don't think anything else does it. I've had men come on to me, and it's repulsed and frightened me, whereas, if I'm in the mood, the same man could come on to me and I'll love it. Sometimes I think it's just the cutest thing in the world to be lied to and manipulated by a guy. I can't think of anything more amusing than having somebody play around with me for the night. That's if I'm feeling very strong and I'm not really afraid of getting lost inside his fantasy. So, to me, I think it's all in your own readiness. But the man I married, I married not only because he's cute and attractive to me, but because he has an incredible spirit that I find really moving and encouraging and affirmative. I found it really difficult when I spent a period of my life as what one friend of mine describes as an old homosexual. I found it really, really difficult that women were hostile to my attitudes as well. They didn't like the fact that I was playing with it rather than taking it seriously. It was a serious game, I wasn't trifling – a serious and possibly deadly game. We all know how that stuff works, but I was sleeping with men I wasn't interested in romantically; I was falling in love with men in a sense that I didn't love at all; I wasn't looking for a mate or weighing qualities or looking for somebody who would repre-sent me in the world or trying to find somebody who could help me in my career; it was a completely gratuitous and self-centred activity.

When a woman tries to do this in this culture, she's looked on as self-destructive. Whereas, when a man does it, he may be frowned on as childish, but he's not ever considered self-destructive. And it wasn't self-destructive for me at all. It was often punishing, and sometimes painful, but it was mostly very pleasurable and an important transition for me. It was really, really important for my mental development.

There is a bit of collaborationism in almost all heterosexual matings. But the spiritual price of not loving your enemy is much greater than the spiritual price of loving your enemy. The challenge is to be able to love your enemy and not to join him as an enemy.

I could live without a man, I could probably even live without television. Actually, I think most women in America could probably live without men more easily than they could live without television. I could live without men, but I would probably fight to the death not to have to. I really like living, I like contradiction. Contradiction was my wet-nurse, I like all the confusion and difficulty of a heterosexual world, though I'd like that world to be a better one, I'd like its contradictions to be less destructive.

Sarah Fox-Pitt: I rebelled against a single point of view about relationships. Later on, when I went to live in Italy, the doors were open wide, and of course typically, as an English girl, one roamed, and I became somebody's mistress. I remember my mother saying before I left, of course, Italy will change you irrevocably, and she was quite right. At the time, I didn't really understand what she meant, but I know now. It put me out of touch with her, out of touch with her values, as well as showing me a different way of life in all sorts of respects.

Baroness Plowden: It's quite a long time now since I've divided people into men and women. I have both men and women friends. I still work with a great many people. I think I always believed that you couldn't make friends with people (and I suppose I meant men as well as women) unless you walked in the rain with them and got really cold. Therefore you had to know them well enough to know they were pleasant people who would survive hardship rather than just people you met at a party and went to bed with. Somebody you only see at a party in the evening can be entirely unreal. You have no idea what they are like, they are just somebody at a party showing one side of themselves. If you spent the day with somebody and you got wet, you'd begin to know more what they were like.

906

People's expectations of marriage are different. When it goes wrong, or something appears to go wrong, they say, oh, to hell with this, why should I go on with this, this is enough. Occasionally, in my dentist's waiting room, I read some of the questions from women who write saying I've discovered my husband slept with somebody ten years ago and I now say I won't have anything to do with him. They feel they have been betrayed somehow. It seems very peculiar, absolutely childish.

Eve Pollard: I like clever men. I will never forget my first romance. I was in love with a boy in my teenage years, and then, when we got home from our holidays, he wrote me a letter and couldn't spell, and that was it. I was distraught. In a minute this mad passionate longing I had had for this boy was gone completely, because he couldn't spell.

I would rather go out with an interesting woman than a boring man. Great, funny women are the best company you could possibly have, though I have men friends I adore speaking to, too. I don't think men are fascinating just as men, but I've spent most of my working life in the company of men. The classic odds would be ten men and one woman, me, at an editorial meeting. Yet my doctor is a woman, my gynaecologist is a woman, my hairdresser is a woman, and up to recently my dentist was a woman, so I have obviously chosen them because I feel more relaxed, or perhaps they understand me better. Perhaps I can go through short-cuts with women that men possibly wouldn't understand.

I've never been seduced by power. I've been lucky, I've been very close to powerful men for a long, long time, and I've lived always in the middle of London. I know where all the loos are in Harrods better than anybody. But if I had come up from a small town to the big city, and I had met someone who had all the trappings, I can see how it might have happened.

Women can do it for lust, and we do do it for lust. I mean, how can you see someone at a party, think they are wonderful, and go back to bed with them and say this is a romantic entanglement? It may become a romantic entanglement, and probably the woman prays it will; and the man might think, this is just a one-night stand and that's that. The trouble is, and the difference is, that as we get older, however much we try, the looks start fading and all the rest of it. Number one, we want a settled home because the biological time-clock goes on: we want to have a baby, we want to have that in a settled environment. Number two, having a rash of lustful one-night stands is unreal; nobody can fall in and out of love that often and be grown up. At a certain stage, you actually

907

think, I must be maturing. It is crazy to say that every relationship that is sexual is going to be traditionally long-standing and full of love. And it is also crazy to say you are going to go throughout your life leaping into bed with whomever you lust for. What happens is that we take out insurance, often in the form of marriage, which means, in theory, you are both going to try and be faithful, both going to try and love one another and stick to one another so that you have this solid edifice, a home, from which you feel you can go out and conquer the world. Many successful women need that home and that sort of a solid background behind them from which to succeed. They may pretend it is not important, but it gives them a terrific emotional back-up.

If your relationship is not working well, it is out of tune with the 1980s to put up with it, out of tune with the 1980s to compromise, out of tune with the 1980s to say this is not perfect, this is not what I want right now, but I'll try to make the best of it. It is a tragic thing, in many ways. Many men have said to me, I should have stuck with my first wife, I was equally unhappy, bored or whatever with her as I am now with the second. But what I've got is the guilt, the costs, and the feeling of where can I go from here? I cannot embark on a third. On the other hand, I don't see how we will change it. A marriage, a good marriage, is almost like a good firm. The two of you are there, working together. You have this edifice, this house, these children. I think if my husband had a one-night stand, it would mean there was something wrong with our marriage and that he was sexually not interested in me. My sexual pride would be really hurt and I probably would behave quite stupidly. And he would probably stand there for ever and say, I just got drunk and I didn't mean it, I can't remember her name, it doesn't matter. But another danger about women working is that you become slightly asexual, and it's terribly important that you don't get tired and don't think everything else comes before the sexual side of your marriage. It's terribly important to keep that up.

All the time, there is a conflict at home. A conflict of, for instance, who is more important? A conflict of, who gets the telephone first? And who's more successful? All the time. And, of course, in some ways it's got harder. My husband has been an editor for a long time, but I'm slowly catching him up. So there is a conflict all the time. I think it is very healthy, we enjoy it, it's competition. In some ways, you get rid of some of the normal aggressive disagreements in a marriage, professionally. I think he finds it very hard. Sometimes it can destroy a marriage.

Antonia de Portago: I was raised in Paris, and for some reason didn't get along with Frenchwomen so well. But women who live in New York are a special breed. Whatever country they come from – my own included – they came here for a reason. They want to grow, to change their lives and to open their minds, I believe. Everybody here is here for a real purpose. They left very beautiful places because New York has something to offer that other cities don't.

Barbara de Portago: It's one thing, telling a girlfriend everything and listening to her advice, but what I prefer and love most, and even yearn for, is the understanding of a man.

I'd rather be with men. I love men. I breathe men. Where women are concerned, I love women too, very much. The only drawback I have in getting on with women is that I first have to get over the barrier that, well, I am a good-looking woman. So I go out of my way to make them feel comfortable, and once that barrier's crossed and they know I'm really OK, I get on very well with women.

We have no more physical taboos, no more social taboos between men and women. It's a great strain, frankly. I like the barriers. It's like watching a steeplechase, you know. You like to see how far a person will go for you.

I really do think of the man as the conqueror and the woman as being conquered. I like to be conquered. I like to be sought after, wanted, pursued, put on a pedestal, taken off of it.

I was married at seventeen, and then I was married again – I lived with a man for eight years and I married him for ten months. So I have not exactly been what you would call a single person out there in the dating game. I'm just starting. I'm discovering now. Having been so spoiled all my life, the man has always come and got me, and here, in New York City, I found this out very quickly. Never call, never call; let yourself be called. Before, I would tend just to call up and find out how people were, not meaning in any way that I would see them or whatever, but I found out very quickly that you do not call a man. You wait to be called.

Diana Potter: I'm very happy in both companies. I've got more good girlfriends than good men friends, but that's just because it is easier to have more girlfriends than it is men friends. The husband of one of my greatest friends is also one of my greatest friends. He amuses me, and I find him attractive, but I don't find him sexually attractive, mainly because he is hers. I think every time anything like this comes up, I just rationalize and cut it off because of the friendship. Most women do do that, *click*, and do not allow themselves to fall in love.

I find powerful men rather worrying, really. People like Jimmy Gold-smith, or Maxwell, or Conran, I find they go into a sort of aspic bubble. They are so used to telling everybody what to do, they never listen to anybody properly, even at dinner. I mean, Maxwell's a prime example. He just goes on like a sort of truck. No, I am not seduced by powerful men. There are certain television personalities the same thing happens to. A tremendous conceit overcomes powerful or famous men – not all, but a lot of them – which is very unattractive. Wógan hasn't got it yet.

Usha Prashar: I think people have made a decision that, if marriage doesn't work, why suffer it? And that is a very positive development. I think before, because people thought there was a stigma attached to divorce, they would adjust, but one party or the other would be suffering, in most cases the woman. They were the ones who compromised 100 per cent. Of course, they should try to make a success of it, but now, because they have their independence, if it doesn't work they can get out. From the woman's point of view, that is a good thing.

My husband doesn't earn less than I do, but he is not in the public eye. I am. I haven't found that a strain, but I think that depends on the quality of the man. The man has to be very secure in himself. If he is a macho man, and he's got to be superior to the woman, then it is bound to put a strain on the marriage, but if the man is different, then it won't. In my personal experience, that hasn't been the case. If anything, my husband has been a great support, and if anything, he is thrilled when I am in the public eye.

Judith Price: I'm into power. I like powerful people. And I think that is seductive.

I don't trust women. Men are better for me. I don't know if they're better for other people. I can go out to lunch with men, go out to breakfast with them. I can kind of harmlessly flirt with them, tell them unabashedly that I am madly and passionately in love with them and they're terrific. I just feel good about them.

About a year after I was married, I felt totally claustrophobic. I hated being married, I really did. And I thought, at that time, I had a choice.

910

All my friends were having affairs – I could have an affair. I could tell my husband, I am thinking of having an affair and let me tell you why; or go and have an affair. Or do nothing. Instead, I went to my husband and said, you know, I'm thinking of having an affair. There's no question I had it in mind. It was the most risky, the most risky, but he said he was thinking of it, too. It was a very stormy period in our relationship, which we lived through. We talked, and I think that was it. We talked about how unhappy we were, that I got married because I felt obliged, I had to get married. I mean, not that I was pregnant, but I was going to be twenty-three years old. I mean, my God, I had to get married.

I think what my marriage has done is it has made me feel, and this is the girl part in me, more stable. It really has. When I first started my marriage, I could get very emotional about things, and my relationship with my husband has taught me not to get emotional in business decisions. Someone here wants to fire someone else, and I agree with them. I say, you're right, but don't fire them now, or you'll waste four months. Consolidate, then you'll fire them, but not now. Now, maybe ten, eleven years ago, I would have said, yes, yes, get 'em, get 'em.

Colombe Pringle: I love to be seduced. I enjoy it, I'm very thankful to men who seduce me.

Marjorie Proops: There are far more temptations for men. If a man goes off to work, he sees young, attractive girls who, in themselves, will regard somebody else's man as a conquest. Not necessarily a sexual conquest, but it's a bit of fun to get a man to be unfaithful to his wife, and a little triumph. And you've got to be a very strong man indeed to resist. In fact, this is why I say to so many of the women who write despairing letters when they discover their husbands have been unfaithful, even though the husbands are full of regret and remorse and everything else – when they say, shall I leave him, I write back and say, no, regardless of that little aberration. It is no more than a slight illness he has suffered. Just help him to get better.

More men abandon their wives than vice versa. But an increasing number of women are leaving their husbands, because women are much more independent and stronger than they were. They are not so afraid to be on their own as they were. But generally, I think men get bored. They are tired of the sort of routine of going home to the same female, lack of excitement, lack of stimulation; they need new stimulants to arouse them.

911

Bob Maxwell is very affectionate, very loving. If he walked in here now, he would put his arm round me and kiss me. And my head would be on his shoulder and he would be loving and I respond to that. That's the sort of man I personally respond to: somebody who is warm, somebody who is loving, somebody who is loving towards me.

My husband has been retired for many years, but before he retired he was a successful businessman in the building industry. He was a director of a big London company, and we were both involved very much in each other's jobs and lives during that period. He supported me and I supported him. I couldn't have done my job without his support, and he tells me he couldn't have done his, at any rate as well, without mine. So we always had that between us. I think there could have been tension when he retired and I was working still. I think that was the real testing time in our marriage. But he is a man with a great sense of humour and reality, and he waves me goodbye in the morning and says, don't worry about a thing, dear, I'll look after the shopping and all that kind of thing. And, indeed, he does. He runs the house. And he's not proud about admitting it. He makes jokes about it, and he sometimes rings me up at the the office and says, I'm going to Harrods, is there anything special you fancy for dinner? And this is absolutely wonderful.

Andrée Putman: An amazing amount of men are absolutely unable to deal with life if they are not beautifully assisted by women. Many women can exist perfectly well after the tyrant disappears. There are many, many tyrants.

The reason I get along with men rather better is that, as a woman, I resent the fragility of so many women around me. I cannot totally respect women who are fearful of men, who really believe men are more intelligent, more reasonable, more organized. I don't get along with that kind of woman. The ones who are terrified do not have the kind of personality which impresses me, and instead of pitying them and being incredibly generous and open and spending maybe a lot of energy helping them, I want to shake them and say, why did you say that, why did you act as a loser in such and such a situation in front of men? Because I like them, I think women are incredibly courageous. It's not a lack of courage that stops them succeeding, it's a lack of confidence. Everything is organized still to make them feel weak and fragile. Many of the media images of women show women as fragile, as objects of seduction: weak, unreal, immature.

I don't believe in that naïve idea: the beautiful wedding and the thirty-five, forty years together holding hands. This dream should not be given to young women. I have a very beautiful daughter of twenty-two, who is a complete human being; she has suffered a lot, she has had all kinds of difficult experiences and is not dreaming about a happy wedding, and I'm responsible for that. She will have great love affairs and she will get married, maybe several times, but she doesn't have that naïve approach to life: you know, you must prepare yourself for that love which is going to be eternal and fulfilling. The last couple I thought were going to last for ever, a couple near me that had every chance to survive, exploded yesterday: that's the news of the week. I don't believe in couples very much, except if there is an amazing proportion of friendship. One of the two is hurt usually. One of the two loves more than the other.

Mary Quant: I do think flirtation is a tremendously good thing. It's through flirtation that so much of that sort of fun between the sexes can continue without any damage or causing any problems, or any complexities, or going any further at all. It just renews everything and makes everyone feel so good without breaking relationships or anything.

I would like us to move to a situation where people, when they married, made a contract, like you do in business, so that from the beginning it would be stipulated exactly how things were to be divided up if they separated. So that they wouldn't make that decision to part without knowing exactly what was going to go, exactly what they were going to keep, and exactly what their circumstances were going to be. So that the break-up wasn't made worse by prolonged battles and rows and whatever – everything from property to cats, let alone children. And the couple should spell out some of the really major important things; like whether or not they want children, which are almost the point of marriage as against a friendly ongoing relationship. These things should be set out more when you get married.

Charlotte Rampling: Previously I was happier in the company of men, but now it doesn't matter. Before, women were always jealous of me, so I had few women friends, right from school age, because I had a French education for three years, and when I was thirteen I went back to an English private school. And for some reason, whether or not it was because of that, I was always excluded. They always pretended they liked me but would do things behind my back. They would say, we are not going to the cinema this weekend, and I would go alone to the cinema and find all my group of friends there. That sort of thing. So I

913

was very wary about the treachery of women, and this made me go much more towards men, to find friendships among men. Not sexual friendships, but just friendships that I needed. Women betrayed me a lot. But now it's different. I am no longer possibly in competition so much with them. Now, at least, and it's very rewarding, I know five or six women I am becoming very close to, and that's nice.

When my sister died in rather tragic circumstances when she was twenty-three, and I was just twenty-one, my mother had a very severe stroke, a telepathic stroke, because they were so linked. My sister was in the Argentine, and my mother had a stroke at the time my sister died from a brain haemorrhage. My mother became ill in England, and then, a few hours later, we got the call about my sister. It was really spooky. So then my mother was very ill for a few years, and my father was concerned that I shouldn't come home any more, it was so upsetting to see my mother in that state. He said, go and live your life, and please don't feel you have to come home and look after your mother; I'll look after her and put her in a hospice; I'll get her through this. He just dedicated his life to my mother. I remember when there was a thing in the newspapers about me living with two men. I married one of them, really because of my parents and to disprove the story. The story was actually true, but I didn't want my parents to think it was. The whole press got on top of it. I actually loved them both – well, love, I mean I was twenty-two and I was having a good time. It only lasted about a year but it was a wonderful sort of adventure. They were friends and not jealous of each other. It was very strange. I got pregnant by one, so I married him. It was a wonderful time, but I couldn't tell anybody about it. It was made into such a shabby press scandal, and my mother was just getting better, so then I married the man. I knew I shouldn't have, it could never have worked. We were just young and having a good time. But I married him because I got pregnant and didn't want to upset my father any more and wanted to squash the rumours.

At the moment, I am in a marriage where we are equally successful, and this is something which is very rare. People always say, my goodness, you have been with this man for ten years, how on earth can it happen? You are both successful, both very busy, both well known, how can it work? I think it works *because* of that. Or a great chunk of it works because of that. We both work the same way in our fields, we are very *marginale*, as they say in French. Jean-Michel does things which are off the beaten track, I do things which are off the beaten track. So our careers are the same; they converge, they don't collide. I think, however much you love somebody, one of the most difficult things in life must be to sense you are a failure and your partner is successful.

Esther Rantzen: I get accused of surrounding myself with bright young men. But there are just as many bright young women. It's just that people like those images. It amuses them to think of me, a forty-six-year-old woman, I suppose slightly bossy, gathering a bouquet of bright young men around her. But in my bouquet, if it is my bouquet, I have some very bright young women as well.

I went to dinner in the States, and one couple had been married more than fifteen years, but all the other men were on their second, third or fourth wives. This was explained to me by our host by saying that American men, when they reach a certain stage of success, dump whoever they are with at that time and go for the testimonial woman, the woman who is actually a testimonial to their success. She needs to be blonde, long-legged and entirely admiring. It's not nearly as restful and charming to go home to the old lady who has known him since he was a struggling not very attractive pauper, and who therefore criticizes him and sees him only too clearly, as wanting to be lapped in anodyne praise. Maybe that is why I find men of that kind unattractive. My husband and I have a completely different kind of relationship, based on seeing each other almost too clearly. But we can rely on each other's judgement, and we do. We support each other through problems, because of the clarity of our vision and because of the way we are partners, real partners of equal strength. And you can't beat that. The centre of your life is your own home when the front door shuts. And there, what you need is a relationship based on mutual regard. I don't know if the Queen wears the crown in bed. In other words, I don't know whether, when she goes home, everything she says is a royal proclamation or whether she defers to her husband. I am not suggesting that we become little women, but I am suggesting we become partners. And when you are in a relationship in which you ask each other advice, when it's quite clear you respect each other, then the outward image of success, who earns the money, doesn't matter.

I've got the model of my parents' marriage to look at. They had all the problems that could have led to a divorce, in the sense that, like every couple, they hit rocky times. Their life was not at all plain sailing, either financially, or professionally for my father. They had tough times, and they stayed together. It wouldn't have occurred to them not to. I think it was part of putting the children as the priority. You are not going to do something like deprive them of their parents. You might be arguing and rowing but the children need both parents. That's absolutely fundamental in my life: the child needs a father and a mother. Since I came from a background in which I depended on both of them, I believe my chidren will, too. Now, I know it's possible for two people to make each other's lives sheer misery. I am my husband's second wife. I know that a house can become a prison and a relationship which once was love can turn into such hatred that it becomes destructive to everybody involved, including the children. So there's no way I am saying everybody should stay together.

Mirella Ricciardi: My father always used to say, being a good Neapolitan, there is no friendship between men and women, it doesn't exist. If two people, a man and a woman, stay together long enough, they either split or they become lovers, but there is no such thing as friendship. As Lorenzo, my husband, says, if I don't fuck I don't have fun.

I am more at ease with women, because I always feel men are judging you, constantly looking at you, your physical appearance, the way you talk, the *way* you are saying it, rather than what you are saying. They are constantly looking, checking you out, whereas women don't give a damn, they just listen to you; they just decide they like you or they don't like you, whether you're fat or thin, or small or grey-haired or ugly. It is amazing how the physical appearance of a woman affects a man, and that puts me off terribly. Whether I am considered beautiful or ugly will affect a man's relationship with me. One day, when I stop being a photographer, I want to make a film about two people who meet blindfolded and have an affair without ever seeing each other, and explore what happens. It is really awful how the physical aspect can change your attitude towards somebody.

Fidelity is an unnatural condition in the male. He's not capable of it, and if he says he is, there is something the matter with him; he is not a true man. No man is built physiologically to stay with one woman. I don't believe it. If he does it, he does it because he reasons with his head or because he is not totally a true, complete man. Just look at the animals. I have accepted this, and so have been able to understand men much more than a lot of my women friends, because I know that asking a man to be faithful to one woman for his whole life is an unnatural demand. It will have an effect on him and ultimately it will backfire, because one day he is just going to say, *merde!* and he is going to explode. Any woman who expects her man to be faithful to her all his life is totally unrealistic and needs a real dose of good sexual education to be able to understand what actually makes a man tick, and that, if he doesn't have his freedom and cannot express his self sexually, he becomes a totally warped and torpid person, a tortured person.

I am seduced by intelligence. I don't give a shit about the way he looks. I

916

like to feel he is warm, that he is natural, that he is not putting on a seductive game with me. Obviously, if he does also have attractive things about him, like the curve of his neck or the way his hair curls, or his hands – but I have loved men who are just so physically unattractive, yet I would rather have them any day than some beautiful guy I see walking down the beach at Malibu. The man who is ugly and intelligent also has to be a good lover, because if he is ugly he is going to have problems getting me into bed. I have had ugly people in bed and beautiful ones in bed, and I must say the quality of the love-making has varied. But remember, I am a very visual person. I once had a long affair with a black guy, which was the most outrageous thing any colonial girl has ever done. But he was so totally beautiful that it really enhanced the quality of the love-making. In other words, in love, the physical act of love, there comes a point when you don't want any more intellectual stimulus. I can't stand, for instance, these people who fuck you with their heads. It is such a turn-off for me, I can't tell you. They seduce you with their head, but then they have to fuck. If they start bringing their intellect into the bed, and start playing games with you, and start doing all the erotica – *ugh!* as far I am concerned, forget it. I know there are lots of women who love it, but I think they pretend to love it.

I think our way of life is an unnatural one. I think the world is going fast towards its own destruction, and one of the very obvious ways of destruction is Aids, which is Nature's way of dealing with the problem of sexual liberation. Because when we don't listen and we abuse, Nature will do what it has to do, and is doing it now, this very minute. Same thing with ecology, and the same thing with marriage. The couples are not working together because our way of life is an unnatural one. And when you go back to primitive people, the couples work. Among people who haven't been affected by the race to God knows where, the race to destruction, you don't see marriages not going well. People grow up, people grow old together. I talk from my own personal observations. I am not somebody who has read about it; I feel it. Our world, our way, our civilization – we have to learn, we have to cope with it before it's too late. My daughter has had to go to a psychiatric ward, she has been unbelievably ill this year, and has landed me with her friend, whom she met at the psychiatric ward. This friend is twenty-one years old and is an alcoholic. You ask how it is a sweet, lovely, pretty, intelligent, sensitive little thing is an alcoholic at twenty-one, and she tells you, and you understand and think, well, obviously I'd be an alcoholic, too. It's not very complicated to see what's going on around. And where things go wrong is when you get away from the dictates of Nature. I'm a great believer in Nature. If you are sick, go back to the natural way, drink water, stop eating too much, don't smoke, don't drink alcohol – that's all unnatural. Aids came from an unnatural way of fucking. That was not how it was meant to be done. It took years and centuries, but we finally became sexually liberated, and now, because of Aids, everybody is so scared of having any kind of relationship with anybody that they are not having relationships, and that, too, is unnatural. I think of my girls, aged twenty-two and twenty-six. What are they going to do? Become celibate? What about their natural sexual urges? They are going to put on weight, they are going to have pre-menstrual tension. Why? Because they are not leading a natural sexual life. If they lead a natural sexual life, they risk getting Aids.

Nancy Richardson: I'm much more fun with men for the simple reason that they all talk to me. I want someone to talk to me. The women won't necessarily talk honestly with me. As I look over my professional associations at *House and Garden*, there is not anyone on the staff who will speak really honestly with me, because they perceive me as a threat. The men are more honest, but I'm not a threat to them.

My husband and I share the view that it's not at any cost that we will proceed in life, it must be within a moral framework. But somebody has to play vice-president, somebody has to play the wife, and as my husband has this financial ability that far outstrips mine, I am under a lot of pressure. He says to me, I'll bolt, I'll leave, if you start a magazine now. I'll leave you, because I know what you do when you're working hard, I'll find another wife. So that is a terrible pressure from an honest man you love who is the father of your children, a terrible pressure.

Before I was married, sex meant so much to me. I felt extremely incomplete unless I had a man. Now, with children and the pressures of a career, Frank Richardson comes back like mad in his forties and I find myself tired. If I decided to have work-outs every afternoon, I'd be more interested in my husband. Sex is a very fragile thing; the more you do, the more you want to do, and the less you do, the less you want to do. I watch my husband being extremely interested at a time when I feel tired even when he has had an even more exhausting day than I have. We're seeing a lot of divorced men and women in their forties – the Sid Bass and Mercedes Kellogg thing. I think men at this so-called mid-life thing go through a great deal in terms of a psychological adjustment. Men feel like babies then, they feel as if they are seventeen, for heaven's sake. The man I am married to, I'd be crazy, not just for financial reasons, but I'd be crazy to let something that's going well go down the tubes because I'm not there. That's one reason I won't let Condé Nast take advantage of me.

Men don't like their wives being successful. But we are going to have to see a new breed of men and women. There is going to be the new man who is not going to mind, and there is going to be the new woman who, if she happens to be better at something than her man, is not going to grind it in his face. It's the etiquette of marriage that's going to improve as we get a better view of each other as male and female. We're going to have the grace not to make it into a problem.

Stella Richman: Five years ago, in my own restaurant, it would be 33 per cent women and 66 per cent men together. I noticed in the last year an extremely curious thing, I'm trying to fathom out why, it's all men again. Women are no longer invited out to the courtesy, the obligatory lunch. A friend of mine, an Englishwoman who arrived from America yesterday, came to join us and she said, my God, there's not a woman in the place except us. And this is a funny thing. I think men's confidence has been eroded by women coming into their world. So now, sub-consciously – I don't think it's thought out or planned – they think, we can have a meal without a bloody woman there. They've gone back to the old boys' club bit.

It's horses for courses, and I know quite a few young men under thirty who, to my surprise, can't have an affair with somebody unless they are in love with her. It leads to terrible disasters because they think they keep hearing wedding bells. I think, in that way, women are more mature.

Women tend to put a lot of store by the word faithful; and I don't know whether it's a delusion or not that they want only one man. Now I think this is probably not true if they really scratched the surface. It's very hard for two people to take those vows and think each of them is going to give the other everything they need for the rest of their lives.

When I want something badly enough, of course I would use my femininity; I'd be a damn fool not to. Sometimes you have to take a decision: whatever I do with this chap, I've got to play it dead straight, because no other way is going to work. And sometimes you get a pleasure out of using your femininity. If you're out to score Brownie points in a business or work situation, it's fair to use everything within your power to use, provided you don't hurt anybody. That's where I draw the line. And when you're young, very young, and you're in a powerful position, you're more ruthless than you are as the years go by a bit. I never found it necessary to walk over corpses. But, thinking about it, I've only ever used my femininity if a man was attractive enough to use it on.

After the break-up of my last marriage, I got terribly fed up with people who said, well, she can look after herself. Of course one does, because in the final issue anyone can really. But it's to do with loneliness as well as the things we can be more explicit about. I would love a time in my life when somebody would say, stop worrying about this or that, I'll do it all for you. It may be that this will never happen to me because of the sort of person I am, but I would love it to happen. But it would have to be somebody very strong.

Having been for years and years the owner of premises which have ladies' toilets, the dialogues you overhear are, to me, shattering; in California and in London. Four friends out for the night, two husbands, two wives, and the women go off to powder their noses in the cliché sense, and if you're sitting on one of the loos, you're shocked by the intimate details two so-called friends – and I query the word friends – discuss with each other in between the smoked salmon and the next course.

There's a famous restaurant in LA where I stayed in the loo longer than I had to because I was so riveted by this boring dialogue two gorgeous young women were having, remaking up for the third time and giving themselves a shot, I may say. But the things they were saying about their men – it's like they were talking about objects. Not Fred, or Bill, or Harry, or whoever, but objects that were there to serve them. I find that very distasteful. Maybe I'm old-fashioned. I don't think I would discuss with my best friend what went on between me and my husband in the bedroom in my three marriages. It's an army joke, what she did last night: that's a different world, you pay for something, you get a service which is good or not good, and you joke about it with the boys. But with wives and close girlfriends, women more than men, I tell you, the women of the famous, I find it unbelievable.

Angela Rippon: I worked for a company called Westward Television, an ITV company in the West Country. I was a producer and a director, and this was in my late twenties. My secretary was a woman, but the film crews were men. During the day, I was in charge of that group of people: men old enough to be my father were answerable to me, and my decisions were final decisions. If I said shoot that, do this, do that, they did it. And they didn't question that because they recognized my authority and position as the director. They also recognized my ability to do the job, and I hope they appreciated that. But in the evening, when we went out for dinner, the men would still very helpfully open the door for me, which I was grateful for, pull a chair up for me to sit down for dinner. I was the director, so they recognized the authority of my position, but equally they remembered that I was a woman. It was important to them, not only to be good at their job, but also to maintain their masculinity while I retained my femininity. And I have always tried to do that. I have never tried to emulate men by losing my femininity. Men have been at this power game for centuries, they know all the rules because they wrote most of them, and they play by their own rules. I've worked in television now for twenty-one years, and have observed in those years how men play the game. I have learned the rules and I have played by those rules. Not once, I think, have I lost my femininity any more than the men lose their masculinity. I have still been very feminine, I hope, in the way that I dress, in the way I think, but I've played the game according to their rules.

I enjoy men's company very much. I've worked with men most of my life, and there might have been a time when I would have said I enjoy the company of men more than of women. I think that now I am reaping the benefit of what essentially is women's evolution in society. I think other women, over the years, have felt uncomfortable in my company because they were not as confident and they would somehow edge away. Which would make any kind of relationship with women very difficult sometimes. But now there are more and more women becoming much more confident of their role in society. It is much easier for women who already have a career to relate very easily to more women because we are all feeling much more equal. It is becoming a much more egalitarian society, not just in terms of education and opportunity, but socially as well.

If you are unfortunate enough to marry a man whose ego is bigger than any other part of his anatomy, then, as a successful woman, you've got a real problem. I don't have that problem. I have been married for twenty years and have known my husband since I was seventeen. I knew him when I was at school. As my career has developed and grown, he has developed and grown with me. So it's not as if he was suddenly dumped into a situation that was created before he had anything to do with it. My marriage, my relationship with my husband, and my career, and his career, have all gone along at a steady pace since we were seventeen, and we have grown together. My career has gone in one direction, his has gone in another. I think it comes back to individuals. If you are pretty weak, then you are not going to stay the course. If you are fairly strong and the relationship and understanding you have between you is very strong, then it's going to take a darned sight more than the fact that your wife goes out to work to destroy the marriage. And if it does, well, it wasn't much of a marriage in the first place.

My husband is very successful at what he does, and I am successful at what I do. There are no jealousies between us. He is not jealous of the fact that I am nationally known and he isn't. He is not interested in what I do. He isn't jealous of my success because he is not jealous of my career and what I do for a living because he's busy doing his own thing. Likewise, I am not jealous of his successes and his abilities. We have, I think, a very good working relationship. So it's not going to be that that's going to separate us. We spend a lot of time apart, but it wouldn't say much for the relationship if being apart for a couple of months was going to destroy it.

I can't stand men who love themselves, or preen. I met somebody at a party last night who was incredibly good-looking, and afterwards I went out to dinner with some of the friends I was with, and one of the women said, oh, isn't so and so devastatingly good-looking, and doesn't he know it? And I thought, yes, that's exactly what made me have a totally negative approach to him. He is incredibly good-looking, and he knows it. And he preens, and he postures, and he poses. And I wouldn't care if he looked like Robert Redford, that is an absolute switch-off, if he loves himself.

Shirley Ritchie: I've dealt with a lot of marriages in this country in the last twenty years. I have a very strong view, and that is that people are getting married too young without having the faintest idea what they are doing. You have a couple of nineteen-year-olds who all their lives have lived at home, so even if it is assumed, at this stage, that they are earning their own money and giving their mum £10 a week or whatever, they have all the rest of their money for clothes, for going to discos, for going to pubs, for going to the cinema, anything they like. They spend their entire life having a super social life as a couple. They go to the pub, meet up with a crowd of people; they go to the disco, meet up with a crowd of people; they go home, they are there with mum and dad and Auntie Sue. Then comes the wedding, it's absolutely fabulous. But then they find themselves in a flat, haven't got any money, can't go out. For the first time in their lives, they have to sit down and talk to each other, and they very often find that they don't like what they've got. Within two to three years, the marriage dies. Second marriages, when they know what they are looking for and what married life is all about, frequently last. It's the young marriages that collapse in the first few years.

Over the years, society's views of divorce have changed. It's no longer a stigma. The idea of somebody living alone is wholly acceptable, and especially of women going off and doing things on their own: travelling alone and going out to restaurants alone and so on. Thirty years ago, if a woman divorced her husband, she might be condemning herself to a social wilderness. Also, in the old days, when you were sixty and you had been married for thirty years, you would think, well, there's probably only another five years to go, I can cope with it. But if you've got another twenty-five to think about, because people live longer now, you reckon you might as well find something more enjoyable for that, even if just for a bit of peace and quiet.

Hélène Rochas: When I was married, my husband would not allow me to do anything in the house at all. I really was the 'woman as object' and I'm delighted to have been so, it was marvellous. I don't want to forget that position today. I was very happy. I rebelled against it because, when a particular piece of work is finished, then you can stop playing Pygmalion. I had my own ideas, and after about the age of twenty I knew what I wanted. At that stage, I must say, there were a few arguments.

Once a woman becomes a good friend of mine, I don't regard her husband in the same light as another man. I base all my emotional relationships on loyalty. For me, it's indispensable. I hate lies, and for that reason I suppose I can have very good relationships with other women. It's more difficult to be friends with a woman, because there is always the element of competition, but with a man there's the edge between flirting and friendship. I love the company of men; I like being with one woman friend or two, but three women together is difficult. In any case, I much prefer a *tête-à-tête* to anything else. Whenever there is a third party, people are not so natural. At a cocktail party, there are always the same questions, what are you doing in the holidays, et cetera, even from people I've known for twenty or thirty years, and it remains on a very superficial level. When you are on your own with someone, you can discover what they are really like suddenly, though it's rare.

Anita Roddick: I don't understand why everybody wants a marriage to last so long. Why do we have to get awards for being married fifty years, sixty years, seventy years? I've never understood longevity being a plus for a marriage. Marriages don't last so long now because people know they can effect change. People are not taking second best, people know that life is short. When politics are such that the world can blow up tomorrow, people just want the best for themselves. If you want to get divorced, then you just get divorced. For myself, I like the exclusivity of marriage, the sense of continuity, the sense of family, the sense of growing old, the sense of shorthand, the friendship. Nobody told me about that when I met my husband. Everyone told me about the lust and the love and the sexual side, but nobody told me about this great friendship that comes later on, when lust and passion go. Everybody's worried when passion goes – you know, not making love every day. But there's something absolutely comforting in the cuddle, the touch, the holding hands. I suppose, really, it's like a dress rehearsal for your old age. And I love that, I love that.

When I think of who affects me, who makes my heart miss a beat, it would be people who break the rules, who challenge themselves, who have done something brilliant, who have gone beyond themselves and contributed. People like Bob Geldof would have me breathless; because he's done it, he's absolutely effected change in a generous, humane way. It would be people like Laurens van der Post. The only time I am ever still, absolutely still mentally, with my heart beating, is when I listen to somebody like Laurens van der Post. I think there is essential goodness there, and that's such an attraction. Not a sexual attraction, but almost a falling-in-love attraction. But I've never got the hots for power at all.

Deborah Rogers: When you're involved, as I was, in a relationship that's going bad, or that is in lots of ways damaging to you, obviously you know quite well what it is, yet you go on. Afterwards, you wonder what it was that kept you absolutely locked into it. I suppose your reasons for loving somebody are not always very clear to you, but the reasons in my case were never the power of the bad element. I think it was because I always believed in the qualities I saw there, and I thought I would somehow be strong enough to bring them out in him. I think this is something some women do feel: that they have the key, that they alone can actually bring out whatever is the goodness in this particular beast. It's not always that they're held in the thrall of somebody's violence or vileness, it's much more because they think they can help unlock some other quality that's there.

You choose to hang on because you have your reasons. They may seem completely batty to other people, but whatever your reasons, they're valid to you, it's your choice. You can just as well say to somebody, I'm going tomorrow, or get out. You don't, because you still believe in his good qualities. So I think there is a sort of crusading salvation thing in a lot of women. It isn't awfully nice, either, because the missionary spirit isn't always entirely beneficial.

Selwa Roosevelt: One of the things I have been acutely aware of is, if a woman has had a very good relationship with her mother – looks up to her, admires her, but has a healthy, good relationship – they are healthier mentally than women who've idolized their fathers. Now, that is the one generality I would make just by observing all my friends. My friends who have had the worst problems as adult women – I can think of three who are alcoholics, two who became lesbian – were all women who had devastating fathers, very attractive, whom they worshipped. Now that is something I'm absolutely convinced of. It isn't that they shouldn't love their fathers, but that they must have that basically healthy respect and relationship with the mother to appreciate their own femininity. And that, I think, is what makes for a healthy woman.

I would rather discuss intimate subjects with men. I don't have that kind of relationship with my women friends. I think what my women friends like about me is that I'm very loyal and I'm there when they're in trouble and they need help. I'm a coper. And a lot of my women friends like to come to me for advice or help. I don't tend to go to them for advice or help. But I go to men, to my men friends, when I'm really in trouble. I feel more comfortable with them. And I trust them, really. However, I have had women friends I've given a confidence that they would go to the grave with before they'd repeat it, so women, too, can be very good with each other.

I've found in England that Englishwomen were very amoral, by and large. I have lovely English women friends, so I don't want to dump them all, but I do find American women are very moral. I like my English women friends, and when you know them a long time, they're terrific, but they're suspicious of women, and not as comfortable as women as American women are. In this country, women are more old-fashioned about their relationships with men. I'm not talking about Hollywood, or the actresses, and the people you see in *People Magazine*. That's another world, a very fast world. I see a lot of that world, but I also see ordinary nice people, and they don't carelessly break up homes. They might have an affair, but it's a big deal to go after someone's husband. I see it happen, of course, it happens every day, but it's not something that an American woman, I think, can do with

925

impunity, without feeling guilty and feeling terrible, whereas I think in England it's a little bit more casual.

One thing people lose sight of is modern transportation and mobility. In the old days, people would live and marry within a few miles of each other, and spend their whole life without going anywhere. Now we get on planes and go round the world without thinking about it. That does affect the stability of our society, and I think that's what affects marriages.

If I compromise, it's because I'm a person who believes in getting along with people and I like to see if I can find a way to make human relations better. I'm not a confrontational person, but I would not compromise because I'm a woman. My husband has to compromise, too. I am not an easy woman to live with. I'm a very strong woman, and he's very understanding and tolerant.

I like tender men, and the men I have loved in my life have all been very tender and very loving.

Kimberly Du Ross: Nobody knows how to deal with each other any more. It's like, how aggressive should you be? How aggressive shouldn't you be? Should you call him? Should he call you? All that. Nobody knows. It's a complete oblivion out there. Nobody knows how to deal with anyone.

It's a horrible idea that somebody is completely self-sufficient. That's total isolationism, and sounds very depressing to me. I love people, I like to be around people. I think to have a great lover is fantastic – a great friend and lover, somone you can be totally on the same wavelength with and someone you can talk about everything with, your other half – is bliss, bliss. It's just so hard to find.

Juliet Mitchell-Rossdale: In some ways, it's easier to be with women because you share a certain history, a certain expectation of life. There's an immediate identification, I think, from women to women. But precisely that ease of identification might mean that you don't have so much to talk about, and therefore somebody you are less identified with, and who sees the world differently and experiences the world in some sense differently, can be more fun, more enjoyable, more stimulating to talk to. But women who say how they don't like talking to other women and aren't comfortable with them probably just haven't done it, haven't tried it very much, and still don't think of women being as important as men and therefore only want people they think important to hear them. They don't know much about other women, and don't respect their opinions. Their own particular narcissism is only flattered if it's a man – whom they see as more important – listening to them.

The expectation of a marriage one hundred years ago would be about fifteen years, of which most would be spent in child-producing and -rearing, so there wasn't that much time for the marriage. People were either working a twelve- to sixteen-hour day in a factory, both men and women, or they were in a bourgeois family, producing children and leading quite segregated lives. There's been a terrific emphasis on the marriage in our century, so the couple have to sustain what a whole network of relationships or work situations sustained in the past. You might have seen much more of the person on the factory bench than you saw of your wife or of your husband, or you might have seen much more of your cousins, aunts and sisters and children than you saw of your husband, according to social class. Everything in this century has been put on the marital couple. It's asked to sustain an enormous amount of emotional intensity, which it probably wasn't asked to do before, and that's hard. I think that's partly the problem, and the prospect of sustaining this for forty or fifty years. It's an awful lot for two people to bear.

Yvette Roudy: Friendship between a man and a woman at some point fatally reaches the stage of physical attraction, and so sexuality is then expressed. I have male friends, and when you have friendships with someone of the opposite sex, you admit the existence of sexuality. Knowing that, you always have to accept that idea at the back of your mind. That kind of strain does not exist between women, who are therefore freer and don't have this unsaid feeling between them, although this does not exclude the possibility of sexuality between women, even if it's not admitted.

Power is fascinating. As power is usually held by men and not women, then naturally it is fascinating for a woman to be seduced by male power. A man with power has an extra plus in his chances of seducing a woman, but it's true for women, too. When I had certain responsibilities and functions, I realized that, for me, it was also a plus in my seductiveness. Too few women have power, and when the day comes that they do have it, it will be a great step for equality.

Joan Ruddock: Until my generation, there was no certain control over one's own fertility. To begin with, there was an enormous penalty for women because if you were to behave sexually on a par with men or men's desires, you would be constantly pregnant by many different men. So that is the first obvious deterrent, as it were, to women's sexual behaviour. Secondly, in terms of environment, there is always the economic situation. If women are to suffer that possibility of pregnancy, and if there is not freely available abortion, which there isn't in many societies, there is the question of who will support the result of this sexual behaviour. And the third factor, I suspect, in the environment is attitudes to women and how they should behave, particularly the idea prevalent until my generation that women were only acceptable as marital partners if they hadn't had sexual experience on a fairly wide level. But once you move beyond that, once you move to my generation, to the 1960s, where first of all you could control your fertility pretty accurately, attitudes about women being virgins at marriage changed, and women became more economically independent, then there is a spectrum. I think that there are, in terms of percentages, a few women (I'm not saying I'm one) who will have exactly the same attitudes as men, or some men (not all men have this attitude), that sexual experience can be valued for itself, take it or leave it, here today, gone tomorrow. Then, I think, there is a broader group of women who will want to have lots of sexual experiences but will want a degree of involvement, albeit they accept that the involvement will be of a limited duration. And then, I think, there is the much larger pool of women, undoubtedly the majority, in my view, who really do feel that sexual involvement must have emotional involvement, that they cannot be separated. There is a confusion there, because I believe you can have emotional and sexual involvement in a fairly short term, and they can be very creative and fulfilling relationships. But I think, for most women, conditioning dictates (and perhaps, again, real emotions and real attitudes dictate) that relationships involving sex should actually be a lifetime or close to a lifetime, that they should result in marriage.

I don't accept that the average, intelligent woman accepts the position of domination of the husband, but I have certainly seen it being a problem where women have been more successful than their husbands. In my own case, fortunately perhaps, our relationship has been one of real equality from the beginning. We are both scientists, of the same kind of age, same attitudes. I haven't had any children, I have worked all my life in paid employment, and it has never occurred to me that I would do all the domestic duties; they were always shared. My public life is, in fact, something of a burden at times for my husband, but it has not been a burden in the sense of a competitive one.

A lot of the work I've done, having quit my science a long time ago, has been in the field of counselling. Over the years, I have either interviewed or seen case histories of tens of thousands of people with marriages on the rocks, and absolutely the most common thing said is that the other partner doesn't understand, doesn't listen. It's all to do with lack of communication. Sometimes it's the fact that their sexual relationship isn't satisfactory, maybe it's never been satisfactory since children came. But in general it is communication, the fact they don't share ideas. The marriage began with interest in each other, because they were new people; they had to discover, to find out, to share, to develop. Then the discovery stopped and there was no continuing exchange, no observation of phenomena that could be discussed and exchanged, no interest, and routine set in. In many cases, conversation virtually ceases, conversation becomes a matter of, have you put the milk bottles out, have you shut the windows and doors? Purely the routine of domestic situation. In my experience, that is where most relationships come apart. Why does it happen? I suppose, if I knew that, I would be able to write a bestselling book or open a clinic. I don't know why. I am no expert. It could be a mass of things. It could be that, in the past, people's lives were physically demanding in mechanical work and earning a living and providing was actually extremely absorbing, and there would be more children. People now have more time in which, theoretically, they could be together, and they should be doing things and being interested. And they are surrounded by forces of materialism, television, all kinds of things, that block communication, and all kinds of pursuits that are actually not conducive to strengthening relationships. If you look at the marriage breakdown among unemployed people, it is extremely high, and that's where people are thrown together constantly and have no resources. So it's the other side of the coin: having no resources and no choices and absolutely nothing to do in a completely sterile environment.

For most of us, the expectations are too high. We expect wonderful things to come of this relationship without putting any effort into it, and it does go on seemingly for ever. Objectively and logically it probably is statistically unlikely that you can choose a partner at the age of twenty and twenty-two and expect to be together in a thriving relationship fifty years later. I'm not surprised at the rate of marital breakdown. I think it's regrettable, and I think there are many people who, at a very early stage in relationships, don't either have the ability or the time to make the effort to analyse their problems and work on the marriage. There's no reason why the next go they have at marriage is going to be more successful if they haven't found out what went wrong the first time. So I think there are people, and quite a lot of them, who could usefully do something about the first relationship that begins to break down. But having said that, I doubt that, given free choice about options to get out of marriage, statistically we could expect a very much better position than we have today, given resources, counselling, opportunity and a more realistic outlook. Because there is not a realistic outlook. But given all the plus factors and the positive forces, I suspect that marital breakdown would perhaps run at the rate of 25 per cent.

Eve Ruggieri: I have been attracted to men who were ugly, but when they talked, lived, existed, they were fascinating, and I am sensitive to that. It's charisma which bowls you over. You don't know where it comes from, but it is irresistible. Power is nothing at all, it's a soap bubble. People who have power don't see where they are going; they're blind, they don't know where they are going or who they are. People who are powerless, but who dream of power, are pathetic, too. What is fascinating are the people with power behind the throne, the *éminences grises*, like Mazarin and Talleyrand, who had the intelligence to refuse ultimate power while having it at the same time. It's a much more interesting kind of career, because you can still be yourself to some extent. When you are at the pinnacle, you are manipulated, deceived and abused, and that is not interesting, neither is the person.

Carol Rumens: We do repeat the patterns of our childhood in our adult relationships an awful lot. That's probably one of the problems of making progress in society. Women can be attracted to men who don't have a lot of time for them or who are going to treat them badly, and I'm sure it's because it's become a natural way of relating to an adult. Probably there's a certain excitement in it as well, in the other person not being predictable, not always there when you need them. I can understand it. I had a man whom I was very attracted to, who wasn't faithful. He was just a person who wanted lots of relationships, and so I had some experience of that, because for about two years I pursued him and considered myself in love with him, and the love absolutely wasn't returned. I was just an occasional partner, one of many. I think there's an element of addiction in it, actually. You get addicted to a certain person, and it's very hard to break out of, but quite self-destructive, and I'm glad I got over it and got out.

Women have an absolute need to understand and experience various relationships and see how they feel and how things work in relation to men. It's part of anybody's natural growing-up process, and to marry with no experience at all is a recipe for divorce as far as I'm concerned.

A lot of women consider they're changing, growing up, moving on, developing; it's a sense of quest in Western societies, I think, for people to feel they're not static in their lives. Most people feel they're on some kind of journey into self-knowledge, and relationships are a part of that, discovering other people is part of that. Most people live much longer than they used to, so you make a promise to love, honour and obey for the rest of your life, and you find you're with somebody for fifty years maybe, which is an awful long time. I think some idea of a shorter marriage contract is quite reasonable.

I must admit I feel more at ease with men, and I don't know why that should be. I've never really had a close woman friend. I watch my two daughters growing up together, and this idea of sisterhood which the feminists have a great thing about, and which may well exist with adult women, I've never seen in operation between my two girls, who were rivals from an early age, and still are. And I have not felt a great sense of sisterliness in general with other women, but it might be something that's wrong with me. I don't know, I can only speak for how I feel. I went to an all-girls school, and I think, with playground rivalry at a very early age, I had experience of women or girls not getting on, of a lot of tensions and mutual criticisms. If that had included boys as well, I'd probably feel differently about men, but I feel they're somehow remote from some of the sorts of tension and criticism you might get with women. In a way, women understand your weaknesses better, perhaps, and I feel more exposed.

Doris Saatchi: Power is very attractive, but I'm much more interested in how the individual behaves with that power. Most powerful men are not very attractive because they have been so single-minded to achieve that power that they are not wide, broad people, so they're not very interesting really, and they're focused on themselves for the most part. I'm far more attracted to someone who thinks I'm fascinating than to someone who, with half his brain, is thinking about what he is going to do at the board meeting tomorrow.

I try not to be romantic. I love being emotional, I love the emotions. I really think that's all we've got left that's going to fool and surprise us, and I love that.

Altaf Al-Sabah: My marriage wasn't exactly arranged, but at the same time, in our family, we have to get married within the family. There are certain restrictions. I knew that I had to get married to one of my cousins; I was not allowed to get married to anybody else. It didn't worry me. It has advantages. People know who you are, they take care of you, they respect you.

I look forward to seeing my daughters grow and get married. It will take away a lot of the fears I have for myself, because I will not be alone. I think that is why family life is quite rewarding in old age. You will look through the eyes of your children and forget the fears you have for yourself.

Melissa Sadoff: I prefer men if the women are not educated. I don't mean educated in the sense of university degrees, but educated in life. I have met many wise old women who were not educated at university, but they were utterly, utterly interesting to talk to. They had been through the university of life, they were wise, they were very intelligent – maybe not academic, but intelligent - and I like interesting women. If a woman speaks to me only about washing machines and the price of butter and where the children go to school, I don't enjoy that type of woman at all.

I love a man who, no matter how much he loves to work, knows the seductive side of life and can combine the pleasures of life with work. I also like a man who treats a woman like a woman.

Ghida Salaam: A great-aunt of mine was the first woman in Lebanon and Palestine to take off the veil. She would not have been able to take off the veil had her father not encouraged her, not supported her. He could very easily have disowned her, shut her up. I believe that, in every strong and concerted step that either a man or a woman takes, there has to be tremendous interaction, tremendous co-operation between both sexes.

Khairat Al-Saleh: When an Arab man seeks the company of a woman, in most cases he is seeking it because she is the opposite sex, because she is a woman, and because of the sexual connotations and implications – not because of friendship or comradeship. So I cannot say really that Arab men prefer the company of Arab women. If they seek the company of their equals among women, then their immediate reactions are fear and a sense of threat and the possibility of being overwhelmed.

There isn't really enough love in marriages any more. Human beings are losing the capacity to love – all over the world, everywhere. We are in too much hurry, too much rush; the pressures are so tremendous that we cannot really dwell upon ourselves. If you do not know yourself, how can you know another human being? There is a lack of knowledge, and if there is a lack of knowledge, that will inevitably lead to a lack of love. How can you love somebody you don't know?

I have lived without the love of a man for some years, but that does not mean that I do not need the love of a man. You see, you can live without love, you can exist without love, but you do not live fully. I think human relations are so essential that it is my loss, a tremendous and terrible loss, to live without that love. But sometimes you don't meet the right person. Maybe some women, the so-called feminists, are content to live without the love of a man, but I have never really considered things like that. I believe in love, in human relations, I believe in the meeting of men and women, and I regard love as really sacred, essentially holy.

Bushra Salha: Arab men living in England tend to stick together at parties, which didn't happen in Lebanon. It might have happened occasionally, but here it happens systematically. I don't know if it is the Western influence.

I feel more at ease with men, but having said that, there is something about a very close relationship with a woman that you cannot describe, that you cannot get – at least, until now I haven't got it – with a man.

Naomi E. Sargant: Unless a man is terribly ugly, looks are not a consideration. I mean, one is very rarely going to be off with a god-like film star; that's not real life, and it wasn't when one was young any more than when one is older. So, within the limits of what one recognizes as a reasonable physiology, it is much more their mind and their sense of humour and something about their eyes that get me into bed. You are going to have to be prepared to intellectually fuck them. It's not worth it otherwise. And if you are going to regret the next morning that you've gone to bed with them, then there really isn't any point, I don't think.

Dame Cicely Saunders: I've only really been in love with three people in my life, and they were all Poles. They have something in the way of sensitivity and loss. Poles know a lot about loss. That probably says something about me, needing to be needed and so on, but my husband isn't somebody whose loss stands out with him. He's now frail and old, and he's got major medical problems which are quite a burden for him and for me to try and help him carry. But that's how he is.

There are two different problems in failed marriages. I think that people who divorce after a year or two are people who go into it without adequate preparation and thought. The people who split up after thirty years, like my parents did, are people who were not suited in the first place, who worked terribly hard for years to try and make it, and finally didn't have the energy to go on any longer. I think we get a terrible lot of temptation pushed at us all the time to be the acquisitive society, and acquisition doesn't pay off in the end. Giving does much better.

It is part of the macho image and so on for a man to be a success sexually, to have plenty of conquests. A woman is much more concerned, at least in my environment, to have one good relationship, and that's it. We see the end of some bad marriages, but we see the end of many more good marriages here, and we see death parting people after forty or fifty years together. Working in our situation gives you a very good view of human nature and its capacity to bring good out of things. It really does. If you want to know about marriage, you should look at the end of it, not at the beginning. You see that marriage is a good thing, faithfulness a good thing. It pays off.

Sylvia Scafardi: In 1929, I met Ronald Kidd whom I lived with till his death in 1942. The first reaction to each other, in my case and his case, too, was physical. Of course, I wouldn't have been attracted to the man if there hadn't been the complete rapport from the point of view of what he cared about, what mattered to him, what interested him. But I could see the seriousness and vitality of the man, and obviously these are fundamentally physical, because men are fundamentally physical, in their physique, in their attitude.

When I met Ronald, what I liked straight away was his strong neck, and I loved the way his ears lifted a little when he smiled. But what attracts you in the man is the man wanting you and you wanting him, and the chemistry of the thing. You can't explain it, it's there or it isn't. It's just a feeling in the air. Of course, sometimes that feeling can be purely physical, and if it's not backed up by something congenial or something in the temperament, then I think you squash it or he squashes it and that's that.

When I was green and a virgin and on the stage, I met Wilfrid Lawson. He was powerful, and he expected me to fall for him. He had a little

934

gash in his face, and he was a real toughie – Albert Finney type. It was an absolutely rubbishy show, and I used to dance on in a chiffon nightie edged with swansdown and he, of all people, had to play the juvenile part. Of course, he was much too old, much too meaty and powerful an actor, but his first remark to me in the wings was, are my trousers too tight? Of course, I was absolutely innocent and looked at them, and I thought, well, they bloody are. At the end of the show, we were supposed to go to bed together. It was absolute rubbish. Then he and his wife moved into digs where I was. I didn't know he drank, he never smelt of drink, but when he used to come in from the pub, he would be the rajah, his attitude rather was that we were in the harem. But he was a delightful man, and he never ever swore in front of me, and he obviously expected me to fall for him, but I didn't. His wife was a dear who liked me and knew she could trust me. One woman knows about another. I was years, years younger. She was the fair type, the little cheeks already wrinkled, and she dyed her hair, of course. Girlie, he used to call her, but she was already fading. I would not have dreamed of letting Girlie down, nor would I have dreamed of letting myself down. So that was my experience of power, and although I was really at the stage where I was dying to have a man, I would never ever have dreamed of doing it.

I think marriages would have broken up just as much in Victorian times if it had been possible, if society had accepted that either partner could rat on it so simply and easily. Men and women clashed and women put up with it or men visited the prostitute and so on. I think marriages have been as torn, unhappy and difficult as they are today, but today they can be broken up; you tear it all up and start again. It's just the opportunity. I think it's crackers to go into a marriage in a completely unthinking way, hoping for the best. I don't think that's a way to start a marriage, because there's no sense in it. It's just going to make a lot of unpleasantness and trouble. But I think it's a good thing that, if people are so daft, they shouldn't be tied together. Once the situation is hopeless, it's better to separate, and today it doesn't seem to matter much, but I think the attitude is perhaps not very happy to start with.

Alexandra Schlesinger: Our society is built on Hollywood: the sort of happy-ending principle where you come in pursuit of happiness and marry the person you love. So you start out with unrealistic motives. Then it is self-perpetuating.

I don't think either men or women are faithful in twentieth-century cosmopolitan marriages. I mean, the statistics are that something like

70 per cent of both men and women, if they are married, have an affair. An element of trust is terribly important. But if someone goes off and has an affair, I don't think people get terribly upset by that.

Anne Seagrim: It was much easier just to have a light-hearted relationship with a Frenchman than with an Englishman. The Englishman is either scared off, or was by me, or much too intense, too rapid. There was no halfway of doing it. That's not to say that I didn't have affairs of the heart, lots of them, and I was sort of unofficially engaged; but then the war came and my young man went away, and when he came back we were still very fond of each other but we had grown apart.

After the war, I met C. P. Snow, and through unfortunate circumstances we didn't get married and bitterly regretted it ever after. I never looked at anyone else. Thirty-four years I knew him. I couldn't say I was totally content, no, of course not, absolutely not. But there was no question of anyone else.

I was made terribly sad by being secretary to the Windsors. It was the saddest period of my life; they were so isolated. All this glamour and glitter weren't any compensation. It was a very exciting job to have done, but I couldn't possibly have lasted longer because it was so terribly depressing. One was isolated oneself. But I thought more for their isolation, I was borne down by the sadness of their situation. They had no purpose, no place in life. People were criticizing them for doing nothing, but they weren't allowed to do anything. Everything they did was criticized; either they were being childish and frivolous or they were trying to curry favour with the authorities and trying to get back into good public opinion. Tragic, absolutely tragic. He had such a tremendous aura as a person. With the duchess, one felt much more on an equal footing. But she didn't have that aura. I liked her very much indeed, and admired her guts, I really did. She had tremendous courage. And she was very fair, extremely fair.

Jenny Seagrove: I'm not very comfortable in groups of men, and I'm very choosy about the men I talk to intimately, or have a deep relationship with, whether it's platonic or sexual.

I've been with a man for five and a half years; I lived with him for three years and then we got married. He's a man who developed my thoughts and looked after me. I physically earned the money, but he's almost a kind of mentor. In fact, he's taken over my thoughts and it's got to the stage where I now have rejected that and my marriage is actually at an end. I've said now wait a minute, when I'm away from you I'm actually a full human being who can speak for herself and make decisions for herself, but when I'm with you, you think for me, you talk for me, you decide everything for me, and I'm not having that any more. So while I've been slowly growing in confidence, in one way, my confidence has also been decreasing – until I made this decision that I wanted to leave this man, in order to find myself. It's a strange thing. I'm twenty-nine and I've talked to a lot of girlfriends who have had a relationship or been married to an older man, who's done exactly that, who has taken over their identity, and at the age of around twenty-nine, and this is absolutely true, they've suddenly realized they've grown up and have to leave that person, have to make decisions for themselves. They suddenly find a confidence and a need to express themselves without being dominated. They've had a father/child relationship, and suddenly the child is grown up, and either the relationship has to change or has to end. Mine was a very complicated relationship because I was the more successful in the world's terms; my husband needed some kind of status in our family terms, and it grew from there. He has an extraordinary perception of the world and life; he's a very talented person. But he developed in me a fear that I couldn't actually work as an actress or as a human being without consulting him. He became the driving force in our private life.

It became too claustrophobic and too painful really. I had to get out. I understand that he needed a status, needed some kind of fulfilment. It's just that he seemed to be living his life through me, and I found that ultimately it wasn't healthy for either of us.

For a man to have an affair in marriage is much less dangerous than a woman having an affair, because if a woman has an affair with someone, there is a giving. To sleep with someone is to give them something, it's like being discovered, like being exposed, being opened up, you feel so vulnerable.

I always fall for older men. For maturity. Young men bore me to death. They all seem to be going through this need to prove themselves.

Emma Sergeant: I'm fairly allergic to the idea of marriage right now. I would love to have children eventually, but as late as possible. I'd love to have a husband and a house, but the trouble with painting is it takes so much time. Every winter I have to go off and do a four-month expedition so I can really put in a solid block of work, because back in

London one is trying just to organize things, and where I live becomes an office rather than a studio. So I have to live a very selfish life – a painter has to. It's not a nine-to-five job, and your mind has to be clear, without chains, you have to be able to float away from the domestic life and to have time to think up ideas. Whereas, if you're married, it's not like that; it's the husband's life you have to worry about, fitting in with other people. Picasso never had to worry about fitting in with anybody.

We all get territorial if we have some man around us and see a gorgeous girl walking in, but in the end, the older you get, the more you realize personality is important. I'm sure men love looking at pretty girls, and there's nothing better for a party than hundreds of pretty girls, but in the end it's personality that keeps somebody by you. And you find the more strong, independent and determined you are to do what you want to do, the more attractive it is to other people.

Delphine Seyrig: My experience is that there are a lot of things I can share with women that I cannot share with men. Men, in my experience, cannot share a great many things with other men, except in the Church, in the army and in sports. Otherwise, I find men are very lonely, and very isolated from each other.

How can one believe in marriage? I don't believe in much. I don't know what marriage is any more. It made sense as a sort of law in the past for women to be able to have a roof over their heads and be supposedly protected but actually they were greatly imprisoned.

Clare Short: There is a part of me still looking for that wonderful, strong, brilliant, kind, perfect man who will make me happy. Instinctively in a way, even though I'm old enough to know they don't exist.

I got married when I was very young – I don't know why, looking back – and went through a relationship that was pretty painful, and in some ways we grew up together though in other ways it was very unsatisfactory. That lasted five or seven years, but by the time I came out at the other end I'd hit all the questions of what it meant to be a woman and to wish to be a person in your own right. And it's full of conflicts.

I like people who are very irreverent. It's because my life is so political. I couldn't fancy someone who had views and values totally different from mine. And then I like to be fancied. I think that's the way that female sexuality is constructed. One of the things which turn me on, is if you think someone really fancies you. I don't think I've been seduced by power. My experience of getting anywhere near to power, or so-called power, is of it being unimpressive and a charade, and discovering that the myths we all have about these powerful people who run everything are laughable, and they are all just ordinary people.

There were all sorts of people who treated each other extremely badly or didn't like each other much who remained married for ever. And then, of course, if you remain with someone for ever, you get through the bad patches and you get fond of each other, in your sixties and seventies or whatever. The reason it's changed is that the options are different. Contraception is there, the economic possibilities for women are there, and so the marriages have to survive in their own right; and marriage is hard. I don't think there is any such thing as a happy marriage. Any marriage has lots of clashes, tensions and hurt in it. As it becomes an economic option and socially acceptable for marriages to end, more will do so. Probably there's a learning process in it, and people who have married once or twice, as I have, start to understand that it is no solution to seek more and more new marriages. Whatever marriage you have, it's going to hit those problems.

Alexandra Shulman: I love men's forearms. I think it's a very chemical thing, my actual attraction to a man.

Rosemary Anne Sisson: One is always just a tiny bit on show to men, and that is part of the pleasure. That's probably why I enjoy the company of men, that there is a certain feminine standard which I ask of myself when I'm with men. I'm sure this is why there's this little extra pleasure both for me and for them.

I must have a dozen at least, if not two dozen men friends, who are either fellow-writers or actors. A good example is Edward Woodward, whom I've known since he was in my first play. He's one of the most attractive and sexily attractive men I've ever known, and I found it a great mercy I never fell in love with him. I can't think why I didn't except that he was married and so something in my mind forbade it. So I love him dearly, but he's like a brother to me, like a dear, dear brother.

I didn't meet the man I loved enough to marry. If I had, I would not have written until the children were grown up. So I have absolutely no sympathy with people who marry and have children and then grumble that they're not their own person any more. When you marry and have

939

children, that's a marvellous, wonderful thing, and I've never had it, but I've had great compensations. I didn't meet any eligible men because of the war breaking out. All the boys I knew and who might well have been the ones I would marry, went off to war. Some were killed – at least three of our close friends were killed – and two lost legs. And after the war, then, in a way, it was beginning to be too late; I was very choosy by then. I was still marriageable, but I wasn't prepared to marry just for the sake of marrying. I had about five proposals, and one I came quite close to – he was going to be a vicar, a minister, and absolutely delightful when he was courting me, writing lovely letters every day. Then, unfortunately, he sent me one of his sermons, and it was dreadful. I thought, he's not as clever as I am, and if I'm going to marry a man, he's got to be cleverer, stronger, wiser, better than I am. I couldn't bear to be married to a fool.

I like men who are strong and kind, but also very intelligent, and if I can get that combination, I do find that quite irresistible. I really don't think I am at all seduced by power, because I've known some cowboys who didn't have nine dollars in their pockets and who were strong and kind and funny, and I found them very very attractive indeed. The man I don't like is the little man who tries to assert his strength. That was another proposal I turned down, and I said, no, I couldn't marry you, you're not as strong as I am. And he took hold of me and said, yes, I am, I'm just as strong as you are; and I kicked him on the shins and said, if you don't let me go I'll scream. This was in the middle of Knightsbridge. I kicked him on the shins and screamed at the top of my voice and he let me go very quickly.

People are really, truly, dreadfully self-indulgent. They've been brought up to think there is a cure for everything, and they don't believe in death. I think it's most extraordinary. As soon as a marriage gets difficult, they think, oh, I don't like this, this is getting difficult. Whereas I think once you marry, you marry until death do you part. All marriages go through bad stages, and you have to thole it, as my parents used to say. Thole it. My parents lived to a Golden Wedding through obviously very difficult times, and times when they almost hated each other. But they were married and loved each other, too; and to see that, to reach that, is what marriage is all about.

Ginette Spanier: Nobody takes any trouble about marriage. They will spend hours working out a problem in their business, but if something goes wrong with their marriage, it's off and out. They don't give it very much thought, *c'est fini*. That I have always found very strange.

940

Obviously marriage is very difficult. But that people are willing to work at their work and not at their marriage seems very strange to me.

My husband was French. He was a brilliant doctor, he was very tall and good-looking, but everywhere we went, people are such beasts, they would say to him, doesn't it make you feel small, being M. Spanier? My real name is Jenny Sideman. Spanier was my maiden name that I kept for working. I could have killed them. He promised me he didn't suffer from it at all. Maybe he did a little bit. That used to happen constantly, and it really made me cross, but I can't say it brought any dissension in our marriage. Of course, we were the opposite of each other. I have a terrible vitality and he was very calm, as doctors are.

I'm sure power is an aphrodisiac. I've seen it all around me, with French girls especially – not Americans, but French girls. If somebody says, I'll send a limousine, the word limousine is as if they had something falling from heaven. I knew Marlene Dietrich terribly well. If she wanted to impress somebody, she hired a limousine. The trappings of power are fascinating.

Koo Stark: I get attracted to people I find mentally stimulating. If somebody's excited and interested in something, their passion about their own subject will make me attracted to them or what they're interested in. I get swept up easily by other people's excitement. Recently Norman Parkinson was a great influence on my life in terms of changing my career and photography and giving me a lot of courage to try something new. And the writer Graham Greene – I met him recently – he's suddenly become very influential in my life. I met him this summer in Antibes. I had an idea I wanted to talk to him about, and I'd worked with him before as an actress. So we met up again for lunch, and I was discussing my idea and he turned round and said to me, I think you ought to write. I said, no, no, I couldn't possibly write. And he said, well, I'm telling you you can, and I'll tell you how to go about it, and if you need any help, you can come to me. And it was exactly the same sort of encouragement I got from Norman Parkinson when I said I couldn't possibly take any pictures. People like that are very secure in themselves, and they're very generous with others.

Gloria Steinem: Some of the roughest, toughest, most masculine men are homosexual. The paradigm of a love and sex relationship is the passive, dominant paradigm, it is a female/male paradigm. So until fairly recently, you got both lesbians and homosexual men, in couples,

941

playing roles. One would have to be the female, the other one would have to be the male, which was obviously crazy on the face of it since it just wasn't biologically possible. More recently, you get lesbian women and gay men having more equal relationships because the paradigm of what a sex or love relationship is is beginning to change. I would not venture to say what causes homosexuality. I just think homosexuality is as natural as heterosexuality. We are all probably bisexual, it's just a question of training, opportunity and so on. But when you see men who behave in a very feminine way, studies show that frequently their childhood has been one in which men, their father or whoever, were very cruel. So, as children, they said to themselves, if this is what it means to be a man, I am not going to be a man, it's too painful. I am not going to go out and shoot small animals and beat people up because I don't want to do that. So the only way out of doing that was to behave like a woman, because that was the only other model of behaviour.

There was a wonderful study of sexuality done in, I think, Seattle, and whereas most sexuality studies are done at a particular point in time, this one was done over a four-year period and included a massive sample. What they often discovered was that, out of a heterosexual married couple, perfectly happy in year one, and maybe even homophobic besides, one of them was living in a gay relationship in year three; and conversely, out of a gay male couple in year two who said they would never be heterosexual, one of them was married in year four. So sexuality really seems to be a continuum, not a box. In different times, different circumstances, we have different people. People love each other for a whole panoply of reasons. Once I was giving a lecture, and a woman in the audience got up and said this wonderful thing that really made sense. She said, look, human beings are the only animals who seem to experience sexual pleasure, and orgasm, and sexual intensity, as much when they can't conceive as when they can. All the other animals seem to have periods of oestrum, of heat, when they are focused on sex. Human beings uniquely don't. So, for human beings, sexuality is a mark of our differentness from the other animals, like our cerebral cortex, our ability to reason. Sexuality for human beings is uniquely and naturally not just a way we procreate, but also a way we communicate, also the way we reach out to each other and express love and caring. So I think it's wrong to label people gay or whatever. We have to use these labels for the moment and to make them honourable, if you know what I mean. As long as they are dishonourable, they can be used to stigmatize, but the truth of the matter is probably that people are sexual, period. And under some circumstances, they may love one of their own gender, and under others, someone of the opposite gender.

I used to be seduced by power because I thought the only way I could ever have power was through men. But I don't think that any more. I discovered that two things fell away as I began to do work I cared about myself. One was that I didn't have to make men fall in love with me any more, which is the way women show power. Men go to bed with women and that's a sign of power; they've got her, they go to bed. Obviously that doesn't work for a woman because she's the one, theoretically, being conquered. So women get men to fall in love with them. That's where we get our feeling of power. And secondly, there's shopping, which is one of the few places women have power, because they are consumers. In the department store, people are nice to you because you are spending money. But I no longer need to get men to fall in love with me, and I no longer need to go shopping. I don't get a kick out of either any more.

Lady Arabella Stuart: Englishmen are so different from other men, and I feel that must be more to do with their schooling and upbringing and the attitudes that have been instilled into them than with biological make-up. Why should being English in itself make any difference? I find them very odd, Englishmen. I don't really get on with them very well, never have done. They don't respond to me and I don't respond to them. I've got remarkably few and, even in the past, I've had remarkably few very close men friends who are English. Most of my friends have been foreign, or Jewish, or American, but not English, except maybe for Mark, who is very untypical. I've really come to the conclusion that they don't like women much at all.

It's very un-English to stay on good terms with a woman you've once had a romance with. They just don't want to be bothered, they just love saying how boring somebody's got, or how they've lost their looks, and I used to feel really depressed. I used to feel, at one time, that if you met an Englishman you knew, and he even quite liked you or found you quite attractive, if he was on the other side of the road, he'd find it too much trouble to cross. I have long periods of being quite lonely and depressed, and once I went to stay for the weekend with my sister who was living in Brussels. But the minute I got over the Channel, things changed. People looked at one with interest, and one just felt a completely different attitude. They were curious about one, wondering why one is on one's own, interested in one, in a very nice, encouraging way, which in England one doesn't get. I find very little response from Englishmen – I don't know why.

After I was married, for about ten years I literally never had lunch with

943

a man, or talked to a man alone for any length of time. As soon as one was happily married anyway, people completely lost interest. So if one's confidence had always been reinforced by having people fond of one or attracted, to have that suddenly cut off is very difficult because one is left totally dependent on this one man, which is a very difficult situation really. I think perhaps I was rather extreme in my experience, but it must happen to other Englishwomen, too.

There are things I like very much about men, a sort of ideal man; I like them when they're very solid, very un-neurotic, very masculine. Most Englishmen I know tend to be very neurotic, and that's boring for women. If you're depressed, you don't dare tell them because, goodness, they might get even more depressed. I find women are always trying to protect them and make life easier for them and support them, whereas I like men to be like a rock. You could get angry with them, and you don't worry that they're going to be wounded or hurt or be too vicious back. That's what I think men should be like: less concerned with feelings probably than women, because that gets to be a bit of a bore in the end, too emotional. But there aren't many Englishmen who are like that.

Whether you find somebody sexually attractive or not is not anything to do with looks, it's something deeper. I remember just kissing somebody hello or goodbye because he worked in a friend's shop, and it was somebody I'd never even thought of as to whether I would find him attractive – he wasn't attractive-looking, he was just a friend of a friend. But I got this curious sort of shock on a casual goodbye kiss, and realized that sometimes there's a very strong magnetic attraction that you're only aware of at very close quarters, and it's nothing to do with anything visual. It's just a sort of attraction that's very strong. It's not something you can tell across a room. It's physical magnetism, a draw between two people. It's more to do with touch than looks.

Friendship between a man and a woman is rather rare, and therefore very precious, but there are so many obstacles. If the man is heterosexual, usually he's married to somebody else. It's quite a difficult thing, that, and incredibly nice if it does happen, but it's quite unusual to have a close friendship with a heterosexual man that isn't a love affair. So on the whole, friendship with women tends to be easier and more straightforward.

I would never willingly threaten any other woman, and, when I've been threatened, as I have frequently, I don't become tough, I just want to back away. I really can't bear that sort of confrontation, so I just give

944

up, I suppose, in rather a defeatist way. I really don't want to compete. I'm too proud, really, I think.

Our parents were much more stoical, and on the whole they put up with things. I remember my mother telling me that she once said to my father that she wasn't at all happy, and my father said, why should you be happy, how many people are happy, for goodness' sake? So this feeling that we all have now, that one deserves a degree of happiness and one is justified in ending a marriage for such a reason, is really quite new. People don't put up with unsatisfactory relationships any more, which on the whole is a good thing, but it's also rather sad in a way, because quite often things that seemed unsatisfactory in one period, if you could just manage to live through them, could be put behind you.

Imogen Stubbs: When I was at school, I used to think I could never go out with someone who didn't wear drainpipe jeans, and I meant it, I really did. I thought, God, how could anyone go out with someone who wore flares, or wore glasses, or had a beard. It's one of those teenage things. You imagine you would only go out with someone who looks like Paul Newman. Now I distrust good looks and I distrust the kind of ego that goes with very good looks.

If I married someone, I'd like to think that I wouldn't have clandestine affairs. If I felt that way, and didn't love the person any more, and things were going wrong, I would be very honest about it. Whereas the number of husbands I know who have affairs and things – I find it so disheartening and sad that so many men, although they still love their wives, need that kind of diversion. Maybe it's just with society and conditioning, women have never been able to have that same freedom; it's sort of acceptable for men to have affairs while it's still very taboo for women to cheat on their husbands. Women want to be loyal to their husbands, because if you have children you know what you're putting at risk by having an affair; you know the whole security, your whole set-up is going to tumble if you lose the trust that keeps the family together. Because you're with the children and you're in your home the whole time, and in conventional nuclear families, the wife is totally aware of what it means for a husband and wife to split up.

I've never been in a situation where someone has been unfaithful to me with my knowledge. I'm sure they might well have. I'm desperately jealous. I'd like to think I could forgive, but there's nothing more awful than broken trust, nothing. I think I'm ruthless, I don't think I could forgive someone, however much I loved them. I would be so disappointed in them – more than just disappointed, I'd probably be so angry. I think I would have enormous guilt if I betrayed someone. I love someone very much at the moment, and when you're in that situation, you can't imagine infidelity or not loving each other or wanting to go with other people, so it's hard even to talk about it.

I believe that the person you marry or fall in love with is someone who takes over from your mother, the sort of person who cares about your small triumphs in the way someone who's followed you from the moment you're born does. I think the person you love must be the person who understands what makes you happy and what makes you sad. It must be someone able to share sensibilities, someone who doesn't laugh at you when you become honest about the things that really move you. What's important in life is to find the right person, to be really in love with someone, to find someone who really understands things and shares them with you and lives your small life with you instead of wanting to share your big life with everyone.

Andrea von Stumm: From kindergarten onwards, I was brought up in schools where there were boys and girls, and it was probably a very good thing because I have a great facility for normal friendship with a man. I find it very irritating today when people give the impression that, when a woman and man talk, you have two armies facing each other and preparing for some battle.

Women are, generally speaking, perhaps less direct, less honest; they are more like cats and men are more like dogs. Women are very feline and there is this competitiveness that I don't think men feel so much. Women can be together, and the moment a man walks into the room there is immediately some kind of distraction: who's going to please this man? It's a game, perhaps it's instinct.

A man should be a fatherly figure, someone who says sometimes no, who slaps you when necessary, but one who trusts you and whose love is unconditional. If something really happens, he fights for you first and asks questions afterwards. However, I wouldn't like a man to dominate me, as in the Arab countries, where you are really at the mercy of men and have absolutely no margin of freedom. That is not what I understand by being dominated. I want to look up to someone. I very much agree with the definition of love which encompasses admiration.

Men can be intelligent, funny and very interesting, but they must have some goodness of the heart; without it, I don't feel attracted. I don't want to see a man a second time if I feel he is cold or a bastard, however attractive he might be. But certainly, physically speaking, the appearance, and then the hands, the voice, the attitude – from the first three minutes you can almost say this is someone I might have an affair with. I'm also seduced by power, because power means personality. I'm seduced by strong personality. I'm seduced by the idea, also, in every respect, of being dominated. I'm one of these women who likes to be dominated – I'm talking about more subtle ways of domination.

Janet Suzman: If one is examining the minutiae, the details of life, you have to explain yourself, or explain your motives to a man. You keep on saying, you see, what I feel is – whereas you don't have to do that with a woman. They seem to understand in any case.

Conny Templeman: I would probably stick to my mother's advice: don't get married. I'm not against marriage. I think if I have children and it poses a problem, I'll get married. I'm not against marriage and I'm not for it. I'm just now learning to drive, and I've just become aware of the difficulties and advantages, so maybe marriage will loom its head like the driving licence. I have a friend who married because the insurance on their bicycles was cheaper if they were married.

Lisa St Aubin de Terán: The most common reason for marriage failure is that people want too much out of the relationship without really putting very much in. Most people are not really prepared to give a lot of themselves, but they want to get a lot. One can marry and marry and marry and marry, but, over and over again, marriages will fail, I think. It is not just marriage, it is not an isolated factor that marriages are breaking down: I think the whole social system, at least in England and North America, is breaking down quite seriously, and the fact that marriages don't last is just one factor of a much more complex social disintegration. An enormous number of traditional values have been destroyed and taken away and not been replaced by enough other values, so there is a general sense of not only not knowing what is expected or wanted of one, but not having a sense of purpose, not having a sense of belonging and doing something worthwhile. I notice this very much with my own children: from very early on there is a great confusion about what their role is and what they're meant to be doing, what is expected of them, what they are heading towards. They're heading towards a kind of shipwreck, really, where they drift on their own, I feel. People talk a lot about freedom, and individual freedom,

947

without thinking very much about what freedom really means and whose freedom we are talking about. I think one is never free, no mother is ever free. Mothers are less free than others, but nobody is really free or can be free of everybody and everything. Yet one is brought up, from an early age, to believe one can be. So there is conflict when one realizes it is just not working out.

Fiona Thyssen: It is more difficult to have a male friend. Unfortunately, you cannot exclude the sexual element in a relationship. I remember reading, some years ago, that a man was never interested in a woman intellectually unless he was also interested in her as a woman. I find the same thing, and it took me a long time to admit it: if I am interested in a man intellectually, he also has to be an appealing man, he has to be nice, you have to want to see him and talk to him. It certainly plays a role.

There have always been many homosexuals. It's been a famous part of history as far back as we know. One of the theories why certain groups of early *Homo sapiens* disappeared was because they were all homosexuals and didn't breed. They didn't know about breeding, didn't know which place to put it in to have a child, and didn't really know the difference between males and females; which seems hard to believe, because the animal instinct is very well organized. But I find it totally normal that there should be large groups of homosexuals. It has never disturbed or upset me. But there are now probably more than there were thirty or forty years ago. Thirty years ago, if you were borderline, there was a lot of social pressure not to be homosexual. So you suppressed it very easily. Today, if you are borderline and have the opportunity to try both, you probably would try both because it's acceptable. I was taught that you are bisexual until a certain age, then you make a choice; whether it's subjective, biological or psychological, you make a choice. I would have thought that, unless you have suppressed one part of yourself very severely all your life, you would be very unlikely to switch at thirty or forty or fifty, but I am sure there are people who do. There is no universal norm. There must be people who don't fit into any categories who do suddenly decide at sixty that they would rather be a lesbian or whatever. My guess is that most people know much earlier on.

I have had some of the most unattractive boyfriends anyone could imagine. It may be a question of who is attracted to me, because I've never been able to figure out a pattern; they haven't been tall, short, fat, old, young, rich, poor, anything. The only thing they have all had in common is that they hunted me, hunted me. I hate to think of it, but I have a terrible suspicion that I have been attracted to the people who have been attracted to me. Otherwise there would be some logical pattern. There isn't.

I felt, ultimately, only really comfortable in the presence of my husband. I had a tremendous need for my husband, because I was very insecure underneath this very smooth façade. I didn't look to other people for security – I only looked to my husband. I put my husband on a pedestal and chose to play a subservient role. I didn't find it abnormal. I had no wish or desire or need to establish myself as an individual.

In the last few years, having come to London after rather an enclosed life in Switzerland, I've been staggered to see these very predatory women everywhere in London. That absolutely freaked me. First of all, I find it very unfeminine. But, of course, in a society where there are so many gay men, there are very few normal heterosexual males around unless you are prepared to be predatory, so you see they have already adjusted to a changing social environment. But I don't think it is part of their nature to be like that. I still think that the woman must surely feel more desirable if she is sitting there, looking absolutely beautiful, and the hunter comes up and hunts her and seduces. This is an affirmation of her desirability. At the moment, she is going out and doing the hunting. Her whole role is so altered, she has no way of knowing how desirable she is. There's a whole breed of very predatory ladies around town who are not very much admired or liked by anybody, males or females.

My basic very naïve theory is that the best hunter brings home the meat.

Claire Tomalin: I grew up passionately preferring the company of men. My father was away, I had no brother, both my grandfathers died before I was born. I had a vision of men as being this amazing thing – they would arrive and somehow make everything all right – and I romanticized them. I grew up during the war, so everyone's father was away. I used to go to school at that time, and I can remember the American soldiers saying to me, have you got a big sister? I thought that these were amazingly glamorous creatures, and I suppose I've rather retained romantic feelings about men. I regret that I haven't been better at friendships with women. I think I've got better as I've got older, and I have three beloved daughters.

I realized, when I was first widowed, that if you only see men, other women are suspicious of you and women actually control social life very much. So it's rather a mistake not to get on with them. But that's rather cynical. I don't mean to be.

As you get older, your friendships with men probably become desexualized so that, perhaps, they all become much more the same. When you're in your twenties, thirties, forties, when you meet a man, there's always perhaps a slight feeling something might happen between us, a possibility of some adventure here. When you're in your fifties, or when you're really settled down, that changes. You can't imagine it's going to change, just as it's quite hard to imagine back to what it was like when you really did feel all that sense of possible adventure. It's certainly changed for me. It's wonderfully relaxing, because you can then allow really warm friendships with both men and women on rather the same basis.

There are fashions in sexual behaviour as in all other sorts of behaviour. I think feminism moved quietly in the direction of lesbianism because a lot of women, young women, were really exhausted by the pressures of the demands of conventional sexual behaviour. I feel I've had a rather happy and fortunate life, being absolutely conventional, really, but I think a lot of young women thought they wanted a rest. I think a lot of them aren't wildly lesbian, they just want a bit of peace, they want to have quiet gentle friendships and don't want to be forced into sexual competition or having to do things for men that they don't have to, economically, any more. They've been released from the feeling my mother's generation had, which was that the one thing you had to do was get a husband and hold on to him.

I haven't been in love with very many men in my life, but they have probably all been intellectuals, and I have to say that I have fallen in love with men, on the whole, because they've fallen in love with me. I've been quite passive and I have succumbed. Somebody sees you, and sees you in a wonderful way, in a sort of magic light, and then you begin to feel wonderful and you think, why is this? And then you realize this great beam is coming towards you from somebody, and you are somehow transformed by it, and then you respond to it. I don't think I have ever gone out and pursued a man.

I don't want any protection. I very strongly feel and know – I'm somebody who tends to look ahead – that the likelihood is one is going to end one's life alone and having to take responsibility. Men die younger than women somehow. Their hearts aren't so good, they're not so resistant, they're not so strong. But I've always thought, at the back of my mind, that I will have to fight my own battles, and I have fought my own battles for such a long time. My husband was a sweet, lovely, polite and charming man, but he was always running off, and I was often alone bringing up the children, and then he was killed. Now, although I live with Michael, this is my house and we're not married. I do love him very much, and I can't say I don't depend on him; I do depend on his love, and if he dies, that feeling of that other necessary person goes and nothing will replace him, so I feel extremely tenderly towards him. On the other hand, I don't think I require his protection; I don't think he requires mine either.

Lili Townsend: In the early part of my life, most of my friends were men. They were my buddies. I like scuba diving and riding and climbing, and those kind of high-risk macho sports. That is something across the sexes, where people want to risk themselves physically, to be on the edge of their strength and their courage, in order to push through their limits of fear. So I think I sought men's company for that particular edge. I lived for three years on a small boat with a man, and it was really two against the world in the sense we were equal partners in surviving the oceans. He was the leader and I was the first mate, and I learned to be a very good first mate and how to take orders, because it was a question of survival. I had never taken orders at an instant level like that, and it was hard for me to adjust to because I'm a rather headstrong person, but when I saw the safety of the boat, of our lives, depended essentially on the skipper's reactions, I was able, for the first time, to take with comfort second place and to understand that the first mate has a whole set of duties that are equally important to the survival of the whole. After that sea experience, and when I began studying in the healing arts, I became much more aware of the depth of my friendships with women, and the depth of those friendships helped me see the depth of myself. I think we put before us the mirrors we need, we put those people right in front of us who express what we need to get through, which is why we often attract opposites in our relationships.

The reason for the breakdown in relationships is that what women want is intimacy and what men are afraid to give is that part of themselves which involves going into an area where there are enormous doubts and questions. Men have not explored the inner nature of their psyche, and it's most dangerous and frightening for them to be somewhere where they really don't have all the answers. They're much better off sticking with their traditional positions rather than taking a chance in a relationship with a woman where they can explore their feminine side. So relationships that seem to be evolving now have to do with both sides

951

being able to take risks in the area of expressing the truth of their hearts to each other. Expressing real trust.

My first husband was a very strong person by whom I was quite dominated. My second husband was quite the opposite. A classic psychological reaction: I married someone who was not strong, and though I didn't realize it in the beginning, it was to my detriment, because I was the person ultimately who made the decisions and also who created the wealth and had all the ideas. I became the mother in a sense, because the man I married was an alcoholic, which I didn't see in the beginning either. I realize now, with hindsight, that my father was an alcoholic. In the most gentlemanly and delightful way, he was sloshed a great deal of the time. So I never had a meaningful relationship with the male model, the archetype. My second husband was very much in that frame: a man who was charming and delightful, and yet he was putting a veil down between him and the world, and I became partners with him in the creation of an illusion. In the end, being married to someone like that totally destroyed my life. The strength I had built up on the physical level, in the material sense and certainly emotionally, all evaporated because I was married to a weak man. I had to leave the relationship with the last of the strength I had. And I had to find the strength in myself through it. I think I needed to experience those depths before I could understand the lessons.

There is no way to compare and quantify my marriages, because they were really both important to me. I was a furious, furious person by the time I got out of my relationship with the strong man. He told me for years that I was a beautiful dumb blonde, and I had to thank him ten years later by saying, you know, if you hadn't told me I was a beautiful dumb blonde all those years, it wouldn't have been necessary for me to go out in the business world and prove I was a genius. If the relationship had been balanced and working, I wouldn't have had to go to those lengths.

A man's spirit is what seduces me, what attracts me, because I've experienced all the other aspects of men. Any kind of relationship without a basis in spirit is not interesting to me at this time. The spiritual aspect makes the sexual part happen. That's the sexiest thing in the world to me.

Unity is the goal, not separation. Certainly the women I have spent time with are quite self-sufficient. Yet we all yearn for the safety of an intimate relationship. Certainly I have that as an ideal, although I have never seen it; I have hardly ever seen a relationship that really works.

Polly Toynbee: I feel more comfortable with women, though I don't think I did when I was a teenager, because it was so tied up with the status thing: if you were seen to be going out with a group of other girls, you were a failure. It was terribly important that you had boys around. It may just be that, being married, the whole status thing falls away anyhow. But naturally, I tend to fall in more easily with women, though it's taken me some time to realize that this was the case, and at Oxford, certainly, I think I had many more close friends who were men than women. I rather despise myself for that, because it was probably much more about status, about some feeling of power: you felt a more powerful person if you had quite a lot of men around you than if you had a lot of women about you. It was more the prevailing teenage adolescent culture than what I really thought. If I count up my best friends today, they are all women, and the people I ring up and talk to most, and the people I feel most relaxed with, are women.

There are quite a lot of men who actually really like to be surrounded by women, but that's because the women aren't going to talk about anything serious at all. They treat them like geishas. I know one prominent politician whose relaxation is to surround himself by women with whom he will absolutely not talk about anything serious. If you sit next to him at dinner, he will never ever discuss an even remotely serious subject. It's all got to be gossip and silliness, that's where he consigns women. On the other hand, if you happen to meet him across a table in a committee, then he will treat you as an equal, and that's different.

I think, on the whole, that very few women are naturally promiscuous, though they might be encouraged into it either by neuroses or by an anxious seeking after some sort of social status when they're very young. Probably most women have a pretty simple and romantic idea about fidelity. And an awful lot of men don't. But, again, to what extent that's the culture, I don't know.

Englishmen are absolutely terrified, petrified of women. It's partly the public school, it must be, because I can't see why they should be so different from men in other countries. But then men in other countries show their fear differently; often they show it in the opposite way, by excessive gallantry instead of that rather curt and frigid way that Englishmen behave. It's all about palaver, about how wonderful, how beautiful you are, all this kissing your hand, opening the door. That's a kind of fear, too. I find this exaggerated courtliness even worse to cope with, very unnerving – because I'm not that used to it. But probably, in most cultures, they express it differently. Men just are very bad at talking to women. It's just so culturally imprinted, probably at their mother's knee, that women aren't in the same category, they are somewhere else, and best of all in the kitchen and dealing with other aspects of their lives, not conversations and companionship. I think that's the hardest thing to get across: that men and women should be equal companions, in marriage or as friends.

The idea of getting married to somebody and not knowing what you're in for, having no idea at all, is horrifying, and I think it's actually an obscenity the way Barbara Cartland describes it entirely in mercenary terms. That's the way you get the man, my dear, she says; a man should go out and have experience of older women. Who these respectable or unrespectable women are, I don't know, but the women shouldn't, the women should be absolutely virginal, because that's the way to get him. She sees it in very mercenary terms, not at all in terms of the individual relationship. She's thought to be romantic. She's the most unromantic creature I've ever come across. I'd be appalled to think of getting married to someone without knowing them that well.

Looking back on the men in my life, I can't see any linking factor whatever. I think they've got to be very interesting. You've got to be able to suffer hours of conversation with them without getting bored. There's nothing worse than a boring man. I think they've got to be reasonably confident people, but only at about the same level as me. I wouldn't want somebody who felt a great deal more confident. Certainly not somebody who felt more insecure.

Kathleen Turner: Up to about six or seven years ago, I would have said automatically I prefer the company of men. It is not so any more. I don't know whether it's because women are taught to mistrust each other and to compete for men's attention against each other. There is definitely some of that in our upbringing. But I've managed to lose a great deal of that, partly, of course, because of the building of my confidence. I am going to get attention now, so I don't have to worry so much about grabbing it or competing for it. And that's probably helped a lot. But I find now that my closest friendships are with women, because there is a great deal, a great deal, that men do not understand.

If you see a woman dressing as a man or seeming to emulate a man, it does not mean they are not having an absolutely fucking wonderful time, that they have lost any of their satisfaction. I'm sure some of them frighten men away. I am sure I do. I frighten the hell out of men half the time. Ask my husband. Because any woman who comes up and says,

954

no, no, no, I'll do it my way, is frightening to men. It's nothing that a man would not say, but it frightens men.

My husband does not wish, thank God, to compete in terms of attention or recognition. It certainly bothers him that, when I give a public appearance, which I do occasionally for charities, he is Mr Turner, although he handles it very, very well. I think his problem is feeling that my work takes so much time, I am away every night instead of at home to have dinner with him. That is difficult for him. It's a real crisis. But it would be impossible for him to say, I don't want you to work. I am who I am, I do my work. But it is difficult for him to find my work essential and not threatening.

In my marriage with my husband – we've spoken about this – we choose to be only for each other, because, of course, in my field there are very attractive men, some of the most attractive in the world. For my own state of mind, I must keep a separation between my work and myself. I'm dying here tonight and every night, I cannot carry this emotion with me outside the theatre. To form a liaison within this would be the bridge for that emotion. So I can't do it, I just can't do it. I don't want to take the character home, to take that emotional involvement home. That's my choice. However, before my commitment to my husband, I didn't feel that I had to be in love to have a sexual partner. I mean, the attraction is undeniable; there are men out there that are just goddam gorgeous and you want to grab them, you want to have a wonderful time with them. But I did not think I was in love with them. This is maybe somewhat unusual. In a way, everyone would like there to be involvement, to have every sexual encounter turn into a beautiful love. It doesn't have to be that way. I don't think the testing-ground of love is the sexual encounter.

I've always been attracted to Jewish men, I don't know why. My only two real boyfriends before my husband were Jewish, and my husband's Jewish. They're smart. Jewish men are encouraged to feel they have an identity their whole lives. They are Jews, they are members of a race, members of a tradition.

I will do anything to keep my marriage working out except give up my work. But, short of that, I think I would do almost anything. I think, actually, that the marriage has added a great deal to my ability to do my work. I feel so much more cherished and secure and confident than I've ever felt. And that's essentially because of the marriage.

955

Jill Tweedie: I feel completely comfortable in the presence of women. All women, no matter how much I dislike them. I think I feel very comfortable with men, but there's more of an edge, of course. You are more aware of something in the air. It is different, and also one is frightened to some extent that they are going to be impossible in some way. Now, impossible can vary in various ways from the time you are twenty to the time you are eighty, but either they are going to say something intolerable and cruel, or they are going to create some scene or other, or there's going to be sex. You know, there's an air of danger. Which has its interest, of course, too.

Before feminism, there was only room for one and a half in marriage. There still isn't room for two grown adult human beings.

At the penalty of frightful things, women have had to be monogamous through the years. Maybe it isn't so good for us. Marriage does not make women as healthy and long-lived and all these things it does for men. They've done quite a lot of surveys on marriage, and they've found that men benefit from marriage, women do not.

Men are still very bad at relationships. A lot of men use their wives as funnels to their outside world, even to their children. They say to the wife the things the wife says to the children. Often it is the mother who interprets the father to the children. She says, your father is like this, your father is like that. He doesn't say it. He loses, or never had, all ability to make and keep friends and human contacts. One of the things, of course, that feminists have seemed to be rather harsh about, but I think can only end up doing men good, is to say, go away and find your own friends and don't come and cry on my shoulder. You have to work on yourself. You can't always come to women and put all your sadness and all your misery, and be buoyed up and sent back into the world feeling good, feeling better and all that. Quite a lot of women are now saying that's too exhausting. You must do the work yourself. And it will be good for men when they do that.

I don't believe men are violent by nature. What I do believe is that there is something very unfortunate about the fact that it is only women who raise children. I believe that if parents shared the raising of children, we would see a real difference in the way the adult male regards and feels for women. When a child is very small, the parents are huge, they become giants. And you are absolutely dependent, and it is very frightening to be dependent like that. And, very often, a boy grows up surrounded by huge women, and they have frightened and humiliated him. I'm not talking now about them being nasty to him, I mean

956

conditioned as being little and having giants around. And he will grow up and will seek, to a lesser or greater extent, his revenge on these giants. If they were man and woman, equally, then he would come to terms with it. But they are not, they are women. Many men grow up and think inside, I'll get my own back on the giant, and she is a woman.

Marie-Claire Valène: Beauty alone can be seductive for me. I'm as capable of considering a man as an object as a man is a woman. I'm very sure about that, and it's a sort of power. I can very easily have a man simply because I find him handsome. For me, there are no problems about that. I'm no more dependent on him than he would be on a woman whom he has simply because he finds her beautiful.

Joan Vass: I happen to know several families where they have three or four sons, and all the boys are homosexuals. America is full of families like this now. Lesbian women are so quiet and restrained, and in England, they have lived quietly for centuries, and in the United States, as well, their communities are very low-key, they don't make waves. But now we have this gay liberation. Homosexual men used to behave very *sotto voce*, but now a lot of them make wild gestures in order to be known and acknowledged.

When you marry, you should believe that you're marrying for good. You should absolutely work at it, and you should not divorce until it's impossible not to. I think you must marry very seriously, and you must marry not because it would be a good first marriage, not because it would be convenient, you marry because you desire it more than anything in the world. Marriage is very serious. I think people divorce too easily. I'm divorced.

Sara Vass: I don't like men who are shorter than me. I don't consider them for me as even a possibility. They might well be totally wonderful, they could be the best lovers, the most generous, wonderful, loving, terrific, sensual, strong-centred person in the world, but I personally find it very difficult to consider someone shorter than I am.

There was this man, a lawyer, who was very bright, very funny, and who was mad about me, absolutely wild about me, and in fact was negotiating for my hand with my family. Very nice, very funny, but I had this feeling he was covered all over his body with hair. I would say to myself, when he comes over, I'll hug him hello and feel under his shirt, and I

957

couldn't bear it. Eventually it looked like there was no out, this would be the night we would sleep together or not. And I drank a lot of cognac, because I sat there after dinner thinking, why? Why was I suddenly having to get myself prepared for this? It was like going into a bullfight. And we got to my home and he took off his shirt, and he was covered with hair. I locked myself in my guest room, and I couldn't tell him, because I thought it would be too insulting and so awful. How could I say, an intelligent woman like me, you have all this hair and it makes me ill, I was terrified you would be, and you are. That was about six or seven years ago. He went to California and is now making deals for movies. But I ran into him about three weeks ago, and he took me aside and he said, I want you to know that you drove me completely crazy. I was wild about you, and I don't really understand what happened. I've been seeing a psychiatrist for seven or eight years, and I have to know what happened that night, what did I do?

Diana Vreeland: Women have such a sense of competition that I was always awed and aroused by them.

Virginia Wade: I'd much rather be with a sensitive man than with a macho man. I don't know whether that's because I've always been surrounded in the tennis world with all these terrific physical specimens, and you just get your fill of them. But I am much more attracted to the artistic type.

Women have got used to accepting that their horizons are not as high as men's. I basically think women are competitive, I think everybody's competitive. But they get afraid to put themselves on the line in certain areas, and so they get competitive in ridiculous things like clothes or really female talk, which just gets very, very boring. If I go to a party, I would rather sit and talk to the men than women, although I've got plenty of very intelligent women friends. But I hate to get into that women-talk thing. It's nonsense when you're just talking about the children and that sort of stuff. I just feel that they missed out on so much else, that that's all they are left to talk about.

I would say the majority of men like to control women. They get nervous if a woman tries to have fairly aggressive or progressive ideas, it makes them very insecure. The male ego is more fragile. If you get rejected as a man, it is much more of a blow to your self-image. I think there is a real lack of communication between the sexes, and this is manifested by the total crop of failures as far as relationships go. Society still expects people to fall in love; you have to fall in love, and then you have to get married and play the role. And I think people are not really capable of doing that.

I don't know now whether I would like to get married. I wouldn't want to put up with playing games, that's for sure. I don't think one actually has to get married any more. You can, but I don't know what it means.

Michaela Walsh: I'm fascinated by the use of power and the ability to empower other people. I don't care about power myself, in terms of directing other people. I don't have any desire to sit on a pinnacle of power where I control others; it doesn't have any fascination for me. I am interested in the empowerment of other people, and the use of money, the use of influence as a way of doing that.

Tracy Ward: I am not sure that marriage should be around any more. I'd be delighted if marriage was abolished. I really don't think it necessary. Although I, for myself, would love to get married, I know I would.

I love women, and my women friends are my greatest friends and will be there for ever and ever, amen, as far as I am concerned. But to go to a movie, have a laugh, I would rather be with a man, funnily enough.

Marina Warner: I don't believe you should need to be married, I don't believe women should aim at marriage, and I don't believe marriage is in any way a solution to anything. But my upbringing was so focused on that, that I never could escape that need. It was a deep emotional need for me, to be married, to have somebody want to marry me and to have the security of that symbolic pledge. So, as I have been married twice, I am attracted to people who want to marry me, which is pathetic for a feminist, absolutely pathetic. It was personal qualities in Johnnie's case. I was attracted by him, he is very good with children, he is terribly nice to my son. So that was very important to me. I had had a number of liaisons before I was married to Johnnie, in which the men were competitive with the child. They wanted more attention, or they didn't want me to put him first, and I'm afraid I believe that the child must come first. Not that the child must be the prince in the castle, but the child is a dependant and I am not. So there is no reason why a man should cut in with his needs over a child, because he can fend for himself, a child cannot. A distressed child in the middle of the night is

959

more important than a man with a hard-on. A lot of men won't take that. A lot of men want you to shut the door. They say it is good for the child. It happens with many many men, it happens within marriage.

I think love is a very unexamined subject. We know very little about love, not sexual love only, but just love. One of the curious effects of this Freudian revolution, which in many ways is a wonderful revolution, has been that we have slightly forgotten what we mean by love, what we want from love, as we examine the Oedipal structures, sexual desires, neurotic attachments. The Greeks had a more sophisticated inquiry into different types of love.

Heather Watts: I lived with one man for twelve years, and I've lived alone for four years, and it's becoming increasingly difficult for me to imagine not having my own place. I'm used to it. It's hard for me to imagine going back to the other thing. Being married to somebody and living with him for forty years – I'm not sure I'll ever do that. I believe in commitment, loyalty, love for somebody else, that goes on no matter what, but to reduce it to who does the laundry and who takes out the garbage – I'm not sure. I could see myself having children, at least a child, without being married and living in the same place with a man.

Arabella Weir: Most mothers will prefer their sons over their daughters. Mine did. Mine showed preferential treatment to my brothers, and she's a feminist, but she showed preferential treatment because relationships between men and women are usually better than those between the same sex.

I don't believe that platonic, truly platonic relationships exist between two heterosexual people. It's only platonic because you don't find him attractive. If you found him attractive, and he found you attractive, it wouldn't be a platonic relationship, unless you were both committed to someone else.

All the men I know are much more faithful than the women. It's the women I know who have had love affairs and one-night stands, not the men. The men have behaved badly within their marriages or relationships in other ways, but on the whole, as far as I can see, it's a myth purported by men that they are the ones who want the variety, and I think they've used it to suppress and terrify women into submission. But, from my experience, it has been women who have wanted to lead a

960

more interesting life, not men. I mean, I've slept with people for lust, and I don't need to feel loved and adored, but all the men I've known do.

Katharine Whitehorn: Maybe men don't equate sex with love, but the extent to which they do is something which varies according to upbringing. This Latin American idea that every woman is either a madonna or a whore, and that's the way you're brought up – good women you don't do it with, bad women you do – and then you get all these basket cases who can't do it with anybody they don't despise because that's the way it's been set up for them. Now, I think that's absurd. But I think you could have a difference between two cultures: one where, say, in the course of thirty years of marriage, a man might go off the rails once or twice, be ashamed of it. It would not be a major part of his life, he would keep bloody quiet about it. And you could have a culture where, of course, it's assumed that any gentleman has a mistress and that's supposed to be once a week, and his wife is supposed to know about it, supposed to put up with it. French *belle époque* is one thing, middle-class respectable Scotland in Edwardian times would be very different. I think what you can expect out of a relationship is what everybody has been brought up to expect, and you might have been brought up to expect something very different in one context from another.

I am attracted by strength, however defined, and gentleness. You know, he that can do hurt and will do none, the Gary Cooper figure, the cowboy who won't behave like a brute. And interest in me, which I think actually most women find seductive.

Shelley Vaughan Williams: When Rupert was three and a half, I had to start my life again. I was living in South America and pregnant with a third baby, which I lost through the shock of my husband's death. My in-laws and family were very loving, and I guess, as a young widow, I had all their support. I had felt I had been loved all my life and that now was my turn to stand on my own two feet and provide for Rupert and Lionel. I wanted to bring them up in the way that I thought they should be brought up, each one differently perhaps, because they are terribly individual. That was when I started my first company, because I would never, as an employee, have earned the sort of money I wanted to earn for my sons. I started off on my kitchen table and worked day and night, day and night, so hard, until I could afford an *au pair* girl, Maria Teresa, who was like a gazelle, Spanish, who used to break all the crockery, but it didn't matter because she was so full of love I knew the boys would be safe with her. And I used to make sure, when the boys started going to nursery school, that I was always at home a quarter of an hour before they got home, so they would feel I had been home all day, even if it meant working after they went to bed. My second marriage was desperately unhappy and nearly destroyed me in every sort of way, and that was hard to take, but I'm all right now. Everything always happens at the same time, and during that marriage I had a terrible car crash, I went through the windscreen. There's a runner in the window of a car, and that tore my eyelids off, but it wrapped itself round my face so the glass didn't go in my face. I broke my arm and leg, my sternum and my wrist, and I was totally alone because the boys were at school and my second husband deposited my son at the hospital and then took a plane and went away. It was a year before I could properly walk, and I went out to Barbados on my own and was determined to water-ski. Because I'd got a scar, I felt terribly self-conscious, and a year to the day from my accident I walked to where all those other people were who I thought weren't wounded – but everybody is walking wounded in some way. And this tall black Negro said, you want something, lady? And I said, I'm going to water-ski, but I've had a bad car accident and I'm terrified, but the thing I most want to do in all the world is to get up on those water-skis. So he said, you just keep looking with those lovely eyes at my lovely eyes, and I'll get you up on the water-skis. I must have gone down about fifteen times, but he just kept saying, just keep looking at my lovely eyes, and in the end I got up and I went round, looking at that man's eyes. I'll never forget him. Those are the sort of people you love all your life though you may never see them again.

I don't think that a really strong man, a really masculine man who is sensitive and intelligent, is any more interested in one-night stands or going rogue steer than the equal of him in a woman. But there are a hell of a lot of people who are. I heard Rupert and Lionel on the telephone when they were about fourteen, and boys of fourteen can be very arrogant and crass, and I didn't know who was on the other end of the phone, but they were talking in a way that it had to be a girl, and in such a terrible way, and they thought they were being funny and great. And I sat them down, I was so angry. I said, listen, I don't know who that girl was, and I don't want to know, but if she's like that, then by God she needs your respect more than any other woman you're with, because she's obviously lost and has no love around her, and she's terribly vulnerable, and therefore, out of respect for yourself, you can't cheat on her like that and treat her as trash. I'm sure you'll think I'm crazy and you don't know what I mean, and I'm not saying it well, because I'm so upset. But they said, yes, we do understand.

The expectations we have of each other are ridiculous. Noël Coward said that American women expect the same perfections from their husbands as Englishwomen expect from their butlers. I think it was also Noël Coward who said that most marriages collapse out of boredom. If women are not immaculate and fastidious in their marriages, that is killing, and the same with men.

For a woman to lose the touch of a man who loves her is a supreme separation. We each need each other in a physical way, but that's only the manifestation of everything else you feel about that person, and for me that would come after all the other things.

I think I feel more comfortable with men, although, having said that, 90 per cent of them are pretty awful. But I'd rather go into a room full of major-generals than I would into a women's bridge party.

Jeanette Winterson: For some men, it's almost a nervous twitch to have to ask every woman they meet to go to bed with them to reinforce themselves. It's an insecurity in them, and it's not something I feel threatened by. But it can be a bit boring. Because it's not what you always want.

Men have got it wrong when they empire-build night and day and, equally, women who take on male roles and have no time for the heart. Because the heart atrophies very quickly, and suddenly you have everything but you don't have yourself and you don't have anyone to share it with. I would never want to get in that position, so I always try to keep a balance in what I do. Even if it means sacrificing some things that attract me professionally perhaps, if I think it's going to cost me emotionally, I won't do them.

Male and female are actually totally unknown to each other, and that's what's frightening. It's because we're all so blasé about that fear that, in a sense, we treat each other quite badly, because nobody wants to admit they're fearful, and they don't know how to act and what to do, and they feel silly. I think those are enormous hurdles in a heterosexual courtship. With women, it doesn't come up like that, because you do know, and also women find it easier to say, look, I haven't got a clue here and I'm scared and all the rest of it, so you find there's a great warmth and understanding which can be generated very quickly. Also, you're not having to play mother which, for a lot of women, is very important, because they don't always want to do that. And with men, if you want to build a very caring relationship, you do have to an extent to help them.

I'm quite monogamous in as much as I wouldn't hurt my partner just for the sake of it, so I'd have to fall in love. Even though there are men that attract me, I wouldn't do anything about it, just as I wouldn't do anything about women that attract me, other than my lover, because I don't want to cause pain needlessly. But I'd be prepared to dismantle the whole world if I fell in love, that's a different matter.

Anna Wintour: I have so many great girlfriends in their thirties who are unmarried and quite desperate about it. They're very successful, very attractive. One can only assume that they're frightening men. Maybe they're too strong, too demanding. Men are put off by them.

My own experience of marriage is great. I'd rather see my husband than anybody in the world. We've never had a bad patch, we don't know what having a bad patch is. I think, in previous relationships I've had, there were so many bad patches that I knew there was no reason ever to get married.

Personally, I feel that if a marriage needs work, then it's not a marriage.

Enid Wistrich: What you do with your marriage and sex life is part of what you are yourself. You can be selfish with it, or you can be foolish with it, or you can be steadfast with it and make something of it.

I think power is an aphrodisiac, actually. Because there's something about a man who has power which exudes something. I don't know what it is, but it is something you should resist, because it's an awful thing to be seduced by power.

Priscilla Woolworth: I have a lot of good girlfriends, but with women a lot I feel it's not always comfortable because there is always this hint of competition, of jealousy and mistrusting.

If you ignore your husband to take care of your children, there's going to be problems. It's very important for a wife really to be with her husband and travel with him. The man, the one providing security, financial security for the family, he's the power, the security in the family, and you have to be by his side in it. I couldn't wish for anything more than to be with someone to take care of. It gives me so much pleasure, to make someone happy, to take care of a man, to cook something he loves. It's so wonderful to relax, to go to the country, to do things and really take care of each other And he gives back things to you. Each has different ways of giving to another, but I think it's so important for a woman to take care, to obey, to serve.

Women can be very seduced by power, because men who are in power know how to manipulate you – very well. I went to this dinner at the White House a few weeks ago, and was sitting next to Donald Regan, and I was completely seduced by him. Not because of his looks or whatever, but the power, the way he talked, he was just incredible. It was an incredible force, and I can understand how women just go crazy, because it's very seducing.

8
Differences

'*On ne nait pas femme: on le devient*'
– Simone de Beauvoir, *Le Deuxième sexe* (1949)

'*Thus far women have been the mere echoes of men. Our laws and constitutions, our creeds and codes, and the customs of social life are all of masculine origin. The true woman is as yet a dream of the future*'
– Elizabeth Cady Stanton, Speech to the International Council for Women (1888)

'*Instead of getting hard ourselves and trying to compete, women should try and give their best qualities to men – bring them softness, teach them how to cry*'
– Joan Baez, quoted in Tracy Hotchner, 'Sexism Seen But Not Heard', *Los Angeles Times*, 26 May 1974

'*Where love is absent there can be no woman*'
– George Sand, *Lelia*, vol. 1 (1833)

Lolicia Aitken: It's not that women are discriminated against, it's because their self-image is that they are the feminine violets who are not able to go for things, not able to cope. It's all to do with nursery problems that the boy must be tough and not cry, which is idiotic in the same way, and the girl must be feminine and soft, sweet and tender. That's role playing.

Maria Aitken: Women are just as lustful as men. The greatest aphrodisiac for men and for women is newness.

I do think the most attractive man I have ever known had a great proportion of female, if one can call it that, in the sense of being completely relaxed about the macho question, and being intuitive and not having a self-image, which is really the key to it all.

In all my life, I have noticed with men that they take twice, three times, as long to get ready as I do and that they look in the mirror more. They look in the mirror for different reasons, too. They look and rather enjoy what they see mostly. Women look to check up that everything hasn't gone wrong. Very few women actually look into the mirror to gloat; it's simply a quick appraisal of the situation to see if everything is OK. But I don't think that is why men look, because they very rarely adjust things afterwards. They just look.

I can't imagine being a man because I am a mother, and men are not only my friends but very pivotal in my life, for friendship, sexually living with, as friends. I can't believe men have such a happy combination of the earthy part of one's life and the intellectual part of one's life. I don't see it in men, or very few of them. They don't permit themselves the pleasure; they become rather a Hampstead joke if they do.

I don't know about other women, but I think reading pornography can be terrific, but looking at it is never the same. Women are more imaginative, probably have to be. A presentable, powerful or charming man does not go out with an ugly girl, *ergo* he doesn't need to fantasize much, he goes out with beautiful girls. Women often go out with extremely plain men who happen to be witty or powerful or charming or whatever. So we have had fantasy at our fingertips for a very long time. Whatever one needs to blind one a little to the realities of the situation, women have been practising for ever.

Our sexual needs probably are different. I did my best to disprove that for some years, but I actually think they are different. I was taught a sort of feminine cosiness by men, taught to settle down by men who were rather mature. So I stopped being a sort of female equivalent of a tomcat but, looking back on it, I think it was rather a fake. It was a need to show I was not a little feminine thing; I wanted to choose and have affairs whenever I thought I wanted. In fact, I think I wanted far fewer than I had. It is quite interesting to look back on it. I was brainwashed. It is a myth that women are happy to settle down with one man and men require variety. Actually, women would like variety too, but I do think the urge in us is more easily deflected by activity and needn't be specifically solved by sex. We can channel it into cooking or whatever.

Madeleine L. H. Alatas: I went to the roughest business school in America, the top business school, very much having been brought up in Europe and coming straight out of the Arab world because I left Saudi Arabia to do it in fifteen months, to get my MBA, and arrived with Michel and a nanny and everything. A friend, who also grew up in Europe, was sharing a house with me and we were both quite, as I would say, not feminine but woman-like in the sense that we knew we had other roles besides simply being a brain power, and a lot of charm goes a long way. In other words, we weren't above, if you got a very tough question, being able to smile at the professor and throw him off for five minutes until you could really think of the answer. These women would never do it. They would never, ever use femininity to gain an advantage, whereas what's wrong with it? We always used to say they were asexual rather than saying they were masculine. They were nothing, they were neuter, they were cardboard. They were asexual, completely without any type of capability or sensitivity.

Saudi women have much more power than American women ever thought of having: real power, power to make decisions and to influence decisions. Albeit they do it vicariously, they do it through filters. They learn to manipulate at a very early age. They learn to make a man think it's all his idea and in actual fact it's not. And the men laugh, they have a sense of humour. They can laugh at themselves about that.

When I went to the Arab world, everybody said, my God, a twenty-one-year-old in Saudi Arabia, financial adviser to the SIDF and all this type of thing, how on earth did you get in that position? Weren't the Arabs awful to you? And all this *rubbish*. I find, in England, it is much worse. Englishmen feel terribly intimidated and very threatened. The Arab men, because I was unique, felt very protective towards me. They fell over backwards, they made sure everyone was, you know – has he been nice to you? Is he polite to you? Tell us, we'll protect you. They were fascinated. It was like a racehorse for them. Anyone who had guts and spirit, they admired. And rewarded, whether it was a man, woman or child, and particularly a woman, because a woman rarely got the opportunity to show guts or a type of skill against a watermark that they had to set themselves, that the men had to come up against all the time. So they loved seeing a woman succeed.

One is born a female, but that's biological, nothing to do with being a real woman. I call a real woman somebody who is multi-faceted, someone who is many-dimensional and, in each one, comes to a certain level, not just passing but above average. And it goes back to all the roles a woman has to practise every day of her life.

In men, you find, to a much greater extent, this peculiar mix of tremendous arrogance, the need to prevail: not survive, but prevail, push somebody underneath their thumb. And insecurity, tremendous insecurity. As a matter of fact, you'll find that in the most powerful men. It's an odd mix between arrogance and insecurity, and the more powerful they are, the more extreme it becomes. Women, on the other hand, generally, unless provoked, are not as focused as men, unless they've been wounded or hurt or aggravated. There must be some event that triggers off this mechanism of focusing, determination, sheer drive. If you see a woman who's that determined, that focused, and can target everything, one of the questions you ask inwardly to yourself is, my God, what the hell happened to her that she is that focused? Because women, by nature, are not so, they have so many roles to play. A woman has the role of a mother, a friend, a lover, a wife, a mistress. You have to be all things to all people, and if you have a career, you have to do all that, so you're not focused, you're kind of distracted. You cannot have a balanced woman in England that's successful that I know of. But then, again, define success. It's not necessarily achievement. Success can be having proper balance, equilibrium. I would define success as being able to achieve what you wanted to do without depriving yourself of something intrinsically valuable.

A man is emotionally much more vulnerable, and as a mother I can say that. A boy requires much more loving, much more confidence instilled. You can do it, appealing to the better nature: a boy is much more within himself, requires much more affection than a girl. Girls are kind of independent, they're like cats. They love you, yes, but they can stand on their own two feet.

I think a woman never really grows old. Neither do men, in a funny way. I've seen personalities come through. I find some women who are forty-five, forty-six, most attractive. I mean, if I was a man, I would think they were devastating, much more attractive than some little flirt of a girl who doesn't know, who is not a woman. I don't mean biologically, but in the sense she hasn't been able, like a diamond, to build a facet. That's what fascinates me about women: how well they polish their diamond, how many facets they have. And what fascinates me about men is the extremes.

Jan Amory: I don't think men are as treacherous, as Machiavellian, and I don't think they are as manipulative. A woman might say, if you don't leave your wife, I'm not sleeping with you any more, though it depends on the woman. I think the woman calls the shots, usually, in that. If she can.

The society we live in is trying to make us feel that men can be women and women can be men. But I feel men are different, not just because of a biological thing. Men are meant to be stronger. What can women depend on if it isn't a strong man?

Men are better actors. Men are probably less confident than women, but they pretend to be more confident. Frankly, a lot of confidence of men and women depends on financial power. You can get a woman who is terribly able to do an awful lot of things, and she doesn't have any money and therefore lacks confidence. Whereas, if she was given a million dollars and was just as able and no more, she'd have a terrific amount of confidence. It's unfortunate that money makes people confident, at least in America. But I think men in America are very insecure as well. A European man who doesn't have much money but has a tremendous amount of background is very secure. Whereas an American man, who relatively speaking comes from a good background

– you can't compare it to a European background – is not as secure without the money behind him.

I think men can go to bed with a woman purely to satisfy themselves, the way a woman will eat a chocolate bar. Women, unfortunately, even on a one-night stand, can tend to be emotional, and that's the problem. Men know this and take full advantage. It's the exceptional man that can really give you his emotional feelings early on in the relationship. Men really need sex the way you brush your teeth and get up in the morning. Women need love; men don't need love as much. I think men just like to have their orgasm, feel better, and get on with it. If, by chance, they fall in love doing it, then they get married. That's how blasé men really are. I don't think they think in the beginning at all, the way women do, of let's fall in love first.

Adèle Anderson: I know some very sexually driven women, and I know some very non-sexual men. I think women are just as sexually responsive as men, and can be just as sexually driven, but they probably wouldn't go from partner to partner; they just like to have a partner, whereas a man seems to be after one – then, where's the next one? It's like going along the fence and poking it through different holes.

I think men are much more visually stimulated than women. Women are stimulated by laughter. I've certainly got one friend, if somebody can make her laugh, that's fine, it doesn't matter what he looks like. Power stimulates women. Witness the women who go from one millionaire husband to another. Power, achievement. They are visually stimulated as well, of course, otherwise there wouldn't be *Playgirl* magazine and you wouldn't be able to buy those calendars. It's a well-known fact that the part of a man that turns women on most is his bum, not his penis or his face, but his bottom. That seems to turn women on most of all. Perhaps women have a greater capacity of acceptance, in that, if they marry when they're twenty and they get to forty, the man will often go and look for another twenty-year-old, right; the woman, if she's then divorced, probably wouldn't marry a twenty-year-old man, she'd marry another forty-year-old man. She's more pragmatic, more of a realist really.

I feel much more of a full-bodied character. I've developed a warmth and understanding I never had before. I do feel that women have a much greater capacity for gentleness and understanding, and actually not getting so worked up about things. The funny thing is that I was a very weak male, and I'm a very strong woman. All my energies got released and I've achieved far more careerwise, relationshipwise and in terms of general and spiritual well-being than I ever would have if I had remained as I was. So, yes, it was a release of energy.

Dr Swee Chai Ang: My grandfather had four wives at the same time. He wasn't even a Muslim, he was Chinese. He said it was company for the women in the house, arguing with each other, fighting for attention. They had no existence outside of their husband. Now, that is crazy. I find that attitude unbearable, and I understand why my mother walked out.

It is entirely possible to get a group of women and bring them up as men, and subject them to a military training and bring them up like army boys and condition them. There will be no difference, in a sense, except when they have their period and that sort of thing. It is possible, and I know in some countries it's like that. I'm sure there would be differences if we really studied carefully, but whether that difference is 5 per cent or 10 per cent or 50 per cent, I don't know. Right now, when we look at a woman and a man, the difference is 100 per cent, but I think our task is really to find out whether, in actual fact, when you strip down all the conditioning, the difference is 20 per cent or 5 per cent. Her biological structure is different, she's got more fat distribution, and so on and so forth; the man is more muscular, the bones are bigger. But, apart from that, is there actually a psychological difference? If you strip away all the culture influences, then I think probably not.

Let's take an extreme case. If a woman has had a baby, she is lactating, probably she sees things differently because, at the time, she is full of female hormones and producing milk. She is protective, she is nurturing, she gets aggressive if anything happens to her baby, but otherwise she is very gentle towards the baby. To make a man behave like that, you would have to pump in whole quantities of female hormones. So there is that difference. Of course, after the baby grows up, you revert to your original self. That is so obvious, even in animals. If you see a cat delivering babies, she is totally different; she is a mother cat. After the babies are grown up, she becomes an ordinary cat, she goes out and chases after rats and that sort of thing.

Lady Elizabeth Anson: Unfortunately there is the bitch side of the woman, which is stronger and therefore more unkind than whatever one would call it in the male.

I do think men are more logical. I don't like to admit it, but I think they are.

I have many friends who are homosexuals. In fact, most of my very close men friends are, and I think they have that seventh sense and intuition that a heterosexual male doesn't have. I find them wonderful to work with, because a lot of people I work with on the artistic level of my business are homosexuals, and they have that understanding, that certain amount of something, so that one doesn't actually need to spell everything out and talk it all over. You don't have to go into laborious detail. I think that is one thing that women – and homosexuals – do have.

My wedding dress was made by a marvellous woman called Maureen Baker who did Princess Anne's wedding dress. A man sees a dress as something static, I think, and doesn't really understand that you are going to have to run upstairs or dance a jig or sit for hours in a theatre, or get in and out of cars that are difficult. They are not practical about that side of it. A woman would think about all those things.

Beatrice Aristimuno: In sensibilities, men and women are completely different. We don't feel the same things at the same time in the same way. A man could say something that could leave me crying for twenty minutes and thinking, my God, what he has just told me, it's awful. In fact, to him, it might not mean anything, it might have no importance, and there you see the real difference between men and women.

Pamela Armstrong: A study was done of women who were given babies to look after, and when they were told what sex they were, they were absolutely comfortable and felt quite able to relate to the child. It was as if they knew what was expected of them. But when they were given a baby and weren't told whether it was a boy or a girl, they were extremely uncomfortable and didn't know what to do with it. That has to say something about the manner in which we condition our children. Because something about knowing what the sex was made the woman feel she understood the appropriate behaviour around that particular child – as if there is a different kind of behaviour needed around boy babies from around girl babies.

There is a form of massage called rolfing. It's actually painful and has to do with massaging the ligaments and the bone; it's very very deep and painful, but apparently very good. I was talking to someone who was a specialist in this form of massage, and he said it was extraordinary that, when he massaged Scandinavian men, they reacted differently from British men, who reacted differently from American men. When he massaged American men, it was fine all over their bodies, but when he came to their forearms, he found that the same amount of pressure caused immense anxiety and pain in the American men and would trigger off memories of childhood. For some reason, their forearms were very sensitive, as if that was where they stored all their anxieties. They found it almost intolerable to be massaged there. When he massaged British men, he could massage them all over, no problem, but when he got to their jaws, they had the same reaction as the American men to their forearms, and in the Scandinavians it was the shoulders. So what that seemed to be saying is that different nations carry their tensions in their bodies in different places. It's quite interesting that the American macho man, being brought up to be punchy and aggressive, appears to carry his tension in his forearms. With the British men it's the jaw, and they're taught to have stiff upper lips and we carry all our tension in our faces, we don't let it show. And, in the Scandinavians, it's across the shoulders, for whatever reason. So I think that shows that men have pain, men have emotions, but triggering it can be different, and it can be different for different nations. They do actually have pain, and I'm sure they have irrational emotions in the same way women do, but they're conditioned not to show it. I've seen men going through very difficult emotional situations at work, and men and women are exactly the same when it comes to expressing emotions. Some people express it, and some people don't. It has much more to do with the nature of the personality than it has to do with their sexuality.

Debbie Arnold: Because women's instinct is to have children, a woman is fussy about who she sleeps with, because deep down inside all you're looking for is someone to make babies with. That's why you take so long to find someone special, someone you want to be with. Whereas a man can really sleep with anyone. It doesn't matter, he's almost been programmed to give as many people babies as he can.

Men think completely differently from women. Completely and utterly. Women, I find, my girlfriends and I, are very honest. The amount of trouble we have with men. We're always on the phone saying, oh, he did this, and he did that, and how could he do this? I think a man would rather lie to a woman than be honest and hurt her. He'd rather lie around a situation, thinking it was best if she never knew, whereas a woman, most of my girlfriends and me, especially, would be very definite and say, look, I didn't see you tonight because I was seeing somebody else. I wouldn't lie about it. I feel men would.

I like the way men are handier than women. I like the way they can do things around the house. That's a good masculine trait. I don't know many women that are as handy. I also like the way they take on the traditional role, not necessarily of the breadwinner but as the protective partner. That is very important, that they look after you, and a real man does look after a woman, he really does make you feel safe. I feel that men who don't bother to look after women aren't men.

A man can go to bed with a woman and that's it, it doesn't mean anything to him. It does to a lot of women. I don't care how much they say it doesn't mean anything to them, it does. Even though they might try and talk themselves into the fact that it doesn't mean anything, it's bound to. It's a completely different feeling to let someone make love to you. It's not a physical need that, oh, gosh, I've just got to have somebody, that I think men have. It's a release for a man; it's not a release for a woman. Women need loving as opposed to a quick screw, and men can get away with just a quick screw. Well, that's what all the men I've been involved with tell me. They can go off with other women and it doesn't mean anything. I don't know any of my girlfriends who have been involved and in love with men who can actually go off and have a quick screw and go back to the fella.

Women are basically stronger than men: emotionally much stronger. When a man totally falls in love with a woman, he is much worse than a woman is when she's totally in love with a man. And when they break up, I think a man suffers worse, really. If he's really in love, I think he suffers, deep down, probably more emotional turmoil than a woman, who I feel suffers it more on the surface and can easily pull herself together, pick herself back up again. Women are more emotional on the surface. Surface emotions.

Leslie Ash: My father is a very strong, selfish man, and he really likes women in their place. He likes to get up, to have his breakfast, to go out and play golf, to gamble, he likes to do all these things. He likes to come home and to have dinner, and he likes my mother, he likes to have sex. And then he likes to go to sleep and, really, he couldn't care less what my mother did during the day. So much so that, in fact, they have split up.

A woman *can* survive on her own. My sister's been on her own for a long time, and she's got a child and she's brought that child up on her own. But I know that, deep down, my sister would love to be able to be with a man and have that sort of family thing. Any woman who wants to survive on her own must be a very sad person. Maybe it's because I can't really bear being on my own. I don't like my own company that often. It drives me mad sometimes.

There are lots of exercises we do in acting when we're actually getting characters together, or thinking of where this person would live and what sort of character they are. One thing we do is we actually draw a house where you think this person would live, and then you draw the trees and you have to include a lake and a duck or something like that. My teachers always used to look at it and say, well, you've put a fence in front of the house, you obviously feel this character either likes being fenced in or likes keeping people out. I always remember, with this exercise, that men used to draw large ducks in the pond and there would only be one duck. It seemed to me that they were the duck, the big duck in the pond, the big fish in the pool. They did it totally unconsciously, but they would always draw a big duck, one duck in a pond.

Women can express themselves through childbirth, through the creation of life. Whereas, with men, it's bottled up inside them. That's why you meet so many crazy, strange men in your life. Some men are violent, some men very weak, because they've got it so bottled up they can never let it go, and men become very nervous people. Certain men. They must have a hell of a lot bottled up inside them, men. And that's what I always love about going to bed with a man: when a man actually reaches his climax, suddenly he's just a child, almost child-like – he lets go.

I find men get embarrassed a lot more than women do. Men might not often show their embarrassment, or they show it in a lot of different ways, by either being annoyed, or they go red, or just don't talk, or get coy or whatever. A woman may go like that, and giggle, but that's about it with a woman. A man can actually show his embarrassment by being violent. Quite often, violence starts off from being embarrassed. If a woman actually gets one up, that's when the woman gets hit, because of this embarrassment.

Diana Athill: There is a precariousness over many years in your situation; you depend on keeping your man. If you're out of that situation, it doesn't apply. I've known some perfectly unjealous women.

The most neurotically jealous people I've known have been men, actually. I think silly women get jealous because their self-confidence is threatened. When the love is withdrawn, you think it's going away; you collapse because you haven't got what you feel makes you worthwhile. Once you're out of that bind – once a woman is able to earn her own living, do her own thing or feel confident in herself – I don't think she is any more jealous than a man. And think of all those sensible shrewd French ladies allowing their husbands to have it off, knowing not to fuss. I think a lot of English people do it, too, I just think they don't talk about it so much. I think wisdom teaches you, whether you're a man or a woman, not to be too jealous.

There is certainly more aggressiveness in most men, they are more willing to fall into aggressive attitudes. I think men are pretty horrible in many ways, they really are quite violent, and women much less so. There are occasions when you really feel it. For instance, I went into a restaurant not long ago, and there was a rugger-club reunion or something going on and something like ten rather large men with slight grunts in their voices. They were actually quite frightening to look at. You thought, yes, they're really a not very nice kind of animal. If you got them individually, they would all have been perfectly all right, I'm sure, but there was something rather frightening about them. Of course, women can be a little frightening, too, in that way. They can actually be much more damaging in some ways in a gang, in a gaggle. If you hear women talking in a girls' gaggle, if they've got a little drunk, they're really slicing people up, but clearly there's no physical threat. Men, there's the possibility there, always, always. And although the *Guardian*'s women's-page attitude in which every woman they talk about is quivering with fear of rape goes rather far, there is something in it. For instance, in my fairly limited acquaintance, I know three women who have been raped, one of whom was seventy. Two by burglars, and one by a nut who chased her upstairs in a hotel. I don't know very many people, and three out of those few is quite a lot.

On that miserable subject of rape, quite a lot of men try to say, well, after all, what about it? Whereas women know that it's not sex that they're talking about, they know it is outrage, aggression. And an awful lot of men, nice men who have never thought of doing it, think, why should anyone be so flustered just because some poor chap is desperate for it? It isn't that, you see. Men don't understand it, so they have a different attitude to their own violence, naturally. Men are sometimes more frightened of being emotional than women because they've been brought up: men don't cry, you know, men don't do this, men don't do that. A nice warm person who's been brought up easily and well, there's very little difference in the emotions. I know men who adore their children, for instance, as physically, as warmly as any woman, because something in their upbringing has allowed them to do it.

I've known a lot of animals in my time. I'm very interested in animal behaviour. I think we are animals, and I do see a continuum. I know people who get so angry when you say this, they can hardly bear it, but I still feel it's there. I still feel that the woman – basically, at some quite deep level – is the creature designed to produce the infant, and the male is designed to be a bit more aggressive. I can't help feeling that this is as true of people as it is of dogs, lions, cows, horses, to a certain extent. I don't think it ought necessarily to go on being true, because now we're conscious, we speak and we think, we can change it a bit as it goes on. But I'm sure it's there, and I don't think we can change it totally. I think that's pie in the sky, myself, to believe you can. I really do think it can't be done. I don't see why it should be done.

Leila Badawi: A man will see himself as the centre of the world, the world is made up in his own image. A woman is more inclined to see other people as centres of many separate worlds, and perhaps try to project herself into other people's worlds.

Joan Bakewell: I don't want to generalize, because to attribute to women characteristics called feminine is to accept a dichotomy that's been invented by men. But women have a certain relationship to their presence on the planet which is, I suspect, to do with their potential to bear children or the fact that they have borne children, which roots them in a sounder way to the purpose of life. I don't know what the purpose of life is, and I'm not enchanted by anyone who says they do, but I do feel that women have something fruitful about them. They seem to understand their own natures, they listen to their bodies and they're not in flight from themselves. Very often, men are pursuing some fantasy of school, or their fathers, or their nation. Women are slightly more rooted in themselves. That's not to say they're more introspective, but they just have a presence; they've had to. But, also, they seem to have it naturally.

Women are more a prey, women seek to please more than men. I think Simone de Beauvoir would say that little girls are brought up to please; and, she would say, to please men. And I do think there is a tendency in women to be eager to please which is not altogether healthy. It's nice to please somebody, but not at the loss of your own integrity, and that's something, at the moment, that women could lose, are beginning to lose, but a characteristic women have. Men aren't eager to please, and don't.

We're in the shadow of the received behaviour that a woman's voice at a table is perhaps not so listened to as a man's. We're still in that era, and therefore women do lack the confidence. A lot of men have got confidence who shouldn't have it. A lot of deeply second-rate men are behaving as though they're cock of the walk, and there are plenty of them in publishing, I'm sure. There are certainly plenty of them in television. They do not deserve the confidence, but the confidence itself is a quality that helps towards the job. You see extremely capable women being slightly craven about wasting their confidence or riding easily into a situation. They don't ride easily at the moment, there's a certain tension. I can see it in young women who are beginning to be very assertive in television. There are plenty of them in their twenties and thirties, but there's just a slight anxiety about their behaviour, while young men in their twenties just sit there. They're born to it, they inherit it.

The experience of sex is more directional for a man – the erection and ejaculation. Whereas, for a woman, I think her whole body is involved, and also her body is entered; it is the place that is entered, and therefore occupied. I do think that makes the woman the cradle of these events and therefore very much caught up in them. And women do need and want affection. Men need and want affection, too, but they are not allowed by society to need it to the extent that women are. Small boys have it beaten out of them quite early on and cease to be able to express it. Women are not ashamed of their attachments and feelings. There is something wonderfully graciously honest about women who are not afraid to say, I am in love and it hurts. Men don't say this. I don't know whether they say this to each other. I very much doubt it.

Elisabeth Barillé: I think it was Freud who said that your anatomy is your destiny. The fact of having a woman's body influences the way I write but I can't really analyse that, it's unconscious. I can only say that differences are surely biological. I always come back to novels, and I find it very difficult to write for a male character as Flaubert did the other way round with *Madame Bovary*. As a novelist, I can't write through a male character. All I can say is that having a female body leads me towards a particular smelting of the novel. In my present novel, I describe childbirth. If I were a man, perhaps I wouldn't.

Dame Josephine Barnes: The man who has his little affairs on the side, he doesn't tell his wife. Women, on the whole, don't have affairs on the side and not tell their husbands. I think many more women are faithful to their husbands than husbands are faithful to their wives. We are much more candid than men, much more outgoing and truthful. I think men are more devious, more deceitful, I really do.

Josephine Barstow: Instinctively, one feels that women's feet are closer to the earth, they are buried in the earth. And men's feet are a little way above the earth, which means that they find it more difficult to be realistic, thereby causing pain. Obviously there are men whose feet are in the earth, and those are the men, as a woman, one looks for. One learns, as one gets older, to try and avoid the men whose feet are rather too high above the earth. This lack of contact with reality leads to the aggression and everything else that often comes out in the masculine personality.

I wish, in a way, that more women could perceive sex in a masculine way. The difficulty about sex, as far as women are concerned, is that it has other connotations, that it leads towards the desire to possess. Male sexuality doesn't do that. Male sexuality possesses in the act, but that's enough. But a woman then has to make it into something else, unless she trains herself not to, and it is very hard for most women to train themselves not to do that. Whether it's actually a desirable state, ultimately I'm not sure. The way the hormones work is one of the dilemmas of being alive, and the male and female hormones do actually affect the personality and the brain differently, making one respond and react and want different things.

Jennifer Bartlett: Women can have children and men can't. And I think that that possibility, which you are aware of from the age of eleven, twelve or thirteen as a physical reality, makes you take things more seriously. Things have a very specific consequence. If you fuck around, there's a chance you get pregnant. If you decide to take the pill, you may get cancer or heart disease. There is always a physical consequence.

More often than not, if a woman says she will do something, she will do it, and if a man says he'll do it, it may get done or it may not. I would trust women's sense of responsibility more, their sense of obligation, or greater guilt, than I would most men's. That's just something I've found. I like to do business with women.

Nathalie Baye: It is not that a woman is superior, but she has a strength, which is that she is closer to everyday life than a man, to the realities of life. I think it is very difficult to be a man. He's told he is responsible, the boss, he has to succeed, he has to have a job. A woman is closer to natural things, perhaps, but that again comes from the fact that she gives birth and is more lucid than men.

A man can make love with a woman for whom he has no feelings at all. It is rarer for a woman to do the reverse, but a woman has a power over man, sadly. She can simulate desire or satisfaction if she wants to. A man can't. Even if a man loves a woman, but is not sexually excited, then he can't make love to her. In this sense, a woman is stronger than a man. She can live with a man and love him for various reasons, but not love him physically, even though she will have physical relations with him. For a man, it is more difficult.

Gilberte A. Y. Beaux: If you look at the animal world, you have a lot of male animals who are polygamous, but there are others who live all the time with their females. I would think that every person is different. I would not make any generalization. Some women probably have the same attitude as men to sex and vice versa. We have, in fact, both sexes in ourselves, so it depends on the person, I guess, and also the environment.

Rotraut Lisa Ursula Beiny: Women desire security, and that's why women also want to be married. It's not so important for a man. And I sometimes think, because they want security, they are not such big gamblers; and often, to create a large business, you have to gamble. Obviously there are exceptions, but I think women prefer security and don't want to take such great risks. In creating this business, for instance, my father had to take enormous risks and gambles that I don't think I would have been able to take. I am very good following on, but would I have been able to create it and to take all these risks? I think that is something women are not so likely to do.

For me, sex and love go together. There may be women this doesn't apply to, but on the whole, I think, for women, it is love and sex, and for men I think it is sex and that's it. Obviously there are exceptions, but I think that is how it goes.

Jeanne-Louise Bieler: I know so many men who are emotional that I

983

start to think it's something typically male rather than female. Women who are really emotional are those not in a career, not in a job. Professional women are less emotional than men, much less.

I have two girls and, of course, I always had certain ideas of femininity and equally of equality and so on. Nevertheless, one day I was walking through the fields with a little boy, and we saw a big truck and stopped and looked at it. Suddenly I realized that I had never done that with my daughters, and I thought you are conditioning them like everyone else, and I was shocked at my own attitude. So, you see, if you're convinced that you do all the things you should, you don't – not yet. And I am a convinced feminist, yet I make mistakes like that, but the majority of women who are not so feminist make these mistakes ten times more than I do.

Rebecca Blake: It's not necessarily a difference of perception, it's a difference in the execution. For instance, say a man was photographing a woman. If there was an energy exchange, it could possibly veer off and become a sexual energy exchange and it could be a flirtation. OK? I think, when I do a photography session, if there is an eroticism or a passion or whatever expressed in the image, it is less specific, it's amorphous. It's not as specific as what a man would do in terms of the kind of response he would get from a woman. My pictures may still be erotic, but in a sense the experience that takes place during a shoot session is one in which I encourage the subjects, male or female, to express themselves and talk to me, and for them to realize I would never abuse that trust in any way. In a sense, when I'm shooting, I think I become androgynous.

Emily Bolton: I've been very lucky, having been in *Tenko*, because I got so many letters from men saying they just love watching *Tenko*, and I thought, this is rather strange, because it is about women, it's only about women. Why should a man want to watch? In many cases, I have asked men, and they said, well, it's just so refreshing to see women in a different situation, not the situation we are used to seeing, like in the kitchen with the apron on, with the babies. That's the image we grow up with. And now women were actually making decisions in a particular situation. It was a camp, it was survival. And they enjoyed seeing women like that. I think they were able to see that there's always that survival element, and women are mentally very strong in that sense.

Betty E. Box: There was a good deal of curiosity about me, because I was the only woman film producer, possibly in the world, at that time. Certainly, in the English-speaking world, I was the only woman film producer, and I used to get rather bored because I always had the press on to me saying, what does it feel like, being a woman film producer? And I said, what is it like to be a male film producer? I'm just a film producer. I went through my press-cuttings book the other day, turning out some old files. It was full of stories about the only woman film producer, and why I was different from everybody else. Personally, I think I was just the same.

A lot of women do have to put up with things they shouldn't have to put up with, but I've never mixed with that sort of women, which is possibly a drawback. Maybe I should have done more. I don't think we are that different. I see a great deal of femininity in men, in my husband, in Ralph Thomas, whom I worked with a great deal. I don't mean this unkindly. They have the intuition women are supposed to have, they have a pleasure in looking nice themselves. I find that a lot of women have some of the masculine attributes. I don't think we're all that different. I never had any maternal instinct, never, never wanted children, and it's something perhaps I don't understand. I always said, oh, well, every one of my films is a child, it takes about nine months to get a film out and each one of these is my production. I think we all have the feminine, the masculine in our make-up, I think it's there very strongly. I can remember my mother telling me that, when my older brother had his first little sailor suit, he went to the lady next door to show it off and held up one hand and said, if only I had a gold bracelet like you have, wouldn't it look beautiful? And I think men like beautiful things and wearing nice clothes just as much as women do.

Heather Brigstocke: A lot of men have been able to channel all of their energies into what they have done, whether they have been married or not. If they've been married, they've had a support system, so they haven't had to think about what am I going to have for supper, they've been able to be utterly single-minded. I don't think you'd find many geniuses in what we now term single-parent families, who had to have the supper ready for their children when they got home. They may have lived in squalor and poverty and deprivation, but they weren't responsible for physical nurturing.

One of the reasons why I support single-sex schools for girls is precisely because girls are innately different. Today, for instance, I was having lunch with seven of my head girls, and we were discussing the school and planning all sorts of things when I suddenly said, oh, I've just bought the most marvellous knitting pattern! And I went out to the car and got the pattern and the wool for everyone to look at. It's fun to talk about these things; women should have the self-confidence to enjoy them, be proud of them. But I don't think most men will ever get excited about knitting or sewing, just as I will never get excited about golf.

Dianne Brill: Women have different emotions from men. When you feel pleasure, when you feel pain, it just goes right by men. Women are more sensitive to it, and sometimes that is shown off as being a weakness because: there she is crying in the corner again. And a man says, you're in a bad mood today, or, it's that time of the month, or whatever, and dismisses it, but in the meantime those things the woman is feeling are very real.

Suzanne Brøgger: A basic difference is that women have a different perception of time. I believe that the feeling of time for women is cyclical not linear. But women are brought up in a society which emphasizes linear thinking and progress and going from point to point to reach the goal and become No 1, which I think is a male-orientated way of perceiving. So I think men are probably better designed for all kinds of professions that have to do with going from one point to reach the goal and become No 1. And that line of work is not necessarily pleasing to a woman, whose cyclical feeling of time will be more content or find great satisfaction in making a Gobelin, or something that takes a million years to do. Penelope was weaving her tapestry waiting for Odysseus; she unwove it every night and continued the next day. That, I think, would be a disaster for a man, it would be waste for him. A woman can find pleasure in embroidery and other kinds of creativity which take more patience. I, myself, feel much closer to the conception of time that the peasants have: the years, the seasons of the years, that recur like the wheel, not linear industrialized time.

Janet Brown: I've often thought that women are basically not tougher – that's not the right word – but they have a greater strength. For example, I watched a woman the other evening on television. She had two or three very badly disabled children and was able to talk sensibly and matter-of-factly about what had to be done or what it was possible to do for these children – with them falling around, not even able to keep their heads up or walk properly, and her propping them up. And I thought, what has given this woman the strength to be able to start every

986

day of her life now when she's living a life of that kind? And to be able to talk in a normal, tolerant, matter-of-fact, even way? I think women have colossal strength at times. We're very much survivors.

Tina Brown: I don't think the sexes are the same at all. I think women are instinctively much more nurturing. It's for the woman to think imaginatively about the emotional life in a relationship. I play that role, even though my husband and I are really quite equal in terms of what we both do. It's for me to think we really must try and spend three weeks away together, and it's me who thinks about when, and me who gets the diary out and insists we make time. But I've noticed this with women across the board: it's always they who say we really must think about Christmas now. Women think in that much more caring, strategic way.

Joan Juliet Buck: In the men I have been involved with, apart from my husband, I see, first of all, a tremendous fear of intensity, of commitment, a fear of things getting out of hand, getting too strong, too big, and a fear of things getting too romantic along with a desire to protect the wonderful future timetable of general affairs. In the women who are my close friends, I see a longing for commitment, a longing for intensity, a longing for romance. The men whom I know very well, when really strong things happen – and strong love affairs happen – they try and do that male thing of, OK, now this is called 'L'Amour', so let's put it in a bottle and market it and we'll make a lot of money. The man wants to be able to know what to do with it. And the woman just wants to be swept away, dominated, annihilated – happily never recovering. I think a man's looking for God and a woman is looking for God in man.

In America, a woman who is my age and isn't married has to justify it by feminism. In the rich New York circles, I've seen women of any generation trade up husbands, marry rich, and then marry better and better. All that is protection from the outside world. There's a lot of work discrimination against women in England, but then women in England tend not to be educated, and the educated ones seem ready to accept any kind of insult employers or society are going to hurl at them. People in England aren't willing to take responsibility. There's a huge thing of just blaming everything on the government. I saw it when I used to go canvassing for a politician, and it's something about the British character. Here, in France, there's the legend of the divorced mother of two who goes out to work and is very brave. Also in France, there is the wonderful tradition of people who have love affairs for forty years and are married to the wrong people; and then one of the partners dies and finally they marry and are very old people. But women here take responsibility. In America, they do whatever the current ethos tells them they should do. I'm appalled, in America, at the amount of unqualified personalities having careers that formerly used only to be open to people who had more spirit, more drive, more intelligence, more guts, and more hunger than others. Now very average women, who should actually be at home taking care of kids, having human lives, are out in the workplace trying to forge empires, and it doesn't work because not all women are made to do that.

Averil Burgess: A whole lot of fascinating studies have been done in the education world about the achievement and non-achievement of women. And there's a very well-known one about attributing failure. When women fail, they attribute it instantly to their own deficiency. When men fail, the first reaction is to attribute it to bad luck or other people. And this is simply a different gut reaction between the two. Whether it's ineradicable, I wouldn't like to say, but it is the case that women instantly take failure as a personal thing: I have failed, I have fallen short in this job. A man thinks, golly I was unlucky there, so-and-so has done me down.

It is difficult to be sure of innate differences, because conditioning is very important. I certainly see differences which, if not innate, are a result of very early conditioning. Girls are much more at ease verbally. Verbal skills develop much more rapidly in girls than in boys. On the other hand, boys develop special skills very much more rapidly than girls. And I think without any form of conditioning, if you put a couple of girls together, they will talk to each other; if you put a couple of boys together, they will start playing with whatever toys and tools are around. And this appears to me to be an almost fundamental difference between the sexes, which I do not believe is purely the result of conditioning. At the same time, I think a lot more could be done to equalize this. In the female education world, we've placed a lot of emphasis recently on girls to be more confident in mathematics and science. We ought to make a far more conscious effort to place more emphasis on getting boys to be confident in personal relationships. The equalization has tended to go in one direction. But if one could modify the early conditioning of boys by making them more aware of the needs of others, and the need to talk to others, to learn about them and so on, then it might be very much happier. But I would not go all the way with feminists in saying there are no innate differences at all. There are, perhaps, intellectual differences, I'm not sure about that. Certainly there are emotional and psychological differences which affect learning

988

and what somebody is interested in. Mothers who don't give their little boys guns to play with will find their little boys make guns for themselves and little girls will care for dolls or what have you. The role of family education and school education should in some way be to bridge the gap, in some way to strengthen the weak sides of both sexes, but co-existence has to be based, not on identity, but on appreciation of a difference.

Liz Calder: Emotion is a very powerful thing which everybody has. Women are less ashamed of their own feelings and bring them into account. Women are more responsive, and will react perhaps more quickly and won't have so many preconceived ideas, so can be more flexible and reactive; but they are also capable of profound logic.

I think men regard their own sexual natures, and indeed their own sexual lives, as almost sacred, as something which they are almost a servant of; they serve it. I think, with women, the need to express oneself sexually is probably as great, but it's usually focused towards the object of one's affections.

Carmen Callil: I have got a lot of men friends, and they're just as emotional or unemotional as my women friends. I don't think women are more emotional than men; I think they're probably less so, come to think of it. We've all got to talk about the worlds we live in, and I live in the world of publishing and writing, where men tend to be less conventional. The men in publishing and men who write are not conventional, macho men. I've had men who worked for me weeping that their cat's died that morning; I've had women saying, my boyfriend's left me, I'm miserable; I've never had a man saying, my wife's left me, I'm miserable. So perhaps there's a slight tendency for men not to bring their love-life into work, but frankly I don't encourage anyone to bring their love-life into work. I think women are superior to men. They're so much more interesting. It's very hard to find an interesting man. Women are extremely interesting because they do so many things, see so many things and know so many things. That's why the men friends I have I really value. They're like precious gold, because there aren't enough of them around. Whereas whole loads of women are interesting, and women laugh a lot more. Your average man, in my experience, never laughs at himself, whereas all women I know laugh at themselves.

I wouldn't know if it were inherent, but most of the men I've worked with, or for, are much more used to having things done for them than women. They seem to be much sloppier and less obsessive about detail. I know some exceptions to that, but I always say to the men who work for me, they remind me of my brothers, who had my mother going around picking up their trousers and underpants.

I have travelled all over the world, and it's an utter bore travelling by yourself because men accost you all the time. It's not the same for a man. Women don't accost men all the time, and if they do, men are powerful enough to deal with it.

I really do feel sorry for men. I don't think they have such a good time. I've always felt sorry for men. I think they're limited. They're not brought up properly so that they can see how wonderful the world is. They just do very tiny little things and they've got tiny little obsessive minds and they don't laugh at themselves. That's a very great generalization. I know lots of men who are different from that, but they don't have such a good time as women.

Angela Carter: I don't believe there is such a thing as femininity. I really don't believe it. I don't believe there is an essential womanliness that women have that men don't.

Women are more likely to internalize and it comes out as neuroses or suicide, or suicide attempts or depression, and maybe we do it because we are nicer than men, and we'd rather become neurotic than hit somebody over the head.

Men don't have the menopause, they don't have the sense of the terminal, of being able to have children as a state that will be terminated. I don't know what knock-on effect this has psychologically, I don't theorize about this. I get on with my work.

Anna Carteret: I think a lot of the difference between men and women is conditioning. My mother instilled into me a sort of submissive, subordinate attitude. You know, you must put your husband first. I believe she still thinks it. She still can't quite accept that my career is as important to me as his is to him, which sometimes means putting it before my children, which sounds cold and heartless. But men put their career before their children at the drop of a hat, and they're not criticized for it. My husband is in America now for three months, and he wouldn't dream of turning down a job because of his children, whereas if I'm offered a job for three months in America, I have to furiously weigh up whether the job is worth the amount of hassle and possible neglect of the children. I also have to pay someone to look after them. It's me that has to do all that. I'm not saying my husband is awful. I think most men are like that.

In *Juliet Bravo*, there are many situations which, of course, are based on real life. Acting in *Juliet Bravo* helped me to see that women have an ability to draw people out. I don't know whether you call it a sixth sense or an intuition, but they do have a way of discerning and finding things out from people which perhaps men don't. Men aren't as good at opening themselves, so they don't encourage the other person to open up. Women operate a lot through feeling, which is a much-despised word in business. It's built up as being emotional, woolly, clouding the main issue, but in fact I believe a lot in instinct and feelings. I think they're often much more truthful, or they lead you to the truth more than the intellect.

I think men have a tendency to be far more single-minded, and this helps them to concentrate on one thing and get to the light at the end of the tunnel, get to the top of their profession, whereas women are used to operating on many different levels. This very flexibility and adaptability in women could be used to advantage in professional jobs, and in businesses and executive management, and it should become an asset rather than a liability.

Barbara Cartland: I think, in the old days, it was part of a woman's make-up to be compassionate and understanding: loving children, thinking of old people. That's all been rather swept on one side in this effort to be pseudo men. Women are harder than the men now, much harder. I think men are much cleverer than women. Mrs Thatcher is an exception. She's a very exceptional person. I've known Margaret for a very long time. I used to speak for her when she was at Alexandra Palace, in 1966, so I'm not making anything up now. I said in my biography, if we ever have a woman Prime Minister, which is very unlikely, it will be Margaret Thatcher. She was always brilliant. She had a man's brain, which you can say is a reincarnation. She ought to have been a man in another incarnation. She has a man's brain; she looks at things from a man's point of view, which is very different from a woman's point of view. Really successful men have terrific one-point concentration and terrific vitality and terrific go-getting. You can't explain it any other way: a go-getting idea. They're terrifically self-centred and egotistical, and yet they get what they want by sheer power of thought and energy. Men are much easier to live with, for the simple reason that they're very loyal. They make up their minds about something and stick to it, they don't shrivel about. I find women very difficult to work with. You can say to a man, damn you, do this properly, and a man doesn't take umbrage. A woman will take umbrage at once.

I think women are born women, and born being feminine, sweet, loving children, loving a man and wishing to be faithful. What has happened is that they've been pressured by all of the modern world into thinking they must do something different. Why? If a woman does the same job as a man, she should have the same wages, but very few women are as strong as men, therefore a woman is not such a viable employee as a man. One or two things women do better than men, one of them being, surprisingly enough, making envelopes. It always seemed to me extra-ordinary that you should want women to make envelopes.

I think men are far more romantic than women. Women should really make the romance in a man's life, but they've ceased doing that. They're not keen on making romance. They just complain all the time. Love can be a tremendous thing to a man, but actual sex can be just a passing phase. To a woman, it's always an emotional experience, and that is why I disapprove of women who are promiscuous, because they affect their characters and personalities.

Luciana Castellina: Between men and women there is a biological difference, a psychological difference and an historical difference. The point is not to deny the difference, the point is to establish that the difference is not derogatory.

Charlotte Chandler: As a general rule, women tend to be more conservative, more cautious, because they feel less able to dominate the environment.

Actually, a great many women have much more experience than any man is ever going to have. The attractive young woman, who feels that she can freely be involved in sex, gets so many offers, she simply has to accept, whereas a man has actually to go forward and face being rejected, and he may not have anything near the number of sexual experiences a young woman has these days.

Alexandra Chapman: Women have good sense. They are much more in touch with reality. They have their feet on the ground. Because they have to deal with reality every day. I don't think a woman would have invented the new French 10-franc coin, which looks exactly like a 50-centime piece and people are constantly confusing them at the market. Women tend to listen better than men do, because they have had to, for centuries. This is an ingrained thing: women make good listeners. For the rest, I think every woman is different. I have known women who are very maternal; I have know women who were not maternal at all. I have known women who were masculine in their dress and thinking; I have known women who wear fluffy lace dresses like Scarlett O'Hara.

Shirley Conran: We all know that masculine and female qualities should not be so called and every person is a mixture of both. The whole thing is simply a question of indoctrination. Behind us stand our parents. We are all very influenced by what our mothers did and what our fathers did. Now, who influenced the people who influenced us? The people who influenced their early lives: ancestors. And I happen to know that my mother and father were taught a great deal of rubbish. But I'm quite certain that my grandparents didn't do that on purpose. They didn't say right, I am going to indoctrinate your head with this rubbish. They just did it because they thought it was correct at the time. I tried not to influence my sons at all. I think it was the most sensible thing I could do. We're coming out of the Dark Ages.

I think, on the whole, that men are perhaps more badly indoctrinated than women. I would hate to have been brought up to be a little man, and not to cry and be a brave soldier, and not be allowed to show any emotion because it was unmanly. And my generation was brought up like that. I would quite like to be a man brought up by me.

The word aggression has got warped. There's nothing wrong with being aggressive, but no woman would like to be called aggressive. No man would mind being called aggressive, he'll rather simper, and look quite pleased with himself, as if you had said, my, my, what a huge chest you've got or something. You know, it's considered almost a compliment. There are too many words women are frightened of having applied to themselves because they have been brainwashed into thinking these qualities are unfeminine. I'd like to know what feminine is.

Genevieve Cooper: The survival instinct might be stronger in women sometimes, because it's you and the baby. Women have had to learn how to look after themselves and a child, if necessary, and that's consciously always there and keeps a lot of women from being as giving and loving as they may appear to be. In my experience, men can be a hell of a lot more susceptible and sensitive than women. I think most women are tougher than men think, and in my experience it's men who are less self-sufficient than women. Women are very self-sufficient. They've been taught to be in some ways; they've been taught to sew and cook and most men haven't. But also, emotionally, they're very self-sufficient. That's borne out by statistics. Widows live longer and are happier than widowers, who die early and usually very unhappily. Men need people more than women do – in my experience.

I haven't had children, but feminists who had the view that it was all conditioning and have now had children, a boy and a girl, change their minds. They do feel that little boys are different, and little girls are different from an early age. I think it's a mixture of both. The preoccupations of both sexes are different, obviously, which will make their characters slightly different. A woman's biological years, which more or less finish when she's forty, will mean that she does have to cram much more urgency into everything until she's forty-five. She has to cram more into her life at the beginning than a man, so it makes her concerns very different.

If the son grows up identifying strongly with his mother, he is likely to be a far more passive and gentle person, and not necessarily simply expect women to do everything his mother did. Most of the men I've been attracted to are men who, for one reason or another, have been brought up by mothers, sometimes mothers alone without fathers, or with lots of sisters, because it's very clear that those are the men who like women. It's very clear instantly to a woman, when you meet a man, whether he likes women as a race or whether he doesn't like women as a race. You can almost divide them in two, and the men I've gone for have always been the first kind. There are a lot of women who seem to be masochistic, who will never go for that person, they will always go for the ones who, for some reason, do not like women, thereby provoking a behaviour they already expect.

Women will talk about being desperately upset about something; men won't talk about it, but it's there. That's the difference, I think. Men are taught to repress their feelings and women are taught not to repress their feelings, so that's led us to believe that men don't think or feel, but I don't think that's true at all.

Michelle Coquillat: Of course, you find enormous differences caused by the cultural environment. For instance, it is interesting to realize that men have decided they have an enormous ability to learn technical and mathematical languages and so on. It seems to be more difficult for women, but for cultural reasons, because they are set aside from the very beginning, from the time they are six or seven years old, and if they are not fantastically gifted, they will never make it. Therefore, of course, men's and women's consciousness probably will be different because they have different vocabulary, different concepts. But this is essentially cultural.

A certain difference comes from our biological make-up. I don't deny that men are physically stronger, that this strength gives them a different view of the world, different attitudes. Also, most of the time, they have better health. For instance, they can eat and drink more without being affected by it. The difference between a man and a woman is enormous for that reason. Being taller gives them another view of the world. Men and women are told that they have different glands and therefore must have different behaviours. Undoubtedly, the fact of being physically stronger, stronger muscles and so forth, of being less affected by long journeys, being less tired, being able to work longer, all gives another perception of the world. Men themselves are different, too, because you have very strong men who are weak physically. For instance, in the nineteenth century the great Romantic vision of the creative artist was the very small, fragile, feminine-looking man – Chateaubriand, Lamartine, all these young men killing themselves at twenty-one because they were unable to stand the difficulty of the world. But this is accepted in the society of men; it is not considered as being inferior. There's no stereotype. What is wonderful about men is that they tolerate all the spectrum of types of men. You can be a small man with great ideas and perfectly accepted; you can be a tall man with no ideas and be accepted; you can be a sportsman with no brain and so forth. Therefore the spectrum of creative possibilities for men is enormous, and I think this is what we should try to get for women. This is why a lot of men think the feminist women are jealous of men. This is not it; it is just that they have set for themselves no standards, there's an enormous range of possibilities. Women don't have this, and this is where I think there is a great disadvantage. It is very hard for a woman to be dwarfish or ugly. If a man is like this, and has a great intelligence and a fantastic job, it's not going to affect his life that much.

Susan Crosland: Because of the nature of women's lives, unless they are career women and in an office, they have more time – if they are at home, which most of them are – more time to reflect and go over things

995

in their minds. And women who are based at home tend – this is a generalization – to get things out of proportion, and therefore to be illogical, because they keep going over the thing in their mind, whereas the man puts it out of his mind. There is a sex difference here, perhaps, in that the man, in my experience, tends to go on to the next thing. He listens to what the problem is, but he doesn't want to go on agonizing about the problem. Take a decision, that's the end of it; go on to the next thing, go on to your office, but don't go on over and over the thing. And women, by thinking so much about a thing, actually should have cleared it up, but in fact get it out of proportion.

There you are, in your teens, with this bloody mess. I don't like my period and I've never liked my period. I knew nothing about it until it happened. It was traumatic, literally traumatic, and I still don't like my period. From the age of twelve or so, you're dealing with the fact that you are bleeding once a month. My youngest daughter said, can you imagine how a *man* would feel?

Mary Crowther: An attractive, elegant woman, who is also intelligent and quick, is far more noticeable and sought after than the male equivalent. I suppose because they're such a rare commodity.

The reason there are fewer female politicians, or female surgeons, or whatever, is partly lack of confidence. Women don't think they can be as good as men. There's also an element of choice, that women choose not to lead the mad lives many men lead.

If you want to be fulfilled by being a doctor, you can get that fulfilment in other ways, without doing surgery. For men, it's different. Why should it be different, having said that? I don't know. Perhaps because of the ethos of surgery as well. Surgery is very much a boys' club. Surgery is very crude. The environment is very crude. It's a male-dominated field, needing a lot of physical stamina. Women have that. Women can get up in the middle of the night, they have children, they look after children, they are quite as capable of doing that as men. But there is a sort of bravura about it that doesn't appeal to women. It's sweaty and it's coarse.

There's this great dichotomy in women that they're very good at practical things whereas men are far better at abstract things. Women can be very careful, very painstaking, very gentle, very soft, but the other side of the coin is the instinctive wrath, if you like, or anger in women, which I guess is an old protective instinct for looking after children, but it's an anger far steelier, far more vengeful than male anger. A man can go and get a gun and shoot someone – you can have Joseph Stalin in any society. If you don't like it, get rid of it, exterminate it. But women don't usually do that. Their anger is directed in far crueller ways. But men have the power to break you through money – if you upset them, they destroy your business or whatever. Men have other ways of getting even with people who cross them. But women don't usually have that sort of power, and so they have to use other devices, and it's usually on a personal level: things that are said or acts against men. It's very odd, for example, where you hear of marriages when men and women don't sleep together and don't talk to each other for years. It's usually women who initiate that rather than men. Women switch off. Men just fumble along from day to day.

I'm sure there are biological differences, quite apart from sexual ones, which affect the ways in which men and women think. From the earliest ages after birth, even before children can have perceived conditioning, there are distinct differences in the motor capacity of little male and female babies and tasks they can do, so there probably are biological differences. Whether that's a hormonal effect, whether it comes after birth, I don't know, but there are differences. Women are far better with their hands, doing fine tasks, far more diligent. Little girls are far better numerically at doing arithmetic than men, yet, in terms of mathematics and the more abstract field of numbers, men are better than women. Men do think in a different way, and I'm sure it's not conditioning.

Jennifer D'Abo: Women in this country still have a credibility gap. Men always feel that you have emotional problems, suffer more from stress, have families to worry about; you get to a certain age and you're unpredictable, et cetera. There's always a feeling that women don't have the strength men have. Now I don't think that's true. I think women have more stamina.

I would employ women much more easily than men do. I think I'm tolerant of women's problems more than men are. I employ a lot of women. For instance, our warehouse, distribution system and computer system is run by a woman, an extremely competent, ex-commodity broker, brilliant girl, ten years younger than me. She came to me and said, I want to have a baby, but I don't want to have it and upset you. I said, well, have it in August, the warehouse is at its lowest in August – which she did. She takes the baby into the office and takes days off, and all I've ever said is, you do your job in your own time. Now, how many

997

men would say that? I'm more flexible. I would rather have her on fewer days a year doing a better job than any man I've ever found to do it.

Béatrice Dalle: When women are together, it's only to criticize other people, or discuss blokes and clothes, how badly dressed other women are. It makes you sick. But with men it's not the same, you don't talk shit. That's why I don't have girlfriends. I get pissed off with them.

Alma Daniel: Now we are recognizing that there is a male and female part in each one of us. Whether we happen to be in a male body or a female body, we have both of these aspects within us. And the challenge, right now, is to learn how to bring these two aspects into some kind of harmony, so that I can have a masculine aspect and be in a feminine body without being lesbian or homosexual; and a man can recognize this feminine aspect in a male body, without being considered gay. I think we are coming to terms with our various sides and our various aspects.

Conditioning is a process that takes place over many, many generations, and centuries. And that has to do with cellular changes. That's my theory. By dint of repetition of ways of being, which have been repeated and repeated and repeated, those ways of being become innate. They do experiments where one generation of rat learns how to do a maze, OK? The next generation of rat knows how to run that maze. Now, how does that generation of rat learn that? Was it culturally endowed? Was it genetically endowed? Are there some genetic differences within the sexes? Perhaps so, perhaps so, for the purpose of procreation. Why do women tend to be monogamous and men not? Doesn't it have to do with child-bearing, and knowing who the father is, and having a father there? Whereas men don't have that necessity. And yet this tendency is something that has been encouraged over centuries, it seems to me.

There must be differences. That's what makes for fun, that's what makes for some enjoyment in the situation. If we were all identical, there wouldn't be much challenge and there wouldn't be much stimulation. But some of these gendered differences are getting less. In the playground, I see fathers with their children, and where are the mothers? Working? Yes, in many cases. There are house-husbands who have taken on the traditional female roles, and I must think that this has to do not only with the imperatives of their situation, but with some natural impulse on their part to be nurturing.

998

Sister Camille D'Arienzo: No matter how we got our separate perceptions and gifts and creativity and strength, if we joined forces in a common goal for the good of the world, what we offer as a pair, man and woman, is far more than we can offer separately. And what I look for in the Church is the recognition of our complementarity. Don't tell me that God created us all equally, but somehow men are more equal than women. That's nonsense. Don't tell me that women cannot hear and love and follow the Lord. I've seen too many do it. Don't tell me that women can't administer. They've run the school systems and the hospital systems and the health-care agencies. Don't tell me they are not brave. They've gone out there on battlefields to nurse the dying. They will face ecclesiastical hierarchy in ways that men simply can't, because they have too much vested in the system. So women have the courage. They have vision, they have imagination, they have generosity. All women? Of course not. I'm speaking of those who feel called and who are disposed to do this. The only way any person, man or woman, can be inferior to the other is by making those choices which somehow diminish the amount of grace in the world. When I say the amount of grace I mean the amount of goodness, the quality of life, the virtues of caring. I think inferiority is a matter of will, I don't think it is a matter of physical composition. Physical composition is not important to me.

The most irrational construct of our lifetime is the making of weapons of destruction. Now, if nuclear weapons are a testimony to the rationality of man, we have to redefine the term rational. Am I afraid that women feel and express feelings? Would I be afraid that some women, at some point of the month, behave in ways that are not as sanely acceptable? First of all, I don't believe that that holds in most instances. But it would be better to be irrational two days a month than thirty days when you planned another Pentagon enterprise.

Mandy Rice Davies: The one thing I find that women have that men lack in a serious degree is common sense.

Women's autobiographies tend to talk about the men in their lives; whereas, in men's autobiographies, the woman is nearly always the background, and the foreground of that autobiography is the career, what he has done. That's quite interesting. That tells a lot.

Régine Deforges: Men have much more self-esteem and pride. Women can be proud but they are much less vain. Men hold on to their rank. I know lots of women who don't give a fig where they are sat at a dinner, but a man will be mortified if he isn't given the right position.

When it comes to crimes of passion or premeditated crime, then a man will do something violent and liberating; a woman who kills is hiding her crime. I think that murderesses must be much more interesting than murderers. It's much more complex. A man will kill calculatingly, or through impulse; women, too, but *before* getting to that point a woman is more timid in violence. A man will fight in the street. I am a combative type, but I do not see myself giving someone a punch in the face in the street.

Male sexuality is external and immediately perceptible. You can see it. There is calm, then suddenly something explodes. Female sexuality is the opposite. It is internalized.

Dr Mary Jordan-DeLaurenti: If you go into a group of all males, you will see the aggressiveness, sometimes even the violence, in that group. If you go into a group of all females, you will see a lot of chatter, a lot of interaction, a getting down to things that are really important to them. I don't think it is society's conditioning. Experiments have been done with injections of oestrogen and injections of testosterone. The testosterone has made people more aggressive, much more aggressive. But I know that conditioning is critical to the influence. I consider my husband to be one of the most sensitive human beings I know and have met, and most accepting of women in general and of me in particular. But I see the male characteristics in him: things like never admitting defeat, never giving in when he's wrong, those kinds of things that I think are perhaps conditioning. But a lot of it is a mixture of conditioning with the biological.

Women have intuition, a strong sensitivity to pick up signals that men don't have the sensitivity to pick up. We understand the total person more than men do, we get right into it. I think we bring that sensitivity to an organization. I have had this business now for eleven years, and when I go into an organization that has all males in it, I believe it's dominated by some of the worse characteristics of the male or what I call too much testosterone. A like thing can be said if you go into an environment of all females, that the environment is dominated by some of the worse characteristics. It's when they're blended that the best of both come out. The advantages of being a female are in being able to contribute something different from what the males contribute: not only sensitivity to people – that, I think, we have – but also a different perception of issues. We perceive issues differently from the way men perceive issues, and we bring a whole different point of view. For years, these men have thought one way, made decisions one way, and a woman will ask a question that they think is completely out of the ordinary or off the wall, and they start thinking a whole different way.

Lady Camilla Dempster: Men are unbelievably aggressive, which doesn't get them anywhere. Whereas women might think, OK, too bad, let's go on to the next thing. And women are much more ready to admit their failings. I don't think it's humility, I think they are much less buttoned up. But that goes back to the English upper-class thing of never showing your feelings to anybody except your dog.

Women have compassion and men don't. Men try and say that women are sentimental, which they are – more obviously sentimental than men – and try to say their compassion is nothing more than sentimentality. But I don't think that's true. And I do think women are kinder and much less aggressive. I think they've worked out that life is much easier if you don't lose your temper all the time.

Women react quicker and maybe are not so rational. But I do think their instinct that they work on irrationally is usually right. It might sound irrational, but if you wait and see if they are right or not, they usually are.

Sylvia Deutsch: Women are much more down to earth, and men can't stand being on their own so much. A woman has her children, her friends; a man needs someone to dominate or at least be at his side in order to exist. There is something I have noticed, and that's that stupid women have never been so successful as at the moment – as opposed to all these women who impose themselves and who frighten men and who make them feel unmanned by their intelligence. The more stupid a woman is, the more successful she is, because she reassures the man, and I've known examples of men married to or connected with intelligent women – not, I may add, the Valkyrie type – and these men have all turned towards stupid ugly women because their own Pygmalion side is appeased. When he can't dominate, a man is lost.

You need more energy to live in a male world made for men. In the business world, men have a ready-made position, whereas women have to make their own position. Even over twenty-four hours, a woman has much more to do because her home has to be well kept. A woman automatically has to be a housewife: the children have to be well dressed and have the right things to eat. So what with the house, animals if there are any, the children, the man whom you have to amuse, excite, all that, in addition to work, a woman has more to do than a man, and in more areas. For a man, it's his work, home and sometimes extra-conjugal relationships but, apart from his work, his life is very passive, whereas a woman has to be active in work, at home and with her children. And since it's more often the woman who seduces, then, yes, a woman needs to work harder, or perhaps be more cunning.

The way the brain is constructed is different in men and women, and we are biologically very different. I've always been fascinated by the way man and woman have been made to go together, and it is probably those differences which make us closer. They are moral and physical differences, and also cultural. For thousands of years, men have underlined the difference, and if you look at how various civilizations have imposed the difference, the woman has been inferior, the subject; and, apart from a few exceptions resulting from a quite unusual combination of circumstances or of exceptional intelligence, men have created this difference because they needed to reassure themselves. Now that there is a *certain* equality – I don't believe there is total equality – man feels lost, he is deeply disturbed. He needed that difference to feel sure of himself, to give himself confidence.

Kay Dick: A lot of men and women today put themselves into image positions which aren't really true. They say, I'm a man, therefore I must react in a certain way; I'm a woman, therefore I must react in a certain way. A lot of them do, in order to be, quote, trendy. But the people one likes react as people, they're half and half. My theory is that most people are bisexual. I don't mean in sexual behaviour, I mean in temperament, in emotional outlook. There's always something of the man in a woman, or something of the woman in a man – at least in the nicest people.

Anne Dickson: Men don't know they have feelings, and so they are much more prone to behaving in a really cock-eyed way. They don't know they are responding to some kind of distress in themselves. It is as people we have feelings. It's not: men have feelings and women have feelings. Again, because of this sexist division, they say women are irrational, men are rational. Men have no idea that they have deep feelings. And they certainly don't want to express them, and they are still operating in whatever position they have from an apparently

1002

rational viewpoint, but that rational viewpoint is rooted in emotion – in anger, sometimes, in resentment, frustration, fear, all sorts of things – and is never expressed.

I am not a mother, but nevertheless my ability to conceive, menstruation and all that, are really important parts of being a woman, and that is a connection with the earth which I don't think I would have if I were a man. At this particular time, too, I love the extremes of being a woman. I love the fact that I can be both totally emotional and yet utterly dispassionate and rational about things, and I love the feminine extremes, like being able to dress up in feathers and sequins, then appear in jeans. I just love all the options at different levels. Had I lived two hundred years ago, I still think I would have had the rhythm and everything, but I would probably have been married and had lots of children, and that would have been different. But there is a tremendous power in being a woman. I love the power, and it is not power *over*. Men don't really have a lot of power, except in the world; they have a lot of oppressive power and money power, but women have a lot more power in themselves, and some of that comes from the connection with the earth and the rhythms and the seasons. They are very much a part of Nature. There's that ancient quality about that power that women have, and I don't think they lose it, even though you might look at many women and wonder where the hell it is. As Doris Lessing said in one of her books, women were the keepers of secrets, and they are – and that's one of the reasons. There's a great secret power in women, and it's really exciting that more of that is being discovered, but it's not being discovered for the first time. Women know, they know about living and about dying, which I don't think men do. Women are cut off from dying now, because we have been stereotyped. Again, this is sexism. We've only been told to be loving, we've forgotten about the death that's involved in giving birth as well. But women have a fundamental grasp of the really important life issues, and of the soul. They have a tremendous spiritual power, and that's what real power is, and I don't think men have it. Men try and subdue it in women, and want it from women, want to touch it and take some of it for themselves. But I don't think they actually have it.

Margaret Drabble: I think that women's capacity to cope is something to do with knowing that your mind has got to take in a lot of things at once. With me, I know it's having to work while I had small children, and so you're listening to somebody, you're thinking about the supper. I'm so used to sitting in a committee meeting and writing my shopping list, thinking, if I get to the deli on the way home, can I get this? Men don't have to worry about that kind of thing, so their minds don't react as quickly. That is both a terrible worry to a woman, and also a great advantage, because it keeps the brain moving.

Because of the menstrual cycle and the bodily instincts, it could be argued that women have more sense of bodily reality than men. There's a wonderful bit in one of Saul Bellow's novels, where he says that women are used to seeing their own blood and men aren't, but men are terrified of blood and therefore they fight wars. Which I suppose the feminists have now taken up: the whole idea of menstruation being a natural process and fighting war unnatural, and blood being unnatural in war but natural in the menstrual cycle. It's not proven, but I do think it's interesting.

I've never felt unhappy with my situation at all, but that's because I have the kind of life that's ideally suited to a woman. The advantages are that one has a very flexible way of looking at things. One learns to do plenty of things at once, to keep an eye, an ear open for everything that's happening, which means that, if something goes wrong in one's career structure, it's not a terrible setback, a terrible loss of face, it's just, OK, something else. That flexibility is a very strong card. Professional men on the whole, in this country, expect to march up through the hierarchy, and if they don't make the next step, that's really bad. Women don't even notice they haven't made it. A lot of women don't even notice, because they're so busy thinking about new things. I was talking to a friend who's a botanist. She is full of a new career, and she's my age, in her late forties. She said, well, it's extraordinary, she now has more ideas and more offers of jobs than she's ever had, because she's able to think of anything, whereas a man in her position would now be running the administrative part of the Natural History Museum, he'd be a civil servant. She's completely free to go off for a year to the rain forests of Borneo, which is what she's doing next year. She doesn't have the structure to worry about.

I've got two boys and one girl, and I look at how they've grown up, and I really can't tell what makes the difference, but I think a lot of it is conditioning. It would have been very interesting in my own family if there had been an older boy instead of three big girls, to see where my mother would have put her sympathies, her ambition. My children are very different. My elder son is a very academic boy, therefore he could have a conventionally successful career if he chose. My daughter's all over the place, full of wild ideas and very gifted, but in a much more diffuse way. My younger son, he knows what he is doing. It's interesting because I can see the danger to me of trying to impose on my elder boy the masculine career that was closed to me. I can see I could do that.

Some women are very unkind. Women can be very unkind and hard, and they can be domestically appallingly behaved and ruin the lives of the men to whom they happen to be married. The ideal of the nurse is this loving tender angel of the bedside. In fact, some nurses are very sadistic, as though they're taking revenge for their status on the patients. And I remember my father on his deathbed saying, don't let any women near me, I've had enough of them. That was in hospital, and I thought that was very interesting that he had had enough of so-called kind women nurses and matrons. He wanted young men by his bedside, because he said they were kinder. So, to assume that all women are naturally tender and loving is not true at all.

Princess Elizabeth of Yugoslavia: We are more emotional than men. But men can make irrational mistakes and decisions because of their own ego problems. They can often take the most ridiculous steps for face-saving, or out of pride, which is very dangerous. This is why I think it is dangerous to have too many men politicians.

Sally Emerson: Women are much more vulnerable. They've got to be, to have children. That's why women are made that way, to have that amount of love and sympathy for the child and to bring it up while always also looking after it and making sure it's all right. And never to be concerned about yourself. You've got to have that ability to be selfless, which means you must be emotionally vulnerable. Also, this business of falling in love and staying with one man. Nature's worked out that it is better for the human race that women, when they fall in love, really fall in love and just want that one man. They settle down to have children and look after them, and they don't just abandon them.

Men are much more ruthless. If a man, a strong-minded man, decides he wants a woman, he'll just take that woman. He won't consider the family or the children or anything else. You see it time and again. Whereas, if a woman decides she wants a man, she will actually think about the children and the wife, and she will stay in some bed-sitting room year in, year out, waiting for the phone to ring. Men don't do that, they just immediately break up the marriage. It wouldn't matter with men if it was a best friend. If they wanted the woman, that would be that, I think.

Women tend to be much kinder, much more understanding, much more sympathetic. I don't know that they're superior. I think men tend to be much cleverer. Men have much better brains than women, in the sense of rational, intellectual brains. They can work things out better. Women may be more intuitive and instinctive, but when it comes to an argument, men, on the whole, are a lot better than women. There are just standard truths about men and women. Men tend to be less interested in people, or what's going on in people's lives – you could call it gossip – and much more interested in public events. They're interested in the intellectual public events and women are interested in private events, passions, instincts and intuitions.

Very often, even in the best novels, there is a sense of women being seen from the outside, as these rather mysterious creatures. They don't come over to me as a real friend, as I experience somebody I know well who is a woman. None of these characters do, particularly in *War and Peace*, although they're marvellous characters. But the men are real people who are developing and expanding. I find it very difficult to do the men in my books. My women are much much better. But – this is interesting – sometimes I find it difficult writing women because I get this sense of seeing them from the outside, seeing them through men's eyes, when I'm writing, because we're living in such an obviously male society, and have been for so long. I find I'm slipping into the same way of looking, because that is the way the society looks. It happens more and more to me, not just in my writing but in general. As you pass through life, you absorb more of it, and more of its conventions. I have to shake myself out of it.

Men have to pound off and do better and better in their careers, and I think most conventional men in the conventional world have a rough time; and a rougher time, increasingly, as women become tougher, because they don't then even have women saying, oh, you're marvellous, you're working so hard for me. I think they have a raw deal. Women just come back and say, oh, well, I've been doing my job and looking after the child and we went for walk in the park; and they don't really respect men for doing their work. There isn't that sense of, you've earned all the money for me. It's just, you happen to be doing that, but I wish you'd come and look after the child more. They don't get the rewards they used to have. Women may have problems nowadays, but the real problem nowadays is being a man.

Shirley Eskapa: I wouldn't say men believe women are irrational as much as illogical when, in fact, women are much more logical than men.

1006

Women form their conclusions so quickly, and their inner computer moves so rapidly, that they're never sure how they come to the conclusions. They make conclusions without being aware of having made deductions, because they have to in their own lives all the time. Women have to balance so much. They have to make so many decisions at so many levels, and very often simultaneously. Men don't understand why people react as they do. They don't understand why personality conflicts should take place. For example, if you're talking about a man at his workplace, are you not talking about him at home? Women understand that sort of thing. But very often, to get their point of view across, they have to be manipulative, simply because, by and large, men are much thicker than women.

The compassion of women is very real. It extends to men and extends to women in need or women as equals, but never to a woman competitor. That's why I wrote *Woman versus Woman*. What I tried to show in that book is that the wife or the other woman each sees the other as an enemy and as a threat, and then all their ingenuity, all their intellect, is brought to bear on that woman enemy. They can be much more cruel to a woman competitor or a woman threat than any man. I am convinced of that, and my work's borne it out. Women can interpret the behaviour of other women in all areas much better than men can. If I'm dealing with a man who is my superior, I am only dealing with him on an unequal footing because he can't understand what I'm on about, because women are not transparent to most men. But any woman can see through me. One glance and they know everything about me. Women have to do that to survive, absolutely to survive.

No matter how liberated, once a woman is involved with a man, that man in her life becomes infinitely more important than she becomes in his life. This is the other thing I realized when I was doing my book, the most damning discovery I made. I asked men, did you think your wife would leave you? Have you ever thought what you would do if your girl-friend left you? They had never thought of it. Every single woman I spoke to – every single one – told me that, at some level of their consciousness, they had this profound fear that their man would leave. Now I can only believe this is true because the responsibility for the maintenance of the family lies with the woman. Because it is much, much easier for a man to find a replacement than it is for a woman. Women know this.

Marcia Falkender: Men and women are very different in every way. Men don't agonize, they live much more on the surface of life rather than recognizing what it's all about. They have to in a sense, because it's their role – or was traditionally their role – to provide. And it's that role, imposed upon them, that has produced what they are: mainly that they are not very deep in the sense women are. Women are much more introspective about life and finding and believing and working out what it is all about. I don't think men are like that at all. And a woman can't actually accept that what for her is a very big moment in life, isn't necessarily going to be for a man. A man can't see that relationships necessarily are something you have to work at and have to get right. I mean, it can wait, can't it? Surely you can talk about that next year, or next month, or tomorrow – we'll go through it then. But a woman feels you should try to do this as you go along, you shouldn't get it out of sync. She likes life to be tidier, in that sense. A man is much more likely just to skate over it to get what he wants. He's engaged in something else. He's quite happy to sacrifice some of the other things in life as he goes along if it's a question of his employment. I don't think a woman is quite so happy to. She'll balk at it, and she'll probably choose the personal end of it rather than the other. They are very different, and to try and pretend women can be like men, and therefore you can have some equality of the sexes on those grounds, is nonsense. They complement each other rather beautifully, and that's what makes life worth living. If you start to try and break them down so that they are both going to be exactly like each other, it would end up as sheer horror.

Women totally lack confidence in everything they do, it's one of their problems. And that's because they take life far too seriously. Everything in life matters for them, because in a sense it really does. Women understand what we are here for, I think, more than men do. I know men are the philosophers and the great writers, but the woman has the realities of life. She bears the children and therefore knows what life is really about. And she can't be bothered with all the rubbish that goes with position and keeping your place, and keeping to forms, and all that sort of thing. She gets so taken up with realities, the knowledge that she does have to keep all of that going, that it diverts her from practising the art of being whatever men feel it is to be a top person. I find, in top people's lives, that if you go to a committee meeting and don't address the chairman as Mr Chairman every five minutes, you are not a good committee member. It's rubbish. Now, a woman won't be bothered with all that. She'll sometimes remember to say, well, Mr Chairman, or she'll remember there are certain forms and procedures to be followed. But, on the whole, it's not important, so she won't actually keep to it. A man always keeps to those forms because they are part of the sort of dance of his life. It's how he manages to make it go. He'll spend hours doing all that, even if nothing comes out at the end of it. It's part of the structures of being the chairman, the managing director, it's more the form than the substance. And although they pretend they are all for action and getting things done, when you have sat with them long enough, you realize that just isn't so. The action and what's being done is never happening where *they* pretend it's happening. It's either happened because somebody else did it for them and told them afterwards, or it's happened in the space of two seconds – they got to their office and took the one call that, by coincidence, came as they walked in and was the most important call of that day, or that week, or even that year. So it's nothing to do with all these forms that they have going on, and all these structures they keep going. But they love it. If you strip them of all of that, and strip them of the titles and all the paraphernalia of their lives and all the hours they spend just talking, you reduce them to nothing. Now, a woman can't put up with that. She finds that a waste of time because her life has to be very much geared to doing other things as well. Very often she is a wife and mother as well as being a public person and carrying a job. And therefore all of it has to be got through, and it has to be got through efficiently. And if she is sitting in a committee and they are wasting hour after hour discussing and getting nowhere, she becomes impatient and cuts through it all and forgets the procedures, and forgets this committee or that committee has got to decide it before you go on from this to that. She sees that you don't really need to go to the Lord Mayor's Banquet every year at exactly the same time, dressed in exactly the right gear, and you don't have to keep up the act of being whatever you think you are. I think it's that that singles the woman out from the man and makes it much more difficult for her to cope with his world. She regards it, I think, with a little bit of scepticism and thinks it a bit false. Because reality, for her, isn't like that. Reality, for her, is the home and looking after it and making life work privately and personally as well as making things happen in her working life. And if she's got children, it's also making sure they are OK, too. Of course, some don't have children, and they are the fortunate ones in respect of carrying a job – the unfortunate ones in respect of living.

The difference is partly biological, otherwise there would have been no reason to have constructed male and female as they are. It must be biological. Having a child takes a long time; giving a child takes all of one second. So, by definition, it has to be a very different role, and the role you have must, by definition, also make you a different creature. In the animal world, it's the same. There's a difference between a woman who hasn't had children and a woman who has had children, though I think the woman who hasn't had children has an instinctive knowledge of what it could be about, there's a solidarity of feeling there. It does change you, however, there's no doubt about it. The protective side is always very dominant in women, because that's the role Nature gave them. Maybe that's why men see them more as staff officers and more as the supportive characters than the lead role. Because women do have a protective instinct about them. They want to make everything all right, they want it to be stable and safe, and they want to form a protective barrier around everything that's happening. Women don't naturally make war, for instance. They would not want to expose sons, or brothers, or lovers, or husbands to going to war. It's that wish to protect that makes them very different in their attitudes to the big issues.

As regards the Falklands War, I rather suspect that Mrs Thatcher didn't think it was the Third World War, which it wasn't. And I think, if it had been fighting Russia or fighting a first-rate country with a vast experience of fighting wars and a well-trained army, Mrs Thatcher's courage might have been a little less. It was a wonderful operation. I wouldn't decry it for a moment. Like everyone else, on the day it happened I said, what are the Argentines doing, marching into the Falkland Islands? We must do something. I think most of us never thought it would get as far as doing anything. Certainly, if Argentina had been Western Germany or Israel or somewhere like that, no one, for one minute, would have decided to go to war with them, because they'd have known they would have been hammered. So I think that warlike instinct was political, not necessarily a masculine trait. I think she has certain fighting instincts in the way a woman fights for her own, not the way a man fights for acquisition. I don't think women naturally fight for acquisition. They like to possess things, but they are not going to want to possess things just for the sake of possessing. On the whole, they aren't that acquisitive. They are acquisitive just to make their own patch and their own near to them safe and get things for them. But they don't do it in the way a man does. His is a much more aggressive and nastier role.

Esther B. Ferguson: History has always shown that women simply share more. You can't bond if you can't talk about the bad things and the good things, and men will not tell you what's wrong with them, what their hurts are, and present their vulnerabilities. We women will, flat out in a minute, tell you. I can do this, I can't do that, what our problems are, where our hurts are. And when you do that, you can bond.

Annie Flanders: When your hormones are acting up, no matter how rational and strong you want to be, you just sometimes become irrational.

For many years, I would have gone along with saying women are more intuitive, but since the women's movement, and since more equality between men and women, there is a younger generation of men, not a lot of them, who have been brought up not to take on this macho role, and to feel free, to be warm, to cry, to be sensitive. I think they also are intuitive. There's a change in some of the younger men.

Christina Foyle: They're very different, men and women. You need men because they are very able. You've got to have a few good men in a big business, you don't often find women with the ability men have. After all, what woman could design a car? Very few have. They do paint pictures and they write, but men are way ahead, really. But then women are far more honest, I think, far more trustworthy. We employ far more women here, because you can't trust men as you can trust women, in my experience. Women are very trustworthy, but they have their place, really. I mean, men are brilliant and they can do all kinds of marvellous things women never can do.

I think that the frightful thing about men, the one ghastly thing, is that they're so violent, so horrible. If you look all over the world, whether it's in Beirut or Ceylon, they're always fighting and using ghastly weapons. And they're so horrible, but women are not. That's why I'm glad we've got Mrs Thatcher. Men have got this awful streak, and I don't know how it will ever be solved. There are 50,000 men in prison and 500 women. Men are criminal, women are not.

I think that men are more selfish than women. They do what they want to do, and good luck. Most women don't, and they ought to. I think probably men want far more affairs than women, naturally they do; they always have. They enjoy it more, you know. It's always been the same.

Lynne Franks: A man's sexual needs are purely physical, a woman's sexual needs are generally emotional. So although one can meet women who seem to have been very promiscuous, if one really sat down to it and asked, would you sacrifice promiscuity for a fabulous relationship, both emotionally and sexually, with one man, they would. Most women really want to be loved and held and cared for, not by a whole series of people, but by one. I read a very funny book by the *Cosmopolitan* columnist Irma Kurtz, and she analysed it very well: men basically can put it anywhere, and women can't.

Rebecca Fraser: All men are always interested in one-night stands; this would be my guess. And women by and large are not.

Teri Garr: People all say, oh, girls develop faster, they are smarter, faster, or something like that. I don't think that's necessarily true. Some do, some don't. It's another prejudice, another thing that's put on our minds like, you know, black people like watermelon, and we go, oh, yeah. It's just a pre-conditioned idea, it's bullshit.

Pamela Gems: In my own personal history, I see men equally oppressed, for different reasons. That's not to say that there aren't men who aren't absolute monsters, but I see as many women who are monsters, witches – bad witches – that destroy children's psyches before they are out of the cradle with their coldness and hatefulness. But I think that the male dilemma is particularly acute. I have had men say to me, in a way you're lucky, you have a cause. It's true.

The more I talk to my sons and other men, and the more I talk to women, the more I think we see things differently. I say this particularly after having seen women, often younger than me, going for what I would call the masculine style of behaviour that is gaining pace, living a free sexual life, exercising the right to choose a partner, to ditch a partner, the right to choose not to breed from a partner, the desire to have a child but not to want to marry – you know, all these radical choices women have been making. And the concomitant unhappiness has been very defeating for a lot of women. I've seen that unhappiness. I know women, very well-known women, who've spent years in the London Clinic trying to breed. I know a woman who had a hysterectomy because she wanted to be an artist. Is art to be at the cost of mutilation? That can't be right. My own perception now is that women and men are far more different than I used to think, when I grew up with brothers. Particularly sexually. Particularly where sexual loyalty is concerned. I suppose I was nearly into my forties before I realized that to expect sexual loyalty from a man is to expect an abnormal man. You know, there was something bloody well wrong with him if he didn't lust after something that was absolutely fascinating out there in the street. It's very hard for women to accept that, because most women do breed at some point in their lives, and it changes you utterly. You are hostages to fortune then. You are dependent on the goodwill of the world; particularly, if you are wise, on a man, and if you are very wise, on the father of your children. We haven't discovered any really good substitute for the family unit, boring and reactionary and traditional as it's regarded. Children have a right to their own genetic inheritance. Take the surrogacy case in America – the woman who had a baby then couldn't give it up. The father lost all his relations in the Holocaust, so he badly needs a child. One can imagine his need. His wife has multiple sclerosis, so it would obviously be unwise for her to have a child. So they found a surrogate and the surrogate couldn't give up the child. What judgement does one make? The father is middle class, the child would have a very good life with him. The mother is working class, rather shaky background, without culture. Do you simply say, it is better for the child to be with the father? It's quite simple for me, because I am a woman. You cannot take a child away from its mother. It's an insanity. She can't give up the child and the child has a right to her. But the judge will give that child to the father, to what he thinks is the best environment and consider he's solved it. There's a surrogate case in England where twins were born and the woman didn't want to give them up. She's accepted £5,000 and the judge has ruled that the father may adopt the children and the mother must now be deprived of them. In other words, she must legally stay by her bond. It's nothing to do with what happens in the uterus and the bonding between a mother and child. If you start to break those laws, we might as well give up. Really I believe that. I think it's terribly dangerous not to honour the fact of natural family. You might as well go to the Nazis. You cannot say, look, you're a poor woman, you're a working-class woman, you can hardly afford to bring up your three children; we're an infertile middle-class family, we'll give you £10,000, please have a baby for us. I would love to have a baby for you; I already have my children and I need the £10,000. But now I have the baby and the milk's coming through, of course I can't give him up, he *is* me. I can't give up my arms and my legs. This is the difference between a man and woman. But most judges are still men, and the few female judges are in the masculine mode. Otherwise they wouldn't have got there.

Sarah Giles: I look at women who have slept around a lot. They have the same look as women who have taken too much cocaine or something. They look raddled. Whereas men – they just look like big macho gorillas, they look better and better.

Victoria Glendinning: Women are capable of great kindness but also of great unkindness. A great deal has been written about boys at public schools and prep schools, and the torture they go through. I went to a girls' boarding school, and the cruelty to unpopular girls and new girls and girls who were somehow different was much subtler and much less obvious, and probably the teachers never noticed it, but it was ingeniously cruel, so I think women are far more capable of both extremes than men.

Men say women are more irrational because women are working on a different system of reason. Women are more irrational in men's terms because men's terms are so very limited. Women are totally rational within the premises of their own argument, which a man doesn't see or recognize. Women aren't more irrational, it's just that they are using a different set of variables, or values, from the man. I think men, on the whole, can be as hurt, as touchy, as demanding, as needy as women. Anybody I've been close to, I've seen him cry. Maybe I made him cry. Quite often.

I think men have been made infantile by the service industry of women. On a perfectly superficial level, in a previous generation and still now, there are men who can't get their own dinners, as it were, and don't like coming back to an empty house. It always makes me laugh when a man says he hates coming back to an empty house, because that means the woman has to come back to an empty house. Somebody has to. That means that women are more grown-up. I think, to retain our hold on men, we have allowed them to remain infantile. The price of men growing up would be us not having a hold on them.

In the realm of politics, men like to have the last word and they like to have a say. Men tend to talk longer. When one is talking about the future of the SDP or something like that, the men tend to say more than the women and to keep on longer and want what they say to be it. And if you put forward different things, they try and find ways of knocking it down. Politics is the only topic where I find myself silenced in a rather humiliating way. I don't know why. I think politics is the weakest area for women in this country. We may have a woman PM, but she's a typical example of the woman who has done it the man's way, only more so. Or has revealed a side of women that most women use as a weapon without actually showing it. I do think it's true that women have characteristics that are most usually attributed to men. They need to have them to get through their lives; and men tend to have the characteristics which are traditionally attributed to women, a kind of dependence, and habit, and needing. There was the whole business of protecting women from life which went on in my parents' generation – women can't bear this, women mustn't know about that. But it had always been women who washed the dirty underpants, who cleaned up the shit, who changed the nappies, cleaned up the blood. They were never spared anything, and yet there was this myth that they were more delicate and mustn't hear these things. All the time, they were doing these things, cleaning up these things, and all the time it was the men who couldn't bear to see these things. There is a sense in which Margaret Thatcher has blown the gaff on that and shown the underneath toughness of women that, in a way, I myself don't admire. There is a side of women that is evil, and I think she sort of personifies it.

A lot of women live almost like my dog Sophie – in the moment, for the moment. And I do a lot of the time. A great many men have said to me that there's another person watching them doing what they're doing almost. It's as if they're measuring themselves all the time. Women find it harder to step outside their consciousness.

I feel that one has a certain amount of energy, and if you're very lucky you have quite a lot of it. But it's the same laser beam of energy we put on feeding the baby, doing the garden, painting the house, writing the book, thinking about Hegel. You just switch on the laser beam. I think what has happened to women is that we're very diffused in that way; even the ones with the most energy tend, if they're great writers, to run the farm as well. It's very hard not to get involved with everything. Whereas men are able to blank out huge areas of life, partly, again, because of history, because somebody else is looking after it. A merchant banker only thinks of tomorrow's meeting, because he doesn't have to think about what's for dinner. Partly it's necessity. I don't know how much this diffusiveness is necessity on a woman's part and how much her natural thing. I think women are rather imperialistic. Although we might say, I should love someone to take over the whole responsibility of the domestic side, I never want to cook the dinner again; seeing somebody else cook the dinner, you say, I wouldn't put so much turmeric in that if I were you. There is this incredible emotional imperialism, and physical imperialism, which means that, if they have energy, it can go out in a great many directions into a great deal.

Isabel Goldsmith: Many more women than men are stupid, but they are always stupid in a more charming way. Stupid men are so heavy and plodding, but stupid women have always got something. They always have a view of things that strikes one as rather unusual or funny, or, by its simplicity, sometimes is just charming. There is always something charming about women's stupidity which there isn't with men. Men find stupid women so much more relaxing. I always thought, if I had had a choice of how I'd want to be, I'd be not particularly intelligent. Just enough to go through life in a practical way, with good sense and incredible beauty. I really would have liked that.

Francine Gomez: The problem with women is that they mix their private lives and their professional lives, because their private lives are very important to them. Men consider professional life much more important, the private comes second, so they never take all their problems to the office. Women are not so regular. When they have love affairs going badly, they are depressed and you have to help them get out of it; and when they feel happy, they are marvellous.

Angela Gordon: Men have more of a sense of humour. Women are good at what I'm not keen on, and that is things like soft features. It's a terrible thing to say, isn't it? But it seems, in my experience, to be true. Women aren't hard-nosed enough when it comes to news. Nor are they very humorous when it comes to writing, generally speaking. I'm committing a great calumny saying this, but it's true in my experience.

Felicity Green: In all the areas of perception, women look at the same object with different eyes. Their evaluation is not different. If men and women look at a great painting, their evaluation of that painting may well be similar, if not identical. But I find, in discussing painting or writing with friends, one finishes up discussing different areas of appreciation with men and with women. Women tend to be less tangible, less technical, more emotional, more interpretative, less analytical. These are generalizations, and they probably come from observation among my own friends who come from my own background. It may well not apply if you are talking among academics, if you are talking among financiers. Most of my conversational stimulus comes from people in the media, people in my own working environment, and therefore I am probably discussing these things with people who begin from a similar position to myself. Certainly male journalists eye the world with a very different consciousness from women journalists, very different.

We live in a vast area of indecision and change. But for man to display indecision or lack of conviction militates against him in the society he has built up. Women don't have this handicap, this muddle about what they feel and feel they can say. It has been my experience that women carry their emotions much nearer the surface and, by and large, are prepared to peel off that surface and expose what lies beneath without feeling they are losing anything, without jeopardizing their position in their home, in their job, in society. Personally, I am happy to say, I have never cried in the office but I've been in the company of quite a few young women who, in circumstances not totally outrageous, were reduced to tears. So what? Lend them my handkerchief and, you know, in five minutes they pull themselves together. Imagine if a man were to cry in the office? It's unthinkable. I doubt he would ever be able to hold his head up again. I think it was Katharine Whitehorn who was talking about reporting wars, and the difference between male reporters and female reporters, and said, if you had more female reporters there would be a great deal less bang-bang and a lot more splat, which is what you get when people are demolished. It has become a cliché, a truism, but certainly, as far as journalism is concerned, if you give a woman writer a story, she wants to know who it's about, and if you give a man a story, it's often a question of where it is. Women have this preoccupation with flesh and blood and personality, and people and humanity. We are more emotional, and we are prepared to be more emotional without feeling we are giving anything up.

Menie Grégoire: Lots of differences are acquired, but there's one main biological difference, an essential one: the fact that women can have children. The priority we give to sentiment and feeling comes from this, in my opinion. They go side by side.

Laura Gregory: Intuition in women is exceptional. Loyalty: their loyalty is unprecedented. If you are good and fair to them, nothing will cloud their judgement. Whereas a man will sway with the wind, he'll sway with the boss, because he is terrified all the time of losing his job, losing his friends. Women probably have fewer friends. If you say to a man, how many friends do you have? Oh, I've got loads of chums and mates. If you say to a woman, how many friends have you got, she will probably look at you and say about four, or three, maybe even two. So those friends really are friends, not mates. A woman doesn't consider mates to be friends, they are just acquaintances.

Elsa Gress: Much has been accomplished politically and culturally, at least in this part of the world, and it is time for women to use the advantages and rights they have rather than stress minor discrimination and insist on extra privileges. The differences that do exist between the sexes are unimportant, and in many case delightful when looked at as part of the human heritage.

Baroness Grimond: Men excel at analysis. If you have a committee in which there are women, taking opposite or different points of view, the women instinctively try to arrive at some kind of synthesis or working arrangement. Whereas men (some men, not all) have to have some kind of opposition; they are stimulated by division, and this makes them perform better. I see this inside our party. There are certain groups who have to be always opposing, and this is their way of boosting themselves. Now, this could be conditioning. Perhaps it is, perhaps it comes from millions of years of having to defend your tribe. I just don't know. I think the biological difference may well make us temperamentally different.

Miriam Gross: When I observe my daughter, she's so different from my son. All her friends – the girls, I mean – talk about friendships, who's the most popular person. They analyse each other's characters and are interested in relationships even very early on. The boys, not particularly at all. There's a very profound difference between them which is not environmental. Little boys go around making machine-gun noises and shouting and banging into the furniture from the earliest age, whatever you do, and little girls, they may not play with dolls naturally, but they're interested in each other's characters and other people's characters. Obviously, one is generalizing, but by and large I think there is a biological element that makes women more interested in relationships, both for themselves and in general, and of course society adds to it.

Valerie Grove: I've got three daughters and a son, and the character of the boy was different from Day 1 without doing anything at all. In fact, the household and family were geared to female toys and female things, and from the moment he walked at nine months, earlier than any of the girls, he stomped and marched, straight-backed, with soldierly bearing, and he was interested immediately in things we hadn't got – aeroplanes, helicopters, guns.

Jerry Hall: I actually think that women are the stronger of the species. That's why they're chosen to have children, too. Because if men had to have children, they'd probably die. We're not as strong physically, but women can suffer pain more. When men are sick, they're really sick. The end of the world. When a woman is sick, she can get up and do things a man wouldn't. Women have much greater intuitive powers. All of my family are very intuitive, we always know when something is wrong with one of the others. We have very strong feelings from great distances. My twin sister and I have such a strong intuitive feeling together because we're twins. We slept in the same bed until we were sixteen, we spent every single day together. We always knew we had a special thing. We would know exactly what the other was thinking. If a friend said let's do this, anything like that, we always knew what the other was going to say. And when we left home, when I went to Paris and she stayed in Texas, when something was wrong with her, I would feel it, and when something was wrong with me, she would feel it. Once I was at a fashion show and fainted, and I'd never fainted before, I don't faint. I woke up with a terrible pain in my side, so I thought I was having an appendicitis, and they took me to the hospital and I had a very high temperature. They gave me tests for three days, my temperature went away after a day. They couldn't find anything wrong with me, though they thought it was very strange, and so they sent me home. Then I called my mother, because I didn't want to call her until I knew what was wrong, and she said, oh, I'm so glad you called, because the other day Terry had an appendicitis attack. She fell down, they had to take her to the hospital and take her appendix out.

Lucy Hughes-Hallett: I think that women, for sometimes rather negative reasons, are freer to shape their own lives. For instance, when I was growing up, it was very clear that a young man of my background – well-to-do middle-class – ought to be going into a certain kind of job. Had I wanted to be a journalist, as a man, as a boy, my parents would have been very concerned about it: there would have been a lot of pressure on me to choose a more secure profession. People limit themselves. I think a lot of men would have felt that, as they were probably going to have to support a wife and children in the future, so they ought to think about something, some work, which would bring in the kind of salary which would make that possible, whereas journalism is always a bit dicey, you don't know what's going to happen. So, in that way, I was much freer. I was able to take risks I wanted to take. In the same way now, I think, for a man, status – professional, social and financial status – is terribly important, and men, however much they might dislike it, are involved in a kind of competition. They are under pressure to prove themselves in certain conventional ways, and women can ignore all that.

I think men now feel less proud of being street-fighting men; they have been made aware that there are other values. And women, once they get an opportunity to get out into the workplace, can be very aggressive, very competitive, very assertive. Women can express feelings more easily, because women are more accustomed to that and have less shame about it. But whether that means they have more feelings, I'm not sure. There is one difference which seems to be very deep-rooted: that of sexual behaviour, that men are naturally promiscuous. Of course, nowadays women are more relaxed, more prepared to take their pleasure without emotional involvement.

Mira Hamermesh: I think the whole tack of men and women not being different is the wrong tack. There are differences between me and my sister, between us as the same gender, as individuals, and there are bound to be differences between the opposite sexes, and bound to be differences between nationalities. Not to acknowledge them almost inhibits a proper way of exploring some truth, because you are already being sent in a particular direction. You know, it's like, when did you stop beating your wife? Differences matter, but I'm not sure those differences are the only thing that matters.

Katharine Hamnett: I think women can go without orgasm for a much longer time than men can. Men have wet dreams, so obviously they need to have an orgasm much more frequently than women. And if you just look at animal life: female cats only fuck when they're on heat, male cats all the time, whenever they find a female on heat. There's one egg and a billion sperm. I think men actually need to fuck more than women do. In Nature, all male mammals do, but the females know they have to take more responsibility about their sexuality. They're left carrying the baby, so somehow one is programmed slightly differently.

Claire Harrison: Women will really worry a bit more about the people around them, whereas men will think, to a great extent, about themselves. I find that men who are very nurturing have had a very strong relationship with their own mothers, or some mother-figure, whereas men who have grown up with a less attached relationship with the female parent tend to be a bit less concerned, perhaps slightly less sensitive.

Nicky Hart: Men seem able to divorce emotional attachment and orgasm. This is the main problem for me in sorting out my own arguments for equality, because women do get somehow emotionally attached to men through sex, whereas men don't to women. It implies that men will have more power and freedom because they will have less emotional involvement.

Romaine Hart: Films that women make are on a much more personal level, about people, about relationships, about love, about all kinds of things that affect women and life and people. Men make films about violence, about war, about all the things they have been involved in. That is the difference between them. There are some men who make films about relationships, but mainly they're European men. They're not too often American men, or they're younger.

Quite often, men can't laugh at themselves. Women, I think, are more able to laugh at themselves, because they don't have this sense of ego and sense of self. Women have to laugh at themselves, do laugh at themselves.

Women have more common sense and more ability to get to the heart of the matter. There are wonderful exceptions to this – like Mrs Thatcher – but, on the whole, women certainly are much more able to take the centre out of a thing and get to the heart of it. I'm on a lot of committees, but I always think of the simple practical thing and I'm always surprised that none of the men on that committee have even thought of that. They're so busy paddling their own canoe or having their own particular hobbyhorse or going down their own avenue that they don't think in broad terms of the overall position and pick out the one central thing. I think I do that because I'm a woman.

In the right atmosphere, the right situation, the right environment, when they're feeling happy, or they've had a drink, or whatever, either sex would be happy to step out of line. But a man would probably do it first.

Bettina von Hase: If you look like the back of a bus, you can have the greatest mind or be the sweetest person, yet no man will be interested, forget it. That's a very crass statement, but it happens to be true in most cases, and it's incredibly maddening. I mean, women aren't attracted by looks at all. They are an added bonus. Women are very attracted by power, by personality. Funnily enough, I don't think, in general, they are as attracted by money as men always think they are, but they are attracted by – I don't know – an authority, by someone who feels passionate about something, a man who's honest with himself. If he happens to be good-looking into the bargain, that's rather great.

Nikki Haskell: I've seen men who are very irrational. I was married to a man who was very irrational. But I think that if women are irrational, it is because they don't know how to deal with situations. It's like men go through basic training before they go in the army. They learn how to fight, they learn how to protect themselves. Women never do that. There's no self-protection. There's no training for a woman.

Men are more pragmatic than women. I think the minute a man gets involved in a relationship, he knows the woman is going to want to get married. So everything he does is a lot more practical. He sets things up in a more practical manner so that he doesn't get caught, unless he wants to get caught. With a woman, it's a totally emotional thing. And if she finds someone who cares for her, all she is thinking about is getting married. That's the way I look at it. So a man is more practical in his overall approach, where a woman does it out of gut instinct.

Olivia de Havilland: There is such a thing as a masculine mind, the mind that has the sense of architecture. Now, I know some women who have masculine minds. Bette Davis is one, and I respect her mentality deeply and get along with her where other people can't. The reason is that I know how her mind is going to work. It will go straight to the point, like that, and she is fearless in defending her position, ferocious. And I watch all this and am really fascinated because I respect the way her mind works, I can see the quality of her thinking. She gets right to the point of things, she has a sense of architecture in situations. I don't understand a woman's mind, anyway. I really don't. I don't pay much attention to them and what they have to say. I really don't, as a general rule, have much respect for women's minds. They are appallingly inaccurate, superficial, and I think they lack judgement, I really do.

Kitty Hawks: Maybe emotions don't frighten women. When we get stuck on somebody, we want them around and don't mind showing our dependence. In fact we revel in it most of the time. I mean, I have seen men who are absolutely crazy about women and you watch them not reaching out to her, not showing that emotion, whereas women will hug guys and put their arms around them. It gets worse as you get older.

My femininity, my perception of myself as a successful sexual being, is not defined by whether or not I can get it up. And if it were, it would be a much trickier proposition. The sexual act does not define our sense of ourselves to the same degree it does with men. I've always felt sorry for them because of that. If they go out on their first date, and they're nervous and it doesn't work, they feel so awful about themselves, much more than we feel about them. I mean, we are not deriding them and making fun of them and saying how pathetic that they couldn't do this. But it's somehow bred into them, that need to prove themselves, to have as many women as they can. Who knows how all this is going to change now? Certainly Aids has changed the sexual behaviour of an awful lot of people. I think there's a closer link between the man who needs to prove himself sexually and prove himself, period. I don't think women need to prove as much.

Brooke Hayward: I'd say, and I base this on discussions with many, many men, that men really don't have the emotional attachment to sex that women do. For the obvious reason that women's bodies are, more or less, being invaded. So women have to be more protective, and more discriminating. Men have a more aggressive and less protective view about their bodies.

Cynthia Heimel: Women are more rational than men, because women take into account emotions, women take into account psychological motivation. What I've noticed about men is that they are much cruder in their knowledge of psychology, in their intuitive understanding of psychology and maybe even their formal understanding, and that plays such an important part that I find women more objective, much more logical, much more intelligent about the workings of human beings.

Men never know why they do the things they do. They don't understand their own motivations, they don't understand what makes them tick nearly as well as women do. Women are so used to having to watch other people, having to be aware of the different motivations, the different needs of other people, that they know what is going on much more than men do.

People are less threatened by women most of the time, and that fosters the closeness of humanity that men can't feel, can't have. I think that if you're feeling a cycle every month, and if you have babies, you do ebb and flow with Nature. You have that intense bond with your children. I suppose men feel an intense bond, but I don't know that it's as biologically imperative. I do feel sorry for men that they can't feel that, because having children is probably the most wonderful thing that can happen.

Marie Helvin: I don't think it is possible for men to be as honest as

1023

women. I really don't. Women think more about things in general. They'll look at a television programme or a painting and will think about it more than a man does. They think about things in a different way. I don't mean they'll think deeper, but in most cases it goes beyond what the average man would think or how he would feel about, let's say, a painting. I like men very much, but I do think there is something lacking, or maybe not lacking, it's just that it isn't there. And women have it. Is it a sense? I can't define it, but there is something that sets them apart up here.

A woman's emotional feelings are stored in her sexual organs. If she is feeling depressed, they're the first place it is going to affect. Men just don't have that in their balls, it's just not there.

Anouska Hempel: There is a biological difference, there absolutely is. You have a family full of boys, and a family full of girls: you can see the difference very early on, without the conditioning. As a mother with six children, two boys and four daughters, I have to tell you, you see the difference very early on. Little children react in a very different way. A boy and a girl in a room together will work the room in a very different way. The girls already have a sort of deviousness in them that I don't think they are aware of. Women have more inner strength on a survival level than men; obviously, with childbirth and all the suffering things women are supposed to have. Perhaps the greatest difference, from my point of view, is that women will listen and give somebody the benefit of the doubt more than a man ever will, on whatever level. He comes with a mind that answers, that is black, that is white, that's red, that area's grey.

Emotion leads women to be much more creative, it gives them much more of an ability to be creative. If you've been through a great tragedy or some terrible disappointment, or if you are high and flying on something, you will probably be higher or lower than a man will be. Now, if you are creative and artistic or whatever, those periods of highs and lows have to be constructive. Your sensitivity is more sensitive on both ends of the scale than a man's.

Beth Henley: When I write men characters and women characters, I always try to perceive them, their past, their wants, as those of an individual instead of saying, well, a man is going to be this and a woman is going to be that, like a woman is going to be shy and retiring. I might want a woman to be violent and angry or a man to be gentle. I really try

1024

to look at all the aspects of human nature depending on the individual. I think that's the only way to write real characters instead of trying to say these qualities are male and these female, and write the characters like that.

Val Hennessy: I think women aren't happy with the concept of a one-night stand. Women like some sort of continuity with the man they're making love to. If you really fall in love with a man, you don't simply want to sleep with him, you also actually would like to cook him a nice meal and make him laugh and share the books you enjoy with him. You'd like to take him to a particular beauty spot that you've enjoyed in the country and share it with him. I think women have this immense need to share all aspects of their experience, and not simply the sexual aspect, whereas a lot of men are quite happy with the casual one-night stand. I think this is particularly illustrated by gay men. I find it quite impossible to understand the way that gay men I've met will boast quite cheerfully about having had sex with four different men in one day, or one night. They'll pick somebody up they never ever met before, go back to some flat they've never ever been to before, do the most intimate things with this total stranger and then never see him again. They have no wish to see him again, and they will do the same with somebody else on the same day. Now, if you speak to gay women, this is almost unheard of. They have rather similar relationships to those heterosexual women would have. It's a partnership. They see the person repeatedly, they share things, they cook together, they go shopping together, it's a shared, loving, tender, close relationship, and this is not so with gay men. I think this could be a male characteristic. In the same way as gay men will be very promiscuous, there are heterosexual men also who are happy to have these casual relationships which require no depth, which actually require no deep giving, and, in fact, not giving deeply of yourself prevents you from being hurt if the relationship doesn't work out. That, to me, is a very profound difference between the sexes. I'd like to say not all men are like this, and I have men friends who are very conscious of longing to have long-term relationships and they've been unfortunate in not having discovered the person with whom they can have one.

Carolina Herrera: Men are the most irrational people in the world. It's absolutely out of this world how they react, and how they can be manipulated by women.

I'm not afraid of getting older and I never lie about my age. I'm not afraid of being alone either. That is another difference between men and women. Men are not accustomed to being alone; they do not know how to be alone. They have to have someone in the house or they have to be out.

Elizabeth Hess: I don't think ambition and aggression are simply the result of emulating men. I think women are genuinely ambitious and aggressive and are out there doing it because that's who they are. There are some men certainly that have been role models in terms of their success, but I don't think these women think of themselves as simply emulating a male model. The male model doesn't really want to move over and let them in. They are having to carve out their own territory. The same thing is true when it comes to sex. There are a tremendous number of single women out there finding that their sexual appetites are very similar to those of men. It's not just men who have access to the jobs they want, the sex they want, women are also out there in the same battlefield wanting the same things. I don't think it's simply that women are becoming more like men; I think women are being given the space to be who they are. The differences, in certain areas, are not that distinct.

Min Hogg: My masculine side comes out because I'm the one who does all the work when the others are having babies. I can't see any answer to that one that really works. We've had six babies in my office, and whenever any of them go, we don't bring in someone. They come back, but when they're away, it's my responsibility.

If there's trouble, men will almost always put it back to Mummy, because, they say, I can't, I can't. Women don't say that. Men need much more massage of yes, you can, yes, you can. You're a wonderful boy, a wonderful boy, works tremendously well. A man loves flattery, needs it. I do lay it on much thicker if I'm commissioning a man to do something than I would need to with a woman. Much thicker. And these are ordinary men, not homosexuals.

Marie-Hélène du Chastel de la Howarderie: Women usually feel more what you're talking about, whereas men, they pretend to.

Men seem to stick to something more easily than a woman. Women always have to hesitate. That's probably because of this connection between the two sides of the brain. I don't know, but they always have to go over things backwards and forwards. Men stick to something much better.

Arianna Stassinopoulos Huffington: I'm kind of reluctant to talk about women in general, because I've met so many different women who have demonstrated every conceivable characteristic. Even talking about myself, I see certain ways in which I am different from most men. I was thirty-five when I married, but now I'm married I feel that my relationship with my husband is the most important thing in my life. It's become the pivot around which my life revolves, and that I wouldn't have thought would be the case at all when I was single and very much a career woman and very much in my work. It doesn't mean that my work isn't terribly important to me now, but ultimately my marriage and my relationship with my husband comes first. Now, that's not anything to do with ideology or how it should be, or anything that comes from a mental decision, it is simply the way my heart tells me I want my life to be, it's just a heart decision. I feel I'm now acting more from my heart and less from my mind. Now, there are people who will say that this is a woman's characteristic. I don't know. I see a lot of men who act from their heart, and a lot of women who act from their mind. I used to act almost entirely from my mind – I was as cerebral a creature as you would hope to find. So I feel what's happening is that a lot of women and a lot of men in their own lifetimes evolve the masculine and feminine part in themselves, and that fascinates me. That's why I hesitate to talk about women doing this and men doing that. I feel we are moving towards an era where men will develop more and more the feminine in them, the intuitive, the supportive and the nurturing part, and women will develop more the assertive part of them, keeping it at the same time hand in hand with the nurturing of the family, whereas ten or twenty years ago they felt they had to reject the nurturing and the family in order to achieve the more assertive part of their personality.

Simply by virtue of the way men and women are built, there is a difference that is fundamental. If you take the sexual act, women are somehow made to be more receptive. That doesn't mean that they cannot be also assertive and everything, but there is a fundamental receptivity in the female make-up and a fundamental assertiveness in the male make-up. All this can become pathological, and you get the assertiveness becoming aggressiveness and the receptivity becoming a kind of masochistic surrendering, but there is no question that there are fundamental differences. Now, these differences do not in my opinion affect anything a woman can or cannot do, but they do affect our basic psychological make-up and we cannot ignore that. In the same way, when you look at statistics and say there are only so many women in this area and only so many in that area, you forget that so many women still choose primarily to be mothers and wives, and that many women who enter the workforce do it not because of any grand reasons of achieving equality with men, but because they need the money.

Being vulnerable, surrendering to life, is so important, and I feel that, as a woman, it is easier to do that. It takes a more exceptional man who can allow himself to be vulnerable and allow himself to surrender to the process of life and still be able to make a difference, and make things happen, and contribute and be assertive. That combination comes easier to a woman than to a man, and therefore we are very blessed. We don't have to be so exceptional to achieve the magical combination.

Caroline Huppert: In general, I believe more in acquired differences, and, though I don't know where it comes from, I think women are much more tenacious. Men are much more laid back whereas women have more trouble in relaxing. That can be a fault, of course. At work, a woman can fly into a temper, a man rarely. A woman can't stand having her word doubted; she gives the maximum in everything she does, 150 per cent.

I think a woman feels more than a man that time is against her, and that makes her less confident. It's not so much that she lacks confidence in herself: she thinks that things are going too fast for her, and it's true, she has less time to do things. In the same time-span, she has to have a career, have children, and then suddenly she is old and no one wants to know. Professional success for a woman depends on youth; it is rare to start a career when you are fifty-five. By that age you rely on an acquired reputation, and by then you are getting on. For a man, it's different. Perhaps he has not had much success until then, but there can be some kind of a miracle and he can suddenly take off. A woman knows that she has many years, but the useful ones are few. That is why women are tense; more so than men.

Angela Huth: To be a fly on the wall of two women having lunch is something absolutely extraordinary. I think one or two playwrights have tried to do something about this. It is really very odd, listening to women talk to each other. They tell each other everything, they don't stop anywhere. They are terribly indiscreet about themselves, about their husbands, about their sex lives, about what they feel about

1028

everything. Women are a bit exhausting. That's the reason I really like being with men better on the whole.

I think women are more hysterical. The emotions are bubbling nearest the surface in women, perhaps, and tumble out more quickly than with men. One of the most moving things in the world is a man who cries because it so rarely happens. And I have always thought it must be something really important to make a man cry: the death of his child or his wife, or some real huge thing in his life. In fact, I think there are a lot of other things that men would like to cry for, and just don't because they are conditioned. Men are conditioned not to cry. Women cry all the time and therefore the currency of their tears is less than men's.

I feel rather sorry for men, particularly today. They really are having a bashing from all these tough old women, and thank goodness it is beginning to go the other way. I think a great man is greater than a great woman. Of course, there are many, many wonderful and marvellous women, and this is a hopeless thing on which to generalize, and I will be in trouble for saying I think men are greater. But I do, I do. They don't have to be famous or anything, but there is a quality of greatness about some men that is very touching, very moving in a way, for me, that is not the same ever with a woman.

Sheila Innes: It's a grave mistake of women, as they rise in the ranks, to pretend that they are men in skirts. That's wrong. Women are different. I happen to think that, in management terms, women have enough gifts, enough insight, and enough sensitivity, to be better managers than men. But if you want equality, you have to agree that you can't have the frills as well. Equality of opportunity means who finds the seat first as well as having the opportunity of a seat on the board.

Angela Janklow: Man is just one step away from beast, period. If you look at the animal kingdom, the males rule it; with the exception of bees, where the queen rules. But the queen is a big fat bald blob of nothing. She is immobile, huge, gross, nothing. I want boy children because they still will always have the greater possibilities. In my lifetime, they will have the greater possibility for power and sovereignty, and to get what they want. I just think it's easier for a man to get what he wants than it is for a woman.

If you can weaken the other side, you have a better chance of winning, and men are certainly proficient at that. But women are, too, and there

1029

are certain sexual innuendoes that can destroy a man. Women are more sensitive mentally, since they have been put down for so long and are using their minds rather than their bodies.

Tama Janowitz: I do find that men, for the most part, are much less verbal than women, especially when it comes to talking about emotions. My brother and I are relatively close in age, but he's very different and he's very sort of macho and not really able to talk about his feelings and, to me, this seems more biological than environmental because if it was all environment then he would be a much more feminine kind of male, more talkative, more artistic and more like me. He's really not.

Dr Lukrezia Jochimsen: If something is denied to women, then they are very uneasy about coming back for a second, third or even a fourth time, while men, if there is a no, they think OK, this is the first no, I have to change my tactics, I have to change my strategy, and then come back again, and then try harder. Women, when once told no, think that is rather definite and accept it and don't come back. It is a female way of dealing with the facts of life.

Sally Jones: Often women will look at a male-dominated area and say, you have to be wonderful to do that job. What they don't do is look at some of the individual men in that area and see that often there will be a man at the top of the organization who is absolutely lousy at what he is doing. There will only be real equality when you can have a woman at the top of an organization who is absolutely lousy at what she is doing. At the moment, most of the women I see in really excellent top jobs – and there are only one or two of them – have to be very much better than their male counterparts, and they have to have extra confidence. A lot of women are almost too perfectionist, they expect more from themselves than they would of a man in a similar position. Because they somehow think, well, a woman's not expected to get there, therefore she has to be doubly good, much better than her male colleagues. So she will really go absolutely flat out and sometimes sacrifice her social life, her personal life, to a great extent, in order to try to prove she is better than her male colleagues and to instil the confidence in herself. I have several friends in merchant banking, and there they all say the women are the ones who spend the most masochistic amounts of time at work. They perhaps go in at six in the morning and stay there often till twelve o'clock at night; they'll be the ones who go to the printers and bring back the flotation proposals, et cetera, in the middle of the night and put themselves out in a way no man would. And it's simply because they feel very much more under threat as women, because there are so few of them there, and they feel everybody is watching them like a hawk.

There is a great feeling now that people should have their cake and eat it, that you shouldn't need to choose between marriage, children and your job, that the two should be in some ways dove-tailed and it should be workable. In practice, it often brings an awful lot of guilt and harassment on the woman who is trying to dove-tail everything together. I see it all the time at work: women who are perhaps juggling three or four different careers. They might be the wife of a successful man whom they have to entertain for, they might have a child, or several children, they might have their own fairly high-flying sort of job. And so they are running from pillar to post all day long. They never stop, because if they are not doing their job, they are on the phone making sure the child-minder's there or the nanny's happy or the car's just got back from having its MOT. Men are probably conditioned to think that theirs is really only one job, that they are the breadwinner, the hunter, the provider, and that's all they need to do. If they are suddenly, through divorce or death or for whatever reason, thrust into the position where they are having to do a lot of different functions, they often cope far worse because they have never thought they were going to have to. I think, also, one of the skills which has made me be able to do a lot of different things is the capacity at any one time to concentrate absolutely on something, say, for an hour, and then switch immediately to something else and back again, but giving a lot of concentration to whatever it is I am doing. I think a lot of men prefer to have an entire day doing the same work, that they find it more difficult to switch. I don't know whether I am being sexist in this. I can give tunnel vision for fifteen minutes on something; if I'm reading something on the train frequently I'll look up and it's my stop and I have to leap out, because I get so buried in it. I can totally bury myself in whatever it is I am doing. So I tend to have spurts. I'll do a couple of hours on something; then I'll leave off and write an article and spend a couple of hours doing that as hard as I can; and then, almost as a relaxation, a couple of hours playing sport. Playing real tennis, the end of the world could happen and I would be absolutely focused and concentrating on that one thing.

Rana Kabbani: Women are long-suffering, both physically and emotionally, I think. It's common knowledge that they can bear more pain than men. But I think they also have more stamina inside themselves. It's because they have been conditioned to think they should suffer and be still, they should be stoic. Although it is generally considered that men are stoic, it's really women who are.

Men and women are equally treacherous, but if you had to decide who was more treacherous, it would be men. Men have far more capacity to deceive and lie and be unfaithful than women do, I think. They get away with it, it's easier, there's no stigma attached. If a man takes away another man's wife, he is a hero; he is not, you know, a slut. Whereas if a woman takes away another woman's husband, she is a Jezebel.

Dillie Keane: I do think there is a difference between men and women. But I have yet to discover what it is. There is an enormous biological difference which is bound to make a difference on the psyche. Also we are conditioned from Day 1. Even from the way you carry a baby. Girl babies tend to be carried like that, in the arms. Boy babies are bounced on the end of the knee. There's automatically a distance thing: you are rougher with boy children, and more gentle with girls. But whether you can divide the conditioning from the biological thing – it's very difficult.

Caroline Kellett: It think it is possible for a man to be in love with a woman all his life, or part of his life, and to love, or to have physical relationships with, many women. Whatever the feminists say, I think the act of love-making between a man and woman has a very much higher emotional content for a woman than it does for a man. It's possible, it's par for the course, that men can derive totally detached, abstract, physical stimulation and satisfaction from any number of relationships. And the women who are able to be promiscuous and say that their emotions aren't involved are in the minority and very often far more psychologically disturbed than they'd like to admit. A woman can love one man for her entire life and be faithful to him, and that's another part of her genetic conditioning, which, again, is against the feminist argument. That safeguards the continuation of the race. If we were meant to be promiscuous and have any number of relationships and have contraception completely wrapped up, what would happen to reproduction? That's not the way things should be.

Tessa Kennedy: Men are better on the whole in dress design, because women inevitably see themselves in the thing. I remember talking to Pierre Balmain about that a long time ago, and he said, if he'd been a woman, he would always have to design a dress that he knew he would look good in, but being a man, he never had those restrictions. Whatever his figure, he could always design something that a woman, any woman, would look good in. I think he was right in a way, because if you have larger hips, you design in a way that will cover larger hips, and you wouldn't necessarily think of those women who look like clothes-horses – thin, like Twiggy – who just go straight down. You're less restricted if you're a male dress designer; you don't think of any particular female body, you just think about clothes as a whole.

Men have cycles, too. They work with the moon. Definitely. The same as women, I'm sure. You can more or less count it, the days they're going to be crazy lunatics. But I'm sure women are more emotional, because, again, they can use those emotions and there are a lot of good actresses, too, who aren't acting professionally, I should say, but they act in their lives to get what they want.

My husband hates it when I'm not jealous. That's the one thing my grandmother always taught me as a child, that you must never be jealous, that the most ugly thing is a jealous woman. Whereas he's unbelievably jealous, even if I talk to somebody on the telephone. At home he presses the button to hear who I'm talking to and presses it back again and comes rushing up: who's that on the telephone? And, I mean, in my business I talk to more men than women probably.

Mary Kenny: Little boys and little girls are very different right from the start. If you deny a little boy a gun, he finds a piece of wood in the garden and makes a gun from it. I interviewed a woman not very long ago who had been in a Nazi concentration camp, and she had actually never had any dolls, and she had made a doll out of old Nazi flags.

What I admire about men is that they can dismiss unimportant things from their mind much more easily than women, and that is very efficient from an evolutionary point of view, because it's very wasteful to worry about little things all the time. It's time-consuming. On the other hand, sometimes little things are part of the caring side of life.

I don't think women are capable of the absolute quality of concentration that men are capable of. Men can achieve – and that's very often visible in chess – this huge act of concentration, where their entire being is concentrated on creating something, and women never, or very seldom, achieve this very high level of concentration. The evolutionary explana-tion is that women have this thing known as the atavistic ear, and the atavistic ear is that, at the back of the mind, a woman is always listening

1033

for a baby's cry, so that whatever she is doing, she always realizes there is a child somewhere to be fed or looked after. She always has this thought in her mind, and this distracts her from total concentration.

Very often, it's a mistake for women to imitate men. Very often, this is very much against the interests of women. For example, at the moment we happen to have a great argument about whether there should be women priests in the Anglican Church. The feminists are saying, why shouldn't women be priests? I'm sure that if women became priests, they would simply have to work a great deal harder and probably have a much less pleasant life and not really reap any benefit from it.

Griselda Kerr: A woman's voice naturally comes across much less assertively than a man's. The conferences I've spoken at, or lectures I've given – I used to always hear myself coming across as a kind of young girl, not as the curator of the Royal Academy's collection, and used to think how amateur I sounded, although what I was saying was based on quite a lot of knowledge. Whereas if a man had given that same speech, it would have come across terrifically authoritatively.

Women very often have a more lateral viewpoint than men. I find this again and again, even in my own married life: that my husband always has much greater clarity of vision from A to B, but I somehow see things east to west much more as I progress through life.

Soraya Khashoggi: Let's face it: a man can't have a baby. I had nine. Women are very good at repetitive, boring jobs within the home. Men have no patience for it. That's nothing to do with conditioning. It's actually genetic, it's biological. Of course, there are exceptions. John Lennon was a house-husband. He stayed five years, I believe, looking after the little boy, while his wife went to work. They chose to reverse roles. I would imagine there are very few families that that would work in. But, basically, the structure of the family today is the same as it was right at the beginning of time when man went out, hunted the animal, brought it home to the cave and skinned it. That was the end of his job. Then the woman had to cook it, and from the skin she had to make clothes and keep her children warm.

How can we be the same when we are born different? We are born with a uterus and the facility to have children, and men are born with an extra piece on their body that we don't have. We are biologically different, therefore emotionally and sexually different. We can't be the

1034

same. I defy the woman who says she is the same as a man, and that she can pick up a guy and go to bed with him and have a one-night stand. I know women do it. It's an accepted part of the twentieth century that women do it, but basically women want a family-structured society and that kind of behaviour is not conducive to family life. Men don't think of that. Usually, if it's a one-night stand, they don't even remember what she looks like the next morning. Most men tell me that they prefer the woman to get out in the middle of the night so they don't have to look at her in the morning.

Lesley Kingcome: If there's a crisis, a woman copes with it better than a man. And I think that strange. I used to think, in my youth, that you needed a man around to cope in a crisis. You actually need a woman around to cope with a crisis. I have two sons and a daughter. I believe my daughter would rise to the occasion whatever the crisis, more easily than my sons. I respect all three enormously, I think they are absolutely marvellous, but I'm not such a believer in men and their ability to cope.

Rhoda Koenig: Women are more anchored to reality than men. Despite the stereotype of women as irrational, I have found that women are much more aware of their feelings, and of other people's feelings, than men, and men are often so shuttered off from their feelings and other people's. And I have a picture of them blundering around, these huge animals, in an unpropitious environment and bumping into each other in the dark. Women are much more earthy, and their bodies are controlled by the feeling, the mood.

The main thing I keep running into over and over is men being terrified of expressing their feelings, or not even knowing what their feelings are, or if they have any. And of being terribly threatened by criticism. Women are much more able to take criticism, personal criticism, in their stride.

Irma Kurtz: I've passed the age of sexual surmise, which is the real danger between men and women. Unattached young women will look at men as a possible mate, even the most ambitious women. A woman's ego is not the same as a man's. It's fractured. Also there is the business of having children, the biological urge to have children. Some women have it stronger than others, but it's a dangerous thing to deny. And it changes our relationships with men, because the men are going to be the fathers of those children. I do not believe the female ego is the same. I think we are very different, men and women.

Men's great fear, I'm sure, is fear of failure. The woman's fear is fear of not being loved. Now, it's very difficult to come into a work arena when you are afraid of not being loved, because you are going to have to make yourself unpopular at some point, somehow, with somebody. A man's fear of failure overrides that, he'll go ahead and do it because he would rather succeed than anything else. This is true, even in sex life, all the way through a man's career; it's true still, I'm afraid. How do you react to fear? People always over-react to the things they are afraid about. Men over-react to the fear of failure, and look what happens to them: they get strokes and heart attacks, they make fools of themselves. They run off with their secretaries sometimes, that's another over-reaction to a fear of failure. Women over-react, too, to their fear of not being loved. They say, goddammit, I don't care, and get wildly aggressive. They are also filling a space because a lot of those women are not married and many of them don't have children.

We really ought to make every effort to understand the biological differences. Why do our sexual encounters have an abrasive element? It seems imperative that we keep that tension between the sexes or we won't want to make love. You don't – forgive me for being uncouth – fuck friends, that's the fact of the matter. So it could be that Nature has made us this way and keeps us this way even if we've done away with the sabre-toothed tiger and the guy doesn't have to go out any more and hunt for the dinosaur meat.

Verity Lambert: When I was running Thames's drama department, I felt it was important to try to keep a balance, in terms of producers, of men and women. In other words, there would be different points of view, and I found, when I was hiring, that it was extremely difficult for me to keep that balance – not because I wanted to hire more men, but because the women who'd got to that position were so good that they outstripped the men. Women, on the whole, are more responsible, more organized, and they take more care – they're more meticulous. I think that, if they get a job, they really work harder, and that is because, to get on as a woman, you have got to be as good as or even better than any man.

What I've operated on most of my life is my instincts. If I like this, I can say it's well written, the characters are interesting and things like this, but initially it's really a gut feeling, which is instinct. If someone asks me to define what makes that different from another piece of perhaps well-written stuff that I don't feel so strongly about, it's almost impossible except to say, instinctively, I feel that's going to work, I have a feeling for it. I don't think men operate in quite the same way. They are more logical in that sense, and they'll think it through. And the interesting thing is that men are, on the whole, more entrepreneurial, and more imaginative in that entrepreneurial sense. So that can kind of counterbalance their logic. You don't find many women entrepreneurs, actual entrepreneurs.

Marghanita Laski: I would have thought that women were, of necessity, more timid than men because they are less well able to defend themselves, they are generally speaking less strong. When women are properly trained, like policewomen, like air stewardesses, they don't seem to be any more timid than men; it's just those of us who are smaller and not trained and weaker and who can't defend ourselves against attack. We're also trained in timidity by society at certain periods and in certain classes. A Victorian upper-class girl was trained to cast down her eyes and blush and be timid; a Victorian working-class girl wasn't, because it wouldn't advantage her. She was trained to be tough and fight her way.

If people want to exchange roles, I wouldn't wish to see any condemnation of that, I would like to see people able to do it, but I think, generally speaking, playing our own roles is better. My hands are better suited to fine needlework, my husband's hands are better suited to carpentry.

Sara Leighton: They say men are the greatest casualties in divorces, more men commit suicide after divorce, and one thing I have noticed, if a relationship breaks up, if the woman is left, she is philosophical, because partly it's her lot, she's indoctrinated to the fact that that is going to happen. But if it happens to men, their pride is so great. In the old days, they used to join the Foreign Legion or shoot big game or sometimes shoot themselves. They collapse more at the end of a relationship than a woman does, if they're not the ones to walk out, because they have their masculine pride to cope with.

Catherine Leroy: Some picture editors would look at my photographs and say, only a woman could do those photographs, which is total bullshit. I don't think, as a photographer, as a journalist, I have a different eye. If my name didn't come up in the caption as a woman, I defy them to say a woman did those photographs.

Maureen Lipman: For me, as a woman, to bring up my daughter is considerably harder than bringing up my son. And that's because she knows my act. From the word go, at three months old, that child looked me in the eye and said, I'm never going to take any shit from you; and frightened the life out of me, actually. And I always feel I am being judged by my girl. If my daughter wants something, she wheedles and whinges for it. I don't know if that is conditioning, or if it's tribal, instinctive, from so many generations back that it's nothing to do with me. I don't think I've behaved any differently towards her from how I have towards him. But there's a world of difference between them. The tendency is immediately there to wrap her arms round her father and look at me, to learn the word daddy before she learns the word mummy, although that's easier to say. And the boy, it's the opposite. He is an open book, he's not learned to be secretive like a girl. Girls learn to play it close to the chest. They learn from an early age to say one thing and mean another. If they want something, they go for it by a diverse route. I haven't taught her that. Except subliminally, maybe I have, because my mother taught it to me. So when the feminists say the only difference is conditioning, they are probably right, but we are going to have to talk about another fifty generations, or certainly twenty generations, before we get it right.

Cecilie Løveid: A woman is not so warm as a man is, because she is nearer death. She has life and death in herself, and the man hasn't. A woman has a softness, but she is also strong; she can be cruel, she can also kill.

Blanche Lucas: The most irrational thing in the world is to assume that emotions are inferior and that only inferior people have them. That's the most irrational thing in the world, and that is what so many men suffer from. Men think that emotions are something weakening, that only weak and foolish people have emotions. Men believe – not all men, of course, I'm generalizing hopelessly – that objectivity exists, that 100 per cent objectivity exists. Well, it might be that it doesn't exist, and that in itself is an irrationality of the first order. Men are terribly irrational because they blot out so much. Then they make a theory about what remains.

I always think of men as having been singled out by Nature to spread their seed. Their duty is to go and spread their seed wherever they possibly can. It's a duty that Nature puts upon them, and they have to do it. Women don't have this sort of urgency. I sometimes wonder why this is not explained to more boys. Perhaps it is, but I've never heard of anyone explaining it to them. Because it would be so nice for them to know that the fact they feel so randy all the time has nothing whatever to do with wickedness, it's simply that they were made to do this. Women don't have to learn that lesson in quite the same way. Because they, in fact, don't have this urge that Nature puts upon men.

Jenny Lumet: Men are very romantic, and people think women are romantic, but women have been taught from the day they were born to catch a husband. Note the word catch. And they're very practical about it, very pragmatic about something that should be completely out of the window. Love is crazy, it makes no sense, and I think a lot of women are planning it, and planning it. I don't think men do.

Anna McCurley: Women depend on the five senses plus the sixth sense, which is really a combination of the five senses, tallying up and giving you an answer. A man tends to go straight for something. He sees a preconditioned pattern, he goes for it. What they call instinct isn't really; it's responses. A woman gathers these at random, she gathers them into a little bundle. I do. At least, it's the only way I can describe it. I gather all these little instincts into a bundle, put them together, and that's the answer to somebody or something – my response. And it's done with all sorts of things that may be irrational to men. It might just be the set of the head, the colour of the eyes, it might be the smell of somebody. It can be all sorts of things.

Sheena McDonald: I think women are much less possessive and much keener on the greater good than on the personal advancement. Because they are practical. I think women are tribal, men individualist.

Physiologically, making love is good for women. It makes their skin glow, their blood race. It's bad for men. They collapse afterwards. One can see why Orientals choose to conserve their semen. They reckon that inadvertent loss is not a good idea at all. One can understand why.

Nobody is consistent, and for any of the fine, generous things I might say about anybody, I have been and can be as malicious and unkind to men and women as anybody is and everybody is; and for all the good times, the nice times I have with people, I can also be incredibly petty-minded and unfair, and this isn't a matter of displaying a masculine or feminine characteristic; it's a human characteristic. I do think the difference between men and women is not so much to do with their intellect and thought processes, I think the main difference between men and women is their sexuality and it's to do with the design of the species. Despite our apparent sophistication in this modern world, we are still lumped with these rather primitive physical desires, and man's is to seed as widely and regularly as possible and women's is to look after themselves, preserve the temple, or the womb or however you want to put it.

I think that a woman who is in love is a very powerful force indeed, and it does consume a great deal of her conscious life. When love fails, men are much more obsessed by it. They find it very much harder to accept a love that's failed than women do. Women are much more practical and philosophical, and quite pragmatic about love affairs that haven't worked out. Men are much more romantic, in a way, idealistic and self-deluding, and they seem to have a much greater capacity for hurting themselves than women do. Women are much more self-preservative. I think, when things go wrong, women are much better at recouping their losses and regathering their strength and setting off. Women cope better.

Susan McHenry: What is useful to observe about the differences between men and women is that our differences as individuals from each other are more important than our differences as a gender from each other. If we can respond to people as individuals, even when they don't seem to be acting like individuals, I think that will get us a very long way towards co-operating and collaborating with each other.

Women tend – and this I really think is cultural as opposed to biological – women tend to be more concerned with relationships and how people are getting along. Men tend to be more task-orientated, more instrumental, more XYZ. What we need is both of these styles and both of those concerns, and what has been happening is that men have been trying to learn those sensibilities and women have been studying instrumental approaches. What it will all boil down to in the end is for individuals to use the proper balance: whatever is right for them to be successful and get the things done that they need to get done.

Deirdre McSharry: In ancient societies, pagan societies, the arrangements for women were very like what they are in the twentieth century. There was a pair-bonding, the so-called marriage, where women

1040

brought their cattle and possessions with them, and when the marriage broke down (and there were clauses, in fact sixteen clauses, on which a marriage, a bonding, could be broken, one of them bad breath) the woman could then remove her children and cattle and retire to her bit of the forest. So, really, all our current notions of maleness and femaleness and what is appropriate behaviour and superiority is based on the last 400 or 500 years – which, in the scheme of things, is very very recent. Anybody who knows anything about ancient societies knows there was not this huge difference between men and women, there really wasn't. It's quite a modern invention.

The tragedy of very many men is that, when they retire, that's it, they die, because there isn't anything else. They have been so single-mindedly concentrating on the career, that when the career stops there is nothing, whereas even the most successful women, and I know a few, who have lost their jobs or something has happened, can immediately console themselves, with families, or gardens, or clothes, or food, or buy a house, or do something else.

Women are more vulnerable, but at least we feel. We don't suffer from an absence of feeling, and an awful lot of men do, young men and middle-aged men, and that's worse. It is better to suffer and know you're living in this world and that you're feeling than to become as so many people are – and when I say people, it's shorthand for men. They have no feelings, they're cut off. Terrible things happen to them, and they can't even feel it.

Norris Church Mailer: My first husband is a nuclear engineer, and he is a very bright man, but when we separated he didn't know how to wash clothes, he didn't know where to go to pay bills, he didn't know how to do any of these things. I spent a week with a list, showing him how to run the dishwasher and that sort of thing. It's not that men can't do it, it's just that most men are never faced with having to do it.

Alice Mason: Part of what inhibits a woman from being a success is not that anyone stops her; what stops her is that she puts so much energy in a man. A man never puts that energy in a woman ever. He puts his energy in his work. He never sits and waits for a phone call, or is excited about a date, or spends all the time talking to other women about this big romance like girls do. So girls waste half their energy on men. That, I think, is the problem. I think any woman can do almost anything regardless. I don't know about in Saudi Arabia, or somewhere like that, but in a country where a woman is free, she can do anything she has a mind to do.

Eventually everyone is alone, everyone, unless you die in a car crash together. Women are really superior to men, basically because men cannot be alone, they really can't. They need a woman for whatever reason, and it doesn't have to be sex. They need her to keep their home. They're doing what they have to do, and they have to come home, to have a home, and the woman usually makes the home. They really need someone to plan their social life, what they're doing. I am not saying there aren't a few men out there who don't, but really, on the whole, that's what men need. Women don't need that because they are already making their home and have a career, and what can a man do for them? If they don't need him to give them their name, or their apartment, or their this and that, they don't need him. And companionship is the most boring thing in the world. People say it is interesting. It is not interesting. There is nothing worse than companionship: every day knowing you have to see the same person and talk to them and find out his day and tell him your day. What is more boring? I really believe that so strongly. I think every woman should get to know that they have an option out there. I also think it's just terrible for a woman that suddenly she is an older woman and is still looking for a man. I can't think of anything worse. I mean, it's all right that a man is still looking for a woman, they are children anyway.

Margaret Matheson: ITV and BBC drama is all run by podgy middle-aged men and the drama they produce reflects that. There's very little really stimulating original thinking going on in the preparation of what is served up to the nation as drama. And I think there would be more if there were more women running the show. There will be, but progress is unbearably slow. Men are perfectly able to be witty, delightful, bright, creative and so on, it's just that there are lots who aren't. I'm tending to talk around the business I know; I don't know really a tremendous lot about how a bank is run; I know a little bit about how the law is run, and that is pretty male-dominated. The point is that the tendency in any profession or business is towards complacency. We all know that, it's a fact of life. People move more slowly once they've got more secure, and life should be as dangerous as possible. It is automatically more dangerous for women, because, regrettably, women are still the minority in the kind of jobs we're talking about. So (everybody's said this a hundred times) you have to work harder. I feel this is too boring to state because it's been said too many times before in women's maga-zines, but it is a fact that, if a woman does her job badly, the chances are

1042

a group of men will sit around and say, well, she's doing so badly because she can't handle the home and the job, or because she has terrible menstruation problems. It's boring, really, it's tiresome. Of course, it's also true, but it's such a truism as to be tedious to go on about.

I think most women do have – whatever posh words one wants to give it – maternal instincts, and I don't mean simply as it applies towards their children. This is why they make good organizers: a sense of wanting to make people feel good, wanting to create good circumstances for people to live in, wanting to help; if someone falls over, wanting to pick them up. And, it's not a popular view with the feminists, but I think there is perhaps a condition of being male that does tend to want to dominate. Those are characteristics inherent in gender rather than solely a result of conditioning, though, of course, they're developed by society's conditioning.

It's terribly easy, once you're older and you've got children, to think that the reason why women are good at working together and dealing with people is because they are used to dealing with children – and if you can deal with children you can deal with anyone. But actually, it goes back way before that. I think it is a condition, I think it is something one has as a woman and maybe men haven't. Men do, perhaps, seem to have this desire to want to be cock of the roost. They want to have big pricks and have everybody think they're great. Women don't. It doesn't mean women are not ambitious or not keen to create a more just world, it's just to do with the fact that women appear to me to have a less egotistical, more sensible approach to life.

Sonia Melchett: Women are clearer-minded than men. I've sat on various boards: I was on the board of the NSPCC, and I've been a magistrate; there's usually two men and one woman sitting on the magistrates' bench. I find, on the whole, that women think more clearly than men. They can take a more detached view. I really think they cut corners more. Men can ramble on for ages on committees; they like the sound of their own voices. I think women, because their lives are so fragmented and busy and going in different directions, often see things slightly more clearly than men.

Women are more compassionate, slightly more tolerant than men – tolerant of people's weaknesses. Men are a bit more single-minded, they see things very much white or black. I think women see the grey areas, and I think they can teach men a little bit of tolerance that it's not always one thing or the other. And women are survivors; they have to learn the art of survival. I think they can teach men a little bit about survival, a little bit of subtlety in their approach. Men are much more straight-forward than women. I'm not saying that women can teach men to be devious, but they can teach them how to be a bit more subtle and a bit more tolerant. Women have the stamina for survival: each thing they go through, like giving birth, is almost like dying a little, and they're possibly braver about pain and illness. It's quite well known that men make terrible invalids.

I do feel strongly that the influence of women on world peace is enormous. I'm not, myself, at the moment, for total nuclear disarma-ment. I'm quite a realist as well as being romantic, but I do think that women's influence on the nuclear situation in the world has been enormous and for the good. The way they influence men's thinking on this has been very strong. Women can have an enormous effect on calming down men's aggressive instincts, and the more women that get into politics the better from this point of view. They are a very good force for peace in the world. This is a very old-fashioned thing to say, but I really do believe that a woman can help a man, the feminine side of a woman can influence a man. I really believe very strongly in that partnership. I'm afraid it's not a very modern women's lib. thing to say, but I do believe the ideal partnership is between quite an aggressive male and a feminine female. They can be really complementary, and it's not just the woman being conciliatory, calming down, and so on, but the man giving the woman the courage and the guts to go out and do things. I believe we were meant to be complementary and I think we should be. Of course, having said that, there are so many different aspects, there are lesbians and gays, and I'm all for total tolerance of everyone who wants to lead that kind of a life, but the ideal situation is a very male man and a very female woman.

My birth sign is Virgo and I am very close to the elements and feel happy in water. And I can always tell if it is going to be full moon even if I'm nowhere near a diary – I go slightly mad if the moon is full. And I feel that I need the earth under my feet constantly, otherwise I'd equally feel like going mad. I like to feel I'm walking on fields. Women are much more earth creatures, and I wouldn't want not to be.

Lady Menuhin: Men are monolithic on the whole. Their strength lies in that, and they topple over if given a big enough push. Women don't. Women come back like these Japanese dolls that you hit. They come back on a spring, and if they don't, then they don't know how to manage their lives.

Kate Millett: I don't know of any differences between men and women beyond the biological, physical ones. I don't know of any inherent psychological differences. We have every proof of enormous cultural differences, social differences, conditioned differences, but we have no proofs of any inherent, innate psychological ones. But, through our conditioning, we have become enormously different. We live in two different cultures. You can't quote the animal kingdom; the animal kingdom is a mess. It can prove almost anything; it's like quoting the Bible.

With all the stereotyping and conditioned behaviour between men and women, we divide up the good and evil qualities in human nature. Men are active, women passive; women are nurturing, men aggressive, and so on. Well, there's a lot of good in nurturing, there's some good in aggression, so everybody gets to, not a whole person, but half a one, like a semi-person. You can see how this would stunt the human spirit and unbalance human personality. So, in a male-dominated society, traits that are regarded as less valuable and important are assigned to women. Now, a lot of that is crazy. The caring of children is extremely important, but is regarded as unimportant, so we get it. All the way along, it's illogical, irrational, arbitrary, stupid. It's limiting, and it completely suppresses the human spirit, the growth of the individual, the development of an entire psyche. It's a dumb, comically stupid, painfully tragic system.

Cristina Monet: A hole is more passive than a penis. The penis has to go into the hole. So the way men and women are built determines that, on a simplistic, biological level, the man is more likely to be the aggressor in sexual ritual. I don't mean necessarily in life, but in terms of sexual ritual and sorts of eroticism, male aggression has to be connected with the ritual. And there is, to my mind, a certain vegetative bovine contentment, if you're a motherly woman, that comes with mothering and with being the one who carries the child inside. She carries this thing in her. The child knows her smell, suckles at her breast. I don't think man can replace that. Somebody has to hunt and somebody has to be home with the baby. The one from whose tits milk flows will be the one to sit at home. I don't see that this is a terrific mystery.

Bel Mooney: The argument that women and men are fundamentally different is, in some way, appealing to me, in some ways repellent. It's appealing because I think women are far more in touch with their own emotions: they talk to each other. Two women over a business lunch will start talking about how they feel about things, whereas men wouldn't. I see it all the time in my own life. But I reject the kind of Greenham Common-type feminism which says women are an inherently better, superior group. We are more peaceful, more loving, the earth-mother argument – I rather reject that, because we've all known extremely tough, aggressive women, and there were some very cruel women in history, like Catherine the Great of Russia. And there's Margaret Thatcher. She's not cruel, but you know what I mean – tough. So it seems to be rather dangerous to lump the two sexes in categories, because we all know men who are enormously gentle and loving. But I suppose if one was to make a sweeping generalization, given that there are exceptions, that there are tough women and gentle men, on whether women are more vulnerable, more emotional, I would say, yes, we are, and that must be something innate.

I say we can create our own destiny. We may have wombs, but we've also got minds, so don't let's go too far down the path to the uterus in the earth. Nevertheless, we are different physically, and it is a complex mechanism. Women have miscarriages, we have an enormous turmoil. I know, from childbirth and miscarriage and all sorts of things that happened to me, the turmoil you're thrown into. And my husband, grieve as he might, be concerned as he might, can come nowhere near to my feeling.

Sara Morrison: Men and women do have different roles, not only in the traditional sense but in that women are the support system, the infrastructure of the human race. Women are drearily practical, much more practical than men. In the Stone Age, men went out hunting with their clubs. They may have been taking on lions and tigers, but the women were the ones making certain the pot didn't boil over on the fire, or the child who cut his knee was mopped up and the dog that was sick was attended to. Women's natural attitude to life makes them very practical, because they have always had to do eleven things at once. They have never had the narrow focus of the male sex: beating the breast, the Tarzan thing, has never come their way because that's not their role. But whether that's biology or whether it's a certain sort of process in their mind, I'm not sure. I've watched women operate, and they think very often, outside their professional knowledge, of the one thing that might go wrong; it's a sort of automatic reflex. Their physical frailty does make a difference, because, paradoxically, they get less over-tired physically but more easily stressed. And that's biology. They get stressed in the sense of feeling very weary, which is not physical exhaustion. They think more laterally, they exclude less of the rest of life when looking at one thing. They notice all the details; they don't just look in the vertical and totally ignore the other things which might influence the vertical they are looking at.

Women are much more resilient, they honestly are. They bounce back from adversity far more quickly. There are those chauvinists who will say that women are resilient because they have less depth and look at things more superficially; are more hit and run in their mentality, therefore, of course, can rise above better because they haven't actually taken on all the full significance of the horror that has struck. Absolute tripe. What they've got is a certain sort of balance. They know perfectly well that sod's law does apply, and anything that can go wrong will, and therefore they almost take it for granted and have a certain sort of bounce and resilience. I think the times I've felt most resentment among male colleagues is when one does make ghastly remarks which one rather hates oneself for, like: it'll all be all right on the night, worse things happen at sea, it's not really as bad as you think it is. And you can see a look of such dislike sweeping over their faces: there she goes again, trying to cheer us up, mopping our tears, putting bandages on our knees. Actually, very often, I'm right. But at that particular moment, men do love wallowing. A man's morale, when it goes for a burton, goes for a very long time. I always rather envy them having the time to be gloomy.

I asked one of my male colleagues recently to accept a touch of feminine logic about something – you know, as a joke. And, equally as a joke, he said, yes, if it wasn't a contradiction in terms. I said, hang on a moment, what I am actually going to tell you is to start from the other direction and look at the business in reverse and imagine everything that can go wrong and then start your planning. He said, how typical, you're being frightfully perverse. I said, I'm not, I'm just being prudent and safe, and that's what I call feminine logic. He said, that's what I call straight perversity.

Kathy Myers: When you think of the difference between two kinds of women, say Edwina Currie and Dolly Parton, on every level – physical, mental, intellectual, political – there are as many differences between those two as there are between Selina Scott and Charles Bronson. I wouldn't know how to judge the difference. Class is just as axiomatic in British culture. Class sorts out people into their reference groups as sharply as gender. Class is almost inconquerable in this country. As recessions get worse, the differences between social classes become more pronounced. I almost think we have a caste system in this country. The difference between me and men is not as pronounced as the difference between, say, a working-class woman and a middle-class woman. There are really very few points of reference, and the fact that you are a woman is not necessarily enough to cross that boundary. I think a day-to-day-basis class difference determines my codes of conduct and my behaviour and the way I deal with people more than gender.

The average British public schoolboy has no concept of nurturing, he has never nurtured anything in his life, he wouldn't know where to begin. But the schooling system doesn't allow for it, so it would be hard to say whether that's a natural inadequacy or simply because of the way boys are educated in this country. I have a few quite classically male characteristics in the sense that I am completely capable of separating my private life from my work life. When I work, whatever problems I have at home are completely suspended, and I really can lose myself in my work. That's a male characteristic, but it's possessed by a woman, which is me. So you can have male characteristics in both men and women. But it doesn't mean to say that a lot of men have a lot of feminine characteristics. I also have a dislike of emotional conversations. I much prefer to keep things on an analytic level, which has to do with the way my parents brought me up. I don't like mushy conversations, I start to panic. I don't like talking about romance. I'd much rather go out for the day, mountain climbing with somebody, than sit there and talk about how much we love each other, which I find excruciatingly embarrassing, and I start looking for the door. And if I get depressed or run down, I go out for a run or ring up a girlfriend and say, why don't we go out and do something? I don't like what's seen as being feminine, sitting and waiting. I can't sit and wait for anything. Not even a bus. I cycle everywhere because I can't wait for buses. You can say that's just a personal thing or that it's not a traditionally feminine way of going about things.

Lynda Myles: Men are often far less observant than women. They're not as finely tuned. I think so-called female intuition is about reading signals much more closely, and that, again, may be to do with years of children, watching infants, working out what an infant wants, what's wrong with an infant.

Women work much harder. I mean, I've had, at several times, quite a large staff: forty at a film festival and about forty or fifty in Berkeley, largely women. And I like working with them, partly because I think they work much harder, and they're better. We've always had to be better. We can't afford to do anything dumb because we're rejected much faster. So, on balance, I'd rather work with women. I think their egos are much less obtrusive than the male egos.

I find with the male temperament sometimes, under pressure during a shoot, it's very like having a five-year-old with tantrums.

Lynn Nesbit: A lot of men are very envious that women can bear children. Many women, I among them, are envious that men can keep fathering children.

Women have had to be more intuitive. We have a tortuous path to weave through the world if we want both to be successful professionally and also keep our female identity. We look at nuances more, we have to be more aware of responses, what I call sub-text: not just what people say, but what they think or feel. I've thought a lot more about men than I have about women. One of the unfortunate aspects men have in the workplace is this whole thing of male bonding and camaraderie and a kind of adolescent back-slapping. In their search for their own masculine identity, they often revert to gymnasium adolescent tittering: oh, look at that girl, look at those tits. They express their insecurity that way, and it really is a huge waste of time. I've seen it a great deal in business.

One of the biggest complaints I hear from contemporary women is that men are too busy for sex, or too involved, or that it's not that big a concern in their lives. What I do think is a big concern in men's lives is conquering. Maybe they'll see an attractive woman, they'll want to have a brief affair or fling. But that is not coming out of real sexual need; it comes out of their need to reaffirm their sense of masculinity. I am not sure whether there are, statistically, any more men who are homosexual today than there ever were. Probably there aren't, but now, because we are living in a more open society, people express it more. In one sense, you could say that homosexual men express qualities thought to be feminine. They are intuitive, more emotional, more interested in the arts. But that would seem a further argument for saying these particular qualities are neither masculine nor feminine. These are just human qualities; some people have them and some people don't.

Women are much more open to the way men look than men are to the way women look. Women are much more accepting about different appearances; not every man has to be extraordinarily good-looking before women can feel attracted and love them. Too many men

1049

approach women in their psycho-sexual life in a stereotypical way. I don't know how we can ever overcome men's stereotypical approach to sexuality in women.

Julia Neuberger: Often men have a more analytical approach to life and they're able to work out an idea more quickly and more directly than women. Women think differently, and I have no idea whether this is because one is used to looking after children and making lists. I find myself sitting in a meeting and writing down on a piece of paper, remember to buy half a pint of cream on the way home, that sort of thing. I have no idea whether it's the bitty nature of one's life as a woman, or whether men actually do have a more powerful analytical capacity and women think rather differently, less logically, more emotionally.

There are some things I choose not to do. I don't like officiating at circumcisions, it makes me faint. But I have been there and done the service on two occasions, on both of which I collapsed, and at the second one the father and I both passed out at the same time, and the poor doctor actually doing the circumcision didn't know which of us to rescue first. So, since the guy who's doing the actual operation can do the service, I'm not going to be there. I also find the funerals of small children very difficult, but I'm not sure that my male colleagues find them any easier. It just happens, I think because I'm a woman and people think of me as being a mother of young children, that when a young child dies, I am very often asked to do it. I find that a terribly terribly difficult thing to do.

I have quite often to counsel or sit with people who are dying. Sometimes they are in quite considerable pain, although normally pain relief can be provided. The women find it much less disturbing than the men. Facing death? No, I don't think there's a difference there, but the toleration of the pain, the actual pain, the women seem able in some way, even if there is no actual drug, to blot it out mentally, the men not. For the men, pain is enveloping.

Nanette Newman: If you put very tiny children, a boy and a girl, together, you will see in the girl certain traits, certain characteristics that are so totally and utterly female that they have to have been there right from the beginning. There are certain things women are born with, that they perhaps might leave dormant and not develop, but I think they're always there and that some women are just better at being female than others – cleverer and able to use it to their very best advantage. But there are certain things you're actually born with.

Because women are different from men and can produce children, there is this streak of wanting to protect. It is an animal instinct that will always be there; no amount of liberation is ever going to stamp that out. And perhaps, in times of stress, this makes women particularly capable of coping. I don't think you can generalize about women in regard to courage or facing death. Some women are magnificent, some wimps – just like men.

I know more vulnerable women than I do men. And I think they are more shattered by things going wrong in their lives in an emotional way.

I think women are more easily hurt because of their emotional response to things. Our hearts rule our heads. Men are much more capable of being logical than women – particularly in matters of love and sex.

Emma Nicholson: I never really thought about women, largely because I come from such a female background, until Mrs Thatcher appointed me three and a half years ago to look after the women of the party. I said then, why me? I'm a professional woman, I'm not actually in the women's group, I'm not in the women's organization. To which they replied, I must have a go, I was far and away the best qualified for it. And so I have been focusing my attention on women for three and a half years for the very first time. My view is that women tend to take criticism more personally and let it defeat them while men won't let it defeat them. Let me give an example. There are men and women who want to get into Parliament. Many women, when constituencies turn them down, come and say to me, I'm not going on, this is too difficult. The men don't say that, they try again. I know I have this weakness myself. It's very easy to take a rejection as a rejection of you as a human being and not merely as a signal that you and that job may not be right for each other. Therefore women need more encouragement to keep taking the chances that are now offered to them.

Girls are more vulnerable. They get hurt more easily and carry hurt for longer. I met a woman the other day who was about seventy-five, and for all her working life she had been a school matron in a boys' school, and now she had been called back out of retirement to be school matron in a girls' school temporarily. She had been doing it for about a year or so, and I asked, for want of anything better to say, because we were short of conversation, which did she enjoy most? She said that it was awful working with girls, awful compared to boys. If boys were nasty to each other, she ticked them off and she got it all sorted out, and they forgot it and went off and were the best of friends. Little girls bore grudges for ever. They were impossible to work with and you couldn't get things sorted out, they were always getting at each other, being nasty to each other, and it was almost impossible for them to forget a grievance, a grudge, to forget something that had happened to them. Women have very long memories.

The thing that is built in to men that women don't have is a much higher level of aggression. Perhaps aggression sounds too harsh a word, but it's the way I identify it when I look at political audiences, for instance. If I've got an audience of all women, they will hear you out right to the very end, perhaps give a polite smile, a polite laugh if you make a joke, and perhaps, at the very end, they will ask some polite questions. If you have an audience of men, you can get them bouncing in five minutes if you are a really good speaker, either with anger, or surprise, or laughter, and they will pound you with questions, and that is what I term an in-built level of aggression. It's that which makes so many male criminals. One in three men in Britain under twenty-five has now got a criminal conviction. Only 1,400 of the prison population are women, 47,000 are men, and that proportion never really varies. I think the males have a lovely bouncy aggression, and that is what spurs them on, whereas the woman will be calmer and quieter and hold back. So there are tremendous biological differences.

Christine Ockrent: Thank God we are different. I'm very much against the confusion of sexes and genders; it's the ruin of a culture.

Women have a much wiser instinct towards power. I think they have a basic feeling that power is a very relative phenomenon, that social climbing is a very relative thing. It all goes back to giving birth and having that very deep instinct about life and death.

Jane O'Grady: Men are outside the world, and somehow they're able to look in.

There's something that infuriates me about men. Very often you see men who are confident for absolutely no reason. The other day, this man was going on and on, he was so boring. He was standing there as if for some reason I should be delighted to be talking to him, I couldn't think why. And so many men are like that, with very little to offer, whereas women are more diffident, they daren't put themselves forward, are afraid of being laughed at. That's weakness as well, but they probably have been very much put down, whereas men have been pushed forward so much.

Sometimes women are infuriatingly emotional. I like the way men can be single-minded. It's a great virtue of theirs. I like the way they can work without being so subject either to their bodies or their emotions. I wish I could be more like that myself.

I think women have a more diffuse sexuality. I feel it's healthier in a way. Men are turned on in a very fetishistic way, it seems. Maybe they're not, but they obviously are turned on by some of these things in sex shops. I once went to a sex shop, purely to see what it was like, and these things were just slabs of butcher's meat – those fake vaginas and things hanging up. I suppose there must be the odd woman that's turned on by them, but somehow women are swept away in something much more like music or a state of rapture.

Kitty O'Hagan: I find men much more competitive in a group and women tend to be more supportive in a group.

Men are much more manipulative, more political. They are interested more in the end, whereas I'm terribly interested in the means, and I find that generally about women: they are genuinely interested in what they are doing and they don't do it for what they might get out of it at the end.

I'm never very sure if men have an instinct, too. If they do, they very rarely front it. It becomes, oh, it's women's intuition, as if it didn't exist, and it does exist. I'm sure there must be a male intuition as well. I suppose they call it a hunch. They tend not to go with it in business. I feel that a woman's intuition is something one must follow, because that's right, that's what it's about. Men feel as though a hunch is risky, whereas I feel a hunch is a certainty, that's what I would rely on. I would be worried if I didn't have a feeling about it, whatever the decision.

Fifi Oscard: I don't think women become irrational, and I don't think the monthly experience alters women's ability or makes them more beset by emotions than men. I've seen a lot of men who behave like utter idiots because of some emotional experience.

Edna O'Shaughnessy: Biological, psychological, social and historical forces, the myths of our country and our literature all form us. At the back of our minds, there's the knight of the Round Table who rode on his horse for his lady; and to say anatomy is destiny is not enough either, because there are psychological differences, too. Moreover, men's and women's experiences in society are not the same. All this is filtered through each person's intimate family relations, which are the most important of all. Development may go right, and it may go wrong. A phallic, harsh, macho man who believes that to be a man is to be unfeeling, callous, domineering, is, I think, a distortion of masculinity; in the same way that the woman who believes a woman should be propitiating, agreeing, suffering is also a distortion. It seems to me that, a man, to be a full person, even though his fundamental identification is masculine, fundamentally with his father, must also have in his inner world an identification with the first woman he knew, his mother. A woman, too, needs to identify with both parents. Every developmental outcome is the result of a complex matrix: the immediate environment which impinges on us, the balance of our own love and hate, our anxiety, the strengths and weaknesses of our characters, and our defences in this complex scene. Homosexuality or bisexuality is, for some people, the solution to these complicated forces, but I see such solutions as a falling short of what is destiny in the best sense, which I think is ultimately heterosexuality. Not all of us manage so clear a resolution.

Kathy O'Shaughnessy: Men are brought up in such tight-lipped, repressed ways, where you are not allowed to cry and you've got to be tough. It promotes ambition, certainly, but it also promotes an ability to emotionally distance things. It's an emotional hazard. My female friends whom I really like and admire most, tend to be more vibrant, stronger personalities; it's as if they are liberated from something.

Diana Parker: In my professional experience, men seem to have a much more free and easy attitude to one-night stands than women, and it's rare for me to interview a female client and for her to say that, yes, she had a string of lovers during her marriage and none of them lasted more than a week or so. It's much more common for a woman to say that she's had a steady lover for a period of time.

I had a client who had had served upon her a divorce petition making all sorts of heinous allegations. One of the allegations was that she had, on a particular date, taken a knife and attempted to pierce her husband's

1054

chest with it. I asked the question, did you do this? She said, no, but he pierced my heart, so I was going to pierce his heart. In other words, it's not a question of reason against emotion, it's a question of the interplay of reason and emotion. Someone might say that was a completely irrational response, that there was no tie-up at all, that it was a purely emotional response, but none the less it had a logical explanation.

Molly Parkin: Now that I'm older, and have so many male friends, gay or otherwise, and having had two husbands and thousands of lovers, I do see that there really is very little difference emotionally between male and female. Perhaps the greatest difference is really in the conditioning of society, but that's equalling itself out now. Women have top-flight jobs and they lose them. They get the sack and they're upset in the same way as men, but they don't feel it as so much of a blow to their ego in a sense. I think women are more resilient because they've got these other things in their life, because they've got children in their life. Whereas there is more pride involved, macho pride, with a man, which women haven't got. Women are humbler in the best sense of the word.

Judith De Paul: A lot of the difference between men and women is conditioning. If I could get female kids from the age of three to five, I could train them into having as many if not more tools than most men. Women must have an opportunity to understand and be attracted to strategic types of game, strategic types of thinking. And, in particular, they have to be taught how to be aggressive and feel comfortable about it. Women tend to equate an aggressive personality with lack of femininity, and that's not true at all. Being aggressive can be very sexy. I've never wanted to be a man. I've always felt being a woman was a much greater advantage to me than the other way around. But I've learned all their tricks and all the rules.

Penny Perrick: A woman has to perform on two fronts. She not only has to demonstrate intelligence, but she has to demonstrate sex appeal as well. A man can conquer without having that whole list of attributes that a woman has to have.

Men have more energy, which Jeffrey Archer said is the one essential quality for success. They're certainly not born with it: the mortality rate of infant males is higher than that of infant females. Men get ill more, they die earlier, they're more prone to certain diseases, but they have more energy because their lives aren't as tiring, because they don't have to perform on two fronts the way women do. And I feel that this, more than anything else, holds women back.

Lorie Scott Peters: Men aren't as intelligent as women in some ways, because they're driven by their penises; as opposed to women, who are driven by their intuition.

Women have more compassion than men, and that's what the world needs right now, because we've gotten a little bit too cold. I think that it would be a great thing for America one day to have a female president, because she would be an asset. If she felt a little flighty or uptight because she had her period, well, then she just shouldn't be planning any meetings that day, but that's not something to judge a woman by.

I forced myself to go out and be successful and survive, but there are a lot of people out there who are going to get left behind because they don't know how to run a business. And a lot of them are men who just took over daddy's business. They're busy still running around, driving fancy fast cars, little penis-mobiles, in cravats. And the women are out there getting their education and learning to be intelligent and learning how to survive in the business world.

Davina Phillips: I think women are overtly more emotional. We show our emotions more because we have been told to hide our emotions less. But I actually think that men are very, very emotional, more emotional than women. Their emotions are more fragile. A man can have his pride hurt much more easily. You just have to look at the question of infidelity. A woman doesn't like her man to be unfaithful to her, but she copes with it, she accepts it, she'll love him anyway; whereas a man can sometimes just find it impossible ever to go to bed again with a wife who's been unfaithful or ever to forgive her. He always feels angry and resentful. I think it's because he feels hurt, deeply hurt. How could she do that intimate thing with another man, and to him of all people? I think, also, that when men fall in love, they are so totally swept up by the relationship. I've also seen men who have been let down by a woman, really strong, tough men, absolutely devastated, crying, incapable of functioning in their work, or eating. It doesn't happen very often, but when it does, it is really genuine.

Lynn Phillips: I agree with Aristophanes in the *The Symposium* that men and women were hermaphrodites split apart by an evil god, and the culture that I imagine and the kind of sexuality I imagine rejoins them.

Biology is every bit as important as desire makes it, so desire is the main issue. But you have to understand the biology. You can't be afraid of the biological differences. Testosterone is a deadly poison if taken excessively. There's evidence that hormones change the way people think, the types of thought people tend towards. What one craves, first of all, is to live in a society where exceptions are free to be exceptions, a society where people are free to develop along their own best lines. Secondly, one wants a society in which differences are valued in a non-hierarchical way. I really do believe that everyone is created equal, but that doesn't mean everyone is as good at driving a tractor as everyone else, or as good an artist as everybody else. There are all kinds of eccentric and aberrant personalities who, under different conditions, can save your species. I don't think we know enough about chance to say what's valuable and what isn't except in the narrowest of circumstances. Someone who is lazy in one situation may turn out to have the best kind of energy in another; somebody who is psychopathic in one situation, in conditions of war can turn out to be a fabulous person to have in your front line; all those wacko guys roaming the city committing random acts of violence, in the middle of really ugly conventional war can become heroes. So I find myself in visceral revolt against the kind of contempt which is showered on people because of their differences or because the way they are different isn't immediately profitable or doesn't seem to measure up or be handy.

What is traditionally considered female culture comes from two worlds: from the world of eroticism and from the world of motherhood. It's nurturing, life-affirming, it rules by a benevolent interaction rather than the rule of law, and it's devoted to pleasure in the most generous and mutual sense: sensual pleasure, respectful pleasure and mutual pleasure. The female culture is allowed a full range of feeling, though its more power-hungry moments tend to be covert. Masculine culture isn't. You're really not allowed to be completely silly if you're a guy, and girls are. A woman is allowed to hold on to her childhood, to hold on to a child's way of seeing the world a lot longer than most men, except for male artists, who become so scared of becoming women that they have to go out and kill big fish. I had a real insight into an absolute give-away of the phallocentricity of American culture the other day. We were watching the Mets game, and watching this game I realized that the most important player on every team was the pitcher. He's the only person who plays the whole game. He also has to bat, he also has to run, he does a full day's work in every game. Now, normally, in an American media event, the media always have to locate the star and make them special, but this hasn't been done in baseball for the pitcher, and I started to wonder why, and I thought, of course, it's the bat that's the real hero, and the sex symbol. It isn't the job that's being done, that's being assessed; it's an image of masculine power that finally floats above – and I use the word floats with reference to the old Mid-Western song, shit floats. It's more or less, here you have the pitcher, holding the ball, the batter holding the bat; the pitcher's job is female, they have to understand the batter and try to play to his weakness; but the batter is the man with the stick, and if you want to push it further you can talk about the ball being the clitoral image. But I don't think Americans even know that there is such a thing as a clitoris, for the most part, so I don't think that works. A clitoris just doesn't have the same impressive physical reality. You know, looking down a prairie, you can always see a tower but you can't see a button. A lot of our culture is still geared to producing a frontier mentality. Our insistence on flattery, our dread of critical self-scrutiny, I think derive from the fact that the latter tends to be a de-energizing activity. It may in the long run help you direct your energy better, but it cuts down the level of pure megalomaniacal enthusiasm and it slows you down. So Americans don't like it, are afraid of it, feel it weakens them.

Sarah Fox-Pitt: I suppose men in general are able to deal with their emotions more directly than women. I think they are able to compartmentalize their lives probably more successfully than women, but I know very many emotional men who, in the old-fashioned sense, might have been considered to have very feminine traits. I don't actually see that there's such a tremendous difference. Men possibly sometimes are able to make quicker decisions than women, not necessarily better decisions. By tradition, they have been better trained in this role than women. For instance, I have had treatment from both male and female gynaecologists, and there is no question that a woman in this position has a much better understanding of the mechanics and emotions of the female metabolism and body. The woman has experienced the change in the body when carrying a child, the man has not. The body's sensitivities are different, and it requires a super-empathy to get close to the feelings, physical and emotional, of someone else's body.

Baroness Plowden: The kind of things that women like doing together, talking about together, may be different from the kind of things that men like talking about together. But it's probably made worse by men's expectations of the way women should behave. And therefore women don't develop to the extent that they would otherwise. If men know that you know about something, then they'll ask you about it. But they will never assume that you know about something that they don't know about. People will ask me now what I think about broadcasting, or what I think about the Peacock Report, and things like that, but if they didn't know that I knew about those things, they wouldn't ever say, what do you do, what are you interested in, or what are you doing? They would say, how many children have you got, or, where do you live?

Eve Pollard: Women are the great compromisers. Women spend their lives trying to keep everybody happy, so women are much better at finding a middle road than men. Women are also the great absolutists. Women, when they believe, believe black is black and white is white, whereas men, because they have been so well educated into being political, talk about the grey truth. We haven't learned, as somebody once told me, to play cricket yet, so we want to be very strong in our beliefs. I also think that women are more honest, more open. Women think they can influence people with words, men think they can influence people with action. I think, also, there is a vulnerability about women, even those hard, tough women that people would look at and think, my God, nothing can get through to her. There is a deep vulnerability about women, and we're scared at the moment to let it show. The woman who pretends she really doesn't want to go to her child's prize day, the woman who pretends she doesn't actually have to go to the hairdresser's, the woman who pretends she is as tough, if not tougher, than the men in her office, is hiding her vulnerability. At the moment, we are keeping it cloistered as far as we can. It will take another fifty, hundred years before we can let those things out.

Women can be just as unfaithful and just as lusty and bawdy as men. The trouble is, always other things get in our way. First of all, there's our hormones that change our moods. Secondly, there is the worry about our reputation, which we have got to care about. And thirdly, women don't think about sex half so often, whereas men apparently think about sex every six minutes or so. I also think we are not stimulated as quickly. A man can be stimulated by a pretty girl walking down a street. A woman, particularly an intelligent woman, needs a man to be attractive, and to be brainy, and in my case, you need him to make you laugh.

Antonia de Portago: The life we lead puts us into two special categories, and some things are expected of men and not expected from women, so therefore there is a tremendous difference everywhere in everything we do. Do you see many women in the streets whistling at men who pass by, and shouting, hey, pretty buns, or whatever? Women don't do that. We are seen as women every second of the day. I find this very annoying, myself. It's not being paid attention, it's not being chased either. It's a horrible sexist, vulgar thing.

Women live much longer than men. They resist pain much more, they resist stress much more. They are intrinsically stronger than men, in their brain, in their resistance to pain and in lots of things. But they have been conditioned for such a long time to behave in a certain way. Just as in the nineteenth century, a woman was not a woman if she didn't faint a couple of times a month.

Virility is such an immense problem with men. If they're not virile, that's the end of it, they are not a man any more. They go into a deep depression and have to get all sorts of treatment and their whole life crumbles. Whereas lots of women go around frigid and without any orgasms and still function. But, for a man to be impotent, is the worst thing on earth for him.

Women have a far better respect for life than men. Men will say, we have to die for our country. A woman will never accept, I think, that her son or her husband or her brother has died for his country.

Diana Potter: There are a few idiot women who do take themselves rather seriously, but men really take themselves much more seriously. For example, when you go to a meeting with men and women at the table, every man will have his say. The one or two women won't speak unless there is something to be said. And men are much more pompous than women, much more pompous.

I think men are fundamentally unfaithful. And women are fundament-ally faithful. I was talking to my boss the other day and saying the one thing I don't like about homosexuality is the great promiscuity. I've just been reading Joe Orton's diaries – four boys in a day – and I just find it slightly distasteful. And so he said, oh, all men are like that. Basically he thinks the difference between men and women is that. And he's got a point, actually.

Emily Prager: I think men are very exterior-orientated; they have exterior plumbing and tend to be outward-thinking. I think women are much more interior-thinking, they're more hidden in some way.

DIFFERENCES

Men are tremendously vulnerable, and actually in some ways it's much easier to fuck up (excuse me) the upbringing of a man than a woman, because even as little tiny boys they seem to stray away from emotion. It's very simple to give boys almost nothing if you are a parent and think you can get away with it. Boys are either loved to death by their mothers in a seductive manner, where they can do anything they want, or they're kind of ignored. There doesn't seem to be any middle ground.

Men and women have a different sense of time. I think men think in linear time; they see things as going towards the horizon, towards an end, a final end. Whereas women, because of having periods and stuff, actually experience the sense of rebirth every month: things come to an end, it's a tragedy, and it starts again. This is one of the things that makes them better able to deal with tragedy, better able to deal with emotion. Women think in circular time and men think in linear time.

If a woman fucks a man, she's a slut. If a man fucks around, he's a Don Juan, and it's just a different attitude to women, always a different attitude. It's strange, and as people become parents, they go back to it, they're dragged back to it. I've watched my friends, friends who went through the 1960s, and the minute they have babies they're dragged back to these points of view. They don't want their children to turn into monsters, and the demons are in their heads all the time.

Men develop habits, they seem to develop the things they like, and once they've developed those things then they are completely loyal to them. If I were to be asked what any of my former boyfriends were doing at this time in the morning, I could probably say exactly what they were doing. It doesn't matter who they're with, where they are, they will be taking a shower in a certain way, or shaving in the shower or whatever. The rituals they assign themselves become very fixed, unless they're uprooted and have to change. Women are much more adaptable. They adapt to new boyfriends, new habits, and this is something they're expected to do, something they're brought up to do, but I also think they have it in them to do that, because if you try to change a man, no matter how much you want to, it's unbelievably difficult. It's almost impossible. Men always are predictable. That's why they always get into trouble. If men break a pattern, it's really obvious, it's really funny. I can never understand why they don't see this, because they're so predictable that, when they deviate from something, it's like a big signpost.

Judith Price: Women outlive men because they have this vulnerability. This crying nonsense releases tension.

I don't think men let the problems with their wives affect their business. If they did, we'd all be in a great recession. Women cry and bring it into their business life. But I don't know of one man, even, let's say, a homosexual man, who comes into the office crying. Men don't cry in the office. It's not a sign of strength. Women, for some reason, are told, if you cry you'll get your way. They cry. Trust me, they cry.

Colombe Pringle: The biological difference is important, it's essential. Why should we be the same? What would be the interest? Our bodies are different, we think differently, we feel differently, we live differently, we wake up differently, we do everything differently.

Marjorie Proops: It's inevitable that attitudes which are very deeply ingrained in some people will every now and again emerge, so that you will get men who patronize women. But, as time goes on, fewer and fewer women will put up with this situation. When I was writing a column – an ordinary column as distinct from an agony column – we used to call it the battle of the sexes. You no longer see any reference to the battle of the sexes, do you? And I think that's because the battle is largely won. There will always be conflict between men and women, and I've always maintained that men will never understand women fundamentally any more than women will ever understand men fundamentally. No man is ever going to know what it is like to menstruate or have PMT or give birth to a child. No woman is ever going to know what it's like to get an erection. This fundamental physiological difference between the sexes is never going to change. Our understanding can be limited only to attitudes, not to deep emotional feelings. Until men and women realize and then accept the fact that there is a limit to their understanding of each other, then the conflicts will continue and might even become more violent.

Mary Quant: For a start, I'm happy with the shape and being of the female, and I want them to decorate and exaggerate that femaleness and that being: to bring out everything that's essentially attractive, young, female about that being, about that cat-like creature. I think a man is more tempted to look at a woman and turn her into another shape altogether and defy what she is. Looking at some of the famous designers of the past, they would turn a woman into a balloon, or a cube or a diamond or two triangles with a waist in the middle – whatever. They try and defy the natural shape. They design from the outside in and we design from the inside out. We know what makes us feel better, and we know what works. I feel it's like designing a more and more delicious parcel to be unwrapped. You know, to have the bow pulled and the thing to unravel. I would find it far more difficult to design for men because I'm used to working from the inside out.

A male baby is so male. You have less influence on its personality than, before you have the child, you believe you do. You don't actually make its personality, you can only polish it better or worse, spoil it one way or another, damage it one way or another, but its individuality and sexuality are there. I remember noticing that male babies have very smelly feet – quite soon.

Esther Rantzen: If I say to my children, what do you want for your birthday, the girls say, with one voice, a pony, and the boy says, instantly, a computer. They are not getting either, but this is what they have decided. If I say to the girls, would you share his computer, they say no. If I say to the boy, do you want a pony, he shrieks no. But I didn't actually programme my son to enjoy every machine he comes across. He is instantly magnetically attracted to it, plays with it, understands it, enjoys it, spends hours on his dad's computer. This has nothing to do with me. I don't understand machines unfortunately, even though a lot of my life I have to work with them. Equally, my girls are instinctively drawn to dolls and little animals, and imaginative stories about ponies and things. And this difference, I think, manifested itself at a very early age. I must say it is very hard to be a mother and believe that boys and girls are, fundamentally, identical. Because the truth strikes one as incontrovertible. There are influences, of course, there are expectations, absolutely. But I am not someone who says to my son, stiff upper lip, boys don't cry. Because I don't believe in that. Nor, indeed, do I say to my girls, you are going to marry a prince, because I don't believe in that, either. I've never given them gender expectations. I've tried not to condition them. Because I don't feel that I was, as a child, myself. Conditioning is fine as long as it doesn't limit people, so I try not to limit them.

Barbara Chase-Riboud: I think women are more resilient to pain than men. They have to be because, if men went into labour, the population would decrease by 100 per cent.

Men are terribly emotional. Men simply hide their feelings very well. Men are more emotional than women. If they weren't that way, there wouldn't be so many wars. War is totally emotional, it's certainly not rational. It's total irrationality taken to the nth degree.

Geniuses are very one-track-minded people. Totally egotistical. But totally. They have a kind of vision of life and of their work which is so didactic and so totally single-minded. Most women are simply incapable of that kind of concentration.

Mirella Ricciardi: I am sure our menstrual cycle makes us different, but I think men have got their own biological problems and cycles that they have to deal with, so that compensates for the biological cycles of the women. I do find that the biological system of the woman does hamper her. She is emotionally affected by her biological rhythms, and her emotions affect her decisions and her clear thinking. I think she is much more sensitive to situations, and it is often much more difficult for her to be ruthless – as ruthless as maybe she should be sometimes.

Women, when they are faced with a problem, will deal with it much more in depth than a man. I would feel much more at ease dealing with a good female psychiatrist than a male, because a female, in her very nature, is made to understand deeper and go further than men. I am a great believer in Nature. I am a great Nature watcher, and I have watched animals dealing with each other, and I then very often trace the human behaviour back to the animal behaviour. I've even got to a point where I see why the human behaviour has developed the way it has, away from the natural animal behaviour, which is the one we all go back to in cases of crisis. For instance, when you get attacked, your reaction is that of an animal. You become like a chimpanzee, no different. So studying animals and studying female behaviour of animals, among monkeys, elephants, dogs, cats, lions, I see a great similarity towards the instinctive behaviour of women. And this is what I try to be. I don't want to kill that in me, I want to try and keep it.

Nancy Richardson: Having been pregnant three times, and having given birth three times at home, with midwives and no anaesthetic, I can say that there is a strong biological difference. You just feel a certain way. I would hate to be President of the United States and be pregnant; the age for a woman to be President would have to be put up over fifty just to make sure she didn't slide a new baby in when she was forty-eight.

Men can divorce sex from love, and from the time they are children. A woman will do it progressively as she gets older. If I were divorced now, I would separate good sex from a good loving relationship, with no effort. I feel I have that kind of independence from the sentimental side of it now that I never had before. But men have it at twenty. So men and women are different there. But maybe it's because society hasn't afforded the women the opportunity. The cumulative, historic experience is not present for women the way it is for men, because society is always organized on the double standard.

Stella Richman: I think men's confidence has a lot to do with the dark-blue silk suit, a lot to do with how much they can drink. A lot of it is falsely based with men. Truly. When you own a restaurant, you see a lot of things. My late husband always used to say, you can tell a man's character from the way he behaves to a waiter, and that's very true.

Men are much more able to be promiscuous without a conscience than women are. I think women have to delude themselves a bit that it's not just here today and gone tomorrow. Men can do that much more easily, without thinking, oh, my God, was that really me last night? I think, if they've enjoyed it and it's been good, they're quite content to go on to the next thing or go back to their wives or their mistresses. Women carry too much guilt about with them, handed down from generation to generation. They've been brought up for better or worse to think that you give yourself to one chap and that's the way you should stay.

Angela Rippon: I don't see why women should always have to apologize for being different. Men are different from each other. I know men who would not work in a slaughter-house, but there are men who do that for a living. Now, is the man who is very happy to work in the City at a stockbroker's desk any less of a man because he doesn't have that kind of attitude which allows him to go in, kill an animal, cut it up, see its blood and guts spewing all over the place? Is he any different? Of course he is not. He just has a different outlook on life. I know men who go into the army because they feel that regime and way of life is absolutely right for them. I know other men who would run a mile rather than go into the army or any of the armed services, because essentially, as individuals, they have a different outlook on life, a different set of values. And they have, perhaps, different physical attributes as well as mental attributes. Exactly the same applies to women. I am sure I know a couple of women who would work in a slaughter-house, but I know many who wouldn't want to. So, on those basic levels, people are different. But if you insist on breaking it down further and saying men and women, yes, there are certain things that are different, there are bound to be. But I don't know that it is that clearly defined. Obviously I can't talk about motherhood because I don't have children and I haven't seen it in operation. Do I have different attitudes from a lot of the men I see? I suspect I probably have, but then I have a different attitude from a lot of the women I meet as well. The list of the most wanted people in the world includes an awful lot of women who will kill in cold blood. Now, do we say that those therefore are special, and individual, and unique women? Or are they exactly the same as male assassins? Or are we going to put assassins in a different group from the rest of society? I suspect it's been a very easy way of assuming or finding an excuse for differences by saying there are biological differences.

Shirley Ritchie: If men are more determined in one direction than women it's because they're not being interrupted by children and all the things women have to cope with. But that's conditioning, not a basic state. You put a woman into the same situation, and I don't think you'd find any difference.

It is for crimes of violence that people get sent to prison, and I think men on the whole are more violent than women. I think, too, that the opportunity to commit large fraud, which also gets people sent to prison, is available to more men than it is to women. Thirdly, I think that there is, or has been until very recently, an artificial leaning away from sending women to prison, because they have got children who might suffer if they were away from them. You get a chap, a man who has been shoplifting ten times, the court would not hesitate a second about sending him to prison. A woman goes shoplifting ten times: she has a child, the court will bend over backwards to keep her out one more time. But otherwise, I can't think really of any reason why there shouldn't be as many women in prison as there are men.

Hélène Rochas: Women can abandon everything for love; for men that's rarer.

Women always expect more. A man can always envisage a short affair with a woman and then wonder how he can get rid of her afterwards, but a woman wants to have some kind of display afterwards, a phone call, for instance, otherwise she's furiously hurt. But there's a contradiction here which is very funny, because most men want to keep everything in their lives; it's rare that a man doesn't keep in touch with an old affair, his wife, his mistress, his previous mistress. His dream is to have his house full of these women. A woman can leave everything, children and all, when she is in love. There are fewer men who abandon their families than women. A woman in love is monstrous. She will sacrifice everything.

Anita Roddick: Men are too preoccupied with image: image of failure, image of success. I've never found a man who is willing to ask for help unless it's from a very good friend. For a man, certainly the men I work with, and certainly my husband, it's almost an admission of defeat that they have to ask for help. They do, but in the most roundabout way. Whereas I haven't got the time to waste. Women are much more like Inspector Clouseau. We are more curious, and I think we are willing to learn more. We are like sponges. And men are more conditioned to see asking questions as an indication of failure.

Deborah Rogers: Men get tired and have hangovers. I don't think a woman is any less likely, or any more likely, to lose her judgement because it's a certain day of the month than any man. Look what happens to men if they're in love with somebody who has abandoned them, or who is unfaithful to them; men become just as unhinged by this.

Selwa Roosevelt: My husband marvels at the fact that I can't tell the difference between north, south, east and west. But I'm convinced that, basically, more women cannot grasp direction. Now, I don't say that men can't but I think more women cannot. And my husband is always amazed when he says, turn right, and somehow I hesitate.

Men are more rational. They're probably emotionally as vulnerable, but they know how not to show it, because they're trained. Showing emotion for a man is a non-masculine trait. And it's too bad because, of course, I don't see any problem with it at all.

Women are easily offended. Women are more sensitive. You really have to be more careful with your women friends. They're not live and let live the way men are. If you do something that one of your men friends doesn't like, he doesn't hold it against you the rest of your life. He forgets it immediately, especially if you try to make up.

I don't know that I really understand male sexuality, but women are far more romantic, so romance is a very important part of sex in their lives. I just don't think women look upon sex as something clinical, the way some men do. I know one man, for example, who is a very good friend of ours, who is a real Don Juan. The thing for him is the conquest. And then he's totally bored with the person after he has conquered her. And that's sadistic. Now, I don't think many women are like that. I can't think of a single woman who simply wants to collect trophies: male admirers by the dozen. But most women I know value a deep, romantic relationship with a man. It might go on for years and years, but that, for a woman, is something very important. And to flit from man to man is not normal for a woman. I don't mean she couldn't be unfaithful, there are lots of cases of famous women who have had lovers for twenty years. But that's it, that would be their lives, that one love affair. The moral standard is not really different after all, if one has one affair. It's the same moral lapse as if one has ten affairs. So, I'm not looking at it from a moral point of view. It's more that, for a woman, it is not a satisfying pattern to jump from man to man. It never will be, and there is a difference there. I think men really enjoy having lots of women, basically. It's curiosity, probably, and challenge and conquest.

Kimberly Du Ross: When I was in art school eight years ago, androgyny was something they were making films about. Six years later, the big theme is androgyny, with *Victor/Victoria*, but that whole idea's been around for years. The Greeks had it before us. It's just suddenly become fashionable and trendy to discuss androgyny, but it's really been around with us for ages.

Women, in general, maybe have more psychic intuition than men. We're also made up of more water. We're 90 per cent water, men are less. So we're much more affected by the tides and the full moons, and that whole astrological idea, and the menstrual cycle and everything, so we tend to be much more psychically intuitive than men, and that may come in to their art.

Some women are born with innate sex appeal, and some women aren't, and there's nothing they can do about it. It's their blood and whether they dress like men or act like men it's going to come through no matter what. Greta Garbo was meant to have this great feminine allure. Well, she was sexually androgynous, and there are women who can try to look like a man and act like a man, but there is some innate sexual appeal which is totally womanly which will glow through no matter what they do; they can't help it.

Juliet Mitchell-Rossdale: Social customs, by which I mean the deepest unconscious ones as well – psychological aspects – use the biological differences as part of the way they articulate the difference between the sexes. Anthropological studies show that women are very female in one culture and more like men in another, so it's the social living of a difference that uses the biology. I don't personally think that girls are less physically outgoing in a biological way. I suspect that we put the

1068

aggression of girls to a different sort of use, and quite possibly there's something innate that facilitates it. But you could have a society which disregarded that difference and made the girl the one that did the outgoing aggression. It's been known in societies, because of early articulation of this difference in the use of aggression, women's aggression tends to be more turned in into forms of severe depression, self-attacking; it's turned in on themselves in self-attacking ways. And so women are much more depressed than men, depression being the hiding of the aggression. When women are deviants, it is regarded as a psychological problem. When men are deviants it is a criminal problem. Men use their aggression outwardly and attack others and so they are imprisoned. Therefore you have more men in prisons and more women in psychiatric units. The social expectation of masculinity being identified to some degree with a certain sort of violence, and femininity being identified with a certain sort of masochism and passivity, has led to a situation in which women's way of protesting can only be turning on and attacking themselves, and that leads to psychiatric forms of illness.

Whether there is a stereotyped sex difference is hard to say, because individual differences, I think, dominate. And, again, I would take this back to very early infancy and childhood, and different relationships of boys and girls to the mother, which then come up in later life. Old stereotypes, like men needing more sex than women, I think have been proved to be rubbish. It was part of an image of masculinity, just as promiscuity was seen to be an image of masculinity but not of femininity. Those expectations of sexual differences were very tied to social ways that men were not economically dependent on women. And, of course, promiscuity doesn't go with economic dependence; it's not very suitable, if you're economically dependent on someone, to be promiscuous. Whereas, if you are economically independent, you can, of course, be promiscuous. So I think those particular sex stereotypes are very tied to economic conditions, and change with change in economic conditions. It's rubbish to say men have an innate need to spread their seed. I think it's compelling in some men and not in others. It's to do with images of masculinity that start in infancy, it's not innate or biological.

Until now, women have put more value on the private sphere of life, on some forms of self-cultivation, of creativity, of leisure, of nice things around them, of what they would see as a decent sort of balanced life; and they are not prepared to be just a successful career person to the detriment of their personal life. All women, from childhood, are encouraged more to see their life as a rounded whole or even not to see their life as involving work but as involving self-fulfilment in some senses within a home or relationship environment. So when they now get jobs, they don't want to lose the other side. And men have been brought up, in some sense, to think that sort of self-cultivation isn't important, and that they can, in fact, go hell-for-leather to do just the top jobs. And that will bring the self-respect, the respect of peer groups and status and all the rest of it.

Yvette Roudy: I think the difference between men and women is much more cultural than biological. As proof, there are many studies to show that women who were pioneers, or who succeeded, often did so because they had fathers who had no sons and therefore raised their daughters as they would have their sons. In the Middle Ages, in France, Christine de Pisan is such a case, sometimes called the first feminist. Her father brought her up, educated her, gave her cultural insight and ambition, and, when she was widowed with children, instead of retiring into a convent, she began to write and earned her living as a writer. There, culture was important, and I believe strongly in cultural conditioning. You can also see it in certain boys who have been brought up by their mothers, and in those cases the effects are not perhaps always positive. A human being brought up with the idea that nothing is forbidden and everything possible, but who has to work hard, knowing it depends on him- or herself, can reach the limits of his or her capabilities. For another, who is told, be careful; life and the world is hard, difficult, dangerous; protect yourself – that way leads to people who are afraid and who doubt their own abilities.

Joan Ruddock: There is a spectrum of human behaviour and a spectrum of attitudinal difference, and we tend to have the majority of women at one end of the spectrum and the majority of men at the other. But, towards the middle, you have men and women who come very close, where it is difficult to distinguish. I have male friends who hardly differ in their attitudes from my attitudes. It sounds an extraordinary thing to say, but I could almost see them being of the other sex. It is that close that I'm not desperately conscious of their maleness, though they may be attractive and that could be seen to be a sexual thing. What I recognize in society is that, because of the environment, because of conditioning, you expect most men to place themselves at a point in the spectrum, and you expect most women to place themselves, and it's partly to do with placing yourself as well as being placed.

There are so many men who are completely irrational, completely emotional, but it is expressed in different ways. It's not labelled and it's just excused. There are plenty of men who are considered thrusting, ambitious, aggressive, go-getting, which is, in my view, as unacceptable as many men would say women are unacceptable because of their emotional behaviour. It is just different, so I acknowledge difference. But I feel it is quite wrong to classify that as the weak and the strong. I observe a great deal of weakness in men and a great deal of strength in women, and so the popular concept of the difference between men and women is not borne out in my experience, but it is borne out in the labelling and the way in which people are placed. In my experience, it's far less complicated working with a large number of women than if you have a mixed workforce. In a mixed workforce, I actually think most of the trouble comes from the men, because the men are assertive and want to maintain position over the women. That seems to me where the problem lies. There is also sexual tension. I do think it is sometimes not possible to handle that, because, if you are in a hierarchical situation and all the men are at the top, then the women don't have any choices, but if there are as many female as there are male heads of department, then to some extent you can accept that factor, you can be aware of it, but also cope with doing what you're doing and set that aside. But, in my experience it's the men who feel they have to keep exerting their position and actually make it clear, as they see it, that they have a higher status than the women.

Eve Ruggieri: I think people have both types of sexuality. Just because one type predominates does not mean that the other is not there, too. A man who does not recognize his feminine characteristics and know how to use them is depriving himself of a great asset, and a woman who muzzles her masculine characteristics – the spirit of domination, competition and decison-making – will deny herself the chance of furthering her career.

Given that a woman carries a child for nine months, she is more attached to a continuity in her affections than men. There is a nice saying that misunderstanding between a couple comes from the fact that the man is looking at the future and the woman is looking at the man. As a generalization, that sums it up. Of course, there are minorities for whom it is not true, such as feminists. They are valuable because they make evolution possible, but they are not representative of female behaviour as a whole.

Carol Rumens: I certainly think, for myself, that sometimes I'm more aware of things, more sensitive, more emotional, than the majority of men I know in certain situations. I would perhaps take a remark more personally. If somebody's late, or doesn't ring when they say they'll ring, those sort of things are more important to me than they are to most men, I think. There's a sense of women concentrating very much on how people relate to each other, and even with women who are successful, even with women who have a career they take seriously, there's a big stress on relationships.

Doris Saatchi: I decided, a short time ago, that the key to men's behaviour – and I love the mystery of the differences, because they are total, there's no question about it, we are different – the key to men's behaviour is that they are basically competitive. It is in the genes. And they are competitive in absolutely every aspect of their lives, whether it's love, business, sport, money, recreation, and that goes back to when the male went out and did the hunting and brought home the food while the female lit the fire and suckled the babies, and that was how the animal survived. Today, it's just been translated into the stock market and winning the woman of your choice, but it's really no different.

Melissa Sadoff: I think men and women are completely different, not just visually, not just biologically, but our brain is different. We have the same type of nerve centre and so forth, but our reflexes, our emotions will be different. If a man is confronted by a prowler, his natural instinct would be to stand up and fight. A woman's natural instinct would be more or less to run away or scream. It is just a natural reaction. We're not sophisticated enough yet to say we have a brain in our head and we are going to use it. We allow the brain to use us and tell us what to do.

A man needs several women, many women, not only for a short span of time, but throughout his lifetime. I come back again to how different we are, mentally and biologically. Women need a romance and need one man, maybe. They would probably never change that one man if there is no good reason to do so. A man, no matter how loyal and how much he loves his wife, in my opinion – particularly an intelligent man who is well travelled, who knows life such as life is, full of exciting projects and exciting adventures – that man would need a different woman every year, every six months, who is to say, maybe every month. I cannot find anything immoral or amoral about it.

Our sexual needs are different, totally. A man needs to be stimulated all the time, so does the woman. However, unless she is a nymphomaniac, she would be very happy to be stimulated only by one man. As long as she is in love with him, and she can be in love with him for ever and ever, as long as she has that romantic image of the man, she will be faithful to him as long as she lives. However, no matter what she does, unless she really is superb, she is not enough, she is going to start ageing eventually. It is so silly of us women to think that a man doesn't enjoy beauty, doesn't enjoy excitement, doesn't enjoy youth. There are all sorts of women. Some are much sexier than others. If a man is a real man, he will fall under the charms of this other woman. We would have to be all-round women, or what I call women for all seasons, to please a man for ever, and even that would be very difficult.

Naomi E. Sargant: I believe men and women are different, but not in ways that matter in relation to our capacity to do most of the jobs that confront us. There is a major difference which affects how people interpret what people have done, which is basically whether they have had children or not. I don't believe it's their capacity to have children; it's actually more pragmatic. If they've taken a chunk of their life out to have children, and live in a different sort of way while they are having children, that affects the way in which they view everything. Secondly, of course, it affects their ability to carry on a voraciously demanding career. You simply can't do it at a given point. I can do it again now because I had the kids relatively early. I had all of mine in my mid twenties and my youngest is twenty-three. I don't think there are differences which intrinsically prevent men and women from doing jobs equally well. You get some extremely intuitive men and some totally non-intuitive men. You get people, men or women, who are extremely good with people or who are not. I tend to cry when under pressure, and I am intense. It isn't that I wish to, it's just, as they laughingly say, my tear ducts work easily. A man may bang the table, but it's the same kind of emotion coming out.

Dame Cicely Saunders: Women work harder and have more endurance, and they are better people. Men would never survive if it weren't for women. Women have to work harder because they have to bring up families, to support husbands emotionally and all the rest of it. If she wants a career as well, then it's doubly hard work. What a lot of women could well say is, I don't need a husband, I need a wife.

Women are much more up and down; there's a sort of undulation of their physical and emotional capacity. But women are much tougher at enduring adversity, physical as well as mental. The very ill man is not as tough as the very ill woman. And because we're made to be able to cope

1073

with pregnancy and all the rest of it, we are well latched into life. I think the whole view of evolution thinks about man the mighty hunter and never about the woman sitting at home in the cave or out on the plain bringing up the children, and right from there women have had a different relationship with survival. Physically, life is fairly unfair to women, so we get a bit more used to life being unfair than men do. I remember being told in school, of course life is unfair and the sooner you get used to it the better. I think women do get used to it, and perhaps get too used to it and accept it.

Anne Seagrim: Too many people seem to think they have to break up something, and that annoys me very much indeed. There was a case quite near here of a woman of forty-five. She's just left her family because she wants to fulfil herself. I think that's rubbish. And it's this sort of attitude, I think, which gets in the way of women understanding what they are like. They don't understand that they are different and can't do exactly the same as men.

Jenny Seagrove: Myths grow up that women are more sentimental, and this, that and the other. But, in my heart, I believe that men are more sentimental and more romantic than women, and women are perhaps a little bit more practical.

Men are desperately vain. The number of men who come into my dressing room and, instead of talking to me, they're looking in the mirror, doing their hair! They're obsessed with their hair. My husband used to take five minutes in the morning to comb his fringe. And he'd go out and the wind would blow it. Drove me mad.

I do think that sex for men and women is different. Inevitably. I've often heard some of my girlfriends saying about their husbands, oh, I wish he'd just cuddle me, and not as a prelude to sex. They just want to be held, they don't want to have to go through all that hassle. They're perfectly normal people with perfectly normal sexual appetites, who have a good time, but it's just the need of another body next to them and not perhaps any more. I think it is different for men.

Emma Sergeant: Women do grow up, whereas men stay boys. Having such a powerful father, I love older men and love being with them, but I notice that older men just have young boys' problems, except they're older, that's all. Whereas women, I think, do grow up more painfully, and they mature and really do change.

I have found myself sustaining more discomfort and longer hours of work than I know a lot of men do. Women are capable of sustaining more pain than men, and that is a fact. I'd like to see some men go through childbirth. And women have really too much imagination to line up, be troops and go to war.

I'm trying to sell my present studio, and the man I'm selling it to is a sweet friend of mine, but, you know, the one thing he is obsessed with is his suntan and his clothes. He's not going to buy this place unless he can work out where he's going to put his summer and winter wardrobes. I stick my clothes in a trunk, I put them anywhere, it doesn't worry me. To me, clothes are something you put on. You feel good, but you don't prink around in front of the mirror too long because you don't have time, you've just got back from work. I have found more men who are more vain, and absolutely pedantic about the cut of their suit, and they piss around like girls in a harem while they go off shopping together.

I know a lot of men who have a very strong feminine aspect. I'm not talking about homosexuals, I'm talking about men who have got strong mother complexes. They give the impression of being such tough old playboy figures, but in fact they're like little old women underneath – they worry, they dither, they don't make their minds up. There are very few men I know whom I can really call men, who go for exactly what they want, who are clear about their ideas and clear about achieving them. I find men full of just the same vagaries, the same indecision as women.

I think women have always been more predatory than men. A man may think he's being the conqueror, but it's the woman who's spotted the man first. She may do her coy act and pretend she's not interested or shy, but that woman always encourages the man first; just the eye contact, whatever. The man knows he's got his chance, and then goes in for it, and if she makes it difficult for him after that, that's her prerogative. Therefore I do think women are more aggressive that way than men. But that's a very subtle aggressiveness and part of the woman's make-up. It's a great shame to take the man's little conquest away from him. Any woman who comes on too strong with a man is immediately undervaluing herself and taking away from her own femininity. And therefore she doesn't stand much chance of attracting men over a long term.

A woman's orgasm is a more elusive thing, it is a state of mind. Most women have to have that state of mind, that very strong attraction for one man, that very strong romance-and-flirt set-up, so that makes the whole thing conducive to her orgasm. Whereas a man, it's a much quicker, more animal thing. And that is the difference between men and women that should never be denied. A woman is a creature of imagination and dreams.

Delphine Seyrig: I think each individual is slightly different biologically from another one, and there is an infinity of nuances between male and female. I don't think it's that definite. But it's very important for women to realize that their mind is just as good as a man's, and that their power of thinking is certainly as good, and that they're probably far more capable of expressing emotions in ways other than battle. Women probably have difficulty in surviving emotionally in a patriarchal society because emotions have been so distorted from childhood. Men seem to survive. We *are* in a patriarchal society, and I don't think that's contested. Within that framework, there are a lot of women trying to understand the structure, this male structure, and trying to clarify it, trying to identify how women are situated within that structure. Within that male structure, women are subjugated in every sense of the word. Women are the best agents to perpetuate the male structure because they are in charge of small children, yet they're not responsible. They're in charge of children, but they're in charge of bringing them up adapted to this society. If a woman brings up her little boy to cry whenever he feels emotion, she will not make a man adapted to this society, and if she brings up her little girl to be strong, as my mother wanted me to be, well, I could see that society around my mother was not saying the same thing as my mother was, and I chose very early between my mother's vision of what I should be and society's vision. And I could see that my interest in society was to adapt, but not do what my mother felt I should do. My mother was right, in some ways, except that she herself had given up her independence to be a married woman who accompanied her husband and lived his life. She stopped living her life after she was married. I could tell, at a very early age, it was safer to adapt. I'm putting this in an adult's words but I was then between two and four years old, and already something was decided within me: that I was going to be a real little girl, playing a little girl's role and not a boy's role, because boys are boys and girls are girls. But my mother didn't teach me that, society did. Kindergarten taught me that. I knew it was better to be a cute little girl with bows in her hair than a little tomboy. Women are the ones bringing up children, but the responsibility they have is to make them into happy young men and happy young women. And, to be a happy young woman, you have to adapt, because otherwise you will be rejected; and, to be a young man, you have to be a happy young man according to the rules or you will be rejected. So what they are doing is bringing up their children to fit into the world. The fact that women bring up children is not a guarantee of liberated adults, because they know that to be liberated from a society also means being rejected by society.

Hanan Al-Shaykh: Men can see a problem from all sides. They can see a thing when they are determined to do something, they think about the end-result and how they are going to deal with this matter. But sometimes women just think in one direction. Because her emotions are so intense and great, she forgets other aspects.

You find women who are much in love, but they are searching for something else. They are not satisfied and happy to be in love and to be wives. It's not the whole story. It is true that, for a woman, love-making is dramatic; she gives it all her thought, her emotions. And it will remain with her, and she will think about it for days, and maybe nights. Whereas, for men, there is just five minutes, maybe half an hour, and then he forgets. But, at the same time, it is not a woman's total life, because there are many women who are in love, but if they don't achieve other things, they are not very happy.

Alexandra Shulman: People are always saying, that's a typical way for a woman to react. It's not true. There isn't a typical way for a woman to react. I think there is a kind of instinctive reaction that is knocked out of boys who go to English boarding schools which doesn't happen to girls. Girls are not made to feel that it is wet to show your feelings or your emotions in the way men are. They're not made to feel that it's wrong to need other people in a way that a lot of boys are taught at school.

Showing their emotions doesn't mean to say they become irrational. It's a question of whether or not you think an emotional response is an irrational response. I don't personally think so. An emotional response in certain situations is a totally viable response to have. And perhaps more relevant than an intellectual response.

Women have a more kaleidoscopic view in the way, when you were a child, you looked down those kaleidoscopes and saw all the patterns, all the fragments that made up into a pattern. That's how women view life: as a series of fragments that all fit into a pattern; and men just see one great big lump. Women are also more capable in general, not always, of smoothing situations over, of submerging their particular ego for the sake of the general situation, so they would generally rather make life easier and more pleasant. You always notice at dinner parties that, if there's a kind of argument started, it is always the women who are willing to try and smooth things over: you know, let's not spoil the party, kind of thing, whereas the men, they're champing at the bit.

Rosemary Anne Sisson: I think women remain faithful longer than men, even when all hope is gone. I've watched my friends go through break-up of marriages and that is very upsetting. I wrote a play about Henry VIII and Catherine of Aragon, and to the very end of her days Catherine could not believe that her husband would not come back to her. She loved him to the end, and the more she loved him, the more angry it made him, because he wanted to be free. And I watched that played out with my married friends. So I think that what Jane Austen claimed in *Persuasion*, that it is the gift of women to be faithful when all hope is gone, and to be loving when all hope is gone, is a feminine trait.

Ginette Spanier: I equate sex with love. Mostly men equate it with just having a good time, a roll in the hay. I suppose life is easier for a man, but I've seen some very unhappy men.

Koo Stark: There are certain things which are primal, which you can't escape from. If you're a mother, you would kill for your child, you will die for your child. That's not the same as aggressiveness, but it is terrifying in its force. The same if you're in love with somebody. If you're really in love with a man, you would do anything for him, anything. A passionate woman, a woman whose passions have been aroused, is really a force to be reckoned with.

I've been passionate. It gives you enormous strength, far from making you weak. Women have been typically portrayed as being in love and soppy and weak, and incapable of getting out of bed in the mornings and facing the day, because they're so much in love, and swooning all over the screen. I think it's the opposite. Any kind of passion gives you enormous strength – huge strength. It doesn't necessarily have to be your husband, or your lover, or your child. It can be an issue, it can be anything that rouses your passions. A bitter or unhappy woman is probably one of the most dangerous things in the world. Women are dangerous people, far more dangerous than an unhappy or bitter man in my experience.

Men expect different things out of life from women. A man will expect to get his career together first, and he makes that decision quite young in his schooling years, about what direction he wants to take and where he wants to go. If he's going to choose a profession, he chooses it usually by the time he's in his mid teens or late teens, and knows vaguely which direction his life is going to take, in what area of the world he wants to live. A wife and children aren't as important. They'll figure probably in his life, but they're not as important as his career and base. It's very rarely that a man will consider marrying until he has a secure future, or as secure as one can be, whereas women tend still in this day and age, by and large, to go for: well, I can do whatever I want to do and it's all a temporary measure until I get married. I can travel a bit, or I might want to do a secretarial course or take a temporary job here, or pursue my painting or my writing. But the be-all and end-all, the ultimate goal, is not to have a successful career but to have a happy home life, a husband and children.

Gloria Steinem: I believe that the individual difference is bigger than the group difference. That is, the individual difference between two men, or between two women, or between two black people, is greater than the differences between males and females as groups. The difference between two five-year-old boys is bigger than the difference between boys and girls as groups. So what we need to do is throw away the labels and try to let individuals be their real selves. Behaviour in the animal kingdom varies completely from species to species. A lioness takes care of the cubs, but male penguins hatch the eggs and cough up the contents of their gullet to feed the baby penguins. I mean, you can find everything. The male suprematists always choose apes, and usually apes in captivity, in order to demonstrate. But if they used elephants they could come out with something completely different: the female elephants are very often the leaders of the pack. So you can take the differences, and you can argue female superiority and you can argue male superiority. But the truth is that we share much more than what differentiates us. It's the individual difference that's the important one, not the group differences. In any group difference you take, no matter what it is – upper body strength, aggressive behaviour in teenage boys or whatever – you will always have at least 30 per cent of men and 30 per cent of women that overlap. So why make such a big deal out of the two polar opposites? I don't think there is such a thing as male and female aspects. There are human aspects and we have them in different mixes. Masculine or feminine are culturally imposed ideas.

Women are connected to children and men are not. Men are external authorities, making the money and so on. Children learn by what they see, and that's what they see. However, we are breaking the cycle now. Now we have all these children's stories and songs saying to little boys, it's all right to cry. Men should not have to grow up with problems of stress and heart attacks and heaven knows what, just because they have been taught not to release their emotions. The male role, the masculine role, is killing men. This image of John Wayne, of rock-like inflexibility and being right all the time and earning a lot of money: it's impossible; it's not a human image.

Pamela Stephenson: John Cleese actually said to me once that he didn't think women are as funny as men, but I think he didn't mean intrinsically that they couldn't be. I think he meant that, because of some biological or instinctive reason, and to do with the fact they have families, that they feel they must be the ones that hold the family together; at the end of the day, the guy can be out there pissed as a newt, being the clown, but it's the woman who has actually to remain sober so she can return to the children in one piece – or something like that. That she can't achieve the state of madness necessary to produce great comedy. Now, I think that's absolutely untrue. I just know it's untrue. Plenty of women have proved it. But the fact is that women tend to have to be truly schizophrenic in a sense. I know, now that I've had children, that I have to be a mother: that that's a whole different personality from what I have to do when I switch off that role, when I'm on stage and have to forget I'm a mother. It is a very difficult thing.

Lady Arabella Stuart: I've noticed that women who lose their fathers in childhood, as I did, are often left with an uneasy attitude to men in general. Watching a man friend with four daughters, I see how important it is for a girl to have a loving father, to give her a sense of herself as a lovable female. If they don't have this, they seem to remain forever lacking in self-esteem, and diffident. It's as if their first relationship with a man ended in disaster. They found themselves abandoned, and this leaves them with an insatiable yearning for masculine affection and companionship – not necessarily physical – and with a lack of confidence that they will ever achieve or retain it. I can't think that the death of either parent would have a similar effect on a man.

I find women much more supportive and much more honest, and therefore more interesting to talk to. Because they're more realistic. Biologically, I think they just become more realistic because they have to deal with things like childbirth which makes them much more closely tied in with the facts of Nature and life. I find them better at confronting death or birth, or any of those things, and less scared than men, and less apt to live in fantasies. Women are, on the whole, much more concerned with appearances than men are. I don't mean with their own appearance, but with how they are viewed by other people. Whereas most men don't give a damn. I first became aware of this when I was getting divorced. I realized that I wanted very much to behave well, and to be seen to have behaved well. Whereas my ex-husband didn't give a damn what people thought of him. Men's vanity seems to be confined to their looks. I used to notice how upset men were by Mark's drawings, even when they had commissioned them themselves, for a Christmas card or some such thing. (Another odd quirk, a sort of vanity in itself. No woman would pay someone to caricature her and be silly enough to expect to like the result.) But it's as if some women, myself included, carry around a sort of ideal image of themselves which they are reluctant to give up. They waste too much time agonizing over a trivial thing that happened yesterday, an inept remark that might have hurt someone's feelings. Men don't have these hang-ups, and it gives them a lot more power.

I remember reading a remark of Enid Bagnold's, that esteem makes a good substitute for love as one gets older. And I think that is very true. I discussed this with a friend at the time, who said, I'd rather be thought good than beautiful any day. (In fact she was both.) But I can't imagine any man saying that. Yet esteem seems a reasonably realistic thing to aspire to as one gets older, rather than staying attractive.

Imogen Stubbs: I like people who know what they want. I always remember my aunt used to get very cross if she said, do you want tea or coffee, and I would say, I don't mind. She loathed people dithering and putting the responsibility on her, and I somehow find it more a male trait to know one's own mind. That's easier for men than women, I don't know why. That's why I probably find more masculine women attractive. But here I am, condemning people who don't make up their minds, when I have always been terribly scatty and fluffy-brained, and disorganized and hopeless with money, and I've got away with it.

There is a kind of pomposity which is quite staggeringly male, and I think that comes from boys being indulged by their mothers or parents. I've never come across that kind of pomposity in women. There is a kind of passion in some men I've met that I've never come across in women. There's a strength in certain male actors that it's hard to find a parallel with in female actors. Women actors have other things, but Anthony

Hopkins has something about him, a kind of presence, which seems to me very male and terribly powerful. Maybe Redgrave has the female equivalent.

Andrea von Stumm: Physically and emotionally, I would say that men are good sprinters and women are good long-distance runners.

Janet Suzman: I think there's some astonishing faithfulness in women which is not at all prevalent in men, or, at least, it's terribly, terribly rare if it happens. Women commit themselves emotionally probably too much for their own good. Maybe this is biological, because they jolly well have to with children. If the mother doesn't commit herself to the child, the poor child is lost, so there's that instinctive commitment anyway.

There is a kind of atavism in a child about the word father, a kind of response. Where is it got from? Nursery school or somewhere, I don't know. It makes the male father figure seem slightly more mysterious, probably because he is not seen as much as the mother. He is a gift-bearer, a benign and rare influence on his life. It seems a very powerful one indeed. And that's very likely, because a woman is seen by a child at her worst, and at her best, consistently throughout the day. He sees the whole spectrum of somebody angry, somebody loving, somebody yelling, somebody looking terrible, somebody looking good, whatever. So the mystery falls away, and what he sees is actually a human being simply coping with the day – his day, too, the child's day. Maybe that is the thing that allows him to judge women. I'm saying him, with a more jaundiced eye, and perhaps the male, being less accessible, seems stronger, gentler and quieter.

Conny Templeman: There are exceptions, but men, though they're in front socially, seem behind emotionally and spiritually.

I find men assume a lot. They assume they have the right to a certain position, to a certain voice, to a certain role, and women don't make that kind of assumption.

Lisa St Aubin de Terán: Women are, in fact, stronger than men psychologically. They are more able to deal with stress and continual problems, and are able to work more than men. Not with physical strength, but with psychological strength. They have the power of endurance, and I think, in extreme situations, it is the women who can actually pull through. They are more capable of holding things together. Nowadays, a lot of women are working, but they haven't given up what they used to do. They are still mothers, they still run a house. They have just added to that workload and they are quite capable of doing that. A lot of men would find it truly impossible to do the same amount. Maybe this is because one has a different kind of concentration, a concentration that is more complex. I notice that I can write and answer the telephone, pay the milkman, have people interfering, coming into the room, and it doesn't spoil my concentration. Whereas I notice a lot of men need to have really intense concentration to be able to produce anything. The butterfly mind is extremely useful.

I don't actually put a huge amount of effort into my writing if effort is translated as time. I tend to spend most of my time just mulling things over in my head, and the actual amount of time I spend at the typewriter is very small, whereas most of my male colleagues are drudging away. Again, I have the advantage of being able to carry the threads while I'm out doing other things, apparently leading a normal, rather indolent life. But I am, in fact, writing a book in my head, which is just in one compartment, and so by the time I've sat down to write I have actually got everything in my head and it's like a dictation. In fact, I have many different compartments which run simultaneously. One of them is the next book, and another is the next after that. I carry about five or six in my head at a time. Eventually I just say it aloud on to the typewriter as I go along, because I've got it all in my head.

There's no long-lasting element of sexual failure for a woman. The man, even if he fails once, although 10,000 times he hasn't, that one failure is chalked up against him, as it were. So, in that, there is a definite advantage sexually for a woman. A woman can actually allow herself to be far more sensual than a man, because she doesn't tire. She can be sensual all her life, every minute of the day, whereas, a man, there's just so much energy and so much actual sexual prowess, and then, however masculine he is, he gets tired. Another difference is that women tend to dream or day-dream of a kind of perfection, and so even a very inadequate partner can be something quite wonderful because one is imagining this, but then, again, the fantasy can suddenly end. Over and over again, a girl can be going out with somebody, or living with somebody, and then, literally from one day to the next, because the back-up of all this romance and imagination can be switched off for the moment and the person is so below what this ideal has been, it's all gone, all broken off. Often men find it very hard to deal with, because nothing has materially changed. But the mental back-up has gone and there is nothing from that point. He could stand on his head, he could be an Adonis; it would make no difference, it's gone. The back-up of the ideal situation is very much in the head.

Fiona Thyssen: Once you get to university, a woman's voice is as easily heard as a man's, I would have thought. If there is reticence in a woman not speaking out, it is probably more genetic, or maybe social. Women are quieter by nature. They are not as raucous and as loud as men, unless, of course, they drink, in which case they are absolutely obnoxious.

Martha Tiller: Act like a lady, think like a man and work like a dog: I think that has to be our motto. In business situations particularly, I stop many times in the course of the day before responding in a feminine emotional manner to the situation. I stop and say, now how would a man think and act in this situation? And it helps me in my own little way to feel and hopefully appear more professional, not emotional. I try to base decisions on sound, well-thought-out, logical business practices, not on exciting, intense, emotional impulses. Most successful men have had a mentor, and I think a mentor is one of the great missing links for women. At this point in time, there are not many women mentors another woman can look up to.

Women, in addition to being emotional, tend to be very jealous of one another. A man may inside begrudge the success of a colleague, but in the good-old-boy network, he will support that colleague, contribute to his cause, pat him on the back, help him. Many women are reluctant to do that.

I'm glad I don't have a daughter. They are very cognisant of designer labels. I lived in New York for years before I knew what a designer was.

Lili Townsend: The masculine traits are dynastic, patriarchal qualities, and everything that has to do with creation of the dynasty, with the creation of strength, wealth, support, brings out in men their aggressive nature. Certainly, at some level, that aggressive nature is, has been, part of the structure of life, the firm solid structure that the male has built. The female has feathered the nest. What we're seeing is the emergence of change, but I still think the structure is basically a male function. The system makes a great deal of sense like that. We can see it in Nature, where, essentially, the male is involved with protection and the female involved with life, the giving of life.

The successful person is one who has balanced the male and female aspects of their being. The success of this new way of thinking, I think, is for us each to cherish the parts we are not.

Polly Toynbee: The differences between human beings, between the intelligent and the unintelligent, between different interests, between people of different cultures, are far greater than the differences between a man and woman of the same class and the same culture – they have much more in common. Yet, arbitrarily, we decide that the differences in sex are really the most important. The first thing, when a child is born: is it a boy or a girl? From then onwards, everything that happens to it is determined by that. We are artificially reinforcing what's there in Nature. I suspect that what's there in Nature is quite strong, but not very strong, and that if we were able to do away with cultural bias, we would find it all falling away; and so there would be a lot of men who would be much gentler, and a lot of women who would be much fiercer. I'm just going through a certain crisis myself, about this. I've had three daughters and I have a son who is now twenty months old. Now, I didn't think I brought up my daughters with any particular bias towards being girls, and I've brought him up exactly the same as I brought up the girls. Of course, he's just a baby, but already he is possessed by tractors, cars, engines. My husband is entirely hopeless with his hands and isn't remotely interested in machines, so it's not that he sits and watches his father mending or even cleaning cars, but something has triggered off in his mind, already at this age, the idea that tractors are really very exciting things, much more exciting than lots of other things. And this didn't happen with my daughters, and I don't know where that comes from. I suppose, if I was a real extremist, I'd say, well, he's already been watching a lot of television and looking at the wrong sort of books, he's already been culturally contaminated. Nevertheless it makes me think that there must be some differences, though quite how maleness should attach itself to machinery is a mystery. Feminists fantasize that this or that society was once a perfect matriarchy, but I don't think there is any evidence that there's ever been any such society except in fantasy literature.

A wonderful piece of research was done where some researchers got young mothers of six-month-old children, put them one by one in a room with a camera, and gave them a baby to hold; and the baby was dressed in blue; then they gave them another baby to hold which was dressed in pink, and they were told that one was a boy and one was a girl, but they never knew which was which. They filmed how these young mothers treated them, and the babies in blue were picked up, bounced up and down – lovely strong legs, fine boy – and the babies in pink were held very close and cooed to and rocked. It's very difficult to decide how much of the difference between male and female is biological, but what we do know is that a very large amount of it is cultural.

I doubt if there is a biological urge that is significantly different between women and men. You get highly-sexed women and lowly-sexed women, highly-sexed men and lowly-sexed men. I doubt if there is a very fundamental difference. I think the biggest difference is between how both of them respond to the pressures of sexual success, and that's a cultural difference, a conditioned difference.

Abir Dajani Tuqan: Women are less emotional sometimes than men. Men crack up more easily. Men feel they have to control themselves, but in actual fact they are more irrational, I think. Women let themselves go. They can afford to scream while men have to control themselves. I think women are very, very rational. They have to be, because they have to take care of the children.

Kathleen Turner: Women are in many ways so much more level-headed, so much more in touch with the reality, that they don't force their projections of what the world should be quite as much as men. Part of this is due to the fact that a woman, in having a child – and now I am projecting, since I have no children – but the having of a child, I think, would create an essential feeling of responsibility that's inescapable, a feeling that perhaps a man manages to escape all his life, if he cares to.

Marie-Claire Valène: One isn't a woman, one becomes one. There are real biological differences, of course. I won't enlarge on them. But the differences are cultural. The perception of men and women is the same, but the differences are cultural and acquired. I don't have children, but with my brothers, friends, cousins and so on, I've never seen any difference, never felt it. They can be stronger, but they are equally weak. They are physically stronger because they can carry heavier weights, they are muscularly stronger, taller, but that doesn't modify their perception. They might be more aggressive, but that might be an acquired characteristic, an *idée reçue* about their virility. But, I've noticed, the more intelligent a man is, the less aggressive he is.

Diana Vreeland: I think men have more masterly minds. Men are also usually more creative, educated and sensible than women.

Women are apt to be more nervous than men and feel more privileged. Men work as a matter of course, women expect something exceptional and wonderful might happen to them.

Michaela Walsh: A woman has a different experience from a man in bringing life into the world, so what is important to her is quite different. I've seen many women who are highly motivated in their career, respond to children and to something that may be life-threatening to children, in a way that is very different from men.

Marina Warner: One of the things that is very important to think about is that people are different at different ages, and that when we think of women being different from men, we are tending to think of women between five years old and forty, woman sexed through actual incipient fertility and ebbing fertility. We should look more perhaps at the changing pattern of woman's whole life and what the differences are between old women and old men. I think that there is a difference and that this is physiologically grounded. I am very against biological determinism, because I do think that biology doesn't exist in a void, it must always exist within a social structure. But I think that where men and women come from, in terms of hormones, probably does contribute to the difference between them. After all, what we mean by a man is very often connected to ideas of physical strength and physical aggression, and there are hormonal secretions that men have that are to do with aggression which don't exist in the same quantities in the female body. The other thing is the way desire manifests itself in a man and is released in a man, because it is so much shorter; there is some greater difference than just the biological difference. It is to do with gratification of a certain kind that must come faster. But it is terribly dangerous and actually rather unpleasant and somehow fascist to build ideas about sexual difference on such things. You get into terrible trouble then, I think.

One of the reasons men don't have to look after their looks the way women have to in our society is because that's not the currency in which they deal sexually. We all know how amazed we are when we see some enormously fat old man with a gorgeous young woman, but it is a very common surprise.

Heather Watts: I find women, by nature, much bitchier than men, and much cattier to each other. I think men behave in a more civilized manner than women.

Arabella Weir: I'm always stunned at what men will believe when you tell them things. I'm always amazed. So fragile are their egos that they will grab the opportunity to believe you and not question it.

I think all the women I see and all the women I've known who have had to cope with hardship have done so much better than the men. Most men I know who have had to cope with hardship have behaved very childishly, or have become drunks, or have become drug addicts, or have got new women immediately to cope with everything for them. Women, possibly because they have to be, because they're usually in charge of the children, seem to be much more capable. They seem to suffer crises much more easily. When a man has a crisis, on the whole he tends to give up his whole body and soul to a crisis, whereas a woman will get through it, probably because she has to.

Felicity White: I think the London businessman who has a one-night stand after a New York party feels that he is off on a trip, he has cut free. Whatever he feels about his wife, he feels that his peer group somehow expect him to score at a party. A woman, in the same situation, is more likely to pick and choose. She either will have a one-night stand or she won't. Whereas the man is more likely to do his level best, and if he doesn't, well, it's been a really bad party.

Both of the sexes have compassion, but women are far more prepared to show it. I also think they are far more prepared to say what they think and to risk opprobrium, or whatever is going to come at them, and to answer it back and argue their case. I think, also, they are better at dealing with criticism, although they absolutely loathe it. They will answer a criticism and say, I did it for these reasons, rather than trying always to be the perfect person and wheedle their way out. So they are far more up-front. Now, whether that is something inherent in a woman, or whether that's something that is there at the moment because of the way society runs and the way they have had to fight for their place in society, I don't know, but I fear it is the latter. Because of the way women are brought up, because of the way we are expected to run a home and do all the things that go with that, plus a career, we have learned to think about ten paces ahead the whole time. Men don't, and it's very difficult to actually explain it to men.

1088

DIFFERENCES

Katharine Whitehorn: There are vast differences between men and women, but I think the differences between people are, in the majority of cases, greater than the differences between men and women when you remove the programming. If I can put it this way: we're none of us all-male and all-female, and if the women's movement has done nothing else, it has stopped people drawing a dotted line down the middle with male on one end and female on the other; and if you were slightly less male then you must be more female, and slightly less female then you must be more male. At least they now admit there is a vast central androgynous area, and I would say that, in an enormous number of cases, a lawyer is more like another lawyer of a different sex than a lawyer is like a businessman of the same sex or whatever.

There is one thing which I think is enormously important, and that is the gang feeling of men. There is a book called *Managers and Magic* by Graham Cleverley, and a lot of it is quite jokey. He is equating modern management practices with the things primitive tribes do – the ritual meal is the business lunch and so on – but he has a very penetrating chapter on women. He says that primitive tribes think women are weakening; and that it's not just that you stay away from your wife the night before a battle because you might be exhausted from making love to her, but all the other things that go with female magic – lactating, menstruating. All these things are, at some very deep level of men, felt to be weakening to them. If you want to take, not an anthropological but a Freudian parallel, the struggle of a man to get away from under his mother's dominance to be a man is something which shapes him for life, in a way. Cleverley also said that the reason the demands for women's equality will never get anywhere is that they are based on logic and reason when they are up against much more, something fundamental and deeper. He cites one well-authenticated case of a Bantu warrior in 1895, who found that a menstruating woman had walked across his tribal blanket, and he was so upset that he killed her and died of fright in a fortnight. One of the women war correspondents in Vietnam couldn't understand why they hated her so much until she realized that the men resented the presence of a woman. It was a particularly nasty war, you weren't allowed to win it, you were in very hostile territory, they were having a lousy time, and the only thing that held them together was that they were strong warriors together. And then you get some girl in khaki coming in among them and taking that away, and they couldn't bear it, which I suppose is understandable. I feel we are very much up against this male bonding, but it can be eroded.

I'm very interested in two things: menstruation and menopause. There was a book written called *The Wise Wound*, by Penelope Shuttle and

1089

Peter Redgrove. It was a terrible title but a very interesting book, suggesting that the things associated with menstruation – the main one of which is that you are *hors de combat* for sex for five days or whatever it is – were actually an enormous advantage to women. And there was an Ellen Goodman article in America recently, headed, 'Menopause, an Advantage that Men Have to Do Without'. She says there comes a point when a woman knows she can't have any more children, so that's it, that bit is over. So she's now getting on with the next bit. But the temptation of a man to try to be twenty again and beget more children stays practically the whole of his life. And the extent to which people underestimate the terrifying energy of the post-menopausal woman would be more apparent, I think, if we didn't have our career structure entirely set up on the male plan.

A man might want happiness, but what does happiness consist of? Maybe it consists of being managing director. The Peter Principle, that a man must go on being promoted until he gets to his maximum level of inefficiency, doesn't apply to women, I don't think. A woman, from her upbringing, is much more likely to say, no, I've got a job I like, the hours fit and the money is enough, and I don't want to take the next one up. I said this to the woman who runs the Citizens' Advice Bureau network and she said, well, now, you've forgotten the Paula Principle. The Paula Principle is that a woman is offered a job and she says, oh, I don't think I could. And maybe she's expecting to be asked again or given three weeks to think it over or come to terms with it, but she will probably feel diffident about taking it. But if it's offered to a man of the same ability, and he can't actually do it any better than she can, he will say, yes, because he feels he has to.

One of the things women have done in civilization, all civilizations – one of our jobs, as it were – has been to contain the overwide spreading of the male seed. This was really brought home to me in a thing Martin Amis wrote to do with the spread of Aids which was related to homosexual behaviour. It was very interesting. When you get male homosexuals, and there is no halfway meeting between the male and the female principles, there can be ninety sexual contacts a week. Imagine taking ninety people to the opera. Male homosexuals are extra-ordinarily promiscuous, even when they have a very steady relationship as well. It's as if you have sorted out the male principle entirely, and it's like that. I don't know much about lesbians, and I guess that a lot of people described as lesbians are not necessarily particularly sexually active, because more of our reproductive urge goes into things connected with lactation and babies. I did not experience this myself. I didn't mind breastfeeding, and I did it because it was the best thing for the

1090

baby, but I have talked to women who actually got a sexual thrill from the physical act of breastfeeding and were very reluctant to give it up, even when the children were coming up to a year old. It is quite obvious that our biological mechanisms provide us with a variety of satisfaction along the reproductive cycle, whereas men, through sheer biology, have just the one. Obviously, spiritually, mentally, they have all the others as well, but biologically, however enlightened you are, you cannot as a man get a physical charge out of breastfeeding.

Shelley Vaughan Williams: I thought before, as I think now, that there is a delightful difference between the sexes, and it's the strength and the weakness of the two that, if they're put together in a loving instead of in a combative, competitive way, it takes you right up, gives you wings, and you fly, both of you.

A lot of men hide behind desks. I've never interviewed or received anybody from behind a desk, because I think it puts the desk between you psychologically, and I think a lot of men use the desk almost consciously, particularly when dealing with women.

Jeanette Winterson: There are enormous biological differences, and there should be, because, in a sense, it's set up for us to interact. That ought to work for the benefit of both sexes, and if we were exactly the same, it would be terrible. But I am concerned that there have been so many attributes simply ascribed to women over the years, that they are more loving, more nurturing – you know, naturally they will want children, they are weaker or whatever, they can't make their minds up. There's an endless stream of things that have just been pasted on layer by layer until it's built into an enormous legend about what a woman is. That has to be carefully scrutinized. The differences are there, but we have to be sure they are real differences and not made-up ones.

Women have periods, and this is quite crucial in the way they operate. Contrary to the belief that it makes women completely irrational and off-the-wall for a few days of the month, I think it actually makes them terribly clear-sighted. I do my best work around that time. I don't know why, but I know that it is the case. If I have a problem, I will solve it around that time. I find it very creative, I know this experience is shared with a number of women. I think we always have a sense that our bodies are undergoing a change, which perhaps men don't so much. And that gives you perhaps a rather more precarious outlook on the world, but also a very sensitive one, because you feel the changes in yourself, and

1091

so, perhaps, you're more able to respond to changes in your life outside.

I think men are very concerned with how things work: building a world that you can see and touch and is concrete. And I think, to a large extent, women look behind those things, perhaps into motives, perhaps into personalities, into the way things actually work, and into people more. Which is why, I think, women make very good personal-relations people and they're good in advertising. If it's to do with human nature, women are more likely to be able to see into that and use the information, because they look beyond the surface. We have to, because so often in the past our way forward has been via men, so we have learned to look into the heart. Men have very rarely had to do that, because they can just crash and bang through the world and it quite often works for them simply because they are male.

Women often do the listening, so they pick up things about human nature which they can then apply in other situations, whereas men are often doing the talking. If you go into a bar and see couples or groups, it's often the men who are talking and the women who are listening and putting in comments here and there. And that's not always passive – women are picking up so much. Because, if you're talking all the time, you're not hearing, and that's where the skill comes from. I've known men who are equally skilled, but they're unusual.

Anna Wintour: Women are stronger than men in many ways, and I think they're only just beginning to know their strength. In the years I've been working, except on very special occasions, I can't think of a woman who's said, I can't come to work today because my husband's just left me, or I'm having a rotten time.

Enid Wistrich: In the eighteenth century, for example, there was not this inhibition on men to cry. It was acknowledged that a man could cry, and it's often said that Nelson wept, or Winston Churchill, who was in some ways an eighteenth-century man, wept when he was moved. I think it is a conditioning thing, I don't think it's an inherent thing.

I've noticed that, if you give women a job to do with other women, they look for co-operation, how to do it together. If you give a group of men a job, they look for one to take the lead, or one takes the lead and wants to boss the others and tell them what to do. I actually think this is quite a basic difference between the way men and women work. Men look for hierarchy: hierarchical positions and authority, and clearly defined authority. It's almost the difference between a circle, which is what women will look for – people moving across, talking to each other and working together – and a triangle, which is what men will look for, with one at the top and others in a hierarchy.

Priscilla Woolworth: When a woman is in love, it shows. If a man is in love, he smiles, but his physique is not changed. But a woman: her eyes glisten, everything – her hair, everything – is more beautiful.

Biographies

Jenny Agutter was born in 1952 in Taunton, Somerset. With a father in the army, she spent much of her childhood overseas. At nine she returned to England to board at the Elmhurst Ballet School, and when she was eleven she was cast in the leading role of the Disney film *Ballerina*. Her first major success was as Roberta in *The Railway Children*, which brought her the Variety Club of Great Britain's Most Promising Actress Award. She has since received an Emmy for her role in *The Snow Goose* and the British Academy of Film and Television Arts Award as Best Supporting Actress in Peter Shaffer's *Equus*. Her first major American film, *Logan's Run*, took her to Los Angeles in 1975, and she spent the next few years travelling extensively to make films before returning to England in 1982 as a member of the Royal Shakespeare Company. Her most recent filming has been in episodes of *Murder She Wrote* and *The Twilight Zone*, and in the suspense feature *The Dark Tower*. She has just completed a season in Hollywood as Kate in Charles Marowitz's *Shrew*. Jenny Agutter is also an accomplished photographer and in 1983 she published *Snap*, a photographic tribute to London and Los Angeles.

Lolicia Aitken was born in 1947 in Belgrade, an only daughter. She was educated at Lausanne University in Switzerland and obtained a Masters degree in economics in 1968. She founded her own economic consultancy business in 1970 in Lausanne. She married Jonathan Aitken the MP in 1979. Her twin daughters were born in 1980 and her son in 1982. She lives in London.

Maria Aitken was educated at Oxford University, where she was the first elected woman member of OUDS. At Oxford she appeared in *Dr Faustus* with Richard Burton. Her numerous parts in the theatre include those in *A Little Night Music* at the Adelphi, *Travesties* at the RSC, *Blithe Spirit* and *Bedroom Farce* at the National, *Private Lives* at the Duchess Theatre and *The Women* at the Old Vic. In television she has been in *Armchair Thriller* (Thames); *Company & Co*, *Ripping Yarns* (BBC); *Bedroom Farce* and *Poor Little Rich Girls* (Granada). She hosted her own chat show, *Private Lives*, on BBC. Her film appearances include those in *Dr Faustus*, *Mary Queen of Scots*, *Half Moon Street* and *Melba*. She has also directed several plays, including *Private Lives* at the Oxford Playhouse and *The Rivals* at the Court Theatre, Chicago. Most recently she has filmed a drama-documentary called *Lizzie* in the Amazon basin and has appeared in 1987 in a revival of Noël Coward's *The Vortex*. She has published *A Girdle Round the Earth*, a book about adventuresses.

Lady Penelope Aitken MBE (1955) JP was born in 1910. She married Sir

William Aitken in 1939. She is the mother of Maria Aitken, the actress, and of Jonathan Aitken, the politician.

Shirin Akiner BA PhD (London) was born in Dhaka, Bangladesh. The daughter of a Bengali diplomat, her childhood was spent in travel. She studied music in Moscow under David Oistrakh and in Amsterdam. She is now the first holder of the post of lecturer in Central Asian Studies at the School of Oriental and African Studies, University of London. She has been consultant on documentary films shot in the USSR, China, Pakistan and Turkey. She is widowed and has one son.

Baria Alamuddin is Lebanese and was educated in Beirut. She graduated from the American University of Beirut in 1972 with a degree in journalism, mass media and political science. She has been editor of the Lebanese television news programme and of *Al Assayad* magazine and, since 1986, editor-in-chief and chairman of Media Services Syndicate. She is a freelance journalist, specializing in interviews with heads of state. She is also visiting lecturer on journalism to Lebanon and London Universities and a Middle East political adviser to Lebanese and British television. Baria Alamuddin is married and has two daughters.

Madeleine L. H. Alatas graduated from the University of Pennsylvania with an MA in business administration. Since 1984, she has been consultant on assignments in consumer goods and banking for McKinsey & Company Inc., London. During her career as a business consultant, she has been involved in several major negotiations between US and European companies and Saudi Arabia, including setting up Alatas-Big Lift and work for the Hay Group. Besides English, she speaks French and Arabic.

Jan Amory was born in 1946 in New York. She graduated from Hewitt School and Briarcliff College. She is married to Minot Amory and has one son, aged six, from a previous marriage. She is expecting a second child at the age of forty. She owns a summer home in Newport, Rhode Island.

Adèle Anderson was born in 1952. She graduated from Birmingham University in 1972 with a BA Hons. in drama. In 1973, she underwent a sex change from male to female. She worked as a civil servant and a secretary from 1974 to 1983. Between 1982 and 1983, she sang jazz in various night-clubs before joining the group Fascinating Aïda in 1984. She is co-author of the book *Fascinating Who?* published in 1986. She is currently recording with Warren Wills (ex-Bouncing Czeck), and in 1985 she made a fleeting appearance in Trevor Nunn's début film, *Lady Jane*.

Dr Swee Chai Ang was born in Malaysia in 1948. She has been made a permanent resident of the United Kingdom under the 1951 Convention of United Nations. She is a Bachelor of Medicine and Surgery, a Master of Science in Occupational Medicine (University of Singapore) and a Fellow of the Royal College of Surgeons of England. She has worked as an orthopaedic registrar in various hospitals in the United Kingdom since 1977. In 1982, she was volunteer orthopaedic surgeon on the British Christian Aid War Relief Team to the Lebanon and co-founded a British charity to raise funds for an Accident and Emergency Centre in Beirut. She won the Guinness Award for Selfless Service Towards the War Victims of Lebanon in 1982, and the Gold Medal of the Arab League Red Crescent Societies in 1983.

Lady Elizabeth Anson was born in 1941. She founded 'Party Planners' with £25 when she was eighteen years old. She has organized parties for Princess Margaret, Mick Jagger, Jocelyn Stevens and many other celebrities. She married Geoffrey Adam Shakerley in 1972, and she lives in London.

Beatrice Aristimuno was born in 1956 in Venezuela. She studied in France and

Switzerland and, after a year at fashion design school in Paris, started work in public relations for Norwegian designer Per Spook and later for Jean-Louis Scherrer. Between 1982 and 1984, she was a freelance fashion editor for *Harper's Bazaar*, *Vogue*, and *Femme* in Milan. She also trained as a press assistant for Gianni Versace, and in 1985 went back into public relations work for Poiray Jerella. In 1987, she became responsible for the Italian fashion company Via Appia.

Pamela Armstrong was born in North Borneo in 1951. After obtaining a diploma in communication studies at Central London Polytechnic, she joined Capital Radio as a researcher and presenter. She has worked as a presenter and reporter for *London Today* (Yorkshire Television) and *Well Being* (a Channel Four health programme). In 1983, she joined ITN as a presenter of *News at Ten*.

Debbie Arnold was born in Sunderland, the daughter of Eddie Arnold, the late impressionist, and Mary Arnold, a theatrical agent. She started her acting career in television and has appeared in over two hundred shows. Among her successes are her role opposite Omar Sharif in *The Sleeping Prince*, and her parts in *The Body in the Library*, in the *Miss Marple* TV series, *Minder on the Orient Express*, *C.A.T.S. Eyes* and BBC TV's *Don't Wait Up*. She is a top voice-over artiste, as well as an excellent mimic, and her voice is often heard on both TV and radio.

Leslie Ash was born in Mitcham, Surrey, and educated at Virgo Fidelis Convent, South London, and at the Italia Conti Stage School. Her appearances in theatre, television and film have been numerous and include, in the theatre, *The Bottom Drawer*; in television, *The Gentle Touch* (LWT), *La Ronde*, *Blankety Blank*, *The Two Ronnies* (BBC), *Shelley* (Thames); and in films, *Quadrophenia*, *The Curse of the Pink Panther*, *The Nutcracker* and *Shadey*.

Diana Athill was born in 1917 and spent her childhood in Norfolk, which remains her family's home. After leaving Oxford, where she read English, she went to London and got a job with the BBC which lasted for the duration of the Second World War. In 1946, she drifted by chance into publishing, which has remained her profession ever since. She has been a director of André Deutsch since the publishing firm was founded in 1952. Her own publications are: *An Unavoidable Delay* (1960); *Instead of a Letter*, an autobiography (1963); *Don't Look at Me like That* (1968); and *After a Funeral* (1986).

Leila Badawi went to school in Malaysia and Nigeria before attending St Paul's Girls' School in London. She obtained a Bachelor of Science Honours degree in molecular biology from King's College, London, and became a freelance journalist. She has been a delegate to several conferences, including the symposium on the 'Common Forms and Principles of Islamic Art' in Istanbul in 1983 and the Aga Khan Award for Architecture in 1984. She worked for two years as assistant marketing manager in London for a major Arab book publisher, and she contributed to a number of Middle East and UK publications, including the *Guardian*. She has been a speaker on *Reflections*, the BBC World Service religious programme. Leila Badawi is married with one son.

Joan Bakewell was born in 1933 and educated at Newnham College, Cambridge, where she gained a BA in history and economics. She has presented many programmes for the BBC, including *Meeting Point* (1964), *Film 72* and *Film 73*, and *Arts UK:OK?* (1980). Her publications include *The Complete Traveller* (1977), and many articles for *Punch* and the *Radio Times*. From 1978 to 1981 she was television critic of *The Times*, and since 1981 she has been arts correspondent to BBC Television. She was married to Michael Bakewell until the marriage was dissolved in 1972, and has two children.

Elisabeth Barillé was born in Paris in 1960. She has degrees in English (Sorbonne) and Russian (L'Institut des Langues Orientales). She is a qualified freelance journalist and contributes to *Paris-Match*, *Depêche-Mode*, *Femme* and *Geo* among others. She is literary editor of *L'Eventail* and is a writer herself. Her first novel, *Corps de jeune fille*, was published in 1986.

Dame Josephine Barnes DBE (1974) **FRCP FRCS FRCOG** was born in 1912. She was educated at Oxford High School, at Lady Margaret Hall, Oxford (Hon. Fellow, 1980), where she obtained a First Class Honours degree in physiology, and at University College Medical School. She is the consulting obstetrician and gynaecologist at Charing Cross Hospital and Elizabeth Garrett Anderson Hospital. Since 1974, she has been president of the Women's National Cancer Control Campaign. Her publications include *Gynaecological Histology* (1948), *The Care of the Expectant Mother* (1954) and *Essentials of Family Planning* (1976). She lives in London and has three children.

Josephine Barstow CBE (1985) was born in 1940. She was educated at Birmingham University (BA), and then studied at the London Opera Centre. She has given pleasure to opera lovers in Europe, Canada and the United States with her performances in *Die Fledermaus*, *La Traviata*, *Aïda*, *Tosca*, *Peter Grimes* and many others. In 1985, she was awarded the Fidelio Medal by the Association of International Opera Directors. She is married to Ande Anderson, and together they run a farm, raise cattle and breed Arabian horses.

Jennifer Bartlett was born in Long Beach, California, in 1941. She received a Bachelor of Arts degree in 1963 from Mills College, Oakland, a Bachelor of Fine Arts from the Yale School of Art and Architecture in 1964 and a Master of Fine Arts from Yale in 1965. She has won many awards for her art, including the Harris Prize from the Art Institute of Chicago (1976 and 1986) and the American Insitute of Architects Award (1986). She has had over fifty one-person exhibitions over the past twenty-five years (including one at the Tate Gallery, London) and has taken part in countless group exhibitions. Her many commissions include work for the courthouse of the Georgia capital, the Institute of Scientific Research in Philadelphia, Philip Johnson's AT & T building and the Volvo Corporation Headquarters in Göteborg, Sweden. She was an instructor at the New York School of Visual Arts between 1972 and 1977.

Nathalie Baye was brought up in Paris and Menton. She trained as a dancer but, after being offered the part of Joelle in Truffaut's *La Nuit américaine*, she made her career in cinema. She has starred in twenty-nine films and has had many television and stage roles. She has twice won the César for the best supporting actress (in *Sauve qui peut* and *Une Etrange Affaire*), and in 1982 she won the César for the best actress in *La Balance*.

Gilberte A. Y. Beaux, born Gilberte Lovisi in 1929, acquired a diploma of higher education from the Institut Technique de Banque in 1954. She started her banking career as a secretary for Seligman & Cie in Paris in 1946, and rose through the echelons of banking to become, in 1962, director of Compagnie Financière de Paris (COFPA); after which she joined L'Union Financière de Paris for five years as director and then moved to Génèrale Occidentale, where she is now director-general of the group. At the same time, she was involved in banking in Switzerland, Luxemburg and in the Caribbean; and she was also administrator of General Occidental Inc. USA. She is a member of numerous committees in the financial world. She is married with one child.

Rotraut Lisa Ursula Beiny was born in

1932 in Germany. She arrived in England in 1939 via Czechoslovakia and Poland. She won a scholarship to study dentistry at the London Hospital and obtained a First Class Honours degree BDS. She has worked as a dentist in London and Libya. In 1953, she married David Beiny and accompanied him during his National Service in Egypt and Libya. She became director of the Antique Porcelain Co., London, in 1959, and president of the same company in New York. In the past few years, she has spent her time running the Antique Porcelain Company in London, New York and, for a short while, in Zürich. She has two children.

Jeanne-Louise Bieler was born in 1941 in Switzerland. She obtained a law degree from the University of Geneva and, after a career in management, was appointed director of the Geneva Tourist Office in 1986. She is the first woman to be appointed director. She was vice-president of the American Women's Club of Geneva in 1975, and, from 1981 to 1984, was president of the Geneva Association of University Women.

Christine Bogdanowicz-Bindert is a senior vice-president in the corporate finance division of Shearson Lehman Brothers Inc., New York. She holds a Master's degree in economics from the Catholic University of Louvain, and a Master's degree in advanced government studies from the College of Europe in Bruges, Belgium. Prior to joining Lehman Brothers, she worked as an economist at the International Monetary Fund (IMF) in Washington; and from 1980 to 1985 she was senior vice-president for International Government Advisory Services, responsible for government accounts in Latin America and Africa. She also teaches an international banking course at Fordham and Columbia Universities in New York. She has had numerous articles published in professional publications as well as newspapers and magazines, and has been on many radio and television programmes. She speaks French, German, Polish and Spanish in addition to English.

Rebecca Blake was born in Antwerp, Belgium. She studied to be a concert pianist at New York's High School of Music and Art and received her Bachelor's degree from New York University. After a career in painting, she became a distinguished photographer whose work has been published by *Vogue*, *Esquire* and *Harper's Bazaar* among others. Her advertising clients include Revlon, Yves St Laurent, Nikon, Warner Brothers, Twentieth Century-Fox and Columbia Pictures. Her work is also used on many album covers and posters (she conceived and directed Prince's video *Kiss*). Her latest book, *Forbidden Dreams*, was published in 1984. The Rebecca Blake Studio in New York opened in 1972.

Emily Bolton was born in South America, on the island of Aruba. At twelve, she won a scholarship to study at the Conservatoire in The Hague. She decided she wanted to act, however, and her screen credits to date include *Passage to England*, *Tales of 1001 Nights*, *The Enigma Files*, *Anna Karenina*, *Moonraker* and *Empire State*. For three years, she played the role of Christina Campbell in BBC Television's top-rated *Tenko* series.

Betty E. Box OBE (1958) began her film career in 1942. From 1945 she worked as assistant producer in Sydney Box's feature film organization; in 1947, she moved to Gainsborough Pictures as producer, and in 1950 she was offered a long-term contract by the J. Arthur Rank Organization. She had many box-office successes, including *Doctor in the House*, *Deadlier than the Male* and *Tale of Two Cities*. She has been a director of Ulster TV since its formation. She is married to film producer Peter Rogers of *Carry On* fame.

Francesca Braschi is one of the latest of the young socialites to become a designer on the American fashion scene with her own label. She is the only daughter of Count and Countess Pier Arrigo Braschi of Rome, San Marino and New York. Her family is of twelfth-century Italian nobility and her distinguished lineage includes Pope Pius VI.

Liz Brewer started her own company in the mid 1960s. She specializes in personal promotions and marketing. Her clients have recently included the Western Australian Government for the Defence of the Americas Cup; Richard Branson with the marketing of his private island; and the Abbeyfield Society, for whom she successfully secured a multi-million-dollar sponsorship deal with Alan Bond and his Bond Corporation. She is a society hostess known for her spectacular parties. She is married to polo player John Rendall and has one daughter.

Heather Brigstocke was born in 1929 and educated at Abbey School, Reading, and at Girton College, Cambridge (MA). From 1951 to 1953, she taught classics at Francis Holland School, London, and she became headmistress of this school in 1965. Since 1974, she has been high mistress of St Paul's Girls' School. She is also a governor of the Royal Ballet School, of Wellington College and of Forest School among other institutions. She has four children.

Dianne Brill is one of the hottest young designers on the New York fashion scene. She has created as much of a stir with her looks and style as with her acclaimed menswear collections. At the age of twenty-six, with only one year in the business, she has been nominated the Most Promising Designer by the judges of the Cutty Sark Award.

Suzanne Brøgger was born in Copenhagen in 1944 and brought up in South-East Asia. She studied Russian at the University of Copenhagen. She is the author of several books, including *Deliver Us from Love*, *Misleading Loves*, *Crème Fraiche*, *Brøg* and *The Dear Whiz*. She has won the Laureate, among several prizes, and is the vice-chairman of the Danish Tibetan Cultural Society. She has one daughter.

Janet Brown was born in Glasgow. She is a comedienne, famous for her impersonations, particularly that of Margaret Thatcher, whom she has met twice. She made her name in the comedy series *Who Do You Do?*, where she was the only comedienne in the whole series. She has been a guest on many shows, including the *Mike Yarwood Show*, the *Tommy Cooper Show*, the *Dick Emery Show*, *Parkinson*, *All Star Secrets*, *Breakfast Time* and *TV AM*. After the success of a special show for Thames Television, she started on a new series, *Janet and Company*. She recently appeared on the *Johnny Carson Show* in the United States, and in 1985 she went on a tour of Australia. Janet Brown's autobiography was published in 1986 and came out in paperback in 1987.

Tina Brown is editor-in-chief of *Vanity Fair* magazine. She was editor of the *Tatler* from 1979 to 1983. After receiving an MA in English from Oxford University, she was named Most Promising Female Journalist of the Year and awarded the Catherine Pakenham Prize for her contributions to the *New Statesman*. She joined *Punch* in 1978, and was Young Journalist of the Year for her column in *Punch* and her work in the *Sunday Telegraph* magazine. She has published two books, *Loose Talk* (1979) and *Life as a Party* (1983), and two of her plays have been produced (*Under the Bamboo Tree* won the *Sunday Times* Drama Award). She is married to Harold Evans and their son was born in 1986.

Victoria Brynner has been, since early childhood, an intrepid traveller. She is a model by profession and since 1985 has worked for Boucheron and recently finished an advertising campaign for Canon in Japan. She also works for *Le Figaro* magazine and for the Box Office Agency. Very often she is herself behind the camera, and she also takes acting lessons.

BIOGRAPHIES

Joan Juliet Buck was born in Los Angeles. Her family moved to Paris in 1952, and to London in 1957. After beginning a degree in Paris, she transferred to Sarah Lawrence College in New York in 1967 to study anthropology. She dropped out of college to write and be a junior editor on *Glamour* magazine. She returned to Europe and was briefly, in 1972, features editor of English *Vogue* before becoming London correspondent of *Women's Wear Daily* at the age of twenty-four. She decided to abandon journalism, moved to LA, and began writing scripts and her first novel. In 1976, she married the writer John Heilpern and, having moved between Europe and the United States several more times, writing for the *Observer* and American *Vogue*, she published her first novel, *The Only Place To Be*, in 1982 and her second, *Daughter of the Swan*, in 1987. She is divorced, has no children and lives in New York and Paris.

Averil Burgess was born in 1938 in Liverpool, of pure Welsh stock. She read history at London University, then taught in a variety of schools before moving to the Girls' Public School Trust in 1969. She was head of history, then second mistress at Wimbledon High School and was appointed headmistress of South Hampstead High School in 1975. She was married for fourteen years, but is now divorced and has no children.

Liz Calder was born in Middlesex in 1938. She took a degree at Canterbury University, New Zealand, and married Richard Calder on graduating. They spent six years travelling in North and South America with their two children. She joined Victor Gollancz in the early 1970s, and worked there for nine years before moving to Jonathan Cape. In 1986, she left to become one of the four founding directors of Bloomsbury Publishing. She has been a member of the Arts Council Literature Panel, is a founding director of the Groucho Club and a founding member of BAND (Book Action for Nuclear Disarmament).

Carmen Callil was born in 1938 and educated at Melbourne University (BA). She began her career in publishing in 1965 as an editorial assistant at Hutchinson Publishing Co. She was publicity manager of Panther Books and Granada Publishing, and worked for André Deutsch before founding Carmen Callil Ltd, a book publicity company, in 1972. She is the founder of Virago Press and is currently chairman of Virago and managing director of Chatto & Windus and the Hogarth Press. She is also a director of Channel Four.

Angela Carter was born in 1940. She went to Bristol University. Her novels include *The Magic Toyshop* (1967), which won the John Llewellyn Rhys Prize; *Several Perceptions* (1968), which won the Somerset Maugham Award; and *Nights at the Circus* (1984), for which she was awarded, jointly, the James Tait Black Memorial Prize. She is also the author of *The Sadeian Woman* (1979). She was fellow in creative writing at Sheffield University from 1976 to 1978. She also contributes to the *Guardian* and *New Society* among many publications. She has one son.

Anna Carteret started her acting career in repertory theatres before joining the National Theatre Company, where she has played many leading roles. She has numerous television credits and has spent three years at the BBC playing Inspector Kate Longton in *Juliet Bravo*. She recently appeared in *The Beaux' Stratagem* at the Lyric Theatre, Hammersmith. In 1981, she set up the group Raving Beauties Ltd with Sue Jones-Davies and Fanny Viner. Their first show, *In the Pink*, won the Lysistrata Prize for the Best Feminist Show.

Barbara Cartland published her first novel at the age of twenty-one, and it ran into five editions. She is now the bestselling author in the world (*Guinness Book of Records*). She is famous for her romantic novels and she has also written biographies of Charles II, Elizabeth, Empress of Austria and Metternich, among others. She has married twice and has three children. She lives in Hertfordshire and is actively involved in many organizations, including the St John Ambulance Brigade. She advocates virginity for girls and honey for everyone.

Luciana Castellina was born in 1929. She obtained her law degree at the University of Rome and entered the Italian Communist party (PCI) in 1947. She was secretary of the Communist Students' Organization and later editor of the weekly paper of the Italian Communist Youth Federation (*Nuova Generazione*). During the 1960s, she worked as a journalist on the daily paper *Paese Sera* and the weekly *Rinascita*. She was also co-chairwoman of the Italian Women's Union (UDI). In 1969, she left the PCI and set up the magazine *Il Manifesto*, which was also a political group close to the '68 students' and young workers' movement. In 1971, the magazine became a daily and the political group later became a party (the PDUP) and took part in the elections. Luciana Castellina became a member of the Italian Parliament in 1976, 1979 and 1983, and she has been a member of the European Parliament since 1979. The PDUP merged with the PCI at the end of 1984.

Charlotte Chandler has always wanted to write and her first efforts were published in children's poetry magazines when she was a child. She has always been a freelance and her first article, an interview with Juan Perón, was bought by *Playboy* magazine. This was followed by an interview with Groucho Marx, which, in turn, led to her first book, *Hello, I Must be Going* about Groucho Marx. It became a bestseller in the United States and *The Ultimate Seduction* followed, published in the United States and the United Kingdom. She is the author of the play *Confessions of a Nightingale*, based on her conversations with Tennessee Williams.

She founded the American Friends of the Cinémathèque Française, an organization devoted to film preservation, and is on the board of the Film Society of Lincoln Center in New York where she lives.

Alexandra Chapman was born in Nazi-occupied Holland. She has lived in the United States and Germany and, since 1966, she has lived in Paris with her two cats. She obtained a Bachelor of Arts degree in French literature and, after twenty years in international publishing (Doubleday, Time-Life, the *Reader's Digest*) she opened her own literary agency in 1984. She has co-authored a travel guide with George Oakes called *Turn Right at the Fountain*.

Tina Chow was born in Cleveland, Ohio. She has modelled in Tokyo, Paris and London, and is launching her own designer jewellery project in 1987. She is married to Michael Chow (artist, actor and restaurateur) and to three restaurants. She has two children.

Felicity Waley-Cohen was born in 1948. She was educated in England, Switzerland and Vienna. She set up the Felicity Samuel Gallery in 1972, and ran it until 1981. She helped to initiate the Patrons of New Art at the Tate and has been chairman since 1982. She retired in April of this year. She has been a trustee of the Tate Foundation since it was set up in 1986. She is married and has three sons and a daughter.

Shirley Conran was born in 1932. She was educated at St Paul's Girls' School, London, and the Southern College of Art, Portsmouth. She married Terence Conran in 1955. She was fabric designer and director of Conran Fabrics between 1956 and 1962. She was women's editor of the *Observer* colour magazine (1964) and of the *Daily Mail* (1969). Between 1972 and 1974, she was 'Life and Style' editor for *Over 21* magazine. She wrote *Superwoman* in 1975, followed by *Superwoman Year Book* (1976), *Superwoman in Action* (1977), *Action Woman* (1979) and the bestselling *Lace*

(1982). She is divorced and has two sons.

Genevieve Cooper, former deputy editor of *You* magazine and former editor of the *Sunday Times* colour supplement, is now deputy editor of the London *Standard*.

Michelle Coquillat, after obtaining a post-graduate degree in the arts, taught in the United States for eight years before moving to Paris. She works alongside Yvette Roudy, the government representative for women's rights. She published a study of Simone de Beauvoir in 1981 and *La Poétique du mâle* in 1982. In 1983, her study of women, power and influence, *Qui sont elles?*, was published.

Fleur Cowles is an artist and writer. She has had over forty exhibitions in the last eighteen years. She has written nine books, illustrated several others and contributed to *I Can Tell It Now* (1964) and *Treasures of the British Museum* (1971). She was the originator and editor of *Flair* magazine, USA, and associate editor of *Look* magazine, USA. She is a Chevalier of the Légion d'Honneur, France, and a Chevalier of the Southern Cross, Brazil (in 1973 she was promoted to the rank of Commander). She has been awarded the Order of Bienfaisance, Greece; the Queen's Coronation Medal, UK; and the Ribbon of La Dama of the Order of Isabel la Católica, Spain. She is a member and trustee of several boards and committees, including the International World Wildlife Fund, Geneva, and the Jersey Wildlife Preservation Trust.

Susan Crosland is widely read for her witty and perceptive character studies of such public figures as Michael Heseltine, King Juan Carlos and Martha Gellhorn. She was married to Tony Crosland, the cabinet minister, and in 1982, five and a half years after being tragically widowed, she wrote his remarkable and bestselling biography. The two published selections of her journalism are *Behind the Image* (1974) and *Looking Out, Looking In* (1987).

Mary Crowther was born and educated in Adelaide, Australia. She studied medicine at the University of Adelaide Medical School, before moving to London to take a surgical course at the Royal College of Surgeons. She won a research appointment at St Bartholomew's Hospital, London, to work in the Williamson Laboratory for Cancer Research. She got her MD Research Degree in 1980 and was senior house officer in gynaecology at Barts for a year, followed by a year as senior house officer in obstetrics at Queen Charlotte's Maternity Hospital. Now a consultant gynaecologist and obstetrician, she was formerly lecturer/honorary senior registrar in the Department of Obstetrics and Gynaecology at Barts. She is writing a book on gynaecological cancers, and has contributed several research papers to scientific journals, textbooks on cancer and teaching aids for medical students. She married Dr Frank Weiss, an economist, in 1987.

Jennifer D'Abo started her business career in 1976 with the purchase of a local grocery store which she turned into a thriving concern and sold in 1977. She went on to revive the fortunes of Burlington's, and in 1980 she acquired Jean Sorelle, a toiletry manufacturing business in Peterborough. Having made the company into a successful business, she sold it in 1983. In 1981, she formed a consortium with institutional backing which purchased Ryman Group from the Burton Group PLC. She is now chairman of Ryman. In 1985 she made a bid for the Selincourt Group. Jennifer D'Abo is also a director of the London Docklands Development Corporation and Channel Four. She has two children.

Maryam D'Abo was born in London in 1960. Having lived in Paris and Geneva she then moved to England, where she went to art school and drama school before beginning a career in modelling

1103

and acting. She has acted in the theatre in France and has had roles in *White Nights*, *Out of Africa* and the latest James Bond movie, among others.

Béatrice Dalle was born in 1964 in Brest. Her first film, *'37, 2° Le Matin*, directed by Jean-Jacques Beineix, made her into a star. In 1986, she appeared in Françis Huster's *On a volé Charlie Spencer*.

Alma Daniel was born in 1935 in New York. At seventeen she became a reporter and columnist for the *Long Island Daily Press*; at twenty-three she was a Madison Avenue account supervisor for a PR firm, and at twenty-eight she 'retired' to have three children. In 1977, she established the Human Potential Counseling Service, and she now teaches healing, meditation, ethics and other methods of spiritual development. She is a Second Degree Reiki healer and is trained in Swedish massage. In 1983, she established the Flotation Tank Association. She is divorced and now lives and works with her partner, Timothy Wyllie.

Sister Camille D'Arienzo has been a Sister of Mercy since 1951. She lectures on a variety of topics, including women and the life of the Church, and has contributed articles to *America* and *Commonweal*. Occasionally a visiting professor at the University of Michigan, she is a tenured associate professor in the Television Radio Department of Brooklyn College, an associate editor of the *Tablet* and Catholic commentator for WINS Radio. She received the Lillian Block Award for religious news writing in 1984, and the Teresa Avila Award in 1986 for courageous use of the media in challenging Church and society. She made two trips to Central America between 1981 and 1985.

Mandy Rice Davies, when she was sixteen, ran away from Birmingham to London, where she took up modelling, cabaret dancing and acting. She became notorious for her part in the Profumo Affair, after which she left England in

1963. She went on a world cabaret tour, earning two gold discs along the way, and, in 1966, she married an Israeli whom she met on tour. She settled in Israel and opened a chain of successful clubs and restaurants, running a fashion show and pursuing a successful career in theatre and films. In 1980, she returned to England to launch her autobiography. She appeared in Tom Stoppard's *Dirty Linen* in the West End, the BBC series *Birds of Prey* and starred in the 1982 national tour of Agatha Christie's *The Hollow*. Her most recent appearance on screen was as Mum in *Absolute Beginners* and her novel, *Today and Tomorrow*, was published in 1986. She now lives in London with her daughter.

Régine Deforges was born in Montmorillon, France. She has been a librarian, bookbinder, editor, scriptwriter, film director and writer and opened several bookshops in Paris and the provinces. In 1968 she set up her own publishing company, L'Or du Temps, and the first book she published, *Irène*, attributed to Aragon, was seized within forty-eight hours of being in the shops. She became the champion of controversial and radical authors, but numerous law-suits and heavy fines eventually forced her to abandon her company. In 1976, she started another publishing company bearing her own name, specializing in fiction and erotica, which she again had to abandon in 1978. Alongside her publishing activities, she herself has written numerous books. In 1982, she published *La Bicyclette bleu*, the first volume in an ambitious trilogy that was completed in 1985. Sales for the trilogy have subsequently passed the five million mark in the French language. She wrote and produced her first film, *Contes pevers*, in 1980.

Dr Mary Jordan-DeLaurenti was born in Pennsylvania. She went into a convent when she was seventeen and was a nun with the Sister Servants of the Immaculate Heart of Mary in Scranton from 1955 to 1969, including the time she attended Marywood College. She received her PhD in educational administration from the University of Notre Dame, and in 1970 she left the convent, becoming the dean of the College of Continuing Education at Lewis University in Joliet, Illinois. In 1973, she went to work for General Motors in Flint, Michigan, as a training consultant. She was also an adjunct professor at the University of Michigan School of Business. She then moved to Martin Marietta-Aerospace in Orlando in 1974 as a training manager. Here she met her husband Robert; they were married six weeks after they met. After a job with Boeing Aerospace, she set up her own company in 1975: Jordan-DeLaurenti Inc., a Dallas-based management consultancy. Her husband now works for the company as secretary/treasurer. She is the first woman member of the Chief Executive Officers Club of Dallas, composed of CEOs whose companies' sales exceed one million dollars. In 1985, the company launched a new military training division.

Lady Camilla Dempster was born in 1950, daughter of the 11th Duke of Leeds. In 1977, she married Nigel Dempster. She has two daughters and lives in London. She reviews books for the *Literary Review* and other periodicals.

Sylvia Deutsch was born in Paris and lived for fourteen years in Senegal. She did one year of studies at Sciences Politiques before working as a political campaign organizer. She married at twenty-two and took over the family business in real estate and race horses when she was twenty-three. She took up art dealing because her husband was a drug-addict. She is now divorced and has one daughter. She recently started to design jewellery and her first line of jewellery was launched in 1987.

Kay Dick was born in London and spent her childhood in Switzerland. She worked in publishing and broadcasting, as a journalist and as a bookseller, before becoming a full-time writer. Her novels include *By the Lake*, *Young Man*, *An Affair of Love*, *Sunday*, *Solitaire* and *The Shelf*. Her non-fiction works are *Pierrot*, *Friends and Friendship* and *Ivy and Stevie*. Kay Dick also reviews regularly in *The Times*, *Punch*, the *Standard* and the *Spectator*. She lives in Brighton and her hobbies are friends and walking the dog.

Anne Dickson is an author, educationalist and counsellor. For ten years she has specialized in assertiveness training and human sexuality. She is author of *A Woman in Your Own Right*, a bestselling book about the techniques of assertive behaviour, and *The Mirror Within*, a book about women and sexuality.

Dame Jean Conan Doyle OBE (1948), daughter of Sir Arthur Conan Doyle, was born in 1912. Educated at Granville House, Eastbourne, she joined the RAF in 1938. She served in the United Kingdom from 1939 to 1945 and in Germany between 1947 and 1950. Between 1963 and 1966, she was an honorary ADC to the Queen and director of the Women's Royal Air Force. She was a governor of the Royal Star and Garter Home between 1968 and 1982. She divides her time between her homes in London and Kent.

Margaret Drabble CBE (1980) was born in 1939 and educated at the Mount School, York, and Newnham College, Cambridge. Her first novel, *A Summer Birdcage*, was published in 1962. Since then she has written many acclaimed books, including *The Garrick Year*, *The Millstone* (filmed as *A Touch of Love* in 1969), *The Needle's Eye*, and, most recently, *The Radiant Way*. In 1976, she edited *The Genius of Thomas Hardy*, and in 1986 the fifth edition of *The Oxford Companion to English Literature*. She has received many awards, including the E. M. Forster Award from the American Academy of Arts and Letters in 1973. She was chairman of the National Book League between 1980 and 1982. She is now married to Michael Holroyd and lives in London.

She has three children, two sons and a daughter.

Maureen Duffy was born in 1933 and educated at Trowbridge High School for Girls and King's College, London (BA). Her publications include *That's How It Was* (1962), *The Paradox Players* (1967) and *Change* (1987). She has also published collections of poetry: *Lyrics for the Dog Hour* (1968), *Evesong* (1975) and *Memorials of the Quick and the Dead* (1979). She was chairman of the Greater London Arts Literature Panel between 1979 and 1981 and co-founder of the Writers' Action Group. Since 1982, she has been chairman of the Authors' Lending and Copyright Society, and she is also president of the Writers' Guild of Great Britain.

Princess Elizabeth of Yugoslavia was just four years old when her father, Prince Paul of Yugoslavia, who was ruling the country until his young nephew, King Peter, could take over, lost the monarchy and had to go into exile with his family. Princess Elizabeth spent most of her youth in France until, at the age of twenty-three, she eloped to New York with clothing manufacturer Howard Oxenberg. They were married for seven years and have two daughters, Catherine and Christina. Her second husband was Neil Balfour, a British banker and aspiring politician, and they have a son. She now lives in New York where she promotes the famous La Prairie Clinic in Clarens, Switzerland. She is engaged to a Peruvian senator.

Sally Emerson read English at Oxford and edited the university magazine, *Isis*. In 1972, she won the *Vogue* Talent Contest for writers and worked on New York *Vogue*. She won the *Radio Times* Young Journalist of the Year award in 1974. She has written for papers, including *The Times*, the *Sunday Times* and the *Illustrated London News*; she also edited the literary magazine *Books and Bookmen*. Her first novel, *Second Sight*, was published in 1980 and her latest novel, *Firechild*, was published in 1987.

Shirley Eskapa was educated at the University of Witwatersrand, Johannesburg, where she took a degree in sociology and psychology and a postgraduate degree in international relations. Her first short story was published in 1961. Her work has appeared in various magazines, including *Cornhill*, the *Telegraph* magazine, *Fair Lady* and *Woman*. She is the author of two thrillers, *Blood Fugue* and *The Secret Keeper*. These were followed by *Woman versus Woman*, published in 1984, and she has just completed another novel, *The Seduction*. She is married with three children and divides her time between London and Monaco.

Kathryn Falk was born in Harrisburg, Illinois, and raised in Michigan. She has lived in New York for over twenty years. She is the publisher of three magazines which reach over 90,000 readers world-wide: *Rave Reviews*, a bimonthly magazine covering fiction and non-fiction; *Romantic Times*, on romantic fiction; and *Fiction Writers*, a magazine for aspiring and published writers. She is the author of four non-fiction books: *Miniature Needlepoint and Sewing Projects for Dollhouses*; *The Complete Doll House Building Book*; *Love's Leading Ladies* and *How to Write a Romance and Get It Published*. She is currently working on a new travel book called *How to Plan a Fantasy Holiday and Get There*. She is engaged to Kenneth Rubin, a plastics manufacturer and importer and author of a book about antique coin-operated machines. They live in a 150-year-old carriage house in Brooklyn Heights.

Marcia Falkender CBE (1970) was created Baroness Falkender of West Haddon in 1974. She was awarded a BA Honours degree in history by the University of London, Queen Mary College. Since 1956, she has been the personal and political secretary to Lord Wilson of Rievaulx, and since 1986 she has worked as a political columnist for the *Mail on Sunday*. In 1972, she wrote *Inside Number 10*, and in 1983, *Downing Street in Perspective*.

Esther B. Ferguson was born in 1943, and educated at the University of South Carolina, where she gained a BA in political science and art history. At the same time as she was pursuing her full-time curriculum, Mrs Ferguson managed the Broadcast Resource Center, Columbia, SC, a national non-profit broadcast TV centre that distributed educational video cassettes. She was also involved in other organizations: she was commissioner of the South Carolina Arts Commission (1977–9) and arts editor and host of *Review*, a live arts and current events programme broadcast weekly on South Carolina Educational TV (1977–9). From 1982 to 1983, she was president of the American Philharmonic Orchestra in New York. She is currently a member of the Board of Overseers at William Penn College, and in 1983 she was awarded a Doctor of Laws degree for her long-time involvement in management and fund-raising for the non-profit sector. At the age of forty she had raised ten million dollars.

Annie Flanders began her career as a fashion co-ordinator and buyer. In 1966, she founded the innovative New York boutique, Abracadabra, which provided young cottage industry designers with a showcase. In 1976, she created the 'Style' section of the *Soho Weekly News*, and in 1982 started *Details* magazine with Bill Cunningham, Stephen Saban, Lesley Vinson and Ronnie Cooke. The Council of Fashion Designers presented Annie Flanders and *Details* with the Award for Creative Achievement in 1984 for developing a fresh approach to fashion journalism.

Lorraine Stanley-Ford was born in London in 1948. Both her parents were professional ballroom dancers. She left school after O-Levels and had a series of brief and unsatisfactory jobs, including work with the Customs and Excise and selling encyclopedias to the American Forces in West Germany. After taking a diploma in hotel management, she joined the Excelsior Hotel at Heathrow as a trainee and in 1971 became a stewardess with BOAC airlines. In 1982, she changed direction again and started work as a copy runner on the sports desk of LBC Radio. In 1986, she was officially appointed motor-sport reporter for LBC. She married briefly in 1975 (for four months) and is now single.

Christina Foyle is the managing director of Foyles Bookshop and daughter of its founder, William Alfred Foyle. At the age of nineteen, she launched her now famous literary luncheons; the speakers have included Emperor Haile Selassie, George Bernard Shaw, General de Gaulle, President Beneš, Christian Dior, Sir Thomas Beecham, Harold Macmillan, Eleanor Roosevelt, Charles Chaplin, the Archbishop of Canterbury, Field Marshal Montgomery, Harold Wilson, Lord Mountbatten and Cardinal Hulme. She has her own art gallery and lives in Beeleigh Abbey in Essex. She was awarded an Honorary Doctorate by the University of Essex.

Lynne Franks runs the PR consultancy firm Lynne Franks Ltd. She was brought up in Southgate, North London, and after school went to Pitman's Secretarial College before joining *Petticoat* magazine as a secretary. She then went to Freeman's Mail Order to write a staff magazine. After meeting Katharine Hamnett, she started working as her public relations person and eventually set up her own company. She is a Buddhist and a socialist (she has worked for the Labour Party PR team) and supports the Greenham Common women. Her husband, Paul Howie, is co-managing director of Lynne Franks Ltd. She has two children.

Rebecca Fraser is twenty-nine. She was an editor at Quartet Books and the editorial director of Robin Clark until

1986. She has illustrated five books, including *The Peace-Seeker's Tale* by Claud Cockburn. Her first book, a biography of Charlotte Brontë, will be published in 1987. She has been working as a journalist on the *London Daily News*.

Gisèle Galante was born in Neuilly-sur-Seine, a suburb of Paris, in 1956. She studied law at Nanterre University for five years, obtaining a Master's degree in criminal law. In 1979, she passed the French Bar examination and started her apprenticeship, which lasted three years. Afterwards she changed career and started work as a journalist for *Paris-Match*, *Elle* and *Canal Plus*, the fourth French TV channel. She has spent the last four years travelling and interviewing over a hundred personalities. In 1984, she spent six months in Los Angeles interviewing film stars for *Elle* magazine. She is the daughter of Olivia de Havilland.

Teri Garr came from a vaudeville family. She began her career by studying ballet dancing and her first acting break was a part in the original production of *West Side Story*. After attending California State University as a speech and drama major, she played a number of roles before her breakthrough role as Gene Hackman's girlfriend in *The Conversation*, directed by Francis Coppola. Among the many other films she has appeared in are *Close Encounters of the Third Kind*, *Young Frankenstein*, *One from the Heart* and *Tootsie*.

Pamela Gems began writing for the theatre when she arrived in London in the early 1970s. She had plays produced at the Cockpit Theatre, the Almost Free Theatre, the Roundhouse and the Soho Poly Theatre, among others. Her first commercial success was *Dusa, Fish, Stas and Vi*. *Queen Christina*, *Piaf* and *Camille* all received their premières at the Royal Shakespeare Company. Her most recent plays are *Pasionaria* and *The Danton Affair*, directed by Ron Daniels for the Royal Shakespeare Company.

Susan George began her acting career at an early age, co-starring in the original stage production of *The Sound of Music* and appearing in over a dozen TV plays and series by the time she was twelve. She was seventeen when she made *The Strange Affair* with Michael York. Other films include *Twinky* with Charles Bronson and Trevor Howard; *Spring and Port Wine* with James Mason; *Dirty Mary, Crazy Larry* with Peter Fonda; and *Straw Dogs* in which she played Amy, her highly acclaimed role as Dustin Hoffman's wife. More recently she made *Jigsaw Man* with Laurence Olivier and starred in *The Country Girl* at the Apollo Theatre. Susan George and her husband, Simon MacCorkindale, recently set up Amy International Productions to produce their own films and plays. She is also a poet and a songwriter; in 1987 a book of her poems, *Songs to Bedroom Walls*, was published and her first album was released.

Sarah Giles is the daughter of Frank Giles, former editor of the *Sunday Times*. She worked on *Vogue* and the *Tatler* in London before being appointed editor-at-large on *Vanity Fair* magazine in New York.

Alexandra M. Giurgiu is the director of international operations at Lifeboat Associates Inc., a software distributor and publisher. She received her Bachelor of Science degree in operations research from Columbia University School of Engineering in 1979, and in 1983 received a Master of Science degree in industrial engineering from the same university. Between 1979 and 1984, she worked for Chemtex Inc., a company specializing in services for plants in developing nations, as an assistant manager, manager of the sales proposal department and a senior officer in the contract administration and finance department. She has also been a freelance correspondent of the French entrepreneurial magazine, *Défis*. She is fluent in the French, Italian, Spanish, Romanian and English languages.

Victoria Glendinning was born and brought up in the North of England. She was educated at St Mary's School, Wantage, and Millfield School and read modern languages at Somerville College, Oxford. Before becoming a writer, she was a teacher and a social worker. In the mid 1970s, she was an editorial assistant on *The Times Literary Supplement*, and has since then contributed book reviews and feature articles to newspapers and magazines on both sides of the Atlantic. Her books are *A Suppressed Cry* (1969); *Elizabeth Bowen: Portrait of a Writer* (1977); *Edith Sitwell: A Unicorn among Lions* (1981); *Vita: The Life of Vita Sackville-West* (1983); and *Rebecca West: A Life* (1987). She has been twice married and has four grown-up sons.

Lady Annabel Goldsmith was born in 1934 as Lady Annabel Vane Tempest Stewart, the second daughter of the 8th Marquess of Londonderry, sister of the 9th Marquess. She married Mark Oswald Birley in 1953 and had three children. In 1978, she married Sir James Goldsmith, and has three more children. She lives in Richmond, Surrey.

Isabel Goldsmith is the eldest child of Sir James Goldsmith, born of his first marriage to Isabel Patino. She was brought up in France and England, and lived in Paris until 1983 when she moved to London. She married Arnaud de Rosnay in 1973 and divorced in 1976. She is now working in the business of her maternal family and is a keen art collector.

Francine Gomez was born in 1932. She started her career as an interior designer before joining Waterman in 1969 as head of new products. She has been director of Waterman since 1972 and she is head of the Waterman operations in Great Britain, Benelux and Italy. Alongside her professional career, she has been involved with committees concerned with economic development in France and, in particular, the Languedoc Roussillon region.

She is a member of the European Business Council and has been awarded the Chevalier of the Légion d'Honneur and the Chevalier of the L'Ordre National du Mérite. She is the author of *On ne badine pas avec la politique*. She has been married twice and has two children from her first husband.

Angela Gordon began her career as a Thomson trainee on the *Edinburgh Evening News*. In 1980, she won Scotland's Young Journalist of the Year Award and was runner-up for the Catherine Pakenham Memorial Award for Women Journalists. She has worked on the 'Peterborough' column for the *Daily Telegraph*, has been diary editor for *The Times* and news editor on the *Observer*, and in 1987 she became assistant editor on the *Observer*. She has also worked on *Wogan*, CBS, Granada, *What the Papers Say* and on programmes for Channel Four, Yorkshire Television and LWT. She is a regular Radio 4 presenter as well as having interviewed on *Start the Week* and *Midweek* and presented for *Newsstand* and *Newsquiz*.

Felicity Green's first journalistic job was fashion editor for *Woman and Beauty* magazine. After two years with W. S. Crawford Advertising Agency, she became assistant editor on *Woman's Sunday Mirror*. She moved on to be assistant editor on both the *Sunday Mirror* and the *Daily Mirror*, and was named the Woman's Page Journalist of the Year. After being made executive director for the Mirror Group's women's pages, she was appointed publicity director in 1973, the first woman main board member in Fleet Street. In 1977, she became managing director of the Vidal Sassoon Corporation in Europe. In 1980, she went to the *Daily Express* as associate editor, and for the past two years she has been a senior lecturer on journalism at St Martin's School of Art. She was the first woman to be appointed to the Board of the National Film Finance Corporation and the National Film Development Council; she was contributing editor on *Working Woman* magazine and was appointed editorial consultant to the Daily Telegraph Group in 1986. She has also co-authored a bestselling book on colour with Mary Quant.

Menie Grégoire obtained a BA Honours degree in history and spent ten years studying Freudian psychoanalysis at the French Institute of Psycho-analysis. She originated two daily radio programmes in 1967 and 1973, which she ran for several years. She is now a daily radio commentator on RLT net-work and presents the daily French television programme, *Living with Our Times*. She has been a staff writer and editor on *Marie-Claire* magazine and on the women's pages for *France-Soir* magazine. She has also been assistant secretary-general for the Liaison Com-mittee of French Women's Associa-tions, a member of the board for the French Family Planning Association, a consultant for the National Committee on Women's Labour and a member of the Supreme National Committee on Sex Education. She has written several books, including the bestselling *What It Means To Be A Woman* (1964). She is married with three children.

Laura Gregory began her career in market research for the National Maga-zine Company. She joined Crinnan Jewellery in Old Bond Street as a pro-moter before working for video produc-tion companies in a variety of roles from PA to producer. In 1979, she set up Gregory Lunn Challenge Video with director Roger Lunn. In 1983, they moved back into film with Gregory Lunn Challenge Company, and now have a reputation as one of the top film production companies. Credits include the much-acclaimed *Guess* jeans com-mercials.

Katya Grenfell started her career as a picture restorer. Following this, she became Franco Zeffirelli's assistant and worked on such films as *The Champ* and the Viennese production of *Carmen*. She then married the con-ductor Oliver Gilmour and had a daughter. She went to New York to study photography and worked for various publications, including the *Telegraph*, the *Tatler* and *Harpers and Queen*. She took the still photographs for the Merchant Ivory productions *A Room with a View* and *Maurice*, and is currently working on a book called *Naked London*.

Elsa Gress was born in Denmark in 1919. She is a literary historian by train-ing, and was awarded in 1944 a gold medal for a dissertation on the emerg-ence of classicism in English literature before completing her MA. After the war, she was able to travel to England and later won a scholarship to the United States, from where she was expelled for writing critical articles in the Danish press. Within the space of three years, she made her appearance as an essayist with *Incursions* (1945), as a dramatist with *If* (1946), a play for radio, and as a novelist with *Interlude* (1947). She has since written many novels and memoirs, and has been awarded numerous prizes. Since 1975, she has been a member of the Danish Academy. She lives with her husband, the American painter Clifford Wright, on the island of Møn, where they have established Decenter, an informal set-up for Danish and foreign writers, actors, painters, musicians and dancers. She has three children.

Baroness Grimond was educated pri-vately in England and briefly at the Collège Sévigné, Paris, and the Schwarzwald Gymnasium, Vienna. She married Joseph Grimond (later Lord Grimond) in 1938, and had a daughter and three sons (one deceased). She was a magistrate for Richmond, Surrey Bench, between 1955 and 1959. In 1970, she unsuccessfully contested West Aberdeenshire as a Liberal candidate. She was made Honorary Sheriff of Orkney in 1956 and in 1974. She also became a member of the Orkney Island's Council. In 1981, she joined the Liberal Party working party on Local Government Finance, and from

1984 to 1986 she was a member of the Joint SDP-Liberal Alliance Commission on Defence and Disarmament. She is chairman of the Liberal Party Defence and Disarmament Panel. During the 1970s, she was a regular *Guardian* columnist.

Amy Gross was born in Brooklyn, New York, in 1942. She graduated from Connecticut College in 1963 with a BA Honours degree in zoology, and in 1978 became features writer and consulting editor of *Mademoiselle* magazine, New York. She joined US *Vogue* in 1983 as features editor and is currently writing a book on women's surgery. She married Alan Fraser in 1974.

Miriam Gross was born in Jerusalem in 1939. She obtained a BA Honours degree in English at St Anne's College, Oxford, in 1961. She was deputy literary editor of the *Observer* between 1964 and 1981. She was women's editor of the *Observer* for four years before becoming the editor of *Book Choice* (Channel Four) in 1986 and arts editor of the *Daily Telegraph* in the same year. She was the editor of *The World of George Orwell* and *The World of Raymond Chandler*. She is married and has two children.

Pamela Gross was born in New York in 1962. She graduated from Harvard University with a BA degree in English and philosophy. She now works in RCA Records International Department. She has lived in New York, London, the South of France and Cape Cod.

Flora Groult was born in Paris. She is the daughter of André Groult, a well-known furniture designer of the 1920s and 1930s, and Nicole Groult, the fashion designer. She studied at the Académie Jullian and at the Ecole des Arts Décoratifs in Paris. She has written fourteen books, the first three with her sister, Benoit Groult. She is currently writing a biography of the French painter, Marie Laurencin. She has been twice married, once divorced, and lives in Paris and London.

Valerie Grove was born in 1946 in South Shields, the eldest daughter of a newspaper cartoonist, and moved to London with her family when she was fourteen. She won an exhibition to Girton College, Cambridge, where she read English. From 1968 to 1987, she worked on the London *Evening Standard* as a feature writer, women's editor, columnist and literary editor. She now writes for the *Sunday Times*. She is the author of two books: *Where I was Young – Memories of London Childhoods* and *The Compleat Woman*, interviews with women who have combined motherhood with a distinguished working life for twenty-five years or more. She herself is married to journalist Trevor Grove and they have four children: three daughters and one son.

Georgina Hale was nominated for Best Comedy Performance for her portrayal of Josie in Nell Dunn's *Steaming*. Her first performance in the theatre was as Juliet in *Romeo and Juliet* and her appearances on the stage have been numerous. Her most recent appearance has been as Crystal in *The Women* at the Old Vic. Her many television appearances include Jean in *Budgie* (LWT); Violet in *Upstairs, Downstairs* (LWT); Electra in *Only Make Believe* (BBC); and Ruth Ellis in *The Lady-killers* (Granada). Her films include Ken Russell's *The Devils*, *The Boy Friend* and *Mahler*; *The French Lieutenant's Woman*; and, most recently, *Castaway*.

Jerry Hall was born in 1956. In 1973, she went to Paris to start modelling and she has been on the cover of over one hundred magazines during the last fourteen years. She has been in eight films since 1974, has launched several beauty campaigns, has made numerous television appearances and appeared in over twenty-five television commercials. She has made two videos with Bryan Ferry, and in 1976 sang on stage with him at the Bottom Line, New York. She is the author of *Tall Tales* (1984). She has lived with Mick Jagger for the past ten years and has two children.

Lucy Hughes-Hallett was born in 1951. She has been working as a journalist since 1975. She was on the staff of British *Vogue* for five years as arts editor and feature writer, winning the Catherine Pakenham Memorial Award in 1979. Since then her work has appeared in a number of publications, including the *Observer*, *The Times*, the *Guardian*, *The Times Literary Supplement* and *Time Out*. From 1983 to 1987, she was the television critic on the London *Evening Standard*, to which paper she still contributes. She is currently working on a book about the legend of Cleopatra.

Mira Hamermesh is a British filmmaker and artist who trained at the internationally recognized Polish Film School. Her documentary work focuses on aspects of oppression and injustice, subjects painfully close to her own early experiences as a Polish Jew whose parents died in the Holocaust. Her most extraordinary achievement is the film she made for Channel Four, *Maids and Madams*, about South Africa. She researched the project for three years, but was refused a work permit to make the film by the South African Embassy and so decided to travel there as a tourist and make the film using local film crews. She wrote and directed *Maids and Madams*, and Associates Film Productions provided production back-up and resources. The film has won several prizes: the Villy de Luca prize, the special prize awarded by the TV documentary jury at the Prix Italia 1986 competition; first prize in the documentary section at Festicon, the Netherlands; the International Current Affairs Award at the Royal Television Society Awards for Journalism (1986); and the special jury prize at Banff (1986).

Katharine Hamnett was born in 1947 in Gravesend, Kent. She was educated at Cheltenham Ladies' College and at St Martin's School of Art under Bernard

Neville. She went freelance, then set up a company, then went bust. She had her first child in 1976, and three years later she came back into the world of fashion, this time as a one-woman band, and built up a fashion business that has gone from strength to strength to the empire it has become today. She now has a turnover of £4 million and is still expanding.

Claire Harrison was born in 1962. When she was twelve she moved to Italy with her mother and Italian stepfather, and was then sent to school in Switzerland before going to Columbia College to read English literature. She is about to go to New York Graduate Film School.

Nicky Hart was born in 1960. After obtaining a BA Honours degree in art history and philosophy at University College, London, she joined Linda Seifert Associates (a literary agency specializing in film and television writers and directors) as an associate agent in 1984. Her clients include Alex Cox, Chris Bernard, Conny Templeman, Richard Lowenstein and Chris Menges. She has also assisted in the production of several films.

Romaine Hart is one of a third generation of cinema owners. She inherited the old Islington Rex cinema in 1970 and reopened it, completely refurbished, as the Screen on the Green. In 1977, she opened the Screen on the Hill and, in 1984, the Screen on Baker Street and the Screen on the Electric, Portobello Road. She has served for five years on the Board of the National Film Finance Corporation and is currently a member of the British Screen Advisory Council. She is also a director of Friday Productions, a company providing film development finance. She has established a reputation for bringing fine films to the public, such as *My Beautiful Laundrette*, *My Brilliant Career*, *Newsfront* and *Desert Hearts*.

Bettina von Hase was born in Bonn, West Germany, in 1957. She went to

1112

school in West Germany and England before taking an MA in modern history at Lady Margaret Hall, Oxford. She began working for Reuters in 1978 as a trainee, then as a foreign correspondent at the Vienna bureau, and then as a Reuters news agency editor in London. She was a production assistant to film producer David Puttnam in 1981, and became assistant field producer on CBS News for two years. In 1983, she was appointed producer of ARD German TV in the New York bureau, and since 1986 she has been the Burda TV correspondent in London. She speaks English, French, German and Italian. She is single.

Nikki Haskell was born in Chicago and raised in Beverly Hills. After attending UCLA and Chicago's Art Institute, she did some modelling in New York before entering the world of real estate in 1961. She married before returning to New York on a permanent basis, and was later divorced. She earned her Californian broker's licence in Los Angeles, and then headed for Wall Street. One of the first women stockbrokers on Wall Street, she joined the respected firm of Drexel Burnham Lambert in 1966 and won the Broker of the Year Award for her first year. She entered the field of entertainment in the 1970s when she co-produced the feature film *Aces High*. She moved on to become the celebrity host of cable television's programme *In*, on which she interviewed the celebrities and socialites of the New York scene. The show earned a cult following and was renamed *The Nikki Haskell Show* in 1980. She has expanded the scope of the show, which now covers international cultural events, and in 1982 *The Nikki Haskell Show* went national over the Satellite Program Network.

Olivia de Havilland was born in Tokyo in 1916. She was educated in California. Among her most important films are: *Gone with the Wind* (1939); *The Dark Mirror* (1946); *The Heiress* (1949); and *Airport '77*. In 1967, she was awarded the American Legion Humanitarian

Medal, and in 1981, the Freedoms Foundation Exemplar American Award. She has two children and lives in France.

Kitty Hawks received her BA in political science from Smith College in 1967 and went on to work in advertising as a special projects consultant and as assistant to the chairman of the New York City Board of Corrections. In 1972, she joined David Susskind Productions as a reader and film consultant before moving to First Artists Productions as a story editor. In 1974, she became a film agent for International Creative Management, and in 1979 went to the UCLA School of Architecture and Urban Planning to study the history of architecture and architectural design. From 1983 to 1985, she was the interior design consultant for Michael Graves Architect, and since 1985 has been the corporate creative director for Perry Ellis International.

Brooke Hayward is the daughter of Leland Hayward, the theatrical agent, and Margaret Sullavan, the Hollywood and Broadway actress. She grew up in California. Her autobiography *Haywire* was published in 1977. She is currently contributing editor of *Architectural Digest* and also writes for *House and Garden*.

Cynthia Heimel was born in Philadelphia, Pennsylvania. She had a variety of jobs after school, including work as an ice-cream truck driver, a gas station attendant, a sandwich maker, summer camp counsellor and art school model. She married in 1968, and her son was born in 1970. She moved to England in 1971, and back to New York in 1973, where she now lives with her son. She has written freelance articles for *Vogue*, *Harper's Bazaar*, *Vanity Fair*, *Rolling Stone*, *New York* magazine and *American Photographer*. She has been a columnist for the *Distant Drummer* (a Philadelphia alternative newspaper); a community organizer and newsletter writer for Albany, Deptford; a columnist and editor on the *Soho Weekly*

News in New York; and a staff writer for *New York* magazine. Recently she has been a columnist for the *Daily News* Sunday magazine, for the *Village Voice* and for *Playboy*. She has written two books: *Sex Tips for Girls* (1983) and *But Enough about You* (1986).

Marie Helvin, the daughter of an American father of French and Danish descent and a Japanese mother, grew up in Hawaii. Her modelling career started in Japan, where she spent three years before moving to Europe. She has worked for many of the world's leading couturiers and photographers, including Saint-Laurent, Kenzo, Valentino, Helmut Newton and David Bailey. She has written for the *Independent*, the *Sunday Telegraph* and *Time Out* among others, and her book *Catwalk – The Art of Model Style*, was published in 1985. She is currently working on another book and is co-presenting *Frocks on the Box* on ITV. In 1975, she married David Bailey; they are now separated and she lives and works in London.

Margaux Hemingway was born in Portland, Oregon. She is the granddaughter of Ernest Hemingway. She became one of the highest-paid models in the 1970s and went on to make films such as *Lipstick*. She has been working on a documentary on the life of her grandfather, and this year has completed a film in Italy.

Anouska Hempel is the designer and owner of Blakes Hotel and Restaurant in Chelsea, London. She is also a couturier.

Beth Henley was born and raised in Jackson, Mississippi. Her father was a lawyer and her mother was active in the local theatre. At Southern Methodist University, she continued writing and acting. A year of graduate work and teaching followed at the University of Illinois in Champaign before she moved to Los Angeles to be with Stephen Tobolowsky, director, writer, actor and collaborator. Her first play, *Crimes of the Heart*, was produced in 1980 and won the Best American Play of the 1980–1 season (awarded by the New York Drama Critics Circle). She was subsequently awarded the Pulitzer Prize, the first woman to be so honoured in twenty-three years. She has written several plays and screenplays since then, and a film adaptation of *Crimes of the Heart*, directed by Bruce Beresford and starring Diane Keaton, Sissy Spacek and Jessica Lange, was released this year.

Val Hennessy was winner of the Enid Blyton Busy Bee of the Month Prize in 1952 (PDSA). She was an undistinguished pupil of Gravesend Grammar School for Girls, and an undistinguished student at Goldsmiths'. College, University of London. She was sacked from the teaching profession. Spent two nights in custody following arrest in the Committee of 100 demonstration in Whitehall with Bertrand Russell. Is now one of Fleet Street's leading journalists.

Carolina Herrera is a designer, businesswoman, mother and wife. In 1971, she was named in the 'Best Dressed List', and in 1981 entered the 'Best Dressed Hall of Fame'. In 1986, she was called one of the 'Ten Most Elegant Women in the World' by *Elle* magazine. DeBeers Diamonds elected her as one of 'Twenty Women of Quality' in 1984. In 1979 the Red Cross presented her with the Red Cross Medal for her consistent efforts on their behalf.

Dr Leah Hertz was born in Israel in 1937. She was educated at the Hebrew University, Jerusalem, London City University and Darwin College, Cambridge, where she read law. She is an entrepreneur, academic and author. She is the founder and managing director of an international group of companies specializing in textiles, distribution and construction; a Senior Visiting Fellow at the London City University Business School and the author of *In Search of a Small Business*

Definition (1982) and *The Business Amazons* (1986) among others. She is the first woman national vice-president of the Conservative Small Business Bureau; a councillor for the London Borough of Barnet; a promoter of the Young Enterprise organization; a member of the National Export Education Co-ordinating Committee; a national co-ordinator of the Women into Public Life Campaign and an activist in the campaign to free dissidents in Russia. She has been a British citizen for the last twenty-six years, is married with two daughters and is a Karate Black Belt.

Elizabeth Hess is a writer living in New York City. She has written on feminism and art for numerous publications, including the *Washington Post*, the *Village Voice*, *Art in America*, *Art News*, *Mother Jones* and *Ms*. She is the author of *Re-Making Love: The Feminization of Sex*.

Min Hogg was born in 1938. She attended the Central School of Art between 1956 and 1959. From 1961 to 1962, she worked as a features editor on *Queen* magazine and became the home editor for the *Observer* newspaper in 1962. She was an agent for Cartoonists and Photographers for eight years before joining *Harpers and Queen* as fashion editor in 1974 and *Sheba* magazine as fashion editor in 1979. In 1981 she moved to the *World of Interiors* to be editor-in-chief. She has lived in London all her life, except for the war, when she lived in Wales and Surrey.

Marie-Hélène du Chastel de la Howard-erie was born in Belgium in 1958. She went to the Lycée Français in Brussels, received a BSc degree in mathematics and physics and an MSc in theoretical mathematics and logic. She took a course in financial accounting at Fordham University in 1984. Her present job is as an assistant security analyst in the telecommunications industry. She has travelled extensively through South America and Europe and speaks fluent French, English and Spanish.

Jeny Howorth had an uncomplicated birth under the sign of Gemini in 1963. She left school with a talent for music and French she found difficult to exploit. From the age of seventeen, having discovered that her bodily assets had developed into a marketable product, she began modelling and hasn't looked back. In her own words: 'Keep eating the garlic. Twenty-three years of sunshine, that's how it's been. That's how it's going to be.'

Arianna Stassinopoulos Huffington is a writer, lecturer and broadcaster. She studied economics at Cambridge University and in 1971 she became president of the Cambridge Union. Her books include: *The Female Woman*; *After Reason*, a book on politics and culture; *Maria Callas: The Woman Behind the Legend*; and *The Gods of Greece*. She is much in demand as a lecturer and a public speaker on such topics as: 'The Art of Living and the Games of Life'; 'Callas and Picasso, a Study in Genius'; 'Politics and Culture'; 'The Modern Leadership Crisis'; 'The Fourth Basic Instinct'; and 'The Quest for Self-Discovery from Plato to Today'. She lives in Washington, DC, with her husband Michael Huffington, and is currently working on a major biography of Pablo Picasso.

Caroline Huppert was born in 1950 in Paris. She set up La Compagnie du Manoir in 1976, which produced or co-produced six plays, directed by herself, between 1973 and 1978, including *On ne badine pas avec l'amour* with Isabelle Huppert, Didier and Sabine Haudepin. In 1980, she directed *Monsieur Beaucaire*, the operetta by André Messager, at the Grand Théâtre de Nancy. She has directed several plays for television, for which she also wrote or adapted the screenplays. She co-wrote, adapted and directed *Signé Charlotte* and *La Chambre d'Ami* and is at present directing *Taxi*, an FR3 programme produced by Philippe Alfonsi, and working on a *série noire* for television.

Isabelle Huppert made her début in film

in 1971 in *Faustine ou le bel été*. Her films include *César et Rosalie* (1972); *Les Valseuses* (1973); *Le Juge et l'assassin* (1975); *La Dentellière* (1976); *Violette Nozière* (1978); *Sauve qui peut la vie* (1979); *Passion* (1981); *Coup de torchon* (1981); *Cactus* (1985); and *The Bedroom Window* (1986).

Angela Huth is a novelist, playwright, critic and broadcaster. Her plays have been mostly for radio and television, though her first stage play, *The Understanding* (1982), starred Ralph Richardson and Celia Johnson. *The Trouble with Old Lovers*, her new stage play, was produced in 1987. She has recently written a book for children and a work of non-fiction, *The English Woman's Wardrobe*, which she also made into a documentary film for BBC Television. At present she is at work on a second collection of short stories. She is married to James Howard-Johnston, a don at Corpus Christi College, Oxford, where they live with their six-year-old daughter Eugenie. Her eldest daughter is the writer Candida Crewe.

Sheila Innes was born in 1931. She graduated from Lady Margaret Hall, Oxford, with a BA Honours degree in modern languages and an MA. From 1955 to 1961 she was the BBC radio producer of the World Service, and since 1984 she has been controller of BBC Educational Broadcasting. She is a member of the Council for Educational Technology and Research and the European Broadcasting Union Educational Working Party. In 1986, she was elected Fellow of the Royal Society of Arts. Her recreations include listening to classical music and jazz, sketching and photography.

Angela Janklow is the daughter of the literary agent Morton Janklow, whose clients include Nancy Reagan and Judith Krantz. She lives in New York and is a contributor to *Vanity Fair*.

Tama Janowitz, the daughter of a poet

and a psychiatrist, was born in San Francisco and raised in Manhattan. She majored in fiction at Barnard College, New York, where she won several prizes, and, on leaving, won the Guest Editor Award on *Mademoiselle* magazine. In 1978, she won a fellowship to do an MA programme at Hollins College, Virginia, where she wrote her first novel, *American Dad*, at the age of twenty-three. She has been awarded a fellowship to the Fine Arts Work Centre and, in 1981, a grant from the National Endowment for the Arts, and her stories have appeared in many magazines. *Slaves of New York*, stories about the downtown arts scene in New York published in 1981, won her instant fame, and Andy Warhol took out an option on the Stash and Eleanor stories to make a film. She was recently appointed writer-in-residence at Princeton University for a year.

Margaret Jay was educated at school in London and read politics, philosophy and economics at Somerville College, Oxford. She joined BBC Television as a research assistant after graduating and has been involved in broadcast journalism ever since. In 1966, she was a Ford Foundation 'Young Leaders' fellow in the United States and she has worked as a political assistant on Capitol Hill for several years. In 1981, she became the first woman reporter on the BBC *Panorama* programme and stayed there until 1986, when she moved to Thames Television as a reporter on *This Week*. She is a member of the District Health Authority for Paddington and North Kensington, and is trustee of the UK AIDS Foundation. She is involved with various other charities and voluntary activities. She married Peter Jay in 1961, but divorced in 1986. They have three children.

Dr Lukrezia Jochimsen was born in 1936 in Nuremberg. She read philosophy and sociology at the Universities of Hamburg and Muenster. In 1961 she obtained her doctorate *magna cum laude* in sociology. In 1962, she published a study of gipsies in West

Germany, and in 1970 a report on the primary school system in Germany. She started working for television in 1970, and in 1975 was a member of the *Panorama* team. Her most recent publication is about women and socialism. Since 1985, she has been a correspondent for ARD German Television in London. She has one son and is working and living together with film documentarist Lucas Maria Boehmer.

Sally Jones is sports presenter and reporter for BBC *Breakfast Time*, the first ever networked woman sports presenter. After obtaining a BA Honours degree in English at St Hugh's College, Oxford, she worked in the United States on an educational documentary about Texas in the 1920s. She was a BBC news trainee from 1978 to 1979, then moved to Westward TV in Plymouth as a reporter on the regional news programme. In 1981, she went to HTV Wales in Cardiff, as a reporter then a presenter on the daily news programme. Before joining *Breakfast Time*, she presented Central TV's evening news show *Central News*, and also reported for the show and for Central's political programme *Central Lobby*. She has worked as a guest newscaster for *TV-AM*, as a reporter for ITN and Channel Four, and as a presenter on Thames TV's *World of Sport*. She writes a weekly sports column for *Today* newspaper, as well as many features and sports articles for this and other newspapers and magazines. She has written six books, among them the bestselling *Legends of Cornwall* and the children's book *The First Team at Tennis*. She is an accomplished sportswoman and has won five Blues for tennis, squash, cricket, netball and modern pentathlon. She speaks French, German and conversational Welsh. She is single and has no children.

Rana Kabbani was born in Damascus in 1958 and was brought up in New York City and Djakarta. At sixteen, she went to Washington and studied literature at Georgetown University, graduating with a BA degree in 1977. During the first years of the war in Lebanon, she was teaching fellow at the American University of Beirut, later moving to Paris, where she worked as an art critic. She came to Britain in 1980 and read English at Jesus College, Cambridge, where she received her PhD degree. She has translated Mahmoud Darweesh from the Arabic, *Sand and Other Poems* (1986), and is the author of *Europe's Myths of Orient* (1986). She lives and writes in London.

Elaine Kaufman was born in New York. She is the proprietor of Elaine's Restaurant on Second Avenue and 88th Street, a famous meeting place for the literati and media stars of New York.

Dillie Keane was born in 1952. She is the oldest surviving member of the group Fascinating Aïda which she formed with Marilyn Cutts and Lizzie Richardson in 1983. She studied music at Trinity College, Dublin, but did not graduate due to illness. She went on to study drama at LAMDA from 1975 to 1978, and did some acting and piano playing before Fascinating Aïda saved her from a hasty marriage. She is co-author of the book *Fascinating Who?*

Caroline Kellett is a freelance writer, consultant and stylist. After graduating from Oxford University (Wadham College) with a BA Honours degree in history, she worked for *Vogue* from 1981 to 1986 as fashion features editor. She is at present writing her first novel.

Tessa Kennedy is one of Britain's leading designers. Among her recent projects was the new *Atlantis II* for Stavros Niarchos and a night-club for Regine. After boarding school in England, she attended the Ecole des Beaux-Arts in Paris. She eloped in 1957, subsequently married Dominic Elwes in Cuba, and has three sons by him. She is now married to Elliott Kastner, with whom she has had a son and a daughter.

Mary Kenny was born in Dublin in 1944. She has been a Fleet Street journalist for twenty years. She is the author of *Women X Two: How to Cope with a Double Life*, a book about working mothers, and *Abortion: The Whole Story* published in 1986. She was one of the founder members of the Irish Feminist Movement in the 1970s. Mary Kenny is married to journalist Richard West and has two sons.

Patsy Kensit, at seventeen years old, already has a long career as an actress behind her. Her early work was mainly in television, *Prince Regent*, *The Legend of King Arthur* and *Great Expectations*, and she starred with Jenny Seagrove as the young Diana in the BBC Television serialization of R. F. Delderfield's *Diana*. Her most recent television success was as Effie in *Silas Marner* (BBC) with Ben Kingsley. In 1986, she starred in *Absolute Beginners*. Other feature films include *The Great Gatsby*, *Hanover Street*, and *The Blue Bird* with Elizabeth Taylor. She has recently been filming with Christopher Lambert in *Priceless Beauty*. She has also had a successful career as a singer/songwriter in a group formed by her brother, Eighth Wonder. She wrote the song 'Having It All' which she sings in *Absolute Beginners*. Her first album, *Will You Remember?*, was issued in 1985.

Griselda Kerr was born in 1950. She was educated at St Mary's School, Wantage, the Sorbonne and Queen's Secretarial College. She worked as a cook and a temporary secretary before going to the British Academy and then the Royal Academy where she was secretary to the clerk for three years, then press officer and assistant secretary. In 1981, she became the secretary of the Royal Academy Trust and in 1982 director of the Royal Academy Trust Appeal. She has one child.

Princess Yasmin Aga Khan received her BA from Bennington College. She is a vice-president of the Alzheimer's Disease and Related Disorders Association (ADRDA) in Chicago. She is also the president of the Alzheimer's

Disease International and has been a leading force in establishing a worldwide network to find a cause and cure for the disease. In addition to her work with ADRDA, she serves as a National Council member of the Salk Institute, and she is on the Boston University School of Medicine Board of Visitors. She is on the Honorary Council of Musica Sacra, serves on the Board of Trustees of Bel Canto Opera and is an advisory board member of the Opera Ensemble of New York.

Soraya Khashoggi was born in Leicester, of an Irish Catholic background maternally and a New Zealand father. She was educated at the School of the Holy Child, Middlesex. She converted to Islam when she was sixteen and married Adnan M. Khashoggi in 1960. She went to live in Riyadh and Beirut, where she attended the American University and studied political science. She also gained a BA in French literature at Lausanne. During the war in Lebanon, she brought her family to England, where she now lives. She is divorced and is the mother of nine children, five boys and four girls. She is a professional photo-journalist who specializes in Third World and showbusiness. She has photographed forty-two heads of government. She dislikes Greenham Common women, Women's Lib and CND, agreeing with their beliefs but not their methods. Her biggest dislike is drugs, and she advocates the death penalty for pushers.

Lesley Kingcome owns and runs a successful and prestigious furniture manufacturing and interior design business. She owns shops in Walton Street and the Fulham Road, a cleaning division on an industrial estate in Chelsea, and workshops in the heart of Devon. She started her business as a part-time hobby with negative capital and a friendly bank manager; she herself delivered the furniture she designed and built. Today she undertakes seven-figure turn-key projects in the Middle East, and her furniture graces the homes of internationally famous figures in politics, entertainment and sport as well as embassies and consulates, European royal houses and some of London's best hotels.

Rhoda Koenig is the literary editor of *New York* magazine. She is also a contributor to *Vogue*, the *New Republic* and other publications.

Irma Kurtz was born in New York. She was educated at Columbia University and then took a variety of jobs in order to travel: she was a cook on a yacht, an English teacher at Berlitz in Paris and a waitress. She came to London in the late 1960s and has stayed ever since. She now lives in Soho. She has written four books and is a freelance journalist as well as an agony aunt for *Cosmopolitan* in the United Kingdom, the United States, Australia and Japan. She has a teenaged son.

Verity Lambert was born in 1935 and educated at Roedean and at the Sorbonne, Paris. She joined BBC Television as a drama producer in 1963 and was the first producer of *Doctor Who*. In 1970, she joined LWT and produced *Budgie* and *Between the Wars*, and in 1974 she went to Thames Television where she was director of drama (1981–2) and director from 1982 to 1985. Among her numerous credits are: *Rumpole of the Bailey*; *Edward and Mrs Simpson*; *The Naked Civil Servant*; and *The Flame Trees of Thika*. As director of production for Thorn EMI Screen Entertainment, from 1982 to 1985 she was responsible for *Morons from Outer Space*, *Dreamchild*, *Restless Natives* and *Clockwise* among others. In 1973 she married Michael Bucksey. She is currently director of Cinema Verity Ltd, and governor of the British Film Institute.

Marghanita Laski was born in 1915 and educated at Ladybarn House School, Manchester, and at Somerville College, Oxford (MA). Novelist, critic, journalist, her credits are numerous. Among her best-known works are *The Victorian*

Chaise-Longue (1953), *Jane Austen and Her World* (1969), *George Eliot and Her World* (1973) and *Kipling's English History* (1974). From 1980 to 1984 she was chairman of the Literature Advisory Panel; in 1980 she became chairman of the Drama Advisory Panel; and she is a member of the Arts Council of Great Britain. She is married and has two children.

Frances Lear is the editor-in-chief of *Lear's*, a magazine for women over forty. She began working at seventeen and has devoted the past twenty-five years to issues of interest to women. She is divorced, has two daughters and lives in New York.

Sara Leighton was born in London in the mid 1930s. She was educated at a convent and then at drama school. She turned her talents to painting. Annigoni called his pupil 'the most beautiful woman in the world'. She has travelled and painted extensively in Africa, South America and Arabia. In 1980, she published her autobiography, *Of Savages and Kings*.

Catherine Leroy set out in 1966 at the age of twenty-one with a Leica and a one-way ticket to Saigon. In less than two years, her intrepid reporting made her not only one of the most published photographers of the war, but also put her personally in the news. She was captured by the North Vietnamese Army in 1968, managed to talk her way out and came back with a unique document of the NVA in action that put her on the cover of *Life* magazine. Her two and a half years in Vietnam won her numerous awards. Since then she has taken her camera to most areas of conflict, including Lebanon, where her coverage of the civil war won her the Robert Capa Award in 1976; she was the first woman to obtain it. She is unmarried and lives in Paris.

Doris Lessing was born in Persia in 1919. From 1929 to 1949 she lived in Southern Rhodesia. She has been married twice and has three children. Her numerous novels include: *Retreat to Innocence* (1956); *The Golden Notebook* (1962), which won the Prix Medicis in 1976 for the French translation, *Le Carnet d'or*; *The Memoirs of a Survivor* (1975, filmed in 1981); *The Marriages Between Zones Three, Four and Five* (1980); and *The Good Terrorist*, which won the W. H. Smith Literary Award in 1986.

Maureen Lipman studied at LAMDA. She was with the National Theatre at the Old Vic for two years, then joined the RSC, where she played Celia in *As You Like It*. West End appearances include Candida, Maggie in *Outside Edge*, for which she was nominated for the SWET award, Best Comedy Performance, and Martin Sherman's *Messiah* – SWET Award nomination for Best Actress. Recently she won the Olivier Award for Best Comedy Performance as Miss Skillen in *See How They Run* at the Shaftesbury Theatre. Television performances include the award-winning *Evacuees* by Jack Rosenthal, *Rogue Male*, Jane Lucas in *Agony* (BAFTA award nomination for Best Comedy Performance), *Smiley's People*, *Couples*, *The Knowledge*, Alan Bennett's *Rolling Home* (BAFTA award nomination for Best Actress), Jane in Ayckbourn's *Absurd Person Singular*, Marge in *Absent Friends* and Sheila Haddon in the recently televised series *All at Number 20*. She is Julie in BBC's autumn 1987 film *Shift Work* and Miss Minchin in LWT's serial *The Little Princess*. Her film credits to date are *Educating Rita* (BAFTA award nomination for Best Supporting Actress) and *Water* with Michael Caine. She recently published her first book, *How Was It For You*, which has been serialized for BBC Radio's *Woman's Hour*. She is married to writer Jack Rosenthal and has two children: the actress is twelve and the pool shark is nine. In her spare time she lies down a lot.

Lady Lothian is the daughter and granddaughter of doctors. She married the Marquess of Lothian in 1943 and has four daughters and two sons, all married, and fifteen grandchildren. She launched her famous 'Women of the Year' lunches in 1955, and by 1980 they had raised £103,438 for the Greater London Fund for the Blind, of which she is chairman. The 'Women of the Year' lunches have seen guests as varied as Margaret Thatcher, Shirley Williams, Princess Anne, Polly Styrene, Mary Whitehouse and Germaine Greer, and its enduring fellowship enlists the support of women from HM Queen Elizabeth to Mikki Doyle, women's editor of the *Morning Star*. She was current affairs columnist for the *Scottish Daily Express* between 1960 and 1970. She devised the *Shadow Cabinet* series for Birmingham ATV and the *Wise Women* series for Thames TV.

Cecilie Løveid, born in 1951, made her literary début in 1972 and has written poetry, prose and plays for radio and the theatre. She is among the most innovative and imaginative of Norway's young authors. In 1983, she was awarded the international radio play prize, the Prix Italie, for *Gull Eaters*, and in 1984 the prestigious Aschehoug Prize for her total *oeuvre*. *Sea Swell*, her first novel to be translated into English, has also been translated into Danish, Swedish and German. She lives with her husband and her two children in an old wooden house by the sea.

Blanche Lucas was for many years a senior partner specializing in family division work with a leading firm of solicitors in London, where she is now a consultant.

Jenny Lumet is the daughter of film director Sidney Lumet (of *Serpico* and *Twelve Angry Men* fame) and granddaughter of Lena Horne, the jazz singer. She left New York University after a year, 'because it was silly', and is now a freelance writer, a hostess at the infamous 'The Tunnel' night-club in New York, and a dedicated party girl.

Gillian Lynne was educated at Baston School in Kent and at the Arts Educational School. From 1944 to 1951 she was the leading soloist at Sadler's Wells Ballet, and then, from 1951 to 1953, she was the star dancer at the London Palladium. During her varied career, she has directed and choreographed ballets, musicals, operas and films. Her productions include *Parsifal* (1979); *Tomfoolery* (1980); *Cats* (1983); *Cabaret* (1986); and, most recently, *The Phantom of the Opera*. She has also staged television shows for Ray Charles, Perry Como, Harry Secombe and John Curry among others. She is married to the actor Peter Land and they live in London.

Anna McCurley has been Conservative MP for Renfrew West and Inverclyde since 1983. She was born in 1948. After obtaining an MA from Glasgow University, she received a diploma in secondary education from Jordanhill College of Education. She was a teacher of history between 1966 and 1972, and then returned as a college methods tutor to Jordanhill College for two years. She was a Strathclyde regional councillor between 1978 and 1982, and was appointed a member of the Scottish Select Committee in 1984. Her recreations are music, cookery and painting in oils.

Sheena McDonald was born in 1954. She was educated at George Watson's Ladies' College and at both Bristol and Edinburgh Universities. She works for Scottish Television in Glasgow, where she is principal news and arts presenter. She lives in Edinburgh. Having recently and unprecedentedly fallen in love, all stated views are now subject to possible radical revision.

Mary McFadden spent her early years on a cotton plantation near Memphis, Tennessee. She was educated at the Traphagan School of Design, Ecole Lubec, Paris, the New School for Social Research, and Columbia University. From 1962 to 1964, she served as director of public relations for Christian Dior in New York. She has also worked for

South African, US and French *Vogue*. During her extensive travels, which included Africa, she collected unusual textile designs and from these created tunics which were instantly bought by Henri Bendel. Her subsequent designs won her many awards and *Vogue* ranked her among the top twelve designers in America. Her designs have included furs, shoes, sportswear, furnishing fabrics and wallpaper. She is a member of the National Endowment for the Arts Design Program Policy Panel, a member of the advisory board of Steuben Glass and serves on the Professional Committee at Cooper-Hewitt Museum among many other commitments.

Susan McHenry was born and brought up in Louisville, Kentucky, and graduated from Radcliffe College, Harvard University. She also received an MA from Boston University. She joined the editorial staff of *Ms.* magazine in 1978. Her responsibilities include overseeing the magazine's art and media coverage as well as the regular columns on consumer economics, personal finance, employment, entrepreneurship and other work options for women. She also contributes to *Ms.* as a writer and has won the Front Page Award from the Newswomen's Club of New York for best magazine column.

Donna McKechnie won the Tony Award for Best Actress in a musical for her role of Cassie. She has been seen in seven other Broadway shows, including *Promises, Promises, Company* and *Stephen Sondheim – A Musical Tribute*, which also transferred to London's West End. She has many Off Broadway and regional credits to her name, and has guest-starred on several television shows. Recently she was in *The Little Mermaid* on Faerie Tale Theatre and HBO's *Musical Comedy III*.

Deirdre McSharry is editor-in-chief of *Country Living*. She was women's editor of the *Sun* before moving to *Cosmopolitan* and has written for a wide range of magazines and newspapers. She was voted Magazine Editor of the Year in 1981. She has a home in Kent and has a keen interest in rural conservation, architecture and arts and crafts.

Norris Church Mailer is a painter and screenwriter. She lives in Brooklyn, New York, with her husband, Norman Mailer, and sons John and Matthew.

Alice Mason was born in 1932 in Pennsylvania. She arrived in New York at the age of twenty and entered the residential real-estate brokerage business two years later. At twenty-six, she set up her own firm. She specializes in the uppermost strata of the co-operative market and is considered the première broker in New York in this field. She is also an acclaimed hostess. In 1960, her only child was born, Dominique Richard, who now manages the company Alice F. Mason Ltd and is herself a broker.

Margaret Matheson became director of production for Zenith Productions in 1984. From story editor at the BBC, she went to Granada Television as a researcher and reporter on news and documentaries, and then she became associate producer on the films *Caesar and Cleopatra* and *Hallmark of Fame*. After working as a producer for EMI, she joined the BBC as producer of the *Play for Today* series. In 1980, she moved to Independent Television as producer, and then became controller of drama at Central Independent Television. In 1983 she was made chairman of the British Film Institute Production Board.

Homayoun Mazandi was born in Tehran. In 1959, she married Yousof Mazandi, the founder, proprietor and editor of the *Iran Tribune* and *Financial Investor*. He is now living in the United States. In 1974, she moved to England, and she has become one of London's most celebrated hostesses. She writes poetry and is interested in Persian philosophy. She has two children, a son and a daughter.

Sonia Melchett was born in India where her father was a doctor in the British Army. After leaving school, she worked for the BBC and in the Control Commission in Germany. She married Julian Mond, later Lord Melchett, by whom she had a son and two daughters. He died in 1973. She worked as a magistrate and is currently on the Council of the English Stage Company and the National Theatre. She has contributed widely to magazines in Britain and the United States, and has written two books: *Tell Me, Honestly* and *Someone is Missing*. She is now married to the historian and writer, Andrew Sinclair.

Lady Menuhin was born and brought up in London, the daughter of an Irish diplomat father, and an English mother who was a highly successful pianist. As Diane Gould, she attended the Ballet Rambert School and went on to dance with Massine, Nijinska and Balanchine in Paris. In 1947, she married Yehudi Menuhin. They have two sons: Gerard, a writer, and Jeremy, a well-known pianist. Her book, *Fiddler's Moll*, was published in 1984.

Kate Millett was born in St Paul, Minnesota, in 1934. She received a BA degree in English from the University of Minnesota at Minneapolis and a BA Honours degree with First Class Honours from St Hilda's College, Oxford. Her PhD in comparative literature from Columbia Uni-versity was granted with Distinction. She has been an English instructor at the University of North Carolina, at Waseda University in Tokyo, and at Barnard College in New York City, and a kindergarten teacher in East Harlem. In 1979, she became an instructor in the Department of Sociology at Bryn Mawr College, Pennsylvania, before becoming Distinguished Visiting Professor at Sacramento State University, California, in 1973. In 1974, she went to Berkeley University as a lecturer. She is a leading writer on feminism and sexual politics whose publications include *Sexual Politics* (1970), *The Prostitution*

Papers (1971), *Flying* (1974), *Sita* (1976), *The Basement* (1979) and *Going to Iran* (1981). She produced and directed a film called *Three Lives* – biographical portraits of three women – and has had sixteen one-woman shows of her sculpture and drawings in the United States, Tokyo, Berlin, Amsterdam and Paris. She has been chairwoman of the Educational Committee of the National Organization for Women in New York City for five years, was a founding member of Columbia's Women's Liberation and is a member of Redstockings, New York Radical Women, Downtown Radical Women and Radical Lesbians.

Cristina Monet is a writer and a singer. She went to Radcliffe College, Harvard, to read history and literature after attending the Central School of Drama in London. She has done some acting and has written for the *Literary Review* and *Vanity Fair*, but for a while she pursued a career as a singer after Ze Records produced her first record, *Disco Clone*. Her most successful record was an album called *Sleep It Off*. She is married to Michael Zilkha and they have a baby daughter.

Bel Mooney was born in 1946. She was educated at University College, London. In 1968, she married Jonathon Dimbleby, and they have two children. During her career as a freelance journalist, she has written for numerous publications and has also been a columnist for the *Daily Mirror* (1979–80); the *Sunday Times* (1982–3); and the *Listener* (1984–6). Her work in television includes the interview series *Mothers by Daughters* (1983) and *Fathers by Sons* (1985). She is the author of *The Year of the Child* (1979); *Liza's Yellow Boat* (1980); *The Windsurf Boy* (1983); *I Don't Want To!* (1985); *Father Kissmass and Mother Claws* (with Gerald Scarfe, 1985); and *The Stove Haunting* (1986) among others.

Sara Morrison is an executive director of the General Electric Company (GEC), dealing with such issues as employee welfare, community developments and public affairs. Her career has included work for the National Consumer Council, the National Association of Youth Clubs and the Volunteer Centre. She was a Wiltshire county councillor for twelve years until 1971, when she was appointed vice-chairman of the Conservative Party. She was chairman of the National Council for the Employment of Disabled People from 1981 to 1984, and she has also been chairman of the National Council for Voluntary Organizations, a member of the Annan Committee of Enquiry into Broadcasting, a director of Fourth Channel TV Company and a non-executive director of the Abbey National Building Society and the Imperial Group. She is also a member of the Video Appeals Committee. Sara Morrison has two grown-up children and two grandchildren.

Kathy Myers took a BA degree at the University of Cambridge and then a PhD in advertising. She has been editor of *City Limits* media section and, as a freelance journalist, has written for the *Guardian* and the *Independent*. She has written a book called *Understains: the Sense and Seduction of Advertising*, and is co-producer of Channel Four's *Media Show*.

Lynda Myles was born in 1947 in Scotland. She graduated from Edinburgh University in 1970 with a BA Honours degree in philosophy and became a scriptwriter for Scottish Television soon after. She was a BBC trainee radio producer, director of the Edinburgh International Film Festival, the curator of film for the University of Berkeley and a film consultant for Channel Four before becoming developing producer for David Puttnam's Enigma Films. In 1986, she became an independent producer, and is now senior vice-president creative affairs for Europe for Columbia Pictures. She is co-author, with Michael Pye, of *The Movie Brats*.

Lynn Nesbit is a literary agent and

senior vice-president of International Creative Management. She graduated from Northwestern University with a BA in speech in 1960. She attended the Radcliffe Publishing Course and then joined the Sterling Lord Agency. In 1965, she moved on to form a literary department for what later became International Creative Management, which now has offices in Los Angeles, New York, London and Paris. The firm represents film directors, playwrights, screenwriters, actors, actresses and authors. Lynn Nesbit also serves on the Board of Trustees for *Partisan Review* magazine, the New York Institute for Humanity and the Literature Council for the National Endowment for the Arts.

Julia Neuberger is a rabbi of the South London Liberal Synagogue. She was educated at Newnham College, Cambridge, and at the Leo Baeck College in London; she is now an associate fellow of both colleges. She is chairman of the ULPS Rabbinic Conference and of the ULPS Service of the Heart Liturgy Committee; a member of the National Committee of the SDP; a council member of the Council for Arms Control; the honourable president of the Social Democrats for Gay Rights; a trustee and board member of the Anchor Housing Association and chairman of the Cambridge University Shelter Group, among many other roles and responsibilities. She has taught at the Leo Baeck College, at Cambridge University and at the Royal College of Nursing (where she is a member of the Committee on Ethics); she visits schools throughout the country and lectures occasionally at universities in Britain and abroad. She has published various articles and has contributed to several books. She occasionally appears on TV and broadcasts on radio.

Nanette Newman was born in Northampton. She trained at the Royal Academy of Dramatic Art and entered films immediately after. She has won acclaim for her roles in many films, including *The Wrong Box*, *The Stepford Wives* and *The Raging Moon*, for which she won a Best Actress Award from the Variety Club. She was also voted Best Actress by the readers of the *Evening News* for her performance in *International Velvet*. Television credits include parts in *Stay with Me till Morning* and *Jessie*, and she has twice had her own programme – a talk show and a children's series, *The Fun Food Factory*. She is the author of several children's books, including *That Dog*, *The Pig Who Never Was* and *Pigalev*; and a series of children's sayings and a number of cook books. *The Summer Cookbook* won the Bejam Cookery Book of the Year Award. She is married to film director and author Bryan Forbes and they have two daughters.

Emma Nicholson MP is the daughter of Sir Godfrey Nicholson, Conservative MP, and Lady Katherine Lindsay, the vice-chairman of Dr Barnardo's. She attended the Royal Academy of Music before training with International Computers as a software programmer, instructor and computer systems analyst. She has worked for John Tyzak, as a computer consultant, and McLintock, Mann & Whinney Murray, as a computer and general management consultant. Between 1973 and 1985 she was director of fund-raising for Save the Children Fund and is currently employed as a fund-raising consultant by the World Association of Girl Guides and Girl Scouts. In 1986, she was appointed by Prince Edward as his deputy chairman to the Duke of Edinburgh's Award 30th Anniversary Project. She has also been appointed fund-raising consultant to the Children's Medical Charity. In 1979, she achieved the highest Conservative vote ever recorded in Blyth, and in 1983 was appointed national vice-chairman of the Conservative Party by the Prime Minister, with special responsibility for women. She was the successful candidate for Torridge and West Devon in the 1987 General Election. She is married to businessman Michael Caine.

Mavis Nicholson was born in 1930 in

Briton Ferry, South Wales. She married her husband, Geoff Nicholson, one year after leaving Swansea University. She began her career as a copywriter in advertising. She was then a full-time mother until her three sons were at school. She returned to work as a freelance writer for magazines like *Nova* and she wrote a book called *Help Yourself*. Seventeen years ago, she landed a job at Thames Television as an interviewer on the afternoon programme *Good Afternoon*, which became *Afternoon Plus* then *A Plus* and now *Mavis on 4* on Channel Four. She writes a regular column for *Family Circle*.

Béatrice Nivois was born in Marseille in 1964. She has a diploma in journalism and mass communication and is working for a diploma in history and geography. She worked for a year for French regional television (FR3), and caused a great sensation by appearing nude in French *Playboy*.

Christine Ockrent was born in Brussels in 1944. She is a journalist and film producer. She studied at the University of Cambridge and the Institut d'Etudes Politiques de Paris; she is also an eligible fellow of the Harkness Foundation, New York. She has worked in the Information Office of the European Economic Community in Paris, for NBC News (European Production Unit) as a researcher and for CBS News as assistant producer, associate producer and producer-correspondent. In 1976, she became the executive producer of the weekly magazine *Vendredi* for FR3, then a freelance producer for ABC News. In 1981, she became the chief editor and newscaster for the morning news on Europe 1 radio network, and in 1981 she joined Antenne 2, French television, as editor-in-chief of the anchor evening news. In 1985, she became editor-in-chief and commentator for RTL.

Jane O'Grady is a freelance journalist and a supply teacher. She studied philosophy at University College, London.

Kitty O'Hagan was born in Scotland in 1947. She graduated from Aberdeen University with an MA in psychology. She moved to London and worked as a quantitative researcher, a qualitative researcher, a senior planner with Ogilvy & Mather and is now in senior management as a board director of GGK London, a new advertising agency. She has just completed a film on the nature of communication with women in the advertising medium. Kitty O'Hagan was married for fifteen years; she is now divorced and has two sons.

Fifi Oscard is the president of the Fifi Oscard Agency, one of the largest talent and literary agencies in New York. She was born of French parents in New York in 1920. She attended Barnard College and, in the early 1940s, married Harold Steinmetz, a lawyer and businessman who died in 1984. She began her career in 1949 as a talent and literary agent, purchased the Lucille Phillips Agency in 1959 and has constantly expanded the agency's services. Her clients have included Bernadette Peters, Warren Beatty, Jack Palance, Orson Welles, Alexander Scourby, Geraldine Chaplin and Debbie Reynolds. She sits on the board of the Mercantile Library, the New York Centre for Visual History and the French-American Film Workshop. She has endowed the Julliard School with an annual dramatic scholarship in memory of her mother, Helen Berthet Oscard. She has two children.

Edna O'Shaughnessy was born in 1924, in South Africa. She studied a variety of courses at the University of Witwatersrand, including philosophy. She continued her studies at Oxford. She trained in psychoanalysis for children at the Tavistock Clinic and for adults at the British Institute of Psychoanalysis. She is married with one son and two daughters.

Kathy O'Shaughnessy was born in 1958 in Hampstead, London. She went to South Hampstead School for Girls,

Camden School for Girls and Lady Margaret Hall, Oxford, where she graduated in 1981 with a First Class BA Honours degree in English. She did a year's MPh on Byron at Oxford, and then left to work as deputy literary editor on the *Literary Review*. In 1986, she went to *Vogue* as the arts editor.

Clare Park was born in London in 1956. She trained at the Ballet Rambert, but when she was twenty she changed career. She travelled extensively as a model and developed her skill as a photographer while working with some of the world's top photographers. In 1984, she won the *Vogue*/Sotheby Cecil Beaton photographic award. She has had several exhibitions and is currently working on a book with the London Festival Ballet.

Diana Parker MA MPh is a solicitor. She is a member of the Solicitors' Family Law Association (SFLA) Working Party on the Law Commission Report on Illegitimacy; of the SFLA Working Party on SFLA Code of Practice and the SFLA Main Committee. She has published numerous articles on family law in both professional journals and newspapers in Britain and abroad.

Molly Parkin was a painter for ten years. One of her works is in the bowels of the Tate Gallery. She was then a successful journalist for ten years. One of her jobs in Fleet Street was as fashion editor of the *Sunday Times*. This was followed by ten years and more as a writer of novels, such as *Bite of the Apple*, *Fast and Loose*, *Full Up*, *Love All*, *Love Bites*, *Purple Passages* and *Switchback*, and also published a collection of her journalism, *Good Golly Ms Molly*. Her latest activity has been as Cupid in Matthew Hawkins's ballet *A Different Set of Muscles*.

Judith De Paul was born in New York of Russian and Italian parents. She made her dancing début at the age of seven, but trained as a singer at the School of Performing Arts in New York and was a soprano with the Metropolitan Opera from the age of twenty-two to thirty-one. After this she started acting and won two Emmies in 1980 for her performances in television films. She has been a television producer since 1978 and in 1985 she went to London and formed her own company, Silver Chalice Productions. Among her successes are the *Gilbert and Sullivan* series, a six-hour mini series on Mountbatten and *Orpheus and the Underworld*. Silver Chalice Productions also represent US companies like MTM (responsible for *Lou Grant* and *Hill Street Blues*). She was married for seven years to an Italian painter with whom she is still friends. She lived in an apartment in the Grosvenor House Hotel in London until April 1987 when she moved to New York.

Penny Perrick was born in 1941. She is literary editor of the *Sunday Times* and a weekly columnist on *The Times*. She started her career as a *Vogue* talent contest finalist which led to jobs on *Vogue* as copywriter and fashion editor. She has been a columnist on the *Sun*, the editor of *The Times* 'Diary' and has had various posts on the *Sunday Times*. She is author of *Late Start: Careers for Wives*, *The Working Wife's Cook Book* and *Womanpower*. She has been married twice and has two grown-up children.

Lorie Scott Peters is a freelance executive producer. She has a BA in fine arts from Washington University and has worked as a freelance producer for a wide range of top American and British commercial production companies. She has also worked as a staff executive producer for Movie Box, which, under her supervision, became one of the top ten French production companies.

Davina Phillips was born in York, England, in 1941. Her father, David Arthur Taylor, was killed in action while flying with the RAF. She left school at fifteen to look after her half-brother and half-sister and began a small dressmaking business to help support the family. A photograph of her in an amateur photographic magazine led to her joining the Jean Bell modelling agency. She was given a part in the film *Jason and the Argonauts* following a modelling assignment for Christian Dior in Rome, and went on to take small parts in four films and three television plays. She married when she was twenty-three and had two children. Seven years later, she was divorced and set up a house-renovation company, Davina Taylor Developments. She recently bought the Royal College of Needlework to restore and refurnish. In addition to her own children, she adopted two more from her mother's third marriage and is supporting three children in India through the Save the Children Fund.

Lynn Phillips was born in Manhattan, where she now lives. She is a screen and television writer whose credits include a year on *Mary Hartman, Mary Hartman*. She recently co-authored the book *How to be a Mogul* and has contributed satires to the new *Realist* newsletter and the *National Lampoon* magazine. She is currently writing a screenplay about the rise and self-destruction of the Nazi socialite, Magda Goebbels. She has also worked as a journalist, film editor, window dresser, political propagandist and organizer. She has lived in various East and West Coast American cities.

Sarah Fox-Pitt was born in 1941. Her father's military career included Royal Household Service to both the Duke of Windsor and Her Majesty the Queen. She was educated in England and France and received her BA Honours degree in the history of art from the Courtauld Institute, London University, in 1972. She was a part-time secretarial assistant to Lord Fisher of Lambeth from 1962 to 1965. Between 1967 and 1968, she was an apprentice restorer of paintings at the Gabinetto di Restauro della Galleria degli Uffizi, in Florence. In 1972 she researched for the TV series *Romantic v. Classic Art*; the following year, she worked in the sales department of Petersburgh Press, and

in 1974 she became senior research assistant at the Tate Gallery Library and Archive, a post she held until 1982 when she became head of the Tate Gallery Archive of Twentieth-Century British Art. She is the author of several articles on twentieth-century art and the Tate Gallery Archive.

Baroness Plowden DBE (1972) was educated at Downe House. She married Baron Plowden in 1933, and they have two sons and two daughters. She has always been actively involved in all areas of education and is currently vice-president of the Pre-School Playgroups Association and president of the National Association of Adult Continuing Education. From 1975 to 1980, Lady Plowden was chairman of the Independent Broadcasting Authority. She is also president of the National Marriage Guidance Council.

Eve Pollard is currently editor of *You*, the *Mail on Sunday* colour magazine. Previous jobs include editor of the *Sunday* magazine; editor-in-chief of *Elle*, which she launched in the United States; features editor and presenter at *TV-AM*; assistant editor of the *Sunday People*; woman's editor of the *Sunday Mirror* and woman's editor of the *Observer* magazine. She has appeared regularly on television, and in 1987 she devised the series *Frocks on the Box*. She has been a commentator at Royal Ascot and has worked for the BBC on two royal weddings. In 1971, her book *Jackie*, a biography of Jacqueline Onassis, was published. She is married to Nicholas Lloyd, editor of the *Daily Express*, and has two children.

Antonia de Portago is a singer, songwriter and actress. She was trained for two years by Stanley Zareff in New York, and for five years by Renée Doria of the Opéra de Paris. She has had several stage roles, is the lead-singer of Antonia and the Operators and has appeared with Blondie's Debbie Harry, B52's Fred Schneider, the Contortions and James White and the Blacks. She has made several

1127

records and has been a co-hostess and performer on television and radio. At the moment she is organizing an album against cruelty to animals for SOS Animals, a non-profit organization of which she is president.

Barbara de Portago is the fashion director and curator of Woolite American Home Products in New York. She took classical studies at the Sorbonne in Paris before going to the Lester Polakov Studio of Design in New York. She also did voice training for three years at the Herbert Berghof Studios, New York. She worked as a theatrical set and costume designer, then as a co-hostess with Bud Palmer on the TV talk show *World Events*. She was a lifestyle editor on *AM New York* before becoming a lecturer on 'Growing Up in the Palace of Versailles' for the Keedick Lecture Bureau and for Ross Associates, New York. In 1985, she was an official greeter at the Musée et Fondation Claude Monet at Giverny in France; director of special projects for the New York Academy of Art; and a trustee of the Franklin Trust, creating public awareness for America's national monuments. She is a working chairman and committee member of a number of charitable organizations and a well-known society hostess. As well as English, she speaks French, Spanish, German and Italian.

Diana Potter was born in 1934. She attended various schools, including the Assumption Convent in Sidmouth, before going to Queen's College, Harley Street, London, in 1951 for a year. In 1953, she studied for a Lambeth diploma in theology at King's College, London. After various secretarial jobs and a year at Crawford's Advertising Agency, she took over the 'Spice of Life' column in *Woman's Own*. A year later she became Eliza Kendall's assistant at *Vogue*, and in 1959 joined *Harper's Bazarre* as beauty editor and fashion writer. In 1962 she became director of BBC afternoon programmes, children's programmes, design programmes and BBC News. In 1968, she joined Rediffusion/Thames Television as director of *Magpie*, then worked as a producer of the *Good Afternoon* programme and an executive producer of various adult education and religious programmes. From 1981 to 1985, she was the executive producer of Thames *Telethon* (a twenty-four-hour fund-raising programme) and she is currently executive producer in the Current Affairs and Documentaries Department, working on the next *Telethon* (1988).

Emily Prager attended the English School in Hong Kong and has lived in Taiwan and London. She studied anthropology at Barnard College in the United States. She was the co-author of *World War II Resistance Stories*, and the author of *I Hate Physio Games Handbook*. Her most recent book, *Visits from the Foot Binder*, is her first novel. She has been a contributing editor for *National Lampoon* magazine and for *Viva*, and has written a column for *Penthouse*. As an actress-comedienne, she has been in several Off Broadway plays and was in the soap *Edge of Night* for four years. She lives in New York.

Usha Prashar was born in 1948 in Nairobi, Kenya. She was educated in Nairobi and in Yorkshire at the Wakefield Girls' High School and took a BA Honours degree in political science at Leeds University and a diploma in social administration at Glasgow University. From 1972 to 1975, she was conciliation officer at the Race Relations Board; in 1977, she became director of the Runnymeade Trust; and between 1984 and 1986, she was a research fellow at the Policy Studies Institute. In 1986, she was appointed director of the National Council for Voluntary Organizations (NCVO). She is or has been a member of eighteen different bodies, including the Arts Council of Great Britain, the Greater London Arts Association, the Roundhouse Trust (director), the Child Poverty Action Group and the Anti-Racism Consortium.

BIOGRAPHIES

Judith Price is president and publisher of *Avenue* magazine in New York City. *Avenue* has won international recognition as one of America's most effectively designed magazines. She graduated from the University of Pennsylvania where she majored in economics and attended Columbia University graduate faculties in economics. She started *Avenue* nearly ten years ago after being an executive at Time Inc., Chase Manhattan Bank and Pan American World Airways. She is the author of *Executive Style: Achieving Success through Good Taste and Design* and *The Office Style Book*. She is a member of the American Economic Association, the Committee of Two Hundred, the President's Advisory Board of the Museum of Modern Art and the President's Council of the Museum of the City of New York. She currently lives in Manhattan with her husband.

Colombe Pringle was born in Paris, the daughter of Michael Pringle, an English banker, and Flora Groult, a French writer. After studying for her Baccalauréat, she worked as a Woman Friday for Daisy Galard, the producer of the television programme *Dim Dam Dom*. In 1968, she went as an apprentice to Mafia boutique. In 1971, she had her first child and married Philippe Royer, a painter, with whom she still lives. She again went to work as an assistant to Daisy Galard, who had become the editor-in-chief of *Elle* magazine, and in 1975 she had another son. She was involved in the Marché St-Honoré development directed by Andrée Putman and opened her own boutique, Toiles; Michel Klein, Adeline André and Pablo and Delia were among her first designers. She went to China to purchase stock for an exhibition by Galeries Lafayette, and on her return she began to write articles for *Elle*. She became a full-time journalist and reporter for them in 1980 and was later appointed joint editor-in-chief. In 1985, she had a daughter and began to write a book. In 1986, she became editor of French *Vogue*.

Marjorie Proops OBE (1969) was born in London. After brief training at art school, she became a fashion and commercial artist, joining the *Daily Mirror* as fashion artist shortly before the Second World War. She wrote magazine articles during the war, and in 1945 joined the *Daily Herald* as fashion correspondent and became woman's editor. In 1954, she went back to the *Daily Mirror* as a columnist and she started writing advice columns for the Mirror Group in the late 1950s and for the *Daily Mirror* in the late 1960s. In addition to writing the 'Dear Marje' page in the *Daily Mirror*, she is now a director and an assistant editor on the paper. She is also a frequent broadcaster on radio and television. In 1969, she was made an Officer of the British Empire and a rose was named Marjorie Proops. She served on the Committee for One-Parent Families, is a member of the Royal Commission on Gambling and is President of the National Campaign Against Solvent Abuse. She is also a member of the Council for Action Against Alcohol Abuse. Marjorie Proops is married to a building engineer. They live in southwest London and have one son and two grandchildren.

Andrée Putman was born in Paris. She studied piano at the Paris Conservatoire, but then changed career and began writing an interior design column for *Elle* magazine. She moved into industrial design in the 1960s and co-founded Créateurs et Industriels in the 1970s, working with designers like Issey Mihake and Castelbajac. A few years ago, she discovered Eileen Gray, and in 1978 she founded Ecart International to specialize in exact re-editions of furnishings made by Mallet-Stevens, Fortuny, Gaudi, Herbst, Lartigue, Dufet and Frank. Work includes the office of Jack Lange, French Minister of Culture, the Museum of Contemporary Art in Bordeaux, the Ministry of Finance in Paris, the Museum of Modern Art in Rouen, fifteen boutiques for Yves Saint-Laurent, Morgan's Hotel in New York, the

1129

interior of the Palladium Nightclub in New York and the Novotel Hotel in Toronto.

Mary Quant OBE (1966) **RDI** (1969) was born in 1934 and was educated at thirteen schools and then Goldsmiths' College of Art, London. She has been a director of the Mary Quant group of companies since 1955. Her innovative designs have won her fame and many awards, including the Maison Blanche Rex Award (1964), the *Sunday Times* International Award (1964), and the Annual Design Medal from the Institute of Industrial Artists and Designers in 1966. She is the author of *Quant by Quant* (1966). Mary Quant is married to Alexander Plunket Greene and they have one son.

Charlotte Rampling started her career as a model before quickly being taken up by films. Her first film, *The Knack*, directed by Richard Lester, was produced in 1964. Her films include *Georgy Girl* (1966), *The Long Duel* (1967), *Asylum* (1972), *The Night Porter* (1973), *Zardoz* (1973), *Farewell My Lovely* (1975), *Stardust Memories* (1980), *The Verdict* (1982), *Viva la vie* (1984), *Max My Love* (1986), *Angel Heart* (1986) and *Mascara* (1986). She lives in Croissy-sur-Seine with her husband and children.

Esther Rantzen was born in 1940. She was educated at Somerville College, Oxford, where she obtained an MA. She has been a television producer and presenter since 1968, and has always been concerned with social issues, producing and presenting such programmes as *That's Life*, *Drugwatch*, *Childwatch* and *The Lost Babies*. She was BBC TV Personality of 1975, is chairman of Childline, president of Meet-a-Mum Association and vice-president of a number of charitable organizations, including Contact-a-Family (families of disabled children). She is co-author of *Kill the Chocolate Biscuit* (1981) and *Baby Love* (1985);

and author of *Ben: The Story of Ben Hardwick*. She is married to Desmond Wilcox and has three children.

Barbara Chase-Riboud is a graduate of Yale University and she holds an honorary doctorate from Temple University. Among her numerous awards are a John Hay Whitney Fellowship and a National Endowment for the Arts Fellowship, as well as the Janet Heidinger Kafka Prize for the best novel written by an American woman in 1979, *Sally Hemings*, an international bestseller with more than a million and a half copies in print in eight languages. Her other works include *Valide* and *Portrait of a Nude Woman as Cleopatra*. She has travelled widely in Africa and the Near and Far East. She was the first American woman to be admitted to the People's Republic of China after the Revolution.

Mirella Ricciardi was born and brought up in Kenya, East Africa, where her Italian father and French mother moved in 1929 after a year-long foot safari across what was then the Belgian Congo. She took up photography at the age of twenty-one in Paris, where she studied with Harry Meerson. Her book *Vanishing Africa*, a pictorial tribute to the vanishing tribes of East Africa, brought her international recognition and has enabled her to take assignments across the world. Her autobiography *African Saga* was published in 1983. She has been married for thirty years, has two daughters and spends much of her time travelling away from home.

Nancy Richardson has been a journalist since 1967. She was senior editor of the US *House and Garden*, where she had a monthly column, 'All About Style', until she resigned in 1987 to write a book on antiques. She is married and has three children under twelve.

Stella Richman was born in 1922 and educated in London. She started her television career working in the script department at ATV. She went on to become the first woman executive in television and its first woman producer. At ATV she produced such popular series as *Love Story*, to which contributors included Edna O'Brien and Doris Lessing, and *The Power Game*. While controller of programmes for London Weekend Television, she was responsible for putting *Upstairs, Downstairs* and *Budgie* on the air. She has also been chairman and owner of the White Elephant Club in Mayfair since 1960.

Angela Rippon was born in 1944 in Devon. She left school at seventeen to work on the local daily newspaper and soon moved to the local Sunday paper where she worked as a general reporter for three years. In 1966, she joined BBC Plymouth as a reporter and presenter, then went to Westward Television as producer and editor/presenter of the weekly woman's programme. In 1973, she went to the BBC as news reporter for the BBC's national news. She became presenter of BBC2's *News Extra*, and in 1976 she began working as a newsreader for BBC's *Nine O'Clock News*. She won the Radio and Television Industries Award for Newsreader of the Year in 1976, 1977 and 1978 – the only newsreader ever to have achieved this distinction. In 1981, she left to become a founder member of the *TV-AM* consortium. She has worked as arts and entertainment editor for WNEV TV's Channel 7 in Boston, presented her own late-night magazine programme on BBC Radio 2, appeared on numerous television shows, chaired a BBC quiz programme (*Masterteam*), presented six documentaries for BBC1 and written, presented and directed the *Rippon Reports* for television. She has written several books, including a series for young children, and made several recordings (including *Shape Up and Dance with Angela Rippon*, which went gold). Angela Rippon lives in Devon with her husband, Christopher Dare, whom she married in 1967.

Shirley Ritchie QC (1979) was born in 1940 and educated at Rhodes University, South Africa (BA, LlB). She was called to the South African Bar in 1963, and the Bar, Inner Temple, three years later. She has been a recorder of the Crown Court since 1981. She is married to Robin Hamilton Corson Anwyl and has two children.

Hélène Rochas met the young dress designer Marcel Rochas at a very young age. They were married within a few months and he gave her as a wedding gift his first perfume, 'Femme'. Her *salon* became open to the world of the arts, literature and fashion and she was nominated one of the ten best-dressed women in the world. Her husband died when she was still young and she became director of their business concerns. Her perfume 'Madame Rochas' placed her in the same league as Coco Chanel, Jeanne Lanvin and Nina Ricci. In 1970, she left the firm of Rochas, although it was under her advice that a new range of beauty care was created. In 1984, the new president of Rochas, Claude Buchet, persuaded her to return and be part of the creative board.

Anita Roddick was born Anita Lucia Parella in 1942 to an Italian immigrant family. From Bath College of Education, where she did her teacher training, she went to Paris, where she worked in the newspaper cuttings library of the *New York Herald Tribune* and in the embassies of Malaysia and Australia. After a year of teaching back in England, she went to Geneva, where she joined the Women's Department of the International Labour Organization at the United Nations. At the age of twenty-five, she set off to travel around the world. During her travels to the Polynesian Islands, Tahiti, Australia and Africa, she became acquainted with natural ingredients for skin and hair care. A few years after returning to England, she opened her first shop in Brighton, selling twenty-five skin and hair preparations. Today, the Body Shop is a fast-growing franchised chain of 80 shops in the United Kingdom and 167 in twenty-seven other countries.

She is married and has two daughters.

Deborah Rogers is one of London's leading literary agents.

Selwa Roosevelt was born in Kingsport, Tennessee, where she lived until her marriage to Archibald Roosevelt, a grandson of President Theodore Roosevelt, in 1950. She is a graduate of Vassar College, where she took her degree in international relations with Honours. In the 1950s, she wrote a column for the *Washington Star* called 'Diplomatically Speaking', but interrupted her career to accompany her husband on diplomatic missions overseas. She has lived in Istanbul, Madrid and London. In 1961, she was a special assistant to Roger Stevens, then head of the National Cultural Center, and since 1967 she has worked as a freelance writer for the *Washington Post*. She served on the Citizens' Advisory Board of Duke University Comprehensive Cancer Center for seven years and has written many medical articles, particularly about cancer and cancer research. She has served as chief of protocol for five years and has been awarded by the Department of the Army the Outstanding Civilian Service Medal. In 1985, she was given the Betty Ford Award by the Susan Komen Foundation in Dallas for the advancement of breast cancer research. She lives in Washington with her husband, who is a director of international relations for the Chase Manhattan Bank.

Kimberly Du Ross was born in 1957. She studied psychology at Boston College and painting at the Rhode Island School of Design. She spent a year in Paris at the École des Beaux-Arts before receiving her BFA Degree from Rhode Island School. She has been living in New York since then, and her work has been exhibited in America and Italy.

Juliet Mitchell-Rossdale was born in New Zealand in 1940, but has lived in London since 1944. She was a lecturer in English literature at the Universities of Leeds and Reading. She has written numerous essays in literary criticism and in the political theory of women's oppression, and is one of Britain's foremost feminist thinkers. Her published work includes *Women: The Longest Revolution* and *Psychoanalysis and Feminism* (1974). Juliet Mitchell-Rossdale is now a psychoanalyst practising in London, where she lives with her husband and daughter.

Yvette Roudy was born in 1929 into a working-class family. Married at an early age to Pierre Roudy, she followed him to Glasgow where she acquired a fluency in English. She is the translator into French of Betty Friedan's *The Feminine Mystique*. Her militant socialism and feminism were nurtured by Marie-Thérèse Eyquem and Colette Audry in 1964 within the Democratic Feminist Movement. In 1975, *La Femme en marge* was published with a preface by François Mitterrand. Her feminist political activities led to her being nominated in 1977 as national secretary for feminist action for the Socialist Party. In 1979, she was elected to the European Parliament, where she created a commission for the rights of women. As minister in charge of women's rights under the Maurois government, she continues her fight for the rights of women.

Joan Ruddock MP was born in 1943 and educated at Pontypool Grammar School for Girls and Imperial College, University of London (BSc, ARCS). She has been active in politics and pressure groups, and a member of anti-racist concerns throughout her working life. From 1968 to 1973, she worked for Shelter and from 1973 to 1977 was a director of the Oxford Housing Aid Centre. She is currently the organizer of the Reading Citizens' Advice Bureau. One of her foremost concerns is CND, of which she was chairperson until 1985, and is now vice-chairperson. In 1984, she was given the Frank Cousins Peace Award, TGWU. She was elected Labour MP for Deptford in the 1987 General Election. She is married to Dr

Keith Ruddock and lives in London.

Eve Ruggieri was born of musical parents in Limoges. She studied literature at the Centre Universitaire Méditerranéen de Nice and won first prize at the Conservatoire de Nice for her piano playing. She began her career in radio and television by working as a producer for France Inter and La Première Chaine de Television. In 1979, she produced and presented on Antenne 2 a programme intended to introduce classical music to the general public. She has set up musical co-productions between Europe and America. She has written and produced plays and cassettes. In 1986, Alpha brought out Eve Ruggieri's *History of the World* on cassette.

Carol Rumens was born in London in 1944. Her poetry is highly acclaimed and she has published five collections: *A Strange Girl in Bright Colours*, *Unplayed Music*, *Star Whisper*, *Direct Dialling* and *Selected Poems*, which is published simultaneously with the novel, *Plato Park*. She is poetry editor of the *Literary Review* and a Fellow of the Royal Society of Literature. She has two daughters and lives in London.

Doris Saatchi was born in Memphis, Tennessee. She grew up in the 1950s in a well-to-do suburb of New York City. Following her education at Smith College and the Sorbonne, she emigrated to London and there married Charles Saatchi in 1973. Together they have formed a large collection of contemporary art. She now lives in London and New York and is a contributing editor to *House and Garden* (US) and a frequent contributor of articles on the art world, interior design and architecture to various American and British publications.

Altaf Al-Sabah is a member of the National Council of the Arts in Kuwait and is a co-founder and director of the Al-Sadu Centre, a private foundation for the preservation of traditional Bedouin weaving. She has an MA degree in anthropology from the American University of Beirut and has taught anthropology at Kuwait University. She has edited a book on Bedouin culture and is supervising the research and publication of an anthropological reader on Kuwaiti society and culture.

Melissa Sadoff, who was born in Central Europe, began writing philosophical articles at the age of twelve. At fourteen she published a series of essays in Yugoslavia on Aristotle and Seneca. Two years later, she began touring Central Europe as a concert pianist. In 1960, having emigrated to New York City and become a US citizen, she married and moved with her husband to the West Coast. Here she became a partner in a theatrical, film and television company, and worked as associate producer on several film and television projects. Her handbook *Woman as Chameleon: How to be an Ideal Woman* was published in 1987. She is now married to Lord Stevens and divides her time between the United States, England and France.

Ghida Salaam was born in Lebanon in 1963 and lived there until the age of eighteen. As a result of the deteriorating situation in her country's civil war, she decided to pursue her higher education in the United States. She obtained BSc and MSc degrees in international politics and economics from Georgetown University's School of Foreign Service. Having been brought up in the Middle East in a family that has been involved in politics for decades, she has travelled extensively throughout the region and met key political leaders. She speaks fluent Arabic, French, English and Spanish and is currently holding a position as a newsdesk assistant in the London Bureau of the American Broadcasting Corporation (ABC News).

Khairat Al-Saleh was born in Jerusalem but spent most of her childhood in Damascus. She went to Egypt for a BA degree in English literature. In 1970, she came to Great Britain and acquired a diploma in drama and poetry and completed an MPh in dramatic literature. She has written extensively in both Arabic and English and some of her poetry has been broadcast by the BBC Arabic World Service. She is the co-author-editor of an Arabic course for English-speaking students at the Linguaphone Institute. This has been translated into several languages. In 1985, her first book for younger readers, *Fabled Cities, Princess and Jinn*, was published. As well as being a writer, she paints and has taken part in several exhibitions.

Bushra Salha was born in Lebanon in 1946. She was educated at the American Girls' School in Sidon and at Beirut College for Women. She graduated in 1967 with a BA degree in political science and history. She worked as a consultant interior designer at the hotel Le Vendôme in Beirut in 1975–6. She moved to London in 1976. She attended the Styles of Art Course at Sotheby's in 1979, the Christie's Fine Arts course in 1981 and the Modern Art Studies course in 1982. She studied with Roger Bevan at the New Academy for Art Studies in 1983. She is currently working in London as an art adviser and freelance journalist. She is married and is the mother of one daughter and three sons.

Naomi E. Sargant is senior commissioning editor in charge of educational programming at Channel Four. Prior to joining Channel Four, as Naomi E. McIntosh, she was a professor of applied social research at the Open University. Graduating in sociology from Bedford College, London, she spent twelve years as a market and social researcher at the Gallup Poll before joining Enfield College of Technology as a senior lecturer in market research. Her most recent appointments in the public sector were as chairman of the National Gas Consumers' Council, and as a member of the Commission on Energy and the Environment and the National Con-

sumer Council. She has written widely both on the subject of evaluation and on adult and higher education generally: notably *The Door Stood Open* (with Woodley), *A Degree of Difference* and *Access to Higher Education in England and Wales* (with Woodley and Griffiths). She is married with three sons.

Dame Cicely Saunders OBE (1969) **DBE FRCP FRCS** was born in 1918 and educated at Roedean School, St Anne's College, Oxford, and St Thomas's Hospital Medical School. In 1967, she founded St Christopher's Hospice. She was medical director there from 1967 to 1985 and is currently chairman. She has been awarded several honorary degrees and prizes, and her publications include *Care of the Dying* (1960) and *Living with the Dying* (1983).

Sylvia Scafardi is eighty-four years old. She founded the National Council of Civil Liberties in the 1930s. She has acted on stage with Laurence Olivier.

Alexandra Schlesinger was born in 1936 in Manhattan. She attended school in New York and Pennsylvania and graduated from Radcliffe College in 1958. She lived abroad for four years after college. She has had a variety of jobs, including flower arranging and assistant at the *New York Review of Books*, and is presently painting. She has been married twice, now to Arthur Schlesinger, and is the mother of two sons.

Anne Seagrim was born in 1914 at Les Vertues, France. She was educated in France and then came to London to acquire secretarial skills. Between 1935 and 1965, her secretarial appointments have been numerous and have included working for Imperial Chemical Industries, Lord Hardwicke, and Dr C. P. Snow at the English Electric Company. Between 1950 and 1954, she worked for HRH the Duke of Windsor in Paris and New York, during which time she took part in the preparation of the manuscript for *A King's Story*. She then went on to work for the managing director of

Northern Aluminium, being seconded only briefly to work on the Duke of Edinburgh's Study Conference on Industrial Relations, and then working for Field Marshal the Earl Alexander of Tunis on his appointment as chairman of Northern Aluminium. Between 1965 and 1984, she was the Winston Churchill Memorial Trust administrator and was appointed honorary Churchill fellow upon her retirement. She paints as a hobby and has had several individual and group exhibitions.

Jenny Seagrove was born in Kuala Lumpur, where she spent the first nine years of her life. She trained at the Bristol Old Vic Theatre School. She graduated in 1979, not only as an actress but also as recipient of the Recommended Certificate of the Society of British Stage Fight Directors. It was her performance in the title role of Diana in the BBC serialization of the R. F. Delderfield novel that first won her widespread recognition in Britain. She starred as Emma Harte in the Channel Four production of *A Woman of Substance*. On the big screen, Jenny Seagrove won acclaim for her roles in *Local Hero*, *A Shocking Accident* and *Moonlighting*. Her stage work in regional theatre ranges from Jan in Alan Ayckbourn's *Bedroom Farce* to Mrs de Winter in Daphne du Maurier's *Rebecca*. She originally planned to become a veterinary surgeon.

Susan Seidelman was brought up in Philadelphia and attended New York University's Graduate School of Film and Television. She made her directing début with *And You Act Like One, Too*, a twenty-eight-minute satire about a woman in a domestic rut which won a Student Academy Award from the Academy of Motion Pictures, Arts and Sciences. She also directed *Deficit* and *Yours Truly, Andrea G. Stern* which won the Silver Plaque at the Chicago Film Festival, a blue ribbon at the American Film Festival and the Special Merit Award for Best Fiction at the Athens International Film Festival. In 1980, she began *Smithereens*, which was

very successful when it opened in 1982. *Desperately Seeking Susan* is Susan Seidelman's first film for a major Hollywood Studio.

Emma Sergeant is an artist. She painted pub signs for Tolly Cobbold before attending a foundation year at Camberwell School of Art in 1978. She then obtained a BA degree from the Slade School of Art, and in 1981 she won the Imperial Tobacco National Portrait Gallery Competition. In 1982, she was commissioned by the National Portrait Gallery to paint Sir Laurence Olivier and Lord David Cecil. In 1983, she won the prize at the Slade for the best figurative composition. She had her first solo show at Agnew's Art Gallery in 1984 and in 1986 her exhibition *Out of Afghanistan – Paintings for UNICEF* was also shown at Agnew's Art Gallery.

Delphine Seyrig was born in Beirut in 1932, the daughter of an archaeologist. An accomplished actress in film, theatre and television, she has acted in Paris and London. Her roles in Alain Resnais's *Last Year in Marienbad* (1960) and *Muriel* (1964) won her recognition. In 1977, she won the Grand Prix National du Cinéma. She has been directed in films by Joseph Losey, François Truffaut, Luis Buñuel, Marguerite Duras and Chantal Akerman. She is head of the Centre Audiovisuel Simone de Beauvoir, which was created in 1981, and devotes much of her time to cataloguing films by and about women.

Hanan Al-Shaykh was born in Lebanon in 1945 and spent her early life in Beirut, then in Cairo, where she continued her studies and wrote her first novel, *Suicide of a Dead Man*. She then returned to Beirut and worked as a journalist on the leading Arabic newspapers and presented her own television programme. She has lived in the Arabian Gulf and at present lives in London, continuing to write novels and short stories which have brought her increasing fame in the Arab World. *The*

Story of Zahra was her first major novel to be translated into English. Because of its courageous and frank treatment of personal, sexual and political subjects, it has been banned in several Arab countries, but despite this has had a wide circulation and has put her in the forefront of young writers widening the frontiers of the Arabic novel. She is married and has two children.

Clare Short MP is Labour member for the Ladywood constituency in Birmingham, where she herself was born. The daughter of an Irish immigrant teacher, she was educated at a Roman Catholic grammar school and went into the Civil Service. She left the Home Office to run a community centre in Birmingham, and then became director of Youthaid before entering the Commons. She is involved in the Kinnock New Deal as a front-bench spokeswoman in the employment team, and concentrates her energy on fighting for the low paid, the unemployed and would-be immigrants. One of her most publicized battles was the unsuccessful Bill to get the Page Three nudes out of Britain's newspapers.

Alexandra Shulman was born in London and educated at St Paul's Girls' School and Sussex University, where she did a BA Honours degree in social anthropology. She worked for Hannibal and then Arista Records, and left to join *Over 21* magazine. In 1982, she joined *Tatler* magazine, and in 1986 became its features editor. She writes freelance profiles and a weekly television review for *The Times*.

Rosemary Anne Sisson was born in London and brought up in Sussex. The home was near a Battle of Britain airbase, and during the Second World War she worked as an aircraft plotter with the Royal Observer Corps in Horsham. She took her BA Honours degree in English at University College, London, and her MLit at Newnham College, Cambridge. After the war she lectured at the Universities of Wisconsin, London and Birmingham, and was

drama critic of the *Stratford-upon-Avon Herald* for three years. The success of her play, *The Queen and the Welshman*, led to a full-time writing career which, to date, spans nine stage plays, five films, nine novels, six television dramatizations, countless individual television plays and series, three television documentaries, several radio plays and a variety of other works from the framework for *Dawn to Dusk*, delivered by Prince Andrew at the Royal Tournament, to the Son et Lumière production of *The Heart of the Nation* at the Horse Guards Parade. She has also had six children's books published. She has travelled extensively in Europe, the Middle East, Australia and the United States, and while writing the full-length animation feature *The Black Cauldron*, she made annual trips to the Disney Studios in Hollywood. A former chairman of the Writers Guild, Rosemary Anne Sisson was presented with the Guild's Laurel Award in 1985 for her service to writers.

Lady Anne Somerset was born in 1955. She read history at King's College, London, and graduated in 1976. After a period of time working as research assistant to various historians, in 1980 she published her first book, *The Life and Times of William IV*. This was followed in 1984 by *Ladies in Waiting*, a study of women at the English Royal Court from Tudor times to the present day. She is now writing a biography of Queen Elizabeth I.

Ginette Spanier went from being a saleswoman in the gift department of Fortnum & Mason in 1930 to sales manager of Pembaron, a bag factory, in 1932, and directrice of Marjorie Castle, ready-to-wear American clothes, in 1937. She married during the war and returned to Paris after its liberation by bicycling through German lines. In Paris, she worked for the US Army as Chief of Civilian Personnel, Signal Corps, and in 1945 she received the Medal of Freedom from the US Army and was sent to the Nuremberg Trials by Signal Service. In 1947, she became directrice of Pierre Balmain Haute Couture. She worked for Balmain for twenty-nine years, and in 1975 became directrice of Nina Ricci's Ready to Wear Boutique. During the years following the war, Ginette Spanier lectured in England and the United States. She returned to England in 1981 to live and, in addition to many articles, has written three books: *It isn't All Mink*; *And Now It's Sables*; *Long Road to Freedom*.

Koo Stark was born in New York in 1956. She went to the Academy of Dramatic Art in New York before pursuing a career in acting and photography. She moved to London when she was fourteen and has featured in films for ITV, BBC and Thames Television, and has also played at the National Theatre. She has had four solo photographic exhibitions in London, and is contributing to a travelling exhibition for the Council for the Privileged in Rural England. Her work has been shown at the National Portrait Gallery and the Hamilton Gallery. She has been working as a professional photographer since 1985.

Gloria Steinem has, for more than a decade, been the most persuasive spokesperson for the feminist movement in America. At the same time, she has gained a reputation as a journalist. Her work has appeared in *New York* magazine, where she was a founding editor and the political columnist until 1971, and numerous other national publications as well as many abroad. She is considered to be one of the most influential women in the United States. She also travels as a speaker and feminist organizer. Though a Midwesterner 'by birth and by accent', she now lives in New York City.

Pamela Stephenson was born in New Zealand to two scientists. She went to university but spent most of the time waitressing in Sydney night-clubs so as to get to drama school instead. She travelled extensively after this, before

arriving in Britain, where she played a number of forgettable parts. She made her name in *Not the Nine O'Clock News,* and some of her mentionable movies include *History of the World Part One* with Mel Brooks, *Superman III* and *Finders Keepers.* In 1985 she starred in *Saturday Night Live* for a season in New York and she appeared in *The Pirates of Penzance* at Drury Lane. Her first live one-woman show was *Small but Perfectly Formed.* Since then, she has toured Britain with *Naughty Night Nurses without Panties Down Under Number Two,* and in 1987 has toured *Shocking Behaviour.*

Lady Arabella Stuart was born in 1934. She is half-Scottish, half-American. She writes under the name of Arabella Boxer. She is food editor of *Vogue,* writes on cookery and travel for *Vogue,* the *Sunday Times* magazine and many others; has written ten cookbooks and won the Glenfiddich Food Writer of the Year Award in 1975 and 1978. She also worked as a part-time silversmith from 1974 to 1980. Arabella Stuart has been married and divorced and has two grown-up children.

Imogen Stubbs was brought up on a barge in Chiswick. With a father in the Royal Navy, she travelled a great deal as a child and was formally educated at St Paul's Girls' School and Oxford University, on a scholarship to Exeter College. After obtaining a first-class Honours degree in English, she was a waitress in a London cocktail bar before going to RADA. In 1984, she left RADA and went to the Wolsey Theatre, Ipswich, where she played Sally Bowles in *Cabaret* and Polly in *The Boy Friend.* She has recently spent a season with the Royal Shakespeare Company in Stratford, where she has won acclaim in *The Two Noble Kinsmen, Richard II* and *The Rover* with Jeremy Irons. She has also appeared in Conny Templeman's film *Nanou.*

Andrea von Stumm was born in Germany, brought up in Paris and educated in Switzerland. She gained a BA in modern history from the London School of Economics. She worked for Naim Attallah for one year. She has also worked on the development of *Departures* magazine and on *Sat 1* – Munich Television.

Christine Sutherland grew up in Poland and France; she was married and lived in the United States where, as Christine Hotchkiss, she was an editor and free-lance writer and published two biographies, *Home to Poland* and *A Boy Called Tony*. She was the London editor of *American Horizon* and *American Heritage* for nine years. In 1984, she published the acclaimed biography *The Princess of Siberia*, and her biography of Marie Walewska (1979) has been translated into several languages. She is married to David Sutherland, a Scot, and lives in London and Scotland.

Janet Suzman was born in 1939. She has had an extensive career in the theatre, on television and in film. She has played in *The Duchess of Malfi*, *The Good Woman of Setzuan*, *The Relapse*, *The Taming of the Shrew*, Beatrice in *Much Ado About Nothing*, Celia in *As You Like It*, Cleopatra, Helen and Clytemnestra in *The Greeks* (RSC), the title role in *Saint Joan*, *The Three Sisters*, *Family Reunion*, Lady Macbeth, Hedda Gabler and Nicola in *The Singing Detective* (BBC TV); and, on film, *A Day in the Death of Joe Egg*, *Nicholas and Alexandra*, *Priest of Love*, *Nijinsky* and *The Draughtsman's Contract*. She won an Academy Award Nomination for Best Actress in 1971, and an *Evening Standard* Drama Award for Best Actress in 1973 and 1976. She has one son.

Conny Templeman was brought up in Peru and England. After taking a degree in literature at the University of East Anglia, she travelled round Europe to write, working as a waitress, painter and cleaning lady. She made her first short film *Home* for the British Film Institute in 1976, and went on to make a film for the Equal Opportuni-ties Commission. She joined the National Film and Television School and, while still a student, wrote *Nanou*, a 35mm feature film which she later went on to direct in 1985 for Simon Perry. With *Nanou*, Conny Templeman was the first British woman director to be invited to the Venice Film Festival in thirty years.

Lisa St Aubin de Terán won the Somerset Maugham Award for her first novel, *Keepers of the House* (1982), and the John Llewellyn Rhys Memorial Prize for her second, *The Slow Train to Milan* (1983). Her third novel, *The Tiger*, was published in 1984. She lives alone with her children in Italy.

Fiona Thyssen was spotted by photographer Norman Parkinson when she was seventeen years old. She became one of the most famous models of the 1950s. In 1956 she married Baron Heini Thyssen and went to live in Switzerland. They were divorced seven years later. She has two children.

Martha Tiller has spent over twenty years in the communications and public-relations world. After graduating from the University of Texas, she apprenticed in New York with CBS and Goodson Todman Productions before marrying and returning to Texas. She worked for the Texas Fine Art Association, was special assistant to former President Lyndon Johnson and then became the press and social secretary for Mrs Johnson. In 1977, she was named the director of public affairs for the Dallas advertising and public-relations firm, Glenn, Bozell & Jacobs. In 1972, she was selected as Outstanding Young Woman of Texas and she received 1982's Best of Texas Award from the Texas Public Relations Association. Martha Tiller is now president and founder of her own Dallas-based public-relations firm.

Claire Tomalin was born in 1933 and educated at Dartington Hall School and Newnham College, Cambridge (MA). From 1974 to 1977, she was literary editor of the *New Statesman*, and from 1979 to 1986 was literary editor of the *Sunday Times*. Her publications include *The Life and Death of Mary Wollstonecraft* (1974), *Shelley and His World* (1980) and *Parents and Children* (1981). She currently writes for a wide variety of periodicals.

Lili Townsend was born in New York City in 1937. She grew up in Long Island and married early after attending a private girls' school. Her son, Clarke Ohrstrom, was born in 1961 and is a financial analyst for a real-estate firm and a professional motor-cycle racer. Lili's ten-year career in fashion was marked by the opening of the Rive Gauche boutique of Yves Saint-Laurent and, later, Valentino of Rome. She was also director of advertising for Georg Jensen. In 1976, she set out to spend three years in the Atlantic and the Caribbean on her boat, *The Venus*, and in 1979 she began multi-discipline studies in the field of holistic medicine. She has since served as a healer, counsellor and teacher. Currently she is organizing human dolphin interactions in the Florida Keys and lives in Santa Fe, New Mexico, where she practises spiritual therapy.

Polly Toynbee was born in 1946. She was educated at Badminton School, Holland Park Comprehensive and St Anne's College, Oxford. Since 1977, she has been a columnist on the *Guardian*. She won the Catherine Pakenham Award for Journalism in 1975 and the British Press Award in 1977. She has been a reporter and feature writer for the *Observer* and an editor on the *Washington Monthly*. She is the author of *Leftovers* (1966); *A Working Life* (1970); *Hospital* (1977); *The Way We Live Now* (1981); and *Lost Children* (1985). She is a member of the SDP National Committee and Policy Committee and stood as an SDP candidate for Lewisham East in 1983. She is married to Peter Jenkins and has one son, two daughters and a stepdaughter.

Abir Dajani Tuqan was born in Jaffa,

Palestine. She was educated in Switzerland and read law at London University. She qualified as a barrister at Middle Temple and has worked in the Civil and Criminal Chambers in London. She has been a legal consultant in Kuwait and a lecturer on women's rights in the Sharia. She has published various articles and was the co-producer for Costa-Gavras's film *Hannah K*. She is married to Usama Tuqan and has three children.

Kathleen Turner is an actress. Her film credits include *Body Heat, Crimes of Passion, Prizzi's Honour, Romancing the Stone, Jewel of the Nile, The Man with Two Brains, Peggy Sue Got Married* and *Julia, Julia*. Stage credits include *Gemini* on Broadway, *Travesties* and the *Seagull* for the Manitoba Theatre Center in Winnipeg, *Candida, A Midsummer Night's Dream* at Arena Stage, *Toyer* at the Kennedy Center and, most recently, Marguerite Gautier in Pam Gems's *Camille* at the Long Wharf Theater, Connecticut.

Jill Tweedie was born in 1936 and educated at a variety of girls' schools, She is a freelance writer for the press, radio and television and has been a columnist with the *Guardian* since 1969. She was named Woman Journalist of the Year in the IPC National Press Awards, 1971. She is married to Alan Brien and has three children. She is the author of *In the Name of Love* (1979); *It's Only Me* (1980); *Letters from a Faint-hearted Feminist* (1982); *More from Martha* (1983); and two novels: *Bliss* (1984) and *Internal Affairs* (1986). She also contributes to various European and American anthologies.

Marie-Claire Valène was born in 1933. Both her mother and father were doctors. She had an unconventional childhood interrupted by the Second World War and by her parents' involvement in the French Resistance movement. Alongside her conventional studies after the war, she won a place at the Ecole Nationale Supérieure d'Art

Dramatique de la Rue Blanche, from which she finished with the first prize for the dramatic arts. As early as 1956, she became interested in theatre direction and administration. In London, she was a leading lady in *The French Mistress*, and at the same time met Joan Littlewood. She returned to France and worked on several production. In 1963, she became the first woman director to win the Prix des Jeunes Compagnies for her production of *La Nuit des erreurs*, a French translation of *She Stoops to Conquer* by Oliver Goldsmith. In 1974, she created the Cultural Centre of French Polynesia in Tahiti. From 1976 to 1979, she was director of the Cultural Centre in Créteil, and finally, in 1980, she became director of the Théâtre des Champs-Elysées in Paris.

Joan Vass was born in New York City in 1925. She graduated from the University of Wisconsin as a philosophy major and did graduate work in the area of aesthetics at the University of Buffalo and the New School of Social Research, New York City. She was curator at the Museum of Modern Art, editor at Harry N. Abrams and established her own business in 1974. She has won the Coty Award for Knits, the Prix de Cachet and the Extraordinary Women in Fashion Award in 1978. She is married to Gene Vass and they have four children.

Sara Vass received her BA degree in art history in 1969. She was the co-ordinator and publicist of *Art Now '75* and *Art Now '76* in Washington, DC, before becoming co-ordinator of special events in the Office of the Mayor. In 1982, she joined Rea Lubar Inc. in New York as an account executive, and in 1983 she became vice-president of the company. In 1984, she was appointed special consultant and events and media co-ordinator for Daniel J. Edelman Inc., New York, and the following year was press and creative co-ordinator for People for the American Way. She then worked in the same capacity for *Child* magazine, Taxi Publishing Inc., and in 1985 became director of public infor-

mation for the Cooper Union for the Advancement of Science and Art. She has been a consultant for various media projects in Washington, appeared as a rotating interviewer and co-host on *Panorama* television programme, and between 1969 and 1970 she created, marketed and broadcast a daily programme of music and interviews for WHFS-FM, Washington. She was rated at one time the number-one female disc jockey in DC.

Diana Vreeland has inspired the world of high fashion for the past half-century, first as fashion editor of *Harper's Bazaar*, then as editor-in-chief of *Vogue*, and for the last few years as special consultant to the Costume Institute of the Metropolitan Museum of Art in New York City.

Virginia Wade was born in 1945 in England. She was brought up in South Africa, but the family returned to England when she was fifteen. She went on to Sussex University, where she graduated with a BSc in mathematics and physics. She was involved with tennis from an early age; while still at school, she was invited to play on England's Wightman Cup Team. In 1968, she won the first-ever US Open Championship against Billie Jean King. It was the first of seven 'Grand Slam' titles she would win. She was named Player of the Year in 1977 by the Women's Tennis Association, reaching the million-dollar mark in career earnings by 1981. She was the first women ever elected to the Wimbledon Committee (1982). She remains active as a player, coach and tennis broadcaster, and has had two books published: her autobiography, *Courting Triumph* (1978), and *Ladies of the Court* (1984), a historical book marking the women's centenary at Wimbledon. She divides her time between London and New York.

Michaela Walsh is the president and founder of Women's World Banking, an independent non-profit financial institution set up in 1979 to provide women with access to credit. She spent seventeen years in the financial world and seven years with the Rockefeller Brothers Fund on questions concerning innovation and alternative futures. Her attention is currently focused on building bridges between the banking community and small businesses as a means to strengthen the economic status of women on an international scale. She has travelled widely and participated on several boards and committees concerning women, finance and enterprise development.

Tracy Ward was born in 1958. She attended several boarding schools and lived in Paris for a year after school, studying French and modelling. She went to Italy for a year before obtaining a diploma in art history from a London art college. She then worked in Christie's in London and as an art dealer in New York. In 1983, she returned to train as an actress. Her work as an actress includes a solo cabaret, plays at the Nottingham Playhouse and in the West End and various television appearances, among them in *Mussolini*, *If Tomorrow Comes*, *Dr Who* and *C.A.T.S. Eyes*. She married Harry Worcester in June 1987.

Marina Warner was born in London in 1946. She was educated at several Catholic convents and at Lady Margaret Hall, Oxford. She worked for the *Daily Telegraph* magazine and for *Vogue* as features editor between 1969 and 1972. During this period, she won the *Daily Telegraph* Young Writer of the Year Award. She is now a distinguished writer and critic. Among her books are the internationally acclaimed, *Alone of All Her Sex: The Myth and Cult of the Virgin Mary* and *Joan of Arc: The Image of Female Heroism*. She has also written children's books and two novels, *In a Dark Wood* and *The Skating Party*. Her other books include *The Dragon Empress: The Life and Times of Tz'U-Hsi, Empress Dowager of China 1835–1908*. She broadcasts regularly for radio and television and reviews for the *Independent*.

She is married to the painter John Dewe Matthews and has a son. They live in London.

Heather Watts joined the New York City Ballet in 1970, was promoted to soloist in May 1978, and became a principal dancer in October 1979. A native of California, she went to New York at the age of thirteen on a Ford Foundation scholarship to the School of American Ballet, the official school of the New York City Ballet. She was seventeen when she began to assume solo and principal parts, and her versatility of technique has enabled her to dance roles as diverse as the Novice in *The Cage* and the ballerina in Tchaikovsky Suite No. 3's *Theme and Variations*. In 1985, Miss Watts received both L'Oreal Shining Star Award and the prestigious *Dance* Magazine Award. She was also one of the recipients of the New York Public Library's first annual Lions of the Performing Arts Awards.

Arabella Weir was trained at New College of Speech and Drama and gained a London University diploma in dramatic art. Her leading roles in television productions include Prish in *Honest, Decent and True* (1985), Liz Morrison in *Blood Hunt* (1985) and Annie in *The Corner House* (1986). Her film credits include *The French Lieutenant's Woman* (1980) and *The Frog Prince* (1984). She has also played a wide variety of parts in the theatre.

Felicity White was born and educated in Sussex. She took a BA degreee in classics and ancient history at University College, London. She taught English in Bombay, India, in 1974, and attended the University of Salonika in Greece for three months. In 1980, she qualified as a solicitor, and in 1986 was a founding partner in Bazley White & Co. In 1987 she published her first book, *Divorce and Separation*. She is married with one daughter and lives in London.

Katharine Whitehorn was born in

London and educated at several schools including Roedean, and Newnham College, Cambridge. She has been a columnist on the *Observer* since 1960 and associate editor since 1980. Her publications include *Only on Sundays* (1966), *How to Survive Children* (1975) and *How to Survive Your Money Problems* (1983). She has written for *Woman's Own* and the *Spectator* among other journals. She is married to Gavin Lyall and has two sons.

Shelley Vaughan Williams is the chairman of trustees of the Jersey Scriptorium (an educational charitable trust). She is chairman of Catherine Productions (film, theatre and television); consultant to Orbit Productions Inc. in Washington; managing director of SVW Associates (fine art consultants) and co-director of Strabo Investment Management (international financial consultants). She is a freeman of the Worshipful Company of Printer-Stainers, London, and a freeman of the City of London. She is currently engaged with François Xavier Lovat on a book celebrating the bicentennial of the Constitution of America.

Jeanette Winterson was born in Lancashire in 1959. She went to school on and off and worked at a variety of jobs, including assisting an undertaker and caring for a megalomaniac. She read English at Oxford and now writes full-time. Her first novel, *Oranges are Not the Only Fruit*, won the 1985 Whitbread First Novel Award. Her latest novel, *The Passion*, was published in 1987. She lives with her lover (a woman) in North London.

Anna Wintour is the daughter of ex-*Standard* editor Charles Wintour. She took over the editorship of *Vogue* in 1986 following the retirement of Beatrix Miller who had been editor for twenty-one years. Her work on US *Vogue*, and prior to that on the monthly *New York*, already established her as an innovative force in publishing. Anna Wintour lives in Kensington, but retains a house in New York, dividing her time between

London and her family who still live in the United States.

Enid Wistrich was born in 1928 and educated at St Paul's Girls' School and at the London School of Economics (BScEcon, PhD). She has undertaken academic research into areas of politics and public policy. From 1969 to 1972, she was the senior research officer at the LSE. She served as a local councillor on Hampstead Metropolitan Borough Council (1962–5) and on Camden Council (1964–8 and 1971–4). Her publications include *I Don't Mind the Sex, It's the Violence*: *film censorship explored* (1978) and *The Politics of Transport* (1983). She is currently principal lecturer in public administration at Middlesex Polytechnic. She is also chairman of Hampstead Community Health Council. She is married and has a grown-up daughter and son.

Priscilla Woolworth was born in 1962 in New York City. She grew up in the South of France and Paris and went to a convent in Oise. She did her A-Levels at a boarding school in England and majored in art history at college. She is an aspiring actress and lives in New York. She speaks fluent French.

APPENDIX
The Brain:
A Comparative Study

Reports of differences between the brains of men and women, and the research being carried out in this area, proved to be so fascinating that it was decided to include the following summary, based on research material provided by Dr Anna Paterson MK BSc PhD, who is currently engaged on a book on The Endocrine System of Behaviour.

It is only too easy to construct biological stereotypes for man and woman by using impeccable scientific data from such areas of research as genetics, anatomy, psychology and neurophysiology. For example, we might define woman as the baseline creation, physically more resilient, less prone than man to congenital and infantile trauma and less affected by adult stress. She is found to mature earlier, both in terms of sexual competence and social adaptability, and is characterized by a high degree of verbal dexterity combined with a low level of aggressivity. The counter-image of man then becomes an elegant but dangerous variation on the female theme. While the male is more vulnerable and slower to develop, adult man grows to be bigger and stronger than woman. His brain becomes more split up into compartments and he tends to develop non-verbal abstract skills, his high level of aggressiveness making him less capable of coping with group tasks of co-operation.

Here we have a basic blueprint that might be matched against most human societies. Woman lives peaceably with others. She communicates and imparts verbal skills to her children, using her fine motor control, which happens to be better than a man's (and also makes her better than a man at threading needles, painting inside outlines, making microchips), to care for the ill and the very young, and especially for the weak and therefore the precious male children. She needs to draw on her physical strength to give birth as well as to work.

Aggressive and taciturn man, on the other hand, abstracts his environment into maps and reduces the phenomena he observes into

1143

mechanical constructs even as he elevates the muddled cadences of speech into the ordered sequences of music. As he roams and fights, he takes risks in the secure knowledge that there will always be enough women around (since women survive better). For him, the reproduction of the species means a quick and easily repeated task.

There will be readers who, as they cast an eye over these notions of reality, find that they comfortably support their belief in the status quo. There will be others who are likely to stop reading in disgust at this point, feeling that anything that might now be added is already invalidated by such an array of clichés. In other words, we are badly in need of a few more items of biological wisdom to bring a balance to the emerging picture.

To begin with, we have the old nature *versus* nurture debate, and no contemporary biologist is going to argue with this juxtaposition. The vast genetic system and the environment in which that system exists are in a constant state of interaction. The twenty-three gene pairs that control the biological system known as a human being are overwhelmingly non-sexual. It is only one pair, the twenty-third, that determines the genetic sex of an individual. The fundamental human shape might be said to be female, for, in the absence of androgen (male) hormones, nature produces a female. The male genitals, the male skeletal and muscular growth, the pattern of fat deposition, the tendency to grow bald and so forth, are all governed by hormones, even as hormones are directly involved in maintaining typically female characteristics.

In general, therefore, hormones are secreted in response to internal or external changes in the environment. Two systems – the nervous and the hormonal – interact. Together they form the biological basis for the commonplace observation that nurture may indeed influence various aspects of nature.

Secondly, we come to the principle of biological variation which means that the factors able to influence a biological state are so numerous that no individual behaviour can ever be totally steady and predictable. It is only the *most likely* outcome of a particular factor (being female, having high blood pressure, drinking gin at breakfast and so forth) that can be predicted. As biological studies make clear, the qualities of 'male' and 'female' are somewhat vague approximations to the sets of characteristics most often encountered. There is no good reason for anyone to express surprise at coming across a female theoretical physicist with solitary habits or a male hat-maker who loves gossip and has lots of dear friends.

As for the brain itself, brain power is at the very core of the variability of behaviour seen in all organisms that possess this organ. The more complex the brain, the less predictable the behaviour of its owner. Every species, and every sub-group within the species, will be found to have characteristic brains, but the very function of the nervous system is planned so as to leave scope for learning new and individual responses.

The organization of the brain may be seen in terms of a large, well-managed but democratically run institution. Individual employees are grouped into small teams responsible for specific tasks. Each employee has several lines of communication – with team-mates, with area management groups and with various levels of senior management all the way up to the board of directors. All levels of management are also in direct contact, and board members, while maintaining degrees of specialization, sustain a network of interconnecting hotlines. They may delegate certain major projects to subcontractors, but their work is constantly monitored and adjusted according to the circumstances imposed by both internal and external events.

If we translate this image into brain terminology, individual employees become the nerve cells (neurons), which are formed into task-orientated interconnected groups (nuclei). The input and output lines between nerve cells are the nerve fibres, and these, like telephone lines, are capable of transmitting small electrical impulses in frequency coded sequences. The nuclei, which, with their connections, make up the main bulk of the brain, function in a way that is partly hierarchical. Blood pressure regulation, for instance, or fluid intake or co-ordination of the muscles in one part of the body, are controlled from the centres formed by one or several nuclei. Groups of functions are then co-ordinated by higher-level nuclei, while the 'board of directors' integrates all incoming information, compares it with past experience, sorts it, stores it, and issues general directives. This essentially supervisory function resides in the cortex, the multi-layered sheet of nerve cells that covers the brain's surface. When it comes to delegation, however, the most striking example is the control of posture and balance and the accuracy of muscular movements, all of which are handled by a remarkable bio-computer: the cerebellum, or 'little brain'.

The body has a left and a right side, both constructed in essentially the same way. The brain, too, is bilaterally symmetrical. But neither brain nor body are entirely symmetrical, and functional asymmetry is especially pronounced in the cortex as it covers the right and the left halves (the hemispheres) of the brain. This would seem to be laying down the basis for a truly 'split personality', but corresponding cell groups on either side of the midline of the brain are linked by special bundles of nerve fibres (commissures), of which the biggest and most important is that known as the corpus callosum. For reasons not fully understood, though their importance may be assumed, the right cortex controls the left-hand side of the body, and vice versa, information being received back by the brain along the same lines.

The asymmetry of brain and body is a subtle matter. Both

hemispheres can do most of the same things as these relate to the opposite side of the body; but then we find that the left hemisphere is, in most people, the dominant side for the manipulation and understanding of language and a variety of fine motor skills, while the right side is predominant in comprehending spatial tasks and the abstract ordering of sounds in music. We might therefore say that, in the higher reaches of the central nervous system, two apparently paradoxical forms of organization prevail. While symmetrically placed nuclei send out their output fibres across the midline to contact structures on the other side, subtle changes in layout have led to the asymmetrical concentration of certain nuclei on one side or the other. It is in such subtleties as these that sex differences in the nervous system are expressed.

The role of hormones in brain and body is, of course, of central importance, and the most obvious illustration of this comes from the effects of castration. It seems that there has been, since the dawn of history, an awareness of the uses of castration as a prime technique of behaviour-modifying surgery. Its de-masculinizing effects depend to quite an extent on when it is carried out. To obtain eunuchs, oxen or inoffensive male cats, the operation needs to be done before 'adolescence' – that is to say, before the burst of sexual maturation in the young male. This, in turn, depends to a large extent on an increased output of the testicular hormone, testosterone. It is not that castration cancels out maleness, for testosterone and related androgens (male hormones) have been circulating at earlier critical phases of development. Moreover, androgens are also secreted (if less vigorously) by another gland, the adrenal, which is present in both men and women. (Therefore those who say that, 'There is a little of the masculine in all women,' are only citing a biological truism; as are those who say, vice versa, that, 'There is something of the female in all men,' for oestrogen-like compounds also circulate in men's bodies.) Castration in the grown male will tend to have fewer effects, and most behavioural changes can probably be accounted for by the psychological trauma. Attempts to treat violent criminals, especially sex offenders, with castration have been remarkably unpredictable in their results.

The equivalent in women of removing the testicles of the male would be to perform an ovarectomy. In effect, and in a physiological sense, this happens to every grown woman at the menopause. None of the consequences, however, may be said to eliminate a woman's essential femininity (unless sexual drive is seen as an essential component of being female). Ovarectomies in pre-pubertal girls are practically unheard of, but if they were carried out they would certainly prevent the development of mature female characteristics at puberty.

The male and female sex hormones are therefore inescapably important. During the earliest months of our foetal life, they mark us for all

our days. The critical role of foetal testosterone (and related compounds) in promoting the attributes of maleness has been shown by
many studies. During the burst of growth at adolescence, it is the
completion of the body characteristics of the sexes that occurs.

Growth patterns are, in fact, given their relative shapes by such socio-
economic factors as nutrition, medical care and the physical demands
made on a growing child. Absolute differences between the sexes then
direct development. The average child today begins its final period of
sexual differentiation at about the age of ten. Girls grow rapidly
between ten and thirteen, and tend to become bigger than boys, their
mean age for starting menstruation being between twelve and thirteen
in Western Europe. Boys are later developers, and are also more
vulnerable to adverse circumstances ('easily thrown off their growth
curves') and to illness. This is a trend which persists into adulthood,
especially if we discount those disorders in women that relate directly to
pregnancy and labour. The male starts his main adolescent growth at
about thirteen, and this is then relatively rapid so that the final male
product will, in physical measures – height, skeletal and muscular bulk,
blood and lung volume, strength and so forth – be on average 10 per
cent bigger than the female. The years of growth last approximately till
sixteen for girls and eighteen for boys, and glands differentiate during
this period, so that not only testes and ovaries but also pituitary and
adrenal glands, for instance, acquire sexual characteristics.

It follows that the brain must also be affected during all the pre- and
post-natal bursts of growth and differentiation. But we do not know
how and to what extent. There is, however, an obvious target in the
brain for hormones: a region that specializes in the management of the
hormone-producing glands – the pituitary, whose widespread effects
on body glands are again mediated by hormones. The pituitary is part of
a bigger group of nuclei, collectively termed the hypothalamus. Other
nuclei in the group control functions relating to sexual and emotional
responses and food and drink intake. We might summarize the hypothalamic function as imparting a sense of gratification or aversion,
according to circumstances. It may be assumed (though it is an
unproven assumption) that it is in this region that many sexual preferences and behaviours are first defined.

The hypothalamus, especially in primates, ranks only as minor
management. Its activities are constantly monitored, suppressed or
stimulated by the complex hierarchy of brain regions. It is not even that
it has an exclusive interest in hormonal and emotional matters, for other
centres show analogous characteristics. Yet whereas we have so far been
talking mainly of 'hard-wired biology', it has also been said that one of
the prime features of the gland and nervous system is flexibility – an
adaptability to the environment. Outside influences can bring about

changes by slow evolutionary processes in the long term, or, in the relative short term, through learning by individuals or groups. Primates are notable for having freed themselves over the long term from the dominance of regular cycles of sexual behaviour. Thus, in a sense, the brains of human and related species may be said to have become emancipated from the chronological tyranny of sex. Another feature of long-term change is the tendency of species whose females undergo long pregnancies, often combined with a long commitment to bringing up young, to have 'hidden ovulation'. That is to say, they provide no signals to males to show they are fertile. One theory has it that this mechanism protects the female against constant vulnerability. It may also be said to make for male polygamy.

Many social circumstances, including the short-term behavioural changes that come about through learning, affect both the brain and hormonal secretions. Studies of monkeys in social groups seem to indicate that status is of primary importance: whereas hormones change the sexual signals, status determines the degree of sexual activity. While, in other species, the behavioural and hormonal effects of status and such other determinants as stress may be changed by manipulating the social structure, subordinate monkeys never recover the sexual initiative, even after all their competitors are removed. In other words, learning a 'role' can result in entrenched changes of response.

Aggression is another example where both brain and hormones come into play. Aggressive behaviour is part of a system of related responses that may be termed agonistic: threat and attack, counter-attack and defence, advancing and running away, proclaiming victory and conceding defeat, dominating and submitting, together with the rituals and signals that may be more or less regarded as signifying any of these things. In mammals, agonistic behaviours occur more frequently in males than in females, the simplest explanation being that female animals have never had much time for such matters. It is the female animal which has to make the greater investment in being a parent, and, in most cases, this means not only bearing and feeding her young, but also seeing to such other time-consuming tasks as nest-building and socializing offspring. The tasks the male takes on are more often concerned with defence against predators and combating intruders within territorial limits. In other words, females may well have aggressive potential, but the restraint of aggression is necessary for successful breeding.

Monogamy is a comparative rarity in the animal world. The polygamous males create their own social hierarchy on the basis of coming out on top in agonistic encounters. While female/female competition is also common, male/female contests are not. Subordinate males then create their own niches in the social order by signalling that they accept their status. They often do this by adopting females signals (postures) of a sexual nature.

Interpreting male and female relations in human societies in such bleak socio-biological terms is another exercise that may be slipped into all too easily. It seems of far greater interest to ask how, and to what degree human beings are capable of freeing themselves from such brutal biological constraints. To alter our biology from first principles is not practicable. To alter individual and collective behaviour is, in principle, a distinct possibility. Biological systems are, above all else, adaptable, but it remains impossible at present to forecast the nature of the results of any adaptation. For one thing, it would be useful to know something about the immediate physiological mechanisms which trigger social behaviours. In fact, we know very little in this area, and not for want of trying. The simplest ideas – that genetic sex and/or sex hormones are required to account for social and sexual behaviour – have been investigated to exhaustion. It is only very recently that research has begun to take account of the highly complex nature of the problem and to ask, among other questions, how it is that laboratory conditions may change the very object under study, how previous experience affects current responding, or how one set of behaviours interacts with other sets.

Environment matters a great deal. In laboratory stock monkeys, for example, an experimental brain operation known as an amygdalectomy (the removal of the amygdala, an 'emotional' brain area) has reportedly led to a lack of aggression combined with several other symptoms including hypersexuality and failures of recognition (inappropriate responses). When this syndrome attracted attention, amygdalectomy became part of the stock-in-trade of pyscho-surgeons, as a suitable intervention for violent patients or offenders. However, monkeys operated on in this way which were kept in approximately natural colonies showed only one of the many features of the original syndrome: the failures of recognition. These had a catastrophic effect on their lives within the group, since the inability to react appropriately to any kind of normal social signal led to what can only be called a 'severe social maladjustment'. Beatings and literally fatal social ostracism were the consequences. We might mention as an aside here that an association between sexual arousal and aggression has never been disproved; quite the other way about. In human tests using the 'Buss aggression machine' – in which the test subject believes himself or herself to be administering painful electric shocks to someone else unseen – men tend to turn up the current intensity higher than women, though both sexes deliver stronger shocks if they are also sexually aroused.

Previous experience also comes into it, as any amateur thinker on behaviour might anticipate. Yet only recently have animal experiments

1149

which take this into account been described. The possibility of hormone secretion being affected by experience would imply that the brain, having taken stock of an immediate situation, must signal the glands to adjust output. The feedback of hormones on the brain may then reinforce certain behavioural responses. Experiments on the human experience of winning or losing (in boxing and tennis) suggest that male testosterone levels rise after winning and fall after losing. Analogous observations of male and female rats show that, while both sexes will fight, especially if pretreated with testosterone, their responses to victory and defeat are different. When they were subsequently placed in renewed agonistic situations, the hormone-treated males submitted if their previous experience had been one of defeat (or vice versa), while the females responded to the hormone treatment with aggression, irrespective of what the outcome of previous fights had been. One might tentatively conclude that, while the male rat's brain was 'reminded' of earlier events by rising testosterone levels, the female brain did not react to this example of hormonal 'imprinting'. One might, even more hesitantly, detect in these results a hormonal basis for male hierarchies. It is known that, in animals at least, male social status is associated with characteristic secretion patterns from both the testis and adrenal glands. This is not necessarily to say, however, that the glandular output is nature's given class distinction. If dominant males are removed, sub-ordinate males can often adjust their behaviour along with their glandular secretions to their new status.

It may be that social rank order is perceived as more or less stressful to individuals, or certain groups of individuals. Where the stress factor is great, both dominant and submissive group members may be less flexible in responses to social change. Males are characteristically more prone than females to stress-related physiological symptoms – often pathologically so. Stress affects both the nervous and the hormonal systems, one effect being a brain-initiated shift in adrenal hormonal secretion which is critical to the outcome of agonistic encounters. In different circumstances, the adrenal stress hormones can promote or suppress aggression. Yet females are less subject to violent swings in stress hormonal secretion, a feature that probably has some connection with a reluctance to start a fight and also (perhaps paradoxically) with a greater endurance of pain.

The most surprising aspect of the differences between male and female brains is that there have been so few real investigations into them. From Aristotle on, those who look for patterns in nature have been struck by differences between the sexes. It is something that has worked both ways. Aristotle, and innumerable followers, were con-vinced of such imponderables as differences in timing of the entry of the soul – always later in the female. Thomas Aquinas accepted this line of thought more than 700 years later on the grounds that the female was *mas occasionatus*, an incomplete man. After two millennia of the refinement of ideas, female thinkers have stepped forward to assure us of 'females...having a cranium of almost superior race' (Montessori); and that 'if the frontal lobes are considered the seat of intelligence, it must also be pointed out that the frontal area of the brain is more developed in women' (Greer). The fact of the matter is that the frontal lobes are neither of these things. The sheer mass of opinionated nonsense combined with the paucity of acceptable facts is enough to induce despair.

When we come to discuss the cerebral (as opposed to the cultural) basis of sexual differences in behaviour and mental capacity, then there are two intellectually respectable lines of inquiry open to us. The first involves a systematic inquiring into the physiology, pharmacology and so on of animal behaviour; the second is the more holistic approach of neuropsychologists in recording the responses and abilities of human beings under carefully controlled conditions. Present-day studies of animals have been vitalized by changes in the social perception of the quality of femaleness. Not only have the past few years seen a marked increase in such investigations, but the basis for asking questions has changed as the possibility has emerged that hormones may not be the ultimate sex determinants.

In a sense, the most interesting results are those that are most fundamental. If it can be shown, for instance, that the relative weights of the brains of men and women really are different, and that the number of neurons, or connections between neurons, really do vary, then at least there is something definite on which to centre new arguments. Differences of this order are therefore being looked for and being found, although they usually turn out to be slight and generally inconsistent. Male brains are in fact heavier than female brains once the ratio to overall body weight is accounted for. This difference is detectable by about two years of age, and it continues at a level of approximately 10 per cent throughout the whole of life. On the other hand, investigations into the corpus callosum suggest that the female has the edge in size where this important inter-hemispheric connection is concerned, and that this particular sex difference starts during the foetal stage – is, in other words, independent of, though not necessarily unaffected by, life outside the uterus.

Other human studies have proved to be rather less conclusive, but studies of animal brains, which are naturally easier to come by, do, on the whole, support the notion that certain differences exist between the sexes. The hypothalamic area provides several examples, but the most convincing work to have been done is on the thickness and organization of the cerebral cortex. Here, differences have been found, but they require interpretation. To take an example, male and female rats, when raised in isolation or with access to social play areas, are alike in showing increased cortical development in response to environmental complexity. Yet, when comparisons are made, the males produce more extensive interconnections in the visual cortex in comparison with the females, while the females develop more in those regions concerned with memory and orientation.

Among the most critical differences between males and females of any species may well be those that are biorhythmical; that is to say, where the important thing is not so much what happens as when it happens. In mammalian species, including the human, there is an important centre for the control of rhythmically recurring body function, notably hormone secretion, which is lodged in a small hypothalamic nucleus (known as the supracharismatic nucleus). Its organization in rats takes different forms according to gender, and the same conclusion seems to apply to humans. One study of the sexual behaviour of rats (which happens to be rhythmic in both males and females) and its dependence on hormones, reached the significant conclusion that each sex could potentially perform like the other in the presence of appropriate hormones, but that, in the female, the timing of bursts of hormone secretion was critical. While primate brains seem relatively less affected by the turning on and off of hormonal output, there are many examples to show how these ancient mechanisms remain active. Two much-discussed examples of derangements of normal behaviour come to mind: first, those seen in many women during the menopause, and secondly, those that happen in a smaller population of both sexes during winter when the rhythm of light and dark shifts towards darkness.

As neuropsychological testing has shown, men and women possess different abilities in problem-solving. The differences are often quite small, and the function being measured hard to define, but the unmistakable trend is there. To simplify the trend considerably, it might be said that males are right-hemisphere orientated and therefore good at spatial, constructional tasks; and that women are left-hemisphere types with predominantly verbal minds. But then we must add that, hidden behind these statements, there remain endless contradictions and oddities together with ill-understood feelings.

In the United States, repeated studies of highly gifted children (aged between twelve and fourteen) have revealed undeniable differences in aptitude. The tests spanned a decade, and, in many cases, follow-up studies were also applied. In this population segment, consisting, of course, of individuals who were of more than average ability, a balanced ratio of boys and girls were tested, yet boys outnumbered girls in mathematical ability by a proportion that increased with increasing scores. (The boy/girl ratio was 2:1 at a score of 500+; 4:1 at 600+; while, at 700+, an exceedingly rare level of mathematical reasoning at any age, it stood at 13:1.) Tests of verbal skills taken simultaneously showed no essential differences between the sexes. Between four and five years later, retesting showed an essentially unchanged pattern, except for the added twist that the boys now also increased their scores over the girls on the verbal test as well. By this later stage, more boys than girls were engaged in science and mathematics, which seems to give the first set of test results a predictive status. This was not, moreover, a phenomenon that could be explained away on the grounds of sex preference shown by teachers and so forth. It was demonstrated that, while the boys did better at the standard nationwide tests, the girls were awarded better marks at school.

As was argued quite reasonably, all of this concerned a group of children for whom socio-economic and cultural factors did not seriously affect performance. Their attitudes to and expectations from science and mathematics did not differ greatly, while the 'socializing effect' (responses to the expectations of others) was not significantly different. Interestingly enough, a study of adult scientists carried out by the same study team showed the personality traits of male and female scientists to be similar. It is therefore in the context of the general population that males possess the 'personalities of scientists' more often than females.

All this research led to the pursuit of biological correlates to match against the test results. Since a link had been established between late maturation in children and a better development of abstract 'spatial' thinking, and since the adolescent growth burst comes later in boys, the hormonal hypothesis seemed likely. There is also the theory that the higher androgen level in male foetuses promotes right-hemisphere dominance at the expense of the left hemisphere. Whatever the truth of this, the fact remained that most children tested were pre-adolescent so that any effects of puberty could be expected to show up in the follow-up test group.

And then, as soon as the tested children were compared with the population at large, a number of other strange clues emerged. For one thing, it was relatively twice as common for test children to be either left-handed or ambidextrous; for another, atopic disease (allergies, asthma and so on) was about a third more common. They also tended to be short-sighted (myopia being almost four times over the average). Since males in general tend to be more subject than females to atopic disease and certain other immune disorders, and also tend to be left-handed more often, a pattern emerged that remains so far inexplicable.

We could go on listing many odd findings. The sexes differ, for instance, in their proneness to cerebral vascular occlusion, so that men tend to suffer from strokes affecting the left hemisphere more often than the right, and the areas affected tend to be larger than in women. Women who take strong oestrogen analogues while pregnant may, against expectation, produce boys with 'decreased assertiveness, aggressiveness, athletic skill and grace'. Maternal stress during pregnancy may produce a homosexual boy child as a consequence. There is by now a growing body of research into (though not as yet a growing understanding of) the biological bases of sex and gender. Biological correlates may be expected to emerge, but not necessarily biological determinants.

Males and females do, in general, act and think differently, no doubt by a process of biology begetting culture begetting biology and so on. 'Maleness' and 'femaleness' can therefore, in the gender sense of the terms, be changed. The behavioural technology exists to achieve it, and a cultural drive towards using that technology seems to be growing. On the other hand, it would seem a pity to throw out the baby (adventure, abstract thought, music, machinery) with the murky bathwater (predation, aggression, exploitation of females, status-ridden competitiveness), but the action may come to be seen as necessary. There is no doubt that the single most significant move would be to tie the male to the care of children. The next few generations are likely to present a fascinating picture of many women doing things that previously only a few could try. Biological evolution may, in itself, be relied on to adapt to the changes in behaviour.

Sources for the Appendix

The most comprehensive source of 'technical' background information used in compiling this paper was:

De Vries, G.J., De Bruin, J.P.C., Uylings, H.B.M. and Corner, M.A. (eds.), *Sex Differences in the Brain*, *Progress in Brain Research*, vol. 61, Elsevier, Amsterdam, 1984,

from which the most extensively used papers were:

Sodersten, P., 'Sexual differentiation: do males differ from females in gonadal hormones?'
De Jonge, F.H. and Van de Poll, N.E., 'Relationship between sexual and aggressive behaviour in male and female rats: effects of gonadal hormones'
Keverne, E.B., Eberhart, J.A., Yodyingyuad, U. and Abbott, D.H., 'Social influences on sex differences in the behaviour and endocrine state of talapoin monkeys'

Swaab, D.F. and Hofman, M.A., 'Sexual differentiation of the human brain'

Kimura, D. and Harshman, R.A., 'Sex differences in brain organization for verbal and non-verbal functions'

Benbow, C. Persson, and Benbow, R.M., 'Biological correlates of high mathematical reasoning ability'.

Other sources included:

Barash, D.P., *Sociobiology and Behaviour*, Hodder & Stoughton, London, 1982

Brain, P.F. and Benton, D. (eds.), *The Biology of Aggression*, NATO Advanced Study Institute Series, Sijthoff & Noordhoff, Amsterdam, 1981

Holloway, R.L. and Lacoste, M.C., 'Sexual dimorphism in the human corpus callosum: an extension and replication study', *Human Neurobiology*, 5, 1986

Kimura, D., 'Male brain, female brain: the hidden difference', *Psychology Today*, 1985.